national
STATISTICS

2002 edition

United Kingdom

No 138

KT-583-179

Annual Abstract
of Statistics

Editor: Ramona Insalaco

London: The Stationery Office

Contact points
For enquiries about this publication,
contact the Editor, Ramona Insalaco
Tel: 020 7533 6147
E-mail: ramona.insalaco@ons.gov.uk

To order this publication, call
The Stationery Office
on **0870 600 5522.** See also back cover.

For general enquiries,
contact the National Statistics
Public Enquiry Service on **0845 601 3034**
(minicom: 01633 812399)
E-mail: **info@statistics.gov.uk**
Fax: 01633 652747
Letters: Room 1.001, Government Buildings,
Cardiff Road, Newport NP10 8XG

You can also find National Statistics on the
internet - go to **www.statistics.gov.uk**

About the Office for National Statistics
The Office for National Statistics (ONS) is the
government agency responsible for compiling,
analysing and disseminating many of the United
Kingdom's economic, social and demographic
statistics, including the retail prices index, trade
figures and labour market data, as well as the
periodic census of the population and health
statistics. The Director of ONS is also the
National Statistician and the Registrar General
for England and Wales, and the agency
administers the statutory registration of births,
marriages and deaths there.

A National Statistics publication
Official statistics bearing the National
Statistics logo are produced to high professional
standards set out in the National Statistics Code
of Practice. They undergo regular quality
assurance reviews to ensure that they meet
customer needs. They are produced free from
any political interference.

CONTENTS

CONTENTS

CONTENTS

CONTENTS

CONTENTS

CONTENTS

CONTENTS

CONTENTS

CONTENTS

UNITS OF MEASUREMENT

Length

1 millimetre (mm)		= 0.0393701 inch
1 centimetre (cm)	= 10 millimetres	= 0.393701 inch
1 metre (m)	= 1,000 millimetres	= 1.09361 yards
1 kilometre (km)	= 1,000 metres	= 0.621371 mile
1 inch (in.)		= 25.4 millimetres or 2.54 centimetres
1 foot (ft.)	= 12 inches	= 0.3048 metre
1 yard (yd.)	= 3 feet	= 0.9144 metre
1 mile	= 1,760 yards	= 1.60934 kilometres

Area

1 square millimetre (mm²)		= 0.00 55 square inch
1 square metre (m²)	= one million square millimetres	= 1.19599 square yards
1 hectare (ha)	= 10,000 square metres	= 2.47105 acres
1 square kilometre (km²)	= one million square metres	= 247.105 acres
1 square inch (sq. in.)		= 645.16 square millimetres or 6.4516 square centimetres
1 square foot (sq. ft.)	= 144 square inches	= 0.092903 square metre or 929.03 square centimetres
1 square yard (sq. yd.)	= 9 square feet	= 0.836127 square metres
1 acre	= 4,840 square yards	= 4,046.86 square metres or 0.404686 hectare
1 square mile (sq. mile)	= 640 acres	= 2.58999 square kilometres or 258.999 hectares

Volume

1 cubic centimetre (cm³)		= 0.0610237 cubic inch
1 cubic decimetre (dm³)	= 1,000 cubic centimetres	= 0.0353147 cubic foot
1 cubic metre (m³)	= one million cubic centimetres	= 1.30795 cubic yards
1 cubic foot (cu. ft.)		= 0.0283168 cubic metre or 28.3168 cubic decimetres
1 cubic yard (cu. yd.)	= 27 cubic feet	= 0.764555 cubic metre

Capacity

1 litre (l)	= 1 cubic decimetre	= 0.220 gallon
1 hectolitre (hl)	= 100 litres	= 22.0 gallons
1 pint		= 0.568 litre
2 pints	= 1 quart	= 1.137 litres
8 pints	= 1 gallon	= 4.54609 cubic decimetres or 4.546 litres
36 gallons (gal.)	= 1 bulk barrel	= 1.63656 hectolitres

Weight

1 gram (g)		= 0.0352740 ounce
1 hectogram (hg)	= 100 grams	= 3.5274 ounces or 0.220462 pound
1 kilogram (kg)	= 1,000 grams or 10 hectograms	= 2.20462 pounds
1 tonne (t)	= 1,000 kilograms	= 1.10231 short tons or 0.9842 long ton
1 ounce avoirdupois (oz.)		= 28.3495 grams
1 pound avoirdupois (lb.)	= 16 ounces	= 0.45359237 kilogram
1 hundredweight (cwt.)	= 112 pounds	= 50.8023 kilograms
1 short ton	= 2,000 pounds	= 907.18474 kilograms or 0.90718474 tonne
1 long ton (referred to as ton)	= 2,240 pounds	= 1,016.05 kilograms or 1.01605 tonnes
1 ounce troy	= 480 grains	= 31.1035 grams

Energy

Energy	British thermal unit (Btu)	= 0.252 kilocalorie (kcal) = 1.05506 kilojoule (kj)
	Therm	= 100,000 British thermal units = 25,200 kcal = 105,506 kj
	Megawatt (Mw)	= 10^6 watts
	Gigawatt hour (GWh)	= 10^6 kilowatt hours = 34,121 therms

Food and drink

Food and drink	Butter	23,310 litres milk	= 1 tonne butter (average)
	Cheese	10,070 litres milk	= 1 tonne cheese
	Condensed milk	2,550 litres milk	= 1 tonne full cream condensed milk
		2,953 litres skimmed milk	= 1 tonne skimmed condensed milk
	Milk	1 million litres	= 1,030 tonnes
	Milk powder	8,054 litres milk	= 1 tonne full cream milk powder
		10,740 litres skimmed milk	= 1 tonne skimmed milk powder
	Eggs	17,126 eggs	= 1 tonne (approximate)
	Sugar	100 tonnes raw sugar	= 95 tonnes refined sugar
	Beer	1 bulk barrel	= 36 gallons irrespective of gravity

Shipping

Shipping	Gross tonnage	= The total volume of all the enclosed spaces of a vessel, the unit of measurement being a ton of 100 cubic feet.
	Deadweight tonnage	= Deadweight tonnage is the total weight in tons of 2,240 lb. that a ship can legally carry, that is the total weight of cargo, bunkers, stores and crew.

ACKNOWLEDGEMENTS

The Editor would like to thank the following people for their help in producing this book:

Production team: Mario Alemanno

Nicola Amaranayake

Andrew Corris

Michael Crawley

Kevin Laverty

Mark Nevill

Mayur Patel

David Penny

Matthew Richardson

Brian Yin

Contributors

The Editor also wishes to thank all her colleagues in the ONS, the rest of the Government Statistical Service and all contributors in other organisations for their generous support and helpful comments, without whose help this publication would not be possible.

INTRODUCTION

Welcome to the 2002 edition of the *Annual Abstract of Statistics*. This compendium draws together statistics from a wide range of official and other authoritative sources. Their help is gratefully acknowledged.

Regional information, supplementary to the national figures in this *Annual Abstract*, is published in *Regional Trends,* published by The Stationery Office (TSO).

The five Parts of the *Annual Abstract*, illustrated in the contents, align with their equivalents in *UK 2002: The Official Yearbook of Great Britain and Northern Ireland,* so that the two books can be consulted as complementary volumes, painting a picture of the UK in words and figures.

Current data for many of the series appearing in this *Annual Abstract* are contained in other ONS publications, such as *Economic Trends, Monthly Digest of Statistics, Population Trends, Health Statistics Quarterly* and *Financial Statistics*. All are published by TSO.

The name and telephone number of the organisation providing the statistics are shown under each table. In addition, a list of Sources is given at the back of the book, which sets out the official publications or other sources to which further reference can be made.

All the data series published in the *Annual Abstract* are contained on a database, and almost all are stored with a four letter identification code (e.g. LUJS). These codes appear at the start of most columns or rows of data and can be quoted if you contact us requiring any further information about the data.

Definitions and Classification

Time Series
So far as possible annual totals are given throughout, but quarterly or monthly figures are given where these are more suitable to the type of series.

Explanatory notes
Most sections are preceded by explanatory notes which should be read in conjunction with the tables. Definitions and explanatory notes for many of the terms occurring in the *Annual Abstract* are also given in the *Annual Supplement* to the *Monthly Digest of Statistics*, published annually in the January editions. Detailed notes on items which appear in both the *Abstract* and *Financial Statistics* are given in an annual supplement to the latter entitled *Financial Statistics: Explanatory Handbook*. The original sources listed in the Sources may also be consulted.

Standard Industrial Classification
A Standard Industrial Classification (SIC) was first introduced into the United Kingdom in 1948 for use in classifying business establishments and other statistical units by the type of economic activity in which they are engaged. The classification provides a framework for the collection, tabulation, presentation and analysis of data about economic activities. Its use promotes uniformity of data collected by various government departments and agencies.

Since 1948 the classification has been revised in 1958, 1968, 1980 and 1992. One of the principal objectives of the 1980 revision was to eliminate differences from the activity classification issued by the Statistical Office of the European Communities (Eurostat) and entitled 'Nomenclature générale des activités économiques dans les Communautés Européennes', usually abbreviated to NACE. In 1990, the European Communities introduced a new statistical classification of economic activities (NACE Rev 1) by regulation. The regulation made it obligatory for the UK to introduce a new Standard Industrial Classification SIC(92), based on NACE Rev 1.

UK SIC(92) is based exactly on NACE Rev 1 but, where it is thought necessary or helpful, a fifth digit has been added to form subclasses of the NACE 1 four digit system. There are 17 sections, 16 subsections, 60 divisions, 222 groups, 503 classes and 253 subclasses. Full details are available from *UK Standard Industrial Classification of Economic Activities 1992* (TSO 1997, price £25.00) and *Indexes to the UK Standard Industrial Classification of Economic Activities 1992* (TSO 1997, price £22.50).

Regional classification. Some tables have been reclassified using the Government Office Regions. This has changed from the Standard Statistical Regions. For further advice please contact the Office for National Statistics Geographic Support Service (01329 813536).

Revisions to contents

Some of the figures, particularly for the latest year, are provisional and may be revised in a subsequent issue of the *Annual Abstract*.

Symbols and conventions used

Change of basis
Where consecutive figures have been compiled on different bases and are not strictly comparable, a footnote is added indicating the nature of the difference.

Units of measurement
The various units of measurement used are listed opposite the inside back cover.

Rounding of figures
In tables where figures have been rounded to the nearest final digit, the constituent items may not add up exactly to the total.

Introduction

Symbols

The following symbols have been used throughout:

.. = not available or not applicable (also information suppressed to avoid disclosure).

- = nil or less than half the final digit shown.

Contact point

The Editor welcomes any feedback on the content of the *Annual Abstract*, including comments on the format of the data and the selection of topics. Comments and requests for general information should be addressed to:

Ramona Insalaco
Social Analysis and Reporting Division
Room B5/06
Office for National Statistics
1, Drummond Gate
London SW1V 2QQ

or

E-mail: annual.abstract@ons.gov.uk

January 2002

1 Area

Area

The United Kingdom comprises Great Britain and Northern Ireland. Great Britain comprises England, Wales and Scotland only.

Physical Features

The United Kingdom (UK) constitutes the greater part of the British Isles. The largest of the islands is Great Britain. The next largest comprises Northern Ireland and the Irish Republic. Western Scotland is fringed by the large island chain known as the Hebrides, and to the north east of the Scottish mainland are the Orkney and Shetland Islands. All these, along with the Isle of Wight, Anglesey and the Isles of Scilly, have administrative ties with the mainland, but the Isle of Man in the Irish Sea and the Channel Islands between Great Britain and France are largely self-governing, and are not part of the United Kingdom. The UK is one of the 15 member states of the European Union (EU).

With an area of about 243 000 sq km (94 000 sq miles), the United Kingdom is just under 1 000 km (about 600 miles) from the south coast to the extreme north of Scotland and just under 500 km (around 300 miles) across at the widest point.

- Highest mountain: Ben Nevis, in the highlands of Scotland, at 1 343 m (4 406 ft)

- Longest river: the Severn, 354 km (220 miles) long, which rises in central Wales and flows through Shrewsbury, Worcester and Gloucester in England to the Bristol Channel

- Largest lake: Lough Neagh, Northern Ireland, at 396 sq km (153 sq miles)

- Deepest lake: Loch Morar in the Highlands of Scotland, 310 m (1 017 ft) deep

- Highest waterfall: Eas a'Chual Aluinn, from Glas Bheinn, in the highlands of Scotland, with a drop of 200 m (660 ft)

- Deepest cave: Ogof Ffynnon Ddu, Wales, at 308 m (1 010 ft) deep

- Most northerly point on the British mainland: Dunnet Head, north-east Scotland

- Most southerly point on the British mainland: Lizard Point, Cornwall

- Closest point to mainland continental Europe: Dover, Kent. The Channel Tunnel, which links England and France, is a little over 50 km (31 miles) long, of which nearly 38 km (24 miles) are actually under the Channel.

1.1 Area of the United Kingdom, 2000

	sq km		sq km
UNITED KINGDOM	242 910	Worcestershire County	1 761
GREAT BRITAIN	229 334	*Herefordshire and Worcestershire*	3 923
		Former county of Shropshire	3 487
ENGLAND AND WALES	151 201	*Former county of Staffordshire*	2 716
ENGLAND	130 422	**EAST**	19 120
NORTH EAST	8 592	Luton UA	43
		Peterborough UA	344
Darlington UA	197	Southend-on-Sea UA	42
Hartlepool UA	94	Thurrock UA	164
Middlesbrough UA	54		
Redcar and Cleveland UA	245	Bedfordshire County	1 192
Stockton-on-Tees UA	204	Cambridgeshire County	3 056
		Essex County	3 469
Durham County	2 232	Hertfordshire	1 639
Northumberland	5 026	Norfolk	5 372
Tyne and Wear (Met County)	540	Suffolk	3 798
Tees Valley	794	*Former county of Bedfordshire*	1 235
Tees Valley less Darlington	597	*Former county of Cambridgeshire*	3 400
Former county of Durham	2 429	*Former county of Essex*	3 675
NORTH WEST	14 165	**LONDON**	1 580
Blackburn with Darwen UA	137	Inner London	322
Blackpool UA	35	Outer London	1 258
Halton UA	74		
Warrington UA	176	**SOUTH EAST**	19 096
Cheshire County	2 081	Bracknell Forest UA	109
Cumbria	6 824	Brighton and Hove UA	82
Greater Manchester (Met County)	1 286	Isle of Wight UA	380
Lancashire County	2 897	Medway UA	192
Merseyside (Met County)	655	Milton Keynes UA	309
		Portsmouth UA	40
Former county of Cheshire	2 331	Reading UA	40
Former county of Lancashire	3 069	Slough UA	27
		Southampton UA	50
YORKSHIRE AND THE HUMBER	15 411	West Berkshire UA	704
		Windsor and Maidenhead UA	198
East Riding of Youkshire UA	2 415	Wokingham UA	179
Kingston upon Hull, City of UA	71		
North East Lincolnshire UA	192	Buckinghamshire County	1 568
North Lincolnshire UA	833	East Sussex County	1 713
York UA	271	Hampshire County	3 689
		Kent County	3 543
North Yorkshire County	8 038	Oxfordshire	2 606
South Yorkshire (Met County)	1 559	Surrey	1 677
West Yorkshire (Met County)	2 034	West Sussex	1 988
The Humber	3 511	*Former county of Berkshire*	1 257
Former county of North Yorkshire	8 309	*Former county of Buckinghamshire*	1 877
		Former county of East Sussex	1 795
EAST MIDLANDS	15 627	*Former county of Hampshire*	3 779
		Former county of Kent	3 735
Derby UA	78		
Leicester UA	73	**SOUTH WEST**	23 829
Nottingham UA	75		
Rutland UA	394	Bath and North East Somerset UA	351
		Bournemouth UA	46
Derbyshire County	2 551	Bristol, City of UA	110
Leicestershire County	2 084	North Somerset UA	373
Lincolnshire	5 921	Plymouth UA	80
Northamptonshire	2 367	Poole UA	65
Nottinghamshire County	2 085	South Gloucestershire UA	497
		Swindon UA	230
Former county of Derbyshire	2 629	Torbay UA	63
Former county of Leicestershire	2 551		
Former county of Nottinghamshire	2 160	Cornwall and the Isles of Scilly	3 559
		Devon County	6 562
WEST MIDLANDS	13 004	Dorset County	2 542
		Gloucestershire	2 653
Herefordshire, County of UA	2 162	Somerset	3 452
Stoke-on-Trent UA	93	Wiltshire County	3 246
Telford and Wrekin UA	290		
		Bristol/Bath area	1 331
Shropshire County	3 197	*Former county of Devon*	6 705
Staffordshire County	2 623	*Former county of Dorset*	2 653
Warwickshire	1 979	*Former county of Wiltshire*	3 476
West Midlands (Met County)	899		

1.1
continued

Area of the United Kingdom, 2000

	sq km		sq km
WALES	20 779	Dumfries and Galloway	6 439
Blaenau Gwent	109	Dundee City	65
Bridgend	251	East Ayrshire	1 252
Caerphilly	278	East Dunbartonshire	172
Cardiff	140	East Lothian	678
Carmarthenshire	2 395		
		East Renfrewshire	173
Ceredigion	1 795	Edinburgh, City of	262
Conwy	1 130	Eilean Siar (Western Isles)	3 134
Denbighshire	838	Falkirk	299
Flintshire	438	Fife	1 323
Gwynedd	2 548		
		Glasgow City	175
Isle of Anglesey	714	Highland	25 784
Merthyr Tydfil	111	Inverclyde	162
Monmouthshire	850	Midlothian	356
Neath Port Talbot	442	Moray	2 238
Newport	190		
Pembrokeshire	1 590	North Ayrshire	884
		North Lanarkshire	474
Powys	5 196	Orkney Islands	992
Rhondda, Cynon, Taff	424	Perth and Kinross	5 311
Swansea	378	Renfrewshire	261
Torfaen	126	Scottish Borders	4 734
The Vale of Glamorgan	331		
Wrexham	504	Shetland Islands	1 438
		South Ayrshire	1 202
		South Lanarkshire	1 771
SCOTLAND	78 133	Stirling	2 196
		West Dunbartonshire	162
Aberdeen City	186	West Lothian	425
Aberdeenshire	6 318		
Angus	2 181		
Argyll and Bute	6 930	**NORTHERN IRELAND**	13 576
Clackmannanshire	157		

Source: Office for National Statistics

2 Parliamentary elections

2.1 Parliamentary elections[1]

Thousands and percentages

	26 May 1955	8 Oct 1959	15 Oct 1964	31 Mar 1966	18 June 1970[1]	28 Feb 1974	10 Oct 1974	3 May 1979	9 June 1983	11 June 1987	9 April 1992	1 May 1997	7 June 2001
United Kingdom													
Electorate	34 852	35 397	35 894	35 957	39 615	40 256	40 256	41 573	42 704	43 666	43 719	43 846	44 403
Average-electors per seat	55.3	56.2	57.0	57.1	62.9	63.4	63.4	65.5	66.7	67.2	67.2	66.5	67.4
Valid votes counted	26 760	27 863	27 657	27 265	28 345	31 340	29 189	31 221	30 671	32 530	33 614	31 286	26 367
As percentage of electorate	76.8	78.7	77.1	75.8	71.5	77.9	72.5	75.1	71.8	74.5	76.7	71.4	59.4
England and Wales													
Electorate	30 591	31 109	31 610	31 695	34 931	35 509	35 509	36 695	37 708	38 568	38 648	38 719	39 228
Average-electors per seat	55.9	56.9	57.8	57.9	63.9	64.3	64.3	66.5	67.2	68.8	68.8	68.0	68.9
Valid votes counted	23 570	24 619	24 384	24 116	24 877	27 735	25 729	27 609	27 082	28 832	29 897	27 679	23 243
As percentage of electorate	77.0	79.1	77.1	76.1	71.2	78.1	72.5	75.2	71.8	74.8	77.5	71.5	59.3
Scotland													
Electorate	3 388	3 414	3 393	3 360	3 659	3 705	3 705	3 837	3 934	3 995	3 929	3 949	3 984
Average-electors per seat	47.7	48.1	47.8	47.3	51.5	52.2	52.2	54.0	54.6	55.5	54.6	54.8	55.3
Valid votes counted	2 543	2 668	2 635	2 553	2 688	2 887	2 758	2 917	2 825	2 968	2 931	2 817	2 313
As percentage of electorate	75.1	78.1	77.6	76.0	73.5	77.9	74.5	76.0	71.8	74.3	74.2	71.3	58.1
Northern Ireland													
Electorate	873	875	891	902	1 025	1 027	1 037	1 028	1 050	1 090	1 141	1 178	1 191
Average-electors per seat	72.8	72.9	74.2	75.2	85.4	85.6	86.4	85.6	61.8	64.1	67.1	65.4	66.2
Valid votes counted	647	576	638	596	779	718	702	696	765	730	785	791	810
As percentage of electorate	74.1	65.8	71.7	66.1	76.0	69.9	67.7	67.7	72.9	67.0	68.8	67.1	68.0
Members of Parliament elected: (Numbers)	630	630	630	630	630	635	635	635	650	650	651	659	659
Conservative	344	364	303	253	330	296	276	339	396	375	336	165	166
Labour	277	258	317	363	287	301	319	268	209	229	271	418	412
Liberal Democrat	6	6	9	12	6	14	13	11	17	17	20	46	52
Social Democratic Party	-	-	-	-	-	-	-	-	6	5	-	-	-
Scottish National Party	-	-	-	-	1	7	11	2	2	3	3	6	5
Plaid Cymru	-	-	-	-	-	2	3	2	2	3	4	4	4
Other[2]	3	2	1	2	6	15	13	13	18	18	17	20	20

1 The Representation of the People Act 1969 lowered the minimum voting age from 21 to 18 years with effect from 16 February 1970.
2 Including the Speaker.

Source: University of Plymouth for the Electoral Commission: 01752 233205

2.2 Parliamentary by-elections

	June 1987 - April 1992	General[1,2] Election June 1987	April 1992 - April 1997	General[1,2] Election April 1992	May 1997 - June 2001	General[1,2,3] Election May 1997
Numbers of by-elections	24		18		17	
Votes recorded						
By party (percentages)						
Conservative	23.8	33.7	21.4	40.1	27.0	25.1
Labour	38.9	41.1	39.5	36.2	29.7	40.1
Liberal Democrat[2]	19.1	18.6	24.6	16.4	22.1	14.4
Social Democratic Party[2]	3.2	-	-	-	-	-
Scottish National Party	4.8	1.8	5.2	3.1	6.0	4.1
Plaid Cymru	2.3	0.6	0.5	0.2	2.5	2.3
Other	7.9	4.2	8.8	4.1	12.7	14.1
Total votes recorded						
(percentages)	100.0	100.0	100.0	100.0	100.0	100.0
(thousands)	878	1 130	625	808	435	723

1 Votes recorded in the same seats in the previous General Election.
2 The Social Democratic Party was launched on 26 March 1981. An SDP candidate contested a parliamentary seat for the first time at a by-election at Warrington on 16 July 1981. In the 1987 General Election the Liberals and the SDP contested the election jointly as the Liberal/SDP Alliance. Subsequently the Alliance split into its constituent parties and the Liberals are now known as the Liberal Democrats. The SDP effectively ceased to exist when its two remaining MPs lost their seats at the 1992 General Election.

3 Proportions of 'other' votes inflated by the fact that votes were cast for the retiring Speaker as 'The Speaker seeking re-election' and not as a party candidate.

Source: University of Plymouth for the Electoral Commission: 01752 233205

3 International development

International development

Overseas development assistance
(Tables 3.1 and 3.2)

The UK development assistance programme is administered by the Department for International Development (DFID) to promote the economic development of recipient countries. It is managed within financial years, the money being voted annually by Parliament. Since 1992 the statistics relating to the programme are also published on a financial year basis and on a calendar year basis for both international aid comparisons and for national purposes such as the balance of payments.

Aid flows can be measured before (gross) or after (net) deduction of repayments of principal on past loans. These tables show only the gross figures.

Assistance is provided in two main ways: *bilateral*, that is directly to governments of recipient countries or to institutions in the United Kingdom for work on behalf of such countries, or *multilateral*, that is to international institutions for their economic development programmes. Table 3.1 shows the main groups of multilateral agencies, the International Development Association being the largest in the World Bank Group.

Bilateral assistance takes various forms:

Project aid is finance for investment schemes primarily designed to increase the physical capital of the recipient country, including contributions for local and recurrent costs.

Sector-wide programmes (typically in education, health or agriculture) comprise a combination of assistance including direct budgetary aid and technical co-operation.

Programme aid is financial assistance to fund imports, sector support programmes or budgetary expenditure, usually as part of a World Bank/IMF co-ordinated structural adjustment programme.

Technical co-operation is the provision of know-how in the form of personnel, training, research and associated costs.

Grants and other aid in kind are used to provide equipment and supplies, and support to the development work of UK and international voluntary organisations.

Humanitarian assistance comprises food aid and other disaster relief.

Aid and Trade Provision is a special allocation to soften the terms of credit to developing countries by mixing aid funds with private export credits.

The *Commonwealth Development Corporation* invests in productive public or private sector projects in developing countries.

Other Government Departments' expenditure covers debt relief, drug-related assistance and support to voluntary organisations.

Most of the expenditure not allocable by region in Table 3.2, is for assistance provided through organisations in the United Kingdom.

Fuller statistics of the UK's development assistance effort are published annually in *Statistics on International Development* (obtainable from Statistics Department, Abercrombie House, East Kilbride, Glasgow G75 8EA). International comparisons are available in the OECD Development Assistance Committee's annual report. The latest is *2001 Report: Development Co-operation* (available from The Stationery Office).

3.1 UK Gross public expenditure on aid (GPEX)

£ Thousands

		1992 /93	1993 /94	1994 /95	1995 /96	1996 /97	1997 /98	1998 /99	1999 /00	2000 /01
Bilateral Assistance										
DFID										
Project or Sector Aid	LUJS	122 834	119 832	121 812	121 456	106 361	96 448	118 870	176 213	181 336
Programme Aid	LUJW	136 771	121 027	113 510	83 494	96 299	84 784	133 574	140 374	251 597
Technical Co-operation Projects	LUOS	398 637	401 560	430 447	446 788	457 060	486 307	478 546	512 256	575 365
Grants & Other Aid in Kind	LUOT	155 889	171 688	149 556	184 315	191 152	173 354	188 444	168 820	177 382
Humanitarian Assistance	LUOU	142 813	179 601	205 368	141 410	121 886	94 680	126 058	226 200	179 607
Debt Relief	LUOV	20 099	23 698	28 144	27 337	23 529	23 161	25 659	23 140	21 188
Aid and Trade Provision	LUOW	93 071	84 700	59 987	71 988	61 978	60 710	56 898	37 790	27 645
CDC Investments	LUOX	223 301	183 354	215 295	279 986	189 082	249 062	166 716	269 052	194 194
Other Government Departments	LUOY	60 475	22 796	33 034	61 606	34 224	170 171	87 147	100 721	141 585
Total Bilateral Assistance	LUOZ	1 353 889	1 308 257	1 357 153	1 418 381	1 281 571	1 438 678	1 381 911	1 654 566	1 749 899
Multilateral Assistance										
European Community	LUPA	476 065	529 823	612 080	693 690	636 418	557 287	754 548	757 867	727 999
World Bank Group	LUPB	249 682	229 613	227 728	206 877	174 398	189 851	175 254	170 631	277 121
International Monetary Fund	LUPC	10 000	20 000	90 000	30 000	20 000	20 000	18 000	17 000	–
UN Agencies	LUPD	122 366	142 527	127 880	116 772	130 775	141 281	130 986	176 970	244 872
Regional Development Banks	LUPE	91 933	76 413	71 212	69 513	58 833	60 411	66 295	67 179	54 667
Other	LUPF	21 360	17 829	27 904	27 036	30 665	30 846	31 216	35 514	39 948
Total Multilateral Assistance	LUPG	971 406	1 016 205	1 156 804	1 143 887	1 051 089	999 676	1 176 299	1 225 161	1 344 608
Administrative Costs	LUPH	58 823	65 329	70 314	72 198	82 133	91 627	99 879	106 704	127 865
Total Gross Public Expenditure on Aid	LUPI	2 384 119	2 389 790	2 584 270	2 634 465	2 414 793	2 529 981	2 658 090	2 986 431	3 222 373

Source: Department for International Development: 01355 843612

3.2 Total bilateral gross public expenditure on aid (GPEX): by main recipient countries and regions

£ Thousands

		1992 /93	1993 /94	1994 /95	1995 /96	1996 /97	1997 /98	1998 /99	1999 /00	2000 /01
Main recipients										
India	LUPJ	116 108	102 367	98 622	154 730	111 789	113 919	110 315	107 262	128 816
States of Former Yugoslavia[1]	ZBXN	37 003	51 803	43 511	38 905	42 639	20 667	3 934	65 585	21 127
Uganda	LUPN	34 707	40 551	46 615	40 590	49 207	59 324	64 261	90 286	93 111
Tanzania	LUPK	62 457	32 499	31 633	29 900	56 414	51 436	78 085	75 099	110 597
Bangladesh	LUPM	64 934	56 068	57 441	54 282	44 329	39 078	67 361	71 794	76 920
Mozambique	LUPV	34 177	34 744	25 068	22 026	26 610	48 311	28 902	70 630	43 304
Indonesia	LUPZ	32 679	34 885	51 404	57 265	38 472	48 689	25 420	58 714	28 324
Ghana	LUPL	41 736	26 190	23 530	26 305	28 474	30 428	62 907	52 032	75 200
Malawi	LUPP	27 378	27 015	41 174	35 720	44 876	30 651	52 628	49 337	56 941
South Africa	LUPT	11 558	14 504	15 706	17 666	23 214	28 371	35 110	47 838	36 755
Zambia	LUPO	47 978	47 752	56 629	58 915	40 529	46 742	33 511	46 676	93 296
Bolivia	ZBXO	9 262	6 514	5 820	32 747	4 965	27 515	11 365	39 785	9 837
Dominican Republic	ZBXP	55	4 545	4	20 303	2 852	2 204	253	35 209	646
Kenya	LUPR	37 514	31 503	30 691	29 378	26 438	30 025	42 163	32 926	62 608
Sierra Leone	ZBXQ	6 483	4 003	8 345	8 963	10 841	3 293	9 153	30 044	35 142
Russian Federation	LUPW	11 795	20 749	32 753	30 884	32 205	33 617	30 887	27 728	26 114
China	LUPS	34 914	33 630	28 344	32 803	30 956	38 616	39 190	26 260	56 766
Pakistan	LUPY	35 063	48 197	63 487	60 234	59 365	32 703	27 654	23 477	16 342
Montserrat	LUPU	3 271	5 689	5 815	6 568	14 441	37 867	31 096	22 639	20 811
Zimbabwe	LUPX	44 268	41 390	35 394	20 191	21 007	13 715	29 394	17 363	14 716
Total Main Recipients	LUQD	693 340	664 598	701 986	778 375	709 623	737 171	783 589	990 684	1 007 373
Total Other Countries	LUQE	660 549	643 659	655 167	640 006	571 948	701 507	598 322	663 882	742 526
Regional Totals										
Africa	LUQF	526 833	457 991	475 626	437 146	445 153	450 324	575 036	634 760	778 369
America	LUQG	118 685	114 208	132 407	192 769	107 291	271 336	170 124	240 361	176 664
Asia	LUQH	424 574	410 387	415 812	465 945	401 402	391 681	350 756	381 654	417 763
Europe	LUQI	99 362	134 713	137 995	129 941	137 934	115 134	84 471	191 891	114 153
Pacific	LUQJ	28 715	14 935	16 291	14 053	12 458	26 890	20 251	7 248	4 631
World Unallocated[2]	LUQK	155 720	176 022	179 023	178 527	177 333	183 313	181 273	198 651	258 319
Total Bilateral GPEX	LUQL	1 353 889	1 308 257	1 357 153	1 418 381	1 281 571	1 438 678	1 381 911	1 654 566	1 749 899

1 The totals for the period prior to 1998/99 include amounts for the successor states of the Former Yugoslavia. The figures for 1999/00 and 2000/01 include humanitarian assistance to Kosovo.

2 World Unallocated comprises block grants to the British Council, VSO, CSOs, Research Institutions and Commonwealth Organisations based in the UK, and some ATP Technical Co-operation.

Source: Department for International Development: 01355 843612

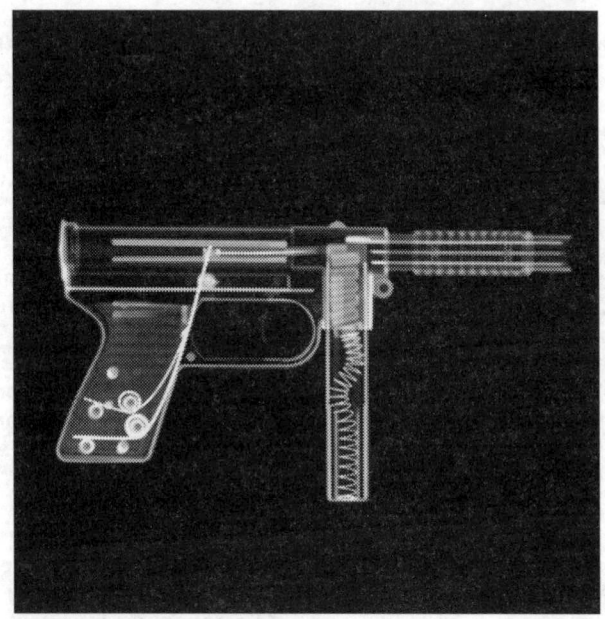

4 Defence

Defence

This section includes figures on Defence expenditure, on the size and role of the Armed Forces and on related support activities.

Much of the material in this section can be found in *UK Defence Statistics 2001 (The Stationery Office)*.

Formation of the armed forces *(Table 4.1)*
This table shows the number of units which comprise the "teeth" elements of the Armed Forces and excludes supporting units.

The aircraft and helicopters which comprise both the Joint Force Harrier squadrons and the Joint Helicopter Command squadrons are excluded.

The figures for the Royal Marines include two Artillery regiments and two Engineer regiments which are now also assigned to 3 Commando Brigade. The Infantry figures include two in role Parachute Battalions. One of the Infantry battalions are based in Great Britain as the Province Reserve Battalion. The Queen's Colour Squadron is part of the Field Squadrons, which since 1994 has had a war role.

Defence expenditure *(Table 4.2)*
The "estimate" figures for the latest year are derived from Supply Estimates. These figures and the outturn figures in the rest of the table are the latest agreed at the time of going to press.

The "Adjusted Defence Budget" takes account of major definitional changes in defence spending and of major transfers of responsibility to and from Government Departments. It therefore provides a more consistent and reliable guide to trends. This is the basis upon which defence spending figures are presented in the Ministry of Defence (MOD) Department Report, the Statement on the Defence Estimates and certain Treasury publications. It excludes the element of receipts from the sale of the Married Quarters Estate that were appropriated onto Defence Votes.

Service personnel *(Tables 4.3 to 4.6 and 4.10)*
The Regular Forces consist entirely of volunteer members serving on a whole-time basis.

Locally Entered Personnel are recruited outside the United Kingdom for whole-time service in special formations with special conditions of service and normally restricted locations. The Brigade of Gurkhas is an example.

The Regular Forces are supported by Reserves and Auxiliary Forces. There are both regular and volunteer Reserves. Regular Reserves consist of former Service personnel with a Reserve liability. Volunteer Reserves are open to both former Service personnel and civilians. The call out liabilities of the various reserve forces differ in accordance with their roles.

All three Services run cadet forces for young people and the Combined Cadet Force, which is found in certain schools where education is continued to the age of 17 or above, may operate sections for any or all of the Services.

Service manpower strengths *(Table 4.3)*
This table excludes reserve personnel mobilised for service in the former Yugoslavia.

Full-Time Reserve Service personnel represent reserves serving full-time in regular posts. This was made possible by the Reserve Forces Act 1996. None existed before 1998.

Royal Air Force (RAF) Full-Time Reserve Service figures comprise Full Commitment, Limited Commitment and Home Commitment.

Home Service battalions of the Royal Irish Regiment. Up until 1 July 1992, this was the Ulster Defence Regiment.

The figures for the Territorial Army include Officer Training Corps and non-regular permanent staff.

The figures for cadet forces for each service include the Combined Cadet Force. Naval Service figures include officers and civilian instructors. The Army and Royal Air Force figures exclude officers and civilian instructors.

Deployment of Service personnel *(Table 4.6)*
The figures for Service personnel in England, Wales, Scotland and Northern Ireland are obtained from a different source from that used to compile the United Kingdom total. Consequently the sum of the national figures can differ from the United Kingdom total. The figures for Northern Ireland include all personnel who are serving on emergency tours of duty but exclude the former Ulster Defence Regiment, now the Home Services element of the Royal Irish Regiment. The figures for overseas countries include service personnel who are on loan to countries in the areas shown. Royal Navy and Royal Marines personnel on board ship are included in the United Kingdom figure if the ship was in home waters on the situation date or otherwise against the appropriate overseas area. All Defence Attaches and Advisers and their staffs are included under "Other Locations" and not identified within specific areas.

Service married accommodation and Defence land holdings *(Table 4.7)*
Accommodation is provided for Service families in the United Kingdom and abroad, partly by building to approved standards and partly by renting accommodation. Permanent holdings in the United Kingdom include a small number of unfurnished hirings taken on from local authorities and the Scottish Special Housing Association which are not recorded separately.

The table also presents statistics of land and foreshore in the United Kingdom owned or leased by the Ministry of Defence or over which it has limited rights under grants or licences. Land declared as surplus to Defence requirements is also included.

Civilian personnel *(Table 4.8)*
This table gives an analysis of the number of civilians employed in the various management areas. The attribution of civilian staff can change according to

circumstances so that figures for successive years may not always be comparable. The figures include UK based civilians serving overseas. Other civilian staff are engaged overseas to work locally as circumstances demand.

Prior to April 1995 all part-timers were counted as half of full time. From that date they are counted as the number of hours worked as a proportion of normal conditioned hours. The average part timer works about 60% of full time.

The Centre includes all MOD Police. From 1991 it includes staff in the Meteorological Office (transferred from 'Air Force'), staff in the Chemical Defence Establishment (transferred from 'Procurement Executive'), and all personnel serving overseas in support of the services (other than in British Army on the Rhine (BAOR) or RAF Germany). Communications staff are excluded after 1993 and the Metrological staff after 1995. From 1996, those staff in the procurement executive are included in the Centre.

Prior to becoming Trading Funds the Defence Evaluation Agency and the Hydrographic Office were included in Procurement Executive.

As from 1 April 2000 a new top level budget was formed in the Centre called Defence Logistics Organisation, replacing the top level budgets CinC Fleet Support, Quarter Master General and RAF Logistics Command.

The Devonport and Rosyth Dockyards were contractorised with effect from 6 April 1987. The Atomic Weapons Establishment was contractorised with effect from 1 April 1992.

Health *(Tables 4.9 and 4.10)*
The Services operate a number of hospitals in this country and in areas abroad where there is a significant British military presence. These hospitals take as patients, members of all three Services and their dependants; in addition, the hospitals in the United Kingdom take civilian patients under arrangements agreed with the National Health Service. Medical support is also supplied by Service medical staff at individual units, ships and stations.

UK regular forces - deaths *(Table 4.10)*
No further data on health indicators are currently available as the data are under review. This table will be revised in future if more data becomes available.

Deaths includes deaths occurring on or off duty. Rates per thousand have been calculated by taking the number of episodes in each year and dividing by the average strength for the year.

Defence services and the civilian community *(Table 4.11)*
The Royal Navy Fishery Protection squadron operates within the British fishery limits under contract to the Department for Environment, Food and Rural Affairs. Boardings carried out by vessels of the Executive Environment and Rural Affairs Department and the Department of Agriculture for Northern Ireland are not included.

Search and rescue operations *(Table 4.12)*
This table covers incidents in which Rescue Coordinating Centres (RCCs) in the United Kingdom coordinated search and rescue (SAR) action in which elements of the Armed Forces were involved. The table also includes urgent medical incidents in which the Forces SAR facilities gave assistance (e.g. inter-hospital transfers). More than one element of the SAR services are called to the same incident. Consequently, the number of callouts is likely to be greater than the number of incidents.

Persons rescued refers to civilian or military personnel who were removed from a hazardous environment or were transported from the scene by SAR Units in order to receive urgent medical attention. People assisted by Mountain Rescue Teams, but subsequently transported from the scene by helicopter, are credited as having been rescued by the helicopter unit concerned. The total incidents figure also includes any HM Coastguard incidents under the control of ARCC Kinloss.

The Ministry of Defence helps the civil community in a variety of ways, for example by providing assistance in time of natural disasters or other emergencies and by undertaking community projects which are of training value to the Services. In some cases facilities established primarily for defence purposes also provide benefits to the general public.

Service assistance may be provided during an industrial dispute at the request of the civil ministries in order to maintain services essential to the life of the community (e.g. maintenance of emergency fire services).

4.1 Formation of the UK armed forces
As at 1 April

Numbers

		Front Line Units	1991	1992	1993	1994	1995	1996	1997	1998	1999	2000	2001
Royal Navy[1]													
Submarines	KCGA	Vessels	28	23	23	23	16	15	15	15	15	16	16
Carriers and assault ships	KCGB	Vessels	5	5	5	5	5	5	5	5	6	6	6
Cruisers, Destroyers and Frigates	KCGC	Vessels	48	44	40	37	35	36	35	35	35	32	32
Mine counter-measure	KCGE	Vessels	37	34	35	18	18	18	18	19	20	21	23
Patrol ships and craft	KCGF	Vessels	30	25	25	34	32	32	34	28	24	24	23
Fixed wing aircraft[2]	KCGG	Squadrons	3	3	3	3	3	3	3	3	3	1	1
Helicopters[3]	KCGH	Squadrons	17	17	17	17	15	15	15	12	12	9	9
Royal Marines	KCGI	Commandos	3	3	3	3	3	3	3	3	3	3	3
Regular Army													
Royal Armoured Corps[4,5]	KCGJ	Regiments	19	19	14	12	11	11	11	11	11	11	10
Royal Artillery[4]	KCGK	Regiments	22	21	18	16	16	16	16	15	15	15	15
Royal Engineers[6]	KCGL	Regiments	13	13	13	12	10	10	10	10	10	11	11
Infantry	KCGM	Battalions	55	55	48	45	41	41	40	40	40	40	46
Special Air Service	KCGN	Regiments	1	1	1	1	1	1	1	1	1	1	1
Army Air Corps[3]	KCGO	Regiments	4	5	6	6	5	5	5	5	5	–	–
Royal Air Force													
Strike/attack	KCGP	Squadrons	11	9	8	6	6	6	6	6	5	5	5
Offensive support[2]	KCGQ	Squadrons	5	5	5	5	5	5	5	5	5	2	2
Air defence	KCGR	Squadrons	11	9	7	6	6	6	6	6	5	5	5
Maritime patrol	KCGS	Squadrons	4	4	3	3	3	3	3	3	3	3	3
Reconnaissance	KCGT	Squadrons	5	5	5	5	5	5	5	5	5	5	5
Airborne early warning[7]	KCGU	Squadrons	1	1	1	1	1	2	2	2	2	2	2
Air transport and tankers and helicopters[2]	KCGV	Squadrons	15	16	16	15	14	14	13	14	14	8	9
Search and rescue	KCGX	Squadrons	2	2	2	2	2	2	2	2	2	2	2
Ground based air defence	KCGY	Squadrons	7	6	5	5	5	6	6	6	4	4	4
Field	KCGZ	Squadrons	5	5	5	5	5	5	5	5	5	5	6

1 Only active vessels are shown from 1995 onwards. All vessels are included before then.
2 From 2000 excludes aircraft transferred to the Joint Force Harrier squadron.
3 From 2000 excludes helicopters transferred to the Joint Helicopter command.
4 Figure for 1994 includes one training regiment.
5 From 2000 includes one Armoured Regiment which is committed to the new Joint Nuclear Biological and Chemical Regiment.
6 From 2000 includes an additional Close Support Regiment formed as a result of the Stategic Defence Review.
7 Figure for 2001 includes an embedded Operational Conversion Unit at the Sentry Operation Establishments.

Source: Ministry of Defence/DASA (Tri-Service): 020 7218 1546

4.2 UK Defence expenditure

£ millions

		1990 /91	1991 /92	1992 /93	1993 /94	1994 /95	1995 /96	1996 /97	1997 /98	1998 /99	1999 /00	2000[1] /01
Total expenditure at outturn prices *of which:*	KDAA	22 298	24 562	23 762	23 424	22 519	21 517	22 041	20 910	22 475	22 549	23 538
Expenditure on personnel	KDAB	8 811	9 934	10 504	9 835	9 313	8 524	8 633	8 259	8 553	8 509	8 754
of the Armed Forces	KDAC	4 811	5 499	5 634	6 907	6 490	6 150	6 223	5 938	6 286	6 257	6 500
of the retired Armed Forces[2]	KDAD	1 406	1 613	1 950	..	..	..	..	..	..	..	..
of civilian staff	KDAE	2 594	2 822	2 920	2 928	2 823	2 374	2 409	2 321	2 267	2 252	2 255
Expenditure on equipment[3]	KDAF	8 838	9 758	8 711	9 207	8 819	8 537	9 100	9 003	9 889	9 715	10 008
Sea systems	KDAG	2 955	3 142	2 891	2 589	2 441	2 110	2 190	2 142	2 319	..	..
Land systems	KDAH	1 927	2 157	1 846	1 806	1 642	1 576	1 806	1 658	1 665	..	..
Air systems	KDAI	3 197	3 574	3 152	3 246	3 184	3 356	3 507	3 843	4 572	..	..
Other	KDAJ	759	885	822	1 566	1 552	1 495	1 597	1 360	1 333	..	..
Other expenditure	KDAK	4 649	4 870	4 547	4 382	4 387	4 456	4 308	3 648	4 033	4 325	4 775
Works, buildings and land	KDAL	2 067	2 090	1 780	2 073	2 402	2 065	1 904	1 253	1 759	1 799	1 918
Miscellaneous stores and services[4]	KDAM	2 582	2 780	2 767	2 309	1 985	2 391	2 404	2 395	2 274	2 526	2 857
Adjusted defence budget at 2000/01 prices[5]	GPWI	29 652	30 743	27 910	27 008	26 405	24 478	24 628	23 161	23 419	22 973	23 538

1 Estimate.
2 Includes financial assistance to pre-1973 war widows.
3 The split between sea, land and air is no longer available, due to a change in accounting practice.
4 From 1995/96, military aid to overseas countries has been excluded from NATO definitions.
5 Adjusted to 2000/01 prices using the GDP deflator.

Source: Ministry of Defence/DASA (Procurement): 0117 913 4585

4.3 UK Defence: service manpower strengths
As at 1 April

Thousands

		1991	1992	1993	1994	1995	1996	1997	1998	1999	2000	2001
UK service personnel												
Full-time trained strength	ZBTR	281.6	278.3	267.1	248.4	226.3	211.6	197.4	194.0	191.1	190.5	188.8
Trained Naval Service	ZBTS	55.2	55.8	55.3	52.4	48.2	45.6	41.7	40.5	39.3	38.9	38.5
UK regulars	ZBTT	55.2	55.8	55.3	52.4	48.2	45.6	41.7	40.4	39.1	38.3	38.0
Full-time reserve service	ZBTU	..	..	..	..	..	..	..	0.1	0.3	0.3	0.5
Trained Army	ZBTV	143.7	140.5	132.9	121.8	108.7	103.6	101.5	100.9	99.9	100.4	100.2
UK regulars	ZBTW	136.5	133.4	126.5	116.1	104.5	99.5	97.8	97.5	96.3	96.5	96.3
Full-time reserve service	ZBTX	..	..	..	..	..	..	..	..	0.2	0.5	0.6
Gurkhas	ZBTY	7.2	7.2	6.5	5.6	4.2	4.0	3.8	3.4	3.4	3.4	3.4
Trained Royal Air Force	ZBTZ	82.7	82.0	78.9	74.2	69.4	62.5	54.2	52.7	51.9	51.2	50.1
UK regulars	ZBUA	82.7	82.0	78.9	74.2	69.4	62.5	54.2	52.7	51.8	51.0	49.8
Full-time reserve service	ZBUB	..	..	..	..	..	..	..	..	0.1	0.2	0.3
Untrained UK regulars	ZBUC	23.7	22.3	14.2	11.8	11.2	14.3	17.2	19.7	21.5	21.9	21.5
Naval Service	ZBUD	6.9	6.4	4.1	3.4	2.7	2.8	3.5	4.1	4.6	4.6	4.4
Army	ZBUE	11.1	12.0	8.1	6.9	7.2	9.3	11.1	12.4	13.4	13.6	13.2
Royal Air Force	ZBUF	5.7	4.0	2.0	1.5	1.3	2.2	2.7	3.2	3.5	3.7	3.9
Locally Entered Personnel (excluding Gurkhas)	ZBUG	1.4	1.3	1.3	1.2	0.6	0.6	0.4	0.4	0.4	0.4	0.3
Royal Irish Regiment Home Service batallions	ZBUH	6.1	6.0	5.6	5.4	5.3	5.0	4.8	4.6	4.4	4.2	3.8
Reserve personnel	ZBUI	340.8	341.0	334.2	334.1	329.6	327.3	323.6	318.6	306.4	293.7	288.4
Regular Reserves	ZBUJ	258.7	260.8	258.3	262.2	264.1	264.6	259.5	254.7	247.5	241.3	234.7
Naval Services	ZBUK	28.5	27.5	22.0	23.3	23.3	23.9	24.1	24.8	24.7	24.2	23.5
Army	ZBUL	187.7	188.6	190.1	192.5	195.3	195.5	190.1	186.0	180.4	175.2	169.5
Royal Air Force	ZBUM	42.5	44.8	46.1	46.4	45.5	45.2	45.4	43.9	42.4	41.9	41.6
Volunteer Reserves	ZBUN	82.1	80.2	75.9*	71.9	65.5	62.7	64.1	63.9	58.9	52.4	53.7
Royal Naval Reserve and Royal Marine Reserve[1]	ZBUO	7.0	7.0	5.6	4.6	3.7	3.5	4.3	4.4	4.5	4.8	4.8
Territorial Army	ZBUP	73.3	71.3	68.5	65.0	59.7	57.3	57.6	57.0	51.8	44.8	46.3
Royal Auxilliary Air Force	ZBUQ	1.8	1.8	1.8	2.3	2.1	1.9	2.2	2.5	2.6	2.7	2.6
Cadet Forces	ZBUR	134.7	137.2	135.9	135.7	133.9	134.7	133.1	132.0	132.9	136.4	142.1
Naval Service	ZBUS	27.0	28.8	27.1	26.7	26.5	26.9	26.3	25.9	24.5	24.1	23.8
Army	ZBUT	64.6	64.8	65.1	65.2	63.7	65.4	65.1	64.9	65.7	68.5	66.4
Royal Air Force	ZBUU	43.1	43.6	43.7	43.8	43.7	42.4	41.8	41.2	42.7	43.7	51.9

1 Figures before 1997 do not include University Royal Navy Units.

Source: Ministry of Defence/DASA (Tri-Service): 020 7218 4535

4.4 Intake of UK regular forces from civilian life: by service

Numbers

		1990 /91	1991 /92	1992 /93	1993 /94	1994 /95	1995 /96	1996 /97	1997 /98	1998 /99	1999 /00	2000 /01
All services:												
Male	KCJB	26 782	24 357	13 067	10 616	11 154	15 495	19 121	20 169	22 545	22 374	20 363
Female	KCJC	4 428	3 550	1 750	1 333	1 853	2 175	3 038	3 336	3 431	3 159	2 606
Total	KCJA	31 210	27 907	14 817	11 949	13 007	17 670	22 165	23 505	25 976	25 533	22 969
Naval service:												
Male	KCJE	5 712	5 570	1 888	1 272	961	2 007	3 397	3 966	4 106	4 250	3 990
Female	KCJF	1 199	1 013	384	250	340	353	562	634	661	703	633
Total	KCJD	6 911	6 583	2 272	1 532	1 301	2 360	3 959	4 600	4 767	4 953	4 623
Army:												
Male	KCJJ	15 955	15 544	10 289	8 764	9 491	11 510	13 480	13 374	14 988	14 740	13 396
Female	KCJK	1 547	1 594	1 098	812	1 193	1 376	2 042	2 005	1 975	1 743	1 318
Total	KCJI	17 502	17 138	11 387	9 576	10 684	12 886	15 522	15 379	16 963	16 483	14 714
Royal Air Force:												
Male	KCJM	5 122	3 243	890	580	702	1 978	2 250	2 829	3 451	3 384	2 977
Female	KCJN	1 675	943	268	261	320	446	434	697	795	713	655
Total	KCJL	6 797	4 186	1 158	841	1 022	2 424	2 684	3 526	4 246	4 097	3 632

Source: Ministry of Defence/DASA (Tri-Service): 020 7218 1546

4.5 Outflow of UK regular forces: by service[1]

Numbers

		1990 /91	1991 /92	1992 /93	1993 /94	1994 /95	1995 /96	1996 /97	1997 /98	1998 /99	1999 /00	2000 /01
All Services:												
Male	KDNA	36 017	30 057	31 138	29 699	31 046	25 746	29 325	21 775	24 459	23 767	22 415
Female	KDNB	3 062	2 748	2 517	2 429	2 994	3 118	3 675	2 483	2 976	2 739	2 419
Total	KDNC	39 079	32 805	33 655	32 128	34 040	28 864	33 000	24 258	27 435	26 506	24 834
Naval Service:												
Male	KDND	7 428	6 105	4 655	4 613	5 504	4 314	6 191	4 650	4 925	5 164	4 460
Female	KDNE	680	662	455	493	681	631	940	621	606	632	550
Total	KDNF	8 108	6 767	5 110	5 106	6 185	4 945	7 131	5 271	5 531	5 796	5 010
Army:												
Male	KDNI	21 582	18 304	20 993	19 633	20 234	13 935	13 758	13 103	15 282	14 520	13 816
Female	KDNJ	1 242	1 147	1 336	1 288	1 651	1 508	1 596	1 275	1 733	1 570	1 326
Total	KDNK	22 824	19 451	22 329	20 921	21 885	15 443	15 354	14 378	17 015	16 090	15 142
Royal Air Force:												
Male	KDNL	7 007	5 648	5 490	5 453	5 308	7 497	9 376	4 022	4 252	4 083	4 139
Female	KDNM	1 140	939	726	648	662	979	1 139	587	637	537	543
Total	KDNN	8 147	6 587	6 216	6 101	5 970	8 476	10 515	4 609	4 889	4 620	4 682

1 Comprises all those who left the Regular Forces and includes deaths.

Source: Ministry of Defence/DASA (Tri-Service): 020 7218 1546

4.6 Deployment of UK service personnel[1]
As at 1 July

Thousands

		1990	1991	1992	1993	1994	1995	1996	1997	1998	1999	2000
UK Service personnel, Regular Forces:												
In United Kingdom	KDOB	215.9	207.9	210.7	204.3	192.1	182.2	177.4	171.6	173.4	171.7	170.3
England[2]	KDOC	179.6	173.3	174.2	167.1	156.5	149.4	146.6	142.6	144.6	144.3	143.0
Wales[2]	KDOD	5.3	5.2	5.2	5.1	4.8	5.2	4.3	3.3	3.2	3.3	3.2
Scotland[2]	KDOE	19.3	18.2	18.8	19.4	18.4	16.9	15.5	13.9	14.2	14.9	15.1
Northern Ireland	KDOF	11.5	11.2	12.6	12.5	12.3	9.9	10.5	11.5	11.0	9.0	8.4
Overseas	KDOG	88.9	89.3	78.9	65.5	56.2	50.0	48.5	42.6	43.1	47.1	43.0
Germany[3,4,5]	KDOH	63.2	69.7	60.0	45.6	37.2	33.4	20.8	21.2	20.3	18.0	19.5
Elsewhere in Continental Europe[4,5]	KDOI	6.8	–	–	–	–	–	11.7	6.2	6.9	15.2	8.2
Gibraltar	KDOJ	1.8	1.0	1.0	1.3	1.5	0.6	0.6	0.5	0.5	0.6	0.6
Cyprus	KDOL	4.8	5.2	4.8	4.7	4.1	4.4	4.0	3.9	3.6	3.6	3.5
Mediterranean, Near East and Gulf	KDOM	1.3	1.1	2.2	2.8	2.4	0.6	0.5	0.3	1.2	1.3	1.1
Hong Kong	KDON	2.1	2.3	2.1	1.9	1.7	0.9	0.9	–	–	–	–
Elsewhere in the Far East	KDOP	0.5	0.5	2.1	0.3	0.3	0.3	0.3	1.5	0.3	0.3	1.0
Other locations[2,6]	KDOQ	8.4	9.5	6.7	8.8	8.9	9.4	9.8	9.0	10.4	8.2	9.1
Total	KDOA	303.1	297.2	289.6	270.9	248.3	232.2	225.9	214.2	216.5	218.8	213.2
Locally entered service personnel:[7]												
United Kingdom	KDOS	1.4	1.4	1.3	1.4	1.5	1.8	1.7	2.1	2.1	2.0	2.1
Gibraltar	KDOT	0.1	0.1	0.2	0.2	0.2	0.2	0.2	0.2	0.4	0.4	0.3
Hong Kong	KDOV	5.5	5.5	5.2	4.4	3.7	1.8	1.6	0.7	–	–	–
Brunei	KDOW	0.9	0.8	0.8	0.8	0.7	0.9	0.7	1.0	0.9	0.8	0.8
India/Nepal	KDOX	1.1	1.3	1.3	1.2	0.2	0.5	0.7	0.9	0.5	0.5	0.5
Total	KDOK	8.9	9.1	8.8	7.9	7.1	5.1	4.9	4.7	4.0	3.7	3.7

1 Figures may not add to totals because of rounding.
2 Up to 1992 the England, Wales and Scotland national figures include personnel who were UK based but temporarily deployed in the South Atlantic. These have also been included in the Overseas numbers against 'Other locations'.
3 Prior to 1994, personnel serving in Northern Ireland on emergency tours of duty but remaining under the command of the Commander-in-Chief, British Army of the Rhine, are included in these numbers. Personnel serving on emergency tours of duty in other overseas areas are included in the numbers for that area.

4 These figures include personnel stationed in Berlin and Sardinia.
5 From 1991-1995, figures for the Federal Republic of Germany and elsewhere in Continental Europe were combined.
6 These figures include Defence Attaches/Advisers and their staffs.
7 Including Gurkhas.

Source: Ministry of Defence/DASA (Tri-Service): 020 7218 1546

4.7 Family accommodation and defence land holdings
As at 1 April

			1991	1992	1993	1994	1995	1996	1997	1998	1999	2000	2001
Married accommodation													
United Kingdom: total	KDPA	Thousands	73.6	72.3	71.8	71.1	69.7	72.1	68.6	67.3	65.5	64.8	59.2
Land holdings		Thousand											
United Kingdom		hectares											
Land[1]	KDPF	"	224.8	225.4	224.1	223.5	221.0	222.6	221.0	220.0	220.2	219.9	222.1
Foreshore[1]	KDPH	"	18.0	18.0	18.4	18.5	18.4	18.5	18.6	18.6	18.6	18.6	20.8
Rights held	KDPJ	"	121.3	120.7	100.2	100.4	122.3	124.3	124.5	124.5	124.8	124.8	124.8
Defence land													
Used for agricultural purposes	KDPL	"	109.9	109.3	107.1	107.6	107.9	107.4	96.2	103.5	114.5	92.2	98.6
Used for grazing only	KDPM	"	63.9	62.6	62.4	61.3	61.8	60.7	51.9	59.6	65.5	50.3	66.6
Full agricultural use	KDPN	"	46.0	46.7	44.6	46.3	46.1	46.7	44.3	43.9	49.0	41.9	32.0

1 Freehold and leasehold.

Source: Ministry of Defence/DASA (Tri-Service): 020 7218 1546

4.8 UK Defence civilian manpower strengths[1,2]
As at 1 April

Thousands: Full-time Equivalent

		1991	1992	1993	1994	1995	1996	1997	1998	1999	2000	2001
Ministry of Defence civilians												
Centre												
Non-industrial	KDQE	21.8	22.9	23.7	18.9	17.3	20.0	21.2	20.6	20.0	18.1	17.7
Industrial	KDQF	0.7	0.8	0.8	0.8	0.7	0.9	1.1	1.1	1.0	0.9	0.9
Defence Logistics Organisation												
Non-industrial	ZBTJ	..	..	..	..	..	..	..	..	..	19.0	17.0
Industrial	ZBTK	..	..	..	..	..	..	..	..	..	11.3	8.2
Naval Service												
Non-industrial	KYCW	14.9	14.9	15.5	15.8	15.2	13.7	12.6	12.2	11.6	3.6	3.5
Industrial	KYCX	15.8	15.2	14.1	13.0	12.0	9.7	9.0	8.0	6.8	2.7	2.6
Army												
Non-industrial	KDQK	21.4	21.2	22.0	22.5	22.1	21.4	20.7	20.5	20.3	15.4	15.5
Industrial	KDQL	17.0	17.0	15.1	14.9	14.5	13.7	13.2	11.8	10.3	5.7	5.6
Royal Air Force												
Non-industrial	KDQM	10.2	10.7	10.3	10.3	10.1	9.9	10.0	10.1	10.6	5.6	5.6
Industrial	KDQN	7.7	7.7	7.2	7.0	6.7	6.5	6.4	6.1	7.1	3.4	3.3
Procurement Executive												
Non-industrial	KDQO	22.0	21.0	16.4	15.3	15.1	–	–	–	–	–	–
Industrial	KDQP	8.6	8.1	4.1	3.1	2.5	–	–	–	–	–	–
Total UK based	KDQB	140.2	139.5	129.2	121.6	116.1	109.9	109.2	104.0	100.9	100.3	80.0
Non-industrial	KDQC	90.3	90.7	87.9	82.8	79.8	77.1	77.9	75.7	74.5	75.2	59.4
Industrial	KDQD	49.9	48.8	41.3	38.8	36.3	32.7	31.3	28.3	26.4	25.1	20.6
Locally engaged overseas	KDQA	28.9	27.0	26.6	20.7	16.9	16.9	15.7	15.0	14.8	14.7	13.3
Non-industrial	KDQT	9.9	9.7	9.6	7.3	6.4	7.1	7.0	6.7	6.7	6.7	7.0
Industrial	KDQU	19.1	17.3	17.0	13.4	10.5	9.8	8.7	8.2	8.0	8.0	6.3
Total	KFHT	169.1	166.5	155.8	142.3	133.0	126.8	124.9	119.0	115.7	114.7	93.3
Trading funds[3]	GQHI	..	..	..	..	..	14.0	15.1	13.6	13.0	14.2	18.4
Non-industrial	KYCU	..	..	..	..	..	12.1	13.4	12.3	11.9	13.1	..
Industrial	KYCV	..	..	..	..	..	1.9	1.7	1.3	1.1	1.1	..

1 Individuals on temporary and geographic (T&G) promotion are classed as non- industrial.
2 The figures refer to personnel above the line.
3 The split between industrial and non-industrial is no longer available.

Source: Ministry of Defence/DASA (Civilian): 020 7218 6019

4.9 Strength of uniformed UK medical staff[1]
As at 1 April

Numbers

		1991	1992	1993	1994	1995	1996	1997	1998	1999	2000	2001
Qualified doctors:												
Naval Service	KDMA	267	263	270	268	262	238	211	209	209	211	215
Army	KDMB	649	530	522	490	473	431	434	431	437	452	422
Royal Air Force	KDMC	371	375	368	359	334	273	223	207	197	185	183
All Services	KDMD	1 287	1 168	1 160	1 117	1 069	942	868	847	843	848	820
Qualified dentists:												
Naval Services	KDME	77	75	76	75	73	62	65	64	65	60	56
Army	KDMF	194	183	178	168	154	145	139	140	141	144	132
Royal Air Force	KDMG	120	121	119	115	110	104	87	80	85	78	69
All Services	KDMH	391	379	373	358	337	311	291	284	291	282	257
Support staff:[2,3]												
Naval Services	KDMI	1 254	1 308	1 361	1 401	1 352	1 294	1 025	946	935	963	998
Nursing services	ZBTL	..	..	..	..	..	..	..	..	299	282	268
Support	ZBTM	..	..	..	..	..	..	..	..	636	681	730
Army	KDMJ	4 941	4 297	4 288	3 761	3 381	3 284	3 017	3 094	3 002	2 991	3 037
Nursing services	ZBTN	..	..	..	..	..	..	..	..	667	658	658
Support	ZBTO	..	..	..	..	..	..	..	..	2 335	2 333	2 379
Royal Air Force	KDMK	1 974	1 948	2 038	1 837	1 795	1 404	1 213	1 194	1 225	1 286	1 335
Nursing services	ZBTP	..	..	..	..	..	..	..	..	296	334	336
Support	ZBTQ	..	..	..	..	..	..	..	..	929	952	999
All Services	KDML	8 169	7 553	7 687	6 999	6 245	5 982	5 255	5 234	5 162	5 240	5 370

1 Includes staff employed at units (including ships) and in hospitals.
2 Includes all members of the Nursing Services/Nursing Corps.

3 From 1999, figures for support staff have been split so that nurses are separate from other support staff.

Source: Ministry of Defence/DASA (Tri- Service): 020 7218 1546

4.10 UK regular forces - deaths

		1975	1980	1985	1990	1994	1995	1996	1997	1998	1999	2000
Deaths												
Total Number	LUIC	422	370	319	320	219	207	146	165	165	143	153
Male	LUID	414	367	314	314	212	198	144	156	157	140	149
Female	LUIE	8	3	5	6	7	9	2	9	8	3	4
Rates per thousand												
Tri-service	LUIF	1.24	1.11	0.96	1.03	0.87	0.88	0.65	0.79	0.78	0.68	0.73
Navy	LUIG	0.81	1.07	0.81	0.80	0.66	0.61	0.54	0.86	0.60	0.58	0.58
Army[1]	LUIH	1.45	1.16	0.90	1.10	1.06	0.99	0.77	0.87	0.91	0.76	0.85
RAF	LUII	1.21	1.05	1.18	1.06	0.65	0.82	0.48	0.47	0.66	0.50	0.60

1 Includes Gurkhas, except for 1975.

Source: Ministry of Defence/DASA (Medical Statistics): 01225 472963

4.11 UK Defence services and the civilian community

		1990	1991	1992	1993	1994	1995	1996	1997	1998	1999	2000
Military aid to civil ministries during industrial disputes												
Service personnel deployed (man weeks)	KCMN	–	–	–	–	–	1 827	256	389	1 394	–	–
Fishery protection												
Vessels boarded	KCMO	1 992	2 284	2 465	2 540	2 080	1 878	2 224	1 758	1 829	1 777	1 658

Source: Ministry of Defence/DASA (Tri-Service): 020 7218 1546

4.12 Search and rescue operations at home

Numbers

		1991	1992	1993	1994	1995	1996	1997	1998	1999	2000
Call outs	**GPYC**	2 058	2 306	2 145	2 024	2 300	2 164	1 942	1 898	1 915	1 940
of Royal Navy helicopters	**GPXO**	465	544	606	560	667	512	495	463	499	499
of Royal Air Force helicopters	**GPXP**	1 333	1 475	1 260	1 215	1 393	1 392	1 258	1 257	1 238	1 278
of Contractorised and other helicopters	**GPXQ**	74	92	47	26	24	27	16	20	–	–
of Royal Air Force Nimrod aircraft	**GPXR**	83	64	73	74	78	69	79	71	65	71
of other fixed wing aircraft[1]	**GPXS**	6	1	2	3	6	1	2	1	–	–
of HM ships and auxilliary vessels[1]	**KCMG**	5	5	8	6	7	1	4	4	–	–
of Royal Air Force mountain rescue teams	**KCMH**	92	125	149	140	125	162	88	82	113	92
Persons rescued: total	**KCMI**	1 564	1 432	1 508	1 391	1 448	1 598	1 259	1 245	1 163	1 297
By rescue service											
Royal Navy helicopters	**GPXT**	330	318	406	369	426	371	358	285	343	348
Royal Air Force helicopters	**GPXU**	1 072	1 015	952	893	958	1 116	878	937	800	925
Royal Air Force mountain rescue teams	**GPXV**	36	23	97	49	44	101	16	12	20	24
Other	**GPXW**	126	76	53	80	20	10	7	11	–	–
By type of rescue											
Rescue	**GPXX**	433	365	479	464	275	307	219	317	302	272
Medrescue	**GPXY**	841	794	764	766	828	919	711	667	621	703
Medivac	**GPXZ**	183	193	194	123	220	275	224	209	201	236
Recovery	**GPYA**	21	29	32	25	44	38	54	43	31	29
Other	**GPYB**	86	51	39	13	81	59	51	9	8	57
Search and rescue incidents: total	**KCMM**	1 765	1 976	1 856	1 775	2 011	1 900	1 738	1 687	1 707	1 779

1 Not permanently on stand-by.

Source: Ministry of Defence/DASA (Logistics): 01225 4687699

5 Population and vital statistics

Population and vital statistics

This section begins with a summary of population figures for the United Kingdom and constituent countries for 1851 to 2026 and for Great Britain from 1801 (Table 5.1). Table 5.2 analyses the components of population change. Table 5.3 gives details of the national sex and age structures for years up to the present date, with projected figures up to the year 2021. Legal marital condition of the population is shown in Table 5.4. The distribution of population at regional and local levels is summarised in Table 5.5.

In the main, historical series relate to census information, while mid-year estimates, which make allowance for under-enumeration in the census, are given for the recent past and the present (from 1961 onwards).

Population *(Tables 5.1 - 5.3)*
Figures shown in these tables relate to the population enumerated at successive censuses, (up to 1951), mid-year estimates (from 1961 to 2000) and population projections (up to 2026).

Definition of resident population
The estimated population of an area includes all those usually resident in the area, whatever their nationality. HM Forces serving abroad are excluded from, but non-UK Armed Forces stationed here are included within the estimates of resident population. Students are taken to be resident at their term-time addresses.

The current series of estimates are updated annually. Starting with estimates derived from results of the 1991 Census of Population, allowance is made for subsequent births, deaths, migration, aging of the population and for estimated underenumeration in the 1991 Census.

Table 5.4 shows the population estimates by marital status. The 1991 figures for England and Wales have been rebased using 1991 Census results. Rebased population estimates by marital status for England and Wales for 1991-1995 were published in an ONS First Release in October 1997 and are available from the Population Estimates Unit.

Projected resident population of the United Kingdom and constituent countries *(Tables 5.1 - 5.3)*
These projections are prepared by the Government Actuary, in consultation with the Registrars General, as a common framework for use in national planning in a number of different fields. New projections are made every second year on assumptions regarding future fertility, mortality and migration which seem most appropriate on the basis of the statistical evidence available at the time. The population projections in Tables 5.1 - 5.3 are based on the estimates of the population of the United Kingdom at mid-2000 made by the Registrars General.

Geographical distribution of the population *(Table 5.5)*
The population enumerated in the censuses for 1911-1951 and the mid-year population estimates for later years, are provided for standard regions of the United Kingdom, for metropolitan areas, for broad groupings of local authority districts by type within England and

Wales, and for some of the larger cities. Projections of future sub-national population levels are prepared from time to time by the Registrar General, but are not shown in this publication.

Migration into and out of the United Kingdom *(Tables 5.7 and 5.8)*
A migrant into the United Kingdom is defined as a person who has resided abroad for a year or more and on entering has declared the intention to reside here for a year or more; and vice versa for a migrant from the United Kingdom. The estimates shown are derived from the International Passenger Survey (IPS), a sample survey covering the principal air and sea routes between the United Kingdom and overseas but excluding routes to and from the Irish Republic. Migration between the Channel Islands and the Isle of Man and the rest of the world has been excluded from these tables from 1988. It is also highly likely that the data exclude asylum seekers and persons admitted as short-term visitors who are subsequently granted an extension of stay for a year or more for other reasons, for example as students or on the basis of marriage. After taking account of persons leaving the United Kingdom for a short-term period who stay overseas for periods longer than originally intended, adjustment is needed to net migration ranges from about 10 thousand in 1981 to 96 thousand in 2000, an average of approximately 34 thousand. The overall net inflow for 2000, including migration with the Irish Republic, is about 183 thousand.

Acceptances for settlement in the United Kingdom *(Table 5.9)*
This table presents in geographic regions, the statistics of individual nationalities, arranged alphabetically within each region. The figures are on a different basis from those derived from IPS (Tables 5.6 and 5.7) and relate only to people subject to immigration control. Persons accepted for settlement are allowed to stay indefinitely in the United Kingdom. They exclude temporary migrants such as students and generally relate only to non-EEA nationals. Settlement can occur several years after entry to the country.

Applications received for asylum in the United Kingdom excluding dependants *(Table 5.10)*
This table shows statistics of applications for asylum in the United Kingdom. Figures are shown of the main applicant nationalities by geographic region. The basis of assessing asylum applications, and hence of deciding whether to grant asylum in the United Kingdom, is the 1951 United Nations Convention on Refugees.

Marriages *(Table 5.11)*
The figures in this table relate to marriages solemnised in the constituent countries of the UK. They take no account of the growing trend towards marrying abroad.

Divorces *(Tables 5.12 and 5.13)*
A marriage may be either *dissolved* following a petition for divorce and the granting of a decree absolute, or *annulled*, following a petition for nullity and the awarding of a decree of nullity. The first group of decrees are known as dissolutions of marriage and the second as annulments of marriage. In Table 5.12 the term 'divorce' includes *both* types of decrees, although strictly speaking, it should refer only to dissolutions.

Births *(Tables 5.14, 5.15 and 5.16)*
For Scotland and Northern Ireland the number of births relate to those registered during the year. For England and Wales the figures up to and including 1930-32 are for those registered while later figures relate to births occurring in each year.

All data for England and Wales and for Scotland include births occurring in those countries to mothers not usually resident in them. Data for Northern Ireland, and hence UK, prior to 1981 include births occurring in Northern Ireland to non-resident mothers; from 1981, such births are excluded.

Deaths *(Tables 5.18 and 5.19)*
The figures relate to the number of deaths registered during each calendar year. However, from 1993 onwards, the figures for England and Wales represent occurrences. This change has little effect on annual totals.

Cause of death (Table 5.19)
Changes in coding practices for England and Wales, particularly coding of underlying cause of death, from January 1993 have led to some differences in the pattern of cause of death (eg. pneumonia) as compared with previous years. These changes result in a return to the rules in place prior to 1984 and bring England and Wales back into line with Scotland, Northern Ireland, and other countries. For further details, see the Introduction to *Mortality Statistics:* cause 1993 (revised) and 1994, Series DH2, no. 21, HMSO (1996).

In Scotland, causes of death have been coded using the latest, tenth, revision of the International Statistical Classification of Diseases and Related Health Problems (ICD-10) since 1 January 2000. All cause of death information for 2000 presented in this table is based on the revised classification. To assist users to assess any discontinuities arising from the introduction of the revised classification, a bridge-coding exercise was carried out on all deaths registered in 1999 and data for that year are presented in the table on both ICD9 and ICD-10 bases. For further information about ICD-10 and the results of the bridge-coding carried out by the General Register Office for Scotland, consult their Annual Report for 2000 or log on to their website at: www.gro-scotland.gov.uk.

ICD-10 was implemented into mortality coding in England and Wales and in Northern Ireland on 1 January 2001. Similar bridge-coding exercises are being undertaken.

Infant and maternal mortality *(Table 5.20)*
On 1 October 1992 the legal definition of a stillbirth was altered from baby born dead after 28 completed weeks gestation or more, to one born after 24 completed weeks of gestation or more. The 258 stillbirths of 24 to 27 weeks gestation which occurred between 1 October and 31 December 1992 are excluded from this table.

Life tables *(Table 5.22)*
The interim life tables are constructed from the estimated populations in 1998-2000 and the deaths occurring in those years for England and Wales and registered in those years for Scotland and Northern Ireland.

Adoptions *(Tables 5.23 and 5.24)*
These tables are included in this volume for the first time. The figures relate to the date the adoption was entered in the Adopted Children Register. Figures based on the date of court order are available for England and Wales from the volume *Marriage, divorce and adoption statistics 1999* (no. 27 in the FM2 series) available on the National Statistics website *www.statistics.gov.uk* or from the enquiry point in the ONS shown at the foot of the tables.

Population and vital statistics

5.1 Population summary

Thousands

	United Kingdom			England and Wales			Wales	Scotland			Northern Ireland		
	Persons	Males	Females	Persons	Males	Females	Persons	Persons	Males	Females	Persons	Males	Females
Enumerated population: census figures													
1801	..	..	..	8 893	4 255	4 638	587	1 608	739	869	..	..	..
1851	22 259	10 855	11 404	17 928	8 781	9 146	1 163	2 889	1 376	1 513	1 442	698	745
1901	38 237	18 492	19 745	32 528	15 729	16 799	2 013	4 472	2 174	2 298	1 237	590	647
1911	42 082	20 357	21 725	36 070	17 446	18 625	2 421	4 761	2 309	2 452	1 251	603	648
1921[1]	44 027	21 033	22 994	37 887	18 075	19 811	2 656	4 882	2 348	2 535	1 258	610	648
1931[1]	46 038	22 060	23 978	39 952	19 133	20 819	2 593	4 843	2 326	2 517	1 243	601	642
1951	50 225	24 118	26 107	43 758	21 016	22 742	2 599	5 096	2 434	2 662	1 371	668	703
1961	52 709	25 481	27 228	46 105	22 304	23 801	2 644	5 179	2 483	2 697	1 425	694	731
Resident population: mid-year estimates													
	DYAY	BBAB	BBAC	BBAD	BBAE	BBAF	KGJM	BBAG	BBAH	BBAI	BBAJ	BBAK	BBAL
1965	54 350	26 368	27 982	47 671	23 151	24 521	2 693	5 210	2 501	2 709	1 468	716	752
1966	54 643	26 511	28 132	47 967	23 296	24 671	2 702	5 201	2 496	2 704	1 476	719	757
1967	54 959	26 673	28 286	48 272	23 451	24 821	2 710	5 198	2 496	2 702	1 489	726	763
1968	55 214	26 784	28 429	48 511	23 554	24 957	2 715	5 200	2 498	2 702	1 503	733	770
1969	55 461	26 908	28 553	48 738	23 666	25 072	2 722	5 209	2 503	2 706	1 514	739	776
1970	55 632	26 992	28 641	48 891	23 738	25 153	2 729	5 214	2 507	2 707	1 527	747	781
1971	55 928	27 167	28 761	49 152	23 897	25 255	2 740	5 236	2 516	2 720	1 540	755	786
1972	56 097	27 259	28 837	49 327	23 989	25 339	2 755	5 231	2 513	2 717	1 539	758	782
1973	56 223	27 332	28 891	49 459	24 061	25 399	2 773	5 234	2 515	2 719	1 530	756	774
1974	56 236	27 349	28 887	49 468	24 075	25 393	2 785	5 241	2 519	2 722	1 527	755	772
1975	56 226	27 361	28 865	49 470	24 091	25 378	2 795	5 232	2 516	2 716	1 524	753	770
1976	56 216	27 360	28 856	49 459	24 089	25 370	2 799	5 233	2 517	2 716	1 524	754	770
1977	56 190	27 345	28 845	49 440	24 076	25 364	2 801	5 226	2 515	2 711	1 523	754	769
1978	56 178	27 330	28 849	49 443	24 067	25 375	2 804	5 212	2 509	2 704	1 523	754	770
1979	56 240	27 373	28 867	49 508	24 113	25 395	2 810	5 204	2 505	2 699	1 528	755	773
1980	56 330	27 411	28 919	49 603	24 156	25 448	2 816	5 194	2 501	2 693	1 533	755	778
1981	56 357	27 412	28 946	49 634	24 160	25 474	2 813	5 180	2 495	2 685	1 543	757	786
1982	56 325	27 394	28 931	49 613	24 148	25 466	2 806	5 167	2 490	2 677	1 545	757	788
1983	56 384	27 433	28 952	49 681	24 190	25 491	2 807	5 153	2 484	2 669	1 551	759	792
1984	56 513	27 513	29 000	49 810	24 270	25 540	2 806	5 146	2 482	2 664	1 557	761	796
1985	56 693	27 613	29 080	49 990	24 369	25 621	2 810	5 137	2 479	2 658	1 565	765	800
1986	56 859	27 698	29 160	50 162	24 456	25 706	2 820	5 123	2 474	2 649	1 574	768	805
1987	57 015	27 789	29 227	50 321	24 546	25 775	2 833	5 113	2 470	2 643	1 582	773	809
1988	57 166	27 875	29 290	50 487	24 641	25 846	2 854	5 093	2 461	2 632	1 585	774	812
1989	57 365	27 988	29 377	50 678	24 750	25 928	2 869	5 097	2 463	2 634	1 590	776	814
1990	57 567	28 116	29 452	50 869	24 872	25 998	2 878	5 102	2 466	2 636	1 596	778	818
1991	57 814	28 248	29 566	51 100	24 995	26 104	2 891	5 107	2 470	2 637	1 607	783	824
1992	58 013	28 365	29 648	51 277	25.099	26 178	2 899	5 111	2 473	2 638	1 625	793	831
1993	58 198	28 477	29 720	51 439	25 198	26 241	2 906	5 120	2 479	2 642	1 638	801	838
1994	58 401	28 595	29 805	51 621	25 304	26 317	2 913	5 132	2 486	2 646	1 648	805	842
1995	58 612	28 731	29 881	51 820	25 433	26 387	2 917	5 137	2 489	2 647	1 655	809	846
1996	58 807	28 860	29 948	52 010	25 557	26 453	2 921	5 128	2 486	2 642	1 669	816	853
1997	59 014	28 992	30 022	52 211	25 684	26 527	2 927	5 123	2 484	2 638	1 680	823	857
1998	59 237	29 128	30 108	52 428	25 817	26 611	2 933	5 120	2 484	2 636	1 689	827	861
1999	59 501	29 299	30 202	52 690	25 985	26 705	2 937	5 119	2 486	2 634	1 692	829	863
2000	59 756	29 459	30 297	52 943	26 142	26 801	2 946	5 115	2 485	2 630	1 698	832	866
Resident population: projections (mid-year)[2]													
2001	59 987	29 605	30 382	53 174	26 286	26 888	2 949	5 109	2 484	2 625	1 705	836	869
2006	60 946	30 209	30 738	54 136	26 878	27 259	2 971	5 078	2 478	2 600	1 732	853	880
2011	61 956	30 807	31 149	55 151	27 469	27 682	3 000	5 047	2 470	2 576	1 759	868	890
2021	64 105	31 953	32 151	57 329	28 621	28 707	3 067	4 973	2 439	2 534	1 803	893	910
2026	64 992	32 384	32 608	58 267	29 078	29 188	3 088	4 911	2 407	2 504	1 814	899	915

1 Figures for Northern Ireland are estimated. The population at the Census of 1926 was 1 257 thousand (608 thousand males and 649 thousand females).
2 These projections are 2000-based. See chapter text for more detail.

Sources: Office for National Statistics: 01329 813233;
General Register Office for Scotland;
General Register Office (Northern Ireland);
Government Actuary's Department: 020 7211 2622

5.2 Population changes

| | Population[1] at start of period | Average annual change | | | | |
		Overall annual change	Births	Deaths[2]	Excess of births over deaths	Net migration and other adjustments[3]
United Kingdom						
1901 - 1911	38 237	385	1 091	624	467	-82
1911 - 1921	42 082	195	975	689	286	-92
1921 - 1931	44 027	201	824	555	268	-67
1931 - 1951	46 038	213	793	603	190	22
1951 - 1961	50 225	258	839	593	246	12
1961 - 1971	52 807	312	962	638	324	-12
1971 - 1981	55 928	42	736	666	69	-27
1981 - 1991	56 357	146	757	655	103	43
1991 - 2000	57 814	216	738	636	102	114
2000 - 2001[4]	59 987	192	676	627	50	143
2001 - 2011	60 372	201	680	614	66	135
2011 - 2021	62 382	211	704	628	76	135
England and Wales						
1901 - 1911	32 528	354	929	525	404	-50
1911 - 1921	36 070	182	828	584	244	-62
1921 - 1931	37 887	207	693	469	224	-17
1931 - 1951	39 952	193	673	518	155	38
1951 - 1961	43 758	244	714	516	197	47
1961 - 1971	46 196	296	832	560	272	23
1971 - 1981	49 152	48	638	585	53	-5
1981 - 1991	49 634	147	664	576	89	58
1991 - 2000	51 100	205	653	560	93	112
2000 - 2001[4]	53 174	193	603	553	50	143
2001 - 2011	53 560	202	608	541	66	136
2011 - 2021	55 580	215	633	554	80	136
Scotland						
1901 - 1911	4 472	29	131	76	54	-25
1911 - 1921	4 761	12	118	82	36	-24
1921 - 1931	4 882	-4	100	65	35	-39
1931 - 1951	4 843	13	92	67	25	-12
1951 - 1961	5 096	9	95	62	34	-25
1961 - 1971	5 184	5	97	63	34	-30
1971 - 1981	5 236	-6	70	64	6	-11
1981 - 1991	5 180	-7	66	63	3	-10
1991 - 2000	5 107	1	60	61	0	1
2000 - 2001[4]	5 109	-6	52	58	-6	0
2001 - 2011	5 096	-6	51	57	-6	0
2011 - 2021	5 034	-8	50	58	-8	0
Northern Ireland						
1901 - 1911	1 237	1	31	23	8	-6
1911 - 1921	1 251	1	29	22	7	-6
1921 - 1931	1 258	-2	30	21	9	-11
1931 - 1951	1 243	6	28	18	10	-4
1951 - 1961	1 371	6	30	15	15	-9
1961 - 1971	1 427	11	33	16	17	-6
1971 - 1981	1 540	0	28	17	11	-11
1981 - 1991	1 543	6	27	16	12	-5
1991 - 2000	1 607	10	24	15	9	1
2000 - 2001[4]	1 705	6	21	15	6	-1
2001 - 2011	1 716	5	21	15	6	-1
2011 - 2021	1 769	4	21	16	5	-1

1 Census enumerated population up to 1951; mid-year estimates of resident population from 1961 to 2000 and mid-2000-based projections of resident population thereafter.

2 Including deaths of non-civilians and merchant seamen who died outside the country. These numbered 577 000 in 1911-1921 and 240 000 in 1931-1951 for England and Wales; 74 000 in 1911-1921 and 34 000 in 1931-1951 for Scotland; and 10 000 in 1911-1926 for Northern Ireland.

3 Changes in census visitor balance, in Armed Forces, asylum seekers, etc.

4 The population at the beginning of the period is the mid-year estimate for 2000.

Sources: Government Actuary's Department: 020 7211 2622;
Office for National Statistics: 01329 813233;
General Register Office for Scotland;
General Register Office (Northern Ireland)

5.3 Age distribution of the resident population

Thousands

		United Kingdom													
		Population enumerated in Census			Estimated mid-year resident population					Projected mid-year resident population[1]					
		1901	1931	1951	1961	1971	1981	1991	2000	2001	2006	2011	2016	2021	2026
Persons: All ages	KGUA	38 237	46 038	50 225	52 807	55 928	56 357	57 814	59 756	59 987	60 946	61 956	63 038	64 105	64 992
Under 1	KGUK	938	712	773	4 274[3]	899	730	794	686	671	672	682	699	706	692
1 - 4	KABA	3 443	2 818	3 553	..	3 654	2 726	3 094	2 890	2 852	2 694	2 701	2 763	2 819	2 803
5 - 9	KGUN	4 106	3 897	3 689	3 819	4 684	3 677	3 674	3 863	3 788	3 532	3 376	3 393	3 472	3 535
10 - 14	KGUO	3 934	3 746	3 310	4 267	4 232	4 470	3 501	3 885	3 929	3 808	3 552	3 397	3 413	3 493
15 - 19	KGUP	3 826	3 989	3 175	3 748	3 862	4 735	3 739	3 683	3 727	3 995	3 874	3 619	3 463	3 480
20 - 29	KABB	6 982	7 865	7 154	6 570	7 968	8 113	9 298	7 717	7 614	7 701	8 232	8 377	8 003	7 596
30 - 44	KABC	7 493	9 717	11 125	10 529	9 797	10 956	12 221	13 751	13 912	13 701	12 714	12 161	12 511	12 921
45 - 59	KABD	4 639	7 979	9 558	10 605	10 202	9 540	9 500	11 083	11 262	12 009	12 763	13 668	13 461	12 518
60 - 64	KGUY	1 067	1 897	2 422	2 788	3 222	2 935	2 888	2 884	2 863	3 247	3 829	3 530	4 004	4 569
65 - 74	KBCP	1 278	2 461	3 689	3 977	4 764	5 195	5 067	4 917	4 917	4 996	5 484	6 397	6 649	6 878
75 - 84	KBCU	470	844	1 555	1 885	2 159	2 677	3 139	3 237	3 277	3 363	3 405	3 586	4 027	4 761
85 and over	KGVD	61	–	13 185	–	9 123	–	24 118	1 162	1 175	1 226	1 344	1 448	1 576	1 745
School ages (5-15)	KBWU	–	–	7 649	..	9 704	9 086	7 855	8 501	8 480	8 148	7 662	7 471	7 568	7 720
Under 18	KGUD	–	–	13 248	..	15 798	14 472	13 185	13 534	13 492	13 101	12 578	12 358	12 471	12 601
Pensionable ages [2]	KFIA	2 387	4 421	6 828	7 747	9 123	10 035	10 602	10 789	10 830	11 239	11 948	12 079	12 251	13 385
Males: All ages	KGWA	18 492	22 060	24 118	25 528	27 167	27 412	28 248	29 459	29 605	30 209	30 807	31 404	31 953	32 384
Under 1	KGWK	471	361	397	2 194[3]	461	374	407	351	344	344	349	358	361	355
1 - 4	KBCV	1 719	1 423	1 818	..	1 874	1 400	1 588	1 481	1 461	1 380	1 383	1 415	1 444	1 436
5 - 9	KGWN	2 052	1 967	1 885	1 956	2 401	1 889	1 888	1 979	1 941	1 808	1 728	1 736	1 777	1 809
10 - 14	KGWO	1 972	1 892	1 681	2 185	2 175	2 295	1 800	1 994	2 015	1 951	1 818	1 737	1 746	1 787
15 - 19	KGWP	1 898	1 987	1 564	1 897	1 976	2 424	1 925	1 894	1 916	2 047	1 983	1 850	1 770	1 779
20 - 29	KBCW	3 293	3 818	3 509	3 288	4 024	4 103	4 738	3 962	3 909	3 933	4 188	4 254	4 059	3 848
30 - 44	KBCX	3 597	4 495	5 461	5 237	4 938	5 513	6 141	6 994	7 089	7 022	6 523	6 220	6 370	6 561
45 - 59	KBUU	2 215	3 753	4 493	5 137	4 970	4 711	4 732	5 519	5 608	5 994	6 415	6 924	6 858	6 386
60 - 64	KGWY	490	894	1 061	1 250	1 507	1 376	1 390	1 411	1 401	1 594	1 879	1 733	1 981	2 286
65 - 74	KBWL	565	1 099	1 560	1 605	1 999	2 264	2 272	2 287	2 296	2 375	2 628	3 074	3 192	3 322
75 - 84	KBWM	196	335	617	675	716	922	1 152	1 273	1 302	1 394	1 470	1 589	1 808	2 147
85 and over	KGXD	23	36	70	105	126	141	215	315	322	367	442	512	587	669
School ages (5-15)	KBWV	–	–	3 895	..	4 982	4 666	4 038	4 360	4 349	4 173	3 921	3 822	3 873	3 950
Under 18	KGWD	–	–	6 753	..	8 108	7 430	6 776	6 942	6 918	6 710	6 439	6 325	6 382	6 449
Pensionable ages [2]	KFIB	785	1 471	2 247	2 385	2 841	3 327	3 639	3 875	3 920	4 136	4 541	5 175	5 587	6 138
Females: All ages	KGYA	19 745	23 978	26 107	27 279	28 761	28 946	29 566	30 297	30 382	30 738	31 149	31 634	32 151	32 608
Under 1	KGYK	466	351	376	2 079[3]	437	356	387	334	327	328	333	341	344	338
1 - 4	KBWN	1 724	1 397	1 735	..	1 779	1 327	1 505	1 409	1 391	1 315	1 318	1 348	1 375	1 368
5 - 9	KGYN	2 054	1 930	1 804	1 863	2 283	1 788	1 786	1 883	1 846	1 724	1 649	1 656	1 695	1 726
10 - 14	KGYO	1 962	1 854	1 629	2 083	2 057	2 175	1 701	1 891	1 914	1 857	1 735	1 659	1 667	1 706
15 - 19	KGYP	1 928	2 002	1 611	1 851	1 887	2 311	1 815	1 789	1 811	1 948	1 891	1 769	1 693	1 701
20 - 29	KBWO	3 690	4 047	3 644	3 282	3 945	4 009	4 560	3 755	3 705	3 769	4 044	4 123	3 945	3 748
30 - 44	KBWP	3 895	5 222	5 663	5 292	4 859	5 442	6 080	6 757	6 824	6 679	6 190	5 941	6 141	6 360
45 - 59	KBWR	2 424	4 226	5 065	5 467	5 231	4 829	4 769	5 564	5 654	6 015	6 348	6 744	6 603	6 133
60 - 64	KGYY	577	1 003	1 361	1 539	1 715	1 559	1 498	1 473	1 461	1 654	1 950	1 796	2 023	2 283
65 - 74	KBWS	713	1 361	2 127	2 372	2 765	2 931	2 795	2 630	2 621	2 621	2 856	3 324	3 457	3 556
75 - 84	KBWT	274	509	937	1 210	1 443	1 756	1 987	1 964	1 975	1 969	1 935	1 996	2 218	2 614
85 and over	KGZD	38	77	154	241	359	462	683	847	852	860	902	936	989	1 076
School ages (5-15)	KBWW	–	–	3 753	..	4 722	4 421	3 817	4 141	4 131	3 975	3 740	3 648	3 696	3 769
Under 18	KGYD	–	–	6 495	..	7 690	7 042	6 409	6 592	6 574	6 391	6 138	6 033	6 088	6 152
Pensionable ages [2]	KFIC	1 601	2 950	4 580	5 362	6 282	6 708	6 963	6 914	6 910	7 103	7 407	6 904	6 664	7 246

5.3 Age distribution of the resident population
continued

		England							Wales					
		Estimated mid-year resident population			Projected population[1]				Estimated mid-year resident population			Projected population[1]		
		1981	1991	2000	2001	2011	2026		1981	1991	2000	2001	2011	2026
Persons: All ages	KCCI	46 821	48 208	49 997	50 225	52 151	55 178	KERY	2 813	2 891	2 946	2 949	3 000	3 088
Under 1	KCCJ	598	663	578	566	579	596	KFAC	36	39	31	31	32	31
1 - 4	KCCK	2 235	2 574	2 422	2 394	2 289	2 404	KFBX	136	154	137	135	127	129
5 - 9	KCCL	3 011	3 035	3 225	3 165	2 853	3 015	KFCA	185	187	187	183	160	169
10 - 14	KCCM	3 666	2 880	3 226	3 270	2 983	2 967	KFCB	222	178	198	199	172	171
15 - 19	KCCN	3 897	3 083	3 043	3 084	3 241	2 951	KFCC	233	188	190	192	190	171
20 - 29	KCEG	6 734	7 790	6 466	6 385	6 929	6 490	KFCD	381	422	351	345	396	345
30 - 44	KCEH	9 175	10 231	11 558	11 707	10 779	11 029	KFCE	536	587	623	628	556	589
45 - 59	KCEQ	7 948	7 920	9 280	9 433	10 709	10 620	KFCF	485	486	567	573	612	569
60 - 64	KCEW	2 449	2 399	2 398	2 379	3 213	3 856	KFCG	158	154	153	153	203	217
65 - 74	KCGD	4 347	4 222	4 088	4 089	4 584	5 754	KFCH	272	284	268	266	295	353
75 - 84	KCJG	2 249	2 645	2 719	2 750	2 850	4 020	KFCI	139	165	179	183	182	252
85 and over	KCKJ	511	763	993	1 004	1 142	1 478	KFCK	29	47	61	62	74	93
School ages (5-15)	KCWX	7 451	6 473	7 075	7 066	6 450	6 568	KFCL	453	399	425	421	368	374
Under 18	KCWY	11 871	10 899	11 280	11 258	10 602	10 743	KFCM	721	665	668	663	602	601
Pensionable ages [2]	KEAA	8 403	8 870	9 021	9 053	10 013	11 252	KFEB	525	576	586	588	642	698
Males: All ages	KEAB	22 795	23 588	24 697	24 838	25 984	27 547	KFEI	1 365	1 407	1 445	1 448	1 484	1 532
Under 1	KEAC	306	340	296	290	296	305	KFEJ	18	20	16	16	16	16
1 - 4	KEAD	1 147	1 322	1 241	1 226	1 172	1 231	KFEK	70	79	70	69	65	66
5 - 9	KEAE	1 547	1 561	1 654	1 623	1 459	1 543	KFEL	95	96	96	93	82	86
10 - 14	KEAF	1 883	1 482	1 656	1 677	1 525	1 517	KFFA	113	92	102	102	88	87
15 - 19	KECA	1 996	1 588	1 569	1 588	1 660	1 508	KFFN	119	97	96	98	97	87
20 - 29	KECB	3 404	3 974	3 320	3 279	3 522	3 281	KFHA	193	214	182	179	203	177
30 - 44	KECC	4 623	5 148	5 899	5 987	5 546	5 606	KFHB	270	294	314	317	284	297
45 - 59	KECD	3 938	3 957	4 630	4 706	5 403	5 436	KFHW	240	242	282	285	305	288
60 - 64	KECE	1 154	1 159	1 178	1 169	1 580	1 940	KFQO	73	74	75	75	100	108
65 - 74	KECF	1 902	1 900	1 911	1 918	2 205	2 791	KFQV	118	128	125	125	142	170
75 - 84	KECG	777	975	1 074	1 098	1 238	1 820	KFUK	48	60	71	73	79	114
85 and over	KECH	119	183	270	277	377	569	KFUL	7	11	16	17	24	36
School ages (5-15)	KECI	3 827	3 330	3 630	3 624	3 299	3 360	KFUV	232	206	217	216	188	191
Under 18	KECJ	6 096	5 604	5 787	5 774	5 426	5 496	KFVE	370	342	342	340	308	308
Pensionable ages[2]	KECK	2 798	3 058	3 256	3 293	3 821	5 181	KFVF	173	199	212	214	245	319
Females: All ages	KEJV	24 026	24 620	25 300	25 387	26 167	27 632	KFVL	1 448	1 484	1 501	1 501	1 515	1 557
Under 1	KEJW	292	324	282	276	282	291	KFYW	18	19	15	15	16	15
1 - 4	KEJX	1 088	1 253	1 181	1 168	1 117	1 173	KFZJ	66	75	67	66	62	63
5 - 9	KEKP	1 464	1 474	1 571	1 542	1 393	1 472	KGCK	90	91	92	89	78	82
10 - 14	KEKQ	1 783	1 399	1 570	1 593	1 457	1 450	KGCM	109	86	96	97	84	83
15 - 19	KEKR	1 901	1 495	1 475	1 496	1 581	1 443	KGCN	114	91	94	94	93	84
20 - 29	KEKS	3 330	3 816	3 146	3 106	3 407	3 209	KGCO	189	208	169	167	194	169
30 - 44	KENR	4 553	5 083	5 658	5 720	5 233	5 424	KGCP	265	294	309	311	272	292
45 - 59	KEOQ	4 009	3 964	4 651	4 727	5 306	5 183	KGGZ	246	244	285	289	307	281
60 - 64	KEOZ	1 295	1 239	1 221	1 210	1 633	1 916	KGIY	85	80	77	78	103	110
65 - 74	KEQJ	2 445	2 323	2 177	2 170	2 379	2 963	KGKR	154	156	143	142	153	183
75 - 84	KEQK	1 472	1 670	1 644	1 651	1 612	2 199	KGTQ	91	105	109	110	103	138
85 and over	KEQL	392	580	723	728	765	909	KGTZ	22	36	45	45	49	57
School ages (5-15)	KEQM	3 625	3 143	3 445	3 442	3 150	3 209	KGVG	221	194	207	205	179	182
Under 18	KEQN	5 775	5 295	5 492	5 484	5 176	5 247	KGVH	351	323	326	324	294	293
Pensionable ages[2]	KEQO	5 605	5 812	5 765	5 760	6 193	6 071	KGVK	352	377	374	374	397	378

5.3 Age distribution of the resident population

continued

Thousands

| | | Scotland | | | | | | | Northern Ireland | | | | | |
| | | Estimated mid-year resident population | | | Projected population[1] | | | | Estimated mid-year resident population | | | Projected population[1] | | |
		1981	1991	2000	2001	2011	2026		1981	1991	2000	2001	2011	2026
Persons: All ages	KGVP	5 180	5 107	5 115	5 109	5 047	4 911	KIOY	1 543	1 607	1 698	1 705	1 759	1 814
Under 1	KHAQ	69	66	54	52	50	46	KIOZ	27	26	22	22	21	19
1 - 4	KHCT	249	259	234	229	201	190	KIPA	106	106	96	95	84	81
5 - 9	KHDN	348	321	322	315	256	246	KIPN	133	131	128	125	108	105
10 - 14	KHDQ	433	313	326	326	280	248	KIPP	148	129	135	135	118	107
15 - 19	KHDT	459	340	322	323	318	254	KIPQ	146	128	127	128	124	105
20 - 29	KHDU	771	834	663	649	663	555	KIPR	227	253	238	234	244	205
30 - 44	KHDV	971	1 088	1 195	1 199	1 011	941	KIPS	273	315	374	379	367	361
45 - 59	KHFK	880	853	952	967	1 100	970	KIPT	227	241	283	289	342	360
60 - 64	KHOZ	260	265	259	257	320	374	KIPU	68	70	73	74	93	122
65 - 74	KHTU	460	441	440	440	461	584	KIPV	116	120	122	122	144	187
75 - 84	KHUO	232	259	264	268	289	370	KIPW	57	69	75	77	84	119
85 and over	KHUQ	49	69	84	84	98	132	KIPX	14	19	24	24	30	42
School ages (5-15)	KHVV	871	698	712	706	594	544	KIPY	311	285	289	287	250	233
Under 18	KIMT	1 377	1 153	1 126	1 114	969	880	KIQL	504	467	460	456	405	377
Pensionable ages [2]	KIMU	882	910	924	927	993	1 086	KIQM	224	246	259	262	300	390
Males: All ages	KIMV	2 495	2 470	2 485	2 484	2 470	2 407	KIQN	757	783	832	836	868	899
Under 1	KIMW	35	34	28	27	26	24	KIQO	14	13	12	11	11	10
1 - 4	KIMX	128	133	120	118	103	97	KIQP	54	54	49	49	43	41
5 - 9	KIMY	178	164	165	161	131	126	KIQQ	69	67	65	64	55	54
10 - 14	KIMZ	222	161	167	167	144	128	KIQR	76	66	69	69	60	55
15 - 19	KINA	234	174	164	164	163	130	KIQS	75	66	65	66	64	54
20 - 29	KINB	390	423	337	331	337	284	KIQT	117	127	123	121	126	106
30 - 44	KINC	483	543	595	597	508	474	KIQU	137	156	184	187	185	184
45 - 59	KIND	424	415	467	475	540	482	KIQV	109	118	140	142	167	179
60 - 64	KINE	118	124	123	122	154	180	KIQW	32	32	35	36	45	58
65 - 74	KINR	194	192	197	197	213	273	KIRJ	50	53	54	55	68	88
75 - 84	KINS	77	91	99	102	119	160	KIRK	21	26	29	30	35	52
85 and over	KINT	11	16	22	22	31	49	KIRL	4	5	6	7	9	16
School ages (5-15)	KINU	446	358	364	362	305	280	KIRM	160	146	148	147	128	120
Under 18	KINV	706	591	576	571	498	452	KIRN	259	239	236	234	208	193
Pensionable ages[2]	KINW	282	299	318	322	363	482	KIRO	75	83	89	91	112	156
Females: All ages	KINX	2 685	2 637	2 630	2 625	2 576	2 504	KIRP	786	824	866	869	890	915
Under 1	KINY	33	32	26	26	24	23	KIRQ	13	13	11	10	10	10
1 - 4	KINZ	121	126	114	111	98	93	KIRR	52	52	47	46	41	39
5 - 9	KIOA	170	157	158	154	124	120	KIRS	65	64	63	61	53	51
10 - 14	KIOB	211	153	159	159	136	121	KIRT	72	63	66	66	57	52
15 - 19	KIOC	225	166	158	158	156	123	KIRU	70	62	62	62	60	51
20 - 29	KIOO	381	411	325	318	326	272	KISH	110	126	115	113	118	99
30 - 44	KIOP	488	545	600	601	503	467	KISI	137	159	190	192	182	177
45 - 59	KIOQ	456	437	485	492	559	488	KISJ	118	123	143	146	175	180
60 - 64	KIOR	142	141	137	135	166	194	KISK	37	38	38	38	48	63
65 - 74	KIOS	265	249	243	242	247	311	KISL	66	67	68	67	76	99
75 - 84	KIOT	155	168	165	166	170	210	KISM	37	44	46	47	50	67
85 and over	KIOU	38	53	61	62	66	84	KISN	10	14	18	18	21	27
School ages (5-15)	KIOV	424	340	348	345	289	264	KISO	151	139	141	140	122	114
Under 18	KIOW	671	562	550	544	471	428	KISP	245	228	224	222	198	184
Pensionable ages[2]	KIOX	600	611	606	605	630	604	KISQ	150	163	170	171	188	234

1 2000-based projections are made as described in the introductory note on page 24.
2 The pensionable age population is that over state retirement age. The 2011 figures take account of planned changes in retirement age from 65 for men and 60 for women at present to 65 for both sexes. This change will be phased in between April 2010 and March 2020.
3 This is for ages 0 - 4.

Sources: Office for National Statistics: 01329 813233; General Register Office for Scotland; General Register Office (Northern Ireland); Government Actuary's Department: 020 7211 2622

5.4 Marital condition (de jure): estimated population

Thousands

| | | United Kingdom[1] | | | | | | | | England and Wales | | | | | | |
| | | Males | | | | Females | | | | Males | | | | Females | | |
		1971	1981	1991[2]		1971	1981	1991[2]		1971	1981	1991		1971	1981	1991
All ages:																
Single	KQCA	12 120	12 168	12 874	KQDP	11 131	10 860	11 231	KRPL	10 507	10 614	11 320	KUBS	9 584	9 424	9 829
Married	KQCB	14 067	13 791	13 237	KQDQ	14 130	13 856	13 364	KRPM	12 522	12 238	11 745	KVCC	12 566	12 284	11 838
Widowed	KQCC	779	793	828	KQDR	3 178	3 331	3 370	KRPN	682	698	731	KVCD	2 810	2 939	2 978
Divorced	KQCD	201	657	1 306	KQDS	321	897	1 598	KRPO	187	611	1 200	KVCE	296	828	1 459
Age groups:																
0 - 14: Single	KQCE	6 912	5 956	5 683	KQDT	6 557	5 646	5 378	KRPP	5 984	5 181	4 991	KVCF	5 672	4 910	4 720
15 - 19: Single	KQCF	1 936	2 400	1 916	KQDU	1 726	2 203	1 778	KRPQ	1 677	2 095	1 677	KVCG	1 491	1 923	1 554
Married	KQCG	39	24	9	KQDV	160	107	36	KRPR	34	20	8	KVCH	142	93	32
Widowed	KQCH	–	–	–	KQDW	–	–	–	KRPS	–	–	–	KVCI	–	–	–
Divorced	KQCI	–	–	–	KQDX	–	–	–	KRPT	–	–	–	KVCJ	–	–	–
20 - 24: Single	KQCJ	1 376	1 618	2 004	KQDY	857	1 150	1 616	KRPU	1 211	1 420	1 764	KVCK	745	1 007	1 421
Married	KQCK	781	542	285	KQDZ	1 251	930	558	KRPV	689	466	249	KVCL	1 113	811	490
Widowed	KQCL	–	1	–	KQYZ	2	2	1	KRPW	–	1	–	KVCM	2	2	1
Divorced	KQCM	3	11	13	KQZA	10	30	32	KRPX	3	10	12	KVCN	9	27	29
25 - 34: Single	KQCN	722	1 020	1 925	KQZB	379	563	1 280	KRPY	637	906	1 718	KVCO	326	496	1 135
Married	KQCO	2 762	2 847	2 393	KQZC	2 980	3 160	2 831	KRPZ	2 450	2 508	2 100	KVCP	2 635	2 791	2 488
Widowed	KQCP	4	5	3	KQZD	14	16	9	KRQA	4	4	2	KVCQ	12	13	8
Divorced	KQCQ	41	163	270	KQZE	68	236	345	KRQB	38	151	245	KVCR	63	218	312
35 - 44: Single	KQCR	366	359	548	KQZF	242	198	322	KRQC	317	316	482	KVEH	201	170	280
Married	KQCS	2 838	2 845	3 002	KQZG	2 871	2 878	3 118	KRQD	2 513	2 519	2 658	KVEI	2 529	2 540	2 760
Widowed	KQCT	15	14	14	KQZH	57	49	41	KRQE	13	12	12	KVEJ	48	41	34
Divorced	KQCU	52	191	423	KQZI	72	240	487	KRQF	48	178	388	KVEK	66	222	444
45 - 54: Single	KQCV	326	293	287	KQZJ	298	203	168	KRQG	279	254	251	KVEL	248	169	144
Married	KQCW	2 924	2 640	2 648	KQZK	2 891	2 598	2 629	KUAR	2 605	2 338	2 347	KVEM	2 570	2 292	2 322
Widowed	KQCX	55	44	37	KQZL	218	176	138	KUBA	47	38	31	KVEN	187	150	118
Divorced	KQCY	50	144	315	KQZM	75	171	361	KUBB	46	134	290	KVEO	69	158	332
55 - 59: Single	KQCZ	140	149	116	KQZN	177	131	82	KUBC	118	128	101	KVEP	148	108	69
Married	KQDA	1 399	1 336	1 186	KQZO	1 293	1 267	1 114	KUBD	1 250	1 192	1 050	KVEQ	1 154	1 130	982
Widowed	KQDB	57	53	40	KQZP	247	216	159	KUBE	49	46	34	KVER	213	186	136
Divorced	KQDC	21	53	103	KQZQ	33	68	117	KUBF	20	49	95	KVES	31	63	107
60 - 64: Single	KQDD	125	115	120	KQZR	208	131	97	KUBG	105	98	104	KVET	174	109	80
Married	KQDE	1 276	1 149	1 121	KQZS	1 098	1 046	1 023	KUBH	1 140	1 029	997	KVEU	985	936	908
Widowed	KQDF	89	74	73	KQZT	382	328	289	KUBI	77	64	63	KVEV	332	284	250
Divorced	KQDG	17	38	76	KQZU	27	55	89	KUBJ	16	35	70	KVEW	25	51	82
65 - 74: Single	KQDH	159	178	177	KQZV	396	315	214	KUBK	132	149	150	KMGN	332	263	176
Married	KQDI	1 567	1 773	1 754	KQZW	1 254	1 431	1 464	KUBL	1 407	1 594	1 574	KMGO	1 133	1 291	1 317
Widowed	KQDJ	258	267	261	KQZX	1 087	1 112	1 002	KUBM	226	234	229	KMGP	959	978	879
Divorced	KQDK	15	46	80	KQZY	28	72	116	KUBN	14	43	74	KMGQ	26	68	107
75 and over: Single	KQDL	58	81	99	KQZZ	291	320	295	KUBO	47	67	81	KMGR	249	270	250
Married	KQDM	480	633	840	KRPI	332	440	592	KUBP	434	573	763	KMGS	304	401	541
Widowed	KQDN	301	336	401	KRPJ	1 172	1 433	1 731	KUBQ	266	300	360	KMGT	1 056	1 285	1 554
Divorced	KQDO	3	11	26	KRPK	7	24	50	KUBR	3	11	25	KMGU	6	23	46

5.4 Marital condition (de jure): estimated population

continued

Thousands

		Scotland								Northern Ireland[1]						
		Males				Females				Males				Females		
		1971	1981	1991		1971	1981	1991		1971	1981	1991[2]		1971	1981	1991[2]
All ages:																
Single	KJPS	1 197	1 149	1 135	KJVG	1 155	1 066	1 029	KJWV	417	406	411	KJYK	392	370	373
Married	KJPT	1 227	1 227	1 159	KJVH	1 243	1 240	1 181	KJWW	318	327	339	KJYL	321	332	350
Widowed	KJPU	79	77	78	KJVI	297	317	306	KJWX	19	18	19	KJYM	71	75	80
Divorced	KJPV	13	42	97	KJVJ	24	62	122	KJWY	1	4	11	KJYN	2	6	18
Age groups:																
0 - 14: Single	KJPW	695	563	492	KJRI	660	535	468	KJWZ	232	212	200	KJYO	224	201	191
15 - 19: Single	KJPX	195	230	173	KJVL	178	214	163	KJXA	64	75	66	KJYP	58	67	61
Married	KJPY	5	4	1	KJVM	15	11	2	KJXB	1	1	–	KJYQ	3	3	1
Widowed	KJPZ	–	–	–	KJVN	–	–	–	KJXC	–	–	–	KJYR	–	–	–
Divorced	KJQQ	–	–	–	KJVO	–	–	–	KJXD	–	–	–	KJYS	–	–	–
20 - 24: Single	KJQR	120	149	184	KJVP	81	109	151	KJXE	45	48	57	KJYT	31	34	46
Married	KJQS	75	60	26	KJVQ	111	93	49	KJXF	18	16	9	KJYU	27	26	16
Widowed	KJQT	–	–	–	KJVR	–	–	–	KJXG	–	–	–	KJYV	–	–	–
Divorced	KJQU	–	1	1	KJVS	1	3	2	KJXH	–	–	–	KJYW	–	–	–
25 - 34: Single	KJQV	61	87	160	KJVT	37	51	113	KJXI	25	27	43	KJYX	16	16	30
Married	KJQW	243	266	224	KJVU	267	290	259	KJXJ	70	73	73	KJYY	77	80	86
Widowed	KJQX	–	1	–	KJVV	2	2	1	KJXK	–	–	–	KJYZ	–	1	1
Divorced	KJQY	3	11	23	KJVW	5	17	29	KJXL	–	1	2	KJZA	–	2	5
35 - 44: Single	KJQZ	35	32	49	KJVX	30	21	32	KJXM	13	11	14	KJZB	11	8	9
Married	KJRW	259	252	265	KJVY	271	262	276	KJXN	67	74	81	KJZC	70	76	83
Widowed	KJRX	2	2	2	KJVZ	7	6	5	KJXO	–	–	–	KJZD	2	2	2
Divorced	KJRY	3	12	31	KJWA	6	17	38	KJXP	–	1	4	KJZE	–	2	6
45 - 54: Single	KJRZ	34	28	26	KJWB	37	25	18	KJXQ	13	10	10	KJZF	13	9	7
Married	KJTD	254	241	232	KJWC	255	244	237	KJXR	64	61	69	KJZG	65	63	70
Widowed	KJTE	6	5	4	KJWD	25	21	15	KJXS	1	1	1	KJZH	6	6	5
Divorced	KJTF	3	9	22	KJWE	6	12	26	KJXT	–	1	3	KJZI	1	1	4
55 - 59: Single	KJTG	16	15	11	KJWF	22	17	10	KJXU	6	5	4	KJZJ	7	6	4
Married	KJTH	120	116	107	KJWG	112	110	105	KJXV	29	28	28	KJZK	27	27	28
Widowed	KJTI	6	6	5	KJWH	27	23	18	KJXW	1	1	1	KJZL	6	6	5
Divorced	KJTJ	1	3	8	KJWI	2	5	9	KJXX	–	–	1	KJZM	–	–	1
60 - 64: Single	KJTK	15	12	11	KJWJ	26	16	12	KJXY	6	5	5	KJZN	8	6	5
Married	KJTL	109	96	99	KJWK	92	88	92	KJXZ	27	24	25	KJZO	21	22	24
Widowed	KJTM	10	8	8	KJWL	40	35	30	KJYA	2	2	2	KJZP	9	9	8
Divorced	KJTN	1	2	5	KJWM	2	4	7	KJYB	–	–	1	KJZQ	–	–	1
65 - 74: Single	KJUY	20	21	18	KJWN	50	39	27	KJYC	8	8	8	KJZR	14	13	10
Married	KJUZ	129	144	143	KJWO	98	113	119	KJYD	31	35	38	KJZS	23	27	31
Widowed	KJVA	27	27	26	KJWP	104	109	95	KJYE	6	6	6	KJZT	24	26	26
Divorced	KJVB	1	2	5	KJWQ	2	4	8	KJYF	–	–	1	KJZU	–	–	1
75 and over: Single	KJVC	7	10	11	KJWR	34	39	34	KJYG	4	4	4	KJZV	9	10	11
Married	KJVD	36	48	62	KJWS	22	31	43	KJYH	11	13	16	KJZW	6	8	10
Widowed	KJVE	28	29	33	KJWT	93	121	141	KJYI	7	7	8	KJZX	23	26	34
Divorced	KJVF	–	1	1	KJWU	–	1	3	KJYJ	–	–	–	KJZY	–	–	–

1 Figures for Northern Ireland are more approximate than those for other countries: at each age/sex the proportions enumerated in the census in the various marital status groups have been applied to the estimated total (all statuses) population.
2 Mid-1991 population estimates by marital status for Northern Ireland are still provisional.

Sources: Office for National Statistics: 01329 813233;
General Register Office for Scotland;
General Register Office (Northern Ireland)

5.5 Geographical distribution of the population

Thousands

		Population enumerated in Census			Mid-year population estimates				
		1911	1931	1951	1961	1971	1981	1991	2000
United Kingdom	KIUR	42 082	46 074	50 225	52 807	55 928	56 357	57 814	59 756
Great Britain	KISR	40 831	44 795	48 854	51 380	54 388	54 815	56 207	58 058
England	KKOJ	33 650	37 359	41 159	43 561	46 412	46 821	48 208	49 997
Standard Regions									
North	KKNA	2 729	2 938	3 009	3 246	3 152	3 117	3 092	3 068
Yorkshire and Humberside	KKNB	3 896	4 319	4 567	4 630	4 902	4 918	4 983	5 058
East Midlands	KKNC	2 467	2 732	3 118	3 108	3 652	3 853	4 035	4 208
East Anglia	KKND	1 191	1 231	1 381	1 489	1 688	1 894	2 082	2 214
South East	KKNE	11 613	13 349	14 877	16 346	17 125	17 011	17 637	18 735
South West	KKNF	2 818	2 984	3 479	3 436	4 112	4 381	4 718	4 975
West Midlands	KKNG	3 277	3 743	4 423	4 762	5 146	5 187	5 265	5 335
North West	KKNH	5 659	6 062	6 305	6 545	6 634	6 459	6 396	6 403
Government Office Regions									
North East	JZBU	..	..	..	..	2 679	2 636	2 603	2 577
North West (including Merseyside)	JZBV	..	..	..	..	7 108	6 940	6 885	6 894
Yorkshire and The Humber	JZBX	..	..	..	..	4 902	4 918	4 983	5 058
East Midlands	JZBY	..	..	..	..	3 652	3 853	4 035	4 208
West Midlands	JZBZ	..	..	..	..	5 146	5 187	5 265	5 335
South West	JZCA	..	..	..	..	6 830	7 245	7 679	8 115
East	JZCB	..	..	..	..	4 112	4 381	4 718	4 975
London	JZCC	..	..	..	..	4 454	4 854	5 150	5 460
South East	JZCD	..	..	..	..	7 529	6 806	6 890	7 375
Wales	KKNI	2 421	2 593	2 599	2 635	2 740	2 813	2 891	2 946
Scotland	KGJB	4 761	4 843	5 096	5 184	5 236	5 180	5 107	5 115
Northern Ireland	KGJC	1 251 *	1 280[3]	1 371	1 427	1 540	1 543	1 607	1 698
Greater London	KKNJ	7 161	8 110	8 197	7 977	7 529	6 806	6 890	7 375
Inner London[1]	KISS	4 998	4 893	3 679	3 481	3 060	2 550	2 627	2 874
Outer London[1]	KITF	2 162	3 217	4 518	4 496	4 470	4 255	4 263	4 501
Metropolitan areas of England & Wales	KITG	9 716	10 770	11 365	11 686	11 862	11 353	11 166	11 135
Tyne and Wear	KGJN	1 105	1 201	1 201	1 241	1 218	1 155	1 130	1 104
West Yorkshire	KGJP	1 852	1 939	1 985	2 002	2 090	2 067	2 085	2 121
South Yorkshire	KGJO	963	1 173	1 253	1 298	1 331	1 317	1 302	1 302
West Midlands	KGJQ	1 780	2 143	2 547	2 724	2 811	2 673	2 629	2 619
Greater Manchester	KGJR	2 638	2 727	2 716	2 710	2 750	2 619	2 570	2 586
Merseyside	KGJS	1 378	1 587	1 663	1 711	1 662	1 522	1 450	1 403
Principal Metropolitan Cities[1]	KITH	3 154	3 906	3 915	4 204	3 910	3 550	3 451	3 434
Newcastle	KGJT	267	286	292	336	312	284	278	270
Leeds	KGJX	446	483	505	710	749	718	717	726
Sheffield	KGJV	455	512	513	581	579	548	529	530
Birmingham	KGKF	526	1 003	1 113	1 179	1 107	1 021	1 007	1 010
Manchester	KGKJ	714	766	703	657	554	463	439	440
Liverpool	KGKM	746	856	789	741	610	517	481	457
Other metropolitan districts[1]	KITI	6 562	6 864	7 450	7 482	7 952	7 803	7 716	7 701
Non-metropolitan districts of England & Wales	KITJ	19 194	21 072	24 196	26 533	29 761	31 475	33 043	34 433
Non-metropolitan cities[1,2]	KITK	..	..	..	4 670	4 715	4 617	4 676	..
Incl. Kingston-upon-Hull	KKNZ	278	314	299	302	288	274	267	..
Leicester	KKOA	227	239	285	286	285	283	285	..
Nottingham	KKNX	260	269	308	311	302	278	281	..
Bristol	KKNV	357	397	443	436	433	401	397	..
Plymouth	KITL	207	215	225	240	249	253	254	..
Stoke-on-Trent	KKOD	235	277	275	276	265	252	253	..
Cardiff	KKOB	182	224	244	289	291	281	294	..
Industrial districts[1,2]	KITM	..	..	..	6 004	6 486	6 713	6 852	..
New Towns[1,2]	KITN	..	..	..	1 552	1 895	2 194	2 382	..
Resort, port and retirement districts[1,2]	KITO	..	..	..	2 828	3 184	3 368	3 626	..
Urban and mixed urban/rural districts[1,2]	KITP	..	..	..	7 240	8 821	9 446	9 964	..
Remoter, mainly rural districts[1,2]	KITQ	..	..	..	4 239	4 661	5 137	5 544	..
City of Edinburgh local government district	KGKU	320	439	467	..	478	446	440	453
City of Glasgow local government district	KGKT	784	1 088	1 090	..	983	774	689	609
Belfast	KGKV	387	438[3]	444	..	..	315	294	283

1 Details of the classification by broad area type are given in recent issues of the ONS annual reference volume "Key Population and Vital Statistics; local and health authority areas" (Series VS). The ten broad area types include all local authorities in England and Wales.

2 The breakdown of non-metropolitan districts by area type has not been provided for the mid-2000 population. This is because the effect of boundary changes due to the major local government reorganisation on 1 April 1995 and 1 April 1996 (particularly in Wales) make the comparison of 1991 and 1996 data with data for earlier years invalid.

3 Figures for Northern Ireland and the City of Belfast relate to the 1937 Census.

Sources: Office for National Statistics: 01329 813233;
General Register Office for Scotland;
General Register Office (Northern Ireland)

5.6 Population by age and ethnic group, United Kingdom[1]
Average over the period Spring 2000 to Winter 2000

Percentages and thousands

Ethnic group	0 to 4	5 to 9	10 to 14	15 to 19	20 to 24	25 to 29	30 to 34	35 to 44	45 to 59	60 to 74	75 and over	%	000's
						Age-group							All ages
Ethnic group													
Black - Caribbean	7	7	8	7	7	5	10	21	14	12	3	100	529
Black - African	12	10	9	8	8	8	12	19	9	3	-	100	440
Black - Other (non-mixed)	13	15	13	10	8	5	12	19	3	2	-	100	129
Black - Mixed	22	20	16	9	7	6	6	8	3	1	1	100	178
Indian	7	7	8	8	8	8	9	18	16	10	2	100	985
Pakistani	12	12	10	10	10	9	9	13	9	5	1	100	675
Bangladeshi	12	13	13	11	12	8	8	10	7	6	1	100	257
Chinese	6	6	5	9	13	9	9	19	17	6	1	100	151
Other - Asian (non-mixed)	5	6	6	6	8	11	12	20	19	5	1	100	242
Other - Other (non-mixed)	8	9	7	8	10	9	10	19	16	3	1	100	219
Other - Mixed	21	14	14	9	6	7	7	9	8	3	1	100	240
All minority ethnic groups	10	10	9	9	9	8	9	16	12	7	1	100	4 045
White	6	6	6	6	6	7	8	15	19	14	7	100	54 670
All ethnic groups[2]	6	7	7	6	6	7	8	15	19	13	7	100	58 731

1 Estimates whose relative standard errors exceed 20% appear in italics and should not be used in any analysis - they are provided as an approximate indication only
2 Includes ethnic group not stated.

Source: Office for National Statistics, Labour Force Survey

5.7 Estimates of migration into and out of the United Kingdom
Analysis by usual occupation[1] and gender

Thousands

	Total			Professional and managerial			Manual and clerical			Not gainfully employed[2]		
	Persons	Males	Females	Persons	Males	Females	Persons	Males	Females	Persons	Males	Females
Inflow												
	KGOA	KGOB	KGOC	KGOD	KGOE	KGOF	KGOG	KGOH	KGOI	KGOJ	KGOK	KGOL
1990	267	135	132	93	61	32	53	26	27	121	48	72
1991	267	122	144	80	51	29	56	23	33	131	48	83
1992	216	99	117	62	39	23	44	17	27	111	43	68
1993	213	101	112	66	41	25	43	21	22	105	39	66
1994	253	126	127	82	49	34	56	31	25	115	46	68
1995	245	130	115	86	57	29	46	20	26	113	53	60
1996	272	130	143	89	53	36	57	25	33	125	52	74
1997	285	143	142	93	59	34	44	24	20	147	60	87
1998	332	167	165	117	68	49	74	37	37	142	63	79
1999	354	181	173	131	77	54	77	41	36	146	63	83
2000	364	191	173	163	98	65	64	34	30	137	60	77
Outflow												
	KGPA	KGPB	KGPC	KGPD	KGPE	KGPF	KGPG	KGPH	KGPI	KGPJ	KGPK	KGPL
1990	231	113	118	75	47	27	56	25	31	100	41	59
1991	239	120	119	82	48	34	50	28	21	108	44	63
1992	227	113	114	82	50	33	47	23	24	98	40	58
1993	216	113	103	70	38	32	45	24	20	101	51	50
1994	191	92	98	55	32	23	48	24	25	87	37	50
1995	192	102	90	62	42	20	42	23	19	88	38	50
1996	216	105	111	84	53	31	46	23	24	86	30	56
1997	225	121	103	86	57	29	48	23	25	91	42	50
1998	199	100	99	79	46	33	41	21	20	79	32	47
1999	245	132	114	97	60	38	70	32	37	79	41	39
2000	278	154	124	128	80	48	59	36	23	90	37	53
Balance												
	KGRA	KGRB	KGRC	KGRD	KGRE	KGRF	KGRG	KGRH	KGRI	KGRJ	KGRK	KGRL
1990	36	22	14	19	14	5	−3	1	−4	21	7	13
1991	28	2	26	−2	3	−5	6	−5	11	24	4	19
1992	−11	−14	3	−21	−11	−10	−4	−6	3	13	3	10
1993	−2	−12	10	−4	3	−8	−2	−4	2	3	−12	15
1994	62	34	28	27	17	11	8	8	−	27	9	18
1995	54	28	26	24	15	9	5	−3	7	25	16	9
1996	56	24	32	5	1	5	11	2	9	39	22	18
1997	60	22	38	8	2	5	−4	1	−5	56	18	38
1998	133	68	66	38	22	16	33	16	17	63	30	32
1999	109	49	60	33	17	16	8	9	−2	67	22	45
2000	87	38	49	35	18	17	5	−2	8	47	22	24

1 Refers to regular occupation before migration.
2 Includes housewives, students, children and retired persons.

Source: Office for National Statistics: 01329 813255

5.8 Estimates of migration into and out of the United Kingdom
Analysis by citizenship and country of last or next residence

Thousands

	All migrants	British citizens						European Union citizens[1] (excluding British)			
			Country of last/next residence						Country of last/next residence		
	Total	Total	European[1] Union	Old[2] Common-wealth	New[3] Common-wealth	United States of America	Other countries	Total	European[1] Union	Other Europe	Other countries
Inflow											
	KEZR	KGLA	KGLB	KGLC	KGLD	KGLE	KGLF	KGLG	KGLH	KGLI	KGLJ
1990	267	106	30	29	22	10	15	37	33	–	4
1991	267	117	39	30	23	10	15	32	29	–	3
1992	216	99	47	22	13	8	10	24	23	–	2
1993	213	92	31	24	19	10	9	25	23	–	2
1994	253	118	45	22	21	16	14	31	27	1	3
1995	245	91	32	16	18	13	13	41	36	–	5
1996	272	104	33	21	22	14	13	54	49	1	4
1997	285	97	36	23	12	8	19	61	56	–	5
1998	332	111	29	33	16	17	17	68	63	–	5
1999	354	116	32	38	15	11	20	60	55	–	5
2000	364	103	29	29	19	8	19	59	53	–	6
Outflow											
	KEZS	KGMA	KGMB	KGMC	KGMD	KGME	KGMF	KGMG	KGMH	KGMI	KGMJ
1990	231	135	34	49	15	22	15	30	25	2	3
1991	239	137	46	42	19	13	18	32	23	2	6
1992	227	133	45	34	15	16	23	17	14	–	3
1993	216	127	45	34	16	16	16	23	21	–	3
1994	191	108	34	28	13	15	18	23	19	–	4
1995	192	118	38	34	13	17	16	20	16	–	4
1996	216	139	52	37	18	16	17	24	18	–	5
1997	225	131	40	37	12	15	26	32	27	1	4
1998	199	111	37	34	7	15	18	26	21	1	4
1999	245	115	37	41	8	14	15	47	41	–	6
2000	278	140	41	48	9	19	23	46	39	1	6
Balance											
	KEZT	KGNA	KGNB	KGNC	KGND	KGNE	KGNF	KGNG	KGNH	KGNI	KGNJ
1990	36	–30	–4	–20	7	–12	–1	7	8	–1	1
1991	28	–20	–7	–12	4	–3	–2	–	5	–2	–3
1992	–11	–34	2	–12	–3	–8	–13	8	9	–	–1
1993	–2	–35	–13	–10	2	–7	–7	2	2	–	–
1994	62	10	11	–6	8	1	–4	8	9	1	–2
1995	54	–27	–6	–17	5	–5	–4	21	21	–	1
1996	56	–36	–19	–16	4	–1	–3	30	31	1	–1
1997	60	–34	–5	–14	–1	–8	–7	29	29	–1	1
1998	133	–	–8	–2	9	2	–1	42	42	–1	1
1999	109	1	–6	–3	7	–3	6	13	14	–	–1
2000	87	–37	–13	–19	11	–12	–4	13	14	–1	–

Source: Office for National Statistics: 01329 813255

5.8 Estimates of migration into and out of the United Kingdom

Analysis by citizenship and country of last or next residence

continued

Thousands

| | Commonwealth citizens | | | | | | | | | | Other foreign citizens | | | | |
| | Country of last/next residence | | | | | | | | | | Country of last/next residence | | | | |
	Total	Aust-ralia	Canada	New Zealand	South Africa	Bangl-adesh, India, Sri Lanka	Pakistan	Other African Common-wealth	Carib-bean Common-wealth	Other count-ries	Total	Euro-pean[1] Union	Other Europe	United States of America	Other coun-tries
Inflow															
	KGLK	KGLL	KGLM	KGLN	KTDK	KGLO	KGLP	KGLQ	KGLR	KGLT	KGLU	KGLV	KGLW	KGLX	KGLY
1990	71	17	3	10	1	11	4	9	2	10	53	6	7	17	22
1991	68	12	4	7	1	10	7	9	2	14	50	6	7	14	23
1992	52	9	2	6	–	7	5	6	2	14	40	2	7	9	21
1993	53	11	3	5	2	9	4	5	–	10	44	2	12	12	18
1994	52	9	2	6	1	7	4	8	–	12	53	6	14	11	22
1995	63	12	5	7	2	8	3	4	–	19	50	2	10	11	26
1996	64	15	3	7	4	8	7	6	1	10	50	–	7	16	27
1997	80	15	5	7	5	16	5	7	1	19	47	–	7	12	28
1998	94	25	5	14	12	10	4	11	2	12	59	4	8	19	28
1999	99	26	2	12	12	14	6	14	3	10	79	3	19	15	42
2000	115	23	6	11	14	21	9	13	1	16	87	2	11	13	61
Outflow															
	KGMK	KGML	KGMM	KGMN	KTDL	KGMO	KGMP	KGMQ	KGMR	KGMT	KGMU	KGMV	KGMW	KGMX	KGMY
1990	31	8	3	5	2	1	1	4	1	5	34	–	4	18	12
1991	34	7	4	5	–	2	2	3	–	10	36	1	3	16	16
1992	29	6	2	5	1	2	1	2	1	7	48	1	11	19	17
1993	32	8	2	4	1	3	1	3	1	7	34	2	3	16	14
1994	29	5	2	4	1	2	3	2	1	7	31	1	9	8	13
1995	27	6	1	4	1	1	1	2	1	6	27	–	5	8	14
1996	29	7	2	3	2	2	–	2	–	8	24	1	6	5	11
1997	34	6	1	5	4	2	2	2	1	12	28	2	5	8	12
1998	29	8	1	3	4	2	1	2	–	6	33	2	6	9	16
1999	38	11	2	6	4	1	–	1	–	13	45	–	9	14	22
2000	44	12	3	8	5	2	2	2	1	9	48	3	11	9	24
Balance															
	KGNK	KGNL	KGNM	KGNN	KTDM	KGNO	KGNP	KGNQ	KGNR	KGNT	KGNU	KGNV	KGNW	KGNX	KGNY
1990	40	9	–	5	–1	10	3	4	2	5	19	6	4	–1	10
1991	34	6	–	2	1	7	5	6	2	4	14	4	4	–2	7
1992	23	4	–	1	–1	5	4	3	1	7	–8	1	–4	–10	4
1993	21	3	1	1	1	6	3	2	–	2	10	–	9	–4	4
1994	23	4	–	2	–	5	1	6	–1	5	22	4	5	4	9
1995	36	6	4	3	1	7	3	2	–1	13	23	2	6	3	12
1996	35	8	1	5	2	6	7	4	1	1	27	–1	1	11	16
1997	46	8	4	3	1	14	4	4	–	8	20	–2	2	4	16
1998	65	17	3	11	7	8	3	9	1	5	26	2	1	11	12
1999	61	15	–	6	8	13	6	13	3	–3	34	3	10	2	19
2000	71	11	3	3	9	19	8	11	–	7	40	–1	–	4	36

1 Figures for the European Union have been revised for all the years in this table to show the Union as it was constituted on 1 January 1995. This includes Austria, Finland and Sweden.

2 Figures for all years include South Africa in the Old Commonwealth.

3 Figures for all years include Pakistan in the New Commonwealth.

Source: Office for National Statistics: 01329 813255

5.9 Acceptances for settlement by nationality
United Kingdom

Number of persons

Geographical region and nationality		All acceptances for settlement				Geographical region and nationality		All acceptances for settlement			
		1997	1998	1999	2000			1997	1998	1999	2000
All nationalities	KGFA	58 720	69 790	97 120	125 090	**Africa(continued)**					
						Egypt	KGGW	330	360	380	480
Europe						Ethiopia	KGGX	210	190	2 170	2 730
European Economic Area						Ghana	KGGY	1 290	1 550	3 480	3 130
Austria	KGFM	–	–	–	..	Kenya	KGHA	500	530	760	1 120
Belgium	KGFB	–	–	–	..	Libya	KGHB	120	160	160	370
Denmark	KGFC	–	10	–	..	Mauritius	KGHC	380	450	460	680
Finland	KGFO	–	–	–	..	Morocco	KGHD	410	430	430	590
France	KGFD	10	30	–	..	Nigeria	KGHE	2 540	2 950	3 180	6 520
Germany	KGFE	10	30	–	..	Sierra Leone	KGHF	470	540	1 060	1 070
Greece	KGFF	10	20	–	..	Somalia	KGHG	990	2 950	3 180	12 290
Iceland	KOSQ	–	–	–	..	South Africa	KGHH	1 290	2 260	2 950	4 300
Italy	KGFG	10	20	–	..	Sudan	KGHI	2 180	470	540	1 520
Luxembourg	KGFH	–	–	–	..	Tanzania	KGHJ	150	220	240	420
Netherlands	KGFI	20	30	–	..	Tunisia	KGHK	70	110	160	130
Norway	KGFQ	10	–	–	..	Uganda	KGHL	690	500	1 400	3 440
Portugal	KGFJ	20	110	–	..	Zambia	KGHM	180	210	240	440
Spain	KGFK	10	20	–	..	Zimbabwe	KGHN	340	410	430	960
Sweden	KGFR	10	–	–	..	Other Africa	KOSU	550	870	1 570	2 060
European Economic Area[1]	KGFL	110	270	10	..	Africa	KGHO	13 200	16 090	27 020	44 460
Remainder of Europe						**Asia**					
Bulgaria	KGFW	160	180	280	300						
Cyprus	KGFN	240	280	430	510	**Indian sub-continent**					
Former Czechoslovakia	KGFX	280	400	500	760	Bangladesh	KGHP	2 870	3 630	3 280	3 680
Of which,						India	KGHQ	4 650	5 430	6 290	8 050
Czech Republic[2]	LQLS	..	240	270	420	Pakistan	KGHR	5 560	7 350	11 860	11 010
Slovakia	LQLT	..	160	230	340						
Hungary	KGFZ	180	180	190	250	Indian sub-continent	KGHS	13 080	16 420	21 440	22 730
Malta	KGFP	60	70	60	80						
Poland	KGGA	570	580	620	830	**Middle East**					
Romania	KGGB	220	240	290	310	Iran	KGHT	1 060	930	1 560	1 920
Switzerland	KGFS	200	250	220	220	Iraq	KGHU	1 610	1 650	2 210	2 710
Turkey	KGFT	4 230	2 360	5 220	5 210	Israel	KGHV	280	300	260	360
Former USSR	KGGC	870	1 180	1 390	2 070	Jordan	KGHW	150	130	140	250
Of which,						Kuwait	KGHX	40	60	60	60
Estonia	LQLU	..	20	20	20	Lebanon	KGHY	640	590	760	990
Latvia	LQLV	..	40	30	60	Saudi Arabia	KGHZ	30	50	60	50
Lithuania	LQLW	..	50	110	130	Syria	KGIA	120	110	140	240
Russia[3]	LQLX	..	860	870	1 180	Yemen	KOSV	150	230	260	290
Ukraine	LQLY	..	140	200	380	Other Middle East	KOSW	90	120	140	210
Other former USSR	LQLZ	..	80	160	300						
Former Yugoslavia	KGFU	590	1 500	6 650	4 440	Middle East	KGIB	4 160	4 180	5 590	7 090
Of which,											
Croatia	LQMA	..	180	320	650	**Remainder of Asia**					
Slovenia	LQMB	..	10	20	20	China	KGIC	1 230	1 550	1 520	1 710
Yugoslavia[4]	LQMC	..	870	5 760	2 640	Hong Kong[6]	KOSX	900	810	490	800
Other former Yugoslavia	LQMD	..	440	550	1 130	Indonesia	KGID	90	120	200	210
Other Europe	KOSO	30	60	130	140	Japan	KGIE	1 760	1 880	1 590	1 720
						Malaysia	KGIF	500	550	510	780
Remainder of Europe	KOSP	7 640	7 300	15 980	15 100	Philippines	KGIG	890	950	1 190	1 910
						Singapore	KGIH	160	120	170	230
Europe	KGGE	7 740	7 570	15 990	15 110	South Korea	KOTE	220	270	300	480
						Sri Lanka	KGII	1 620	2 100	5 370	7 530
Americas						Taiwan	KOSY	80	100	120	180
Argentina	KGGF	50	60	60	80	Thailand	KGIJ	500	540	830	950
Barbados	KGGG	60	100	70	100	Other Asia	KOSZ	420	530	770	1 230
Brazil	KGGH	330	350	410	460						
Canada	KGGI	980	1 050	1 010	1 320	Remainder of Asia	KGIL	8 370	9 520	13 060	17 720
Chile	KGGJ	70	50	50	80						
Colombia	KGGK	240	370	650	810	Asia	KGIM	25 610	30 120	40 090	47 540
Guyana	KGGM	170	180	130	200						
Jamaica	KGGN	1 030	1 120	1 060	2 100	**Oceania**					
Mexico	KGGO	130	120	90	130	Australia	KGIN	1 920	2 200	2 410	2 930
Peru	KGGP	110	100	140	160	New Zealand	KGIO	1 150	1 440	1 670	1 920
Trinidad and Tobago	KGGQ	280	320	280	490	Other Oceania	KOTA	30	50	40	50
USA	KGGR	3 900	3 940	3 760	4 580						
Venezuela	KGGT	50	60	60	80	Oceania	KGIP	3 100	3 690	4 120	4 900
Other Americas	KOSR	390	2 950	750	940						
						British Overseas citizens	KGIQ	540	960	560	630
Americas	KGGU	7 790	10 780	8 520	11 520	Stateless	KGIS	740	580	820	930
Africa						**All nationalities**	KGFA	58 720	69 790	97 120	125 090
Algeria	KGGV	370	710	1 130	1 010						
Angola	KOSS	60	90	520	310						
Congo (Dem. Rep.)[5]	KOST	90	120	2 580	910						

1 Includes Liechtenstein.
2 Includes Czechoslovakian passport holders.
3 Includes Soviet Union passport holders.

4 Includes holders of passports of the former Yugoslavia.
5 Democratic Republic of the Congo, formerly known as Zaire.
6 Includes Hong Kong stateless persons.

Source: Home Office: 020 8760 8289

5.10 Applications[1] received for asylum, excluding dependants, by nationality
United Kingdom

Number of principal applicants

Nationality		1992[2]	1993	1994	1995	1996	1997	1998	1999[3]	2000[3,4]
Europe										
Albania	LQME	100	70	75	110	105	445	560	1 310	1 490
Czech Republic	LQMF	–	5	5	15	55	240	515	1 790	1 200
FYR	ZAFA	..	..	..	..	400	1 865	7 395	11 465	6 070
Poland	DMLX	90	155	360	1 210	900	565	1 585	1 860	1 015
Romania	KEAV	305	370	355	770	455	605	1 015	1 985	2 160
Russia	ZAEQ	..	..	..	..	205	180	185	685	1 000
Turkey	KEAW	1 865	1 480	2 045	1 820	1 495	1 445	2 015	2 850	3 990
Ukraine	ZAER	..	..	..	..	235	490	370	775	770
Other Former USSR	ZAES	270	385	595	795	960	1 345	2 260	2 640	2 505
Other Former Yugoslavia	ZAET	5 635	1 830	1 385	1 565	630	395	585	2 715	2 265
Other	ZAEU	170	245	535	770	1 035	1 575	1 260	200	415
Total	KEAZ	8 435	4 535	5 360	7 050	6 475	9 145	17 745	28 280	22 880
Americas										
Colombia	KEBZ	280	380	405	525	1 005	1 330	425	1 000	505
Ecuador	KYDB	15	60	105	250	435	1 205	280	610	445
Other	KECS	170	305	380	565	330	295	270	420	465
Total	KECT	465	745	890	1 340	1 765	2 825	975	2 025	1 420
Africa										
Algeria	KOTB	150	275	995	1 865	715	715	1 260	1 385	1 635
Angola	KECU	245	320	605	555	385	195	150	545	800
Congo (Dem. Rep.)	KEEH	880	635	775	935	680	690	660	1 240	1 030
Ethiopia	KECW	680	615	730	585	205	145	345	455	415
Gambia	DMMA	10	25	140	1 170	245	125	45	30	50
Ghana	KECX	1 600	1 785	2 035	1 915	780	350	225	195	285
Ivory Coast	DMLZ	310	330	705	245	125	70	95	190	445
Kenya	KOTC	110	630	1 130	1 395	1 170	605	885	485	455
Nigeria	KECY	615	1 665	4 340	5 825	2 900	1 480	1 380	945	835
Rwanda	ZAEV	10	10	100	135	80	90	280	820	760
Sierra Leone	KOTD	325	1 050	1 810	855	395	815	565	1 125	1 330
Somalia	KECZ	1 575	1 465	1 840	3 465	1 780	2 730	4 685	7 495	5 020
Sudan	KEEE	560	300	330	345	280	230	250	280	415
Tanzania	DMMC	30	110	205	1 535	225	90	80	80	60
Uganda	KEEG	295	595	360	365	215	220	210	420	740
Zimbabwe	GRFS	20	40	55	105	130	60	80	230	1 010
Other	ZAEW	230	440	805	1 255	975	905	1 185	2 510	2 635
Total	KEEJ	7 630	10 295	16 960	22 545	11 290	9 515	12 380	18 435	17 920
Middle East										
Iran	KEEK	405	365	520	615	585	585	745	1 320	5 610
Iraq	KEEL	700	495	550	930	965	1 075	1 295	1 800	7 475
Other	ZAEX	875	655	910	755	600	675	745	1 045	1 330
Total	KEGY	1 980	1 520	1 985	2 295	2 150	2 335	2 785	4 165	14 415
Asia										
Afghanistan	DMLY	270	315	325	580	675	1 085	2 395	3 975	5 555
Bangladesh	ZAEY	150	155	310	685	645	545	460	530	795
China	KEGZ	330	215	425	790	820	1 945	1 925	2 625	4 000
India	KEIL	1 450	1 275	2 030	3 255	2 220	1 285	1 030	1 365	2 120
Pakistan	KEIM	1 700	1 125	1 810	2 915	1 915	1 615	1 975	2 615	3 165
Sri Lanka	KEIN	2 085	1 965	2 350	2 070	1 340	1 830	3 505	5 130	6 395
Other	ZAEZ	125	130	265	390	275	265	650	1 225	1 205
Total	KEJO	6 100	5 175	7 515	10 685	7 885	8 570	11 940	17 465	23 230
Other, and nationality not known[5]	KEJP	–	100	125	50	80	105	190	785	450
Grand Total	KEJQ	24 605	22 370	32 830	43 965	29 640	32 500	46 015	71 160	80 315

1 Figures rounded to the nearest 5.
2 Figures do not include overseas applications.
3 May exclude some cases lodged at Local Enforcement Offices between January 1999 and March 2000.
4 Provisional figures.
5 Where the nationality was not known between 1991 and 1994 the most likely nationality was recorded.

Source: Home Office: 020 8760 8297

5.11 Marriages

Numbers

		1989	1990	1991	1992	1993	1994	1995	1996	1997	1998	1999
United Kingdom												
Marriages	KKAA	392 042	375 410	349 739	356 013	341 608	331 232	322 251	317 514	310 218	304 797	301 083
Persons marrying per 1,000 resident population	KKAB	*13.7*	*13.1*	*12.1*	*12.3*	*11.7*	*11.3*	*11.0*	*10.8*	*10.5*	*10.3*	*10.1*
Previous marital status												
Bachelors	KKAC	288 478	276 512	256 538	258 567	245 996	236 619	227 717	221 826	216 237	214 005	211 820
Divorced men	KKAD	92 033	88 199	83 069	87 419	85 824	85 261	85 743	87 113	85 625	82 977	81 750
Widowers	KKAE	11 531	10 699	10 132	10 027	9 788	9 352	8 791	8 575	8 356	7 815	7 513
Spinsters	KKAF	291 516	279 442	259 084	260 252	248 063	237 241	228 462	221 697	216 776	215 399	213 246
Divorced women	KKAG	89 234	85 608	81 224	86 361	84 268	85 220	85 396	87 618	85 648	82 016	80 816
Widows	KKAH	11 294	10 360	9 431	9 400	9 277	8 771	8 393	8 199	7 794	7 382	7 021
First marriage for both partners	KMGH	251 572	240 729	222 369	222 142	210 567	200 910	192 078	185 293	181 135	180 404	178 759
First marriage for one partner	KMGI	76 850	74 496	70 884	74 535	72 925	72 040	72 023	72 937	70 743	68 596	67 548
Remarriage for both partners	KMGJ	63 620	60 185	56 486	59 336	58 116	58 282	58 150	59 284	58 340	55 797	54 776
Males												
Under 21 years	KKAI	19 070	15 930	13 271	11 031	8 767	7 091	6 302	5 497	5 126	5 173	5 234
21-24	KKAJ	102 977	92 270	79 877	74 458	65 129	56 877	49 432	42 488	36 875	32 723	29 390
25-29	KKAK	123 491	122 800	115 637	118 255	114 101	111 108	105 218	101 647	97 345	94 696	90 412
30-34	KKAL	56 442	56 966	56 970	62 470	63 848	65 490	68 245	69 867	70 904	71 096	72 129
35-44	KKAM	51 411	49 984	48 147	51 125	50 553	51 310	53 350	56 513	58 292	59 838	62 114
45-54	KKAN	22 329	21 996	20 915	23 290	23 841	24 136	24 786	26 252	26 472	26 118	26 581
55 and over	KKAO	16 322	15 464	14 922	15 384	15 369	15 220	14 918	15 250	15 204	15 153	15 223
Females												
Under 21 years	KKAP	54 256	45 626	38 305	32 618	26 839	22 903	20 643	18 485	17 254	16 793	16 082
21-24	KKAQ	128 411	119 037	105 505	102 494	93 125	84 171	75 071	66 191	59 549	54 645	50 350
25-29	KKAR	100 531	103 209	99 851	105 223	104 517	102 803	100 644	99 651	97 932	97 181	94 703
30-34	KKAS	41 989	42 794	43 617	48 514	49 546	52 359	54 819	57 752	58 589	59 349	60 446
35-44	KKAT	40 290	38 983	37 582	40 075	40 090	41 213	43 115	45 969	47 267	47 721	50 136
45-54	KKAU	17 172	16 825	16 473	18 504	18 800	19 280	19 720	21 025	21 038	20 708	20 822
55 and over	KKAV	9 393	8 936	8 406	8 585	8 691	8 503	8 239	8 441	8 589	8 400	8 544
England and Wales												
Marriages	KKBA	346 697	331 150	306 756	311 564	299 197	291 069	283 012	278 975	272 536	267 303	263 515
Persons marrying per 1,000 resident population	KKBB	*13.7*	*13.1*	*12.0*	*12.2*	*11.6*	*11.3*	*10.9*	*10.7*	*10.4*	*10.2*	*10.0*
Previous marital status												
Bachelors	KKBC	252 230	241 274	222 823	224 152	213 476	206 077	198 208	193 306	188 268	186 329	184 266
Divorced men	KKBD	84 035	80 282	74 860	78 473	76 986	76 633	76 967	78 003	76 839	74 029	72 617
Widowers	KKBE	10 432	9 594	9 073	8 939	8 735	8 359	7 837	7 666	7 429	6 945	6 632
Spinsters	KKBF	254 763	243 825	224 812	225 608	214 987	206 332	198 603	192 707	188 457	187 391	185 328
Divorced women	KKBG	81 702	77 994	73 408	77 542	75 904	76 857	76 869	78 939	77 098	73 330	71 971
Widows	KKBH	10 232	9 331	8 536	8 414	8 306	7 880	7 540	7 329	6 981	6 582	6 216
First marriage for both partners	KMGK	218 904	209 043	192 238	191 732	181 956	174 200	166 418	160 680	156 907	156 539	155 027
First marriage for one partner	KMGL	69 185	67 013	63 159	66 296	64 551	64 009	63 975	64 653	62 911	60 642	59 540
Remarriage for both partners	KMGM	58 608	55 094	51 359	53 536	52 690	52 860	52 619	53 642	52 718	50 122	48 948
Males												
Under 21 years	KKBI	16 312	13 772	11 416	9 471	7 540	6 175	5 520	4 877	4 574	4 608	4 629
21-24	KKBJ	89 263	79 818	68 547	63 932	55 963	49 073	42 711	36 713	31 907	28 389	25 424
25-29	KKBK	108 834	107 784	100 891	102 942	99 314	96 862	91 607	88 338	84 644	82 135	78 364
30-34	KKBL	50 409	50 600	50 403	55 012	56 129	57 848	60 014	61 582	62 265	62 323	63 212
35-44	KKBM	46 549	45 038	43 013	45 364	44 863	45 514	47 330	50 038	51 654	52 812	54 528
45-54	KKBN	20 365	19 991	18 929	20 925	21 440	21 794	22 349	23 661	23 688	23 385	23 676
55 and over	KKBO	14 965	14 147	13 557	13 918	13 948	13 803	13 481	13 766	13 804	13 651	13 682
Females												
Under 21 years	KKBP	47 529	40 022	33 428	28 541	23 469	20 250	18 343	16 510	15 439	15 065	14 379
21-24	KKBQ	112 048	103 653	91 338	88 553	80 470	72 937	65 126	57 296	51 766	47 446	43 691
25-29	KKBR	88 662	90 629	87 244	91 735	91 134	89 941	87 680	86 838	85 352	84 399	82 250
30-34	KKBS	37 452	38 032	38 425	42 675	43 559	46 119	48 216	50 799	51 405	51 982	52 721
35-44	KKBT	36 678	35 315	33 755	35 660	35 662	36 651	38 367	40 889	41 838	42 245	44 199
45-54	KKBU	15 661	15 290	14 891	16 619	16 969	17 409	17 791	18 992	18 938	18 575	18 572
55 and over	KKBV	8 667	8 209	7 675	7 781	7 934	7 762	7 489	7 651	7 798	7 591	7 703

5.11 Marriages

continued

Numbers

		1990	1991	1992	1993	1994	1995	1996	1997	1998	1999	2000
Scotland												
Marriages	KKCA	34 672	33 762	35 057	33 366	31 480	30 663	30 242	29 611	29 668	29 940	30 367
Persons marrying per 1,000 resident population	KKCB	*13.6*	*13.2*	*13.7*	*13.0*	*12.3*	*11.9*	*11.8*	*11.6*	*11.6*	*11.7*	*11.9*
Previous marital status												
Bachelors	KKCC	26 636	25 549	26 106	24 609	23 004	22 126	21 454	20 994	20 987	21 052	21 201
Divorced men	KKCD	7 108	7 344	8 027	7 879	7 654	7 741	8 048	7 845	7 934	8 142	8 427
Widowers	KKCE	928	869	924	878	822	796	740	772	747	746	739
Spinsters	KKCF	26 940	25 979	26 274	25 103	23 248	22 410	21 799	21 303	21 241	21 308	21 608
Divorced women	KKCG	6 869	7 048	7 935	7 469	7 487	7 542	7 718	7 621	7 754	7 949	8 141
Widows	KKCH	863	735	848	794	745	711	725	687	673	683	618
First marriage for both partners	KEZV	23 529	22 401	22 588	21 214	19 644	18 822	18 071	17 751	17 677	17 680	17 864
First marriage for one partner	KEZW	6 518	6 726	7 204	7 284	6 964	6 892	7 111	6 795	6 874	7 000	7 081
Remarriage for both partners	KEZX	4 625	4 635	5 265	4 868	4 872	4 949	5 060	5 065	5 117	5 260	5 422
Males												
Under 21 years	KKCI	1 626	1 378	1 172	902	680	577	452	406	421	490	364
21-24	KKCJ	9 454	8 572	7 958	6 870	5 693	4 915	4 191	3 494	3 147	2 853	2 720
25-29	KKCK	11 430	11 244	11 587	11 266	10 812	10 209	10 056	9 495	9 439	9 031	8 536
30-34	KKCL	5 061	5 290	6 022	6 214	6 176	6 574	6 574	6 911	6 988	7 179	7 419
35-44	KKCM	4 210	4 383	4 950	4 803	4 864	5 021	5 412	5 649	5 945	6 470	7 018
45-54	KKCN	1 760	1 733	2 083	2 093	2 050	2 124	2 288	2 459	2 412	2 575	2 960
55 and over	KKCO	1 131	1 162	1 285	1 218	1 205	1 243	1 269	1 197	1 316	1 342	1 350
Females												
Under 21 years	KKCP	4 161	3 589	3 060	2 461	1 959	1 728	1 423	1 302	1 289	1 322	1 171
21-24	KKCQ	11 666	10 735	10 503	9 506	8 291	7 264	6 474	5 568	5 248	4 778	4 581
25-29	KKCR	9 755	9 771	10 457	10 368	9 895	9 904	9 818	9 574	9 764	9 539	9 495
30-34	KKCS	3 925	4 331	4 822	5 002	5 145	5 401	5 675	5 927	6 036	6 433	6 463
35-44	KKCT	3 194	3 333	3 847	3 774	3 917	4 025	4 378	4 722	4 726	5 150	5 633
45-54	KKCU	1 351	1 386	1 673	1 606	1 648	1 689	1 794	1 844	1 900	1 994	2 279
55 and over	KKCV	620	617	695	649	625	652	680	674	705	724	745
Northern Ireland												
Marriages	KKDA	9 588	9 221	9 392	9 045	8 683	8 576	8 297	8 071	7 826	7 628	7 584
Persons marrying per 1,000 resident population	KKDB	*12.1*	*11.7*	*11.5*	*11.0*	*10.6*	*10.4*	*10.0*	*9.6*	*9.3*	*9.0*	*8.9*
Previous marital status												
Bachelors	KKDC	8 602	8 166	8 309	7 911	7 538	7 383	7 066	6 975	6 689	6 502	6 463
Divorced men	KKDD	809	865	919	959	974	1 035	1 062	941	1 014	991	966
Widowers	KKDE	177	190	164	175	171	158	169	155	123	135	155
Spinsters	KKDF	8 677	8 293	8 370	7 973	7 661	7 449	7 191	7 016	6 767	6 610	6 540
Divorced women	KKDG	745	768	884	895	876	985	961	929	932	896	933
Widows	KKDH	166	160	138	177	146	142	145	126	127	122	111
First marriage for both partners	KEZY	8 157	7 730	7 822	7 397	7 066	6 838	6 542	6 477	6 188	6 052	6 016
First marriage for one partner	KEZZ	965	999	1 035	1 090	1 067	1 156	1 173	1 037	1 080	1 008	971
Remarriage for both partners	KFBI	466	492	535	558	550	582	582	557	558	568	597
Males												
Under 21 years	KKDI	532	477	388	325	236	205	168	146	144	115	119
21-24	KKDJ	2 998	2 758	2 568	2 296	2 111	1 806	1 584	1 474	1 187	1 113	983
25-29	KKDK	3 586	3 502	3 726	3 521	3 434	3 402	3 253	3 206	3 122	3 017	2 967
30-34	KKDL	1 305	1 277	1 436	1 505	1 466	1 657	1 711	1 728	1 785	1 738	1 779
35-44	KKDM	736	751	811	887	932	999	1 063	989	1 081	1 116	1 167
45-54	KKDN	245	253	282	308	292	313	303	325	321	330	361
55 and over	KKDO	186	203	181	203	212	194	215	203	186	199	208
Females												
Under 21 years	KKDP	1 443	1 288	1 017	909	694	572	552	513	439	381	346
21-24	KKDQ	3 718	3 432	3 438	3 149	2 943	2 681	2 421	2 215	1 951	1 881	1 732
25-29	KKDR	2 825	2 836	3 031	3 015	2 967	3 060	2 995	3 006	3 018	2 914	2 946
30-34	KKDS	837	861	1 017	985	1 095	1 202	1 278	1 257	1 331	1 292	1 366
35-44	KKDT	474	494	568	654	645	723	702	707	750	787	819
45-54	KKDU	184	196	212	225	223	240	239	256	233	256	259
55 and over	KKDV	107	114	109	108	116	98	110	117	104	117	116

Sources: Office for National Statistics: 01329 813339;
General Register Office for Scotland;
General Register Office (Northern Ireland)

5.12 Divorce

Numbers

		1990	1991	1992	1993	1994	1995	1996	1997	1998	1999	2000
United Kingdom												
Decrees absolute granted[1,2]:												
Number	ZBRL	167 555	173 454	175 144	180 018	173 611	170 050	171 729	161 087	160 057	158 746	154 628
Duration of marriage:												
0-4 years	ZBRM	38 624	40 123	39 191	39 530	37 978	36 594	37 016	33 719	33 087	31 047	28 933
5-9 years	ZBRN	46 169	46 884	47 990	50 883	49 215	48 309	48 670	45 040	44 243	43 357	41 621
10-14 years	ZBRO	30 053	31 773	32 261	33 221	31 177	30 257	30 159	29 085	29 706	30 270	30 166
15-19 years	ZBRP	21 761	22 233	22 179	22 324	21 336	21 040	21 379	20 211	20 078	20 147	19 902
20 years and over	ZBRQ	30 932	32 422	33 516	34 055	33 898	33 840	34 487	33 020	32 935	33 916	34 000
Not stated	ZBRR	16	19	7	5	7	10	18	12	8	9	6
Age of wife at marriage:												
16-19 years	ZBRS	45 905	45 356	44 347	43 368	38 464	35 145	33 590	28 987	27 627	25 440	23 505
20-24 years	ZBRT	78 110	80 969	81 574	83 806	80 594	78 341	78 075	72 971	71 416	69 509	66 215
25-29 years	ZBRU	23 260	25 813	27 109	29 213	30 576	31 611	33 634	33 452	34 195	35 585	36 009
30-34 years	ZBRV	9 457	10 180	10 582	11 272	11 716	12 322	13 122	12 968	13 719	14 420	14 892
35-39 years	ZBRW	5 171	5 300	5 531	6 018	5 979	6 172	6 470	6 155	6 571	6 848	6 993
40-44 years	ZBRX	2 749	2 897	3 017	3 260	3 247	3 335	3 507	3 375	3 360	3 557	3 568
45 years and over	ZBRY	2 863	2 877	2 933	3 004	2 952	3 052	3 239	3 094	3 086	3 291	3 352
Not stated	ZBRZ	40	62	51	77	83	72	92	85	83	96	94
Age of wife at divorce:												
16-24 years	ZBSA	16 778	16 150	14 604	13 895	11 845	10 517	9 298	7 371	6 758	5 671	5 115
25-29 years	ZBSB	38 504	39 059	38 186	38 632	35 824	33 354	32 808	28 814	26 968	24 120	21 280
30-34 years	ZBSC	34 326	36 434	38 220	39 879	39 456	38 839	39 497	37 257	36 795	36 052	34 356
35-39 years	ZBSD	26 596	28 097	29 044	30 746	30 000	30 280	31 497	30 641	31 688	32 605	32 588
40-44 years	ZBSE	23 156	23 928	23 756	23 943	22 847	22 791	22 843	22 246	22 810	23 614	23 879
45 years and over	ZBSF	28 139	29 705	31 276	32 841	33 549	34 187	35 684	34 662	34 947	36 578	37 311
Not stated	ZBSG	56	81	58	82	90	82	102	96	91	106	99
Divorces in which there were:												
No children aged under 16[3]	ZBSH	76 614	78 694	77 709	78 803	78 913	78 844	..	..	..	..	..
One or more children aged under 16[3]	ZBSI	90 941	94 760	97 435	101 215	94 698	91 206	..	..	..	..	..
England and Wales												
Decrees absolute granted[1]:												
Number	KKEA	153 386	158 745	160 385	165 018	158 175	155 499	157 107	146 689	145 214	144 556	141 135
Rate per 1,000 married couples	KKEB	*13.0*	*13.5*	*13.7*	*13.9*	*13.4*	*13.1*	*13.8*	*13.0*	*12.9*	*13.0*	*12.7*
Duration of marriage:												
0-4 years	KKEC	36 299	37 779	36 898	37 252	35 695	34 507	34 924	31 767	31 136	29 307	27 474
5-9 years	KKED	42 061	42 735	43 745	46 536	44 769	44 304	44 609	41 260	40 239	39 676	38 206
10-14 years	KKEE	27 310	28 791	29 285	30 156	28 073	27 365	27 332	26 215	26 698	27 384	27 459
15-19 years	KKEF	19 819	20 127	20 160	20 233	19 200	18 943	19 321	18 027	17 934	18 072	17 870
20 years and over	KKEG	27 881	29 294	30 290	30 836	30 431	30 370	30 912	29 408	29 199	30 108	30 120
Not stated	KKEH	16	19	7	5	7	10	9	12	8	9	6
Age of wife at marriage:												
16-19 years	KKEI	41 116	40 594	39 734	38 811	34 069	31 322	29 927	25 579	24 276	22 486	20 930
20-24 years	KKEJ	71 489	74 050	74 701	76 853	73 291	71 360	71 123	66 167	64 453	62 853	59 874
25-29 years	KKEK	21 701	24 025	25 173	27 178	28 360	29 441	31 396	31 022	31 533	32 867	33 282
30-34 years	KKEL	8 909	9 608	9 939	10 593	11 007	11 585	12 335	12 094	12 788	13 507	13 972
35-39 years	KKEM	4 880	5 024	5 200	5 673	5 615	5 800	6 051	5 767	6 153	6 432	6 562
40-44 years	KKEN	2 598	2 727	2 872	3 091	3 064	3 121	3 254	3 156	3 135	3 331	3 378
45 years and over	KKEO	2 693	2 717	2 766	2 819	2 769	2 870	3 021	2 904	2 876	3 080	3 137
Age of wife at divorce:												
16-24 years	KKEP	15 454	14 960	13 482	12 924	10 956	9 783	8 615	6 871	6 298	5 318	4 839
25-29 years	KKEQ	35 121	35 582	34 853	35 362	32 608	30 563	30 075	26 435	24 586	22 173	19 650
30-34 years	KKER	31 295	33 195	34 901	36 300	35 848	35 538	36 274	33 967	33 446	32 837	31 420
35-39 years	KKES	24 421	25 661	26 577	28 162	27 195	27 550	28 727	27 715	28 605	29 663	29 820
40-44 years	KKET	21 263	21 979	21 783	21 891	20 765	20 739	20 774	20 125	20 521	21 325	21 469
45 years and over	KKEU	25 816	27 349	28 782	30 374	30 796	31 316	32 633	31 564	31 750	33 231	33 931
Not stated	KKEV	16	19	7	5	7	10	9	12	8	9	6
Divorces in which there were:												
No children aged under 16[3]	ZBSJ	68 635	70 399	68 960	70 103	69 684	69 632	70 174	66 019	64 738	65 258	64 359
One or more children aged under 16[3]	ZBSK	84 751	88 346	91 425	94 915	88 491	85 867	86 933	80 670	80 476	79 298	76 776

5.12 Divorce
continued

Numbers

		1990	1991	1992	1993	1994	1995	1996	1997	1998	1999	2000
Scotland												
Decrees absolute granted[1]												
Number	KKFA	12 272	12 399	12 479	12 787	13 133	12 249	12 308	12 222	12 384	11 864	11 143
Rate per 1,000 married couples	KKFB	*10.5*	*10.6*	*10.8*	*11.1*	*11.5*	*10.8*	*10.9*	*11.0*	*11.2*	*10.8*	*10.3*
Duration of marriage:												
0-4 years	KKFC	2 208	2 142	2 085	2 092	2 095	1 908	1 914	1 793	1 766	1 588	1 304
5-9 years	KKFD	3 546	3 508	3 610	3 722	3 790	3 399	3 432	3 224	3 360	3 095	2 890
10-14 years	KKFE	2 361	2 484	2 454	2 539	2 592	2 407	2 310	2 385	2 456	2 368	2 168
15-19 years	KKFF	1 617	1 718	1 675	1 745	1 786	1 698	1 709	1 804	1 729	1 686	1 622
20 years and over	KKFG	2 540	2 547	2 655	2 689	2 870	2 837	2 934	3 016	3 073	3 127	3 159
Not stated	ZBSL	–	–	–	–	–	–	9	–	–	–	–
Age of wife at marriage:												
16-19 years	ZBSM	4 040	3 894	3 755	3 768	3 641	3 091	2 939	2 749	2 654	2 374	2 043
20-24 years	ZBSN	5 745	5 845	5 821	5 890	6 197	5 845	5 822	5 714	5 744	5 453	5 142
25-29 years	KKFJ	1 377	1 545	1 685	1 812	1 926	1 887	1 933	2 151	2 314	2 333	2 318
30-34 years	KKFK	497	514	575	612	628	654	697	791	824	829	805
35-39 years	KKFL	275	249	301	312	329	338	393	360	382	379	378
40-44 years	KKFM	139	148	138	152	163	196	234	199	198	208	170
45 years and over	KKFN	159	142	153	164	166	166	198	173	185	192	193
Not stated	KKFO	40	62	51	77	83	72	92	85	83	96	94
Age of wife at divorce:												
16-24 years	KKFP	1 199	1 038	963	844	767	622	583	426	377	301	232
25-29 years	KKFQ	2 938	2 932	2 807	2 775	2 750	2 353	2 269	2 021	1 957	1 597	1 330
30-34 years	KKFR	2 611	2 741	2 785	3 037	3 045	2 747	2 708	2 736	2 767	2 642	2 381
35-39 years	KKFS	1 891	2 037	2 092	2 212	2 390	2 290	2 307	2 469	2 562	2 450	2 298
40-44 years	KKFT	1 614	1 665	1 685	1 771	1 788	1 734	1 761	1 819	1 951	1 929	1 999
45 years and over	KKFU	1 979	1 924	2 096	2 071	2 310	2 431	2 587	2 667	2 687	2 848	2 810
Not stated	KKFV	40	62	51	77	83	72	93	84	83	97	93
Divorces in which there were:												
No children aged under 16[3]	KKFW	6 555	6 521	6 927	6 951	7 390	7 515	..	..	..	..	..
One or more children under 16[3]	KKFX	5 717	5 878	5 552	5 836	5 743	4 734	..	..	..	..	..
Northern Ireland												
Decrees absolute granted[1,2]:												
Number	ZBSO	1 897	2 310	2 280	2 213	2 303	2 302	2 314	2 176	2 459	2 326	2 350
Duration of marriage:												
0-4 years	ZBSP	117	202	208	186	188	179	178	159	185	152	155
5-9 years	ZBSQ	562	641	635	625	656	606	629	556	644	586	525
10-14 years	ZBSR	382	498	522	526	512	485	517	485	552	518	539
15-19 years	ZBSS	325	388	344	346	350	399	349	380	415	389	410
20 years and over	ZBST	511	581	571	530	597	633	641	596	663	681	721
Age of wife at marriage:												
16-19 years	ZBSU	749	868	858	789	754	732	724	659	697	580	532
20-24 years	ZBSV	876	1 074	1 052	1 063	1 106	1 136	1 130	1 090	1 219	1 203	1 199
25-29 years	ZBSW	182	243	251	223	290	283	305	279	348	385	409
30-34 years	ZBSX	51	58	68	67	81	83	90	83	107	84	115
35-39 years	ZBSY	16	27	30	33	35	34	26	28	36	37	53
40-44 years	ZBSZ	12	22	7	17	20	18	19	20	27	18	20
45 years and over	ZBTA	11	18	14	21	17	16	20	17	25	19	22
Age of wife at divorce:												
16-24 years	ZBTB	125	152	159	127	122	112	100	74	83	52	44
25-29 years	ZBTC	445	545	526	495	466	438	464	358	425	350	300
30-34 years	ZBTD	420	498	534	542	563	554	515	554	582	573	555
35-39 years	ZBTE	284	399	375	372	415	440	463	457	521	492	470
40-44 years	ZBTF	279	284	288	281	294	318	308	302	338	360	411
45 years and over	ZBTG	344	432	398	396	443	440	464	431	510	499	570
Divorces in which there were:												
No children aged under 16[3]	ZBTH	1 424	1 774	1 822	1 749	1 839	1 697	1 676	1 573	1 807	1 649	1 051
One or more children aged under 16[3]	ZBTI	473	536	458	464	464	605	638	603	652	677	1 299

1 Includes decrees of nullities.
2 Marital estimates are not available for Northern Ireland - no divorce rate for UK/Northern Ireland.
3 Children of the family as defined by the Matrimonial Causes Act 1973.

Sources: Office for National Statistics: 01329 813339;
General Register Office for Scotland;
Northern Ireland Statistics and Research Agency

5.13 Divorce proceedings

Numbers

							United Kingdom					
		1990	1991	1992	1993	1994	1995	1996	1997	1998	1999	2000
Dissolution of marriage[1]												
Decree absolute/decree granted	ZBXR	167 086	172 997	174 718	179 539	173 178	169 621	171 309	160 733	159 688	158 418	154 273
On grounds of:												
Adultery	ZBXS	45 457	46 161	45 458	45 759	42 743	41 313	41 127	38 652	37 302	35 545	34 082
Behaviour	ZBXT	73 481	77 294	77 648	78 686	75 029	71 733	72 581	68 546	68 685	67 851	65 687
Desertion	ZBXU	1 112	1 185	1 096	1 193	1 185	1 196	1 101	956	828	748	722
Separation (2 years and consent)	ZBXV	35 015	36 041	37 955	41 002	41 144	41 969	42 265	39 398	39 627	40 368	39 763
Separation(5 years)	ZBXW	11 195	11 528	11 806	12 183	12 317	12 699	13 547	12 552	12 697	13 389	13 653
Combination of more than one ground and other	ZBXX	826	788	755	716	760	711	688	629	549	517	366
Decree absolute/decree granted to:												
the wife	ZBXY	119 715	124 472	125 833	128 797	123 256	118 869	119 570	111 912	111 556	109 828	106 958
the husband	ZBXZ	46 981	48 136	48 509	50 407	49 507	50 268	51 247	48 393	47 764	48 236	47 069
both	ZBYA	396	393	379	345	423	490	493	430	369	358	247
Nullity of marriage[2]												
Decree absolute/decree granted	ZBYB	469	457	426	479	433	429	420	354	369	328	355

							England and Wales					
		1990	1991	1992	1993	1994	1995	1996	1997	1998	1999	2000
Dissolution of marriage												
Petitions filed	KKGA	191 615	179 103	189 329	184 471	175 510	173 966	177 970	163 769	165 870	162 775	157 809
Decree nisi granted	KKGM	157 344	153 258	149 126	160 625	154 241	155 739	157 588	148 310	144 231	143 106	143 729
Decree absolute granted	KKGN	152 927	158 301	159 967	164 556	157 756	155 076	156 692	146 339	144 851	144 233	140 783
On grounds of:												
Adultery	KKGB	44 038	44 737	44 128	44 466	41 449	40 178	40 012	37 592	36 319	34 584	33 310
Behaviour	KKGC	69 381	73 266	73 906	74 583	70 932	68 168	68 986	65 047	65 257	64 816	63 182
Desertion	KKGD	1 027	1 082	1 021	1 118	1 062	1 108	1 030	912	790	713	680
Separation (2 years and consent)	KKGE	28 710	29 414	30 995	34 144	33 996	35 030	35 422	32 638	32 394	33 482	32 820
Separation(5 years)	KKGF	8 964	9 031	9 181	9 556	9 589	9 930	10 626	9 592	9 616	10 193	10 498
Combination of more than one ground and other	ZBYC	807	771	736	689	728	662	616	558	475	445	293
Decree absolute granted to[2]												
the wife	ZBYD	109 571	113 947	115 393	118 127	112 415	108 764	109 489	102 173	101 583	100 469	98 227
the husband	ZBYE	42 960	43 961	44 195	46 084	44 918	45 823	46 712	43 739	42 902	43 413	42 311
both	ZBYF	396	393	379	345	423	489	491	427	366	351	245
Nullity of marriage												
Petitions filed	KKGO	665	619	535	634	822	881	702	485	505	549	452
Decree nisi granted	KKGR	430	508	369	365	705	425	332	248	281	495	274
Decree absolute granted	KKGS	459	444	418	462	419	423	415	350	363	323	352
Judicial separation												
Petitions filed	KKGT	2 900	2 588	2 434	2 251	4 358	3 349	2 795	1 078	916	882	650
Decrees granted	KKGW	1 794	1 747	1 452	1 413	1 350	1 543	1 199	589	519	696	540

5.13 Divorce proceedings
continued

Numbers

		Scotland										
		1990	1991	1992	1993	1994	1995	1996	1997	1998	1999	2000
Dissolution of marriage[1]												
Decree granted	ZBYG	12 266	12 395	12 476	12 777	13 125	12 243	12 307	12 220	12 383	11 860	11 142
On grounds of:												
Adultery	ZBYH	1 232	1 198	1 136	1 092	1 099	956	943	909	832	770	610
Behaviour	ZBYI	3 847	3 688	3 407	3 757	3 711	3 203	3 184	3 081	3 005	2 611	2 099
Desertion	ZBYJ	68	82	58	56	103	72	61	33	28	18	34
Separation (2 years and consent)	ZBYK	5 362	5 508	5 823	5 800	6 078	5 846	5 835	5 773	6 121	5 908	5 878
Separation(5 years)	ZBYL	1 757	1 919	2 052	2 072	2 134	2 166	2 284	2 424	2 397	2 553	2 521
Decree granted to[2]												
the wife	ZBYM	8 862	8 930	8 865	9 190	9 278	8 545	8 559	8 266	8 329	7 774	7 191
the husband	ZBYN	3 410	3 469	3 614	3 597	3 855	3 704	3 749	3 956	4 055	4 090	3 952
Nullity of marriage												
Decree granted	ZBYO	6	4	3	10	8	6	1	2	1	4	1

		Northern Ireland										
		1990	1991	1992	1993	1994	1995	1996	1997	1998	1999	2000
Dissolution of marriage												
Petitions filed	ZBYP	2 258	2 591	2 597	2 610	2 875	2 875	2 695	2 808	2 760	2 414	3 005
Decree nisi granted	ZBYQ	2 190	2 344	2 386	2 384	2 535	2 535	2 419	2 532	2 904	2 393	2 456
Decree absolute granted	ZBYR	1 893	2 301	2 275	2 206	2 297	2 302	2 310	2 174	2 454	2 325	2 348
On grounds of:												
Adultery	ZBYS	187	226	194	201	195	179	172	151	151	191	162
Behaviour	ZBYT	253	340	335	346	386	362	411	418	423	424	406
Desertion	ZBYU	17	21	17	19	20	16	10	11	10	17	8
Separation (2 years and consent)	ZBYV	945	1 119	1 137	1 059	1 072	1 093	1 010	991	1 112	978	1 065
Separation(5 years)	ZBYW	474	578	573	555	594	603	637	536	684	643	634
Combination of more than one ground and other	ZBYX	17	17	19	26	30	49	70	67	74	72	73
Decree absolute granted to:												
the wife	ZBYY	1 282	1 595	1 575	1 480	1 563	1 560	1 522	1 473	1 644	1 585	1 540
the husband	ZBYZ	611	706	700	726	734	741	786	698	807	733	806
both	ZBZA	–	–	–	–	–	1	2	3	3	7	2
Nullity of marriage												
Petitions filed	ZBZB	7	5	1	2	5	5	5	7	2	4	3
Decree nisi granted	ZBZC	9	10	3	2	3	5	5	2	6	2	5
Decree absolute granted	ZBZD	4	9	5	7	6	–	4	2	5	1	2
Judicial separation												
Petitions filed	ZBZE	16	23	17	44	57	84	63	70	64	50	54
Decrees granted	ZBZF	16	13	22	6	15	30	22	34	40	31	23

1 The terms Petition filed, Decree nisi granted, Decree absolute and Judicial separation are not used in Scotland. Decree absolute granted to 'both' and 'Combination of more than one ground and other' are not procedures used in Scotland.

2 Information on Decree granted for the wife or husband for Scotland includes nullities (these are identified separately under 'Nullity of marriage'); figures excluding nullities are not available.

Sources: Office for National Statistics: 01329 813339;
General Register Office for Scotland;
Northern Ireland Statistics and Research Agency;
The Court Service (E&W/NI);
Scottish Courts Administration

Population and vital statistics

5.14 Births
Annual averages or calendar years

Thousands

| | Live births | | | | Rates | | | | |
	Total	Male	Female	Sex ratio[1]	Crude birth rate[2]	General fertility rate[3]	TFR[4]	Still-births[5]	Still-birth rate[5]
United Kingdom[6]									
1900 - 02	1 095	558	537	1 037	28.6	115.1	..	..	..
1910 - 12	1 037	528	508	1 039	24.6	99.4	..	..	..
1920 - 22	1 018	522	496	1 052	23.1	93.0	..	..	..
1930 - 32	750	383	367	1 046	16.3	66.5	..	..	..
1940 - 42	723	372	351	1 062	15.0	..	1.89	..	..
1950 - 52	803	413	390	1 061	16.0	73.7	2.21	..	..
1960 - 62	946	487	459	1 063	17.9	90.3	2.80	25	..
1970 - 72	880	453	427	1 064	15.8	82.5	2.36	14	13
1980 - 82	735	377	358	1 053	13.0	62.5	1.83	5	7
	BBCA	KBCZ	KBCY	KMFW	KBCT	KBCS	KBCR	KBCQ	KMFX
1984	729	373	356	1 049	12.9	60.3	1.77	4.2	5.7
1985	751	385	365	1 053	13.3	61.4	1.79	4.2	5.6
1986	755	388	368	1 053	13.3	61.0	1.78	4.1	5.3
1987	775	398	378	1 053	13.6	62.3	1.81	3.9	5.0
1988	787	403	384	1 049	13.8	63.1	1.82	3.9	4.9
1989	777	398	379	1 051	13.6	62.1	1.79	3.7	4.7
1990	798	409	390	1 049	13.9	64.0	1.83	3.7	4.6
1991	792	406	386	1 052	13.7	63.6	1.81	3.7	4.7
1992	781	400	381	1 052	13.5	63.4	1.79	3.4	4.4
1993	762	391	371	1 054	13.1	62.3	1.76	4.4	5.7
1994	750	385	365	1 054	12.9	61.6	1.74	4.4	5.8
1995	732	375	357	1 052	12.5	60.1	1.71	4.1	5.6
1996	732	376	357	1 055	12.5	60.1	1.72	4.1	5.5
1997	727	372	354	1 051	12.3	59.5	1.72	3.9	5.3
1998	717	367	350	1 052	12.1	58.6	1.71	3.9	5.4
1999	700	359	341	1 056	11.8	57.1	1.69	3.7	5.3
2000	679	348	331	1 051	11.4	55.2	1.64	3.6	5.3
England and Wales									
1900 - 02	932	475	458	1 037	28.6	114.7	..	..	..
1910 - 12	884	450	433	1 040	24.5	98.6	..	..	..
1920 - 22	862	442	420	1 051	22.8	91.1	..	..	..
1930 - 32	632	323	309	1 047	15.8	64.4	..	27	..
1940 - 42	607	312	295	1 057	15.6	61.3	1.81	22	..
1950 - 52	683	351	332	1 058	15.6	72.1	2.16	16	..
1960 - 62	812	418	394	1 061	17.6	88.9	2.77	16	..
1970 - 72	764	394	371	1 061	15.6	81.4	2.31	10	13
1980 - 82	639	328	311	1 053	12.9	61.8	1.81	4	7
	BBCB	KMFY	KMFZ	KMGA	KMGB	KMGC	KMGD	KMGE	KMGF
1984	637	326	311	1 049	12.8	59.8	1.75	3.6	5.7
1985	656	337	320	1 054	13.1	61.0	1.78	3.6	5.5
1986	661	339	322	1 052	13.2	60.6	1.77	3.5	5.3
1987	682	350	332	1 053	13.6	62.0	1.81	3.4	5.0
1988	694	355	339	1 048	13.7	63.0	1.82	3.4	4.9
1989	688	352	335	1 051	13.6	62.5	1.80	3.2	4.7
1990	706	361	345	1 048	13.9	64.2	1.84	3.3	4.6
1991	699	358	341	1 052	13.7	63.6	1.82	3.3	4.6
1992	690	354	336	1 053	13.4	63.5	1.80	3.0	4.3
1993	673	346	328	1 056	13.1	62.6	1.76	3.9	5.7
1994	665	341	323	1 055	12.9	61.9	1.75	3.8	5.7
1995	648	332	316	1 051	12.5	60.4	1.72	3.6	5.5
1996	649	333	316	1 055	12.5	60.5	1.73	3.5	5.4
1997	643	330	314	1 051	12.3	59.8	1.73	3.4	5.3
1998	636	326	310	1 051	12.1	59.0	1.72	3.4	5.3
1999	622	319	303	1 055	11.8	57.6	1.70	3.3	5.3
2000	604	310	295	1 051	11.4	55.7	1.66	3.2	5.3

5.14 Births
continued
Annual averages or calendar years

Thousands

| | Live births | | | | Rates | | | | |
	Total	Male	Female	Sex ratio[1]	Crude birth rate[2]	General fertility rate[3]	TFR[4]	Still-births[5]	Still-birth rate[5]
Scotland									
1900 - 02	132	67	65	1 046	29.5	120.6	..	..	..
1910 - 12	123	63	60	1 044	25.9	107.4	..	..	..
1920 - 22	125	64	61	1 046	25.6	105.9	..	..	..
1930 - 32	93	47	45	1 040	19.1	78.8	..	..	..
1940 - 42	89	46	43	1 051	18.5	73.7	..	4	..
1950 - 52	91	47	44	1 060	17.9	81.4	2.41	2	..
1960 - 62	102	53	50	1 060	19.7	97.8	2.98	2	..
1970 - 72	84	43	41	1 057	16.1	83.3	2.46	1	13
1980 - 82	68	35	33	1 051	13.1	62.2	1.80	-	6
	BBCD	KMEU	KMEV	KMEW	KMEX	KMEY	KMEZ	KMFM	KMFN
1984	65	33	32	1 037	12.7	58.4	1.68	0.4	5.8
1985	67	34	33	1 048	13.0	59.5	1.70	0.4	5.5
1986	66	34	32	1 061	12.8	58.5	1.67	0.4	5.8
1987	66	34	32	1 053	13.0	58.8	1.67	0.3	5.1
1988	66	34	32	1 059	13.0	59.1	1.68	0.4	5.4
1989	63	33	31	1 049	12.5	56.8	1.61	0.3	5.0
1990	66	34	32	1 057	12.9	58.8	1.66	0.3	5.3
1991	67	34	33	1 056	13.1	59.8	1.69	0.4	5.5
1992	66	34	32	1 044	12.9	59.3	1.68	0.4	5.4
1993	63	32	31	1 046	12.4	57.4	1.61	0.4	6.4
1994	62	31	30	1 038	12.0	56.0	1.58	0.4	6.1
1995	60	31	29	1 043	11.7	54.5	1.55	0.4	6.6
1996	59	31	29	1 061	11.6	54.0	1.55	0.4	6.4
1997	59	31	29	1 055	11.6	54.3	1.58	0.3	5.3
1998	57	29	28	1 060	11.2	52.6	1.55	0.4	6.1
1999	55	28	27	1 050	10.8	50.8	1.51	0.3	5.2
2000	53	27	26	1 051	10.4	49.0	1.47	0.3	5.6
Northern Ireland[6]									
1900 - 02	..	..	..	..	..	..	..	..	..
1910 - 12	..	..	..	..	..	..	..	..	..
1920 - 22	31	16	15	1 048	24.2	105.9	..	..	..
1930 - 32	26	13	12	1 047	20.5	78.8	..	..	..
1940 - 42	27	14	13	1 078	20.8	73.7	..	..	..
1950 - 52	29	15	14	1 066	20.9	81.4	..	..	..
1960 - 62	31	16	15	1 068	22.5	111.5	3.47	7	23
1970 - 72	31	16	15	1 074	20.4	105.7	3.13	3	14
1980 - 82	28	14	13	1 048	18.0	87.5	2.59	-	8
	BBCE	KMFO	KMFP	KMFQ	KMFR	KMFS	KMFT	KMFU	KMFV
1984	27	14	13	1 069	17.6	83.4	2.50	0.2	5.8
1985	27	14	13	1 054	17.5	82.1	2.45	0.2	6.4
1986	28	15	13	1 076	17.8	82.7	2.44	0.1	4.4
1987	28	14	13	1 055	17.5	81.2	2.39	0.2	6.1
1988	28	14	13	1 056	17.4	80.6	2.35	0.1	5.0
1989	26	13	13	1 063	16.2	75.5	2.19	0.1	5.1
1990	26	13	13	1 049	16.5	76.5	2.21	0.1	4.4
1991	26	13	13	1 066	16.2	75.1	2.16	0.1	4.7
1992	25	13	12	1 040	15.6	72.7	2.08	0.1	4.9
1993	25	13	12	1 025	15.1	70.3	2.01	0.1	5.2
1994	24	12	12	1 053	14.6	68.0	1.94	0.2	6.3
1995	24	12	11	1 078	14.3	66.4	1.91	0.1	6.1
1996	24	12	12	1 032	14.6	67.6	1.95	0.2	6.2
1997	24	12	12	1 048	14.3	66.3	1.92	0.1	5.4
1998	24	12	12	1 039	14.0	64.9	1.89	0.1	5.1
1999	23	12	11	1 084	13.6	62.9	1.85	0.1	5.7
2000	22	11	10	1 070	12.7	58.7	1.74	0.1	4.3

Note: Figures may not add up due to rounding.
1 Males per 1,000 females.
2 Rate per 1,000 population and produced using whole numbers.
3 Rate per 1,000 women aged 15 - 44.
4 Total period fertility rate is the average number of children which would be born to a woman if she experienced the age-specific fertility rates of the period in question throughout her child-bearing life span. UK figures for the years 1970-72 and earlier are estimates.

5 On 1 October 1992 the legal definition of a stillbirth was changed from a baby born dead after 28 completed weeks gestation or more to one born dead after 24 completed weeks gestation or more. Between the 1 October and 31 December 1992 in the UK there were 258 babies born dead between 24 and 27 completed weeks gestation (216 in England and Wales, 35 in Scotland and 7 in Northern Ireland). If these babies were included in the stillbirth figures given, the stillbirth rate would be 4.7 for the UK and England and Wales while Scotland and Northern Ireland stillbirth rate would remain as stated.
6 From 1981, data for the United Kingdom and Northern Ireland have been revised to exclude births in Northern Ireland to non-residents of Northern Ireland.

Sources: Office for National Statistics: 01329 813339;
General Register Office for Scotland;
General register Office (Northern Ireland)

5.15 Birth occurrence inside and outside marriage by age of mother

Thousands

	Inside marriage						Outside marriage					
	All ages	Under 20	20 - 24	25 - 29	Over 30	Mean[1] age (Years)	All ages	Under 20	20 - 24	25 - 29	Over 30	Mean[1] age (Years)
United Kingdom[2]												
	KKEY	KKEZ	KKFY	KKFZ	KKGX	KKGY	KKGZ	KKIC	KKID	KKIE	KKIF	KKIG
1961	890	55	273	280	282	27.7	54	13	17	10	13	25.5
1971	828	70	301	271	185	26.4	74	24	25	13	12	23.8
1981	640	36	193	231	180	27.3	91	30	33	16	13	23.4
1986	596	21	159	231	185	27.9	158	45	60	31	22	23.7
1987	598	18	153	235	192	28.1	178	48	68	37	26	23.9
1988	589	16	144	234	195	28.2	198	51	76	42	29	24.1
1989	570	14	130	228	198	28.4	207	49	79	46	32	24.3
1990	576	13	121	233	209	28.6	223	51	83	53	37	24.5
1991	556	10	109	224	213	28.9	236	50	87	58	41	24.8
1992	540	9	98	216	218	29.1	241	46	86	62	46	25.1
1993	520	8	87	204	221	29.3	242	44	84	64	50	25.4
1994	510	7	78	194	231	29.6	240	41	80	65	55	25.7
1995	486	6	69	180	232	29.8	246	42	79	66	60	25.9
1996	473	6	61	170	237	30.1	260	45	80	69	66	26.0
1997	460	6	55	159	240	30.3	267	47	79	71	71	26.1
1998	447	6	51	149	243	30.5	270	49	77	70	74	26.2
1999	428	6	47	136	239	30.7	272	49	77	68	77	26.3
2000	411	5	44	126	237	30.9	268	47	77	66	78	26.4
Great Britain												
	KKIH	KKII	KKIJ	KKIK	KKIL	KKIM	KKIN	KKIO	KKIP	KKIQ	KKIR	KKIS
1961	859	53	264	270	272	27.7	53	13	17	10	13	25.5
1971	797	68	293	261	176	26.4	73	24	25	13	12	23.8
1981	614	34	186	223	171	27.2	89	29	32	16	13	23.3
1986	572	20	153	222	177	27.9	155	44	59	30	22	22.9
1987	574	17	147	227	184	28.0	174	46	66	36	25	23.4
1988	566	16	138	226	186	28.2	194	49	74	42	29	23.6
1989	549	13	125	220	190	28.4	202	48	77	45	32	24.2
1990	554	12	116	225	201	28.6	218	49	81	52	36	24.6
1991	535	10	105	216	205	28.9	231	48	85	57	41	24.8
1992	520	9	94	208	210	29.1	235	45	84	61	46	25.1
1993	500	7	84	196	213	29.3	236	42	82	62	49	25.4
1994	492	7	75	188	222	29.6	235	41	78	63	53	25.7
1995	468	6	66	173	223	29.8	240	40	77	65	59	25.9
1996	455	6	59	163	227	30.1	254	44	78	68	65	26.0
1997	442	6	53	152	231	30.3	261	46	76	69	69	26.2
1998	430	6	49	143	233	30.5	263	48	74	68	73	26.3
1999	412	6	46	131	230	30.7	265	48	74	67	76	26.4
2000	396	5	43	121	228	30.9	261	46	74	65	77	26.5

1 The mean ages presented in this table do not take into account the changing population distribution of women.

2 From 1981, data for the United Kingdom have been revised to exclude births in Northern Ireland to non-residents of Northern Ireland.

Sources: Office for National Statistics: 01329 813339; General Register Office for Scotland; Northern Ireland Statistics and Research Agency

5.16 Live births by age of mother

Numbers

All live births - United Kingdom[1,2]

Age-group:	Under 20	20 - 24	25 - 29	30 - 34	35 - 39	40 - 44	45 and over	All ages
	KMDV	KMDW	KMDX	KMDY	KMDZ	KMES	KMET	KMBZ
1990	62 997	203 444	285 909	176 732	58 375	10 294	548	798 364
1991	59 702	196 193	282 069	182 637	60 539	10 449	577	792 269
1992	54 922	184 359	277 315	189 020	63 768	10 802	553	780 799
1993	51 463	171 096	267 413	193 565	66 235	11 123	582	761 526
1994	47 874	157 468	259 367	202 880	70 871	11 432	536	750 480
1995	47 646	147 056	246 017	204 601	73 945	12 008	585	731 882
1996	50 793	141 090	238 857	210 490	78 335	12 832	638	733 163
1997	52 851	133 257	229 429	212 162	84 508	13 731	618	726 622
1998	54 822	127 230	218 072	212 876	88 729	14 453	640	716 888
1999	54 921	124 036	204 808	208 986	91 272	15 210	695	699 976
2000	52 060	120 304	191 583	202 893	95 400	16 032	708	679 029

Age-specific fertility rates - United Kingdom[1,2]

Age-group:	Under 20	20 - 24	25 - 29	30 - 34	35 - 39	40 - 44	45 and over	All ages
	KMBR	KMBS	KMBT	KMBU	KMBV	KMBW	KMBX	KMBY
1990	33.1	90.8	122.8	86.4	31.0	5.0	0.3	64.0
1991	32.9	88.9	119.9	86.5	32.0	5.0	0.3	63.6
1992	31.8	85.5	117.6	87.0	33.2	5.5	0.3	63.4
1993	30.8	81.8	114.3	86.8	33.8	5.8	0.3	62.3
1994	28.8	78.2	112.1	88.4	35.4	6.0	0.3	61.6
1995	28.3	75.7	108.5	87.2	35.9	6.4	0.3	60.1
1996[1]	29.6	76.2	106.7	88.6	36.9	6.8	0.3	60.1
1997	30.2	75.4	104.6	88.9	38.7	7.1	0.3	59.5
1998	30.7	74.1	102.0	89.7	39.5	7.4	0.3	58.6
1999	30.7	72.4	98.8	88.9	39.5	7.6	0.4	57.1
2000	29.1	69.3	94.9	87.6	40.2	7.7	0.4	55.2

All live births - England and Wales

Age-group:	Under 20	20 - 24	25 - 29	30 - 34	35 - 39	40 - 44	45 and over	All ages
	KGSA	KGSB	KGSC	KGSD	KGSE	KGSF	KGSG	KGSH
1990	55 541	180 136	252 577	156 264	51 905	9 220	497	706 140
1991	52 396	173 356	248 727	161 259	53 644	9 316	519	699 217
1992	47 861	163 311	244 798	166 839	56 650	9 696	501	689 656
1993	45 121	151 975	235 961	171 061	58 824	9 986	539	673 467
1994	42 026	140 240	229 102	179 568	63 061	10 241	488	664 726
1995	41 938	130 744	217 418	181 202	65 517	10 779	540	648 138
1996	44 667	125 732	211 103	186 377	69 503	11 516	587	649 485
1997	46 372	118 589	202 792	187 528	74 900	12 332	582	643 095
1998	48 285	113 537	193 144	188 499	78 881	12 980	575	635 901
1999	48 375	110 722	181 931	185 311	81 281	13 617	635	621 872
2000	45 846	107 741	170 701	180 113	84 974	14 403	663	604 441

Age-specific fertility rates - England and Wales

Age-group:	Under 20	20 - 24	25 - 29	30 - 34	35 - 39	40 - 44	45 and over	All ages
	KGSI	KGSJ	KGSK	KGSL	KGSM	KGSN	KGSO	KGSP
1990	33.3	91.4	122.6	86.9	31.1	5.0	0.3	64.2
1991	33.0	89.3	119.4	86.7	32.1	5.1	0.3	63.6
1992	31.7	86.2	117.3	87.2	33.4	5.5	0.3	63.5
1993	31.0	82.7	114.1	87.0	34.1	5.9	0.3	62.6
1994	29.0	79.4	112.1	88.7	35.8	6.1	0.3	61.9
1995	28.5	76.8	108.6	87.3	36.2	6.5	0.3	60.4
1996	29.8	77.5	106.9	88.6	37.2	6.9	0.3	60.5
1997	30.2	76.6	104.8	88.8	38.9	7.3	0.3	59.8
1998	30.7	75.5	102.2	89.9	39.8	7.5	0.3	59.0
1999	30.8	73.7	99.2	89.2	39.8	7.7	0.4	57.6
2000	29.2	70.6	95.4	88.0	40.5	7.9	0.4	55.7

5.16 Live births by age of mother

continued

Numbers

All live births - Scotland[1]

Age-group:	Under 20	20 - 24	25 - 29	30 - 34	35 - 39	40 - 44	45 and over	All ages
	KGTA	KGTB	KGTC	KGTD	KGTE	KGTF	KGTG	KGTH
1990	5 603	16 953	24 203	14 379	4 143	603	24	65 973
1991	5 523	16 723	24 163	15 206	4 589	686	31	67 024
1992	5 206	15 405	23 571	15 973	4 877	674	23	65 789
1993[1]	4 750	13 923	22 758	16 088	5 049	697	23	63 337
1994	4 303	12 637	21 851	16 705	5 346	736	26	61 656
1995	4 280	11 913	20 395	16 803	5 799	811	26	60 051
1996	4 544	11 026	19 511	17 038	6 126	891	32	59 296
1997	4 835	10 607	18 782	17 455	6 740	936	19	59 440
1998	4 802	9 804	17 477	17 207	6 893	1 027	43	57 319
1999	4 755	9 440	16 011	16 722	7 034	1 096	41	55 147
2000	4 599	8 962	14 676	16 233	7 395	1 133	29	53 076

Age-specific fertility rates - Scotland[1]

Age-group:	Under 20	20 - 24	25 - 29	30 - 34	35 - 39	40 - 44	45 and over	All ages
	KGTI	KGTJ	KGTK	KGTL	KGTM	KGTN	KGTO	KGTP
1990	31.9	82.4	117.2	76.7	24.5	3.5	0.2	58.8
1991	33.3	82.3	116.5	78.3	26.8	4.0	0.2	59.8
1992	33.1	77.6	113.6	80.7	27.8	4.1	0.1	59.3
1993	31.2	72.4	109.7	79.7	28.0	4.3	0.1	57.4
1994	28.4	68.2	106.1	81.2	28.9	4.5	0.2	56.0
1995	28.1	66.7	100.8	80.5	30.5	5.0	0.2	54.5
1996	29.6	64.6	97.9	81.6	31.4	5.4	0.2	54.0
1997	30.9	65.5	97.0	83.5	33.9	5.5	0.1	54.3
1998	30.4	62.7	94.2	82.6	34.1	6.0	0.3	52.6
1999	30.0	60.7	90.4	81.3	34.2	6.2	0.2	50.8
2000	29.1	57.4	86.9	80.5	35.4	6.1	0.2	49.0

All live births - Northern Ireland[2]

Age-group:	Under 20	20 - 24	25 - 29	30 - 34	35 - 39	40 - 44	45 and over	All ages
	KMDF	KMDG	KMDH	KMDI	KMDJ	KMDK	KMDL	KMDM
1990	1 853	6 355	9 129	6 089	2 327	471	27	26 251
1991	1 783	6 114	9 179	6 172	2 306	447	27	26 028
1992	1 855	5 643	8 946	6 208	2 241	432	29	25 354
1993	1 592	5 198	8 694	6 416	2 362	440	20	24 722
1994	1 545	4 591	8 414	6 607	2 464	455	22	24 098
1995	1 428	4 399	8 204	6 596	2 629	418	19	23 693
1996	1 582	4 332	8 243	7 075	2 706	425	19	24 382
1997	1 644	4 061	7 855	7 179	2 868	463	17	24 087
1998	1 735	3 889	7 451	7 170	2 955	446	22	23 668
1999	1 791	3 874	6 866	6 953	2 957	498	19	22 957
2000	1 615	3 601	6 206	6 547	3 031	496	16	21 512

Age-specific fertility rates - Northern Ireland[2]

Age - group:	Under 20	20 - 24	25 - 29	30 - 34	35 - 39	40 - 44	45 and over	All ages
	KMDN	KMDO	KMDP	KMDQ	KMDR	KMDS	KMDT	KMDU
1990	29.2	100.4	148.0	107.6	47.4	9.6	0.6	76.5
1991	28.7	97.2	146.4	105.3	45.8	9.0	0.6	75.1
1992	30.2	90.1	141.3	103.1	43.0	8.8	0.6	72.7
1993	26.1	83.1	136.0	104.2	44.0	8.9	0.4	70.3
1994	25.4	74.8	130.8	104.9	44.4	9.2	0.4	68.0
1995	23.4	73.3	128.2	102.8	45.6	8.4	0.4	66.4
1996	25.6	73.5	128.3	108.2	45.4	8.4	0.4	67.6
1997	26.5	70.8	123.3	109.2	46.5	8.8	0.3	66.3
1998	27.9	69.5	117.9	108.2	47.1	8.2	0.4	64.9
1999	28.9	70.5	111.6	104.7	46.0	8.9	0.4	62.9
2000	26.1	65.7	103.3	98.9	46.3	8.5	0.3	58.7

1 The 'All ages' figure for Scotland includes births to mothers whose age was not known. There were 65 such births in 1990, 103 in 1991, 60 in 1992, 49 in 1993, 52 in 1994, 24 in 1995, 128 in 1996, 66 in 1997, 66 in 1998, 48 in 1999 and 49 in 2000.

2 Data for the United Kingdom and Northern Ireland have been revised to exclude births in Northern Ireland to non-residents of Northern Ireland.

Sources: Office for National Statistics: 01329 813339;
General Register Office for Scotland;
General Register Office (Northern Ireland)

5.17 Legal abortions
Total by age for residents

	England and Wales										
	All ages	Under 15	15	16 - 19	20 - 24	25 - 29	30 - 34	35 - 39	40 - 44	45 and over	Not stated
1986	147 619	924	2 970	33 819	45 316	28 656	18 005	12 977	4 521	409	22
1987	156 191	907	2 858	35 167	49 256	31 243	18 960	12 639	4 757	390	14
1988	168 298	859	2 709	37 928	54 067	34 584	20 000	12 681	5 047	412	11
1989	170 463	803	2 580	36 182	54 880	36 604	21 284	12 713	5 020	388	9
1990	173 900	873	2 549	35 520	55 281	38 770	22 431	12 956	5 104	404	12
1991	167 376	886	2 272	31 130	52 678	38 611	23 445	13 035	4 901	408	10
1992	160 501	905	2 095	27 589	49 052	38 430	23 870	13 252	4 844	452	12
1993	157 846	964	2 119	25 806	46 846	38 139	24 690	13 885	4 889	494	14
1994	156 539	1 080	2 166	25 223	44 871	38 081	25 507	14 156	5 008	440	7
1995	154 315	946	2 324	24 945	43 394	37 254	25 759	14 352	4 868	457	16
1996	167 916	1 098	2 547	28 790	46 356	39 311	28 228	16 118	5 027	428	13
1997	170 145	1 020	2 414	29 947	44 960	40 159	28 892	16 858	5 413	482	-
1998	177 871	1 103	2 656	33 236	45 766	40 366	30 449	18 174	5 576	511	34
1999	173 701	1 066	2 537	32 807	45 004	38 492	29 139	18 341	5 755	502	58
2000	175 542	1 048	2 700	33 218	47 099	37 852	28 735	18 589	5 794	459	48

	Scotland									
	All ages	Under 15	15	16 - 19	20 - 24	25 - 29	30 - 34	35 - 39	40 - 44	45 and over
1986	9 628	74	236	2 529	2 985	1 744	1 081	708	249	22
1987	9 460	70	210	2 417	2 996	1 729	1 082	697	242	17
1988	10 128	65	218	2 529	3 304	1 970	1 107	663	257	15
1989	10 209	53	209	2 561	3 202	1 968	1 229	706	266	15
1990	10 219	54	186	2 539	3 242	2 063	1 161	700	253	21
1991	11 068	77	203	2 571	3 486	2 253	1 445	743	262	28
1992	10 818	73	174	2 377	3 389	2 291	1 444	799	254	17
1993	11 076	92	193	2 300	3 368	2 447	1 492	891	264	29
1994	11 392	78	215	2 312	3 486	2 431	1 648	877	315	30
1995	11 143	79	233	2 169	3 399	2 438	1 609	887	296	33
1996	11 978	87	236	2 362	3 571	2 603	1 801	960	331	27
1997	12 109	85	204	2 431	3 444	2 651	1 854	1 093	322	25
1998	12 485	73	213	2 707	3 426	2 749	1 807	1 149	339	22
1999	12 167	69	182	2 635	3 354	2 553	1 810	1 180	361	23
2000[1]	11 993	93	181	2 610	3 354	2 403	1 767	1 176	381	28

1 Data are provisional.

Sources: Office for National Statistics; Scottish Executive

5.18 Deaths: analysis by age and gender
Annual averages or calendar years

Numbers

	All ages[1]	Under 1 year	1-4	5-9	10-14	15-19	20-24	25-34	35-44	45-54	55-64	65-74	75-84	85 and over
Males														
1900 - 02	340 664	87 242	37 834	8 429	4 696	7 047	8 766	19 154	24 739	30 488	37 610	39 765	28 320	6 563
1910 - 12	303 703	63 885	29 452	7 091	4 095	5 873	6 817	16 141	21 813	28 981	37 721	45 140	29 397	7 283
1920 - 22	284 876	48 044	19 008	6 052	3 953	5 906	6 572	13 663	19 702	29 256	40 583	49 398	34 937	7 801
1930 - 32	284 249	28 840	11 276	4 580	2 890	5 076	6 495	12 327	16 326	29 376	47 989	63 804	45 247	10 022
1940 - 42	314 643	24 624	6 949	3 400	2 474	4 653	4 246	11 506	17 296	30 082	57 076	79 652	59 733	12 900
1950 - 52	307 312	14 105	2 585	1 317	919	1 498	2 289	5 862	11 074	27 637	53 691	86 435	79 768	20 131
1960 - 62	318 850	12 234	1 733	971	871	1 718	1 857	3 842	8 753	26 422	63 009	87 542	83 291	26 605
1970 - 72	335 166	9 158	1 485	1 019	802	1 778	2 104	3 590	7 733	24 608	64 898	105 058	82 905	30 027
1980 - 82	330 495	4 829	774	527	652	1 999	1 943	3 736	6 568	19 728	54 159	105 155	98 488	31 936
1990 - 92	312 521	3 315	623	372	396	1 349	2 059	4 334	6 979	15 412	40 424	87 849	106 376	43 032
	KHUA	KHUB	KHUC	KHUD	KHUE	KHUF	KHUG	KHUH	KHUI	KHUJ	KHUK	KHUL	KHUM	KHUN
1980	332 370	5 174	792	609	659	2 022	1 940	3 786	6 698	20 577	55 176	107 089	96 301	31 547
1981	329 145	4 759	771	517	666	2 008	1 919	3 761	6 544	19 740	53 770	104 950	97 881	31 859
1982	329 971	4 555	760	456	632	1 966	1 971	3 661	6 462	18 867	53 531	103 426	101 281	32 403
1983	328 824	4 230	695	469	609	1 834	1 899	3 601	6 537	18 238	54 493	100 469	103 038	32 712
1984	321 095	3 995	725	423	580	1 708	1 999	3 595	6 425	17 647	53 715	95 420	102 513	32 350
1985	331 562	4 003	728	393	583	1 612	2 031	3 452	6 728	17 316	52 502	97 458	109 241	35 515
1986	327 160	4 219	653	384	444	1 676	2 067	3 668	6 712	16 814	50 352	95 987	108 123	36 061
1987	318 282	4 105	657	377	470	1 612	2 125	3 776	6 793	15 950	47 675	93 348	105 773	35 621
1988	319 119	4 110	680	433	460	1 525	2 160	3 983	6 860	16 016	46 001	91 893	107 082	37 916
1989	320 193	3 799	699	414	398	1 537	2 118	3 968	6 832	15 560	43 693	90 304	109 450	41 421
1990	314 601	3 614	674	376	406	1 487	2 197	4 354	6 991	15 507	41 983	88 458	107 451	41 103
1991	314 427	3 377	636	395	404	1 417	2 049	4 270	7 102	15 493	40 256	88 014	107 416	43 598
1992	308 535	2 954	559	346	377	1 144	1 932	4 379	6 845	15 236	39 033	87 075	104 261	44 394
1993[2]	317 796	2 746	582	325	401	1 072	1 907	4 442	6 672	15 631	38 734	90 160	105 693	49 431
1994	303 333	2 660	497	319	400	1 041	1 829	4 741	6 661	14 983	36 469	86 896	98 982	47 855
1995	310 722	2 595	447	314	388	1 115	1 810	4 748	6 754	15 644	36 068	85 459	103 324	52 056
1996	305 323	2 562	489	267	352	1 104	1 693	4 746	6 789	15 796	35 033	81 333	102 090	53 069
1997	300 414	2 391	456	300	364	1 111	1 712	4 583	6 667	15 689	33 707	77 870	101 365	54 199
1998	300 160	2 327	463	283	343	1 058	1 539	4 684	6 902	15 825	33 778	75 718	101 468	55 772
1999	300 368	2 318	456	257	319	1 085	1 553	4 516	6 946	15 849	33 338	73 736	101 795	58 200
2000	290 186	2 120	380	253	326	1 042	1 491	4 397	7 081	15 470	32 556	69 499	98 075	57 496
Females														
1900 - 02	322 058	68 770	36 164	8 757	5 034	6 818	8 264	18 702	21 887	25 679	34 521	42 456	34 907	10 099
1910 - 12	289 608	49 865	27 817	7 113	4 355	5 683	6 531	15 676	19 647	24 481	32 813	46 453	37 353	11 828
1920 - 22	274 772	35 356	17 323	5 808	4 133	5 729	6 753	14 878	18 121	24 347	34 026	48 573	45 521	14 203
1930 - 32	275 336	21 072	9 995	3 990	2 734	4 721	5 931	12 699	15 373	24 695	39 471	59 520	56 250	18 886
1940 - 42	296 646	17 936	5 952	2 743	2 068	4 180	5 028	11 261	14 255	23 629	42 651	70 907	71 377	24 658
1950 - 52	291 597	10 293	2 098	880	625	1 115	1 717	5 018	8 989	18 875	37 075	75 220	92 848	36 844
1960 - 62	304 871	8 887	1 334	627	522	684	811	2 504	6 513	16 720	36 078	73 118	105 956	51 117
1970 - 72	322 968	6 666	1 183	654	459	718	900	2 110	5 345	15 594	36 177	75 599	109 539	68 024
1980 - 82	330 269	3 561	585	355	425	733	772	2 099	4 360	12 206	32 052	72 618	117 760	82 743
1990 - 92	328 218	2 431	485	259	255	520	714	1 989	4 340	9 707	25 105	61 951	115 467	104 994
	KIUA	KIUB	KIUC	KIUD	KIUE	KIUF	KIUG	KIUH	KIUI	KIUJ	KIUK	KIUL	KIUM	KIUN
1980	329 149	3 938	596	409	442	771	811	2 157	4 460	12 583	32 349	73 672	116 461	80 500
1981	328 829	3 402	599	352	424	738	737	2 083	4 309	12 275	31 625	72 476	117 458	82 351
1982	332 830	3 342	561	304	410	689	767	2 057	4 312	11 759	32 183	71 705	119 362	85 379
1983	330 277	3 126	568	318	374	719	698	1 914	4 318	11 384	32 197	69 266	118 940	86 455
1984	323 823	3 005	537	304	344	665	722	1 932	4 269	10 947	32 262	66 432	116 649	85 756
1985	339 094	3 027	574	314	355	626	729	1 852	4 397	10 581	32 010	68 505	122 445	93 679
1986	333 575	2 961	561	275	307	635	769	1 882	4 387	10 211	29 954	67 313	120 663	93 657
1987	326 060	2 972	550	265	288	614	733	1 974	4 454	10 177	29 037	65 570	117 266	92 160
1988	330 059	2 951	552	264	251	612	745	1 915	4 615	9 887	28 154	65 020	117 731	97 362
1989	337 540	2 743	551	271	268	598	773	1 955	4 506	9 834	27 324	64 575	120 975	103 167
1990	327 198	2 658	489	249	273	534	700	1 967	4 463	9 718	26 350	62 019	116 357	101 421
1991	331 754	2 448	512	280	264	538	738	2 005	4 295	9 699	24 952	62 200	116 924	106 899
1992	325 703	2 187	455	249	228	489	704	1 994	4 262	9 705	24 013	61 635	113 119	106 663
1993[2]	340 685	2 084	436	239	283	465	659	2 121	4 204	9 973	23 900	63 767	114 905	117 649
1994	324 303	1 989	410	205	232	406	626	2 053	4 285	10 081	22 401	62 069	106 816	112 730
1995	334 771	1 931	370	224	250	449	592	2 140	4 203	10 389	22 093	60 988	110 247	120 895
1996	330 701	1 904	355	214	224	493	589	2 140	4 215	10 301	21 406	57 889	109 578	121 393
1997	329 332	1 862	333	215	239	487	574	1 960	4 323	10 412	20 999	55 687	108 276	123 965
1998	329 012	1 752	347	213	215	486	568	1 971	4 289	10 430	20 874	54 200	107 135	126 532
1999	331 694	1 727	338	195	240	473	553	1 924	4 372	10 430	21 045	52 240	106 841	131 316
2000	318 180	1 671	277	177	203	449	535	1 961	4 509	10 459	20 533	48 994	101 711	126 701

United Kingdom

5.18 Deaths: analysis by age and gender
Annual averages or calendar years
continued

Numbers

	All ages[1]	Under 1 year	1-4	5-9	10-14	15-19	20-24	25-34	35-44	45-54	55-64	65-74	75-84	85 and over
							England and Wales							
Males														
1900 - 02	288 886	76 095	32 051	7 066	3 818	5 611	7 028	15 869	21 135	26 065	31 600	33 568	23 835	5 144
1910 - 12	257 253	54 678	24 676	5 907	3 348	4 765	5 596	13 603	18 665	24 820	32 217	38 016	24 928	6 036
1920 - 22	240 605	39 796	15 565	5 151	3 314	4 901	5 447	11 551	17 004	25 073	34 639	42 025	29 685	6 455
1930 - 32	243 147	23 331	9 099	3 844	2 435	4 354	5 580	10 600	14 041	25 657	41 581	54 910	39 091	8 624
1940 - 42	268 876	19 393	5 616	2 834	2 051	3 832	3 156	9 484	14 744	25 983	46 948	68 791	51 779	11 158
1950 - 52	266 879	11 498	2 131	1 087	778	1 248	1 947	4 990	9 489	23 815	46 948	75 774	69 496	17 677
1960 - 62	278 369	10 157	1 444	812	742	1 523	1 624	3 278	7 524	22 813	54 908	77 000	73 180	23 364
1970 - 72	293 934	7 818	1 259	860	677	1 524	1 788	3 079	6 637	21 348	56 667	92 389	73 365	26 522
1980 - 82	290 352	4 168	657	452	555	1 716	1 619	3 169	5 590	16 909	47 144	92 485	87 338	28 551
1990 - 92	275 550	2 926	545	325	338	1 157	1 757	3 717	6 057	13 258	34 977	77 063	94 672	38 757
	KHVA	KHVB	KHVC	KHVD	KHVE	KHVF	KHVG	KHVH	KHVI	KHVJ	KHVK	KHVL	KHVM	KHVN
1980	291 869	4 471	668	517	546	1 745	1 613	3 203	5 710	17 693	48 053	94 188	85 300	28 162
1981	289 022	4 119	651	447	573	1 734	1 576	3 181	5 535	16 889	46 858	92 189	86 774	28 496
1982	290 166	3 914	652	391	546	1 669	1 668	3 122	5 526	16 144	46 521	91 079	89 940	28 994
1983	289 419	3 654	604	391	514	1 580	1 635	3 071	5 581	15 632	47 315	88 622	91 531	29 289
1984	282 357	3 443	610	348	501	1 484	1 728	3 033	5 512	15 113	46 904	83 728	90 983	28 970
1985	292 327	3 510	638	328	503	1 374	1 738	2 953	5 776	14 838	45 704	85 695	97 362	31 908
1986	287 894	3 724	573	325	380	1 429	1 746	3 104	5 767	14 370	43 637	84 437	96 201	32 201
1987	280 177	3 637	578	309	404	1 389	1 811	3 218	5 823	13 678	41 367	82 021	94 060	31 882
1988	280 931	3 649	587	374	402	1 279	1 802	3 367	5 855	13 701	39 791	80 870	95 306	33 948
1989	281 290	3 368	606	371	337	1 325	1 782	3 380	5 947	13 407	37 680	79 012	97 027	37 048
1990	277 336	3 207	593	333	338	1 295	1 889	3 714	6 060	13 342	36 405	77 604	95 539	37 017
1991	277 582	2 966	554	341	354	1 208	1 760	3 687	6 160	13 316	34 853	77 227	95 815	39 341
1992	271 732	2 606	487	302	322	969	1 621	3 751	5 952	13 117	33 674	76 357	92 662	39 912
1993[2]	279 561	2 407	510	276	340	912	1 596	3 813	5 784	13 416	33 347	78 881	93 754	44 525
1994	267 555	2 367	432	278	331	843	1 550	4 065	5 769	12 923	31 320	76 270	88 230	43 177
1995	274 449	2 305	391	269	340	910	1 533	4 043	5 880	13 487	30 973	74 970	92 291	47 057
1996	268 682	2 272	441	236	291	925	1 409	4 064	5 843	13 565	30 066	71 046	90 708	47 816
1997	264 865	2 137	412	267	325	947	1 442	3 940	5 707	13 484	28 907	68 024	90 207	49 066
1998	264 707	2 070	413	240	291	875	1 292	4 013	5 895	13 595	29 052	66 099	90 450	50 422
1999	264 299	2 075	405	218	275	902	1 270	3 847	5 934	13 620	28 689	64 296	90 431	52 337
2000	255 547	1 886	335	217	284	872	1 224	3 755	6 048	13 367	27 898	60 593	87 126	51 942
Females														
1900 - 02	269 432	60 090	30 674	7 278	4 010	5 265	6 497	15 065	18 253	21 474	28 424	35 307	29 118	7 977
1910 - 12	242 079	42 642	23 335	5 883	3 519	4 522	5 256	12 742	16 363	20 611	27 571	38 489	31 363	9 782
1920 - 22	229 908	29 178	14 174	4 928	3 456	4 719	5 533	12 244	15 142	20 580	28 633	41 010	38 439	11 871
1930 - 32	233 915	16 929	8 013	3 338	2 293	3 969	5 039	10 716	13 022	21 190	33 798	50 844	48 531	16 234
1940 - 42	253 702	14 174	4 726	2 265	1 695	3 426	4 198	9 470	12 093	20 413	36 814	60 987	61 891	21 550
1950 - 52	252 176	8 367	1 727	732	520	893	1 365	4 131	7 586	16 161	31 875	65 087	81 154	32 579
1960 - 62	266 849	7 409	1 103	527	444	591	700	2 147	5 576	14 389	31 083	63 543	93 548	45 789
1970 - 72	284 181	5 677	1 020	562	396	620	806	1 814	4 585	13 417	31 222	65 817	96 952	61 293
1980 - 82	290 026	3 064	511	301	365	635	670	1 821	3 740	10 420	27 606	63 023	103 676	74 194
1990 - 92	288 851	2 161	420	227	217	455	625	1 718	3 765	8 347	21 466	53 783	101 752	93 914
	KIVA	KIVB	KIVC	KIVD	KIVE	KIVF	KIVG	KIVH	KIVI	KIVJ	KIVK	KIVL	KIVM	KIVN
1980	289 516	3 428	518	349	373	667	696	1 861	3 771	10 757	27 857	64 087	102 728	72 424
1981	288 868	2 902	529	302	368	650	642	1 821	3 742	10 513	27 211	62 762	103 554	73 872
1982	291 695	2 861	485	253	353	588	672	1 781	3 708	9 990	27 751	62 221	104 745	76 287
1983	290 189	2 727	489	269	332	629	597	1 655	3 708	9 786	27 792	59 913	104 844	77 448
1984	284 524	2 594	454	260	302	575	621	1 676	3 658	9 343	27 764	57 813	102 744	76 720
1985	298 407	2 631	497	260	308	544	630	1 583	3 803	9 111	27 664	59 285	108 099	83 992
1986	293 309	2 589	491	248	272	562	674	1 646	3 834	8 761	25 785	58 360	106 463	83 624
1987	286 817	2 635	489	237	246	525	639	1 708	3 897	8 774	25 000	56 858	103 354	82 455
1988	290 477	2 621	498	232	218	542	650	1 670	4 025	8 448	24 104	56 567	103 666	87 236
1989	295 582	2 440	472	241	226	531	650	1 678	3 925	8 406	23 336	55 932	106 000	91 745
1990	287 510	2 357	434	220	230	472	616	1 702	3 875	8 337	22 511	53 770	102 440	90 546
1991	292 462	2 192	439	248	222	462	644	1 729	3 703	8 369	21 303	54 156	103 268	95 727
1992	286 581	1 933	387	214	199	432	615	1 722	3 717	8 336	20 585	53 423	99 548	95 470
1993[2]	299 238	1 835	374	194	246	394	575	1 802	3 625	8 614	20 423	55 245	100 947	104 964
1994	285 639	1 753	364	187	204	357	535	1 771	3 669	8 688	19 039	53 921	94 197	100 954
1995	295 234	1 677	333	196	210	382	502	1 859	3 644	9 001	18 891	52 987	97 162	108 390
1996	291 453	1 687	320	175	196	430	507	1 852	3 658	8 852	18 244	50 195	96 679	108 658
1997	290 416	1 663	297	177	209	426	490	1 718	3 737	9 016	17 949	48 293	95 508	110 933
1998	290 308	1 555	309	177	189	407	480	1 724	3 678	9 066	17 927	46 894	94 713	113 189
1999	291 819	1 546	300	168	215	385	470	1 668	3 786	9 029	18 031	45 100	93 878	117 243
2000	280 117	1 491	246	156	179	384	466	1 688	3 874	9 090	17 635	42 174	89 310	113 424

5.18 Deaths: analysis by age and gender
continued
Annual averages or calendar years

Numbers

	All ages[1]	Under 1 year	1-4	5-9	10-14	15-19	20-24	25-34	35-44	45-54	55-64	65-74	75-84	85 and over
								Scotland						
Males														
1900 - 02	40 224	9 189	4 798	1 083	672	1 069	1 292	2 506	2 935	3 591	4 597	4 531	3 117	834
1910 - 12	35 981	7 510	3 935	962	595	826	910	1 969	2 469	3 325	4 356	5 113	3 182	813
1920 - 22	34 649	6 757	2 847	710	489	747	791	1 616	2 128	3 314	4 785	5 624	3 928	911
1930 - 32	32 476	4 426	1 771	610	365	568	706	1 352	1 848	2 979	5 095	6 906	4 839	1 010
1940 - 42	36 384	3 973	1 011	449	321	668	888	1 643	2 090	3 348	5 728	8 556	6 317	1 337
1950 - 52	32 236	1 949	349	175	105	200	265	693	1 267	3 151	5 574	8 544	8 094	1 871
1960 - 62	32 401	1 578	222	121	102	146	185	456	1 013	2 986	6 682	8 505	7 980	2 425
1970 - 72	32 446	944	168	119	93	178	233	396	875	2 617	6 641	10 176	7 383	2 624
1980 - 82	31 723	451	80	56	71	206	233	423	776	2 280	5 601	10 152	8 804	2 591
1990 - 92	29 421	287	57	34	40	137	230	485	744	1 730	4 402	8 611	9 311	3 353
	KHWA	KHWB	KHWC	KHWD	KHWE	KHWF	KHWG	KHWH	KHWI	KHWJ	KHWK	KHWL	KHWM	KHWN
1980	31 669	481	93	65	78	190	223	421	778	2 316	5 628	10 248	8 571	2 577
1981	31 700	435	71	50	66	208	250	439	816	2 330	5 506	10 193	8 788	2 548
1982	31 801	436	77	53	69	220	225	410	733	2 195	5 669	10 015	9 052	2 647
1983	31 196	380	67	53	65	185	178	406	764	2 131	5 769	9 414	9 204	2 580
1984	30 731	389	87	53	65	172	202	429	696	2 017	5 493	9 337	9 222	2 569
1985	31 147	342	57	49	58	174	208	390	759	1 959	5 486	9 339	9 569	2 757
1986	31 111	334	66	44	49	177	238	436	757	1 967	5 354	9 169	9 574	2 946
1987	30 384	331	54	46	47	163	212	415	779	1 870	5 131	9 058	9 383	2 895
1988	30 195	324	64	39	42	181	246	475	808	1 915	4 997	8 763	9 314	3 027
1989	31 025	331	62	24	45	150	246	445	719	1 721	4 889	9 028	9 922	3 443
1990	29 617	297	62	31	50	138	240	502	745	1 734	4 512	8 635	9 499	3 172
1991	29 312	299	59	42	34	150	211	441	757	1 741	4 382	8 657	9 209	3 330
1992	29 334	265	51	28	36	123	238	511	731	1 716	4 313	8 541	9 225	3 556
1993[2]	30 504	240	50	39	37	107	225	490	725	1 817	4 375	9 031	9 470	3 898
1994	28 416	212	42	27	48	133	212	538	715	1 684	4 114	8 575	8 446	3 670
1995	28 791	197	37	30	30	152	195	563	698	1 746	4 144	8 449	8 604	3 946
1996	29 223	206	41	23	46	139	212	556	755	1 845	4 087	8 259	8 926	4 128
1997	28 305	186	32	22	27	114	208	521	788	1 794	3 876	7 909	8 791	4 037
1998	28 132	183	37	34	39	134	200	524	843	1 796	3 828	7 746	8 585	4 183
1999	28 605	161	31	23	33	138	215	545	818	1 820	3 773	7 569	8 908	4 571
2000	27 511	173	33	24	28	115	198	512	842	1 716	3 789	7 224	8 523	4 334
Females														
1900 - 02	39 891	7 143	4 477	1 162	747	1 058	1 246	2 625	2 732	3 130	4 485	5 273	4 305	1 508
1910 - 12	36 132	5 854	3 674	981	618	836	910	2 149	2 473	2 909	3 960	5 636	4 588	1 552
1920 - 22	34 449	5 029	2 602	687	489	711	889	1 947	2 266	2 828	4 157	5 587	5 443	1 814
1930 - 32	32 377	3 319	1 602	527	339	568	666	1 508	1 812	2 731	4 380	6 630	6 178	2 117
1940 - 42	33 715	2 852	921	373	283	595	656	1 382	1 672	2 528	4 630	7 674	7 613	2 536
1950 - 52	31 525	1 432	284	115	84	185	293	714	1 127	2 188	4 204	8 157	9 310	3 431
1960 - 62	30 559	1 107	170	80	63	72	87	287	762	1 897	4 115	7 752	9 991	4 177
1970 - 72	30 978	694	118	69	46	73	74	231	608	1 769	4 036	7 823	10 112	5 324
1980 - 82	32 326	337	49	37	44	74	73	213	493	1 456	3 565	7 781	11 333	6 871
1990 - 92	31 747	190	45	20	29	49	72	218	458	1 093	2 966	6 630	11 079	8 898
	KIWA	KIWB	KIWC	KIWD	KIWE	KIWF	KIWG	KIWH	KIWI	KIWJ	KIWK	KIWL	KIWM	KIWN
1980	31 630	350	51	41	44	77	90	222	547	1 511	3 587	7 673	10 988	6 449
1981	32 128	345	46	35	43	68	69	213	453	1 414	3 556	7 935	11 144	6 807
1982	33 221	317	50	35	45	78	60	203	479	1 444	3 552	7 735	11 867	7 356
1983	32 258	266	51	33	33	67	76	201	504	1 317	3 568	7 558	11 340	7 244
1984	31 614	283	62	32	37	72	78	205	475	1 320	3 703	6 979	11 134	7 234
1985	32 820	282	55	37	34	63	76	207	481	1 179	3 563	7 449	11 604	7 790
1986	32 356	247	50	16	24	50	77	188	441	1 181	3 372	7 251	11 476	7 983
1987	31 630	232	44	21	34	60	70	195	429	1 160	3 301	7 032	11 262	7 790
1988	31 762	219	33	22	21	54	63	197	470	1 115	3 250	6 879	11 361	8 078
1989	33 992	223	56	23	27	54	104	224	470	1 156	3 279	7 052	12 100	9 224
1990	31 910	213	32	16	34	46	68	204	468	1 099	3 109	6 685	11 233	8 703
1991	31 729	174	54	22	31	57	74	225	463	1 070	2 974	6 542	11 059	8 984
1992	31 603	184	50	23	21	45	73	225	442	1 109	2 816	6 663	10 944	9 008
1993[2]	33 545	172	45	34	27	55	60	258	460	1 089	2 793	6 918	11 330	10 304
1994	30 912	170	29	11	19	33	74	229	495	1 102	2 723	6 617	10 008	9 402
1995	31 709	178	26	16	26	50	70	231	435	1 100	2 601	6 449	10 452	10 075
1996	31 448	159	24	31	21	49	67	218	453	1 172	2 573	6 206	10 256	10 219
1997	31 189	130	23	28	21	43	71	199	496	1 128	2 480	5 985	10 164	10 421
1998	31 032	137	26	28	19	55	68	198	485	1 106	2 416	5 955	9 913	10 626
1999	31 676	115	26	20	17	65	58	201	467	1 128	2 431	5 837	10 198	11 113
2000	30 288	132	20	10	21	46	56	222	510	1 086	2 324	5 512	9 875	10 474

5.18 Deaths: analysis by age and gender
Annual averages or calendar years
continued

Numbers

Northern Ireland

	All ages[1]	Under 1 year	1-4	5-9	10-14	15-19	20-24	25-34	35-44	45-54	55-64	65-74	75-84	85 and over
Males														
1900 - 02	11 554	1 958	985	280	206	367	446	779	669	832	1 413	1 666	1 368	585
1910 - 12	10 469	1 697	841	222	152	282	311	569	679	836	1 148	2 011	1 287	434
1920 - 22	9 622	1 491	596	191	150	258	334	496	570	869	1 159	1 749	1 324	435
1930 - 32	8 626	1 083	406	126	90	154	209	375	437	740	1 313	1 988	1 317	388
1940 - 42	9 383	1 258	322	117	102	153	202	379	462	751	1 290	2 305	1 637	405
1950 - 52	8 197	658	105	55	36	50	77	179	318	671	1 169	2 117	2 178	583
1960 - 62	8 080	499	67	38	27	49	48	108	216	623	1 419	2 037	2 131	816
1970 - 72	8 786	396	58	40	32	76	83	115	221	643	1 590	2 493	2 157	881
1980 - 82	8 420	211	37	20	26	77	92	144	202	539	1 414	2 518	2 346	795
1990 - 92	7 550	102	21	13	18	55	73	132	178	423	1 044	2 175	2 393	922
	KHXA	KHXB	KHXC	KHXD	KHXE	KHXF	KHXG	KHXH	KHXI	KHXJ	KHXK	KHXL	KHXM	KHXN
1980	8 832	222	31	27	35	87	104	162	210	568	1 495	2 653	2 430	808
1981	8 423	205	49	20	27	66	93	141	193	521	1 406	2 568	2 319	815
1982	8 004	205	31	12	17	77	78	129	203	528	1 341	2 332	2 289	762
1983	8 209	196	24	25	30	69	86	124	192	475	1 409	2 433	2 303	843
1984	8 007	163	28	22	14	52	69	133	217	517	1 318	2 355	2 308	811
1985	8 088	151	33	16	22	64	85	109	193	519	1 312	2 424	2 310	850
1986	8 155	161	14	15	15	70	83	128	188	477	1 361	2 381	2 348	914
1987	7 721	137	25	22	19	60	102	143	191	402	1 177	2 269	2 330	844
1988	7 993	137	29	20	16	65	112	141	197	400	1 213	2 260	2 462	941
1989	7 878	100	31	19	16	62	90	143	166	432	1 124	2 264	2 501	930
1990	7 648	110	19	12	18	54	68	138	186	431	1 066	2 219	2 413	914
1991	7 533	112	23	12	16	59	78	142	185	436	1 021	2 130	2 392	927
1992	7 469	83	21	16	19	52	73	117	162	403	1 046	2 177	2 374	926
1993[2]	7 731	99	22	10	24	53	86	139	163	398	1 012	2 248	2 469	1 008
1994	7 362	81	23	14	21	65	67	138	177	376	1 035	2 051	2 306	1 008
1995	7 482	93	19	15	18	53	82	142	176	411	951	2 040	2 429	1 053
1996	7 418	84	7	8	15	40	72	126	191	386	880	2 028	2 456	1 125
1997	7 244	68	12	11	12	50	62	122	172	411	924	1 937	2 367	1 096
1998	7 321	74	13	9	13	49	47	147	164	434	898	1 873	2 433	1 167
1999	7 464	82	20	16	11	45	68	124	194	409	876	1 871	2 456	1 292
2000	7 128	61	12	12	14	55	69	130	191	387	869	1 682	2 426	1 220
Females														
1900 - 02	12 735	1 537	1 013	317	277	495	521	1 012	902	1 075	1 612	1 876	1 484	614
1910 - 12	11 397	1 369	808	249	218	325	365	785	811	961	1 282	2 328	1 402	494
1920 - 22	10 415	1 149	547	193	188	299	331	687	713	939	1 236	1 976	1 639	518
1930 - 32	9 044	824	380	125	102	184	226	475	539	774	1 293	2 046	1 541	535
1940 - 42	9 229	910	305	105	90	159	174	409	490	688	1 207	2 246	1 873	572
1950 - 52	7 896	494	87	33	21	37	59	173	276	526	996	1 976	2 384	834
1960 - 62	7 463	371	61	20	15	21	24	70	175	434	880	1 823	2 417	1 151
1970 - 72	7 809	295	45	23	17	25	20	65	152	408	919	1 959	2 475	1 407
1980 - 82	7 917	160	26	17	17	23	29	65	127	329	881	1 813	2 752	1 678
1990 - 92	7 620	80	20	12	9	16	17	53	117	267	672	1 538	2 636	2 182
	KIXA	KIXB	KIXC	KIXD	KIXE	KIXF	KIXG	KIXH	KIXI	KIXJ	KIXK	KIXL	KIXM	KIXN
1980	8 003	160	27	19	25	27	25	74	142	315	905	1 912	2 745	1 627
1981	7 833	155	24	15	13	20	26	49	114	348	858	1 779	2 760	1 672
1982	7 914	164	26	16	12	23	35	73	125	325	880	1 749	2 750	1 736
1983	7 830	133	28	16	9	23	25	58	106	281	837	1 795	2 756	1 763
1984	7 685	128	21	12	5	18	23	51	136	284	795	1 640	2 770	1 802
1985	7 867	114	22	17	13	19	23	62	113	291	783	1 771	2 742	1 897
1986	7 910	125	20	11	11	23	18	48	112	269	797	1 702	2 724	2 050
1987	7 613	105	17	7	8	29	24	71	128	243	736	1 680	2 650	1 915
1988	7 820	111	21	10	12	16	32	48	120	324	800	1 574	2 704	2 048
1989	7 966	80	23	7	15	13	19	53	111	272	709	1 591	2 875	2 198
1990	7 778	88	23	13	9	16	16	61	120	282	730	1 564	2 684	2 172
1991	7 563	82	19	10	11	19	20	51	129	260	675	1 502	2 597	2 188
1992	7 519	70	18	12	8	12	16	47	103	260	612	1 549	2 627	2 185
1993[2]	7 902	77	17	11	10	16	24	61	119	270	684	1 604	2 628	2 381
1994	7 752	66	17	7	9	16	17	53	121	291	639	1 531	2 611	2 374
1995	7 828	76	11	12	14	17	20	50	124	288	601	1 552	2 633	2 430
1996	7 800	58	11	8	7	14	15	70	104	277	589	1 488	2 643	2 516
1997	7 727	69	13	10	9	18	13	43	90	268	570	1 409	2 604	2 611
1998	7 672	60	12	8	7	24	20	49	126	258	531	1 351	2 509	2 717
1999	8 199	66	12	7	8	23	25	55	119	273	583	1 303	2 765	2 960
2000	7 775	48	11	11	3	19	13	51	125	283	574	1 308	2 526	2 803

1 In some years the totals include a small number of persons whose age was not stated.
2 See chapter text.

Sources: Office for National Statistics: 01329 813223; General Register Office for Scotland; General Register Office (Northern Ireland)

5.19 Deaths: analysed by cause
International Statistical Classification of Diseases, Injuries and Causes of Death
Ninth Revision, 1979

Numbers

		England and Wales							
		1993[1]	1994	1995	1996	1997	1998	1999	2000
	ICD 9 code								
Total deaths	KHEA	578 799	553 194	569 683	560 135	555 281	555 015	556 118	535 664
Deaths from natural causes [2]	KHEB	559 649	534 354	550 936	541 429	536 422	536 396	537 166	516 804
Infectious and parasitic diseases[3]	KHEC	001-139	3 257	3 318	3 682	3 636	3 496	3 410	3 613	3 767
Intestinal infectious diseases	KJZZ	001-009	194	222	277	339	384	418	476	547
Tuberculosis of the respiratory system	KHEH	010-012	423	418	353	310	289	283	299	279
Other tuberculosis, including late effects	KHEI	013-018,137	193	180	161	166	148	170	138	148
Whooping cough	KHEK	033	–	3	2	2	1	4	2	2
Meningococcal infection	KHEM	036	173	149	196	235	242	210	217	199
Measles	KHEP	055	4	1	1	–	3	3	3	1
Malaria	KHER	084	4	11	4	11	12	8	13	17
Syphilis	KHES	090-097	6	11	9	6	9	3	9	1
Neoplasms	KHET	140-239	142 535	141 747	141 297	139 459	137 618	138 306	136 181	134 793
Malignant neoplasm of stomach	KHEU	151	7 548	7 590	7 077	6 756	6 613	6 442	6 139	5 779
Malignant neoplasm of trachea, bronchus and lung	KHEV	162	32 614	32 143	31 627	30 810	29 976	30 199	29 493	29 029
Malignant neoplasm of breast	KHEW	174-175	13 115	12 918	12 623	12 246	12 047	11 835	11 670	11 433
Malignant neoplasm of uterus	KWUP	179+182	1 308	1 241	1 329	1 303	1 291	1 296	1 231	1 333
Malignant neoplasm of cervix	KWUQ	180	1 483	1 370	1 339	1 315	1 225	1 158	1 107	1 106
Leukaemia	KHEY	204-208	3 559	3 507	3 540	3 464	3 587	3 551	3 680	3 570
Benign and unspecified neoplasms	KHEZ	210-229,239	1 544	1 580	1 784	1 647	1 624	1 605	1 656	1 733
Endocrine, nutritional and metabolic diseases and immunity disorders	KHFA	240-279	7 924	7 430	7 883	7 502	7 383	7 542	7 560	7 247
Diabetes mellitus	KHFB	250	6 266	5 938	6 240	5 994	5 890	5 938	5 963	5 773
Nutritional deficiencies	KHFC	260-269	85	66	80	70	65	72	59	60
Other metabolic and immunity disorders[3]	KMBO	270-279	1 119	1 052	1 138	1 048	1 038	1 169	1 150	1 054
Diseases of blood and blood-forming organs	KHFD	280-289	1 974	1 898	1 929	1 986	2 008	1 937	1 855	1 791
Anaemias	KHFE	280-285	786	660	711	724	681	641	584	554
Mental disorders	KHFF	290-319	7 780	8 042	9 149	9 296	9 725	10 430	11 173	10 866
Diseases of nervous system and sense organs	KHFG	320-389	9 143	9 010	9 724	9 772	9 772	10 035	10 192	9 632
Meningitis	KHFH	320-322	218	170	209	245	224	216	182	206
Diseases of the circulatory system	KHFI	390-459	257 989	242 213	243 390	237 669	228 446	226 677	219 087	207 228
Rheumatic heart disease	KHFJ	393-398	1 834	1 719	1 714	1 682	1 481	1 629	1 638	1 551
Hypertensive disease	KHFL	401-405	3 052	2 800	2 882	3 026	3 084	3 122	3 324	3 184
Ischaemic heart disease	KHFM	410-414	146 302	135 440	133 861	129 047	122 432	121 037	115 119	108 417
Diseases of pulmonary circulation and other forms of heart disease	KHFN	415-429	21 341	25 795	26 891	26 170	26 609	26 377	26 462	25 139
Cerebrovascular disease	KHFO	430-438	61 172	58 768	59 957	59 723	57 747	57 516	56 051	52 516
Diseases of the respiratory system	KHFP	460-519	90 981	81 485	91 298	88 630	92 517	90 192	97 755	92 461
Influenza	KHFQ	487	439	62	251	179	347	129	585	509
Pneumonia	KHFR	480-486	54 624	48 917	55 318	54 137	56 719	54 631	59 273	56 329
Bronchitis, emphysema	KHFS	490-492	5 715	4 969	4 907	4 249	4 116	3 523	3 452	2 981
Asthma	KHFT	493	1 701	1 516	1 459	1 349	1 439	1 366	1 364	1 272
Diseases of the digestive system	KHFU	520-579	18 399	18 635	19 466	19 946	20 406	21 025	21 698	22 134
Ulcer of stomach and duodenum	KHFV	531-533	4 222	4 111	3 999	4 111	3 959	3 935	4 011	4 007
Appendicitis	KHFW	540-543	124	113	101	102	125	144	133	139
Hernia of the abdominal cavity and other intestinal obstruction	KHFX	550-553,560	1 855	1 814	1 975	1 967	2 106	2 042	2 126	2 117
Chronic liver disease and cirrhosis	KHFY	571	2 979	3 244	3 612	3 789	4 107	4 494	4 718	4 770
Diseases of the genito-urinary system	KHFZ	580-629	6 727	6 812	7 118	6 752	6 757	6 946	7 299	7 270
Nephritis, nephrotic syndrome and nephrosis	KHGA	580-589	3 401	3 246	3 283	3 057	2 930	2 946	2 952	2 901
Hyperplasia of prostate	KHGB	600	275	283	273	235	247	207	200	188
Complications of pregnancy, childbirth, etc	KHGC	630-676	36	50	45	41	35	43	30	38
Abortion	KHGD	630-639	3	6	8	4	2	7	5	7
Diseases of the skin and subcutaneous tissue	KHGE	680-709	1 019	1 107	1 088	1 075	1 025	1 070	1 152	1 266
Diseases of the musculo-skeletal system	KHGF	710-739	3 559	3 406	3 646	3 517	3 559	3 566	3 554	3 407
Congenital anomalies	KHGG	740-759	1 338	1 301	1 290	1 227	1 283	1 247	1 194	1 165
Certain conditions originating in the perinatal period	KHGH	760-779	259	147	148	149	131	124	116	83
Birth trauma, hypoxia, birth asphyxia and other respiratory conditions	KHGI	767-770	169	133	116	114	99	94	72	53
Signs, symptoms and ill-defined conditions	KHGJ	780-799	6 729	7 754	9 783	10 772	12 292	13 846	14 707	13 656
Sudden infant death syndrome	KMBP	798-0	391	371	315	345	327	236	222	180
Deaths from injury and poisoning[2]	KHGK	E800-E999	16 354	16 091	16 049	16 061	16 311	16 201	16 517	16 525
All accidents	KHGL	E800-E929	10 396	10 219	10 156	10 479	10 661	10 351	10 625	10 771
Motor vehicle accidents	KHGM	E810-E825	3 437	3 279	3 123	3 184	3 184	2 946	3 003	2 889
Suicide and self-inflicted injury	KHGN	E950-E959	3 719	3 619	3 570	3 445	3 424	3 614	3 690	3 479
All other external causes	KHGO	(E930-E949)+ (E960-E999)	2 239	2 253	2 323	2 137	2 226	2 236	2 202	2 275

Note: On 1 January 1986, a new certificate for deaths within the first 28 days of life was introduced. It is not possible to assign one underlying cause of death from this certificate. The 'cause' figures in this table exclude all deaths at ages under 28 days.
1 See chapter text.
2 Within certain main categories only selected causes of death are shown.

3 Deaths assigned to HIV & HIV-related diseases are included in ICD 270-279 for England and Wales up to 1992. Northern Ireland has always assigned such deaths to the Chapter on Infectious Diseases (001-139). England and Wales adopted this practice from 1993.

Source: Office for National Statistics: 01329 813223

5.19 Deaths: analysed by cause

continued

International Statistical Classification of Diseases, Injuries and Causes of Death

Ninth Revision, 1979

Numbers

	ICD 9 code	ICD 10 code	Scotland						
			1995	1996	1997	1998	1999[1] ICD9	1999[1] ICD10	2000
Total deaths			60 500	60 654	59 494	59 164	60 281	60 281	57 799
I.Certain infectious and parasitic diseases	001-139	A00-B99	326	493	431	486	498	601	476
Tuberculosis	010-018,137	A15-19,B90	56	53	71	58	65	64	66
Meningococcal infection	036	A39	15	12	12	20	14	14	18
Viral hepatitis	070	B15-19	15	15	15	22	17	14	14
Human Immunodeficiency Virus (HIV) disease[2]	042-044	B20-24	112	79	41	32	23	28	23
II. Neoplasms	140-239	C00-D48	15 462	15 414	15 054	14 907	14 966	15 327	15 255
Malignant neoplasms	140-208	C00-97	15 224	15 171	14 889	14 752	14 789	15 008	14 958
Malignant neoplasms of lip, oral cavity and pharynx	140-149	C00-14	270	231	251	255	248	248	232
Malignant neoplasm of oesophagus	150	C15	762	723	734	730	776	780	708
Malignant neoplasm of stomach	151	C16	758	699	710	680	650	657	649
Malignant neoplasm of colon	153	C18	1 144	1 189	1 065	996	1 018	1 017	1 052
Malignant neoplasm of rectum and anus	154	C19-21	587	561	634	664	680	680	564
Malignant neoplasm of liver and intrahepatic bile ducts	155	C22	212	236	228	244	243	243	254
Malignant neoplasm of pancreas	157	C25	538	560	556	607	574	570	633
Malignant neoplasm of larynx	161	C32	115	99	91	128	109	106	112
Malignant neoplasm of trachea, bronchus and lung	162	C33-34	4 221	4 125	4 106	3 984	3 961	3 906	3 948
Malignant melanoma of skin	172	C43	111	119	118	144	131	127	115
Malignant neoplasm of breast	174-175	C50	1 249	1 200	1 161	1 147	1 136	1 165	1 122
Malignant neoplasm of cervix uteri	180	C53	147	138	144	145	122	120	117
Malignant neoplasm of of other parts of the uterus	179,182	C54-55	98	105	106	110	138	135	128
Malignant neoplasm of ovary	183.0	C56	368	408	413	405	403	397	409
Malignant neoplasm of prostate	185	C61	776	743	708	677	769	790	773
Malignant neoplasm of kidney, except renal pelvis	189.0	C64	316	309	265	299	304	298	303
Malignant neoplasm of bladder	188	C67	508	505	486	469	449	460	425
Malignant neoplasm of lymphoid,haematopoietic and related tissue	200-208	C81-96	927	993	922	963	964	1 016	990
III. Diseases of the blood and blood-forming organs and certain disorders involving the immune mechanism	280-289	D50-89	129	181	200	222	204	129	114
IV. Endocrine, nutritional and metabolic diseases[2]	240-279	E00-90	738	721	727	797	870	911	828
Diabetes mellitus	250	E10-14	461	525	510	574	670	700	616
V. Mental and behavioural disorders	290-319	F00-99	1 583	1 595	1 611	1 725	1 901	2 330	2 309
Mental and behavioural disorders due to use of alcohol	291,303,305.0	F10	228	271	292	329	358	334	330
Mental and behavioural disorders due to use of drugs	304,305.2-.9	F11-16,F18-19	158	183	143	182	230	230	245
VI-VIII. Diseases of the nervous system and the sense organs	320-389	G00-H95	832	852	900	894	971	1 393	1 315
Meningitis	320-322	G00-03	18	14	17	6	19	21	15
IX. Diseases of the circulatory system	390-459	I00-99	27 079	26 723	25 911	25 153	24 787	25 284	23 657
Ischaemic heart diseases	410-414	I20-25	14 977	14 647	14 013	13 419	13 337	13 368	12 412
Other heart diseases	420-423,425-429	I30-33,139-52	1 772	2 178	2 100	2 092	1 875	1 993	1 707
Cerebrovascular diseases	430-438	I60-69	7 748	7 128	6 959	6 900	6 785	7 183	6 803
X. Diseases of the respiratory system	460-519	J00-99	7 668	7 859	7 891	8 011	8 870	6 881	6 547
Influenza	487	J10-11	33	45	83	12	62	62	131
Pneumonia	480-486	J12-18	4 021	4 155	4 028	4 064	4 526	2 490	2 312
Chronic lower respiratory diseases	490-494,496	J40-47	2 784	2 684	2 764	2 831	3 137	17 661	3 009
Asthma	493	J45-46	120	122	113	120	119	117	131
XI. Diseases of the digestive system	520-579	K00-93	2 252	2 438	2 428	2 578	2 787	2 829	2 922
Ulcer of the stomach, duodenum and jejunum	531-534	K25-28	368	344	307	319	341	322	351
Chronic liver disease	571	K70,K73-74	607	722	767	806	896	855	956
XII. Diseases of the skin and subcutaneous tissue	680-709	L00-99	80	75	87	94	90	94	89
XIII. Diseases of the musculo-skeletal system and connective tissue	710-739	M00-99	303	252	268	284	295	398	405
Rheumatoid arthritis and osteoarthrosis	714-715	M05-06,M15-19	168	106	130	139	141	186	175
XIV. Diseases of the genito-urinary system	580-629	N00-99	928	839	904	890	936	961	844
Diseases of the kidney and ureter	580-594	N00-29	686	613	652	644	619	657	563
XV. Pregnancy, childbirth and the puerperium	630-676	O00-07	6	6	4	5	7	8	8
XVI. Certain conditions originating in the perinatal period	760-779	P00-96	178	181	140	165	137	129	170
XVII. Congenital malformations, deformations and chromasomal abnormalities	740-759	Q00-99	176	192	182	176	157	163	154
Congenital malformations of the nervous system	740-742	Q00-07	19	21	24	23	13	13	25
Congenital malformations of the circulatory system	745-747	Q20-28	75	97	84	81	59	56	56
XVIII. Symptoms, signs and abnormal clinical and laboratory findings not elsewhere classified	780-799	R00-99	365	336	383	398	355	365	322
Sudden infant death syndrome	798.0	R95	48	43	52	37	41	41	33
Other ill-defined and unknown causes	798.1-9,799	R96-99	211	202	220	223	123	118	105
XX. External causes of morbidity and mortality	E800-999	V01-Y98	2 395	2 497	2 373	2 379	2 450	2 478	2 384
Accidents	E800-929	V01-X59,Y85,Y86	1 377	1 371	1 299	1 303	1 359	1 407	1 341
Transport accidents	E800-848	V01-99	446	377	398	399	344	345	345
Falls	E880-888	W00-19	641	624	620	613	713	714	675
Poisonings	E850-869	X40-49	25	20	30	38	30	30	34
Intentional self-harm	E950-959	X60-84,Y87.0	623	597	599	649	637	637	648
Assault	E960-969	X85-Y09,Y87.1	103	129	86	94	121	121	93
Event of undetermined intent	E980-989	Y10-Y34, Y87.2	213	249	275	229	237	251	230

1 See Chapter text re: Bridge coding exercise.

2 Pre-1996, HIV-related deaths were derived using a combination of ICD codes and GROS defined supplementary codes. From 1996-1999 HIV was assigned the new ICD9 codes 042-044 (HIV Infection). In ICD10 HIV is assigned codes B20-24.

Sources: Office for National Statistics: 01329 813223;
General Register Office for Scotland

5.19
continued

Deaths: analysed by cause
International Statistical Classification of Diseases, Injuries and Causes of Death
Ninth Revision, 1979

Numbers

			Northern Ireland							
			1993	1994	1995	1996	1997	1998	1999	2000
		ICD 9 code								
Total deaths	KHKA		15 633	15 114	15 310	15 218	14 971	14 993	15 663	14 903
Deaths from natural causes[1]	KHKB		14 871	14 325	14 516	14 528	14 276	14 331	14 942	14 296
Infectious and parasitic diseases	KHKC	001-139	55	39	44	54	61	53	47	73
Intestinal and infectious diseases	KHKD	001-009	–	2	1	1	–	–	1	4
Tuberculosis of the respiratory system	KHKE	010-012	9	6	13	–	8	4	7	3
Other tuberculosis, including late effects	KHKF	013-018,137	6	3	1	3	3	2	–	4
Whooping cough	KHKG	033	–	–	–	–	–	–	–	–
Meningococcal infection	KHKH	036	4	4	4	5	4	6	4	9
Measles	KHKI	055	–	1	–	–	–	–	–	–
Malaria	KHKJ	084	1	–	–	–	–	–	1	–
Syphilis	KHKK	090-097	1	–	–	–	–	–	–	1
Neoplasms	KHKL	140-239	3 705	3 665	3 585	3 715	3 669	3 769	3 654	3 647
Malignant neoplasm of stomach	KHKM	151	194	201	170	200	171	215	187	180
Malignant neoplasm of the trachea, bronchus and lung	KHKN	162	812	768	752	816	773	775	781	792
Malignant neoplasm of breast	KHKO	174-175	339	338	329	309	267	299	286	289
Malignant neoplasm of uterus	KWUT	179+182	32	37	28	28	35	34	26	33
Malignant neoplasm of cervix	KWUU	180	33	38	19	45	26	33	36	30
Leukaemia	KHKQ	204-208	84	94	83	92	107	93	104	91
Benign neoplasms and neoplasms of unspecified nature	KHKR	210-229,239	55	47	51	60	53	121	67	60
Endocrine, nutritional and metabolic diseases	KHKS	240-279	75	74	86	81	106	85	118	122
Diabetes mellitus	KHKT	250	44	45	43	49	77	55	93	89
Nutritional deficiencies	KHKU	260-269	–	1	2	–	1	1	3	2
Other metabolic and immunity disorders	KHKV	270-279	25	20	38	28	17	26	20	22
Diseases of blood and blood-forming organs	KHKW	280-289	29	29	29	22	20	24	24	122
Anaemias	KHKX	280-285	8	15	10	11	9	14	9	13
Mental disorders	KHKY	290-319	56	91	78	100	138	145	190	207
Diseases of nervous system and sense organs	KHKZ	320-389	189	187	224	236	235	240	284	245
Meningitis	KHLA	320-322	15	4	1	7	8	4	3	6
Diseases of the circulatory system	KHLB	390-459	7 137	7 011	6 929	6 633	6 505	6 367	6 423	5 777
Rheumatic heart disease	KHLC	393-398	47	30	47	29	38	29	35	33
Hypertensive disease	KHLD	401-405	67	79	94	75	73	72	68	75
Ischaemic heart disease	KHLE	410-414	4 245	4 168	4 086	3 856	3 764	3 654	3 568	3 235
Diseases of pulmonary circulation and other forms of heart disease	KHLF	415-429	678	633	641	655	635	680	768	637
Cerebrovascular disease	KHLG	430-438	1 722	1 738	1 690	1 653	1 646	1 602	1 680	527
Diseases of the respiratory system	KHLH	460-519	2 756	2 398	2 656	2 749	2 664	2 627	3 161	942
Influenza	KHLI	487	17	3	9	6	8	2	5	39
Pneumonia	KHLJ	480-486	1 814	1 595	1 781	1 817	1 775	1 727	2 130	2 026
Bronchitis, emphysema	KHLK	490-492	151	116	104	137	99	108	93	75
Asthma	KHLL	493	58	30	42	31	32	44	38	33
Diseases of the digestive system	KHLM	520-579	445	424	449	483	450	499	507	531
Ulcer of stomach and duodenum	KHLN	531-533	97	100	87	102	95	80	80	89
Appendicitis	KHLO	540-543	1	3	6	–	4	2	3	5
Hernia of the abdominal cavity and other intestinal obstruction	KHLP	550-553,560	43	50	39	52	42	47	49	44
Chronic liver disease and cirrhosis	KHLQ	571	66	66	71	88	68	104	92	101
Diseases of the genito-urinary system	KHLR	580-629	261	250	251	254	243	265	242	292
Nephritis, nephrotic syndrome and nephrosis	KHLS	580-589	171	165	162	168	175	164	155	182
Hyperplasia of prostate	KHLT	600	5	3	7	3	4	5	4	1
Complications of pregnancy, childbirth, etc	KHLU	630-676	–	–	–	1	–	1	–	–
Abortion	KHLV	630-639	–	–	–	–	–	–	–	–
Diseases of the skin and subcutaneous tissue	KHLW	680-709	33	27	37	29	25	36	27	21
Diseases of the musculo-skeletal system	KHLX	710-739	35	31	40	35	44	30	54	40
Congenital anomalies	KHLY	740-759	116	87	91	72	59	70	93	57
Certain conditions originating in the perinatal period	KHLZ	760-779	62	69	93	68	67	64	69	62
Birth trauma, hypoxia, birth asphyxia and other respiratory conditions	KHMA	767-770	22	29	27	28	24	21	21	18
Signs, symptoms and ill-defined conditions	KHMB	780-799	40	44	55	88	92	149	161	180
Sudden infant death syndrome	KHMC	7980	6	7	9	15	8	4	3	–
Deaths from injury and poisoning[1]	KHMD	E800-E999	639	688	663	598	593	569	609	607
All accidents	KHME	E800-E929	391	430	391	402	427	381	430	364
Motor vehicle accidents	KHMF	E810-E825	152	172	140	121	153	129	134	138
Suicide and self-inflicted injuries	KHMG	E950-E959	129	138	122	124	120	126	121	163
All other external causes	KHMH	(E930-E949) (E960-E999)	119	120	150	72	45	62	58	80

1 Within certain main categories only selected causes of death are shown.

Sources: Office for National Statistics: 01329 813223; General Register Office (Northern Ireland)

5.20 Infant and maternal mortality

	Deaths of Infants under 1 year of age per thousand live births												Maternal deaths per thousand live births[2]			
	United Kingdom			England and Wales[1]			Scotland			Northern Ireland			United Kingdom	England and Wales	Scotland	Northern Ireland
	Total	Males	Females	Total	Males	Females	Total	Males	Females	Total	Males	Females				
1900 - 02	142	156	128	146	160	131	124	136	111	113	123	103	4.71	4.67	4.74	6.03
1910 - 12	110	121	98	110	121	98	109	120	97	101	110	92	3.95	3.67	5.65	5.28
1920 - 22	82	92	71	80	90	69	94	106	82	86	95	77	4.37	4.03	6.36	5.62
1930 - 32	67	75	58	64	72	55	84	94	73	75	83	66	4.54	4.24	6.40	5.24
1940 - 42	59	66	51	55	62	48	77	87	66	80	89	70	3.29	2.74	4.50	3.79
1950 - 52	30	34	26	29	33	25	37	42	32	40	45	36	0.88	0.79	1.09	1.09
1960 - 62	22	25	19	22	24	19	26	30	22	27	30	24	0.36	0.36	0.37	0.43
1970 - 72	18	20	16	18	20	15	19	22	17	22	24	20	0.17	0.17	0.17	0.12
1980 - 82	12	13	10	11	13	10	12	13	10	13	15	12	0.09	0.09	0.14	0.06
1990 - 92	7	8	6	7	8	6	7	8	6	7	8	6	0.07	0.07	0.10	-
	KKAW	KKAX	KKAY	KKAZ	KKBW	KKBX	KKBY	KKBZ	KKCW	KKCX	KKCY	KKCZ	KKDW	KKDX	KKDY	KKDZ
1979	12.9	14.4	11.3	12.8	14.4	11.1	12.8	13.9	11.8	14.8	15.6	13.9	0.11	0.12	0.10	0.04
1980	12.2	13.4	10.6	12.0	13.3	10.7	12.1	13.6	10.4	13.4	15.1	11.5	0.11	0.11	0.15	0.07
1981	11.2	12.7	9.5	11.1	12.6	9.4	11.3	12.3	10.2	13.2	14.7	11.6	0.09	0.09	0.19	0.04
1982	11.0	12.3	9.5	10.8	12.2	9.4	11.4	12.9	9.8	13.6	14.8	12.4	0.07	0.07	0.09	0.07
1983	10.1	11.3	8.9	10.1	11.3	8.9	9.9	11.3	8.5	12.1	13.9	10.1	0.09	0.09	0.12	0.15
1984	9.6	10.7	8.4	9.5	10.6	8.3	10.3	11.7	8.9	10.5	11.4	9.6	0.09	0.08	0.12	0.11
1985	9.4	10.4	8.3	9.4	10.4	8.2	9.4	10.0	8.7	9.6	10.6	8.5	0.07	0.07	0.13	0.07
1986	9.5	10.9	8.1	9.6	11.0	8.0	8.8	9.9	7.7	10.2	11.0	9.2	0.07	0.07	0.11	–
1987	9.1	10.3	7.9	9.2	10.4	7.9	8.5	9.7	7.2	8.7	9.6	7.7	0.06	0.07	0.03	0.04
1988	9.0	10.2	7.7	9.0	10.3	7.7	8.2	9.5	6.8	8.9	9.6	8.2	0.06	0.06	0.12	0.07
1989	8.4	9.5	7.2	8.4	9.6	7.3	8.7	10.2	7.2	6.9	7.4	6.3	0.08	0.08	0.06	–
1990	7.9	8.8	6.8	7.9	8.9	6.8	7.7	8.8	6.6	7.5	8.1	6.8	0.08	0.08	0.06	–
1991	7.4	8.3	6.3	7.4	8.3	6.4	7.1	8.7	5.3	7.4	8.3	6.4	0.07	0.06	0.13	0.04
1992	6.6	7.4	5.7	6.6	7.4	5.8	6.8	7.9	5.7	6.0	6.4	5.6	0.07	0.07	0.11	–
1993	6.3	7.0	5.6	6.3	7.0	5.6	6.5	7.4	5.6	7.1	7.8	6.3	0.06	0.05	0.11	–
1994	6.2	6.9	5.4	6.2	6.9	5.4	6.2	6.8	5.6	6.1	6.5	5.6	0.08	0.08	0.15	–
1995	6.2	6.9	5.4	6.1	6.9	5.3	6.2	6.4	6.1	7.1	7.5	6.6	0.07	0.07	0.10	–
1996	6.1	6.8	5.4	6.1	6.9	5.4	6.2	6.7	5.5	5.8	6.7	4.8	0.07	0.07	0.10	0.04
1997	5.8	6.4	5.3	5.9	6.5	5.3	5.3	6.1	4.5	5.6	5.5	5.8	0.06	0.06	0.07	–
1998	5.7	6.3	5.0	5.7	6.4	5.0	5.6	6.2	4.9	5.6	6.1	5.1	0.07	0.07	0.09	0.04
1999	5.8	6.4	5.1	5.8	6.5	5.1	5.0	5.7	4.3	6.4	6.8	5.9	0.05	0.05	0.13	–
2000	5.6	6.1	5.0	5.6	6.1	5.1	5.7	6.4	5.1	5.1	5.5	4.6	0.07	0.06	0.15	–

5.20 Infant and maternal mortality

continued

Deaths per thousand live births

		Analysis by sex of infant													
		1987	1988	1989	1990	1991	1992	1993	1994	1995	1996	1997	1998	1999	2000
Total															
United Kingdom:															
Stillbirths[3]	KHNQ	5.0	4.9	4.7	4.6	4.7	4.3	5.7	5.8	5.6	5.5	5.3	5.4	5.3	5.3
Perinatal[3]	KHNR	9.0	8.8	8.3	8.1	8.1	7.7	9.0	8.9	8.9	8.7	8.3	8.3	8.2	8.1
Neonatal	KHNS	5.0	4.9	4.7	4.5	4.4	4.3	4.2	4.1	4.2	4.1	3.9	3.8	3.9	3.9
Post neonatal	KHNT	4.1	4.1	3.7	3.3	3.0	2.3	2.2	2.1	2.0	2.0	2.0	1.9	1.9	1.7
England and Wales:															
Stillbirths[3]	KHNU	5.0	4.9	4.7	4.6	4.6	4.3	5.7	5.7	5.5	5.4	5.3	5.3	5.3	5.3
Perinatal[3]	KHNV	8.9	8.7	8.3	8.1	8.0	7.6	8.9	8.9	8.7	8.6	8.3	8.2	8.2	8.2
Neonatal	KHNW	5.1	4.9	4.8	4.6	4.4	4.3	4.2	4.1	4.1	4.1	3.9	3.8	3.9	3.9
Post neonatal	KHNX	4.1	4.1	3.7	3.3	3.0	2.3	2.1	2.1	2.0	2.0	2.0	1.9	1.9	1.7
Scotland:															
Stillbirths[3]	KHNY	5.1	5.4	5.0	5.3	5.5	4.9	6.4	6.1	6.6	6.4	5.3	6.1	5.2	5.6
Perinatal[3]	KHNZ	8.9	8.9	8.7	8.7	8.6	8.5	9.6	9.0	9.6	9.2	7.8	8.7	7.6	8.4
Neonatal	KHOA	4.7	4.5	4.7	4.4	4.4	4.6	4.0	4.0	4.0	3.9	3.2	3.6	3.3	4.0
Post neonatal	KHOB	3.8	3.7	4.0	3.3	2.7	2.2	2.5	2.2	2.2	2.2	2.1	2.0	1.7	1.8
Northern Ireland:															
Stillbirths[3]	KHOC	6.1	5.0	5.1	4.4	4.7	4.9	5.2	6.3	6.1	6.3	5.4	5.1	5.7	4.3
Perinatal[3]	KHOD	9.8	9.3	8.2	7.6	8.4	8.2	8.8	9.7	10.4	9.4	8.2	8.1	10.0	7.3
Neonatal	KHOE	4.8	5.4	4.0	4.0	4.6	4.1	4.9	4.2	5.5	3.7	4.2	3.9	4.8	3.8
Post neonatal	KHOF	3.8	3.6	2.9	3.5	2.8	1.9	2.1	1.9	1.6	2.0	1.4	1.7	1.6	1.3
Males															
United Kingdom:															
Perinatal[3]	KHOG	9.7	9.5	9.3	8.8	8.7	8.3	9.7	9.6	9.4	9.1	8.7	8.8	8.7	8.7
Neonatal	KHOH	5.7	5.5	5.4	5.0	4.9	4.8	4.7	4.6	4.6	4.6	4.2	4.2	4.3	4.2
Infant mortality	KHOI	10.3	10.2	9.5	8.8	8.3	7.4	7.0	6.9	6.9	6.8	6.4	6.3	6.4	6.1
England and Wales:															
Perinatal[3]	KHOK	9.8	9.4	9.2	8.8	8.6	8.1	9.5	9.6	9.3	9.0	8.7	8.8	8.6	8.7
Neonatal	KHOL	5.7	5.5	5.4	5.1	4.8	4.7	4.6	4.6	4.6	4.6	4.2	4.3	4.3	4.2
Infant mortality	KHOM	10.4	10.3	9.6	8.9	8.3	7.4	7.0	6.9	6.9	6.9	6.5	6.4	6.5	6.1
Scotland:															
Perinatal[3]	KHOO	8.9	9.7	10.0	9.1	9.8	9.8	10.8	9.6	10.1	10.0	8.1	9.6	8.4	9.5
Neonatal	KHOP	5.3	5.3	5.3	4.7	5.5	5.5	4.5	4.4	4.1	4.3	3.4	4.0	3.8	4.5
Infant mortality	KHOQ	9.7	9.5	10.2	8.8	8.7	7.9	7.4	6.8	6.4	6.7	6.1	6.2	5.7	6.4
Northern Ireland:															
Perinatal[3]	KHOS	10.5	10.9	8.7	8.7	7.9	8.6	10.3	10.4	10.4	10.1	8.5	8.9	10.5	8.0
Neonatal	KHOT	5.3	6.0	4.5	4.8	5.5	4.5	5.9	4.3	5.7	4.3	4.3	4.4	5.5	4.2
Infant mortality	KHOU	9.6	9.6	7.4	8.1	8.3	6.4	7.8	6.5	7.5	6.7	5.5	6.1	6.8	5.5
Females															
United Kingdom:															
Perinatal[3]	KHOW	8.1	8.0	7.4	7.4	7.5	7.0	8.2	8.2	8.3	8.2	7.9	7.7	7.8	7.5
Neonatal	KHOX	4.3	4.3	4.0	4.0	3.8	3.8	3.6	3.6	3.7	3.6	3.5	3.3	3.4	3.5
Infant mortality	KHOY	7.9	7.7	7.2	6.8	6.3	5.7	5.6	5.4	5.4	5.4	5.3	5.0	5.1	5.0
England and Wales:															
Perinatal[3]	KHPA	8.0	8.0	7.4	7.4	7.5	7.0	8.3	8.1	8.1	8.2	7.9	7.7	7.8	7.6
Neonatal	KHPB	4.3	4.3	4.0	4.0	3.9	3.9	3.6	3.6	3.6	3.6	3.6	3.3	3.5	3.5
Infant mortality	KHPC	7.9	7.7	7.3	6.8	6.4	5.8	5.6	5.4	5.3	5.4	5.3	5.0	5.1	5.1
Scotland:															
Perinatal[3]	KHPE	9.0	8.1	7.3	8.2	7.4	7.1	8.3	8.4	9.2	8.4	7.5	7.9	6.7	7.2
Neonatal	KHPF	4.1	3.7	4.1	4.1	3.2	3.7	3.5	3.6	3.9	3.5	2.9	3.2	2.8	3.5
Infant mortality	KHPG	7.2	6.8	7.2	6.6	5.3	5.7	5.6	5.6	6.1	5.5	4.5	4.9	4.3	5.1
Northern Ireland:															
Perinatal[3]	KHPI	9.2	7.6	7.6	6.4	9.0	7.9	7.2	8.9	10.5	8.6	8.0	7.3	9.5	6.5
Neonatal	KHPJ	4.4	4.7	3.5	3.2	3.7	3.6	3.9	4.1	5.2	3.1	4.0	3.4	4.1	3.4
Infant mortality	KHPK	7.7	8.2	6.3	6.8	6.4	5.6	6.3	5.6	6.6	4.8	5.8	5.1	5.9	4.6

1 From 1937 to 1956 death rates are based on the births to which they relate
  in the current and preceding years.
2 Deaths in pregnancy and childbirth.
3 Deaths per 1,000 live and stillbirths. See chapter introduction.

Sources: Office for National Statistics: 01329 813223;
General Register Office for Scotland;
General Register Office (Northern Ireland)

5.21 Death rates per 1,000 population[1]
United Kingdom
Analysis by age and gender

	All ages	0-4	5-9	10-14	15-19	20-24	25-34	35-44	45-54	55-64	65-74	75-84	85 and over
Males													
1900 - 02	18.4	57.0	4.1	2.4	3.7	5.0	6.6	11.0	18.6	35.0	69.9	143.6	289.6
1910 - 12	14.9	40.5	3.3	2.0	3.0	3.9	5.0	8.0	14.9	29.8	62.1	133.8	261.5
1920 - 22	13.5	33.4	2.9	1.8	2.9	3.9	4.5	6.9	11.9	25.3	57.8	131.8	259.1
1930 - 32	12.9	22.3	2.3	1.5	2.6	3.3	3.5	5.7	11.3	23.7	57.9	134.2	277.0
1940 - 42	..	..	..	..	..	..	..	..	..	..	..	..	..
1950 - 52	12.6	7.7	0.7	0.5	0.9	1.4	1.6	3.0	8.5	23.2	55.2	127.6	272.0
1960 - 62	12.5	6.4	0.5	0.4	0.9	1.1	1.1	2.5	7.4	22.2	54.4	123.4	251.0
1970 - 72	12.4	4.6	0.4	0.4	0.9	1.0	1.0	2.4	7.3	20.9	52.9	116.3	246.1
1980 - 82	12.1	3.2	0.3	0.3	0.8	0.9	0.9	1.9	6.3	18.2	46.7	107.1	224.9
1990 - 92	11.1	2.0	0.2	0.2	0.7	0.9	0.9	1.8	4.6	14.3	38.7	92.9	195.7
	KHZA	KHZB	KHZC	KHZD	KHZE	KHZF	KHZG	KHZH	KHZJ	KHZK	KHZL	KHZM	KHZN
1979	12.4	3.8	0.3	0.3	0.9	1.0	1.0	2.1	6.9	19.2	48.8	112.0	236.0
1980	12.1	3.4	0.3	0.3	0.8	0.9	0.9	2.0	6.5	18.7	47.2	108.6	227.0
1981	12.3	3.2	0.3	0.3	0.9	0.9	1.0	2.0	6.4	18.4	47.5	110.6	239.5
1982	12.0	2.9	0.3	0.3	0.8	0.9	0.9	1.8	6.1	17.9	46.4	106.4	225.0
1983	12.0	2.7	0.3	0.3	0.8	0.8	0.9	1.8	5.9	18.0	46.3	104.6	221.0
1984	11.7	2.6	0.3	0.3	0.7	0.9	0.9	1.7	5.7	17.5	44.9	100.9	212.8
1985	12.0	2.6	0.2	0.3	0.7	0.8	0.9	1.8	5.6	17.5	45.0	104.8	223.4
1986	11.8	2.6	0.2	0.2	0.7	0.9	0.9	1.7	5.5	17.0	43.6	102.0	217.1
1987	11.5	2.5	0.2	0.3	0.7	0.9	0.9	1.7	5.2	16.4	42.0	97.3	194.3
1988	11.5	2.5	0.2	0.3	0.7	0.9	0.9	1.7	5.1	16.0	41.2	96.6	193.9
1989	11.5	2.3	0.2	0.2	0.7	0.9	0.9	1.7	4.9	15.3	40.4	97.0	199.0
1990	11.2	2.2	0.2	0.2	0.7	0.9	1.0	1.8	4.8	14.8	39.5	94.3	187.8
1991	11.1	2.0	0.2	0.2	0.7	0.9	0.9	1.8	4.7	14.2	38.7	93.3	203.5
1992	10.9	1.8	0.2	0.2	0.6	0.9	0.9	1.7	4.4	13.8	37.9	91.2	195.8
1993	11.2	1.7	0.2	0.2	0.6	0.9	1.0	1.7	4.4	12.8	36.8	92.7	213.3
1994	10.6	1.6	0.2	0.2	0.6	0.9	1.0	1.7	4.1	12.8	36.8	90.3	190.5
1995	10.8	1.5	0.2	0.2	0.6	0.9	0.9	1.7	4.2	13.5	38.4	91.3	188.0
1996	10.6	1.6	0.1	0.2	0.6	0.9	1.0	1.7	4.2	12.4	35.4	86.5	195.5
1997	10.4	1.5	0.1	0.2	0.6	0.9	1.0	1.6	4.1	11.8	33.9	83.4	191.9
1998	10.3	1.5	0.1	0.2	0.6	0.9	1.0	1.6	4.1	11.7	33.1	82.0	188.1
1999	10.3	1.5	0.1	0.2	0.6	0.9	1.0	1.6	4.1	11.2	32.3	81.1	190.0
2000	9.9	1.4	0.1	0.2	0.6	0.8	1.0	1.6	4.0	10.8	30.4	77.0	182.5
Females													
1900 - 02	16.3	47.9	4.3	2.6	3.5	4.3	5.8	9.0	14.4	27.9	59.3	127.0	262.6
1910 - 12	13.3	34.0	3.3	2.1	2.9	3.4	4.4	6.7	11.5	23.1	50.7	113.7	234.0
1920 - 22	11.9	26.9	2.8	1.9	2.8	3.4	4.1	5.6	9.3	19.2	45.6	111.5	232.4
1930 - 32	11.5	17.7	2.1	1.5	2.4	2.9	3.3	4.6	8.3	17.6	43.7	110.1	246.3
1940 - 42	..	..	..	..	..	..	..	..	..	..	..	..	..
1950 - 52	11.2	6.0	0.5	0.4	0.7	1.0	1.4	2.3	5.3	12.9	35.5	98.4	228.8
1960 - 62	11.2	4.9	0.3	0.3	0.4	0.5	0.8	1.8	4.5	11.0	30.8	87.3	218.5
1970 - 72	11.3	3.6	0.3	0.2	0.4	0.4	0.6	1.6	4.5	10.5	27.5	76.7	196.1
1980 - 82	11.4	2.3	0.2	0.2	0.3	0.4	0.5	1.3	3.9	9.9	24.8	67.2	179.5
1990 - 92	11.1	1.6	0.1	0.2	0.3	0.3	0.4	1.1	2.9	8.4	22.2	58.5	154.6
	KHZO	KHZP	KHZQ	KHZR	KHZS	KHZT	KHZU	KHZV	KHZW	KHZX	KHZY	KHZZ	KHZI
1979	11.6	2.8	0.2	0.2	0.3	0.4	0.6	1.4	4.3	10.2	25.6	70.8	187.1
1980	11.4	2.7	0.2	0.2	0.3	0.4	0.5	1.3	4.0	10.0	25.0	67.7	181.3
1981	11.6	2.5	0.2	0.2	0.3	0.4	0.5	1.3	3.9	10.0	25.5	70.4	190.6
1982	11.5	2.3	0.2	0.2	0.3	0.4	0.5	1.2	3.8	9.9	24.8	66.8	179.4
1983	11.4	2.1	0.2	0.2	0.3	0.3	0.5	1.2	3.6	9.8	24.7	65.1	177.2
1984	11.2	2.0	0.2	0.2	0.3	0.3	0.5	1.2	3.5	9.7	24.3	62.6	170.2
1985	11.7	2.0	0.2	0.2	0.3	0.3	0.5	1.2	3.4	9.9	24.7	64.8	178.4
1986	11.5	2.0	0.2	0.2	0.3	0.3	0.5	1.1	3.3	9.5	24.0	63.2	172.4
1987	11.2	2.0	0.2	0.2	0.3	0.3	0.5	1.1	3.3	9.4	23.3	60.8	159.9
1988	11.3	1.9	0.2	0.2	0.3	0.3	0.5	1.2	3.2	9.2	23.2	60.4	162.3
1989	11.5	1.8	0.2	0.2	0.3	0.3	0.5	1.1	3.1	9.1	23.2	61.4	164.7
1990	11.1	1.7	0.1	0.2	0.3	0.3	0.5	1.1	3.0	8.8	22.4	58.9	156.7
1991	11.2	1.6	0.2	0.2	0.3	0.3	0.4	1.1	2.9	8.4	22.3	58.9	156.9
1992	11.0	1.4	0.1	0.1	0.3	0.3	0.4	1.1	2.8	8.1	22.0	57.8	150.3
1993	11.5	1.3	0.1	0.2	0.3	0.3	0.5	1.1	2.9	7.5	21.6	58.0	162.3
1994	10.9	1.3	0.1	0.1	0.2	0.3	0.4	1.1	2.8	7.6	21.7	57.5	148.4
1995	11.1	1.2	0.1	0.1	0.3	0.3	0.4	1.1	2.7	8.0	22.6	59.8	150.4
1996	11.1	1.2	0.1	0.1	0.3	0.3	0.5	1.1	2.7	7.3	21.2	56.8	153.7
1997	11.0	1.2	0.1	0.1	0.3	0.3	0.4	1.1	2.7	7.1	20.6	55.2	153.9
1998	10.9	1.2	0.1	0.1	0.3	0.3	0.4	1.0	2.7	7.0	20.3	54.4	153.3
1999	11.0	1.2	0.1	0.1	0.3	0.3	0.4	1.0	2.7	6.9	19.7	54.3	157.1
2000	10.5	1.1	0.1	0.1	0.3	0.3	0.5	1.0	2.7	6.6	18.6	51.8	149.5

1 The figures 1978 to 1980 incorporate the revised intercensal estimates for England and Wales and Northern Ireland, but the old series for Scotland.

Sources: Office for National Statistics: 01329 813223; General Register Office for Scotland; General Register Office (Northern Ireland)

5.22 Life tables

	Interim life tables, 1998-00							
	United Kingdom				**England and Wales**			
	Males		Females		Males		Females	
Age(x)	l_x	$e^0{}_x$	l_x	$e^0{}_x$	l_x	$e^0{}_x$	l_x	$e^0{}_x$
0 years	100 000	75.1	100 000	80.0	100 000	75.4	100 000	80.2
5 years	99 258	70.7	99 408	75.5	99 256	70.9	99 406	75.7
10 years	99 193	65.7	99 357	70.5	99 193	66.0	99 357	70.7
15 years	99 110	60.8	99 299	65.5	99 112	61.0	99 298	65.7
20 years	98 832	55.9	99 168	60.6	98 849	56.2	99 174	60.8
25 years	98 416	51.2	99 010	55.7	98 457	51.4	99 019	55.9
30 years	97 964	46.4	98 827	50.8	98 025	46.6	98 841	51.0
35 years	97 464	41.6	98 579	45.9	97 542	41.8	98 597	46.1
40 years	96 840	36.9	98 199	41.1	96 939	37.1	98 223	41.3
45 years	95 909	32.2	97 560	36.3	96 041	32.4	97 602	36.5
50 years	94 442	27.7	96 557	31.7	94 615	27.9	96 627	31.9
55 years	92 113	23.3	94 991	27.2	92 368	23.5	95 092	27.3
60 years	88 241	19.2	92 512	22.8	88 616	19.3	92 675	23.0
65 years	82 134	15.4	88 624	18.7	82 664	15.6	88 882	18.9
70 years	72 744	12.1	82 463	14.9	73 437	12.2	82 864	15.0
75 years	59 174	9.2	72 740	11.5	59 961	9.3	73 275	11.6
80 years	42 306	6.9	58 972	8.6	43 064	7.0	59 608	8.7
85 years	24 577	5.1	41 096	6.3	25 151	5.2	41 735	6.3
90 years	10 424	3.9	21 940	4.6	10 753	3.9	22 419	4.7

	Interim life tables, 1998-00							
	Scotland				**Northern Ireland**			
	Males		Females		Males		Females	
Age(x)	l_x	$e^0{}_x$	l_x	$e^0{}_x$	l_x	$e^0{}_x$	l_x	$e^0{}_x$
0 years	10 000	72.8	10 000	78.2	10 000	74.5	10 000	79.6
5 years	9 928	68.4	9 944	73.7	9 927	70.0	9 938	75.1
10 years	9 920	63.4	9 938	68.7	9 917	65.1	9 931	70.1
15 years	9 910	58.5	9 932	63.7	9 908	60.1	9 927	65.2
20 years	9 871	53.7	9 915	58.8	9 870	55.4	9 909	60.3
25 years	9 810	49.0	9 895	53.9	9 819	50.6	9 892	55.4
30 years	9 744	44.3	9 873	49.1	9 773	45.9	9 874	50.5
35 years	9 677	39.6	9 843	44.2	9 719	41.1	9 852	45.6
40 years	9 592	34.9	9 797	39.4	9 659	36.4	9 818	40.7
45 years	9 467	30.4	9 718	34.7	9 564	31.7	9 749	36.0
50 years	9 283	25.9	9 591	30.1	9 407	27.2	9 645	31.4
55 years	8 966	21.7	9 403	25.7	9 164	22.8	9 484	26.9
60 years	8 461	17.9	9 097	21.4	8 768	18.7	9 226	22.5
65 years	7 712	14.4	8 624	17.5	8 127	15.0	8 830	18.4
70 years	6 635	11.3	7 882	13.9	7 144	11.7	8 207	14.6
75 years	5 199	8.6	6 783	10.7	5 767	8.9	7 248	11.2
80 years	3 550	6.5	5 317	7.9	4 041	6.6	5 831	8.3
85 years	1 962	4.8	3 546	5.6	2 241	4.9	3 959	6.0
90 years	776	3.5	1 777	3.8	856	4.0	2 056	4.2

Note Column l_x shows the number who would survive to exact **age**(x), out of 100,000 or 10,000 born, who were subject throughout their lives to the death rates experienced in the three-year period indicated.

Column $e^0{}_x$ is 'the expectation of life', that is, the average future lifetime which would be lived by a person aged exactly x if likewise subject to the death rates experienced in the three-year period indicated. See introductory notes.

Source: Government Actuary's Department: 020 7211 2622

5.23 Adoptions by date of entry in Adopted Children Register: by age and gender

	All ages		Under 1		1-4		5-9		10-14		15-17	
	Numbers	Percentages	Numbers	Percentages	Numbers	Percentages	Numbers	Percentages	Numbers	Percentages	Numbers	Percentages
Great Britain **Persons**												
	GQSF	GQSG	GQSH	GQSI	GQSJ	GQSK	GQSL	GQSM	GQSN	GQSO	GQSP	GQSQ
1996[1]	6 542	100	302	5	1 728	26	2 539	39	1 579	24	393	6
1997	5 777	100	251	4	1 743	30	2 105	36	1 353	23	325	6
1998	4 877	100	211	4	1 615	33	1 743	36	1 066	22	242	5
1999	4 805	100	230	5	1 762	37	1 653	34	919	19	241	5
2000	5 333	100	275	5	2 158	40	1 673	31	993	19	234	4
Males												
	GQSR	GQSS	GQST	GQSU	GQSV	GQSW	GQSX	GQSY	GQSZ	GQTA	GQTB	GQTC
1996	3 288	100	160	5	892	27	1 317	40	741	23	178	5
1997	2 840	100	139	5	888	31	1 017	36	656	23	140	5
1998	2 449	100	108	4	838	34	849	35	549	22	105	4
1999	2 361	100	113	5	887	38	803	34	443	19	115	5
2000	2 662	100	140	5	1 097	41	830	31	477	18	118	4
Females												
	GQTD	GQTE	GQTF	GQTG	GQTH	GQTI	GQTJ	GQTK	GQTL	GQTM	GQTN	GQTO
1996[1]	3 254	100	142	4	836	26	1 222	38	838	26	215	7
1997	2 937	100	112	4	855	29	1 088	37	697	24	185	6
1998	2 428	100	103	4	777	32	894	37	517	21	137	6
1999	2 444	100	117	5	875	36	850	35	476	19	126	5
2000	2 671	100	135	5	1 061	40	843	32	516	19	116	4
England and Wales **Persons**												
	GQTP	GQTQ	GQTR	GQTS	GQTT	GQTU	GQTV	GQTW	GQTX	GQTY	GQTZ	GQUA
1996	5 962	100	253	4	1 598	27	2 310	39	1 435	24	366	6
1997	5 307	100	225	4	1 606	30	1 914	36	1 265	24	297	6
1998	4 387	100	195	4	1 489	34	1 545	35	938	21	220	5
1999	4 316	100	196	5	1 627	38	1 477	34	802	19	214	5
2000	4 942	100	251	5	2 018	41	1 550	31	908	18	215	4
Males												
	GQUB	GQUC	GQUD	GQUE	GQUF	GQUG	GQUH	GQUI	GQUJ	GQUK	GQUL	GQUM
1996	2 988	100	143	5	822	28	1 184	40	674	23	165	6
1997	2 610	100	122	5	824	32	917	35	619	24	128	5
1998	2 214	100	100	5	775	35	755	34	489	22	95	4
1999	2 114	100	96	5	816	39	712	34	389	18	101	5
2000	2 452	100	127	5	1 022	42	759	31	434	18	110	4
Females												
	GQUN	GQUO	GQUP	GQUQ	GQUR	GQUS	GQUT	GQUU	GQUV	GQUW	GQUX	GQUY
1996	2 974	100	110	4	776	26	1 126	38	761	26	201	7
1997	2 697	100	103	4	782	29	997	37	646	24	169	6
1998	2 173	100	95	4	714	33	790	36	449	21	125	6
1999	2 202	100	100	5	811	37	765	35	413	19	113	5
2000	2 490	100	124	5	996	40	791	32	474	19	105	4

Sources: Office for National Statistics: 01329 813339;
General Register Office for Scotland

5.23 Adoptions by date of entry in Adopted Children Register: by age and gender
continued

	All ages		Under 1		1-4		5-9		10-14		15-17	
	Numbers	Percentages	Numbers	Percentages	Numbers	Percentages	Numbers	Percentages	Numbers	Percentages	Numbers	Percentages
Scotland												
Persons												
	GQUZ	GQVA	GQVB	GQVC	GQVD	GQVE	GQVF	GQVG	GQVH	GQVI	GQVJ	GQVK
1996[1]	580	100	49	8	130	22	229	39	144	25	27	5
1997	470	100	26	6	137	29	191	41	88	19	28	6
1998	490	100	16	3	126	26	198	40	128	26	22	4
1999	489	100	34	7	135	28	176	36	117	24	27	6
2000	391	100	24	6	140	36	123	31	85	22	19	5
Males												
	GQVL	GQVM	GQVN	GQVO	GQVP	GQVQ	GQVR	GQVS	GQVT	GQVU	GQVV	GQVW
1996	300	100	17	6	70	23	133	44	67	22	13	4
1997	230	100	17	7	64	28	100	43	37	16	12	5
1998	235	100	8	3	63	27	94	40	60	26	10	4
1999	247	100	17	7	71	29	91	37	54	22	14	6
2000	210	100	13	6	75	36	71	34	43	20	8	4
Females												
	GQVX	GQVY	GQVZ	GQWA	GRFK	GRFL	GRFM	GRFN	GRFO	GRFP	GRFQ	GRFR
1996[1]	280	100	32	11	60	21	96	34	77	28	14	5
1997	240	100	9	4	73	30	91	38	51	21	16	7
1998	255	100	8	3	63	25	104	41	68	27	12	5
1999	242	100	17	7	64	26	85	35	63	26	13	5
2000	181	100	11	6	65	36	52	29	42	23	11	6

1 Includes one female with age not stated.

Sources: Office for National Statistics: 01329 813339;
General Register Office for Scotland

5.24 Adoptions by date of entry in Adopted Children Register

Numbers

		1990	1991	1992	1993	1994	1995	1996	1997	1998	1999	2000
United Kingdom	**GRFT**	7 498	8 207	8 400	7 851	7 096	6 600	6 711	5 927	4 998	4 949	5 505
England and Wales	**GRFU**	6 533	7 170	7 341	6 854	6 240	5 797	5 962	5 307	4 387	4 316	4 942
Scotland	**GRFV**	821	815	823	805	664	640	580	470	490	489	391
Northern Ireland	**GRFW**	144	222	236	192	192	163	169	150	121	144	172

Sources: Office for National Statistics: 01329 813339;
General Register Office for Scotland;
General Register Office (Northern Ireland)

6 Education

Education

Educational establishments in the United Kingdom are administered and financed in several ways. Most schools are controlled by local education authorities (LEAs), which are part of the structure of local government, but some are 'assisted', receiving grants direct from central government sources and being controlled by governing bodies which have a substantial degree of autonomy. Outside the public sector, completely, are non-maintained schools run by individuals, companies or charitable institutions.

For the purposes of UK education statistics, schools fall under the following broad categories:

**Mainstream state schools
(Grant-aided mainstream schools in Northern Ireland)**
These schools work in partnership with other schools and local education authorities and they receive funding from LEAs. Since 1 September 1999, the categories (typically in England) are:

Community - schools formerly known as 'county' plus some former Grant-maintained (GM) schools;

Foundation - most former GM schools;

Voluntary Aided - schools formerly known as 'aided' and some former GM schools;

Voluntary Controlled - schools formerly known as 'controlled'.

Non-maintained mainstream schools consisting of

(a) Independent schools
Schools which charge fees and may also be financed by individuals, companies or charitable institutions. These include Direct Grant schools, where the governing bodies are assisted by Departmental grants and a proportion of the pupils attending them do so free or under an arrangement by which local education authorities meet tuition fees. City technology colleges (applicable in England only) are also included as independent schools.

(b) Non-maintained schools
Run by voluntary bodies who may receive some grant from central government for capital work and for equipment, but their current expenditure is met primarily from the fees charged to the LEAs for pupils placed in schools.

Special schools
Provide education for children with special educational needs (SEN) who cannot be educated satisfactorily in an ordinary school. Maintained special schools are run by LEAs, while non-maintained special schools are financed as shown at (b) above.

Pupil Referral Units
Pupil Referral Units (PRUs) operate in England and Wales and provide education outside of a mainstream or special school setting, to meet the needs of difficult or disruptive children.

Schools in Scotland are categorised as Education Authority, Grant-Aided, Opted-out/Self-governing (these three being grouped together as 'Publicly funded' schools), Independent schools and Partnership schools.

The home Government Departments dealing with education statistics are:

Department for Education and Skills (DfES);

National Assembly for Wales (NAfW);

Scottish Executive (SE);

Northern Ireland Department of Education (DENI);

Northern Ireland Department for Employment and Learning (DELNI).

Each of the home Education Departments in Great Britain, along with the Northern Ireland Department of Education, have overall responsibility for funding the schools sectors in their own country.

Up to March 2001, further education (FE) courses in FE sector colleges in England and in Wales were largely funded through grants from the respective Further Education Funding Councils. In April 2001, however, the Learning and Skills Council (LSC) took over the responsibility for funding the FE sector in England, and the National Council for Education and Training for Wales (part of Education and Learning Wales – ELWa) did so for Wales. The LSC in England is also responsible for funding provision for FE and some non-prescribed higher education in FE sector colleges; it also funds some FE provided by LEA maintained and other institutions referred to as 'external institutions'. In Wales, the National Council – ELWa, funds FE provision made by FE institutions via a third party or sponsored arrangements. The Scottish FEFC (SFEFC) funds FE colleges in Scotland, while the Department for Employment and Learning funds FE colleges in Northern Ireland.

Higher education courses in higher education establishments are largely publicly funded through block grants from the HE funding councils in England and Scotland, the Higher Education Council – ELWa in Wales, and the Department of Employment and Learning in Northern Ireland. In addition, some designated HE (mainly HND/HNC Diplomas and Certificates of HE) is also funded by these sources. The FE sources mentioned above fund the remainder.

Statistics for the separate systems obtained in England, Wales, Scotland and Northern Ireland are collected and processed separately in accordance with the particular needs of the responsible Departments. Since 1994/95 the Higher Education Statistics Agency (HESA) has undertaken the data collection for all higher education institutions (HEIs) in the UK. This includes the former Universities Funding Council (UFC) funded

UK universities previously collected by the Universities Statistical Record. There are some structural differences in the information collected for schools, further and higher education in each of the four home countries and in some tables the GB/UK data presented are amalgamations from sources that are not entirely comparable.

Stages of education
There are five stages of education: nursery, primary, secondary, further and higher education, and education is compulsory for all children between the ages of five (four in Northern Ireland) and sixteen. The non-compulsory fourth stage, further education, covers non-advanced education, which can be taken at both further (including tertiary) education colleges, higher education institutions and increasingly in secondary schools. The fifth stage, higher education, is study beyond A levels and their equivalent which, for most full-time students, takes place in higher education institutions.

Nursery education
In recent years there has been a major expansion of pre-school education, with an increased emphasis on children beginning school with a basic foundation in literacy and numeracy. Many children under 5 attend state nursery schools or nursery classes within primary schools. Others may attend playgroups in the voluntary sector or in privately run nurseries. In England and Wales many primary schools also operate an early admissions policy where they admit children under 5 into what are called 'reception classes'.

Primary education
The primary stage covers three age ranges: nursery (under 5), infant (5 to 7 or 8) and junior (up to 11 or 12) but in Scotland and Northern Ireland there is generally no distinction between infant and junior schools. Most public sector primary schools take both boys and girls in mixed classes. It is usual to transfer straight to secondary school at age 11 (in England, Wales and Northern Ireland) or 12 (in Scotland), but in England some children make the transition via middle schools catering for various age ranges between 8 and 14. Depending on their individual age ranges middle schools are classified as either primary or secondary.

Secondary education
Public provision of secondary education in an area may consist of a combination of different types of school, the pattern reflecting historical circumstance and the policy adopted by the local education authority. Comprehensive schools largely admit pupils without reference to ability or aptitude and cater for all the children in a neighbourhood, but in some areas they co-exist with grammar, secondary modern or technical schools. In 2000/01, 87 per cent of pupils in England attended comprehensive schools while all secondary schools in Wales are comprehensive schools. The majority of education authority secondary schools in Scotland are comprehensive in character and offer six years of secondary education; however in remote areas there are several two-year and four-year secondary schools. In Northern Ireland, post primary education is provided by secondary intermediate and grammar schools.

Special schools
Special schools (day or boarding) provide education for children who require specialist support to complete their education, for example because they have physical or other difficulties. Many pupils with special educational needs are educated in mainstream schools. All children attending special schools are offered a curriculum designed to overcome their learning difficulties and to enable them to become self-reliant.

Further education
The term further education may be used in a general sense to cover all non-advanced courses taken after the period of compulsory education, but more commonly it excludes those staying on at secondary school and those in higher education, i.e. courses in universities and colleges leading to qualifications above GCE A Level, SCE H Grade, GNVQ/NVQ level 3, and their equivalents. Since 1 April 1993 sixth form colleges have been included in the further education sector.

Higher education
Higher education is defined as courses that are of a standard that is higher than GCE A level, the Higher Grade of the Scottish Certificate of Education, GNVQ/NVQ level 3 or the Edexcel (formerly BTEC) or SQA National Certificate/Diploma. There are three main levels of HE course: (i) postgraduate courses are those leading to higher degrees, diplomas and certificates (including postgraduate certificates of education and professional qualifications) which usually require a first degree as entry qualification; (ii) first degrees which includes first degrees, first degrees with qualified teacher status, enhanced first degrees, first degrees obtained concurrently with a diploma, and intercalated first degrees; (iii) other undergraduate courses which includes all other higher education courses, for example HNDs and Diplomas in HE. As a result of the 1992 Further and Higher Education Act, former polytechnics and some other higher education institutions were designated as universities in 1992/93. Students normally attend HE courses at higher education institutions, but some attend at further education colleges. Some also attend institutions which do not receive public grant (such as the University of Buckingham) and these numbers are excluded from the tables.

6.1 Number of schools or departments[1] by type and establishments of further and higher education

Academic years

		1990 /91	1995 /96	1997 /98	1998 /99	1999[2] /00	2000[3] /01
United Kingdom:							
Public sector mainstream							
Nursery[4,5]	KBFK	1 364	1 486	1 681	2 369	2 864	3 228
Primary[6]	KBFA	24 135	23 441	23 230	23 125	23 036	22 902
Secondary[7]	KBFF	4 790	4 463	4 434	4 418	4 405	4 337
of which 6th form colleges	KPGM	116	..	..	..	..	..
Non-maintained mainstream[1]	KBFU	2 508	2 436	2 499	2 482	2 457	2 414
Special - all	KBFP	1 830	1 565	1 517	1 522	1 523	1 498
maintained	KPVX	..	1 456	1 419	1 428	1 426	1 401
non maintained	KPGO	..	109	98	94	97	97
Pupil referral units	KXEP	..	315	332	325	325	338
Universities (including Open University)[8]	KAHG	48	89	88	88	88	90
All other further and higher education institutions	KJPQ	588	609	596	581	574	559
Higher education institutions	KPVY	..	66	63	58	58	60
Further education institutions	KSNY	..	543	533	523	516	499
of which 6th form colleges	KPGP	..	110	108	107	105	105
England:							
Public sector mainstream							
Nursery	KBAK	566	547	533	520	514	506
Primary	KBAA	19 047	18 480	18 312	18 234	18 158	18 069
Secondary[7]	KBAF	3 897	3 594	3 567	3 560	3 550	3 481
of which 6th form colleges	KPGS	114	..	..	..	..	..
Non-maintained	KBAU	2 289	2 266	2 244	2 231	2 204	2 205
Special - all	KBAP	1 380	1 263	1 229	1 209	1 197	1 175
maintained	KPGT	..	1 191	1 164	1 148	1 134	1 113
non maintained	KPGU	..	72	65	61	63	62
Pupil referral units	KXEQ	..	291	309	298	295	308
Universities (including Open University)[8]	KAHM	37	72	71	70	70	72
All other further and higher education institutions	KJPR	460	503	491	482	475	457
Higher education institutions	KPXA	..	50	48	47	47	46
Further education institutions	KPWC	..	453	443	435	428	411
of which 6th form colleges	KPGV	..	110	108	107	105	105
Wales:							
Public sector mainstream							
Nursery	KBBK	54	52	47	46	42	41
Primary	KBBA	1 717	1 681	1 673	1 660	1 644	1 631
Secondary[7]	KBBF	230	228	228	229	228	229
of which 6th form colleges	KPGY	2	..	..	..	..	..
Non-maintained	KBBU	71	62	57	54	55	54
Special (Maintained)	KBBP	61	54	50	48	47	45
Pupil referral units	KZBF	..	24	23	27	30	30
Universities[8]	KAHS	1	2	2	2	2	2
All other further and higher education institutions	KJQP	38	31	30	28	28	30
Higher education institutions	KSNZ	..	5	4	4	4	6
Further education institutions	KPGZ	..	26	26	24	24	24
Scotland:							
Public sector mainstream							
Nursery[5]	KBDK	659	796	1 010	1 712	2 213	2 586
Primary	KBDA	2 372	2 332	2 300	2 291	2 293	2 278
Secondary	KBDF	424	405	401	392	389	389
Non-maintained[1]	KBDU	131	87	176	175	176	129
Special - all	KBDP	343	201	191	218	228	230
maintained	KYCZ	343	164	158	185	195	195
non-maintained	KYDA	..	37	33	33	33	35
Universities[8]	KAHX	8	13	13	14	14	14
All other further and higher education institutions	KJRA	64	56	56	52	52	53
Higher education institutions	KPWE	..	9	9	5	5	6
Further education institutions	KPHB	..	47	47	47	47	47
Northern Ireland:							
Grant aided mainstream							
Nursery[4]	KBEK	85	91	91	91	95	95
Primary[6]	KBEA	999	948	945	940	941	924
Secondary	KBEF	239	236	238	237	238	238
Non-maintained	KBEU	17	21	22	22	22	26
Special (Maintained)	KBEP	46	47	47	47	50	48
Universities	KIAD	2	2	2	2	2	2
Colleges of education	KIAE	2	2	2	2	2	2
Further education colleges	KIAG	24	17	17	17	17	17

1 From 1997/98 non-maintained mainstream schools in Scotland with more than one department have been counted once for each department e.g. a school with nursery, primary and secondary departments has been counted 3 times. The 2000/01 figure for Scotland shows primary and secondary only.

2 Revised to include 1999/00 data for Wales and updated nursery schools and non-maintained special schools data for Scotland.

3 Provisional.

4 Excludes voluntary and private pre-school education centres in Northern Ireland (304 in total in 2000/01).

5 Nursery schools figures for Scotland prior to 1998/99 only include data for Local Authority pre-schools. Data thereafter include partnership pre-schools.

6 From 1995/96, includes Preparatory Departments in Northern Ireland Grammar Schools (22 in total in 2000/01).

7 From 1993/94 excludes sixth form colleges in England and Wales which were reclassified as further education colleges on 1 April 1993.

8 From 1993/94 includes former polytechnics and colleges which became universities as a result of the Further and Higher Education Act 1992.

Source: Education Departments: 01325 392756

6.2

Full-time and part-time pupils in school[1] by age[2,3] and gender
United Kingdom
All schools at January [4]

		1991	1992	1993	1994	1995	1996	1997	1998	1999	2000	2001[5]
Age at previous 31 August[6]												
Number (thousands)												
England[7]	KBIA	7 617	7 712	7 842	7 883	8 013	8 110	8 195	8 261	8 310	8 346	8 374
Wales	KBIB	482	487	493	498	504	..	..	501	513	512	512
Scotland[2]	KBIC	821	826	832	841	845	846	848	850	844	874	882
Northern Ireland[3]	KBID	341	343	346	349	351	353	354	352	352	349	348
United Kingdom	KBIE	9 260	9 368	9 513	9 571	9 714	9 813	9 905	9 973	10 019	10 081	10 116
Boys and girls												
2 - 4[8]	KBIF	1 012	1 045	1 082	1 103	1 135	1 145	1 149	1 150	1 154	1 184	1 187
5 - 10	KBIG	4 346	4 356	4 392	4 462	4 517	4 581	4 627	4 666	4 661	4 629	4 597
11	KBIH	714	735	727	713	718	717	742	747	762	783	771
12 - 14	KBII	1 975	2 021	2 112	2 179	2 179	2 158	2 151	2 180	2 211	2 256	2 297
15	KBIK	691	664	638	651	700	721	717	701	706	705	732
16	KBIL	295	308	313	259	259	279	289	289	283	285	287
17	KBIM	197	206	215	180	181	191	206	216	218	213	219
18 and over	KBIN	32	34	35	23	24	22	22	24	25	27	27
Boys												
14	KBIO	344	332	338	367	376	371	365	368	367	381	384
15	KBIP	355	341	327	333	358	368	366	358	361	359	374
16	KBIQ	144	151	154	128	127	136	141	140	137	138	139
17	KBIR	96	100	104	88	88	92	100	104	104	101	105
18 and over	KBIS	17	18	18	12	13	12	12	13	13	14	15
Girls												
14	KBIT	326	314	322	347	358	355	349	350	352	364	365
15	KBIU	336	323	311	318	342	353	351	344	345	346	358
16	KBIV	151	156	159	131	132	142	148	149	146	147	148
17	KBIW	100	106	111	92	93	99	106	112	114	111	114
18 and over	KBIX	15	16	16	11	11	10	10	11	11	13	12

1 From 1 April 1993 excludes 6th form colleges in England and Wales which were reclassified as further education colleges.
2 Figures for Scotland are estimates using proportions of the stage rolls.
3 In Northern Ireland, a split is not collected by age but is available by year group and so this is used as a proxy.
4 In Wales and Scotland, as at the previous September.

5 Provisional.
6 1 July for Northern Ireland and 31 December for Scotland.
7 From 1992, figures for independent schools in England include pupils aged less than 2.
8 Includes the so-called "rising 5s" (i.e. those pupils who become 5 during the autumn term.

Source: Education Departments: 01325 392756

6.3 Number of pupils and teachers: pupil/teacher ratios[1] by school type
United Kingdom
At January[2]

		1996[3]	1997[3]	1998[3]	1999[3]	2000[3,4]	2001[4,5]
All schools or departments							
Total							
Pupils (thousands)							
Full-time and full-time							
equivalent of part-time	KBCA	9 580.8	9 663.7	9 741.3	9 782.6	9 828.3	9 867.7
Teachers[6] (thousands)	KBCB	532.3	533.0	533.6	540.4	545.6	553.1
Pupils per teacher[6]:							
United Kingdom	KBCC	18.0	18.1	18.2	18.2	18.1	17.9
England	KBCD	18.2	18.3	18.5	18.4	18.3	18.1
Wales	KBCE	18.7	18.8	19.1	18.8	18.7	18.4
Scotland	KBCF	15.5	15.8	15.8	15.4	15.4	15.6
Northern Ireland	KBCG	17.2	17.1	17.1	17.1	16.8	16.6
Public sector mainstream schools or departments							
Nursery							
Pupils (thousands)							
Full-time and full-time							
equivalent of part-time	KBFM	61.8	61.5	61.7	61.1	75.3	88.8
Teachers[6] (thousands)	KBFN	2.9	2.9	3.0	3.0	3.1	3.4
Pupils per teacher[6]	KBFO	21.3	21.3	20.7	20.6	24.2	26.5
Primary[7]							
Pupils (thousands)							
Full-time and full-time							
equivalent of part-time	KBFB	5 144.9	5 184.9	5 213.8	5 202.5	5 167.9	5 130.5
Teachers[6] (thousands)	KBFD	226.9	227.0	225.4	226.7	228.0	229.6
Pupils per teacher[6]	KBFE	22.7	22.8	23.1	22.9	22.7	22.3
Secondary[8]							
Pupils (thousands)							
Full-time and full-time							
equivalent of part-time	KBFG	3 677.4	3 742.7	3 741.1	3 793.3	3 859.0	3 915.5
Teachers[6] (thousands)	KBFH	228.1	228.5	228.7	230.4	232.9	237.0
Pupils per teacher[6]	KBFI	16.1	16.2	16.4	16.5	16.6	16.5
Special schools							
Pupils (thousands)							
Full-time and full-time							
equivalent of part-time							
all	KBFQ	114.1	114.2	114.5	..	..	..
maintained	KPGE	107.7	107.8	108.4	108.5	107.4	106.5
non-maintained[9]	KPGF	6.4	6.4	6.0	..	..	..
Teachers[6] (thousands)							
all	KBFS	18.6	18.3	18.1	..	..	..
maintained	KPGG	17.1	16.8	16.7	16.9	17.0	17.0
non-maintained[9]	KPGH	1.5	1.4	1.4	..	..	..
Pupils per teacher[6]							
all	KBFT	6.2	6.2	6.3	..	..	..
maintained	KPGI	6.3	6.4	6.5	6.4	6.3	6.3
non-maintained[9]	KPGJ	4.4	4.4	4.4	..	..	..

1 'All schools' pupil/teacher ratios exclude Pupil Referral Units and non-maintained special schools.
2 In Scotland and Wales the school census date is September whereas for the rest of the United Kingdom it remains at January.
3 Includes revised data.
4 Nursery schools for Scotland refer to pre-school education centres and are not therefore directly comparable with earlier years.

5 Provisional.
6 Figures of teachers and of pupil/teacher ratios take account of the full-time equivalent of part-time teachers.
7 Includes preparatory departments attached to grammar schools in Northern Ireland.
8 Includes voluntary grammar schools in Northern Ireland.
9 England and Scotland only.

Source: Education Departments: 01325 392756

6.4 Full-time and part-time pupils with special educational needs (SEN)[1], 2000/01[2]
United Kingdom
By type of school

Thousands and percentages

	United Kingdom	England[3]	Wales	Scotland	Northern Ireland
All schools					
Total pupils	10 109.9	8 374.1	512.3	871.7	351.9
SEN pupils with statements	300.8	258.2	17.0	16.7	8.8
Incidence (%)[4]	3.0	3.1	3.3	1.9	2.5
Maintained schools[5]					
Nursery[6,7]					
Total pupils	146.1	45.0	2.4	88.8	9.9
SEN pupils with statements	1.1	0.6	-	0.4	0.1
Incidence (%)[4]	0.8	1.3	1.0	0.5	0.6
Placement (%)[8]	0.4	0.2	0.1	2.6	0.6
Primary[9]					
Total pupils	5 297.7	4 406.2	285.8	425.2	180.4
SEN pupils without statements[10]	996.6	927.0	58.1	11.5	-
SEN pupils with statements	88.2	75.3	6.2	4.2	2.5
Pupils with statements - incidence (%)[4]	1.7	1.7	2.2	1.0	1.4
Pupils with statements - placement (%)[8]	29.3	29.1	36.3	25.0	28.7
Secondary					
Total pupils	3 916.9	3 231.8	210.4	319.1	155.6
SEN pupils without statements[10]	628.5	586.3	32.4	9.8	-
SEN pupils with statements	96.2	82.1	6.7	5.0	2.4
Pupils with statements - incidents (%)[4]	2.5	2.5	3.2	1.6	1.5
Pupils with statements - placement (%)[8]	32.0	31.8	39.5	30.1	26.8
Special[11,12]					
Total pupils	107.7	91.0	3.8	8.3	4.7
SEN pupils with statements	101.6	87.4	3.7	6.7	3.9
Incidence (%)[4]	94.3	96.1	97.2	80.4	82.9
Placement (%)[8]	33.8	33.9	21.5	39.9	43.9
Pupil referral units[11,13]					
Total pupils	9.7	9.3	0.4	..	..
SEN pupils with statements[10]	1.9	1.8	0.1	..	..
Incidence (%)[4]	20.0	19.4	34.0	..	..
Placement (%)[8]	0.6	0.7	0.9	..	..
Other schools					
Independent					
Total pupils	626.1	586.2	9.5	29.2	1.3
SEN pupils with statements[10]	6.9	6.6	0.3	-	..
Incidence (%)[4]	1.1	1.1	3.0	0.1	..
Placement (%)[8]	2.3	2.6	1.7	0.3	..
Non-maintained special[11]					
Total pupils	5.7	4.6	..	1.1	..
SEN pupils with statements	4.8	4.5	..	0.3	..
Incidents (%)[4]	85.1	96.1	..	31.8	..
Placement (%)[8]	1.6	1.7	..	2.1	..

1 For Scotland, pupils with a Record of Needs.
2 Provisional.
3 Estimates have been made for January 2001 because the data for SEN are known to be incomplete.
4 Incidence of pupils - the number of pupils with statements within each school type expressed as a proportion of the total number of pupils on roll in each school type.
5 Grant-Aided schools in Northern Ireland.
6 Includes pupils in Voluntary and Private Pre-School Centres in Northern Ireland funded under the Pre-School Expansion Programme which began in 1998/99.
7 Nursery school figures for Scotland are for 1999/00.

8 Placement of pupils - the number of pupils with statements within each school type expressed as a proportion of the number of pupils with statements in all schools.
9 Includes nursery classes (except for Scotland, where they are included with Nursery Schools) and reception classes in primary schools.
10 UK totals are slight undercounts as data are not available for Wales and not applicable for Northern Ireland.
11 England and Wales figures exclude dually registered pupils.
12 Including general and hospital special schools.
13 England and Wales only.

Source: Education Departments: 01325 392756

6.5 GCE, GCSE and SCE[1] qualifications obtained at a typical age[2,3], and GCE, GCSE, SCE and GNVQ/GSVQ qualifications obtained by students of all ages

United Kingdom

Percentages and thousands

| | Pupils in their last year of compulsory education[2] | | | | | Pupils/students in education[3] | | | |
| | | | | | | % achieving GCE A Levels and equivalent | | | |
	5 or more grades A*-C[4]	1-4 grades A*-C[4]	Grades D-G[5] only	No graded results	Total (=100%) (Thousands)	2 or more passes[6,7]	1 pass[8]	1 or more passes	Population aged 17 (thousands)
Students at a typical age (percentages and thousands)									
1995/96[9]									
All	45.2	25.9	21.3	7.5	696.4	29.5	8.0	37.5	648.3
Males	40.4	25.4	25.4	8.7	355.7	26.7	7.3	34.0	333.6
Females	50.2	26.4	17.0	6.3	340.7	32.5	8.8	41.3	314.6
1996/97									
All	46.2	25.5	20.9	7.4	713.3	29.6	7.4	37.0	723.5
Males	41.4	25.3	24.9	8.5	363.5	26.5	6.7	33.2	372.4
Females	51.3	25.7	16.7	6.3	349.7	33.0	8.1	41.1	351.0
1997/98									
All	47.5	25.2	21.1	6.5	698.4	33.5	6.5	40.1	751.0
Males	42.3	25.4	24.9	7.5	356.1	29.9	6.0	35.9	384.9
Females	52.8	25.0	17.1	5.3	342.3	37.4	7.2	44.5	366.1
1998/99									
All	49.1	24.8	20.3	5.9	703.6	33.7	6.7	40.3	744.2
Males	43.8	25.2	24.1	6.9	359.6	30.1	6.1	36.2	381.4
Females	54.6	24.3	16.3	4.8	344.0	37.4	7.3	44.7	362.8
1999/00									
All	50.4	24.5	19.7	5.5	703.7	34.5	6.5	41.0	732.2
Males	45.0	25.0	23.6	6.4	357.7	30.5	6.0	36.6	376.0
Females	55.9	23.9	15.7	4.5	346.0	38.6	7.1	45.6	356.3

| | GCSE and SCE S Grade/Standard Grade (SG) | | | | GCE A Level and SCE/NQ Higher Grade | | |
	5 or more grades A*-C[4,10]	1-4 grades A*-C[4,10]	Grades D-G[5,11] only	No graded results[12]	2 or more passes[6,7]	1 pass[8]	Total 1 or more passes
Students of all ages (thousands)							
1995/96							
All	331.4	371.7	236.5	40.0	204.5	78.2	282.6
Males	151.3	175.3	130.9	20.0	95.2	33.8	129.0
Females	180.1	196.4	105.6	20.0	109.3	44.3	153.6
1996/97							
All	333.6	358.7	240.5	41.8	219.3	76.6	295.9
Males	152.3	169.6	133.5	20.7	101.2	33.2	134.3
Females	181.0	189.1	107.0	21.2	118.1	43.4	161.6
1997/98							
All	335.3	336.4	233.9	37.4	260.4	70.3	330.6
Males	152.8	162.3	129.5	18.3	119.2	30.5	149.7
Females	182.5	174.1	104.5	19.2	141.2	39.8	181.0
1998/99							
All	341.0	323.7	229.8	31.2	257.9	69.9	327.8
Males	162.3	150.6	128.1	15.6	118.4	30.6	149.0
Females	178.7	173.2	101.7	15.6	139.5	39.3	178.8
1999/00							
All	357.7	311.6	224.4	30.3	258.8	65.6	324.4
Males	162.8	150.9	125.3	15.2	118.0	28.7	146.6
Females	194.9	160.7	99.1	15.1	140.9	36.9	177.7

1 From 1999/00 National Qualifications (NQ) were introduced in Scotland. NQs include Standard Grades, Intermediate 1 & 2 and Higher Grades. The figures for Higher Grades combine the new NQ Higher and the old SCE Higher.

2 Pupils aged 15 at the start of the academic year, pupils in year S4 in Scotland.

3 Pupils in schools and students in further education institutions aged 16-18 at the start of the academic year in England, Wales and Northern Ireland as a percentage of the 17 year old population. Pupils in Scotland generally sit Highers one year earlier and the figures tend to relate to the results of pupils in year S5/S6.

4 Standard Grades 1-3 in Scotland.

5 Grades D-G at GCSE and Scottish Standard Grades 4-7.

6 3 or more SCE/NQ Higher Grades in Scotland.

7 Includes Advanced level GNVQ/GSVQ which is equivalent to 2 GCE A Levels or AS equivalents/3 SCE/NQ Higher grades.

8 2 AS levels or 2 Highers in Scotland, count as 1 A Level pass. Includes those with 1.5 A level passes.

9 Great Britain only.

10 Includes GNVQ/GSVQ Intermediate Part 1, Full and Language unit which are equivalent to 2, 4 and 0.5 GCSE grades A*-C/SCE Standard grades 1-3 respectively. Figures include those with 4.5 GCSEs.

11 Includes GNVQ/GSVQ Foundation Part 1, Full and Language unit which are equivalent to 2, 4 and 0.5 GCSE grades D-G/SCE Standard grades 4-7 respectively.

12 Figures for Scotland include students in Year S4 only. Time series has been revised.

Source: Education Departments: 01325 392756

6.6 Students in further[1] education by country, mode of study[2], gender and age,[3] during 1999/00

United Kingdom (home and overseas students)   Thousands

	United Kingdom		England[4]		Wales		Scotland[5]		Northern Ireland	
	Full-time	Part-time	Full-time	Part-time	Full-time	Part-time	Full-time	Part-time	Full-time	Part-time
All										
Age under 16	9.9	66.0	7.9	33.8	0.6	4.1	1.3	25.5	0.1	2.6
16	255.6	79.4	226.4	54.5	13.9	4.0	7.8	14.8	7.4	6.1
17	214.2	88.4	188.8	65.6	11.1	4.5	7.5	13.5	6.9	4.7
18	109.6	91.7	94.4	72.8	5.7	5.0	5.4	10.8	4.0	3.0
19	47.5	81.5	41.5	65.6	2.4	4.8	2.5	8.8	1.1	2.3
20	28.1	69.7	25.1	57.0	1.2	4.2	1.4	6.8	0.4	1.7
21	21.1	61.9	19.1	51.5	0.8	3.6	1.1	5.3	0.2	1.5
22	18.0	60.2	16.4	50.5	0.6	3.5	0.8	4.9	0.1	1.3
23	16.6	62.3	15.3	52.4	0.6	3.6	0.7	4.9	0.1	1.4
24	15.6	64.2	14.5	54.4	0.4	3.5	0.6	4.9	0.1	1.3
25	14.7	65.0	13.7	55.4	0.4	3.6	0.6	4.7	-	1.3
26	14.3	67.2	13.3	57.3	0.4	3.8	0.5	4.9	-	1.2
27	14.0	70.6	13.1	60.4	0.4	3.9	0.5	5.1	-	1.2
28	13.8	73.9	12.9	62.9	0.4	4.2	0.5	5.6	-	1.3
29	13.4	73.3	12.5	62.4	0.4	4.1	0.5	5.6	-	1.2
30+	225.2	1885.4	212.5	1595.5	5.9	117.7	6.7	147.5	0.2	24.8
Unknown	4.7	54.3	4.6	50.7	0.1	3.2	-	0.1	-	0.4
All ages	1036.3	3015.2	932.0	2502.7	45.3	181.5	38.2	273.7	20.7	57.3
Males										
Age under 16	5.5	35.0	4.4	19.0	0.4	2.2	0.7	12.3	0.1	1.6
16	127.4	41.1	111.6	29.5	7.1	2.0	4.7	6.9	4.0	2.7
17	104.6	49.0	91.9	37.4	5.3	2.7	3.9	6.8	3.4	2.1
18	57.1	50.2	49.4	39.5	2.8	2.9	2.7	6.4	2.1	1.5
19	26.4	41.6	23.1	32.9	1.3	2.7	1.4	5.0	0.7	1.0
20	15.5	32.7	13.9	26.4	0.7	2.1	0.7	3.5	0.2	0.6
21	11.1	27.1	10.1	22.4	0.3	1.6	0.6	2.5	0.1	0.6
22	9.3	25.4	8.5	21.3	0.3	1.5	0.4	2.1	-	0.5
23	8.5	25.9	7.9	21.7	0.2	1.5	0.3	2.1	-	0.5
24	8.1	26.5	7.5	22.6	0.2	1.4	0.3	2.1	-	0.4
25	7.4	26.9	6.9	23.1	0.2	1.4	0.3	2.0	-	0.4
26	6.9	27.7	6.5	23.9	0.1	1.5	0.2	1.9	-	0.3
27	6.8	29.1	6.5	25.2	0.1	1.5	0.2	2.0	-	0.3
28	6.7	30.1	6.3	25.8	0.1	1.6	0.2	2.2	-	0.4
29	6.4	30.0	6.1	25.9	0.1	1.6	0.2	2.2	-	0.4
30+	108.1	730.5	103.8	620.9	1.8	44.7	2.5	57.6	0.1	7.2
Unknown	2.5	22.4	2.5	20.8	-	1.4	-	-	-	0.1
All ages	518.2	1251.1	466.9	1038.2	21.1	74.3	19.5	117.8	10.8	20.7
Females										
Age under 16	4.3	31.0	3.5	14.9	0.3	1.9	0.5	13.2	-	1.0
16	128.2	38.3	114.9	25.0	6.8	2.1	3.1	7.9	3.5	3.3
17	109.6	39.4	96.9	28.2	5.8	1.9	3.5	6.7	3.5	2.6
18	52.5	41.5	45.0	33.3	2.9	2.1	2.7	4.4	1.9	1.6
19	21.1	39.9	18.4	32.7	1.1	2.1	1.1	3.8	0.5	1.2
20	12.6	37.1	11.2	30.6	0.6	2.1	0.6	3.3	0.1	1.0
21	10.0	34.9	9.0	29.2	0.4	2.0	0.5	2.8	0.1	0.9
22	8.7	34.8	7.9	29.2	0.3	2.0	0.4	2.7	-	0.9
23	8.1	36.5	7.3	30.7	0.3	2.1	0.4	2.8	-	1.0
24	7.5	37.7	7.0	31.8	0.2	2.1	0.3	2.9	-	0.9
25	7.3	38.1	6.8	32.3	0.2	2.1	0.3	2.7	-	0.9
26	7.4	39.5	6.8	33.4	0.3	2.3	0.3	2.9	-	0.9
27	7.1	41.5	6.6	35.2	0.3	2.4	0.3	3.1	-	0.9
28	7.1	43.9	6.6	37.1	0.3	2.6	0.3	3.4	-	0.9
29	7.1	43.3	6.5	36.5	0.3	2.5	0.3	3.4	-	0.9
30+	117.1	1155.0	108.7	974.6	4.0	73.0	4.2	89.9	0.2	17.5
Unknown	2.2	31.9	2.1	29.9	-	1.8	-	-	-	0.3
All ages	518.1	1764.1	465.1	1464.5	24.2	107.1	18.8	155.9	10.0	36.5

1 Further education figures are whole year counts and differ from the higher education tables which use annual snapshots. Data for Northern Ireland however, are on a snapshot basis.

2 Full-time includes sandwich, and for Scotland, short full-time. Part-time comprises both day and evening, including block release (except Scotland) and open/distance learning.

3 Ages as at 31 August 1999 (1 July in Northern Ireland and 31 December in Scotland).

4 Excludes approximately 175,650 students in FE institutions in England since the information cannot be broken down in this way. External institutions and specialist designated colleges are also excluded.

5 Figures for Scotland further education institutions are enrolments rather than headcounts.

Source: Education Departments: 01325 392756

6.7 Students in further education[1] by country, mode of study[2], gender and subject group, during 1999/00[3]

United Kingdom - Home and overseas students

Thousands

	United Kingdom		England[3]		Wales		Scotland[4]		Northern Ireland	
	Full-time	Part-time	Full-time	Part-time	Full-time	Part-time	Full-time	Part-time	Full-time	Part-time
All persons										
Subject group										
Medicine & Dentistry	-	-	-	-	-	-	-	-	-	-
Allied Medicine	100.2	157.8	97.7	145.8	-	-	1.1	10.3	1.4	1.8
Biological Sciences	1.0	2.3	0.8	0.2	-	-	0.2	2.1	-	-
Agriculture	35.4	155.6	33.8	145.7	-	-	1.5	9.4	0.1	0.5
Physical Sciences	13.6	6.6	13.6	5.4	-	-	-	0.9	-	0.3
Mathematical and Computing Sciences	127.7	351.0	123.3	276.4	-	-	2.8	63.8	1.6	10.8
Engineering & Technology	49.8	111.6	42.2	86.9	-	-	5.6	20.7	1.9	4.0
Architecture	26.3	49.2	20.6	39.8	-	-	3.1	7.8	2.6	1.6
Social Sciences	16.6	72.0	10.8	46.3	-	-	5.1	23.0	0.7	2.6
Business & Financial	99.3	277.0	87.3	220.4	-	-	6.9	43.8	5.1	12.7
Documentation	8.4	21.6	7.3	12.1	-	-	0.7	9.1	0.4	0.4
Languages	21.3	83.5	20.6	66.3	-	0.1	0.6	15.1	-	1.9
Humanities	6.4	9.9	6.2	7.0	-	-	0.2	2.8	-	-
Creative arts	68.4	75.7	60.7	54.5	0.1	-	5.1	17.9	2.5	3.3
Education[5]	17.7	44.8	15.0	26.7	-	0.4	2.1	15.2	0.6	2.5
Combined, gen	148.7	207.1	141.4	156.5	0.2	4.2	3.3	31.7	3.8	14.8
Unknown	295.6	1 389.6	250.6	1 212.8	45.0	176.8	-	-	-	-
All subjects	1 036.3	3 015.2	932.0	2 502.7	45.3	181.5	38.2	273.7	20.7	57.3
Males										
Subject group										
Medicine and Dentistry	-	-	-	-	-	-	-	-	-	-
Allied Medicine	32.8	61.4	32.6	56.3	-	-	0.1	5.0	0.1	0.2
Biological Sciences	0.4	0.9	0.3	-	-	-	0.1	0.8	-	-
Agriculture	15.7	56.3	14.9	51.3	-	-	0.8	4.8	-	0.3
Physical Sciences	9.6	3.9	9.6	3.3	-	-	-	0.4	-	0.1
Mathematical and Computing Sciences	60.5	129.3	57.4	100.1	-	-	1.9	25.6	1.3	3.5
Engineering & Technology	46.4	102.1	39.3	81.0	-	-	5.3	17.4	1.8	3.6
Architecture	25.0	45.3	19.5	37.2	-	-	2.9	6.5	2.6	1.6
Social Sciences	2.2	10.6	1.4	5.9	-	-	0.8	4.5	0.1	0.2
Business & Financial	43.3	100.2	39.4	80.9	-	-	2.2	16.1	1.7	3.3
Documentation	4.3	8.4	3.7	4.6	-	-	0.4	3.7	0.2	0.1
Languages	8.8	29.3	8.5	23.0	-	-	0.3	5.5	-	0.7
Humanities	3.0	4.1	2.9	3.1	-	-	0.1	1.1	-	-
Creative arts	24.9	14.5	22.5	9.4	-	-	1.7	4.7	0.8	0.4
Education[5]	10.7	16.9	9.1	9.4	-	0.1	1.2	6.4	0.4	0.9
Combined, gen	71.6	80.9	68.0	58.4	0.1	1.5	1.7	15.2	1.8	5.8
Unknown	159.0	586.9	138.1	514.2	21.0	72.7	-	-	-	-
All subjects	518.2	1251.1	466.9	1038.2	21.1	74.3	19.5	117.8	10.8	20.7
Females										
Subject group										
Medicine & Dentistry	-	-	-	-	-	-	-	-	-	-
Allied Medicine	67.4	96.4	65.1	89.5	-	-	1.0	5.3	1.3	1.6
Biological Sciences	0.6	1.4	0.5	0.2	-	-	0.1	1.2	-	-
Agriculture	19.7	99.3	18.9	94.4	-	-	0.6	4.6	0.1	0.3
Physical Sciences	4.0	2.7	4.0	2.0	-	-	-	0.5	-	0.1
Mathematical and Computing Sciences	67.1	221.7	65.9	176.3	-	-	0.9	38.2	0.3	7.2
Engineering & Technology	3.4	9.5	3.0	5.9	-	-	0.4	3.3	0.1	0.4
Architecture	1.3	3.9	1.1	2.5	-	-	0.2	1.3	-	0.1
Social Sciences	14.4	61.4	9.5	40.5	-	-	4.3	18.6	0.7	2.4
Business & Financial	56.0	176.7	47.9	139.5	-	-	4.7	27.7	3.4	9.5
Documentation	4.1	13.2	3.6	7.5	-	-	0.3	5.4	0.2	0.3
Languages	12.5	54.2	12.2	43.3	-	-	0.3	9.6	-	1.3
Humanities	3.4	5.7	3.3	4.0	-	-	0.1	1.8	-	-
Creative arts	43.5	61.2	38.3	45.1	-	-	3.4	13.2	1.7	2.9
Education[5]	7.0	27.9	5.9	17.3	-	0.3	0.9	8.7	0.2	1.6
Combined, gen	77.1	126.2	73.4	98.0	0.1	2.7	1.6	16.5	2.0	9.0
Unknown	136.5	802.7	112.5	698.6	24.0	104.1	-	-	-	-
All subjects	518.1	1764.1	465.1	1464.5	24.2	107.1	18.8	155.9	10.0	36.5

1 Further education figures are whole year counts and differ from the higher education tables which use annual snapshots. Data for Northern Ireland however, are on a snapshot basis.

2 Full-time excludes sandwich, and for Scotland, short full-time. Part-time comprises both day and evening, including block release (except Scotland) and open/distance learning.

3 Provisional. Includes estimated breakdowns by subjects for students in further education institutions in England but excludes approximately 175,650 students in further education institutions in England since the information cannot be broken down in this way. External institutions and specialist designated colleges are also excluded.

4 Figures for Scotland further education institutions are enrolments rather than headcounts. Due to a reclassification of subject groupings, subject categories for Scotland cannot be directly compared with previous years.

5 Includes ITT and INSET.

Source: Education Departments: 01325 392756

6.8 Students in higher[1] education by level, mode of study[2], gender and age[3], 2000/01[4]
United Kingdom (home and overseas students)

Thousands

	Postgraduate level						First degree		Other undergraduate		Total higher education[5]	
	PHD's and equivalent		Masters and others		Total postgraduate							
	Full-time	Part-time	Full-time	Part-time	Full-time	Part-time	Full-time	Part-time	Full-time	Part-time	Full-time[5]	Part-time[5]
All Persons												
Age under 16	-	-	-	-	-	-	-	-	-	0.1	0.1	0.1
16	-	-	-	-	-	-	0.4	-	0.6	0.4	1.0	0.4
17	-	-	-	-	-	-	9.9	-	4.1	1.2	14.1	1.2
18	-	-	-	-	-	-	145.5	0.5	22.9	6.3	168.5	6.9
19	-	-	0.1	0.1	0.1	0.1	202.9	2.3	31.4	11.2	234.6	13.7
20	0.1	-	1.1	0.2	1.2	0.2	210.8	3.9	26.6	12.3	238.6	16.4
21	0.8	-	13.7	1.2	14.5	1.2	138.7	4.9	17.8	11.2	171.1	17.4
22	2.7	0.1	17.8	3.7	20.5	3.8	61.0	4.5	12.1	10.9	93.6	19.2
23	4.2	0.2	15.5	5.3	19.7	5.5	30.2	4.0	9.1	11.4	59.0	20.9
24	4.6	1.1	12.0	6.2	16.5	7.4	18.2	3.5	6.9	12.0	41.6	22.9
25	3.8	2.2	9.4	7.0	13.2	9.1	12.6	3.4	5.5	12.0	31.3	24.6
26	3.0	2.1	7.4	7.3	10.5	9.4	9.9	3.4	4.8	12.7	25.1	25.5
27	2.6	2.1	6.1	7.9	8.7	10.0	8.2	3.3	4.1	13.3	21.0	26.6
28	2.2	1.9	5.5	8.3	7.7	10.2	7.2	3.3	3.8	13.8	18.6	27.4
29	1.8	1.8	4.6	8.4	6.4	10.3	6.5	3.3	3.4	14.1	16.3	27.7
30+	12.1	25.5	31.1	146.8	43.2	172.3	59.5	55.1	37.7	302.2	140.5	530.2
Unknown	-	0.1	0.3	2.0	0.3	2.1	0.5	0.3	0.4	7.3	1.2	9.7
All ages	38.1	37.2	124.5	204.4	162.6	241.6	922.0	95.7	191.2	452.6	1276.3	791.0
Males												
Age under 16	-	-	-	-	-	-	-	-	-	0.1	-	0.1
16	-	-	-	-	-	-	0.2	-	0.3	0.2	0.4	0.2
17	-	-	-	-	-	-	4.4	-	1.8	0.6	6.2	0.6
18	-	-	-	-	-	-	65.9	0.3	10.6	3.9	76.6	4.3
19	-	-	0.1	0.1	0.1	0.1	93.7	1.3	15.0	6.9	108.8	8.3
20	-	-	0.5	0.1	0.5	0.1	98.0	2.2	11.9	6.8	110.4	9.2
21	0.5	-	5.7	0.5	6.1	0.5	67.8	2.8	7.5	5.8	81.5	9.0
22	1.6	-	8.0	1.5	9.6	1.5	31.9	2.5	5.2	4.9	46.6	8.9
23	2.5	0.1	7.1	2.2	9.6	2.3	16.4	2.1	3.9	4.8	29.9	9.2
24	2.6	0.6	5.7	2.6	8.3	3.2	9.7	1.6	2.9	4.9	20.9	9.8
25	2.1	1.3	4.5	2.9	6.6	4.2	6.5	1.5	2.2	4.8	15.3	10.5
26	1.7	1.2	3.6	3.0	5.3	4.2	4.9	1.4	1.9	5.2	12.1	10.8
27	1.5	1.2	3.1	3.4	4.6	4.6	4.0	1.4	1.5	5.5	10.1	11.6
28	1.3	1.1	2.8	3.7	4.0	4.8	3.5	1.4	1.4	5.9	9.0	12.1
29	1.1	1.0	2.4	4.0	3.5	5.0	3.0	1.3	1.3	6.1	7.7	12.4
30+	7.3	14.9	16.3	71.3	23.6	86.2	21.9	17.9	11.3	121.2	56.9	225.6
Unknown	-	-	0.2	1.1	0.2	1.2	0.2	0.1	0.2	2.9	0.6	4.2
All ages	22.1	21.6	59.8	96.3	81.9	117.9	432.1	37.9	78.8	190.3	593.1	346.7
Females												
Age under 16	-	-	-	-	-	-	-	-	-	0.1	-	0.1
16	-	-	-	-	-	-	0.2	-	0.3	0.2	0.5	0.2
17	-	-	-	-	-	-	5.6	-	2.3	0.6	7.9	0.6
18	-	-	-	-	-	-	79.6	0.2	12.3	2.4	91.9	2.7
19	-	-	0.1	-	0.1	-	109.2	1.0	16.4	4.4	125.8	5.4
20	-	-	0.6	0.1	0.6	0.1	112.8	1.7	14.7	5.4	128.2	7.3
21	0.3	-	8.1	0.7	8.4	0.7	70.8	2.2	10.3	5.5	89.6	8.3
22	1.2	-	9.8	2.3	10.9	2.3	29.1	2.1	7.0	6.0	47.0	10.4
23	1.8	0.1	8.4	3.1	10.1	3.2	13.8	1.9	5.2	6.6	29.2	11.7
24	1.9	0.5	6.3	3.7	8.2	4.2	8.5	1.9	4.0	7.1	20.7	13.2
25	1.7	0.9	4.9	4.1	6.6	5.0	6.1	1.9	3.3	7.2	16.0	14.1
26	1.3	0.9	3.8	4.3	5.2	5.2	4.9	1.9	2.9	7.5	13.0	14.7
27	1.2	0.9	3.0	4.4	4.2	5.4	4.2	1.9	2.6	7.8	11.0	15.0
28	1.0	0.8	2.7	4.6	3.7	5.4	3.7	1.8	2.3	8.0	9.7	15.3
29	0.7	0.8	2.1	4.4	2.9	5.2	3.5	2.0	2.1	8.1	8.5	15.3
30+	4.8	10.6	14.8	75.5	19.6	86.1	37.5	37.2	26.3	181.1	83.5	304.6
Unknown	0.1	-	0.1	0.9	0.1	0.9	0.2	0.2	0.2	4.5	0.6	5.6
All ages	15.9	15.6	64.8	108.1	80.7	123.7	489.9	57.9	112.3	262.2	683.2	444.4

1 Includes Open University students. Part-time figures include dormant modes, those writing up at home and on sabbaticals, which are not included in HESA SFR 48.

2 Full-time includes sandwich, and for Scotland, short full-time. Part-time comprises both day and evening, including block release (except Scotland) and open/distance learning.

3 Ages as at 31 August 2000 (1 July in Northern Ireland and 31 December in Scotland).

4 Provisional. Figures are for students on courses at a particular point during the year. Therefore students starting courses after this date will not be counted. Figures for higher education students in further education institutions (except Northern Ireland) relate to 1999/00.

5 Includes data for FE institutions in Wales which cannot be split by level.

Source: Education Departments: 01325 392756

6.9 Students in higher[1] education by type of course, mode of study[2], gender and subject group, 2000/01[3,4]

United Kingdom - Home and overseas students

Thousands

	PHD's & equivalent		Masters and others		Total postgraduate		First degree		Other undergraduate		Total higher education[5]	
	Full-time	Part-time	Full-time	Part-time	Full-time	Part-time	Full-time	Part-time	Full-time	Part-time	Full-time[5]	Part-time[5]
All persons												
Subject group												
Medicine & Dentistry	2.3	3.5	2.9	5.3	5.2	8.8	30.0	0.1	0.2	0.1	35.3	9.0
Allied Medicine	1.8	2.0	3.2	16.0	5.0	18.0	53.3	23.7	56.1	44.4	114.5	86.1
Biological Sciences	6.0	3.7	4.1	4.8	10.1	8.4	65.1	3.0	2.5	1.7	77.7	13.2
Agriculture	0.9	0.6	1.2	1.2	2.1	1.8	10.3	0.4	4.7	2.2	17.2	4.4
Physical Sciences	6.1	3.2	4.5	3.2	10.7	6.3	44.9	2.0	1.5	2.8	57.1	11.1
Mathematical and Computing Sciences	2.4	1.6	10.1	8.0	12.4	9.6	72.3	5.5	18.4	22.5	103.0	37.6
Engineering & Technology	5.8	4.2	9.4	9.7	15.2	13.9	73.0	7.0	13.0	28.5	101.3	49.5
Architecture	0.4	0.6	4.2	5.3	4.6	5.9	20.2	5.6	3.7	9.8	28.5	21.3
Social Sciences	4.1	4.4	21.1	20.8	25.2	25.3	109.2	10.8	11.6	24.3	145.9	60.3
Business & Financial	1.4	2.2	19.0	44.6	20.4	46.8	107.8	11.4	34.0	75.8	162.3	134.1
Documentation	0.2	0.3	3.1	3.4	3.3	3.7	18.1	0.8	2.6	1.4	23.9	5.8
Languages	2.3	2.5	4.5	4.2	6.8	6.8	56.5	3.1	4.0	16.2	67.2	26.1
Humanities	2.3	2.7	3.8	5.6	6.1	8.4	31.4	2.8	0.7	9.1	38.2	20.3
Creative arts	0.6	0.9	5.5	3.8	6.1	4.7	79.3	3.2	15.8	7.0	101.1	14.9
Education[6]	0.9	3.9	25.4	38.6	26.3	42.5	43.0	4.6	3.3	15.7	72.6	62.8
Combined, gen	0.6	0.8	2.4	29.4	3.0	30.2	99.2	9.8	14.1	173.6	116.3	213.6
Unknown[5]	-	-	-	0.4	-	0.4	8.4	2.0	5.0	17.4	14.1	21.0
All subjects	38.1	37.2	124.5	204.4	162.6	241.6	922.0	95.7	191.2	452.6	1 276.3	791.0
Males												
Subject group												
Medicine and Dentistry	1.0	2.0	1.3	2.5	2.3	4.5	13.6	0.1	0.1	-	15.9	4.6
Allied Medicine	0.8	0.8	1.1	4.1	1.8	4.9	12.6	2.8	8.5	4.3	23.0	12.0
Biological Sciences	2.6	1.7	1.6	1.6	4.2	3.2	24.2	1.1	1.2	0.6	29.6	5.0
Agriculture	0.5	0.4	0.7	0.6	1.1	1.0	3.8	0.2	2.3	1.2	7.3	2.3
Physical Sciences	4.1	2.2	2.6	1.9	6.7	4.1	27.5	1.1	0.9	1.6	35.1	6.8
Mathematical and Computing Sciences	1.8	1.2	7.1	5.3	8.9	6.5	55.0	4.1	13.7	13.1	77.6	23.7
Engineering & Technology	4.6	3.6	7.5	8.4	12.1	12.0	61.5	6.4	11.3	26.3	85.0	44.7
Architecture	0.3	0.4	2.5	3.5	2.8	3.9	14.5	4.5	3.0	8.4	20.4	16.8
Social Sciences	2.2	2.4	9.3	8.6	11.4	11.0	43.1	4.2	2.7	5.3	57.2	20.4
Business & Financial	0.9	1.5	10.7	24.5	11.6	25.9	50.9	4.9	14.6	30.2	77.1	61.0
Documentation	0.1	0.1	1.1	1.2	1.2	1.3	6.9	0.2	1.3	0.5	9.4	2.1
Languages	1.0	1.1	1.5	1.4	2.4	2.5	15.6	0.9	1.3	6.4	19.3	9.8
Humanities	1.4	1.6	1.8	2.6	3.2	4.2	14.6	1.1	0.3	3.3	18.1	8.6
Creative arts	0.3	0.5	2.3	1.6	2.5	2.1	31.9	1.0	7.6	2.5	42.0	5.6
Education[6]	0.4	1.8	7.5	11.3	7.9	13.1	9.9	1.1	1.7	4.7	19.5	18.9
Combined, gen	0.3	0.5	1.3	16.9	1.6	17.4	42.6	3.5	5.8	74.4	50.0	95.3
Unknown[5]	-	-	-	0.2	-	0.2	3.8	0.6	2.5	7.8	6.6	9.2
All subjects	22.1	21.6	59.8	96.3	81.9	117.9	432.1	37.9	78.8	190.3	593.1	346.7
Females												
Subject group												
Medicine & Dentistry	1.3	1.6	1.6	2.8	2.9	4.4	16.4	-	0.1	0.1	19.4	4.4
Allied Medicine	1.0	1.2	2.1	11.9	3.2	13.1	40.7	20.9	47.6	40.1	91.5	74.1
Biological Sciences	3.4	2.0	2.6	3.2	6.0	5.2	40.9	1.9	1.3	1.1	48.1	8.2
Agriculture	0.4	0.3	0.6	0.6	1.0	0.9	6.5	0.2	2.4	1.0	9.9	2.1
Physical Sciences	2.0	1.0	1.9	1.3	3.9	2.3	17.5	0.8	0.6	1.2	22.0	4.3
Mathematical and Computing Sciences	0.5	0.4	3.0	2.7	3.5	3.1	17.2	1.4	4.7	9.4	25.4	13.9
Engineering & Technology	1.2	0.7	1.9	1.3	3.1	1.9	11.5	0.7	1.7	2.2	16.3	4.8
Architecture	0.2	0.2	1.6	1.8	1.8	2.0	5.7	1.1	0.6	1.5	8.1	4.5
Social Sciences	1.9	2.0	11.9	12.2	13.8	14.3	66.1	6.7	8.9	19.0	88.7	39.9
Business & Financial	0.5	0.7	8.3	20.2	8.8	20.9	56.9	6.5	19.5	45.6	85.2	73.0
Documentation	0.1	0.1	2.0	2.2	2.1	2.3	11.2	0.5	1.2	0.9	14.5	3.8
Languages	1.3	1.4	3.1	2.8	4.4	4.3	40.9	2.2	2.7	9.8	48.0	16.3
Humanities	0.9	1.2	1.9	3.0	2.9	4.2	16.8	1.7	0.4	5.9	20.1	11.7
Creative arts	0.3	0.4	3.3	2.2	3.6	2.6	47.4	2.1	8.2	4.6	59.2	9.3
Education[6]	0.5	2.1	17.9	27.3	18.4	29.4	33.1	3.5	1.6	11.0	53.1	43.9
Combined, gen	0.3	0.4	1.1	12.4	1.4	12.8	56.6	6.3	8.3	99.2	66.3	118.3
Unknown[5]	-	-	-	0.2	-	0.2	4.6	1.4	2.5	9.7	7.5	11.8
All subjects	15.9	15.6	64.8	108.1	80.7	123.7	489.9	57.9	112.3	262.2	683.2	444.4

1 Higher education institutions include Open University students. Part-time figures include dormant modes, those writing up at home and on sabbaticals, which are not included in HESA SFR48.

2 Full-time includes sandwich, and for Scotland, short full-time. Part-time comprises both day and evening, including block release (except Scotland) and open/distance learning.

3 Provisional. Figures for higher education students in further education institutions (except for Northern Ireland) relate to 1999/00. Includes estimated breakdowns by subjects for students in further education institutions in England.

4 Figures for students (other than Scotland FE institutions) are snapshots counted at a particular point in the year (December for UK HE institutions and FE institutions in Wales, November for FE institutions in England and Northern Ireland). Students starting courses after these dates will not therefore be counted. Figures for Scotland are whole year enrolments (rather than headcounts) for 1999/00.

5 Includes data for FE institutions in Wales which cannot be split by level.

6 Including ITT and INSET.

Source: Education Departments: 01325 392756

6.10 Students[1] obtaining higher education qualifications[2,3] by type of course, gender and subject group, 1999/00

United Kingdom

Thousands

	Sub-degree[4]	First degree	Postgraduate			Total higher education
			PHD's and equivalent	Other	Total	
All persons						
Subject group						
Medicine & Dentistry	-	6.0	1.0	2.0	3.0	9.0
Subjects Allied to Medicine	21.5	17.8	0.6	4.5	5.1	44.4
Biological Sciences	1.1	18.4	1.8	3.0	4.7	24.3
Vet. Science, Agriculture & related	1.1	2.9	0.3	0.9	1.2	5.3
Physical Sciences	0.8	13.2	1.8	2.5	4.3	18.3
Mathematical & Computer Sciences	5.0	15.3	0.7	5.5	6.2	26.5
Engineering & Technology	4.6	20.6	1.7	6.3	8.0	33.2
Architecture, Building & Planning	1.5	6.6	0.1	3.2	3.3	11.4
Social Sciences	5.7	32.9	1.1	16.3	17.4	56.0
Business & Financial Studies	10.1	31.9	0.4	21.4	21.8	63.8
Librarianship & Info Science	0.4	4.6	0.1	2.4	2.4	7.4
Languages	1.5	16.6	0.7	2.9	3.5	21.6
Humanities	1.1	10.4	0.6	2.8	3.5	14.9
Creative Arts & Design	2.7	21.3	0.1	3.8	4.0	28.0
Education[5]	4.5	11.9	0.4	26.6	27.0	43.4
Combined, gen.	10.7	34.9	0.1	6.8	7.0	52.6
All subjects	72.5	265.3	11.5	110.9	122.5	460.3
Males						
Subject group						
Medicine and Dentistry	-	2.9	0.5	0.9	1.4	4.3
Subjects Allied to Medicine	2.3	3.6	0.3	1.2	1.4	7.3
Biological Sciences	0.5	6.9	0.8	1.1	1.9	9.3
Vet. Science, Agriculture & related	0.6	1.3	0.2	0.5	0.7	2.6
Physical Sciences	0.6	8.0	1.3	1.4	2.7	11.3
Mathematical & Computer Sciences	3.6	11.3	0.5	3.8	4.3	19.2
Engineering & Technology	4.2	17.3	1.4	5.1	6.5	28.0
Architecture, Building & Planning	1.1	5.0	0.1	2.1	2.1	8.2
Social Sciences	1.7	13.2	0.6	7.3	7.9	22.8
Business & Financial Studies	4.4	14.8	0.3	11.8	12.1	31.3
Librarianship & Info Science	0.2	1.7	-	0.8	0.8	2.7
Languages	0.5	4.6	0.3	0.9	1.2	6.3
Humanities	0.4	4.6	0.4	1.3	1.7	6.8
Creative Arts & Design	1.3	8.5	0.1	1.6	1.7	11.5
Education[5]	1.4	2.7	0.2	7.6	7.8	11.9
Combined, gen.	4.1	14.8	0.1	4.0	4.1	22.9
All subjects	26.7	121.2	7.1	51.3	58.4	206.4
Females						
Subject group						
Medicine & Dentistry	-	3.1	0.5	1.1	1.6	4.7
Subjects Allied to Medicine	19.3	14.2	0.3	3.4	3.7	37.1
Biological Sciences	0.6	11.6	0.9	1.9	2.9	15.0
Vet. Science, Agriculture & related	0.5	1.6	0.1	0.4	0.5	2.7
Physical Sciences	0.3	5.1	0.5	1.1	1.6	7.0
Mathematical & Computer Sciences	1.5	4.0	0.1	1.7	1.8	7.3
Engineering & Technology	0.5	3.2	0.3	1.2	1.5	5.2
Architecture, Building & Planning	0.4	1.6	0.1	1.1	1.2	3.2
Social Sciences	4.0	19.7	0.5	9.0	9.5	33.2
Business & Financial Studies	5.7	17.1	0.1	9.6	9.7	32.5
Librarianship & Info Science	0.2	2.9	-	1.6	1.6	4.7
Languages	1.0	12.1	0.4	1.9	2.3	15.4
Humanities	0.7	5.7	0.2	1.5	1.8	8.2
Creative Arts & Design	1.4	12.8	0.1	2.2	2.3	16.5
Education[5]	3.1	9.2	0.2	19.0	19.2	31.5
Combined, gen.	6.7	20.2	-	2.8	2.9	29.7
All subjects	45.8	144.1	4.4	59.6	64.1	253.9

1 Includes students on Open University courses.
2 Excludes qualifications from the private sector.
3 Includes higher education in higher education institutions in the UK only. Higher education qualifications in further education institutions (approximately 6% of the total number of students) are excluded.
4 Excludes students who successfully completed courses for which formal qualifications are not awarded.
5 Including ITT and INSET.

Source: Education Departments: 01325 392756

6.11 Qualified teachers: by type of school and gender

Thousands

	Public sector mainstream schools		Non-maintained mainstream schools	All special schools	Total
	Nursery and primary	Secondary[1]			
All full-time teachers					
Great Britain					
1990/91	200.3	223.2	44.9	18.2	486.6
1995/96	203.3	212.2	48.6	16.6	480.6
1996/97[2]	202.8	211.4	48.2	16.3	478.7
1997/98[2]	201.3	209.8	49.1	16.0	476.2
United Kingdom					
1998/99[2]	210.8	221.7	50.5	16.7	499.7
1999/00[3]	211.1	223.0	51.2	16.6	502.0
of which:					
England and Wales[4]	181.4	190.3	48.4	13.8	433.9
Scotland	21.5	22.6	2.7	2.1	48.9
Northern Ireland[3]	8.1	10.2	0.1	0.7	19.2
Full-time male teachers					
Great Britain					
1990/91	35.8	116.0	20.6	5.8	178.2
1995/96	33.8	103.4	21.1	5.3	163.5
1996/97[2]	33.0	101.7	20.6	5.1	160.4
1997/98[2]	31.9	99.4	20.7	5.0	157.1
United Kingdom					
1998/99[2]	33.0	103.4	20.8	5.1	162.4
1999/00[2]	32.6	102.9	21.1	5.0	161.6
of which:					
England and Wales[4]	29.6	87.8	19.9	4.4	141.8
Scotland	1.5	10.9	1.1	0.4	13.9
Northern Ireland[3]	1.5	4.3	-	0.1	5.9
Full-time female teachers					
Great Britain					
1990/91	164.5	107.1	24.3	12.4	308.4
1995/96	169.5	108.8	27.4	11.3	317.0
1996/97[2]	169.8	109.7	27.6	11.2	318.3
1997/98[2]	169.3	110.3	28.5	11.0	319.1
United Kingdom					
1998/99[2]	177.8	118.3	29.6	11.6	337.8
1999/00[2]	178.5	120.1	30.2	11.6	340.4
of which:					
England and Wales[4]	151.8	102.5	28.5	9.4	292.2
Scotland	20.1	11.7	1.6	1.6	35.0
Northern Ireland[3]	6.6	5.9	0.1	0.6	13.2
All part-time teachers[5]					
Great Britain					
1990/91	..	..	..	..	30.0
1995/96	18.7	17.6	8.9	1.5	46.7
1996/97	17.8	15.7	9.4	1.4	44.3
1997/98	18.0	16.2	10.7	1.4	46.4
United Kingdom					
1998/99[2]	19.7	16.8	9.8	1.5	47.8
1999/00[3]	20.0	17.3	10.2	1.6	49.0

1 From 1993/94 excludes sixth form colleges in England and Wales which were reclassified as further education colleges on 1 April 1993.
2 Includes revised data for England and Wales.
3 Provisional. Includes 1998/99 data for Northern Ireland.
4 A gender breakdown of public sector teachers in England and Wales is only available from the Database of Teachers Records (DTR) where some in service teachers may be shown as not in service because their service details are not recorded. Complete coverage of teachers in England and Wales is available from the Form 618G survey, and published in "Statistics of Education: Teachers England and Wales".
5 Full-time equivalents of part-time teachers.

Source: Education Departments: 01325 392756

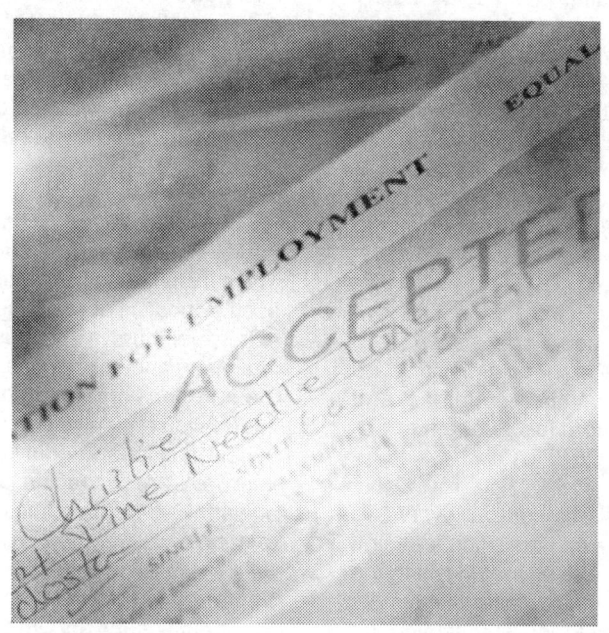

7 Labour market

Labour market

Labour Force Survey
(Tables 7.1 to 7.3, 7.6, 7.9, 7.10, 7.12 and 7.15 to 7.17)

Background

The LFS is the largest regular household survey in the United Kingdom. LFS interviews are conducted continuously throughout the year. In any 3 month period, a nationally representative sample of approximately 120,000 people aged 16 or over in around 61,000 households are interviewed. Each household is interviewed five times, at 3 monthly intervals. The initial interview is done face-to-face by an interviewer visiting the address. The other interviews are done by telephone wherever possible. The survey asks a series of questions about respondents' personal circumstances and their labour market activity. Most questions refer to activity in the week before the interview.

The concepts and definitions used in the LFS are agreed by the International Labour Organisation (ILO) - an agency of the United Nations. The definitions are used by European Union member countries and members of the Organ-isation for Economic Co-operation and Development (OECD).

The Labour Force Survey was carried out every two years from 1973 to 1983. The ILO definition was first used in 1984. This was also the first year in which the survey was conducted on an annual basis with results available for every spring quarter (representing an average of the period from March to May). The survey moved to a continuous basis in spring 1992 in Great Britain and in winter 1994/5 in Northern Ireland, with average quarterly results published 4 times a year for seasonal quarters: spring (March to May), summer (June to August), autumn (September to November) and winter (December to February). From April 1998, results are published 12 times a year for the average of 3 consecutive months.

The LFS collects information on a sample of the population. To convert this information to give estimates for the population the data must be grossed. This is achieved by calculating weighting factors (often referred to simply as weights) which can be applied to each sampled individual in such a way that the weighted-up results match estimates or projections of the total population in terms of age distribution, sex, and region of residence. Estimates in the previous edition of this volume were derived using grossing control totals based on 1992-based population projections. These projections became progressively out of step with population estimates and have been superseded by figures which are more accurate and which relate to latest geographies. Therefore, all LFS data for autumn 1993 onwards have been regrossed using the best available population figures for any given period. See LFS User Guide volume 10 - Regrossing of LFS Data and 'LFS: regrossing and seasonal adjustment' in *Labour Market Trends*, May 2000. Whilst regrossing LFS data to the most up-to-date population estimates has resulted in an improvement in accuracy it has inevitably led to changes between the old and new series. These differences are in the absolute totals of the old and new series rather than in rates.

Strengths and limitations of the LFS

The LFS produces coherent labour market information on the basis of internationally standard concepts and definitions. It is a rich source of data on a wide variety of labour market and personal characteristics. It is the most suitable source for making comparisons between countries. The LFS is designed so that households interviewed in each three month period constitute a representative sample of UK households. The survey covers those living in private households and nurses in National Health Service accommodation. Students living in halls of residence have been included since 1992 as information about them is collected at their parents' address.

However the LFS has its limitations. It is a sample survey and is therefore subject to sampling variability. The survey does not include people living in institutions such as hostels or residential homes. 'Proxy' reporting (when members of the household are not present at the interview, another member of the household answers the questions on their behalf) can affect the quality of information on topics such as earnings, hours worked, benefit receipt and qualifications. Around one third of interviews are conducted 'by proxy', usually by a spouse or partner but sometimes by a parent or other near relation.

Sampling Variability

Survey estimates are prone to *sampling variability.* The easiest way to explain this concept is by example. In the September to November 1997 period, ILO unemployment in Great Britain (seasonally adjusted) stood at 1,847,000. If we drew another sample for the same period we could get a different result, perhaps 1,900,000 or 1,820,000.

In theory, we could draw many samples, and each would give a different result. This is because each sample would be made up of different people who would give different answers to the questions. The spread of these results is the sampling variability. Sampling variability is determined by a number of factors including the sample size, the variability of the population from which the sample is drawn and the sample design. Once we know the sampling variability we can calculate a range of values about the sample estimate that represents the expected variation with a given level of assurance. This is called a confidence interval. For a 95% confidence interval we expect that in 95% of the samples (19 times out of 20) the confidence interval will contain the true value that would be obtained by surveying the entire population. For the example given above, we can be 95% confident that the true value was in the range 1,791,000 to 1,903,000.

Unreliable estimates

Very small estimates have relatively wide confidence intervals making them unreliable. For this reason, the ONS does not publish LFS estimates below 10,000.

Non-Response

Non-response can introduce bias to a survey, particularly if the people not responding have characteristics that are different from those who do respond. The LFS has a response rate of around 80 per cent to the first interview, and over 90 per cent of those who are interviewed once go on to complete all five interviews. These are relatively high levels for a household survey. Any bias from non-response is minimised by *weighting* the results.

Weighting (or grossing) converts sample data to represent the full population. In the LFS, the data are weighted separately by age, sex and area of residence to population estimates based on the Census. Weighting also adjusts for people not in the survey and thus minimises non-response bias.

Labour Force Survey Concepts and Definitions

Discouraged workers - a sub-group of the economically inactive population, defined as those neither in employment nor unemployed (on the ILO measure) who said they would like a job and whose main reason for not seeking work was because they believed there were no jobs available.

Economically active - people aged 16 and over who are either in employment or ILO unemployed.

Economic activity rate - the percentage of people aged 16 and over who are economically active.

Economically inactive - people who are neither in employment nor unemployed. This group includes, for example, all those who were looking after a home or retired.

Employment - people aged 16 or over who did at least one hour of paid work in the reference week (whether as an employee or self-employed); those who had a job that they were temporarily away from (on holiday, for example); those on Government-supported training and employment programmes (from spring 1983); and those doing unpaid family work (from spring 1992).

Employees - the division between employees and self-employed is based on survey respondents' own assessment of their employment status.

Full Time - the classification of employees, self-employed and unpaid family workers in their main job as full-time or part-time is on the basis of self-assessment. Up until autumn 1995, people who were on government work-related training programmes are classified as full-time or part-time according to whether their usual hours of work per week were over 30 or 30 and under; from winter 1995/96 onwards, the full-time/part-time classification for this group has been changed to self-assessment, in line with the other groups outlined above. People on Government-supported training and employment programmes who are at college in the survey reference week are classified, by convention, as part-time.

Government-supported training and employment programmes - comprise all people aged 16 and over participating in one of the Government's employment and training programmes (Youth Training, Training for Work and Community Action), together with those on similar programmes administered by Training and Enterprise Councils in England and Wales, or Local Enterprise Companies in Scotland.

Hours worked - respondents to the LFS are asked a series of questions enabling the identification of both their usual hours and their actual hours. Total hours include overtime (paid and unpaid) and exclude lunchbreaks.

ILO unemployment - the International Labour Office (ILO) measure of unemployment used throughout this supplement refers to people without a job who were available to start work in the two weeks following their LFS interview and who had either looked for work in the four weeks prior to interview or were waiting to start a job they had already obtained. This definition of unemployment is in accordance with that adopted by the 13th International Conference of Labour Statisticians, further clarified at the 14th ICLS, and promulgated by the ILO in its publications.

ILO unemployment (rate) - the percentage of economically active people who are unemployed on the ILO measure.

ILO unemployment (duration) - defined as the shorter of the following two periods: (a) duration of active search for work; and (b) length of time since employment.

Part-Time - see full-time

Second jobs - jobs which LFS respondents hold in addition to a main full-time or part-time job.

Self-employment - See Employees

Temporary employees - in the LFS these are defined as those employees who say that their main job is non permanent in one of the following ways: fixed period contract; agency temping; casual work; seasonal work; other temporary work.

Unpaid Family Workers - the separate identification from spring 1992 of this group in the LFS is in accordance with international recommendations. The group comprises persons doing unpaid work for a business they own or for a business that a relative owns.

Distribution of workforce *(Table 7.4)*

Claimant unemployed - those people who were claiming unemployment-related benefits (Unemployment Benefit, Income Support or National Insurance credits) at Employment service local offices on the day of the monthly count. The seasonally adjusted claimant unemployment series allows for all relevant changes which, unless adjusted for, would distort comparisons over time.

Labour market

Workforce jobs (formerly workforce in employment) - comprises employee jobs, self-employment jobs (from the Labour Force Survey), HM Forces and government supported trainees.

HM Forces (provided by Ministry of Defence) - represent the total number of UK service personnel, male and female, in HM Regular Forces, wherever serving and including those on leave.

Self-employed jobs - estimates are based on the results of the Labour Force Survey. The Northern Ireland estimates are not seasonally adjusted.

Government-supported trainees - include all participants on government training and employment programmes who are receiving some work experience on their placement but who do not have a contract of employment (those with a contract are included in the employee jobs series). The numbers are not subject to seasonal adjustment.

Persons employed in local authorities *(Table 7.8)*
The full-time equivalents for local authorities are derived by applying factors to the numbers of part-time workers in three groups based on average hours worked in each group nationally.

Jobseekers allowance claimant count
(Tables 7.13 and 7.14)
This is a count of all those people who are claiming unemployment-related benefits at Employment Service local offices and who have declared that they are unemployed, capable of, available for, and actively seeking work during the week in which their claim is made. All people claiming unemployment-related benefits on the day of the monthly count are included in the claimant count, irrespective of whether they are actually receiving benefits.

Average earnings index *(Tables 7.21 and 7.22)*
The Average Earnings Index (AEI) is designed to measure changes in the level of earnings i.e. wage inflation in Great Britain. Average earnings are calculated as the total wages and salaries paid by firms, divided by the number of employees paid. Like all indices, changes are measured against a base year, whose index value is set to 100. The current base year is 1995 for Table 7.21 and March 1996 for Table 7.22.

The Average Earnings Index was the subject of two reviews at the beginning of 1999. These were, *"Review of Methodology for the Average Earnings Index"* R Chambers and D Holmes, University of Southampton December 1998, and *"Review of the Revisions to the Average Earnings Index"* report submitted by Sir Andrew Turnbull and Mervyn King, The Stationery Office, March 1999. They made a number of recommendations for change in the methodology underpinning the index, and set out a long-term project for development. Work to implement the recommendations is underway and regular updates on progress will be published in the ONS' journal Labour Market Trends.

The AEI is published monthly in the Labour Market Statistics First Release. The main indicator of growth, the headline rate, is based on the annual change in the seasonally adjusted index values for the latest 3 months compared with the same period a year ago. The use of a 3-month average reduces the level of volatility seen in the data on a month-on-month basis.

Strengths of the AEI
The AEI, based on monthly survey data, is a timely indicator of changes in the level of earnings.

Limitations of the AEI
The index is not adjusted for any changes in the composition of the workforce such as changes in the share of full-time and part-time workers, or in the share of skilled and unskilled workers. Similarly, the index does not account for changes in the number of hours worked, or any temporary factors that affect earnings.

The sample of the Monthly Wages and Salaries Survey on which the AEI is based is not designed to provide information on the level of earnings. The sample is not completely representative of the economy as firms with fewer than 20 employees are excluded, as are the earnings of self employed persons.

The AEI only covers earnings in Great Britain as earnings information is not collected for Northern Ireland and regional data are not available.

Vacancies at jobcentres *(Table 7.27)*

Vacancy - This is a job opportunity notified by an employer to a Jobcentre.

Unfilled vacancy - (also known as "Stock of vacancies")
This is the number of vacancies which have not been filled or cancelled on the count date.

Inflow of vacancy - (also known as "Notified vacancies")
This is the number of job opportunities notified by employers to Jobcentres in the period between two successive count dates.

Outflow of vacancy - This is a derived statistic which represents the total of vacancies filled plus cancelled between count dates. This concept can also be expressed as "vacancy stock" at the beginning of the period plus notified vacancies (inflows) minus "vacancy stock" at the end of the period.

Placings - This is the number of Jobseekers placed into employment by individual Jobcentres.

Earnings *(Table 7.19 - 7.25)*
The total gross remuneration employees receive before any statutory deductions (tax, national insurance). Income in kind and pension funds are excluded.

7.1 Summary for United Kingdom labour force
Spring each year. Not seasonally adjusted.

Thousands

| | All aged 16+[1] | All aged 16 and over | | | | Economic activity rate 16-59/64 (%)[2] | Employment rate - all aged 16+ (%)[3] | Employment rate 16-59/64 (%)[4] | ILO unemployment rate (%)[5] |
		Total economically active	Total in employment	ILO unemployed	Economically inactive				
All	BEAJ	BEAM	BEAP	BEAS	BEAV	BEAY	BEBK	BEBN	BEBQ
1991	45 226	28 813	26 400	2 414	16 413	79.8	58.4	73.0	8.4
1992	45 310	28 581	25 812	2 769	16 728	78.8	57.0	71.1	9.7
1993	45 400	28 447	25 511	2 936	16 954	78.4	56.2	70.2	10.3
1994	45 488	28 455	25 717	2 738	17 032	78.2	56.5	70.6	9.6
1995	45 641	28 486	26 026	2 460	17 155	78.0	57.0	71.1	8.6
1996	45 835	28 663	26 323	2 340	17 172	78.2	57.4	71.6	8.2
1997	46 036	28 852	26 814	2 037	17 184	78.2	58.2	72.6	7.1
1998	46 253	28 892	27 116	1 776	17 361	78.0	58.6	73.1	6.1
1999	46 431	29 194	27 442	1 752	17 237	78.4	59.1	73.6	6.0
2000	46 581	29 412	27 793	1 619	17 169	78.7	59.7	74.3	5.5
2001	46 832	29 470	28 066	1 404	17 362	78.4	59.9	74.6	4.8
Men	BEAK	BEAN	BEAQ	BEAT	BEAW	BEAZ	BEBL	BEBO	BEBR
1991	21 871	16 401	14 887	1 514	5 470	87.7	68.1	79.6	9.2
1992	21 924	16 187	14 321	1 865	5 737	86.3	65.3	76.3	11.5
1993	21 985	16 021	14 035	1 986	5 964	85.6	63.8	74.8	12.4
1994	22 049	16 000	14 173	1 826	6 050	85.2	64.3	75.3	11.4
1995	22 156	16 009	14 397	1 612	6 146	84.7	65.0	76.1	10.1
1996	22 283	16 052	14 503	1 549	6 230	84.6	65.1	76.4	9.6
1997	22 412	16 098	14 792	1 306	6 314	84.4	66.0	77.5	8.1
1998	22 547	16 096	14 999	1 098	6 450	83.9	66.5	78.1	6.8
1999	22 657	16 234	15 138	1 095	6 423	84.1	66.8	78.4	6.7
2000	22 754	16 327	15 336	991	6 427	84.3	67.4	79.1	6.1
2001	22 917	16 318	15 459	859	6 600	83.8	67.5	79.3	5.3
Women	BEAL	BEAO	BEAR	BEAU	BEAX	BEBJ	BEBM	BEBP	BEBS
1991	23 354	12 412	11 512	900	10 942	71.0	49.3	65.8	7.2
1992	23 386	12 395	11 491	904	10 991	70.6	49.1	65.4	7.3
1993	23 415	12 426	11 476	949	10 989	70.6	49.0	65.1	7.6
1994	23 438	12 456	11 544	912	10 983	70.6	49.3	65.3	7.3
1995	23 486	12 477	11 629	849	11 009	70.6	49.5	65.6	6.8
1996	23 553	12 611	11 820	791	10 942	71.1	50.2	66.5	6.3
1997	23 624	12 754	12 022	732	10 871	71.4	50.9	67.2	5.7
1998	23 707	12 796	12 117	679	10 911	71.5	51.1	67.6	5.3
1999	23 774	12 960	12 304	657	10 813	72.1	51.8	68.3	5.1
2000	23 826	13 084	12 457	628	10 742	72.5	52.3	68.9	4.8
2001	23 915	13 153	12 607	546	10 762	72.4	52.7	69.3	4.2

1 Population in private households, and from 1992, student halls of residence.
2 Economically active of working age as a percentage of all persons of working age.
3 Total employed as a percentage of all persons 16 and over.
4 Total employed of working age as a percentage of all persons of working age (men 16-64, women 16-59).
5 Total ILO unemployment as a percentage of all economically active.

Source: Labour Force Survey, Office for National Statistics

7.2 Employment status, full-time/part-time, second jobs, temporary employees
United Kingdom
Spring each year. Not seasonally adjusted.

Thousands

	All in employment[1,2]					Total employment[2]		Employees[2]		Self-employed[2]		Workers with second jobs[4]	Temporary employees
	Total	Employees	Self employed	Unpaid family workers	Government supported training and employment programmes[3]	Full-time	Part-time	Full-time	Part-time	Full-time	Part-time		
All													
	BEAP	BEBT	BEBW	BEBZ	BECD	BECG	BECJ	BECM	BECP	BECS	BECV	BECY	BEDE
1992	25 812	22 018	3 227	181	386	19 753	6 052	16 835	5 180	2 683	544	988	1 220
1993	25 511	21 812	3 184	151	364	19 377	6 128	16 569	5 241	2 605	578	1 057	1 274
1994	25 717	21 929	3 301	146	342	19 423	6 286	16 543	5 379	2 692	607	1 164	1 410
1995	26 026	22 235	3 361	140	290	19 685	6 337	16 773	5 459	2 733	628	1 306	1 550
1996	26 323	22 643	3 300	127	254	19 748	6 574	16 927	5 715	2 652	648	1 311	1 591
1997	26 814	23 121	3 351	118	224	20 088	6 723	17 267	5 852	2 660	689	1 274	1 712
1998	27 116	23 554	3 280	102	179	20 335	6 776	17 645	5 906	2 560	718	1 207	1 668
1999	27 442	23 976	3 202	101	163	20 573	6 863	17 952	6 020	2 510	691	1 301	1 639
2000	27 793	24 396	3 139	109	149	20 820	6 967	18 269	6 123	2 443	694	1 209	1 653
2001	28 066	24 665	3 147	97	157	21 023	7 031	18 430	6 231	2 487	653	1 204	1 656
Men													
	BEAQ	BEBU	BEBX	BECA	BECE	BECH	BECK	BECN	BECQ	BECT	BECW	BECZ	BEDF
1992	14 321	11 577	2 438	55	251	13 307	1 009	10 905	670	2 260	179	451	517
1993	14 035	11 370	2 384	43	237	12 993	1 039	10 680	690	2 184	200	477	563
1994	14 173	11 421	2 480	49	223	13 056	1 114	10 672	748	2 267	212	515	621
1995	14 397	11 620	2 549	42	187	13 226	1 169	10 804	815	2 316	232	550	719
1996	14 503	11 832	2 470	42	160	13 254	1 249	10 926	905	2 233	237	555	711
1997	14 792	12 130	2 486	37	139	13 460	1 330	11 128	1 001	2 233	253	561	788
1998	14 999	12 443	2 411	28	117	13 651	1 345	11 433	1 008	2 139	271	531	748
1999	15 138	12 617	2 378	35	109	13 746	1 389	11 556	1 058	2 118	258	552	783
2000	15 336	12 915	2 293	37	91	13 920	1 413	11 835	1 078	2 021	271	513	765
2001	15 459	12 990	2 330	36	103	14 030	1 420	11 880	1 107	2 078	247	497	768
Women													
	BEAR	BEBV	BEBY	BECB	BECF	BECI	BECL	BECO	BECR	BECU	BECX	BEDD	BEDG
1992	11 491	10 441	789	126	135	6 445	5 042	5 930	4 510	423	365	537	702
1993	11 476	10 441	800	108	127	6 384	5 089	5 889	4 551	422	378	580	711
1994	11 544	10 508	820	97	119	6 366	5 172	5 871	4 632	425	395	649	788
1995	11 629	10 615	813	98	103	6 459	5 168	5 969	4 644	417	396	757	831
1996	11 820	10 810	830	85	94	6 494	5 326	6 000	4 810	419	411	757	880
1997	12 022	10 991	865	81	85	6 628	5 393	6 139	4 851	428	437	713	924
1998	12 117	11 112	869	73	62	6 683	5 431	6 212	4 897	421	448	676	921
1999	12 304	11 359	825	66	55	6 827	5 475	6 396	4 961	391	433	749	856
2000	12 457	11 481	845	72	58	6 900	5 554	6 434	5 045	422	423	696	888
2001	12 607	11 675	818	60	54	6 993	5 610	6 550	5 124	410	407	707	888

1 See chapter text for definitions.
2 People whose main job is full or part-time.
3 Those on employment and training programmes are classified as in employment. Some of those on programmes may consider themselves to be employees or self employed so appear in other categories.

4 Second jobs reported in LFS in addition to person's main full or part-time job.

Source: Labour Force Survey, Office for National Statistics

7.3 Employment
United Kingdom
By age and gender. At Spring each year. Not seasonally adjusted.

Thousands and percentages.

	All aged 16 and over	16-59/64	16-17	18-24	16-24	25-34	35-49	50-64 (m) 50-59 (f)	65+ (m) 60+ (f)
Thousands									
All									
	BEAP	BEDH	BEDK	BEDN	BEDQ	BEDT	BEDW	BEDZ	BEEC
1992	25 812	24 996	648	3 814	4 462	6 720	9 176	4 638	816
1993	25 511	24 738	551	3 579	4 130	6 809	9 218	4 581	773
1994	25 717	24 936	558	3 432	3 990	6 930	9 327	4 688	782
1995	26 026	25 230	579	3 330	3 909	7 042	9 476	4 802	796
1996	26 323	25 552	631	3 283	3 914	7 081	9 653	4 906	771
1997	26 814	26 012	668	3 231	3 899	7 236	9 725	5 152	803
1998	27 116	26 341	665	3 199	3 864	7 212	9 870	5 395	775
1999	27 442	26 627	648	3 208	3 856	7 145	10 044	5 581	816
2000	27 793	26 966	645	3 275	3 919	7 026	10 286	5 734	827
2001	28 066	27 253	639	3 300	3 939	6 862	10 503	5 950	813
Men									
	BEAQ	BEDI	BEDL	BEDO	BEDR	BEDU	BEDX	BEEA	BEED
1992	14 321	14 021	332	1 998	2 329	3 846	4 980	2 866	300
1993	14 035	13 780	276	1 879	2 155	3 860	4 973	2 792	255
1994	14 173	13 909	284	1 819	2 103	3 931	5 041	2 835	264
1995	14 397	14 109	292	1 776	2 068	3 999	5 150	2 893	288
1996	14 503	14 238	321	1 736	2 057	4 008	5 207	2 965	266
1997	14 792	14 523	328	1 731	2 059	4 080	5 263	3 121	269
1998	14 999	14 725	332	1 714	2 045	4 086	5 355	3 238	274
1999	15 138	14 851	321	1 718	2 039	4 018	5 447	3 346	288
2000	15 336	15 049	322	1 757	2 079	3 956	5 603	3 412	287
2001	15 459	15 194	319	1 769	2 088	3 864	5 701	3 541	265
Women									
	BEAR	BEDJ	BEDM	BEDP	BEDS	BEDV	BEDY	BEEB	BEEE
1992	11 491	10 975	316	1 817	2 133	2 874	4 197	1 771	515
1993	11 476	10 958	275	1 701	1 976	2 949	4 244	1 790	518
1994	11 544	11 026	274	1 614	1 887	3 000	4 287	1 853	518
1995	11 629	11 121	287	1 554	1 841	3 044	4 326	1 910	508
1996	11 820	11 315	309	1 547	1 856	3 072	4 446	1 940	505
1997	12 022	11 488	340	1 500	1 840	3 155	4 461	2 031	534
1998	12 117	11 616	333	1 486	1 819	3 126	4 515	2 156	501
1999	12 304	11 776	327	1 490	1 817	3 127	4 597	2 235	528
2000	12 457	11 916	322	1 518	1 840	3 070	4 684	2 323	540
2001	12 607	12 059	320	1 531	1 851	2 998	4 802	2 409	547
Rates[1]									
All									
	BEBK	BEBN	BEEF	BEEI	BEEL	BEEO	BEER	BEEU	BEEX
1992	57.0	71.1	46.9	64.9	61.5	74.0	79.7	63.3	8.0
1993	56.2	70.2	41.6	63.0	58.9	74.1	79.1	62.0	7.6
1994	56.5	70.6	43.0	62.7	58.9	74.7	79.2	62.5	7.7
1995	57.0	71.1	43.1	63.1	59.0	75.6	79.5	63.1	7.8
1996	57.4	71.6	44.3	64.6	60.2	75.8	79.8	63.5	7.6
1997	58.2	72.6	45.8	65.3	60.9	77.8	80.0	64.5	7.9
1998	58.6	73.1	45.7	65.2	60.8	78.5	80.7	65.4	7.6
1999	59.1	73.6	44.9	65.3	60.7	79.5	81.0	66.1	8.0
2000	59.7	74.3	44.8	66.4	61.5	80.4	81.7	66.6	8.1
2001	59.9	74.6	43.8	66.2	61.1	80.4	81.9	68.0	7.9
Men									
	BEBL	BEBO	BEEG	BEEJ	BEEM	BEEP	BEES	BEEV	BEEY
1992	65.3	76.3	46.9	66.6	62.8	83.6	86.6	66.2	8.5
1993	63.8	74.8	40.5	64.8	60.2	83.0	85.4	64.1	7.1
1994	64.3	75.3	42.7	65.0	60.7	83.6	85.6	64.3	7.4
1995	65.0	76.1	42.4	65.8	61.0	84.5	86.3	64.9	8.0
1996	65.1	76.4	44.0	66.9	61.9	84.5	85.9	65.8	7.3
1997	66.0	77.5	44.0	68.5	62.9	86.3	86.3	67.2	7.3
1998	66.5	78.1	44.6	68.4	63.0	87.3	87.1	67.8	7.4
1999	66.8	78.4	43.4	68.6	62.9	87.7	87.4	68.5	7.7
2000	67.4	79.1	43.7	69.9	63.9	88.8	88.4	68.6	7.7
2001	67.5	79.3	42.7	69.5	63.4	88.7	88.2	70.2	7.0
Women									
	BEBM	BEBP	BEEH	BEEK	BEEN	BEEQ	BEET	BEEW	BEEZ
1992	49.1	65.4	47.0	63.1	60.1	64.1	72.9	59.0	7.8
1993	49.0	65.1	42.6	61.1	57.6	65.0	72.8	58.9	7.9
1994	49.3	65.3	43.3	60.2	57.0	65.6	72.8	59.8	7.9
1995	49.5	65.6	43.8	60.2	56.9	66.3	72.6	60.5	7.8
1996	50.2	66.5	44.6	62.3	58.4	66.9	73.6	60.3	7.7
1997	50.9	67.2	47.8	62.0	58.8	69.1	73.7	60.7	8.2
1998	51.1	67.6	46.9	61.9	58.5	69.4	74.1	62.2	7.7
1999	51.8	68.3	46.4	61.9	58.4	71.0	74.6	62.8	8.1
2000	52.3	68.9	45.9	62.7	58.9	71.6	74.9	64.0	8.3
2001	52.7	69.3	44.9	62.6	58.6	71.7	75.6	64.9	8.4

1 Total in employment as a percentage of all persons in the relevant group.

Source: Labour Force Survey, Office for National Statistics

7.4 Distribution of the workforce
At mid-June each year

Thousands, seasonally adjusted

		1991	1992	1993	1994	1995	1996	1997	1998	1999	2000	2001
United Kingdom												
Claimant unemployed	KAMO	2 275	2 711	2 902	2 625	2 294	2 135	1 571	1 345	1 263	1 094	963
Males	KAMP	1 730	2 084	2 235	2 016	1 756	1 625	1 206	1 027	968	835	734
Females	KAMQ	545	627	667	609	538	509	364	317	295	259	229
Workforce jobs	KAMR	27 103	26 406	26 050	26 198	26 492	27 640	28 198	28 563	28 871	29 064	29 229
Males	KAMS	15 077	14 486	14 141	14 201	14 366	14 757	15 173	15 335	15 475	15 528	15 559
Females	KAMT	12 026	11 920	11 909	11 998	12 126	12 883	13 025	13 228	13 396	13 536	13 670
HM Forces	KAMU	297	290	271	250	230	222	210	210	209	207	204
Males	KAMV	278	270	252	232	214	206	195	194	192	190	188
Females	KAMW	19	20	19	18	16	16	15	16	16	17	17
Self-employment jobs	KAMX	3 756	3 441	3 446	3 548	3 608	3 625	3 620	3 499	3 487	3 397	3 411
Males	KAMZ	2 828	2 573	2 537	2 630	2 680	2 681	2 632	2 534	2 525	2 451	2 480
Females	KANA	928	868	910	918	928	943	989	964	963	946	931
Employees jobs	KANB	22 682	22 335	22 006	22 084	22 414	23 598	24 195	24 722	25 042	25 337	25 496
Males	KANC	11 747	11 430	11 150	11 139	11 316	11 749	12 240	12 529	12 676	12 812	12 820
Females	KAND	10 935	10 905	10 857	10 945	11 097	11 849	11 955	12 192	12 365	12 526	12 676
of whom												
Total, production and construction industries	KANF	5 895	5 524	5 200	5 180	5 228	5 282	5 406	5 531	5 377	5 316	5 211
Total, all manufacturing industries	KANG	4 362	4 137	3 951	3 967	4 069	4 121	4 185	4 204	4 054	3 950	3 828
Government-supported trainee	KANH	369	340	326	317	240	195	173	133	133	123	117
Males	KANI	225	213	203	199	156	121	106	77	81	75	72
Females	KANJ	144	128	124	118	84	74	66	56	52	48	45
Great Britain												
Claimant unemployed	KANN	2 176	2 607	2 798	2 527	2 207	2 048	1 509	1 287	1 212	1 053	923
Males	KANO	1 654	2 004	2 155	1 940	1 687	1 559	1 157	982	928	803	704
Females	KANP	522	603	643	587	519	489	352	305	284	249	220
Workforce jobs	KANQ	26 446	25 758	25 403	25 539	25 809	26 959	27 495	27 847	28 147	28 321	28 477
Males	KANR	14 708	14 128	13 783	13 837	13 993	14 390	14 794	14 947	15 086	15 125	15 154
Females	KANS	11 738	11 630	11 620	11 701	11 816	12 570	12 701	12 900	13 061	13 196	13 323
HM Forces	KANT	297	290	271	250	230	222	210	210	209	207	204
Males	KANU	278	270	252	232	214	206	195	194	192	190	188
Females	KANV	19	20	19	18	16	16	15	16	16	17	17
Self-employment jobs	KANW	3 660	3 354	3 362	3 463	3 515	3 539	3 529	3 411	3 402	3 304	3 318
Males	KANX	2 748	2 501	2 464	2 556	2 603	2 610	2 558	2 461	2 455	2 373	2 402
Females	KANY	912	853	898	907	913	930	971	950	946	931	916
Employee jobs	KANZ	22 140	21 792	21 460	21 525	21 839	23 019	23 597	24 108	24 416	24 697	24 848
Males	KAOA	11 471	11 156	10 875	10 860	11 031	11 463	11 943	12 225	12 365	12 494	12 500
Females	KAOB	10 669	10 636	10 585	10 665	10 808	11 556	11 654	11 883	12 050	12 203	12 349
of whom												
Total, production and construction industries	KAOC	5 755	5 389	5 068	5 048	5 094	5 148	5 264	5 389	5 234	5 172	5 069
Total, all manufacturing industries	KAOD	4 258	4 036	3 852	3 866	3 965	4 017	4 078	4 097	3 949	3 846	3 726
Government-supported trainees	KAOE	348	322	310	301	224	179	159	118	122	112	106
Males	KAOF	211	201	192	189	145	111	97	67	74	68	64
Females	KAOG	137	121	118	112	79	68	61	51	48	45	42

Note: Because the figures have been rounded independently totals may differ from the sum of the components. Also the totals may include some employees whose industrial classification could not be ascertained.

Source: Earnings and Employment Division, Office for National Statistics: 01633 812079

7.5 Employee jobs
Analysis by industry based on the Standard Industrial Classification 1992
At June in each year

Thousands, not seasonally adjusted

			United Kingdom						Great Britain					
		SIC 1992	1996	1997	1998	1999	2000	2001		1996	1997	1998	1999	2000	2001
All sections	KAOH	A - Q	23 601	24 156	24 680	25 004	25 299	25 448	KAPN	23 024	23 560	24 068	24 380	24 661	24 803
Index of production and construction industries	KAOI	C - F	5 270	5 382	5 514	5 364	5 305	5 203	KAPO	5 137	5 241	5 372	5 222	5 162	5 062
Index of production industries	KAOJ	C - E	232	231	220	204	189	188	KAPP	4 239	4 292	4 303	4 142	4 025	3 902
of which, manufacturing industries	KAOK	D	4 117	4 175	4 196	4 048	3 945	3 821	KAPQ	4 013	4 067	4 089	3 943	3 841	3 719
Service industries	KAOL	G - Q	18 051	18 460	18 844	19 323	19 674	19 947	KAPR	17 623	18 021	18 390	18 856	19 195	19 458
Agriculture, hunting and forestry and fishing	KAOM	A/B	280	314	322	318	320	298	KAPS	264	298	306	302	305	282
Agriculture hunting and forestry	KPHI	A	270	304	311	305	309	287	KOVW	254	288	295	290	294	271
Agriculture hunting & related activities	KPHJ	01	261	295	303	297	303	281	KOVX	245	279	287	282	288	265
Fishing	KPHK	B	10	10	12	13	11	11	KOVY	10	10	11	12	11	11
Mining and quarrying	KPHL	C	75	76	75	73	70	70	KOVZ	73	75	72	71	68	69
Mining and quarrying of energy producing materials	KPHM	CA	44	46	46	45	43	44	KOWA	43	46	45	45	43	44
Mining	KAPG	10/12	..	..	..	..	..	..	KOWB	13	15	13	14	13	13
Extraction of crude petroleum	KPHN	11	..	..	..	..	..	..	KOWC	30	32	32	30	30	31
Mining and quarrying except of energy producing materials	KPHO	CB(13/14)	31	30	29	28	27	26	KOWD	30	29	27	27	25	25
Energy and water supply industries	KAOO	C/E	232	231	220	204	189	188	KOWE	226	225	214	199	184	183
Manufacturing	KPHP	D	4 117	4 175	4 196	4 048	3 945	3 821	KOWF	4 013	4 067	4 089	3 943	3 841	3 719
Manufacture of food products Beverages and tobacco	KPHQ	DA	464	490	502	499	494	488	KOWG	444	471	482	479	475	469
Of food	KPHR	151 to 158	..	..	..	..	..	..	KOWH	388	413	420	425	421	414
Of beverages and tobacco	KPHS	159/16	..	..	..	..	..	..	KOWI	57	58	62	54	54	56
Manufacture of textiles and textile products	KPHT	DB	347	344	334	293	262	237	KOWJ	323	321	311	274	246	224
Of textiles	KPHU	17	184	183	177	161	151	142	KOWK	174	173	166	152	143	134
Of made-up textile articles except apparel	KPHV	174	..	..	..	..	..	..	KOWL	34	33	35	34	34	33
Of textiles excluding made-up textile	KPHW	Rest of 17	..	..	..	..	..	..	KOWM	140	139	131	118	109	102
Of wearing apparel,dressing and dyeing of fur	KPHX	18	163	161	157	132	111	95	KOWN	150	148	145	122	103	89
Manufacture of leather and leather products including footwear	KPHY	DC	43	38	34	30	27	24	KOWO	42	37	34	30	27	23
Of leather and leather goods	KPHZ	191/192	..	..	..	..	..	..	KOWP	16	13	13	11	11	10
Of footwear	KPIA	193	..	..	..	..	..	..	KOWQ	26	24	20	19	16	13
Manufacture of wood and wood products	KPIB	DD(20)	86	88	86	84	85	84	KOWR	83	85	83	81	82	80
Manufacture of pulp paper and paper products,publishing and printing	KPIC	DE	466	466	474	469	469	459	KOWS	459	459	468	462	462	453
Of pulp paper and paper products	KPID	21	116	111	109	104	100	96	KOWT	114	108	107	102	98	94
Publishing printing and reproduction of recorded media	KPIE	22	349	355	365	365	369	363	KOWU	345	351	361	360	364	359
Manufacture of coke refined petroleum products and nuclear fuel	KPIF	DF(23)	29	30	27	27	26	27	KOWV	29	30	27	27	26	27
Manufacture of chemicals,chemical products and man-made fibres	KPIG	DG(24)	252	252	258	250	240	236	KOWX	248	248	254	246	236	232
Manufacture of rubber and plastics	KPIH	DH(25)	240	251	253	243	235	224	KOWY	233	244	246	236	229	217
Manufacture of other non-metallic mineral products	KPII	DI(26)	145	148	145	140	144	143	KOWZ	141	144	141	135	138	137
Manufacture of basic metals and fabricated metal products	KPIJ	DJ	576	573	556	537	529	513	KOXA	571	567	550	530	523	506
Of basic metals	KPIK	27	142	138	137	126	118	113	KOXB	142	138	137	125	118	113
except machinery	KPIL	28	434	435	418	411	411	400	KOXC	429	429	413	405	405	393

7.5 Employee jobs
Analysis by industry based on the Standard Industrial Classification 1992
continued   At June in each year

Thousands, not seasonally adjusted

		SIC 1992	United Kingdom							Great Britain					
			1996	1997	1998	1999	2000	2001		1996	1997	1998	1999	2000	2001
Manufacture of Machinery and Equipment not elsewhere classified	KPIM	DK(29)	390	389	389	369	356	346	KOXD	383	382	382	363	349	340
Manufacture of electrical and optical equipment	KPIN	DL	498	507	518	503	493	478	KOXE	489	497	506	492	480	466
Of office machinery and computers	KPIO	30	42	40	48	52	52	50	KOXF	41	39	46	50	50	48
Of electrical machinery and apparatus	KPIP	31	180	184	190	187	180	173	KOXG	177	181	187	185	177	170
Of electric motors etc control apparatus and insulated cable	KPIQ	311 to 313	..	..	..	..	..	..	KOXH	100	103	108	108	103	99
Of accumulators, primary cells, batteries, lamps and electrical equipment	KPIR	314 to 316	..	..	..	..	..	..	KOXI	77	78	79	76	74	70
Radio television and communication equipment	KPIS	32	132	134	133	125	130	125	KOXJ	128	129	127	120	124	119
Of electronic components	KPIT	321	..	..	..	..	..	..	KOXK	53	52	51	50	52	53
Of radio TV and telephone apparatus, sound and video recorders	KPIU	322/323	..	..	..	..	..	..	KOXL	74	77	77	71	72	66
Of medical precision and optical equipment, watches	KPIV	33	144	150	147	139	131	130	KOXM	142	149	145	137	129	129
Manufacture of transport equipment	KPIW	DM	387	388	407	393	372	352	KOXN	376	376	395	380	359	339
Of motor vehicles and trailers	KPIX	34	230	231	238	223	204	187	KOXO	227	227	234	219	199	182
Of other transport equipment	KPIY	35	157	157	169	170	169	165	KOXP	149	149	161	161	160	157
Manufacturing not elsewhere classified	KPIZ	DN(36/37)	195	209	213	211	213	211	KOXQ	191	206	209	207	209	206
Electricity gas and water supply	KPJA	E	157	154	145	131	119	117	KOXR	110	121	126	125	126	124
Electricity gas steam and hot water supply	KPJB	40	..	..	..	..	..	..	KOXS / KOXT	152 / 100	150 / 102	142 / 98	127 / 97	116 / 88	114 / 87
Collection purification and distribution of water	KPJC	41	..	..	..	..	..	..	KOXU	52	48	43	30	27	27
Construction	KPJD	F(45)	921	976	1 098	1 112	1 171	1 195	KOXW	898	949	1 069	1 080	1 137	1 160
Services	KPJE	G - Q	18 051	18 460	18 844	19 323	19 674	19 947	KOXX	17 623	18 021	18 390	18 856	19 195	19 458
Wholesale and retail trade; Repair of motor vehicles, motorcycles and personal household goods	KPJF	G (50 - 52)	4 096	4 221	4 283	4 333	4 370	4 479	KOXY	4 007	4 128	4 184	4 230	4 265	4 373
Sale maintenance and repair of motor vehicles, retail of automotive fuel	KPJG	50	591	584	578	576	575	567	KOXZ	578	572	564	563	560	552
Sale of motor vehicles, motorcycles and parts, motorcycle repair and sale of automotive fuel	KPJH	501/503 - 505	..	..	..	..	..	..	KOYA	337	345	350	346	338	340
Maintenance and repair of motor vehicles	KPJI	502	..	..	..	..	..	..	KOYB	184	172	157	158	169	161
Wholesale trade and commission trade except motor vehicles	KPJJ	51	1 067	1 142	1 137	1 168	1 187	1 196	KOYC	1 046	1 121	1 115	1 145	1 164	1 174
Wholesale on a fee of contract basis	KPJK	511	..	..	..	..	..	..	KOYD	45	46	49	58	60	61
Wholesale agricultural raw materials and live animals	KPJL	512	..	..	..	..	..	..	KPLD	22	24	26	24	23	23
Wholesale food beverages & tobacco	KPJM	513	..	..	..	..	..	..	KPLE	203	207	197	205	206	205
Wholesale household goods	KPJN	514	..	..	..	..	..	..	KPLF	239	260	259	252	263	267
Wholesale of non-agricultural intermediate products waste & scrap	KPJO	515	..	..	..	..	..	..	KPLG	246	245	244	238	246	240
Wholesale machinery eqpt. & supplies	KPJP	516	..	..	..	..	..	..	KPLH	212	244	254	262	256	260
Other wholesale	KPJQ	517	..	..	..	..	..	..	KPLI	78	97	86	106	110	116
Retail trade except of motor vehicles and motorcycles; repair of personal and household goods	KPJR	52	2 439	2 495	2 568	2 588	2 609	2 715	KPLJ	2 383	2 436	2 504	2 523	2 542	2 647
Non-specialised stores selling mainly food beverages & tobacco	KPJS	5211/5221-4,5227	..	..	..	..	..	..	KPLK	911	915	984	969	977	1 027
Other non-specialised stores second hand shops & sales not in stores	KPJT	5212/525-526	..	..	..	..	..	..	KPLL	278	320	341	336	324	335

7.5
Employee jobs
Analysis by industry based on the Standard Industrial Classification 1992

continued   At June in each year

Thousands, not seasonally adjusted

		SIC 1992	United Kingdom							Great Britain					
			1996	1997	1998	1999	2000	2001		1996	1997	1998	1999	2000	2001
Alcoholic & other beverages, tobacco	KPJU	5225 to 5226	..	..	..	..	..	..	KPLM	47	61	62	71	70	74
Pharmaceutical & medical goods cosmetics & toilet articles	KPJV	523	..	..	..	..	..	..	KPLN	141	132	98	88	92	96
Clothing footwear & leather goods	KPJW	5242/5243	..	..	..	..	..	..	KPLO	245	271	296	341	354	383
Textile furniture lighting equipment electrical household appliances radio and TV paints glass hardware and household goods not elsewhere classified	KPJX	5241/5244-46	..	..	..	..	..	..	KPLP	288	291	259	267	276	281
Books newspapers and stationery, other retail in specialised stores	KPJY	5247/5248	..	..	..	..	..	..	KPLQ	394	379	376	386	373	379
Repair of personal and household goods	KPJZ	527	..	..	..	..	..	..	KPLR	18	19	21	19	21	20
Hotels and restaurants	KPKA	H	1 502	1 532	1 601	1 652	1 688	1 692	KPLS	1 473	1 502	1 566	1 616	1 651	1 654
Hotels camp sites short-stay accom.	KPKB	551/552	..	..	..	..	..	..	KPLT	370	356	372	371	370	375
Restaurants	KPKC	553	..	..	..	..	..	..	KPLU	398	406	431	478	493	489
Bars	KPKD	554	..	..	..	..	..	..	KPLV	469	507	522	535	559	548
Canteens and catering	KPKE	555	..	..	..	..	..	..	KPLW	236	233	242	232	228	242
Transport, storage and communication	KPKF	I	1 374	1 395	1 423	1 474	1 536	1 593	KPLX	1 351	1 371	1 399	1 448	1 510	1 566
Land transport, transport via pipelines	KPKG	60	502	497	517	520	526	539	KPLY	492	487	507	509	515	528
Transport via railways	KPKH	601	..	..	..	..	..	..	KPLZ	80	46	50	49	50	50
Other land transport and via pipelines	KPKI	602/603	..	..	..	..	..	..	KPMA	412	441	457	460	465	478
Water transport	KPKJ	61	26	23	20	20	19	17	KPMB	25	22	19	20	18	16
Air transport	KPKK	62	62	73	82	88	92	94	KPMC	61	72	81	87	91	93
Supporting and auxiliary transport activities, activities of travel agents	KPKL	63	322	338	334	361	388	401	KPMD	317	334	329	356	383	396
Travel agencies and tour operators	KPKM	633	..	..	..	..	..	..	KPME	88	96	98	121	132	137
Post and telecommunications	KPKN	64	462	464	470	485	512	542	KPMF	455	456	462	477	503	533
National post and courier activities	KPKO	641	..	..	..	..	..	..	KPMG	266	259	278	275	280	313
National post activities	KPKP	6411	..	..	..	..	..	..	KPMH	211	220	221	215	215	246
Courier activities	KPKQ	6412	..	..	..	..	..	..	KPMI	55	39	57	60	65	67
Telecommunications	KPKR	6420	..	..	..	..	..	..	KPMJ	189	197	185	201	223	220
Financial intermediation	KPKS	J	1 016	1 040	1 054	1 074	1 066	1 058	KPMK	1 002	1 026	1 040	1 060	1 052	1 043
Financial intermediation except insurance and pension funding	KPKT	65	605	608	607	619	600	584	KPML	597	599	597	610	591	574
Insurance and pension funding except compulsory social security	KPKU	66	210	225	228	232	228	231	KPMM	208	222	226	230	226	228
Activities auxiliary to financial intermediation	KPKV	67	200	207	219	222	238	243	KPMN	198	205	216	220	235	241
Except insurance and pension funding	KPKW	671	..	..	..	..	..	..	KPMO	51	69	81	79	91	95
Auxiliary to insurance and pension funding	KPKX	672	..	..	..	..	..	..	KPMP	147	136	135	141	144	146
Real estate renting & business activities	KPKY	K	3 071	3 269	3 422	3 562	3 640	3 710	KPMQ	3 038	3 233	3 382	3 517	3 592	3 659
Real estate activities	KPKZ	70	281	299	299	314	345	355	KPMR	279	296	296	311	341	351
Activities with own property, letting of own property	KPLA	701/702	..	..	..	..	..	..	KPMS	158	160	168	188	214	223
Activities on a fee or contract basis	KPLB	703	..	..	..	..	..	..	KPMT	121	136	129	123	127	128

7.5

Employee jobs
Analysis by industry based on the Standard Industrial Classification 1992

continued   At June in each year   Thousands, not seasonally adjusted

			United Kingdom							Great Britain					
		SIC 1992	1996	1997	1998	1999	2000	2001		1996	1997	1998	1999	2000	2001
Renting of machinery and equipment without operator & of personal & household goods	KPLC	71	119	133	135	149	155	158	KPMU	117	131	134	147	153	155
Construction and civil engineering machinery	KOUU	7132	..	..	..	..	..	..	KPMV	34	36	40	39	41	40
All other goods and equipment	KOUV	Rest of 71	..	..	..	..	..	..	KPMW	83	96	94	108	112	115
Computer and related equipment	KOUW	72	262	304	357	409	430	431	KPMX	260	302	353	405	426	426
Research and development	KOUX	73	93	92	95	98	101	98	KPMY	92	91	94	97	99	96
Other business activities	KOUY	74	2 315	2 441	2 536	2 592	2 609	2 669	KPMZ	2 290	2 413	2 505	2 557	2 573	2 631
Legal, accounting, book-keeping & auditing activities	KOUZ	741	..	..	..	..	..	..	KPNA	646	649	697	651	665	667
Legal activities	KOVA	7411	..	..	..	..	..	..	KPNB	207	215	221	234	238	236
Accounting, book-keeping auditing, tax consultancy	KOVB	7412	..	..	..	..	..	..	KPNC	169	146	170	179	195	200
Market research business and consultancy activities	KOVC	7413/7414	..	..	..	..	..	..	KPND	191	197	205	200	200	199
Management activities of holding companies	KOVD	7415	..	..	..	..	..	..	KPNE	79	91	101	38	32	32
Architectural engineering activities and related technical consultancy, technical testing	KOVE	742/743	..	..	..	..	..	..	KPNF	357	340	317	324	323	332
Advertising	KOVF	744	..	..	..	..	..	..	KPNG	85	88	89	84	83	89
Industrial cleaning	KOVG	747	..	..	..	..	..	..	KPNH	420	408	358	454	422	418
Public administration and defence, compulsory social security	KOVH	L(75)	1 414	1 366	1 399	1 409	1 396	1 406	KPNI	1 354	1 307	1 341	1 351	1 338	1 347
Education	KOVI	M(80)	1 867	1 872	1 852	1 986	2 100	2 149	KPNJ	1 802	1 808	1 788	1 921	2 034	2 083
Health and social work	KOVJ	N	2 588	2 615	2 617	2 589	2 605	2 588	KPNK	2 496	2 522	2 524	2 495	2 511	2 492
Human health, veterinary activities	KOVK	851/852	..	..	..	..	..	..	KPNL	1 511	1 585	1 584	1 591	1 618	1 607
Social work activities	KOVL	853	..	..	..	..	..	..	KPNM	985	937	940	905	893	885
Other community social and personal service activities, private households with employed persons, extra-territorial organisations and bodies	KOVM	O - Q	1 124	1 151	1 193	1 244	1 272	1 272	KPNN	1 098	1 124	1 167	1 217	1 244	1 242
Sewage and refuse disposal; sanitation	KOVN	90	84	92	132	108	92	88	KPNO	82	90	130	105	90	85
Activities of membership organisations	KOVO	91	211	210	212	214	221	218	KPNP	202	201	205	207	213	210
Recreational cultural and sporting activities	KOVP	92	574	588	577	628	655	666	KPNQ	562	575	564	615	641	651
Motion picture video radio TV news agencies and entertainment activities	KOVQ	921 to 924	..	..	..	..	..	..	KPNR	166	167	165	201	214	217
Library archives museums and other cultural activities	KOVR	925	..	..	..	..	..	..	KPNS	80	81	80	77	85	88
Sporting activities and other recreational activities	KOVS	926/927	..	..	..	..	..	..	KPNT	316	328	319	336	342	346
Other service activities, private households with employed persons, extra territorial organisations	KOVT	93/95/99	256	261	272	295	304	300	KPNU	253	258	269	291	300	296
Washing, dry cleaning of textile and fur products	KOVU	9301	..	..	..	..	..	..	KPNV	50	48	54	46	43	44
Hairdressing, other beauty treatment, physical and well-being activities	KOVV	9302/9304	..	..	..	..	..	..	KPNW	92	88	96	97	99	98

*Sources: Department of Manpower Services (Northern Ireland);
Earnings and Employment Division, ONS: 01633 812079*

7.6 Weekly hours worked[1]
United Kingdom
At Spring each year. Not seasonally adjusted.

Hours

	All workers' weekly hours[2]		Average actual weekly hours of work		
	Total (millions)	Average	Full-time employment[2,3]	Part-time employment[3]	Second jobs[4]
All					
	BEFA	BEFD	BEFG	BEFJ	BEFM
1991	908	34.4	39.3	15.2	9.6
1992	856	33.3	38.4	14.8	9.3
1993	852	33.5	38.8	14.9	9.2
1994	866	33.8	39.2	15.2	9.1
1995	884	34.1	39.5	15.3	9.1
1996	890	33.9	39.5	15.3	8.8
1997	897	33.5	39.0	15.2	9.3
1998	905	33.4	39.0	15.2	9.0
1999	918	33.5	39.0	15.5	8.9
2000	923	33.3	38.7	15.6	8.8
2001	937	33.5	38.8	15.9	9.3
Men					
	BEFB	BEFE	BEFH	BEFK	BEFN
1991	596	40.1	41.2	14.8	10.6
1992	554	38.9	40.3	14.3	10.3
1993	548	39.3	40.8	14.4	10.2
1994	558	39.6	41.2	14.9	9.8
1995	571	39.9	41.6	14.7	10.0
1996	573	39.7	41.5	14.7	9.7
1997	577	39.1	41.1	14.8	10.6
1998	584	39.0	41.0	14.9	9.6
1999	587	38.9	40.9	14.9	9.5
2000	590	38.5	40.6	15.0	9.1
2001	596	38.6	40.6	15.5	9.9
Women					
	BEFC	BEFF	BEFI	BEFL	BEFO
1991	312	27.1	35.3	15.2	8.6
1992	302	26.4	34.6	14.9	8.5
1993	304	26.5	34.9	15.0	8.5
1994	308	26.8	35.2	15.3	8.5
1995	312	26.9	35.1	15.4	8.5
1996	317	26.8	35.3	15.4	8.2
1997	319	26.6	34.9	15.3	8.3
1998	321	26.5	34.8	15.3	8.5
1999	332	27.0	35.2	15.6	8.5
2000	333	26.8	34.9	15.7	8.7
2001	341	27.1	35.1	16.0	8.9

1 Average hours actually worked in the reference week which includes hours
  worked in second jobs.
2 Main and second job.

3 People whose main job is full-time or part-time.
4 Second jobs reported in the LFS in addition to persons' main full time job.

Source: Labour Force Survey, Office for National Statistics

7.7 Civil Service staff
Analysis by ministerial responsibility[1,2]
At 1 April each year

Full-time equivalents[3] (thousands)

		1991	1992	1993	1994	1995	1996	1997	1998	1999	2000	2001
Agriculture, Fisheries and Food	BCDA	11.0	11.0	11.0	11.0	10.6	10.8	10.1	10.8	11.7	10.8	11.4
Cabinet Office	KPQI	2.0	2.0	6.0	12.0	11.7	12.3	7.8	6.2	7.6	6.9	6.9
Chancellor of the Exchequer's Departments:												
Customs and Excise	BCDC	27.0	27.0	25.0	25.0	24.1	23.2	23.1	23.4	22.5	21.9	21.7
Inland Revenue	BCDD	67.0	70.0	68.0	64.0	59.1	56.5	54.0	53.4	61.3	66.3	66.9
Department for National Savings	BCDE	7.0	6.0	6.0	6.0	5.4	4.7	4.3	4.1	0.1	0.1	0.1
Treasury and others	BCDF	10.0	10.0	5.0	5.0	4.3	6.0	5.1	5.1	5.0	5.5	5.5
Total	BCDB	111.0	113.0	105.0	99.0	92.9	90.3	86.4	86.0	89.0	93.8	94.2
Education	BCDG	3.0	3.0	3.0	2.0	2.5	..	..	..	..	–	–
Employment	BCDH	50.0	58.0	58.0	55.0	49.6	..	..	..	..	–	–
Education and Employment	KTDI	..	..	..	..	..	40.8	34.1	33.6	34.6	36.5	38.3
Energy	BCDI	1.0	1.0	..	..	..	..	..	..	..	–	–
Environment	BCDJ	26.0	23.0	18.0	10.0	9.4	10.9	9.6	..	..	–	–
Environment, Transport & Regions	JYXS	..	..	..	..	..	..	..	21.2	21.3	23.2	25.4
Foreign and Commonwealth	BCDK	10.0	10.0	10.0	8.0	7.5	7.1	6.6	5.4	5.5	5.5	5.5
International Development	JYXU	..	..	..	..	..	..	..	1.1	1.2	1.2	1.3
Health	BAKR	7.0	7.0	7.0	7.0	6.2	4.8	4.7	4.6	4.8	7.0	7.2
Home	BCDL	45.0	50.0	52.0	51.0	51.4	50.8	50.4	50.7	50.0	53.6	60.1
Legal Departments	KPQJ	29.0	29.0	30.0	29.0	28.7	27.8	26.3	25.4	24.4	24.9	25.0
National Heritage	KPQK	–	1.0	1.0	1.0	1.0	1.0	1.0	..	..	–	–
Culture, Media and Sport	JYXT	..	..	..	..	..	..	..	0.6	0.6	0.6	0.6
Northern Ireland	KPQD	–	–	–	–	0.2	0.2	0.2	0.2	0.2	0.2	0.2
Scotland	BCDN	13.0	13.0	14.0	13.0	12.1	11.7	11.8	12.0	13.6	13.6	13.7
Social Security	BAKS	80.0	81.0	86.0	90.0	89.2	91.5	93.1	87.2	81.6	83.5	81.9
Health and Social Security	KAZL	–	–	–	–	–	–	–	–	–	–	–
Trade and Industry	KAZM	13.0	13.0	13.0	12.0	11.1	11.2	10.3	10.4	10.5	11.0	11.4
Transport	BCDR	15.0	15.0	15.0	14.0	12.9	11.3	11.4	..	..	–	–
Wales	BCDS	2.0	2.0	3.0	2.0	2.2	2.1	2.2	2.1	2.3	2.7	3.2
Total civil departments	BCDU	418.0	431.0	431.0	418.0	400.8	384.6	366.0	357.6	358.8	375.1	384.4
Defence	BCDW	141.0	140.0	130.0	122.0	116.1	109.9	109.2	104.2	100.8	100.3	98.3
Total all departments	BCDX	559.0	571.0	560.0	540.0	516.9	494.5	475.2	461.7	459.6	475.4	482.7
of whom												
Non-industrial staff	BCDY	495.0	509.0	509.0	494.0	474.1	458.7	439.3	430.5	428.9	446.0	453.8
Industrial staff	BCDZ	64.0	61.0	52.0	46.0	42.0	35.9	36.0	32.8	30.7	29.4	28.9

1 The figures include non-industrial and industrial staff but exclude casual or seasonal staff and employees of the Northern Ireland Civil Service.
2 A comprehensive list of Machinery of Government changes is listed on the Cabinet Office's website at www.civil-service.gov.uk/statistics
3 Figures included are measured as 'full-time equivalent' staff. Part-time staff are recorded as a proportion of full-time employees according to the proportion of a full week that they work.

Source: Cabinet Office: 020 7276 1532

7.8 Persons employed in local authorities[1]

Thousands (Full-time equivalents)[2]

		1990	1991	1992	1993	1994	1995	1996	1997	1998	1999	2000
England												
Education	ATAM	857.0	849.4	835.8	712.1	692.8	698.4	691.8	691.8	693.9	707.3	730.9
Construction	BCHC	93.7	85.7	77.1	70.9	67.4	63.5	58.8	55.0	51.9	52.3	51.2
Transport	BCHD	2.4	1.9	1.5	1.4	1.4	1.4	1.4	1.4	1.4	..	..
Social services	BCHE	236.0	235.6	232.3	225.8	233.3	234.3	230.6	227.3	221.3	215.9	213.5
Public libraries and museums	BCHF	33.6	33.3	32.4	31.9	31.8	32.7	31.5	31.4	31.1	31.5	31.1
Recreation, parks and baths	BCHG	77.2	75.7	72.7	68.6	67.2	65.2	63.6	60.7	59.8	58.1	57.2
Environmental health	BCHH	19.1	18.8	19.6	19.0	18.5	17.4	17.2	17.4	16.9	17.2	17.7
Refuse collection and disposal	BCHS	29.9	27.1	23.6	21.8	20.5	25.1	24.5	24.6	24.0	23.7	21.9
Housing	BCHT	64.5	65.5	65.4	65.5	65.7	68.0	66.8	65.5	64.7	65.4	65.1
Town and country planning	BCHU	22.9	23.1	23.1	22.5	22.2	25.9	27.1	27.3	26.8	27.7	27.7
Fire service												
regulars	BAIV	34.5	34.5	34.3	34.2	33.9	33.8	33.6	33.3	33.1	34.0	33.9
others	BAIW	6.0	5.7	5.8	5.7	5.7	5.8	5.7	5.6	5.6	6.3	6.2
Other services[3]	BCHM	243.7	244.7	238.0	226.7	217.0	191.3	183.8	177.9	173.1	178.1	177.8
Total of above	BCHN	1 720.5	1 701.0	1 661.6	1 506.1	1 477.4	1 462.8	1 436.4	1 419.2	1 403.6	1 417.5	1 434.2
Police Service												
police: all ranks	BCHO	120.2	120.9	120.8	121.4	121.0	118.8	118.4	118.5	119.2	119.2	117.0
cadets	BAIX	0.3	0.3	0.3	0.2	0.1	0.1	0.3	0.3	0.1	–	..
traffic wardens	BAIY	4.5	4.7	4.9	4.9	4.7	4.5	4.3	4.1	3.5	3.3	2.8
civilians	BAIZ	42.2	44.0	44.9	46.7	46.9	48.1	49.8	50.0	50.3	50.5	50.8
Magistrates courts	BAJA	9.4	10.0	10.0	10.0	9.9	10.0	9.9	9.2	8.9	9.0	8.9
Probation staff												
officers	BAJB	6.5	6.5	6.9	7.1	7.2	7.2	6.9	6.9	6.2	6.8	7.1
others	BAJC	7.0	7.3	7.5	7.9	8.0	8.5	7.2	7.1	5.4	7.1	7.5
Total law and order	BAJD	190.1	193.7	195.3	198.2	197.8	197.2	196.8	196.1	193.6	195.9	194.1
Agency staff	BAJE	1.3	1.5	1.1	1.4	1.6	0.9	0.8	0.8	0.8	–	..
Total (excluding special employment and training measures)	BCHR	1 911.9	1 896.2	1 858.0	1 705.7	1 676.8	1 660.9	1 634.0	1 616.1	1 598.0	1 613.4	1 628.3

		1990	1991	1992	1993	1994	1995	1996	1997	1998	1999	2000
Wales												
Education	ATAN	54.3	55.6	53.8	48.2	47.9	48.7	50.6	49.5	49.9	51.6	50.7
Construction	BCGC	7.4	7.0	6.5	5.9	5.8	5.9	6.0	5.5	5.5	5.7	5.6
Transport	BCGD	–	–	–	–	–	–	–	–	..	..	..
Social services	BCGE	15.0	15.0	16.0	16.0	17.0	18.3	18.5	19.0	18.8	19.2	19.2
Public libraries and museums	BCGF	1.6	1.7	1.7	1.7	1.7	1.7	1.5	1.6	1.5	1.6	1.6
Recreation, parks and baths	BCGG	5.8	5.9	5.8	6.0	6.0	6.3	5.8	6.4	6.1	6.1	6.0
Environmental health	BCGH	1.4	1.4	1.5	1.5	1.5	1.5	1.6	1.5	1.3	1.4	1.5
Refuse collection and disposal	BCGI	1.6	1.7	1.6	1.6	1.5	2.2	2.9	2.9	2.9	2.8	2.6
Housing	BCGJ	2.8	2.9	3.0	3.1	3.1	3.4	3.3	3.6	3.6	3.8	3.6
Town and country planning	BCGK	1.5	1.6	1.7	1.8	1.8	2.2	1.9	2.0	2.0	2.1	2.0
Fire service												
regulars	BAKT	1.8	1.8	1.8	1.8	1.8	1.8	1.9	1.9	1.9	1.9	1.9
others	BAKU	0.3	0.4	0.4	0.4	0.4	0.3	0.3	0.3	0.3	0.4	0.4
Other services	BCGM	19.0	18.8	18.7	23.5	19.8	15.6	14.2	14.6	14.0	15.1	15.1
Total of above	BCGN	112.9	114.3	112.5	111.5	108.1	107.9	108.5	108.8	107.8	111.7	109.9
Police Service												
police: all ranks	BCGO	6.5	6.6	6.6	6.6	6.5	6.4	6.4	6.6	6.6	6.6	6.6
cadets	BAKV	–	–	–	–	–	–	–	–	..	..	..
traffic wardens	BAKW	0.2	0.2	0.2	0.2	0.2	0.2	0.2	0.2	0.2	0.2	0.2
civilians	BAKX	2.0	2.1	2.1	2.1	2.2	2.2	2.5	2.4	2.4	2.8	2.7
Magistrates courts	BAKY	0.6	0.6	0.6	0.7	0.7	0.7	0.6	0.6	0.6	0.7	0.6
Probation staff												
officers	BAKZ	0.4	0.4	0.4	0.4	0.4	0.4	0.4	0.4	0.3	0.4	0.4
others	BALA	0.3	0.3	0.4	0.4	0.4	0.4	0.4	0.4	0.3	0.4	0.4
Total law and order	BALB	10.1	10.2	10.3	10.4	10.4	10.3	10.5	10.6	10.4	10.3	10.1
Agency staff	BALC	–	–	–	–	–	–	–	–	..	..	..
Total (excluding special employment and training measures)	BCGR	122.9	124.4	122.8	121.9	118.5	118.2	119.0	119.4	118.2	122.0	120.0

7.8 Persons employed in local authorities[1]

continued

Thousands (Full-time equivalents)[4]

		1990	1991	1992	1993	1994	1995	1996	1997	1998	1999	2000
Scotland												
Education	ATAO	89.2	87.1	87.5	80.0	77.1	77.6	74.7	73.6	75.5	76.7	78.7
Construction	BCMC	23.4	23.5	23.1	22.9	22.0	21.7	20.7	20.6	20.5	20.4	20.5
Transport	BCMD	0.7	0.8	0.8	0.8	0.9	0.9	0.9	0.9	0.9	0.9	0.9
Social Services	BCME	36.2	36.2	36.8	37.3	38.3	39.1	38.4	37.9	37.0	34.6	34.6
Public libraries and museums	BCMF	4.4	4.4	4.5	4.6	4.7	4.7	4.2	4.2	4.2	4.1	4.0
Recreation, leisure and tourism	BCMG	13.8	13.6	13.3	13.7	13.9	13.9	11.4	11.4	11.3	11.3	11.3
Environmental health	BCMH	2.3	2.5	2.5	2.7	2.7	2.6	3.4	3.4	3.3	3.1	3.0
Cleansing	BCMI	8.4	8.2	8.1	8.2	8.1	8.0	7.3	7.2	7.2	7.2	7.2
Housing	BCMJ	7.3	7.3	7.2	7.4	7.8	7.9	7.9	8.4	8.5	8.5	8.5
Physical planning	BCMK	2.0	2.0	2.1	2.2	2.2	2.2	3.7	3.4	3.3	3.3	3.3
Fire service	BCML	5.1	5.2	5.2	5.3	5.3	5.2	5.8	5.6	5.7	5.7	5.7
Other services[3]	BCMM	44.3	46.8	48.1	48.0	52.1	51.5	40.7	40.7	38.5	39.0	38.1
Total of above	BCMN	237.1	237.6	239.2	233.1	235.1	235.3	219.1	217.3	215.9	214.8	215.8
Police service												
police (all ranks)	BCMO	13.7	13.9	13.9	14.2	14.2	14.4	13.7	14.2	14.3	14.4	14.4
others[5]	BCMP	4.7	4.6	4.8	5.1	5.2	5.2	5.2	5.3	5.4	5.4	5.4
Administration of district courts	BCMQ	0.2	0.2	0.1	0.2	0.2	0.2	0.2	0.2	0.2	0.2	0.2
Total (excluding special employment measures) and training	BCMR	255.7	256.3	258.0	252.6	254.7	255.1	238.2	237.0	235.8	234.8	235.8

1 Figures are based on surveys undertaken on behalf of central and local government by the ONS and the Scottish Executive and the Convention of Scottish Local Authorities (COSLA).

2 Based on the following factors to convert part-time employees to approximate full-time equivalents: for teachers and lecturers in further education, 0.11; teachers in primary and secondary education and all other non-manual employees, 0.53; manual employees, 0.41.

3 Including civil/central services departments (eg engineers and finance) and all services not shown separately.

4 Based on the following factors to convert part-time employees to approximate full-time equivalents: for lecturers and teachers, 0.40; non-manual staff (excluding teachers), 0.58; manual employees, 0.46.

5 Includes civilian employees of police forces and traffic wardens.

Sources: Office for National Statistics: 0117 987 8675;
Home Office;
Scottish Executive;
Scottish Joint Staffing Watch.

7.9 Duration of ILO unemployment
United Kingdom
At Spring each year. Not seasonally adjusted.

Thousands

	All ILO unemployed	Less than 3 months	3 months & less than 6 months	6 months & less than 1 year	1 year & less than 2 years	2 years & less than 3 years	3 years & less than 4 years	4 years & less than 5 years	5 years or more	All 1 year or more Number	All 1 year or more As % of total
All											
	BEAS	BEFP	BEFS	BEFV	BEFY	BEGB	BEGE	BEGH	BEGK	BEGN	BEGQ
1991	2 414	834	466	434	276	113	67	41	179	676	28.0
1992	2 769	668	500	607	529	174	75	37	179	993	35.9
1993	2 936	600	474	599	612	287	109	57	196	1 262	43.0
1994	2 738	610	389	488	514	310	166	81	178	1 248	45.6
1995	2 460	570	388	423	405	243	144	102	183	1 076	43.8
1996	2 340	602	381	421	344	190	130	85	185	933	39.9
1997	2 037	600	319	325	289	149	84	72	198	791	38.8
1998	1 776	595	327	265	218	109	68	42	149	587	33.1
1999	1 752	623	328	277	211	88	44	39	139	522	29.8
2000	1 619	605	308	249	198	79	36	32	111	456	28.2
2001	1 404	529	265	223	163	88	29	18	88	386	27.5
Men											
	BEAT	BEFQ	BEFT	BEFW	BEFZ	BEGC	BEGF	BEGI	BEGL	BEGO	BEGR
1991	1 514	455	288	281	189	76	50	31	142	488	32.3
1992	1 865	396	320	409	380	125	55	28	152	740	39.6
1993	1 986	348	313	385	439	212	84	43	160	938	47.2
1994	1 826	346	230	313	361	236	124	63	152	936	51.2
1995	1 612	301	240	268	280	182	115	79	144	801	49.7
1996	1 549	332	236	268	234	144	105	68	159	711	45.9
1997	1 306	323	195	198	195	104	63	58	167	588	45.0
1998	1 098	313	190	172	139	77	48	35	124	421	38.4
1999	1 095	341	203	171	143	61	31	31	113	379	34.6
2000	991	325	184	144	137	52	27	25	94	335	33.8
2001	859	285	158	134	111	63	19	14	73	280	32.6
Women											
	BEAU	BEFR	BEFU	BEFX	BEGA	BEGD	BEGG	BEGJ	BEGM	BEGP	BEGS
1991	900	378	178	153	87	36	17	10	37	188	20.9
1992	904	272	180	198	149	49	20	..	28	254	28.1
1993	949	251	161	214	173	74	25	15	37	323	34.1
1994	912	264	159	176	152	74	42	18	26	313	34.3
1995	849	270	148	155	125	61	28	23	39	275	32.4
1996	791	271	144	152	109	46	24	17	26	222	28.1
1997	732	277	124	127	94	45	20	14	31	203	27.8
1998	679	282	137	93	80	32	21	..	25	166	24.5
1999	657	282	126	106	69	27	13	..	25	143	21.7
2000	628	279	124	104	61	27	..	..	17	121	19.3
2001	546	244	107	89	52	24	11	..	14	106	19.4

1 See chapter text for definitions.

Source: Labour Force Survey, Office for National Statistics

7.10 ILO Unemployment
United Kingdom
By age group and gender. At Spring each year. Not seasonally adjusted.

Thousands and percentages

	All aged 16 and over	16-59/64	16-17	18-24	16-24	25-34	35-49	50-64 (m) 50-59 (f)	65+ (m) 60+ (f)
All	**Thousands**								
	BEAS	BEGT	BEGW	BEGZ	BEHC	BEHF	BEHI	BEHL	BEHO
1992	2 769	2 738	123	694	817	781	714	426	32
1993	2 936	2 902	112	755	867	801	748	487	33
1994	2 738	2 712	122	650	771	766	712	464	25
1995	2 460	2 443	122	586	708	693	654	388	17
1996	2 340	2 321	143	536	679	661	619	361	19
1997	2 037	2 015	144	464	608	537	546	324	23
1998	1 776	1 757	133	413	546	485	449	276	20
1999	1 752	1 732	142	400	541	437	478	276	19
2000	1 619	1 602	147	377	524	378	433	268	17
2001	1 404	1 390	114	346	461	331	401	197	15
Men									
	BEAT	BEGU	BEGX	BEHA	BEHD	BEHG	BEHJ	BEHM	BEHP
1992	1 865	1 850	71	469	541	517	459	333	15
1993	1 986	1 974	62	504	566	530	500	378	12
1994	1 826	1 816	66	434	499	510	455	352	10
1995	1 612	1 604	69	383	452	450	408	294	..
1996	1 549	1 538	87	360	446	417	401	273	11
1997	1 306	1 294	79	302	381	340	342	232	11
1998	1 098	1 088	73	259	332	291	264	201	..
1999	1 095	1 086	88	247	336	256	293	201	..
2000	991	984	81	235	316	221	253	193	..
2001	859	851	69	216	285	192	227	147	..
Women									
	BEAU	BEGV	BEGY	BEHB	BEHE	BEHH	BEHK	BEHN	BEHQ
1992	904	888	52	224	276	264	255	93	16
1993	949	928	49	251	300	271	248	109	21
1994	912	896	56	216	272	256	257	112	15
1995	849	839	53	203	256	243	246	95	..
1996	791	783	56	177	233	244	218	88	..
1997	732	720	65	162	227	197	204	92	11
1998	679	668	60	154	214	193	185	76	10
1999	657	646	53	152	206	181	184	75	10
2000	628	618	66	142	207	156	180	74	10
2001	546	539	46	130	176	139	174	50	..
All	**Rates[1]**								
	BEBQ	BEHR	BEHU	BEHX	BEIA	BEID	BEIG	BEIJ	BEIM
1992	9.7	9.9	16.0	15.4	15.5	10.4	7.2	8.4	3.7
1993	10.3	10.5	16.8	17.4	17.3	10.5	7.5	9.6	4.1
1994	9.6	9.8	17.9	15.9	16.2	9.9	7.1	9.0	3.1
1995	8.6	8.8	17.4	15.0	15.3	9.0	6.5	7.5	2.1
1996	8.2	8.3	18.5	14.0	14.8	8.5	6.0	6.9	2.4
1997	7.1	7.2	17.7	12.6	13.5	6.9	5.3	5.9	2.7
1998	6.1	6.3	16.7	11.4	12.4	6.3	4.4	4.9	2.5
1999	6.0	6.1	17.9	11.1	12.3	5.8	4.5	4.7	2.3
2000	5.5	5.6	18.6	10.3	11.8	5.1	4.0	4.5	2.0
2001	4.8	4.9	15.2	9.5	10.5	4.6	3.7	3.2	1.8
Men									
	BEBR	BEHS	BEHV	BEHY	BEIB	BEIE	BEIH	BEIK	BEIN
1992	11.5	11.7	17.7	19.0	18.8	11.9	8.4	10.4	4.9
1993	12.4	12.5	18.5	21.1	20.8	12.1	9.1	11.9	4.6
1994	11.4	11.5	18.8	19.3	19.2	11.5	8.3	11.0	3.7
1995	10.1	10.2	19.2	17.7	17.9	10.1	7.3	9.2	..
1996	9.6	9.7	21.3	17.2	17.8	9.4	7.2	8.4	4.0
1997	8.1	8.2	19.4	14.8	15.6	7.7	6.1	6.9	4.1
1998	6.8	6.9	18.1	13.1	14.0	6.7	4.7	5.8	..
1999	6.7	6.8	21.5	12.6	14.1	6.0	5.1	5.7	..
2000	6.1	6.1	20.1	11.8	13.2	5.3	4.3	5.4	..
2001	5.3	5.3	17.7	10.9	12.0	4.7	3.8	4.0	..
Women									
	BEBS	BEHT	BEHW	BEHZ	BEIC	BEIF	BEII	BEIL	BEIO
1992	7.3	7.5	14.0	11.0	11.5	8.4	5.7	5.0	3.1
1993	7.6	7.8	15.1	12.9	13.2	8.4	5.5	5.7	3.9
1994	7.3	7.5	16.9	11.8	12.6	7.9	5.6	5.7	2.9
1995	6.8	7.0	15.5	11.6	12.2	7.4	5.4	4.7	..
1996	6.3	6.5	15.3	10.2	11.1	7.4	4.7	4.3	..
1997	5.7	5.9	16.0	9.8	11.0	5.9	4.4	4.3	2.1
1998	5.3	5.4	15.3	9.4	10.5	5.8	3.9	3.4	2.0
1999	5.1	5.2	14.0	9.3	10.2	5.5	3.9	3.3	1.9
2000	4.8	4.9	16.9	8.5	10.1	4.8	3.7	3.1	1.7
2001	4.2	4.3	12.5	7.8	8.7	4.4	3.5	2.0	..

1 Total ILO unemployment as a percentage of all economically active persons in the relevant age group.

Source: Labour Force Survey, Office for National Statistics

7.11 Claimant count[1] by age and duration
Computerised claims
United Kingdom

Thousands, not seasonally adjusted

		1996	1997	1998	1999	2000
Annual averages						
Males						
All ages						
All durations	GEZG	1 601.0	1 216.3	1 031.0	954.6	834.0
Up to 6 months	GEZH	667.1	569.4	541.1	530.6	488.8
Over 6 and up to 12 months	GEZI	300.6	200.6	188.5	166.8	143.2
All over 12 months	GEZJ	633.4	446.3	301.4	257.1	202.0
All over 24 months	GEZK	372.7	269.7	169.8	128.9	102.4
Aged 18 to 24						
All durations	GEZL	378.1	284.6	237.5	205.2	182.2
Up to 6 months	GEZM	203.8	172.5	159.8	160.9	149.6
Over 6 and up to 12 months	GEZN	81.0	53.2	44.2	34.3	28.3
All over 12 months	GEZO	93.5	58.9	33.5	10.0	4.4
All over 24 months	GEZP	35.3	22.1	10.7	2.3	0.5
Aged 25 to 49						
All durations	IACI	957.7	729.1	619.4	582.9	506.2
Up to 6 months	IACK	363.5	313.7	303.2	291.3	266.9
Over 6 and up to 12 months	IACN	173.7	118.2	117.3	107.4	92.8
All over 12 months	IACQ	420.6	297.2	198.9	184.3	146.5
All over 24 months	IACT	257.5	185.6	112.4	88.0	70.5
Aged 50 and over						
All durations	IACW	255.6	193.0	165.8	158.0	137.7
Up to 6 months	IACZ	91.2	74.3	70.3	70.6	65.0
Over 6 and up to 12 months	IADC	45.1	28.6	26.6	24.6	21.6
All over 12 months	IADF	119.2	90.1	69.0	62.8	51.1
All over 24 months	IADI	80.0	62.0	46.7	38.6	31.5
Females						
All ages						
All durations	GEZR	506.9	373.5	321.8	296.3	260.6
Up to 6 months	GEZS	267.4	216.3	203.0	195.5	177.9
Over 6 and up to 12 months	GEZT	102.1	62.1	54.5	48.1	41.3
All over 12 months	GEZU	137.4	95.2	64.2	52.7	41.4
All over 24 months	GEZV	67.0	48.9	30.9	22.9	18.2
Aged 18 to 24						
All durations	GEZW	164.9	121.8	101.5	88.9	79.2
Up to 6 months	GEZX	100.1	80.1	72.4	71.1	65.6
Over 6 and up to 12 months	GEZY	33.6	21.6	17.3	14.0	11.7
All over 12 months	GEZZ	31.1	20.1	11.8	3.8	1.9
All over 24 months	GEYU	9.9	6.6	3.3	0.8	0.2
Aged 25 to 49						
All durations	IACJ	253.3	181.7	157.4	147.1	127.9
Up to 6 months	IACL	127.8	100.8	96.1	90.3	80.7
Over 6 and up to 12 months	IACO	52.3	29.9	27.0	24.7	21.3
All over 12 months	IACR	73.3	51.1	34.3	32.1	25.9
All over 24 months	IACU	37.2	27.5	16.9	13.4	10.9
Aged 50 and over						
All durations	IACX	81.5	62.8	56.7	54.0	47.5
Up to 6 months	IADA	33.0	28.6	28.6	28.2	26.0
Over 6 and up to 12 months	IADD	15.6	10.2	9.9	9.1	7.9
All over 12 months	IADG	32.9	23.9	18.1	16.7	13.6
All over 24 months	IADJ	20.0	14.9	10.7	8.7	7.1

1 Count of claimants of unemployment-related benefits; computerised claims only.

Sources: Office for National Statistics: 020 7533 6094;
Benefits Agency

7.12 ILO unemployment rates
At Spring each year. Not seasonally adjusted.

Percentages

		1994	1995	1996	1997	1998	1999	2000	2001
United Kingdom	BEBQ	9.6	8.6	8.2	7.1	6.1	6.0	5.5	4.8
North East	BENU	12.5	11.4	10.8	9.8	8.1	10.1	9.1	7.4
North West	BENV	10.3	9.0	8.4	6.8	6.6	6.2	5.3	5.1
Yorkshire and Humber	BENY	9.9	8.7	8.1	8.0	7.0	6.5	6.0	4.9
East Midlands	BENZ	8.3	7.4	7.4	6.3	4.9	5.2	5.1	4.9
West Midlands	BEOA	10.0	8.9	9.2	6.8	6.3	6.8	6.2	5.0
East	BEOB	8.2	7.5	6.1	5.8	5.0	4.1	3.6	3.6
London	BEOC	13.1	11.5	11.3	9.1	8.2	7.6	7.0	5.8
South East	BEOD	7.1	6.4	6.0	5.2	4.3	3.6	3.3	3.0
South West	BEOE	7.5	7.8	6.3	5.2	4.5	4.7	4.1	3.5
England	BEOF	9.5	8.6	8.1	6.8	6.0	5.8	5.2	4.6
Wales	BEOG	9.4	8.8	8.3	8.3	6.7	7.0	6.1	5.7
Scotland	BEOH	10.0	8.4	8.7	8.5	7.4	7.4	7.6	5.8
Northern Ireland	BEOI	11.6	11.0	9.5	7.5	7.2	7.2	7.0	6.2

Source: Labour Force Survey, Office for National Statistics

7.13 Claimant count rates[1,2]
Seasonally adjusted annual averages

Percentages

		1990	1991	1992	1993	1994	1995	1996	1997	1998	1999	2000
United Kingdom	BCJE	5.5	7.6	9.2	9.7	8.8	7.6	7.0	5.3	4.5	4.2	3.6
North East	DPDM	9.1	10.5	11.3	12.1	11.7	10.8	10.0	8.1	7.2	7.0	6.3
North West	IBWC	7.0	8.6	9.8	10.0	9.3	8.1	7.5	5.9	5.1	4.6	4.1
Yorkshire and the Humber	DPBI	6.3	8.2	9.4	9.7	9.1	8.1	7.6	6.1	5.4	5.0	4.4
East Midlands	DPBJ	4.8	6.9	8.6	9.0	8.3	7.1	6.5	4.7	4.0	3.7	3.5
West Midlands	DPBN	5.5	8.0	9.8	10.3	9.4	7.7	6.9	5.3	4.6	4.5	4.0
East	DPDP	3.3	6.0	8.1	8.8	7.6	6.2	5.7	4.0	3.2	2.9	2.5
London	DPDQ	4.7	7.6	9.9	10.9	10.1	8.9	8.2	6.2	5.0	4.5	3.8
South East	DPDR	2.8	5.4	7.4	8.1	6.9	5.6	4.9	3.3	2.6	2.3	1.9
South West	DPBM	4.0	6.5	8.7	9.0	7.7	6.5	5.9	4.2	3.4	3.1	2.5
England	VASQ	5.0	7.3	9.1	9.7	8.7	7.5	6.8	5.1	4.3	3.9	3.4
Wales	DPBP	6.4	8.5	9.5	9.8	8.9	8.1	7.7	6.2	5.4	5.0	4.4
Scotland	DPBQ	7.7	8.2	8.9	9.2	8.7	7.5	7.3	6.2	5.5	5.1	4.6
Northern Ireland	DPBR	12.7	12.9	13.7	13.6	12.6	11.2	10.7	8.1	7.3	6.4	5.3
Great Britain	DPAJ	5.3	7.5	9.1	9.6	8.7	7.5	6.9	5.3	4.4	4.1	3.6

1 The number of unemployment-related benefit claimants as a percentage of the estimated total workforce (the sum of claimants, employee jobs, self-employed, participants on work-related government training programmes and HM Forces) at mid-year.
2 Seasonally adjusted and excluding claimants under 18, consistent with current coverage.

Source: Labour Market Statistics, Office for National Statistics: 020 7533 6094

7.14 Claimant count[1,2]
Analysis by Government Office Regions
Seasonally adjusted

Thousands

	North East	North West	Yorkshire and the Humber	East Midlands	West Midlands	East	London	South East	South West	England	Wales	Scotland	Great Britain	Northern Ireland	United Kingdom
	DPDG	IBWA	DPAX	DPAY	DPBC	DPDJ	DPDK	DPDL	DPBB	IBWK	DPBE	DPBF	DPAG	DPBG	BCJD
1987 Jan	191.3	429.4	283.1	184.1	316.5	185.6	381.6	238.1	188.3	2 393.9	159.1	334.7	2 891.8	123.1	3 014.9
Apr	187.3	417.5	276.9	178.6	303.9	174.0	364.2	222.8	180.2	2 304.0	152.0	332.0	2 789.6	121.5	2 911.1
Jul	179.5	396.9	263.1	169.3	287.5	161.4	348.8	205.5	168.9	2 182.4	145.5	317.8	2 644.2	119.8	2 764.0
Oct	172.3	379.5	249.1	159.3	271.6	149.6	331.0	189.5	158.2	2 059.3	139.4	303.7	2 503.2	117.8	2 621.0
1988 Jan	164.7	363.6	237.6	150.7	256.1	138.3	313.7	171.7	150.4	1 943.7	132.9	294.6	2 374.3	114.3	2 488.6
Apr	158.8	347.1	229.2	143.1	241.4	124.0	299.8	154.6	140.1	1 835.6	128.7	283.5	2 250.3	112.1	2 362.4
Jul	151.7	328.4	216.1	134.1	224.4	110.8	277.6	140.1	129.6	1 713.8	120.9	270.4	2 104.1	110.3	2 214.4
Oct	146.2	319.0	207.0	127.2	210.0	101.4	265.4	130.8	122.3	1 629.0	117.1	265.0	2 011.4	108.6	2 120.0
1989 Jan	140.3	301.4	192.6	116.8	190.9	89.5	242.3	114.6	109.2	1 495.9	108.1	254.2	1 859.9	107.4	1 967.3
Apr	132.3	283.0	178.6	106.6	171.9	80.2	221.3	103.4	99.9	1 375.7	99.4	238.9	1 715.5	105.1	1 820.6
Jul	124.4	269.7	171.3	101.7	163.0	78.4	216.1	100.6	95.5	1 322.0	93.2	226.3	1 640.2	102.8	1 743.0
Oct	118.0	256.5	164.5	97.8	155.9	76.8	204.8	99.7	91.5	1 265.2	88.5	217.7	1 571.7	100.0	1 671.7
1990 Jan	112.5	243.7	159.5	93.8	151.1	74.3	199.4	95.5	86.5	1 215.7	84.4	207.9	1 508.6	97.3	1 605.9
Apr	109.3	238.0	154.0	92.7	145.0	75.3	194.7	95.1	86.5	1 189.9	82.8	200.8	1 474.2	96.0	1 570.2
Jul	109.1	237.7	156.1	96.1	147.1	83.8	203.9	107.2	94.1	1 234.7	83.2	194.3	1 512.6	94.4	1 607.0
Oct	112.3	248.0	165.0	104.8	157.3	98.2	226.6	127.5	106.4	1 345.5	88.7	197.3	1 632.1	93.8	1 725.9
1991 Jan	116.7	261.8	176.4	113.1	171.0	112.5	255.8	149.7	122.2	1 478.8	95.0	200.9	1 775.1	96.0	1 871.1
Apr	126.2	285.9	197.5	132.0	203.5	138.5	303.2	190.5	146.9	1 723.9	108.8	212.7	2 045.7	97.9	2 143.6
Jul	130.5	305.4	211.9	145.5	225.4	158.9	342.3	221.3	165.7	1 906.8	115.5	220.1	2 242.5	98.8	2 341.3
Oct	133.2	318.2	219.6	154.5	240.0	172.4	368.9	240.9	178.6	2 025.9	119.3	224.0	2 369.6	100.5	2 470.1
1992 Jan	133.9	325.4	222.7	160.4	250.6	183.3	389.8	258.4	188.4	2 112.6	121.3	228.0	2 462.2	102.2	2 564.4
Apr	135.7	332.8	227.6	168.0	260.0	196.0	409.6	277.7	199.0	2 205.5	123.4	231.8	2 561.6	103.4	2 665.0
Jul	136.7	335.2	232.4	172.1	266.1	205.1	426.2	288.9	206.6	2 268.9	124.1	235.2	2 628.6	104.6	2 733.2
Oct	141.4	343.6	240.2	178.8	277.4	218.6	448.0	308.4	215.3	2 371.1	129.2	242.4	2 743.3	105.1	2 848.4
1993 Jan	146.2	348.3	247.5	185.2	286.2	229.5	464.6	325.2	222.6	2 454.4	131.4	245.3	2 832.0	105.5	2 937.5
Apr	148.0	345.2	246.5	183.6	285.1	228.2	469.5	321.4	220.0	2 446.6	130.3	243.2	2 821.0	104.5	2 925.5
Jul	148.5	338.0	240.9	180.8	278.7	223.5	466.3	314.0	214.4	2 404.4	129.3	241.2	2 775.6	102.5	2 878.1
Oct	147.5	331.1	237.8	177.8	271.5	216.6	460.4	306.6	208.4	2 356.8	127.8	236.6	2 722.1	101.8	2 823.9
1994 Jan	145.6	325.1	233.7	174.7	262.3	210.0	451.4	296.7	203.6	2 302.3	126.7	236.0	2 665.8	100.2	2 766.0
Apr	141.6	314.5	227.4	170.7	252.0	200.4	440.4	280.9	194.5	2 221.7	123.3	231.7	2 577.4	98.9	2 676.3
Jul	139.1	304.2	222.7	166.3	242.3	191.0	428.1	268.1	188.1	2 148.8	119.0	227.4	2 496.3	97.2	2 593.5
Oct	136.0	291.7	215.9	160.1	230.5	180.5	415.4	251.1	178.9	2 059.0	112.9	218.1	2 391.1	93.8	2 484.9
1995 Jan	133.0	280.1	210.6	153.2	218.5	172.3	401.4	237.9	171.4	1 977.5	108.3	209.3	2 296.0	91.3	2 387.3
Apr	130.0	270.8	206.8	148.1	211.0	167.1	395.0	229.7	166.0	1 923.8	106.2	200.3	2 231.0	88.6	2 319.6
Jul	128.2	266.1	204.6	145.3	206.9	165.0	390.2	225.1	162.5	1 892.8	106.7	195.3	2 195.9	87.6	2 283.5
Oct	126.4	260.9	200.7	142.3	201.3	160.7	383.2	219.1	159.4	1 852.7	105.4	193.5	2 152.9	85.8	2 238.7
1996 Jan	123.1	255.8	197.0	140.0	196.5	157.2	376.8	213.3	155.6	1 814.6	104.0	193.2	2 112.5	85.9	2 198.4
Apr	121.7	254.9	195.7	137.7	194.2	153.5	367.9	207.6	152.3	1 785.1	104.6	194.9	2 085.0	86.1	2 171.1
Jul	116.9	248.2	188.8	131.8	187.6	146.8	357.5	198.9	146.8	1 722.5	101.8	191.9	2 017.0	86.4	2 103.4
Oct	110.5	238.4	181.1	124.9	177.8	138.5	341.6	185.5	137.9	1 635.0	98.2	186.3	1 920.7	81.7	2 002.4
1997 Jan	101.2	218.6	166.6	111.9	160.1	123.7	313.2	163.6	125.5	1 484.4	90.2	174.0	1 748.6	71.1	1 819.7
Apr	95.1	201.4	154.8	102.5	147.3	110.7	285.1	144.2	112.2	1 353.7	82.5	162.4	1 598.2	65.0	1 663.2
Jul	92.5	188.6	148.3	94.9	137.9	102.2	264.1	130.8	100.7	1 259.9	78.1	152.4	1 490.5	61.3	1 551.8
Oct	90.4	177.6	142.1	87.7	131.7	94.2	246.4	120.4	93.1	1 183.3	73.6	146.5	1 403.7	60.7	1 464.4
1998 Jan	87.8	170.6	137.2	82.6	126.1	88.5	234.5	112.4	88.5	1 128.2	71.0	141.8	1 341.0	59.9	1 400.9
Apr	84.1	165.5	134.1	80.0	122.5	85.2	229.3	108.0	85.1	1 093.8	69.2	138.6	1 301.6	57.9	1 359.5
Jul	81.7	163.7	133.3	80.0	121.2	83.7	225.0	105.4	84.1	1 078.1	68.5	138.3	1 284.9	57.2	1 342.1
Oct	82.1	160.9	131.0	79.9	121.3	82.0	219.4	102.5	81.8	1 060.9	68.1	136.9	1 265.9	56.1	1 322.0
1999 Jan	82.8	159.6	129.6	78.6	122.7	80.3	215.0	101.1	80.9	1 050.6	68.0	135.9	1 254.5	55.9	1 310.4
Apr	82.2	157.4	126.9	78.3	123.2	79.0	207.4	98.9	78.5	1 031.8	67.0	133.8	1 232.6	55.0	1 287.6
Jul	80.0	153.4	122.2	75.9	119.8	76.5	201.8	94.3	74.9	998.8	63.6	128.8	1 191.2	49.9	1 241.1
Oct	76.9	150.0	118.4	73.8	115.8	73.6	196.6	91.2	71.4	967.7	61.1	126.2	1 155.0	46.6	1 201.6
2000 Jan	76.0	145.6	114.4	72.5	112.4	70.1	189.8	86.9	67.5	935.2	59.4	123.6	1 118.2	44.2	1 162.4
Apr	73.4	140.3	108.9	70.4	108.7	66.7	181.3	81.8	64.2	895.7	57.7	119.2	1 072.6	42.4	1 115.0
Jul	71.7	135.0	104.8	68.6	106.7	62.8	171.8	77.8	61.1	860.3	56.7	113.1	1 030.1	41.0	1 071.1
Oct	69.9	131.3	103.0	68.0	106.4	60.7	165.1	74.2	58.2	836.8	56.5	112.2	1 005.5	41.3	1 046.8
2001 Jan	66.5	127.2	99.5	65.7	104.5	56.6	158.7	68.8	54.0	801.5	54.9	109.1	965.5	40.8	1 006.3
Apr	63.2	125.3	98.0	65.3	101.5	55.2	152.4	67.0	53.7	781.7	52.8	105.5	940.0	40.0	980.0
Jul	61.4	121.2	95.4	63.2	96.9	54.1	150.5	65.2	52.3	760.1	50.1	102.2	912.3	39.3	951.6
Oct	61.8	121.5	93.7	62.1	95.4	53.6	155.0	64.9	51.0	758.9	49.2	104.4	912.5	38.7	951.1

1 The figures are based on the number of claimants receiving unemployment related benefits and are adjusted for seasonality and discontinuities to be consistent with current coverage.

2 The latest national and regional seasonally adjusted claimant count figures are provisional and subject to revision in the following month.

Source: Labour Market Statistics, Office for National Statistics: 020 7533 6094

7.15 Economic activity: by age and gender
United Kingdom
At Spring each year. Not seasonally adjusted.

Thousands and percentages

	All aged 16 and over	16-59/64	16-17	18-24	16-24	25-34	35-49	50-64 (m) 50-59 (f)	65+ (m) 60+ (f)
All	**Thousands**								
	BEAM	BEIP	BEIS	BEIV	BEIY	BEJB	BEJE	BEJH	BEJK
1992	28 581	27 734	771	4 508	5 279	7 501	9 890	5 064	847
1993	28 447	27 640	663	4 334	4 997	7 610	9 966	5 068	806
1994	28 455	27 648	679	4 082	4 761	7 696	10 039	5 152	807
1995	28 486	27 673	701	3 916	4 617	7 735	10 130	5 191	813
1996	28 663	27 873	773	3 819	4 593	7 742	10 272	5 267	790
1997	28 852	28 026	812	3 695	4 507	7 773	10 271	5 476	825
1998	28 892	28 097	798	3 612	4 410	7 697	10 319	5 671	795
1999	29 194	28 359	790	3 608	4 398	7 582	10 522	5 858	835
2000	29 412	28 568	792	3 651	4 443	7 403	10 720	6 002	844
2001	29 470	28 643	753	3 647	4 400	7 193	10 904	6 147	827
Men									
	BEAN	BEIQ	BEIT	BEIW	BEIZ	BEJC	BEJF	BEJI	BEJL
1992	16 187	15 871	403	2 467	2 870	4 363	5 439	3 200	316
1993	16 021	15 754	338	2 382	2 721	4 390	5 473	3 170	267
1994	16 000	15 725	350	2 252	2 602	4 441	5 496	3 187	274
1995	16 009	15 713	362	2 158	2 520	4 449	5 558	3 186	296
1996	16 052	15 776	408	2 096	2 504	4 425	5 608	3 239	277
1997	16 098	15 818	407	2 032	2 440	4 421	5 605	3 353	280
1998	16 096	15 813	405	1 973	2 377	4 378	5 619	3 439	283
1999	16 234	15 937	409	1 966	2 375	4 274	5 741	3 548	297
2000	16 327	16 034	404	1 992	2 396	4 177	5 856	3 605	294
2001	16 318	16 045	388	1 985	2 373	4 056	5 928	3 688	273
Women									
	BEAO	BEIR	BEIU	BEIX	BEJA	BEJD	BEJG	BEJJ	BEJM
1992	12 395	11 863	368	2 041	2 409	3 138	4 452	1 864	532
1993	12 426	11 887	324	1 952	2 276	3 220	4 492	1 898	539
1994	12 456	11 923	329	1 830	2 159	3 255	4 543	1 965	533
1995	12 477	11 960	340	1 758	2 097	3 286	4 572	2 004	517
1996	12 611	12 098	365	1 723	2 089	3 316	4 664	2 028	513
1997	12 754	12 208	405	1 663	2 067	3 352	4 666	2 123	545
1998	12 796	12 284	393	1 640	2 033	3 320	4 700	2 232	511
1999	12 960	12 422	380	1 642	2 023	3 308	4 781	2 310	538
2000	13 084	12 534	388	1 660	2 047	3 227	4 863	2 397	550
2001	13 153	12 598	365	1 661	2 027	3 137	4 976	2 459	555
All	**Rates[1]**								
	BEJN	BEAY	BEJQ	BEJT	BEJW	BEJZ	BEKC	BEKF	BEKI
1992	63.1	78.8	55.9	76.7	72.7	82.6	86.0	69.1	8.4
1993	62.7	78.4	50.0	76.3	71.3	82.8	85.5	68.5	7.9
1994	62.6	78.2	52.3	74.5	70.3	83.0	85.2	68.6	8.0
1995	62.4	78.0	52.2	74.2	69.7	83.0	85.0	68.2	8.0
1996	62.5	78.2	54.4	75.2	70.6	82.9	84.9	68.2	7.8
1997	62.7	78.2	55.7	74.7	70.4	83.6	84.5	68.5	8.1
1998	62.5	78.0	54.8	73.7	69.4	83.8	84.3	68.8	7.8
1999	62.9	78.4	54.7	73.5	69.2	84.4	84.9	69.4	8.1
2000	63.1	78.7	55.0	74.0	69.7	84.7	85.1	69.8	8.2
2001	62.9	78.4	51.6	73.1	68.2	84.3	85.1	70.2	8.0
Men									
	BEJO	BEAZ	BEJR	BEJU	BEJX	BEKA	BEKD	BEKG	BEKJ
1992	73.8	86.3	56.9	82.3	77.4	94.9	94.6	73.9	8.9
1993	72.9	85.6	49.7	82.1	76.0	94.4	94.0	72.8	7.5
1994	72.6	85.2	52.5	80.5	75.1	94.5	93.3	72.3	7.6
1995	72.3	84.7	52.4	80.0	74.4	94.1	93.2	71.5	8.2
1996	72.0	84.6	56.0	80.7	75.3	93.3	92.5	71.8	7.6
1997	71.8	84.4	54.6	80.4	74.5	93.5	91.9	72.2	7.6
1998	71.4	83.9	54.4	78.8	73.2	93.5	91.4	72.0	7.7
1999	71.6	84.1	55.3	78.5	73.2	93.3	92.1	72.6	8.0
2000	71.8	84.3	54.8	79.2	73.7	93.8	92.4	72.5	7.9
2001	71.2	83.8	51.9	78.0	72.1	93.2	91.7	73.1	7.2
Women									
	BEJP	BEBJ	BEJS	BEJV	BEJY	BEKB	BEKE	BEKH	BEKK
1992	53.0	70.6	54.7	70.9	67.9	70.0	77.3	62.1	8.1
1993	53.1	70.6	50.2	70.2	66.4	71.0	77.1	62.5	8.2
1994	53.1	70.6	52.1	68.3	65.2	71.2	77.1	63.4	8.1
1995	53.1	70.6	51.9	68.1	64.8	71.6	76.7	63.5	7.9
1996	53.5	71.1	52.7	69.4	65.7	72.2	77.3	63.1	7.9
1997	54.0	71.4	56.9	68.7	66.0	73.4	77.0	63.4	8.4
1998	54.0	71.5	55.3	68.3	65.4	73.7	77.2	64.3	7.8
1999	54.5	72.1	54.0	68.3	65.0	75.1	77.6	64.9	8.2
2000	54.9	72.5	55.2	68.6	65.6	75.3	77.8	66.0	8.4
2001	55.0	72.4	51.3	68.0	64.2	75.1	78.3	66.3	8.5

1 Total economically active (see chapter text for definitions) as a percentage of all persons in the relevant age group.

Source: Labour Force Survey, Office for National Statistics

7.16 Economically inactive: by age and gender
United Kingdom
At Spring each year. Not seasonally adjusted.

Thousands and percentages

	All aged 16 and over	16-59/64	16-17	18-24	16-24	25-34	35-49	50-64 (m) 50-59 (f)	65+ (m) 60+ (f)
	Thousands								
All									
	BEAV	BEKL	BEKO	BEKR	BEKU	BEKX	BELA	BELD	BELG
1992	16 728	7 439	609	1 368	1 978	1 581	1 616	2 264	9 289
1993	16 954	7 602	663	1 349	2 012	1 576	1 687	2 327	9 352
1994	17 032	7 690	619	1 396	2 015	1 578	1 742	2 355	9 343
1995	17 155	7 810	643	1 364	2 007	1 584	1 794	2 425	9 345
1996	17 172	7 790	649	1 261	1 911	1 594	1 828	2 457	9 382
1997	17 184	7 818	646	1 253	1 899	1 523	1 883	2 514	9 367
1998	17 361	7 929	657	1 292	1 949	1 487	1 916	2 576	9 433
1999	17 237	7 818	655	1 302	1 957	1 403	1 872	2 586	9 419
2000	17 169	7 744	649	1 284	1 932	1 338	1 872	2 602	9 425
2001	17 362	7 911	707	1 341	2 048	1 340	1 915	2 609	9 451
Men									
	BEAW	BEKM	BEKP	BEKS	BEKV	BEKY	BELB	BELE	BELH
1992	5 737	2 511	305	532	837	235	312	1 127	3 226
1993	5 964	2 661	342	518	860	262	352	1 187	3 304
1994	6 050	2 735	316	546	863	259	393	1 220	3 315
1995	6 146	2 828	328	540	868	281	409	1 270	3 318
1996	6 230	2 866	321	501	822	319	455	1 270	3 365
1997	6 314	2 926	339	496	835	309	491	1 290	3 388
1998	6 450	3 038	339	531	871	302	526	1 340	3 412
1999	6 423	3 006	330	539	869	306	492	1 339	3 418
2000	6 427	2 987	334	523	857	278	485	1 367	3 440
2001	6 600	3 110	360	559	918	298	536	1 358	3 489
Women									
	BEAX	BEKN	BEKQ	BEKT	BEKW	BEKZ	BELC	BELF	BELI
1992	10 991	4 928	305	837	1 141	1 347	1 304	1 136	6 063
1993	10 989	4 941	321	830	1 152	1 315	1 336	1 140	6 048
1994	10 983	4 955	302	850	1 152	1 320	1 349	1 135	6 028
1995	11 009	4 982	315	824	1 139	1 303	1 385	1 155	6 026
1996	10 942	4 924	328	761	1 089	1 275	1 373	1 188	6 017
1997	10 871	4 892	307	757	1 064	1 214	1 391	1 224	5 978
1998	10 911	4 890	318	760	1 078	1 185	1 390	1 237	6 021
1999	10 813	4 812	324	764	1 088	1 098	1 380	1 247	6 001
2000	10 742	4 758	315	761	1 076	1 060	1 387	1 235	5 985
2001	10 762	4 801	347	782	1 129	1 042	1 379	1 251	5 961
	Rates[1]								
All									
	BELJ	BELM	BELP	BELS	BELV	BELY	BEMB	BEME	BEMH
1992	36.9	21.2	44.1	23.3	27.3	17.4	14.0	30.9	91.6
1993	37.3	21.6	50.0	23.7	28.7	17.2	14.5	31.5	92.1
1994	37.4	21.8	47.7	25.5	29.7	17.0	14.8	31.4	92.0
1995	37.6	22.0	47.8	25.8	30.3	17.0	15.0	31.8	92.0
1996	37.5	21.8	45.6	24.8	29.4	17.1	15.1	31.8	92.2
1997	37.3	21.8	44.3	25.3	29.6	16.4	15.5	31.5	91.9
1998	37.5	22.0	45.2	26.3	30.6	16.2	15.7	31.2	92.2
1999	37.1	21.6	45.3	26.5	30.8	15.6	15.1	30.6	91.9
2000	36.9	21.3	45.0	26.0	30.3	15.3	14.9	30.2	91.8
2001	37.1	21.6	48.4	26.9	31.8	15.7	14.9	29.8	92.0
Men									
	BELK	BELN	BELQ	BELT	BELW	BELZ	BEMC	BEMF	BEMI
1992	26.2	13.7	43.1	17.7	22.6	5.1	5.4	26.1	91.1
1993	27.1	14.4	50.3	17.9	24.0	5.6	6.0	27.2	92.5
1994	27.4	14.8	47.5	19.5	24.9	5.5	6.7	27.7	92.4
1995	27.7	15.3	47.6	20.0	25.6	5.9	6.8	28.5	91.8
1996	28.0	15.4	44.0	19.3	24.7	6.7	7.5	28.2	92.4
1997	28.2	15.6	45.4	19.6	25.5	6.5	8.1	27.8	92.4
1998	28.6	16.1	45.6	21.2	26.8	6.5	8.6	28.0	92.3
1999	28.4	15.9	44.7	21.5	26.8	6.7	7.9	27.4	92.0
2000	28.2	15.7	45.2	20.8	26.3	6.2	7.6	27.5	92.1
2001	28.8	16.2	48.1	22.0	27.9	6.8	8.3	26.9	92.8
Women									
	BELL	BELO	BELR	BELU	BELX	BEMA	BEMD	BEMG	BEMJ
1992	47.0	29.4	45.3	29.1	32.1	30.0	22.7	37.9	91.9
1993	46.9	29.4	49.8	29.8	33.6	29.0	22.9	37.5	91.8
1994	46.9	29.4	47.9	31.7	34.8	28.8	22.9	36.6	91.9
1995	46.9	29.4	48.1	31.9	35.2	28.4	23.3	36.5	92.1
1996	46.5	28.9	47.3	30.6	34.3	27.8	22.7	36.9	92.1
1997	46.0	28.6	43.1	31.3	34.0	26.6	23.0	36.6	91.6
1998	46.0	28.5	44.7	31.7	34.6	26.3	22.8	35.7	92.2
1999	45.5	27.9	46.0	31.7	35.0	24.9	22.4	35.1	91.8
2000	45.1	27.5	44.8	31.4	34.4	24.7	22.2	34.0	91.6
2001	45.0	27.6	48.7	32.0	35.8	24.9	21.7	33.7	91.5

1 Total economically inactive (see chapter text for definitions) as a percentage of all persons in the relevant age group.

Source: Labour Force Survey, Office for National Statistics

7.17 Economically inactive: by reason
United Kingdom
At Spring each year. Not seasonally adjusted.

Thousands

	Total economically inactive	Does not want job[1]	Wants job[1] but not seeking in last 4 weeks								Wants job[1] and seeking work but not available to start[2]		
			Total	Availability to start work in next 2 weeks		Discouraged workers[3]	Long term sick/ disabled	Looking after family/ home	Students	Other	All	Students	Other
				Available	Not available[2]								
All[4]													
	BEKL	BEMK	BEMN	BEMQ	BEMT	BEMW	BEMZ	BENC	BENF	BENI	BENL	BENO	BENR
1995	7 810	5 510	2 017	889	1 128	105	518	763	256	374	283	173	109
1996	7 790	5 450	2 113	864	1 249	102	574	768	280	389	227	138	89
1997	7 818	5 394	2 174	753	1 421	89	686	738	288	373	249	145	104
1998	7 929	5 492	2 176	707	1 468	73	750	738	270	345	261	145	116
1999	7 818	5 456	2 108	663	1 446	70	751	674	264	349	253	140	113
2000	7 744	5 391	2 125	645	1 479	65	770	649	264	378	229	126	102
2001	7 911	5 678	2 001	596	1 405	36	731	630	276	328	231	117	115
Men													
	BEKM	BEML	BEMO	BEMR	BEMU	BEMX	BENA	BEND	BENG	BENJ	BENM	BENP	BENS
1995	2 828	1 969	726	298	428	62	321	49	137	157	133	85	48
1996	2 866	1 950	807	319	488	59	356	68	151	173	109	67	41
1997	2 926	1 965	842	254	587	52	414	69	149	159	119	79	40
1998	3 038	2 029	880	261	619	45	470	74	143	148	130	80	50
1999	3 006	2 037	856	258	598	42	461	71	136	146	113	68	45
2000	2 987	2 020	866	248	618	36	467	64	130	169	101	64	36
2001	3 110	2 159	838	241	597	24	448	67	141	159	113	63	49
Women													
	BEKN	BEMM	BEMP	BEMS	BEMV	BEMY	BENB	BENE	BENH	BENK	BENN	BENQ	BENT
1995	4 982	3 541	1 291	591	700	44	197	714	119	217	149	88	61
1996	4 924	3 500	1 306	545	761	42	218	700	129	216	119	71	48
1997	4 892	3 430	1 333	499	833	38	273	669	139	214	130	66	64
1998	4 890	3 463	1 296	446	850	28	280	664	127	197	131	65	66
1999	4 812	3 420	1 252	405	847	29	291	603	128	202	140	72	68
2000	4 758	3 371	1 259	397	862	29	302	584	134	209	128	62	66
2001	4 801	3 519	1 163	355	808	12	284	563	135	169	119	54	65

1 According to responses to LFS question.
2 Not available to start work in next two weeks including a few people who could not state whether or not they were available.
3 People whose reason for not seeking work was that they believed no jobs were available.
4 All persons of working age (men 16-64, women 16-59).

Source: Labour Force Survey, Office for National Statistics

7.18 Labour disputes
United Kingdom

Thousands and numbers

		1994	1995	1996	1997	1998	1999	2000
SIC 1992								
Working days lost through all stoppages in progress: total	KBBZ	278	415	1 303	235	282	242	499
Analysis by industry								
Mining, quarrying, electricity, gas and water	DMME	1	1	2	2	..	..	3
Manufacturing	DMMF	58	65	97	86	34	57	52
Construction	DMMG	5	10	8	17	13	49	49
Transport, storage and communication	DMMH	110	120	884	36	139	50	97
Public administration and defence	DMMI	11	95	158	29	28	35	50
Education	DMMJ	70	67	128	28	6	25	50
Health and social work	DMMK	5	16	8	7	16	5	122
Other community, social and personal services	DMML	11	23	3	5	30	7	36
All other industries and services	DMMM	8	16	15	25	15	12	40
Analysis by number of working days lost in each stoppage								
Under 250 days	KBFC	11	11	14	12	8	11	12
250 and under 500 days	KBFJ	6	10	13	6	11	13	9
500 and under 1,000 days	KBFL	24	19	13	17	11	16	21
1,000 and under 5,000 days	KBFY	53	82	61	72	48	69	71
5,000 and under 25,000 days	KBFZ	68	195	123	101	118	133	85
25,000 and under 50,000 days	KBGS	..	29	54	26	..	..	..
50,000 days and over	KBGT	117	68	1 025	..	86	..	301
Working days lost per 1 000 employees all industries and services	KBHA	12	18	55	10	11	10	20
Workers directly and indirectly involved: total	KBHB	107	174	364	130	93	141	183
Analysis by industry								
Mining, quarrying, electricity, gas and water	DMMN	–	2	1	..	1	..	1
Manufacturing	DMMO	23	33	34	28	14	31	28
Construction	DMMP	1	2	3	13	2	18	16
Transport, storage and communications	DMMQ	37	54	146	24	39	42	39
Public administration and defence	DMMR	8	28	32	20	4	17	29
Education	DMMS	29	30	122	15	4	28	17
Health and social work	DMMT	2	4	5	5	2	..	28
Other community, social and personal services	DMMU	2	10	2	1	22	2	13
All other industries and services	DMMV	5	11	21	23	4	2	12
Analysis by duration of stoppage								
Not more than 5 days	KBHM	75	142	208	108	57	129	82
Over 5 but not more than 10 days	KBHN	5	11	133	7	32	8	9
Over 10 but not more than 20 days	KBJQ	1	2	4	14	1	3	8
Over 20 but not more than 30 days	KBJR	6	2	3	..	..	..	..
Over 30 but not more than 50 days	KBJS	..	10	16	1	1	..	83
Over 50 days	KBJT	20	7	1	..	1	..	1
Numbers of stoppages in progress: total	KBLG	205	235	244	216	166	205	212
Analysis by industry								
Mining, quarrying, electricity, gas and water	DMMW	1	5	6	1	1	..	3
Manufacturing	DMMX	71	68	67	53	36	37	38
Construction	DMMY	4	9	11	11	13	20	16
Transport, storage and communications	DMMZ	54	56	72	68	57	91	116
Public administration and defence	DMNA	27	26	22	23	10	17	7
Education	DMNB	13	27	35	35	19	21	18
Health and social work	DMNC	7	17	9	7	6	4	10
Other community, social and personal services	DMND	15	19	12	8	17	8	13
All other industries and services	DMNE	14	14	11	12	7	8	5
Analysis of number of stoppages by duration								
Not more than 5 days	KBNH	176	199	196	184	130	179	187
Over 5 but not more than 10 days	KBNI	14	12	20	15	21	8	14
Over 10 but not more than 20 days	KBNJ	6	9	7	8	3	9	5
Over 20 but not more than 30 days	KBNK	5	6	6	2	4	4	1
Over 30 but not more than 50 days	KBNL	1	2	10	6	3	3	3
Over 50 days	KBNM	3	7	5	1	5	2	2

NOTES These figures exclude details of stoppages involving fewer than ten workers or lasting less than one day except any in which the aggregate number of working days lost is 100 or more.

There may be some under-recording of small or short stoppages; this would have much more effect on the total of stoppages than of working days lost.

Some stoppages which affected more than one industry group have been counted under each of the industries but only once in the totals.

Stoppages have been classified using *Standard Industrial Classification (SIC) 1992.*

The figures for working days lost and workers involved have been rounded and consequently the sum of the constituent items may not agree with the totals.

Classifications by size are based on the full duration of stoppages where these continue into the following year.

Working days lost per thousand employees are based on the latest available mid-year (June) estimates of employee jobs.

Source: Labour Market Statistics, Office for National Statistics: 01928 792825

7.18
continued

Labour disputes
United Kingdom

Thousands and numbers

		1994	1995	1996	1997	1998	1999	2000
SIC 1980								
Working days lost through all stoppages in progress: total	KBBZ	278	415	1 303	235	282	242	499
Analysis by industry								
Coal extraction	KBCH	–	..	..	..	..	..	..
Other energy and water	KBCI	–	..	..	..	..	..	..
Metals, minerals and chemicals	KBCJ	8	..	..	..	..	..	..
Engineering and vehicles	KBCK	36	..	..	..	..	..	..
Other manufacturing industries	KBCL	15	..	..	..	..	..	..
Construction	KBCM	5	..	..	..	..	..	..
Transport and communication	KBCN	87	..	..	..	..	..	..
Public administration, sanitary services and education	KBCO	92	..	..	..	..	..	..
Medical and health services	KBDZ	1	..	..	..	..	..	..
All other industries and services	KBEZ	35	..	..	..	..	..	..
Analysis by number of working days lost in each stoppage								
Under 250 days	KBFC	11	11	14	12	8	11	12
250 and under 500 days	KBFJ	6	10	13	6	11	13	9
500 and under 1,000 days	KBFL	24	19	13	17	11	16	21
1,000 and under 5,000 days	KBFY	53	82	61	72	48	69	71
5,000 and under 25,000 days	KBFZ	68	195	123	101	118	133	85
25,000 and under 50,000 days	KBGS	..	29	54	26	..	..	..
50,000 days and over	KBGT	117	68	1 025	..	86	..	301
Working days lost per 1,000 employees all industries and services	KBHA	12	18	55	10	11	10	20
Workers directly and indirectly involved: total	KBHB	107	174	364	130	93	141	183
Analysis by industry								
Coal extraction	KBHC	–	..	..	..	..	..	..
Other energy and water	KBHD	–	..	..	..	..	..	..
Metals, minerals and chemicals	KBHE	2	..	..	..	..	..	..
Engineering and vehicles	KBHF	17	..	..	..	..	..	..
Other manufacturing industries	KBHG	4	..	..	..	..	..	..
Construction	KBHH	1	..	..	..	..	..	..
Transport and communication	KBHI	25	..	..	..	..	..	..
Public admin., sanitary services and education	KBHJ	39	..	..	..	..	..	..
Medical and health services	KBHK	1	..	..	..	..	..	..
All other industries and services	KBHL	18	..	..	..	..	..	..
Analysis by duration of stoppage								
Not more than 5 days	KBHM	75	142	208	108	57	129	82
Over 5 but not more than 10 days	KBHN	5	11	133	7	32	8	9
Over 10 but not more than 20 days	KBJQ	1	2	4	14	1	3	8
Over 20 but not more than 30 days	KBJR	6	2	3	..	..	..	..
Over 30 but not more than 50 days	KBJS	..	10	16	1	1	..	83
Over 50 days	KBJT	20	7	1	..	1	..	1
Numbers of stoppages in progress: total	KBLG	205	235	244	216	166	205	212
Analysis by industry								
Coal extraction	KBLR	–	..	..	..	..	..	..
Other energy and water	KBLS	–	..	..	..	..	..	..
Metals, minerals and chemicals	KBLT	14	..	..	..	..	..	..
Engineering and vehicles	KBLU	42	..	..	..	..	..	..
Other manufacturing industries	KBLV	16	..	..	..	..	..	..
Construction	KBLW	4	..	..	..	..	..	..
Transport and communication	KBLX	52	..	..	..	..	..	..
Public admin., sanitary services and education	KBLY	55	..	..	..	..	..	..
Medical and health services	KBLZ	2	..	..	..	..	..	..
All other industries and services	KBNG	21	..	..	..	..	..	..
Analysis of number of stoppages by duration								
Not more than 5 days	KBNH	176	199	196	184	130	179	187
Over 5 but not more than 10 days	KBNI	14	12	20	15	21	8	14
Over 10 but not more than 20 days	KBNJ	6	9	7	8	3	9	5
Over 20 but not more than 30 days	KBNK	5	6	6	2	4	4	1
Over 30 but not more than 50 days	KBNL	1	2	10	6	3	3	3
Over 50 days	KBNM	3	7	5	1	5	2	2

NOTES These figures exclude details of stoppages involving fewer than ten workers or lasting less than one day except any in which the aggregate number of working days lost is 100 or more.

There may be some under-recording of small or short stoppages; this would have much more effect on the total of stoppages than of working days lost.

Some stoppages which affected more than one industry group have been counted under each of the industries but only once in the totals.

Stoppages have been classified using *Standard Industrial Classification (SIC) 1980*, although data are only available for this industrial classification to 1994

The figures for working days lost and workers involved have been rounded and consequently the sum of the constituent items may not agree with the totals. Classifications by size are based on the full duration of stoppages where these continue into the following year.

Working days lost per thousand employees are based on the latest available mid-year (June) estimates of employee jobs.

Source: Labour Market Statistics, Office for National Statistics: 01928 792825

7.19 Average earnings and hours of manual employees by industry division
Full time employees on adult rates: pay unaffected by absence: Great Britain
At April

	Agriculture, Hunting and Forestry	Fishing	Mining and Quarrying	Manufacturing	Electricity, Gas and Water Supply	Construction	Wholesale and Retail Trade; repair of motor vehicles, cycles, personal and household goods
Standard Industrial Classification: Revised 1992							
Full-time manual men							
Weekly earnings							
	KOTK	KOTL	KOTM	KOTN	KOTO	KOTP	KOTQ
1996	241.2	..	367.8	323.6	399.7	308.2	264.1
1997	252.1	..	400.5	337.5	401.2	324.8	275.1
1998	260.3	..	408.3	352.6	418.6	342.3	292.2
1999	272.4	..	396.0	354.6	440.5	351.3	299.4
2000	270.6	..	393.6	364.0	453.3	369.1	308.1
Hours worked							
	KOTZ	KPFV	KOUA	KOUB	KOUC	KOUD	KOUE
1996	47.5	46.5	50.8	44.2	42.6	45.8	44.4
1997	47.8	47.0	52.0	44.5	42.1	46.9	44.0
1998	47.0	..	50.1	44.3	42.5	46.9	44.3
1999	47.5	..	51.7	43.5	42.8	46.4	43.9
2000	45.8	..	48.7	43.6	41.5	46.6	43.8
Hourly earnings							
	KOUN	KPFW	KOUO	KOUP	KOUQ	KOUR	KOUS
1996	5.06	..	7.15	7.29	9.38	6.71	5.91
1997	5.27	..	7.70	7.58	9.45	6.92	6.26
1998	5.54	..	8.14	7.96	9.85	7.29	6.59
1999	5.75	..	7.66	8.15	10.30	7.56	6.84
2000	5.91	..	8.08	8.35	10.93	7.92	7.03
Full-time manual women							
Weekly earnings							
	KOYL	KPFX	KOYM	KOYN	KOYO	KOYP	KOYQ
1996	177.9	..	..	205.0	..	..	185.4
1997	186.9	..	..	214.1	..	..	194.1
1998	185.7	..	..	224.2	..	..	203.6
1999	199.0	..	..	231.7	..	..	215.3
2000	225.1	..	..	240.0	..	..	213.4
Hours worked							
	KOYZ	KPFY	KOZA	KOZB	KOZC	KOZD	KOZE
1996	41.3	..	..	40.7	..	..	40.0
1997	40.9	..	42.6	40.8	38.1	43.8	40.3
1998	42.0	..	..	40.7	..	..	40.3
1999	41.8	..	..	40.4	..	..	39.9
2000	41.9	..	..	40.4	..	..	39.2
Hourly earnings							
	KOZN	KOZO	KOZP	KOZQ	KOZR	KOZS	KOZT
1996	4.33	..	..	5.04	..	..	4.63
1997	4.50	..	..	5.26	..	5.54	4.81
1998	4.43	..	..	5.52	..	..	5.06
1999	4.74	..	..	5.74	..	..	5.44
2000	5.37	..	..	5.94	..	..	5.45
Full-time manual adults							
Weekly earnings							
	KPBO	KPFZ	KPBP	KPBQ	KPBR	KPBS	KPBT
1996	234.7	..	366.5	300.8	398.5	307.0	253.5
1997	245.4	..	398.9	314.6	399.6	323.4	264.3
1998	251.7	..	403.8	329.9	416.2	340.9	280.3
1999	264.1	..	392.5	333.7	439.5	350.9	287.7
2000	265.6	..	392.3	343.5	452.8	368.6	295.2
Hours worked							
	KPCT	KPGA	KPCU	KPCV	KPCW	KPCX	KPCY
1996	46.9	46.5	50.8	43.5	42.6	45.8	43.9
1997	47.1	47.0	51.9	43.8	42.0	46.8	43.5
1998	46.4	..	49.9	43.7	42.4	46.9	43.8
1999	46.8	..	51.6	43.0	42.7	46.4	43.4
2000	45.4	..	48.7	43.1	41.4	46.5	43.2
Hourly earnings							
	KPDV	KPGB	KPDW	KPDX	KPDY	KPDZ	KPFA
1996	5.00	..	7.15	6.88	9.36	6.70	5.75
1997	5.20	5.42	7.69	7.18	9.42	6.90	6.08
1998	5.42	..	8.07	7.56	9.81	7.27	6.40
1999	5.65	..	7.61	7.77	10.29	7.56	6.66
2000	5.86	..	8.06	7.98	10.93	7.92	6.84

7.19 Average earnings and hours of manual employees by industry division
Full time employees on adult rates: pay unaffected by absence: Great Britain
continued — At April

	Hotels and restaurants	Transport, Storage and Communication	Financial Inter-mediation	Real Estate, Renting and Business	Public Administration and Defence; compulsory social security	Educa-tion	Health and Social work	Other community, social and personal service activities
Standard Industrial Classification: Revised 1992								
Full-time manual men								
Weekly earnings								
	KOTR	KOTS	KOTT	KOTU	KOTV	KOTW	KOTX	KOTY
1996	203.3	314.9	373.8	275.6	275.4	243.5	241.3	264.4
1997	213.9	328.4	381.6	292.4	281.2	268.7	250.7	280.2
1998	227.0	344.0	394.8	302.7	289.0	277.9	264.4	289.0
1999	230.5	359.6	377.9	312.3	307.5	285.2	267.7	300.8
2000	240.3	367.0	386.0	322.8	311.0	289.6	283.6	301.2
Hours worked								
	KOUF	KOUG	KOUH	KOUI	KOUJ	KOUK	KOUL	KOUM
1996	42.1	47.6	42.5	46.4	42.4	41.7	41.8	44.0
1997	41.9	48.5	42.1	46.7	42.3	41.5	42.4	44.3
1998	42.5	48.0	42.5	46.4	41.9	41.7	42.1	44.8
1999	42.1	47.5	39.9	45.5	42.2	40.8	41.8	44.8
2000	41.8	47.4	39.8	44.8	41.3	40.2	41.8	43.4
Hourly earnings								
	KOUT	KOYE	KOYF	KOYG	KOYH	KOYI	KOYJ	KOYK
1996	4.83	6.60	8.76	5.94	6.50	5.83	5.78	6.03
1997	5.10	6.77	9.07	6.27	6.66	6.48	5.92	6.33
1998	5.34	7.17	9.28	6.53	6.90	6.67	6.26	6.47
1999	5.48	7.56	9.46	6.86	7.30	7.00	6.41	6.72
2000	5.74	7.75	9.72	7.20	7.56	7.22	6.91	6.95
Full-time manual women								
Weekly earnings								
	KOYR	KOYS	KOYT	KOYU	KOYV	KOYW	KOYX	KOYY
1996	156.7	286.7	..	199.6	214.6	167.3	175.5	166.6
1997	160.5	278.3	..	205.3	218.5	197.1	178.5	176.0
1998	170.8	292.7	..	211.9	232.2	203.7	187.2	178.1
1999	180.5	311.5	..	221.5	232.3	223.0	199.5	197.4
2000	184.7	320.3	..	234.6	239.2	226.9	204.2	204.6
Hours worked								
	KOZF	KOZG	KOZH	KOZI	KOZJ	KOZK	KOZL	KOZM
1996	39.4	42.4	37.9	41.6	39.6	38.6	39.1	40.0
1997	39.2	42.2	37.5	41.8	39.4	38.8	39.1	39.7
1998	39.4	42.0	..	41.4	39.6	38.3	39.3	39.6
1999	39.3	41.5	..	40.4	38.6	38.0	39.1	39.8
2000	39.2	41.7	..	40.4	38.4	37.9	39.2	39.3
Hourly earnings								
	KOZU	KOZV	KOZW	KOZX	KOZY	KOZZ	KPBN	KTDJ
1996	3.98	6.29	..	4.81	5.43	4.35	4.49	4.17
1997	4.07	6.52	6.14	4.92	5.57	5.05	4.56	4.45
1998	4.30	6.98	..	5.08	5.89	5.32	4.75	4.50
1999	4.55	7.52	..	5.48	6.09	5.86	5.10	4.94
2000	4.72	7.69	..	5.82	6.38	6.00	5.24	5.25
Full-time manual adults								
Weekly earnings								
	KPBU	KPBV	KPBW	KPBX	KPBY	KPBZ	KPCR	KPCS
1996	182.4	312.5	349.7	264.6	264.7	220.0	199.7	241.8
1997	190.6	324.8	355.6	278.2	271.4	244.3	208.1	249.1
1998	203.6	340.0	367.3	289.1	280.7	254.8	218.9	258.3
1999	210.3	355.7	353.6	298.2	296.9	266.0	227.8	273.8
2000	217.1	363.3	359.6	308.7	301.3	270.3	237.2	274.1
Hours worked								
	KPCZ	KPDO	KPDP	KPDQ	KPDR	KPDS	KPDT	KPDU
1996	40.9	47.3	41.7	45.7	41.9	40.8	40.1	43.0
1997	40.7	48.1	41.3	45.9	41.8	40.6	40.5	42.9
1998	41.2	47.6	41.6	45.6	41.6	40.7	40.5	43.3
1999	41.0	47.0	39.7	44.7	41.7	40.0	40.2	43.5
2000	40.7	46.9	39.5	44.1	40.8	39.5	40.0	42.2
Hourly earnings								
	KPFB	KPFC	KPFD	KPFE	KPFF	KPFG	KPFT	KPFU
1996	4.46	6.58	8.34	5.80	6.32	5.39	4.99	5.63
1997	4.67	6.76	8.61	6.07	6.50	6.02	5.14	5.82
1998	4.93	7.16	8.84	6.33	6.76	6.27	5.40	5.97
1999	5.12	7.56	8.92	6.67	7.15	6.66	5.66	6.29
2000	5.33	7.74	9.11	7.00	7.41	6.86	5.95	6.51

Source: New Earnings Survey, Office for National Statistics: 01633 819024

7.20 Average weekly and hourly earnings and hours of full-time employees on adult rates: Great Britain

At April

	All Industries				Manufacturing industries			
			Average hourly earnings				Average hourly earnings	
	Average weekly earnings[1]	Average hours	including overtime	excluding overtime	Average weekly earnings	Average hours	including overtime	excluding overtime
	£		£	£	£		£	£
All adults								
	KBRZ	KBSA	KIUY	KIUZ	KBSD	KBSE	KIVO	KIVP
1996	351.7	40.2	8.71	8.72	349.2	41.9	8.29	8.22
1997	367.6	40.3	9.10	9.13	361.7	42.0	8.60	8.53
1998	384.5	40.2	9.53	9.54	384.5	41.8	9.17	9.10
1999	400.1	40.0	10.01	10.03	395.3	41.4	9.55	9.49
2000	410.6	39.8	10.32	10.28	407.0	41.3	9.84	9.72
All men								
	KBSH	KBSI	KIVQ	KIWR	KBSL	KBSM	KIWS	KIWT
1996	391.6	41.7	9.34	9.39	380.0	42.7	8.86	8.81
1997	408.7	41.8	9.74	9.82	392.7	42.8	9.16	9.12
1998	427.1	41.7	10.20	10.26	416.8	42.6	9.75	9.72
1999	442.4	41.4	10.68	10.75	424.6	42.0	10.10	10.06
2000	453.3	41.2	11.00	11.00	436.0	42.0	10.37	10.26
Manual men								
	KFHX	KFHY	KIWU	KIWV	KFJT	KFJU	KIWW	KIWX
1996	301.3	44.8	6.70	6.51	323.6	44.2	7.29	7.05
1997	314.3	45.1	6.97	6.79	337.5	44.5	7.58	7.34
1998	328.5	45.0	7.30	7.10	352.6	44.3	7.96	7.71
1999	335.0	44.4	7.54	7.36	354.6	43.5	8.15	7.92
2000	343.9	44.3	7.78	7.51	364.0	43.6	8.35	8.04
Non-manual men								
	KFJX	KFJY	KIWY	KIWZ	KFMU	KFMV	KIXO	KIXP
1996	464.5	39.1	11.83	11.87	479.6	39.9	11.95	12.00
1997	483.5	39.1	12.33	12.39	489.2	39.8	12.28	12.32
1998	506.1	39.1	12.90	12.94	525.9	39.8	13.17	13.23
1999	525.5	39.0	13.49	13.52	541.6	39.6	13.68	13.73
2000	533.9	38.8	13.74	13.72	550.6	39.5	13.92	13.91
All women								
	KBTF	KBTG	KIXQ	KIXR	KBTJ	KBTK	KIXS	KIXT
1996	283.0	37.6	7.51	7.50	246.7	39.3	6.27	6.23
1997	297.2	37.6	7.88	7.88	258.8	39.2	6.60	6.56
1998	309.6	37.6	8.23	8.22	274.5	39.2	7.01	6.97
1999	326.5	37.5	8.71	8.70	292.1	39.0	7.49	7.46
2000	337.6	37.4	9.02	8.98	303.5	38.9	7.80	7.74
Manual women								
	KFMY	KFMZ	KIXU	KIXV	KFPS	KFPT	KIXW	KIXX
1996	195.2	40.2	4.81	4.72	205.0	40.7	5.04	4.92
1997	201.1	40.2	4.99	4.90	214.1	40.8	5.26	5.13
1998	210.8	40.2	5.23	5.14	224.2	40.7	5.52	5.39
1999	221.9	39.9	5.56	5.48	231.7	40.4	5.74	5.62
2000	227.9	39.8	5.74	5.63	240.0	40.4	5.94	5.78
Non-manual women								
	KFRY	KFRZ	KIXY	KIYA	KFUY	KFUZ	KIYB	KIYC
1996	302.4	37.1	8.16	8.14	289.4	37.9	7.64	7.61
1997	317.8	37.1	8.56	8.55	300.0	37.8	7.94	7.92
1998	330.1	37.0	8.90	8.89	317.2	37.9	8.38	8.36
1999	346.9	37.0	9.37	9.36	341.5	37.9	9.02	9.01
2000	357.5	36.9	9.67	9.62	352.4	37.8	9.34	9.31

1 Excluding those whose pay was affected by absence.

Source: New Earnings Survey, Office for National Statistics: 01633 819024

7.21 Average earnings index: all employees: main industrial sectors
Great Britain
Analyses by industry based on Standard Industrial Classification 1992

1995 = 100

Unadjusted

	Annual averages	Jan-uary	Feb-ruary	March	April	May	June	July	August	Sept-ember	Oct-ober	Nov-ember	Dec-ember
Whole economy (Divisions 01 - 93)													
LNMM													
1999	119.0	115.7	118.7	122.5	117.4	117.8	119.0	119.3	117.6	117.6	118.1	119.1	124.9
2000	124.3	123.2	125.3	129.3	122.5	122.4	123.3	123.6	122.5	122.2	122.7	124.0	131.1
2001	..	128.6	133.8	134.7	128.4	127.6	129.2	128.8	127.8	127.6	..	..	..
Manufacturing industries (Divisions 15 - 37)													
LNMN													
1999	118.3	115.1	116.7	120.7	117.5	116.7	117.1	118.7	117.0	117.4	119.0	120.3	123.7
2000	123.8	121.8	122.1	126.1	122.8	122.7	122.4	124.0	121.8	122.6	123.9	125.8	129.6
2001	..	126.3	128.3	132.7	129.0	128.4	128.2	129.3	127.4	127.9	..	..	..
Production industries (Divisions 10 - 41)													
LNMO													
1999	117.8	114.7	116.3	120.4	117.3	116.4	116.6	118.2	116.5	116.8	118.3	119.5	122.8
2000	122.9	121.2	121.6	125.4	122.0	121.9	121.8	123.0	120.9	121.6	122.8	124.7	128.4
2001	..	125.4	127.9	131.8	128.1	127.3	127.5	128.1	126.3	126.6	..	..	..
Service industries (Divisions 50 - 93)													
LNMP													
1999	119.2	115.9	119.5	123.1	117.3	118.2	119.6	119.5	117.7	117.4	117.7	118.6	125.2
2000	124.5	123.7	126.5	130.2	122.4	122.3	123.5	123.5	122.8	121.9	122.3	123.4	131.6
2001	..	129.5	135.8	135.4	128.1	127.2	129.1	128.4	127.7	127.2	..	..	..
Private sector services (unadjusted) (Divisions 50-99)													
JJGF													
1999	121.4	115.9	119.5	123.1	117.3	118.2	119.6	119.5	117.7	117.4	117.7	118.6	125.2
2000	127.2	123.7	126.5	130.2	122.4	122.3	123.5	123.5	122.8	121.9	122.3	123.4	131.6
2001	..	129.5	135.8	135.4	128.1	127.2	129.1	128.4	127.7	127.2	..	..	..

Seasonally adjusted

	Annual averages	Jan-uary	Feb-ruary	March	April	May	June	July	August	Sept-ember	Oct-ober	Nov-ember	Dec-ember
Whole economy (Divisions 01 - 93)													
LNMQ													
1999	119.0	115.8	116.6	117.3	117.5	118.3	119.0	119.4	119.9	120.3	121.0	121.3	121.9
2000	124.5	122.9	122.8	123.4	122.8	123.2	123.5	124.2	125.0	125.4	126.0	126.6	127.7
2001	..	128.0	131.0	128.5	128.7	128.8	129.5	129.7	130.4	131.0	..	..	..
Manufacturing industries (Divisions 15 - 37)													
LNMR													
1999	118.3	115.8	116.0	116.6	117.0	117.2	117.8	118.5	119.2	119.5	120.2	120.5	121.1
2000	123.7	122.2	121.3	121.7	122.2	123.2	123.1	123.7	124.1	125.0	125.3	126.1	126.9
2001	..	126.9	127.6	128.2	128.6	129.0	129.3	129.4	130.0	130.3	..	..	..
Production industries (Divisions 10 - 41)													
LNMS													
1999	117.8	115.5	115.6	116.2	116.7	116.8	117.2	117.9	118.6	118.9	119.6	119.8	120.4
2000	122.9	121.7	120.7	120.9	121.2	122.3	122.2	122.8	123.2	124.1	124.4	125.1	125.7
2001	..	125.9	126.8	127.2	127.5	127.8	128.3	128.3	128.8	129.1	..	..	..
Service industries (Divisions 50 - 93)													
LNMT													
1999	119.3	115.7	116.7	117.5	117.6	118.9	119.4	119.8	120.1	120.6	121.2	121.5	122.1
2000	124.7	123.1	123.0	123.7	123.0	123.3	123.6	124.4	125.4	125.6	126.3	126.8	127.9
2001	..	128.3	132.0	128.6	128.7	128.7	129.4	129.6	130.4	131.1	..	..	..
Private sector services (seasonally adjusted) (Divisions 50-93)													
JJGH													
1999	121.5	115.7	116.7	117.5	117.6	118.9	119.4	119.8	120.1	120.6	121.2	121.5	
2000	127.3	123.1	123.0	123.7	123.0	123.3	123.6	124.4	125.4	125.6	126.3	126.8	
2001	..	128.3	132.0	128.6	128.7	128.7	129.4	129.6	130.4	131.1	..	..	

Note: The Average Earnings Index has been revised. More information is available on the website, www.statistics.gov.uk, and helpline.

Source: Office for National Statistics: 01633 819002

7.22 Average earnings index[1] excluding bonus payments: all employee jobs: by industry (unadjusted)

Great Britain

March 1996 = 100

	Agriculture[2], forestry and fishing	Mining and quarrying	Food products, beverages and tobacco	Textiles	Clothing, leather and footwear	Wood, wood products and other manufacturing n.e.c.	Pulp, paper products, printing and publishing	Chemicals and chemical products	Rubber and plastic products	Other non-metallic mineral products	Basic metals	Fabricated metal products (excluding machinery)	Machinery and equipment n.e.c.
SIC 1992 Class	(01,02,05)	(10-14)	(15,16)	(17)	(18-19)	(20,23,36,37)	(21,22)	(24)	(25)	(26)	(27)	(28)	(29)
	LOTJ	LOTK	LOTL	LOTM	LOTN	LOTO	LOTP	LOTQ	LOTR	LOTS	LOTT	LOTU	LOTV
1997	..	104.8	103.6	105.1	105.0	107.0	104.4	105.2	105.4	105.1	107.7	104.8	105.1
1998	..	108.8	108.1	107.3	109.2	111.6	108.5	111.5	110.5	109.4	113.0	108.3	109.4
1999	..	109.8	110.0	111.2	111.8	114.7	112.8	119.0	113.7	113.1	115.8	109.3	111.8
2000	..	112.7	114.6	114.5	109.3	121.6	116.1	124.2	117.6	119.1	124.1	111.5	117.0
1997 May	..	104.7	103.1	104.0	105.2	106.2	102.9	104.2	104.4	104.4	107.0	104.0	104.5
Jun	..	104.7	103.3	105.1	105.5	106.7	103.8	105.0	104.8	105.2	107.1	104.4	105.6
Jul	..	105.0	103.8	105.6	105.6	107.1	104.2	105.1	105.5	105.4	108.1	104.8	105.6
Aug	..	104.8	103.8	105.8	105.2	106.5	105.0	105.4	105.8	105.5	107.4	104.7	105.7
Sep	..	104.6	103.9	105.4	104.9	106.8	105.6	105.5	106.1	105.5	108.6	105.1	105.2
Oct	..	104.0	103.9	105.6	104.8	107.4	106.4	105.9	106.0	106.0	108.0	105.3	105.2
Nov	..	104.8	104.6	106.6	105.2	109.1	106.5	106.4	106.7	106.6	109.0	106.3	105.7
Dec	..	106.1	105.6	107.0	105.3	110.0	106.4	107.5	107.1	107.2	109.2	106.7	106.8
1998 Jan	..	106.4	105.9	106.4	105.8	110.7	105.8	108.2	107.7	107.7	109.5	106.9	107.0
Feb	..	106.8	105.9	105.3	106.5	110.6	105.5	109.0	108.0	108.0	110.0	107.0	107.4
Mar	..	106.8	105.9	105.0	107.7	111.2	105.6	109.1	108.6	108.0	110.3	107.1	107.6
Apr	..	108.0	106.6	105.8	108.6	111.8	106.4	109.6	109.6	108.2	112.0	108.0	108.5
May	..	108.7	107.7	106.3	109.1	112.6	107.4	110.0	110.4	108.6	113.1	108.6	109.0
Jun	..	108.9	108.4	107.5	109.4	112.1	108.0	110.9	110.5	109.1	113.5	108.8	109.5
Jul	..	108.7	108.8	107.7	109.8	112.2	108.3	111.3	110.4	109.8	114.4	108.9	110.1
Aug	..	108.4	108.2	108.2	109.7	111.4	108.7	111.8	110.5	110.1	114.6	108.7	110.5
Sep	..	108.7	108.2	107.8	109.8	111.3	109.3	111.7	111.2	110.2	114.8	108.8	110.4
Oct	..	109.3	108.0	107.9	109.4	110.9	110.1	112.1	111.5	110.0	114.1	108.2	110.1
Nov	..	110.0	109.0	108.7	109.8	111.8	110.7	112.9	111.7	110.3	113.7	108.4	110.0
Dec	..	110.6	109.9	108.7	109.8	111.9	111.1	114.5	111.7	110.5	113.4	108.5	110.0
1999 Jan[4]	..	110.7	110.1	108.6	110.2	111.6	111.4	115.3	111.7	110.4	111.7	108.6	109.9
1999 Feb[4]	..	109.8	109.6	107.5	110.0	111.1	111.1	115.6	111.6	110.1	110.9	108.0	109.7
Mar	..	109.1	109.1	107.4	110.5	111.3	110.7	115.5	111.4	110.5	111.4	107.7	109.6
Apr	..	108.8	108.9	107.9	110.4	111.8	110.7	116.6	111.4	111.4	112.0	108.1	110.1
May	..	109.1	109.3	109.2	110.9	112.6	111.2	117.4	111.8	112.2	114.0	108.7	110.7
Jun	..	109.4	109.5	110.6	111.0	113.4	111.8	118.5	112.2	112.6	115.2	109.5	111.3
Jul	..	109.4	109.8	111.6	111.4	114.3	112.1	118.7	112.5	113.0	117.0	110.0	111.7
Aug	..	109.7	110.0	112.3	111.1	115.0	112.7	119.1	113.3	113.6	117.2	109.8	112.0
Sep	..	109.8	110.3	112.3	111.5	116.0	113.4	119.8	114.2	114.1	117.4	110.0	112.0
Oct	..	110.3	110.6	113.0	112.1	116.8	114.2	120.2	115.6	114.4	117.2	110.0	112.4
Nov	..	110.9	110.8	113.7	113.6	117.7	114.6	121.1	116.8	114.6	118.4	110.7	113.4
Dec	..	111.0	111.2	114.4	114.1	118.3	115.2	122.2	117.1	115.2	119.1	110.1	114.3
2000 Jan	..	111.3	111.8	113.4	112.0	118.1	114.8	122.9	116.9	116.3	120.5	110.0	114.4
Feb	..	111.4	112.4	112.4	110.9	118.3	114.5	123.0	115.5	117.8	120.5	110.0	114.6
Mar	..	112.1	113.1	111.8	108.6	118.6	114.1	122.9	115.0	118.5	120.6	110.6	115.1
Apr	..	112.1	114.6	112.0	108.7	119.3	114.4	123.3	114.7	119.3	120.6	110.4	116.0
May	..	112.0	115.8	112.6	107.2	119.2	115.0	123.6	115.7	120.2	121.4	110.8	116.3
Jun	..	111.9	116.1	113.5	107.6	119.6	115.2	123.7	117.0	120.6	122.8	111.0	117.1
Jul	..	112.3	114.8	114.7	108.0	120.3	115.6	123.8	118.3	120.1	125.8	111.9	117.8
Aug	..	112.5	113.9	115.2	108.2	121.4	115.7	124.0	118.6	119.0	126.7	111.4	118.0
Sep	..	112.7	113.7	115.6	109.0	122.3	116.9	124.2	118.9	118.5	127.1	111.2	117.5
Oct	..	113.0	113.9	116.2	109.7	123.4	117.7	124.3	118.7	118.3	125.4	111.6	117.4
Nov	..	114.0	114.7	117.4	111.3	124.7	118.5	124.8	119.4	118.3	126.2	112.7	117.9
Dec	..	114.1	115.5	117.1	112.0	125.9	118.3	126.0	119.3	118.9	125.9	113.2	118.4
2001 Jan	..	113.9	116.2	117.2	112.5	126.7	118.4	127.1	119.7	119.4	125.8	113.1	118.7
Feb	..	113.7	116.4	116.7	113.3	126.8	118.2	127.8	119.6	120.5	124.9	113.1	119.1
Mar	..	114.5	116.7	117.6	113.4	127.1	118.3	128.7	119.9	120.7	125.9	113.7	119.7
Apr	..	115.1	118.0	117.5	113.9	128.4	119.1	128.8	120.1	121.1	126.3	115.0	120.3
May	..	115.5	119.3	118.1	113.8	129.9	120.0	129.0	121.2	120.9	127.2	116.5	120.6
Jun	..	115.8	120.1	118.6	113.6	131.5	120.7	129.3	122.1	121.3	127.3	118.2	121.1
Jul	..	116.4	120.0	119.2	114.0	131.9	120.8	130.1	122.8	121.1	127.9	118.7	121.5
Aug	..	116.1	119.8	118.9	114.1	131.9	121.1	130.5	122.5	121.1	128.5	118.3	121.2
Sep	..	116.0	119.5	119.1	114.4	131.6	122.1	130.4	122.7	121.0	128.6	117.6	120.9

7.22 continued

Average earnings index[1] excluding bonus payments: all employee jobs: by industry (unadjusted)

Great Britain

March 1996 = 100

	Electrical and optical equipment	Transport equipment	Electrici-ty, gas and water supply	Construct-ion	Wholesale trade	Retail trade and repairs	Hotels and restaur-ants	Transport, storage and communi-cation	Financial intermedi-ation	Real estate, renting and business activities	Public administr-ation	Education, health and social work[3]	Other services
SIC 1992 Class	(30-33)	(34,35)	(40,41)	(45)	(51)	(50,52)	(55)	(60-64)	(65-67)	(70-74)	(75)	(80-85)	(90-93)
	LOTW	LOTX	LOTY	LOTZ	LOUA	LOUB	LOUC	LOUD	LOUE	LOUF	LOUG	LOUH	LOUI
1997	105.7	101.6	101.0	103.4	104.9	97.9	106.3	103.9	106.7	104.1	101.0	104.6	106.2
1998	110.1	106.3	103.9	110.4	110.8	101.8	110.8	107.9	113.3	110.3	103.5	107.6	114.8
1999	116.5	110.7	102.1	115.0	113.8	103.0	117.4	109.5	118.0	115.2	106.0	112.9	121.9
2000	124.2	116.4	100.3	121.7	118.2	105.9	124.4	113.3	124.4	121.3	109.8	117.6	130.4
1997 May	105.0	100.9	100.4	102.1	104.1	98.1	104.5	102.4	105.5	103.1	100.0	103.8	104.6
Jun	105.6	100.9	101.2	102.4	104.5	97.6	104.9	102.5	106.5	103.5	99.8	104.1	103.4
Jul	106.4	101.4	101.6	103.1	104.9	98.2	106.2	102.9	107.2	104.2	99.9	104.6	103.8
Aug	106.6	101.2	101.0	103.1	105.2	98.6	106.9	103.7	107.7	104.3	100.5	105.6	105.2
Sep	106.5	101.5	101.0	103.7	105.5	99.0	107.1	105.1	107.9	104.5	101.1	106.5	107.1
Oct	106.2	101.7	101.1	104.2	105.7	98.8	107.2	105.2	108.1	104.6	101.9	106.3	108.5
Nov	106.6	103.0	102.1	105.3	105.9	98.4	107.1	105.8	108.2	105.0	102.5	105.4	109.3
Dec	107.1	104.0	102.5	106.0	106.9	98.2	108.8	106.3	108.7	105.8	102.9	104.8	110.2
1998 Jan	107.1	104.5	102.5	106.4	107.4	98.5	109.9	107.0	109.3	107.0	102.6	104.8	110.7
Feb	107.5	104.8	102.2	106.8	107.9	99.0	110.4	107.3	110.0	108.2	102.5	104.9	110.9
Mar	107.7	105.0	102.3	107.1	107.8	99.2	109.5	107.3	110.7	108.8	102.8	104.5	111.6
Apr	108.6	105.7	103.2	107.7	108.8	99.8	109.3	108.6	111.3	109.2	102.9	104.9	112.9
May	109.0	106.0	103.9	108.3	109.9	101.1	109.9	109.1	112.3	109.7	102.9	105.6	113.7
Jun	109.4	106.5	104.1	109.0	111.0	102.1	110.4	107.5	113.2	110.1	102.9	106.7	113.7
Jul	110.0	107.0	104.3	110.1	111.6	102.9	110.9	106.1	113.8	110.4	103.4	107.7	114.1
Aug	110.4	107.0	104.3	111.0	111.9	103.0	110.8	105.9	113.9	110.1	103.8	108.9	115.6
Sep	110.7	106.5	104.6	111.9	112.0	103.3	110.8	108.0	114.1	110.4	103.7	109.8	116.7
Oct	111.0	106.2	104.5	112.4	112.1	102.8	110.7	108.3	114.4	110.5	104.1	109.9	117.0
Nov	111.6	106.4	104.5	113.3	112.2	102.5	111.0	109.3	114.9	111.3	104.3	109.5	117.0
Dec	112.5	107.0	104.5	113.5	112.5	102.6	112.7	108.9	115.4	112.0	104.7	109.5	117.3
1999 Jan[4]	112.9	107.3	103.7	113.6	112.5	103.4	113.7	109.3	115.8	113.1	104.8	109.8	117.2
1999 Feb[4]	113.2	107.5	102.5	113.0	112.4	103.1	113.8	109.5	115.7	113.7	104.8	110.2	117.1
Mar	113.5	107.7	101.4	113.0	112.4	102.1	112.9	109.8	115.9	114.2	105.0	109.9	117.3
Apr	114.0	108.9	102.2	113.0	113.1	101.6	113.4	109.8	116.5	114.6	105.0	110.4	117.7
May	114.6	109.7	103.8	113.3	113.6	102.1	115.2	108.6	117.6	115.2	105.1	111.2	118.3
Jun	115.1	110.3	104.9	113.4	113.8	103.2	117.1	107.8	118.2	115.8	105.6	112.7	119.5
Jul	116.0	110.5	103.7	113.9	113.8	103.2	118.0	108.1	118.6	116.0	105.9	113.4	121.2
Aug	116.9	111.1	102.2	114.3	114.0	103.7	119.0	108.6	118.6	115.4	106.1	114.4	122.6
Sep	118.0	111.5	101.0	115.5	114.3	104.0	118.7	109.9	118.6	115.0	105.9	114.7	123.8
Oct	118.7	112.1	100.8	116.5	114.4	103.9	118.7	109.8	118.2	114.6	106.4	114.8	124.5
Nov	119.3	112.8	100.9	117.8	114.3	103.3	118.2	110.0	118.5	115.1	107.2	114.5	125.8
Dec	119.4	113.3	101.2	118.0	114.6	102.8	120.8	110.5	119.3	115.6	107.6	114.3	126.9
2000 Jan	119.8	113.7	101.8	118.2	115.3	104.0	121.8	111.7	121.3	117.2	108.0	114.6	128.7
Feb	120.3	113.4	101.3	118.5	116.4	104.7	122.8	112.1	122.0	118.5	109.0	114.8	130.3
Mar	121.3	114.3	100.3	119.6	117.1	105.2	121.2	111.9	122.6	119.5	109.3	114.8	130.1
Apr	122.0	115.0	99.4	120.0	117.6	104.7	122.8	111.0	122.1	119.5	109.3	115.4	129.5
May	122.7	115.7	99.5	120.3	118.0	105.6	123.2	111.6	122.9	120.0	108.3	116.1	128.7
Jun	123.5	115.9	100.2	120.7	118.4	106.3	124.3	112.5	123.4	120.4	108.6	117.3	129.8
Jul	124.2	116.0	100.1	121.7	118.2	106.8	124.0	113.0	124.1	121.2	108.7	117.8	130.5
Aug	124.9	115.9	100.1	121.9	117.9	106.5	125.5	113.5	124.3	121.3	109.0	118.7	131.4
Sep	125.5	115.9	99.8	121.8	118.1	106.8	125.8	113.6	124.6	121.6	109.3	119.1	131.0
Oct	125.8	116.5	99.7	122.0	118.6	106.5	126.0	114.3	125.1	121.9	109.8	119.2	130.7
Nov	126.2	118.2	99.9	123.5	119.1	106.0	125.1	114.7	126.0	122.7	111.1	118.9	129.9
Dec	126.6	119.6	100.8	124.6	119.3	105.3	126.2	115.3	127.0	123.9	111.8	119.0	130.6
2001 Jan	127.2	120.4	101.6	125.5	119.3	105.9	125.7	115.7	127.9	125.2	112.4	119.4	131.2
Feb	128.2	120.2	101.9	125.8	119.4	106.4	125.9	116.2	128.8	126.3	112.5	119.6	132.2
Mar	129.2	120.3	101.3	126.7	119.6	106.7	125.3	117.1	129.7	126.9	112.7	119.7	131.8
Apr	130.4	121.2	101.3	127.2	120.3	107.2	127.0	117.9	130.7	127.2	113.2	121.1	131.2
May	130.8	122.2	101.5	128.1	120.7	108.5	128.2	118.9	131.7	127.6	113.5	122.7	131.1
Jun	131.4	122.8	102.2	129.1	121.1	109.7	129.5	118.9	131.8	128.3	114.2	124.4	131.8
Jul	131.6	123.0	102.6	130.2	121.2	109.9	130.3	119.0	132.0	128.4	114.6	125.3	133.2
Aug	132.2	122.6	103.8	129.9	121.8	110.2	131.5	118.5	132.0	128.5	115.0	126.3	134.6
Sep	132.8	122.4	103.7	129.8	122.1	110.4	132.3	118.4	131.8	128.4	115.7	126.9	135.0

Note: The Average Earnings Index has been revised. More information is available on the website, www.statistics.gov.uk, and helpline below.

1 Users should note that data contained in this table are not comparable with those previously published in Table 18.11 (prior to March 1999). Excluding bonuses and averaging the data over a three month period renders the data fundamentally different to the previous indices published for the same industries, but which included bonuses and related to single months only.

2 As a result of a discontinuity in the reporting of data for the agricultural sector, this series is not available.

3 The index for the sector "Education, health and social work" is based on a sample which excludes representatives of the private health and social work sector until June 1998. Monthly movements in the index for this sector therefore exclude health and social work up to May 1998.

4 As a result of a change in the survey questionnaire, the series excluding bonuses are subject to a discontinuity between January and February 1999.

Source: Office for National Statistics: 01633 819002

7.23 Gross weekly and hourly earnings of full-time adult employees
Great Britain
At April

	Gross weekly earnings					Gross hourly earnings				
	Lowest decile	Lower quartile	Median	Upper quartile	Highest decile	Lowest decile	Lower quartile	Median	Upper quartile	Highest decile
	£	£	£	£	£	£	£	£	£	£
All men										
	KBYD	KBYE	KBYF	KBYG	KBYH	KIYD	KIYE	KIYF	KIYG	KIYH
1992	170.2	219.3	295.9	401.9	544.1	4.12	5.17	6.97	9.79	14.04
1993	174.7	226.0	304.6	417.3	567.2	4.22	5.35	7.25	10.28	14.55
1994	179.9	231.1	312.8	427.3	581.7	4.33	5.44	7.39	10.51	14.96
1995	182.0	237.1	323.2	442.7	600.8	4.33	5.55	7.60	10.90	15.60
1996	189.0	245.2	334.9	460.7	632.0	4.50	5.75	7.91	11.40	16.32
1997	198.6	256.4	349.7	480.0	656.9	4.71	6.00	8.24	11.89	17.01
1998	203.9	265.3	362.8	499.0	685.1	4.88	6.24	8.57	12.34	17.75
1999	211.1	274.5	374.3	517.3	711.6	5.09	6.50	8.92	12.96	18.63
2000	220.0	283.9	386.6	532.8	728.8	5.32	6.73	9.25	13.40	19.17
Manual men										
	KFZY	KFZZ	KGAK	KGAL	KGAM	KIYN	KIYO	KIYP	KIYQ	KIYR
1992	157.6	197.4	250.7	316.7	397.3	3.82	4.62	5.72	7.16	8.68
1993	160.9	201.2	256.4	324.0	407.1	3.87	4.72	5.89	7.35	8.98
1994	165.9	206.1	261.8	331.6	414.2	3.99	4.82	5.95	7.46	9.10
1995	166.9	211.1	271.8	347.1	437.5	3.97	4.86	6.09	7.66	9.43
1996	173.8	218.4	280.0	358.9	452.5	4.11	5.01	6.32	7.99	9.83
1997	182.4	228.8	292.5	373.9	472.8	4.32	5.25	6.60	8.28	10.17
1998	190.0	238.0	305.0	392.7	494.2	4.50	5.48	6.87	8.67	10.72
1999	194.9	244.8	312.8	399.0	500.6	4.68	5.69	7.11	8.95	11.04
2000	201.3	252.0	320.5	410.5	508.6	4.89	5.89	7.29	9.18	11.33
Non-manual men										
	KGAS	KGAT	KGAU	KGAV	KGAW	KIYX	KIYY	KIYZ	KIZA	KIZB
1992	188.0	257.6	353.4	473.3	641.2	4.77	6.51	9.05	12.57	17.11
1993	194.9	266.3	365.9	489.7	671.8	4.93	6.77	9.47	13.03	17.83
1994	200.4	274.4	376.0	503.9	688.5	5.03	6.90	9.67	13.30	18.20
1995	204.1	280.1	384.6	519.5	712.7	5.11	7.06	9.93	13.83	19.07
1996	211.1	287.9	399.4	544.0	752.4	5.28	7.28	10.28	14.38	19.87
1997	220.7	301.0	415.9	565.8	780.8	5.49	7.60	10.72	14.94	20.81
1998	225.5	309.1	430.7	586.1	823.4	5.62	7.79	11.09	15.54	21.74
1999	233.5	321.1	449.1	612.2	862.6	5.90	8.14	11.59	16.24	22.90
2000	243.0	331.9	460.7	626.3	868.9	6.12	8.39	11.96	16.63	23.17

As percentages of the corresponding median

All men										
	KBZH	KBZI	KBZJ	KBZK	KBZL	KBZM	KBZN	KBZO	KBZP	KBZQ
1992	57.5	74.1	100.0	135.8	183.9	59.1	74.2	100.0	140.5	201.4
1993	57.4	74.2	100.0	137.0	186.2	58.2	73.8	100.0	141.8	200.7
1994	57.5	73.9	100.0	136.6	186.0	58.6	73.6	100.0	142.2	202.4
1995	56.3	73.4	100.0	137.0	185.9	57.0	73.0	100.0	143.4	205.3
1996	56.4	73.2	100.0	137.5	188.7	56.9	72.7	100.0	144.2	206.3
1997	56.8	73.3	100.0	137.3	187.8	57.2	72.8	100.0	144.3	206.4
1998	56.2	73.1	100.0	137.6	188.8	56.9	72.7	100.0	143.9	207.1
1999	56.4	73.3	100.0	138.2	190.1	57.1	72.9	100.0	145.3	208.8
2000	56.9	73.4	100.0	137.8	188.5	57.5	72.8	100.0	144.9	207.3
Manual men										
	KGBS	KGBT	KGBU	KGBV	KGBW	KGBX	KGBY	KGBZ	KGCH	KGCI
1992	62.9	78.7	100.0	126.3	158.5	66.8	80.8	100.0	125.2	151.7
1993	62.8	78.5	100.0	126.4	158.8	65.7	80.1	100.0	124.8	152.5
1994	63.4	78.7	100.0	126.7	158.2	67.1	81.0	100.0	125.4	152.9
1995	61.4	77.7	100.0	127.7	161.0	65.2	79.8	100.0	125.8	154.8
1996	62.1	78.0	100.0	128.2	161.6	65.0	79.3	100.0	126.4	155.6
1997	62.4	78.2	100.0	127.8	161.6	65.5	79.5	100.0	125.5	154.1
1998	62.3	78.0	100.0	128.8	162.0	65.5	79.8	100.0	126.2	156.1
1999	62.3	78.3	100.0	127.6	160.0	65.9	80.0	100.0	125.8	155.2
2000	62.8	78.6	100.0	128.1	158.7	67.0	80.8	100.0	125.9	155.4
Non-manual men										
	KGCJ	KGCQ	KGCR	KGCS	KGCT	KGCU	KGCV	KGCW	KGCX	KGCY
1992	53.2	72.9	100.0	133.9	181.4	52.7	71.9	100.0	138.9	189.1
1993	53.3	72.8	100.0	133.8	183.6	52.1	71.5	100.0	137.6	188.3
1994	53.3	73.0	100.0	134.0	183.1	52.0	71.4	100.0	137.5	188.2
1995	53.1	72.8	100.0	135.1	185.3	51.5	71.1	100.0	139.3	192.0
1996	52.9	72.1	100.0	136.2	188.4	51.3	70.8	100.0	139.9	193.2
1997	53.1	72.4	100.0	136.0	187.7	51.2	70.9	100.0	139.4	194.1
1998	52.4	71.8	100.0	136.1	191.2	50.7	70.2	100.0	140.1	196.0
1999	52.0	71.5	100.0	136.3	192.1	50.9	70.2	100.0	140.0	197.5
2000	52.8	72.0	100.0	135.9	188.6	51.2	70.2	100.0	139.1	193.8

7.23
continued

Gross weekly and hourly earnings of full-time adult employees
Great Britain
At April

	Gross weekly earnings					Gross hourly earnings				
	Lowest decile	Lower quartile	Median	Upper quartile	Highest decile	Lowest decile	Lower quartile	Median	Upper quartile	Highest decile
	£	£	£	£	£	£	£	£	£	£
All women										
	KCBK	KCBL	KCBM	KCBN	KCBO	KIZC	KIZD	KIZE	KIZF	KIZG
1992	129.1	161.4	211.3	295.9	387.1	3.43	4.26	5.57	7.81	10.90
1993	134.0	168.2	221.6	309.1	402.3	3.55	4.44	5.86	8.19	11.30
1994	139.1	174.6	229.4	320.1	417.8	3.66	4.58	6.02	8.39	11.59
1995	141.1	179.5	237.2	332.5	430.7	3.70	4.69	6.24	8.87	12.30
1996	146.7	186.8	248.1	347.3	449.4	3.84	4.87	6.55	9.31	12.97
1997	154.5	196.1	260.5	364.7	472.1	4.03	5.11	6.84	9.79	13.54
1998	161.0	203.6	270.0	379.1	493.5	4.22	5.32	7.10	10.20	14.16
1999	169.5	213.3	284.0	398.2	521.2	4.47	5.59	7.47	10.75	14.98
2000	177.1	223.1	293.6	412.9	536.6	4.66	5.82	7.73	11.13	15.36
Manual women										
	KGCZ	KGDA	KGDB	KGDC	KGDD	KIZM	KIZN	KIZO	KIZP	KIZQ
1992	105.7	126.6	156.6	199.2	253.5	2.87	3.33	4.00	4.92	6.00
1993	109.6	130.5	162.2	205.8	263.7	2.95	3.41	4.12	5.12	6.25
1994	114.1	134.7	165.4	212.0	272.0	3.05	3.51	4.20	5.23	6.39
1995	114.8	137.4	171.0	222.1	282.6	3.02	3.56	4.32	5.37	6.61
1996	119.0	142.8	178.7	230.8	291.4	3.15	3.68	4.49	5.61	6.85
1997	122.4	148.7	185.4	237.3	300.0	3.25	3.83	4.66	5.81	7.16
1998	128.9	156.3	193.9	248.6	312.5	3.43	4.02	4.87	6.08	7.44
1999	140.4	164.7	201.4	260.9	327.8	3.73	4.27	5.08	6.37	7.93
2000	145.0	171.0	210.0	266.5	332.5	3.88	4.45	5.27	6.56	8.05
Non-manual women										
	KGDJ	KGDK	KGDL	KGDM	KGDN	KIZW	KIZX	KIZY	KIZZ	KJAN
1992	140.5	174.4	227.6	315.9	401.6	3.78	4.68	6.07	8.42	11.60
1993	146.4	182.5	238.4	329.6	414.1	3.93	4.90	6.35	8.83	11.98
1994	152.0	188.9	247.0	342.5	430.3	4.06	5.05	6.52	9.04	12.25
1995	155.6	194.7	256.2	355.6	445.3	4.13	5.22	6.83	9.61	13.09
1996	161.7	203.0	268.7	372.2	471.1	4.31	5.44	7.16	10.08	13.75
1997	171.4	212.8	283.3	390.7	495.1	4.53	5.68	7.53	10.61	14.38
1998	176.2	219.3	291.5	405.6	513.5	4.68	5.86	7.77	11.01	14.88
1999	184.0	230.3	305.0	422.3	540.9	4.92	6.14	8.16	11.52	15.78
2000	191.9	238.0	315.0	436.5	558.7	5.10	6.37	8.40	11.93	16.12

As percentages of the corresponding median

All women										
	KGEO	KGEP	KGEQ	KGER	KGES	KGET	KGEU	KGEV	KGEW	KGEX
1992	61.1	76.4	100.0	140.0	183.2	61.6	76.5	100.0	140.2	195.7
1993	60.5	75.9	100.0	139.5	181.5	60.6	75.8	100.0	139.8	192.8
1994	60.6	76.1	100.0	139.5	182.1	60.8	76.1	100.0	139.4	192.5
1995	59.5	75.6	100.0	140.2	181.5	59.3	75.2	100.0	142.1	197.1
1996	59.1	75.3	100.0	140.0	181.1	58.6	74.4	100.0	142.2	198.1
1997	59.3	75.3	100.0	140.0	181.2	58.9	74.7	100.0	143.1	198.0
1998	59.6	75.4	100.0	140.4	182.8	59.4	74.9	100.0	143.6	199.4
1999	59.7	75.1	100.0	140.2	183.5	59.8	74.8	100.0	143.9	200.4
2000	60.3	76.0	100.0	140.6	182.8	60.3	75.4	100.0	144.1	198.7
Manual women										
	KGDT	KGDU	KGDV	KGDW	KGDX	KGDY	KGDZ	KGEA	KGEB	KGEC
1992	67.5	80.8	100.0	127.2	161.9	71.8	83.3	100.0	123.0	150.0
1993	67.6	80.5	100.0	126.9	162.6	71.6	82.8	100.0	124.3	151.7
1994	69.0	81.4	100.0	128.2	164.4	72.6	83.6	100.0	124.5	152.1
1995	67.1	80.3	100.0	129.9	165.2	69.9	82.4	100.0	124.3	153.0
1996	66.5	79.9	100.0	129.1	163.0	70.2	82.0	100.0	125.1	152.6
1997	66.0	80.2	100.0	128.0	161.8	69.7	82.2	100.0	124.7	153.6
1998	66.5	80.6	100.0	128.2	161.2	70.4	82.6	100.0	124.9	152.7
1999	69.7	81.8	100.0	129.5	162.8	73.4	84.0	100.0	125.4	156.1
2000	69.0	81.4	100.0	126.9	158.3	73.5	84.5	100.0	124.4	152.7
Non-manual women										
	KGED	KGEE	KGEF	KGEG	KGEH	KGEI	KGEJ	KGEK	KGEL	KGEM
1992	61.7	76.6	100.0	138.8	176.4	62.3	77.1	100.0	138.7	191.1
1993	61.4	76.6	100.0	138.3	173.7	61.9	77.2	100.0	139.1	188.7
1994	61.5	76.5	100.0	138.7	174.2	62.3	77.5	100.0	138.7	187.9
1995	60.7	76.0	100.0	138.8	173.8	60.5	76.4	100.0	140.7	191.7
1996	60.2	75.6	100.0	138.5	175.3	60.2	76.0	100.0	140.7	192.1
1997	60.5	75.1	100.0	137.9	174.8	60.2	75.4	100.0	140.9	191.0
1998	60.4	75.2	100.0	139.1	176.2	60.2	75.5	100.0	141.7	191.5
1999	60.3	75.5	100.0	138.4	177.3	60.3	75.3	100.0	141.2	193.4
2000	60.9	75.6	100.0	138.6	177.4	60.7	75.8	100.0	142.1	191.9

Source: New Earnings Survey, Office for National Statistics: 01633 819024

7.24 Gross weekly and hourly earnings of full-time adults
Northern Ireland
April of each year

	Gross weekly earnings[1]					Gross hourly earnings[1]				
	Lowest decile	Lower quartile	Median	Upper quartile	Highest decile	Lowest decile	Lower quartile	Median	Upper quartile	Highest decile
	£	£	£	£	£	p	p	p	p	p
All men										
	KCIF	KCIG	KCIH	KCII	KCIJ	KCIK	KCIL	KCIM	KCIN	KCIO
1993	147.1	195.0	274.3	393.6	534.2	368.3	465.6	636.0	964.2	1 256.6
1994	152.8	198.6	279.4	405.3	546.4	382.1	473.5	652.2	1 006.9	1 288.2
1995	161.0	205.3	285.6	419.4	548.5	394.6	491.2	674.6	1 043.5	1 371.6
1996	163.0	213.7	296.9	424.0	549.8	399.4	512.3	695.7	1 073.9	1 402.8
1997	171.1	222.2	307.1	449.6	575.8	414.8	522.1	724.4	1 106.2	1 452.0
1998	175.4	227.4	322.1	455.1	596.1	435.8	548.8	763.0	1 137.2	1 497.5
1999	183.9	237.0	328.9	467.7	607.6	457.0	572.3	778.4	1 167.1	1 545.9
2000	190.1	247.3	342.4	491.3	636.3	476.3	601.0	799.8	1 204.6	1 596.9
Manual men										
	KCIP	KCIQ	KCIR	KCIS	KCIT	KCIU	KCIV	KCIW	KCIX	KCIY
1993	135.9	172.2	218.2	281.9	356.0	339.8	412.2	513.3	627.0	761.8
1994	141.6	175.4	222.0	291.0	366.2	349.9	418.8	513.9	634.9	799.9
1995	149.7	181.5	230.9	299.4	383.3	359.7	435.5	527.0	664.6	826.5
1996	150.6	187.2	240.7	310.1	389.9	369.9	448.0	563.7	684.6	860.6
1997	158.4	192.9	249.4	321.4	402.7	385.0	460.0	570.5	709.5	882.0
1998	165.0	200.9	262.9	340.5	422.8	408.3	487.3	595.3	767.3	940.7
1999	175.6	216.4	270.4	355.0	454.6	435.5	515.0	624.5	786.0	994.7
2000	180.0	225.5	279.8	363.9	457.0	445.0	535.7	650.0	814.5	987.3
Non-manual men										
	KCIZ	KCJO	KCJP	KCJQ	KCJR	KCJS	KCJT	KCJU	KCJV	KCJW
1993	168.6	251.9	356.5	488.7	611.5	435.6	636.0	923.2	1 176.4	1 476.6
1994	174.8	253.8	366.4	501.5	615.2	445.9	641.7	956.2	1 222.5	1 461.7
1995	183.4	260.7	383.4	511.0	628.9	470.3	660.6	987.7	1 292.8	1 601.8
1996	192.5	268.4	387.1	506.4	617.2	482.4	682.5	1 013.0	1 322.7	1 612.2
1997	198.3	277.4	403.0	533.1	666.6	491.4	690.9	1 048.2	1 363.0	1 638.2
1998	200.5	284.2	418.4	543.8	685.9	500.0	715.7	1 074.7	1 404.5	1 739.5
1999	200.0	296.8	424.0	546.8	680.6	502.8	740.4	1 103.6	1 461.9	1 779.4
2000	209.1	306.0	456.6	580.0	730.8	543.3	767.7	1 165.1	1 519.9	1 917.3

As percentages of the corresponding median

All men										
	KCJX	KCJY	KCJZ	KCKA	KCKB	KCKC	KCKD	KCKE	KCKF	KCKG
1993	53.6	71.1	100.0	143.5	194.8	57.9	73.2	100.0	151.6	197.6
1994	54.7	71.1	100.0	145.1	195.6	58.6	72.6	100.0	154.4	197.5
1995	56.4	71.9	100.0	146.8	192.1	58.5	72.8	100.0	154.7	203.3
1996	54.9	72.0	100.0	142.8	185.2	57.4	73.6	100.0	154.4	201.6
1997	55.7	72.4	100.0	146.4	187.5	57.3	72.1	100.0	152.7	200.4
1998	54.5	70.6	100.0	141.3	185.1	57.1	71.9	100.0	149.0	196.3
1999	55.9	72.0	100.0	142.2	184.7	58.7	73.5	100.0	149.9	198.6
2000	55.5	72.2	100.0	143.5	185.9	59.5	75.1	100.0	150.6	199.6
Manual men										
	KCKH	KCKI	KCKT	KCKK	KCKL	KCKM	KCKN	KCKO	KCKP	KCKR
1993	62.3	78.9	100.0	129.2	163.6	66.2	80.3	100.0	122.2	148.4
1994	63.8	79.0	100.0	131.1	165.0	68.1	81.5	100.0	123.5	155.7
1995	64.8	78.6	100.0	129.7	166.0	68.3	82.6	100.0	126.1	156.8
1996	62.6	77.8	100.0	128.8	162.0	65.6	79.5	100.0	121.4	152.7
1997	63.5	77.3	100.0	128.9	161.5	67.5	80.6	100.0	124.4	154.6
1998	62.8	76.4	100.0	129.5	160.8	68.6	81.9	100.0	128.9	158.0
1999	64.9	80.0	100.0	131.3	168.1	69.7	82.5	100.0	125.9	159.3
2000	64.3	80.6	100.0	130.1	163.4	68.5	82.4	100.0	125.3	151.9
Non-manual men										
	KCKQ	KCKS	KFZW	KCKU	KCKV	KCKW	KCKX	KCKY	KCKZ	KCLA
1993	47.3	70.7	100.0	137.1	171.5	47.2	68.9	100.0	127.4	159.9
1994	47.7	69.3	100.0	136.9	167.9	46.6	67.1	100.0	127.8	152.9
1995	47.8	68.0	100.0	133.3	164.0	47.6	66.9	100.0	130.9	162.2
1996	49.7	69.3	100.0	130.8	159.4	47.6	67.4	100.0	130.6	159.2
1997	49.2	68.8	100.0	132.3	165.4	46.9	65.9	100.0	130.0	156.3
1998	47.9	67.9	100.0	130.0	163.9	46.5	66.6	100.0	130.7	161.9
1999	47.2	70.0	100.0	129.0	160.5	45.6	67.1	100.0	132.5	161.2
2000	45.8	67.0	100.0	127.0	160.1	46.6	65.9	100.0	130.4	164.6

7.24
continued

Gross weekly and hourly earnings of full-time adults
Northern Ireland
April of each year

	Gross weekly earnings[1]					Gross hourly earnings[1]				
	Lowest decile	Lower quartile	Median	Upper quartile	Highest decile	Lowest decile	Lower quartile	Median	Upper quartile	Highest decile
	£	£	£	£	£	p	p	p	p	p
All women										
	KCDS	KCDT	KCDU	KCDV	KCDW	KCDX	KCDY	KCDZ	KCFF	KCFG
1993	118.0	147.6	202.9	298.1	392.7	311.5	383.2	528.9	753.5	1 074.1
1994	120.4	149.0	201.5	303.7	399.0	321.3	398.0	545.5	809.4	1 138.4
1995	130.2	162.9	217.4	320.5	423.2	345.1	424.3	583.8	885.5	1 203.8
1996	133.3	165.5	226.2	331.9	434.8	354.5	431.0	595.8	893.6	1 256.9
1997	137.5	170.0	231.3	334.4	450.9	360.0	441.6	602.6	906.2	1 285.5
1998	148.1	181.4	243.9	348.0	465.2	390.2	471.5	652.5	950.9	1 304.5
1999	151.3	191.9	257.8	374.3	485.9	404.3	494.7	683.3	1 026.6	1 410.6
2000	162.9	203.9	271.8	400.4	512.5	435.3	536.5	713.4	1 091.7	1 440.2
Manual women										
	KCFH	KCFI	KCFJ	KCFK	KCFL	KCFM	KCFN	KCFO	KCFP	KCFQ
1993	103.9	121.6	142.9	173.7	218.7	276.2	314.6	371.0	431.0	533.1
1994	101.7	122.2	146.8	175.1	213.7	279.5	322.2	376.7	444.1	545.4
1995	109.1	131.5	161.0	193.7	247.7	287.6	343.0	401.7	483.0	616.2
1996	110.9	132.5	161.1	197.1	248.7	293.9	345.7	408.0	496.2	599.7
1997	113.4	138.3	160.0	201.8	250.8	308.3	354.4	413.7	500.0	593.0
1998	120.0	146.5	172.9	213.6	258.4	309.0	385.7	440.0	549.0	631.2
1999	136.1	151.3	175.1	219.0	275.8	360.0	397.2	451.3	546.8	633.8
2000	144.0	163.7	195.0	240.1	282.3	395.1	435.5	509.7	592.9	713.9
Non-manual women										
	KCFR	KCFS	KCFT	KCFU	KCFV	KCFW	KCFX	KCFY	KCFZ	KCHA
1993	129.6	169.2	229.4	332.3	402.2	334.8	442.0	595.3	837.0	1 127.7
1994	132.3	169.7	227.1	334.4	411.9	363.2	458.5	606.7	893.3	1 197.2
1995	139.1	176.9	241.4	346.3	435.8	375.2	473.9	650.1	943.0	1 269.6
1996	145.3	182.5	253.0	364.7	437.0	385.0	490.2	675.6	997.3	1 302.6
1997	149.7	188.6	254.0	364.3	451.3	389.0	501.6	679.4	996.7	1 342.9
1998	156.6	200.2	270.9	383.8	475.5	412.8	530.7	725.0	1 028.2	1 373.9
1999	167.4	211.5	289.3	409.2	500.9	442.1	569.7	773.3	1 137.8	1 459.0
2000	174.3	219.9	299.1	426.8	517.4	458.7	590.2	793.3	1 170.2	1 507.1

As percentages of the corresponding median

All women										
	KCHB	KCHC	KCHD	KCHE	KCHF	KCHG	KCHH	KCHI	KCHJ	KCHK
1993	58.2	72.8	100.0	146.9	193.5	58.9	72.5	100.0	142.5	203.1
1994	59.8	73.9	100.0	150.7	198.0	58.9	73.0	100.0	148.4	208.7
1995	59.9	74.9	100.0	147.4	194.7	59.1	72.7	100.0	151.7	206.2
1996	58.9	73.2	100.0	146.7	192.2	59.5	72.3	100.0	150.0	211.0
1997	59.4	73.5	100.0	144.6	194.9	59.7	73.3	100.0	150.4	213.3
1998	60.7	74.4	100.0	142.7	190.7	59.8	72.3	100.0	145.7	199.9
1999	58.7	74.5	100.0	145.2	188.5	59.2	72.4	100.0	150.2	206.5
2000	59.9	75.0	100.0	147.3	188.6	61.0	75.2	100.0	153.0	201.9
Manual women										
	KCHL	KCHM	KCHN	KCHO	KCHP	KCHQ	KCHR	KCHS	KCHT	KCHU
1993	72.7	85.1	100.0	121.6	153.0	74.4	84.8	100.0	116.2	143.7
1994	69.3	83.2	100.0	119.3	145.6	74.2	85.5	100.0	117.9	144.8
1995	67.8	81.7	100.0	120.3	153.9	71.6	85.4	100.0	120.2	153.4
1996	68.8	82.2	100.0	122.3	154.4	72.0	84.7	100.0	121.6	147.0
1997	70.9	86.4	100.0	126.1	156.8	74.5	85.7	100.0	120.9	143.3
1998	69.4	84.7	100.0	123.5	149.4	70.2	87.7	100.0	124.8	143.5
1999	77.7	86.4	100.0	125.1	157.5	79.8	88.0	100.0	121.2	140.4
2000	73.9	84.0	100.0	123.1	144.8	77.5	85.4	100.0	116.3	140.1
Non-manual women										
	KCHV	KCHW	KCHX	KCHY	KCHZ	KCIA	KCIB	KCIC	KCID	KCIE
1993	56.5	73.8	100.0	144.9	175.3	56.2	74.2	100.0	140.6	189.4
1994	58.3	74.7	100.0	147.2	181.4	59.9	75.6	100.0	147.2	197.3
1995	57.6	73.3	100.0	143.5	180.5	57.7	72.9	100.0	145.1	195.3
1996	57.4	72.1	100.0	144.2	172.7	57.0	72.6	100.0	147.6	192.8
1997	58.9	74.3	100.0	143.4	177.7	57.3	73.8	100.0	146.7	197.7
1998	57.8	73.9	100.0	141.7	175.5	56.9	73.2	100.0	141.8	189.5
1999	57.9	73.1	100.0	141.5	173.2	57.2	73.7	100.0	147.1	188.7
2000	58.3	73.5	100.0	142.7	173.0	57.8	74.4	100.0	147.5	190.0

1 Those whose pay in the survey period was not affected by absence. Weekly earnings figures refer to April in each year and are gross before deductions, generally excluding the value of incomes in kind but including bonus, overtime and commission payments for the pay period.

Sources: Department of Enterprise, Trade and Investment (Northern Ireland);
028 9052 9897

7.25 Average earnings by age group of full-time employees whose pay for the survey pay period was not affected by absence: Great Britain

At April 2000

	Gross weekly earnings								Average weekly hours		Average hourly earnings excluding overtime pay
	Average		As a percentage of the median			As a percentage of the median		Percentage earning under £250			
	Total	Overtime pay	Lowest decile	Lower quartile	Median	Upper quartile	Highest decile		Total	Overtime	
	£	£	per cent	per cent	£	per cent	per cent				£
All males											
Under 18	141.7	8.4	63.3	81.5	126.4	125.2	158.3	94.6	40.9	1.8	3.43
18 to 20	204.9	13.7	67.2	82.2	188.6	125.1	157.6	80.0	40.8	1.9	4.89
21 to 24	284.3	18.7	64.9	79.5	259.7	128.4	158.3	45.6	40.8	2.1	6.86
25 to 29	382.0	25.4	61.1	76.3	340.7	130.4	170.2	21.5	40.9	2.3	9.22
30 to 39	464.1	29.9	58.3	74.6	405.3	133.3	181.2	12.7	41.3	2.6	11.20
40 to 49	505.3	28.6	56.3	73.0	437.6	134.9	185.4	10.6	41.0	2.6	12.37
50 to 59	483.7	26.8	57.1	73.1	403.4	140.6	194.9	14.2	41.2	2.6	11.78
60 to 64	402.8	27.5	61.5	77.2	328.5	139.0	192.1	23.7	42.1	2.9	9.55
All ages	448.9	27.2	55.6	72.8	383.9	137.7	188.6	17.8	41.2	2.5	10.88
Manual males											
Under 18	139.6	10.5	64.0	80.0	125.0	124.1	157.4	95.2	41.7	2.3	3.29
18 to 20	202.7	16.6	65.1	80.2	187.1	128.2	161.0	78.8	41.8	2.4	4.72
21 to 24	272.2	27.2	62.8	78.5	257.3	125.8	155.0	46.5	42.8	3.2	6.18
25 to 29	321.5	39.4	65.2	80.0	298.9	127.8	160.3	29.4	43.8	4.0	7.09
30 to 39	359.6	51.2	63.4	78.8	336.5	127.1	155.8	19.8	44.7	4.9	7.75
40 to 49	366.6	52.1	63.9	78.9	342.9	127.1	156.9	18.0	44.6	5.1	7.95
50 to 59	346.5	46.5	65.0	79.3	324.7	126.4	156.0	21.9	44.3	4.8	7.59
60 to 64	310.9	38.7	66.0	81.0	288.9	126.3	157.2	31.6	44.0	4.3	6.86
All ages	340.0	45.6	62.0	78.4	317.2	128.5	159.5	25.5	44.2	4.6	7.43
Non-manual males											
Under 18	..	..	..	..	..	..	..	..	..	..	..
18 to 20	208.0	9.6	72.4	85.6	190.2	122.0	152.2	81.8	39.5	1.2	5.16
21 to 24	294.0	11.8	66.0	79.1	263.8	129.4	160.3	44.9	39.1	1.2	7.43
25 to 29	421.5	16.2	59.2	76.6	373.8	129.4	171.5	16.4	39.0	1.2	10.69
30 to 39	536.7	15.0	57.0	75.4	469.5	133.2	184.0	7.7	39.0	1.0	13.74
40 to 49	598.1	12.8	55.6	75.3	521.9	132.6	183.9	5.7	38.5	0.9	15.52
50 to 59	593.9	11.1	52.1	72.2	508.8	135.2	190.1	8.1	38.6	0.8	15.37
60 to 64	524.3	12.7	54.4	72.6	423.2	140.8	198.3	13.3	39.5	1.1	13.35
All ages	530.1	13.4	51.7	71.1	459.7	135.7	188.3	12.0	38.8	1.0	13.62
All females											
Under 18	141.4	5.2	58.1	73.5	137.5	121.1	148.4	95.9	38.6	1.0	3.64
18 to 20	184.6	5.4	72.9	85.1	174.0	120.3	147.3	89.1	38.2	0.7	4.79
21 to 24	249.6	6.7	69.3	82.1	231.0	127.7	155.1	59.4	38.2	0.8	6.48
25 to 29	323.8	7.6	63.2	77.7	296.5	128.8	162.9	33.7	37.6	0.7	8.55
30 to 39	372.8	7.8	58.7	74.3	329.9	137.9	177.2	26.8	37.5	0.7	9.90
40 to 49	357.5	7.0	58.2	74.3	310.0	145.1	183.1	32.2	37.1	0.7	9.59
50 to 59	333.3	6.1	60.8	76.8	287.7	147.3	185.8	36.7	36.9	0.6	8.97
60 to 64	292.6	5.5	64.3	78.8	251.1	133.8	190.7	49.5	37.3	0.7	7.78
All ages	335.2	7.0	59.9	75.7	291.6	140.7	183.1	36.4	37.4	0.7	8.91
Manual females											
Under 18	..	..	..	..	..	..	..	..	..	..	..
18 to 20	172.7	5.4	73.6	86.3	163.0	117.8	145.0	92.4	38.8	0.8	4.40
21 to 24	210.3	10.4	71.8	83.4	194.7	124.8	156.2	77.8	40.4	1.4	5.13
25 to 29	239.7	13.6	66.8	79.5	223.1	125.3	156.5	63.3	40.1	1.7	5.88
30 to 39	241.6	14.1	67.4	79.8	225.1	126.5	158.2	62.5	39.8	1.8	5.99
40 to 49	230.1	16.1	69.1	81.5	212.8	127.2	156.2	67.1	39.9	2.0	5.65
50 to 59	222.7	13.7	70.8	82.9	204.5	125.9	157.4	71.5	39.5	1.7	5.54
60 to 64	208.1	10.8	73.2	83.2	196.7	121.2	145.0	79.4	39.3	1.6	5.24
All ages	226.8	13.6	68.8	81.2	209.3	126.8	158.5	69.3	39.8	1.7	5.60
Non-manual females											
Under 18	138.0	4.2	59.8	72.3	133.4	123.7	143.3	95.8	38.3	0.9	3.58
18 to 20	188.3	5.4	73.6	85.5	177.3	120.4	147.9	88.0	37.9	0.7	4.92
21 to 24	256.3	6.1	68.9	81.4	239.7	127.6	152.0	56.2	37.8	0.6	6.72
25 to 29	335.6	6.7	65.1	78.1	307.2	126.8	162.0	29.6	37.3	0.6	8.94
30 to 39	392.6	6.9	60.2	74.8	350.5	134.2	172.7	21.4	37.2	0.5	10.52
40 to 49	381.9	5.2	58.8	73.3	339.9	138.4	174.7	25.4	36.5	0.4	10.40
50 to 59	357.4	4.5	61.9	76.5	312.5	146.8	178.8	29.2	36.4	0.4	9.76
60 to 64	326.0	3.4	65.0	79.1	282.1	132.4	183.3	37.7	36.5	0.3	8.85
All ages	355.0	5.8	60.5	75.6	312.3	139.5	178.9	30.5	36.9	0.5	9.55

Source: New Earnings Survey, Office for National Statistics: 01633 819024

7.26 Trade unions[1,2]
United Kingdom
At end of year

Percentages

		1989	1990	1991	1992	1993	1994	1995	1996	1997	1998	1999
Number of trade unions	KCLB	338	327	306	315	302	281	271	261	257	243	241
Analysis by number of members:												
Under 100 members	KCLC	18.6	17.7	15.7	14.3	15.9	16.4	15.5	13.0	16.0	16.9	18.5
100 and under 500	KCLD	21.9	22.3	23.2	22.9	24.8	23.1	23.2	27.2	22.2	21.4	20.2
500 and under 1,000	KCLE	6.5	7.6	6.9	9.8	7.6	8.9	10.0	8.0	12.1	10.7	9.5
1,000 and under 2,500	KCLF	16.3	15.6	17.0	17.1	15.2	15.3	15.1	17.2	14.8	13.2	14.0
2,500 and under 5,000	KCLG	8.9	9.5	9.5	8.9	8.9	9.3	8.9	7.7	7.8	9.5	9.5
5,000 and under 10,000	KCLH	6.2	5.2	5.9	6.0	6.3	6.4	5.9	5.7	5.8	6.2	5.3
10,000 and under 15,000	KCLI	2.1	2.1	1.6	1.6	2.0	2.1	3.0	2.7	2.7	2.1	1.6
15,000 and under 25,000	KCLJ	3.8	3.4	3.3	3.8	3.0	2.8	2.6	2.3	2.3	2.9	4.1
25,000 and under 50,000	KCLK	7.1	7.6	7.2	6.3	7.0	7.1	7.4	7.7	7.4	8.2	7.8
50,000 and under 100,000	KCLL	1.8	1.8	2.3	2.9	3.0	2.5	2.6	1.9	2.3	2.5	2.1
100,000 and under 250,000	KCLM	3.8	4.3	4.6	3.5	3.3	3.6	3.0	3.1	3.1	2.5	2.1
250,000 and over	KCLN	3.0	2.8	2.9	2.9	3.0	2.5	3.0	3.4	3.5	4.1	4.5
All sizes	KCLP	100	100	100	100	100	100	100	100	100	100	100
Membership[3]												
Analysis by size of union:												
Under 100 members	KCLQ	–	–	–	–	–	–	–	–	–	–	–
100 and under 500	KCLR	0.2	0.2	0.2	0.2	0.2	0.2	0.2	0.3	0.2	0.2	0.2
500 and under 1,000	KCLS	0.1	0.2	0.2	0.2	0.2	0.2	0.2	0.2	0.3	0.2	0.2
1,000 and under 2,500	KCLT	0.9	0.8	0.9	1.0	0.9	0.9	0.9	0.9	0.8	0.7	0.7
2,500 and under 5,000	KCLU	1.0	1.1	1.1	1.1	1.1	1.1	1.1	0.9	0.9	1.1	1.1
5,000 and under 10,000	KCLV	1.3	1.2	1.3	1.5	1.5	1.6	1.4	1.3	1.3	1.4	1.2
10,000 and under 15,000	KCLW	0.8	0.8	0.6	0.6	0.8	0.9	1.3	1.2	1.1	0.9	0.7
15,000 and under 25,000	KCLX	2.5	2.0	1.8	2.3	1.8	1.7	1.5	1.3	1.3	1.6	2.3
25,000 and under 50,000	KCLY	8.6	9.0	8.3	8.0	8.6	8.9	9.1	8.8	8.1	8.4	8.2
50,000 and under 100,000	KCLZ	4.2	4.3	4.9	7.0	7.3	5.9	5.9	3.9	4.5	4.5	3.8
100,000 and under 250,000	KCMA	20.0	22.3	22.9	18.6	18.2	19.3	16.3	15.2	15.3	11.9	9.9
250,000 and over	KCMB	60.3	58.1	57.8	59.4	59.2	59.3	62.0	66.0	66.1	69.1	71.7
All sizes	KCMC	100	100	100	100	100	100	100	100	100	100	100
Total membership (thousands)	KCMD	10 174	9 960	9 555	9 171	8 848	8 297	8 111	7 982	7 842	7 894	7 940

1 The statistics relate to all organisations of employees known to Certification Officer with head offices in the United Kingdom that fall within the appropriate definition of a trade union in the 1992 Trade Union and Labour Relations Act.

2 Included in the data are home and overseas membership figures of contributory and non-contributory members. Employment status of members is not provided and the figures may therefore include some people who are self-employed, unemployed or retired.

3 This table was revised in 2001, so that statistics presented here are on a consistent basis with the GB table produced by the Certification Officer in his Annual Report and with tables produced in the annual Labour Market Trends Trade Union article. There is a break in the time series for the figures in this table between the years 1988 (contained within previous publications) and 1989. GB data for 1989-95 are DTI analysis of annual returns, with 1996-1999 as published in the Certification Officer's Annual Report. Data for Northern Ireland for 1989-1991 are DTI analysis of annual returns, with 1992-1999 from the Certification Officer's Annual Report.

Source: Department of Trade and Industry: 020 7215 5780

7.27 Vacancies at jobcentres in the United Kingdom[1,2,3]
Seasonally adjusted

Thousands

	January	February	March	April	May	June	July	August	September	October	November	December
Numbers of vacancies remaining unfilled DPCB												
1991	140.0	138.9	133.9	119.8	110.2	105.6	106.0	109.2	112.5	109.6	111.8	117.4
1992	117.0	118.2	118.2	117.1	118.8	119.8	120.2	118.6	113.1	112.9	114.4	117.0
1993	119.0	120.3	124.3	123.6	125.9	124.8	129.2	129.8	129.5	133.2	136.3	138.2
1994	140.4	142.7	143.4	146.2	149.1	154.9	158.8	165.0	165.4	175.3	176.9	177.6
1995	175.2	174.3	177.5	186.0	185.4	182.9	181.8	181.7	184.5	181.7	185.2	186.7
1996	190.4	189.3	196.9	201.2	209.2	220.7	233.0	238.8	247.4	248.7	257.5	265.5
1997	272.6	279.2	279.6	279.4	277.3	283.9	288.0	295.2	297.2	293.7	275.2	278.2
1998	275.0	285.0	286.3	288.2	298.1	300.1	302.8	302.7	301.5	302.9	304.4	303.2
1999	305.3	300.8	298.5	295.7	304.6	305.6	307.8	315.8	314.7	336.5	338.5	347.4
2000	340.3	341.7	344.6	355.7	354.3	357.2	362.9	361.6	365.6	364.5	374.3	376.5
2001	395.7	391.6	394.9	387.8	..	..	..	..	..	..	..	..
Inflow of vacancies DRYW												
1991	185.4	167.8	168.0	182.8	182.2	163.9	165.6	168.7	170.7	168.3	164.9	167.1
1992	166.4	166.9	171.7	166.0	166.2	176.4	173.3	164.0	167.1	171.3	164.7	173.8
1993	180.2	175.9	181.5	179.3	180.2	183.5	190.5	183.4	191.5	189.6	193.9	197.2
1994	199.2	199.5	199.1	203.7	205.2	212.2	208.3	223.6	216.6	219.1	223.1	226.8
1995	218.2	219.5	215.2	205.4	227.7	223.1	225.6	230.9	226.5	231.9	232.9	222.1
1996	228.9	222.2	219.8	231.7	221.4	219.5	224.4	223.1	221.7	203.4	230.2	232.8
1997	202.9	239.3	242.9	239.1	236.2	226.2	226.4	220.8	227.6	222.6	217.9	216.2
1998	184.2	218.5	219.2	216.3	218.2	225.0	222.0	221.4	221.8	229.9	223.1	219.4
1999	237.7	222.8	221.8	229.6	224.4	226.2	231.2	234.0	230.2	235.0	235.3	236.7
2000	227.9	226.1	228.8	225.3	213.2	222.3	220.6	219.0	225.6	221.3	220.2	222.8
2001	224.9	233.2	232.8	237.6	..	..	..	..	..	..	..	..
Outflow of vacancies DRZL												
1991	176.4	168.7	172.4	197.5	197.1	168.3	165.0	164.9	168.7	170.2	159.9	160.8
1992	169.7	165.6	170.5	168.4	168.6	174.1	172.5	164.1	170.5	169.8	160.8	170.6
1993	178.8	173.6	176.6	180.1	181.0	184.0	185.6	182.0	189.8	186.4	191.0	195.3
1994	196.8	196.7	198.3	202.3	203.4	205.8	202.8	217.1	214.8	210.8	221.6	227.0
1995	219.0	220.6	214.1	195.1	229.0	225.0	224.6	230.4	225.5	237.1	229.7	219.2
1996	225.6	222.1	213.8	222.7	212.9	211.1	214.3	218.4	213.9	200.9	220.9	229.8
1997	208.5	232.1	238.0	236.8	234.1	220.9	225.0	215.0	216.8	224.2	232.5	219.9
1998	207.2	208.7	213.1	214.0	209.0	222.3	219.3	221.2	218.5	228.7	220.4	223.5
1999	236.9	224.4	220.9	232.3	219.4	225.2	227.6	226.5	229.0	219.6	233.6	231.1
2000	240.6	223.6	224.1	218.9	213.9	218.6	214.6	219.2	221.8	217.1	211.8	220.4
2001	212.1	237.6	226.1	241.1	..	..	..	..	..	..	..	..
Number of placings DTQR												
1991	129.4	122.5	127.6	148.4	148.4	123.9	123.2	120.9	122.1	122.7	114.8	115.9
1992	124.6	119.7	123.6	122.6	123.0	126.5	126.5	119.6	125.9	127.6	120.6	130.2
1993	134.3	132.1	131.7	134.0	134.9	136.3	139.0	136.1	144.1	140.6	146.4	148.2
1994	149.5	150.6	151.5	156.6	157.7	161.9	157.7	169.6	166.4	162.3	170.3	173.2
1995	166.2	169.1	164.6	145.8	179.8	173.6	174.4	178.5	172.5	183.5	179.7	167.4
1996	176.1	164.6	151.5	152.8	151.6	148.2	149.7	153.6	148.9	135.4	150.4	159.3
1997	147.9	157.7	163.6	164.0	151.8	143.1	138.6	127.1	126.4	123.1	120.2	116.9
1998	109.0	113.9	115.5	114.1	110.5	115.9	115.8	116.4	117.8	121.4	118.0	117.2
1999	119.8	120.3	116.7	126.5	118.1	121.0	123.0	121.8	122.7	120.3	123.1	122.6
2000	121.1	116.4	115.7	111.4	108.1	109.5	107.3	109.9	111.3	109.9	107.1	108.4
2001	110.2	108.6	109.1	117.5	..	..	..	..	..	..	..	..

Note: Vacancies notified to and placings made by jobcentres do not represent the total number of vacancies/engagements in the economy. Latest estimates suggest that about a third of all vacancies are notified to jobcentres: and about a quarter of all engagements are made through jobcentres. Inflow, outflow and placings figures are collected for four or five-week periods between count dates; the figures in this table are converted to a standard 4 $^{1}/_{3}$ week month.

1 Excluding vacancies on government programmes except vacancies on Enterprise Ulster and Action for Community Employment (ACE) which are included in the seasonally adjusted figures for Northern Ireland.

2 The latest national seasonally adjusted vacancy figures are provisional and subject to revision in the following month.

3 Publication of the jobcentre vacancy statistics has been deferred. Figures from May 2001 are affected by the introduction of Employer Direct. This major change involves transferring the vacancy taking process from local Jobcentres to regional Customer Service Centres, as part of Modernising the Employment Service. ONS and the Employment Service will continue to monitor and review the data with the aim of publishing the series as soon as it is possible to produce a consistent measure.

Source: Labour Market Statistics, Office for National Statistics: 020 7533 6094

8 Personal income, expenditure and wealth

Personal income, expenditure and wealth

Average incomes of households *(Table 8.1)*

Original income is the total income in cash and kind of the household before the deduction of taxes or the addition of state benefits. The addition of cash benefits (retirement pensions, child benefit, etc) and the deduction of income tax, council tax, water charges, domestic rates and employees' national insurance contributions give disposable income. By further allowing for taxes paid on goods and services purchased, such as VAT, an estimate of "post-tax" income is derived. These income figures are derived from estimates made by the Office for National Statistics, based largely on information from the Family Expenditure Survey (FES), and published each year in *Economic Trends*.

A retired household is defined as one where the combined income of retired members amounts to at least half the total gross income of the household, where a retired person is defined as anyone who describes themselves as "retired" or anyone over the minimum NI pension age describing themselves as "unoccupied" or "sick or injured but not intending to seek work."

Children are defined as persons aged under 16 or aged between 16 and 18, unmarried and receiving non-advanced further education.

Distribution of total incomes *(Table 8.2)*

The information shown in Table 8.2 comes from the Survey of Personal Incomes for the financial years 1995/96, 1996/97, 1997/98 and 1998/99. This is an annual survey that covers approximately 125 000 individuals across the whole of the UK. It is based on administrative data held by Inland Revenue offices on individuals who could be liable to tax.

The table relates only to those individuals who have some tax liability. The distributions cover only incomes as computed for tax purposes and above a level which for each year corresponds approximately to the single person's allowance. Incomes below these levels are not shown because the information about them is incomplete.

Investment income from which tax has been deducted at source is not always known to local tax offices. Estimates of missing bank and building society interest and dividends from United Kingdom companies are included in these tables. The missing investment income is distributed, in a manner consistent with information from the Family Expenditure Survey and the National Accounts, to individuals for whom there is no investment income already reported by the tax office.

Superannuation contributions are estimated and included in total income. They have been distributed among earners in the Survey of Personal Incomes sample by a method consistent with information about the number of employees who are contracted in or out of the State Earnings Related Pension Scheme and the proportion of their earnings contributed.

Family Expenditure Survey *(Tables 8.3 - 8.5)*

The Family Expenditure Survey, introduced in 1957, covers all types of private households in the United Kingdom. It is a continuous survey with fieldwork carried out in every month of the year. In 1999-2000 around 7,000 households in the UK provided information. The main purpose of the survey is to provide a source for the weighting pattern for the Index of Retail Prices, so it is primarily concerned with household expenditure on goods and services. However, it does have several other important uses.

Although the survey is primarily concerned with the expenditure of private households, much additional information is collected about income and the characteristics of co-operating households. Consequently, the survey provides a unique fund of important economic and social data.

Like all surveys based on a sample of the population, its results are subject to sampling error, and to some bias due to non-response.

The results of the survey are published in an annual report, the latest being *'Family Spending 2000-2001'*. The report includes a list of definitions used in the survey, items on which information is collected and a brief account of the fieldwork procedure.

8.1 Average incomes of households before and after taxes and benefits[1], 1999/00
United Kingdom

	Retired households		Non-retired households								
	1 adult	2 or more adults	1 adult	2 adults	3 or more adults	1 adult with children	2 adults with 1 child	2 adults with 2 children	2 adults with 3 or more children	3 or more adults with children	All house-holds
Number of households in the population (thousands)	3 624	2 863	4 346	5 108	2 068	1 546	1 807	2 051	957	965	25 334
Average per household (£ per year)											
Original income	3 526	10 302	15 201	31 877	37 334	6 721	32 914	34 900	28 740	41 588	22 004
Disposable income	7 727	15 053	12 989	26 098	31 813	11 224	27 173	28 735	26 470	36 297	20 225
Post-tax income	6 389	11 730	10 196	21 098	24 714	8 857	21 825	23 113	21 262	28 967	16 134

1 Redistribution of Income, included in the Effects of taxes and benefits upon household income, 1999/00, article published in the April 2001 edition of *Economic Trends*.

Source: Office for National Statistics: 020 7533 5772

8.2 Distribution of total incomes before and after tax
United Kingdom
Years ended 5 April

| | 1996/97 Annual Survey | | | | | 1997/98 Annual Survey | | | |
| | Number of individuals (000s) | £ million | | | | Number of individuals (000s) | £ million | | |
		Total income before tax	Total tax	Total income after tax			Total income before tax	Total tax	Total income after tax
Lower limit of range of income					**Lower limit of range of income**				
All incomes[1]	25 700	427 000	75 800	351 000	All incomes[1]	26 200	461 000	79 500	381 100
Income before tax £					Income before tax £				
3 765	259	1 010	6	1 000					
4 000	567	2 400	49	2 360	4 045	509	2 170	21	2 150
4 500	589	2 800	100	2 700	4 500	560	2 660	74	2 580
5 000	896	4 710	180	4 530	5 000	678	3 580	127	3 450
5 500	810	4 660	220	4 430	5 500	841	4 840	190	4 650
6 000	1 640	10 700	680	9 990	6 000	1 640	10 700	600	10 100
7 000	1 570	11 800	910	10 900	7 000	1 540	11 600	820	10 800
8 000	3 080	27 800	2 690	25 100	8 000	3 050	27 400	2 440	25 000
10 000	2 830	31 100	3 770	27 300	10 000	2 850	31 200	3 520	27 700
12 000	3 470	46 700	6 630	40 100	12 000	3 530	47 500	6 270	41 200
15 000	3 980	69 000	10 900	58 000	15 000	4 260	73 800	11 100	62 700
20 000	3 770	90 800	16 000	74 800	20 000	3 260	102 700	17 200	85 500
30 000	1 550	57 500	12 600	44 800	30 000	1 730	63 7000	13 100	50 600
50 000	491	32 400	9 270	23 100	50 000	582	38 400	10 600	27 700
100 000 and over	154	33 800	11 840	22 000	100 000	135	18 000	5 850	12 100
					200 000 and over	51	22 400	7 560	14 900
Income after tax £					Income after tax £				
3 765	326	1 280	99	1 270					
4 000	705	3 070	77	2 990	4 045	629	2 710	33	2 680
4 500	707	3 520	150	3 370	4 500	683	3 350	112	3 240
5 000	1 040	5 720	240	5 470	5 000	812	4 470	186	4 280
5 500	1 020	6 200	350	5 850	5 500	1 000	6 050	281	5 770
6 000	1 920	13 500	1 000	12 500	6 000	1 960	13 600	885	12 700
7 000	1 920	15 800	1 390	14 400	7 000	1 900	15 600	1 270	14 300
8 000	3 820	38 700	4 310	34 400	8 000	3 750	37 600	3 840	33 800
10 000	3 180	40 300	5 400	34 900	10 000	3 230	40 500	5 100	35 400
12 000	3 560	56 300	8 550	47 800	12 000	3 760	58 800	8 390	50 400
15 000	3 660	75 700	12 800	62 900	15 000	4 030	82 800	13 300	69 500
20 000	2 640	77 800	14 900	62 900	20 000	3 070	89 100	15 900	73 200
30 000	861	42 500	10 900	31 600	30 000	1 030	50 100	12 300	37 900
50 000	237	22 700	7 100	15 600	50 000	291	27 700	8 460	19 200
100 000 and over	72	23 900	8 570	15 300	100 000	63	12 800	4 350	8 420
					200 000 and over	23	15 500	5 150	10 400

8.2 Distribution of total incomes before and after tax
United Kingdom
continued   Years ended 5 April

| | 1998/99 Annual Survey | | | | | 1999/00 Annual Survey | | | |
| | | £ million | | | | | £ million | | |
	Number of individuals (000s)	Total income before tax	Total tax	Total income after tax		Number of individuals (000s)	Total income before tax	Total tax	Total income after tax
Lower limit of range of income					**Lower limit of range of income**				
All incomes[1]	26 900	498 000	88 000	409 000	All incomes[1]	27 000	527 400	92 000	435 400
Income before tax £					Income before tax £				
4 195	322	1 400	9	1 390					
4 500	552	2 620	57	2 560	4 335	736	3 440	24	3 420
5 000	580	3 050	112	2 930	5 000	1 070	5 920	113	5 810
5 500	873	5 030	183	4 850	6 000	3 120	21 800	930	20 900
6 000	1 640	10 600	561	10 100	8 000	2 980	26 800	2 090	24 800
7 000	1 560	11 700	821	10 900	10 000	2 780	30 700	3 100	27 600
8 000	3 120	28 000	2 400	25 600	12 000	2 450	31 700	3 770	28 000
10 000	2 730	30 000	3 290	26 700	14 000	2 170	32 500	4 240	28 200
12 000	3 650	49 100	6 290	42 800	16 000	1 940	32 900	4 590	28 300
15 000	4 460	77 200	11 400	65 800	18 000	1 570	29 700	4 450	25 300
20 000	4 460	107 600	17 900	89 700	20 000	4 761	115 300	18 660	96 600
30 000	2 060	75 900	15 300	60 600	30 000	2 386	88 230	16 980	71 200
50 000	702	46 400	12 800	33 600	50 000	800	52 891	14 133	38 763
100 000	160	21 300	6 940	14 300	100 000	178	23 700	7 550	16 200
200 000 and over	62	27 600	9 980	17 700	200 000 and over	69	31 700	11 400	20 400
Income after tax £					Income after tax £				
4 195	394	1 730	14	1 710					
4 500	701	3 420	91	3 330	4 335	802	3 780	28	3 750
5 000	725	3 990	175	3 810	5 000	1 250	7 060	155	6 900
5 500	1 010	6 060	260	5 800	6 000	3 820	28 100	1 470	26 600
6 000	1 990	13 700	839	12 900	8 000	3 600	35 600	3 220	32 300
7 000	1 840	15 000	1 210	13 800	10 000	3 320	41 100	4 670	36 400
8 000	3 740	37 100	3 630	33 500	12 000	2 730	40 700	5 330	35 300
10 000	3 280	41 000	5 010	36 000	14 000	2 360	41 100	5 810	35 300
12 000	3 940	61 600	8 610	53 000	16 000	1 870	37 400	5 680	31 700
15 000	4 220	86 400	13 600	72 800	18 000	1 470	33 100	5 220	27 900
20 000	3 390	98 800	17 500	81 300	20 000	3 739	108 400	18 470	89 900
30 000	1 250	60 400	14 500	45 900	30 000	1 528	72 580	16 474	56 120
50 000	352	33 400	10 200	23 200	50 000	414	38 466	11 355	27 140
100 000	76	15 400	5 290	10 100	100 000	86	17 200	5 780	11 500
200 000 and over	28	19 300	7 060	12 300	200 000 and over	32	22 800	8 300	14 500

1 All figures have been independently rounded.

Source: Board of Inland Revenue: 020 7438 4335

8.3 Sources of gross household income
United Kingdom

		1990	1991	1992	1993	1994 /95	1995 /96	1996 /97	1997 /98	1998[1] /99	1999[1] /00	2000[1,2] /01
Number of households supplying data	KPDA	7 046	7 056	7 418	6 979	6 853	6 797	6 415	6 409	6 630	7 097	6 637
Average weekly household income by source (£)												
Wages and salaries	KPCB	212.50	222.00	222.70	228.30	237.90	245.00	256.30	280.20	309.20	315.40	336.70
Self-employment	KPCC	32.10	29.70	29.60	29.20	35.30	32.90	37.50	32.90	37.20	46.00	44.50
Investments	KPCD	19.00	23.70	20.80	18.00	16.20	18.10	17.80	18.70	18.80	21.80	20.00
Annuities and pensions (other than social security benefits)	KPCE	15.50	17.30	19.60	21.90	23.50	26.00	26.00	28.90	30.30	32.80	35.00
Social security benefits	KPCF	35.30	40.10	45.00	48.90	49.90	52.40	54.10	55.00	55.80	58.00	60.10
Imputed income from owner/rent-free occupancy[1]	KPCG	18.60	24.50	..	..	..	..	..	..	..	..	..
Other sources	KPCH	4.50	5.30	5.20	6.70	6.50	6.60	5.30	5.20	5.70	5.90	6.20
Total	KPCI	337.60	362.70	342.90	353.00	369.30	380.90	396.90	420.80	457.00	479.90	502.50
Sources of household income as a percentage of total household income												
Wages and salaries	KPCJ	63	61	65	65	64	64	65	67	68	66	67
Self-employment	KPCK	10	8	9	8	10	9	9	8	8	10	9
Investments	KPCL	6	7	6	5	4	5	5	4	4	5	4
Annuities and pensions (other than social security benefits)	KPCM	5	5	6	6	6	7	7	7	7	7	7
Social security benefits	KPCN	11	11	13	14	14	14	14	13	12	12	12
Imputed income from owner/rent-free occupancy[1]	KPCO	6	7	..	..	..	..	..	..	..	..	..
Other sources	KPCP	1	2	2	2	2	2	1	1	1	1	1
Total	KPCQ	100	100	100	100	100	100	100	100	100	100	100

1 Income based on weighted data.
2 Data are provisional.

Sources: Family Expenditure Survey,;
Office for National Statistics: 020 7533 5756

8.4 Availability in households of certain durable goods
United Kingdom

Percentage

		1990	1991	1992	1993	1994 /95	1995 /96	1996 /97	1997 /98	1998[1] /99	1999[1] /00	2000[1,2] /01
Number of households supplying data	KPDA	7 046	7 056	7 418	6 979	6 853	6 797	6 415	6 409	6 630	7 097	6 637
Car	KPDB	67	68	68	69	69	70	69	70	72	71	72
One	KPDC	44	45	45	46	45	47	43	44	44	43	44
Two	KPDD	19	19	19	19	20	19	22	21	23	21	22
Three or more	KPDE	4	4	4	4	4	4	5	5	5	6	6
Central heating, full or partial	KPDF	79	81	82	83	84	85	87	89	89	90	91
Washing machine	KPDG	86	87	88	89	89	91	91	91	92	91	92
Refrigerator or fridge/freezer	KPDH	98	98	99	99	99	99	..	..	..	..	..
Fridge/freezer or deep freezer	KPDI	80	82	84	87	86	87	91	90	92	91	94
Refrigerator	KPDJ	..	..	..	..	..	..	49	51	52	53	..
Dishwasher	GPTL	..	..	..	..	18	20	20	22	23	23	25
Television	KPDK	98	98	98	..	..	..	..	..	..	..	..
Telephone	KPDL	87	88	88	90	91	92	93	94	95	95	93
Home computer	KPDM	17	18	19	..	..	..	27	29	33	38	44
Video recorder	KPDN	61	65	69	73	76	79	82	84	85	86	87
Internet access	ZBUZ	..	..	..	..	..	..	..	..	10	19	32

1 Percentages based on grossed number of households.
2 Data are provisional.

Sources: Family Expenditure Survey,;
Office for National Statistics: 020 7533 5756

8.5 Households and their expenditure at current prices
United Kingdom

		1990	1991	1992	1993	1994 /95	1995 /96	1996 /97	1997[1] /98	1998[1,2] /99	1999[1,2] /00	2000[1,2] /01
Number of households supplying data	KPDA	7 046	7 056	7 418	6 979	6 853	6 797	6 415	6 409	6 630	7 097	6 637

Average weekly household expenditure on commodities and services (£)

		1990	1991	1992	1993	1994 /95	1995 /96	1996 /97	1997[1] /98	1998[1,2] /99	1999[1,2] /00	2000[1,2] /01
Housing	KPEV	44.40	50.20	47.40	44.90	46.40	48.30	49.10	51.50	57.20	57.00	63.90
Fuel and power	KPEW	11.10	12.30	13.00	13.20	13.00	12.90	13.40	12.70	11.70	11.30	11.90
Food	KPEX	44.80	46.10	47.70	50.00	50.40	52.90	55.20	55.90	58.90	59.60	61.90
Alcoholic drink	KPEY	10.00	10.80	11.10	12.00	12.30	11.40	12.40	13.30	14.00	15.30	15.00
Tobacco	KPEZ	4.80	5.20	5.40	5.60	5.60	5.80	6.10	6.10	5.80	6.00	6.10
Clothing and footwear	KCWC	16.00	15.80	16.40	17.40	17.10	17.20	18.30	20.00	21.70	21.00	22.00
Household goods	KCWH	20.00	20.10	21.90	23.10	22.70	23.50	26.70	26.90	29.60	30.70	32.60
Household services	KCWI	12.30	13.00	13.40	15.40	15.10	15.10	16.40	17.90	18.90	18.90	22.00
Personal goods and services	KCWJ	9.50	10.00	10.20	11.00	10.80	11.60	11.60	12.50	13.30	13.90	14.70
Motoring expenditure	KCWK	33.80	34.10	35.70	36.30	36.20	37.00	41.20	46.60	51.70	52.60	55.10
Fares and other travel costs	KCWL	6.20	5.60	7.20	7.00	6.60	6.20	7.50	8.10	8.30	9.20	9.50
Leisure goods	KCWM	11.30	12.10	13.30	13.30	13.90	13.20	15.20	16.40	17.80	18.50	19.70
Leisure services	KCWN	21.50	22.20	27.60	25.60	31.20	32.10	34.00	38.80	41.90	43.90	50.60
Miscellaneous	KCWO	1.40	1.60	1.80	2.10	2.30	2.40	2.20	2.00	1.20	1.40	0.70
Total	KCWP	247.20	259.00	271.80	276.70	289.90	289.90	309.10	328.80	352.20	359.40	385.70

		1990	1991	1992	1993	1994 /95	1995 /96	1996 /97	1997[1] /98	1998[1,2] /99	1999[1,2] /00	2000[1,2] /01

Expenditure on commodity or service as a percentage of total expenditure

		1990	1991	1992	1993	1994	1995	1996	1997[1]	1998[1,2]	1999[1,2]	2000[1,2]
Housing	KPFH	18	19	17	16	16	17	16	16	16	16	17
Fuel and power	KPFI	5	5	5	5	5	5	4	4	3	3	3
Food	KPFJ	18	18	18	18	18	18	18	17	17	17	16
Alcoholic drink	KPFK	4	4	4	4	4	4	4	4	4	4	4
Tobacco	KPFL	2	2	2	2	2	2	2	2	2	2	2
Clothing and footwear	KPFM	7	6	6	6	6	6	6	6	6	6	6
Household goods	KCWQ	8	8	8	8	8	8	9	8	8	9	8
Household services	KCWR	5	5	5	6	5	5	5	5	5	5	6
Personal goods and services	KCWS	4	4	4	4	4	4	4	4	4	4	4
Motoring expenditure	KCWT	14	13	13	13	13	13	13	14	15	15	14
Fares and other travel costs	KCWU	3	2	3	3	2	2	2	3	2	3	2
Leisure goods	KCWV	5	5	5	5.	5	5	5	5	5	5	5
Leisure services	KCWW	9	9	10	9	11	11	11	12	12	12	13
Miscellaneous	KPFR	1	1	1	1	1	1	1	1	–	–	–
Total	KPFS	100	100	100	100	100	100	100	100	100	100	100

1 Rented unfurnished includes Local Authority and Housing Association (furnished and unfurnished) and privately rented (unfurnished). Rented furnished only includes privately rented (furnished) Owner-occupied includes shared owners (who part own and part rent).

2 Averages based on grossed number of households. Expenditure based on weighted data and including children's expenditure.

Sources: Family Expenditure Survey,;
Office for National Statistics:020 7533 5756

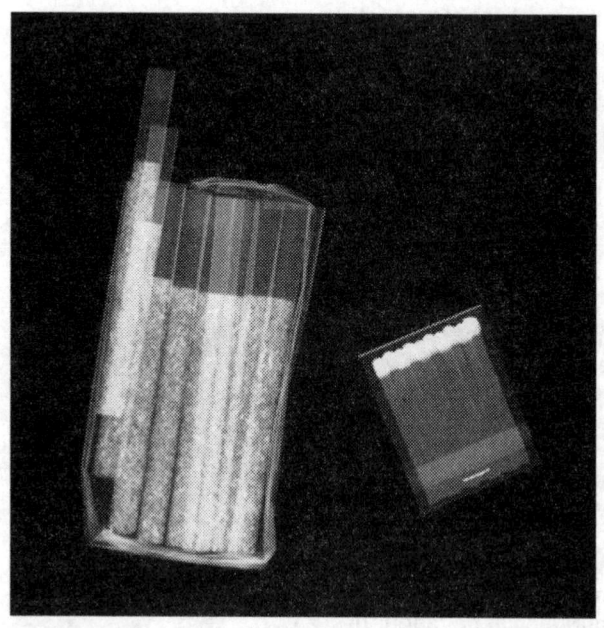

9 Health

Health

Occupational ill health *(Tables 9.6 and 9.7)*

There are a number of sources of data on the extent of occupational or work-related ill health in Great Britain. For some potentially severe lung diseases caused by exposures which are highly unlikely to be found in a non-occupational setting, it is useful to count the number of death certificates issued each year. This is also true for mesothelioma, a cancer affecting the lining of the lungs and stomach, for which the number of cases with non-occupational causes is likely to be larger (although still a minority). **Table 9.7** shows the number of deaths for *mesothelioma* and *asbestosis* (linked to exposure to asbestos), *pneumoconiosis* (linked to coal dust or silica), *byssinosis* (linked to cotton dust) and some forms of *allergic alveolitis* (including farmer's lung). For asbestos-related diseases the figures are derived from a special register maintained by HSE.

Most conditions which can be caused or made worse by work can also arise from other factors. The remaining sources of data on work-related ill health rely on *attribution* of individual cases of illness to work causes. In the Occupational Disease Intelligence Network (ODIN), this is done by specialist doctors - either occupational physicians or those working in particular disease specialisms (covering musculoskeletal, psychological, respiratory, skin, audiological and infectious disease). **Table 9.6** presents data from ODIN for the last three years. It should be noted that not all cases of occupational disease will be seen by participating specialists; for example, the number of deaths due to mesothelioma (shown in Table 9.7) is known to be greater than the number of cases reported to ODIN.

Injuries at work *(Table 9.8)*

The appropriate 'responsible person' is required to report injuries arising from workplace activities to HSC or the local authority under the Reporting of Injuries, Diseases and Dangerous Occurrences Regulations 1995 (RIDDOR 95). This includes fatal injuries, non-fatal major injuries, as defined by the Regulations, and other injuries causing incapacity for work for more than 3 days. As of 1 April 2001, cases could be alternatively reported to an Incident Contact Centre (ICC), based at Caerphilly.

HSE gets to know about virtually all workplace fatalities. However, it is known that employers and others do not report all non-fatal reportable injuries. To estimate the level of under-reporting by employers, HSE place questions each year with the Labour Force Survey (LFS), asking respondents if they have suffered a workplace injury in the past year.

The results from the LFS show that in Great Britain employers now report 44% of reportable injuries. Although the reporting level is higher now than in 1990, LFS results are indicating that the rate of improvement in non-fatal injury rates is slowing more recently. The self-employed report fewer that 1 in 20 reportable injuries.

9.1 Hospital and family health services
England and Wales

			England						Wales				
			1996	1997	1998	1999	2000		1996	1997	1998	1999	2000
Hospital services[1]													
Average daily number of available beds	KNMY	Thousands	199	194	190	186	186	KNHY	15.6	15.2	14.9	14.7	14.6
Average daily occupation of beds:													
All departments	KNMX	"	162	157	157	154	156	KNHX	12.2	12.0	11.8	11.8	11.7
Psychiatric departments	KNMW	"	41	39	37	34	34	KNGZ	3.0	2.9	2.7	2.6	2.5
Persons waiting for admission at 31 March[2]	KNMV	"	1 048	1 158	1 298	1 037	1 007	KNGY	65.0	69.9	61.8	75.4	61.1
Finished consultant episodes	KNLZ		..	..	..	..	..						
Day case admissions	KNLY	"	2 907	3 071	3 421	3 593	..	KNBZ	173.5	186.9	191.0	195.0	216.2
Ordinary admissions	KIBS	"	8 369	8 459	8 563	8 604	..	KNEO	516.4	521.1	522.7	516.3	513.8
Out-patients													
New cases	KNLX	"	11 293	11 529	11 778	12 136	12 466	KNBY	667.1	693.3	691.3	694.1	699.2
Total attendances	KNLW	"	40 872	41 635	42 154	43 041	43 569	KNBX	2 569.5	2 643.3	2 667.4	2 706.2	2 737.2
Accident and Emergency:													
New cases	KOTH	"	12 484	12 794	12 811	13 167	12 953	KTCO	798.4	826.6	831.0	868.0	853.7
Total attendances	KOTI	"	14 126	14 364	14 280	14 629	14 293	KTCP	975.3	997.9	982.0	1 026.4	986.2
Ward attendances	KOTJ	"	1 027	1 034	1 068	1 073	1 078	KTCQ	..	..	..	..	..
Family health services[3]													
Medical services:													
Doctors on the list[4]	KNKX	Numbers	..	..	..	..	..	KNBR	1 736	1 753	1 749	1 761	1 775
Number of UPEs[5]	LQZZ		26 855	27 099	27 392	27 591	27 704	ZCMA	1 739	1 756	1 755	1 770	1 880
Number of patients per doctor	KNKW	"	1 885	1 878	1 866	1 845	1 853	KNBQ	1 724	1 706	1 713	1 694	1 695
Paid to doctors[6]	KNKV	£ millions	2 857.0	3 131.0	3 242.0	3 348.0	..	KNBP	170.5	179.4	186.0	201.3	213.0
Pharmaceutical services:[7,8]													
Number of prescription forms	KWUK	Millions	282.9	287.4	291.1	293.6	300.0						
Number of prescription items	KWUL	"	484.9	500.2	513.2	529.8	552.0	KNBO	38.0	39.6	40.7	42.1	44.0
Total cost	KWUM	£ millions	4 534.2	4 919.8	5 231.4	5 619.9	5 966.0	KNBN	325.6	351.9	372.7	403.9	434.0
Average total cost per prescription	KWUN	£	9.40	9.80	10.20	10.60	11.00	KNBK	8.56	8.89	9.17	9.60	10.00
Income from patients	KWUO	£ millions	295.7	320.9	341.3	366.7	387.0	KNBM	16.9	18.8	19.6	21.6	23.0
Dental services:													
Principals on an FHSA/HA list at 30 September[9]	KIAZ	Numbers	15 280	15 509	15 820	16 089	16 276	KIBG	834	863	879	913	928
Number of adult courses of treatments	KIBA	Thousands	24 580	25 268	26 171	25 915	26 353	KIBH	1 357	1 446	1 514	1 525	1 557
Number of adult patients accepted into continuing care provision at 30 September[10]	KIBB	"	19 524	19 383	16 721	16 649	16 813	KIBI	1 177	1 184	1 043	1 055	1 074
Number of children accepted into capitation at 30 September[10]	KIBC	"	7 270	7 367	6 775	6 821	6 845	KIBJ	426	434	405	408	411
Gross expenditure[11]	KIBD	£ thousands	1 323 074	1 347 577	1 437 727	1 477 423	1 554 885	KIBK	72 248	76 816	82 262	86 093	91 498
Paid by patients[11]	KIBE	"	382 995	388 436	419 621	431 189	453 062	KIBL	19 483	20 665	22 293	23 456	24 634
Paid out of public funds[11]	KIBF	"	940 078	959 141	1 018 106	1 046 234	1 101 823	KIBM	52 765	56 151	59 969	62 637	66 864
General ophthalmic services:													
Sight tests[12,13]	KNJL	Thousands	6 808	6 991	6 992	9 399	9 567	KNBD	464	477	477	631	659
Pairs of spectacles for which NHS vouchers redeemed[13]	KNJK	"	3 967	3 935	3 777	3 662	3 575	KNBC	287	300	288	275	273
Cost of services (gross)[11]	KNJJ	£ millions	237.2	241.4	239.6	281.0	292.0	KNBA	17.2	17.8	17.7	20.1	21.0
Paid out of public funds:[11]													
For sight testing	KNJH	"	97.5	102.8	103.5	146.1	156.0	KMZZ	6.7	7.1	7.2	9.8	10.0
For cost of vouchers[10]	KNHZ	"	139.8	138.6	136.0	134.4	136.0	KMZX	9.5	9.8	9.6	9.4	10.0

1 Data shown reflect data for the financial year commencing the year in the heading (for example the figure under 1996 reflects 1996/97 data). Out-patient figures do not include accident and emergency figures or ward attenders which are given separately as follows: Information on general practitioner maternity clinics was not collected separately from 1992/93 in England.

2 People awaiting elective admission at NHS Trusts in England and Wales, as an inpatient or a day case.

3 Welsh FHS expenditure and income is based upon cash payments and receipts in each financial year, as accrued gross expenditure is not available in a common format for all years shown in this series. Welsh Dental Services data excludes refunds of dental charges.

4 For Wales, Principals providing unrestricted services as at 1 October

5 UPE's include Unrestricted Principals, PMS Contracted GP's and PMS salaried GP's. UPE data are at 1 October.

6 For Wales, includes PFMA but excludes GPFH drugs and payments to providers.

7 Welsh data is based on pricing bureau totals of prescriptions dispensed in a calendar year and paid during the financial year. Data shown reflects data for the year commencing the year in the heading (eg. the figure under 1996 reflects 1996/97 data). Financial year is from 1 April to 31 March.

8 The data cover all prescription items dispensed by community pharmacists and appliance contractors, dispensing doctors and prescriptions submitted by prescribing doctors for items personally administered. Total cost refers to the cost of the drug less discounts and includes on cost allowance, dispensing fees, container allowance, oxygen payments and VAT. The figures for income from patients are for financial years. Figures include charges retained by pharmacists, received by dispensing doctors, income from pre-payment certificates, and recoveries from patients.

9 Principals only. Assistants and vocational trainees are not included. Some dentists may have a contract with more than one Family Health Service /Health Authority. These dentists have been counted once only.

10 Figures for 1998 onwards are affected by the shortening of the registration period to 15 months.

11 In England, figures are based on provisional outturn figures. Gross expenditure and patient figures have been adjusted from previous publications to include refunds of dental charges. In Wales, figures are for financial years and are based on the Appropriation account.

12 Number of NHS sight tests paid for by FHSAs/HAs in the period.

13 Data given are for financial years and reflect the year commencing the year in the table heading (eg. the figures for 1999 represents 1999/2000 data).

Sources: Department of Health: 020 7972 2231;
National Assembly for Wales: 029 2082 5080

9.2 Hospital and primary care services
Scotland

		Unit	1990	1991	1992	1993	1994	1995	1996	1997	1998	1999	2000
Hospital and community services													
In-patients[1,2]:													
Average available staffed beds	KDEA	Thousands	52.1	50.6	48.7	46.7	44.2	42.4	40.6	38.4	36.8	35.2	33.5
Average occupied beds:													
All departments	KDEB	"	42.5	41.2	39.5	38.1	35.9	34.3	32.8	30.9	29.5	28.2	26.9
Psychiatric and learning disability	KDEC	"	17.0	16.3	15.5	14.6	13.2	12.6	11.7	10.8	10.0	9.1	8.3
Discharges or deaths[3]	KDED	"	896	912	920	942	952	960	973	965	977	975	965
Outpatients:[2,4]													
New cases	KDEE	"	2 381	2 403	2 426	2 457	2 503	2 577	2 666	2 675	2 715	2 734	2 766
Total attendances	KDEF	"	5 925	5 971	6 005	6 086	6 145	6 241	6 338	6 272	6 331	6 424	6 451
Medical and dental staff:[5]	JYXO	Numbers	7 936	7 890	8 069	8 078	8 317	8 524	8 774	9 098	9 157	9 367	9 324
Whole-time	KDEG	"	5 475	5 481	5 625	5 767	5 937	6 102	6 433	6 707	7 052	7 202	6 889
Part-time	KDEH	"	1 881	1 862	1 883	1 730	1 827	1 854	1 819	1 886	1 613	1 685	1 971
Honorary	JYXN	"	580	547	561	582	563	579	534	522	506	495	496
Professional and technical staff[6]:													
Whole-time	KDEI	"	9 291	9 387	9 759	9 953	10 062	10 452	10 584	10 740	10 884	11 261	11 261
Part-time	KDEJ	"	2 727	2 782	3 127	3 434	3 753	4 075	4 370	4 738	4 928	5 218	5 483
Nursing and midwifery staff[7]:													
Whole-time	KDEK	"	34 364	34 302	34 053	33 284	32 956	32 693	32 560	32 218	32 156	32 356	32 397
Part-time	KDEL	"	28 781	29 887	30 709	30 459	30 532	30 580	29 917	29 736	29 178	29 242	29 067
Administrative and clerical staff[8]:													
Whole-time	KDEM	"	13 223	13 718	14 447	15 125	15 723	15 815	15 155	14 707	14 564	14 541	14 433
Part-time	KDEN	"	4 985	5 276	5 815	6 113	6 624	7 005	6 986	7 174	7 265	7 456	7 663
Domestic, transport, etc. staff[9]:													
Whole-time	KDEO		12 468	11 622	10 805	10 205	9 574	9 037	8 596	8 187	8 090	7 972	7 848
Part-time	KDEP		16 685	16 167	15 753	15 403	14 464	14 105	13 554	13 082	12 716	12 424	12 272
Cost of services (gross)[10]	KDEQ	£ millions	2 195.6	2 503.6	2 768.0	2 940.5	3 050.5	3 269.5	3 430.6	3 610.3	3 856.0	4 309.7	4 862.6
Payments by patients[10]	KDER	"	1.3	1.5	2.0	2.3	0.4	–	–	–	–	–	–
Payments out of public funds[10]	KDES	"	2 194.3	2 502.1	2 766.0	2 938.2	3 050.1	3 269.5	3 430.6	3 610.3	3 855.9	4 309.7	4 862.6
Primary care services													
Medical services													
Doctors on the list[11]:													
Principals[12]	KDET	Numbers	3 359	3 379	3 421	3 456	3 490	3 524	3 573	3 625	3 660	3 697	3 707
Assistants	KDEU	"	16	24	31	22	25	28	22	22	27	20	25
Average number of patients per principal doctor[13]	KDEV	"	1 593	1 580	1 556	1 542	1 524	1 506	1 488	1 468	1 450	1 441	1 425
Payments to doctor[14]	KDEW	£ millions	222.2	247.2	263.8	275.3	291.7	311.9	333.2	356.4	365.9	377.5	404.7
Pharmaceutical services[15]													
Prescriptions dispensed	KDEX	Millions	42.42	44.31	46.10	48.18	49.27	51.08	54.62	56.64	58.52	60.36	62.34
Payments to pharmacists (gross)	KDEY	£ millions	298.2	329.8	370.2	406.1	434.9	474.2	543.4	588.4	627.2	693.7	731.0
Average gross cost per prescription	KDEZ	£	7.030	7.440	8.030	8.430	8.825	9.283	9.950	10.390	10.717	11.492	11.730
Dental services[16]													
Dentists on list[17]	KDFA	Numbers	1 645	1 676	1 702	1 772	1 763	1 764	1 772	1 798	1 854	1 833	1 831
Number of courses of treatment completed	KDFB	Thousands	3 057	2 485	2 569	2 647	2 723	2 711	2 825	3 406	3 349	3 406	3 395
Payments to dentists (gross)[18]	KDFC	£ millions	99.9	132.8	133.6	128.4	136.1	137.3	139.2	154.9	157.5	160.6	162.9
Payments by patients	KDFD	"	48.0	41.6	40.5	40.0	42.2	41.7	41.4	45.9	47.4	48.8	50.6
Payments out of public funds[19]	KDFE	"	51.8	91.3	93.2	88.4	93.9	95.6	97.8	109.0	110.1	111.8	112.3
Average gross cost per course	KDFF	£	33.1	40.0	39.0	37.0	38.0	38.0	40.1	36.5	38.0	38.0	37.0
General ophthalmic services													
Number of sight tests given[19]	KDFG	Thousands	417	477	537	568	614	618	635	656	657	850	861
Number of pairs of glasses supplied[20]	KDFH	"	320	374	404	463	473	461	474	488	485	494	439
Cost of services (gross)	KDFI	£ millions	13.7	16.4	19.7	22.2	24.4	25.8	27.7	29.1	29.8	32.0	33.1
Payments by patients	KDFJ	"	–	..	..	..	..	..	..	..	..	..	..
Payments out of public funds:													
For sight testing and dispensing	KDFK	"	13.7	16.4	19.7	22.2	24.4	25.8	27.7	29.1	29.8	32.0	33.1

1 Excludes joint user and contractual hospitals.
2 In year to 31 March.
3 Includes transfers out, and emergency inpatients treated in day bed units.
4 Including attendances at accident and emergency consultant clinics.
5 At 30 September. Figures exclude officers holding honorary locum appointments. There is an element of double counting of "heads" in this table as doctors can hold more than one contract. For example, they may hold contracts of different type, e.g. part time and honorary. Doctors holding two or more contracts of the same type, e.g. part time, are not double counted. Doctors, whose sum of contracts amounts to whole time, are classed as such.
6 Comprises Scientific and Professional, Professions Allied to Medicine and Technical staff
7 Excludes nurse teachers, nurses in training and students on '1992' courses. Between 1992 and 1993 the criterion for excluding nursing staff on low hours was changed from 0.25 hours to 2 hours. This partially accounts for any decrease in staff numbers between these two years.
8 Comprises Senior Management and Administrative and Clerical staff.
9 Comprises Ambulance, Works, Ancillary, Trades and Health Care Assistant staff.
10 These figures are for Health Boards only and do not include the 2 NHS Trusts in 1992/93, 17 in 1993/94, 39 in 1994/95 and 47 in 1995/96. Estimated from financial years

11 At 1 October.
12 Unrestricted principals in post.
13 Unrestricted principals: establishment.
14 Data relate to financial year, eg 1997 data are for year ending 31 March 1998. As 1994/95 data are unavailable for Dumfries & Galloway Health Board, 1993/94 data have been substituted for that board only.
15 For prescriptions dispensed in calendar year by all community pharmacists (including stock orders), dispensing doctors and appliance suppliers.
16 From 1990, when the new dental contract came into effect, the statistics available centrally changed significantly. From 1991, data refers to financial year (eg 1991 data is for year ending 31 March 1992).
17 Comprises principals only.
18 Before 1991 excludes capitation payments; from 1991 includes capitation, continuing care, weighted entry and item of service fees.
19 This figure represents sight tests paid for by health boards, hospital eye service referrals and GOS(s) ST (v) claimants.
20 Includes hospital eye service.

Source: Common Services Agency and The Scottish Office: 0131 551 8899

9.3 Hospital and general health services
Northern Ireland

		Unit	1991	1992	1993	1994	1995	1996	1997	1998[1]	1999[1]	2000[1]
Hospital services[1]												
In-patients:												
Beds available[2]	KDGA	Numbers	12 600	11 712	10 878	10 356	10 054	9 475	9 007	8 819	8 639	8 571
Average daily occupation of beds	KDGB	*Per cent*	*77.0*	*78.0*	*78.0*	*78.0*	*78.0*	*79.0*	*81.0*	*82.0*	*82.0*	*82.0*
Discharges or deaths[3]	KDGC	Thousands	269	275	290	298	304	300	306	338	332	333
Out-patients[4]:												
New cases	KDGD	"	799	819	836	873	937	933	952	962	980	994
Total attendances	KDGE	"	1 963	1 969	1 967	2 051	2 087	2 072	2 083	2 091	2 106	2 113
General health services												
Medical services[1]												
Doctors (principals) on the list[5,6]	KDGF	Numbers	913	935	953	991	1 005	1 028	1 039	1 042	1 054	1 066
Number of patients per doctor	KDGG	"	1 922	1 808	1 779	1 743	1 731	1 698	1 690	1 693	1 679	1 662
GrossPayments to doctors[7]	KDGH	£ thousand	53 675	56 529	60 975	62 849	65 130	67 872	69 889	71 385	78 604	82 471
Pharmaceutical services[8]												
Prescription forms dispensed	KDGI	Thousands	10 145	10 498	11 291	11 152	12 017	12 802	12 855	13 116	13 453	13 666
Number of prescriptions	KDGJ	"	16 755	17 496	18 660	18 560	19 893	21 203	21 430	22 754	23 249	23 985
Gross cost[9]	KDGK	£ thousand	128 334	146 925	165 638	173 064	197 579	219 978	229 852	248 845	266 535	278 405
Charges[9]	KDGL	"	4 876	5 582	6 175	6 299	6 255	6 028	6 607	6 853	8 183	8 499
Net Cost[9]	KDGM	"	123 458	141 343	159 463	166 764	191 324	213 950	223 245	240 096	258 353	269 906
Average gross cost per prescription	KDGN	£	8	8	9	9	10	10	11	11	11	12
Dental services[8,10]												
Dentists on the list[5]	KDGO	Numbers	533	523	541	568	581	596	609	634	660	674
Number of courses of paid treatment	KDGP	Thousands	704	780	801	825	832	928	1 053	1 088	1 097	1 128
Gross cost[11]	KDGQ	£ thousand	44 059	47 701	43 904	46 318	48 780	51 512	53 733	56 835	58 712	61 251
Patients[11]	KDGR	"	9 926	11 036	10 378	11 231	11 530	11 870	12 433	13 686	14 358	15 078
Contributions (Net cost)[11]	KDGS	"	34 132	36 665	33 525	35 086	37 250	39 642	41 300	43 149	44 354	46 173
Average gross cost per paid treatment	KDGT	£	42	61	55	56	59	56	51	52	54	54
Ophthalmic services[8]												
Number of sight tests given[12]	KDGU	Thousands	135	142	169	182	196	212	227	237	298	305
Number of optical appliances supplied[13]	KDGV	"	110	114	133	139	146	153	159	161	157	160
Cost of service (gross)[14]	KDGW	£ thousand	5 607	5 555	7 363	7 127	8 568	9 555	10 271	10 452	11 365	11 975
Health and social services[15]												
Medical and dental staff:												
Whole-time	KDGZ	Numbers	2 262	2 226	2 209	2 358	2 053	2 107	2 156	2 196	2 231	2 224
Part-time	KDHA	"	560	511	554	694	1 154	1 094	1 041	1 009	1 014	580
Nursing and midwifery staff:												
Whole-time	KDHB	"	13 451	12 381	11 445	11 047	10 896	10 578	10 114	10 117	10 135	9 926
Part-time	KDHC	"	7 144	7 417	7 952	8 662	9 169	8 943	9 015	8 287	8 813	7 591
Administrative and clerical staff:												
Whole-time	KDHD	"	6 398	6 573	6 696	7 006	7 078	7 055	6 915	7 019	7 230	7 373
Part-time	KDHE	"	1 831	1 924	2 050	2 186	2 306	2 518	2 708	2 776	2 910	2 972
Professional and technical staff:												
Whole-time	KDHF	"	2 673	2 695	2 695	2 786	2 862	2 939	2 933	3 014	3 177	3 642
Part-time	KDHG	"	559	636	710	804	921	985	1 060	1 146	1 226	1 283
Social services staff(excluding casual home helps):												
Whole-time	KDHH	"	3 641	3 607	3 550	3 480	3 470	3 441	3 349	3 262	3 319	3 017
Part-time	KDHI	"	1 695	1 707	1 766	1 933	2 110	2 250	2 394	2 241	2 358	991
Ancillary and other staff:												
Whole-time	KDHJ	"	5 551	4 954	4 679	4 364	3 982	3 812	3 569	3 423	3 426	2 207
Part-time	KDHK	"	4 728	4 862	4 767	4 609	3 685	3 558	3 482	3 558	3 913	4 505
Cost of services (gross)[16]	KDHL	£ thousand	889 422	947 354	1 002 326	1 043 745	1 111 507	1 120 563	1 153 741	1 292 348	1 422 920	1 576 657
Payments by recipients	KDHM	"	12 322	12 569	13 189	20 629	32 685	40 725	49 498	59 484	65 533	71 411
Payments out of public funds	KDHN	"	877 100	934 785	989 137	1 023 116	1 078 822	1 079 838	1 104 243	1 232 864	1 357 387	1 505 246

1 Financial Year.
2 Average available beds in wards open overnight during the year.
3 Includes transfers to other hospitals.
4 Includes consultant outpatient clinics and Accident and Emergency departments.
5 At beginning of period.
6 Doctors include assistants.
7 These costs refer to the majority of non-cash limited services: further expenditure under GMS is allocated through HSS Boards on a cash limited basis.
8 From 1995 onwards figures are taken from financial year.
9 Prior to 1992, headings read, 'Payments to Pharmacists (Gross)', 'Payments by Patients', 'Payments out of Public Funds'.
10 Due to changes in the Dental Contract which came into force in October 1990 dentists are now paid under a combination of headings relating to Capitation and Continuing Care patients. Prior to this, payment was simply on an item of service basis, which made statistics such as 'Number of courses of treatment completed' and Average gross cost per course' relevant and meaningful. This is no longer the case.

11 Prior to 1992, headings read 'Payments to Dentists (Gross)', 'Payments by Patients', 'Payments out of Public Funds'.
12 Excluding sight tests given in hospitals and under the school health service and in the home.
13 Relates to the number of vouchers supplied and excludes repair/replace spectacles.
14 Gross cost is defined as net ingredient costs plus on-cost, fees and other payments.
15 Manpower figures refer to 31 December. From 1981, figures for medical and dental staff exclude some joint appointees, information for whom is not held on the computor payroll.
16 Figures relate to the costs of the hospital, community health and personal social services, and have been estimated from financial year data.

Sources: Central Service Agency Northern Ireland: 028 9053 5682;
Dept of Health, Social Services & Public Safety Northern Ireland: 028 9052 2509;
(For figures on Hospital Services: 028 9052 2800)

9.4 Health and personal social services: workforce summary
Great Britain

Numbers or whole-time equivalent

		1991	1992	1993	1994	1995	1996	1997	1998	1999	2000
Health service staff and practitioners at 30 Sep:											
Medical staff: total	KDBC	53 019	53 987	55 632	56 736	60 172	62 176	64 316	67 408	69 089	70 939
Hospital medical staff: total	KDBD	49 620	50 793	52 476	53 787	57 299	59 592	61 937	65 088	66 812	68 767
Consultant	KDBE	17 435	17 846	18 251	18 808	20 246	21 066	21 699	23 139	24 250	25 067
Staff grade[1]	KADJ	516	819	1 230	1 536	2 037	2 440	2 785	3 458	3 868	4 423
Associate specialist	KDBF	949	960	1 032	1 013	1 128	1 223	1 340	1 439	1 527	1 572
Registrar group[2]	KWUG	..	..	..	..	..	11 898	12 435	12 863	13 299	13 372
Senior registrar	KDBG	3 912	3 994	4 130	4 281	4 540	..	..	..	..	..
Registrar	KDBH	7 237	7 132	7 103	7 273	7 294	..	..	..	..	..
Senior house officer	KDBI	13 311	13 863	14 586	14 942	15 661	16 616	17 353	17 760	17 518	17 945
House officer	KADK	3 781	3 798	3 792	3 781	4 003	4 025	4 163	4 287	4 364	4 518
Hospital practitioner	KDBL	208	183	183	178	197	212	198	220	230	231
Clinical assistant	KDBM	2 255	2 189	2 162	1 964	2 182	2 094	1 924	1 907	1 744	1 638
Other staff[3]	KDBK	17	10	8	11	11	18	38	16	11	1
Community health medical staff[4]	KDBN	3 399	3 194	3 156	2 948	2 873	2 584	2 379	2 320	2 278	2 172
Dental staff: total	KDBO	2 954	2 971	2 973	2 947	3 070	3 127	3 078	3 193	3 147	3 107
Hospital dental staff: total	KDBP	1 478	1 546	1 573	1 597	1 687	1 737	1 696	1 807	1 816	1 781
Consultant	KDBQ	498	541	521	537	549	556	524	570	581	580
Staff grade[1]	KADL	5	13	24	39	54	67	86	99	113	118
Associate specialist	KDBR	71	70	69	62	69	65	62	68	70	73
Registrar Group[2]	LQMZ	..	..	..	..	..	..	..	309	314	295
Senior registrar	KDBS	123	122	135	124	123	138	169	..	..	..
Registrar	KDBT	189	188	184	178	186	183	125	..	..	..
Senior house officer	KDBU	266	300	353	394	446	490	491	531	496	497
Dental house officer	KDBV	145	143	126	101	86	68	58	59	68	60
Hospital practitioner	KDBX	15	15	17	20	17	23	22	21	23	21
Clinical assistant	KDBY	165	154	142	141	158	145	152	144	146	136
Other staff[3]	KDBW	1	2	2	2	–	3	6	5	6	–
Community health dental staff[4]	KDBZ	1 476	1 425	1 400	1 350	1 383	1 390	1 382	1 386	1 331	1 326
Total non-medical staff[5]	KWUH	912 028	906 236	899 234	876 630	859 213	851 185	894 309	757 143	772 059	888 276
Nursing and midwifery staff:[6,7] (excluding agency): total	KDCA	483 507	467 723	446 056	429 214	353 842	356 109	353 933	355 887	362 554	421 634
qualified	KSBR	298 299	300 698	295 245	291 070	292 248	264 744	262 732	299 010	267 575	309 642
unqualified	KSBS	114 474	115 431	116 360	116 138	116 053	89 998	90 595	91 447	94 408	111 922
learners[8]	KSBT	59 615	44 879	27 560	13 945	7 580	..	..	2 177	1 962	2 054
unknown	KSBV	11 115	6 714	6 891	8 061	5 768	937	606	435	491	69
All Professional & Technical staff[5] (excluding works)	KSBM	103 572	107 367	109 463	111 597	100 350	105 496	107 158	110 350	114 011	131 946
Health care assistants	KWUI	..	..	..	..	..	18 025	19 260	21 992	22 708	24 916
Support staff	KWUJ	..	..	..	..	..	75 876	72 514	71 004	69 826	78 511
Ancillary, Works & Maintenance[5]	KSBN	132 321	123 100	118 867	110 577	102 669	..	..	13 916	13 579	15 107
Administrative & Clerical staff[5]	KSBO	165 467	179 300	180 820	186 446	180 132	178 461	177 957	164 931	170 306	194 150
Ambulance staff[5]	KSBP	21 369	21 744	21 424	21 379	15 681	16 330	16 424	16 041	16 195	19 214
Others[5,9]	KSBQ	5 696	7 165	639	1 250	8 759	6 834	3 337	832	938	743

9.4
Health and personal social services: workforce summary
Great Britain

continued

		1991[10]	1992	1993	1994	1995	1996	1997	1998	1999	2000
Family Health services:[11]											
General medical practitioners:											
Analysis by type of practitioners at 1 October											
Total											
All Practitioners	GPYL	..	..	..	..	..	..	..	..	37 135	37 573
All Practitioners (excluding GP Retainers)	LQZN	33 462	33 834	34 134	34 421	34 594	34 825	35 205	35 611	35 954	36 226
Unrestricted Principals & equivalents (UPE's)	LQZO	30 712	31 065	31 447	31 767	31 945	32 164	32 477	32 801	33 050	33 186
of which GMS UP's	LQZP	30 712	31 065	31 447	31 767	31 945	32 164	32 477	32 414	32 140	31 869
PMS contracted	LQZQ	..	..	..	..	..	..	..	324	837	1 046
PMS salaried	GRGB	..	..	..	..	..	..	..	63	71	271
Restricted principals	LQZS	151	152	161	156	137	126	111	106	97	94
Assistants	LQZT	471	521	539	626	684	890	891	750	690	671
GP Registrars[12]	LQZU	2 102	2 067	1 956	1 841	1 790	1 605	1 678	1 830	1 903	2 028
of which GMS[11]	LQZV	2 102	2 067	1 956	1 841	1 790	1 605	1 678	1 796	1 825	1 920
Salaried Doctors (Para 52 SFA)	LQZW	..	..	..	..	..	..	..	60	118	159
PMS Other[13]	LQZX	..	..	..	..	..	..	..	12	46	37
Associates	LQZY	26	29	31	31	38	40	48	52	50	51
GP Retainers	GPYM	..	..	..	..	..	..	..	..	1 181	1 347
General dental practitioners: total[14]	KDCQ	18 037	18 019	18 467	18 600	18 736	19 147	19 598	20 216	20 840	21 316
General Dental Service	GPYN	18 037	18 019	18 467	18 600	18 736	19 147	19 598	20 216	20 750	21 124
Personal Dental Service	GPYO	..	..	..	..	..	..	..	..	90	192
Ophthalmic medical practitioners [10,15]	KDCT	862	837	789	735	752	766	830	855	814	765
Ophthalmic opticians [10,15]	KDCU	6 841	6 997	7 124	7 179	7 445	7 652	7 847	8 160	8 422	8 359
Personal Social Services staff [16]:											
Total	KDDE	237 280	235 240	232 911	237 752	233 861	233 655	229 439	223 500	221 700	217 200
Management, administration and ancillary staff[17]	KADS	28 049	29 433	..	..	..	..	..	..	..	..
Home help service	KSBU	58 591	58 004	57 593	59 391	56 961	55 430	53 573	50 417	47 227	42 583
Field Social Workers[18]	KSBX	25 537	26 509	28 850	29 820	31 926	32 140	32 990	33 400	33 900	34 700
Day care establishments staff	KADV	28 442	28 596	30 221	31 270	31 109	31 605	30 839	30 300	30 800	30 800
Residential care staff	KADW	83 001	78 918	74 038	72 155	68 651	67 975	65 422	62 100	59 200	30 800
All other staff[17]	KADX	5 355	5 049	..	..	..	..	..	..	..	..

1 New grade introduced in 1989.
2 Includes Specialist Registrar (SpR), Senior Registrar and Registrar. The SpR grade was introduced formally on 1 April 1996.
3 Figures include Senior Hospital Medical/Dental Officers (SHMO) without an allowance and other ungraded staff.
4 Whole-time equivalent. Figures exclude locums and occasional seasonal staff.
5 A new system for classifying NHS non-medical staff was used for the first time in September 1995 non-medical workforce census classifying staff according to what they do (known as new occupation codes). However in order to provide comparative information with earlier years, payscale based estimates were produced using data from organisations providing both payscale and occupation code information for at least 95 per cent of their non-medical staff. These estimates only provide a broad indication of 1995 levels of staff and therefore should be used with caution. For further information on the 1995 non-medical workforce see the Department of Health's statistical bulletin on non-medical staff in England (1985 - 95). These are England and Wales figures only from 1995.
6 Excludes bank nurses.
7 Nursing total includes qualified, unqualified and others only.
8 1999 and 2000 figures exclude Scotland learners.
9 Due to changes in the collection procedure in 1991 a category of 'other staff' was introduced for these locally determined payscales. In previous years these staff were included in their respective main staff groups. Includes learners from 1996.

10 Figures for England and Wales relate to 31 December. Figures for Scotland relate to 31 March of the following year.
11 GP Registrars in GMS Partnerships.
12 GP Registrars were formerly referred to as Trainees.
13 PMS other includes 2 Salaried Restricted Principals who are working in salaried GP's in Scotland.
14 Includes principals, assistants and Vocational Dental Practioners and PDS dentists not working in the GDS. Some dentists may have a contract with more than one Family Health Service Authority/Health Authority. These dentists have been counted only once.
15 OMPs and OOs holding contracts with FHSAs/HAs and/or Scottish Health Boards to carry out NHS sight tests. OOs with contracts with more than one Health Board and/or a Health Board and a FHSA/HA will be counted more than once.
16 Figures are for England only.
17 Breakdown for England not available in this form from 1993.
18 Includes care managers from 1993.

Sources: Scottish Health Service Common Services Agency;
Department of Health: 020 7972 2231;
National Assembly for Wales

9.5 Notifications of infectious diseases

Numbers

		1990	1991	1992	1993	1994	1995	1996	1997	1998	1999	2000
United Kingdom												
Measles	KHQD	15 642	11 723	12 318	12 018	23 517	9 017	6 866	4 844	4 540	2 951	2 865
Mumps	KWNN	5 297	3 836	3 169	2 726	3 143	2 400	2 182	2 264	1 917	2 000	3 367
Rubella	KWNO	15 736	9 702	9 150	12 300	9 650	7 674	11 720	4 205	4 064	2 575	2 064
Whooping cough	KHQE	16 862	6 279	2 750	4 718	4 837	2 399	2 721	3 669	1 902	1 461	866
Scarlet fever	KHQC	9 505	6 876	5 978	7 341	8 031	6 863	6 101	4 639	4 708	2 956	2 544
Dysentery	KHQG	3 042	11 527	20 620	7 577	7 538	5 498	2 643	2 427	1 934	1 630	1 613
Food poisoning	KHQH	59 721	59 497	72 139	76 711	91 128	92 604	94 923	105 579	105 060	96 866	98 076
Typhoid and Paratyphoid fevers	KHQB	294	288	298	277	390	386	291	249	252	278	205
Hepatitis	KWNP	9 864	9 856	9 616	6 142	4 285	3 823	2 876	3 601	3 781	4 365	4 530
Tuberculosis	KHQI	5 898	6 078	6 442	6 565	6 230	6 176	6 238	6 367	6 605	6 701	7 100
Malaria	KWNQ	1 565	1 652	1 253	1 281	1 219	1 363	1 743	1 549	1 163	1 038	1 166
England and Wales[1]												
Measles	KHRD	13 302	9 680	10 268	9 612	16 375	7 447	5 614	3 962	3 728	2 438	2 378
Mumps	KWNR	4 277	2 924	2 412	2 153	2 494	1 936	1 747	1 914	1 587	1 691	2 162
Rubella	KWNS	11 491	7 174	6 212	9 724	6 326	6 196	9 081	3 260	3 208	1 954	1 653
Whooping cough	KHRE	15 286	5 201	2 309	4 091	3 964	1 869	2 387	2 989	1 577	1 139	712
Scarlet fever	KHRC	7 187	5 217	4 645	5 855	6 193	5 296	4 873	3 569	3 339	2 086	1 933
Dysentery	KHRG	2 756	9 935	16 960	6 841	6 956	4 651	2 312	2 274	1 813	1 538	1 494
Food poisoning	KHRH	52 145	52 543	63 347	68 587	81 833	82 041	83 233	93 901	93 932	86 316	86 528
Typhoid and Paratyphoid fevers	KHRB	271	281	282	268	370	370	276	241	243	276	204
Viral hepatitis	KWNT	9 005	8 860	8 993	5 557	3 722	3 296	2 437	3 186	3 183	3 424	3 541
Tuberculosis[2]	KHRJ	5 204	5 436	5 799	5 921	5 591	5 608	5 654	5 859	6 087	6 144	6 572
Malaria	KWNU	1 493	1 553	1 189	1 198	1 139	1 300	1 659	1 476	1 110	1 005	1 128
Total meningitis	KHRO	2 572	2 760	2 571	2 082	1 800	2 285	2 686	2 345	2 072	2 094	2 432
Meningococcal meningitis	KHRP	1 138	1 117	1 067	1 053	938	1 146	1 164	1 220	1 152	1 145	1 164
Meningococcal septicaemia	KWNV	277	273	277	398	430	707	1 129	1 440	1 509	1 822	1 614
Ophthalmia neonatorum	KHRI	440	433	424	340	268	245	246	224	198	163	176
Scotland												
Measles	KHSE	2 006	1 701	1 747	1 911	6 192	1 307	1 055	762	700	434	395
Mumps	KWNW	833	723	601	458	546	371	368	282	251	216	199
Rubella	KWNX	3 702	2 171	2 645	2 048	2 916	1 258	2 449	818	745	548	349
Whooping cough	KHSF	1 291	838	236	493	639	399	186	545	225	214	93
Scarlet fever	KHSD	1 546	1 084	808	911	1 319	1 065	750	645	883	438	301
Dysentery	KHSH	235	1 526	3 486	607	446	575	176	124	103	82	95
Food poisoning[3]	KHSI	6 757	6 318	7 877	7 170	8 291	9 297	10 234	10 144	9 186	8 517	9 263
Typhoid and Paratyphoid fevers	KHSB	20	7	15	7	18	16	14	6	6	2	1
Viral hepatitis	KWNY	546	556	319	290	296	405	360	359	490	863	943
Tuberculosis[4]	KHSL	563	546	559	554	546	478	509	433	457	496	469
Malaria	KWUC	68	91	50	75	74	58	70	57	30	20	27
Meningococcal infection	KWUD	216	178	207	207	201	190	201	271	313	329	301
Erysipelas	KHSC	125	155	128	130	118	125	84	95	66	64	41
Northern Ireland												
Measles	KHTD	334	342	303	495	950	263	197	120	112	79	92
Mumps	KHTR	187	189	156	115	103	93	67	68	79	93	1 006
Rubella	KHTQ	543	357	293	528	408	220	190	127	111	73	62
Whooping cough	KHTE	285	240	205	134	234	131	148	135	100	108	61
Scarlet fever	KHTC	772	575	525	575	519	502	478	425	486	432	310
Dysentery	KHTG	51	66	174	129	136	272	155	29	18	10	24
Food poisoning	KHTH	819	636	915	954	1 004	1 266	1 456	1 534	1 942	2 033	2 285
Typhoid and Paratyphoid fevers	KHTB	3	–	1	2	2	–	1	2	3	–	–
Infective hepatitis	KHTO	313	440	304	295	267	122	79	56	108	78	46
Tuberculosis	KHTI	131	96	84	90	93	90	75	75	61	61	59
Malaria	KWUE	4	8	14	8	6	5	14	16	23	13	11
Acute encephalitis/meningitis	KHTM	158	172	118	122	144	116	105	91	64	99	129
Meningococcal septicaemia	KWUF	2	23	27	34	39	42	67	56	87	145	123
Gastro-enteritis (children under 2 years)	KHTP	1 157	1 091	1 070	1 379	888	1 072	745	896	1 371	1 121	1 205

1 The figures show the corrected number of notifications, incorporating revisions of diagnosis, either by the notifying medical practitioner or by the medical superintendent of the infectious diseases hospital. Cases notified in Port Health Authorities are included.

2 Formal notifications of new cases only. The figures exclude chemoprophylaxis.

3 Scotland's food poisoning includes 'otherwise ascertained' for the first time in 1995.

4 Figures include cases of tuberculosis not notified before death.

Sources: Information and Statistics Division, NHS in Scotland;
General Register Office (Northern Ireland);
PHLS Communicable Diseases Surveillance Centre: 020 8200 6868

9.6 Estimated number of cases of work-related disease reported by specialist physicians to ODIN[1]

Great Britain

	All physicians			Disease specialist physicians			Occupational physicians		
	1998	1999	2000	1998	1999	2000	1998	1999	2000
Musculoskeletal disorders					(MOSS)			(OPRA)	
Upper limb	4 958	5 174	5 043	1 644	1 872	1 752	3 314	3 302	3 291
Spine/ back	2 263	2 715	2 293	648	768	636	1 615	1 947	1 657
Lower limb	494	626	372	252	168	144	242	458	228
Other	264	300	216	96	120	48	168	180	168
Total number of diagnoses	7 979	8 815	7 924	2 640	2 928	2 580	5 339	5 887	5 344
Total number of individuals[2]	7 666	8 635	7 792	2 544	2 844	5 568	5 122	5 791	5 224
Mental ill health[3]					(SOS-) (MI)			(OPRA)	
Stress/ anxiety/ depression	..	5 523	6 327	..	3 024	2 820	2 125	2 499	3 507
Other	..	1 464	912	..	1 224	756	313	240	156
Total number of diagnoses	..	6 987	7 239	..	4 248	3 576	2 438	2 739	3 663
Total number of individuals[2]	..	6 566	6 555	..	3 996	3 420	2 113	2 570	3 135
Respiratory disease					(SWO-) (RD)			(OPRA)	
Asthma	807	1 129	797	409	663	494	398	466	303
Malignant mesothelioma	701	1 018	964	685	991	909	16	27	55
Benign pleural disease	625	1 243	1 080	600	1 205	1 056	25	38	24
Other	876	1 028	1 013	590	687	722	286	341	291
Total number of diagnoses	3 009	4 418	3 854	2 284	3 546	3 181	725	872	673
Total number of individuals[2]	2 934	4 298	3 787	2 246	3 474	3 114	688	824	673
Skin disease					(EPI-) (DERM)			(OPRA)	
Contact dermatitis	3 587	3 933	3 400	1 991	2 291	2 063	1 596	1 642	1 337
Skin neoplasia	347	339	480	347	339	468	-	-	12
Other	645	678	518	304	288	241	341	390	277
Total number of diagnoses	4 579	4 950	4 398	2 642	2 918	2 772	1 937	2 032	1 626
Total number of individuals[2]	4 456	4 850	4 310	2 567	2 830	2 684	1 889	2 020	1 626
Audiological disease					(OSSA)			(OPRA)	
Sensorineural hearing loss	932	714	627	582	436	279	350	278	348
Other	367	289	170	367	265	170	-	24	-
Total number of diagnoses	1 299	1 003	797	949	701	449	350	302	348
Total number of individuals[2]	982	756	648	632	454	300	350	302	348
Infections[4]					(SI-) (DAW)				
Diarrhoeal diseases	..	..	..	1 020	481	367	..	..	..
Other	..	..	..	118	141	194	..	..	..
Total number of diagnoses	..	..	..	1 138	622	561	..	..	..
Total number of individuals[2]	..	..	..	1 138	622	561	..	..	..

1 Occupational Disease Intelligence Network. Comprises the following schemes: OPRA: Occupational Physicians Reporting Activity; MOSS: Musculoskeletal Occupational Surveillance Scheme; SOSMI: Surveillance of Occupational Stress and Mental Illness; SWORD: Surveillance of Work-related and Occupational Respiratory Disease; EPIDERM: Occupational skin disease surveillance by dermatologists; OSSA: Occupational Surveillance Scheme for Audiologists; SIDAW: Surveillance of Infectious Disease At Work.

2 Individuals may have more than one diagnosis.
3 Reports to SOSMI began in January 1999.
4 Infections are not covered by OPRA. A change in SIDAW reporting requirements in mid-1999 reduced the reporting of diarrhoeal diseases.

Source: Health and Safety Executive: 0151 951 4556

9.7 Deaths due to occupationally related lung disease
Great Britain

		1989	1990	1991	1992	1993	1994	1995	1996	1997	1998	1999
Asbestosis (without mesothelioma)[1]	KADY	155	164	163	150	173	174	166	196	190	165	171
Mesothelioma [1]	KADZ	909	895	1 023	1 097	1 152	1 246	1 318	1 320	1 355	1 535	1 595
Pneumoconiosis (other than asbestosis)	KAEA	318	328	287	274	281	276	287	223	230	268	321
Byssinosis	KAEB	25	19	16	21	11	7	6	3	5	5	6
Farmer's lung and other occupational allergic alveolitis	KAEC	8	6	8	4	12	10	10	1	5	8	9
Total	KAED	1 415	1 412	1 497	1 546	1 629	1 713	1 787	1 743	1 785	1 981	2 102

1 By definition every case of asbestosis is due to asbestos; the association with mesothelioma is also very strong, though there is thought to be a low natural background incidence.

Sources: Office for National Statistics; Health and Safety Executive: 0151 951 4540

9.8 Injuries to workers by industry and severity of injury
Great Britain
As reported to all enforcing authorities

				Fatal				Major				Over 3 Days[1]		
		Section	SIC (92)	1997 /98	1998 /99	1999 /00		1997 /98	1998 /99	1999 /00		1997 /98	1998 /99	1999 /00
Agriculture, hunting, forestry and fishing[2]	KSYS	A,B	01,02,05	40	46	36	KSZN	745	679	726	KTAZ	1 382	1 298	1 456
Energy and water supply industries[3]	KSYT	C,E	10-14,40/41	18	11	7	KSZO	684	555	506	KTBH	3 339	2 974	2 511
Mining and quarrying[3]	KSYU	C	10-14	14	7	5	KSZP	440	346	313	KTBI	1 920	1 773	1 503
Mining and quarrying of energy producing materials[3]	KSON	CA	10-12	10	5	3	KSZQ	297	213	189	KTBJ	1 359	1 238	1 029
Mining and quarrying except energy producing materials	KSOO	CB	13/14	4	2	2	KSZR	143	133	124	KTBK	561	535	474
Electricity, gas and water supply	KSOP	E	40/41	4	4	2	KSZS	244	209	193	KTBL	1 419	1 201	1 008
Manufacturing	KSOQ	D	15-37	61	69	41	KSZT	8 864	8 233	8 038	KTBM	41 742	39 264	39 460
of food products; beverages and tobacco	KSOR	DA	15/16	6	7	1	KSZU	1 556	1 525	1 536	KTBN	9 918	9 589	9 796
of textile and textile products	KSOS	DB	17/18	4	–	1	KSZV	353	290	262	KTBO	1 606	1 524	1 341
of leather and leather products	KSOT	DC	19	1	–	1	KSZW	43	25	38	KTBP	156	140	132
of wood and wood products	KSOU	DD	20	7	4	1	KSZX	373	346	361	KTBQ	1 168	1 026	1 064
of pulp, paper and paper products; publishing and printing	KSOV	DE	21/22	3	2	3	KSZY	598	503	493	KTBR	2 695	2 496	2 547
of coke, refined petroleum products and nuclear fuel	KSOW	DF	23	1	–	–	KSZZ	39	38	48	KTBS	138	132	121
of chemicals, chemical products and man-made fibres	KSOX	DG	24	2	4	2	KTAE	518	424	428	KTBT	2 054	1 782	1 936
of rubber and plastic products	KSOY	DH	25	2	5	2	KTAF	677	651	653	KTBU	3 618	3 437	3 535
of other non-metallic mineral products	KSOZ	DI	26	6	6	1	KTAG	483	426	428	KTBV	2 287	2 076	2 095
of basic metals and fabricated metal products	KSYV	DJ	27/28	14	22	17	KTAH	1 833	1 656	1 556	KTBW	6 407	6 144	6 119
of machinery and equipment n.e.c.	KSYW	DK	29	5	5	4	KTAI	765	685	638	KTBX	3 441	2 913	2 859
of electrical and optical equipment	KSYX	DL	30-33	2	–	–	KTAJ	513	481	473	KTBY	2 467	2 198	2 284
of transport equipment	KSYY	DM	34/35	5	5	2	KTAK	742	770	721	KTBZ	4 297	4 342	4 100
Manufacturing n.e.c.[4]	KSYZ	DN	36/37	3	9	6	KTAL	371	413	403	KTCA	1 490	1 465	1 531
Construction	KSZA	F	45	80	65	81	KTAM	4 326	4 656	4 749	KTCB	10 265	9 576	10 504
Total service industries	KSZB	G-Q	50-99	75	62	55	KTAN	15 383	14 930	15 296	KTCC	79 045	80 032	82 182
Wholesale and retail trade, and repairs	KSZC	G	50-52	17	15	11	KTAO	3 527	3 158	3 221	KTCD	16 353	15 695	15 568
Hotel and restaurants	KSZD	H	55	1	1	1	KTAP	942	924	874	KTCE	3 234	3 434	3 439
Transport, storage and communication[5]	KSZE	I	60-64	27	25	19	KTAQ	2 771	2 879	2 978	KTCF	17 351	18 626	20 603
Financial intermediation	KSZF	J	65-67	–	–	–	KTAR	131	153	159	KTCG	623	653	579
Real estate, renting and business activities	KSZG	K	70-74	13	13	10	KTAS	1 013	1 050	1 134	KTCH	3 791	3 981	3 879
Public administration and defence	KSZH	L	75	3	2	3	KTAT	2 153	2 001	2 227	KTCI	13 895	14 266	14 908
Education	KSZI	M	80	–	1	–	KTAU	1 589	1 548	1 475	KTCJ	4 850	4 680	4 767
Health and social work	KSZJ	N	85	2	–	–	KTAV	1 966	1 930	1 863	KTCK	14 209	14 148	13 825
Other community, social and personal services activities	KSZK	O-Q	90-99	12	5	11	KTAW	1 291	1 287	1 365	KTCL	4 739	4 549	4 614
Unclassified	KSZL			–	–	–	KTAX	–	–	–	KTCM	–	–	–
All industries	KSZM			274	253	220	KTAY	30 002	29 053	29 315	KTCN	135 773	133 144	136 113

1 Injuries causing incapacity for normal work for more than 3 days.
2 Excludes sea fishing.
3 Includes the number of injuries in the oil and gas industry collected under offshore installations safety legislation.
4 n.e.c.: not elsewhere classified
5 Injuries arising from shore based services only. Excludes incidents reported under merchant shipping legislation.

Source: Health and Safety Executive (HSE): 0151 951 4842

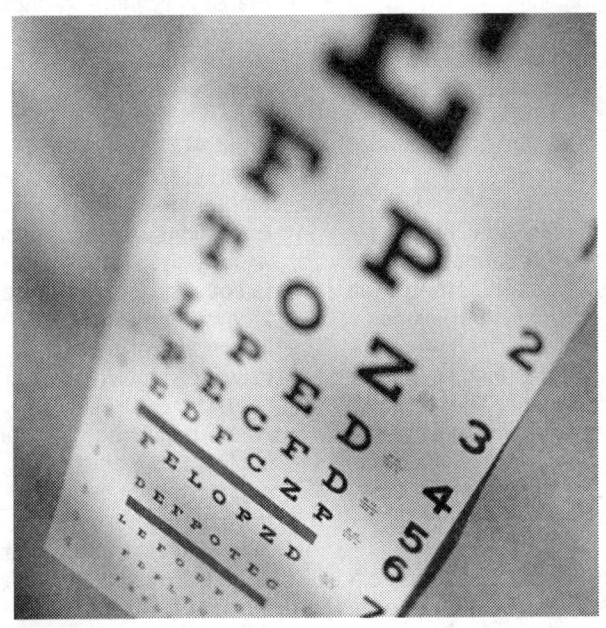

10 Social protection

Social protection

Social security
(Tables 10.2 - 10.8, 10.10, 10.11 and 10.13 to 10.16)
Tables 10.2 to 10.6 and 10.10 to 10.16 give details of contributors and beneficiaries under the National Insurance and Industrial Injury Acts, supplementary benefits and war pensions.

There are three types of contributor:

Class 1   Employed people, that is, people working for employers. Their contributions are paid partly by themselves and partly by their employers. They are covered for all benefits.

Class 2   Self-employed people, that is, people working on their own account. They are covered for all benefits other than unemployment and industrial injuries.

Class 3   Non-employed people, that is, people who do not work for gain. These people pay contributions on a voluntary basis. They are covered for benefits other than unemployment, sickness, industrial injuries and maternity allowances.

Class 4   Payable, in addition to Class 2 by self-employed people, and the amount payable is proportionate to profits or gains between a lower and upper limit in any one year.

An employer must pay a contribution for every employee whose earnings exceed a base level. Most employed people pay the full employee's contribution, but retirement pensioners working for an employer do not and some married women and some widows who are working need not, unless they so wish, contribute except for industrial injuries benefit. Thus the total numbers in the analysis by benefit for which the contributions were payable are less than the total numbers in the analysis by class of contributor.

Sickness benefit, Invalidity benefit and Incapacity benefit (Tables 10.7 and 10.8)
Incapacity Benefit replaced Sickness Benefit and Invalidity Benefit from 13 April 1995. The first condition for entitlement to these contributory benefits is that the claimants are incapable of work because of illness or disablement. Secondly, that they satisfy the contribution conditions which depend on contributions paid as an employed (Class 1) or self-employed person (Class 2). Under Sickness and Invalidity Benefits the contribution conditions were automatically treated as satisfied if a person was incapable of work because of an industrial accident or prescribed disease. Under Incapacity Benefit those who do not satisfy the contribution conditions in this case do not have them treated as satisfied. Class 1A contributions paid by employers are in respect of the benefit of cars provided for the private use of employees, and the free fuel provided for private use. These contributions do not provide any type of benefit cover.

Since 6 April 1983, most people working for an employer and paying National Insurance contributions as employed persons, receive Statutory Sick Pay (SSP) from their employer when they are off work sick. SSP was payable for a maximum of 8 weeks until 5 April 1986, and 28 weeks thereafter. People who do not work for an employer, and employees who are excluded from the SSP scheme, or those who have run out of SSP before reaching the maximum of 28 weeks and are still sick can claim benefit. Any period of SSP is excluded from the tables.

From 14 September 1980, spells of incapacity of 3 days or less do not count as periods of interruption of employment, and are excluded from the tables. Exceptions are where people are receiving regular weekly treatment by dialysis, or treatment by radiotherapy, chemotherapy or plasmapheresis where 2 days in any 6 consecutive days make up a period of interruption of employment, and those whose incapacity for work ends within 3 days of the end of SSP entitlement.

At the beginning of a period of incapacity, benefit is subject to 3 waiting days, except where there was an earlier spell of incapacity of more than 3 days in the previous 8 weeks. Employees entitled to SSP for less than 28 weeks and who are still sick can get Sickness Benefit or Incapacity Benefit Short Term (Low) until they reach a total of 28 weeks provided they satisfy the conditions. After 28 weeks SSP and/or Sickness Benefit (SB), Invalidity Benefit (IVB) was payable up to pension age for as long as the incapacity lasts. From pension age Invalidity Benefit was paid at the person's Retirement Pension rate, until entitlement ceases when RP is paid or at deemed pension age (70 for a man, 65 for a woman). For people on Incapacity Benefit under State pension age there are two short-term rates: the lower rate is paid for the first 28 weeks of sickness and the higher rate for weeks 29 to 52. From week 53 the Long Term rate Incapacity Benefit is payable. The Short Term rate Incapacity Benefit is based on Retirement Pension entitlement for people over State pension age and is paid for up to a year if incapacity began before pension age.

The long-term rate of Incapacity Benefit applies to people under State pension age who have been sick for more than a year. People with a terminal illness or who are receiving the higher rate care component of Disability Living Allowance will get the Long Term rate. The Long Term rate is not paid for people over pension age.

Under Incapacity Benefit, for the first 28 weeks of incapacity, people previously in work will be assessed on the 'own occupation' test - the claimant's ability to do their own job. Otherwise, incapacity will be based on a new 'all work' test which will assess ability to carry out a range of work-related activities. The test will apply after 28 weeks of incapacity or from the start of the claim for people who did not previously have a job. Certain people will be exempted from this test.

The tables exclude all men aged over 65 and women aged over 60 who are in receipt of Retirement Pension, and all people over deemed pension age (70 for a man and 65 for a woman), members of the Armed Forces, mariners while at sea, and married women and certain widows who have chosen not to be insured for Sickness Benefit. In addition, employees of the Post Office are excluded prior to 29 March 1986, and the remainder of Civil Service Departments, British Telecom and fringe bodies prior to 25 August 1986. The tables include a number of individuals who were unemployed prior to incapacity.

The Short Term (Higher) and Long Term rates of Incapacity Benefit are treated as taxable income.

There were transitional provisions for people who were on Sickness or Invalidity Benefit on 12 April 1995. They were automatically transferred to Incapacity Benefit, payable on the same basis as before. Former IVB recipients continue to get Additional Pension entitlement, but frozen at 1994 levels. Also their IVB is not subject to tax. If they were over State pension age on 12 April 1995 they may get Incapacity Benefit for up to 5 years beyond pension age.

Family Credit/ Working Families' Tax Credit
(Table 10.12)
Working Families' Tax Credit (WFTC) replaced Family Credit from 5 October 1999.

Family Credit was, and Working Families' Tax Credit is, available to families with at least one adult in remunerative work for at least 16 hours per week and who are responsible for at least one child under 16 (under 19 if in full time education up to A-level or equivalent standard). The rate of payment of WFTC depends on the number of such children and expenditure incurred on eligible childcare. It is also higher if the worker works for at least 30 hours per week, or if there are disabled children or severely disabled adults in the family. It is tapered away above an income threshold. Further details can be obtained from the Inland Revenue.

Government expenditure on social services and housing *(Table 10.17 - 10.22)*
The tables of general government expenditure on the social services and housing in the United Kingdom comprise a summary table followed by separate tables for each of the social services and housing. The definition of government expenditure used in these tables follows that in Table 9.4 of the *Blue Book 2001 Edition*, and covers both current and capital expenditure of the central government (including the National Insurance Fund) and local authorities. The housing table also includes the capital expenditure of public corporations concerned with housing. As in the Blue Book, government expenditure is measured after deducting fees and charges for services. Expenditure on administration includes the cost of common services (accommodation, stationery and printing, superannuation, etc) some of which is not directly borne by the departments administering each service. Transfers from one part of government to another have been eliminated to avoid double counting. The figures

relate to years ended 31 March. Figures for the latest two years are the most recent estimates available and are subject to revision.

It should be noted that the figures no longer include imputed rents for the use of fixed assets owned and used by general government. In the Blue Book, imputed rents have been replaced by capital consumption. Capital consumption, however, cannot be allocated to individual services and is therefore not included in these tables.

The following notes give brief descriptions of each of the main services shown in the tables.

Education (Table 10.18)
This covers expenditure by the Education Departments, local education authorities and the University Grants Committee on education in schools, training colleges, technical institutions and universities. It includes expenditure on school meals.

The education statistics in Table 10.18 are provided by the Department for Education and Skills. They are not normally able to provide a full set of estimates, from their sources, for the latest financial year. The ONS has in the past made estimates from a variety of sources but, following a review of their accuracy, it has been decided that they do not give a reliable guide to the final outcome and have therefore been withdrawn.

National Health Service (Table 10.19)
This covers expenditure by central government on hospital and community health, family practitioner and other health services. The expenditure by local authorities on the provision of health centres, health visiting, home nursing, ambulance services, vaccination and immunisation, etc. was transferred to central government on 1 April 1974. Only the net costs of providing these services are included in total government expenditure, receipts from patients being shown separately.

Personal social services (Table 10.20)
This covers local authority expenditure on the aged, handicapped and homeless, child care, care of mothers and young children, mental health, domestic help, etc. Also included are central government grants to voluntary approved schools.

Welfare foods (Table 10.20)
This covers the cost of providing welfare foods at reduced prices to children and expectant mothers. Only the net costs of providing these services are included in the total government expenditure, payments by the recipients of the services being shown separately.

Social security (Table 10.21)
This comprises both benefits under the Social Security schemes and non-contributory benefits and allowances, administered by the Department for Work and Pensions. The analysis by type of Income Support is not exact; the estimates are derived from average numbers in receipt of benefit and average amounts

Social protection

paid. Unified housing benefit (rent rebates and allowances) is also included as social security expenditure and not as housing expenditure. This is now mainly administered by local authorities who receive grants from central government.

Housing (Table 10.22)

The table shows, in addition to government expenditure on housing, the capital expenditure of public corporations and the total expenditure of the public sector on housing. The government expenditure figures cover subsidies paid by the housing departments towards the provision of housing by local authorities, new town development corporations and housing associations; subsidies by local authorities to their housing revenue accounts; rent rebates for tenants of housing owned by local authorities and new towns; rent allowances for tenants of privately-owned housing; grants to persons for the reduction of mortgage interest payments; capital expenditure on the provision of houses for letting; capital grants to housing associations; grants by local authorities towards the cost of conversion and improvement of privately-owned houses; net lending by the central government and local authorities for private house purchase and improvement and loans for first time purchasers. The public corporations' figures cover capital expenditure on the provision of houses for letting and lending by the Housing Corporation to housing associations.

10.1 National Insurance Fund
United Kingdom
Years ended 31 March

£ thousands

		1991/92	1992/93	1993/94	1994/95	1995/96	1996/97	1997/98	1998/99	1999/00
Receipts										
Opening balance	KJFB	12 161 227	8 637 594	3 577 671	4 672 345	7 042 118	8 044 941	7 869 121	9 763 346	12 624 962
Contributions		33 156 696	34 331 672	35 090 000	38 712 218	40 874 579	42 806 429	46 754 687	50 023 377	51 851 720
Grant from Consolidated Fund	KOTF	..	..	7 785 000	6 445 000	3 680 000	1 951 500	966 200	3 430	2 200
Compensation for SSP/SMP	KJQM	1 089 811	1 124 500	1 158 289	563 400	474 700	541 800	600 500	576 400	624 906
Transfers from GB	KOTG	125 000	40 000	40 000	145 000	125 000	75 000	150 000	315 000	230 000
Income from investments	KJFE	1 160 026	970 862	488 484	365 096	459 217	488 728	474 296	667 261	724 145
Other receipts	KJFF	19 359	24 813	41 989	60 625	76 487	85 126	97 206	92 292	126 728
Redundancy receipts[1]	KIBQ	19 091	26 942	25 688	25 288	23 899	26 193	24 720	21 210	20 874
Total		47 731 210	45 156 383	48 207 121	50 988 972	52 756 000	54 019 717	56 936 730	61 462 316	66 205 535
Expenditure										
Total benefits		37 430 154	39 823 984	42 366 510	42 270 821	43 198 045	44 517 872	45 321 420	46 822 291	49 550 870
Unemployment	KJFH	1 641 928	1 800 589	1 689 604	1 330 922	1 131 373	605 095	148	..	..
Sickness[2]	KJFI	286 455	378 136	378 407	350 700	14 711	..	..	..	..
Invalidity[2]	KJFJ	5 701 239	6 452 717	7 341 161	8 009 286	599 829	..	..	..	..
Incapacity[2]	JYXL	..	..	..	..	7 622 940	7 992 748	7 739 450	7 574 276	7 205 700
Maternity	KETY	32 071	32 660	34 230	28 230	29 897	34 283	36 715	39 329	40 412
Widows' pensions	KEWU	1 044 749	1 044 397	1 075 990	1 057 395	1 050 693	1 016 822	1 020 713	1 007 653	1 019 916
Guardians' allowances & Child's special allowance[3]	KJFK	1 562	2 091	1 111	1 111	1 842	1 569	1 637	1 834	1 823
Retirement pensions[4]		28 604 996	29 995 404	31 720 928	31 366 872	32 619 571	34 735 720	36 396 421	38 071 687	41 156 649
Pensioners' lump sum payments	KAAW	117 154	117 990	125 079	126 305	127 189	131 635	126 336	127 512	126 370
Other payments	KAAZ	9 682	10 523	35 045	8 879	14 174	17 392	19 037	18 305	19 159
Administration	KABE	1 243 488	1 379 212	1 604 510	1 323 631	1 218 772	1 065 338	1 073 350	1 052 820	847 386
Transfers to Northern Ireland	KABF	125 000	40 000	40 000	145 000	125 000	75 000	150 000	315 000	230 000
Redundancy payments	KIBR	285 291	324 994	271 636	198 523	155 068	133 621	119 961	140 075	173 988
Jobseeker's allowance (Contributory)[5]	LUQW	..	..	..	..	..	341 433	489 460	488 863	475 124
Total		39 093 615	41 578 713	44 317 701	43 946 854	44 711 059	46 150 656	47 173 228	48 837 354	51 296 527
Accumulated funds	KABH	8 637 594	3 577 671	4 672 345	7 042 118	8 044 941	7 869 121	9 763 346	12 624 962	14 909 008

1 The assets of the Redundancy Fund became those of the National Insurance Fund on 31 January 1991.
2 Incapacity Benefit replaced Sickness Benefit and Invalidity Benefit from April 1995.
3 Including figures of Child's special allowance for Northern Ireland.

4 Includes figures for Personal Pensions.
5 Jobseeker's Allowance (Contributory) was introduced in October 1996 and replaced Unemployment Benefit.

Sources: Department for Work and Pensions: 01253 856123 Ext 62436; Department of Health, Social Services and Public Safety (Northern Ireland); 028 9052 2062

10.2 Persons who paid National Insurance contributions in a tax year ending April[1]
United Kingdom

Millions

		Total					Men					Women			
		1997	1998	1999	2000		1997	1998	1999	2000		1997	1998	1999	2000
Total	KABI	25.54	25.30	26.06	26.47	KEYF	14.39	14.27	14.64	14.76	KEYP	11.15	11.03	11.42	11.71
Class 1	KABJ	23.02	22.92	23.75	24.14	KEYG	12.56	12.59	13.02	13.18	KEYQ	10.61	10.50	10.88	11.14
Not contracted out	KABK	13.61	13.71	14.42	14.89	KEYH	7.22	7.47	7.90	8.18	KEYR	6.39	6.24	6.51	6.71
Contracted out	KABL	7.72	7.53	7.65	7.61	KEYI	4.36	4.17	4.15	4.04	KEYS	3.36	3.35	3.50	3.57
Mixed contracted in/out[2]	KABM	1.41	1.44	1.47	1.48	KEYJ	0.70	0.67	0.71	0.70	KEYT	0.71	0.77	0.76	0.78
Class 1 Reduced rate (including standard rate)	KABO	0.29	0.24	0.20	0.16	KEYL	–	–	–	–	KEYV	0.29	0.24	0.20	0.16
Class 2	KABP	2.14	2.01	1.97	1.93	KEYM	1.75	1.60	1.56	1.52	KEYW	0.40	0.41	0.41	0.41
Mixed Class 1 and Class 2	KABQ	0.38	0.38	0.35	0.38	KEYN	0.28	0.28	0.25	0.27	KEYX	0.10	0.10	0.10	0.11
Class 3[3]	KABR	0.14	0.13	0.11	0.10	KEYO	0.08	0.08	0.06	0.06	KEYY	0.06	0.05	0.04	0.04

1 The tax year commences on 6 April and ends on 5 April of the following year. The years shown at the head of the column refer to the end of the tax year.
2 Not included in the above rows
3 Persons who paid a mixture of Class 3 contributions and others are not included in this category.

Source: Board of Inland Revenue 020 7438 6234

10.3 Weekly rates of principal social security benefits
Great Britain

£

		1989 Apr	1990 Apr	1991 Apr	1992 Apr	1993 Apr	1994 Apr	1995 Apr	1996 Apr	1997 Apr	1998 Apr	1999 Apr	2000 Apr	2001 Apr
Unemployment benefit:[1,2]														
Men and women	KJNA	34.70	37.35	41.40	43.10	44.65	45.45	46.45	48.25	..	..	..	..	..
Jobseeker's allowance:[2]														
Personal allowances														
Single														
Aged under 18(Depending	KXDH	..	..	..	..	..	..	..	..	29.60	30.30	30.95	31.45	31.95
on their circumstances)	KXDI	..	..	..	..	..	..	..	..	38.90	39.85	40.70	41.35	42.00
Aged 18 - 24	KXDJ	..	..	..	..	..	..	..	..	38.90	39.85	40.70	41.35	42.00
Aged 25 or over	KXDK	..	..	..	..	..	..	..	..	49.15	50.35	51.40	52.20	53.05
Couple														
Both aged under 18[3]	KXDL	..	..	..	..	..	..	..	..	58.70	30.30	30.95	31.45	31.95
One or both aged 18 or over	KXDM	..	..	..	..	..	..	..	..	77.15	79.00	80.65	81.95	83.25
Dependant children and young people														
Aged under 11	KXDN	..	..	..	..	..	..	..	..	16.90	17.30	20.20	26.60	31.45
Aged 11 - 16	KXDO	..	..	..	..	..	..	..	..	24.75	25.35	25.90	26.60	31.45
Aged 16 - 18	KXDP	..	..	..	..	..	..	..	..	29.60	30.30	30.95	31.75	32.25
Sickness benefit:[1,4]														
Men and women	KJNB	33.20	35.70	39.60	41.20	42.70	43.45	..	..	..	..	..	..	..
Invalidity benefit:[4]														
Invalidity pension	KJNC	43.60	46.90	52.00	54.15	56.10	57.60	..	..	..	..	..	..	..
Invalidity allowance:[4]														
High rate	KJND	9.20	10.00	11.10	11.55	11.95	12.15	12.40	12.90	13.15	13.60	14.05	14.20	14.65
Middle rate	KJNE	5.80	6.20	6.90	7.20	7.50	7.60	7.80	8.10	8.30	8.60	8.90	9.00	9.30
Low rate	KJNF	2.90	3.10	3.45	3.60	3.75	3.80	3.90	4.05	4.15	4.30	4.45	4.50	4.65
Increase for dependants:[4]														
Adult	KJNG	26.20	28.20	31.25	32.55	33.70	34.50	35.25	36.60	37.35	38.70	39.95	40.40	41.75
Each child	KJNH	8.95	9.65	10.70	10.85	10.95	11.00	11.05	11.15	11.20	11.30	11.35	11.35	11.35
Incapacity benefit:														
Short term (Lower) Under pension age	KOSB	..	..	..	..	..	..	44.40	46.15	47.10	48.80	50.35	50.90	52.60
Increase for adult dependant	KOSC	..	..	..	..	..	..	27.50	28.55	29.15	30.20	31.15	31.50	32.55
Short term (Lower) Over pension age	KOSD	..	..	..	..	..	..	56.45	58.65	59.90	62.05	64.05	64.75	66.90
Increase for adult dependant	KOSE	..	..	..	..	..	..	33.85	35.15	35.90	37.20	38.40	38.80	40.10
Short term (Higher)	KOSF	..	..	..	..	..	..	52.50	54.55	55.70	57.70	59.55	60.20	62.20
Increase for dependants:														
Adult	KOSG	..	..	..	..	..	..	27.50	28.55	29.15	30.20	31.15	31.50	32.55
Child[5]	KOSH	..	..	..	..	..	..	11.05	11.15	11.20	11.30	11.35	11.35	11.35
Long term	KOSI	..	..	..	..	..	..	58.85	61.15	62.45	64.70	66.75	67.50	69.75
Increase for dependants:														
Adult	KOSJ	..	..	..	..	..	..	35.25	36.60	37.35	38.70	39.95	40.40	41.75
Child[5]	KOSK	..	..	..	..	..	..	11.05	11.15	11.20	11.30	11.35	11.35	11.35
Incapacity age addition:[6]														
Higher rate	KOSL	..	..	..	..	..	..	12.40	12.90	13.15	13.60	14.05	14.20	14.65
Lower rate	KOSM	..	..	..	..	..	..	6.20	6.45	6.60	6.80	7.05	7.10	7.35
Attendance allowance:														
Higher rate	KJNI	34.90	37.55	41.65	43.35	44.90	45.70	46.70	48.50	49.50	51.30	52.95	53.55	55.30
Lower rate	KJNJ	23.30	25.05	27.10	28.95	30.00	30.55	31.20	32.40	33.10	34.30	35.40	35.80	37.00
Mobility allowance[7]	KJNK	24.40	26.25	29.80	..	..	..	..	..	..	..	..	..	..
Disability living allowance:														
care component														
Higher rate	KXDC	..	..	..	43.35	44.90	45.70	46.70	48.50	49.50	51.30	52.95	53.55	55.30
Middle rate	KXDD	..	..	..	28.95	30.00	30.55	31.20	32.40	33.10	34.30	35.40	35.80	37.00
Lower rate	KXDE	..	..	..	11.55	11.95	12.15	12.40	12.90	13.15	13.60	14.05	14.20	14.65
mobility component														
Higher rate	KXDF	..	..	..	30.30	31.40	31.95	32.65	33.90	34.60	35.85	37.00	37.40	38.65
Lower rate	KXDG	..	..	..	11.55	11.95	12.15	12.40	12.90	13.15	13.60	14.05	14.20	14.65

10.3 Weekly rates of principal social security benefits
Great Britain

continued

£

		1989 Apr	1990 Apr	1991 Apr	1992 Apr	1993 Apr	1994 Apr	1995 Apr	1996 Apr	1997 Apr	1998 Apr	1999 Apr	2000 Apr	2001 Apr
Maternity benefit:														
Maternity allowances for insured women[8]														
Higher rate	KOSN	..	..	..	..	..	..	52.50	54.55	55.70	57.70	59.55	60.20	..
Lower rate[9]	KJNL	33.20	35.70	40.60	42.25	43.75	44.55	45.55	47.35	48.35	50.10	51.70	52.25	..
Standard rate[10]	GPTJ	..	..	..	..	..	..	..	..	..	..	..	..	62.20
Threshold[11]	GPTK	..	..	..	..	..	..	..	..	..	..	..	..	30.00
Guardian's allowance	KJNN	8.95	9.65	10.70	10.85	10.95	11.00	11.05	11.15	11.20	11.30	11.35	11.35	11.35
Widow's benefit:														
Widow's pension	KJNO	43.60	46.90	52.00	54.15	56.10	57.60	58.85	61.15	62.45	64.70	66.75	67.50	72.50
Widowed mother's allowance	KJNP	43.60	46.90	52.00	54.15	56.10	57.60	58.85	61.15	62.45	64.70	66.75	67.50	72.50
Addition for each child	KJNQ	8.95	9.65	10.70	10.85	10.95	11.00	11.05	11.15	11.20	11.30	11.35	11.35	11.35
Retirement pension:[12]														
Single person	KJNR	43.60	46.90	52.00	54.15	56.10	57.60	58.85	61.15	62.45	64.70	66.75	67.50	72.50
Married couple	KJNS	69.80	75.10	83.25	86.70	89.80	92.10	94.10	97.75	99.80	103.40	106.70	107.90	115.90
Non-contributory retirement pension:														
Man or woman	KJNT	26.20	28.20	31.25	32.55	33.70	34.50	35.25	36.60	37.35	38.70	39.95	40.40	43.40
Married woman	KJNU	15.65	16.85	18.70	19.45	20.15	20.65	21.10	21.90	22.35	23.15	23.90	24.15	24.95
Industrial injuries benefit														
Disablement pension at 100 per cent rate	KJNW	71.20	76.60	84.90	88.40	91.60	93.20	95.30	99.00	101.10	104.70	108.10	109.30	112.90
Widow's or widower's pension	KJNX	43.60	46.90	52.00	54.15	56.10	57.60	58.85	61.15	62.45	..	..	..	..
Increase for dependants:[13]														
Adult	KJNY	21.40	23.05	25.55	26.60	27.55	28.05	28.65	29.75	..	..	..	..	..
Child benefit:[14]														
First child	KJOA	7.25	7.25	8.25	9.65	10.00	10.20	10.40	10.80	11.05	11.45	14.40	15.00	15.50
Subsequent children	KETZ	..	..	..	7.80	8.10	8.25	8.45	8.80	9.00	9.30	9.60	10.00	10.35
Family Credit[15]														
(maximum awards payable):[16]														
Families with 1 child														
Birth to September following 11th birthday	KJOB	40.90	44.60	48.00	51.40	53.25	55.15	56.50	58.20	59.70	61.15	64.95	..	..
From September following 11th birthday to September following 16th birthday	KJOC	46.50	50.50	54.40	58.25	60.35	62.45	64.00	65.90	67.60	69.25	70.70	..	..
From September following 16th birthday to day before 19th birthday	KJOD	49.95	54.15	58.35	62.45	64.70	67.00	68.55	70.60	72.45	74.20	75.95	..	..
Increase for each additional child														
Birth to September following 11th birthday	KJOF	7.30	8.25	9.70	10.40	10.75	11.15	11.40	11.75	12.05	12.35	15.15	..	..
From September following 11th birthday to September following 16th birthday	KJOG	12.90	14.15	16.10	17.25	17.85	18.45	18.90	19.45	19.95	20.45	20.90	..	..
From September following 16th birthday to day before 19th birthday	KJOH	16.35	17.80	20.05	21.45	22.20	23.00	23.45	24.15	24.80	25.40	25.95	..	..
War pension:														
Ex-private (100 per cent assessment)	KJOJ	71.20	76.60	84.90	89.00	97.20	98.90	101.10	105.00	107.20	111.10	114.70	116.00	119.80
War widow	KJOK	56.65	60.95	67.60	70.35	72.90	74.70	76.35	79.35	81.00	83.90	86.60	87.55	90.45

10.3 Weekly rates of principal social security benefits
Great Britain
continued

£

		1989 Apr	1990 Apr	1991 Apr	1992 Apr	1993 Apr	1994 Apr	1995 Apr	1996 Apr	1997 Apr	1998 Apr	1999 Apr	2000 Apr	2001 Apr
Income Support:														
Personal allowances[17]														
Single														
aged 16-17 either	KJOW	20.80	21.90	23.65[18]	25.55	26.45	27.50	28.00	28.85	29.60	30.30	30.95	31.45	31.95
or depending on their														
circumstances	KABS	..	28.80	31.15[18]	33.60	34.80	36.15	36.80	37.90	38.90	39.85	40.70	41.35	42.00
aged 18-24	KJOX	27.40	28.80	31.15	33.60	34.80	36.15	36.80	37.90	38.90	39.85	40.70	41.35	42.00
aged 25 or over	KJOY	34.90	36.70	39.65	42.45	44.00	45.70	46.50	47.90	49.15	50.35	51.40	52.20	53.05
Couple														
both aged under 18[3]	KJOZ	41.60	43.80	47.30	50.60	52.40	54.55	55.55	57.20	58.70	60.10	61.90	..	..
one or both 18 or over	KJPA	54.80	57.60	62.25	66.60	69.00	71.70	73.00	75.20	77.15	79.00	80.65	81.95	83.25
Lone parent														
aged 16-17 either	KJPB	20.80	21.90	23.65	25.55	26.45	27.50	28.00	28.85	29.60	30.30	30.95	31.45	31.95
or depending on their														
circumstances	KABT	..	28.80	31.15[19]	33.60	34.80	36.15	36.80	37.90	38.90	39.85	40.70	41.35	42.00
aged 18 or over	KJPC	34.90	36.70	39.65	42.45	44.00	45.70	46.50	47.90	49.15	50.35	51.40	52.20	53.05
Dependant children and young people[15]														
aged under 11	KJPD	11.75	12.35	13.35[20]	14.55	15.05	15.65	15.95	16.45	..	..	..	..	..
aged 11-15	KJPE	17.35	18.25	19.75	21.40	22.15	23.00	23.40	24.10	..	..	..	..	..
aged 16-17	KJPF	20.80	21.90	23.65	25.65	26.45	27.50	28.00	28.85	..	..	..	..	..
aged 18	KABU	27.40	28.80	31.15	33.60	34.80	36.15	36.80	37.90	..	..	..	..	..
Birth to September following 11th birthday	KXDQ	..	..	..	..	..	..	..	..	16.90	17.30	20.20		
From September following 11th birthday to September following 16th birthday	ZBXM												26.60	31.45
	KXDR	..	..	..	..	..	..	..	..	24.75	25.35	25.90		
From September following 16th birthday to day before 19th birthday	KXDS	..	..	..	..	..	..	..	..	29.60	30.30	30.95	31.75	32.25

1 Persons under the age of 18 are entitled to the appropriate adult rate.
2 Jobseeker's allowance, introduced 7 October 1996, has replaced unemployment benefit and income support for the unemployed.
3 From 12 April 1999 the personal allowance for couples where both members are not yet 18 or one of the couples is aged 18 or over depends on the couple's circumstances. They may be entitled to a couple allowance or a single person's allowance dependant on certain criteria.
4 Incapacity benefit introduced from 13 April 1995, has replaced sickness benefit and invalidity benefit.
5 For the first child only, the Child Dependency increase is from 1994, reduced by £1.30 to £9.90 because of child benefit.
6 The rate of age addition depends on age at date of onset of incapacity: higher rate for under age 35 and lower rate for age 35-44.
7 Disability living allowance replaced Mobility allowance from April 1992.
8 Following a EU Directive, employee's maternity benefit is aligned with the state benefit they would receive if off work sick.
9 Women who were either not employed or self-employed received the lower rate.
10 New Standard rate introduced from April 2000.
11 MA Earnings Threshold introduced April 2000.

12 Retirement pensioners over 80 receive 25p addition.
13 An allowance for one adult dependent was payable, where appropriate, with unemployment benefit, sickness benefit, retirement pension, injury benefit and maternity allowance.
14 From October 1991 the first child receives £9.25 and each subsequent child £7.50
15 Age bandings for children's personal allowances were revised on 7 April 1997. Some children have protected rights. Further information is available from the Department for Work and Pensions.
16 Maximum award does not include the 30 hour credit.
17 In addition to personal allowances, a claimant may also be entitled to premiums. The types of premiums are family, lone parent, pensioner, higher pensioner, disability, severe disability and disabled child.
18 From October 1991 the rate is £23.90
19 From October 1991 the rate is £31.40
20 From October 1991 each rate increased by 25p.

Source: Department for Work and Pensions: 0191 225 7373

10.4 National Insurance contributions

	Employee's standard contibutions (%)[1]		Employer's standard contributions (%)[1]	
	not contracted-out rate	contracted-out rate[2]	not contracted-out rate	contracted-out rate[3]
Class 1				
Weekly earnings				
1996/97				
Below 61.00 (LEL)	-	-	-	-
61.00-109.99	2% on first £61.00;	2% on first £61.00;	3.00	-
110.00-154.99	10% on balance	8.2% on balance	5.00	2.00
155.00-209.99			7.00	4.00
210.00-455.00			10.20	7.20
Above 440.00 (UEL)	£39.36	£32.48	10.20	10.20
1997/98				
Below 62.00 (LEL)	-	-	-	-
62.00-109.99	2% on first £62.00;	2% on first £62.00;	3.00	-
110.00-154.99	10% on balance	8.4% on balance	5.00	2.00
155.00-209.99			7.00	4.00
216.00-465.00			10.00	7.00
Above 455.00 (LEL)	£41.54	£35.09	10.00	10.00
1998/99				
Below 64.00 (LEL)	-	-	-	-
64.00-109.99	2% on first £64.00;	2% on first £64.00;	3.00	-
110.00-154.99	10% on balance	8.4% on balance	5.00	2.00
155.00-209.99			7.00	4.00
210.00-485.00			10.00	7.00
Above 485.00 (UEL)	£43.38	£36.64	10.00	10.00
1999/2000				
Below 66.00 (LEL)	-	-	-	-
66.00-83.00	10.0%	8.4%	-	-
83.00-500.00	10.0%	8.4%	12.2	9.2
Above 500.00 (UEL)	£43.40	£36.46	12.2	12.2
2000/01				
Below 67.00 (LEL)	-	-	-	-
67.00-76.00 (PT)	-	See note 4	-	See note 5
76.00-84.00 (ST)	10.0%		-	
84.00-535.00 (UEL)	10.0%		12.2	
Above 535.00 (UEL)	£45.90	£38.41	12.2	12.2
2001/02				
Below 72.00 (LEL)	-	-	-	-
72.00-87.00 (PT/ST)	10.00%	See note 4	-	See note 5
87.00-575.00 (UEL)	10.00%		11.90	
Above 575.00 (UEL)	£48.80	£40.75	11.90	11.90

	1996/97	1997/98	1998/99	1999/00	2000/01	2001/02
Class 2						
Flat rate weekly	£6.05	£6.15	£6.35	£6.55	£2.00	£2.00
Small earnings exception[6] (per annum)	£3,430	£3,480	£3,590	£3,770	£3,825	£3,955
Class 3						
Flat-rate voluntary weekly contributions	£5.95	£6.05	£6.25	£6.45	£6.55	£6.75
Class 4 (Self-employed; profit-related)						
Rate on profits between LPL and UPL	6.0%	6.0%	6.0%	6.0%	7.0%	7.0%
Lower profits limit (LPL)	£6,860	£7,010	£7,310	£7,530	£4,385	£4,535
Upper profits limit (UPL)	£23,660	£24,180	£25,220	£26,000	£27,820	£29,900

Note: LEL: Lower Earnings Limit; UEL: Upper Earnings Limit. PT: Primary Threshold; ST: Secondary Threshold.

1 Married women opting to pay contributions at the reduced rate (3.85%) earn no entitlement to contributory National Insurance benefits as a result of these contributions. No women have been allowed to exercise this option since 1977, but around 200,000 women who have been continually married or widowed and in the labour market since that time have retained their right to pay the reduced rate.

2 The contracted-out rebate for employees' contributions is applied only between LEL and UEL. Earnings below LEL are charged at the appropriate not contracted-out rate (which depends on total earnings). Earnings above the UEL are not subject to employee NICs.

3 The rates shown only apply to Contracted-Out Salary Related schemes. (COSR). Earnings below the LEL and above the UEL are charged at the appropriate not-contracted out rate. The employers' contracted-out rate applies only between the LEL and the UEL.

4 The contracted-out rebate for primary contributions in 2000/01 is 1.6 per cent of earnings between the LEL and the UEL for all forms of contracting-out.

5 The contracted-out rebate for secondary contributions is 3 per cent of earnings between the LEL and the UEL.

6 If earnings from self-employment are below this annual limit and the contributor applies for and is granted a small earnings exception Class 2 contributions need not be paid. Class 2 or 3 contributions may be paid voluntarily.

Source: Board of Inland Revenue: 020 7438 4335

10.5 Social Security Acts: number of persons receiving benefit[1]
Great Britain
At any one time

Thousands

Persons receiving:		1991	1992	1993	1994	1995	1996	1997	1998	1999	2000	2001
Unemployment benefit[2]	KJHA	569.5	685.2	671.9	553.5	426.5	397.8	–	–	–	–	–
Jobseeker's allowance[2,3]	JYXM	–	–	–	–	–	–	1 406.3	1 181.2	1 105.8	972.7	848.3
Sickness and Invalidity benefit[4,5]	KJHB	1 415.6	1 577.3	1 727.0	1 808.6	1 894.1	–	–	–	–	–	–
Incapacity benefit[6]	KXDT	–	–	–	–	–	1 812.8	1 749.2	1 671.2	1 557.1	1 504.3	1 515.2
Attendance allowance[7]	KXDU	957.0	1 092.0	945.0	1 018.0	1 109.0	1 120.6	1 183.2	1 225.6	1 243.8	1 249.6	1 290.0
Mobility allowance[8]	KXDV	659	718	–	–	–	–	–	–	–	–	–
Disability living allowance[9]	KXDW	–	–	1 200.6	1 343.2	1 541.4	1 729.2	1 886.5	1 995.9	2 061.3	2 130.5	2 240.5
Guardians' allowances[10]	KJHE	1.9	1.9	2.0	2.1	2.1	2.2	2.3	2.3	2.3	2.5	2.1
Widows' benefits[11]	KJHF	362.3	351.0	345.3	335.0	323.1	311.6	284.6	277.6	263.7	261.0	255.5
National Insurance retirement pensions[5]:												
Males[11]	KJHH	3 512.8	3 613.7	3 623.6	3 657.5	3 728.7	3 836.6	3 926.7	4 010.6	4 015.3	4 039.4	4 083.9
Females[11]	KJHL	6 515.3	6 683.0	6 680.0	6 727.1	6 777.2	6 948.5	6 983.2	7 031.1	6 925.4	6 928.0	6 959.7
Total[11]	KJHG	10 028.1	10 296.8	10 303.6	10 384.7	10 505.9	10 785.1	10 909.9	11 041.9	10 940.7	10 967.4	11 043.6
Non-contributory retirement pensions[5]:												
Males[11]	KJHI	6.1	6.1	6.1	6.1	6.5	6.1	5.9	5.7	5.1	5.2	5.1
Females[11]	KJHJ	25.3	25.7	24.9	24.1	24.5	23.5	22.5	21.3	18.7	18.3	18.3
Total[11]	KJHK	31.4	31.8	31.0	30.2	31.0	29.6	28.3	27.0	23.8	23.4	23.5
Industrial Injuries disablement pensions assessments[12]	KJHN	200.3	204.3	212.4	225.6	235.2	249.2	257.8	269.1	278.2	280.8	–
Reduced earnings allowance/ Retirement allowance assessments[12]	KEYC	163.7	159.7	156.0	154.3	152.1	154.9	155.6	152.8	153.5	153.5	–
Child benefit[5] Families receiving benefit[10]	KJHO	6 805.0	6 857.0	6 913.0	6 954.7	6 996.0	7 024.1	6 956.1	6 976.1	6 989.4	7 107.8	7 065.9
Family Credit[13]	ZCGF	347	397	488	551	608	693	748	767	791	–	–
Income Support[14]	KABV	5 683.0	5 292.9	5 858.4	5 693.7	5 670.2	5 548.9	3 958.1	3 853.1	3 814.4	3 810.5	3 927.9
Housing Benefit and Council Tax Benefit												
Rent rebate	KABY	2 944.0	3 033.9	3 052.5	3 016.1	2 964.3	2 898.3	2 792.7	2 664.1	2 518.5	2 287.8	2 132.1
Rent allowance[15]	KABZ	1 082.4	1 291.6	1 480.6	1 633.9	1 770.1	1 877.6	1 847.5	1 810.6	1 794.6	1 745.7	1 730.5
Community charge benefit[16]	KACB	6 290.7	6 563.9	–	–	–	–	–	–	–	–	–
Council tax benefit[17]	KJPO	–	–	5 251.8	5 496.5	5 623.9	5 611.2	5 500.3	5 325.7	5 166.1	4 830.1	4 651.9
War pensions[5]	KJHR	249.6	260.1	292.9	309.2	315.4	327.5	320.7	302.0	306.0	295.7	284.3

1 Caseload counts at a specific date in the year which varies from benefit to benefit.
2 Figures are given at May each year.
3 Jobseeker's Allowance introduced 7 October 1996, replacing unemployment benefit.
4 A relatively small number of claims do not result in the payment of benefit but are included here because they indicate notified incapacity for work.
5 Includes overseas cases.
6 Incapacity Benefit replaced Sickness Benefit and Invalidity Benefit from 13 April 1995. Figures are taken at the last day in February.
7 Attendance Allowance figures are based at 31 March until 1995 then at the end of May.
8 Mobility Allowance figures are based at 31 December until 1991 and then 31 March 1992.
9 Figures for 1993-2001 as at May
10 Figure for 1999 as at November. Figure for 2000 as at August. Figure for 2001 as at May.

11 Figure for 1999 as at September. Figure for 2000 as at March. Figure for 2001 as at February.
12 Industrial injuries disablement pension, reduced earnings allowance, retirement allowance assessments starting first Monday in April. Includes an allowance for late returns.
13 Family Credit was replaced by Working Families' Tax Credit from October 1999. See table 10.12 for latest figures.
14 From 9 October 1996 Income Support for the unemployed was replaced by Income-based Jobseeker's Allowance. Figures in this table up to and including 1996 include unemployed Income Support claimants. Figures from 1997 exclude unemployed who will be counted in the Jobseeker's Allowance claims.
15 Rent Allowance figures include housing association tenants.
16 Claimants with partners are treated as one recipient.
17 Community Charge Benefit was replaced by Council Tax Benefit in April 1993. Figure excludes Second Adult Rebate Claims.

Source: Department for Work and Pensions: 0191 225 7373

10.6 Unemployed benefit/jobseekers allowance[1] claimants analysed by benefit entitlement

Great Britain

Thousands

		Jobseekers Allowance November 1996	Jobseekers Allowance May 1997	Jobseekers Allowance May 1998	Jobseekers Allowance May 1999	Jobseekers Allowance May 2000	Jobseekers Allowance May 2001
All Persons							
All with benefit - total	XXDX	1 643.2	1 406.3	1 181.2	1 105.2	972.7	848.3
Contribution-based JSA only	XXDY	293.5	181.1	154.2	158.2	148.2	147.0
Contribution based JSA & income-based JSA	XXDZ	41.5	28.3	23.5	27.1	19.0	18.3
Income-based JSA only payment	XXEA	1 308.2	1 196.8	1 003.6	920.4	805.5	683.1
No benefit in payment	XXEB	158.7	156.2	114.5	118.7	94.6	93.7
Total	XXEC	1 801.9	1 562.4	1 295.8	1 224.5	1 067.3	942.0
Males							
All with benefit - total	XXED	1 264.8	1 096.9	918.2	862.3	755.0	659.4
Contribution-based JSA only	XXEE	189.6	119.5	101.6	109.0	104.2	104.5
Contribution based JSA & income-based JSA	XXEF	37.1	25.4	20.7	24.4	17.2	16.7
Income-based JSA only payment	XXEG	1 038.1	952.0	795.9	728.9	633.6	538.2
No benefit in payment	XXEH	105.6	106.8	75.5	79.2	63.4	61.9
Total	XXEI	1 370.4	1 203.7	993.7	941.5	818.4	721.3
Females							
All with benefit - total	XXEJ	378.5	309.4	263.0	243.4	217.7	188.9
Contribution-based JSA only	XXEK	104.0	61.6	52.6	49.2	44.0	42.5
Contribution based JSA & income-based JSA	XXEL	4.5	3.0	2.8	2.7	1.8	1.5
Income-based JSA only payment	XXEM	270.0	244.8	207.7	191.5	171.9	144.9
No benefit in payment	XXEN	53.0	49.4	39.1	39.5	31.2	31.8
Total	XXEO	431.5	358.8	302.1	283.0	248.9	220.7

10.6
continued

Unemployed benefit/jobseekers allowance[1] claimants analysed by benefit entitlement
Great Britain

Thousands

		Unemployment Benefit[2,3]										
		1985	1986	1987	1988	1989	1990	1991	1992	1993	1994	1995
All Persons												
Unemployment benefit in payment - total	KJIB	872.0	955.0	676.0	521.6	304.4	356.1	641.7	671.1	598.3	471.6	386.5
Unemployment benefit only	KJIC	679.0	768.0	549.0	402.2	220.3	294.0	520.2	548.3	495.6	333.6	266.3
Unemployment benefit and Income Support[4]	KJIF	193.0	187.0	127.0	119.3	82.1	62.0	121.5	122.8	102.7	138.0	120.2
Income Support only in payment[4]	KJIG	1 690.0	1 715.0	1 407.0	1 143.0	995.5	1 044.4	1 464.0	1 746.8	1 823.1	1 714.2	1 515.0
Neither Unemployment benefit nor Income Support in payment[4]	KJIH	461.0	500.0	425.0	347.3	252.0	2 529.0	306.6	374.2	316.9	250.1	215.7
Total	KJIA	3 023.0	3 170.0	2 508.0	2 012.8	1 551.9	1 653.3	2 412.3	2 792.1	2 738.3	2 435.9	2 117.1
Males												
Unemployment benefit in payment - total	KJIJ	541.0	596.0	442.0	328.2	200.5	254.1	472.1	488.4	425.8	326.0	265.4
Unemployment benefit only	KJIK	375.0	435.0	331.0	227.5	128.9	197.3	362.0	378.6	335.3	212.8	168.2
Unemployment benefit and Income Support[4]	KJIN	166.0	161.0	111.0	100.7	71.6	56.9	110.1	109.8	90.5	113.1	97.3
Income Support only in payment[4]	KJIO	1 281.0	1 308.0	1 140.0	886.0	778.2	825.4	1 171.7	1 410.3	1 465.1	1 366.3	1 198.8
Neither Unemployment benefit nor Income Support in payment[4]	KJIP	252.0	275.0	279.0	209.9	157.6	166.8	205.3	255.3	215.2	167.0	144.5
Total	KJII	2 074.0	2 179.0	1 861.0	1 424.1	1 136.3	1 246.3	1 849.4	2 154.0	2 106.1	1 859.2	1 608.7
Females												
Unemployment benefit in payment - total	KJIR	331.0	359.0	250.0	278.0	1 039.0	101.9	169.7	182.7	172.6	145.8	121.1
Unemployment benefit only	KJIS	304.0	333.0	231.0	174.8	92.5	96.8	158.1	169.8	160.4	120.8	98.2
Unemployment benefit and Income Support[4]	KJIV	27.0	26.0	19.0	18.6	11.5	5.1	11.5	12.9	12.2	25.0	22.9
Income Support only in payment[4]	KJIW	409.0	407.0	354.0	258.0	217.3	219.0	291.9	336.5	358.0	347.9	316.2
Neither Unemployment benefit nor Income Support in payment[4]	KJIX	209.0	225.0	184.0	138.3	95.4	86.1	101.4	119.0	101.8	83.1	71.2
Total	KJIQ	949.0	991.0	788.0	588.7	416.7	407.0	562.9	638.1	632.4	576.7	508.4

1 Jobseeker's Allowance replaced Unemployment Benefit and Income Support for unemployed claimants on 7 October 1996. It is a unified benefit with two routes of entry: contribution-based which depends mainly upon national insurance contributions and income-based which depends mainly upon a means test. Some claimants can qualify by either route. In practice they receive income-based JSA but have underlying entitlement to the contribution-based element. Figures quoted as at May of each year apart from 1996 which is November.

2 At November each year.

3 Unemployment Benefit and Income Support for unemployed claimants were replaced by Jobseeker's Allowance on 7 October 1996.

4 Income Support replaced Supplementary Benefit from April 1988.

Source: Department for Work and Pensions: 0191 225 7373

10.7 Sickness benefit, invalidity benefit and incapacity benefit claimants, by age and duration of spell

Great Britain at end of statistical year[1]

Thousands

Age at 31 March[2]		1991	1992	1993	1994	1995[3]	1996	1997	1998	1999	2000	2001
Males												
All durations: All ages	KJJA	1 187.1	1 327.1	1 468.0	1 544.4	1 629.9	1 627.0	1 577.9	1 530.1	1 458.4	1 432.0	1 458.5
Under 20	KJJB	5.7	6.2	7.1	6.8	7.8	8.7	8.8	10.7	10.7	11.2	10.2
20-29	KJJC	61.3	75.7	86.2	97.2	106.0	119.3	118.8	119.1	115.0	114.2	119.1
30-39	KJJD	101.3	125.2	145.7	160.4	189.7	202.6	208.5	216.6	217.6	222.5	234.8
40-49	KJJE	169.5	194.5	228.1	245.2	260.4	274.3	272.4	271.4	271.0	277.0	285.2
50-59	KJJF	347.9	386.6	426.1	441.7	468.7	475.4	473.4	474.1	467.3	469.8	473.5
60-64	KJJG	299.8	319.7	344.7	356.6	362.5	352.1	349.7	344.2	336.0	334.2	334.3
65 and over	KJJH	201.6	219.2	230.1	236.5	234.8	194.6	146.2	94.0	40.7	3.1	1.4
Over six months: All ages	KJJI	1 024.0	1 148.5	1 273.8	1 361.5	1 442.1	1 440.9	1 385.7	1 349.2	1 287.0	1 344.8	1 293.4
Under 20	KJJJ	1.80	2.90	2.80	2.90	3.00	3.90	3.60	4.70	4.90	7.40	4.70
20-29	KJJK	37.7	50.2	59.6	65.7	74.3	86.4	83.1	84.5	81.4	97.8	87.8
30-39	KJJL	71.3	94.5	112.9	126.5	152.1	165.1	166.8	177.2	181.2	203.9	197.6
40-49	KJJM	138.1	159.6	184.8	208.6	219.7	235.9	232.3	234.0	237.6	260.0	253.6
50-59	KJJN	300.8	331.7	367.2	389.2	418.2	426.5	423.8	428.2	423.8	446.8	431.6
60-64	KJJO	273.2	291.1	317.1	332.6	340.2	329.7	330.4	326.8	317.6	325.8	316.7
65 and over	KJJP	201.1	218.5	229.4	236.0	234.6	193.3	145.6	93.7	40.6	3.1	1.4
Females												
All durations: All ages	KJJQ	491.2	570.2	646.1	704.7	776.5	779.1	795.1	810.8	815.5	827.5	865.9
Under 20	KJJR	9.1	9.3	9.5	11.0	12.0	12.5	12.3	13.0	14.1	13.7	13.7
20-29	KJJS	56.1	70.8	75.9	74.9	79.4	88.6	89.0	87.8	85.3	84.6	85.1
30-39	KJJT	73.0	86.7	95.5	108.5	122.4	134.6	137.6	144.7	149.4	153.5	159.1
40-49	KJJU	120.4	140.6	162.6	176.0	200.7	201.9	206.5	209.7	217.2	221.0	232.0
50-59	KJJV	192.7	213.1	244.6	266.6	290.7	285.1	303.3	323.1	333.2	349.9	371.5
60 and over	KJJW	39.9	49.7	58.0	67.7	71.3	56.3	46.4	32.5	16.3	4.8	4.6
Over six months: All ages	KJJX	415.4	483.1	552.9	611.4	673.1	672.9	686.6	701.7	707.9	776.2	768.2
Under 20	KJJY	3.9	3.4	3.6	4.7	4.2	6.2	4.8	5.7	6.1	9.9	6.8
20-29	KJJZ	38.9	47.3	54.0	55.9	60.3	66.3	66.1	65.8	64.2	73.9	66.7
30-39	KJKA	57.7	70.5	79.3	92.3	103.2	113.2	117.5	120.9	126.3	142.4	139.4
40-49	KJKB	102.6	120.0	138.4	151.8	170.8	176.4	179.6	183.3	190.1	208.8	207.2
50-59	KJKC	173.0	193.0	220.8	239.9	263.7	256.6	273.1	294.1	305.2	336.5	343.5
60 and over	KJKD	39.3	48.9	56.8	66.8	70.9	54.3	45.4	31.9	16.0	4.6	4.5

Note Figures are based on a 1 per cent sample up to 1995 and 5% sample thereafter.
1 The end of the statistical year up to 1993/94 was the Saturday before the first Monday in April.
2 Until 1995/96 then at 1 March. From 1995/96 the duration is taken on the last day of February.

3 The statistical year for 1994/95 was extended to 12 April 1995, the day before the introduction of the new Incapacity Benefit which replaced Sickness and Invalidity Benefit from 13 April 1995.

Source: Department for Work and Pensions: 0191 225 7373

10.8 Sickness, invalidity and incapacity benefit: days of certified incapacity

Great Britain analysis by age at end of period[1]

Years starting on first Monday in April[2]

Millions

Age at 31 March[4]		1989 /90	1990 /91	1991 /92	1992 /93	1993 /94	1994[3] /95	1995 /96	1996 /97	1997 /98	1998 /99	1999 /00
Males: All ages	KJKH	327.5	356.0	402.7	445.5	468.8	507.9	596.2	576.3	563.5	538.6	526.7
Under 20	KJKI	1.4	1.6	1.7	1.5	1.6	1.8	3.4	3.1	3.5	3.7	3.3
20 - 29	KJKJ	13.8	16.9	21.6	24.5	27.0	30.4	43.7	42.4	43.2	41.7	38.3
30 - 39	KJKK	24.4	28.1	36.1	41.4	46.6	56.0	72.3	73.9	77.7	78.2	75.8
40 - 49	KJKL	44.8	49.2	57.1	64.6	72.7	78.9	98.5	98.5	97.7	97.6	98.0
50 - 59	KJKM	96.2	100.8	112.8	121.7	129.8	141.4	172.0	170.7	172.2	170.0	161.9
60 - 64	KJKN	85.3	89.3	96.1	102.4	107.3	112.6	127.9	127.8	126.7	124.3	126.0
65 and over	KJKO	61.5	70.1	77.4	80.4	83.9	86.8	78.4	59.9	41.7	23.0	23.4
Females: All ages	KJKP	127.6	147.0	170.8	190.7	211.4	237.5	279.5	285.8	292.8	294.8	315.0
Under 20	KJKQ	2.2	2.3	2.2	2.1	2.4	2.6	4.8	4.1	4.4	4.5	4.0
20 - 29	KJKR	15.2	16.7	19.7	22.1	22.1	23.9	31.9	32.0	32.1	31.3	30.7
30 - 39	KJKS	20.1	21.7	25.6	28.5	32.7	37.6	48.0	49.8	51.4	53.4	54.9
40 - 49	KJKT	29.7	34.9	41.2	46.6	51.5	58.9	72.1	74.0	75.8	77.1	79.1
50 - 59	KJKU	49.0	56.7	63.8	71.3	79.1	88.4	101.0	107.5	115.3	120.0	134.3
60 and over	KJKV	11.5	14.6	18.2	20.1	23.6	26.1	21.7	18.4	13.8	8.4	12.0

1 The end of the statistical year up to 1993/94 was the Saturday before the first Monday in April.
2 Up to and including 1994/95 years start first Monday in April. The 1995/96 year started 13 April and ended 31 March. From 1996/97 years start 1 March

3 The statistical year for 1994/95 was extended to 12 April 1995, the day before the introduction of the new Incapacity Benefit which replaced Sickness and Invalidity Benefit from 13 April 1995.
4 Until 1995/96 then at 1 March.

Source: Department for Work and Pensions: 0191 225 7373

10.9 Widows' benefit (excluding widows' allowance: widows' payment[1])
Great Britain
Number in payment analysed by type of benefit and age of widow

Thousands

		September										
		1991	1992	1993	1994	1995	1996	1997	1998	1999	2000	2001[2]
All widows' benefit (excluding widows' allowance)												
All ages	KJGA	357.2	351.0	345.3	335.0	323.1	311.6	293.2	277.6	263.7	261.0	255.5
Under 30	KJGB	2.1	2.1	2.0	1.9	1.6	1.4	1.2	1.1	1.6	1.5	1.3
30 - 39	KJGC	15.5	15.9	15.0	14.5	13.9	13.5	13.0	12.3	10.8	11.0	10.2
40 - 49	KJGD	61.0	57.8	56.0	53.0	52.8	50.1	44.9	41.3	38.5	38.1	37.2
50 - 59	KJGE	230.8	224.2	219.9	216.7	206.9	202.5	197.3	187.7	181.8	182.2	179.1
60 and over	KJGF	47.7	51.1	52.5	48.8	47.8	44.0	36.8	35.2	31.1	28.4	27.7
Widowed mothers' allowance - with dependant children												
All ages	KJGG	52.4	53.2	53.2	53.3	52.8	51.7	49.5	47.1	44.9	47.0	46.6
Under 30	KJGH	2.0	2.0	1.9	1.7	1.6	1.4	1.2	1.1	1.6	1.4	1.2
30 - 39	KJGI	14.1	14.5	13.8	13.9	13.3	12.9	12.4	11.8	10.4	10.6	9.8
40 - 49	KJGJ	25.3	25.8	27.1	26.9	27.5	26.7	24.6	33.3	22.5	23.3	23.7
50 - 59	KJGK	10.8	10.6	10.2	10.7	10.1	10.2	10.7	10.5	10.3	11.6	11.5
60 and over	KJGL	0.2	0.2	0.2	0.2	0.4	0.3	0.3	0.2	0.2	0.2	0.4
Widowed mothers' allowance - without dependant children												
All ages	KJGM	14.2	10.7	8.3	6.7	6.2	5.6	4.6	3.4	3.1	2.9	2.5
Under 30	KJGN	0.2	0.1	–	0.1	0.1	–	–	–	–	–	–
30 - 39	KJGO	1.6	1.3	1.1	0.8	0.6	0.6	0.5	0.5	0.4	0.4	0.4
40 - 49	KJGP	6.4	5.1	3.9	3.4	3.3	2.8	2.3	1.9	1.4	1.2	1.1
50 - 59	KJGQ	5.8	4.0	2.9	2.2	1.9	2.1	1.7	1.0	1.2	1.1	1.0
60 and over	KJGR	0.3	0.2	0.2	0.2	0.1	0.1	0.1	–	0.1	0.1	–
Widows' pension												
All ages	KJGS	145.9	134.4	122.8	108.1	95.1	84.3	71.9	63.4	57.1	54.5	53.0
40 - 49	KJGT	–	–	–	–	–	–	–	–	–	–	–
50 - 59	KJGU	103.5	89.1	76.5	65.8	54.6	48.4	43.0	37.1	35.7	35.6	34.8
60 and over	KJGV	42.6	45.3	46.3	42.1	40.5	36.0	28.9	26.3	21.4	18.9	18.2
Age-related widows' pension[3]												
All ages	KJGW	144.6	152.7	161.0	166.9	168.9	170.0	167.1	163.7	158.6	156.6	153.4
40 - 49	KJGX	29.2	27.0	25.0	22.7	21.9	20.4	17.8	16.0	14.6	13.5	12.4
50 - 59	KJGY	110.8	120.4	130.3	137.9	140.2	141.9	141.6	139.0	134.6	133.8	131.9
60 and over	KJGZ	4.6	5.2	5.7	6.3	6.8	7.6	7.6	8.7	9.4	9.3	9.2

1 This is an especially high rate of benefit which is payable for the first 26 weeks of widowhood, provided that the widow is under pensionable age (age 60) or, if she is over that age, provided that her husband was not entitled to retirement pension. Widows' allowance was replaced by widows' payment on 11 April 1988.

2 Figures as at March.

3 Figures for widows' basic pension are included in age-related widows' pension.

Source: Department for Work and Pensions: 0191 225 7874

10.10 Child benefits
Great Britain
At 31 December

Thousands

		1991	1992	1993	1994	1995	1996	1997[1]	1998[1]	1999[2]	2000[3]	2001[4]
Families receiving allowances:												
Total	KJMU	6 805	6 857	6 913	6 955	6 996	7 024	6 956	6 976	6 989	7 108	7 066
With 1 child	KJMV	2 898	2 906	2 920	2 941	2 970	2 983	–	–	3 007	3 037	3 042
2 children	KJMW	2 732	2 752	2 772	2 781	2 783	2 794	–	–	2 759	2 815	2 790
3 children	KJMX	878	894	908	920	928	929	–	–	916	938	924
4 children	KJMY	221	226	231	228	231	236	–	–	231	238	233
5 or more children	KJMZ	75	79	81	84	84	82	–	–	76	80	78

1 Figures provided by Child Benefit Centre Management Information Statistics as a new scan was being developed.
2 Figures for 1999 are as at November.
3 Figures for 2000 are as at August.
4 Figures for 2001 are as at May.

Source: Department for Work and Pensions: 0191 225 7373

10.11 Contributory and non-contributory retirement pensions
Great Britain
Numbers in payment analysed by age-group[1]

Thousands (percentages in italics)

		At 30 September										
		1991	1992	1993	1994	1995	1996	1997	1998	1999	2000	2001[2]
Men:												
Age-groups:												
65-69	KJSB	1 124.6	1 095.5	1 063.9	1 053.6	1 079.1	1 142.5	1 200.5	1 249.9	1 267.9	1 288.8	1 287.5
Percentage	KJSC	*31.3*	*30.3*	*29.3*	*28.8*	*28.9*	*29.8*	*30.5*	*31.1*	*31.5*	*31.9*	*31.5*
70-74	KJSD	1 046.0	1 104.0	1 155.3	1 196.2	1 155.0	1 146.6	1 138.2	1 131.1	1 115.4	1 117.5	1 125.9
Percentage	KJSE	*29.1*	*30.5*	*31.8*	*32.7*	*31.0*	*29.9*	*28.9*	*28.2*	*27.7*	*27.6*	*27.5*
75-79	KJSF	761.7	738.5	706.8	681.8	748.8	787.3	831.3	876.6	889.3	867.4	860.5
Percentage	KJSG	*21.2*	*20.4*	*19.5*	*18.6*	*20.1*	*20.5*	*21.1*	*21.8*	*22.1*	*21.5*	*21.0*
80-84	KJSH	437.3	448.9	458.2	468.0	477.4	481.8	471.2	454.5	433.6	457.7	493.6
Percentage	KJSI	*12.2*	*12.4*	*12.6*	*12.8*	*12.8*	*12.6*	*12.0*	*11.3*	*10.8*	*11.3*	*12.1*
85-89	KJSJ	172.9	180.5	189.6	197.4	204.4	209.4	217.2	225.0	231.6	231.1	237.0
Percentage	KJSK	*4.8*	*5.0*	*5.2*	*5.4*	*5.5*	*5.5*	*5.5*	*5.6*	*5.8*	*5.7*	*5.8*
90 and over	KJSL	49.1	53.8	57.2	60.6	64.5	69.4	75.3	79.3	82.6	82.1	84.6
Percentage	KJSM	*1.4*	*1.5*	*1.6*	*1.7*	*1.7*	*1.8*	*1.9*	*2.0*	*2.1*	*2.0*	*2.1*
Total all ages	KJSA	3 591.5	3 621.3	3 630.4	3 657.5	3 729.2	3 837.0	3 933.8	4 016.3	4 020.4	4 044.6	4 089.0
Women:												
Age-groups:												
60-64	KJSO	1 124.2	1 121.1	1 099.1	1 090.6	1 094.3	1 200.6	1 245.0	1 296.2	1 310.5	1 332.2	1 339.4
Percentage	KJSP	*16.9*	*16.7*	*16.4*	*16.2*	*16.1*	*17.3*	*17.8*	*18.4*	*18.9*	*19.2*	*19.2*
65-69	KJSQ	1 484.6	1 472.7	1 447.0	1 436.6	1 437.6	1 461.2	1 458.9	1 442.8	1 398.8	1 396.5	1 392.4
Percentage	KJSR	*22.3*	*21.9*	*21.5*	*21.4*	*21.2*	*21.0*	*20.8*	*20.5*	*20.1*	*20.2*	*20.0*
70-74	KJSS	1 336.9	1 403.8	1 469.3	1 515.9	1 447.3	1 423.7	1 398.6	1 379.6	1 341.5	1 339.8	1 341.9
Percentage	KJST	*20.1*	*20.9*	*21.9*	*22.5*	*21.3*	*20.5*	*20.0*	*19.6*	*19.3*	*19.3*	*19.2*
75-79	KJSU	1 161.5	1 126.0	1 068.0	1 023.0	1 100.6	1 148.7	1 197.2	1 255.7	1 267.3	1 227.9	1 196.0
Percentage	KJSV	*17.5*	*16.8*	*15.9*	*15.2*	*16.2*	*16.5*	*17.1*	*17.8*	*18.3*	*17.7*	*17.1*
80-84	KJSW	864.2	868.0	873.9	882.0	892.9	888.4	861.0	814.6	762.9	786.4	843.3
Percentage	KJSX	*13.0*	*12.9*	*13.0*	*13.1*	*13.2*	*12.8*	*12.3*	*11.6*	*11.0*	*11.4*	*12.1*
85-89	KJSY	438.8	499.2	514.1	521.9	534.3	542.2	545.9	552.3	548.9	539.7	543.5
Percentage	KJSZ	*6.6*	*7.4*	*7.7*	*7.8*	*7.9*	*7.8*	*7.8*	*7.8*	*7.9*	*7.8*	*7.8*
90 and over	KJTA	219.1	231.0	244.9	256.8	271.9	285.3	300.4	311.4	314.1	305.5	321.6
Percentage	KJTB	*3.3*	*3.4*	*3.6*	*3.8*	*4.0*	*4.1*	*4.3*	*4.4*	*4.5*	*4.4*	*4.6*
Total all ages	KJSN	6 648.2	6 721.7	6 716.3	6 727.1	6 779.0	6 950.2	7 006.8	7 052.5	6 944.1	6 928.0	6 978.0

1 Including pensions payable to persons residing overseas.
2 Figures are at 31 March.

Source: Department for Work and Pensions: 0191 225 7874

10.12 Family Credit/ Working Families' Tax Credit[1]

Thousands

		Great Britain As at 31 December								United Kingdom As at 30 December	
		1992	1993	1994	1995	1996	1997	1998		1999	2000
Families in receipt:											
Total	KJTO	459.3	518.3	578.0	646.5	716.7	751.4	779.7	ZCMK	965.0	1 167.6
Two-parent families: total	KJTP	266.5	291.0	324.6	356.9	390.2	388.0	383.4	ZCML	467.2	566.0
With 1 child	KJTQ	66.9	73.3	80.1	89.7	98.6	96.6	95.4	ZCMM	116.7	144.9
2 children	KJTR	100.4	110.1	122.4	135.1	146.1	144.4	141.7	ZCMN	178.3	220.1
3 children	KJTS	61.4	66.9	76.4	83.4	91.1	91.4	89.1	ZCMO	107.7	129.3
4 children or more children	ZIYM	37.9	40.7	45.8	48.6	54.4	55.6	57.3	ZCMP	64.6	71.8
One-parent families: total	KJTW	192.7	227.3	253.4	289.6	326.5	363.4	396.3	ZIYI	497.7	601.5
With 1 child	KJTX	100.1	117.8	133.8	152.2	170.4	189.3	203.4	ZIYJ	259.6	313.6
2 children	KJTY	66.7	79.2	86.0	99.1	111.2	121.8	136.1	ZIYK	169.6	207.5
3 or more children	KJTZ	25.8	30.4	33.5	38.3	45.0	52.3	56.9	ZIYL	68.6	80.5

1 Family Credit was replaced by Working Families Tax Credit in October 1999. The WFTC figures for December 1999 include Family Credit awards made before October 1999 and still current (both FC and WFTC awards last for 26 weeks).

Sources: Board of Inland Revenue: 020 7438 6275; Department for Work and Pensions: 0191 225 7373

10.13 Income support: number of claimants receiving weekly payment[1]
Great Britain
On a day in May

Thousands

		1993	1994	1995	1996	1997[4]	1998[4]	1999[4]	2000[4]	2001[4]
All income support	KACC	3 561	3 689	3 889	3 963	3 958	3 853	3 814	3 811	3 928
All aged 60 and over	KACD	1 760	1 749	1 770	1 753	1 720	1 659	1 624	1 615	1 717
Retirement pensioners	KACE	1 426	1 407	1 417	1 404	1 383	1 338	1 308	1 305	1 406
In receipt of other NI benefit[2]	KACF	72	81	92	89	81	74	67	64	65
Others[5]	KACG	262	261	261	260	256	248	249	246	246
All under 60	KACH	1 801	1 940	2 120	2 211	2 238	2 194	2 190	2 196	2 211
Disabled with contributory benefit[2]	KACK	94	113	146	161	180	195	196	207	210
Disabled without contributory benefit[2]	KFBJ	402	481	570	604	646	685	718	755	807
Lone parent premium not in other groups[3]	KACL	988	1 017	1 040	1 044	1 013	961	936	910	888
Others	KACM	317	328	363	402	398	353	341	324	306

1 Data are extracted from the Annual Statistical Enquiry undertaken in May 1993, and the Quarterly Statistical Enquiries May 1994 to May 2001.
2 Contributory/NI benefits other than Retirement pension are Incapacity Benefit (previously IVB & Sickness Benefit), Widows Pension and Widowed Mothers Allowance.

3 Figures relate to one-parent families headed by a man or a woman, where the claimant is not receiving a pensioner or disability premium.
4 Figures exclude unemployed claimants who transferred to Jobseeker's Allowance from 7 October 1996.

Source: Department for Work and Pensions: 0191 225 7373

10.14 Income support
Great Britain[1]
On a day in May

Thousands

		1993	1994	1995	1996	1997	1998	1999	2000	2001
Number of regular weekly payments	KACN	3 561	3 689	3 889	3 963	3 958	3 853	3 814	3 811	3 928
Total number of persons provided for	KACO	6 146	6 465	6 858	7 004	6 973	6 769	6 689	6 666	6 782
Number of dependants	KACP	2 147	2 296	2 440	2 494	2 464	2 379	2 344	2 317	2 289
Partners	KACQ	438	480	528	546	551	537	531	539	565
Total children under 16 years	KACR	2 020	2 156	2 292	2 340	2 303	2 224	2 188	2 158	2 123
Under 11	KACS	1 543	1 623	1 708	1 728	1 685	1 605	1 557	1 524	1 489
11 - 15 years	KACT	477	533	584	612	618	618	631	634	634
16 - 17 years	KACU	104	112	119	129	134	129	128	131	138
Other dependants										
18 years and over	KACV	24	28	28	25	28	26	28	28	28

1 Data are extracted from the Annual Statistical Enquiry undertaken in May 1992-1993 and the Quarterly Statistical Enquiries undertaken in May 1994 to May 2001. Figures exclude unemployed claimants in receipt of Income Support prior to the introduction of Jobseeker's Allowance in October 1996.

Source: Department for Work and Pensions: 0191 225 7373

10.15 Income support: average weekly amounts of benefit
Great Britain[1]

May

Thousands

		1993	1994	1995	1996	1997[2]	1998[2]	1999[2]	2000[2]	2001[2]
All income support	KACW	54.75	56.16	56.29	57.26	58.03	58.72	61.42	65.72	70.21
All aged 60 and over	KJUB	43.59	42.45	41.18	41.69	42.24	42.29	45.30	48.18	50.73
Retirement pensioners	KACX	38.28	36.14	34.61	34.66	34.90	34.50	36.99	39.50	41.20
In receipt of other NI benefit[3]	KJUD	27.17	27.83	27.28	29.17	30.73	32.42	35.58	40.76	47.31
Others	KACY	77.09	80.97	81.72	83.99	85.57	87.29	91.70	96.20	106.10
All under 60	KACZ	65.65	68.51	68.91	69.61	70.17	71.14	73.36	78.61	85.34
Disabled with contributory benefit[3]	KADC	27.22	29.54	31.96	33.05	33.87	33.56	34.40	36.85	41.78
Disabled without contributory benefit[3]	KADD	59.18	64.14	66.84	68.55	70.38	72.86	75.88	79.25	84.29
Lone parent premium not in other groups[4]	KADE	70.31	74.93	76.63	78.19	79.21	79.67	82.01	91.21	101.44
Others	KADF	70.73	68.44	64.92	63.59	63.24	65.38	66.71	68.37	71.26

1 Data are extracted from the Annual Statistical Enquiry undertaken in May 1993, and from the Quarterly Statistical Enquiries May 1994 to May 2001.
2 Figures exclude unemployed claimants who transferred to Jobseeker's Allowance from 7 October 1996.
3 Contributory/NI benefits other than Retirement pension are Incapacity Benefit (previously IVB & Sickness Benefit), Widows Pension and Widowed Mothers Allowance.
4 Figures relate to one-parent families headed by a man or a woman, where the claimant is not receiving a pensioner or disability premium.

Source: Department for Work and Pensions: 0191 225 7373

10.16 War pensions
Estimated number of pensioners

Great Britain at 31 March in each year

Thousands

		1991	1992	1993	1994	1995	1996	1997	1998	1999	2000	2001
Total	KADG	247.67	249.95	266.92	296.30	309.84	323.74	324.64	317.65	306.06	295.67	284.33
Disablement -												
1914 war; 1939 war and later service	KADH	192.04	196.19	214.53	245.44	260.30	265.37	264.59	259.16	248.93	240.76	231.62
Widows and dependants -												
1914 war; 1939 war and later service	KADI	55.83	53.76	52.39	50.86	49.54	58.37	60.05	58.49	55.85	54.92	52.70

Source: Department for Work and Pensions: 0191 225 7373

Social protection

10.17 Summary of government expenditure on social services and housing
Years ended 31 March

£ millions

		1991 /92	1992 /93	1993 /94	1994 /95	1995 /96	1996 /97	1997 /98	1998 /99	1999 /00	2000 /01
Education[1]	KJAA	29 550	31 576	33 544	35 367	36 810	37 953	39 078	38 761	40 889	..
National health service	KJAB	31 842	35 413	37 259	39 879	40 691	42 383	43 878	47 194	48 362	53 039
Welfare services	CSWL	4 873	6 683	7 700	9 016	10 312	11 521	11 713	11 984	12 168	12 995
Social security benefits	KJAE	69 121	78 846	85 805	87 941	90 534	92 217	92 146	93 929	96 010	95 129
Housing	KJAF	5 547	6 984	5 919	5 634	5 445	4 593	3 415	3 605	2 825	2 947
Total government expenditure	KJAG	140 933	159 502	170 227	177 837	183 792	188 667	190 230	195 147	200 254	..
Current expenditure	KJAH	135 231	151 010	163 289	171 277	177 667	183 842	182 500	191 383	198 404	..
Capital expenditure	KJAI	5 702	8 492	6 938	6 560	6 125	4 825	3 590	4 090	3 628	..
Total government expenditure	KJAG	140 933	159 502	170 227	177 837	183 792	188 667	190 230	195 147	200 254	..
Central government	KJAK	103 304	116 304	126 371	130 819	134 954	137 487	142 133	155 290	160 041	..
Local authorities	KJAL	37 629	43 198	43 856	47 018	48 838	51 180	48 102	40 183	40 213	..
Total government expenditure	KJAG	140 933	159 502	170 227	177 837	183 792	188 667	190 230	195 147	200 254	..
Total government expenditure on social services and housing as a percentage of GDP[2]		23.75	25.86	26.11	25.72	25.22	24.41	23.08	22.44	21.94	..

1 Includes school meals.
2 GDP adjusted to take account of change from rates to community charge.

Source: Office for National Statistics: 020 7533 5990

10.18 Government expenditure on education
Years ended 31 march

£ millions

			1990/91	1991/92	1992/93	1993/94	1994/95	1995/96	1996/97	1997/98	1998[1]/99	1999[1]/00
Current expenditure												
Nursery schools	KEZN	KJBA	6 458	7 247	8 262	8 712	9 094	9 352	9 697	10 405	..	..
Primary schools		KJBB									..	..
Secondary schools	KJBC		7 147	7 787	8 347	8 615	8 875	8 844	9 194	9 322	..	..
Special schools	KJBD		1 121	1 245	1 354	1 420	1 451	1 493	1 578	1 655	..	..
Universities[2]	KJBG		2 265	2 437	3 361	..	..	..	..	..	..	..
Other Higher, Further and adult education[3]	KJBE		4 128	4 454	4 136	..	..	..	..	..	..	..
Higher Education Funding Council[3,4]	CSWM		..	..	..	4 908	5 192	5 472	5 729	5 693	4 757	5 232
Further Education Funding Council[5]	CSWO		..	..	..	3 072	3 200	3 392	3 694	3 718	5 108	4 499
Continuing Education	CSWP		..	..	..	380	294	1 801	1 891	1 960	..	..
Other education expenditure	KJBH		1 325	1 361	1 009	905	963	948	1 277	1 355	4 690	5 429
Related current expenditure:												
School welfare[6]	KJBJ		155	214	270	346	359	328	336	372	..	..
School meals[7]	KJBK		506	556	161	149	147	148	147	138	..	..
Youth service and physical training	KJBL		348	360	393	392	401	396	389	389	..	..
Maintenance grants and allowances to pupils and students[8]	KJBM		1 028	1 379	1 705	1 972	2 204	1 660	1 440	1 289	..	..
Transport of pupils	KJBN		393	442	417	444	486	507	526	584	..	..
Miscellaneous expenditure	KJBO		2	3	8	10	31	31	49	45	..	..
Total current expenditure[9]	KJBQ		24 876	27 485	29 424	31 325	32 697	34 372	35 947	36 925	37 250	39 131
Capital expenditure												
Nursery schools	KEZP	KJBR	353	376	384	414	517	497	482	546	..	..
Primary schools		KJBS									..	..
Secondary schools	KJBT		465	493	518	485	565	482	515	601	..	..
Special schools	KJBU		36	35	32	31	37	51	52	44	..	..
Universities[2]	KJBX		211	231	236	..	..	..	..	..	..	..
Other Higher, Further and adult education[3]	KJBV		230	293	285	..	..	..	..	..	..	..
Higher Education Funding Council[3,4]	CSWQ		..	..	..	406	412	424	74	61	31	..
Further Education Funding Council[5]	CSWR		..	..	..	194	201	187	33	29	44	..
Continuing Education	CSWS		..	..	..	6	8	8	5	–	–	–
Other education expenditure	KJBY		39	33	25	12	45	25	24	30	57	..
Related capital expenditure	KJBZ		26	20	17	23	25	17	20	24	..	..
Total capital expenditure[9]	KJCA		1 359	1 481	1 496	1 571	1 810	1 691	1 205	1 335	1 511	1 758
VAT refunds to local authorities	KJBP		493	584	656	648	860	747	801	818	816	906
Total expenditure												
Central government	KJCB		4 582	4 288	4 722	8 186	9 490	10 853	11 388	12 167	11 202	12 956
Local authorities	KJCC		22 146	25 261	26 853	25 354	25 900	25 954	26 562	26 910	27 559	27 933
Total government expenditure on education[10]	KJAA		26 728	29 550	31 576	33 544	35 367	36 810	37 953	39 078	38 761	40 889
Total government education expenditure as a percentage of GDP[11]			4.72	4.98	5.12	5.15	5.11	5.05	4.91	4.74	4.46	4.48

1 From 1998/99 figures have been taken from HM Treasury Public Expenditure Statistical Analyses. They are not comparable with earlier years which used different sources.

2 Includes expenditure on University departments of Education for England and Wales.

3 Includes tuition fees.

4 Includes expenditure on Higher Education Institutions in Northern Ireland.

5 Includes expenditure on Further Education Institutions in Northern Ireland.

6 Expenditure on the school health service is included in the National Health Service.

7 Expenditure on school meals in England has been recharged across other expenditure headings.

8 Excludes the secondment of teachers on further training. Includes student loans expenditure.

9 Due to rounding constituent figures may not sum to totals.

10 Excludes additional adjustment to allow for Capital consumption made for National Accounts purposes. Fron 1995/96, figures include expenditure on training programmes in England (such as Work Based Training for Young People) reclassified as education. Therefore the figures are not comparable with earlier years.

11 GDP includes adjustments to remove the distortion caused by the abolition of domestic rates.

Sources: Department for Education and Skills;
Office for National Statistics: 020 7533 5990

10.19 Government expenditure on the National Health Service
Years ended 31 March

£ millions

		1990/91	1991/92	1992/93	1993/94	1994/95	1995/96	1996/97	1997/98	1998/99	1999/00	2000/01
Current expenditure												
Central government:												
Hospitals and Community Health Services[1] and Family Health Services[2]	KJQA	25 276	29 061	32 195	35 567	37 698	38 514	39 425	40 993	43 600	48 275	52 599
Administration[3]	KJQB	979	1 119	1 258	–	–	–	–	–	–	–	–
less Payments by patients:												
Hospital services	KJQC	–510	–540	–505	–368	–111	–42	–42	–48	–84	–138	–138
Pharmaceutical services	KJQD	–247	–270	–297	–324	–342	–383	–376	–396	–391	–405	–425
Dental services	KJQE	–441	–477	–470	–440	–464	–494	–447	–475	–470	–483	–506
Ophthalmic services	KJQF	–	–	–	–	–	–	–	–	–	–	–
Total	KJQG	–1 198	–1 287	–1 272	–1 132	–917	–919	–865	–919	–945	–1 026	–1 068
Departmental administration	KJQH	268	293	319	270	256	242	265	245	227	231	324
Other central services	KJQI	738	865	1 301	1 651	2 304	2 538	3 124	3 242	4 980	1 601	..
Total current expenditure	KJQJ	26 063	30 051	33 801	36 356	39 341	40 375	41 949	43 561	46 910	48 055	52 707
Capital expenditure												
Central government	KJQK	1 848	1 791	1 612	903	538	316	434	317	284	307	332
Total government NHS Expenditure												
Central government	KJAB	27 911	31 842	35 413	37 259	39 879	40 691	42 383	43 878	47 194	48 362	53 039
Total NHS expenditure as a percentage of GDP[4]		4.93	5.37	5.74	5.72	5.77	5.58	5.48	5.32	5.43	5.30	5.55

1 Including the school health service.
2 General Medical Services have been included in the expenditure of the Health Authorities. Therefore, Hospitals and Community Health Services and Family Practitioner Services (now Family Health Services) are not identifiable separately.

3 Administration costs are not separately identifiable from 1993/94.
4 GDP adjusted to take account of change from rates to community charge.

Source: Office for National Statistics: 020 7533 5990

10.20 Government expenditure on welfare services[1]
Years ended 31 March

£ millions

		1990/91	1991/92	1992/93	1993/94	1994/95	1995/96	1996/97	1997/98	1998/99	1999/00	2000/01
Personal social services												
Central government current expenditure	KJCG	163	190	202	216	197	140	101	73	53	50	49
Local authorities current expenditure:												
Running expenses	CTKQ	5 022	5 725	6 122	7 113	8 400	9 716	10 947	11 131	11 378	11 563	12 048
Capital expenditure	KJCI	227	200	189	190	235	229	210	204	199	145	128
Total	KJAC	5 626	4 732	6 513	7 519	8 832	10 085	11 258	11 408	11 630	11 758	12 226
Welfare foods service												
Central government current expenditure on welfare foods (including administration)	KJCK	120	142	171	182	185	228	264	306	355	411	411
less Receipts from the public	KJCL	–1	–1	–1	–1	–1	–1	–1	–1	–1	–1	–2
Total	KJAD	119	141	170	181	184	227	263	305	354	410	409
Total government expenditure	CSWL	5 745	4 873	6 683	7 700	9 016	10 312	11 521	11 713	11 984	12 168	12 995
Total government expenditure as a percentage of GDP[2]		1.02	0.82	1.08	1.18	1.30	1.42	1.49	1.42	1.38	1.33	1.36

1 School meals are included in Table 10.18.
2 GDP adjusted to take account of change from rates to community charge.

Source: Office for National Statistics: 020 7533 5990

10.21 Government expenditure on social security benefits
Years ended 31 March

£ millions

		1990 /91	1991 /92	1992 /93	1993 /94	1994 /95	1995 /96	1996 /97	1997 /98	1998 /99	1999 /00	2000 /01
Government current expenditure												
National insurance fund:												
Retirement pensions	EKXK	22 725	25 691	27 076	28 481	28 925	30 162	32 146	33 643	35 711	37 833	39 844
Lump sums to pensioners	KJDB	114	114	115	122	123	124	129	118	120	123	128
Widows and guardians allowances	CSDH	893	884	1 014	1 041	1 034	1 018	974	992	973	990	244
Unemployment benefit	CSDI	892	1 627	1 761	1 623	1 277	1 099	588	1	–	–1	–2
Jobseeker's allowance[1]	CJTJ	–	–	–	–	–	–	379	590	474	462	435
Sickness benefit	CSDJ	222	278	365	294	426	12	–	–	–	–	–
Invalidity benefit	CSDK	4 544	5 461	6 198	7 146	8 042	271	–	–	–	–	–
Incapacity benefit[2]	CUNL	–	–	–	–	–	7 615	7 668	7 471	7 295	6 897	6 685
Maternity benefit	CSDL	35	40	42	32	17	28	32	36	39	40	45
Death grant	CSDM	–	–	–	–	–	–	–	–	–	–	–
Injury benefit	CSDN	–	–	–	–	–	–	–	–	–	–	–
Disablement benefit	CSDO	526	–	–	–	–	–	–	–	–	–	–
Industrial death benefit	CSDP	62	–	–	–	–	–	–	–	–	–	–
Statutory sick pay	CSDQ	966	725	688	688	24	24	24	28	28	28	28
Statutory maternity pay	GTKZ	344	396	416	440	498	476	500	516	552	585	449
Payments in lieu of benefits foregone	GTKV	–	–	–	–	–	–	–	–	–	–	–
Total	ACHH	31 323	35 216	37 675	39 867	40 366	40 829	42 440	43 395	45 192	46 957	46 879
Maternity Fund	GTKO	–	–	–	–	–	–	–	–	–	–	–
Redundancy Fund	GTKN	130	276	321	110	208	128	108	88	116	148	156
Social Fund	GTLQ	123	130	175	189	183	216	203	200	360	920	1 895
Non-contributory benefits:												
War pensions	KJDP	688	844	976	913	1 083	1 247	1 352	1 284	1 262	1 247	1 208
Family benefits:												
Child benefit	KJDQ	4 840	5 433	5 950	6 347	6 294	6 332	6 645	7 095	7 327	8 252	8 414
One parent benefit	KJDR	227	249	275	282	289	310	317	9	–	–	–
Family credit	KAAA	466	626	929	1 208	1 441	1 739	2 084	2 338	2 430	1 927	–788
Family income supplement	KJDS	–	–	–	–	–	–	–	–	–	–	–
Maternity grants	KJDT	–	–	–	–	–	–	–	–	–	–	–
Income support/Supplementary benefits:												
Supplementary pensions	KJDU	–	–	–	–	–	–	–	–	–	–	–
Supplementary allowances	KJDV	–	–	–	–	–	–	–	–	–	–	–
Income support	KAAB	9 106	12 325	15 578	16 997	16 387	16 650	14 438	11 998	11 793	12 236	13 115
Other non-contributory benefits:												
Old persons' pensions	KJDX	38	36	36	36	35	36	30	29	29	28	28
Lump sums to pensioners	KJDY	8	11	13	14	13	13	15	17	17	17	17
Attendance allowance	KJDZ	1 698	1 706	1 553	1 795	1 963	2 194	2 393	2 640	2 682	2 834	2 957
Invalid care allowance	KJEA	229	285	345	442	526	617	736	745	783	821	853
Mobility allowance	KJEB	895	1 063	68	–	–	–	–	–	–	–	–
Disability living allowance	EKXL	–	–	1 973	2 772	3 125	3 802	4 498	5 018	5 367	5 651	6 025
Disability working allowance	EKYE	–	–	3	7	11	19	34	44	49	40	–155
Severe disablement allowance	KJEC	407	596	640	703	776	820	906	1 007	984	1 016	1 024
Industrial injury benefits	EKXM	142	655	668	687	706	731	744	754	–	–	–
RPI Adjustment	KAAC	–	–	–	–	–	–	–	–	–	–	–
Housing benefit	KJED	4 735	6 053	7 670	9 163	10 345	10 773	11 276	11 315	11 311	11 247	11 616
Administration	KJEE	3 206	3 617	3 998	4 273	4 190	4 076	3 998	4 170	4 349	3 737	3 936
Total government benefit expenditure	KJAE	58 261	69 121	78 846	85 805	87 941	90 534	92 217	92 146	93 929	96 010	95 129
Total government benefit expenditure as a percentage of GDP[3]		10.30	11.65	12.78	13.16	12.72	12.42	11.93	11.18	10.80	10.52	9.96

1 Jobseeker's allowance was introduced in October 1996 to replace Unemployment benefit and Income Support for the unemployed.
2 Sickness benefit and Invalidity benefit were replaced by a single incapacity benefit in 1995.
3 GDP adjusted to take account of change from rates to community charge.

Source: Office for National Statistics: 020 7533 5990

10.22 Government and other public sector expenditure on housing
Years ended 31 March

£ millions

		1990 /91	1991 /92	1992 /93	1993 /94	1994 /95	1995 /96	1996 /97	1997 /98	1998 /99	1999 /00	2000 /01
Government expenditure												
Current expenditure												
Central government												
housing subsidies:												
to local authorities	CTMN	1 273	1 144	992	874	814	687	717	711	737	715	704
to public corporations	ADVA	284	260	208	214	228	228	236	244	218	230	363
to housing associations	KJRC	67	40	135	180	207	235	215	216	−22	−111	232
grants to housing associations	KJRD	85	117	59	13	3	1	1	–	–	–	–
Local authorities												
housing subsidies	KJVK	3	–	1	–	–	3	1	1	1	3	3
Grants under the option mortgage scheme	KJRF	–	–	–	–	–	–	–	–	–	–	–
Administration, etc	KGVL	320	373	394	364	405	402	447	509	575	590	573
Total current expenditure	KJRH	2 032	1 934	1 789	1 645	1 657	1 556	1 617	1 681	1 509	1 427	1 875
Capital expenditure												
Investment in housing by local authorities	KGVM	1 322	822	913	780	842	1 009	937	−52	59	−729	−368
Capital grants to housing associations	KJRJ	1 495	2 045	2 583	2 136	1 774	1 329	1 393	1 102	1 021	975	950
Improvement grants	ADCE	863	1 152	1 240	1 287	1 105	846	980	1 157	779	766	836
Net lending for house purchase	KJRL	−596	−782	−211	−402	−141	−136	−719	−816	−168	−82	−84
Capital grants to public corporations	XJRM	774	482	631	439	387	837	386	400	415	431	450
Net lending to public corporations	KJRN	176	−104	39	34	10	7	−1	−57	−10	−10	−11
Total capital expenditure	KJRO	4 033	3 613	5 195	4 274	3 977	3 889	2 976	1 734	2 096	1 351	1 773
Total expenditure												
Central government	KJRP	3 835	3 697	4 595	3 839	3 409	3 313	2 362	1 962	2 359	2 276	2 287
Local authorities	KJRQ	2 230	1 850	2 389	2 080	2 225	2 132	2 231	1 453	1 246	549	660
Total government expenditure	KJAF	6 065	5 547	6 984	5 919	5 634	5 445	4 593	3 415	3 605	2 825	2 947
Public corporations' capital expenditure												
Investment in housing	KGVN	519	673	549	568	560	580	574	452	424	420	400
Net lending to private sector	AAFR	−3	−4	3	1	−1	−5	−1	−1	–	–	–
Total	KJRU	516	669	552	569	559	575	569	451	424	420	400
Total public sector housing expenditure[1]	KJRV	5 631	5 838	6 866	6 015	5 796	5 176	4 777	3 523	3 624	2 824	3 116
Total public sector housing expenditure as a percentage of GDP[2]		1.00	0.98	1.11	0.92	0.84	0.71	0.62	0.43	0.42	0.31	0.33

1 Total government expenditure *less* grants and loans to public corporations *plus* public corporations' capital expenditure.
2 GDP adjusted to take account of change from rates to community charge.

Source: Office for National Statistics: 020 7533 5990

11 Crime and justice

Crime and justice

There are differences in the legal and judicial systems of England and Wales, Scotland and Northern Ireland which make it impossible to provide tables covering the United Kingdom as a whole in this section. These differences concern the classification of offences, the meaning of certain terms used in the statistics, the effects of the several Criminal Justice Acts and recording practices.

Recorded crime statistics *(Table 11.1)*

Crimes recorded by the police provide a measure of the amount of crime committed. The statistics are based on counting rules, revised with effect from 1 April 1998, which are standard for all the police forces in England and Wales and now include all indictable and triable-either-way offences together with a few summary offences which are closely linked to these offences. The new rules have changed the emphasis of measurement more towards one crime per victim, and have also increased the coverage of offences. These changes have particularly impacted on the offence groups of violence against the person, fraud and forgery, drugs offences and other offences.

For a variety of reasons many offences are either not reported to the police or not recorded by them. The changes in the number of offences recorded do not necessarily provide an accurate reflection of changes in the amount of crime committed.

For further information please see the Home Office *Statistical Bulletin 12/01 on Recorded Crime Statistics.*

Court proceedings and police cautions
(Tables 11.3 - 11.7, 11.13 - 11.17, 11.20 - 11.22)

The statistical basis of the tables of court proceedings is broadly similar in England and Wales, Scotland and Northern Ireland; the tables show the number of persons found guilty, recording a person under the heading of the principal offence of which he is found guilty, excluding additional findings of guilt at the same proceedings. A person found guilty at a number of separate court proceedings is included more than once.

The statistics on offenders cautioned cover only those who, on admission of guilt, were given a formal caution by, or on the instructions of, a senior police officer as an alternative to prosecution (excluding Scotland). Written warnings by the police for motor offences and persons paying fixed penalties for certain motoring offences are excluded. There are no statistics on cautioning available for Northern Ireland.

In Scotland there are three criminal courts, the High Court of Justiciary, the Sheriff Court and the District Court. The High Court deals with serious solemn (ie Jury) cases and has unlimited sentencing power. The Sheriff Court is limited to imprisonment of 3 years for solemn cases, or 3 months (6 months when specified in legislation for second or subsequent offences and 12 months for certain statutory offences) for summary cases. The District Court deals only with summary cases and is limited to 60 days imprisonment and level 4 fines. Stipendiary Magistrates sit in Glasgow District Court and have the summary sentencing powers of a Sheriff.

Indictable offences are offences which are:

(a) triable on indictment only (these are the most serious crimes such as murder and rape) and are tried at the Crown Court in England and Wales and the High Court in Scotland;

(b) triable either way offences which may be tried at the Crown Court or Magistrates' Court in England and Wales or the High Court, Sheriff Court or District Court in Scotland; summary offences are those for which a defendant in England and Wales or accused in Scotland would normally be dealt with at the Magistrates' Courts and the Sheriff or District Court in Scotland.

The Criminal Justice Act 1991 led to the following main changes in the sentences available to the courts in England and Wales:

(a) introduction of combination orders,

(b) introduction of the "unit fine scheme" at Magistrates' courts,

(c) abolishing the sentence of detention in a young offender institution for 14 year old boys and changing the minimum and maximum sentence lengths for 15 to 17 year olds to 10 and 12 months respectively, and

(d) abolishing partly suspended sentences of imprisonment and restricting the use of a fully suspended sentence.

The Criminal Justice Act 1993 abolished the "Unit Fine Scheme" in Magistrates' courts which had been introduced under the Criminal Justice Act 1991.

A *charging standard for assault* was introduced in England and Wales on 31 August 1994 with the aim to promote consistency between the police and prosecution on the appropriate level of charge to be brought.

The Criminal Justice and Public Order Act 1994 created several new offences in England and Wales, mainly in the area of Public Order, but also including male rape (there is no statutory offence of 'male rape' in Scotland, although such a crime may be charged as serious assault). The Act also:

(a) extended the provisions of section 53 of the Children and Young Persons Act 1993 for 10 to 13 year olds,

(b) increased the maximum sentence length for 15 to 17 year olds to 2 years,

(c) increased the upper limit from £2 000 to £5 000 for offences of criminal damage proceeded against as if triable only summarily, (d) introduced provisions for the reduction of sentences for early guilty pleas, and (e) increased the maximum sentence length for certain firearm offences.

Provisions within the Crime (Sentences) Act 1997, in England and Wales, and the Crime and Punishment (Scotland) Act 1997, in Scotland, included:

a)   an automatic life sentence for a second serious violent or sexual offence unless there are exceptional circumstances (this provision has not been enacted in Scotland);

b)   a minimum sentence of seven years for an offender convicted for a third time of a class A drug trafficking offence unless the court considers this to be unjust in all the circumstances, and, in England and Wales,

c)   the new section 38A of the Magistrates' Courts' Act 1980 extending the circumstances in which a magistrates' court may commit a person convicted of an offence triable either way to the Crown Court for sentence - it was implemented in conjunction with section 49 of the Criminal Procedure and Investigations Act 1996, which involves the magistrates' courts in asking defendants to indicate plea before the mode of trial decision is taken and compels the court to sentence or commit for sentence any defendant who indicates a guilty plea.

The Crime and Disorder Act 1998 created provisions in relation to reprimands and final warnings, new offences and orders which have been implemented nationally or piloted in certain areas. The Youth Justice and Criminal Evidence Act 1999 introduced a new sentence for young offenders of referral to a youth offender panel.

Section 45 of the Criminal Justice (Scotland) Act 1980 was implemented on 15 November 1983; this introduced unified custodial sentencing for under 21 offenders and abolished borstal training.

The system of Magistrates' courts and Crown Courts in Northern Ireland operates in a similar way to that in England and Wales. A particularly significant statutory development, however, has been the Criminal Justice (NI) Order 1996 which introduces a new sentencing regime into Northern Ireland, largely replicating that which was introduced into England and Wales by the Criminal Justice Acts of 1991 and 1993. The order makes many changes to both community and custodial sentences, while introducing new orders such as the combination order, the custody probation order and orders for release on licence of sexual offenders.

Previous convictions of prisoners
(Tables 11.8 and 11.9)
Standard list offences consist of all the indictable offences plus some of the more serious summary offences. From 1 January 1996 a number of summary motoring offences became standard list offences. Excluding the new standard lists from the analysis presented in the table would slightly alter the percentages with previous convictions.

Information on previous convictions of prisoners published prior to 1995 was based upon Prison Service records. However, details of a prisoner's previous conviction were often not recorded (eg. this information was missing for 44 per cent of the 1990 male receptions under sentence). To overcome this problem the Home Office Offenders Index (a computerised database containing details of convictions for standard list offences) is now being used to provide information on prisoners' previous convictions. Unfortunately, this means that the most up-to-date information on previous convictions is not directly comparable with that previously published. Standard list offences include indictable offences and some of the more serious summary offences so the coverage is not as complete. The published information also does not relate to 'prison receptions' but to those sentenced to immediate custody for standard list offences (which accounted for 82 per cent of those sentenced to custody in 1993).

The problems with non-availability of previous history information are much less acute using the Offenders Index data source. Previous convictions were found for 95 per cent of the 1993 prison population sample. Some of the cases where information is missing, would be accounted for by prisoners who are not sentenced for a standard list offence and have no previous record for such offences.

11.1 Recorded crime statistics
England and Wales

Thousands

		Old counting rules										New counting rules		
		1990	1991	1992	1993	1994	1995	1996	1997	1998[1] /99		1998 /99	1999 /00	2000 /01
Violence against the person	BEAB	184.7	190.3	201.8	205.1	218.4	212.6	239.3	250.8	230.8	LQMP	502.8	581.0	600.9
Sexual offences	BEAC	29.0	29.4	29.5	31.3	32.0	30.3	31.4	33.2	34.9	LQMQ	36.2	37.8	37.3
Burglary	BEAD	1 006.8	1 219.5	1 355.3	1 369.6	1 256.7	1 239.5	1 164.6	1 015.1	951.9	LQMR	953.2	906.5	836.0
Robbery	BEAE	36.2	45.3	52.9	57.8	60.0	68.1	74.0	63.1	66.2	LQMS	66.8	84.3	95.2
Theft and handling stolen goods	BEAF	2 374.4	2 761.1	2 851.6	2 751.9	2 564.6	2 452.1	2 383.9	2 165.0	2 126.7	LQMT	2 191.4	2 223.6	2 145.4
Fraud and forgery	BEAG	147.9	174.7	168.6	162.8	145.3	133.0	136.2	134.4	173.7	LQMU	279.5	334.8	319.3
Criminal damage	BEAH	733.4	821.1	892.6	906.7	928.3	914.0	951.3	877.0	834.4	LQMV	879.6	945.7	960.1
Drug offences[2]	LQMO	..	..	..	..	..	..	..	..	21.3	LQYT	135.9	121.9	113.5
Other offences[2]	BEAI	31.1	34.6	39.4	41.0	47.7	50.7	55.8	59.8	42.0	LQYU	63.6	65.7	63.2
Total	BEAA	4 543.6	5 276.2	5 591.7	5 526.3	5 253.0	5 100.2	5 036.6	4 598.3	4 481.8	LQYV	5 109.1	5 301.2	5 170.8

1 Estimates.
2 Prior to 1 April 1998 the offence of drug trafficking was included in the "Other offences" group. From 1 April 1999, under the new counting rules, drug trafficking became part of a new "Drug offences" group which, with the expanded coverage, now includes possession and other drug offences. For 1998/99, under the old counting rules, drug trafficking - the only drugs offence counted - has been listed under drugs offences.

Source: Home Office: 020 7273 2583

11.2 Police forces: strength
End of year

		1990	1991	1992	1993	1994	1995[1]	1996[1]	1997[1]	1998[1]	1999[1]	2000[1]
England and Wales												
Regular police												
Strength:												
Men	KERB	110 790	110 396	111 027	108 967	108 030	107 022	106 549	105 691	104 606	103 083	101 683
Women	KERC	14 352	14 898	15 841	16 571	17 263	17 688	18 501	19 124	19 659	19 967	20 519
Seconded:[2]												
Men	KERD	1 787	1 670	1 766	1 938	1 881	1 896	1 864	1 814	2 007	2 158	2 077
Women	KERE	161	163	167	182	184	202	209	233	232	256	307
Additional officers:[3]												
Men	KERF	85	73	68	63	97	105	111	200	267	324	361
Women	KERG	5	3	3	12	17	22	57	158	514	582	519
Special constables												
Enrolled strength:												
Men	KERH	10 483	11 592	12 251	13 240	12 772	12 751	12 594	12 483	11 331	10 667	9 120
Women	KERI	5 419	6 480	6 992	7 326	7 060	6 904	6 857	6 680	5 965	5 060	4 367
Scotland												
Regular police												
Strength[4]:												
Men	KERK	12 583	12 566	12 629	12 580	12 634	12 341	12 347	12 495	12 479	12 258	12 058
Women	KERL	1 258	1 357	1 465	1 559	1 679	1 665	1 856	2 019	2 202	2 098	2 115
Central service:[4,5]												
Men	KERM	67	64	70	73	79	96	94	85	85	88	95
Women	KERN	6	6	5	5	4	7	8	4	6	9	13
Seconded:[4,6]												
Men	KERO	98	103	120	109	110	108	105	101	101	85	130
Women	KERP	8	6	10	16	16	16	16	13	10	12	18
Additional regular police:												
Strength	KERR	64	93	90	58	91	90	72	72	97	91	84
Special constables												
Strength:												
Men	KERS	1 475	1 436	1 454	1 466	1 518	1 411	1 336	1 286	1 289	1 229	981
Women	KERT	312	342	393	431	474	467	450	437	444	422	355
Northern Ireland												
Regular police[7]												
Strength:												
Men	KERU	7 535	7 510	7 687	7 646	7 640	7 528	7 531	7 562	7 527	7 406	6 916
Women	KERV	708	707	791	818	853	887	897	923	933	987	978
Reserve[8]												
Strength:												
Men	KERW	4 097	4 069	4 060	4 027	4 052	3 976	3 727	3 587	3 469	3 199	2 959
Women	KERX	449	491	533	545	638	709	675	719	705	641	606

1 Figures for England and Wales are as at 30 September. Figures for Scotland are as at 31 March. Prior to this, the figures were as at 31 December. From 1999, figures for Northern Ireland reflect the position at the end of the financial year, i.e. 1999 and 2000 figures are as at 31 March 2000 and 31 March 2001 respectively. Prior to this, the figures were as at 31 December.
2 NCS, NCIS, other inter-force units and officers in central service.
3 Includes Police Officers on loan to organisations outside the British Police Service such as the Royal Hong Kong police, those on career breaks, and those on maternity leave.

4 'Strength' includes central service and seconded police.
5 Instructors at Training Establishments, etc. formerly shown as secondments.
6 Scottish Crime Squad, officers on courses, etc.
7 Does not include officers on secondment.
8 Includes Part-Time Reserve, 1,072 at 31 March 2001 (690 males and 382 females).

Sources: Home Office: 020 7273 2583;
The Scottish Executive Justice Department: 0131 244 2225;
The Police Service of Northern Ireland: 028 9065 0222 ext 24135

11.3

Offenders found guilty: by offence group
Magistrates' courts and the Crown Court

England and Wales

Thousands

		1990	1991	1992	1993	1994	1995	1996	1997	1998	1999	2000
All ages[1]												
Indictable offences												
Violence against the person:	KJEJ	52.5	47.2	43.6	38.9	37.6	29.1	30.0	34.6	35.7	34.4	34.0
Murder	KESB	0.2	0.2	0.2	0.2	0.2	0.2	0.3	0.3	0.3	0.3	0.3
Manslaughter	KESC	0.2	0.2	0.3	0.2	0.2	0.2	0.3	0.3	0.3	0.3	0.3
Wounding	KESD	50.9	45.5	42.0	37.4	36.1	27.4	28.3	32.7	35.2	33.9	33.5
Other offences of violence against the person	KESE	1.2	1.2	1.1	1.0	1.0	1.2	1.2	1.3	1.3	1.3	1.3
Sexual offences	KESF	6.6	5.5	5.0	4.3	4.5	4.7	4.4	4.5	4.6	4.3	3.9
Burglary	KESG	43.6	46.1	44.3	40.3	38.0	35.3	32.2	31.7	30.8	29.3	26.2
Robbery	KESH	4.8	4.8	5.1	5.1	4.9	5.2	5.9	5.6	5.5	5.6	6.0
Theft and handling stolen goods	KESI	134.3	133.5	127.9	121.6	121.6	116.1	114.5	118.4	125.7	131.2	128.0
Fraud and forgery	KESJ	21.9	21.2	20.0	17.5	18.4	17.2	16.3	17.0	19.8	20.3	19.2
Criminal damage	KESK	11.2	10.2	9.8	9.4	10.0	9.6	9.8	10.5	10.9	10.9	10.2
Drugs	KBWX	24.6	23.5	22.7	21.9	27.8	31.6	34.1	40.7	48.8	48.7	44.6
Other offences (excluding motoring)	KESL	32.3	34.4	36.0	37.8	39.4	42.2	43.5	47.6	49.6	47.9	44.5
Motoring offences	KESM	11.1	11.3	10.7	10.8	12.0	11.2	9.9	9.5	9.0	8.1	7.6
Total	KESA	342.8	337.6	324.9	307.6	314.1	302.2	300.6	320.1	341.7	342.0	325.5
Summary offences[2]												
Assaults[3]	KESO	17.3	16.5	18.0	19.0	21.9	29.3	30.0	32.0	35.3	37.5	37.4
Betting and gaming	KESP	–	–	–	–	–	–	–	–	–	–	–
Offences with pedal cycles	KBWY	2.8	1.9	1.4	1.2	1.0	1.1	1.3	1.5	2.1	1.3	0.8
Other Highways Acts offences	KBWZ	7.9	5.9	4.5	3.6	3.4	2.6	2.8	3.2	3.1	2.9	2.7
Breach of local or other regulations	KESQ	12.6	8.5	8.2	10.5	9.4	6.7	5.9	6.4	5.8	6.5	5.0
Intoxicating Liquor Laws:												
Drunkenness	KESR	37.8	29.4	23.8	18.8	20.2	19.8	24.2	28.8	30.8	28.7	27.2
Other offences	KESS	2.2	1.5	1.2	0.8	0.7	0.7	0.5	0.6	0.6	0.5	0.4
Education Acts	KEST	3.0	2.8	2.0	2.3	2.8	3.1	3.5	3.7	5.0	5.1	5.1
Game Laws	KESU	0.1	1.0	0.8	0.6	0.6	0.4	0.4	0.3	0.4	0.3	0.2
Labour Laws	KESV	1.1	0.1	0.1	0.1	0.1	0.1	–	0.1	0.1	0.1	0.1
Summary offences of criminal damage and malicious damage	KESW	33.9	28.5	24.6	21.6	22.7	22.6	23.4	24.7	26.5	27.9	28.0
Offences by prostitutes	KESX	11.5	10.9	9.8	8.2	7.7	6.8	6.6	6.6	6.0	4.0	4.1
Railway offences	KESY	8.3	5.4	4.7	4.0	5.6	6.2	9.1	11.4	12.6	15.2	17.4
Revenue Laws[2]	KESZ	104.9	115.6	121.6	123.0	126.2	123.8	139.1	143.5	174.7	165.8	175.0
Vagrancy Acts	KETB	1.9	2.1	1.8	1.7	1.9	1.6	2.0	2.0	2.2	2.7	3.3
Wireless Telegraphy Acts[2]	KETC	126.4	138.7	170.3	168.7	162.9	113.8	164.9	77.0	76.6	55.8	105.7
Other summary offences	KETD	95.4	85.6	78.9	69.0	67.8	71.5	74.7	74.7	80.9	79.3	78.1
Motoring offences (summary)[2]	KETA	704.6	713.1	723.1	664.7	638.7	642.4	649.0	649.3	665.2	632.9	607.5
Total	KESN	1 171.8	1 167.5	1 194.8	1 117.7	1 093.5	1 052.4	1 137.4	1 065.8	1 128.0	1 066.5	1 098.2
Persons aged under 18[2,4]												
Indictable offences												
Violence against the person:	KETF	6.5	5.6	5.2	5.1	5.8	4.7	5.3	5.9	5.9	6.2	6.4
Murder	KBXA	–	–	–	–	–	–	–	–	–	–	–
Manslaughter	KBXB	–	–	–	–	–	–	–	–	–	0.2	–
Wounding	KBXC	6.4	5.5	5.2	5.1	5.7	4.7	5.3	5.8	5.9	5.9	6.3
Other offences of violence against the person	KCAA	0.1	0.1	–	–	–	–	–	0.1	0.1	–	0.1
Sexual offences	KETG	0.5	0.4	0.4	0.4	0.4	0.4	0.4	0.5	0.5	0.5	0.5
Burglary	KETH	11.2	10.4	9.5	8.7	8.9	9.1	8.6	8.6	8.5	7.8	6.8
Robbery	KETI	1.4	1.4	1.4	1.5	1.7	2.0	2.4	2.3	2.2	2.0	2.2
Theft and handling stolen goods	KETJ	19.1	17.0	15.2	14.1	14.4	18.2	19.0	19.6	21.9	22.7	21.0
Fraud and forgery	KETK	0.9	0.8	0.6	0.4	0.5	0.6	0.7	0.8	1.0	1.1	1.0
Criminal damage	KETL	2.1	1.8	1.6	1.7	2.0	2.1	2.2	2.3	2.3	2.7	2.6
Drugs	KCAB	1.2	1.2	1.0	0.8	1.1	1.3	1.6	1.8	2.7	3.1	3.7
Other offences (excluding motoring)	KETM	2.5	2.8	2.7	2.4	2.8	3.3	3.8	4.2	4.2	4.3	4.4
Motoring	KETN	0.6	0.7	0.5	0.3	0.3	0.4	0.4	0.4	0.4	0.4	0.6
Total	KETE	46.1	42.0	38.1	35.4	37.9	42.2	44.4	46.4	49.7	50.6	49.2
Summary offences[2]												
Offences with pedal cycles	KETP	0.5	0.3	0.2	0.1	0.1	0.2	0.2	0.2	0.3	0.3	0.2
Breach of local or other regulations	KETR	0.4	0.3	0.2	0.1	0.1	0.2	0.3	0.2	0.2	0.2	0.2
Summary offences of criminal damage and malicious damage	KETS	3.9	2.9	2.5	2.2	2.9	3.4	3.9	4.4	5.2	6.1	6.7
Railway offences	KETT	0.4	0.3	0.2	0.2	0.3	0.4	0.4	0.5	0.5	0.5	0.4
Other summary offences	KETU	16.4	14.1	11.3	8.3	9.7	7.2	8.8	10.1	12.1	11.7	11.3
Motoring offences (summary)[2]	KCAC	16.4	13.7	10.8	8.9	8.6	9.3	10.8	10.8	11.3	12.6	14.5
Total	KETO	38.1	31.6	25.2	19.9	21.7	25.6	30.3	22.0	36.8	39.6	42.2

1 Includes 'Companies', etc.
2 It is estimated that in 1995 there was a shortfall of 75,100 offenders found guilty for certain summary offences.
3 A new charging standard was introduced for assault in 1994 (see Introduction - Law enforcement).
4 Figures for persons aged under 18 are included in the totals above.

Source: Home Office: 020 8760 8270

11.4 Offenders cautioned: by offence group
England and Wales

Thousands

		1990	1991	1992	1993	1994	1995	1996	1997	1998	1999	2000
All ages[1]												
Indictable offences												
Violence against the person	KELB	16.8	19.4	23.5	24.1	23.6	20.4	21.8	23.6	23.5	21.2	19.9
Murder	KCAD	–	–	–	–	–	–	–	–	–	–	–
Manslaughter	KCAE	–	–	–	–	–	–	–	–	–	–	–
Wounding	KCAF	16.5	19.1	23.2	23.8	23.2	20.1	21.4	23.3	22.9	20.6	19.3
Other offences of violence against the person	KCAG	0.2	0.2	0.3	0.3	0.3	0.3	0.4	0.4	0.6	0.6	0.6
Sexual offences	KELC	3.4	3.3	3.4	3.3	3.0	2.3	2.0	1.9	1.7	1.5	1.3
Burglary	KELD	14.3	13.3	14.4	12.8	11.5	10.5	10.2	9.4	8.4	7.7	6.6
Robbery	KELE	0.6	0.6	0.6	0.7	0.6	0.6	0.6	0.6	0.6	0.6	0.6
Theft and handling stolen goods	KELF	99.8	108.5	130.3	117.2	104.8	104.9	93.6	82.8	83.6	75.4	67.6
Fraud and forgery	KELG	4.7	5.6	7.5	8.1	7.6	7.9	7.5	7.2	7.4	7.2	6.2
Criminal damage	KELH	4.2	3.8	4.0	4.1	4.3	3.8	3.1	2.8	2.7	3.0	3.2
Drugs	KCAI	18.7	21.2	27.6	35.1	44.4	48.2	47.5	56.0	58.7	49.4	41.1
Other offences (excluding motoring)	KELI	3.9	4.1	4.8	4.2	4.0	4.0	4.4	5.0	5.0	4.6	4.4
Motoring[2]	KCAJ	..	..	..	..	..	..	..	..	..	..	..
Total	KELA	166.3	179.9	216.2	209.6	209.8	202.6	190.8	189.4	191.7	170.6	150.9
Summary offences												
Assaults[3]	KELK	1.4	1.6	2.4	3.1	4.2	8.1	9.1	9.1	–	17.0	17.2
Betting and gaming	KELL	–	–	–	–	–	–	–	–	–	–	–
Offences with pedal cycles	KCAK	2.6	1.7	1.4	0.9	0.8	0.8	0.9	0.9	0.8	0.6	0.3
Other Highways Acts offences	KCAL	1.5	1.2	1.2	1.0	0.9	0.9	0.8	0.8	0.8	0.7	0.4
Breach of local or other regulations	KELM	1.2	1.3	1.5	1.1	1.1	0.9	0.8	0.9	0.9	0.7	0.5
Intoxicating Liquor Laws:												
Drunkenness	KELN	48.6	46.0	45.0	41.1	37.7	22.9	25.9	25.7	22.8	20.3	18.1
Other offences	KELO	2.8	1.7	1.7	1.2	1.0	1.0	0.9	0.9	0.7	0.4	0.2
Education Acts	KELP	–	–	–	–	–	–	–	–	–	–	–
Game Laws	KELQ	0.2	0.2	0.1	0.2	0.1	0.1	0.1	0.1	0.1	0.1	–
Labour Laws	KELR	–	–	–	–	–	–	–	–	–	–	–
Summary offences of criminal damage and malicious damage	KELS	16.2	17.3	20.5	22.1	23.1	25.1	27.7	27.6	28.3	28.7	26.8
Offences by prostitutes	KELT	4.5	4.1	4.2	4.0	3.6	3.3	3.5	3.5	3.5	2.1	1.3
Railway offences	KELU	0.4	0.3	0.3	0.2	0.2	0.3	0.2	0.1	–	–	–
Revenue Laws	KELV	0.5	0.7	0.8	0.5	0.2	0.2	0.1	0.1	0.1	0.1	–
Vagrancy Acts	KELX	0.5	0.7	1.3	1.5	1.0	1.0	0.6	0.6	1.2	0.8	0.4
Wireless Telegraphy Acts	KELY	–	–	–	–	–	–	–	–	–	–	–
Other summary offences	KELZ	22.5	22.1	25.0	24.9	24.6	24.2	24.7	22.3	37.0	24.1	22.5
Motoring offences[2]	KCAM	..	..	..	..	..	..	..	..	..	..	..
Total	KELJ	102.8	98.9	105.1	101.8	98.7	88.7	95.4	92.7	96.2	95.6	88.1
Persons aged 18 and under												
Indictable offences												
Violence against the person	KEMB	8.5	9.2	10.8	10.8	11.1	9.4	9.4	9.6	9.5	8.5	8.3
Murder	KCAN	–	–	–	–	–	–	–	–	–	–	–
Manslaughter	KCAO	–	–	–	–	–	–	–	–	–	–	–
Wounding	KCAP	8.5	9.2	10.7	10.8	11.1	9.4	9.4	9.6	9.4	8.4	8.2
Other offences of violence against the person	KCCE	–	–	–	–	–	–	–	–	–	–	0.1
Sexual offences	KEMC	1.6	1.4	1.3	1.1	1.1	0.8	0.7	0.7	0.6	0.6	0.5
Burglary	KEMD	13.1	11.7	12.0	10.3	9.6	8.5	8.2	7.5	6.7	6.1	5.4
Robbery	KEME	0.5	0.6	0.6	0.6	0.6	0.5	0.6	0.6	0.5	0.5	0.5
Theft and handling stolen goods	KEMF	63.1	62.3	69.8	58.9	58.6	57.4	48.2	40.9	44.0	39.6	36.9
Fraud and forgery	KEMG	1.5	1.5	1.7	1.5	1.4	1.6	1.5	1.4	1.6	1.7	1.5
Criminal damage	KEMH	3.2	2.6	2.6	2.6	2.8	2.4	2.0	1.8	1.7	1.9	2.1
Drugs	KCCF	4.0	5.0	5.4	6.7	8.5	8.7	7.9	9.7	11.0	9.6	7.9
Other offences (excluding motoring)	KEMI	1.0	1.2	1.4	1.4	1.4	1.3	1.3	1.5	1.5	1.4	1.3
Motoring[2]	KCCG	..	..	..	..	..	..	..	..	..	..	..
Total	KEMA	96.6	95.5	105.6	94.1	95.1	90.6	79.9	73.7	77.2	69.8	64.3
Summary offences												
Offences with pedal cycles	KEMK	1.5	0.9	0.7	0.4	0.5	0.4	0.5	0.5	0.4	0.3	0.2
Breach of local or other regulations	KEMM	0.5	0.5	0.6	0.3	0.4	0.3	0.3	0.3	0.3	0.2	0.2
Summary offences of criminal damage and malicious damage	KEMN	10.4	10.1	10.7	11.4	12.5	12.8	13.8	13.5	14.2	14.7	14.4
Railway offences	KEMO	0.2	0.1	0.1	0.1	0.1	0.1	0.1	0.1	–	–	–
Other summary offences	KEMP	18.0	15.5	16.0	15.3	15.6	10.3	10.8	9.1	13.8	9.9	9.2
Motoring offences[2]	KCCH	..	..	..	..	..	..	..	..	..	..	..
Total	KEMJ	30.5	27.1	28.1	27.5	29.2	30.0	33.2	30.8	32.5	34.2	33.2

1 Includes 'Companies', etc.
2 Not applicable as motoring offences may attract written warning.
3 A new charging standard was introduced for assault in 1994 (see Introduction - Law enforcement).

Source: Home Office: 020 8760 8270

11.5 Offenders found guilty of offences: by age and gender
England and Wales

Magistrates' courts and the Crown Court

Thousands

		1990	1991	1992	1993	1994	1995	1996	1997	1998	1999	2000
Males												
Indictable offences												
All ages	KEFA	295.7	293.5	282.8	268.2	273.2	263.2	261.1	276.5	292.9	291.7	276.5
10 and under 15 years	KEFB	6.0	5.1	4.9	5.5	6.9	7.1	6.6	7.1	8.1	8.9	8.7
15 and under 18 years	KEFC	35.0	32.3	28.9	26.2	28.7	30.2	32.5	33.6	35.2	35.1	33.8
18 and under 21 years	KEFD	65.8	65.3	58.9	53.0	50.3	47.4	46.3	48.4	51.8	52.6	49.9
21 years and over	KEFE	188.8	190.8	190.1	183.4	187.4	178.6	175.6	187.3	197.9	195.0	184.0
Summary offences[1]												
All ages	KEFF	968.9	956.3	959.6	892.0	871.0	862.0	903.6	880.9	929.0	886.6	881.0
10 and under 15 years	KEFG	2.0	1.8	1.8	1.8	2.3	2.9	2.8	3.0	3.9	5.1	5.8
15 and under 18 years	KEFH	27.6	21.7	21.7	16.8	17.7	20.5	24.6	25.9	28.5	30.3	32.2
18 and under 21 years	KEFI	125.1	109.8	97.6	85.7	82.9	84.0	88.4	91.0	96.3	94.8	93.0
21 years and over	KEFJ	808.0	816.9	838.5	787.7	768.2	754.6	787.9	761.0	800.3	756.5	750.0
Females												
Indictable offences												
All ages	KEFK	44.0	41.9	40.0	37.8	39.5	37.5	38.0	42.2	47.3	49.0	47.7
10 and under 15 years	KEFL	0.7	0.6	0.6	0.7	1.0	1.0	1.0	1.0	1.4	1.4	1.5
15 and under 18 years	KEFM	4.4	4.0	3.6	3.1	3.8	4.0	4.2	4.6	5.1	5.2	5.2
18 and under 21 years	KEFN	8.3	8.1	7.3	6.3	6.2	5.7	5.7	6.3	7.1	7.6	7.5
21 years and over	KEFO	30.6	29.2	28.5	27.7	28.6	26.8	27.2	30.4	33.7	34.7	33.5
Summary offences[1]												
All ages	KEFP	185.3	194.1	219.0	213.3	211.5	180.5	222.9	174.9	188.3	171.0	208.3
10 and under 15 years	KEFQ	0.1	0.1	0.1	0.2	0.2	0.4	0.4	0.5	0.6	0.8	0.9
15 and under 18 years	KEFR	2.3	2.0	1.7	1.2	1.5	1.8	2.6	3.4	3.8	3.4	3.3
18 and under 21 years	KEFS	12.6	12.1	11.2	10.0	9.6	10.4	12.1	11.1	12.1	10.8	11.8
21 years and over	KEFT	170.4	179.8	206.0	201.9	200.2	167.9	207.9	160.0	171.7	155.4	192.3
Companies, etc												
Indictable offences	KEFU	3.1	2.2	2.1	1.7	1.4	1.5	1.5	1.3	1.5	1.3	1.3
Summary offences[1]	KEFV	17.6	17.2	16.2	12.5	10.9	9.9	10.9	10.0	10.7	8.9	8.8

1 It is estimated that in 1995 there was a shortfall of 75,100 offenders found guilty for certain summary offences.

Source: Home Office: 020 8760 8270

11.6 Persons cautioned by the police: by age and gender
England and Wales

Thousands

		1990	1991	1992	1993	1994	1995	1996	1997	1998	1999	2000
Males												
Indictable offences												
All ages	KEGA	124.2	131.4	155.0	153.6	153.6	149.3	142.6	143.3	142.9	126.1	109.7
10 and under 15 years	KEGB	36.4	33.0	35.0	31.4	32.3	29.2	25.1	22.9	23.7	22.0	20.3
15 and under 18 years	KEGC	38.1	38.5	41.1	37.1	35.5	35.3	33.0	32.0	32.0	28.7	25.0
18 and under 21 years	KEGD	15.1	18.4	23.8	24.5	25.0	24.8	24.3	25.2	25.7	22.7	20.1
21 years and over	KEGE	34.6	41.4	55.1	60.6	60.7	60.0	60.2	63.2	61.5	52.7	44.3
Summary offences												
All ages	KEGF	88.2	85.3	90.0	86.3	83.6	73.8	79.2	75.7	76.9	76.1	69.6
10 and under 15 years	KEGG	9.8	8.9	9.3	9.4	10.5	10.1	10.3	9.9	10.6	11.7	12.0
15 and under 18 years	KEGH	16.9	14.8	15.1	14.4	14.7	15.4	18.0	16.1	16.1	16.1	14.9
18 and under 21 years	KEGI	9.4	9.7	11.3	11.4	11.3	11.1	13.0	12.9	13.2	13.0	11.9
21 years and over	KEGJ	52.1	51.9	54.3	51.0	47.0	37.1	37.9	36.9	37.0	35.3	30.9
Females												
Indictable offences												
All ages	KEGK	42.1	48.5	61.1	55.9	56.2	53.3	48.2	46.0	48.8	44.5	41.2
10 and under 15 years	KEGL	10.3	11.0	14.3	12.8	15.2	14.0	10.8	9.2	11.1	9.8	10.0
15 and under 18 years	KEGM	11.7	13.1	15.2	12.8	12.4	12.2	10.9	9.5	10.3	9.3	9.0
18 and under 21 years	KEGN	4.2	5.5	7.3	6.7	6.1	6.0	5.6	5.7	5.9	5.7	5.2
21 years and over	KEGO	15.8	19.0	24.4	23.6	22.4	21.1	20.9	21.5	21.4	19.6	17.0
Summary offences												
All ages	KEGP	14.6	13.6	15.1	18.5	15.1	14.8	16.2	17.0	19.2	9.4	18.5
10 and under 15 years	KEGQ	1.1	1.0	1.2	1.3	1.5	1.7	1.8	1.7	2.1	2.5	2.8
15 and under 18 years	KEGR	2.8	2.4	2.5	2.3	2.5	2.7	3.2	3.2	3.7	3.9	3.7
18 and under 21 years	KEGS	2.1	1.9	2.0	2.1	1.9	1.9	2.1	2.3	2.6	2.7	2.5
21 years and over	KEGT	8.7	8.3	9.5	9.8	9.2	8.6	9.1	9.9	10.8	10.3	9.6

Source: Home Office: 020 8760 8270

11.7 Sentence or order passed on offenders sentenced for indictable offences: by gender
England and Wales

Magistrates' courts and the Crown Court

Percentages

		1990	1991	1992	1993	1994	1995	1996	1997	1998	1999	2000
Males												
Sentence or order												
Absolute discharge	KEJB	0.7	0.7	0.8	0.9	0.8	0.8	0.8	0.7	0.7	0.6	0.6
Conditional discharge	KEJC	14.2	16.1	18.0	18.6	17.4	16.2	15.6	15.5	15.3	15.0	14.1
Probation order	KEJD	9.1	9.3	9.1	9.3	10.2	10.0	9.9	10.0	10.0	10.1	10.1
Supervision order	KEJE	1.5	1.4	1.4	2.0	2.4	2.7	2.9	2.7	2.7	2.7	2.4
Fine	KEJF	40.1	36.0	34.2	33.8	31.8	30.0	28.6	28.2	28.4	27.7	25.7
Community service order	KEJG	8.5	9.5	10.3	11.4	11.1	10.6	9.9	9.5	9.3	9.3	9.5
Attendance centre order	KEJH	1.9	1.9	1.8	1.9	2.0	2.0	1.9	1.8	1.7	1.8	1.5
Combination orders	KIJW	..	..	0.3	2.1	2.7	3.0	3.5	3.7	3.8	3.7	3.6
Curfew order	LUJP	..	..	..	..	..	..	0.1	0.1	0.2	0.3	0.5
Care order	KEJJ	0.1	–	..	..	..	..	..	..	..	..	..
Sec 53	LUJQ	–	–	–	0.1	0.1	0.1	0.2	0.3	0.2	0.2	0.2
Young offender institution	KEJK	4.5	4.6	4.3	0.8	4.9	5.6	6.1	6.1	6.0	6.2	5.2
Secure training order	LUJR	..	..	..	..	..	..	..	..	–	0.1	–
Imprisonment												
Fully suspended	KEJL	6.3	6.4	5.4	0.9	0.7	0.7	0.8	0.8	0.7	0.6	0.7
Partly suspended[1]	KAFN	0.4	0.3	0.2	..	..	..	..	..	..	..	..
Unsuspended	KEJM	10.7	11.4	11.6	12.0	13.6	16.0	17.2	17.9	18.2	18.7	21.3
Other sentence or order	KEJN	2.1	2.2	2.5	2.5	2.3	2.2	2.4	3.0	2.6	3.1	4.7
Total number of offenders (thousands) = 100 per cent	KEJA	294.7	291.9	282.5	267.5	272.6	262.9	260.8	275.4	292.4	291.3	277.1
Females												
Sentence or order												
Absolute discharge	KEKB	1.0	0.9	1.0	0.9	0.9	0.8	0.9	0.8	0.7	0.7	0.6
Conditional discharge	KEKC	33.2	35.9	37.5	35.4	34.4	32.4	30.6	29.4	28.7	26.9	24.9
Probation order	KEKD	17.5	17.0	15.9	15.4	17.5	18.0	19.0	19.1	19.1	19.4	19.6
Supervision order	KEKE	1.1	1.1	1.3	1.8	2.4	2.7	2.9	2.9	3.1	2.9	2.8
Fine	KEKF	30.8	27.2	26.2	29.2	25.6	24.1	22.5	21.8	21.3	20.8	20.1
Community service order	KEKG	4.1	4.6	5.3	6.1	6.4	6.6	6.5	6.5	6.5	7.1	7.5
Attendance centre order	KEKH	0.3	0.4	0.4	0.5	0.8	1.0	1.0	1.0	0.9	0.9	0.8
Combination orders	KIJX	..	..	0.2	1.4	2.1	2.4	3.0	3.2	3.4	3.3	3.0
Curfew order	LUJT	..	..	..	..	..	..	–	0.1	0.1	0.3	0.4
Care order	KEKJ	0.1	–	..	..	..	..	..	..	..	..	..
Sec 53	LUJU	–	–	–	–	–	0.1	0.1	0.1	–	0.1	0.1
Young offender institution	KEKK	0.8	0.9	0.8	1.1	1.1	1.5	1.8	1.9	2.2	2.4	2.2
Secure training order	LUJV	..	..	..	..	..	..	..	..	–	–	–
Imprisonment												
Fully suspended	KEKL	5.3	5.9	4.8	1.2	1.1	1.4	1.5	1.6	1.5	1.3	1.3
Partly suspended[1]	KAFP	0.3	0.3	0.2	..	..	..	..	..	..	..	..
Unsuspended	KEKM	3.5	4.1	4.4	5.0	5.9	7.4	8.4	9.4	10.0	11.0	12.2
Other sentence or order	KEKN	1.9	1.8	2.2	1.9	1.7	1.8	2.0	2.2	2.5	3.0	4.7
Total number of offenders (thousands) = 100 per cent	KEKA	43.9	41.9	40.0	37.7	39.5	37.5	38.0	42.1	47.2	49.0	47.8

1 Abolished October 1992.

Source: Home Office: 020 8760 8270

11.8 Offenders sentenced to immediate custody for standard list offences
England and Wales
Between 1995 and 1999: by gender and number of previous convictions

Percentages and numbers[1]

Year and gender	Number of previous convictions[2]					Total sentenced for standard list offences	Total sentenced to custody for all offences
	Nil	1 - 2	3 - 6	7 - 10	11 and over		
1995							
Males	18	14	22	18	27	58 592	75 369
Females	41	20	14	9	15	3 429	3 768
Total	20	14	22	18	27	62 021	79 137
1996[3]							
Males	18	16	21	17	27	78 392 (65 656)	80 240
Females ·	36	18	18	11	17	4 273 (4 057)	4 374
Total	20	16	21	17	27	82 665 (69 713)	84 614
1997							
Males	16	16	23	16	29	85 580	87 620
Females	31	18	22	12	17	5 345	5 473
Total	17	16	23	16	28	90 934	93 093
1998							
Males	20	14	20	15	30	91 800	94 000
Females	37	16	18	10	18	6 400	6 600
Total	22	14	20	15	29	98 200	100 600
1999							
Males	32	22	19	10	17	95 500	97 800
Females	49	23	15	6	7	7 300	7 500
Total	34	22	19	9	16	102 800	105 300

1 The percentages are based on samples of 3 304, 2 975, 6 994, 7 562 and 6 096 males and 163, 160, 379, 459 and 426 females in the years 1995, 1996, 1997, 1998 and 1999 respectively. Percentages are rounded and therefore may not add to 100.
2 Counting one conviction per court appearance.

3 From 1 January 1996 a number of summary motoring offences became standard list offences. The sentencing figures shown in brackets for 1996 exclude those sentenced for these offences. Excluding the new standard list offences from the analysis would slightly alter the percentages with previous convictions.

Source: Home Office: 020 7273 3177

11.9 Population in Prison Service establishments under sentence[1]
England and Wales
On 30 June each year : by gender and number of previous convictions

Percentages and numbers[2]

Year and gender	Previous convictions not found[3]	Number of previous convictions[3]					Number of prisoners
		Nil	1 - 2	3 - 6	7 - 10	11 and over	
1995							
Males	5	16	16	21	16	25	37 479
Females	15	34	18	15	9	9	1 456
Total	6	17	16	21	16	25	38 935
1996							
Males	9	22	16	19	14	20	41 187
Females	17	37	17	14	7	8	1 727
Total	9	22	16	19	14	19	42 914
1997							
Males	9	15	16	20	15	24	46 611
Females	15	36	16	15	8	11	2 063
Total	9	16	16	20	15	24	48 674
1998							
Males	5	16	14	19	15	31	49 793
Females	11	35	17	17	8	13	2 366
Total	5	17	14	19	14	30	52 159
1999							
Males	8	12	15	21	15	28	47 989
Females	16	27	18	17	9	13	2 486
Total	9	13	15	21	15	27	50 475

1 Excludes fine defaulters.
2 The percentages are based on samples of 9 105, 11 882, 11 800, 12 303 and 12 341 males and 1 414 , 1 804, 2 032, 2 291 and 2 472 females in the years 1995, 1996, 1997, 1998 and 1999 respectively. Percentages are rounded and therefore may not add to 100.

3 In some cases it was not possible to find details on previous convictions. This can happen when a prisoner is not sentenced for a standard list offence and has no previous record for such offences.

Source: Home Office: 020 7273 3177

11.10 Receptions and average population in custody
England and Wales

Numbers

		1990	1991	1992	1993	1994	1995	1996	1997	1998	1999	2000
Receptions												
Type of inmate:												
Untried	KEDA	53 135	54 676	49 869	53 565	57 079	55 287	58 888	62 066	64 697	64 572	54 892
Convicted, unsentenced	KEDB	20 410	19 927	21 250	30 098	34 563	32 039	34 987	36 424	43 387	45 893	43 889
Sentenced	KEDE	67 510	72 313	69 832	72 966	83 657	89 173	82 861	87 168	91 282	93 965	93 671
Immediate custodial sentence	KEDF	50 851	53 340	50 006	50 563	61 188	69 016	74 306	80 832	85 908	90 238	91 195
Young offenders	KEDG	14 380	15 028	13 174	13 205	14 956	16 244	17 593	18 743	19 599	21 020	21 322
Up to 18 months	KEDH	11 758	12 447	10 862	11 114	12 739	13 783	14 156	14 893	15 965	17 338	17 158
Over 18 months up to 4 years	KEDJ	2 307	2 270	1 982	1 752	1 882	2 129	2 913	3 254	3 153	3 171	3 447
Over 4 years (including life)	KEDL	315	311	330	339	335	332	524	596	481	511	717
Adults	KFBO	36 471	38 312	36 832	37 358	46 232	52 772	56 713	62 089	66 309	69 218	69 873
Up to 18 months	KEDV	25 363	27 159	25 872	27 643	35 520	40 638	42 673	46 727	50 844	53 814	54 147
Over 18 months up to 4 years	KEDW	8 253	8 199	7 967	6 864	7 744	8 811	10 119	10 972	11 126	10 892	11 199
Over 4 years (including life)	KEDX	2 855	2 954	2 993	2 851	2 968	3 323	3 921	4 390	4 339	4 512	4 527
Committed in default of payment												
of a fine	KEDY	16 659	18 973	19 826	22 403	22 469	20 157	8 555	6 336	5 374	3 727	2 476
Young offenders	KEEA	3 522	4 209	4 282	3 353	3 268	2 846	885	555	568	366	216
Adults	KAFQ	13 137	14 764	15 544	19 050	19 201	17 311	7 670	5 781	4 806	3 361	2 260
Non-criminal prisoners	KEDM	2 314	2 791	3 109	5 073	4 507	3 789	3 128	3 204	3 290	3 271	3 153
Immigration Act 1971	KEDN	916	1 225	1 272	1 837	1 641	1 825	1 857	2 122	2 348	2 443	2 455
Others	KEDO	1 398	1 566	1 837	3 236	2 866	1 964	1 271	1 082	942	828	698
Average population												
Total in custody	KEDP	45 636	45 897	45 817	44 565	48 794	51 047	55 281	61 114	65 298	64 771	64 602
Total in prison service establishments	KFBQ	44 975	44 809	44 718	44 551	48 621	50 962	55 281	61 114	65 298	64 771	64 602
Police cells[1]	KFBN	661	1 088	1 098	14	173	85	–	–	–	–	–
Untried	KEDQ	7 625	7 545	7 387	7 960	9 047	8 352	8 374	8 453	8 157	7 947	7 098
Convicted, unsentenced	KEDR	1 815	1 930	1 987	2 700	3 181	2 954	3 238	3 678	4 411	4 571	4 177
Remanded for medical examination[2]	KEDS	20	17	14	12	15	9	6	8	9	8	..
Others	KEDT	1 795	1 913	1 973	2 688	3 166	2 945	3 232	3 670	4 402	4 563	..
Sentenced	KEDU	35 336	35 034	35 037	33 317	35 753	39 040	43 043	48 413	52 176	51 691	52 685
Immediate custodial sentence	KFBR	34 972	34 665	34 707	32 825	35 308	38 636	42 863	48 272	52 045	51 596	52 620
Young offenders	KFBS	6 173	5 754	5 382	5 054	5 258	5 752	6 700	7 820	8 490	8 344	8 435
Up to 18 months	KFBU	3 143	3 095	2 808	2 671	2 736	2 911	2 930	3 267	3 507	3 394	3 987
Over 18 months up to 4 years	KFBV	2 328	2 033	1 999	1 800	1 902	2 159	2 606	3 019	3 155	3 158	3 373
Over 4 years (including life)	KFBW	699	623	575	583	620	682	1 164	1 534	1 828	1 792	1 075
Adults	KFCO	28 799	28 911	29 326	27 771	30 050	32 884	36 162	40 451	43 556	43 343	44 186
Up to 18 months	KFCP	7 001	7 194	7 170	7 054	8 051	8 845	8 199	9 724	10 308	9 441	9 851
Over 18 months up to 4 years	KFCQ	9 751	9 333	9 416	8 445	9 164	10 184	10 320	10 777	11 707	11 322	14 267
Over 4 years (including life)	KFCR	12 047	12 384	12 740	12 272	12 835	13 855	17 644	19 950	21 541	22 580	20 068
Committed in default of												
payment of a fine	KFCS	364	369	330	492	446	403	180	141	131	95	64
Young offenders	KFEW	80	85	65	77	62	54	22	13	15	9	4
Adults	KFEX	284	284	265	415	384	349	158	128	116	86	60
Non-criminal prisoners	KEEB	200	300	308	574	640	615	626	571	554	558	641
Immigration Act 1971	KEEC	144	222	227	431	487	483	516	485	476	485	576
Others	KEED	56	78	81	143	153	132	111	87	78	73	63

1 Mostly untried prisoners.
2 Under Section 30, Magistrates' Courts Act 1980.

Source: Home Office: 020 7217 5567

11.11 Prison population serving sentences: analysis by age and offence[1]
England and Wales

Numbers

	Total	Age in years							
		15 - 17	18 - 20	21 - 24	25 - 29	30 - 39	40 - 49	50 - 59	60 and over
At 30 June 1995									
Offences									
Males									
Total	37 897	957	4 702	7 202	8 261	10 021	4 386	1 792	576
Violence against the person	8 515	120	871	1 400	1 915	2 529	1 122	414	144
Sexual offences	3 658	19	121	231	456	1 029	936	575	291
Burglary	5 938	257	1 220	1 689	1 418	1 086	197	63	8
Robbery	5 267	184	795	1 132	1 314	1 448	332	52	10
Theft, handling, fraud and forgery	4 613	183	561	827	932	1 187	617	263	43
Drugs offences	3 863	11	188	511	874	1 316	677	241	45
Other offences	4 421	112	578	1 072	1 022	1 083	389	142	23
Offence not known	1 622	71	368	340	330	343	116	42	12
Females									
Total	1 482	31	152	233	324	443	224	59	16
Violence against the person	290	7	32	46	63	69	50	18	5
Sexual offences	12	1	2	1	2	3	2	1	-
Burglary	57	2	12	14	16	9	4	-	-
Robbery	108	9	27	27	19	22	4	-	-
Theft, handling, fraud and forgery	379	5	19	54	96	122	57	22	4
Drugs offences	398	-	36	51	79	143	74	12	3
Other offences	145	3	12	20	27	59	18	4	2
Offence not known	93	4	12	20	22	16	15	2	2
At 30 June 1996									
Offences									
Males									
Total	41 323	1 262	5 101	7 569	8 719	11 259	4 723	2 002	688
Violence against the person	9 236	177	937	1 547	1 986	2 747	1 174	501	167
Sexual offences	3 939	32	120	246	437	1 175	946	628	355
Burglary	6 351	373	1 287	1 753	1 484	1 199	202	49	4
Robbery	5 594	268	978	1 171	1 316	1 445	350	62	4
Theft, handling, fraud and forgery	4 709	180	540	798	893	1 311	678	266	43
Drugs offences	5 273	11	293	746	1 239	1 787	850	286	61
Other offences	4 729	119	600	1 050	1 102	1 248	419	160	31
Offence not known	1 492	102	346	258	262	347	104	50	23
Females									
Total	1 732	57	195	263	373	534	223	77	10
Violence against the person	355	16	51	55	60	89	57	22	5
Sexual offences	12	-	2	3	1	2	4	-	-
Burglary	80	5	23	25	12	11	4	-	-
Robbery	124	17	28	23	32	20	3	1	-
Theft, handling, fraud and forgery	433	7	29	48	115	141	62	27	4
Drugs offences	794	3	32	134	181	267	131	44	2
Other offences	166	5	23	31	32	52	16	7	-
Offence not known	76	7	4	13	15	27	9	1	-
At 30 June 1997									
Offences									
Males									
Total	46 739	1 620	6 078	8 472	9 939	12 503	5 046	2 299	782
Violence against the person	10 045	216	1 039	1 631	2 181	3 014	1 234	549	181
Sexual offences	4 069	39	121	232	465	1 169	934	726	383
Burglary	7 983	448	1 574	2 184	1 938	1 515	245	71	8
Robbery	6 278	437	1 227	1 352	1 370	1 471	337	73	11
Theft, handling, fraud and forgery	5 052	167	605	865	1 020	1 417	638	272	68
Drugs offences	6 486	29	356	892	1 494	2 242	1 027	371	75
Other offences	1 746	142	437	296	324	321	141	64	21
Offence not known	5 080	142	719	1 020	1 147	1 354	490	173	35
Females									
Total	2 066	53	198	372	449	615	271	91	17
Violence against the person	391	18	43	72	61	105	62	22	8
Sexual offences	8	-	1	1	1	3	2	-	-
Burglary	101	4	13	29	31	17	6	1	-
Robbery	161	18	50	29	29	28	5	2	-
Theft, handling, fraud and forgery	455	3	25	78	100	148	71	25	5
Drugs offences	691	4	43	111	173	237	88	31	4
Other offences	68	-	8	12	15	25	4	4	-
Offence not known	191	6	15	40	39	52	33	6	-

11.11

Prison population serving sentences: analysis by age and offence[1]
England and Wales

continued

Numbers

	Total	Age in years							
		15 - 17	18 - 20	21 - 24	25 - 29	30 - 39	40 - 49	50 - 59	60 and over
At 30 June 1998									
Offences									
Males									
Total	49 902	1 627	5 807	8 780	10 590	14 109	5 485	2 608	896
Violence against the person	10 530	235	1 028	1 670	2 215	3 239	1 345	594	204
Sexual offences	4 781	51	140	224	560	1 366	1 113	872	455
Burglary	8 541	432	1 502	2 256	2 179	1 799	298	65	10
Robbery	6 452	449	1 244	1 319	1 427	1 587	350	61	15
Theft, handling, fraud & forgery	5 193	190	556	906	1 071	1 535	587	300	48
Drugs offences	7 103	38	308	944	1 616	2 569	1 092	441	95
Other offences	5 277	137	690	1 087	1 132	1 461	509	215	46
Offence not known	2 025	95	339	374	390	553	191	60	23
Females									
Total	2 367	62	210	425	501	709	332	116	12
Violence against the person	420	11	44	68	80	116	68	27	6
Sexual offences	16	1	1	1	2	5	5	1	-
Burglary	118	6	17	27	32	28	6	2	-
Robbery	177	24	45	33	36	28	8	3	-
Theft, handling, fraud & forgery	514	6	36	97	107	169	72	26	1
Drugs offences	794	3	32	134	181	267	131	44	2
Other offences	218	8	22	42	41	65	30	8	2
Offences not known	110	3	13	23	22	31	12	5	1
At 30 June 1999									
Offences									
Males									
Total	48 956	1 643	5 633	8 245	10 080	14 072	5 552	2 678	1 053
Violence against the person	10 435	250	1 070	1 548	2 033	3 260	1 428	608	238
Sexual offences	4 930	48	99	236	485	1 448	1 133	935	546
Burglary	8 626	447	1 441	2 207	2 230	1 899	322	73	7
Robbery	6 175	410	1 126	1 384	1 272	1 556	353	58	16
Theft, handling, fraud and forgery	5 027	208	585	886	1 065	1 418	529	279	57
Drugs offences	7 303	36	338	866	1 614	2 720	1 132	476	121
Other offences	5 224	185	742	968	1 120	1 422	541	197	49
Offence not known	1 236	59	232	150	261	349	114	52	19
Females									
Total	2 436	67	224	427	491	798	301	108	20
Violence against the person	429	17	65	50	77	125	63	25	7
Sexual offences	17	-	2	1	-	5	7	1	1
Burglary	158	7	27	37	38	41	6	2	-
Robbery	158	15	24	36	33	41	6	3	-
Theft, handling, fraud and forgery	502	11	33	113	99	159	58	24	5
Drugs offences	875	2	50	131	184	340	129	35	4
Other offences	220	13	9	45	43	68	26	16	-
Offence not known	77	2	14	14	17	19	6	2	3
At 30 June 2000									
Offences									
Males									
Total	50 514	1 788	5 911	8 691	10 060	14 454	5 720	2 749	1 140
Violence against the person	10 807	256	1 092	1 658	1 964	3 440	1 480	690	226
Sexual offences	5 070	58	139	261	460	1 424	1 157	937	635
Burglary	8 824	453	1 426	2 165	2 291	2 040	359	77	13
Robbery	6 158	399	1 087	1 343	1 315	1 556	387	57	14
Theft, handling, fraud & forgery	5 422	312	798	1 006	1 118	1 419	483	233	53
Drugs offences	7 526	43	405	949	1 591	2 765	1 188	480	106
Other offences	5 909	225	818	1 180	1 161	1 616	598	236	76
Offence not known	797	43	148	131	160	194	67	38	16
Females									
Total	2 666	65	266	457	563	863	335	102	15
Violence against the person	410	22	46	56	71	122	62	26	6
Sexual offences	20	-	1	1	1	7	5	2	2
Burglary	158	10	24	33	45	40	5	1	-
Robbery	195	13	43	39	39	50	10	1	-
Theft, handling, fraud & forgery	638	7	61	117	154	196	74	24	4
Drugs offences	947	6	58	151	200	354	141	34	2
Other offences	229	5	26	47	40	70	31	9	1
Offence not known	69	2	7	13	12	23	7	5	-

1 Includes persons committed in default of payment of a fine.

Source: Home Office: 020 7217 5567

11.12 Expenditure on prisons
England and Wales
Operating cost and total capital employed, years ending 31 March

£ thousand

		1994 /95	1995 /96	1996 /97	1997 /98	1998 /99	1999 /00	2000 /01
Expenditure								
Staff costs	KWUV	866 600	895 700	948 700	939 700	995 200	1 044 700	1 094 500
Accommodation costs	KXCO	127 100	122 400	113 900	116 200	163 400	149 300	153 700
Other operating costs	KXCP	323 400	369 000	373 900	472 600	538 800	584 300	654 200
Depreciation	KXCQ	90 300	159 300	123 600	160 200	146 100	115 700	117 200
Cost of capital	KXCR	201 800	211 500	225 500	231 300	262 500	254 900	259 900
Total expenditure	KXCS	1 609 200	1 757 900	1 785 600	1 920 000	2 106 000	2 148 900	2 279 500
Income								
Contributions from industries	KXCT	−4 600	−6 400	−6 600	−7 900	−8 300	−10 400	−10 600
Other operating income	KXCU	−3 300	−4 900	−5 300	−8 500	−8 500	−9 600	−10 300
Income from other Government Departments[1]	GDPM	..	..	..	..	..	..	−123 900
Total income	KXCV	−7 900	−11 300	−11 900	−16 400	−16 800	−20 000	−144 800
Net operating costs	KXCW	1 601 300	1 746 600	1 773 700	1 903 600	2 089 200	2 128 900	2 134 700
Total capital employed	KXCX	3 452 000	3 580 700	3 920 900	4 116 900	4 345 100	4 382 600	4 726 200

1 Income from the Youth Justice Board (a non-departmental public body of the
Home Office) for the provision of juvenile custody within the Prison Service.

Source: Home Office: 020 7217 5567

11.13 Crimes and offences recorded by the police
Scotland

Thousands

		1990	1991	1992	1993	1994	1995	1996	1997	1998	1999	2000
Non-sexual crimes of violence against the person[1]	KAFR	18.2	21.7	23.3	19.4	19.8	21.1	21.5	19.2	21.1	23.4	23.3
Serious assault, etc[1]	KAFS	6.3	7.0	7.7	6.5	6.7	6.9	7.0	6.1	6.6	7.2	7.0
Handling offensive weapons	KAFT	5.1	6.2	6.5	5.2	5.3	6.5	6.8	6.0	6.7	7.9	8.2
Robbery	KAFU	4.7	6.2	6.8	5.6	5.3	5.3	5.3	4.5	5.0	5.1	4.4
Other	KAFV	2.2	2.4	2.2	2.1	2.5	2.4	2.5	2.6	2.8	3.3	3.8
Crimes involving indecency	KAFW	6.0	5.8	6.2	6.0	6.0	5.5	5.7	7.1	7.4	6.0	5.8
Sexual assault	KAFX	1.5	1.4	1.6	1.6	1.6	1.6	1.7	2.0	2.2	1.9	1.8
Lewd and indecent behaviour	KAFY	2.6	2.6	2.6	2.7	2.7	2.4	2.5	3.0	3.0	2.4	2.3
Other	KAFZ	2.0	1.8	2.0	1.7	1.7	1.5	1.5	2.2	2.3	1.7	1.6
Crimes involving dishonesty	KAGA	385.2	430.2	415.0	374.9	350.3	321.2	295.4	267.2	275.4	276.2	260.9
Housebreaking	KAGB	101.7	116.1	113.2	97.8	88.4	74.2	64.5	55.5	56.6	53.8	48.7
Theft by opening lockfast places	KAGC	92.4	102.8	92.2	84.8	74.9	66.5	60.5	51.1	51.8	50.2	45.0
Theft of a motor vehicle	KAGD	36.1	44.3	47.4	42.8	42.0	37.5	34.2	28.6	28.4	29.8	26.2
Shoplifting	KAGE	26.8	30.1	29.7	26.7	26.6	28.0	26.9	26.3	29.6	32.0	32.3
Other theft	KAGF	97.8	104.6	98.8	93.3	88.9	87.7	82.6	79.6	80.1	81.1	78.1
Fraud	KAGG	19.6	22.0	22.6	19.1	17.7	17.1	16.1	15.7	18.6	18.6	21.2
Other	KAGH	10.8	10.3	11.1	10.3	12.0	10.2	10.8	10.3	10.2	10.6	9.4
Fire-raising, vandalism, etc	KAGI	86.5	89.7	92.2	84.2	88.5	86.5	89.0	81.0	79.2	79.6	83.2
Fire-raising	KAGJ	4.3	4.8	4.7	4.1	3.6	3.3	3.3	2.8	2.5	2.3	2.4
Vandalism, etc	KAGK	82.1	84.9	87.6	80.1	85.0	83.2	85.7	78.2	76.6	77.2	80.8
Other crimes[2]	KAGL	22.6	25.5	28.2	32.7	35.4	41.3	40.3	46.1	48.5	50.5	49.9
Crimes against public justice[2]	KAGM	12.9	13.3	14.4	14.5	16.0	16.4	16.1	16.6	16.9	18.5	18.4
Drugs	KAGN	9.6	12.0	13.6	18.0	19.3	24.8	24.0	29.4	31.5	31.9	31.4
Other	KAGO	0.2	0.2	0.2	0.2	0.2	0.2	0.1	0.1	0.1	0.1	0.1
Total crimes[2]	KAGQ	518.5	572.9	564.9	517.2	500.1	475.7	452.0	420.6	431.6	435.7	423.2
Miscellaneous offences	KAGR	127.0	122.3	127.5	126.6	133.2	134.4	146.1	155.9	153.7	151.0	153.8
Petty assault[1]	KAGS	39.6	41.0	42.5	41.3	45.1	46.6	47.6	50.1	51.0	54.0	54.8
Breach of the peace	KAGT	57.7	55.3	60.0	61.4	65.5	66.1	70.8	73.1	71.7	71.0	70.0
Drunkenness	KAGU	11.7	10.4	10.4	10.1	10.3	9.7	9.6	9.7	8.5	7.8	7.8
Other	KAGV	18.0	15.6	14.6	13.7	12.3	11.9	18.0	23.1	22.6	18.2	21.3
Motor vehicle offences	KAGW	296.2	305.6	306.4	315.1	330.7	317.5	305.9	331.0	362.1	353.4	345.8
Dangerous and careless driving	KAGX	25.3	23.1	22.5	20.0	21.1	18.7	17.3	16.3	15.8	14.0	12.3
Drunk driving	KAGY	11.4	11.0	11.3	10.9	10.8	10.7	11.8	11.2	10.6	10.8	10.7
Speeding	KAGZ	90.0	100.1	93.6	85.4	85.8	85.1	82.4	91.9	115.5	125.3	116.8
Unlawful use of a motor vehicle	KAHA	70.6	75.7	79.9	85.8	88.7	83.4	79.1	79.1	75.5	77.8	85.2
Vehicle defect offences	KAHB	47.5	46.8	47.8	51.4	56.9	56.3	53.5	60.1	63.6	52.9	48.3
Other	KAHC	51.5	48.9	51.5	61.7	67.4	63.2	61.8	72.3	81.2	72.5	72.5
Total offences	KAHD	423.2	427.9	433.9	441.7	463.9	451.9	452.0	486.9	515.8	504.5	499.6
Total crimes and offences[2]	KAHE	941.7	1 000.8	998.8	959.0	964.0	927.6	903.9	907.5	947.3	940.2	922.8

1 The definition of serious assault was changed in January 1990 to improve consistency between forces. It is estimated that the number of serious assaults that would have been recorded in 1989, using the revised definition, is some 1,150 fewer than actually recorded, with a corresponding rise in petty assaults.

2 Data from 1983 onwards has been revised as a result of a legislative change which came into force on 1 April 1996. From this date "offending while on bail" is no longer regarded as an offence in its own right.

Source: The Scottish Executive Justice Department: 0131 244 2225

11.14 Persons proceeded against
Scotland

Number of persons

		1989	1990	1991	1992	1993	1994	1995	1996	1997	1998	1999
Non-sexual crimes of violence	KEHC	4 197	4 392	4 356	5 141	5 327	4 910	4 969	5 741	5 633	5 290	5 547
Homicide	KEHD	118	100	106	148	150	122	159	159	119	104	110
Serious assault, etc	KEHE	1 432	1 512	1 425	1 546	1 592	1 508	1 298	1 421	1 485	1 453	1 595
Handling offensive weapons	KEHF	1 430	1 427	1 504	2 028	2 028	2 001	2 357	2 946	2 882	2 664	2 741
Robbery	KEHG	786	846	885	949	1 006	990	855	929	848	758	824
Other violence	KEHH	431	507	436	470	371	289	302	286	299	311	277
Crimes of indecency	KEHI	1 371	1 825	1 660	1 563	1 683	1 587	1 452	1 154	1 379	1 496	1 083
Sexual assault	KEHJ	225	233	200	203	229	195	182	194	212	207	184
Lewd and libidinous practices	KEHK	438	440	429	363	370	399	350	376	399	400	408
Other indecency	KEHL	708	1 152	1 031	997	1 084	993	920	584	768	889	491
Crimes of dishonesty	KEHM	40 808	40 329	40 765	40 950	38 601	37 026	35 301	33 695	31 931	30 330	28 315
Housebreaking	KEHN	7 673	7 408	7 258	7 105	6 370	6 126	5 452	4 639	4 054	3 706	3 659
Theft by opening lockfast places	KEHO	3 847	3 586	3 906	3 698	3 640	3 565	3 111	2 906	2 665	2 302	2 107
Theft of motor vehicle	KEHP	3 082	3 226	3 476	3 688	3 480	3 494	3 449	3 497	3 259	2 849	2 531
Shoplifting	KEHQ	6 646	7 098	7 921	8 469	8 262	7 260	7 185	7 840	7 959	8 357	8 424
Other theft	KEHR	11 574	10 765	9 944	9 485	8 565	7 532	7 485	7 170	7 113	6 761	6 198
Fraud	KEHS	3 531	3 753	3 438	3 326	3 519	4 191	4 073	3 566	3 202	2 915	2 415
Other dishonesty	KEHT	4 455	4 493	4 822	5 179	4 765	4 858	4 546	4 077	3 679	3 440	2 981
Fire-raising, vandalism, etc	KEHU	6 937	6 757	6 593	6 651	6 029	5 644	5 808	6 198	5 917	5 475	4 893
Fire-raising	KEHV	229	214	192	213	188	203	177	173	149	150	137
Vandalism, etc	KEHW	6 708	6 543	6 401	6 438	5 841	5 441	5 631	6 025	5 768	5 325	4 756
Other crime	KEHX	9 639	10 749	11 990	12 126	13 751	15 108	16 018	17 243	15 515	14 414	13 940
Crime against public justice	KFBK	6 854	7 272	7 537	7 377	8 407	8 892	9 424	9 748	7 248	6 224	6 218
Drugs offences	KFBL	2 756	3 436	4 413	4 713	5 313	6 185	6 556	7 454	8 219	8 153	7 689
Other	KFBM	29	41	40	36	31	31	38	41	48	37	33
Total crimes	KEHB	62 952	64 052	65 364	66 431	65 391	64 275	63 548	64 031	60 375	57 005	53 778
Miscellaneous offences	KEHZ	63 559	60 781	58 962	60 589	54 497	48 383	50 780	52 714	51 837	47 622	39 751
Simple assault	KEIA	16 858	15 990	15 116	14 715	14 452	13 962	14 809	15 577	15 875	15 165	13 752
Breach of the peace	KEIB	24 830	23 483	21 955	21 148	20 353	19 102	20 613	22 377	22 336	20 732	16 589
Drunkenness	KEIC	3 028	2 930	2 376	2 253	1 803	1 483	1 364	1 160	983	783	523
Other miscellaneous offences	KEID	18 843	18 378	19 515	22 473	17 889	13 836	13 994	13 600	12 643	10 942	8 887
Motor vehicle offences	KEIE	67 392	73 784	76 566	72 055	64 580	66 009	62 840	58 712	60 344	54 605	53 312
Dangerous and careless driving	KEIF	8 603	8 862	7 840	7 177	5 883	5 162	5 273	5 193	5 150	4 199	3 742
Drunk driving	KEIG	8 875	8 997	8 679	8 314	7 812	7 601	7 798	8 313	8 900	7 527	7 236
Speeding	KEIH	13 959	18 202	21 807	19 519	15 405	16 787	15 159	12 645	11 805	12 555	14 321
Unlawful use of vehicle	KEII	20 002	20 881	21 742	22 033	21 951	22 947	21 528	21 124	22 213	20 062	18 597
Vehicle defect offences	KEIJ	5 071	5 035	4 489	4 111	3 308	3 560	3 683	3 548	3 775	2 960	2 363
Other motor vehicle offences	KEIK	10 882	11 807	12 009	10 901	10 221	9 952	9 399	7 889	8 501	7 302	7 053
Total offences	KEHY	130 951	134 565	135 528	132 644	119 077	114 392	113 620	111 426	112 181	102 227	93 063
Total crimes and offences	KEHA	193 903	198 617	200 892	199 075	184 468	178 667	177 168	175 457	172 556	159 232	146 841

Source: Scottish Executive Justice Department: 0131 244 2229

11.15 Persons called to court
Scotland

Number of persons

		1989	1990	1991	1992	1993	1994	1995	1996	1997	1998	1999
Court procedure												
High Court[1]	KEIQ	1 055	1 099	1 227	1 419	1 601	1 228	1 390	1 420	1 356	1 225	1 357
Sheriff Court	KEIU	103 150	101 678	100 028	100 109	96 391	97 579	98 306	100 928	98 867	92 519	89 266
District Court	KEIV	80 153	83 591	87 186	84 704	74 920	68 183	66 037	62 485	61 648	57 182	49 020
Stipendiary Magistrate Court	KEIW	8 745	11 300	11 522	11 732	10 472	10 893	10 649	9 973	9 943	7 794	6 689
Total called to court[2]	KEIZ	193 161	197 722	200 017	198 038	183 674	178 067	176 423	174 844	171 932	158 815	146 474

1 Including cases remitted to the High Court from the Sheriff Court.
2 Includes court type not known.

Source: Scottish Executive Justice Department: 0131 244 2229

11.16 Persons with charge proved: by main penalty
Scotland

Number of persons

Main penalty		1989	1990	1991	1992	1993	1994	1995	1996	1997	1998	1999
Restriction of liberty order[1]	ZBRE	..	..	..	..	..	..	..	..	..	71	206
Supervised attendance order[2]	ZBRF	..	..	..	..	..	..	..	8	73	68	107
Absolute discharge	KEXA	698	869	887	967	989	839	939	1 000	1 064	957	985
Admonition or caution	KEXB	15 552	16 558	17 137	17 441	16 976	16 243	15 857	15 859	15 039	13 893	12 914
Probation	KEXC	3 840	4 268	4 877	5 385	5 722	6 145	6 145	6 435	6 814	7 144	7 340
Remit to children's hearing	KEXD	67	52	81	72	83	124	172	193	219	177	136
Community service order	KEXE	4 056	4 739	5 190	5 473	5 079	5 320	5 339	5 711	5 707	5 246	4 888
Fine	KEXF	133 817	135 273	135 479	131 842	116 918	112 748	110 337	105 384	103 861	94 917	83 479
Compensation order	KEXG	1 771	1 678	1 591	1 575	1 578	1 535	1 527	1 415	1 304	1 298	1 154
Insanity, hospital, guardianship order	KYAN	151	152	148	133	138	133	136	159	162	129	135
Prison	KEXI	9 091	8 796	9 222	10 085	10 832	11 583	11 561	12 134	11 621	11 447	11 591
Young offenders' institution	KEXJ	4 531	4 150	4 318	4 488	4 461	4 472	4 646	4 744	4 557	4 459	4 483
Detention of child	KEXM	19	23	35	22	30	36	48	45	29	20	17
Total persons with charge proved	KEXO	173 593	176 558	178 965	177 483	162 806	159 178	156 707	153 087	150 450	139 826	127 435

1 A community sentence introduced by Section 5 of the Crime and Punishment (Scotland) Act 1995 and available on a pilot basis to 3 Scottish sheriff courts since August 1998.
2 A pilot scheme covering the provisions of the Criminal Procedure (Scotland) Act 1995 replacing fines for 16 & 17 year olds has been operating in a small number of Scottish courts.

Source: Scottish Executive Justice Department: 0131 244 2229

11.17 Persons with charge proved: by age and gender
Scotland

Number of persons

		1989	1990	1991	1992	1993	1994	1995	1996	1997	1998	1999
Males	KEWA	148 157	150 105	150 482	147 692	136 127	136 533	133 330	130 961	129 461	120 482	110 326
Under 16	KEWB	215	173	189	138	138	171	180	149	137	135	75
16 to 20	KEWC	41 206	39 720	38 284	36 494	32 589	30 708	30 113	31 703	31 310	29 310	26 927
21 to 30	KEWD	56 509	59 114	59 532	59 561	56 052	56 517	54 184	52 217	50 684	46 121	41 665
Over 30	KEWE	46 602	48 390	49 802	49 093	45 701	47 788	47 648	45 799	46 281	44 047	40 786
Age not known	KEWF	3 625	2 708	2 675	2 406	1 647	1 349	1 205	1 093	1 049	869	873
Females	KEWG	23 186	24 400	26 340	28 051	25 405	21 650	22 412	21 308	20 246	18 667	16 539
Under 16	KEWH	9	11	18	9	6	8	17	12	11	5	6
16 to 20	KEWI	3 700	3 903	3 927	3 885	3 589	2 939	3 098	3 302	3 424	3 361	3 273
21 to 30	KEWJ	9 110	10 077	10 958	11 998	10 557	9 190	9 284	8 461	8 095	7 456	6 494
Over 30	KEWK	9 261	9 507	10 519	11 409	10 611	9 002	9 439	8 894	8 266	7 531	6 494
Age not known	KEWL	1 106	902	918	750	642	511	574	639	450	314	272
Males and Females	KEWM	171 343	174 505	176 822	175 743	161 532	158 183	155 742	152 269	149 707	139 149	126 865
Under 16	KEWN	224	184	207	147	144	179	197	161	148	140	81
16 to 20	KEWO	44 906	43 623	42 211	40 379	36 178	33 647	33 211	35 005	34 734	32 671	30 200
21 to 30	KEWP	65 619	69 194	70 490	71 559	66 609	65 707	63 468	60 678	58 779	53 577	48 159
Over 30	KEWQ	55 863	57 897	60 321	60 502	56 312	56 790	57 087	54 693	54 547	51 578	47 280
Age not known	KEWR	4 731	3 610	3 593	3 156	2 289	1 860	1 779	1 732	1 499	1 183	1 145
Companies	KEWS	2 212	2 024	2 126	1 717	1 263	991	961	812	737	675	551
Total persons with charge proved[1]	KEWT	173 593	176 558	178 965	177 483	162 806	159 178	156 707	153 087	150 450	139 826	127 435

1 Includes gender unknown.

Source: Scottish Executive Justice Department: 0131 244 2229

11.18 Penal establishments: average daily population and receptions
Scotland

Numbers

		1990	1991	1992	1993	1994	1995	1996	1997	1998	1999	2000
Average daily population												
Male	KEPB	4 587	4 696	5 099	5 466	5 408	5 451	5 673	5 900	5 825	5 817	5 666
Female	KEPC	137	143	158	171	177	175	189	184	193	212	203
Total	KEPA	4 724	4 839	5 257	5 637	5 585	5 626	5 862	6 084	6 018	6 029	5 869
Analysis by type of custody												
Remand	KEPD	751	770	876	948	1 015	998	1 000	947	938	1 012	894
Persons under sentence: total	KEPE	3 961	4 056	4 375	4 686	4 569	4 624	4 861	5 134	5 077	5 016	4 974
Adult prisoners[1]	KEPF	3 201	3 322	3 552	3 795	3 785	3 823	4 026	4 345	4 362	4 318	4 319
Young offenders[1]	KEPI	708	684	769	819	720	719	770	789	715	697	654
Persons recalled from supervision/licence	KEPN	39	39	32	40	37	44	46	46	72	93	128
Others	KEPO	13	12	21	32	28	38	18	20	17	28	31
Persons sentenced by court martial	KEPP	11	12	6	2	1	3	–	1	2	1	–
Civil prisoners	KEPQ	1	1	1	1	1	–	1	1	1	1	1
Receptions to penal establishments												
Remand	KEPR	15 168	13 127	13 546	13 412	14 922	14 253	14 977	14 826	15 098	15 291	13 948
Male	KEPS	14 323	12 360	12 722	12 478	13 985	13 377	13 976	13 850	13 979	14 090	12 918
Female	KEPT	845	767	824	934	937	876	1 001	976	1 119	1 201	1 030
Persons under sentence: total	KEPU	17 134	18 226	19 966	22 157	21 111	19 030	22 155	23 202	22 269	20 741	18 913
Male	KEPV	16 235	17 033	18 856	20 741	19 697	17 737	20 869	21 936	20 862	19 465	17 736
Female	KEPW	899	1 193	1 110	1 416	1 414	1 293	1 286	1 266	1 407	1 276	1 177
Imprisoned: Adults:												
directly	KEPX	7 551	7 951	8 543	9 444	9 349	8 730	10 040	9 698	9 959	9 484	8 713
in default of fine	KEPY	5 182	6 336	6 603	7 956	7 377	6 299	7 432	8 873	7 866	7 154	6 542
in default of compensation order[2]	KEPZ	23	6	40	41	26	13	..	..	..	..	..
Sentenced to young offenders' institution:												
directly	KEQA	2 719	2 356	3 041	3 052	2 855	2 772	3 111	2 784	2 844	2 687	2 498
in default of fine	KEQB	1 653	1 573	1 736	1 660	1 498	1 210	1 567	1 847	1 593	1 411	1 160
in default of compensation order[2]	KEQC	3	2	2	4	6	4	..	..	..	..	..
Persons recalled from supervised release orders	JYYD	3	2	1	–	–	2	5	11	7	5	–
Persons sentenced by court martial	KEQH	10	1	2	7	5	4	4	4	5	3	2
Civil prisoners[3]	KEQI	21	25	34	37	27	25	32	23	10	14	12

1 Figures for 1997-1999 have been revised to improve the treatment of prisoners recalled to prison.

2 From 1996 compensation orders are included in the figures for default of fine.

3 For 1995 and 1996 data is estimated.

Source: The Scottish Executive Justice Department: 0131 244 2225

11.19 Expenditure on penal establishments
Scotland
Years ended 31 March

£ thousands

Expenditure		1990 /91	1991 /92	1992 /93	1993 /94	1994 /95	1995 /96	1996 /97	1997 /98	1998 /99	1999 /00	2000 /01
Manpower and Associated Services	KPHC	110 454	124 898	129 597	135 301	140 009	135 941	143 107	137 890	144 660	170 347	160 242
Prisoner and Associated Costs	KPHD	8 446	8 504	10 274	10 795	11 679	12 373	13 377	16 313	18 891	22 930	23 501
Capital Expenditure	KPHE	12 866	13 032	13 681	11 845	15 636	15 377	22 577	22 136	23 697	28 918	24 283
Gross Expenditure	KPHF	131 766	146 434	153 552	157 941	167 324	163 691	179 061	176 339	187 248	222 195	208 026
Less Receipts:-	KPHG	3 819	3 711	3 542	3 598	3 042	2 800	2 600	2 810	8 160	6 668	7 280
Net Operating Costs	KPHH	127 947	142 723	150 010	154 343	164 282	160 891	176 461	173 529	179 088	215 527	200 746

Source: The Scottish Executive Justice Department: 0131 244 2225

11.20 Disposals given to those convicted by court
Northern Ireland

Numbers

		1988	1989	1990	1991	1992	1993	1994	1995	1996	1997	1998
Magistrates court - all offences												
Prison	KYAO	1 222	1 006	1 009	960	830	1 027	945	1 046	1 003	989	..
Young offenders centre	KYAP	401	368	370	502	588	575	499	483	443	430	..
Training school	KYAQ	170	168	153	177	120	125	193	169	147	148	..
Total immediate custody	KYAR	1 793	1 542	1 532	1 639	1 538	1 727	1 637	1 698	1 593	1 567	..
Prison suspended	KYAS	1 647	1 544	1 513	1 379	1 420	1 529	1 558	1 674	1 722	1 506	..
YOC suspended	KYAT	310	319	310	432	507	447	447	385	444	461	..
Attendance centre	KYAU	139	108	118	90	66	94	89	101	91	66	..
Probations/supervision	KYAV	763	778	854	742	849	881	1 017	1 137	1 134	1 155	..
Community supervision order	KYAW	523	435	575	547	464	536	551	547	591	561	..
Fine	KYAX	28 019	26 306	26 644	19 569	23 418	25 166	24 390	22 726	20 612	21 313	..
Recognizance	KYAY	442	412	399	514	713	858	961	1 001	1 203	1 267	..
Conditional discharge	KYAZ	2 707	2 022	1 982	2 102	1 965	2 021	1 830	1 928	1 679	1 597	..
Absolute discharge	KYBA	1 656	1 305	1 274	845	732	690	661	608	509	424	..
Disqualification	KYBB	4 810	4 106	4 335	4 211	640	6	6	2	5	2	..
Other	KYBC	36	20	28	24	12	7	11	8	10	6	..
Total	KYBD	42 845	38 897	39 564	32 094	32 324	33 962	33 158	31 815	29 593	29 925	..
Crown court - all offences												
Prison	KYBE	536	472	493	493	447	555	471	533	469	475	345
Young offenders centre	KYBF	112	111	106	125	119	130	87	76	106	111	63
Training school	KYBG	5	10	4	13	5	2	5	6	–	4	2
Total immediate custody	KYBH	653	593	603	631	571	687	563	615	575	590	410
Prison suspended	KYBI	313	318	295	238	249	211	277	265	253	220	199
YOC suspended	KYBJ	93	73	78	46	63	37	43	63	71	60	49
Custody probation order	ZAEO	..	..	..	..	..	..	..	..	..	..	175
Combination order	ZAEP	..	..	..	..	..	..	..	..	..	..	13
Attendance centre	KYBK	1	2	–	–	–	–	1	–	–	–	–
Probation/supervision	KYBL	80	72	85	103	95	73	58	60	49	47	70
Community supervision order	KYBM	106	71	105	89	79	48	59	60	54	37	33
Fine	KYBN	35	39	33	23	17	33	23	27	39	40	25
Recognizance	KYBO	7	3	8	7	9	5	16	–	7	10	7
Conditional discharge	KYBR	65	51	37	53	36	19	15	64	30	31	23
Absolute discharge	KYBS	5	1	2	5	8	3	2	1	–	1	6
Disqualification	KYBT	4	8	10	6	2	–	–	–	–	–	1
Other	KYBU	5	3	–	8	6	6	1	2	3	3	6
Total	KYBV	1 367	1 234	1 256	1 209	1 135	1 122	1 058	1 157	1 081	1 039	1 017

Source: Northern Ireland Office: 028 9052 7534

11.21 Persons found guilty at all courts by offence group
Northern Ireland

Numbers

		1987	1988	1989	1990	1991	1992	1993	1994	1995	1996	1997
Violence against the person	KYCT	1 534	1 491	1 424	1 750	1 634	1 558	1 674	1 498	1 685	1 597	1 594
Sexual offences	KEVG	210	228	226	275	193	184	126	148	182	184	130
Burglary	KYBW	1 869	1 553	1 363	1 362	1 208	1 149	1 114	979	951	801	715
Robbery	KYBX	314	296	273	220	162	202	159	168	195	161	166
Theft	KYBY	4 108	3 614	3 298	3 399	3 429	3 158	3 254	3 044	3 128	2 765	2 596
Fraud and forgery	KYBZ	728	688	783	699	648	683	633	568	533	467	491
Criminal damage	KYCA	1 230	1 048	939	1 054	1 019	967	1 145	1 134	1 008	1 076	1 163
Offences against the state	KYCB	321	226	216	233	195	187	184	137	166	147	165
Other indictable	KYCC	319	429	380	287	368	448	606	669	863	899	739
Total indictable[1]	KYCD	10 633	9 573	8 902	9 279	8 856	8 536	8 895	8 345	8 711	8 097	7 759
Summary	KYCE	6 072	6 071	5 113	4 293	4 278	4 115	4 307	4 369	4 137	4 402	4 435
Motoring[2]	KYCF	28 218	28 568	26 116	27 248	20 169	20 808	21 882	21 502	20 124	18 177	18 770
All offences	KYCG	44 923	44 212	40 131	40 820	33 303	33 459	35 084	34 216	32 972	30 676	30 964

1 Excludes indictable motoring offences
2 Includes indictable motoring offences

Source: Northern Ireland Office: 028 9052 7534

11.22 Juveniles found guilty at all courts by offence group[1]
Northern Ireland

Numbers

		1987	1988	1989	1990	1991	1992	1993	1994	1995	1996	1997
Violence against the person	KYCH	55	58	33	44	38	46	43	49	51	75	49
Sexual offences	KAHF	12	15	14	17	8	11	7	8	7	4	8
Burglary	KYCI	274	251	228	232	194	165	155	180	170	137	124
Robbery	KYCJ	11	19	11	10	7	8	4	9	22	13	18
Theft	KYCK	421	419	308	329	328	247	280	283	345	338	334
Fraud and forgery	KYCL	21	6	10	10	10	16	14	14	21	14	11
Criminal damage	KYCM	165	114	119	90	92	82	94	117	116	121	136
Offences against the state	KYCN	16	19	14	6	5	6	1	8	9	6	10
Other indictable	KYCO	8	11	15	10	11	8	2	6	14	24	10
Total indictable[2]	KYCP	983	912	752	748	693	589	600	674	755	732	700
Summary	KYCQ	262	190	186	138	111	113	125	131	180	182	198
Motoring[3]	KYCR	129	100	81	92	71	40	44	74	74	58	57
All offences	KYCS	1 374	1 202	1 019	978	875	742	769	879	1 009	972	955

1 Juveniles are aged 10 - 16 years inclusive.
2 Excludes indictable motoring offences.
3 Includes indictable motoring offences.

Source: Northern Ireland Office: 028 9052 7534

11.23
Prisons and Young Offenders Centres
Northern Ireland
Receptions and average population

		1990	1991	1992	1993	1994	1995	1996	1997	1998	1999	2000
Receptions:												
Reception of untried prisoners	KEOA	1 773	1 851	1 987	2 045	2 043	2 003	2 292	2 188	2 284	2 497	2 197
Reception of sentenced prisoners:												
Imprisonment under sentence of immediate custody[1]	KEOB	953	974	941	1 135	1 029	1 070	1 070	1 062	949	963	1 001
Imprisonment in default of payment of a fine	KEOC	1 264	1 282	1 352	1 221	1 190	1 248	1 374	1 513	1 530	1 423	1 261
Total	KEOD	2 217	2 256	2 293	2 356	2 219	2 318	2 444	2 575	2 479	2 386	2 262
Reception into Young Offender Centres:												
Detention under sentence of immediate custody	KEOE	371	348	371	416	346	371	362	331	347	346	282
Detention in default of payment of a fine	KEOF	309	356	364	353	276	351	373	366	385	417	389
Total	KEOG	680	704	735	769	622	722	735	697	732	763	671
Other receptions:												
Civil committals	KEOI	21	17	10	21	13	45	27	42	70	38	56
Total	KEOL	21	17	10	21	13	45	27	42	70	38	56
Daily average population:												
Total	KEOM	1 785	1 796	1 810	1 934	1 899	1 762	1 639	1 632	1 507	1 244	1 068
Unconvicted[2]	KEON	361	350	414	427	440	322	337	376	383	377	317
Convicted[3]	KEOP	1 424	1 446	1 396	1 507	1 459	1 440	1 302	1 256	1 124	867	751

1 Includes those detained under Section 73 of the Children and Young Persons (NI) Act 1968.
2 Prisoners on remand or awaiting trial and prisoners committed by civil process.
3 Includes those sentenced to immediate custody and fine defaulters.

Source: Northern Ireland Office: 028 9052 7534

12 **Lifestyles**

Lifestyles

Expenditure by the Department for Culture, Media and Sport *(Table 12.1)*

The figures in this table are taken from the Department's Annual Report and are outturn figures for each of the headings shown (later figures are the estimated outturn). The Department's planned expenditure for future years is also shown.

Cinema statistics *(Table 12.3)*

These estimates represent the motion picture projection activity for all individual legal units (i.e. companies, sole proprietorships, partnerships etc.) whose main activity is motion picture projection (i.e. heading 92.13 of the UK Standard Industrial Classification 1992). However, where such activity can be identified, the estimates also include the film exhibition activity of a number of legal units where motion picture projection is not their main activity. The Office for National Statistics does not maintain registers of all sites where film exhibition takes place so the estimates will not be completely comprehensive. It is believed, however, that the estimates cover the great majority of units engaged in cinema activity in Great Britain (i.e. England, Scotland and Wales but not Northern Ireland, the Isle of Man, the Channel Islands or the Republic of Ireland).

These figures are produced by combining information obtained by grossing data from a voluntary quarterly panel with estimates derived from the larger sample approached in the annual inquiry to the service trades.

All financial figures are exclusive of Value Added Tax.

Tourism *(Table 12.5)*

The figures in this table are compiled using data from the International Passenger Survey, the United Kingdom Tourism Survey and the British National Travel Survey.

From 2000 the research methodology of the United Kingdom Tourism Survey has been changed. The result is that the data for 2000 are not comparable with data for earlier years. Data for 1995-1999 will be re-worked on the new basis in due course. For more information contact the English Tourism Council on 020 8563 3011 or visit the StarUK website at www.staruk.org.uk.

The British National Travel Survey has been discontinued and later data are not available beyond the data shown in this table.

Gambling *(Table 12.7)*

The National Lottery figures in this table are the latest expenditure figures at the time of going to press which have been released by OFLOT - the National Lottery regulator, and represent ticket sales for each of the games which comprise the lottery. The figures have been adjusted to real terms using the Retail Prices Index.

The National Lottery commenced on the 19 November 1994, with the first instant ticket being sold in March 1995. Various other games have been started since, the latest being the Lottery Extra game. The sum of the individual games may not agree exactly with the figures for total sales, and also includes the Easy Play games which commenced in 1998, but were dropped in 1999.

The other gambling figures in this table are obtained from the Gaming Board for Great Britain Annual Report. The figures have been adjusted to real terms using the Retail Prices Index.

The money spent at casinos represents the money recorded as having been exchanged for chips. The money spent at bingo clubs refers to licensed clubs only. Prior to 1994-95 the figures for bingo clubs relate to the year ending August.

12.1 Expenditure by the Department for Culture, Media and Sport

£ millions

	Museums, galleries and libraries[1]	The arts (England)	Sports (UK)	Historic buildings, monuments, and sites (England)	The Royal Parks (UK)	Tourism (UK)	Broadcasting and media (UK)	Administration research and other research	National Lottery Commission	European regional development fund	Commemorative services and royal funerals	Spaces for sports and arts	Culture online
	GQIF	KWFP	KWFQ	KWFR	LQYY	KWFS	KWFT	GQIG	LQYZ	JYXQ	JYXP	GQIH	GQII
1991/92	333	212	47	..	..	44	22	8	..	..	–	..	..
1992/93	350	235	50	..	..	46	79	17	..	..	–	..	..
1993/94	335	235	54	164	23	46	85	22	2	..	–	..	..
1994/95	372	195	53	164	24	44	93	21	–	..	3	..	..
1995/96	399	200	54	164	25	45	98	20	–	6	3	..	..
1996/97	336	195	52	162	23	46	97	21	–	16	–	..	..
1997/98	321	196	50	156	22	45	43	21	–	26	3	..	..
1998/99	303	198	49	144	21	45	99	23	–	28	–	..	..
1999/00	326	232	52	146	26	48	104	28	–	38	1	..	..
2000/01[2]	338	239	53	151	23	48	104	27	1	31	–	15	2
2001/02[3]	361	253	67	142	25	47	105	29	1	31	–	60	2
2002/03[3]	386	298	83	152	24	49	110	30	1	31	–	–	–
2003/04[3]	395	338	102	154	24	50	112	30	1	31	–	–	–

1 Includes museums and galleries (England), libraries (UK) and museums library archives (UK).
2 Data are estimated outturn.
3 Data are plans.

Source: Department for Culture, Media and Sport: 020 7211 2189

12.2 Employment in tourism related industries
Great Britain

At June in each year

Thousands, not seasonally adjusted

	Hotels and other tourist accommodation	Restaurants, cafes etc.	Bars, pubs, clubs	Travel agents, tour operators	Libraries, museums, culture	Sport and other recreation	All	Total employees in tourist related industries	Estimated self employment
	KWFV	KWFW	KWFX	KWFY	KWFZ	KWGA	LQZA	KWGB	KWGC
1991	307.9	297.7	435.0	69.7	75.6	316.5	1 685.4	1 502.4	183.0
1992	311.0	303.0	414.2	69.2	74.8	320.8	1 671.0	1 493.0	178.0
1993	317.6	298.0	370.6	69.3	75.6	316.5	1 643.6	1 447.6	196.0
1994	375.3	372.2	399.1	83.7	75.6	355.7	1 663.3	1 455.5	207.8
1995	385.8	386.2	445.1	90.7	77.3	363.5	1 751.6	1 536.6	215.0
1996	428.3	456.6	510.6	97.0	80.5	364.2	1 937.1	1 720.1	217.0
1997	399.2	473.2	558.5	108.2	82.1	371.7	1 992.8	1 774.6	218.2
1998	414.7	486.9	560.0	103.3	81.3	359.3	2 005.5	1 820.5	185.0
1999	409.3	534.7	556.4	129.6	80.1	368.9	2 078.9	1 918.9	160.0
2000	405.8	554.7	576.1	141.7	88.4	384.7	2 151.4	1 981.0	170.4
2001	404.4	550.7	565.8	150.5	89.4	381.0	2 141.8	1 983.3	158.5

Source: Department for Culture, Media and Sport: 020 7211 2189

12.3 Cinema exhibitor statistics
Great Britain

	Sites	Screens	Total no. of admissions	Gross box office takings	Amount paid out for films	Revenue per admission	Revenue per screen
	number	number	millions	£ million	£ million	£	£ thousand
	CKNU	CKNV	CKQE	CKQF	CKQG	CKQH	CKQI
1990	496	1 331	78.6	187.7	69.5	2.39	143.8
1991	537	1 544	88.9	229.7	78.5	2.58	152.4
1992	480	1 547	89.4	243.7	81.9	2.73	153.6
1993	495	1 591	99.3	271.3	95.9	2.73	171.0
1994	505	1 619	105.9	293.5	104.6	2.77	183.5
1995	475	1 620	96.9	286.5	96.3	2.96	176.7
1996	483	1 738	118.7	373.5	144.9	3.15	215.5
1997	504	1 886	128.2	443.2	165.9	3.46	255.0
1998	512	2 168	127.1	437.1	159.1	3.43	201.6
1999[1]	539	2 492	133.8	479.4	175.3	3.58	192.4
2000[1]	509	2 560	137.1	507.1	187.4	3.70	198.1

1 Provisional.

Source: Office for National Statistics: 01633 812264

12.4 Films
United Kingdom

	Production of UK films		Expenditure on feature films				
	Films produced in the UK	Production costs	UK box office	Video rental	Video retail	Subscriptions to movie channels	Box office, video, subscription channels
	number	£ million 1998 prices	£ million current prices	£ million current prices	£ million current prices	£ million current prices	£ million current prices
	KWGD	KWGE	KWHU	KWHV	KWHW	KWHX	KWHY
1990	60	271.8	273	418	374	47	1 112
1991	59	285.3	295	407	440	121	1 263
1992	47	208.6	291	389	506	283	1 469
1993	67	214.0	319	350	643	350	1 662
1994	78	436.0	364	339	698	540	1 941
1995	81	421.0	385	351	789	721	2 246
1996	127	726.0	426	382	803	1 319	2 930
1997	115	558.0	506	369	858	..	1 733
1998	91	487.0	515	437	940	..	1 892
1999	103	570.0	606	408	882	..	1 896
2000	90	792.5	628	444	1 104	..	2 176

Source: Department for Culture, Media and Sport: 020 7211 2189

12.5 Tourism

International tourism

	Visits to the UK by overseas residents	Spending in the UK by overseas residents	Spending in the UK by overseas residents	Visits overseas by UK residents	Spending overseas by UK residents	Spending overseas by UK residents
	Thousands	£ million current prices	£ million constant 1995 prices	Thousand	£ million current prices	£ million constant 1995 prices
	KWGF	KWGG	KWGH	KWGI	KWGJ	KWGK
1990	18 013	7 748	9 853	31 150	9 886	12 021
1991	17 125	7 386	8 627	30 808	9 951	11 775
1992	18 535	7 891	8 784	33 836	11 243	12 678
1993	19 863	9 487	10 188	36 720	12 972	13 184
1994	20 794	9 786	10 050	39 630	14 365	14 852
1995	23 537	11 763	11 763	41 345	15 386	15 386
1996	25 163	12 290	11 954	42 050	16 223	15 897
1997	25 515	12 244	11 542	45 957	16 931	18 652
1998	25 745	12 671	11 573	50 872	19 489	21 847
1999	25 394	12 498	11 133	53 881	22 020	24 676
2000	25 209	12 805	11 102	56 837	24 251	27 281

UK Domestic tourism: one or more nights

	Number of trips	Number of nights spent	Expenditure at current prices	Average nights spent	Average expenditure per trip
	Millions	Millions	£ million	Numbers	£
	KWGL	KWGM	KWGN	KWGO	KWGP
1990	95.3	399.1	10 460	4.2	109.8
1991	94.4	395.6	10 470	4.2	110.9
1992	95.6	399.7	10 665	4.2	111.6
1993	90.9	375.9	12 430	4.1	136.7
1994	109.8	416.5	13 215	3.8	120.4
1995	121.0	449.8	12 775	3.7	105.6
1996	127.0	454.6	13 895	3.6	109.4
1997	133.6	473.6	15 075	3.6	112.9
1998	122.3	437.6	14 030	3.6	114.7
1999	146.1	495.3	16 250	3.4	111.2
	GQGY	GQGZ	GQHA	GQHB	GQHC
2000[1]	175.4	576.4	26 132	3.3	150

Holidays taken by GB residents[2]

	Taking a holiday in GB	Taking a holiday abroad	Taking only one holiday (4+ nights)	Taking two holidays (4+ nights)	Taking 3 or more holidays (4+ nights)
	Percentage	Percentage	Percentage	Percentage	Percentage
	KWGQ	KWGR	KWGS	KWGT	KWGU
1990	38	30	36	15	8
1991	41	30	36	16	8
1992	36	32	35	15	9
1993	37	35	36	16	9
1994	35	36	34	16	10
1995	36	37	35	17	10
1996	35	34	35	15	9
1997	33	35	31	16	10
1998	31	38	34	16	9

1 Due to a change in methodology data for 2000 are not directly comparable with earlier years. Data from 1995 will be re-worked on the new basis in due course.

2 The British National Travel Survey has been discontinued and as a result later data are not available.

Sources: Office for National Statistics: 020 7533 5765;
The National Tourist Boards: 020 8563 3011

12.6 Participation in leisure activities[1]
Great Britain

Percentages

		1987	1990	1993	1996
Sports, games and physical activities					
Walking	KWHB	37.9	40.7	40.8	44.5
Swimming	KWHC	13.1	14.8	15.4	14.8
Cue sports	KWHD	15.1	13.6	12.2	11.3
Keep fit/yoga	KWHE	8.6	11.6	12.1	12.3
Cycling	KWHF	8.4	9.3	10.2	11.0
Darts	KWHG	8.8	7.1	5.6	..
Weight lifting)					1.3
Weight lifting/training)	KWHH	4.5	4.8	5.5	..
Weight training)					5.6
Golf	KWHI	3.9	5.0	5.3	4.7
Jogging	KWHJ	5.2	5.0	4.6	4.5
Football	KWHK	4.8	4.6	4.5	4.8
Any activity other than walking	KWHL	44.7	47.8	47.3	45.6
Selected leisure activities					
Watching TV	KWHM	99	99	99	99
Visiting/entertaining friends or relatives	KWHN	95	96	96	96
Listening to the radio	KWHO	88	89	89	88
Listening to tapes or records	KWHP	73	76	77	78
Reading books	KWHQ	60	62	65	65
Gardening	KWHR	46	48	48	48
DIY	KWHS	43	43	42	42
Dressmaking, needlework, knitting	KWHT	27	23	22	22

1 Percentage aged 16 and over participating in each activity in the four weeks before interview.

Source: Office for National Statistics: 020 7533 5444

12.7 Gambling
United Kingdom

£ millions at 2000/01 prices[1]

		1992 /93	1993 /94	1994 /95	1995 /96	1996 /97	1997 /98	1998 /99	1999 /00	2000 /01
Money spent on gambling										
National Lottery - Total[2]	GQHJ	..	..	1 331	6 009	5 256	5 935	5 429	5 172	4 914
On-line	GQHK	..	..	1 320	4 251	4 288	5 080	4 727	4 388	4 095
Instants	GQHL	..	..	12	1 758	967	855	694	585	526
Thunderball	GQHM	..	..	..	..	..	..	..	198	248
Lottery Extra	GQHN	..	..	..	..	..	..	..	..	47
Lotteries (excluding the National Lottery)[3]	GQHO	58	52	46	91	129	135	168	107	107
Casinos[3]	GQHP	2 538	2 700	2 899	2 908	2 897	2 934	2 791	3 201	3 316
Bingo clubs[3]	GQHQ	969	982	994	1 034	1 078	1 099	1 089	1 108	1 118

1 Adjusted to real terms using the Retail Prices Index.
2 Includes Easy Play tickets which are not shown separately.
3 Great Britain only.

Sources: Department for Culture, Media and Sport: 020 7211 2189;
Gaming Board for Great Britain: 020 7306 6253

12.8 Private households with usual residents[1]: Census 1991[2]

Thousands

| | | Selected tenures of households in permanent buildings | | | |
| | | | | Rented | | |
Household and family type	All households	Owner occupied	From council or new town	Unfurnished	With no car
Great Britain					
All households	21 441	14 288	4 589	765	7 095
Households with no family	6 344	3 297	1 778	363	3 936
One person	5 643	2 922	1 652	327	3 657
Two or more persons	701	375	126	36	280
Households with one family	14 898	10 856	2 760	398	3 113
Married couple family	11 847	9 279	1 719	273	1 889
With no children	5 208	3 994	796	156	1 145
With dependent child(ren)	4 802	3 813	651	85	526
With non-dependent child(ren) only	1 837	1 471	272	32	218
Cohabiting couple family	1 139	720	219	57	224
With no children	718	502	68	41	117
With dependent child(ren)	374	187	139	15	100
With non-dependent child(ren) only	47	31	12	1	7
Lone parent family	1 912	858	823	68	1 000
With dependent child(ren)	1 122	391	567	40	689
With non-dependent child(ren) only	790	467	256	28	311
Households with two or more families	199	134	50	4	46
England and Wales					
All households	19 458	13 252	3 838	717	6 253
Households with no family	5 725	3 053	1 498	341	3 500
One person	5 083	2 703	1 393	306	3 254
Two or more persons	642	351	105	34	247
Households with one family	13 551	10 071	2 298	373	2 713
Married couple family	10 779	8 589	1 411	254	1 645
With no children	4 762	3 714	661	146	1 015
With dependent child(ren)	4 358	3 517	534	78	448
With non-dependent child(ren) only	1 659	1 358	215	30	182
Cohabiting couple family	1 064	682	192	55	199
With no children	672	474	58	40	104
With dependent child(ren)	348	178	124	14	89
With non-dependent child(ren) only	43	29	10	1	6
Lone parent family	1 708	800	694	64	868
With dependent child(ren)	1 004	368	484	38	601
With non-dependent child(ren) only	703	432	210	26	267
Households with two or more families	183	127	42	3	40
Scotland					
All households	1 983	1 036	751	48	843
Households with no family	619	244	281	22	436
One person	560	219	260	20	403
Two or more persons	60	25	21	2	33
Households with one family	1 348	785	463	25	401
Married couple family	1 068	690	307	19	244
With no children	446	280	135	10	130
With dependent child(ren)	444	296	116	7	78
With non-dependent child(ren) only	178	113	56	2	36
Cohabiting couple family	75	38	27	2	25
With no children	45	28	10	1	13
With dependent child(ren)	26	9	15	1	11
With non-dependent child(ren) only	3	2	2	0	1
Lone parent family	204	58	129	4	132
With dependent child(ren)	118	23	83	2	88
With non-dependent child(ren) only	86	35	46	2	44
Households with two or more families	16	7	8	0	6

1 Number of households and family type by selected tenures of households in permanent buildings and with no car.
2 Later figures not available.

Sources: Office for National Statistics: 01329 813800;
General Register Office (Scotland): 0131 314 4254

13 Environment, water and housing

Environment, water and housing

Air Emissions *(Table 13.1 to 13.7)*

Emissions of air pollutants arise from a wide variety of sources. The National Atmospheric Emissions Inventory (NAEI) is prepared annually for the Government and the devolved administrations by the National Environmental Technology Centre (NETCEN), with the work being co-ordinated by DEFRA. Information is available for a range of point sources, including the most significant polluters. However, a different approach has to be taken for diffuse sources such as transport and domestic emissions where this type of information could not be available and estimates for these are derived from statistical information and from research on emission factors for stationary and mobile sources. Although for any given year considerable uncertainties surround the emission estimates for each pollutant, trends over time are likely to be more reliable.

UK national emission estimates are updated annually and any developments in methodology are applied retrospectively to earlier years. Adjustments in the methodology are made to accommodate new technical information and to improve international comparability.

Three different classification systems are used in the tables presented here: a National Accounts basis (Table 13.1); the format required by the Inter-governmental Panel on Climate Change (IPCC) (Table 13.2); and the CORINAIR format used by the United Nations Economic Commission for Europe (UNECE) (Tables 13.3-13.7).

The National Accounts figures in Table 13.1 differ from those on an IPCC basis in that they include estimated emissions from fuels purchased in the UK and used by international shipping and aircraft on international flights (marine and air bunkers). This is intended to bring them closer to the National Accounts treatment, which includes expenditures by residents abroad and excludes expenditures by non-residents.

The IPCC classification in Table 13.2 is used to report greenhouse gas emissions and includes land use change and all emissions from domestic aviation and shipping, but excludes international marine and aviation bunker fuels. Estimates of the relative contribution to global warming of the main greenhouse gases, or classes of gases, is presented weighted by their global warming potential.

The UNECE/CORINAIR classification used in Tables 13.3-13.7 excludes land use change, but includes aviation emissions below 1,000 metres to cover take-off and landing cycles.

In tables 13.3 and 13.5, the figures on emissions from individual large combustion plants (LCPs) for 1991 onwards are totals of those reported by the Environment Agency to DEFRA. For 1970-1990, estimates are made assuming all power station emissions from coal, fuel oil and orimulsion stations are included, plus 79 per cent of refineries' emissions, 12 per cent of iron and steel emissions and 38 per cent of other (Table 13.3), and 88 per cent of refineries' emissions, 11 per cent of iron and steel emissions and 40 per cent of other industrial combustions in fuel extraction and

transformation (Table 13.5). It is not possible to calculate LCP figures from the categories presented in these tables as refineries and other industrial combustion are both included in more than one category.

Emissions of PM[10] *(Table 13.4)*

Emissions of PM[10] includes particles which pass through a size selective inlet with a 50 per cent efficiency cut-off at 10μm aerodynamics diameter.

Emissions of nitrogen oxides *(Table 13.5)*

Most of the figures in this table are based on a single NO_x emission factor for each fuel which is held constant over time. Emissions are expressed as nitrogen dioxide equivalent.

Emissions of carbon monoxide *(Table 13.6)*

Most of the figures in this table are based on a single carbon monoxide emission factor for each fuel held constant over time.

Emissions of volatile organic compounds *(Table 13.7)*

Most of the figures in this table are based on a single volatile organic compound emission factor for each source held constant over time.

Water industry expenditure *(Table 13.8)*

The table is informed by the annual and regulatory accounts of water and sewerage companies and water companies of England and Wales. Figures are given based on current cost rather than historical cost accounting principles. The elements which make up operating expenditure are as follows: manpower costs, other costs of employment, power, local authority rates, water charges, Local Authority sewerage agencies, materials and consumables, hired and contracted services, charge for bad and doubtful debts, depreciation, infrastructure renewals expenditure, infrastructure renewals accrual, exceptional items and other operating costs. Capital expenditure figures are the addition to tangible fixed assets including management and general expenditure but excluding infrastructure renewals expenditure.

Water quality *(Tables 13.9 and 13.10)*

The chemical quality of river and canal waters in the UK is monitored in a series of separate national surveys. The General Quality Assessment (GQA) Scheme used in the surveys provides a rigorous and objective method for assessing the basic chemical quality of rivers and canals based on three determinants – dissolved oxygen, biochemical oxygen demand (BOD), and ammoniacal nitrogen. The GQA grades river stretches into six categories (A-F) of chemical quality and these in turn have been grouped into four broader groups – good (classes A and B), fair (C and D), poor (E) and bad (F). In Scotland river and canal water quality is assessed using the following classes: unpolluted, fairly good, poor and grossly polluted. These classes are not directly comparable with those used in England and Wales and Northern Ireland.

To provide a more comprehensive picture of the health of rivers and canals, biological testing was carried out in parallel with chemical testing in the latest two quinquennial river quality surveys in England and Wales,

Scotland and Northern Ireland. The biological grading is based on the monitoring of tiny animals (invertebrates) which live in or on the bed of the river. Research has shown that there is a relationship between species composition and water quality. Using a procedure known as the River Invertebrate Prediction and Classification System (RIVPACS), species groups recorded at a site were compared with those which would be expected to be present in the absence of pollution, allowing for the different environmental characteristics in different parts of the country. In England and Wales and in Northern Ireland two different summary statistics (known as ecological quality indices (EQI)) were calculated and then the biological quality was assigned to one of six bands based on a combination of these two statistics. In Scotland, a third EQI was also calculated by SEPA and the grading system based on a combination of all three statistics or EQIs. The results for Scotland are not directly comparable for this reason.

Surface and groundwater abstractions *(Table 13.12)*
From 1991 data were collected on a different basis. Figures are therefore not strictly comparable with those in previous years. Some regions report licensed and actual abstracts for financial rather than calendar years. As figures represent an average for the whole year expressed as daily amounts, differences between amounts reported for financial and calendar years are small.

The following changes have occurred in the classification of individual sources:-

Public water supply: The 1991 figures include some private water supply.

Spray irrigation: This category includes small amounts of non-agricultural spray irrigation.

Mineral washing: Included for the first time as a separate category in 1991 survey, but no longer reported from 1999.

Private water supply: was shown as separate category from 1992 and includes private abstractions for domestic use and individual households.

Fish farming, cress growing, amenity ponds: Includes amenity ponds, but excludes miscellaneous from 1991.

Other: was included for the first time as a separate category in 1991 survey. The figure for 1991 included some private domestic water supply wells and boreholes, public water supply transfer licences and frost protection use.

Bathing waters *(Table 13.13)*
Under the EC Bathing Water Directive 76/160/EEC, eleven physical, chemical and microbiological parameters are measured including total and faecal coliforms which are generally considered to be the most important indicators of the extent to which water is contaminated by sewage. The mandatory value for total coliforms is 10,000 per 100 ml, and for faecal

coliforms 2,000 per 100 ml. For a bathing water to comply with the coliform standards, the Directive requires that at least 95 per cent of samples taken for each of these parameters over the bathing season are less than or equal to the mandatory values. In the UK a minimum of 20 samples are normally taken at each site. In practice this means that where 20 samples are taken, a maximum of only one sample may exceed the mandatory value for the bathing water to comply, and where less than 20 samples are taken none may exceed the mandatory value for the bathing water to comply.

The bathing water season is from mid-May to end-September in England and Wales, but shorter in Scotland and Northern Ireland. Bathing waters which are closed for the season are excluded for that year.

The table shows Environment Agency (EA) regions for England and Wales. The boundaries of which are based on river catchment areas and not county borders. In particular, the figures shown for Wales are the EA Welsh Region, the boundary of which does not coincide with the boundary of Wales.

The following changes have occurred to these regions:-

North East: Up to 1998 includes Alnmouth which has been undesignated since. Earls Dyke was closed for the 2001 season.

North West: In 1997 West Kirby was reclassified from the Welsh to the North West region. West Kirby data are presented in the North West region for all years for consistency.

Thames: Two new bathing waters were designated in this region in 2001, these are Shoeburyness and Three Shells.

South West: Bathing waters closed for the 2001 season were Redgate, Dartmouth Castle and Sugary Cove.

Radioactive wastes *(Table 13.14)*
Solid radioactive wastes are not discharged to the environment but stored and conditioned by processes such as supercompaction, cementation or turning into glass. Such wastes cover a wide range of materials and can be classified, according to the nature and quantity of radioactivity associated with them, as high level wastes (HLW), intermediate level wastes (ILW) or low level wastes (LLW). HLW result from the reprocessing of nuclear fuel and are highly radioactive. They contain over 95 per cent of all the radioactivity in wastes from nuclear establishments. Although small in volume, HLW have a high heat output as a result of the energy from radioactive decay. ILW include the irradiated metal cladding for nuclear reactor fuel, reactor components, and chemical process residues and filters. They have a lower radioactivity and heat output than HLW but their radioactivity content exceeds the upper limits for LLW.

The table shows recent trends in the volume of radioactive waste stocks for particular groups of nuclear

Environment, water and housing

sites. Data for HLW and ILW are presented in two physical states – as stored and conditioned. "As stored" is the form in which the waste is currently stored. "Conditioned" is the form of waste suitable for long-term storage and ultimate disposal to deep underground repositories when these become available. There is no simple relationship between as-stored and conditioned volumes of waste, since the effects of conditioning can vary with different wastes. Estimates of conditioned wastes are indicative only and should be interpreted with care.

LLW include concrete, rubble and soil from building demolition, discarded protective clothing and worn out or damaged plant and equipment. Unlike HLW and ILW, LLW do not normally require shielding against radiation emisssions during handling and transport. The table reports LLW volumes in the form in which the wastes will be disposed of in existing facilities or a future repository.

The table excludes waste from defence establishments prior to 1991. Such ILW and LLW will add no more than 20 per cent to the volumes of radioactive waste from civil sources before 1991.

Noise complaints *(Table 13.15)*
The table shows trends in the number of complaints received by local authority Environmental Health Officers. The figures are from those authorities making returns and are calculated per million people based on the population of the authorities making returns.

The relevant Acts referred to in the table are the *Control of Pollution Act 1974* until 1990/91 and the *Environmental Protection Act 1990* for 1991/92 onwards. This is except for noise in the streets where section 62 of the *Control of Pollution Act 1974* applies up until 1996/97 (primarily includes the chimes of ice-cream vendors and the use of loudspeakers other than for strictly defined purposes) and vehicles, machinery and equipment in the street where the *Noise and Statutory Nuisance Act 1993* applies.

Most complaints about traffic noise are usually addressed to highways authorities or Department for Transport, Local Government and the Regions (DTLR) Regional Directors, and will not necessarily be included in the figures. Similarly, complaints about noise from civil aircraft are generally received by aircraft operators, the airport companies, the DTLR or Civil Aviation Authority. Complaints about military flying are dealt with either by Station Commanding Officers or by Ministry of Defence headquarters. The figures in this table will not necessarily include these complaints.

Over time the categories shown in this table have changed. These have included:- From 1990 'other' in Scotland includes barking dogs. From 1997/98 complaints about road works are included with 'vehicles machinery and equipment in streets'. From 1997/98 all complaints about noise in the street are included with 'vehicles machinery and equipment in streets'.

Annual Waste *(Table 13.16)*
Agriculture: The estimate is derived from a survey of agricultural waste commissioned by the DEFRA and relates to Great Britain. It includes all waste streams, e.g. excreta from all livestock (both housed and grazing animals) and other wastes including straw, plastics and packaging, animal carcasses and slurries.

Mining and quarrying: The minerals waste estimate is based on ratios of waste to product.

Sewage sludge: The estimate of sewage sludge arisings has been made on the basis of dry weight (wet weight can be estimated on the basis of 4 per cent solid content on average - giving a total of 26,450,000 tonnes).

Dredged material: The data for dredged material are for all UK waters.

Municipal waste: The UK estimate for municipal waste is based on returns made by Waste Disposal Authorities in England and Wales to a DEFRA/National Assembly for Wales survey.

Commercial and industrial: The figures for these sectors only cover England and Wales, and are estimated from a EA survey.

Demolition and construction: These provisional estimates only cover England and Wales, and are estimated from a DEFRA/EA survey.

Recycling *(Table 13.17)*
The ratios shown reflect the amount of secondary material (scrap) used in the UK in a year as a proportion of consumption in that year. This gives some indication of the extent to which secondary material is displacing raw materials from the feedstock. This definition takes no account of the lifetime of the article being recovered ie that material which is being recycled now and related to current consumption might originally have been delivered to an end market some years ago.

Designated areas *(Table 13.18)*
National Parks, Areas of Outstanding Natural Beauty (AONB's) in England, Wales and Northern Ireland and National Scenic Areas in Scotland are the major areas which have been designated to protect their landscape importance. National Scenic Areas in Scotland are the equivalent of AONB's in England, Wales and Northern Ireland.

Some areas may be in more than one category. All areas shown in the table are at December 2000, except for Green Belt land which relates to 1 January 1997.

The area for Green Belt land is based on a new methodology in which the extent of Green Belt land is captured in digital form. This approach provides much more reliable figures than those previously published in earlier years.

Further details regarding tables 13.2 to 13.7 and 13.9 to 13.18 can be found in DEFRA's annual *Digest of Environmental Statistics*. If you would like to discuss the tables, Adrian Redfern can be contacted at DEFRA on 020 7944 6497.

Permanent dwellings *(Table 13.21)*
Local housing authorities include the Commission for the New Towns and New Towns Development Corporations, the Scottish Special Housing Association, the Northern Ireland Housing Trust and the Northern Ireland Housing Executive. The figures shown for housing associations include dwellings provided by housing associations other than the Scottish Special Housing Association and the Northern Ireland Housing Trust and provided or authorised by government departments for the families of police, prison staff, the Armed Forces and certain other services.

13.1 Estimated atmospheric emissions[1] 1999 on National Accounts basis
United Kingdom

Thousand tonnes

| | Greenhouse gases[2] | Acid rain precursors[3] | Emissions affecting air quality[4] | | | | | | | |
	CO_2, CH_4 & N_2O, HFC PFC, SF_6 KtCO$_2$ equiv	SO_2, NO_x & NH_3 KtSO$_2$ equiv	PM_{10}	CO	NMVOC	Benzene	Butadiene	Lead (tonnes)	Cadmium (tonnes)	Mercury (tonnes)
Agriculture	56 800	590	20.4	71.0	149.0	0.4	0.1	4.3	0.02	-
Mining and quarrying	33 700	90	30.7	155.1	194.0	0.5	0.1	3.2	0.04	0.02
Manufacturing	132 800	450	32.7	724.1	483.5	3.2	0.6	183.7	4.54	3.83
Electricity, gas and water supply	155 700	1 020	19.4	81.4	30.1	0.3	-	17.8	0.51	1.68
Construction	4 700	30	7.5	183.1	65.8	0.6	0.2	2.4	0.01	-
Wholesale and retail trade	15 000	40	5.2	177.9	135.6	1.4	0.4	14.6	0.03	-
Transport and communication	70 300	450	16.6	346.7	114.0	2.6	2.3	19.1	0.21	0.02
Financial intermediation	13 400	30	4.0	203.0	26.0	1.2	0.2	17.2	0.03	-
Public administration	9 000	30	1.3	16.9	2.6	0.1	-	1.5	0.01	0.05
Education, health and social work	11 100	20	2.1	34.7	5.5	0.2	-	4.0	0.02	0.09
Other services	20 000	30	1.3	24.8	16.7	0.2	0.1	5.5	0.66	2.23
Domestic	147 900	410	48.7	2848.8	537.3	20.3	3.1	281.0	0.50	0.63
Totals	670 400	3 190	189.9	4 867.5	1 760.0	31.1	7.3	554.4	6.58	8.55
Of which, emissions from road transport	119 200	550	36.3	3 292.4	472.6	21.0	5.3	327.3	0.37	-

1 The National Accounts basis includes estimated emissions from fuels purchased in the UK and used by international shipping and aircraft on international flights.

2 Carbon dioxide, methane, nitrous oxide, hydro-fluorocarbons, perfluorocarbons and sulphur hexafluoride expressed in thousand tonnes of carbon dioxide equivalent.

3 Sulphur dioxide, nitrogen oxides and ammonia expressed as thousand tonnes of sulphur dioxide equivalent.

4 PM_{10}s are carbon particles in air arising from incomplete combustion. CO is carbon monoxide and NMVOC are non-methane volatile organic compounds including benzene and 1,3-butadiene.

Sources: National Environmental Technology Centre; and Office for National Statistics: 020 7533 5904

13.2 Estimated total emissions[1] of UK greenhouse gases on IPCC basis
United Kingdom

Million tonnes (CO_2 equivalent)

		1992	1993	1994	1995	1996	1997	1998	1999
Emissions weighted by global warming potential									
Carbon dioxide (CO_2(asCO_2))	JZCK	591.9	576.3	572.4	563.4	583.0	558.0	560.3	547.8
Methane (CH_4)	JZCL	74.09	70.99	64.43	64.12	62.66	60.71	58.02	55.27
Nitrous oxide (N_2O)	JZCM	58.10	54.46	58.93	56.31	58.38	60.15	58.24	42.89
Hydrofluorocarbons (HFC)	JZCN	12.35	12.90	13.81	15.21	16.29	18.45	20.18	6.21
Perfluorocarbons (PFC)	JZCO	0.96	0.81	0.98	1.09	0.91	0.66	0.65	0.68
Sulphur hexafluoride (SF_6)	JZCP	0.83	0.89	1.06	1.13	1.27	1.26	1.29	1.31
Total	JZCQ	738.3	716.4	711.6	701.3	722.5	699.3	698.6	654.2

1 Emissions inventories based on the methodology developed by the Intergovernmental Panel on Climate Change (IPCC) are used to report UK emissions to the Climate Change Convention.

Sources: National Environmental Technology Centre; for Department for Environment, Food and Rural Affairs 020 7944 6497

13.3 Estimated emissions of sulphur dioxide (SO$_2$) by source
United Kingdom

Thousand tonnes

By source category (UNECE/CORINAIR94)		Percentage of total in 1999	1970	1980	1990	1991	1992	1993	1994	1995	1996	1997	1998	1999
Power stations	JZCR	65	2 913	3 007	2 723	2 535	2 434	2 083	1 762	1 591	1 320	1 025	1 072	776
Refineries	GPKK	8	242	262	153	161	146	148	135	142	144	134	98	93
Combustion in fuel extraction and transformation	JZCT	1	302	71	42	38	15	13	10	9	10	13	12	15
Domestic	JZCU	4	522	226	108	115	103	113	92	67	71	63	53	53
Commercial, public and agricultural combustion	JZCV	2	451	218	90	85	89	95	80	60	57	47	34	22
Iron and steel	JZCW	4	433	128	88	86	66	75	70	65	58	58	45	42
Other industrial combustion	GPLK	10	1 413	776	370	385	433	427	366	279	227	190	161	114
Production processes	GPLN	1	94	77	48	42	36	33	30	27	27	25	19	17
Extraction and distribution of fossil fuels	GPKD	-	5	5	16	6	7	5	6	6	7	6	6	1
Solvent use	GPKQ	-	2	2	2	2	2	2	2	5	4	5	5	4
Road transport	JZCZ	1	44	42	63	58	62	59	63	51	37	27	23	12
Off-road sources	GPLD	-	35	19	8	8	8	8	7	5	5	5	5	5
Military	GPKX	1	9	9	9	10	9	8	8	8	8	8	6	6
Railways	GPUX	-	14	7	3	3	3	2	2	2	2	1	1	1
Shipping	GPUY	2	35	25	27	30	29	30	29	29	30	27	25	22
Civil Aircraft	GPUZ	-	–	–	–	–	1	1	1	1	1	1	1	1
Waste treatment and disposal	GPVA	-	4	5	5	5	5	3	3	3	2	1	2	4
Total	JZDC	100	6 518	4 880	3 754	3 568	3 447	3 105	2 665	2 348	2 010	1 637	1 567	1 187
Emissions from large combustion plants														
Large plants	ZBZK		3 654	3 485	2 930	2 747	2 674	2 329	1 969	1 756	1 468	1 107	1 207	894
Index (1980=100)	ZBZL		105	100	84	79	77	67	57	50	42	32	35	26

Sources: National Environmental Technology Centre;
for Department for Environment, Food and Rural Affairs 020 7944 6497

13.4 Estimated emissions of PM$_{10}$ by source
United Kingdom

Thousand tonnes

By source category (UNECE/CORINAIR94)		Percentage of total in 1999	1970	1980	1990	1991	1992	1993	1994	1995	1996	1997	1998	1999
Power stations	JZDN	10	67	76	70	70	66	55	49	37	34	23	23	19
Refineries	GQOZ	2	5	5	3	4	4	4	4	4	4	4	4	3
Combustion in fuel extraction and transformation	GQPA	2	16	3	3	3	3	3	3	3	4	4	4	4
Domestic	GQPB	20	223	105	55	58	53	54	45	35	37	34	35	38
Commercial, public & agricultural combustion	JZDP	3	22	11	8	8	7	7	7	6	6	7	5	5
Iron and steel	GQPC	-	8	2	1	1	1	1	1	1	1	1	1	1
Other industrial combustion	GQPD	10	69	32	28	29	31	30	29	26	24	22	20	18
Production processes in industry	GQPE	6	14	12	13	13	13	13	13	13	13	13	12	11
Construction, mining and quarrying	GQPF	13	30	25	34	30	28	29	31	29	27	27	27	25
Road transport[1]	JZDS	20	46	55	63	62	60	57	56	52	49	44	39	36
Other transport	GQPG	6	15	13	12	12	12	12	12	11	12	11	11	11
Waste treatment and disposal	GQPH	1	1	4	3	3	3	2	3	2	2	1	1	1
Agriculture[2]	GQPI	8	11	12	12	13	12	12	12	12	13	13	14	14
Total	JZGA	100	528	355	305	304	292	278	263	232	225	204	197	186

1 Includes emissions from tyre and brake wear.
2 Includes emissions from animal waste.

Sources: National Environmental Technology Centre;
for Department for Environment, Food and Rural Affairs 020 7944 6497

13.5 Estimated emissions of nitrogen oxides (NOx) by source
United Kingdom

Thousand tonnes

By source category (UNECE/CORINAIR94)		Percentage of total in 1999	1970	1980	1990	1991	1992	1993	1994	1995	1996	1997	1998	1999
Power stations	JZGB	21	812	861	781	683	671	568	527	495	449	372	365	338
Refineries	JZGC	2	43	42	40	41	38	35	34	33	33	33	37	29
Combustion in fuel extraction and transformation	JZGD	3	62	45	63	65	65	67	77	50	48	48	52	55
Domestic	JZGE	4	62	64	64	71	69	72	69	66	75	69	71	71
Commercial, public and agricultural combustion	JZGF	2	74	46	37	40	39	38	38	37	39	35	34	32
Iron and steel	JZGG	2	75	25	22	22	22	23	27	26	25	26	24	24
Other industrial combustion	JZGH	9	324	246	197	188	183	181	187	172	165	166	159	145
Production processes	JZGI	-	16	15	13	11	10	10	9	6	6	6	6	6
Extraction and distribution of fossil fuels	GQRZ	-	–	–	1	1	1	–	1	1	1	1	1	1
Road transport	JZGJ	44	769	989	1 306	1 275	1 225	1 147	1 084	997	956	880	786	714
Off-road sources	GQSA	5	120	104	89	92	92	90	88	85	89	87	88	82
Military	GQSB	1	32	32	35	34	31	29	28	28	28	28	22	23
Railways	GQSC	1	25	15	13	13	15	14	13	15	15	12	12	12
Shipping	GQSD	3	62	66	72	75	72	71	66	64	69	66	62	56
Civil aircraft	GQSE	1	4	6	9	9	9	10	10	10	11	11	12	12
Waste treatment and disposal	JZGL	-	6	12	9	9	8	8	9	9	8	4	4	3
Agriculture and managed forestry	JZGM	-	10	15	9	8	6	–	–	–	–	–	–	–
Total	JZGO	100	2 497	2 585	2 761	2 636	2 557	2 363	2 265	2 092	2 017	1 846	1 735	1 605

Emissions from large combustion plants

| Large plants | ZBZM | | 946 | 962 | 852 | 749 | 742 | 636 | 572 | 524 | 471 | 371 | 369 | 333 |
| Index (1980=100) | ZBZN | | 98 | 100 | 89 | 78 | 77 | 66 | 60 | 54 | 49 | 39 | 38 | 35 |

Sources: National Environmental Technology Centre;
for Department for Environment, Food and Rural Affairs 020 7944 6497

13.6 Estimated emissions[1] of carbon monoxide (CO) by source
United Kingdom

Thousand tonnes

By source category (UNECE/CORINAIR94)		Percentage of total in 1999	1970	1980	1990	1991	1992	1993	1994	1995	1996	1997	1998	1999
Power stations	JZGP	1	117	121	114	113	110	100	106	104	102	71	73	61
Refineries	GFVW	-	7	7	6	7	7	7	7	7	7	7	8	7
Combustion in fuel extraction and transformation	JZGQ	1	45	24	22	22	20	20	20	22	23	23	26	27
Domestic	JZGR	5	1 251	622	358	382	347	369	324	260	268	246	239	252
Commercial, public and agricultural combustion	JZGS	-	46	26	22	22	21	21	20	19	19	19	18	18
Iron and steel	GFVX	2	220	63	108	102	106	105	97	98	98	100	102	105
Other industrial combustion	GFVY	1	142	82	79	75	75	74	76	72	65	66	55	68
Production processes	GFVZ	10	367	283	442	425	410	414	431	440	455	463	470	476
Extraction and distribution of fossil fuels	GPWA	-	2	2	7	3	3	2	3	3	3	3	3	1
Road transport	GPWB	69	5 427	5 378	5 235	5 072	4 855	4 525	4 268	4 003	3 961	3 726	3 507	3 293
Off-road sources	GPWC	9	584	512	428	445	453	439	428	407	408	407	407	406
Military	GPWD	-	11	11	13	11	10	10	10	10	10	9	8	8
Railways	GPWE	-	9	6	4	4	5	4	4	4	4	3	3	3
Shipping	GPWF	-	8	9	9	10	9	9	9	8	9	9	8	7
Civil aircraft	GPWG	-	4	6	9	9	9	10	10	10	11	12	12	13
Waste treatment and disposal	GPWH	-	3	45	31	28	27	27	35	25	25	20	21	17
Agriculture and managed forestry	JZGY	-	288	449	266	228	165	4	–	–	–	–	–	–
Total	JZHA	100	8 531	7 647	7 155	6 956	6 633	6 140	5 847	5 492	5 468	5 184	4 960	4 760

Sources: National Environmental Technology Centre;
for Department for Environment, Food and Rural Affairs 020 7944 6497

13.7 Estimated emissions of volatile organic compounds[1] by source
United Kingdom

Thousand tonnes

By source category (UNECE/CORINAIR94)		Percentage of total in 1999	1970	1980	1990	1991	1992	1993	1994	1995	1996	1997	1998	1999
Power stations	JZHB	-	7	8	7	7	7	7	8	8	9	8	6	8
Refineries	GQJF	-	1	1	1	1	1	1	1	1	1	1	1	1
Combustion in fuel extraction and transformation	GQJG	-	2	2	2	2	3	3	3	1	1	1	1	1
Domestic	JZHC	2	293	129	64	67	61	61	48	37	40	37	38	42
Commercial, public and agricultural combustion	GQJH	-	4	3	3	4	4	4	4	4	4	4	4	4
Iron and steel	GQJI	-	2	1	1	1	1	1	1	1	1	1	1	1
Other industrial combustion	GQJK	-	6	6	5	5	4	4	5	5	5	5	5	5
Production processes	GQJL	12	282	298	329	321	320	310	303	308	295	274	252	212
Extraction and distribution of fossil fuels	GQJM	15	74	220	315	321	311	312	332	322	336	336	304	259
Solvent use	GQJN	27	593	581	684	648	608	597	597	562	543	528	510	472
Road transport[2]	JZHG	27	636	760	922	901	865	803	750	687	639	581	523	473
Off-road sources	GQJO	3	70	64	58	59	59	58	58	56	57	56	57	56
Military	GQJP	-	2	2	2	2	2	2	2	2	2	2	1	1
Railways	GQJQ	-	4	3	2	2	2	2	2	2	2	2	2	2
Shipping	GQJR	-	2	2	3	3	3	3	2	2	3	2	2	2
Civil aircraft	GQJJ	-	1	1	2	2	2	2	2	2	2	2	3	3
Waste treatment and disposal	JZHI	1	10	56	43	40	38	38	45	37	36	31	29	24
Agriculture and managed forestry	JZHJ	-	37	58	35	30	22	–	–	–	–	–	–	–
Forests[3]	JZHK	10	178	178	178	178	178	178	178	178	178	178	178	178
Total	JZHM	100	2 203	2 373	2 657	2 592	2 491	2 387	2 340	2 215	2 152	2 050	1 917	1 744

1 Excluding methane.
2 Includes evaporative emissions from the petrol tank and carburettor of petrol-engined vehicles.
3 An order of magnitude estimate of natural emissions from managed and unmanaged forests.

Sources: National Environmental Technology Centre; for Department for Environment, Food and Rural Affairs 020 7944 6497

13.8 Water industry expenditure
England and Wales

£ millions

		1990 /91	1991 /92	1992 /93	1993 /94	1994 /95	1995 /96	1996 /97	1997 /98	1998 /99	1999 /00	2000 /01
Operating expenditure												
Water supply	KQQX	2 377.4	1 953.8	2 024.4	2 108.0	2 209.0	2 347.0	2 304.2	2 331.0	2 386.1	2 426.8	2 403.3
Sewerage services	KQQY	1 963.1	1 580.9	1 635.4	1 757.9	1 755.0	1 763.0	1 780.7	1 856.1	1 971.4	2 069.9	2 087.6
Capital expenditure												
Water supply	KQSX	986.4	1 307.0	1 358.2	1 386.7	1 081.0	1 074.5	1 314.3	1 467.2	1 294.1	1 290.0	935.0
Sewerage	KQSY	475.8	559.0	455.3	410.7	381.0	375.6	479.9	455.2	507.5	488.5	352.0
Sewage treatment and disposal	KQSZ	759.2	968.0	906.0	735.3	763.0	773.0	959.4	1 296.3	1 374.5	1 440.8	1 040.9

Source: Office of Water Services: 0121 625 1312

13.9 Chemical quality of rivers and canals[1]

| | | Length[2] in km | | | | | | | Percentage of total | |
| | | Good | | Fair | | | | | | |
	Years	A	B	C	D	Poor E	Bad F	Total	Good or fair	Poor or bad
England and Wales, Northern Ireland										
Environment Agency Regions										
North West	1988-90	720	620	560	440	650	210	3 190	73	27
	1997-99	2 030	1 470	1 050	610	530	50	5 750	90	10
North East	1988-90	850	1 620	550	450	610	170	4 250	82	18
	1997-99	1 680	2 420	940	610	500	80	6 220	91	9
Midlands	1988-90	450	1 510	1 610	990	1000	130	5 700	80	20
	1997-99	930	2 700	1 840	590	570	40	6 670	91	9
Anglian	1988-90	40	760	1 690	1 190	790	100	4 560	81	19
	1997-99	320	1 290	1 630	870	660	30	4 810	86	14
Thames	1988-90	320	980	1 050	580	560	50	3 530	83	17
	1997-99	590	1 390	860	580	360	20	3 790	90	10
Southern	1988-90	240	710	670	290	240	30	2 180	88	12
	1997-99	370	890	530	210	190	-	2 200	91	9
South West	1988-90	1 640	2 670	1 240	740	360	70	6 720	94	6
	1997-99	2 400	2 480	850	130	190	-	6 040	97	3
Welsh	1988-90	1 780	1 410	430	230	130	40	4 020	96	4
	1997-99	3 440	1 200	240	100	60	10	5 040	99	1
England and Wales	1988-90	6 040	10 290	7 800	4 910	4 330	800	34 160	85	15
	1997-99	11 770	13 840	7 940	3 690	3 060	240	40 530	92	8
Northern Ireland[3]	1989-91	100	640	680	170	60	20	1 680	95	5
	1997-99	200	1 170	680	270	100	10	2 430	96	4

| | | Length[2] in km | | | | | Percentage of total | |
	Year	Unpolluted	Fairly good	Poor	Grossly polluted	Total	Unpolluted or fairly good	Poor or grossly polluted
Scotland								
Former River Purification Board								
Highland	1990	14 020	50	10	-	14 070	100	-
	1995	13 780	20	10	10	13 830	100	-
North East	1990	8 620	50	10	-	8 680	100	-
	1995	8 620	40	-	-	8 660	100	-
Tay	1990	6 230	60	-	-	6 290	100	-
	1995	6 110	30	-	-	6 150	100	-
Forth	1990	2 930	340	150	40	3 470	94	6
	1995	2 830	350	130	30	3 350	95	5
Tweed	1990	2 780	10	-	-	2 790	100	-
	1995	2 750	30	-	-	2 770	100	-
Solway	1990	4 890	70	10	10	4 980	100	-
	1995	4 940	20	-	-	4 960	100	-
Clyde	1990	9 990	630	60	20	10 690	99	1
	1995	9 860	590	70	10	10 530	99	1
Scotland	1990	49 450	1 200	240	70	50 960	99	1
	1995	48 890	1 090	220	60	50 260	99	1

1 Based on the GQA chemical classification system.
2 Lengths are rounded to the nearest 10km and may not sum to totals. Scottish figures for 1990 and 1995 include lengths of rivers on islands which were not included in previous surveys.
3 No canals classified in Northern Ireland.

Sources: Environment Agency;
Environment and Heritage Service;
Scottish Executive

13.10 Biological water quality of rivers and canals[1]

| | | Length[2] in km | | | | | | | Percentage of total | |
| | | Good | | Fair | | | | | | |
	Year	A	B	C	D	Poor E	Bad F	Total	Good or fair	Poor or bad
England and Wales, Northern Ireland										
Environment Agency Regions										
North West	1990	430	1 070	690	330	620	880	4 020	63	37
	1995	960	1 530	900	500	810	260	4 970	78	22
North East	1990	1 340	1 170	520	410	380	310	4 130	83	17
	1995	2 260	1 200	730	520	480	270	5 460	86	14
Midlands	1990	330	810	1 210	770	470	220	3 810	82	18
	1995	970	1 680	1 790	920	360	120	5 840	92	8
Anglian	1990	470	1 420	1 520	480	210	70	4 170	93	7
	1995	1 050	2 020	1 170	350	120	20	4 730	97	3
Thames	1990	720	1 000	690	350	240	110	3 090	89	11
	1995	1 130	1 120	790	350	160	20	3 570	95	5
Southern	1990	400	450	400	130	30	10	1 420	97	3
	1995	980	720	300	160	30	-	2 190	98	2
South West	1990	2 140	2 110	830	220	150	90	5 550	96	4
	1995	3 330	1 900	530	100	50	20	5 940	99	1
Welsh	1990	1 400	1 440	610	240	100	20	3 810	97	3
	1995	2 320	1 680	680	150	30	-	4 860	99	1
England and Wales	1990	7 210	9 480	6 470	2 940	2 200	1 710	30 000	87	13
	1995	13 000	11 860	6 890	3 040	2 040	720	37 560	93	7
Northern Ireland[3]	1991	710	950	410	100	10	-	2 190	100	-
	1995	850	910	440	120	10	-	2 330	100	-
	1999	1 130	2 020	1 100	690	110	10	5 060	98	2

| | | Length[2] in km of rivers and canals biologically classified | | | | | Percentage of total | |
	Year	Good A	Moderate B	Poor C	Very poor D	Total	Good or moderate	Poor or very poor
Scotland[4]								
Former River Purification Board								
Highland	1990	2 010	470	-	-	2 480	100	-
	1995	2 730	70	-	-	2 800	100	-
North East	1990	1 540	420	70	30	2 050	95	5
	1995	2 190	30	40	20	2 270	97	3
Tay	1990	1 240	160	20	-	1 420	98	2
	1995	2 870	130	40	10	3 060	98	2
Forth	1990	680	240	60	40	1 030	90	10
	1995	1 320	390	120	50	1 880	91	9
Tweed	1990	730	100	20	-	840	98	2
	1995	1 350	60	-	-	1 410	100	-
Solway	1990	1 070	130	10	-	1 210	99	1
	1995	1 540	40	10	-	1 590	99	1
Clyde	1990	1 260	460	60	70	1 850	93	7
	1995	2 970	640	60	30	3 700	97	3
Scotland	1990	8 530	1 960	230	140	10 870	97	3
	1995	14 960	1 360	280	110	16 710	98	2

1 Based on the new GQA biological classification system. Figures for 1990 and 1995 are not directly comparable.
2 Lengths are rounded to the nearest 10km and may not sum to totals.
3 No canals are classified in Northern Ireland. The length of monitored rivers more than doubled in 1999.
4 The Scottish biological survey covered about 21 per cent of the freshwaters covered by the chemical classification system.

Sources: Environment Agency;
Environment and Heritage Service;
Scottish Executive

13.11 Water pollution incidents and prosecutions
United Kingdom

		Incidents reported									Incidents substantiated					
		1992	1993	1994	1995	1996	1997	1998	1999		1994	1995	1996	1997	1998	1999
Water region																
North West	JZHN	4 206	4 842	4 776	5 014	4 000	3 433	3 839	6 274	JZIA	3 532	3 717	2 818	2 160	2 201	1 828
North East	JZHO	4 048	4 715	4 761	4 364	4 060	3 955	3 284	3 103	JZIB	3 243	2 576	2 143	2 404	1 993	1 668
Midlands	JZHP	6 301	6 689	6 633	6 310	5 953	5 848	5 376	6 567	JZKR	4 895	4 259	4 305	4 411	4 061	2 806
Anglian	JZHQ	3 369	3 504	3 693	3 416	3 318	3 246	2 945	3 838	JZKS	2 819	2 156	2 417	2 411	2 163	1 724
Thames	JZHR	3 595	3 538	3 763	3 977	3 782	3 525	3 257	3 539	JZKT	2 006	1 972	1 959	1 917	1 819	1 210
Southern	JZHS	1 578	1 853	1 719	2 389	2 507	2 357	2 594	3 303	JZKU	1 316	1 235	1 189	1 174	1 138	1 317
South West	JZHT	4 890	5 142	5 508	5 975	5 273	5 101	4 641	6 017	JZKV	4 340	4 558	3 042	2 847	2 603	2 461
Welsh	JZHU	3 686	4 013	4 438	4 445	3 516	3 234	2 734	4 025	JZKW	3 264	2 990	2 285	2 247	1 885	1 359
England and Wales	JZHV	31 673	34 296	35 291	35 890	32 409	30 699	28 670	36 666	JZKX	25 415	23 463	20 158	19 571	17 863	14 373
Scotland[1]	JZHW	..	..	..	..	..	..	..	..	JZKY	3 170	2 752	2 878	3 356	2 329	2 306
Northern Ireland	JZHX	1 845	1 877	2 216	2 380	2 880	2 681	2 508	2 415	JZKZ	..	..	2 063	1 824	1 644	1 510

1 Data for all years refer to financial years.

Sources: Environment Agency;
Scottish Environment Protection Agency;
Environment and Heritage Service

13.12 Estimated abstractions from all surface and groundwater sources by purpose
England and Wales

Megalitres per day

		1989	1990	1991	1992	1993	1994	1995	1996	1997	1998	1999
Public water supply	JZLA	18 205	18 337	17 562	17 953	16 651	16 735	17 346	17 453	16 820	16 765	16 255
Spray irrigation	JZLB	298	377	366	269	164	283	352	369	292	282	325
Agriculture (excl spray irrigation)	JZLC	115	128	131	129	139	115	103	136	108	111	142
Electricity supply industry[1]	JZLD	33 302	30 768	30 359	37 693	26 581	27 732	25 805	31 294	33 307	34 587	26 515
Other industry	JZLE	8 854	9 275	5 469	5 326	6 017	4 292	7 513	4 960	4 352	4 964	5 428
Mineral washing	JZLF	..	..	173	213	198	222	262	250	297	223	..
Fish farming, cress growing, amenity ponds	JYXG	1 111	1 323	3 882	4 479	3 818	3 985	4 268	4 338	4 211	5 495	4 867
Private water supply	JZLG	..	..	..	53	81	82	98	171	162	175	91
Other	JZLH	..	..	1 254	1 794	93	194	223	531	408	289	526
Total	JZLI	61 885	60 208	59 196	67 909	53 742	53 640	55 970	59 503	59 957	62 891	54 148

1 In South West region in 1991 and 1992, Hydroelectric licences were classified as "Other", in 1993 they were classified as "Other industry" and from
1994 they were classified correctly as "Electricity supply".

Source: Environment Agency

13.13 Bathing water surveys
United Kingdom

		Compliance with EC Bathing Water Directive coliform standards during the bathing season													Percentage complying
		Identified bathing waters						Numbers complying							
		1997	1998	1999	2000	2001		1997	1998	1999	2000	2001			2001
Environment Agency Regions															
United Kingdom	GPKA	486	496	535	545	546	GPKN	429	440	489	514	520	GPLA		95
North East	GPKB	56	56	55	56	55	GPKO	51	47	52	51	55	GPLB		100
North West	GPKC	34	34	34	34	34	GPKP	17	21	23	28	30	GPLC		88
Anglian	GPKE	35	36	36	37	37	GPKR	35	36	34	37	36	GPLE		97
Thames	GPKF	3	3	3	3	5	GPKS	3	3	3	3	5	GPLF		100
Southern	GPKG	75	77	79	79	79	GPKT	67	75	74	77	78	GPLG		99
South West	GPKH	180	183	184	187	187	GPKU	164	167	167	179	184	GPLH		98
England	GPKI	383	389	391	396	397	GPKV	337	349	353	375	388	GPLI		98
Wales	GPKJ	64	68	70	75	75	GPKW	60	64	69	74	70	GPLJ		93
Scotland	GPKL	23	23	58	58	58	GPKY	18	12	51	49	49	GPLL		84
Northern Ireland	GPKM	16	16	16	16	16	GPKZ	14	15	16	16	13	GPLM		81

Sources: Environment Agency;
Scottish Environment Protection Agency;
Environment and Heritage Service, Northern Ireland

13.14 Radioactive waste stocks and arisings
Great Britain

m³

	Stocks						
	1/1/1986	1/1/1987	1/1/1988	1/1/1989	1/1/1991	1/4/1994	1/4/1998
High level waste							
As stored	1 351	1 430	1 463	1 575	1 686	1 639	1 804
Conditioned	436	517	594	674	681	653	717
Intermediate level waste							
As stored	41 887	43 602	47 783	45 313	51 558	61 494	70 948
Conditioned	56 211	59 479	66 020	81 762	78 512	66 102	74 131
Low level waste							
As stored	2 429	2 343	1 002	13 752	6 252	7 882	7 983

Source: Electrowatt Engineering Services (UK) Ltd

13.15 Noise complaints received by Environmental Health Officers

Number per million people

		1986 /87	1987 /88	1988 /89	1989 /90	1990 /91	1991 /92	1992 /93	1993 /94	1994 /95	1995 /96	1996 /97	1997 /98	1998 /99	1999 /00
England and Wales															
Not controlled by the Act:															
Road traffic	JZLJ	41	41	42	47	46	65	59	59	60	66	62	52	39	38
Aircraft	JZLK	19	20	47	48	34	72	73	64	111	48	58	92	109	121
Other	JZLL	54	48	35	59	60	99	105	84	91	90	74	229	..	..
Total	JZLM	114	109	124	154	140	236	237	207	262	204	194	373	..	..
Controlled by the Act:															
Industrial/commercial premises	JZLN	654	670	713	811	913	1 037	1 108	1 120	1 320	1 466	1 455	1 647	1 280	1 368
Road works, construction and demolition	JZLO	153	196	233	180	252	148	191	168	300	229	242	285	248	292
Domestic premises	JZLP	1 269	1 579	1 620	1 855	2 264	2 627	3 137	3 468	3 949	4 895	5 051	5 050	4 330	5 149
Vehicles, machinery & equipment in streets	JZLQ	..	..	..	..	..	..	..	..	249	225	206	300	252	269
Total	JZLR	2 076	2 445	2 566	2 846	3 429	3 812	4 436	4 756	5 818	6 815	6 954	7 282	6 110	7 078
Controlled by Section 62 of the Act:															
Noise in streets	JZLS	55	52	69	60	75	100	76	92	89	109	111	..	..	..
Total complaints received	JZLT	2 245	2 606	2 759	3 060	3 644	4 148	4 749	5 055	6 169	7 128	7 259	..	..	..

		1986	1987	1988	1989	1990	1991	1992[1] /93	1993 /94	1994 /95	1995 /96	1996 /97	1997 /98	1998 /99	1999 /00
Scotland															
Not controlled by the Act:															
Road traffic	JZLU	28	32	36	39	54	51	35	..	..	..	24	21	..	..
Aircraft	JZLV	4	4	5	7	17	8	14	..	..	..	14	7	..	..
Other	JZLW	6	4	6	7	87	128	172	..	..	..	304	229	..	..
Total	JZLX	38	40	47	53	158	187	221	..	..	..	342	257	..	..
Controlled by the Act:															
Industrial/commercial premises	JZLY	437	411	436	501	537	519	560	..	..	..	845	504	..	..
Road works, construction and demolition	JZLZ	90	85	100	129	162	177	89	..	..	..	206	177	..	..
Domestic premises	JYWN	169	202	148	161	210	302	431	..	..	..	754	787	..	..
Vehicles, machinery & equipment in streets	JYXH	..	..	..	..	..	..	..	..	..	..	12	41	..	..
Total	JYWO	696	698	684	791	909	998	1 080	..	..	..	1 817	1 509	..	..
Controlled by Section 62 of the Act:															
Noise in streets	JYXI	32	27	23	24	25	61	33	..	..	..	27	22	..	..
Total complaints received	JYWP	766	765	754	868	1 092	1 246	1 334	..	..	..	2 186	1 788	..	..

1 1992/93 figures cover a period of 15 months from January 1992 to March 1993 due to the change from calendar year to financial year in order to come into line with England and Wales.

Sources: The Chartered Institute of Environmental Health; Royal Environmental Health Institute of Scotland

13.16 Estimated total annual waste arisings by sector
United Kingdom

Sector	Annual arisings (million tonnes)	Date of estimate	Status[1]	Source	Percentage of total arisings
Agriculture	87	1999	NC	DEFRA	20
Minerals (Mining and quarrying)[2]					
Colliery[2]	15	1997	NC	DTLR	4
Coal[2]	9	1997	NC	DTLR	2
China clay[2]	26	1997	NC	DTLR	6
Clay[2]	14	1997	NC	DTLR	3
Slate[2]	7	1997	NC	DTLR	2
Quarrying[2]	47	1997	NC	DTLR	11
Sewage sludge	1	1998/89	C	Water UK[3]	-
Dredged material	41	1997	C	DEFRA	10
Municipal waste	30	1999/00	C	DEFRA	7
of which household	29	1999/00	C	DEFRA	6
Commercial	25	1998/99	C	EA	6
Industrial	50	1998/99	C	EA	12
Demolition and construction	72	2000	C	EA	17
Total	428				100

1 NC = Not classed as a controlled waste under the terms of the Environmental Protection Act (Controlled Waste Regulations) 1992; C = controlled wastes under the terms of the Environmental Protection Act (Controlled Waste Regulation) 1992.

2 1997 estimate used, as 1998 estimate is still provisional.
3 Formerly Water Services Association and Water Companies Association.

Sources: Department for Environment, Food and Rural Affairs 020 7944 6497; Environment Agency; Water UK

13.17 Recycling[1] of selected materials
United Kingdom

Scrap reused as a percentage of consumption

		1985	1986	1987	1988	1989	1990	1991	1992	1993	1994	1995	1996	1997	1998
Ferrous	JYWQ	39	36	38	34	36	38	36	45	42	42	40	44	45	35
Aluminium	JYWR	40	34	34	41	44	39	41	39	29	39	53	44	40	43
Copper	JYWS	43	44	47	49	49	50	49	35	35	32	34	36	37	38
Lead	JYWT	69	66	77	73	71	67	62	64	67	74	71	73	69	66
Zinc	JYWU	22	24	24	24	23	24	24	21	21	20	20	19	19	18
Paper & board	JYWV	28	27	27	27	28	32	34	34	32	34	37	38	38	38
Newsprint	GEKY	..	..	..	..	..	26	26	31	31	33	35	44	47	52
Glass cullet	JYWW	9	..	10	11	12	15	17	20	22	22	22	22	21	22
Plastics	ZBZJ	..	..	..	..	..	..	2	2	2	2	3	3	3	3

1 The ratios shown reflect the amount of secondary material used (scrap collected less exported scrap plus imported scrap) in the UK in a year as a proportion of consumption in that year.

Sources: Iron and Steel Statistics Bureau; Aluminium Federation; Customs and Excise; World Bureau of Metal Statistics; British Paper and Board Industry Federation; The Paper Federation of Great Britain; British Glass Manufacturers Confederation; British Plastics Federation

13.18 Designated areas

	National Parks		Areas of Outstanding Natural Beauty[1]		Green Belt Land		Defined Heritage Coasts length (km)
	Area (thousand hectares)	Percentage of total area in region	Area (thousand hectares)	Percentage of total area in region	Area (thousand hectares)	Percentage of total area in region	
North East	111	13	147	17	53	6	138
North West	261	18	157	11	252	18	6
Yorkshire and the Humber	315	21	92	6	264	17	80
East Midlands	92	6	52	3	80	5	-
West Midlands	20	2	127	10	267	21	-
East	30	2	112	6	237	12	121
London	-	-	-	-	36	22	-
South East	-	-	641	31	356	19	74
South West	165	7	712	30	106	4	638
England	994	7	2 040	16	1 650	13	1 057
Wales	413	20	83	4	-	-	496
Scotland	-	-	1 002	13	155	2	-
Northern Ireland	-	-	285	20	227	16	-

1 The South East includes London.

Source: Department for Environment, Food and Rural Affairs 020 7944 6497

13.19 Stock of dwellings: Estimated annual gains and losses
England

Thousands of dwellings

		1991 /92	1992 /93	1993 /94	1994 /95	1995 /96	1996 /97	1997 /98	1998 /99	1999 /00	2000 /01
Dwelling stock at start of financial year	GRWM	19 671	19 829	19 974	20 120	20 279	20 435	20 582	20 372	20 870	21 008
Gains to dwelling stock:											
Housebuilding completions	GRWN	155.1	142.5	147.7	158.0	154.6	145.9	149.6	138.6	141.8	134.7
Conversions (net gain)[1]	GRWO	12.0	8.3	7.5	9.9	8.9	8.6	2.8	3.2	2.6	2.3
Change of use	GRWP	..	..	..	..	..	..	11.6	11.3	9.4	7.6
Non-permanent dwellings additions	GRWQ	..	..	..	..	..	..	0.2	0.2	0.3	0.2
Losses from dwelling stock:											
Slum clearance (non LA owned dwelling demolished)	GRWR	2.2	2.0	3.9	3.0	2.7	2.9	1.3	1.3	1.3	1.7
Other demolitions[1]	GRWS	6.9	4.3	5.2	5.8	4.8	4.1	12.8	12.3	13.9	16.2
Change of use	GRWT	..	..	..	..	..	..	0.7	1.1	0.5	0.5
Non-permanent dwelling losses	GRWU	..	..	..	..	..	..	0.1	0.2	0.1	0.2
New gain in year	GRWV	158.0	144.5	146.2	159.0	156.0	147.4	149.3	138.5	138.1	126.1
Dwelling stock at end of financial year	GRWW	19 829	19 974	20 120	20 279	20 435	20 582	20 372	20 870	21 008	21 134

1 Figures prior to 1997/98 include change of use, and zero for net non-permanent dwellings.

Source: Department for Transport, Local Government and the Regions: 0117 372 8055

13.20 Renovations
Great Britain

Number of dwellings

		1989	1990	1991	1992	1993	1994	1995	1996	1997[1,2]	1998[2,3]	1999[4,5]
England												
Local authorities and new towns	KGBA	238 957	231 558	179 584	171 202	244 582	297 613	311 640	321 802	..	..	..
Housing associations[6]	KGBB	13 024	10 657	6 425	7 532	6 012	6 881	..	..	..	..	..
Private owners: grants paid[7]	KGBC	89 686	90 864	84 696	82 866	80 734	91 233	93 090	95 230	83 045	94 148	108 575
Wales												
Local authorities	KGBE	8 444	10 843	10 513	9 491	23 264	20 397	16 665	4 705	..	..	..
Housing associations[6]	KGBF	812	399	305	322	300	287	163	147	131	275	..
Private owners: grants paid[7]	KGBG	20 074	26 522	21 228	16 642	16 061	14 619	17 314	17 345	17 030	18 287	15 590
Scotland												
Local authorities and new towns[8]	KGBI	52 549	84 261	70 361	80 753	90 519	117 497	75 845	..	..	..	..
Housing associations[6]	KGBJ	1 122	816	1 680	1 785	1 524	1 229	1 328	767	337	..	..
Private owners: grants paid[7]	KGBK	26 915	23 586	23 478	37 934	21 194	19 697	19 027	15 800	13 585	12 711	12 048
Great Britain												
Local authorities and new towns[8]	KGBM	299 950	326 662	260 458	261 446	358 365	435 507	404 150	..	..	..	..
Housing associations[6]	KGBN	14 958	11 872	8 410	9 639	7 836	8 397	..	..	..	..	..
Private owners: grants paid[7]	KGBO	136 675	140 972	129 402	137 442	117 989	125 549	129 431	128 375	113 660	125 146	136 213

1 Of the 100,075 grants paid in 1997 to private owners and tenants in England and Wales, 41,605 were paid under the Housing Grants, Construction and Regeneration Act 1996 and 58,470 were paid under the Local Government and Housing Act 1989.

2 Revised data.

3 Of the 112,435 grants paid in 1998 to private owners and tenants in England and Wales, 102,615 were paid under the Housing Grants, Construction and Housing Act 1996 and 9,820 were paid under the Local Government and Housing Act 1989.

4 Of the 124,165 grants paid in 1999 to private owners and tenants in England and Wales, 121,512 were paid under the Housing Grants, Construction and Regeneration Act 1996 and 2,653 were paid under the Local Government and Housing Act 1989.

5 Provisional data.

6 Figures for England are of work completed funded by the Housing Corporation and Local Authorities. Figures for Wales are for work completed by the Housing Corporation funded by housing associations only. Figures for Scotland are of work approved under specific housing association legislation. Figures from Scottish Homes not available for 1991.

7 Including grants paid to housing associations under private owner grant legislation. Figures include a small number of grants to tenants in both public and private sectors. Figures for 1999 are provisional.

8 Work approved in Scotland.

Sources: Department for Transport, Local Government and the Regions: 0117 372 8055;
Scottish Executive;
National Assembly for Wales

13.21 Permanent dwellings completed

Numbers

	United Kingdom				England and Wales			
	All dwellings	Local authorities[1]	Private enterprise	Registered Social Landlords[2]	All dwellings	Local authorities[1]	Private enterprise	Registered Social Landlords[2]
	KAAD	KAAE	KAAF	KAAG	KAAH	KAAI	KAAJ	KAAK
1976	324 836	146 444	155 296	23 096	278 727	125 565	138 544	14 618
1977	314 160	139 537	143 972	30 651	276 078	122 742	128 755	24 581
1978	288 689	110 165	152 233	26 291	254 068	97 779	134 645	21 644
1979	251 823	86 316	144 121	21 386	220 788	78 125	125 372	17 291
1980	241 999	88 534	131 989	21 476	214 934	78 539	116 179	20 216
1981	206 632	68 340	118 590	19 702	179 794	58 419	104 012	17 363
1982	182 853	40 091	129 022	13 740	159 407	33 544	113 893	11 970
1983	209 026	39 169	153 038	16 819	181 399	31 633	134 901	14 865
1984	220 492	37 632	165 574	17 286	191 190	31 397	145 282	14 511
1985	207 465	30 420	163 395	13 650	178 284	24 359	142 020	11 905
1986	216 592	25 416	178 017	13 159	187 758	20 535	156 065	11 158
1987	226 234	21 833	191 250	13 151	198 732	17 435	169 895	11 402
1988	242 359	21 448	207 423	13 488	214 156	16 921	185 733	11 502
1989	221 463	19 323	187 542	14 598	190 990	15 332	163 344	12 314
1989/90	215 426	19 297	181 618	14 511	185 223	15 512	157 191	12 520
1990/91	198 074	16 550	162 182	19 342	171 031	13 425	141 166	16 440
1991/92	191 825	10 027	160 664	21 134	165 553	7 447	139 583	18 523
1992/93	178 914	4 432	144 367	30 115	152 451	2 705	123 045	26 701
1993/94	185 960	3 611	145 914	36 435	157 813	1 726	122 779	33 308
1994/95	197 169	2 970	156 547	37 652	168 301	997	133 002	34 302
1995/96	198 126	3 045	156 607	38 474	164 581	954	130 891	32 736
1996/97	185 297	1 538	152 929	30 830	155 945	474	128 388	27 083
1997/98	190 748	1 519	160 675	28 554	157 987	325	134 327	23 335
1998/99	176 592	881	152 809	22 902	146 367	223	125 955	20 189
1999/00	184 706	361	159 941	24 404	150 461	102	132 150	18 209
2000/01	179 160	915	153 633	24 612	143 072	764	124 126	18 182

	Scotland				Northern Ireland			
	All dwellings	Local authorities[1]	Private enterprise	Registered Social Landlords[2]	All dwellings	Local authorities[1]	Private enterprise	Registered Social Landlords[2]
	KAAL	KAAM	KAAN	KAAO	KAAP	KAAQ	KAAR	KAAS
1976	36 527	14 361	13 704	8 462	9 582	6 518	3 048	16
1977	27 320	9 119	12 132	6 069	10 762	7 676	3 085	1
1978	25 778	6 705	14 443	4 630	8 843	5 681	3 145	17
1979	23 782	4 755	15 175	3 852	7 253	3 436	3 574	243
1980	20 611	7 488	12 242	881	6 454	2 507	3 568	379
1981	20 011	7 062	11 021	1 928	6 827	2 859	3 557	411
1982	16 423	3 733	11 523	1 167	7 023	2 814	3 606	603
1983	17 929	3 492	13 166	1 271	9 698	4 044	4 971	683
1984	18 838	2 647	14 115	2 076	10 464	3 588	6 177	699
1985	18 411	2 828	14 435	1 148	10 770	3 233	6 940	597
1986	18 637	2 301	14 870	1 466	10 197	2 580	7 082	535
1987	17 707	2 634	13 904	1 169	9 795	1 764	7 451	580
1988	18 272	2 815	14 179	1 278	9 931	1 712	7 511	708
1989	20 190	2 283	16 287	1 620	10 283	1 708	7 911	664
1989/90	20 609	2 236	16 884	1 489	9 594	1 549	7 543	502
1990/91	19 457	1 801	15 305	2 351	7 586	1 324	5 711	551
1991/92	18 956	1 619	15 528	1 809	7 316	961	5 553	802
1992/93	18 902	778	15 563	2 561	7 561	949	5 759	853
1993/94	20 985	997	17 407	2 581	7 162	888	5 728	546
1994/95	22 136	1 095	18 195	2 846	6 732	878	5 350	504
1995/96	24 360	729	18 934	4 697	9 185	1 362	6 782	1 041
1996/97	20 472	241	17 268	2 963	8 880	823	7 273	784
1997/98	22 580	114	17 977	4 489	10 181	1 080	8 371	730
1998/99	20 587	120	18 714	1 753	9 638	538	8 140	960
1999/00	23 846	69	18 674	5 103	10 399	190	9 117	1 092
2000/01	24 420	107	18 995	5 318	11 668	44	10 512	1 112

1 Including the Commission for the New Towns Development Corporations, the Scottish Special Housing Association, the Northern Ireland Housing Executive.

2 Dwellings provided by housing associations other than the Scottish Special Housing Association and the Northern Ireland Housing Trust and provided or authorised by government departments for families of police, prison staff, the Armed forces and certain other services.

Sources: Department for Transport, Local Government and the Regions: 0117 372 8055; Scottish Executive; National Assembly for Wales; Department for Social Development, Northern Ireland

14 Transport and communications

Transport and communications

Road data (Tables 14.1, 14.5, 14.6 and 14.7)

Figures for 1999 and 2000 have been produced on a new basis and are not directly comparable with earlier figures. For time-series tables, the 1999 values are shown on both the original and the new basis. The reasons for the changes are described below.

In 2000/2001, steps were taken to improve the quality of DTLR's major road network database used in producing traffic estimates. This was done using a geographical information system (GIS), together with Ordnance Survey (OS) data. One result of this work was that it identified inconsistencies in the road length data supplied by local authorities. Preliminary checks showed that this was mainly due to the variety of methods used by them to calculate road lengths. However, local authorities have useful local knowledge of their roads, particularly recent changes to their classification. Therefore, once the network data had been compiled, it was sent to each local authority for final checking. In some instances, this led to discussions with Government Regional Offices and the Highways Agency in order to establish the correct, up-to-date classification of roads. The end result of this extensive work was a much-improved road network database for the whole of Great Britain. It was decided to use this GIS-based information, rather than data supplied by local authorities, for grossing-up average traffic flows, in order to produce traffic estimates.

The road network data was further refined by information collected by DTLR traffic count contractors on the location of relevant speed limit signs. This enabled DTLR to be more confident about the built-up and non built-up lengths of each section of road. The net result of both these improvements has been a reduction in the estimates of principal road traffic, particularly on built-up roads.

Furthermore, DTLR began a review of the expansion factors used to convert the occasional, 12-hour manual count data to estimates of annual average daily flows. Highways Agency data strongly suggested that the expansion factors for some motorways, particularly the busiest ones in the South East and Midlands regions, were too low. Temporary adjustments to the factors have been made and these adjustments have led to a general upward revision to 1999 and 2000 motorway traffic estimates. Further work will need to be done to refine these estimates over the coming year.

One final change to the figures is that the estimates of minor road lengths are also now based on OS data, rather than local authority returns. This has led to an upward revision of minor road lengths of about five per cent. It is believed that the increase in length is mainly due to the inclusion in the OS coding of public road lengths that are surfaced, but unadopted. It may also be due to OS's practice of measuring road lengths from the centre of one junction to the next junction, rather than purely that length that is wholly attributable to one road class. Overall the change is not thought to have much implication for the minor road traffic estimates and so the adjustments to the minor roads traffic estimates for 1999 and 2000 are minimal.

The net result of these improvements has been little change to the estimates of *total* motor vehicle traffic for Great Britain for 1999 and 2000, but some changes to the composition of the overall figure. In general, the new motorway traffic estimates are now higher than before, whilst those for other major roads are lower than before.

The new figures for 1999 and 2000 are already considerably more accurate than those produced for earlier years. In the time available, it has not been possible to consider the changes that ought to be made to estimates prior to 1999. However, adjustments to earlier years will be carefully considered over the coming year, once the review of expansion factors is complete and the 1999 and 2000 values are finalised. DTLR intend to publish a full set of figures on the new basis in their Annual Report next year.

14.1

Passenger transport[1]: by mode
Great Britain

	Road					Rail[3]	Air	All modes[4]
	Buses and coaches[2]	Cars, vans and taxis	Motor cycles	Pedal cycles	All road			
Billion passenger kilometres								
	KCTP	KCTQ	KCTR	KCTS	ZCBD	KCTN	KCTM	KCTT
1990	46	588	6	5	645	40	5.2	690
1991	44	582	6	5	637	39	4.8	681
1992	43	583	5	5	635	38	4.8	678
1993	44	584	4	4	636	37	5.1	678
1994	44	591	4	5	643	35	5.5	684
1995	44	596	4	4	648	37	5.9	691
1996	44	606	4	4	658	39	6.3	703
1997	44	614	4	4	666	42	6.8	715
1998	45	618	4	4	671	44	7.0	722
1999	45	617	5	4	671	46	7.3	725
	GRXK	GRXG	GRXH	GRXI	GRXJ			GRXM
1999	45	614	5	4	668	46	7.3	722
2000	45	613	5	4	666	47	7.6	721
Percentages								
	ZCBE	ZCBF	ZCBG	ZCBH	ZCBI	ZCBJ	ZCBK	ZCBL
1990	7	85	1	1	93	6	0.8	100
1991	6	86	1	1	94	6	0.7	100
1992	6	86	1	1	94	6	0.7	100
1993	6	86	1	1	94	5	0.8	100
1994	6	86	1	1	94	5	0.8	100
1995	6	86	1	1	94	5	0.9	100
1996	6	86	1	1	94	6	0.9	100
1997	6	86	1	1	93	6	0.9	100
1998	6	86	1	1	93	6	1.0	100
1999	6	85	1	1	93	6	1.0	100
	GRXN	GRXO	GRXP	GRXQ	GRXR			GRXU
1999	6	85	1	1	93	6	1.0	100
2000	6	85	1	1	92	7	1.1	100

1 Data for 1999 and 2000 have been produced on a new basis and are not directly comparable with earlier figures. 1999 values are shown on both the original and new basis.
2 Data for 2000 are provisional.
3 Financial years. Former British Rail companies and Urban Rail systems.
4 Excluding travel by water within the United Kingdom (including the Channel Islands), estimated at 0.7 billion passenger kilometres in 2000.

Source: Department for Transport, Local Government and the Regions

14.2 Trips per person per year by main mode[1] and purpose, 1998/2000
Great Britain

Numbers

	Walk	Bicycle	Car/van driver	Car/van passenger	Motor-cycle	Other private	Buses in London
Commuting	18	6	95	18	2	1	2
Business	3	-	26	2	-	-	-
Education	31	1	3	18	-	3	2
Escort education	22	-	19	6	-	-	-
Shopping	63	2	81	49	-	-	4
Other escort	9	-	47	22	-	-	-
Other personal business	28	1	43	23	-	1	1
Visiting friends at home	29	2	51	42	-	-	1
Visiting friends elsewhere	14	-	12	14	-	-	-
Social/entertainment	9	1	24	22	-	1	-
Holidays/day trips	2	2	10	12	-	1	-
Other, including just walk	44	-	1	-	-	-	-
All purposes	271	16	411	228	3	8	13

	Other local bus	Non-local bus	LT Under-ground	Surface rail	Taxi/minicab	Other public	All modes
Commuting	9	-	3	6	2	-	161
Business	-	-	-	1	-	-	36
Education	8	-	-	1	-	-	68
Escort education	-	-	-	-	-	-	48
Shopping	14	-	-	1	2	-	216
Other escort	1	-	-	-	-	-	80
Other personal business	4	-	-	-	1	-	103
Visiting friends at home	4	-	-	1	2	-	134
Visiting friends elsewhere	2	-	-	-	3	-	46
Social/entertainment	2	-	-	-	1	-	62
Holidays/day trips	-	-	-	-	-	-	29
Other, including just walk	-	-	-	-	-	-	46
All purposes	45	2	7	12	12	2	1 030

1 Main mode is that used for the longest part of the trip.

Source: Department for Transport, Local Government and the Regions 020 7944 3097

14.3 Retail Prices Index: real changes in the cost of transport and disposable income
Great Britain

Constant prices

Index 1974=100

	Petrol/oil	All motoring	Rail	Bus and coach fares	Disposable income
	ZCFV	ZCFW	ZCFX	ZCFY	ZCFZ
1975	109.5	104.3	109.1	104.8	100.7
1976	99.9	101.2	124.3	115.0	100.3
1977	92.5	99.9	125.0	114.1	98.3
1978	81.2	99.6	132.0	119.4	105.6
1979	94.1	104.0	128.7	118.3	111.5
1980	102.2	103.8	135.6	127.0	113.4
1981	108.5	103.9	138.5	125.6	112.8
1982	107.4	101.0	146.4	133.2	112.6
1983	109.8	103.3	148.5	134.6	115.3
1984	108.2	100.7	142.0	131.0	119.5
1985	108.5	99.4	142.3	128.9	123.6
1986	91.3	94.7	147.0	135.1	128.9
1987	88.4	96.3	148.3	137.3	133.6
1988	83.4	95.9	151.2	140.1	140.6
1989	82.9	93.9	153.1	140.1	146.7
1990	84.6	90.9	152.1	135.0	152.2
1991	85.9	92.3	158.7	145.5	154.5
1992	85.2	95.0	164.1	150.1	160.2
1993	90.5	97.6	172.9	154.3	165.1
1994	92.4	98.5	176.3	154.5	167.2
1995	93.9	97.0	178.0	154.9	171.6
1996	96.3	97.5	180.3	156.9	175.3
1997	102.7	99.6	178.9	157.5	181.9
1998	104.2	99.3	180.0	157.3	182.1
1999	111.3	100.2	183.8	160.6	188.6
2000	122.4	101.2	181.8	162.2	194.3

Source: Office for National Statistics

14.4 Domestic freight transport: by mode
Great Britain

		1990	1991[1]	1992	1993	1994	1995	1996	1997	1998	1999	2000
Goods moved (Billion tonnes kilometres)												
Petroleum products												
Road[2]	ZBZP	4.9	4.9	4.5	5.0	5.1	5.7	6.1	5.8	5.1	4.9	6.3
Rail	ZBZQ	2.1	2.0	2.0	1.9	1.8	1.8	..	..	1.6[4]	1.5	1.4
Water[3]	ZBZR	45.4	46.0	42.7	41.7	43.0	42.5	45.9	38.3	45.2	48.6	..
of which: coastwise	ZBZS	32.1	31.2	29.4	28.9	28.9	31.4	38.7	33.8	36.4	33.3	..
Pipeline	ZBZT	11.1	11.1	11.0	11.6	12.0	11.1	11.6	11.2	11.7	11.6	11.4
All modes	ZBZU	63.5	64.0	60.2	60.2	61.9	61.1	63.6[5]	55.3[5]	63.6	66.6	..
Coal and coke												
Road[2]	ZBZV	4.2	3.7	3.5	3.1	2.9	2.7	2.5	2.7	2.0	2.2	1.5
Rail	ZBZW	5.0	5.0	5.4	3.9	3.3	3.6	3.9	4.4	4.5[4]	4.8	4.8
Water[3]	ZBZX	1.4	1.8	1.8	1.5	1.4	2.3	0.6	0.6	0.5	0.5	..
All modes	ZBZY	10.6	10.5	10.7	8.5	7.6	8.6	6.9	7.7	7.0	7.5	..
Other traffic												
Road[2]	ZBZZ	127.2	121.4	118.5	126.4	135.7	141.2	145.3	148.6	152.4	149.6	150.2
Rail	ZCAA	8.9	8.3	8.1	7.9	7.9	7.9	11.2	12.5	11.2[4]	11.9	11.9
Water[3]	ZCAB	8.7	9.9	10.4	8.0	7.8	8.3	8.7	9.2	11.2	9.6	..
All modes	ZCAC	144.6	139.6	137.0	142.3	151.4	157.4	165.3	170.3	174.8	171.1	..
All traffic												
Road[2]	KCTA	136.3	130.0	126.5	134.5	143.7	149.6	153.9	157.1	159.5	156.7	158.0
Rail	KCTB	16.0	15.3	15.5	13.8	13.0	13.3	15.1	16.9	17.3[4]	18.2	18.1
Water[3]	ZCAD	55.7	57.7	54.9	51.2	52.2	53.1	55.3	48.1	56.9	58.7	..
Pipeline	KCTE	11.1	11.1	11.0	11.6	12.0	11.1	11.6	11.2	11.7	11.6	11.4
All modes	KCTF	218.9	214.1	207.9	211.1	220.9	227.1	235.9	233.3	245.4	245.2	..
Percentage of all traffic												
Road[2]	ZCAE	62	61	61	64	65	66	65	67	65	64	..
Rail	ZCAF	7	7	7	7	6	6	6	7	7[4]	7	..
Water[3]	ZCAG	25	27	26	24	24	23	23	21	23	24	..
Pipeline	ZCAH	5	5	5	5	5	5	5	5	5	5	..
All modes	ZCAI	100	100	100	100	100	100	100	100	100	100	..

		1990	1991[1]	1992	1993	1994	1995	1996	1997	1998	1999	2000
Goods lifted (Million tonnes)												
Petroleum products												
Road[2]	ZCAJ	74	73	63	67	68	71	75	73	61	61	74
Rail	ZCAK	10	10	10	9	8	6	..	..	..	..	..
Water[3]	ZCAL	68	67	66	64	70	72	71	69	76	72	..
of which: coastwise	ZCAM	44	44	43	42	43	47	54	52	55	52	..
Pipeline	ZCAN	121	105	106	125	161	168	157	148	153	155	151
All modes	ZCAO	273	255	245	265	307	317	303[5]	290[5]	290[5]	288[5]	..
Coal and coke												
Road[2]	ZCAP	62	57	55	48	42	34	32	37	22	28	22
Rail	ZCAQ	75	75	68	49	43	45	52	50	45	44	46
Water[3]	ZCAR	6	6	6	5	4	4	3	4	3	3	..
All modes	ZCAS	143	138	129	102	89	83	87	91	70	75	..
Other traffic												
Road[2]	ZCAT	1 613	1 470	1 437	1 500	1 579	1 596	1 623	1 630	1 646	1 572	1 593
Rail[6]	ZCAU	53	51	45	45	47	50	50	55	57	48[7]	50
Water[3]	ZCAV	78	71	68	65	66	67	67	69	70	70	..
All modes	ZCAW	1 744	1 592	1 550	1 610	1 692	1 713	1 740	1 754	1 773	1 690	..
All traffic												
Road[2]	KCTG	1 749	1 600	1 555	1 615	1 689	1 701	1 730	1 740	1 727	1 661	1 689
Rail	KCTH	138.2	135.8	122.4	103.2	97.3	100.7	101.8	105.4	102.1	91.6[7]	95.3
Water[3]	ZCAX	152	144	140	134	140	143	142	142	149	144	..
Pipeline	KCTK	121	105	106	125	161	168	157	148	153	155	151
All modes	KCTL	2 160	1 985	1 923	1 977	2 087	2 113	2 131	2 135	2 131	2 052	..
Percentage of all traffic												
Road[2]	ZCAY	81	81	81	82	81	80	81	81	81	81	..
Rail	ZCAZ	6	7	6	5	5	5	5	5	5	4[7]	..
Water[3]	ZCBA	7	7	7	7	7	7	7	7	7	7	..
Pipeline	ZCBB	6	5	6	6	8	8	7	7	7	8	..
All modes	ZCBC	100	100	100	100	100	100	100	100	100	100	..

1 Figures for rail from 1991 are for financial years.
2 All goods vehicles, including those under 3.5 tonnes gross vehicle weight. These estimates were revised following a survey in 1993.
3 Figures for water are for UK traffic.
4 Figures for goods moved by rail is a new series from 1998.
5 Excludes rail.
6 Figures for 1997, 1998 and 1999 include petroleum products.
7 Figures for goods lifted by rail have been revised from 1999.

Source: Department for Transport, Local Government and the Regions

14.5 Public road length[1]: by road type
Great Britain

Kilometres

		1990	1991	1992	1993	1994	1995	1996	1997	1998	1999		1999	2000
Trunk motorway	ZCBM	2 993	3 033	3 063	3 061	3 092	3 118	3 181	3 250	3 295	3 316	GSMX	3 404	3 421
Principal motorway	ZCBN	77	68	71	78	76	72	45	45	45	42	GSMY	44	44
Non built-up major roads:														
Trunk	ZCBO	11 142	10 867	10 865	10 803	10 767	10 811	11 046	10 955	10 791	10 837	GSMZ	10 483	10 458
Principal	ZCBP	22 692	23 005	23 014	23 034	23 054	23 207	22 896	22 884	22 954	22 897	GSNA	22 319	22 364
Total	ZCBQ	33 834	33 872	33 879	33 837	33 821	34 019	33 941	33 839	33 745	33 734	GSNB	32 802	32 822
Built-up major roads														
Trunk	ZCBR	1 532	1 455	1 431	1 400	1 344	1 297	1 313	1 314	1 344	1 313	GSNC	1 285	1 284
Principal	ZCBS	12 457	12 575	12 627	12 681	12 737	12 750	12 961	12 950	13 048	13 147	GSND	12 444	12 458
Total	ZCBT	13 989	14 030	14 058	14 081	14 081	14 047	14 274	14 264	14 392	14 460	GSNE	13 729	13 742
Minor non built-up roads:														
B roads	ZCBU	22 048	22 290	22 161	22 093	21 872	21 686	21 293	21 169	21 149	20 952	GSNF	20 828	20 740
C roads	ZCBV	67 096	67 360	67 350	67 448	66 980	67 509	66 903	66 472	66 571	65 811	GSNG	65 811	66 004
Unclassified	ZCBW	81 584	81 773	81 108	80 973	79 450	78 944	78 390	77 318	77 083	76 572	GSNH	83 613	82 958
All	ZCBX	170 727	171 424	170 618	170 514	168 302	168 139	166 585	164 958	164 804	163 335	GSNI	170 252	169 702
Minor built-up roads:														
B roads	ZCBY	7 790	7 816	8 066	8 215	8 475	8 567	8 903	9 195	9 129	9 353	GSNJ	9 264	9 317
C roads	ZCBZ	13 621	13 713	13 984	14 376	15 125	15 065	15 626	16 435	16 582	16 989	GSNK	16 989	17 267
Unclassified	ZCCA	115 004	116 010	118 572	120 050	121 995	123 974	126 267	127 881	129 553	130 684	GSNL	143 159	145 391
All	ZCCB	136 415	137 538	140 622	142 641	145 594	147 606	150 795	153 511	155 264	157 026	GSNM	169 412	171 976
All minor roads	ZCCC	307 142	308 962	311 241	313 155	313 897	315 744	317 380	318 470	320 068	320 361	GSNN	339 664	341 678
All roads	KCTY	358 034	359 966	362 310	364 212	364 966	366 999	368 821	369 867	371 543	371 914	GSNO	389 643	391 707

1 Data for 1999 and 2000 have been produced on a new basis and are not directly comparable with earlier figures. 1999 values are shown on both the original and new basis.

Source: Department for Transport, Local Government and the Regions 020 7944 3095

14.6 Road traffic[1]: by type of vehicle
Great Britain

Billion vehicle kilometres

		1990	1991	1992	1993	1994	1995	1996	1997	1998	1999		1999	2000
Cars and taxis	KCWA	335.9	335.2	338.0	338.5	345.7	353.2	362.4	370.9	375.6	380.1	GSNP	378.4	378.7
Motor cycles etc.	KCWB	5.6	5.4	4.5	4.1	4.2	4.1	4.2	4.1	3.9	4.6	GSNQ	4.5	4.4
Larger buses and coaches	KDZS	4.6	4.8	4.6	4.6	4.7	4.7	4.8	4.9	4.9	5.0	GSNR	5.0	4.8
Light vans[2]	KDZT	39.9	41.7	41.2	41.1	42.5	43.8	45.1	45.6	48.1	49.2	GSNS	49.4	50.5
Goods vehicles:														
2 axles rigid	ZCCD	11.6	11.5	11.4	11.3	12.1	11.4	11.4	11.7	10.9	11.7	GSNT	11.8	11.7
3 axles rigid	ZCCE	1.6	1.5	1.4	1.3	1.4	1.5	1.5	1.8	1.9	1.7	GSNU	1.7	1.6
4 or more axles rigid	ZCCF	1.7	1.5	1.4	1.5	1.5	1.5	1.4	1.4	1.4	1.5	GSNV	1.5	1.5
3 and 4 axles artic.	ZCCG	4.6	4.3	3.9	3.4	3.4	3.3	3.5	3.4	3.1	3.0	GSNW	3.1	2.9
5 axles artic.	ZCCH	4.1	4.3	4.3	4.8	5.3	5.6	6.1	6.5	6.7	6.9	GSNX	7.4	7.2
6 or more axles artic.	ZCCI	1.3	1.4	1.4	1.5	1.7	1.8	2.1	2.4	2.6	3.2	GSNY	3.3	4.4
All	KDZV	24.9	24.5	23.8	23.8	25.5	25.1	26.0	27.1	26.7	28.1	GSNZ	28.8	29.3
All motor vehicles	KCVZ	410.8	411.6	412.1	412.2	422.6	430.9	442.5	452.5	459.2	467.0	GSOA	466.0	467.7
Pedal cycles	KDZW	5.3	5.2	4.7	4.5	4.5	4.5	4.3	4.1	3.9	4.2	GSOB	4.1	4.0

1 Data for 1999 and 2000 have been produced on a new basis and are not directly comparable with earlier figures. 1999 values are shown on both the original and new basis.
2 Not exceeding 3,500 kgs gross vehicle weight.

Source: Department for Transport, Local Government and the Regions 020 7944 3095

14.7 Motor vehicle traffic[1]: by road class
Great Britain

Billion vehicle kilometres

		1990	1991	1992	1993	1994	1995	1996	1997	1998	1999		1999	2000
Motorways	ZCEF	61.6	61.0	61.5	63.9	66.7	70.9	73.7	77.9	81.3	83.6	GRXF	93.4	94.1
Non built-up major roads														
Trunk	ZCEG	59.0	59.5	58.9	59.3	59.8	61.3	63.2	64.8	65.5	68.9	GRXL	67.0	66.7
Principal	ZCEH	55.9	57.5	58.2	58.9	60.0	61.2	62.5	64.2	66.3	65.9	GRXS	61.8	62.1
All	ZCEI	114.8	117.0	117.0	118.1	119.9	122.5	125.8	128.9	131.8	134.9	GRXT	128.9	128.8
Built-up major roads[2]														
Trunk	ZCEJ	10.1	9.9	9.8	9.4	10.0	9.1	9.4	9.3	9.5	9.7	GRXV	9.4	9.4
Principal	ZCEK	68.2	69.5	69.7	68.6	70.1	70.0	71.6	70.4	70.1	70.1	GRXW	66.3	66.3
All	ZCEL	78.3	79.4	79.5	78.0	80.2	79.1	81.1	79.7	76.6	79.8	GRXX	75.7	75.7
Minor roads														
Minor non built-up roads	ZCEM	51.6	50.7	49.7	45.5	44.9	44.8	46.3	48.3	48.5	48.4	GRXY	48.2	48.1
Minor built-up roads	ZCEN	104.4	103.4	104.4	106.8	110.9	113.6	115.7	117.7	118.1	120.4	GRXZ	119.8	121.0
All	ZCEO	156.1	154.2	154.1	152.2	155.9	158.4	161.9	166.0	166.6	168.8	GRYA	168.0	169.1
All roads	KCVZ	410.8	411.6	412.1	412.2	422.6	430.9	442.5	452.5	459.2	467.0	GRYB	466.0	467.7

1 Figures for 1999 and 2000 have been produced on a new basis and are not directly comparable with earlier figures. 1999 values are shown on both the original and the new basis.
2 Built-up roads are those with a speed limit of 40 mph or less, irrespective of whether there are buildings or not.

Source: Department for Transport, Local Government and the Regions 020 7944 3095

14.8 Motor vehicles currently licenced at end of year
Great Britain

Thousands

	Private and light goods		Motor cycles, scooters and mopeds	Public transport Hackney taxation class		Goods vehicles	Special machines/ special conces- sionary	Other vehicles	Crown & exempt vehicles	Special vehicles group	All vehicles	Body type cars	
	Body type cars	Other vehicles		Total	Buses							All	Company cars (%)
	BMBJ	BMBK	BMBB	ZCGQ	KCUD	BMBD	KSBY	BMBF	BMBL	KSBZ	BMBI	ZCGR	ZCGS
1990	19 742	2 247	833	115	73	482	375	71	807	..	24 673	20 230	12.9
1991	19 737	2 215	750	109	72	449	346	65	840	..	24 511	20 253	12.0
1992[1]	19 870	2 198	684	107	72	432	324	59	903	..	24 577	20 444	11.1
1993	20 102	2 187	650	107	73	428	318	55	979	..	24 826	20 755	10.7
1994	20 479	2 192	630	107	75	434	309	50	1 030	..	25 231	21 199	10.4
1995[2]	20 505	2 217	594	..	74	421	274	44	1 169	28	25 369[3]	21 394	10.4
1996	21 172	2 267	609	..	77	413	254	40	1 424	48	26 302	22 238	10.3
1997	21 681	2 317	626	..	79	414	249	38	1 522	48	26 974	22 832	10.5
1998	22 115	2 362	684	..	80	412	243	37	1 558	47	27 538	23 293	10.4
1999	22 785	2 427	760	..	84	415	241	36	1 573	47	28 368	23 975	10.0
2000	23 196	2 469	825	..	86	418	233	34	1 590	46	28 898	24 406	10.3

1 New methods of estimating vehicle stock were introduced in 1992.
2 The vehicle taxation system was subject to substantial revision from 1 July 1995.
3 Contains 44,000 vehicles still taxed in classes abolished from 1 July 1995.

Source: Department for Transport, Local Government and the Regions 020 7944 6386

14.9 New vehicle registrations by taxation class
Great Britain

Thousands

		1990	1991	1992	1993	1994	1995	1996	1997	1998	1999	2000
Total[1]	BMAX	2 438.7	1 921.5	1 901.8	2 073.9	2 249.0	2 306.5	2 410.1	2 597.7	2 740.3	2 765.8	2 870.9
Private and light goods[2]												
Private cars	BMAA	1 942.3	1 536.6	1 528.0	1 694.6	1 809.1	1 828.3	1 888.4	2 015.9	2 123.5	2 100.4	2 174.9
Other vehicles	BMAE	237.6	171.9	166.4	158.8	182.6	195.7	205.0	228.4	244.5	241.6	254.9
Total	KCUG	2 179.9	1 708.5	1 694.4	1 853.4	1 991.7	2 024.0	2 093.4	2 244.3	2 368.0	2 342.0	2 429.8
Motor cycles, etc:												
Up to 50c.c.	KCUH	18.8	13.1	9.1	6.5	6.9	6.3	8.9	14.2	22.6	36.2	49.4
Other	KCUI	75.9	63.6	56.5	51.9	57.7	62.6	80.7	107.1	120.7	132.2	133.5
Total	BMAD	94.4	76.5	65.6	58.4	64.6	68.9	89.6	121.3	143.3	168.4	182.9
Public road passenger vehicles												
Buses, coaches, taxis, etc												
Not over 8 seats[3]	KCUJ	2.9	2.2	2.0	1.8	2.5	1.3	..	..	..	..	..
Over 8 seats	KCUK	4.8	3.0	3.1	3.6	4.2	5.2	6.5	6.6	7.4	8.0	7.5
Total	BMAG	7.7	5.2	5.1	5.4	6.7	6.5	6.5	6.6	7.4	8.0	7.5
Heavy general goods[2] **and farmers**[4]												
Goods vehicles: by weight	KCUL	44.4	28.6	28.7	32.8	41.1	48.0	45.5	41.8	49.1	48.3	50.4
Privately owned agricultural tractors and engines[5]	BMAH	34.2	26.1	24.1	30.0	35.3	33.3	25.7	21.7	15.2	24.9	24.0
Special concession group[6]	KSCB	..	..	..	..	..	33.0	25.7	21.7	15.2	17.3	16.9
Other licensed vehicles[7]	KCUM	2.1	0.7	1.6	1.4	1.3	1.0	1.0	1.5	1.5	1.5	1.2
Special vehicles group[8]	DMNR	..	..	..	..	..	3.3	8.1	8.6	7.6	7.6	6.5
Exempt from license duty												
Crown vehicles	KCUN	4.0	3.2	3.7	3.1	4.1	3.3	1.2	0.7	1.1	1.1	1.0
All other exempt vehicles[1,9]	KCUO	72.2	72.6	78.7	89.4	104.3	118.1	139.1	150.7	146.6	170.4	173.9
Total	KCUP	76.2	75.8	82.3	92.4	108.4	121.4	140.3	151.4	147.7	171.6	174.9

1 Including personal and direct export vehicles.
2 For years up to 1990 retrospective counts within these new taxation classes have been estimated.
3 From 1 July 1995 separate taxation of public transport vehicles with 8 or fewer seats was abolished. After this date new vehicles of this type were registered as PLG.
4 Owned by a farmer and available for hauling produce and requisites for his own farm.
5 Agricultural tractors are excluded unless driven on public roads
6 Various revisions to the vehicle taxation system were introduced on 1 July 1995 and on 29 November 1995. Separate taxation classes for farmers' goods vehicles were abolished on 1 July 1995; after this date new vehicles of this type were registered as HGVs. The total includes 5,900 vehicles registered between 1 January and 30 June in the (now abolished) agricultural and special machines group in classes which were not eligible to register in the special concession group. The old agricultural and special machines taxation group was abolished at end June 1995.

The group includes agricultural and mowing machines, snow ploughs and gritting vehicles. Electric vehicles are also included in this group and are no longer exempt from VED. Steam propelled vehicles were added to this group from November 1995.
7 Includes three wheelers, pedestrian controlled vehicles, general haulage and showmen's tractors and recovery vehicles. Recovery vehicle tax class introduced January 1988.
8 The special vehicles group was created on 1 July 1995 and consists of various vehicle types over 3.5 tonnes gross weight but not required to pay VED as heavy goods vehicles. The group includes mobile cranes, works trucks digging machines, road rollers and vehicles previously taxed as showman's goods and haulage. Figure shown for 1995 covers period from 1 July to 31 December only.
9 Between 1980 and 30 June 1995 electric vehicles were exempt from duty. From 1 July 1995 electric vehicles pay Vehicle Excise Duty (VED) as part of the special concession group.

Source: Department for Transport, Local Government and the Regions: 020 7944 3077

14.10 Private motoring: full car driving licence holders by age and gender
Great Britain

Percentages

	17-20	21-29	30-39	40-49	50-59	60-69	70 or over	Estimated number of licence holders (millions)
				Age				
All adults								
1975/76	28	59	67	60	50	35	15	19.4
1985/86	33	63	74	71	60	47	27	24.4
1989/91	43	72	77	78	67	54	32	28.0
1992/94	48	75	82	79	72	57	33	29.0
1995/97	42	73	81	82	74	64	39	30.6
1998/00	41	74	84	84	78	68	41	32.3
Males								
1975/76	36	78	85	83	75	58	32	13.4
1985/86	37	73	86	87	81	72	51	15.3
1989/91	52	82	88	89	85	78	58	16.9
1992/94	54	83	91	88	88	81	59	17.1
1995/97	48	79	89	89	88	83	65	17.6
1998/00	45	81	90	92	89	84	65	18.3
Females								
1975/76	20	43	48	37	24	15	4	6.0
1985/86	29	54	62	56	41	24	11	9.2
1989/91	35	64	67	66	49	33	15	11.2
1992/94	42	68	73	70	57	37	16	12.1
1995/97	36	67	74	74	61	46	22	13.2
1998/00	37	69	78	77	68	54	22	14.1

Source: Department for Transport, Local Government and the Regions; 020 7944 3097

14.11 Private motoring: households with regular use of cars
Great Britain

Percentages

	No car	One car	Two cars	Three or more cars	Total (millions)
	ZCGA	ZCGB	ZCGC	ZCGD	ZCGE
1990	33	44	19	4	22.1
1991	32	45	19	4	22.4
1992	32	45	20	4	22.6
1993	31	45	20	4	22.9
1994	32	45	20	4	23.1
1995	30	45	21	4	23.3
1996	30	45	21	4	23.5
1997	30	45	21	4	23.7
1998	28	44	23	5	23.9
1999	28	44	22	5	24.1
2000	27	45	23	5	..

	No car	One car	Two or more cars	Total
Government Office Regions, 2000				
Great Britain	27	45	28	100
North East	39	43	18	100
North West	30	45	25	100
Yorkshire and the Humber	32	44	24	100
East Midlands	26	43	31	100
West Midlands	25	46	29	100
East	18	46	35	100
London	37	44	19	100
South East	17	46	37	100
South West	20	47	33	100
England	27	45	28	100
Wales	30	45	25	100
Scotland	34	44	22	100

	No car	One car	Two or more cars	Total
Area type, 1998/00				
London	36	45	19	100
Metropolitan areas	36	42	22	100
Other urban areas with population:				
Over 250,000	32	46	22	100
25,000 - 250,000	29	46	25	100
10,000 - 25,000	25	45	31	100
3,000 - 10,000	18	48	34	100
Rural areas	16	43	40	100
Great Britain	28	45	26	100

Sources: Office for National Statistics;
Department for Transport, Local Government and the Regions

14.12 Vehicles with licences current[1]
Northern Ireland

Numbers

		1990	1991	1992	1993	1994	1995	1996[2]	1997	1998	1999	2000
Private cars, etc	KNKA	481 090	498 471	516 194	515 185	514 760	521 610	540 083	575 923	584 706	608 316	615 180
Cycles and tricycles	KNKB	10 167	9 684	9 023	8 634	8 775	9 142	10 026	10 932	11 663	13 087	14 116
Public road passenger vehicles:												
Taxis up to 4 seats	KNKD	603	656	494	462	623	739	..	..	..	..	..
Buses, coaches, over 4 seats	KNKE	2 183	2 231	2 250	2 217	2 455	1 353	2 090	2 144	2 175	2 204	2 266
Total	KNKC	2 786	2 887	2 744	2 679	3 078	2 092	2 090	2 144	2 175	2 204	2 266
General (HGV) goods vehicles:	KNKF	16 191	13 907	14 286	14 576	14 810	16 338	17 401	18 172	18 312	17 075	17 864
Farmers' goods vehicles[3]	KNKJ	4 962	4 994	5 315	5 498	5 904	2 854	..	..	..	..	..
Agricultural tractors and engines, etc[3]	KNKM	8 021	7 199	6 892	7 201	7 317	9 074	5 911	6 378	5 906	5 505	5 048
Other	KNKN	513	403	343	329	354	1 257	1 019	1 188	1 193	1 446	1 287
Vehicles exempt from duty:												
Government owned	KNKP	5 211	5 120	5 004	4 828	4 818	3 872	3 753	3 705	3 785	4 032	3 822
Other:												
Ambulances	KNKQ	74	98	97	101	104	250	371	389	425	417	452
Fire engines	KNKR	162	250	251	205	194	301	292	291	285	286	290
Other exempt[4]	KNKS	13 937	15 305	18 163	27 089	35 837	47 626	58 340	64 447	66 981	68 277	70 405
Total	KNKO	19 384	20 773	23 515	32 223	40 953	52 049	62 756	68 832	71 476	73 012	74 969
Total	KNKT	543 114	558 318	578 312	586 325	595 951	611 562	639 286	683 569	695 431	720 645	730 730

1 Licences current at any time during the quarter ended December.
2 Due to a revision of taxation classes, 1996 data are not directly comparable with previous years.

3 Owned by a farmer and available for hauling produce and requisites for his farm. From 1 July 1995 farmers goods taxation classes have been abolished
4 Changes in the Mobility Allowance (DSS) have contributed to the increase in Other exempt.

Source: Department of the Environment, Northern Ireland: 028 9054 0801

14.13 New vehicles registrations
Northern Ireland

Numbers

		1990	1991	1992	1993	1994	1995	1996	1997	1998	1999	2000
Private cars, etc	KNLA	68 918	63 739	62 777	65 360	70 765	73 718	77 817	83 968	91 141	89 078	84 973
Cycles and tricycles	KNLB	2 343	2 218	1 993	1 885	1 943	2 362	2 803	3 376	4 307	5 310	6 010
Public road passenger vehicles:												
Taxis[1]	KNLD	..	..	..	..	..	..	..	..	..	..	..
Buses, coaches etc	KNLE	..	..	..	..	..	..	..	..	..	..	..
Total	KNLC	606	620	551	466	1 143	622	724	714	486	568	565
Goods vehicles:												
General haulage vehicles:												
Unladen weight:												
Not over 1.5 tons[2]	KNLH	4 301	6 273	6 236	6 468	6 908	7 357	7 232	8 468	10 107	11 054	12 617
Over 1.5 tons and not over 3 tons	KNLI	..	..	..	..	..	..	..	..	..	..	..
Over 3 tons[3]	KNLJ	4 630	2 619	2 471	2 593	2 668	2 935	3 492	3 521	3 572	3 697	3 502
Total	KNLG	..	..	..	..	..	..	..	..	..	..	..
Agricultural vans and lorries[4]	KNLK	..	..	..	..	..	..	..	..	..	..	..
Tractors for general haulage	KNLL	..	..	..	..	..	..	..	..	..	..	..
Goods vehicles: Total	KNLF	..	..	..	..	..	..	..	..	..	..	..
Agricultural tractors and engines, etc[5,6]	KNLM	1 610	1 177	1 184	1 658	1 558	1 619	1 292	1 364	971	987	1 313
Vehicles exempt from duty:												
Ambulances[7]	KGVE KNLO	332	330	..	..	..	..	..	..	..	..	..
Fire engines[7]	KNLP											
Road construction vehicles	KNLQ	..	..	..	..	..	..	..	..	..	..	..
Other exempt	KNLR	2 181	2 006	2 463	4 550	6 423	8 333	10 520	10 885	10 718	11 083	10 789
Total	KNLN	..	..	..	..	..	..	..	..	..	..	..
Total	KNLS	84 921	78 982	77 675	82 980	91 408	96 946	103 880	112 296	121 302	121 777	119 769

1 From 1990 figure is for Hackneys.
2 From 1990 figure is for light goods.
3 From 1990 figure is for heavy goods.
4 Owned by a farmer and available for hauling produce and requisites for his farm.

5 Agricultural tractors are excluded unless driven on public roads.
6 From 1990 figure is for tractors only.
7 From 1990 figure is for crown vehicles.

Source: Department of the Environment, Northern Ireland: 028 9054 0801

14.14 Local bus services: passenger journeys by area

Millions

		1989/90	1990/91	1991/92	1992/93	1993/94	1994/95	1995/96	1996/97	1997/98	1998/99	1999/00
London	KILS	1 188	1 178	1 149	1 129	1 117	1 167	1 205	1 242	1 294	1 279	1 307
English metropolitan areas	KILT	1 648	1 547	1 478	1 383	1 337	1 331	1 292	1 246	1 232	1 195	1 162
English shire counties	KILU	1 474	1 396	1 333	1 307	1 274	1 277	1 265	1 265	1 247	1 246	1 263
England	ZCER	4 310	4 120	3 961	3 819	3 727	3 775	3 762	3 753	3 773	3 719	3 732
Scotland	KILV	613	585	571	532	525	513	494	467	438	413	434
Wales	KILW	151	145	133	129	133	132	127	130	120	116	114
All outside London	ZCES	3 886	3 672	3 516	3 351	3 268	3 253	3 178	3 108	3 036	2 969	2 973
Great Britain	ZCET	5 074	4 850	4 665	4 480	4 385	4 420	4 383	4 350	4 330	4 248	4 281

Source: Department for Transport, Local Government and the Regions 020 7944 3076

14.15 Local bus services: fare indices by area Current prices

Index 1995=100

		1990/91	1991/92	1992/93	1993/94	1994/95	1995/96	1996/97	1997/98	1998/99	1999/00	2000/01
London	KNEP	71.4	78.2	84.2	90.9	96.2	101.1	105.4	109.3	113.7	117.2	117.2
English metropolitan areas	KILD	74.2	82.9	88.6	92.9	96.4	101.5	106.9	113.3	118.7	124.5	129.7
English shire counties	KILE	80.4	86.6	90.4	93.1	97.0	101.1	106.0	111.5	116.7	121.9	128.6
England	ZCEP	76.7	83.6	88.3	92.5	96.7	101.2	106.1	111.4	116.5	121.4	125.8
Scotland	KILF	76.6	82.5	88.2	91.3	96.9	100.8	108.0	116.5	121.8	125.3	129.9
Wales[1]	KILG	..	..	90.4	93.8	97.4	100.7	104.4	110.1	116.3	122.2	127.5
All outside London	ZCEQ	78.0	84.8	89.4	92.8	96.8	101.2	106.6	112.8	118.2	123.3	129.2
Great Britain	KNEU	76.8	83.6	88.4	92.4	96.7	101.2	106.3	112.0	117.1	121.9	126.4
Retail Prices Index	KNEV	86.4	90.5	93.3	94.9	97.5	100.7	103.1	106.5	109.9	111.6	114.9

1 Figures for Wales before 1992/93 are omitted as insufficient fares data were available.

Source: Department for Transport, Local Government and the Regions: 020 7944 3076

14.16 Road accident casualties : by road user type and severity
Great Britain

Numbers

		1990	1991	1992	1993	1994	1995	1996	1997	1998	1999	2000
Child pedestrians:												
Killed	ZCDH	242	225	180	165	160	132	131	138	103	107	107
KSI	KIJS	5 914	5 097	4 901	4 231	4 610	4 400	4 132	3 954	3 737	3 457	3 226
All severities	ZCDI	22 860	20 708	20 124	18 250	19 263	18 590	18 510	18 407	17 971	16 876	16 184
Adult pedestrians:												
Killed	ZCDJ	1 434	1 263	1 163	1 072	953	897	858	835	803	760	750
KSI	KIJT	11 228	9 733	9 125	8 260	8 114	7 716	7 300	6 925	6 592	6 221	6 112
All severities	ZCDK	36 318	32 229	30 354	28 750	28 129	27 178	26 827	26 223	25 827	24 806	24 481
Child pedal cyclists:												
Killed	ZCDL	59	50	48	37	42	48	54	33	32	36	27
KSI	KIJU	1 490	1 345	1 195	1 146	1 234	1 249	1 231	1 016	915	950	758
All severities	ZCDM	8 720	8 182	7 725	7 386	8 075	8 133	8 217	7 899	6 930	7 920	6 260
Adult pedal cyclists:												
Killed	ZCDN	197	192	156	148	129	164	148	150	126	135	98
KSI	KIJV	3 075	2 800	2 752	2 598	2 710	2 673	2 517	2 542	2 345	2 172	1 954
All severities	ZCDO	17 311	16 201	16 488	16 115	16 097	16 140	15 778	16 181	15 326	14 834	13 630
Motorcyclists[1] and passengers:												
Killed	ZCDP	659	548	469	427	444	445	440	509	498	547	605
KSI	ZCDQ	11 121	8 502	7 338	6 882	6 666	6 615	6 208	6 446	6 442	6 908	7 374
All severities	ZCDR	39 048	30 751	26 891	25 094	24 354	23 524	23 133	24 492	24 610	26 192	28 212
Car drivers and passengers:												
Killed	ZCDS	2 371	2 053	1 978	1 760	1 764	1 749	1 806	1 795	1 696	1 687	1 665
KSI	ZCDT	29 120	25 395	25 124	22 833	23 892	23 461	24 048	23 191	21 676	20 368	19 719
All severities	ZCDU	190 558	179 383	185 662	187 479	195 154	194 027	205 336	211 448	210 474	205 735	206 799
Bus/coach drivers and passengers:												
Killed	ZCDV	19	25	19	35	21	35	11	14	18	11	15
KSI	KCUZ	807	725	655	725	815	836	695	601	631	611	578
All severities	ZCDW	9 954	8 875	9 103	9 307	10 090	9 278	9 345	9 439	9 839	10 252	10 088
LGV drivers and passengers:												
Killed	ZCDX	129	119	117	91	64	69	61	64	67	65	66
KSI	ZCDY	1 627	1 427	1 308	1 082	1 101	1 106	989	928	949	867	813
All severities	ZCDZ	9 728	8 673	8 129	7 420	7 558	7 200	7 215	7 476	7 672	7 124	7 007
HGV drivers and passengers:												
Killed	ZCEA	67	65	70	59	41	57	63	45	60	52	55
KSI	ZCEB	772	695	659	635	571	635	555	573	560	540	571
All severities	ZCEC	3 844	3 603	3 326	3 333	3 370	3 331	3 245	3 302	3 444	3 484	3 597
All road users:[2]												
Killed	ZCED	5 217	4 568	4 229	3 814	3 650	3 621	3 598	3 599	3 421	3 423	3 409
KSI	ZCEE	65 658	56 186	53 485	48 834	50 190	49 154	48 097	46 583	44 255	42 545	41 564
All severities	KCVC	341 141	311 368	310 753	306 135	315 359	310 687	320 578	327 803	325 212	320 310	320 283

Note: KSI = Killed or seriously injured.
1 Includes mopeds and scooters.
2 Includes other motor or non-motor vehicle users, and unknown road user
type and casualty age.

Source: Department for Transport, Local Government and the Regions: 020
7944 3078

14.17 Freight transport by road: goods moved by goods vehicles over 3.5 tonnes[1]
Great Britain

Billion tonne-kilometres

		1990	1991	1992	1993	1994	1995	1996	1997	1998	1999	2000
By mode of working												
Mainly public haulage	KNND	94.7	85.8	86.4	93.2	100.8	106.5	109.1	112.2	114.3	110.9	113.0
Mainly own account	KNNC	36.0	38.8	34.9	35.4	37.0	37.2	37.7	37.4	37.6	38.3	37.5
All modes	KNNB	130.6	124.6	121.3	128.6	137.8	143.7	146.8	149.6	151.9	149.2	150.5
By gross weight of vehicle												
Rigid vehicles:												
3.5-17 tonnes	ZCIL	20.9	20.1	19.0	18.7	19.9	18.7	19.5	19.2	17.8	17.9	15.8
17-25 tonnes	ZCIM	7.4	7.1	6.5	6.6	6.1	5.6	5.3	4.7	4.2	4.3	4.8
25 tonnes and over	ZCIN	12.3	11.3	10.7	11.3	12.4	13.3	13.5	14.3	14.7	15.3	15.4
All rigids	ZCIO	40.6	38.5	36.2	36.5	38.4	37.5	38.3	38.1	36.6	37.5	36.0
Articulated vehicles:												
3.5-33 tonnes	ZCIP	21.8	18.6	16.7	16.5	16.9	15.9	15.9	14.3	14.4	14.0	14.0
33 tonnes and over	ZCIQ	68.3	67.6	68.4	75.6	82.5	90.2	92.6	97.1	100.9	97.7	100.4
All articulated vehicles	ZCIR	90.1	86.1	85.0	92.1	99.4	106.1	108.5	111.4	115.3	111.7	114.4
All vehicles												
3.5-25 tonnes	ZCIS	29.2	28.0	26.3	25.9	26.6	24.7	25.3	24.3	22.5	22.7	21.3
25 tonnes and over	KNNG	101.4	96.6	95.0	102.7	111.2	119.0	121.5	125.2	129.4	126.5	129.2
All weights	ZCIT	130.6	124.6	121.3	128.6	137.8	143.7	146.8	149.6	151.9	149.2	150.5
By commodity												
Food, drink and tobacco	ZCIU	32.8	32.7	33.2	35.9	36.5	37.5	39.3	40.8	42.5	41.5	44.3
Wood, timber and cork	ZCIV	2.4	2.7	2.6	3.1	3.3	3.2	3.8	3.5	3.6	3.8	3.7
Fertiliser	ZCIW	1.6	1.5	1.4	1.5	1.3	1.4	1.5	1.3	1.2	1.4	1.2
Crude minerals	ZCIX	14.5	13.0	12.7	12.6	14.1	13.5	13.5	13.6	13.3	12.7	12.4
Ores	ZCIY	1.2	1.3	1.2	1.6	1.4	1.5	1.3	1.7	1.1	1.3	1.2
Crude materials	ZCIZ	1.7	1.7	2.0	1.7	2.0	1.9	2.1	2.1	2.6	2.6	2.6
Coal and coke	ZCJA	4.2	3.7	3.5	3.1	2.9	2.7	2.5	2.7	2.0	2.2	1.5
Petrol and petroleum products	ZCJB	4.9	4.9	4.5	5.0	5.1	5.7	6.1	5.8	5.2	5.0	6.4
Chemicals	ZCJC	8.0	7.3	6.8	7.2	8.1	7.4	7.7	8.2	7.9	7.4	6.8
Building materials	ZCJD	9.4	8.7	8.0	9.3	10.0	10.7	9.6	11.1	10.7	10.6	10.6
Iron and steel products	ZCJE	7.1	6.9	6.5	6.4	6.7	7.8	7.2	7.9	7.7	6.8	6.8
Other metal products[2]	ZCJF	2.1	1.9	2.0	1.9	2.0	1.7	1.7	1.5	1.7	1.7	1.7
Machinery and transport equipment	ZCJG	6.7	5.9	6.0	5.7	6.8	7.4	7.7	8.4	9.1	8.7	9.1
Miscellaneous manufactures[2]	ZCJH	13.3	12.4	12.0	12.4	13.4	13.3	14.2	14.2	15.9	15.7	15.1
Miscellaneous transactions[3]	ZCJI	20.5	20.0	19.0	21.3	24.3	27.8	28.4	26.8	27.5	27.9	27.1
All commodities	ZCJJ	130.6	124.6	121.3	128.6	137.8	143.7	146.8	149.6	151.9	149.2	150.5

1 Rigid vehicles or articulated vehicles (tractive unit and trailer) with gross vehicle weight over 3.5 tonnes.
2 Includes not elsewhere specified.
3 Includes not elsewhere specified and commodity not known.

Source: Department for Transport, Local Government and the Regions; 020 7944 3093

14.18 Freight transport by road: goods lifted by goods vehicles over 3.5 tonnes[1]
Great Britain

Million tonnes

		1990	1991	1992	1993	1994	1995	1996	1997	1998	1999	2000
By mode of working												
Mainly public haulage	ZCJK	978	862	843	911	980	987	1 011	1 044	1 041	991	1 038
Mainly own account	ZCJL	667	643	620	612	618	622	618	599	589	576	556
All modes	ZCJM	1 645	1 505	1 463	1 523	1 597	1 609	1 628	1 643	1 630	1 567	1 593
By gross weight of vehicle												
Rigid vehicles:												
3.5-17 tonnes	ZCJN	363	331	315	322	317	298	306	294	268	254	229
17-25 tonnes	ZCJO	258	236	219	211	202	162	133	120	106	86	87
25 tonnes and over	ZCJP	325	289	282	307	332	373	371	380	401	408	424
All rigids	ZCJQ	947	857	817	840	852	833	811	793	776	748	741
Articulated vehicles:												
3.5-33 tonnes	ZCJR	192	165	142	144	142	139	138	124	125	113	107
33 tonnes and over	ZCJS	506	484	505	540	604	637	679	726	729	706	746
All articulated vehicles	ZCJT	698	648	646	683	746	776	817	850	854	819	852
All vehicles												
3.5-25 tonnes	ZCJU	632	578	544	541	527	467	447	419	382	346	325
25 tonnes and over	ZCJV	1 013	927	919	982	1 070	1 142	1 181	1 224	1 248	1 221	1 268
All weights	ZCJW	1 645	1 505	1 463	1 523	1 597	1 609	1 628	1 643	1 630	1 567	1 593
By commodity												
Food, drink and tobacco	ZCJX	299	291	290	300	302	308	326	342	346	333	346
Wood, timber and cork	ZCJY	18	21	20	25	24	24	27	26	27	28	26
Fertiliser	ZCJZ	14	13	13	12	10	11	13	10	9	11	10
Crude minerals	ZCKA	354	298	327	310	355	319	320	329	327	297	308
Ores	ZCKB	17	14	15	21	18	18	18	25	18	20	16
Crude materials	ZCKC	13	15	17	14	16	16	18	17	20	20	18
Coal and coke	ZCKD	62	57	55	48	42	34	32	37	26	28	22
Petrol and petroleum products	ZCKE	74	73	63	67	68	71	75	73	61	61	75
Chemicals	ZCKF	53	45	42	47	51	50	51	53	53	47	49
Building materials	ZCKG	178	155	136	153	156	161	142	156	161	159	165
Iron and steel products	ZCKH	55	50	46	45	47	54	52	55	54	48	49
Other metal products[2]	ZCKI	20	16	18	20	17	17	15	16	18	17	16
Machinery and transport equipment	ZCKJ	54	46	47	46	57	61	59	71	73	67	69
Miscellaneous manufactures[2]	ZCKK	86	80	75	81	84	85	88	90	96	91	97
Miscellaneous transactions[3]	ZCKL	348	331	300	332	351	379	393	343	342	340	328
All commodities	ZCKM	1 645	1 505	1 463	1 523	1 597	1 609	1 628	1 643	1 630	1 567	1 593

1 Rigid vehicles or articulated vehicles (tractive unit and trailer) with gross vehicle weight over 3.5 tonnes.
2 Includes not elsewhere specified.
3 Includes not elsewhere specified and commodity not known.

Source: Department for Transport, Local Government and the Regions; 020 7944 3093

14.19 Rail systems summary

		1990 /91	1991 /92	1992 /93	1993 /94	1994 /95	1995 /96	1996 /97	1997 /98	1998 /99	1999[1] /00	2000[1] /01
Passenger journeys (Millions)												
National Rail network[2]	ZCKN	809	792	770	740	735	761	801	846	892	931	957
London Underground	KNOE	775	751	728	735	764	784	772	832	866	927	970
Docklands Light Railway	ZCKO	8	8	7	8	12	14	17	21	28	31	38
Glasgow Underground	ZCKP	14	14	14	14	15	14	14	14	15	15	14
(Nexus) Tyne and Wear Metro	ZCKQ	44	41	39	39	37	36	35	35	34	33	33
West Midlands Metro[3]	ZCKR	..	..	..	..	..	..	..	..	..	5	5
Croydon Tramlink[4]	GEOE	..	..	..	..	..	..	..	..	..	..	15
Altram Manchester Metrolink[5]	ZCKS	..	..	8	11	12	13	13	14	13	14	17
Stagecoach Supertram (Sheffield)	ZCKT	..	..	..	..	2	5	8	9	10	11	11
All rail	ZCKU	1 649	1 605	1 566	1 547	1 577	1 627	1 660	1 771	1 858	1 967	2 061
of which: light rail[6]	GENZ	..	49	54	58	63	68	73	79	85	94	120
Passenger receipts (£ million at current prices)												
National Rail network[2]	KNDL	2 057	2 117	2 154	2 193	2 171	2 379	2 573	2 821	3 089	3 368	3 414
London Underground	KNOA	531	559	589	637	718	765	797	899	977	1 058	1 129
Docklands Light Railway	ZCKV	3	3	3	5	6	9	12	14	20	22	29
Glasgow Underground	ZCKW	6	6	6	7	7	8	8	9	9	10	11
(Nexus) Tyne and Wear Metro	ZCKX	16	18	19	19	19	20	21	22	23	24	24
West Midlands Metro[3]	ZCKY	..	..	..	..	..	..	..	..	..	..	3
Croydon Tramlink[4]	GEOF	..	..	..	..	..	..	..	..	..	..	12
Altram Manchester Metrolink[5]	ZCKZ	..	..	7	10	10	11	13	14	..	..	18
Stagecoach Supertram (Sheffield)	ZCLA	..	..	..	..	2	4	5	6	6	7	7
All rail	ZCLB	2 613	2 703	2 778	2 871	2 933	3 196	3 429	3 785	..	..	4 647
of which: light rail[6]	GEOA	..	21	29	34	37	44	51	56	..	..	93
Passenger kilometres (Millions)												
National Rail network[2]	KNDZ	33 200	32 500	31 700	30 400	28 700	30 000	32 100	34 700	36 300	38 454	39 218
London Underground	KNOI	6 164	5 895	5 758	5 814	6 051	6 337	6 153	6 479	6 716	7 171	7 470
Docklands Light Railway	ZCLC	33	32	33	39	55	70	86	103	144	172	200
Glasgow Underground	ZCLD	40	39	39	41	43	41	40	45	47	49	46
(Nexus) Tyne and Wear Metro	ZCLE	290	277	271	273	271	261	254	249	238	230	229
West Midlands Metro[3]	ZCLF	..	..	..	..	..	..	..	..	..	50	56
Croydon Tramlink[4]	GEOG	..	..	..	..	..	..	..	..	..	..	96
Altram Manchester Metrolink[5]	ZCLG	..	..	53	73	79	81	86	88	117	126	152
Stagecoach Supertram (Sheffield)	ZCLH	..	..	..	..	8	20	29	34	35	37	38
All rail	ZCLI	39 727	38 744	37 854	36 640	35 206	36 810	38 748	41 698	43 597	46 289	47 505
of which: light rail[6]	GEOB	..	310	357	385	412	432	455	474	534	615	771
Route kilometres open for passenger traffic (Numbers)												
National Rail network[2]	ZCLJ	14 317	14 291	14 317	14 357	14 359	15 002	15 034	15 024	15 038	15 038	15 042
London Underground	ZCLK	394	394	394	394	392	392	392	392	392	408	408
Docklands Light Railway	ZCLM	12	14	14	14	22	22	22	22	22	27	27
Glasgow Underground	ZCLN	11	11	11	11	11	11	11	11	11	11	11
(Nexus) Tyne and Wear Metro	ZCLO	56	59	59	59	59	59	59	59	59	59	59
West Midlands Metro[3]	ZCLP	..	..	..	..	..	..	..	..	..	21	20
Croydon Tramlink[4]	GEOH	..	..	..	..	..	..	..	..	..	..	28
Altram Manchester Metrolink[5]	ZCLQ	..	..	31	31	31	31	31	31	31	39	39
Stagecoach Supertram (Sheffield)	ZCLR	..	..	..	7	22	29	29	29	29	29	29
All rail	ZCLS	14 790	14 769	14 826	14 873	14 896	15 546	15 578	15 568	15 582	15 632	15 663
of which: light rail[6]	GEOC	..	73	104	111	134	141	141	141	141	175	202
Stations served (Numbers)												
National Rail network[2]	ZCLT	2 488	2 468	2 482	2 493	2 489	2 497	2 498	2 495	2 499	2 503	2 508
London Underground	KNOO	245	246	246	245	245	245	245	245	246	253	253
Docklands Light Railway	ZCLU	15	15	16	27	27	28	28	29	29	34	34
Glasgow Underground	ZCLV	15	15	15	15	15	15	15	15	15	15	15
(Nexus) Tyne and Wear Metro	ZCLW	44	46	46	46	46	46	46	46	46	46	46
West Midlands Metro[3]	ZCLX	..	..	..	..	..	..	..	..	..	23	23
Croydon Tramlink[4]	GEOI	..	..	..	..	..	..	..	..	..	..	38
Altram Manchester Metrolink[5]	ZCLY	..	..	26	26	26	26	26	26	26	36	36
Stagecoach Supertram (Sheffield)	ZCLZ	..	..	..	9	37	45	45	46	47	47	47
All rail	ZCLL	2 807	2 790	2 831	2 861	2 885	2 902	2 903	2 902	2 908	2 957	3 000
of which: light rail[6]	GSOC	..	61	88	108	136	145	145	147	148	186	224

1 National Rail passenger journeys and passenger kilometres revised by the Strategic Rail Authority.
2 Franchised train operating companies from February 1996 following rail privatisation.
3 West Midlands Metro opened in 1999.
4 Croydon tramlink opened in 2000.
5 Transfer of 20 stations from the national rail network to Manchester Metrolink.
6 Light rail excludes London and Glasgow Underground systems.

Sources: Railtrack Group plc; Shadow Strategic Rail Authority; Transport for London, and various Passenger Transport Executives

14.20 National railways freight[1]
Great Britain

Billion tonne-kilometres

		1990/91	1991/92	1992/93	1993/94	1994/95	1995/96	1996/97	1997/98	1998/99	1999/00	2000/01
Freight moved by commodity												
Coal	ZCGG	5.0	5.0	5.4	3.9	3.3	3.6	3.9	4.4	4.5	4.8	4.8
Metals	ZCGH	2.3	2.4	2.3	2.1	1.7	1.7	..	..	2.1	2.2	2.1
Construction	ZCGI	2.7	2.5	2.5	2.3	2.5	2.3	..	..	2.1	2.0	2.4
Oil and petroleum	ZCGJ	2.0	2.0	2.0	1.9	1.8	1.8	..	..	1.6	1.5	1.4
Other traffic	ZCGK	3.8	3.4	3.3	3.5	3.8	3.9	11.3	12.5	7.1	7.6	7.4
All traffic	KCTB	16.0	15.3	15.5	13.8	13.0	13.3	15.1	16.9	17.3	18.2	18.1

		1990/91	1991/92	1992/93	1993/94	1994/95	1995/96	1996/97	1997/98	1998/99	1999/00	2000/01
Freight lifted by commodity												
Coal	ZCGL	74.7	75.1	67.9	48.9	42.5	45.2	52.2	50.3	45.3	44.3	45.7
Metals	ZCGM	18.0	17.8	15.9	15.8	16.9	15.1	..	..	..	..	..
Construction	ZCGN	20.2	17.7	15.8	16.1	16.8	11.5	..	..	..	..	..
Oil and petroleum	ZCGO	10.0	10.0	9.5	9.0	8.1	6.3	..	..	..	..	..
Other traffic	ZCGP	15.1	15.3	13.2	13.4	13.0	22.6	49.6	55.1	56.8	47.5	49.6
All traffic	KCTH	138.2	135.8	122.4	103.2	97.3	100.7	101.8	105.4	102.1	91.6	95.3

1 Because of changes in the way freight traffic has been estimated following privatisation, figures since 1996/97 are not strictly comparable with those for previous years. The series calculation was revised again from 1998/99 and from 1999/00 due to revisions from freight operators.

Source: Department for Transport, Local Government and the Regions: 020 7944 3094

14.21 Railways: permanent way and rolling stock
Northern Ireland
At end of year

Numbers

		1990	1991	1992	1993	1994	1995	1996	1997	1998	1999	2000
Length of road open for traffic[1] (km)	KNRA	332	332	332	330	331	333	335	335	335	335	356
Length of track open for traffic (km)												
Total	KNRB	553	553	553	504	503	506	506	505	526	526	547
Running lines	KNRC	500	500	500	463	462	464	464	464	484	484	505
Sidings (as single track)	KNRD	53	53	53	41	41	42	42	42	42	42	42
Locomotives												
Diesel-electrics	KNRE	9	9	9	9	11	11	8	6	5	6	6
Passenger carrying vehicles												
Total	KNRF	115	115	114	112	112	112	112	112	120	108	108
Rail motor vehicles:												
Diesel-electric, etc	KNRG	30	30	30	30	30	30	30	30	28	30	30
Trailer carriages:												
Total locomotive hauled	KNRH	28	28	28	28	28	28	28	28	38	21	21
Ordinary coaches	KNRI	26	26	26	26	26	26	26	26	36	19	19
Restaurant cars	KNRJ	2	2	2	2	2	2	2	2	2	2	2
Rail car trailers	KNRK	56	56	56	54	54	54	54	54	54	54	54
Non-passenger carrying vehicles												
Post Office and luggage vans, etc	KNRL	–	–	–	–	–	–	–	–	–	–	–
Trucks and wagons owned												
Total	KNRM	17	17	18	–	–	–	–	–	–	–	–
Merchandise wagons:												
Open	KNRN	–	–	–	–	–	–	–	–	–	–	–
Covered	KNRO	–	–	–	–	–	–	–	–	–	–	–
Rail and timber trucks	KNRP	–	–	–	–	–	–	–	–	–	–	–
Brake vans	KNRQ	–	–	–	–	–	–	–	–	–	–	–
Special wagons	KNRR	17	17	18	–	–	–	–	–	–	–	–
Containers	KNRS	–	–	–	–	–	–	–	–	–	–	–
Rolling stock for maintenance and repair	KNRT	55	55	36	42	41	41	41	41	26	18	18

1 The total length of railroad open for traffic irrespective of the number of tracks comprising the road.

Source: Department for Regional Development, Northern Ireland: 028 9054 0801

14.22 Operating statistics of railways
Northern Ireland

		Unit	1990	1991	1992	1993	1994	1995	1996	1997	1998	1999	2000
Maintenance of way and works														
Material used:														
Ballast	KNSA	Thousand m^2	25.0	22.5	30.2	16.0	33.2	22.5	27.0	51.3	38.5	40.0	47.0
Rails	KNSB	Thousand tonnes	0.91	1.68	2.26	2.00	1.80	1.76	2.12	0.37	2.50	3.00	3.50
Sleepers	KNSC	Thousands	19.00	23.20	31.23	14.60	22.40	22.90	27.50	5.10	32.00	30.00	40.00
Track renewed	KNSD	Km	8.80	10.40	14.00	16.00	12.00	16.00	20.00	2.40	22.50	7.00	29.00
New Track laid	KPGD	Km	..	..	..	..	3.2	2.5	–	–	–	–	21.0
Engine kilometres														
Total[1]	KNSE	Thousand Km	3 200	3 200	3 540	3 640	3 640	4 000	4 100	4 100	4 100	4 100	4 100
Train kilometres:														
Total	KNSF	"	3 844	3 410	3 210	3 210	3 210	3 570	3 670	3 670	3 670	3 670	3 670
Coaching	KNSG	"	3 840	3 406	3 206	3 206	3 206	3 566	3 666	3 666	3 666	3 666	3 666
Freight	KNSH	"	4	4	4	4	4	4	4	4	4	4	4

1 Including shunting, assisting, light, departmental, maintenance and repair.

Source: Department for Regional Development, Northern Ireland: 028 9054 0801

14.23 Main output[1] of United Kingdom airlines

		1990	1991	1992	1993	1994	1995	1996	1997	1998	1999	2000
All services: total	KNTA	20 375	20 166	23 145	25 144	27 714	29 904	32 210	35 538	40 021	42 002	43 379
Percentage growth on previous year	KNTB	7.7	–1.0	14.8	8.5	10.2	7.4	7.7	10.3	12.5	5.0	3.6
Scheduled services: total	KNTC	15 274	15 188	17 065	18 605	20 360	22 016	23 793	26 504	29 756	31 815	32 938
Percentage growth on previous year	KNTD	13.8	–0.6	12.4	9.0	9.4	8.1	8.1	11.4	12.3	6.9	3.5
Non-scheduled services: total	KNTE	5 103	4 978	6 079	6 510	7 265	7 695	8 044	9 034	10 265	10 186	10 440
Percentage growth on previous year	KNTF	–7.2	–2.5	22.0	7.1	13.0	5.9	4.5	7.3	13.3	–0.7	4.1

1 Available tonne kilometres (millions).

Source: Civil Aviation Authority: 020 7453 6246

14.24 Air traffic between the United Kingdom and abroad[1]
Aircraft flights and passengers carried

Thousands

		1990	1991	1992	1993	1994[2]	1995	1996	1997	1998	1999	2000
Flights												
United Kingdom airlines												
Scheduled services	KNUA	271.0	250.5	283.0	290.8	325.8	342.1	373.0	410.3	443.7	480.9	520.3
Non-scheduled services	KNUB	207.9	202.6	236.2	215.2	195.0	204.8	198.0	208.2	218.7	212.6	216.2
Overseas airlines[3]												
Scheduled services	KNUC	294.8	300.4	328.0	336.2	351.3	363.3	390.0	399.6	426.4	467.6	467.6
Non-scheduled services	KNUD	45.5	34.6	33.9	38.0	35.1	31.5	31.3	32.5	34.8	31.7	31.7
Total	KNUE	819.2	788.1	881.1	880.2	907.2	941.7	992.3	1 050.6	1 223.6	1 192.8	1 235.8
Passengers carried												
United Kingdom airlines												
Scheduled services	KNUF	25 316.8	23 271.6	27 138.8	29 798.2	32 578.0	34 934.7	37 902.2	41 854.7	46 747.7	50 148.5	54 522.8
Non-scheduled services	KNUG	19 679.1	19 715.2	23 347.6	24 777.1	19 501.0	20 434.5	26 304.4	28 699.5	31 616.6	32 603.8	33 185.9
Overseas airlines[3]												
Scheduled services	KNUH	28 224.4	26 719.4	29 240.9	31 163.4	35 134.5	34 568.5	36 992.1	39 900.7	42 554.5	46 628.0	46 627.9
Non-scheduled services	KNUI	4 187.9	3 078.8	3 222.6	3 638.0	3 509.5	4 244.2	4 416.3	4 413.0	4 569.7	4 156.5	4 156.5
Total	KNUJ	77 408.2	72 785.0	82 949.9	89 376.7	90 723.0	94 231.9	105 615.0	114 867.9	125 488.5	133 536.8	138 493.1

1 Excludes travel to and from the Channel Islands.
2 Due to the introduction of European licencing, off shore helicopter movements are no longer included in this figure.

3 Includes airlines of overseas UK Territories.

Source: Civil Aviation Authority: 020 7453 6246

14.25 United Kingdom airlines[1]
Operations and traffic on scheduled services: revenue traffic

		Unit	1990	1991	1992	1993	1994	1995	1996	1997	1998	1999	2000
All services													
Aircraft stage flights:													
Number	KNFA	Numbers	617 477	568 122	601 500	601 620	621 272	658 958	702 492	749 806	797 682	835 031	878 582
Average length	KNFB	Kilometres	848	876	916	971	1 023	1 032	1 047	1 079	1 111	1 134	1 156
Aircraft-kilometres flown	KNFC	Millions	523.8	497.7	551.2	584.3	663.2	679.9	735.3	809.2	886.3	946.9	1 016.3
Passengers uplifted	KNFD	"	38.4	34.6	38.2	40.1	43.9	47.5	51.1	56.3	61.7	65.4	70.3
Seat-kilometres used	KNFE	"	79 579.6	74 615.4	86 731.4	94 670.1	104 294.5	115 347.1	124 846.5	136 388.2	151 969.1	160 336.4	170 469.0
Cargo uplifted:[2]													
Total	KNFF	Tonnes	485 535	466 622	507 356	541 986	618 067	643 181	690 806	782 855	831 436	860 291	897 184
Tonne-kilometres used:		Millions											
Passenger	KNFH	"	7 465.6	7 007.9	8 135.2	8 905.3	9 789.2	11 171.5	12 189.6	13 287.2	14 754.9	15 517.7	16 507.0
Freight	KNFI	"	2 388.7	2 379.9	2 644.1	2 919.6	3 378.1	3 567.3	3 831.9	4 454.0	4 663.3	4 924.9	5 159.9
Mail	KNFJ	"	168.6	182.6	161.1	141.5	147.3	151.1	176.0	172.2	177.7	153.0	179.2
Total	KNFG	"	10 023.0	9 570.5	10 940.5	11 966.4	13 314.6	14 889.9	16 197.5	17 913.4	19 595.9	20 595.6	21 846.1
Domestic services													
Aircraft stage flights:													
Number	KNFK	Numbers	300 683	285 346	299 893	300 416	301 652	318 884	331 109	336 218	352 936	354 864	353 525
Average length	KNFL	Kilometres	288.0	301.0	305.7	311.3	314.8	317.0	320.0	330.0	333.1	337.0	343.5
Aircraft-kilometres flown	KNFM	Millions	86.5	86.0	91.6	93.5	94.9	101.1	105.8	111.0	117.6	119.6	121.4
Passengers uplifted	KNFN	"	12.7	11.6	11.6	12.1	13.0	14.0	15.0	15.9	16.6	17.1	18.0
Seat-kilometres used	KNFO	"	5 020.8	4 663.7	4 728.2	4 933.8	5 334.0	5 753.6	6 204.3	6 645.7	6 947.5	7 183.9	7 541.8
Cargo uplifted:[2]													
Total	KNFP	Tonnes	45 818	37 739	35 420	30 660	32 670	33 659	35 432	30 679	31 879	25 964	24 644
Tonne-kilometres used:		Millions											
Passenger	KNFR	"	412.0	382.3	387.4	405.2	417.3	485.0	527.8	568.9	592.6	609.9	640.2
Freight	KNFS	"	8.7	6.7	6.6	5.6	6.3	6.9	7.4	6.1	6.0	6.0	5.8
Mail	KNFT	"	7.6	7.4	7.0	6.5	6.7	6.6	6.4	6.0	6.0	4.0	3.7
Total	KNFQ	"	428.3	396.5	401.1	417.3	430.3	498.5	541.6	581.0	604.7	619.9	649.7
International services													
Aircraft stage flights:													
Number	KNFU	Numbers	316 794	282 776	301 607	301 204	319 620	339 714	371 400	413 588	444 746	480 167	525 057
Average length	KNFV	Kilometres	1 381	1 456	1 523	1 629	1 693	1 703	1 695	1 688	1 729	1 723	1 704
Aircraft-kilometres flown	KNFW	Millions	437.4	411.7	459.5	490.8	541.4	578.8	629.5	698.2	768.8	827.3	894.9
Passengers uplifted	KNFX	"	25.7	22.9	26.5	28.0	30.9	33.5	36.1	40.4	45.1	48.2	52.2
Seat-kilometres used	KNFY	"	74 558.8	69 951.7	82 003.1	89 736.3	99.0	109.6	118.6	129.7	145.0	153.1	162.9
Cargo uplifted:[2]													
Total	KNFZ	Tonnes	439 717.0	428 883.0	471 936.0	511 326.0	585.4	609.5	655.4	752.2	799.6	834.3	184.1
Tonne-kilometres used:		Millions											
Passenger	KNJX	"	7 053.6	6 625.6	7 747.8	8 500.1	9 352.3	10 636.4	11 661.9	12 718.2	14 162.3	14 908.0	13 611.1
Freight	KNJY	"	2 380.1	2 373.2	2 637.4	2 914.0	3 371.8	3 560.4	3 824.5	4 448.0	4 657.2	4 919.0	5 154.1
Mail	KNJZ	"	161.1	175.2	154.0	135.0	140.5	144.4	169.5	166.3	171.7	149.0	175.5
Total	KNJW	"	9 594.7	9 174.0	10 539.3	11 549.1	12 864.6	14 391.2	15 655.9	17 332.5	18 991.2	19 976.0	18 940.7

1 Includes services of British Airways and other UK private companies.
2 Cargo has re-defined as freight and mail.

Source: Civil Aviation Authority: 020 7453 6246

14.26 United Kingdom airlines
Accidents on scheduled fixed wing passenger-carrying services[1]

	Passenger casualties			Crew casualties		Thousand aircraft stage flights per fatal accident	Million aircraft-kms. flown per fatal accident	Thousand passengers carried per passenger killed	Million passenger kms. flown per passenger killed	Fatal accidents		Passengers killed per hundred million passenger-kms.
	Number of fatal accidents	Killed	Seriously injured	Killed	Seriously injured					per 100 000 aircraft stage flights	per hundred million aircraft-kms.	
1950-54	7	194	9	28	4	107.4	61.8	46.1	50.0	0.93	1.62	1.99
1955-59	7	123	28	29	8	158.3	92.1	155.2	158.5	0.63	1.09	0.63
1960-64	5	104	35	21	6	303.7	182.3	373.4	390.6	0.33	0.55	0.25
1965-69	6	273	2	32	2	282.7	194.9	222.2	255.2	0.35	0.52	0.39
1970-74	2	167	5	14	2	897.4	737.6	466.3	657.7	0.11	0.14	0.15
1975-79	1	54	6	9	-	1 797.2	1 481.6	1 697.0	3 240.0	0.06	0.07	0.03
1980-84	-	-	4	-	1	.	.	.	.	.	.	.
1985-89	2	47	79	1	8	1 220.0	1 014.5	3031.0	6 262.9	0.08	0.10	0.02
1990-94	-	-	1	-	9	.	.	.	.	.	.	.
1995-99	1	9	1	3	3	3 700.0	4 026.0	31 265.6	76 539.4	0.03	0.02	0.001
	KCVN	KCVO	KCVP	KCVQ	KCVR							
2000	-	-	1	-	.	.	.	.	.	.	.	.

1 Excluding accidents involving the deaths of third parties only.

Source: Civil Aviation Authority: 01293 573346

14.27 Activity at civil aerodromes
United Kingdom

		1990	1991	1992	1993	1994	1995	1996	1997	1998	1999	2000
Movement of civil aircraft (Thousands)												
Commercial Transport	KNQC	1 420	1 365	1 448	1 487	1 552	1 615	1 686	1 764	1 871	1 959	2 045
Other[1]	KNQD	127	115	112	109	112	124	128	143	162	159	159
Total	KNQB	1 547	1 481	1 561	1 596	1 664	1 739	1 814	1 907	2 033	2 118	2 204
Non-commercial[2]	KNQE	1 708	1 466	1 321	1 523	1 684	1 809	1 281	1 330	1 343	1 263	1 186
Total	KNQA	3 255	2 947	2 881	3 119	3 348	3 548	3 095	3 237	3 376	3 381	3 390
Passengers handled												
Terminal	KNQG	102 417	95 768	106 123	112 278	122 364	129 586	135 998	146 823	158 997	168 478	180 001
Transit	KNQH	1 725	1 525	1 680	1 620	1 578	1 514	1 508	1 427	1 251	1 172	1 177
Total	KNQF	104 142	97 293	107 804	113 898	123 942	131 100	137 506	148 250	160 248	169 650	181 178
Commercial freight handled[3] (Tonnes)												
Set down	KNQJ	625 131	595 886	658 183	696 055	794 860	854 859	891 150	9 870 651	777 311	141 517	1 180 912
Picked up	KNQK	567 919	524 087	581 315	682 186	811 353	862 584	892 206	9 685 061	147 911	59 881	1 145 544
Total	KNQI	1 193 050	1 119 973	1 239 498	1 378 241	1 606 213	1 717 443	1 783 356	19 555 712	925 222	201 398	2 326 456
Mail handled												
Set down	KNQM	76 262	77 082	80 236	85 803	91 212	93 562	101 664	110 355	108 110	112 161	117 999
Picked up	KNQN	95 902	93 390	97 241	101 092	110 817	116 057	127 544	138 002	134 275	134 303	139 673
Total	KNQL	172 164	170 472	177 477	186 895	202 029	209 619	229 208	248 357	242 385	246 464	257 672

1 Local pleasure flights and non-transport charter flights for reward (for example: aerial survey work, crop dusting and delivery of empty aircraft).
2 Test and training flights, scheduled service positioning flights, private, aero-club and official flights, etc.
3 Figures include weight of vehicles carried on vehicle ferry services.

Source: Civil Aviation Authority: 020 7379 7311

14.28 Great Britain ports: foreign, coastwise and one-port traffic[1]

Million tonnes

		1989	1990	1991	1992	1993	1994	1995	1996	1997	1998	1999
Inwards:												
Foreign												
Bulk fuel	ZCHN	64.22	75.07	78.02	76.47	78.54	71.17	67.06	70.48	74.80	77.54	69.93
Other traffic	ZCHO	107.20	104.75	100.10	101.23	105.32	113.76	118.09	117.41	126.62	127.52	128.96
All traffic	ZCHP	171.42	179.82	178.12	177.70	183.86	184.93	185.15	187.88	201.42	205.06	198.88
Coastwise												
Bulk fuel	ZCHQ	44.71	41.26	41.73	38.52	40.21	42.80	47.29	49.10	46.51	48.07	44.65
Other traffic	ZCHR	10.99	10.78	11.50	11.63	10.96	10.81	10.81	10.72	11.09	12.39	11.59
All traffic	ZCHS	55.70	52.04	53.22	50.14	51.17	53.61	58.10	59.82	57.60	60.46	56.24
One-port												
Bulk fuel	ZCHT	13.33	13.86	13.45	14.11	10.06	13.73	10.85	10.86	6.87	10.59	20.22
Other traffic	ZCHU	21.70	20.24	16.40	14.86	13.65	14.85	15.88	14.24	14.97	15.50	16.20
All traffic	ZCHV	35.03	34.10	29.84	28.96	23.71	25.58	26.73	25.10	21.84	26.09	36.42
Total inwards												
Bulk fuel	ZCHW	122.26	130.19	133.19	129.10	128.81	127.70	125.20	130.44	128.19	136.20	134.80
Other traffic	ZCHX	139.89	135.77	128.00	127.71	129.93	139.42	144.78	142.37	152.68	155.41	156.74
All traffic	ZCHY	262.15	265.96	261.19	256.81	258.74	267.11	269.97	272.81	280.87	291.61	291.54
Outwards:												
Foreign												
Bulk fuel	ZCHZ	72.88	80.34	84.70	88.81	94.12	112.10	109.58	103.92	102.53	103.65	106.41
Other traffic	ZCIA	54.18	55.33	58.02	60.89	62.93	66.47	68.72	71.41	76.23	77.50	77.45
All traffic	ZCIB	127.06	135.67	142.71	149.70	157.05	178.57	178.30	175.32	178.76	181.16	183.86
Coastwise												
Bulk fuel	ZCIC	50.43	46.60	46.93	45.45	45.84	48.65	54.69	58.40	54.26	53.19	52.39
Other traffic	ZCID	11.12	11.42	12.21	11.45	11.94	11.60	12.86	12.40	13.14	13.95	13.33
All traffic	ZCIE	61.55	58.02	59.13	56.90	57.78	60.26	67.55	70.80	67.40	67.14	65.72
One-port												
Other traffic	ZCIF	14.62	15.64	14.77	14.66	13.78	12.11	12.06	12.04	11.91	8.52	3.21
All traffic	ZCIG	14.62	15.64	14.77	14.66	13.78	12.11	12.06	12.04	11.91	8.52	3.21
Total outwards												
Bulk fuel	ZCIH	123.32	126.94	131.62	134.26	139.96	160.76	164.27	162.32	156.79	156.84	158.80
Other traffic	ZCII	79.92	82.40	84.99	87.00	88.65	90.19	93.64	95.85	101.28	99.97	93.99
All traffic	ZCIJ	203.23	209.34	216.61	221.25	228.61	250.94	257.91	258.16	258.07	256.81	252.79
Total goods handled	ZCIK	465.39	475.30	477.80	478.06	487.35	518.06	527.89	530.97	538.94	548.42	544.33

1 Includes estimates of traffic at smaller ports from 1995 onwards.

Source: Department for Transport, Local Government and the Regions; 020 7944 3087

14.29 Roll-on/roll-off ferry and Channel Tunnel traffic; road goods vehicles outward to mainland Europe: by country of registration

Thousands

		1990	1991	1992	1993	1994	1995	1996	1997	1998	1999	2000
Powered vehicles:												
United Kingdom	ZCGT	339.0	360.2	373.7	398.0	453.1	486.0	531.1	·543.2	544.3	562.7	544.8
Austria	ZCGU	..	..	..	..	..	9.7	8.6	5.4	10.2	14.9	17.0
Belgium/Luxembourg	ZCGV	37.4	33.8	37.2	29.4	37.1	45.7	41.0	53.6	74.5	96.7	·114.1
Denmark	ZCGW	8.4	6.5	6.9	4.9	5.0	4.5	4.6	5.5	7.3	8.7	9.5
Finland	ZCGX	..	..	..	..	..	0.3	0.2	0.8	0.6	0.7	0.9
Germany	ZCGY	33.8	29.8	30.8	27.7	28.1	28.0	30.4	39.3	52.4	73.1	111.5
France	ZCGZ	131.2	128.7	141.2	144.0	163.2	154.9	181.7	234.2	272.4	319.1	338.8
Greece	ZCHA	2.2	2.3	2.2	1.5	1.3	1.8	2.1	2.6	1.9	2.6	2.9
Irish Republic	ZCHB	21.0	24.3	24.7	35.6	32.4	31.0	30.1	32.3	38.8	44.7	48.5
Italy	ZCHC	15.2	13.7	13.5	13.0	22.7	29.3	28.8	30.4	35.3	45.8	67.8
Netherlands	ZCHD	71.0	69.0	71.9	73.3	76.3	84.6	87.2	107.0	125.4	153.3	185.1
Spain	ZCHE	27.2	25.3	32.4	29.5	35.2	38.4	39.4	45.1	56.3	67.7	81.8
Sweden	ZCHF	..	..	..	..	..	0.7	0.9	8.9	10.3	1.0	1.4
Portugal	ZCHG	2.8	2.5	3.4	3.3	3.7	3.4	3.1	5.1	6.7	9.2	10.7
European Union (excluding UK)	ZCHH	350.2	335.8	364.2	362.2	405.2	432.2	458.1	569.5	692.1	837.3	990.0
Non-European Union	ZCHI	32.8	27.1	29.8	30.2	34.2	29.0	26.3	28.0	33.6	47.4	52.9
Unknown	ZCHJ	1.7	2.4	2.1	5.8	4.0	4.0	2.2	5.7	4.5	6.3	17.7
All countries	ZCHK	723.7	725.5	769.8	796.2	896.5	950.2	1 017.7	1 146.4	1 274.5	1 453.7	1 605.4
Unaccompanied trailers	ZCHL	583.9	601.2	629.3	593.4	701.6	677.4	626.4	740.0	737.5	737.8	712.9
Powered vehicles and unaccompanied trailers	ZCHM	1 307.6	1 326.7	1 399.1	1 389.6	1 598.1	1 627.6	1 644.1	1 886.4	2 012.3	2 191.4	2 318.3

Source: Department for Transport, Local Government and the Regions; 0117 987 8484

14.30 United Kingdom international passenger movements by air and sea
Arrivals plus departures

Thousands

		1990	1991	1992	1993	1994	1995	1996	1997	1998	1999	2000
By air												
EC Europe[1]	ZCDD	45 072	43 163	48 641	51 501	58 080	60 003	60 979	66 127	73 397	79 040	84 963
Other Western Europe[2]	ZCDE	8 040	6 735	8 102	8 507	8 812	9 372	9 481	10 397	11 099	11 252	11 900
Rest of the world	ZCDF	22 661	21 981	25 397	27 281	28 899	31 528	34 400	37 575	40 247	42 610	45 288
All air passenger movements	KMUP	75 772	71 879	82 141	87 289	95 790	100 902	104 861	114 099	124 744	132 903	142 153
By sea												
Republic of Ireland, European continent and Mediterranean Sea area[3]	ZCDG	30 088	31 419	32 882	34 685	36 733	34 321	34 543	36 258	33 226	31 381	28 423
Rest of the world	BMMF	22.0	34.0	27.0	37.0	34.0	33.0	24.0	29.0	23.0	26.0	27.0
Pleasure cruises[4,6]	KMRQ	153	172	138	193	236	207	233	–	–	450	466
All sea passenger movements[6]	KMUO	30 263	31 625	33 046	34 915	37 002	34 562	34 792	36 288[5]	33 249[5]	31 857	28 916

1 Includes Azores, Madeira, Canary and Cape Verde Islands. Austria, Finland, and Sweden joined the EC in 1995, but are included in the EC section for all years to show a consistent time series.
2 Includes Iceland and the Faroe Islands.

3 Prior to 1992, includes passengers between the Isle of Man and the Irish Republic.
4 Cruise passengers, like other passengers are included at both departure and arrival if their journeys begin and end at United Kingdom seaports.
5 Excluding cruise passengers.
6 Provisional data.

Sources: Civil Aviation Authority; Department for Transport, Local Government and the Regions

14.31 Postal services and television licences
United Kingdom
Years ended 31 March[1]

		1991	1992	1993	1994	1995	1996	1997	1998	1999	2000	2001
Letters, etc posted[2](millions)	KMRA	15 902	16 038	16 364	16 651	17 468	18 322	18 101	18 389	17 934	18 738	19 092
of which:												
Registered and insured	KMRB	*21.3*	*20.7*	*21.5*	*21.8*	*21.5*	*23.5*	*25.6*	*28.7*	*31.6*	*30.2*	*32.3*
Airmail (Commonwealth and foreign)[3]	KMRC	467.7	544.5	534.4	545.0	567.1	655.1	684.5	658.4	693.2	672.3	659.2
Business reply and freepost items[4]	KMRD	416.7	428.9	481.3	482.9	477.6	493.1	505.8	524.7	503.6	475.3	487.4
Postal orders												
Total issued (thousands)[5]	KMRH	39 644	39 867	38 401	39 089	37 901	35 542	33 404	31 907	30 289	30 153	30 931
Television licences (thousands)												
in force on 31 March	KMQL	19 546	19 631	20 067	20 413	20 732	21 105	21 305	21 723	22 240	22 625	22 839
of which:												
Colour	KMQM	*18 111*	*18 426*	*19 031*	*19 524*	*19 957*	*20 505*	*20 849*	*21 344*	*21 944*	*22 413*	*22 684*

1 Years ended 31 March for letters, postal orders and telegrams sent. For all other items figures relate to 31 March in each year.
2 Including printed papers, newspapers, postcards and sample packets.
3 Including letters without special charge for air transport.
4 Business reply and Freepost is now known as Response Services.
5 Excluding those issued on HM ships, in many British possessions and in other places abroad. For 1990 to 1998 includes Postal Orders issued Overseas and by Ministry of Defence.

Sources: Royal Mail: 01246 547012; Subscription Services Limited: 01179 219384; Post Office Counters Limited: 020 7921 9384

15 National accounts

National accounts

National accounts (Tables 15.1 to 15.22)
The tables which follow are based on those in the *Blue Book 2001 Edition*. Some of the figures are provisional and may be revised later; this applies particularly to the figures for 1999 and 2000.

The accounts are based on the European System of Accounts 1995 (ESA95). The *Blue Book* contains an introduction to the system of the UK accounts outlining some of the main concepts and principles of measurement used. It explains how key economic indicators are derived from the sequence of accounts and how the figures describing the whole economy are broken down by sector and by industry. A detailed description of the structure for the accounts is provided in a separate ONS publication *United Kingdom National Accounts: Concepts, Sources and Methods* (TSO 1998). Further information on the financial accounts is given in the *Financial Statistics Explanatory Handbook*.

In the tables in this chapter on national income, analyses by industry are based, as far as possible, on the Standard Industrial Classification Revised 1992. The principal aggregate measured in these tables is the **Gross domestic product** (GDP). This is a concept of the value of the total economic activity taking place in UK territory. It can be viewed as incomes earned, as expenditures incurred, or as production. Adding all primary incomes received from the rest of the world and deducting all primary incomes payable to non-residents produces **Gross national income** (previously known as gross national product). This is a concept of the value of all incomes earned by UK residents.

ESA95, the internationally compatible accounting framework, provides a systematic and detailed description of the UK economy. It includes the sector accounts which provide, by institutional sector, a description of the different stages of the economic process from production through income generation, distribution and use of income to capital accumulation and financing; and the input-output framework, which describes the production process in more detail. It contains all the elements required to compile such aggregate measures as GDP, gross national income (GNI) and saving.

Gross domestic product and national income (Tables 15.1, 15.2, 15.3)
Table 15.1 shows the main national accounts aggregates, at current prices and at constant 1995 prices.

Table 15.2 shows the various money flows which generate the gross domestic product and gross national income. The output approach to GDP shows the total output of goods and services, the use of goods and services in the production process (intermediate consumption) and taxes and subsidies on products. The expenditure approach to GDP shows consumption expenditure by households and government, gross capital formation and expenditure on UK exports by overseas purchasers. The sum of these items overstates the amount of income generated in the United Kingdom by the value of imports of goods and services; this item is therefore subtracted to produce gross domestic product at market prices. The income approach to GDP shows gross operating surplus, mixed income and compensation of employees (previously known as income from employment). Taxes are added and subsidies are deducted to produce the total of the income-based components at market prices.

Table 15.2 also shows the primary incomes received from the rest of the world, which are added to GDP and primary incomes payable to non-residents, which are deducted from GDP, to arrive at **Gross national income.** Primary income comprises compensation of employees, taxes *less* subsidies on production and property and entrepreneurial income.

Table 15.3 shows the expenditure approach to GDP at constant 1995 prices. When looking at the change in the economy over time the main concern is usually whether more goods and services are actually being produced now than at some time in the past. Over time changes in current price GDP show changes in the monetary value of the components of GDP and, as these changes in value can reflect changes in both price and volume, it is difficult to establish how much of an increase in the series is due either to increased activity in the economy or to an increase in the price level. As a result, when looking at the real growth in the economy over time it is useful to look at volume (or constant price) estimates of GDP. In constant price series, for all years the transactions are re-valued to a constant price level using the average prices of a selected year, known as the base year, presently 1995.

Industrial analysis (Tables 15.4, 15.5)
The analysis of gross value added by industry at current prices shown in Table 15.4 reflects the estimates based on the Standard Industrial Classification, Revised 1992 (SIC92). The table is based on current price data reconciled through the input-output process for 1992 to 1999. The estimates are valued at basic prices, that is, the only taxes included in the price will be taxes paid as part of the production process, such as business rates, and not any taxes specifically levied on the production of a unit of output, for example VAT.

Table 15.5 shows constant price estimates of gross value added at basic prices by industry. Constant price gross value added (output approach) provides the lead indicator of economic change in the short term. The output analysis of gross value added is estimated in terms of change and expressed in index number form. It is therefore inappropriate to show as a statistical adjustment any divergence of an output measure of GDP derived from it from other measures of GDP. Such an adjustment does, however, exist implicitly.

Sector analysis - Distribution of income accounts and capital account (Tables 15.6-15.13)
The new national accounts accounting framework includes the sector accounts which provide, by institutional sector, a description of the different stages of the economic process from production through income generation, distribution and use of income to capital accumulation and financing.

Tables 15.6-15.12 show the allocation of primary income account and the secondary distribution of income account for the non-financial corporations, financial corporations, government and households sectors. Additionally, Table 15.12 shows the use of income account for the households sector and Table 15.13 provides a summary of the capital account. The full sequence of accounts is shown in the *Blue Book*.

The allocation of primary income account shows the resident units and institutional sectors as recipients rather than producers of primary income. It demonstrates the extent to which operating surpluses are distributed to the owners of the enterprises. The resources side of the allocation of primary income accounts includes the components of the income approach to measurement of GDP. The balance of this account is the gross balance of primary income (B.5g) for each sector, and if the gross balance is aggregated across all sectors of the economy the result is **gross national income.**

The secondary distribution of income account describes how the balance of income for each sector is allocated by redistribution; through transfers such as taxes on income, social contributions and benefits and other current transfers. The balancing item of this account is gross disposable income (B.6g). For the households sector, gross disposable income at constant prices is shown as real household disposable income.

Table 15.12 shows, for the households sector, the use of disposable income where the balancing item is saving (B.8g). For the non-financial corporations sector the balancing item of the secondary distribution of income account, gross disposable income (B.6g) is equal to saving (B.8g).

The summary capital account *(Table 15.13)* brings together the saving and investment of the several sectors of the economy. It shows saving, capital transfers, gross capital formation and net acquisition of non-financial assets for each of the four sectors.

Household and non-profit institutions serving households (NPISH) consumption expenditure at current and constant prices *(Tables 15.14-15.17)*
Household and NPISH consumption expenditure is a major component of the expenditure measure of gross domestic product at current prices *(Table 15.2)* and at constant prices *(Table 15.3)*.

Household final consumption expenditure includes the value of income-in-kind and imputed rent of owner-occupied dwellings but excludes business expenditure allowed as deductions in computing income for tax purposes. It includes expenditure on durable goods, for instance motor cars, which from the point of view of the individual might more appropriately be treated as capital expenditure. The only exceptions are the purchase of land and dwellings and costs incurred in connection with the transfer of their ownership and expenditure on major improvements by occupiers, which are treated as personal capital expenditure.

The estimates of household consumption expenditure include purchases of second-hand as well as new goods, *less* the proceeds of sales of used goods.

The most detailed figures are published quarterly in *Consumer Trends*.

Change in inventories (previously known as value of physical increase in stocks and work in progress) *(Table 15.18)*
This table gives a broad analysis by industry, and, for manufacturing industry, by asset, of the value of entries *less* withdrawals and losses of inventories (stocks).

Gross fixed capital formation *(Tables 15.19-15.22)*
Gross fixed capital formation comprises expenditure on the replacement of, and additions to, fixed capital assets located in the United Kingdom, including all ships and aircraft of UK ownership.

15.1 UK national and domestic product
Main aggregates: index numbers and values
At current and constant 1995 prices

		1992	1993	1994	1995	1996	1997	1998	1999	2000
INDICES (1995=100)										
VALUES AT CURRENT PRICES										
Gross domestic product at current market prices ("money GDP")	YBEU	84.9	89.3	94.8	100.0	106.0	112.8	119.6	125.3	131.2
Gross value added at current basic prices	YBEX	85.4	89.9	95.1	100.0	106.2	112.6	119.0	124.2	129.9
VALUES AT 1995 PRICES										
Gross domestic product at 1995 market prices	YBEZ	90.6	92.9	97.2	100.0	102.6	106.2	109.3	111.7	114.9
Gross national disposable income at 1995 market prices	YBFP	91.8	94.0	98.4	100.0	103.0	108.2	113.1	114.8	118.8
Gross value added at 1995 basic prices	CGCE	90.6	92.8	97.3	100.0	102.7	106.0	109.4	111.6	114.8
PRICES										
Implied deflator of GDP at market prices (expenditure based, "total home costs per unit of output")	YBGB	93.8	96.2	97.5	100.0	103.3	106.2	109.3	112.2	114.2
VALUES AT CURRENT PRICES (£ million)										
Gross measures, before deduction of fixed capital consumption										
at current market prices										
Gross domestic product at current market prices ("money GDP")	YBHA	610 854	642 327	681 327	719 176	762 214	811 067	859 805	901 269	943 412
Employment, property and entrepreneurial income from the rest of the world (receipts *less* payments)	YBGG	128	−191	3 348	2 101	1 204	3 906	12 558	4 019	6 117
Subsidies (receipts) *less* taxes (payments) on production from/to the rest of the world	-QZOZ	−4 319	−4 725	−3 349	−5 220	−4 141	−2 811	−3 683	−3 551	−3 446
Subsidies on production	NHQR	66	215	286	293	253	206	246	370	361
Gross national income at current market prices	ABMX	606 729	637 626	681 612	716 350	759 530	812 368	868 926	902 107	946 448
Current transfers from the rest of the world (receipts *less* payments)	-YBGF	−1 275	−734	−2 309	−2 649	−1 902	−3 209	−4 790	−4 067	−5 377
Gross national disposable income at current market prices	NQCO	605 454	636 892	679 303	713 701	757 628	809 159	864 136	898 040	940 706
adjustment to current basic prices										
Gross domestic product at current market prices	YBHA	610 854	642 327	681 327	719 176	762 214	811 067	859 805	901 269	943 412
Adjustment to current basic prices (*less* taxes *plus* subsidies on products)	-NQBU	−64 420	−66 866	−72 587	−79 268	−82 594	−90 375	−98 487	−106 244	−112 359
Gross value added at current basic prices	ABML	546 434	575 461	608 740	639 908	679 620	720 692	761 318	795 025	831 053
Net measures, after deduction of fixed capital consumption	-NQAE	−77 115	−83 522	−85 161	−86 959	−89 639	−93 531	−96 074	−100 650	−106 047
Net domestic product at current market prices	NHRK	533 739	558 805	596 166	632 217	672 575	717 536	763 731	800 619	837 369
Net national income at current market prices	NSRX	529 614	554 104	596 451	629 391	669 891	718 837	772 852	801 457	840 401
Net national disposable income at current market prices	NQCP	528 339	553 370	594 142	626 742	667 989	715 628	768 062	797 390	834 659
VALUES AT 1995 PRICES (£ million)										
Gross measures, before deduction of fixed capital consumption										
at 1995 market prices										
Gross domestic product at 1995 market prices	ABMI	651 566	667 804	698 915	719 176	738 046	763 472	786 303	803 019	826 144
Terms of trade effect ("Trading gain or loss")	YBGJ	7 284	7 950	4 835	−	2 610	10 677	16 671	19 559	25 105
Real gross domestic income	YBGL	658 850	675 753	703 750	719 176	740 656	774 149	802 974	822 578	851 248
Real employment, property and entrepreneurial income from the rest of the world (receipts *less* payments)	YBGI	138	−201	3 459	2 101	1 170	3 728	11 756	3 686	5 546
Subsidies (receipts) *less* taxes (payments) on production from/to the rest of the world	-QZPB	−2 755	−3 695	−2 679	−5 220	−5 181	−2 576	−3 082	−3 364	−4 375
Gross national income at 1995 market prices	YBGM	656 233	671 857	704 530	716 057	736 645	775 301	811 648	822 900	852 419
Real current transfers from the rest of the world (receipts *less* payments)	-YBGP	−1 312	−545	−2 087	−2 354	−1 601	−2 864	−4 252	−3 389	−4 875
Gross national disposable income at 1995 market prices	YBGO	654 834	671 113	702 443	713 703	735 044	772 437	807 396	819 511	847 544
adjustment to 1995 basic prices										
Gross domestic product at 1995 market prices	ABMI	651 566	667 804	698 915	719 176	738 046	763 472	786 303	803 019	826 144
Adjustment to 1995 basic prices (*less* taxes *plus* subsidies on products)	-NTAQ	−71 802	−73 672	−76 491	−79 268	−80 984	−85 193	−86 432	−88 734	−91 582
Gross value added at 1995 basic prices	ABMM	579 834	594 215	622 424	639 908	657 062	678 279	699 871	714 285	734 562
Net measures, after deduction of fixed capital consumption at 1995 prices	-YBFX	−85 215	−89 925	−88 894	−86 959	−87 163	−88 968	−89 644	−91 305	−96 520
Net national income at 1995 market prices	YBET	570 785	581 431	615 648	629 098	649 497	686 229	721 522	730 498	755 901
Net national disposable income at 1995 market prices	YBEY	572 298	583 362	619 421	631 768	647 654	683 168	717 270	727 109	751 026

Source: Office for National Statistics: 020 7533 6031

15.2 UK gross domestic product and national income
Current prices

£ million

		1992	1993	1994	1995	1996	1997	1998	1999	2000
GROSS DOMESTIC PRODUCT										
Gross domestic product: output approach										
Gross value added, at basic prices										
Output of goods and services, at basic prices	NQAF	1 100 189	1 172 054	1 270 951	1 363 534	1 455 417	1 539 896	1 631 361	1 721 728	1 818 849
less intermediate consumption, at purchasers' prices	-NQAJ	-553 755	-596 593	-662 211	-723 626	-775 797	-819 204	-870 043	-926 703	-987 792
Total	ABML	546 434	575 461	608 740	639 908	679 620	720 692	761 318	795 025	831 053
Value added taxes (VAT) on products	QYRC	41 485	42 429	46 117	48 424	51 389	55 454	58 521	62 475	64 906
Other taxes on products	NSUI	29 033	30 815	33 450	37 995	39 724	43 003	46 933	50 465	54 271
less subsidies on products	-NZHC	-6 098	-6 378	-6 980	-7 151	-8 519	-8 082	-6 967	-6 696	-6 818
Gross domestic product at market prices	YBHA	610 854	642 327	681 327	719 176	762 214	811 067	859 805	901 269	943 412
Gross domestic product: expenditure approach										
Final consumption expenditure										
Actual individual consumption										
Household final consumption expenditure	ABPB	379 758	401 970	422 397	443 367	473 800	503 374	536 525	567 555	594 782
Final consumption expenditure of NPISH	ABNV	10 806	13 981	15 287	16 481	18 385	19 602	21 117	22 671	22 866
Individual government final consumption expenditure	NNAQ	73 412	74 549	77 545	81 093	84 968	87 551	92 271	100 504	106 176
Total actual individual consumption	ABRE	463 976	490 500	515 229	540 941	577 153	610 527	649 913	690 730	723 824
Collective government final consumption expenditure	NNAR	55 783	56 985	58 710	59 938	61 811	61 596	62 610	65 790	68 615
Total final consumption expenditure	ABKW	519 759	547 485	573 939	600 879	638 964	672 123	712 523	756 520	792 439
Households and NPISH	NSSG	390 564	415 951	437 684	459 848	492 185	522 976	557 642	590 226	617 648
Central government	NMBJ	78 275	81 566	84 385	86 791	90 396	92 190	95 298	100 647	105 464
Local government	NMMT	50 920	49 968	51 870	54 240	56 383	56 957	59 583	65 647	69 327
Gross capital formation										
Gross fixed capital formation	NPQX	100 583	101 027	108 314	117 448	125 762	134 396	151 539	155 408	165 247
Changes in inventories	ABMP	-1 937	329	3 708	4 512	1 771	4 388	4 460	4 975	1 855
Acquisitions less disposals of valuables	NPJO	17	-29	113	-121	-158	-26	430	230	-3
Total gross capital formation	NPDN	98 663	101 327	112 135	121 839	127 375	138 758	156 429	160 613	167 099
Exports of goods and services	KTMW	144 091	163 640	180 508	203 509	223 091	231 622	228 801	236 720	265 305
less imports of goods and services	-KTMX	-151 659	-170 125	-185 255	-207 051	-227 216	-231 436	-237 948	-252 584	-281 024
External balance of goods and services	KTMY	-7 568	-6 485	-4 747	-3 542	-4 125	186	-9 147	-15 864	-15 719
Statistical discrepancy between expenditure components and GDP	GIXM	–	–	–	–	–	–	–	–	-407
Gross domestic product at market prices	YBHA	610 854	642 327	681 327	719 176	762 214	811 067	859 805	901 269	943 412
Gross domestic product: income approach										
Operating surplus, gross										
Non-financial corporations										
Public non-financial corporations	NRJT	6 607	8 188	9 111	10 987	10 856	9 758	10 216	10 376	9 101
Private non-financial corporations	NRJK	105 864	116 282	133 037	142 165	157 745	168 871	174 261	178 260	188 526
Financial corporations	NQNV	13 649	17 726	20 708	17 838	17 135	14 806	18 436	14 701	15 548
Adjustment for financial services	-NSRV	-19 086	-19 569	-23 119	-23 215	-22 580	-22 396	-27 998	-30 819	-37 091
General government	NMXV	6 075	5 870	5 991	6 447	6 876	7 316	7 534	7 767	7 761
Households and non-profit institutions serving households	QWLS	31 509	33 026	35 354	38 165	40 160	43 147	48 023	51 197	53 206
Total operating surplus, gross	ABNF	144 618	161 523	181 082	192 387	210 192	221 502	230 472	231 482	237 051
Mixed income	HAXH	39 521	42 340	44 319	46 647	49 011	50 461	50 292	52 464	54 442
Compensation of employees	HAEA	347 713	357 662	369 645	386 718	405 469	432 960	464 258	494 186	521 443
Taxes on production and imports	NZGX	86 196	88 310	94 288	101 633	107 042	115 143	122 741	130 953	137 955
less subsidies	-AAXJ	-7 194	-7 508	-8 007	-8 209	-9 500	-8 999	-7 958	-7 816	-7 724
Statistical discrepancy between income components and GDP	GIXQ	–	–	–	–	–	–	–	–	245
Gross domestic product at market prices	YBHA	610 854	642 327	681 327	719 176	762 214	811 067	859 805	901 269	943 412

Source: Office for National Statistics: 020 7533 6031

15.2 UK gross domestic product and national income
Current prices

continued

£ million

		1992	1993	1994	1995	1996	1997	1998	1999	2000
GROSS NATIONAL INCOME at market prices										
Gross domestic product at market prices	YBHA	610 854	642 327	681 327	719 176	762 214	811 067	859 805	901 269	943 412
Compensation of employees										
receipts from the rest of the world	KTMN	551	595	681	887	911	1 007	840	960	1 014
less payments to the rest of the world	−KTMO	−600	−560	−851	−1 183	−818	−924	−850	−759	−871
Total	KTMP	−49	35	−170	−296	93	83	−10	201	143
less Taxes on production paid to the rest of the world										
plus Subsidies received from the rest of the world	−QZOZ	−4 319	−4 725	−3 349	−5 220	−4 141	−2 811	−3 683	−3 551	−3 446
Subsidies on production	NHQR	66	215	286	293	253	206	246	370	361
Property and entrepreneurial income										
receipts from the rest of the world	HMBN	66 153	72 333	73 702	87 132	91 621	95 337	102 945	99 312	132 983
less payments to the rest of the world	−HMBO	−65 976	−72 559	−70 184	−84 735	−90 510	−91 514	−90 377	−95 494	−127 009
Total	HMBM	177	−226	3 518	2 397	1 111	3 823	12 568	3 818	5 974
Gross national income at market prices	ABMX	606 729	637 626	681 612	716 350	759 530	812 368	868 926	902 107	946 448

Source: Office for National Statistics: 020 7533 6031

15.3 UK gross domestic product
Constant (1995) prices

£ million

		1992	1993	1994	1995	1996	1997	1998	1999	2000
GROSS DOMESTIC PRODUCT										
Gross domestic product: expenditure approach										
Final consumption expenditure										
Actual individual consumption										
Household final consumption expenditure	ABPF	411 204	422 273	435 350	443 367	460 760	478 738	496 491	517 757	538 458
Final consumption expenditure of non-profit institutions serving households	ABNU	12 445	14 723	15 900	16 481	16 691	17 055	18 265	18 769	19 408
Individual government final consumption expenditure	NSZK	77 053	78 616	78 479	81 093	83 112	84 808	86 244	88 475	90 071
Total actual individual consumption	YBIO	500 344	515 535	529 729	540 941	560 563	580 601	601 000	625 001	647 937
Collective government final consumption expenditure	NSZL	61 127	58 579	60 145	59 938	59 590	57 971	58 747	60 585	61 372
Total final consumption expenditure	ABKX	561 511	574 114	589 874	600 879	620 153	638 572	659 747	685 586	709 309
Gross capital formation										
Gross fixed capital formation	NPQR	108 556	108 887	113 961	117 448	122 976	131 667	149 092	150 466	157 766
Changes in inventories	ABMQ	−1 962	360	4 836	4 512	1 830	3 762	4 228	4 977	2 450
Acquisitions less disposals of valuables	NPJP	39	−9	115	−121	−182	−52	399	213	478
Total gross capital formation	NPQU	107 239	109 629	118 912	121 839	124 624	135 377	153 719	155 656	160 694
Gross domestic final expenditure	YBIK	667 959	682 932	708 786	722 718	744 777	773 949	813 466	841 242	870 003
Exports of goods and services	KTMZ	163 745	170 916	186 655	203 509	220 268	238 492	245 761	258 935	285 433
Gross final expenditure	ABME	831 594	853 767	895 441	926 227	965 045	1 012 441	1 059 227	1 100 177	1 155 436
less imports of goods and services	−KTNB	−180 012	−185 954	−196 526	−207 051	−226 999	−248 969	−272 924	−297 158	−328 937
Statistical discrepancy between expenditure components and GDP	GIXS	−	−	−	−	−	−	−	−	−355
Gross domestic product at 1995 market prices	ABMI	651 566	667 804	698 915	719 176	738 046	763 472	786 303	803 019	826 144
of which External balance of goods and services	KTNC	−16 267	−15 038	−9 871	−3 542	−6 731	−10 477	−27 163	−38 223	−43 504

Source: Office for National Statistics: 020 7533 6031

15.4 Gross value added at current basic prices: by industry[1,2]

£ million

		1992	1993	1994	1995	1996	1997	1998	1999	2000
Agriculture, hunting, forestry and fishing	EWSH	9 918	10 544	10 617	11 766	11 735	10 145	9 628	9 460	8 912
Mining & quarrying	EWSL	13 418	13 526	14 788	16 369	19 768	18 115	15 679	17 090	24 244
Manufacturing	EWSP	115 891	120 989	130 767	139 789	146 079	152 305	153 272	152 653	155 531
Electricity, gas & water supply	EWST	14 928	16 271	16 158	15 586	16 280	16 141	15 960	16 009	15 677
Construction	EWSX	30 020	29 166	31 216	33 005	34 587	36 879	39 017	41 142	43 287
Wholesale and retail trade	EWTB	79 606	84 063	88 391	92 865	99 806	109 155	117 683	125 641	130 782
Transport & communication	EWTF	45 108	46 408	49 572	51 340	53 473	57 393	62 134	65 910	68 195
Financial intermediation	EWTJ	131 127	142 004	152 854	159 141	169 690	183 883	208 055	220 625	238 510
Adjustment for financial services	-NSRV	−19 086	−19 569	−23 119	−23 215	−22 580	−22 396	−27 998	−30 819	−37 091
Public administration and defence	EWTN	39 210	39 988	39 597	39 756	39 709	39 659	39 751	39 786	42 091
Education, health & social work	EWTR	64 237	68 536	72 265	76 259	81 107	85 671	90 924	97 777	102 489
Other services	EWTV	22 057	23 535	25 634	27 247	29 966	33 742	37 213	39 751	42 560
All industries including adjustment for financial services	ABML	546 434	575 461	608 740	639 908	679 620	720 692	761 318	795 025	831 053

1 The contribution of each industry to the gross domestic product before providing for consumption of fixed capital. The industrial composition in this table is consistent with the Input-Output analyses. Although the industrial composition for 1989-91 is based on Input-Output analyses also, there are improvements to the underlying data from 1992. Between 1989 and 1991, the data were compiled on a different basis, which lead to step changes in 1991 and 1992.
2 Components may not sum to totals due to rounding.

Source: Office for National Statistics: 020 7533 6031

15.5 Gross value added at 1995 basic prices: by industry
Index numbers

Indices 1995=100

	Weight per 1000[1]			1992	1993	1994	1995	1996	1997	1998	1999	2000
	1995											
Agriculture, hunting & forestry; fishing	18.5	GDQA		111.5	102.5	101.2	100.0	99.1	98.2	99.9	102.2	99.9
Production												
Mining and quarrying												
Mining and quarrying of energy producing materials												
Mining of coal	1.9	CKZP		181.8	142.3	94.6	100.0	95.5	90.3	76.5	69.1	59.3
Extraction of mineral oil and natural gas	21.3	CKZO		68.4	77.5	96.1	100.0	105.6	104.7	107.5	112.2	110.7
Other mining and quarrying	2.3	CKZQ		103.4	105.6	105.3	100.0	88.7	87.3	97.0	103.6	111.0
Total mining and quarrying	25.4	CKYX		78.9	84.2	96.8	100.0	103.3	102.1	104.3	108.2	106.9
Manufacturing												
Food; beverages & tobacco	28.7	CKZA		98.9	99.2	101.7	100.0	100.9	103.2	101.5	100.8	99.6
Textiles & textile products	10.1	CKZB		101.9	101.3	103.6	100.0	98.2	95.9	89.0	81.9	78.2
Leather & leather products	1.4	CKZC		95.8	99.1	98.6	100.0	98.6	103.5	89.5	86.6	79.1
Wood & wood products	2.9	CKZD		97.8	100.0	107.8	100.0	98.1	95.5	94.6	89.7	91.6
Pulp, paper & paper products; publishing & printing	26.3	CKZE		93.0	96.0	98.5	100.0	98.0	98.2	98.9	99.1	99.0
Coke, petroleum products & nuclear fuel	4.7	CKZF		88.6	89.0	89.8	100.0	91.8	93.8	88.3	79.4	82.8
Chemicals, chemical products & man-made fibres	24.1	CKZG		88.5	90.4	95.1	100.0	100.6	102.4	104.0	107.4	111.8
Rubber & plastic products	10.5	CKZH		85.1	88.8	97.9	100.0	98.8	98.5	101.6	100.9	100.2
Other non-metallic mineral products	7.9	CKZI		94.7	99.1	102.7	100.0	96.6	99.3	96.9	95.7	95.8
Basic metals & fabricated metal products	24.6	CKZJ		96.0	95.0	97.3	100.0	99.9	101.1	99.2	95.3	95.5
Machinery & equipment not elsewhere classified	19.2	CKZK		94.7	94.6	99.8	100.0	98.0	95.7	95.8	90.0	89.8
Electrical & optical equipment	26.9	CKZL		79.0	83.4	93.5	100.0	104.9	108.1	114.8	126.0	144.4
Transport equipment	20.5	CKZM		99.9	98.1	100.8	100.0	107.7	112.1	118.2	120.1	115.2
Manufacturing not elsewhere classified	7.6	CKZN		97.2	98.6	101.7	100.0	102.0	104.0	105.3	106.6	104.5
Total manufacturing	215.7	CKYY		92.8	94.1	98.5	100.0	100.7	102.0	102.8	103.1	105.1
Electricity, gas and water supply	24.5	CKYZ		92.9	96.8	97.7	100.0	105.1	105.7	107.5	109.4	113.1
Total production	265.6	CKYW		91.3	93.3	98.3	100.0	101.3	102.4	103.4	104.2	106.0
Construction	52.0	GDQB		97.5	96.3	100.0	100.0	102.7	105.7	107.0	107.8	109.7
Service industries												
Wholesale & retail trade (including motor trade); repair of motor vehicles, personal & household goods	116.9	GDQC		87.7	92.8	97.8	100.0	104.3	107.3	110.8	113.9	117.4
Hotels and restaurants	29.0	GDQD		96.0	98.1	100.8	100.0	102.9	103.5	104.5	104.6	101.7
Transport, storage & communication												
Transport and storage	53.6	GDQF		88.1	89.9	96.9	100.0	101.1	106.6	114.5	116.7	118.7
Communication	28.9	GDQG		79.4	83.5	90.5	100.0	112.7	128.9	139.4	158.8	179.4
Total	82.5	GDQH		84.9	87.6	94.6	100.0	105.2	114.6	123.4	131.7	140.3
Financial intermediation	67.4	GDQI		93.4	95.5	96.5	100.0	103.7	108.5	113.8	115.3	119.8
Adjustment for financial services	−40.2	GDQJ		87.7	88.4	92.5	100.0	106.8	114.1	122.9	125.9	132.1
Real estate, renting & business activities												
Letting of dwellings, including imputed rent of owner occupiers	72.2	GDQL		94.9	96.1	97.4	100.0	101.2	103.2	105.8	107.6	107.9
Other real estate, renting & business activities	111.3	GDQK		82.0	84.1	92.8	100.0	107.4	118.7	131.6	138.3	147.5
Total	183.5	GDQM		86.8	88.9	94.5	100.0	105.1	112.8	121.8	126.7	132.5
Public administration & defence	61.2	GDQO		104.6	102.5	100.9	100.0	99.2	98.4	97.4	96.8	98.0
Education	56.0	GDQP		95.0	95.0	98.7	100.0	101.3	102.4	102.9	103.7	104.1
Health and social work	64.6	GDQQ		89.4	93.5	95.9	100.0	103.2	106.5	110.2	113.7	116.7
Other social & personal services, private households with employees and extra-territorial organisations	42.9	GDQR		83.5	90.5	96.1	100.0	105.4	107.5	112.8	115.0	119.3
Total service industries	663.9	GDQS		89.8	92.5	96.9	100.0	103.6	108.0	112.9	116.3	120.3
All industries	1 000.0	YBFR		91.1	93.2	97.5	100.0	102.9	106.2	109.8	112.3	115.5

1 The weights are in proportion to total gross value added in 1995. The GVA for sections L, M, and N in this table follows the SIC(92) and differs from that shown in table 2.3, which is based on Input-Output groups. Central government expenditure on teachers' pay is included in Education in table 2.4 but in PAD in table 2.3. The administation costs of the NHS are included in PAD in table 2.4 but are included in Health and social work in table 2.3 of the *Blue Book*.

2 The output analysis of gross value added is estimated in terms of change and expressed in index number form. It is therefore inappropriate to show as a statistical adjustment any divergence of an output measure of GDP derived from it from other measures of GDP. Such an adjustment does, however, exist implicitly.

Source: Office for National Statistics: 020 7533 6031

15.6 Non-financial corporations
Allocation of primary income account

£ million

		1992	1993	1994	1995	1996	1997	1998	1999	2000
Resources										
Operating surplus, gross	NQBE	112 471	124 470	142 148	153 152	168 601	178 629	184 477	188 636	197 627
of which UK continental shelf companies gross trading profits	CAGD	8 457	9 375	10 776	12 124	15 702	13 978	11 696	13 663	21 436
of which other private non-financial corporations' gross trading profits	CAED	90 930	100 167	117 450	125 151	133 508	145 693	150 975	154 077	156 291
Property income, received										
Interest	EABC	10 816	7 596	7 566	9 337	9 660	9 874	13 940	10 756	13 980
Distributed income of corporations	EABD	14 962	14 281	16 446	22 367	22 919	26 548	25 086	21 440	23 896
Reinvested earnings on direct foreign investment	HDVR	4 711	7 748	12 138	11 376	13 417	11 747	10 979	16 108	22 610
Attributed property income of insurance policy-holders	FAOF	471	470	338	395	423	386	463	333	406
Rent	FAOG	110	106	108	110	114	118	118	117	117
Total	FAKY	31 070	30 201	36 596	43 585	46 533	48 673	50 586	48 754	61 009
Total resources	FBXJ	143 541	154 671	178 744	196 737	215 134	227 302	235 063	237 390	258 636
Uses										
Property income, paid										
Interest	EABG	29 131	23 247	23 243	26 575	26 047	27 738	33 025	32 965	40 094
Distributed income of corporations	NVCS	52 394	53 461	60 304	71 532	76 136	80 813	78 037	85 645	79 151
of which private non-financial corporations' dividends	RVFT	31 728	32 250	36 365	46 218	51 609	56 250	51 686	60 772	51 900
Reinvested earnings on direct foreign investment	HDVB	62	2 004	4 310	4 662	6 117	5 187	3 117	6 120	12 291
Rent	FBXO	682	734	693	719	815	756	584	469	1 221
Total	FBXK	82 269	79 446	88 550	103 488	109 115	114 494	114 763	125 199	132 757
Balance of primary incomes, gross	NQBG	61 272	75 225	90 194	93 249	106 019	112 808	120 300	112 191	125 879
Total uses	FBXJ	143 541	154 671	178 744	196 737	215 134	227 302	235 063	237 390	258 636

Source: Office for National Statistics: 020 7533 6031

15.7 Non-financial corporations
Secondary distribution of income account

£ million

		1992	1993	1994	1995	1996	1997	1998	1999	2000
Resources										
Balance of primary incomes, gross	NQBG	61 272	75 225	90 194	93 249	106 019	112 808	120 300	112 191	125 879
Social contributions										
Imputed social contributions	NSTJ	3 316	2 966	2 884	3 329	3 209	3 173	3 801	3 535	3 625
Current transfers other than taxes, social contributions and benefits										
Non-life insurance claims	FCBP	6 689	6 044	4 031	4 716	5 508	4 190	4 849	4 151	4 963
Miscellaneous transfers	NRJY	112	256	420	494	537	557	595	611	622
Total	NRJB	6 801	6 300	4 451	5 210	6 045	4 747	5 444	4 762	5 585
Total resources	FCBR	71 389	84 491	97 529	101 788	115 273	120 728	129 545	120 488	135 089
Uses										
Current taxes on income, wealth etc.										
Taxes on income	FCBS	14 246	13 536	15 234	19 005	22 417	27 557	25 590	21 637	25 017
Social benefits other than social transfers in kind	NSTJ	3 316	2 966	2 884	3 329	3 209	3 173	3 801	3 535	3 625
Current transfers other than taxes, social contributions and benefits										
Net non-life insurance premiums	FCBY	6 689	6 044	4 031	4 716	5 508	4 190	4 849	4 151	4 963
Miscellaneous current transfers	FDBI	240	272	311	343	1 455	402	363	373	383
Total, other current transfers	FCBX	6 929	6 316	4 342	5 059	6 963	4 592	5 212	4 524	5 346
Disposable income, gross[1]	NRJD	46 898	61 673	75 069	74 395	82 684	85 406	94 942	90 792	101 101
Total uses	FCBR	71 389	84 491	97 529	101 788	115 273	120 728	129 545	120 488	135 089

1 Gross disposable income equals gross saving.

Source: Office for National Statistics: 020 7533 6031

15.8 General government
Allocation of primary income account

£ million

		1992	1993	1994	1995	1996	1997	1998	1999	2000
Resources										
Operating surplus, gross	NMXV	6 075	5 870	5 991	6 447	6 876	7 316	7 534	7 767	7 761
Taxes on production and imports, received										
Taxes on products										
Value added tax (VAT)	NZGF	37 426	37 958	42 996	43 579	46 918	52 057	54 293	58 664	60 702
Taxes and duties on imports excluding VAT										
Import duties	NMBS	–	–	–	–	–	–	–	–	–
Taxes on imports excluding VAT and import duties	NMBT	–	–	–	–	–	–	–	–	–
Taxes on products excluding VAT and import duties	NMBV	27 036	28 586	31 218	35 482	37 380	40 621	44 815	48 395	52 141
Total taxes on products	NVCC	64 462	66 544	74 214	79 061	84 298	92 678	99 108	107 059	112 843
Other taxes on production	NMYD	15 678	15 066	14 721	15 214	15 929	16 686	17 287	18 013	18 778
Total taxes on production and imports, received	NMYE	80 140	81 610	88 935	94 275	100 227	109 364	116 395	125 072	131 621
less Subsidies, paid										
Subsidies on products	-NMYF	–4 361	–4 403	–4 976	–5 013	–5 845	–5 114	–4 304	–4 366	–3 930
Other subsidies on production	-NMCC	–1 030	–914	–741	–765	–725	–710	–744	–747	–538
Total	-NMRL	–5 391	–5 318	–5 717	–5 778	–6 573	–5 825	–5 049	–5 116	–4 475
Property income, received										
Interest										
from general government	NMYI	4 606	4 055	3 866	3 767	3 901	4 004	4 060	4 068	3 925
from other sectors	NMYJ	4 042	3 965	4 562	4 846	4 997	4 313	4 133	4 661	5 653
Total	NMYL	8 649	7 996	8 385	8 553	9 031	8 575	9 236	9 328	9 578
Distributed income of corporations	NMYM	6 330	6 601	6 754	6 915	6 882	6 527	7 450	6 484	6 746
Property income attributed to insurance policy holders	NMYO	29	28	30	32	28	33	48	29	40
Rent										
from sectors other than general government	NMYR	647	699	658	684	780	721	547	433	1 185
Total property income, received										
from general government	NMYS	4 606	4 055	3 866	3 767	3 901	4 004	4 060	4 068	3 925
from other sectors	NMYT	6 902	6 210	6 561	7 204	7 308	6 683	6 752	6 676	13 624
Total	NMYU	15 655	15 324	15 827	16 184	16 721	15 856	17 281	16 274	17 549
Total resources	NMYV	96 479	97 486	105 036	111 128	117 251	126 711	136 161	143 997	152 456
Uses										
Property income, paid										
Interest										
to general government	NMYW	4 606	4 055	3 866	3 767	3 901	4 004	4 060	4 068	3 925
to other sectors	NMYX	18 515	19 786	22 682	25 947	27 406	29 287	29 956	25 907	26 353
Total	NMYY	23 392	24 056	26 804	30 077	31 905	33 809	34 874	30 648	30 930
Balance of primary incomes, gross	NMZH	73 087	73 430	78 232	81 051	85 346	92 902	101 287	113 349	121 526
Total uses	NMYV	96 479	97 486	105 036	111 128	117 251	126 711	136 161	143 997	152 456

Source: Office for National Statistics: 020 7533 6031

15.9 General government
Secondary distribution of income account

£ million

		1992	1993	1994	1995	1996	1997	1998	1999	2000
Resources										
Balance of primary incomes, gross	NMZH	73 087	73 430	78 232	81 051	85 346	92 902	101 287	113 349	121 526
Current taxes on income, wealth etc.										
Taxes on income	NMZJ	80 291	78 313	85 348	95 042	99 310	107 647	124 060	129 044	140 960
Other current taxes	NVCM	10 299	10 551	11 140	11 937	12 795	13 820	14 993	16 263	17 102
Total	NMZL	90 590	88 864	96 488	106 979	112 105	121 467	139 053	145 307	158 062
Social contributions										
Actual social contributions										
Employers' actual social contributions	NMZM	23 189	24 670	24 913	25 917	27 344	29 038	31 391	33 108	35 253
Employees' social contributions	NMZN	16 525	17 235	19 649	21 091	21 700	24 121	25 690	26 519	27 313
Social contributions by self- and non-employed persons	NMZO	1 281	1 472	1 469	1 541	1 771	1 848	1 760	1 801	1 973
Total	NMZP	40 995	43 377	46 031	48 549	50 815	55 007	58 841	61 428	64 539
Imputed social contributions	NMZQ	5 425	5 396	5 419	5 279	5 299	5 356	5 880	5 823	5 919
Total	NMZR	46 420	48 773	51 450	53 828	56 114	60 363	64 721	67 251	70 458
Other current transfers										
Non-life insurance claims	NMZS	408	361	363	377	371	349	499	410	490
Current transfers within general government	NMZT	54 527	55 891	57 736	58 587	59 458	59 506	60 421	64 775	66 327
Current international cooperation	NMZU	1 907	2 558	1 752	1 233	2 424	1 739	1 384	3 176	2 084
from institutions of the EC	NMEX	1 898	2 558	1 752	1 233	2 424	1 739	1 384	3 176	2 084
Miscellaneous current transfers										
from sectors other than general government	NMZX	178	296	414	461	420	468	382	259	280
Total, other current transfers										
from general government	NMZY	54 527	55 891	57 736	58 587	59 458	59 506	60 421	64 775	66 327
from other sectors	NMZZ	2 493	3 215	2 529	2 071	3 215	2 556	2 265	3 845	2 854
Total	NNAA	57 020	59 106	60 265	60 658	62 673	62 062	62 686	68 620	69 181
Total resources	NNAB	267 117	270 173	286 435	302 516	316 238	336 794	367 747	394 527	419 227
Uses										
Social benefits other than social transfers in kind	NNAD	95 339	102 965	106 295	110 409	113 124	116 934	117 549	120 752	124 991
Other current transfers										
Net non-life insurance premiums	NNAE	408	361	363	377	371	349	499	410	490
Current transfers within general government	NNAF	54 527	55 891	57 736	58 587	59 458	59 506	60 421	64 775	66 327
Current international cooperation	NNAG	2 237	1 961	2 007	2 224	1 814	1 700	1 705	1 667	2 418
to institutions of the EC	NMFA	–	2	7	8	8	31	–1	11	6
Miscellaneous current transfers										
to sectors other than general government	NNAI	4 659	8 467	10 440	10 614	12 549	13 916	15 803	17 280	19 556
GNP based fourth own resource	NMFH	914	1 558	2 071	1 826	2 454	2 458	3 920	4 632	4 379
Total other current transfers										
to general government	NNAL	54 527	55 891	57 736	58 587	59 458	59 506	60 421	64 775	66 327
to other sectors	NNAM	7 304	10 789	12 810	13 215	14 734	15 965	18 007	19 357	22 464
Total	NNAN	61 831	66 680	70 546	71 802	74 192	75 471	78 428	84 132	88 791
Disposable income, gross	NNAO	109 947	100 528	109 594	120 305	128 922	144 389	171 770	189 643	205 445
Total uses	NNAB	267 117	270 173	286 435	302 516	316 238	336 794	367 747	394 527	419 227

Source: Office for National Statistics: 020 7533 6031

15.10 Households and non-profit institutions serving households
Allocation of primary income account

£ million

		1992	1993	1994	1995	1996	1997	1998	1999	2000
Resources										
Operating surplus, gross	QWLS	31 509	33 026	35 354	38 165	40 160	43 147	48 023	51 197	53 206
Mixed income, gross	QWLT	39 521	42 340	44 319	46 647	49 011	50 461	50 292	52 464	54 442
Compensation of employees										
Wages and salaries	QWLW	303 008	311 615	322 179	336 973	352 285	376 926	402 321	428 766	451 032
Employers' social contributions	QWLX	44 656	46 082	47 296	49 449	53 277	56 117	61 927	65 621	70 554
Total	QWLY	347 664	357 697	369 475	386 422	405 562	433 043	464 248	494 387	521 586
Property income										
Interest	QWLZ	32 632	23 503	22 240	26 454	23 826	26 585	30 081	24 280	28 454
Distributed income of corporations	QWMA	25 703	25 225	28 582	32 544	33 777	37 172	37 351	40 226	42 975
Attributed property income of insurance policy holders	QWMC	34 874	35 437	37 301	42 358	47 807	52 144	55 587	53 928	59 197
Rent	QWMD	98	96	97	99	103	105	105	105	105
Total	QWME	93 307	84 261	88 220	101 455	105 513	116 006	123 124	118 539	130 731
Total resources	QWMF	512 001	517 324	537 368	572 689	600 246	642 657	685 687	716 587	759 965
Uses										
Property income										
Interest	QWMG	45 748	36 235	36 965	40 288	38 442	42 042	51 513	47 710	53 366
Rent	QWMH	201	195	198	202	210	216	216	215	215
Total	QWMI	45 949	36 430	37 163	40 490	38 652	42 258	51 729	47 925	53 581
Balance of primary incomes, gross	QWMJ	466 052	480 894	500 205	532 199	561 594	600 399	633 958	668 662	706 384
Total uses	QWMF	512 001	517 324	537 368	572 689	600 246	642 657	685 687	716 587	759 965

Source: Office for National Statistics: 020 7533 6031

15.11 Households and non-profit institutions serving households
Secondary distribution of income account

£ million

		1992	1993	1994	1995	1996	1997	1998	1999	2000
Resources										
Balance of primary incomes, gross	QWMJ	466 052	480 894	500 205	532 199	561 594	600 399	633 958	668 662	706 384
Imputed social contributions	RVFH	480	438	425	455	429	410	478	450	374
Social benefits other than social transfers in kind	QWML	127 663	136 084	142 229	149 151	156 612	165 695	170 931	178 050	187 235
Other current transfers										
Non-life insurance claims	QWMM	13 239	12 496	13 272	14 123	19 360	14 004	15 224	13 901	16 621
Miscellaneous current transfers	QWMN	11 248	15 481	17 013	17 722	20 027	20 478	21 146	21 899	24 522
Total	QWMO	24 487	27 977	30 285	31 845	39 387	34 482	36 370	35 800	41 143
Total resources	QWMP	618 682	645 393	673 144	713 650	758 022	800 986	841 737	882 962	935 136
Uses										
Current taxes on income, wealth etc										
Taxes on income	QWMQ	67 343	65 153	69 530	74 590	75 137	75 914	91 076	97 192	107 251
Other current taxes	NVCO	10 299	10 551	11 140	11 937	12 795	13 820	14 993	16 263	17 102
Total	QWMS	77 642	75 704	80 670	86 527	87 932	89 734	106 069	113 455	124 353
Social contributions										
Actual social contributions										
Employers' actual social contributions	QWMT	34 960	36 850	38 146	39 934	43 916	46 773	51 297	55 365	60 146
Employees' social contributions	QWMU	46 477	45 415	49 615	53 747	59 900	66 890	71 182	73 235	76 111
Social contributions by self and non-employed	QWMV	1 281	1 472	1 469	1 541	1 771	1 848	1 760	1 801	1 973
Total	QWMW	82 718	83 737	89 230	95 222	105 587	115 511	124 239	130 401	138 230
Imputed social contributions	QWMX	9 696	9 232	9 150	9 515	9 361	9 344	10 630	10 256	10 408
Total	QWMY	91 727	92 993	99 329	104 800	114 738	125 525	134 603	141 616	148 501
Social benefits other than social transfers in kind	QWMZ	811	897	880	925	899	880	950	922	848
Other current transfers										
Net non-life insurance premiums	QWNA	13 239	12 496	13 272	14 123	19 360	14 004	15 224	13 901	16 621
Miscellaneous current transfers	QWNB	6 802	7 618	8 108	8 279	8 190	9 059	9 293	9 484	9 709
Total	QWNC	20 041	20 114	21 380	22 402	27 550	23 063	24 517	23 385	26 330
Disposable income, gross	QWND	427 774	455 709	471 834	499 059	526 693	562 454	575 332	604 543	634 967
Total uses	QWMP	618 682	645 393	673 144	713 650	758 022	800 986	841 737	882 962	935 136
Read households' disposable income, at 1995 prices	RVGK	464 011	478 766	486 458	499 059	510 926	533 219	531 086	549 540	573 509

Source: Office for National Statistics: 020 7533 6031

15.12 Households and non-profit institutions serving households
Use of disposable income account

£ million

		1992	1993	1994	1995	1996	1997	1998	1999	2000
Resources										
Disposable income, gross	QWND	427 774	455 709	471 834	499 059	526 693	562 454	575 332	604 543	634 967
Adjustment for the change in net equity of households in pension funds	NSSE	13 265	10 742	10 577	11 690	14 824	15 131	16 105	15 417	15 216
Total resources	NSSF	441 039	466 451	482 411	510 749	541 517	577 585	591 437	619 960	650 183
Uses										
Final consumption expenditure										
Individual consumption expenditure	NSSG	390 564	415 951	437 684	459 848	492 185	522 976	557 642	590 226	617 648
Saving, gross	NSSH	50 475	50 500	44 727	50 901	49 332	54 609	33 795	29 734	32 535
Total uses	NSSF	441 039	466 451	482 411	510 749	541 517	577 585	591 437	619 960	650 183
Saving ratio (per cent)	RVGL	11.4	10.8	9.3	10.0	9.1	9.5	5.7	4.8	5.0

Source: Office for National Statistics: 020 7533 6031

15.13 Summary capital accounts and net lending/net borrowing

£ million

		1992	1993	1994	1995	1996	1997	1998	1999	2000
Non-financial corporations										
Gross saving[1]	RPJV	46 898	61 673	75 069	74 395	82 684	85 406	94 942	90 792	101 101
Capital transfers (net receipts)	GZQW	3 251	3 112	3 168	4 734	3 441	2 317	2 020	2 276	1 158
Gross capital formation[2]	RQBZ	52 331	55 139	59 768	68 934	73 994	85 172	94 994	100 277	101 891
Net acquisition of non-financial assets	RQAX	41	254	214	301	117	195	1 002	694	584
Financial corporations										
Gross saving[1]	RPPS	7 564	8 241	12 232	8 254	4 507	1 781	5 989	−2 353	−16 268
Capital transfers (net receipts)	GZQE	–	−88	−518	–	–	–	–	–	–
Gross capital formation[2]	RPYP	5 638	4 154	7 155	5 517	6 594	6 139	11 361	7 556	11 662
Net acquisition of non-financial assets	RPYO	−49	−203	86	−77	−1	−39	−4	26	13
General Government										
Gross saving[1]	RPQC	−19 248	−31 006	−26 661	−20 726	−17 857	−4 758	16 889	23 349	30 654
Capital transfers (net receipts)	GZQU	−6 107	−6 911	−5 826	−6 953	−4 900	−3 742	−3 616	−3 863	−1 719
Gross capital formation[2]	RPZF	14 028	13 403	13 833	13 902	11 372	9 595	10 782	9 849	11 211
Net acquisition of non-financial assets	RPZE	−312	−497	−485	−143	−467	−372	−967	−696	−643
Households & NPISH										
Gross saving[1]	RPQL	50 475	50 500	44 727	50 901	49 332	54 609	33 795	29 734	32 535
Capital transfers (net receipts)	GZQI	3 277	4 196	3 209	2 752	2 181	2 263	2 117	2 383	2 497
Gross capital formation[2]	RPZV	20 983	23 338	26 065	27 868	30 358	33 302	34 677	38 294	37 712
Net acquisition of non-financial assets	RPZU	320	446	185	−81	337	250	17	−36	9
Net lending(+)/net borrowing(-)[3]										
Non-financial corporations	RQAW	−7 906	4 099	12 941	4 276	6 957	−2 194	−3 649	−12 540	−4 839
Financial corporations	RPYN	1 975	4 202	4 473	2 814	−2 086	−4 319	−5 368	−9 935	−27 943
General government	RPZD	−39 071	−50 823	−45 835	−41 438	−33 662	−17 723	3 458	10 333	18 367
Households sector	RPZT	32 449	30 912	21 686	25 866	20 818	23 320	1 218	−6 141	−2 689
Rest of the world[4]	RQCH	12 553	11 610	6 735	8 482	7 973	916	4 341	18 283	16 452
Statistical Discrepancy[5]	RVFE	–	–	–	–	–	–	–	–	652

1 Before providing for depreciation, inventory holding gains.
2 Comprises gross fixed capital formation and changes in inventories and acquisitions less disposals of valuables.
3 This balance is equal to gross saving *plus* capital transfers *less* gross fixed capital formation, *less* Net acquisition of non-financial assets, *less* changes in inventories.

4 Equals, the current balance of payments accounts, *plus* capital transfers.
5 Series is only available annually.

Source: Office for National Statistics: 020 7533 6031

15.14 Household final consumption expenditure: classified by commodity[1]
At current market prices

£ million

		1992	1993	1994	1995	1996	1997	1998	1999	2000
Durable goods:										
Cars, motorcycles and other vehicles	CCDT	16 824	17 808	19 685	20 787	23 757	26 759	28 375	29 209	28 055
Other durable goods	ABZB	16 942	17 985	19 010	19 879	21 495	23 581	24 771	26 027	27 849
Total durable goods	AEIT	33 766	35 793	38 695	40 666	45 252	50 340	53 146	55 236	55 904
Non-Durable Goods:										
Food (household expenditure)	CCDW	45 683	47 171	47 855	49 790	53 025	53 832	55 192	56 886	58 252
Alcohol and tobacco	CDFH	34 266	35 538	37 139	38 174	40 907	42 991	45 142	48 226	49 652
Clothing and footwear	CDDE	23 009	24 321	26 324	27 431	28 899	30 298	31 478	32 828	33 554
Energy products	CCEC	25 403	26 142	26 856	27 189	28 867	29 085	28 734	29 002	31 234
Other goods	ABZN	45 794	48 023	51 231	54 584	58 949	63 864	68 853	73 245	77 690
Total non-durable goods	ABZR	174 155	181 195	189 405	197 168	210 647	220 070	229 399	240 187	250 382
Services:										
Rental and water charges	ABRG	48 637	52 405	55 990	59 633	62 848	66 975	73 399	77 995	81 954
Catering	CDEY	32 435	35 209	36 340	37 472	40 083	41 477	44 799	47 347	49 178
Transport and communication	ABOZ	34 621	37 876	39 789	41 766	43 881	47 427	51 201	54 827	57 822
Financial services	CEGK	14 437	15 778	15 761	16 053	18 026	20 446	22 587	24 176	26 863
Other services	AEJC	40 178	42 571	44 519	50 156	52 724	55 734	59 625	62 417	65 722
Total services	AELL	170 308	183 839	192 399	205 080	217 562	232 059	251 611	266 762	281 539
Total household final expenditure in the UK by resident and non-resident households (domestic concept)	ABQI	378 229	400 827	420 499	442 914	473 461	502 469	534 156	562 185	587 825
Final consumption expenditure outside the UK by UK resident households	ABTA	10 605	11 890	13 058	13 721	14 377	14 942	16 913	19 682	21 630
Less Final consumption expenditure in the UK by households resident in the rest of the world	CDFD	–9 076	–10 747	–11 160	–13 268	–14 038	–14 037	–14 544	–14 312	–14 673
Final consumption expenditure by UK resident households in the UK and abroad (national concept)	ABPB	379 758	401 970	422 397	443 367	473 800	503 374	536 525	567 555	594 782

1 Data for all series in this table are available in *Consumer Trends* or on the ONS Databank. Some of these quarterly data are published regularly in *UK Economic Accounts* in table A7.

Source: *Office for National Statistics: 020 7533 6031*

15.15 Household final consumption expenditure: classified by commodity[1]
At 1995 market prices

£ million

		1992	1993	1994	1995	1996	1997	1998	1999	2000
Durable goods:										
Cars, motorcycles and other vehicles	CCBJ	17 772	18 796	20 232	20 787	22 990	24 824	26 147	27 092	26 370
Other durable goods	ABZD	16 811	17 772	19 109	19 879	21 429	23 896	26 026	28 928	32 794
Total durable goods	AEIV	34 585	36 569	39 341	40 666	44 419	48 720	52 173	56 020	59 164
Non-Durable Goods:										
Food (household expenditure)	CCBM	48 268	49 263	49 744	49 790	51 405	52 347	52 983	54 334	56 123
Alcohol and tobacco	FCCA	39 131	38 583	38 963	38 174	39 396	39 736	39 752	40 459	40 718
Clothing and footwear	FCCB	23 287	24 416	26 355	27 431	29 100	30 252	31 637	33 929	36 130
Energy products	CCBS	27 983	28 181	27 805	27 189	28 305	27 929	27 648	26 909	27 400
Other goods	ABZP	48 289	49 644	52 413	54 584	57 293	61 099	64 736	69 035	74 128
Total non-durable goods	ABZT	186 406	189 824	195 280	197 168	205 499	211 363	216 756	224 666	234 499
Services:										
Rental and water charges	ABRI	57 194	58 018	58 796	59 633	60 392	61 186	62 019	62 736	63 932
Catering	CCHS	35 832	37 150	37 215	37 472	38 977	39 027	40 656	41 477	41 451
Transport and communication	ABPD	35 699	38 468	40 397	41 766	42 804	44 797	47 393	51 057	53 742
Financial services	CEGM	15 513	16 429	15 903	16 053	17 246	18 729	19 334	20 109	21 230
Other services	AEJZ	44 894	45 694	46 385	50 156	51 004	51 797	52 631	52 606	53 077
Total services	AELN	188 681	195 684	198 696	205 080	210 423	215 536	222 033	227 985	233 432
Total household final expenditure in the UK by resident and non-resident households (domestic concept)	ABQJ	409 371	421 706	433 317	442 914	460 341	475 619	490 962	508 671	527 095
Final consumption expenditure outside the UK by UK resident households	ABTC	11 953	12 093	13 490	13 721	14 077	16 357	18 813	21 837	24 090
Less Final consumption expenditure in the UK by households resident in the rest of the world	CCHX	−10 086	−11 524	−11 457	−13 268	−13 658	−13 238	−13 284	−12 751	−12 727
Final consumption expenditure by UK resident households in the UK and abroad (national concept)	ABPF	411 204	422 273	435 350	443 367	460 760	478 738	496 491	517 757	538 458

1 Data for all series in this table are available in *Consumer Trends* or on the
ONS Databank. Some of these quarterly data are published regularly in *UK
Economic Accounts* in table A7.

Source: Office for National Statistics: 020 7533 6031

15.16 Individual consumption expenditure at current market prices by households, NPISHs[1] and general government
Classified by function (COICOP/COPNI/COFOG)[2]

£ million

		1992	1993	1994	1995	1996	1997	1998	1999	2000
FINAL CONSUMPTION EXPENDITURE OF HOUSEHOLDS										
Food and non-alcoholic beverages	ABZV	45 683	47 171	47 855	49 790	53 025	53 832	55 192	56 886	58 252
Food	ABZW	40 720	42 133	42 665	44 324	47 323	47 996	49 134	50 537	51 550
Non-alcoholic beverages	ADFK	4 963	5 038	5 190	5 466	5 702	5 836	6 058	6 349	6 702
Alcoholic beverages and tobacco	ADFL	16 996	17 697	18 359	18 776	20 227	21 187	22 004	23 890	24 566
Alcoholic beverages	ADFM	6 716	6 938	7 426	7 257	7 962	8 539	8 641	9 349	9 420
Tobacco	ADFN	10 280	10 759	10 933	11 519	12 265	12 648	13 363	14 541	15 146
Clothing and footwear	ADFP	23 598	24 887	26 861	28 030	29 548	30 972	32 357	33 826	34 571
Clothing	ADFQ	19 654	20 853	22 587	23 711	25 211	26 562	27 902	29 377	30 301
Footwear	ADFR	3 944	4 034	4 274	4 319	4 337	4 410	4 455	4 449	4 270
Housing, water, electricity, gas and other fuels	ADFS	69 862	73 890	77 378	81 412	85 975	90 265	96 273	100 658	106 269
Actual rentals for housing	ADFT	14 235	16 222	17 379	17 906	18 784	19 821	21 155	22 320	24 446
Imputed rentals for housing	ADFU	31 102	32 546	34 591	37 479	39 548	42 426	47 336	50 517	52 649
Maintenance and repair of the dwelling	ADFV	6 820	6 836	6 458	6 526	6 958	7 939	8 431	8 721	9 625
Water supply and miscellaneous dwelling services	ADFW	3 328	3 667	4 051	4 290	4 567	4 785	4 979	5 247	4 960
Electricity, gas and other fuels	ADFX	14 377	14 619	14 899	15 211	16 118	15 294	14 372	13 853	14 589
Furnishings, household equipment and routine maintenance of the house	ADFY	22 372	23 809	25 179	26 287	28 013	29 996	31 558	33 562	36 489
Furniture, furnishings, carpets and other floor coverings	ADFZ	7 853	8 459	9 287	9 843	10 726	11 503	12 147	13 012	14 302
Household textiles	ADGG	2 592	2 802	2 843	3 020	3 233	3 412	3 692	4 003	4 376
Household appliances	ADGL	3 974	4 177	4 195	4 405	4 615	5 005	5 102	5 130	5 235
Glassware, tableware and household utensils	ADGM	2 421	2 554	2 751	2 767	2 893	3 168	3 423	3 750	4 127
Tools and equipment for house and garden	ADGN	1 686	1 773	1 889	1 911	2 001	2 184	2 339	2 533	2 762
Goods and services for routine household maintenance	ADGO	3 846	4 044	4 214	4 341	4 545	4 724	4 855	5 134	5 687
Health	ADGP	5 807	5 987	6 668	6 835	7 260	7 583	8 112	8 563	8 955
Medical products, appliances and equipment	ADGQ	3 156	3 348	3 794	3 919	4 207	4 388	4 711	4 995	5 371
Out-patient services	ADGR	1 632	1 586	1 754	1 781	1 829	1 897	2 012	2 116	2 115
Hospital services	ADGS	1 019	1 053	1 120	1 135	1 224	1 298	1 389	1 452	1 469
Transport	ADGT	53 612	56 671	59 970	62 733	68 520	75 546	80 437	84 342	86 827
Purchase of vehicles	ADGU	19 940	20 847	22 657	23 588	26 469	29 445	30 854	31 605	30 313
Operation of personal transport equipment	ADGV	21 142	22 362	22 977	23 861	25 581	28 081	29 886	31 619	33 870
Transport services	ADGW	12 530	13 462	14 336	15 284	16 470	18 020	19 697	21 118	22 644
Communications										
Communications	ADGX	7 355	7 873	8 643	9 067	9 358	10 015	11 050	12 107	12 771
Recreation and culture	ADGY	40 107	42 677	45 552	51 075	55 400	59 975	65 306	69 867	73 929
Audio-visual, photographic and information processing equipment	ADGZ	9 090	9 633	9 620	10 862	11 994	13 531	15 086	16 014	17 425
Other major durables for recreation and culture	ADHL	1 421	1 617	1 818	2 133	2 553	2 862	3 101	3 669	4 176
Other recreational items and equipment; flowers, garden and pets	ADHZ	9 211	9 710	10 646	11 284	12 694	14 414	16 160	17 478	18 624
Recreational and cultural services	ADIA	13 463	14 265	15 251	18 241	19 272	20 037	21 412	22 516	22 901
Newspapers, books and stationery	ADIC	6 922	7 452	8 217	8 555	8 887	9 131	9 547	10 190	10 803
Package holidays	ADID	–	–	–	–	–	–	–	–	–
Education										
Educational services	ADIE	4 787	5 182	5 487	6 197	6 405	7 440	7 813	8 161	8 127
Restaurants and hotels	ADIF	43 006	46 170	48 394	50 383	54 072	56 454	60 701	63 660	65 463
Catering services	ADIG	36 793	39 327	41 040	42 182	45 424	47 498	51 530	54 419	56 005
Accommodation services	ADIH	6 213	6 843	7 354	8 201	8 648	8 956	9 171	9 241	9 458
Miscellaneous goods and services	ADII	45 044	48 813	50 153	52 329	55 658	59 204	63 353	66 663	71 606
Personal care	ADIJ	8 113	8 526	9 353	10 378	11 375	11 905	12 610	13 288	13 965
Personal effects n.e.c.	ADIK	3 560	3 615	3 657	3 898	4 028	4 296	4 444	4 644	4 862
Social protection	ADIL	8 108	8 430	8 413	8 187	8 236	8 259	8 363	8 537	9 106
Insurance	ADIM	14 677	16 477	16 408	16 306	16 532	17 853	19 534	19 796	20 820
Financial services n.e.c.	ADIN	4 584	5 326	5 705	5 853	6 980	7 953	8 615	9 906	11 766
Other services n.e.c.	ADIO	6 002	6 439	6 617	7 707	8 507	8 938	9 787	10 492	11 087
Final consumption expenditure in the UK by resident and non-resident households (domestic concept)	ABQI	378 229	400 827	420 499	442 914	473 461	502 469	534 156	562 185	587 825
Final consumption expenditure outside the UK by UK resident households	ABTA	10 605	11 890	13 058	13 721	14 377	14 942	16 913	19 682	21 630
less Final consumption expenditure in the UK by households resident in the rest of the world	CDFD	−9 076	−10 747	−11 160	−13 268	−14 038	−14 037	−14 544	−14 312	−14 673
Final consumption expenditure by UK resident Households in the UK and abroad(national concept)	ABPB	379 758	401 970	422 397	443 367	473 800	503 374	536 525	567 555	594 782

15.16

continued

Individual consumption expenditure at current market prices by households, NPISHs[1] and general government

Classified by function (COICOP/COPNI/COFOG)[2]

£ million

		1992	1993	1994	1995	1996	1997	1998	1999	2000
CONSUMPTION EXPENDITURE OF UK RESIDENT HOUSEHOLDS										
Final consumption expenditure of UK resident households in the UK and abroad	ABPB	379 758	401 970	422 397	443 367	473 800	503 374	536 525	567 555	594 782
FINAL INDIVIDUAL CONSUMPTION EXPENDITURE OF NPISH										
Final individual consumption expenditure of NPISH	ABNV	10 806	13 981	15 287	16 481	18 385	19 602	21 117	22 671	22 866
FINAL INDIVIDUAL CONSUMPTION EXPENDITURE OF OF GENERAL GOVERNMENT										
Health	QYOT	33 236	35 441	37 272	38 981	41 466	42 657	45 391	50 097	53 837
Recreation and culture	QYSU	3 366	3 547	3 246	3 172	3 173	3 089	3 486	3 777	3 903
Education	QYSE	25 511	23 487	24 202	25 291	25 798	26 692	27 960	30 103	31 168
Social protection	QYSP	11 299	12 074	12 825	13 649	14 531	15 113	15 434	16 527	17 268
Housing	QYXO	–	–	–	–	–	–	–	–	–
Final individual consumption expenditure of of general government	NNAQ	73 412	74 549	77 545	81 093	84 968	87 551	92 271	100 504	106 176
Total, individual consumption expenditure/ actual individual consumption	NQEO ABRE	463 976 463 976	490 500 490 500	515 229 515 229	540 941 540 941	577 153 577 153	610 527 610 527	649 913 649 913	690 730 690 730	723 824 723 824

1 Non-profit institutions serving households.
2 "Purpose" or "function" classifications are designed to indicate the "socio-economic objectives" that institutional units aim to achieve through various kinds of outlays. COICOP is the Classification of Industrial Consumption by Purpose and applies to households. COPNI is the Classification of the Purposes of Non-profit Institutions Serving Households and COFOG the Classification of the Functions of Government. The introduction of ESA95 coincides with the redefinition of these classifications and data will be available on a consistent basis for all European Union member states.

Source: Office for National Statistics: 020 7533 6031

15.17 Individual consumption expenditure at 1995 market prices by households, NPISHs[1] and general government

Classified by function (COICOP/COPNI/COFOG)[2]

£ million at 1995 prices

		1992	1993	1994	1995	1996	1997	1998	1999	2000
FINAL CONSUMPTION EXPENDITURE OF HOUSEHOLDS										
Food and non-alcoholic beverages	ADIP	48 268	49 262	49 744	49 790	51 405	52 347	52 983	54 334	56 123
Food	ADIQ	43 385	44 178	44 339	44 324	45 939	46 859	47 469	48 726	49 970
Non-alcoholic beverages	ADIR	4 908	5 102	5 405	5 466	5 466	5 488	5 514	5 608	6 153
Alcoholic beverages and tobacco	ADIS	19 539	19 255	19 268	18 776	19 299	19 459	19 193	19 863	19 959
Alcoholic beverages	ADIT	6 970	7 066	7 600	7 257	7 778	8 272	8 160	8 727	8 775
Tobacco	ADIU	12 803	12 357	11 668	11 519	11 521	11 187	11 033	11 136	11 184
Clothing and footwear	ADIW	23 644	24 923	26 884	28 030	29 729	30 920	32 360	34 694	36 819
Clothing	ADIX	19 623	20 859	22 593	23 711	25 307	26 299	27 632	29 910	32 178
Footwear	ADIY	4 031	4 068	4 291	4 319	4 422	4 621	4 728	4 784	4 641
Housing, water, electricity, gas and other fuels	ADIZ	79 432	80 872	80 742	81 412	83 212	84 230	84 902	85 241	87 745
Actual rentals for housing	ADJA	16 890	17 685	18 177	17 906	18 070	18 122	18 070	18 049	19 095
Imputed rentals for housing	ADJB	36 171	36 186	36 359	37 479	38 084	38 766	39 722	40 442	40 576
Maintenance and repair of the dwelling	ADJC	7 107	7 098	6 642	6 526	6 666	7 238	7 368	7 480	7 985
Water supply and miscellaneous dwelling services	ADJD	4 081	4 162	4 292	4 290	4 339	4 358	4 273	4 303	4 320
Electricity, gas and other fuels	ADJE	14 994	15 526	15 272	15 211	16 053	15 746	15 469	14 967	15 769
Furnishings, household equipment and routine maintenance of the house	ADJF	22 974	24 426	25 898	26 287	27 271	28 892	29 921	31 627	34 572
Furniture, furnishings, carpets and other floor coverings	ADJG	8 262	8 910	9 767	9 843	10 202	10 633	10 988	11 629	12 771
Household textiles	ADJH	2 586	2 848	2 882	3 020	3 167	3 329	3 559	3 876	4 381
Household appliances	ADJI	3 896	4 089	4 210	4 405	4 638	5 110	5 236	5 335	5 624
Glassware, tableware and household utensils	ADJJ	2 487	2 641	2 827	2 767	2 834	3 083	3 294	3 610	4 018
Tools and equipment for house and garden	ADJK	1 714	1 764	1 883	1 911	1 990	2 156	2 314	2 534	2 789
Goods and services for routine household maintenance	ADJL	4 020	4 148	4 329	4 341	4 440	4 581	4 530	4 643	4 989
Health	ADJM	6 824	6 678	7 096	6 835	6 879	6 818	6 847	6 790	6 693
Medical products, appliances and equipment	ADJN	3 757	3 801	4 083	3 919	3 959	3 884	3 885	3 866	3 891
Out-patient services	ADJO	1 884	1 777	1 863	1 781	1 729	1 698	1 655	1 606	1 519
Hospital services	ADJP	1 183	1 100	1 150	1 135	1 191	1 236	1 307	1 318	1 283
Transport	ADJQ	58 211	59 690	61 583	62 733	66 136	69 581	72 375	74 557	74 261
Purchase of vehicles	ADJR	20 832	21 878	23 192	23 588	25 665	27 496	28 850	30 165	29 894
Operation of personal transport equipment	ADJS	23 860	23 736	23 645	23 861	24 526	25 234	25 774	25 892	25 205
Transport services	ADJT	13 648	14 147	14 746	15 284	15 945	16 851	17 751	18 500	19 162
Communications										
Communications	ADJU	6 760	7 181	8 305	9 067	9 545	10 478	11 738	13 276	14 567
Recreation and culture	ADJV	41 550	43 583	46 379	51 075	54 118	57 878	63 413	69 889	76 475
Audio-visual, photographic and information processing equipment	ADJW	8 530	9 028	9 306	10 862	12 108	13 936	16 954	20 699	25 272
Other major durables for recreation and culture	ADJX	1 572	1 740	1 910	2 133	2 414	2 612	2 765	3 171	3 565
Other recreational items and equipment; flowers, gardens and pets	ADJY	9 328	9 808	10 740	11 284	12 462	14 015	15 669	17 271	18 754
Recreational and cultural services	ADJZ	14 553	15 158	15 827	18 241	18 731	18 876	19 502	19 919	19 769
Newspapers, books and stationery	ADKM	7 538	7 790	8 596	8 555	8 403	8 439	8 523	8 829	9 115
Package holidays	ADMI	–	–	–	–		–	–	–	–
Education										
Educational services	ADMJ	5 730	5 856	5 763	6 197	6 147	6 791	6 758	6 675	6 289
Restaurants and Hotels	ADMK	47 663	49 267	50 211	50 383	52 314	52 688	54 111	54 635	53 807
Catering services	ADML	41 209	42 272	42 727	42 182	43 842	44 217	45 828	46 580	46 023
Accommodation services	ADMM	6 526	7 033	7 484	8 201	8 472	8 471	8 283	8 055	7 784
Miscellaneous goods and services	ADMN	50 309	51 726	51 444	52 329	54 286	55 537	56 361	57 090	59 785
Personal care	ADMO	8 891	9 080	9 805	10 378	10 949	11 026	11 044	11 309	11 927
Personal effects n.e.c.	ADMP	3 878	3 761	3 685	3 898	3 983	4 224	4 278	4 321	4 530
Social protection	ADMQ	9 737	9 433	8 822	8 187	7 865	7 499	7 229	6 991	6 976
Insurance	ADMR	15 772	16 725	16 270	16 306	16 601	17 170	17 758	17 255	17 039
Financial services n.e.c.	ADMS	5 162	5 637	5 818	5 853	6 686	7 278	7 376	8 314	10 388
Other services n.e.c.	ADMT	7 015	7 177	7 044	7 707	8 202	8 340	8 676	8 900	8 925
Final consumption expenditure in the UK by resident and non-resident households (domestic concept)	ABQJ	409 371	421 706	433 317	442 914	460 341	475 619	490 962	508 671	527 095
Final consumption expenditure outside the UK by UK resident households	ABTC	11 953	12 093	13 490	13 721	14 077	16 357	18 813	21 837	24 090
less Final consumption expenditure in the UK by households resident in the rest of the world	CCHX	–10 086	–11 524	–11 457	–13 268	–13 658	–13 238	–13 284	–12 751	–12 727
Final consumption expenditure by UK resident households in the UK and abroad (national concept)	ABPF	411 204	422 273	435 350	443 367	460 760	478 738	496 491	517 757	538 458

15.17
continued

Individual consumption expenditure at 1995 market prices by households, NPISHs[1] and general government

Classified by function (COICOP/COPNI/COFOG)[2]

£ million at 1995 prices

		1992	1993	1994	1995	1996	1997	1998	1999	2000
CONSUMPTION EXPENDITURE OF UK RESIDENT HOUSEHOLDS										
Final consumption expenditure of UK resident households in the UK and abroad	ABPF	411 204	422 273	435 350	443 367	460 760	478 738	496 491	517 757	538 458
FINAL INDIVIDUAL CONSUMPTION EXPENDITURE OF NPISH										
Final individual consumption expenditure of NPISH	ABNU	12 445	14 723	15 900	16 481	16 691	17 055	18 265	18 769	19 408
FINAL INDIVIDUAL CONSUMPTION EXPENDITURE OF GENERAL GOVERNMENT										
Health	EMOA	34 803	36 360	37 372	38 981	40 172	41 069	42 171	43 856	44 873
Recreation and culture	QYXK	3 294	3 892	3 333	3 172	3 200	3 287	3 206	3 407	3 433
Education	EMOB	26 627	25 201	24 986	25 291	25 565	25 811	26 037	26 238	26 430
Social protection	QYXM	12 289	13 068	12 788	13 649	14 175	14 641	14 830	14 974	15 335
Housing	QYXO	–	–	–	–	–	–	–	–	–
Final individual consumption expenditure of general government	NSZK	77 053	78 616	78 479	81 093	83 112	84 808	86 244	88 475	90 071
Total individual consumption expenditure/ actual individual consumption	YBIO	500 344	515 535	529 729	540 941	560 563	580 601	601 000	625 001	647 937

Source: Office for National Statistics: 020 7533 6031

1 Non-profit institutions serving households.
2 "Purpose" or "function" classifications are designed to indicate the "socio-economic objectives" that institutional units aim to achieve through various kinds of outlays. COICOP is the Classification of Industrial Consumption by Purpose and applies to households. COPNI is the Classification of the Purposes of Non-profit Institutions Serving Households and COFOG the Classification of the Functions of Government. The introduction of ESA95 coincides with the redefinition of these classifications and data will be available on a consistent basis for all European Union member states.

15.18
Change in inventories at constant prices[1,2]

£ million

		Manufacturing industries				Electricity, gas and water supply	Distributive trades			
	Mining and quarrying	Materials and fuel	Work in progress	Finished goods	Total		Wholesale[3]	Retail[3]	Other industries[4]	Change in inventories
Value of stocks held at end-December 2000	..	..	..	..	..	..	..	..	..	..
	FADO	FBID	FBIE	FBIF	DHBH	FADP	FAJM	FBYH	DLWV	ABMQ
1991	170	−861	−1 358	−1 346	−3 565	200	−612	−404	−420	−5 349
1992	66	−211	−1 124	−47	−1 382	−100	117	216	−616	−1 962
1993	−45	20	−981	−320	−1 281	−270	802	368	738	360
1994	−267	433	639	548	1 620	−661	1 332	884	1 928	4 836
1995	−123	514	1 144	998	2 656	−205	597	811	776	4 512
1996	−47	−105	−217	6	−316	15	681	638	859	1 830
1997	55	403	−1 332	340	−589	103	1 499	799	1 895	3 762
1998	257	721	−588	367	500	−154	−16	987	2 654	4 228
1999	−215	683	−120	−474	89	−159	596	1 474	3 192	4 977
2000	−114	284	554	−258	580	89	302	993	600	2 450

1 Estimates are given to the nearest £ million but cannot be regarded as accurate to this degree.
2 Components may not sum to totals due to rounding.
3 Wholesaling and retailing estimates exclude the motor trades.
4 Quarterly alignment adjustment included in this series. For description see notes.

Source: Office for National Statistics 020 7533 6031

15.19 Gross fixed capital formation at current purchasers' prices
Analysis by broad sector and type of asset
Total economy

£ million

		1992	1993	1994	1995	1996	1997	1998	1999	2000
Private sector										
New dwellings, excluding land	EQBT	16 246	17 124	18 285	18 860	20 149	22 018	23 321	24 200	25 740
Other buildings and structures	EQBU	18 382	16 252	16 430	18 023	20 752	25 224	28 417	32 064	33 155
Transport equipment	EQBV	7 012	8 115	10 112	10 224	11 316	12 320	15 366	14 596	16 012
Other machinery and equipment and cultivated assets	EQBW	32 013	32 441	35 586	42 157	47 110	49 787	58 338	56 544	59 726
Intangible fixed assets	EQBX	3 290	3 122	2 982	3 179	3 278	3 395	3 555	3 490	3 732
Costs associated with the transfer of ownership of non-produced assets	EQBY	3 926	5 089	5 208	5 173	6 695	7 646	7 481	9 653	10 702
Total	EQBZ	80 869	82 143	88 603	97 616	109 300	120 390	136 478	140 547	149 067
Public non-financial corporations										
New dwellings, excluding land	DEER	172	150	139	162	151	123	49	11	5
Other buildings and structures	DEES	3 332	3 416	3 492	3 781	3 397	2 671	2 465	2 662	2 857
Transport equipment	DEEP	678	516	512	354	225	190	171	130	152
Other machinery and equipment and cultivated assets	DEEQ	873	720	761	857	765	705	758	945	740
Intangible fixed assets	DLXJ	256	279	374	496	585	595	605	625	640
Costs associated with the transfer of ownership of non-produced assets	DLXQ	358	376	349	126	133	267	352	381	432
Total	FCCJ	5 669	5 457	5 627	5 776	5 256	4 551	4 400	4 754	4 831
General government										
New dwellings, excluding land	DFHW	2 407	2 618	2 809	2 642	2 148	1 788	1 856	1 801	2 078
Other buildings and structures	EQCH	9 825	9 757	10 118	10 039	8 693	7 556	8 141	8 039	9 299
Transport equipment	EQCI	730	684	771	717	672	675	758	611	580
Other machinery and equipment and cultivated assets	EQCJ	2 185	2 155	1 879	1 998	1 852	1 452	1 278	1 475	1 359
Intangible fixed assets	EQCK	236	247	257	264	273	259	387	425	467
Costs associated with the transfer of ownership of non-produced assets	EQCL	−1 338	−2 034	−1 750	−1 604	−2 432	−2 275	−1 759	−2 244	−2 434
Total	NNBF	14 045	13 427	14 084	14 056	11 206	9 455	10 661	10 107	11 349
Total gross fixed capital formation	NPQX	100 583	101 027	108 314	117 448	125 762	134 396	151 539	155 408	165 247

Source: Office for National Statistics: 020 7533 6031

15.20 Gross fixed capital formation at current purchasers' prices
Analysis by type of asset
Total economy

£ million

		1992	1993	1994	1995	1996	1997	1998	1999	2000
Tangible fixed assets										
New dwellings, excluding land	DFDK	18 825	19 892	21 233	21 664	22 448	23 929	25 226	26 012	27 823
Other buildings and structures	DLWS	31 539	29 425	30 040	31 843	32 842	35 451	39 023	42 765	45 312
Transport equipment	DLWZ	8 420	9 315	11 395	11 295	12 213	13 185	16 295	15 337	16 746
Other machinery and equipment and cultivated assets	DLXI	35 071	35 316	38 226	45 012	49 727	51 944	60 374	58 964	61 827
Total	EQCQ	93 855	93 948	100 894	109 814	117 230	124 509	140 918	143 078	151 708
Intangible fixed assets	DLXP	3 782	3 648	3 613	3 939	4 136	4 249	4 547	4 540	4 839
Costs associated with the transfer of ownership of non-produced assets	DFBH	2 946	3 431	3 807	3 695	4 396	5 638	6 074	7 790	8 700
Total gross fixed capital formation	NPQX	100 583	101 027	108 314	117 448	125 762	134 396	151 539	155 408	165 247

Source: Office for National Statistics: 020 7533 6031

15.21 Gross fixed capital formation at 1995 purchasers' prices[1]
Analysis by broad sector and type of asset
Total economy

£ million at 1995 prices

		1992	1993	1994	1995	1996	1997	1998	1999	2000
Private sector										
New dwellings, excluding land	**DFDP**	17 311	18 353	19 076	18 860	19 607	20 824	20 967	20 472	21 001
Other buildings and structures	**EQCU**	19 288	18 018	18 018	18 023	19 776	23 802	25 731	27 748	27 524
Transport equipment	**EQCV**	7 722	8 978	10 666	10 224	10 951	11 921	15 178	13 739	15 021
Other machinery and equipment and cultivated assets	**EQCW**	35 179	33 758	36 169	42 157	47 089	51 542	64 472	65 639	70 541
Intangible fixed assets	**EQCX**	3 417	3 154	2 997	3 179	3 298	3 288	3 249	3 078	3 174
Costs associated with the transfer of ownership of non-produced assets	**EQCY**	5 045	5 821	5 705	5 173	6 094	6 199	5 530	5 693	5 374
Total	**EQCZ**	82 917	82 261	92 631	97 616	106 815	117 576	135 127	136 369	142 635
Public non-financial corporations										
New dwellings, excluding land	**DEEW**	185	169	150	162	147	119	46	10	5
Other buildings and structures	**DEEX**	3 993	4 391	3 847	3 781	3 154	2 508	2 225	2 317	2 427
Transport equipment	**DEEU**	621	459	529	354	223	180	159	118	143
Other machinery and equipment and cultivated assets	**DEEV**	823	639	766	857	768	731	801	1 006	790
Intangible fixed assets	**EQDE**	274	294	387	496	571	553	554	553	548
Costs associated with the transfer of ownership of non-produced assets	**EQDF**	351	368	355	126	151	288	363	385	434
Total	**EQDG**	5 863	5 932	6 031	5 776	5 014	4 379	4 148	4 389	4 348
General government										
New dwellings, excluding land	**DFID**	2 568	2 932	3 041	2 642	2 114	1 728	1 733	1 587	1 750
Other buildings and structures	**EQDI**	10 192	10 963	11 287	10 039	8 431	7 391	7 239	6 977	7 854
Transport equipment	**EQDJ**	786	745	804	717	659	693	696	556	540
Other machinery and equipment and cultivated assets	**EQDK**	2 297	2 184	1 857	1 998	1 834	1 464	1 338	1 578	1 460
Intangible fixed assets	**EQDL**	226	231	247	264	293	262	353	373	393
Costs associated with the transfer of ownership of non-produced assets	**EQDM**	-1 756	-2 344	-1 937	-1 604	-2 184	-1 826	-1 542	-1 363	-1 214
Total	**EQDN**	14 233	14 721	15 300	14 056	11 147	9 712	9 817	9 708	10 783
Total gross fixed capital formation	**NPQR**	108 556	108 887	113 961	117 448	122 976	131 667	149 092	150 466	157 766

1 For the years before 1994, totals differ from the sum of their components.

Source: Office for National Statistics: 020 7533 6031

15.22 Gross fixed capital formation at 1995 purchasers' prices[1]
Analysis by type of asset
Total economy

£ million at 1995 prices

		1992	1993	1994	1995	1996	1997	1998	1999	2000
Tangible fixed assets										
New dwellings, excluding land	**DFDV**	20 041	21 492	22 267	21 664	21 868	22 671	22 746	22 069	22 756
Other buildings and structures	**EQDP**	32 881	32 779	33 151	31 843	31 361	33 701	35 195	37 042	37 805
Transport equipment	**DLWJ**	9 279	10 281	11 998	11 295	11 833	12 794	16 033	14 413	15 704
Other machinery and equipment and cultivated assets	**DLWM**	38 429	36 679	38 791	45 012	49 691	53 737	66 611	68 223	72 792
Total	**EQDS**	101 028	101 456	106 207	109 814	114 753	122 903	140 585	141 747	149 057
Intangible fixed assets	**EQDT**	3 917	3 679	3 631	3 939	4 162	4 103	4 156	4 004	4 115
Costs associated with the transfer of ownership of non-produced assets	**DFDW**	3 715	3 889	4 123	3 695	4 061	4 661	4 351	4 715	4 594
Total gross fixed capital formation	**NPQR**	108 556	108 887	113 961	117 448	122 976	131 667	149 092	150 466	157 766

1 For the years before 1994, totals differ from the sum of their components.

Source: Office for National Statistics: 020 7533 6031

16 Prices

Prices

Producer price index numbers *(Tables 16.1 and 16.2)*

The producer price indices were published for the first time in August 1983, replacing the former wholesale price indices. Full details of the differences between the two indices were given in an article published in *British Business*, 15 April 1983. The producer price indices are calculated using the same general methodology as that used by the wholesale price indices.

The high level index numbers in Tables 16.1 and 16.2 are constructed on a net sector basis. That is to say, they are intended to measure only transactions between the sector concerned and other sectors. Within sector transactions are excluded. Index numbers for the whole of manufacturing are thus not weighted averages of sector index numbers.

The index numbers for selected industries in Tables 16.1 and 16.2 are constructed on a gross sector basis i.e. all transactions are included in deriving the weighting patterns, including sales within the same industry.

All the index numbers are compiled exclusive of value-added tax. Excise duties on cigarettes, manufactured tobacco and alcoholic liquor are included as is the duty on hydrocarbon oils.

The indices relate to the average prices for a year. The movement in these prices are weighted to reflect the relative importance of the composite products in a chosen year (known as the base year) currently 1995.

Since July 1995, PPIs have been published fully reclassified to the 1992 version of the Standard Industrial Classification (SIC). From 1998, high level PPIs on the 1980 SIC will also be shown in Tables 16.1 and 16.2.

Further details are available from the National Statistics website: www.statistics.gov.uk/ppi

Purchasing power of the pound *(Table 16.3)*

Changes in the internal purchasing power of a currency may be defined as the 'inverse' of changes in the levels of prices; when prices go up, the amount which can be purchased with a given sum of money goes down. Movements in the internal purchasing power of the pound are based on the consumers' expenditure deflator (CED) prior to 1962 and on the General index of retail prices (RPI) from January 1962 onwards. The CED shows the movement in prices implied by the national accounts estimates of consumers' expenditure valued at current and at constant prices, whilst the RPI is constructed directly by weighting together monthly movements in prices according to a given pattern of household expenditure derived from the Family Expenditure Survey. If the purchasing power of the pound is taken to be 100p in a particular month (quarter, year), the comparable purchasing power in a subsequent month (quarter, year) is:

$$100 \quad \times \quad \frac{\text{earlier period price index}}{\text{later period price index}}$$

where the price index used is the CED for years 1946-1961 and the RPI for periods after 1961.

Index of retail prices *(Table 16.4)*

The retail prices index measures the change from month to month in the average level of prices of goods and services purchased by most households in the United Kingdom. The expenditure pattern on which the index is based is revised each year using information from the Family Expenditure Survey. The expenditure of certain higher income households and households of retired people dependent mainly on social security benefits is excluded.

The index covers a large and representative selection of more than 450 separate goods and services, for which price movements are regularly measured in 147 locations throughout the country. Around 130,000 separate price quotations are used in compiling the index.

The index of retail prices replaced the interim index from January 1956 (indices of the interim index of retail prices for the period 1952 to January 1956 were last published in *Annual Abstract of Statistics* No 103, 1965). A new set of weights was introduced, based on expenditure in 1953-54, valued at January 1956 prices. Between January 1962 and 1974 the weights have been revised each January on the basis of expenditure in the three years ended in the previous June, valued at prices obtained at the date of revision. From 1975 the weights have been revised on expenditure for the latest available year.

Following the recommendations of the Retail Prices Index Advisory Committee, the index has been re-referenced to make January 13, 1987 = 100. Calculations of price changes which involve periods spanning the new reference date are made as follows:

$$\% \text{ change} = \frac{\text{Index for later month}}{\text{(Jan 1987 = 100)}} \times \frac{\text{Index for Jan 1987}}{\text{(Jan 1974 =100)}} - 100$$
$$\text{Index for earlier month (Jan 1974 = 100)}$$

Further details are available from the National Statistics website: www.statistics.gov.uk/rpi

Tax and price index (TPI) *(Table 16.5)*

The purpose and methodology of the TPI were described in an article in the August 1979 issue (No 310) of *Economic Trends* (The Stationery Office). The TPI measures the change in *gross* taxable income needed for taxpayers to maintain their purchasing power, allowing for changes in retail prices. The TPI thus takes account of the changes to direct taxes (and employees' National Insurance contributions) facing representative cross-section of taxpayers as well as changes in the retail prices index (RPI).

When direct taxation or employees' National Insurance contributions change, the TPI will rise by less than or more than the RPI according to the type of changes made. Between Budgets, the monthly increase in the TPI is normally slightly larger than that in the RPI, since all the extra income needed to offset any rise in retail prices is fully taxed.

Index numbers of agricultural prices
(Tables 16.6 and 16.7)
The indices of agricultural prices for the United Kingdom are based on the calendar year 1990 and designed to provide an indication of movements in the purchase prices of the means of agricultural production and of the prices received by producers for their agricultural products. The methodology is comparable with that used for the other member states of the European Community and enables the compilation of indices for the Fifteen, which appear in the Communities Eurostat series of publications.

Prices

16.1 Producer price index numbers of materials and fuels purchased
All manufacturing and selected industries SIC(92)
United Kingdom

1995 = 100

			Annual averages							
			1993	1994	1995	1996	1997	1998	1999	2000
Net sector										
Materials and fuel purchased by manufacturing industry	PLKW	6292000000	90.2	91.9	100.0	98.8	90.6	82.4	83.7	93.3
Materials	PLKX	6292000010	88.8	90.3	100.0	99.7	90.9	81.6	83.0	94.2
Fuels	PLKY	6292000020	106.1	104.6	100.0	91.7	88.3	89.2	89.1	86.7
Materials and fuels purchased by manufacturing industry-seasonally adjusted	PLKZ	6292008900	90.2r	91.9r	100.0r	98.7	90.6	82.4	83.7	93.3
Materials and fuels purchased by manufacturing industry other than food, beverages, petroleum and tobacco	PLLA	6292990000	89.0	91.3	100.0	95.7	89.6	85.8	83.1	85.8
Materials purchased by manufacturing industry other than food, drink and tobacco	RWCJ	6292990010	84.9	88.5	100.0	96.6	90.0	85.2	81.9	85.6
Materials purchased by manufacturing industry other than food and beverages	RWCK	6292990020	106.0	104.6	100.0	91.7	88.2	89.1	89.0	86.6
Materials and fuels purchased by manufacturing industries other than food, beverages, petroleum and tobacco-seasonally adjusted	PLLB	6292998900	89.1r	91.3r	100.0r	95.8	89.7	85.8	83.1	85.8
Gross sector										
All manufacturing	RBBO	6192000000	92.0	94.0	100.0	100.3	96.9	93.2	92.5	96.8
Other mining and quarrying products	RABE	6112140000	93.1	95.7	100.0	101.9	102.9	103.9	105.1	108.2
Manufacture of food products	RBBQ	6192151600	93.1	94.2	100.0	99.8	94.2	90.3	88.9	89.1
Food products and beverages	RABF	6112150000	92.9	94.2	100.0	100.9	96.6	93.3	91.6	91.8
Tobacco products	RABG	6112160000	87.8	90.7	100.0	100.9	95.7	91.0	88.7	91.5
Manufacture of textiles	RBBR	6192171800	88.9	92.1	100.0	99.2	96.3	93.2	89.1	90.1
Textiles	RABH	6112170000	88.6	91.6	100.0	99.1	95.8	92.4	88.4	89.8
Wearing apparel	RABI	6112180000	89.6	92.9	100.0	99.5	97.0	94.6	90.2	90.6
Manufacture of leather	RBBS	6192190000	91.9	94.0	100.0	101.0	98.2	94.9	93.2	95.1
Manufacture of wood and wood products	RBBT	6192200000	88.6	93.7	100.0	99.0	98.1	95.3	93.6	94.6
Manufacture of pulp, paper, publishing and printing	RBBU	6192212200	85.4	88.4	100.0	99.2	93.1	90.4	88.9	92.4
Pulp and paper products	RABL	6112210000	85.5	88.3	100.0	99.1	93.1	90.5	89.0	92.3
Printed matter and recording material	RABM	6112220000	85.3	88.4	100.0	99.3	93.1	90.3	88.9	92.6
Manufacture of coke	RBBV	61922330000	101.5	94.7	100.0	118.1	107.4	78.9	103.5	161.0
Manufacture of chemical products	RBBW	6192240000	91.3	93.5	100.0	98.6	95.9	94.2	93.3	96.0
Manufacture of rubber products	RBBX	6192250000	84.3	87.4	100.0	94.7	90.2	84.2	82.2	87.3
Manufacture of other non-metallic mineral products	RBBY	6192260000	95.4	97.0	100.0	100.6	100.3	100.6	101.1	103.6
Manufacture of basic metals	RBBZ	6192272800	89.0	92.8	100.0	99.3	97.3	94.9	90.8	95.6
Basic metals	RABV	6112270000	88.1	92.2	100.0	98.8	96.3	93.3	88.5	94.4
Fabricated metal products	RABW	6112280000	90.2	93.5	100.0	99.9	98.5	96.8	93.7	97.1
Manufacture of machinery and equipment n.e.c.	RBCA	6192290000	92.7	95.2	100.0	100.8	100.4	99.5	97.7	99.3
Manufacture of electrical and optical equipment	RBCB	6192303300	96.8	98.0	100.0	97.5	92.9	88.0	84.7	84.9
Office machinery and computers	RABY	6112300000	103.0	102.6	100.0	94.4	85.4	77.0	72.3	70.7
Electrical machinery and apparatus n.e.c.	RACB	6112310000	91.3	94.0	100.0	99.4	97.6	95.0	92.5	95.3
Radio, television and communication equipment	RACC	6112320000	95.9	97.3	100.0	98.4	95.0	91.2	88.2	88.2
Medical, precision, optical instruments and clocks	RACD	6112330000	95.2	96.7	100.0	98.8	95.8	92.4	89.9	90.4
Manufacture of transport equipment	RBCC	6192343500	93.5	95.7	100.0	101.9	102.0	102.3	102.0	101.9
Motor vehicles, trailers and semi-trailers	RACE	6112340000	93.1	95.4	100.0	101.9	101.9	101.8	100.4	99.6

16.1
continued

Producer price index numbers of materials and fuels purchased
All manufacturing and selected industries SIC(92)
United Kingdom

1995 = 100

			Annual averages							
			1993	1994	1995	1996	1997	1998	1999	2000
Other transport equipment	RACF	6112350000	94.6	96.5	100.0	101.9	102.3	103.8	106.2	108.5
Manufacturing n.e.c.	RBCD	6192363700	89.6	93.1	100.0	99.9	98.8	96.8	94.7	97.1
Electricity	PQMX	4010990000	103.8	103.8	100.0	96.6	90.7	90.6	90.5	84.2
Gas	PQMZ	4020990000	109.2	107.1	100.0	76.4	79.1	83.3	82.8	90.1
Collected and purified water	PQNB	4100000000	91.3	96.8	100.0	104.9	109.6	115.3	119.7	115.3
Construction materials	RWDZ	6101451000	90.1	94.4	100.0	100.5	102.1	102.9	101.6	103.8
House building materials	RWEA	6101452000	90.2	94.6	100.0	100.7	102.2	103.0	102.1	104.1

SIC (80) Net sector

Materials and fuels purchased by manufacturing industry	DZBR	6200000000	89.7	91.7	100.0	96.4	89.0	84.1	82.0	83.9

Source: Office for National Statistics: 01633 812106

16.2 Producer price index numbers of output
All manufacturing and selected industries SIC(92)
United Kingdom

1995 = 100

			Annual averages							
			1993	1994	1995	1996	1997	1998	1999	2000
Net sector										
Output of manufactured products	PLLU	7209200000	93.8	96.1	100.0	102.6	103.5	104.1	105.3	108.0
All manufacturing excluding duty	FVNP	7209200010	94.2	96.2	100.0	102.3	102.4	102.0	102.1	103.9
All manufacturing excluding duty - seasonally adjusted	FVNQ	7209200890	94.2	96.2	100.0	102.3	102.4	102.0	102.1	103.9
Products of manufacturing industries other than the food, beverages, petroleum and tobacco manufacturing industries -unadjusted	PLLV	7209299000	93.9	96.0	100.0	101.9	102.1	102.0	101.6	102.4
All manufacturing excluding food, beverages, tobacco and petroleum - seasonally adjusted	PLLW	7209299890	93.9r	96.0r	100.0r	101.9	102.1	102.0	101.6	102.4
Gross sector										
Manufactured product	POKE	7109200000	95.6	96.6	100.0	102.0	101.3	99.0	99.6	105.0
Manufactured products excluding food, drink, tobacco and petroleum	POKF	7109299000	94.0	95.8	100.0	101.3	100.6	99.9	99.0	99.7
Other mining and quarrying products	POKW	7112140000	91.1	94.3	100.0	105.0	108.1	111.2	112.3	113.6
Food products, beverages and tobacco	POKH	7111151600	94.7	96.3	100.0	103.1	103.0	102.7	102.6	102.5
Food products, beverages and tobacco including duty	RBGA	7111151680	94.5	96.6	100.0	103.3	103.9	104.7	106.4	107.8
Food products and beverages	POKX	7112150000	95.2	96.8	100.0	103.1	102.9	102.3	102.0	101.5
Food products excluding beverages	RBGD	7112159900	95.9	97.3	100.0	103.1	102.1	101.0	100.8	100.0
Tobacco products	POKY	7112160000	79.4	83.5	100.0	101.2	105.6	114.5	121.6	132.7
Textiles and textile products	POKI	7111171800	94.6 B	95.9 B	100.0 B	102.6	104.7	105.7	104.9	105.4
Textiles	POKZ	7112170000	94.0 B	95.5 B	100.0 B	102.3	104.1	104.9	103.5	103.6
Wearing apparel: Furs	POLA	7112180000	96.0 B	97.0 B	100.0 B	103.3	106.2	107.7	108.5	109.7
Leather and leather products	POKJ	7111190000	93.8	97.4	100.0	102.7	103.3	102.8	101.6	102.3
Wood and wood products	POKK	7111200000	90.2 B	94.0 B	100.0 B	98.8	100.3	98.9	96.4	95.9
Pulp, paper and paper products, recorded media and printing services	POKL	7111212200	91.0	92.9	100.0	103.4	102.0	102.5	102.9	105.6
Pulp, paper and paper products	POLD	7112210000	82.8	85.6	100.0	101.7	97.0	95.8	95.1	98.3
Printed matter and recorded media	POLE	7112220000	95.2	96.6	100.0	104.3	104.6	106.0	106.9	109.4
Chemicals, chemical, products and manmade fibres	POKN	7111240000	91.1	93.4	100.0	98.9	97.3	94.0	92.8	95.3
Rubber and plastic products	POKO	7111250000	91.2	92.3	100.0	101.4	100.8	98.4	96.3	96.4
Other non-metallic mineral products	POKP	7111260000	91.8	95.9	100.0	101.1	103.5	106.5	108.3	110.8
Base metals and fabricated metal products	POKQ	7111272800	90.4	93.6	100.0	101.4	100.7	100.1	96.8	99.0
Base metals	POLJ	712270000	84.5	90.0	100.0	98.8	96.0	93.0	87.3	93.0
Fabricated metal products, except machinery and equipment	POLK	7112280000	94.5 B	96.0 B	100.0 B	103.1	104.0	105.0	103.4	103.3
Machinery and equipment n.e.c.	POKR	7111290000	95.5 B	97.5 B	100.0 B	102.9	105.7	106.7	107.8	109.3
Electrical and optical equipment	POKS	7111343500	104.6	103.8	100.0	97.2	90.9	85.3	81.4	78.6
Office machinery and computers	POLM	7112300000	120.8	115.5	100.0	90.9	74.5	62.1	54.4	47.3
Electrical machinery and apparatus n.e.c.	POLN	7112310000	94.0 B	96.1 B	100.0 B	101.6	102.2	101.4	99.1	98.5
Radio, television and communication equipment and apparatus	POLO	7112320000	99.6	100.2	100.0	95.8	90.1	83.2	79.2	78.1
Medical precision and optical instruments, watches and clocks	POLP	7112330000	97.7 B	99.2 B	100.0 B	104.1	104.9	106.1	107.1	107.0

16.2 Producer price index numbers of output
continued
All manufacturing and selected industries SIC(92)
United Kingdom

							Annual averages			
			1993	1994	1995	1996	1997	1998	1999	2000
Gross sector continued										
Transport equipment	POKT	7111343500	94.5	96.5	100.0	103.0	104.4	106.4	108.0	106.7
Motor vehicles, trailers and semi-trailers	POLQ	7112340000	93.9	96.2	100.0	103.0	104.3	105.9	106.2	103.5
Other transport	POLR	7112350000	96.3 B	97.4 B	100.0 B	102.9	104.9	108.2	114.7	117.8
Furniture: other manufactured goods n.e.c.	POLS	7112360000	95.5 B	96.9 B	100.0 B	103.7	105.1	107.3	108.0	107.8
SIC (80) Net sector										
Output of manufactured products	DZCV	7200000000	94.3	96.3	100.0	102.3	102.7	103.2	103.6	104.7

B = These index values are considered less reliable due to lack of market coverage.

Source: Office for National Statistics: 01633 812106

16.3 Internal purchasing power of the pound (based on RPI)[1,2]
United Kingdom

Pence

									Year in which purchasing power was 100p										
	1981	1982	1983	1984	1985	1986	1987	1988	1989	1990	1991	1992	1993	1994	1995	1996	1997	1998	1999	2000
	BAMN	BAMO	BAMP	BAMQ	BAMR	BAMS	BAMT	BAMU	BAMV	BAMW	BASX	CZVM	CBXX	DOFX	DOHR	DOLM	DTUL	CDQG	JKZZ	ZMHO
1982	92	100	105	110	116	120	125	132	142	155	164	171	173	177	184	188	194	201	204	210
1983	88	96	100	105	111	115	120	126	136	148	157	163	166	170	176	180	185	192	195	200
1984	84	91	95	100	106	110	114	120	129	141	150	155	158	162	167	171	177	183	185	191
1985	79	86	90	94	100	103	108	113	122	133	141	146	149	152	158	161	166	172	175	180
1986	76	83	87	91	97	100	104	109	118	129	136	142	144	147	152	156	161	167	169	174
1987	73	80	83	88	93	96	100	105	113	124	131	136	138	141	146	150	155	160	162	167
1988	70	76	79	83	88	92	95	100	108	118	125	130	132	135	139	143	147	152	155	159
1989	65	70	74	77	82	85	88	93	100	109	116	120	122	125	129	133	137	141	144	148
1990	59	64	67	71	75	78	81	85	91	100	106	110	112	114	118	121	125	129	131	135
1991	56	61	64	67	71	73	76	80	86	94	100	104	105	108	112	114	118	122	124	128
1992	54	59	61	64	68	71	74	77	83	91	96	100	102	104	108	110	114	118	119	123
1993	53	58	60	63	67	70	72	76	82	90	95	98	100	102	106	109	112	116	118	121
1994	52	56	59	62	66	68	71	74	80	88	93	96	98	100	103	106	109	113	115	118
1995	50	54	57	60	63	66	68	72	77	85	90	93	94	97	100	102	106	109	111	114
1996	49	53	56	58	62	64	67	70	75	83	87	91	92	94	98	100	103	107	108	112
1997	47	52	54	57	60	62	65	68	73	80	85	88	89	92	95	97	100	103	105	108
1998	46	50	52	55	58	60	63	66	71	77	82	85	86	88	92	94	97	100	102	105
1999	45	49	51	54	57	59	62	65	70	76	81	84	85	87	90	92	95	98	100	103
2000	44	48	50	52	56	57	60	63	68	74	78	81	83	85	88	90	92	96	97	100

1 To find the purchasing power of the pound in 1995, given that it was 100 pence in 1990, select the column headed 1990 and look at the 1995 row. The result is 85 pence.

2 These figures are calculated by taking the inverse ratio of the respective annual averages of the Retail Prices Index.

Source: Office for National Statistics: 020 7533 5874

Prices

16.4 Retail Prices Index
United Kingdom

13 January 1987=100

	ALL ITEMS (RPI)	mortgage interest payments (RPIX)	All items excluding mortgage interest payments and depreciation[1]	housing	food	seasonal food[2]	Food and catering	Alcohol and tobacco	Housing and household expenditure	Personal expenditure	Travel and leisure	Consumer durables	All items excluding mortgage interest payments & indirect taxes (RPIY)[3]
Weights													
	CZGU	CZGY	DOGZ	CZGX	CZGV	CZGW	CBVV	CBVW	CBVX	CBVY	CBVZ	CBWA	
1993	1 000	952	952	836	856	979	189	113	336	97	265	127	
1994	1 000	956	956	842	858	980	187	111	326	95	281	127	
1995	1 000	958	928	813	861	978	184	111	356	93	256	123	
1996	1 000	958	929	810	857	978	191	113	353	92	251	116	
1997	1 000	961	932	814	864	981	185	114	351	96	254	122	
1998	1 000	955	923	803	870	982	178	105	359	95	263	121	
1999	1 000	958	928	807	872	980	179	100	358	95	268	127	
2000	1 000	960	924	805	882	982	170	95	355	101	279	126	
2001	1 000	954	914	795	884	982	169	97	362	96	276	125	
Annual averages													
	CHAW	CHMK	CHON	CHAZ	CHAY	CHAX	CHBS	CHBT	CHBU	CHBV	CHBW	CHBY	CBZW
1992	138.5	136.4	136.4	134.3	140.5	139.1	132.6	146.8	144.2	126.9	136.8	115.5	135.1
1993	140.7	140.5	140.5	138.4	142.6	141.4	136.1	155.1	141.2	129.5	141.8	115.9	139.0
1994	144.1	143.8	143.8	141.6	146.5	144.8	138.5	161.4	144.4	131.9	145.7	115.5	141.3
1995	149.1	147.9	148.0	145.4	151.4	149.6	143.9	169.0	150.8	133.6	148.4	116.2	144.5
1996	152.7	152.3	152.3	149.3	154.9	153.4	148.9	175.9	153.0	135.1	152.8	117.1	148.2
1997	157.5	156.5	156.4	152.9	160.5	158.5	150.4	183.2	158.4	137.7	159.0	117.3	151.5
1998	162.9	160.6	160.3	156.2	166.5	163.8	153.4	192.3	166.2	139.9	162.8	115.9	154.5
1999	165.4	164.3	163.6	158.9	169.4	166.5	155.4	202.6	167.7	139.6	165.6	112.3	157.1
2000	170.3	167.7	166.4	161.3	175.1	171.4	156.7	210.3	176.2	137.2	170.3	108.0	159.9
Monthly figures													
1998 Aug	163.7	161.1	160.7	156.4	167.3	164.6	154.6	193.4	167.5	138.5	163.5	114.2	155.0
Sep	164.4	161.8	161.4	157.1	168.2	165.4	154.3	193.6	168.4	142.3	163.6	116.8	155.7
Oct	164.5	161.9	161.3	157.1	168.3	165.5	154.7	193.9	168.8	141.7	163.2	115.6	155.7
Nov	164.4	162.0	161.4	157.1	168.2	165.4	154.6	193.5	168.9	142.4	162.7	116.7	155.6
Dec	164.4	162.4	161.9	157.6	168.0	165.2	155.5	195.4	168.6	142.0	162.0	118.0	155.8
1999 Jan	163.4	161.8	161.2	156.8	166.7	164.2	156.1	198.2	165.9	136.3	162.8	110.6	155.1
Feb	163.7	162.3	161.7	157.4	167.0	164.5	156.4	198.6	165.9	138.5	162.6	112.3	155.8
Mar	164.1	163.2	162.6	158.4	167.7	165.0	155.8	200.8	165.5	139.8	164.0	114.2	156.0
Apr	165.2	164.3	163.7	159.0	169.1	166.3	155.4	201.9	166.8	140.3	166.1	113.1	156.9
May	165.6	164.7	164.1	159.4	169.5	166.5	156.1	202.6	167.3	140.8	166.2	114.0	157.4
Jun	165.6	164.7	164.0	159.2	169.6	166.6	155.7	203.4	167.3	140.9	165.9	113.1	157.3
Jul	165.1	164.1	163.4	158.6	169.1	166.3	155.1	204.2	166.9	136.9	166.3	109.6	156.7
Aug	165.5	164.5	163.8	158.9	169.7	166.8	154.7	204.5	167.6	138.3	166.6	110.5	157.2
Sep	166.2	165.2	164.4	159.6	170.9	167.4	154.6	204.5	168.5	141.6	166.5	112.7	157.8
Oct	166.5	165.4	164.4	159.6	171.0	167.7	154.6	204.7	169.2	140.8	167.1	111.6	158.1
Nov	166.7	165.6	164.6	159.7	171.1	167.8	155.1	204.3	170.0	141.1	166.6	112.3	158.3
Dec	167.3	165.9	164.9	160.1	171.8	168.4	155.3	204.0	171.7	140.3	166.8	113.2	158.6
2000 Jan	166.6	165.2	164.1	159.1	171.0	167.8	155.5	205.0	170.8	134.4	167.7	106.3	157.9
Feb	167.5	165.8	164.7	159.7	172.0	168.7	155.6	205.7	171.9	137.1	167.8	108.4	158.6
Mar	168.4	166.4	165.3	160.5	173.2	169.7	155.0	206.0	173.2	138.5	169.2	109.6	159.2
Apr	170.1	167.5	166.4	161.3	175.3	171.5	155.1	210.4	175.9	139.2	170.4	110.0	159.4
May	170.7	168.0	166.8	161.7	175.7	171.9	156.3	211.1	176.3	139.4	170.7	110.1	160.0
Jun	171.1	168.4	167.1	162.0	176.1	172.3	156.6	211.5	176.7	138.7	171.7	109.3	160.4
Jul	170.5	167.7	166.4	161.2	175.2	171.5	157.7	211.4	176.7	133.1	171.5	104.5	159.7
Aug	170.5	167.6	166.2	160.9	175.4	171.7	156.9	212.0	177.1	134.6	170.5	105.6	159.6
Sep	171.7	168.9	167.4	162.2	176.8	172.9	157.2	212.7	178.5	137.5	171.3	108.0	160.9
Oct	171.6	168.7	167.2	162.0	176.6	172.8	157.5	212.9	178.6	137.7	170.6	107.4	160.7
Nov	172.1	169.2	167.7	162.5	177.1	173.2	158.1	212.8	179.0	138.4	171.2	108.2	161.2
Dec	172.2	169.3	167.7	162.5	177.1	173.2	158.4	212.3	179.8	137.7	170.8	108.6	161.3
2001 Jan	171.1	168.1	166.5	161.1	175.8	172.1	158.8	213.3	178.5	132.9	170.3	102.8	160.2
Feb	172.0	169.0	167.3	162.0	176.9	173.0	159.0	214.1	179.2	135.5	170.9	104.9	161.1
Mar	172.2	169.6	168.0	162.7	176.9	173.2	160.4	215.4	178.7	137.1	170.5	106.7	162.1
Apr	173.1	170.8	169.1	163.2	177.9	174.1	160.9	216.6	180.2	136.7	171.5	105.7	162.9
May	174.2	172.1	170.4	164.7	178.6	174.8	163.9	216.9	180.3	137.1	173.0	106.4	164.4
Jun	174.4	172.5	170.8	165.1	178.7	174.9	164.7	217.3	179.8	137.2	173.6	106.3	164.9
Jul	173.3	171.4	169.5	163.6	177.9	174.2	162.9	217.4	179.6	132.3	173.3	102.4	163.9
Aug	174.0	172.0	170.0	164.1	178.7	175.0	162.8	217.7	180.7	134.2	173.3	103.8	164.6

1 This series has been constructed using the index for all items excluding mortgage interest payments prior to February 1995.

2 Seasonal food is defined as items of food the prices of which show significant seasonal variations. These are fresh fruit and vegetables, fresh fish, eggs and home-killed lamb.

3 There are no weights available for RPIY.

Source: Office for National Statistics: 020 7533 5874

16.5 Tax and Price Index
United Kingdom

| | Tax and Price Index: January 1978 = 100 | | | | | January 1987 = 100 | | | | | | | | | | | | |
| | BSAA | | | | | DQAB | | | | | | | | | | | | |
	1983	1984	1985	1986	1987	1987	1988	1989	1990	1991	1992	1993	1994	1995	1996	1997	1998	1999
January	170.7	177.9	184.7	192.9	198.0	100.0	101.4	107.1	113.9	123.6	128.1	128.7	132.1	137.2	141.6	143.6	147.1	150.5
February	171.6	178.8	186.4	193.7	..	100.5	101.8	108.0	114.7	124.3	128.8	129.6	132.9	138.2	142.3	144.2	147.9	150.8
March	171.9	179.4	188.4	194.0	..	100.7	102.3	108.5	115.9	124.9	129.3	130.2	133.4	138.8	143.0	144.6	148.4	151.2
April	171.8	178.8	190.2	192.5	..	99.7	101.4	109.8	118.2	125.4	129.6	131.3	135.3	140.3	141.7	143.8	149.7	151.2
May	172.6	179.6	191.2	192.9	..	99.8	101.9	110.5	119.4	125.8	130.2	131.8	135.8	141.0	142.0	144.4	150.6	151.7
June	173.1	180.1	191.7	192.8	..	99.8	102.3	110.9	119.9	126.5	130.2	131.7	135.8	141.2	142.1	145.0	150.5	151.7
July	174.2	179.9	191.3	192.1	..	99.7	102.4	111.1	120.0	126.2	129.6	131.4	135.1	140.4	141.5	145.0	150.1	151.1
August	175.1	181.8	191.8	192.9	..	100.0	103.7	111.4	121.4	126.5	129.7	132.1	135.8	141.3	142.2	146.0	150.8	151.5
September	176.0	182.2	191.7	194.0	..	100.4	104.3	112.2	122.7	127.0	130.3	132.7	136.1	142.0	143.0	146.9	151.5	152.3
October	176.7	183.5	191.4	194.3	..	100.9	105.4	111.7	123.8	127.5	130.8	132.6	136.4	142.3	143.0	147.1	151.6	152.6
November	177.5	184.1	192.1	196.3	..	101.5	106.0	112.8	123.4	128.1	130.6	132.4	136.5	141.2	143.1	147.2	151.5	152.8
December	178.0	183.9	192.4	197.1	..	101.4	106.3	113.1	123.3	128.2	130.1	132.7	137.2	142.1	143.6	147.6	151.5	153.4

| | Retail Prices Index: January 1974 = 100 | | | | | January 1987 = 100 | | | | | | | | | | | | |
| | CBAB | | | | | CHAW | | | | | | | | | | | | |
	1983	1984	1985	1986	1987	1987	1988	1989	1990	1991	1992	1993	1994	1995	1996	1997	1998	1999
January	325.9	342.6	359.8	379.7	394.5	100.0	103.3	111.0	119.5	130.2	135.6	137.9	141.3	146.0	150.2	154.4	159.5	163.4
February	327.3	344.0	362.7	381.1	..	100.4	103.7	111.8	120.2	130.9	136.3	138.8	142.1	146.9	150.9	155.0	160.3	163.7
March	327.9	345.1	366.1	381.6	..	100.6	104.1	112.3	121.4	131.4	136.7	139.3	142.5	147.5	151.5	155.4	160.8	164.1
April	332.5	349.7	373.9	385.3	..	101.8	105.8	114.3	125.1	133.1	138.8	140.6	144.2	149.0	152.6	156.3	162.6	165.2
May	333.9	351.0	375.6	386.0	..	101.9	106.2	115.0	126.2	133.5	139.3	141.1	144.7	149.6	152.9	156.9	163.5	165.6
June	334.7	351.9	376.4	385.8	..	101.9	106.6	115.4	126.7	134.1	139.3	141.0	144.7	149.8	153.0	157.5	163.4	165.6
July	336.5	351.5	375.7	384.7	..	101.8	106.7	115.5	126.8	133.8	138.8	140.7	144.0	149.1	152.4	157.5	163.0	165.1
August	338.0	354.8	376.7	385.9	..	102.1	107.9	115.8	128.1	134.1	138.9	141.3	144.7	149.9	153.1	158.5	163.7	165.5
September	339.5	355.5	376.5	387.8	..	102.4	108.4	116.6	129.3	134.6	139.4	141.9	145.0	150.6	153.8	159.3	164.4	166.2
October	340.7	357.7	377.1	388.4	..	102.9	109.5	117.5	130.3	135.1	139.9	141.8	145.2	149.8	153.8	159.5	164.5	166.5
November	341.9	358.8	378.4	391.7	..	103.4	110.0	118.5	130.0	135.6	139.7	141.6	145.3	149.8	153.9	159.6	164.4	166.7
December	342.8	358.5	378.9	393.0	..	103.3	110.3	118.8	129.9	135.7	139.2	141.9	146.0	150.7	154.4	160.0	164.4	167.3

| | Percentage changes on one year earlier | | | | | | | | | | | | | | | | |
	1983	1984	1985	1986	1987	1988	1989	1990	1991	1992	1993	1994	1995	1996	1997	1998	1999
Tax and Price Index																	
January	5.2	4.2	3.8	4.4	2.6	1.4	5.6	6.3	8.5	3.6	0.5	2.6	3.9	3.2	1.4	2.4	2.3
February	5.7	4.2	4.3	3.9	2.7	1.3	6.1	6.2	8.4	3.6	0.6	2.5	4.0	3.0	1.3	2.6	2.0
March	4.8	4.4	5.0	3.0	2.8	1.6	6.1	6.8	7.8	3.5	0.7	2.5	4.0	3.0	1.1	2.6	1.9
April	3.5	4.1	6.4	1.2	2.5	1.7	8.3	7.7	6.1	3.3	1.3	3.0	3.7	1.0	1.5	4.1	1.0
May	3.1	4.1	6.5	0.9	2.4	2.1	8.4	8.1	5.4	3.5	1.2	3.0	3.8	0.7	1.7	4.3	0.7
June	3.0	4.0	6.4	0.6	2.5	2.5	8.4	8.1	5.5	2.9	1.2	3.1	4.0	0.6	2.0	3.8	0.8
July	3.1	3.3	6.3	0.4	2.8	2.7	8.5	8.0	5.2	2.7	1.4	2.8	3.9	0.8	2.5	3.5	0.7
August	3.6	3.8	5.5	0.6	2.6	3.7	7.4	9.0	4.2	2.5	1.9	2.8	4.1	0.6	2.7	3.3	0.5
September	4.2	3.5	5.2	1.2	2.4	3.9	7.6	9.4	3.5	2.6	1.8	2.6	4.3	0.7	2.7	3.1	0.5
October	4.0	3.8	4.3	1.5	2.9	4.5	6.0	10.8	3.0	2.6	1.4	2.9	3.5	1.3	2.9	3.1	0.7
November	3.9	3.7	4.3	2.2	2.4	4.4	6.4	9.4	3.8	2.0	1.4	3.1	3.4	1.3	2.9	2.9	0.9
December	4.4	3.3	4.6	2.4	1.9	4.8	6.4	9.0	4.0	1.5	2.0	3.4	3.6	1.1	2.8	2.6	1.3
Retail Prices Index																	
January	4.9	5.1	5.0	5.5	3.9	3.3	7.5	7.7	9.0	4.1	1.7	2.5	3.3	2.9	2.8	3.3	2.4
February	5.3	5.1	5.4	5.1	3.9	3.3	7.8	7.5	8.9	4.1	1.8	2.4	3.4	2.7	2.7	3.4	2.1
March	4.6	5.2	6.1	4.2	4.0	3.5	7.9	8.1	8.2	4.0	1.9	2.3	3.5	2.7	2.6	3.5	2.1
April	4.0	5.2	6.9	3.0	4.2	3.9	8.0	9.4	6.4	4.3	1.3	2.6	3.3	2.4	2.4	4.0	1.6
May	3.7	5.1	7.0	2.8	4.1	4.2	8.3	9.7	5.8	4.3	1.3	2.6	3.4	2.2	2.6	4.2	1.3
June	3.7	5.1	7.0	2.5	4.2	4.6	8.3	9.8	5.8	3.9	1.2	2.6	3.5	2.1	2.9	3.7	1.3
July	4.2	4.5	6.9	2.4	4.4	4.8	8.2	9.8	5.5	3.7	1.4	2.3	3.5	2.2	3.3	3.5	1.3
August	4.6	5.0	6.2	2.4	4.4	5.7	7.3	10.6	4.7	3.6	1.7	2.4	3.6	2.1	3.5	3.3	1.1
September	5.1	4.7	5.9	3.0	4.2	5.9	7.6	10.9	4.1	3.6	1.8	2.2	3.9	2.1	3.6	3.2	1.1
October	5.0	5.0	5.4	3.0	4.5	6.4	7.3	10.9	3.7	3.6	1.4	2.4	3.2	2.7	3.7	3.1	1.2
November	4.8	4.9	5.5	3.5	4.1	6.4	7.7	9.7	4.3	3.0	1.4	2.6	3.1	2.7	3.7	3.0	1.4
December	5.3	4.6	5.7	3.7	3.7	6.8	7.7	9.3	4.5	2.6	1.9	2.9	3.2	2.5	3.6	2.8	1.8

Note: The purpose and methodology of the Tax and Price Index were described in an article in the August 1979 issue of *Economic Trends* . The purpose is to produce a single index which measures changes in both direct taxes (including national insurance contributions) and in retail prices for a representative cross-section of taxpayers. Thus, while the Retail Prices Index may be used to measure changes in the purchasing power of after-tax income (and of the income of non-taxpayers) the Tax and Price Index takes account of the fact that taxpayers will have more or less to spend according to changes in direct taxation. The index measures the change in gross taxable income which would maintain their after tax-income in real terms.

Source: Office for National Statistics: 020 7533 5874

16.6 Index of purchase prices of the means of agricultural production
United Kingdom
Annual averages

1990 = 100

		Weights	1990	1991	1992	1993	1994	1995	1996	1997	1998	1999	2000
Goods and services currently consumed	BYEA	100	100.0	103.4	106.9	111.5	111.0	114.9	122.4	116.7	108.4	106.1	109.5
Seeds	BYEB	4.3	100.0	102.5	111.4	119.0	114.1	133.5	141.6	124.5	127.5	119.7	109.2
Animals for rearing and production	BYEC	0.5	100.0	93.9	100.5	88.1	111.6	139.1	139.2	133.4	127.8	118.7	118.7
Energy, lubricants	BYED	6.8	100.0	103.1	105.8	106.6	104.8	108.0	116.4	115.4	110.5	117.6	137.6
Fuels for heating	KVBA	2.0	100.0	97.8	89.5	96.6	88.9	92.5	110.4	102.1	82.2	92.9	141.5
Motor fuel	KVBB	2.1	100.0	102.4	107.9	109.4	111.5	122.0	133.1	141.5	149.5	162.4	183.4
Electricity	KVBC	2.4	100.0	106.8	116.5	112.3	111.2	107.7	107.2	103.6	99.0	97.2	94.5
Lubricants	KVBD	0.4	100.0	112.6	109.6	110.2	112.4	113.1	112.3	114.4	116.9	128.4	132.5
Fertilisers and soil improvers	BYEE	10.9	100.0	96.6	91.1	85.6	91.0	102.0	112.8	97.9	83.0	79.5	94.3
Straight fertilisers	KVBE	4.4	100.0	94.1	87.6	80.1	87.4	98.4	108.8	93.8	78.9	75.5	89.6
Compound fertilisers	KVBF	6.0	100.0	98.1	92.6	87.9	92.0	103.7	115.0	98.6	82.2	78.3	94.5
Other fertiliser	KVBG	0.5	100.0	100.6	102.8	106.3	111.4	113.2	122.2	124.3	127.4	128.5	132.9
Plant protection products	BYEF	6.6	100.0	108.4	110.1	111.5	117.5	115.9	123.5	124.4	116.1	112.7	107.4
Animal feedingstuffs	BYEG	40.5	100.0	101.1	105.2	112.9	107.8	109.3	119.0	108.5	92.5	86.1	87.1
Feed wheat	KVBI	2.3	100.0	104.6	105.7	107.9	93.5	100.4	102.5	81.0	68.8	66.9	60.5
Wheat feed	ZBUV	0.5	100.0	104.6	105.7	107.9	93.5	100.4	102.5	81.0	68.8	66.9	60.5
Whole barley	KVBJ	1.2	100.0	103.8	105.4	109.7	98.1	101.9	101.3	79.2	68.5	70.5	63.4
Whole oats	KVBL	0.1	100.0	101.5	109.6	124.8	101.0	93.3	100.6	78.7	63.4	68.7	64.3
Maize glutten feed	ZBUW	0.6	100.0	108.3	106.9	109.5	107.7	110.6	126.1	93.2	74.7	77.8	77.4
Oilcake	KVBM	2.5	100.0	97.2	103.9	121.9	110.6	106.4	142.7	138.4	96.3	87.0	107.2
White fish meal	KVBN	0.2	100.0	109.3	112.3	105.2	103.0	118.5	145.5	142.9	156.4	106.8	114.0
Other straight feedstuffs	ZBUX	3.9	100.0	100.2	107.2	113.6	111.1	119.4	126.8	113.1	92.8	84.2	92.2
All straight feedstuffs	KVBH	11.3	100.0	101.6	105.9	113.2	104.8	109.3	121.6	106.3	84.9	80.0	83.9
Compound feedingstuffs for:	KVBP	29.2	100.0	100.8	104.9	112.8	108.9	109.3	118.0	109.3	95.5	88.9	88.3
Cattle and calves	ZBUY	12.3	100.0	98.7	103.9	113.8	108.6	107.6	116.5	108.4	93.6	89.0	89.0
Pigs	KVBS	7.2	100.0	103.4	107.7	115.8	110.7	112.7	120.1	110.7	96.7	87.2	85.3
Poultry	KVBT	8.3	100.0	102.2	104.4	109.0	106.5	107.4	116.2	107.2	95.5	88.7	87.7
Sheep	KVBU	1.4	100.0	98.7	102.9	112.1	116.0	118.4	130.1	122.6	106.1	97.3	100.3
Material and small tools	BYEH	4.4	100.0	111.2	116.0	119.0	121.8	122.3	122.7	122.3	119.7	119.8	122.0
Maintenance and repair of plant	BYEI	10.0	100.0	110.6	119.0	126.2	129.0	132.2	139.3	145.2	149.8	155.1	160.5
Maintenance and repair of buildings	BYEJ	4.9	100.0	102.1	102.1	104.9	109.9	116.4	117.0	118.8	119.8	118.3	120.9
Veterinary services	BYEK	2.4	100.0	105.0	108.3	110.4	111.5	113.4	116.2	119.4	122.9	125.8	127.8
General expenses	BYEL	8.7	100.0	107.2	114.6	122.2	124.0	127.0	129.3	132.0	132.4	135.9	136.3
Goods and services contributing to investment in agriculture	BYEM	100	100.0	105.9	109.8	113.2	115.8	118.8	121.8	125.2	128.0	129.2	131.0
Machinery and other equipment	BYEN	50.9	100.0	106.6	111.7	115.7	117.0	117.7	121.8	123.9	124.8	125.1	123.4
Machinery and plant for cultivation	KVBV	6.2	100.0	109.0	117.2	118.9	119.8	121.2	125.0	128.1	130.7	131.5	132.0
Machinery and plant for harvesting	KVBW	11.2	100.0	106.3	110.8	113.8	113.8	113.8	113.8	113.8	113.8	113.8	113.8
Farm machinery and installations	KVBX	4.7	100.0	105.9	109.8	111.3	112.3	113.9	115.3	116.9	118.6	119.8	120.9
Tractors	KVBY	22.3	100.0	106.4	111.5	117.7	119.0	118.8	125.5	128.7	129.5	130.3	127.4
Other vehicles	KVBZ	6.5	100.0	106.4	111.2	116.4	118.4	119.1	125.1	128.1	128.7	128.9	125.6
Buildings	BYEO	49.1	100.0	105.2	107.8	110.6	114.5	120.0	121.7	126.5	131.3	133.5	138.9
Farm buildings	KVCA	33.6	100.0	104.5	106.5	109.3	113.7	119.4	121.9	126.7	130.7	132.8	138.1
Engineering and soil improvement operations	KVCB	15.5	100.0	106.8	110.8	113.5	116.2	121.4	121.2	126.0	132.7	135.0	140.6

Source: Department for Environment, Food and Rural Affairs: 01904 455253

16.7 Index of producer prices of agricultural products
United Kingdom
Annual averages

1990 = 100

		Weights	1990	1991	1992	1993	1994	1995	1996	1997	1998	1999	2000
All products	BYEP	100	100.0	99.2	100.8	106.0	106.4	116.0	114.3	98.8	90.0	86.3	84.2
All crop products	BYEQ	40.4	100.0	101.2	96.4	96.0	98.0	111.5	103.4	86.0	87.6	83.3	77.9
Cereals	BYER	15.9	100.0	105.8	108.1	111.5	97.2	103.1	104.7	83.9	72.7	70.1	63.6
Wheat for:													
breadmaking	KVDA	3.9	100.0	111.4	116.6	122.5	102.3	106.6	108.6	92.5	83.5	75.3	69.5
other milling	KVDB	0.5	100.0	109.2	110.6	111.4	96.4	101.9	103.6	83.7	72.7	69.6	63.6
feeding	KVDC	6.6	100.0	104.6	105.7	107.9	93.5	100.4	102.5	81.0	68.8	66.9	60.6
Barley for:													
feeding	KVDD	2.9	100.0	103.8	105.4	109.7	98.1	101.9	101.3	79.2	68.5	70.8	63.4
malting	KVDE	1.7	100.0	100.6	102.1	102.0	97.9	109.1	110.8	84.0	71.9	69.7	62.3
Oats for:													
milling	KVDF	0.2	100.0	102.2	108.2	120.6	100.6	92.8	100.3	78.5	63.4	66.3	61.9
feeding	KVDG	0.1	100.0	101.5	109.6	124.8	101.0	93.3	100.6	78.7	63.4	68.5	64.4
Root crops	BYES	5.6	100.0	99.5	86.0	80.6	121.7	177.3	105.2	70.4	106.8	105.8	83.4
Potatoes:													
early	KVDH	0.3	100.0	224.7	100.7	110.1	257.7	197.8	139.1	99.5	194.8	93.9	157.3
main crop	KVDI	3.3	100.0	87.7	72.4	58.3	119.2	214.4	94.4	51.4	112.7	121.2	81.5
Sugar beet	KVDJ	2.1	100.0	101.6	105.5	111.9	107.6	116.0	117.8	96.5	85.8	83.0	76.5
Fresh vegetables	BYET	7.8	100.0	99.6	89.0	96.3	99.7	108.4	109.3	97.3	105.6	99.3	105.1
Cauliflowers	KVDK	0.5	100.0	111.5	95.7	104.4	106.6	97.1	107.7	88.2	100.3	93.3	107.4
Lettuce	KVDL	1.0	100.0	101.8	108.9	105.0	106.2	115.4	112.9	122.2	115.3	106.9	123.7
Tomatoes	KVDM	0.7	100.0	88.8	80.4	75.8	84.8	78.5	98.5	69.2	77.9	72.4	80.1
Carrots	KVDN	0.8	100.0	104.0	67.1	86.0	100.1	122.8	121.0	73.3	108.9	104.7	91.9
Cabbage	KVDO	0.7	100.0	98.5	85.6	106.4	94.5	120.5	112.1	102.4	119.4	113.8	129.1
Beans	KVDP	0.2	100.0	68.0	57.2	82.8	93.1	90.8	87.6	92.9	69.8	81.0	101.2
Onions	KVDQ	0.5	100.0	89.9	78.2	88.1	108.6	122.4	75.5	84.2	108.5	70.3	69.8
Mushrooms	KVDR	1.6	100.0	104.2	96.4	106.0	104.3	107.9	111.6	98.2	100.1	98.9	103.8
Fresh fruit	BYEU	2.1	100.0	104.5	100.5	87.5	87.0	95.8	107.5	98.4	98.4	90.0	90.1
Dessert apples	KVDS	0.7	100.0	117.3	124.7	79.6	74.8	96.4	112.6	97.1	93.5	88.5	78.8
Dessert pears	KVDT	0.1	100.0	90.9	90.3	77.8	78.9	86.6	82.9	78.6	75.3	71.5	67.7
Cooking apples	KVDU	0.3	100.0	99.3	78.0	76.3	86.9	88.5	105.6	112.8	125.5	83.8	82.4
Strawberries	KVDV	0.5	100.0	109.9	105.3	101.2	103.0	91.3	94.1	91.0	85.3	90.3	82.7
Raspberries	KVDW	0.2	100.0	85.9	69.0	95.5	93.1	124.7	156.8	106.1	111.6	102.4	129.8
Seeds	BYEV	1.1	100.0	99.1	101.1	92.2	107.3	143.3	122.7	92.1	89.6	93.0	70.2
Flowers and plants	BYEW	3.8	100.0	97.1	99.3	97.9	104.4	107.2	114.6	114.8	109.0	107.8	108.8
Other crop products	BYEX	4.1	100.0	91.3	73.7	60.3	62.6	63.2	66.8	60.2	58.7	45.0	41.4
Animals and animal products	BYEY	59.6	100.0	97.9	103.8	112.8	112.1	119.0	121.8	107.5	91.6	88.4	88.5
Animals for slaughter	BYEZ	33.8	100.0	94.9	102.1	111.8	109.1	112.7	115.5	102.2	84.7	83.2	87.6
Calves	KVDX	0.3	100.0	92.5	114.8	150.7	145.4	130.9	93.6	96.2	82.0	63.3	53.9
Clean cattle	KVDY	11.7	100.0	100.5	102.7	120.2	114.6	115.1	98.2	89.7	79.6	85.2	83.8
Cows and bulls	KVDZ	2.1	100.0	97.4	131.8	110.0	118.1	117.0	106.6	87.7	81.0	68.5	68.4
Clean pigs	KVEA	7.7	100.0	91.4	102.3	92.2	88.6	105.9	122.1	98.4	71.9	70.0	84.1
Sows and boars	KVEB	0.3	100.0	103.2	121.4	92.0	95.4	121.3	131.0	102.5	53.4	53.5	67.1
Sheep	KVEC	4.3	100.0	84.0	105.1	126.7	135.4	136.6	163.2	148.5	111.4	103.9	113.3
Ewe and ram	KVED	0.3	100.0	87.5	109.9	133.8	125.9	123.5	172.0	178.0	105.0	74.0	91.7
Poultry	KVEE	7.0	100.0	95.3	95.0	101.9	101.5	98.4	108.4	100.0	92.3	88.8	89.9
Chickens	KVEF	5.0	100.0	92.9	94.0	101.5	99.3	94.2	104.8	97.3	85.5	81.5	80.2
Turkeys	KVEG	1.6	100.0	100.8	95.9	102.3	107.2	108.6	117.4	103.2	105.4	104.0	115.5
Cows' milk	BYFA	21.7	100.0	104.6	109.6	117.8	119.3	134.0	134.6	119.0	104.2	98.6	91.3
Eggs	BYFB	3.6	100.0	87.5	86.2	98.8	99.4	90.0	107.6	92.3	85.0	80.3	85.4
Other animal products:													
Wool (clip)	BYFC	0.6	100.0	92.0	87.1	72.7	92.2	102.5	95.4	84.0	60.0	49.3	52.2

Source: Department for Environment, Food and Rural Affairs: 01904 455253

16.8 Commodity price trends[1]
United Kingdom
Calendar years

			1990	1991	1992	1993	1994	1995	1996	1997	1998	1999	2000
Wheat £ per tonne	KVAA	Average ex-farm price[2,3]	109.8	116.5	120.5	124.2	106.4	115.6	112.5	91.8	77.8	75.4	67.9
Barley £ per tonne	KVAB	Average ex-farm price[2,3]	108.8	107.8	113.9	113.6	105.4	107.6	103.7	86.3	79.2	74.2	69.9
Oats £ per tonne	KVAC	Average ex-farm price[2,3]	106.4	105.9	115.1	128.8	108.4	101.4	107.4	82.3	66.4	71.1	64.1
Rye £ per tonne	KVAD	Average ex-farm price[2]	114.60	118.50	115.20	113.40	112.80	107.90	113.90	..	..	..	..
Hops £ per tonne	KVAE	Average farm-gate price	2 922	3 211	3 208	3 357	4 005	3 595	3 360	3 550	3 676	4 033	3 820
Potatoes £ per tonne	KVAF	Average farm-gate price[4]	98.70	93.00	75.20	64.10	125.80	187.70	100.50	66.00	121.60	120.50	..
Sugar beet £ per tonne	KVAG	Producer price[5]	31.50	31.40	38.00	36.50	34.70	38.30	37.70	32.90	31.90	..	..
Oilseed rape	KVAH	Average market price[6]	280.00	248.00	133.00	153.00	185.40	177.70	186.90	160.20	164.30	..	..
Apples £ per tonne	KPUE	Dessert average farm-gate price[7]	501.7	561.2	315.4	297.7	391.4	437.3	493.6	525.0	476.1	405.0	359.8
	KVAI	Dessert average market price	500.0	589.0	414.0	370.0	447.4	465.7	474.7	538.1	..	..	..
	KVAJ	Culinary average market price	408.0	420.0	312.0	327.0	446.4	405.9	462.8	558.4	..	..	..
	KPUJ	Culinary average farm-gate price	269.6	281.3	189.5	230.8	232.3	248.2	286.8	335.1	297.3	209.9	236.0
Pears £ per tonne	KPUG	Average farm-gate price	474.9	546.9	430.9	368.4	466.2	425.1	446.2	432.3	404.0	393.5	264.0
	KVAK	Average market price	485.0	468.0	461.0	380.0	408.3	447.5	441.7	433.1	394.2	..	..
Tomatoes £ per tonne	LQMH	Average farm-gate price[7]	605.5	520.8	426.5	528.9	613.5	505.0	641.2	478.4	513.7	499.6	667.6
	KVAL	Average market price[7]	694.0	604.0	494.0	552.8	675.2	624.0	700.1	655.6	..	..	..
Cauliflowers £ per tonne	KPUI	Average farm-gate price[7]	238.5	246.3	201.5	218.6	222.1	283.3	237.8	225.5	215.4	217.4	242.3
	KVAM	Average market price[7]	296.0	292.0	253.0	296.9	323.5	394.9	442.6	372.0	..	..	..
Cattle (rearing)	KVAN	1st quality Hereford/cross bull calves[8,9]	128.00	119.92	145.44	185.95	182.06	166.32	131.81	146.95	107.86	88.24	79.52
£ per head	KVAO	1st quality beef/cross yearling steers[9]	397.00	397.30	419.49	478.00	471.00	475.00	445.00	427.00	369.00	382.00	400.05
Cattle (fat) p per kg liveweight	KVAP	Clean cattle[10]	106.30	106.92	109.58	128.04	121.71	123.15	105.52	96.89	86.10	92.12	89.68

16.8
Commodity price trends[1]
United Kingdom
continued   Calendar years

			1990	1991	1992	1993	1994	1995	1996	1997	1998	1999	2000
Sheep (store) £ per head	KVAQ	1st quality lambs, hoggets and tegs[8]	33.80	35.50	37.90	35.56	40.02	44.46	46.83	53.42	31.28	28.66	34.50
Sheep (fat) p per kg estimated dressed carcase weight	KVAR KVAS	Great Britain[11] Northern Ireland[12]	174.47 170.94	148.16 179.41	182.12 172.37	218.96 199.50	236.88 221.95	236.40 214.41	283.13 260.46	239.02 228.23	192.46 179.06	180.27 165.71	196.44 182.67
Pigs £ per kg deadweight	KVAT	Average price clean pigs	111.74	102.42	115.12	103.02	99.57	118.84	137.73	110.83	80.65	78.55	94.35
Broilers p per kg carcass weight	KVAU	Average producer price	86.8	81.0	82.7	86.8	86.5	83.8	90.7	85.9	76.6	71.8	..
Milk p per litre	KVAV	Average net return to producers[13]	19.19	19.81	20.94	22.68	23.03	24.96	25.01	22.31	19.44	18.55	17.35
Eggs p per dozen	KVAW	Average producer price[14]	42.60	36.30	36.60	41.90	42.40	38.20	45.70	39.80	36.20	34.00	..
Wool p per kg	KHWQ	Average producer price for clip paid to producers by the British Wool Marketing Board	91.04	81.98	79.82	61.00	97.97	94.08	86.90	74.90	47.80	46.30	49.81

1 This table gives indications of the movement in commodity prices at the first point of sale. The series do not always show total receipts by farmers; for some commodities additional premiums or deficiency payments are made to achieve support price levels.

2 Weighted average ex-farm prices of United Kingdom cereals.

3 Data from 1997 onwards has been revised and is not directly comparable with earlier years.

4 Weighted average price paid to growers for early and main crop potatoes in the United Kingdom, (includes all potatoes and a value for sacks)

5 Returns to growers figures since 1986 prices per 'adjusted' tonne at 16% sugar content.

6 Typical contract price adjusted to delivered basis and 40 per cent oil content.

7 Weighted average wholesale prices for England and Wales. Average farm-gate price for England and Wales, crop year (June-May).

8 Average prices at representative markets in England and Wales.

9 Category change 1988: formerly 1st quality yearling steers beef/dairy cross, now consists of Hereford/cross, Charolais/cross, Limousin/cross, Simmental/cross, Belgian/cross, other continental cross, other beef/dairy cross, other beef/beef cross.

10 Based on Meat and Livestock Commission all clean cattle prices.

11 Average of Great Britain weekly market prices as used to determine the level of ewe premium.

12 Average of Northern Ireland weekly market prices used to determine the level of ewe premium.

13 Derived by dividing total value of output by the total quantity of output available for human consumption.

14 Average price of all Class A eggs weighted according to quantity in each grade.

Source: Department for Environment, Food and Rural Affairs: 01904 455332

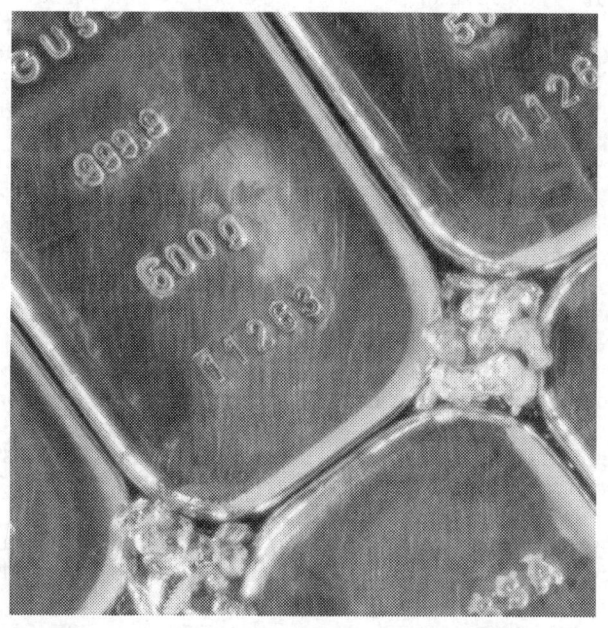

17 Government finance

Government finance

Public sector *(Tables 17.1 to 17.3 and 17.5)*

In Table 17.1 the term public sector describes the consolidation of central government, local government and public corporations. General government is the consolidated total of central government and local government. The table shows details of the key public sector finances' indicators, consistent with the European System of Accounts 1995 (ESA95).

The concepts in Table 17.1 are consistent with the new format for public finances in the *Economic and Fiscal Strategy Report (EFSR),* (published by HM Treasury 11 June 1998). The public sector surplus on current budget in the *EFSR* is equivalent to net saving in national accounts plus capital tax receipts. Net investment is gross capital formation, plus payments less receipts of investment grants, less depreciation. Net borrowing is net investment less surplus on current budget. Net borrowing differs from the net cash requirement (see below) in that it is measured on an accruals basis whereas the net cash requirement is mainly a cash measure which includes some financial transactions.

Details of the public sector net cash requirement and the contributions to the net cash requirement are given in Table 17.2. The net cash requirement indicates the extent to which the public sector borrows from other sectors of the economy and non-residents to finance the balance of expenditure and receipts arising from its various activities. Part of the central government net cash requirement is needed to finance central government on lending to local government and public corporations. Their additional 'contributions' to the public sector are therefore equal to their net cash requirements *less* their direct borrowing from central government.

General government net cash requirement is the sum of the borrowing requirements of central government and local government *less* direct borrowing by local government from central government. The public sector net cash requirement is general government *plus* public corporations' net cash requirement *less* their direct borrowing from central government.

The net cash requirements for local government and public corporations are measured from the financing items rather than as the difference between receipts and payments because this information comes to hand more quickly.

Table 17.3 shows public sector net debt. Public sector net debt consists of the public sector's financial liabilities at face value minus its liquid assets- mainly foreign currency exchange reserves and bank deposits. General government gross debt (consolidated) in table 17.3 is consistent with the definition of general government gross debt reported to the European Commission under the requirements of the Maastricht Treaty. More information on the concepts in table 17.1, 17.2 and 17.3 can be found in a guide to monthly public sector finance statistics, *GSS Methodology Series No 12,* the ONS First Releases *Public Sector Finances* and *Public Sector Accounts* and *Financial Statistics Explanatory Handbook* .

Table 17.5 (Part 1) shows the central government net cash requirement on own account, which is the net measure of all receipts and expenditure on central government funds and accounts, after excluding transactions which do not cross the central government boundary with the rest of the economy. Part 2 shows central government net cash requirement. The table shows the main financial instruments through which central government borrows to finance the net cash requirement. The details of the changes in the financial liabilities and assets of central government in aggregate match the net cash requirement.

Income tax *(Table 17.10)*

Following the introduction of Independent Taxation from 1990-91 the married couple's allowance was introduced. It is payable in addition to the personal allowance and between 1990-91 and 1992-93 went to the husband unless the transfer condition was met. The condition was that the husband was unable to make full use of the allowance himself and in that case he could transfer only part or all of the married couple's allowance to his wife. In 1993-94 all or half of the allowance could be transferred to the wife if the couple had agreed beforehand. The wife has the right to claim half the allowance. The married couple's allowance, and allowances linked to it, were restricted to 20 per cent in 1994-95 and to 15 per cent from 1995-96.

The age allowance replaces the single allowance, provided the taxpayer's income is below the limits shown in the table. From 1989-90, for incomes in excess of the limits, the allowance is reduced by £1 for each additional £2 of income until the ordinary limit is reached (before it was £2 for each £3 of additional income). The relief is due where the taxpayer is aged 65 or over in the year of assessment.

The additional personal allowance could be claimed by a single parent (or by a married man if his wife was totally incapacitated) who maintained a resident child at his or her own expense. Widow's bereavement allowance was due to a widow in the year of her husband's death and in the following year provided the widow had not remarried before the beginning of that year. Both the additional personal allowance and the widow's bereavement allowance were abolished from April 2000.

The blind person's allowance may be claimed by blind persons (in England and Wales, registered as blind by a local authority) and surplus blind person's allowance may be transferred to a husband or wife. Relief on life assurance premiums is given by deduction from the premium payable. From 1984-85, it is confined to policies made before 14 March 1984.

Rateable values *(Table 17.12)*

Major changes to local government finance in England and Wales took effect from 1 April 1990. These included the abolition of domestic rating - replaced by the community charge (replaced in 1993 by the council tax), the revaluation of all non-domestic properties, and the introduction of the Uniform Business Rate. Also in 1990, a new classification scheme was introduced which has resulted in differences in coverage. Further differences are caused by legislative changes which have changed the treatment of certain types of property.

There was little change in the total rateable value of non-domestic properties when all these properties were revalued in April 1995. Rateable values for offices fell and there was a rise for all other property types shown in the table.

With effect from 1 April 2000 all non-domestic properties were revalued. Overall there was an increase in rateable values of over 25% compared to the end of the 1995 list. The largest proportionate increase was for offices and cinemas, with all property types given in the table showing rises.

Central government

The central government embraces all bodies for whose activities a Minister of the Crown, or other responsible person, is accountable to Parliament. It includes, in addition to the ordinary government departments, a number of bodies administering public policy but without the substantial degree of financial independence which characterises the public corporations; it also includes certain extra-budgetary funds and accounts controlled by departments.

The government's financial transactions are handled through a number of statutory funds, or accounts. The most important of these is the Consolidated Fund which is the government's main account with the Bank of England. Up to 31 March 1968 the Consolidated Fund was virtually synonymous with the term 'Exchequer' which was then the government's central cash account. From 1 April 1968 the National Loans Fund, with a separate account at the Bank of England, was set up by the National Loans Act, 1968. The general effect of this Act was to remove from the Consolidated Fund most of the government's domestic lending and the whole of the government's borrowing transactions and to provide for them to be brought to account in the National Loans Fund.

Revenue from taxation and miscellaneous receipts, including interest and dividends on loans made from Votes, continue to be paid into the Consolidated Fund. After meeting the ordinary expenditure on Supply Services and the Consolidated Fund Standing Services, the surplus or deficit of the Consolidated Fund (Table 17.4), is payable into or met by the National Loans Fund.

Table 17.4 also provides a summary of the transactions of the National Loans Fund. The service of the National Debt, previously borne by the Consolidated Fund, is now met from the National Loans Fund which receives (a) interest payable on loans to the nationalised industries, local authorities and other bodies, whether the loans were made before or after 1 April 1968 and (b) the profits of the Issue Department of the Bank of England, mainly derived from interest on government securities, which were formerly paid into the Exchange Equalisation Account. The net cost of servicing the National Debt after applying these interest receipts and similar items is a charge on the Consolidated Fund as

part of the standing services. Details of National Loans Fund loans outstanding are shown in Table 17.7.

Details of borrowing and repayments of debt, other than loans from the National Loans Fund, are shown in Table 17.6.

17.1 Public sector finances[1]
United Kingdom
Not seasonally adjusted

£ millions

		1990 /91	1991 /92	1992 /93	1993 /94	1994 /95	1995 /96	1996 /97	1997 /98	1998 /99	1999 /00	2000 /01
Surplus on current budget[2]												
General Government	ANLW	7 587	−6 942	−29 560	−36 375	−28 552	−22 783	−21 457	289	12 698	21 731	27 082
Public sector	ANMU	2 479	−11 421	−34 242	−40 600	−32 813	−24 673	−23 133	−1 086	11 367	20 983	25 085
Net investment[3]												
General Government	−ANNV	15 325	15 262	16 209	14 308	16 322	13 643	8 776	7 282	7 506	6 526	7 527
Public sector	−ANNW	8 150	10 973	12 356	10 358	10 391	10 259	5 272	4 889	5 867	4 621	6 301
Net borrowing[4]												
General Government	−NNBK	7 738	22 204	45 769	50 683	44 874	36 426	30 233	6 993	−5 192	−15 205	−19 555
Public sector	−ANNX	5 671	22 394	46 598	50 958	43 204	34 932	28 405	5 975	−5 500	−16 362	−18 784
Net cash requirement[5]												
General Government	RUUS	239	13 420	36 577	46 070	38 096	34 489	24 152	1 830	−6 574	−9 594	−37 688
Public sector	RURQ	−776	13 856	36 260	46 131	36 688	31 485	22 728	1 112	−6 960	−8 595	−36 994

1 National accounts entities as defined under the European System of Accounts 1995 (ESA95) consistent with the latest national accounts.
2 Net saving, plus capital taxes.
3 Gross capital formation, plus payments less receipts, of investment grants less depreciation.
4 Net borrowing = net investment minus surplus on current budget.
5 Previously called Public Sector Borrowing Requirement (PSBR).

Source: Office for National Statistics: 020 7533 5984

17.2 Contributions to the public sector net cash requirement
United Kingdom

£ millions

		1990 /91	1991 /92	1992 /93	1993 /94	1994 /95	1995 /96	1996 /97	1997 /98	1998 /99	1999 /00	2000 /01
Central government net cash requirement	RUUW	−2 635	13 020	36 230	49 699	39 123	35 315	25 156	3 542	−4 535	−9 179	−35 216
of which: own account	RUUX	−3 092	11 830	42 312	48 850	39 057	35 628	24 995	2 650	−6 170	−10 592	−37 062
Local government												
Direct borrowing from central government[1]	ABEC	1 472	639	−7 267	−654	−392	473	1 517	955	1 869	1 400	1 119
Net borrowing from other sources	ABEF	1 817	973	1 506	−2 025	−610	−1 611	−2 357	−1 761	−2 166	−486	−1 790
less Transactions in other public sector dept:												
Central government	ABEE	−32	19	−12	43	25	4	2	15	103	−64	−46
Public corporations	AAEJ	−10	3	−14	58	−66	−3	1	−1	4	−1	1
Net cash requirement	ABEG	3 331	1 590	−5 735	−2 780	−961	−1 139	−843	−820	−404	979	−626
General government net cash requirement	RUUI	−776	13 971	37 762	47 573	38 554	33 703	22 796	1 767	−6 808	−9 600	−36 961
Public corporations:												
Direct borrowing from central government	ABEI	−1 015	551	1 185	1 503	458	−786	−1 356	−63	−234	13	727
Net borrowing from other sources	ABES	−216	−357	−621	−745	−779	−633	1 289	−277	−858	747	−187
less Transactions in other public sector debt:												
Central government	ABEK	−230	−225	763	662	1 121	2 281	1 442	374	−675	−291	−119
Local authorities	ABEL	14	−17	118	35	−34	−696	−85	4	−31	33	−35
Net cash requirement	ABEM	−1 015	436	−317	61	−1 408	−3 004	−1 424	−718	−386	1 018	694
Public sector net cash requirement	RURQ	−776	13 856	36 260	46 131	36 688	31 485	22 728	1 112	−6 960	−8 595	−36 994
Public sector net cash requirement excluding privatisation proceeds	RURS	4 569	21 779	44 444	51 561	43 121	33 920	27 162	2 882	−6 890	−8 060	−36 913

1 Excluding market transactions of central government in public sector debt; these transactions are included in 'Net borrowing from other sources.'

Source: Office for National Statistics: 020 7533 5984

17.3 Public sector net debt
United Kingdom

£ millions

		1992 /93	1993 /94	1994 /95	1995 /96	1996 /97	1997 /98	1998 /99	1999 /00	2000 /01
Cental government sterling gross debt:										
British government stock										
Conventional gilts	BKPK	130 642	168 414	186 666	208 943	231 869	232 292	223 105	218 687	204 293
Index linked gilts	BKPL	27 861	34 854	39 207	46 133	51 535	58 729	62 289	65 740	70 316
Total	BKPM	158 503	203 268	225 872	255 075	283 404	291 021	285 394	284 427	274 609
Sterling Treasury bills	BKPJ	5 307	3 483	8 051	10 781	4 996	2 106	4 721	4 453	3 521
National savings	ACUA	44 147	48 330	51 843	56 965	61 754	63 271	63 620	62 546	62 161
Tax instruments	ACRV	2 385	2 133	1 612	1 222	852	705	574	535	491
Other sterling debt[1]	BKSK	10 716	15 045	25 773	26 758	26 571	25 312	26 152	26 773	28 237
Central government sterling gross debt total	BKSL	221 058	272 259	313 151	350 801	377 578	382 416	380 461	378 734	369 019
Central government foreign currency gross debt:										
US$ bonds	BKPG	4 585	4 651	4 241	4 524	4 294	4 180	4 338	4 388	4 924
DM bonds[2]	EYST	2 062	2 018	2 245	2 219	1 828	–	–	–	–
ECU bonds	EYSJ	1 998	1 945	2 045	2 059	1 777	1 606	1 672	1 500	–
ECU/euro Treasury notes	EYSV	1 998	3 890	4 499	4 118	3 199	2 891	3 010	2 701	2 486
ECU/euro Treasury bills	EYSN	2 878	2 723	2 863	2 883	2 488	2 249	2 341	–	–
Other foreign currency debt	BKPH	5 371	1 632	1 018	982	752	537	456	365	291
Central government foreign currency gross debt total	BKPI	18 892	16 860	16 912	16 785	14 338	11 463	11 816	8 954	7 701
Central government gross debt total	BKPW	239 950	289 119	330 063	367 586	391 916	393 879	392 277	387 688	376 720
Local government gross debt total	EYKP	49 897	50 239	50 229	50 552	51 599	51 933	52 742	51 402	52 314
less										
Central government holdings of local government debt	−EYKZ	−41 527	−40 977	−40 707	−41 266	−42 555	−43 397	−45 273	−46 791	−48 021
Local government holdings of central government debt	−EYLA	−81	−124	−149	−153	−155	−170	−273	−77	−31
General government gross debt (consolidated)	BKPX	248 239	298 257	339 436	376 719	400 805	402 245	399 473	392 222	380 982
Public corporations gross debt	EYYD	16 194	23 867	26 916	26 595	26 158	26 044	26 775	26 812	27 740
less:										
Central government holdings of public corporations debt	−EYXY	−15 227	−22 951	−26 279	−25 980	−25 664	−25 668	−26 440	−26 453	−27 181
Local government holdings of public corporations debt	−EYXZ	−11	−69	−3	–	−1	–	−4	−123	−124
Public corporations holdings of central government debt	−BKPZ	−2 617	−2 854	−3 503	−5 723	−7 125	−7 485	−6 529	−6 301	−6 363
Public corporations holdings of local government debt	−EYXV	−1 585	−1 620	−1 586	−890	−805	−810	−779	−121	−106
Public sector gross debt (consolidated)	BKQA	244 993	294 630	334 981	370 721	393 368	394 326	392 496	386 036	374 948
Public sector liquid assets:										
Official reserves	AIPD	27 153	28 908	28 330	30 463	25 547	21 293	22 147	21 498	30 423
Central government deposits[3]	BKSM	1 631	1 775	1 816	1 808	2 067	2 292	1 762	1 879	2 797
Other central government	BKSN	3 386	1 250	–	–	–	–	–	4 756	15 657
Local government deposits[3]	BKSO	6 341	8 762	9 335	10 229	11 276	11 790	12 275	11 758	11 512
Other local government short term assets	BKQG	1 932	2 424	2 621	2 826	3 256	3 693	4 334	3 928	5 755
Public corporations deposits[3]	BKSP	1 166	1 353	2 622	3 089	1 778	1 469	2 029	1 455	1 633
Other public corporations short term assets	BKSQ	1 077	790	943	1 054	964	937	1 300	1 128	1 212
Public sector liquid assets total	BKQJ	42 686	45 262	45 667	49 469	44 888	41 474	43 847	46 402	68 989
Public sector net debt	BKQK	202 307	249 368	289 314	321 252	348 480	352 852	348 649	339 634	305 959
as percentage of GDP[4]	RUTO	32.1	37.2	40.7	42.7	43.7	41.6	39.2	36.4	31.4

1 Including overdraft with Bank of England.
2 Matured on 28 October 1997.
3 Bank and building society deposits.
4 Gross domestic product at market prices from 12 months centred on the end of the month.

Source: Office for National Statistics: 020 7533 5984

17.4 Consolidated Fund and National Loans Fund: revenue and expenditure; receipts and payments

United Kingdom   Years ending 31 March

£ millions

		1990/91	1991/92	1992/93	1993/94	1994/95	1995/96	1996/97	1997/98	1998/99	1999/00	2000/01
Consolidated Fund												
Revenue												
Inland Revenue	KCWZ	82 320.7	79 509.6	76 345.9	77 270.6	87 230.4	97 100.9	103 892.4	117 632.8	128 249.8	139 384.0	149 084.8
Customs and Excise	KCXA	55 336.9	61 826.9	63 398.0	66 885.5	72 485.6	76 668.6	82 351.6	89 839.6	94 018.3	97 291.5	102 168.0
Motor vehicle duties	KCXB	2 971.4	2 945.3	3 196.0	3 752.3	3 805.9	4 043.6	4 217.5	4 543.0	4 666.3	4 893.0	4 642.1
National Non-Domestic Rates	KPOI	..	..	..	..	16 280.3	13 373.4	14 269.3	14 036.9	15 878.3	13 403.8	15 482.0
Miscellaneous receipts	KCXE	21 736.6	27 193.0	30 101.2	22 150.2	16 280.3	10 289.3	12 634.6	14 176.6	10 737.1	8 799.0	29 329.4
Total revenue	KCXF	162 366.1	171 474.8	173 041.2	170 058.6	191 272.0	201 475.8	217 365.4	240 228.9	253 549.8	263 771.3	300 706.3
Expenditure												
Supply services	KCXG	145 763.1	168 702.6	189 961.6	204 376.1	207 465.8	211 403.3	214 226.0	209 440.8	213 439.2	226 989.6	241 685.1
Debt interest[1]	KCXH	10 229.2	8 943.0	10 675.1	13 459.6	16 039.8	18 423.1	20 702.3	21 605.7	21 320.8	18 535.3	16 629.2
Payments to Northern Ireland	KCXI	2 927.7	2 944.9	2 632.1	3 090.3	4 052.6	3 903.5	3 685.2	4 581.5	4 709.3	3 104.4	–
Payments to the European Communities, etc	KCXJ	4 806.1	3 323.3	4 867.1	6 079.5	5 258.2	7 650.7	6 875.3	7 039.9	8 060.7	7 001.8	8 417.1
Other expenditure[2]	KCXL	503.7	276.3	117.7	–453.3	271.6	–14.0	876.2	–53.8	–62.1	223.7	170.1
Total expenditure	KCXM	164 229.8	184 189.7	208 253.6	226 552.2	233 088.0	241 366.5	246 365.0	242 614.1	247 467.9	255 854.8	266 901.5
Deficit met from the National Loans Fund	KCXN	1 863.7	12 715.5	35 212.4	56 493.6	41 816.0	39 890.7	28 999.6	2 385.2	–6 081.9	–7 916.5	–33 804.8
National Loans Fund												
Receipts												
Profits of the Issue Department of the Bank of England - income[3]	KZAW	2 247.3	1 816.5	1 350.8	996.6	955.2	1 275.5	1 200.9	1 604.8	1 600.9	1 327.3	1 603.0
Other miscellaneous receipts	KZAX	–	6.2	66.7	106.6	4.8	4.4	3.6	5.0	5.0	4.4	6.0
Interest on loans	KCXO	5 429.0	5 925.1	5 100.7	4 695.2	4 564.5	4 598.7	4 393.5	5 103.6	4 409.7	4 533.3	6 215.4
Service of the National Debt - balance met from the Consolidated Fund	KCXP	10 229.3	8 943.1	10 675.1	13 459.6	16 039.8	18 423.2	20 702.3	21 605.7	21 320.8	18 535.3	16 629.2
Gilt Edged Official Operations Account Net Income	KJDO	..	..	..	2.0	–	–	–	–	–	127.5	–
Total	KCXQ	17 905.6	16 690.9	17 193.3	19 260.0	21 564.3	24 301.8	26 300.3	28 319.1	27 336.4	24 527.8	24 453.6
Exchange Equalisation Account- sterling capital	KCXR	–1 050.0	300.0	3 574.5	400.0	1 250.0	2 750.0	2 150.0	3 650.0	1 880.0	975.0	–5 205.0
Net borrowing[4]	KCXS	3 684.7	12 112.0	25 907.6	58 939.5	39 848.1	37 688.8	27 547.9	–	–	4 997.3	–
International Monetary Fund- maintenance of sterling holdings	KCXT	–	59.8	47.6	–	–	–	82.1	707.0	181.2	–	–
Profits of the Issue Department of the Bank of England: capital appreciation	KZAY	..	..	..	..	..	..	18.8	21.2	19.3	1.7	2.5
Reduction of National Debt Commissioners' Liability in respect of the National Savings Bank Investment Account	KCXU	–	–	–	–	–	–	–	–	–	–	–
Change in balances and other items	KCXV	–	–	–	–	–	–	–	–	–	–	–
NILO Gilt-Edged operations A/C	KJDL	–	–	–	2 500.0	2 500.0	2 500.0	2 000.0	2 500.0	2 500.0	5 000.0	–
Debt Management Account	GPJW	..	..	..	..	..	..	..	..	..	..	20 000.0
Total	KCXW	20 540.3	29 162.7	46 723.0	81 099.5	65 162.4	42 938.8	58 099.1	35 197.3	31 916.9	35 501.8	39 251.1
Payments												
Service of the National Debt: Interest	KJDM	17 730.6	16 516.3	17 009.5	19 107.0	21 334.7	24 004.0	25 942.5	27 877.8	26 792.1	24 073.7	23 855.8
Management and expenses	KCXY	175.0	174.6	183.8	153.0	229.6	297.8	357.8	441.3	544.3	454.1	597.8
Total	KCXZ	17 905.6	16 690.9	17 193.3	19 260.0	21 564.3	24 301.8	26 300.3	28 319.1	27 336.4	24 527.8	24 453.6
Consolidated Fund deficit met from the National Loans Fund	KCYA	1 863.7	12 714.9	35 212.4	56 493.6	41 816.0	39 890.7	28 999.6	2 385.2	–6 081.9	–7 916.5	–33 804.8
Net repayment[4]	KCYB	–	–	–	–	–	–	–	2 482.1	3 558.2	–	7 083.4
Net lending[5]	KCYC	623.9	–243.1	–6 787.0	–286.6	–974.8	334.1	280.6	–4.2	1 766.3	1 255.9	1 496.5
International Monetary Fund- maintenance of value of sterling holding	KCYD	147.10	–	1 104.30	632.50	226.20	202.10	–	–	–	126.10	21.20
International Monetary Fund- additional subscription	KCYE	–	–	–	–	–	–	–	–	2 826.5	–	–
NILO Gilt-Edged Operations A/C	KJDN	–	–	–	–	2 500.0	2 500.0	2 500.0	2 000.0	2 500.0	2 500.0	–
Discharge of Treasury Liability to the Bank of England Issue Department	KPUK	–	–	–	–	30.7	11.9	18.6	15.1	11.4	8.5	1.2
Debt Management Account	ZAFB	..	..	..	..	..	..	..	..	..	15 000.0	40 000.0
Total	KCYF	20 540.3	29 162.7	46 723.0	81 099.5	65 162.4	42 938.8	58 099.1	35 197.3	31 916.9	35 501.8	39 251.1

1 Payment to National Loans Fund representing its payments for the service of the National Debt *less* its receipts of interest on loans outstanding, etc.
2 Includes net issues to Contingencies Fund.
3 Prior to 1996-97, receipts from the Bank of England for appreciation of the assets of the Issue Department were included in the total ammount for the profits of the Issue Department.
4 See Table 17.6.
5 Minus sign indicates a net issue repayment.

Source: HM Treasury: 020 7270 1586

17.5 Central government net cash requirement
United Kingdom
Years ending 31 March

£ millions

		1990/91	1991/92	1992/93	1993/94	1994/95	1995/96	1996/97	1997/98	1998/99	1999/00	2000/01
Inland revenue	ACAB	82 322	79 353	76 292	77 289	87 255	97 120	103 957	117 632	128 249	139 384	149 085
Customs and excise	ACAC	55 336	61 827	63 398	66 885	72 486	76 670	82 351	89 840	94 019	97 290	102 169
Social security contributions[1]	ABIA	33 013	34 391	35 420	36 985	40 659	42 882	45 121	49 255	53 227	54 606	58 472
Interest and dividends	RUUL	10 997	10 924	9 828	9 595	8 380	9 607	9 082	9 557	9 455	8 637	10 296
Other receipts[2]	RUUM	14 798	16 052	16 529	17 870	17 082	19 289	20 906	20 848	19 618	20 238	44 745
Total cash receipts	RUUN	196 466	202 547	201 467	208 624	225 862	245 568	261 417	287 132	304 568	320 155	364 767
Interest payments	RUUO	17 465	16 538	17 528	19 160	21 998	24 452	27 554	27 807	27 031	24 278	24 011
Privatisation proceeds	ABIF	−5 345	−7 923	−8 184	−5 430	−6 433	−2 435	−4 434	−1 770	−70	−535	−81
Net departmental outlays[3]	RUUP	181 254	205 762	234 435	243 744	249 354	259 179	263 292	263 745	271 437	285 820	303 775
Total cash outlays	RUUQ	193 374	214 377	243 779	257 474	264 919	281 196	286 412	289 782	298 398	309 563	327 705
Own account net cash requirement	RUUX	−3 092	11 830	42 312	48 850	39 057	35 628	24 995	2 650	−6 170	−10 592	−37 062
On lending to local government	ABEC	1 472	639	−7 267	−654	−392	473	1 517	955	1 869	1 400	1 119
On lending to public corporations	ABEI	−1 015	551	1 185	1 503	458	−786	−1 356	−63	−234	13	727
Central government net cash requirement	RUUW	−2 635	13 020	36 230	49 699	39 123	35 315	25 156	3 542	−4 535	−9 179	−35 216

		1993/94	1994/95	1995/96	1996/97	1997/98	1998/99	1999/00	2000/01
Central government funds and accounts									
National Loans Fund:									
Total payments	ACAU	18 973	20 648	24 631	26 581	28 309	29 100	25 786	25 951
Total receipts	ACAQ	19 260	21 593	24 286	26 282	28 318	27 335	24 527	24 454
Less surplus from consolidated fund	ACAP	−56 494	−41 817	−39 889	−28 983	−2 386	6 083	7 859	33 805
Borrowing required	ACAX	56 205	40 871	40 235	29 279	2 376	−4 318	−6 602	−32 309
Surplus of National Insurance Funds[4]	ACAY	903	2 304	674	326	1 798	3 053	2 262	4 329
Departmental balances and miscellaneous	ACAZ	5 585	−539	4 192	3 857	−3 046	−2 947	145	−1 555
Northern Ireland central government debt	ACBA	−20	15	−52	59	−82	−111	−170	−133
Financing of the central government net cash requirement analysed by type of instrument									
Net cash requirement	RUUW	49 699	39 123	35 315	25 156	3 542	−4 535	−9 179	−35 216
Liabilities									
Coin	−EYMW	97	121	74	136	145	219	192	231
Sterling Treasury bills	NAVG	−1 824	4 566	2 730	−5 786	−2 890	2 614	−271	−926
British government securities	ANTA	46 411	21 206	26 607	26 492	6 285	−8 910	−1 202	−14 246
National savings	−AACE	4 111	3 570	5 109	4 821	1 554	365	−1 055	−563
Tax instruments	−AACF	−252	−521	−390	−369	−147	−135	−39	−43
Loans from MFIs	ANTB	3 400	9 028	−292	−1 342	−1 468	2 576	1 291	−1 676
Northern Ireland cg debt	−AACH	−27	−3	−7	−4	−21	−18	−12	−21
ECS liabilities	−AACI	−43	−24	−35	−9	4	−4	–	–
Deposits with cg from other sectors	ANTC	1 242	1 406	1 393	990	156	−1 637	−947	2 980
Government foreign currency debt	−AACL	−1 639	−25	−401	−248	−1 803	−45	−2 221	−1 941
Other government overseas financing	−AACM	−94	−93	−94	−88	−91	−98	−98	−114
Assets									
NILO lending (except PWLB)	ANTD	−124	−122	−97	253	140	−2	−118	−111
Net change in official reserves	AIPA	−1 442	62	705	635	1 902	3	167	−7 072
Deposits with MFIs	ANSZ	−117	−48	13	−325	−224	537	−4 866	−11 714

1 Excluding Northern Ireland contributions.
2 Including some elements of expenditure not separately identified.
3 Net of certain receipts.
4 A negative item represents a surplus, a positive item a deficit.

Sources: HM Treasury;
Office for National Statistics: 020 7533 5984

Government finance

17.6 Borrowing and repayment of debt
United Kingdom
Years ending 31 March

£ millions

		1990/91	1991/92	1992/93	1993/94	1994/95	1995/96	1996/97	1997/98	1998/99	1999/00	2000/01
Borrowing												
Government securities: new issues	KQGA	3 269.3	15 920.7	33 601.1	55 959.2	32 137.5	34 150.3	40 800.8	28 484.4	12 048.0	26 426.5	25 789.8
National savings securities:												
National savings certificates	KQGB	2 658.1	3 549.1	3 453.4	3 381.5	2 187.9	3 425.9	3 695.5	4 435.2	3 028.7	1 962.7	3 086.2
Capital bonds	KQGC	188.7	282.1	524.8	556.2	521.5	504.8	450.8	619.0	469.6	35.4	29.0
Income bonds	KQGD	1 629.1	1 329.1	1 251.2	1 940.8	1 255.7	780.7	1 272.7	1 043.4	1 371.7	653.4	760.5
Deposit bonds	KQGE	–	–	–	–	–	–	–	–	–	–	–
British savings bonds	KQGF	–	–	–	–	–	–	–	–	–	–	–
Premium savings bonds	KQGG	185.9	246.5	378.6	931.5	1 837.2	2 040.6	2 552.5	3 158.8	3 652.8	3 449.4	3 296.0
Save As You Earn	KQGH	88.2	94.3	85.3	76.4	66.5	50.8	34.1	20.7	11.4	5.0	0.3
Yearly plan	KQGI	71.0	87.0	109.9	112.4	116.5	94.1	–	–	5.2	–	–
National savings stamps and gift tokens	KQGJ	11.4	–	–	–	–	–	–	–	–	–	–
National Savings Bank Investments	KQGK	1 491.2	1 215.1	1 227.9	1 370.5	1 368.1	1 312.1	1 478.7	1 282.3	1 085.0	901.6	955.3
Children's Bonus Bonds	KGVO	–	127.0	95.5	91.2	118.9	144.9	352.4	255.3	205.0	58.5	53.4
First Option Bonds	KIAR	–	–	859.4	1 026.0	812.0	826.4	1 139.8	1 152.9	1 001.8	34.3	–
Pensioners Guaranteed Income Bond	KJDW	..	..	..	786.1	1 190.3	2 104.2	2 863.8	1 126.9	201.0	590.7	687.2
Treasurer's account	KWNF	..	..	..	..	..	..	21.1	39.9	17.1	13.6	12.5
Individual Savings Account	ZAFC	..	..	..	..	..	..	..	..	–	257.8	265.9
Fixed Rate Savings Bonds	ZAFD	..	..	..	..	..	..	..	..	–	175.9	284.7
Certificate of tax deposit	KQGL	1 343.1	1 137.7	607.2	470.6	91.2	76.2	109.4	84.1	66.4	121.4	76.5
Nationalised industries', etc temporary deposits	KQGM	25 855.0	20 709.0	19 350.0	28 700.9	29 294.0	36 870.6	53 198.2	46 375.9	39 962.4	40 343.3	56 106.6
British Gas corporation deposits	KQGN	–	–	–	–	–	–	–	–	–	–	–
Sterling Treasury bills (net receipt)	KQGO	–	–	–	–	5 196.1	2 606.1	–	–	3 546.2	–	–
ECU Treasury bills (net receipt)	KQGP	429.2	–	–	–	–	–	–	–	–	–	–
ECU Treasury notes (net receipt)	KDZZ	–	1 066.4	1 396.0	2 073.2	429.8	–	–	–	–	721.1	–
Ways and means (net receipt)	KQGQ	4 107.5	2 530.5	–	9 007.0	8 891.7	1 162.3	511.1	–	183.6	5 599.0	12 126.0
Other debt : payable in sterling : Interest free notes	KQGR	319.1	161.2	1 045.6	796.6	382.6	247.4	99.2	32.4	2 130.9	373.5	972.7
Other debt : payable in external currencies	KHCY	1 939.8	40.0	33 147.7	9 243.9	–	–	2 565.2	–	–	–	–
Total receipts	KHCZ	43 586.6	48 495.7	97 133.6	116 524.0	85 897.5	86 397.4	111 145.3	88 111.2	68 986.8	81 723.1	104 502.6
Repayment of debt												
Government securities : redemptions	KQGS	6 806.0	7 841.5	8 351.8	7 390.5	9 333.3	4 652.7	14 488.4	20 678.9	18 575.5	19 815.8	33 722.2
Statutory sinking funds	KQGT	2.7	2.5	2.5	2.4	2.3	2.2	2.2	2.1	2.0	2.0	2.0
Terminable annuities: National Debt Commissioners	KQGU	–	–	–	–	–	–	–	–	–	–	–
National savings securities:												
National savings certificates	KQGV	2 187.4	1 653.6	1 092.5	2 208.0	1 612.6	2 258.4	3 263.7	4 058.5	3 449.0	2 405.2	4 546.8
Capital bonds	KQGW	23.5	14.6	21.1	398.0	647.7	509.0	698.3	1 160.5	888.3	324.2	375.0
Income bonds	KQGX	831.3	729.0	955.2	1 000.7	1 181.8	1 256.9	1 394.0	1 148.9	880.8	1 686.3	857.0
Deposit bonds	KQGY	138.4	86.8	80.9	71.8	72.3	72.5	64.8	72.6	84.2	70.2	71.1
Yearly Plan	KQGZ	127.5	107.1	99.8	88.9	77.0	101.9	96.3	113.2	120.0	141.8	18.4
British savings bonds	KQHA	–	–	–	–	–	–	–	–	–	–	–
Premium savings bonds	KQHB	194.0	154.3	153.4	181.0	333.0	590.1	869.3	1 203.1	1 398.4	1 923.8	1 872.6
Save As You Earn	KQHC	89.6	103.6	116.9	96.3	92.3	98.7	70.1	68.2	37.1	34.5	22.9
National savings stamps and gift tokens	KQHD	11.1	–	–	0.7	–	–	–	–	–	–	–
National Savings Bank Investments (repayments)	KQHE	1 775.3	1 796.1	2 039.0	1 646.3	1 745.3	1 755.8	1 837.0	2 175.7	2 027.0	1 886.3	1 654.1
Children's Bonus Bonds	KGVQ	–	0.1	1.0	1.2	4.3	0.1	257.8	187.9	183.2	69.3	95.0
First Option Bonds	KIAS	–	–	4.6	1 085.1	969.9	732.7	833.9	1 283.0	1 055.5	298.1	225.2
Pensioners Guaranteed Income Bond	KPOB	–	–	–	–	57.0	104.5	185.0	318.8	897.8	935.3	2 003.8
Treasurer's account	KWNG	..	..	..	..	..	..	1.2	11.8	13.7	16.4	13.9
Individual Savings Account	ZAFE	..	..	..	..	..	..	..	..	–	12.3	39.9
Fixed Rate Savings Bonds	ZAFF	..	..	..	..	..	..	..	..	–	2.8	62.1
Certificates of tax deposit	KQHF	1 192.3	1 116.5	936.9	722.6	612.1	466.0	478.9	229.0	199.9	159.9	120.1
Tax reserve certificates	KQHG	0.1	0.1	–	–	–	–	–	–	–	–	–
Nationalised industries', etc temporary deposits	KQHH	25 833.0	21 186.0	18 477.0	28 098.5	28 557.8	35 263.1	51 979.3	46 835.7	41 776.9	41 089.4	56 004.0
Debt to the Bank of England	KPOC	–	–	–	–	11.0	–	–	–	–	–	–
British Gas Corporation (Repayment of Deposits)	KQHI	–	–	–	–	–	–	–	–	–	–	–
Sterling Treasury bills (net repayment)	KQHJ	140.3	1 191.0	4 882.1	1 547.5	–	–	4 009.6	1 928.5	–	3 014.8	6 194.2
ECU Treasury bills (net repayment)	KJEG	..	..	..	73.3	–	–	–	–	–	2 492.9	–
ECU Treasury notes (net repayment)	KSPA	..	..	..	..	..	439.1	318.3	3.3	13.2	–	1 391.9
Ways and means (net repayment)	KQHK	–	–	6 786.3	–	–	–	–	5 815.4	–	–	–
Other debt: payable in sterling : Interest free notes	KQHL	169.6	268.3	155.8	101.3	225.2	301.3	87.6	1 215.5	850.5	246.4	458.2
Other	KQHM	0.1	0.1	–	–	–	–	–	–	–	–	–
Other debt : payable in external currencies	KQHN	379.7	132.5	27 068.7	12 870.4	514.5	103.6	2 661.7	2 082.7	92.0	98.1	1 835.6
Total payments	KQHO	39 901.9	36 383.7	71 226.0	57 584.5	46 049.4	48 708.6	83 597.4	90 593.3	72 545.0	76 725.8	111 586.0
Net borrowing	KQHP	3 684.7	12 112.0	25 907.6	58 939.5	39 848.1	37 688.8	27 547.9	–	–	4 997.3	–
Net repayment	KHDD	–	–	–	–	–	–	–	2 482.1	3 558.2	–	7 083.4

Source: HM Treasury: 020 7270 1586

17.7 Consolidated Fund and National Loans Fund: assets and liabilities
United Kingdom
At 31 March in each year

£ millions

		1991	1992	1993	1994	1995	1996	1997	1998	1999	2000
Consolidated Fund											
Total estimated assets	KQIA	14 951.0	19 852.9	18 872.0	26 914.5	33 992.4	33 809.0	36 177.4	36 061.0	36 148.0	33 720.0
Subscriptions and contributions to international financial organisations	KQIB	4 329.6	4 315.2	5 009.2	5 438.2	5 898.1	6 470.8	6 528.9	6 660.8	7 059.7	6 903.6
International Bank for Reconstruction and Development	KQIC	224.8	236.3	259.8	274.5	265.2	271.6	265.0	262.5	266.0	267.1
International Finance Corporation	KQID	39.3	39.4	53.1	60.9	62.0	73.1	74.9	72.9	75.6	76.5
International Development Association	KQIE	2 127.3	2 343.3	2 576.0	2 785.4	3 005.5	3 205.8	3 372.7	3 562.2	3 733.3	3 900.0
African Development Bank	KQIF	80.8	91.2	108.1	127.9	141.2	148.3	162.9	180.0	199.1	215.7
Asian Development Bank	KQIG	155.8	173.0	180.9	188.9	201.5	214.6	240.4	272.5	304.6	339.3
Caribbean Development Bank	KQIH	24.6	27.5	29.4	31.2	32.6	34.2	34.1	34.6	36.8	40.7
European Investment Bank	KQII	1 550.3	1 252.8	1 588.9	1 713.7	1 876.4	2 166.6	2 036.5	1 840.7	2 083.1	1 706.6
European Bank for Reconstruction and Development	KPOD	..	22.3	61.3	99.4	146.3	189.4	175.6	164.2	179.2	170.0
Inter-American Development Bank	KQIJ	89.9	89.4	109.8	112.5	107.2	119.6	117.5	219.3	127.8	130.6
International Fund for Agricultural Development	KQIK	34.7	36.9	38.5	40.2	42.7	44.2	46.1	48.8	51.0	53.7
Multilateral Investment Guarantee Agency	KQIL	3.0	3.0	3.5	3.5	3.2	3.4	3.2	3.1	3.2	3.3
Amounts due from overseas governments	KQIM	–	–	–	–	–	–	–	–	–	–
War of 1939-45	KQIN	–	–	–	–	–	–	–	–	–	–
Other	KQIO	–	–	–	–	–	–	–	–	–	–
Loans from Votes	KQIP	2 420.3	4 047.3	6 709.2	11 057.4	13 599.7	12 967.0	13 684.7	14 050.0	11 546.3	3 763.3
Issues of public dividend capital:	KQIQ	1 617.9	1 642.7	4 920.0	7 979.2	11 467.0	12 161.1	12 424.8	13 157.1	16 238.5	21 349.5
British Airways Board	KQIR	–	–	–	–	–	–	–	–	–	–
British Steel Corporation	KQIS	–	–	–	–	–	–	–	–	–	–
Royal Ordnance Factories	KQIT	–	–	–	–	–	–	–	–	–	–
National Enterprise Board	KQIU	–	–	–	–	–	–	–	–	–	–
Royal Mint	KQIV	7.0	7.0	7.0	7.0	7.0	7.0	7.0	7.0	7.0	7.0
Post Office	KQIW	–	–	–	–	–	–	–	–	–	–
Scottish Development Agency	KQIX	–	–	–	–	–	–	–	–	–	–
Welsh Development Agency	KQIY	15.5	13.5	12.6	11.6	10.9	9.8	8.9	8.8	8.6	9.1
British Aerospace	KQIZ	–	–	–	–	–	–	–	–	–	–
British Shipbuilders	KQJA	1 595.4	1 597.4	1 598.3	1 598.3	1 598.3	1 598.3	1 598.5	1 598.3	1 598.3	1 598.3
Patent Office	KIAT		6.3	6.3	6.3	6.3	6.3	6.3	6.3	6.3	6.3
NHS Trusts	KIAU	–	1 325.8	3 279.6	6 336.2	9 603.1	10 173.8	10 349.7	11 078.0	14 158.7	19 227.8
Companies House	KIAV	–	16.9	15.9	15.9	15.9	15.9	15.9	15.9	15.9	15.9
Central Office of Information	KIAW	–	0.3	0.3	0.3	0.3	0.3	0.3	0.3	0.3	0.3
Chessington Computer Centre	KPOE	–	–	–	3.5	3.5	3.5	–	–	–	–
Buying Agency	KWNH	..	..	..	..	0.1	0.4	0.4	0.4	0.4	0.4
Defence Evaluation and Research Agency	KWNI	..	..	..	..	128.8	253.0	274.5	274.5	275.4	275.4
Fire Service College	KWNJ	..	..	..	..	16.7	16.7	16.7	16.7	16.7	16.7
Forensic Science Service	GPVB	..	..	..	..	..	..	..	..	–	18.0
Hydrographic Office	GPVC	..	..	..	..	..	..	..	..	..	13.3
Land Registry	KWNK	..	..	..	..	55.4	55.4	61.5	61.5	61.5	61.5
Medicines Control Agency	KWNL	..	..	..	..	1.6	1.6	1.6	1.6	1.6	1.6
Meteorological Office	KZAZ	..	..	..	..	..	..	58.9	58.9	58.9	58.9
NHS Estates	GPVD	..	..	..	..	..	..	..	..	..	0.4
Registers of Scotland	KZBA	..	..	..	..	..	..	4.3	4.3	4.3	–
Vehicle Inspectorate	KWNM	..	..	..	..	19.1	19.1	20.3	20.3	20.3	20.3
Driving Standards Agency	LQMI	..	..	..	..	..	..	..	3.5	3.5	3.5
Ordnance Survey	GPVE	..	..	..	..	..	..	..	..	..	14.0
Queen Elizabeth II Conference Centre	LQMJ	..	..	..	..	..	..	..	0.8	0.8	0.8
Contingencies Fund - capital	KQJB	942.0	1 097.0	947.0	347.0	447.0	297.0	977.0	577.0	277.0	277.0
Balance on revenue accounts	KQJC	237.2	725.2	477.6	358.7	1 433.6	1 096.1	954.9	1 546.0	1 026.5	1 426.6
Privatisation receipts	KIAX	5 403.9	6 701.0	809.0	1 734.0	1 147.0	817.0	1 607.1	70.1	–	–
Total liabilities	KQJD	128 386.2	–	–	–	–	333 927.9	364 803.0	364 950.8	363 625.5	354 458.6
Liability to balance National Loans Fund	KQJE	125 807.1	142 306.7	182 102.2	240 351.0	286 055.9	331 164.9	362 506.5	362 582.5	361 065.3	351 626.3
Payment from Votes:	KQJF	67.6	66.9	66.1	65.2	64.3	63.4	62.4	61.3	60.2	59.0
Married quarters for Armed Forces	KQJG	67.6	66.9	66.1	65.2	64.3	63.4	62.4	61.3	60.2	59.0
Liability to Post Office Superannuation Fund	KQJH	–	–	–	–	–	–	–	–	–	–
Post-war credits outstanding and interest due - estimated	KQJI	46.1	46.1	46.0	46.0	46.0	45.9	45.9	45.9	45.9	45.8
Revenue paid over in advance of collection	KQJJ	–	8.3	–	83.7	37.0	–	28.2	13.8	177.9	276.2
Inland Revenue	KQJK	–	–	–	–	–	–	–	–	177.9	259.9
Customs and Excise	KQJL	–	–	–	–	–	–	28.2	–	–	–
Broadcast receiving licences	KQJM	–	–	–	–	–	–	–	–	–	–
Vehicle Excise Duty	KQJN	–	8.3	–	83.7	37.0	–	–	13.8	–	16.3

17.7 Consolidated Fund and National Loans Fund: assets and liabilities
United Kingdom
continued At 31 March in each year

£ millions

		1991	1992	1993	1994	1995	1996	1997	1998	1999	2000
Consolidated Fund (*continued*)											
Promissory notes issued by											
Minister of Overseas Development	KQJQ	1 036.4	770.3	979.5	1 002.6	996.7	1 005.8	1 021.9	822.1	963.1	781.9
International Development Association	KQJR	705.3	489.4	673.1	670.5	656.5	663.2	673.6	484.0	612.3	445.6
African Development Fund	KQJS	77.1	92.1	100.7	106.6	93.2	86.2	95.3	95.2	105.6	89.0
Asian Development Bank	KQJT	1.4	0.1	–	–	–	–	–	–	–	1.9
Asian Development Fund	KQJU	108.7	92.1	108.7	131.8	140.5	127.6	136.0	120.5	105.4	87.7
Caribbean Development Bank	KQJV	–	0.1	0.1	1.2	1.3	1.4	1.3	1.3	1.3	1.3
Special Development Fund	KQKC	8.1	8.3	6.9	8.0	9.5	10.6	13.2	15.8	16.4	16.9
European Community/International Development Association Special Action Account	KQJW	–	–	–	–	–	–	–	–	–	–
European Investment Bank	KQJX	61.2	–	–	–	–	–	–	–	–	–
Inter-American Development Bank	KQJY	1.7	1.7	2.6	2.2	1.3	2.0	1.8	1.9	1.0	2.0
Fund for special operations	KQJZ	22.5	22.5	15.4	16.4	13.1	11.3	8.8	6.3	2.6	2.1
International Fund for Agricultural Development	KQKA	16.2	17.8	16.1	18.2	15.8	14.2	12.3	14.2	16.5	18.4
International Bank for Reconstruction and Development	KQKB	34.2	31.9	30.2	24.2	39.2	60.7	71.7	81.9	94.3	104.9
European Bank for Reconstruction and Development	KIAY	–	14.3	20.4	19.9	20.9	21.0	6.1	–	7.7	12.1
United Nations Environment Programme	KJEH	–	–	5.3	3.6	5.4	7.6	1.8	1.0	–	–
Other contributions and instalments due in respect of international subscriptions, etc	KQYX	1 429.0	2 125.1	1 520.7	2 165.8	1 499.6	1 647.9	1 138.1	1 425.2	1 313.1	1 669.2
National Loans Fund											
Total assets	KQKD	198 703.4	214 527.6	248 643.5	306 872.6	349 159.5	390 681.8	419 548.9	418 444.7	421 635.7	426 239.2
Total National Loans Fund loans outstanding	KQKE	56 777.9	55 492.8	48 705.9	48 470.8	47 496.1	46 600.9	46 746.8	46 742.6	48 513.6	49 788.8
Loans to nationalised industries:											
Post Office	KQKF	–	–	–	–	–	–	–	–	–	–
British Coal	KQKG	387.4	257.7	180.0	–	–	–	–	–	–	–
Electricity Council	KQKH	–	–	–	–	–	–	–	–	–	–
North of Scotland Hydro-Electric Board	KQKI	–	–	–	–	–	–	–	–	–	–
Scottish Hydro-Electric	KQKJ	534.9	–	–	–	–	–	–	–	–	–
South of Scotland Electricity Board	KQKK	–	–	–	–	–	–	–	–	–	–
Scottish Power	KQKL	508.6	–	–	–	–	–	–	–	–	–
Scottish Nuclear Ltd	KQKM	203.2	201.3	199.2	196.8	194.1	96.1	–	–	–	–
British Gas Corporation	KQKN	–	–	–	–	–	–	–	–	–	–
British Steel Corporation	KQKO	–	–	–	–	–	–	–	–	–	–
British Airways Board	KQKP	–	–	–	–	–	–	–	–	–	–
Railtrack	KTCR	..	..	..	..	1 287.7	–	–	–	–	–
European Passenger Services	KTCS	..	..	..	..	99.0	761.2	–	–	–	–
Civil Aviation Authority	KQKQ	216.3	271.2	311.9	403.7	453.3	476.1	447.5	420.9	365.7	342.5
British Airports Authority	KQKR	–	–	–	–	–	–	–	–	–	–
British Railways Board	KQKS	938.5	1 040.8	1 923.9	2 445.6	749.2	718.3	601.2	573.7	546.2	518.7
British Transport Docks Board	KQKT	–	–	–	–	–	–	–	–	–	–
British Waterways Board	KQKU	21.6	20.0	19.2	18.6	18.3	18.2	18.2	18.2	18.2	18.2
National Freight Corporation	KQKV	–	–	–	–	–	–	–	–	–	–
National Bus Company	KQKW	–	–	–	–	–	–	–	–	–	–
Scottish Transport Group	KQKX	–	–	–	–	–	–	–	–	–	–
British National Oil Corporation	KQKY	–	–	–	–	–	–	–	–	–	–
British Aerospace	KQKZ	–	–	–	–	–	–	–	–	–	–
British Shipbuilders	KQLA	–	–	–	–	–	–	–	–	–	–
British Telecommunications	KQLB	–	–	–	–	–	–	–	–	–	–
Regional Water Authorities	KQLC	–	–	–	–	–	–	–	–	–	–
Loans to other public corporations:											
New Towns - Development Corporations and Commission	KQLD	1 714.6	1 441.5	1 303.9	1 130.1	1 008.8	314.3	122.2	36.2	8.0	8.0
Scottish Special Housing Association	KQLE	–	–	–	–	–	–	–	–	–	–
Scottish Homes	KQLF	786.4	654.5	401.2	399.4	397.3	395.0	392.5	259.8	190.9	179.0
Housing Corporation (Scotland)	KQLG	–	–	–	–	–	–	–	–	–	–
Housing Corporation (England)	KQLH	1 611.3	1 021.4	986.0	899.0	869.9	926.3	848.7	4.0	4.0	3.0
Housing for Wales	KQLI	125.8	96.6	86.7	86.4	69.2	59.0	–	–	–	–
Covent Garden Market Authority	KQLJ	–	–	–	–	–	–	–	–	–	–
National Enterprise Board	KQLK	–	–	–	–	–	–	–	–	–	–
Land Authority for Wales	KQLL	6.8	8.8	10.3	6.2	3.2	3.2	1.3	1.3	–	–
Scottish Enterprise	KQLM	5.4	4.6	2.7	1.9	1.3	0.6	0.5	0.1	–	–
Welsh Development Agency	KQLN	2.4	1.8	1.5	1.2	0.9	1.1	1.2	1.2	0.9	0.6
Land Registry Trading Fund	KPOF	–	–	–	54.9	–	–	–	–	–	–
Development Board for Rural Wales	KQLO	8.8	8.8	8.8	8.8	8.8	7.9	4.1	4.0	4.0	4.0
Royal Mint	KQLP	–	–	–	–	–	–	–	–	–	2.0
Royal Ordnance Factories	KQLQ	–	–	–	–	–	–	–	–	–	–
The Crown Suppliers	KQLR	–	–	–	–	–	–	–	–	–	–
Crown Agents	KQLS	2.5	2.5	2.3	2.1	2.0	1.9	–	–	–	–
Her Majesty's Stationery Office	KQLT	16.8	10.6	6.7	3.3	–	7.0	–	–	–	–
Urban Development Corporations	KQLU	0.4	0.8	0.7	1.0	–	–	–	–	–	–
Harbour Authorities	KQLV	36.3	33.4	7.1	1.5	0.8	0.7	0.6	0.5	0.4	0.2
Commonwealth Development Corporation	KQLW	–	–	–	–	–	–	–	–	–	–
UK Atomic Energy Authority	KQLX	106.7	111.0	149.8	125.0	147.3	141.0	–	–	–	–
Ordnance Survey	GPVF	..	..	..	..	..	..	..	..	..	15.5

17.7
continued

Consolidated Fund and National Loans Fund: assets and liabilities
United Kingdom
At 31 March in each year

£ millions

		1991	1992	1993	1994	1995	1996	1997	1998	1999	2000
National Loans Fund (*continued*)											
Loans to other public corporations: (*continued*)											
Central Office of Information	KJEI	–	1.3	1.0	0.8	0.5	0.3	–	–	–	–
Registers of Scotland	KZBB	..	..	..	..	..	..	6.4	5.6	5.1	4.5
East of Scotland Water Authority	KZBC	..	..	..	..	..	..	163.0	229.0	288.0	283.0
North of Scotland Water Authority	KZBD	..	..	..	..	..	..	155.0	189.2	242.0	236.5
West of Scotland Water Authority	KZBE	..	..	..	..	..	..	185.0	304.9	425.6	412.4
Loans to local authorities	KQLY	48 087.1	48 742.3	41 464.6	40 979.2	40 440.7	40 969.2	42 134.0	42 951.1	44 742.7	46 099.2
Loans to private sector:											
Shipbuilding Industry Board	KQLZ	–	–	–	–	–	–	–	–	–	–
Shipowners (Ship credit scheme)	KGVR	–	–	–	–	–	–	–	–	–	–
Housing associations	KGVS	14.9	14.6	14.1	13.8	13.2	12.7	0.5	0.5	0.5	0.5
Building societies	KGVT	–	–	–	–	–	–	–	–	–	–
British Nuclear Fuels Ltd	KGVU	–	–	–	–	–	–	–	–	–	–
British Aerospace plc	KGVV	–	–	–	–	–	–	–	–	–	–
Loans within central government:											
Northern Ireland Exchequer	KGVW	1 373.1	1 480.3	1 558.3	1 626.2	1 666.3	1 627.4	1 602.5	1 681.1	1 611.2	1 602.0
Married quarters for Armed Forces	KGVX	67.6	66.9	66.1	65.2	64.3	63.4	62.4	61.3	60.2	59.0
Redundancy Fund	KGVY	–	–	–	–	–	–	–	–	–	–
Other assets:											
Exchange Equalisation Account - capital	KGVZ	11 075.0	10 774.5	7 200.0	6 800.0	5 550.0	2 800.0	650.0	–	–	475.0

Subscriptions and contributions
    to international financial
    organisations:											

International Monetary Fund	KGXE	4 785.5	4 885.3	6 893.0	7 066.4	7 172.2	7 102.6	6 241.2	5 895.6	9 048.1	9 067.4

Gilt-Edged Official
    Operations Account
    -advances outstanding
	KPUF	–	–	–	2 500.0	2 500.0	2 500.0	3 000.0	2 500.0	2 500.0	–

-surplus not paid to the National Loans Fund	KPUH	–	–	–	2.0	–	–	–	141.6	190.8	

Borrowing included in national
    debt but not brought to
    account by 31 March
	KGXF	257.8	1 068.2	3 742.5	1 682.4	385.2	513.4	404.7	568.6	317.9	281.6

Debt Management Account -advances outstanding	GPVG	..	..	..	..	..	..	..	..	..	15 000.0

National Debt Commissioners'
    liability in respect of the
    National Savings Bank's
    Investment Fund
	KCYG	–	–	–	–	–	–	–	–	–	–

Other	KCYH	–	–	–	–	–	–	–	–	–	–
Consolidated Fund liability	KCYI	125 807.1	142 306.7	182 102.2	240 351.0	286 055.9	331 164.9	362 506.2	362 596.4	361 065.3	351 626.3
Total liabilities											
National Loans Fund - national debt outstanding	KCYJ	198 703.4	214 527.6	248 643.5	306 872.6	349 159.5	390 681.8	419 548.9	418 444.7	421 635.7	426 239.2

Source: HM Treasury: 020 7270 1586

17.8
British government and government guaranteed marketable securities[1]
Nominal values of official and market holdings by maturity[2,3]
At 31 March in each year

£ millions

		1991	1992	1993	1994	1995	1996	1997	1998	1999	2000	2001
Total holdings	KQMO	122 437	133 121	162 642	209 507	232 486	262 262	290 259	297 366	291 788	290 630	281 877
Up to 5 years	KQMP	34 933	40 363	46 019	58 437	69 011	81 122	90 357	86 094	95 112	95 131	90 050
Over 5 and up to 15 years	KQMQ	56 309	61 239	72 612	94 308	101 960	111 510	125 401	131 758	124 603	116 910	108 808
Over 15 years (including undated)	KQMR	31 194	31 520	44 010	56 762	61 515	69 630	74 501	79 515	72 074	78 589	83 019
Official holdings:[3]												
Total	THAA	10 892	8 799	4 138	6 239	6 614	7 186	6 858	6 345	6 394	7 560	7 268
Up to 5 years	THAB	4 406	3 478	1 434	1 685	2 007	2 345	2 850	2 499	2 600	2 649	3 462
Over 5 and up to 15 years	THAC	5 415	4 323	1 826	3 194	3 700	3 774	3 041	2 726	2 989	2 791	2 963
Over 15 years (including undated)	THAD	1 071	998	879	1 359	907	1 068	967	1 120	805	2 120	843
Market holdings:												
Total	THAE	111 544	124 323	158 503	203 268	225 872	255 075	283 402	291 021	285 394	283 070	274 609
Up to 5 years	THAF	30 527	36 885	44 585	56 751	67 004	78 777	87 508	83 595	92 512	92 482	86 588
Over 5 and up tp 15 years	THAG	50 894	56 916	70 786	91 115	98 260	107 736	122 360	129 032	121 614	114 119	105 844
Over 15 years (including undated)	THAH	30 123	30 522	43 131	55 403	60 608	68 562	73 536	78 395	71 269	76 469	82 177

1 The government guaranteed securities of nationalised industries only. A relatively small amount of other government guaranteed securities is excluded.

2 Securities with optional redemption dates are classified according to the final redemption date. The nominal uplift of index-linked British government stock has been raised by the amount of accrued capital uplift.

3 Official holdings have changed following the introduction of the central bank sector in the UK national accounts. These holdings now principally include the Debt Management Office, the National Investment and Loans Office and other government departments. The Issue and Banking Departments of the Bank of England are classified within the central bank sector and so as part of market holdings.

Source: Bank of England: 020 7601 4068

17.9 National savings
Year ending 31 March

£ millions

		1990 /91	1991 /92	1992 /93	1993 /94	1994 /95	1995 /96	1996 /97	1997 /98	1998 /99	1999 /00	2000 /01
Department for National Savings												
Receipts												
Total	KQNA	6 408.9	7 704.7	8 485.5	10 336.2	9 246.9	11 596.9	13 353.5	12 565.6	10 212.9	8 731.0	10 169.0
Capital bonds	KQNB	185.6	338.3	476.6	566.4	511.2	500.5	482.7	583.6	238.1	28.9	26.0
National Savings Certificates:												
5yr Fixed Interest	KQNC	696.7	2 119.6	1 894.7	1 929.1	1 083.6	1 519.8	1 805.9	1 753.4	1 174.4	702.9	430.0
5yr Index-linked	KQND	1 503.2	1 500.8	1 600.0	1 434.9	1 083.2	1 949.8	1 871.8	2 640.4	1 734.1	551.0	344.0
2yr Fixed Interest	YZZZ	..	..	..	..	..	..	..	..	..	438.7	1 046.0
2yr Index Linked	ZCEZ	..	..	..	..	..	..	..	..	..	286.0	1 259.0
Yearly Plan	KQNE	74.2	89.3	115.7	118.2	117.5	97.0	0.7	–	–	–	–
Save As You Earn Total	KQNF	83.2	94.1	85.5	76.9	66.7	49.9	33.4	20.3	11.2	5.0	–
Income bonds	KQNH	1 605.6	1 355.9	1 241.2	1 948.9	1 228.9	802.4	1 263.6	1 044.1	1 365.4	642.2	767.7
First Option bonds	KHYZ	–	–	885.0	247.0	95.6	194.3	398.3	149.2	110.1	25.1	–
Investment Account	KQNI	1 515.7	1 247.7	1 107.4	1 392.9	1 393.1	1 299.2	1 478.3	1 270.1	1 045.4	919.0	919.0
Premium Savings bonds	KQNJ	185.7	257.5	384.5	998.2	1 826.2	2 075.7	2 578.1	3 199.6	3 622.9	3 384.0	3 356.0
Ordinary Account	KQNK	559.0	566.0	604.4	636.1	635.6	627.3	643.1	653.0	622.3	642.0	670.0
Children's Bonus bonds	KHCU	–	135.5	90.5	92.6	116.8	144.9	124.3	109.7	73.4	57.6	52.3
5yr Pensioners' bonds	KJRB	..	..	..	895.0	1 088.5	2 336.1	2 651.4	1 104.2	199.1	234.4	72.8
2yr Pensioners' bonds	ZCFA	..	..	..	..	..	..	..	..	..	373.6	432.7
1yr Pensioners' bonds	GQRI	..	..	..	..	..	..	..	..	..	..	196.2
Treasurer's Account	KXCY	–	–	–	–	–	–	21.9	38.0	16.5	13.2	12.3
ISA's	ZCFB	..	..	..	..	..	..	..	..	..	257.4	292.0
Fixed Rate Savings Bond	ZCFC	..	..	..	..	..	..	..	..	..	170.0	293.0
Repayments												
Total	KQNO	7 339.8	6 495.7	5 853.8	8 051.0	7 759.8	8 756.9	11 048.5	13 201.7	11 665.7	10 988.1	12 442.0
Capital bonds	KQNP	23.6	14.9	21.8	345.3	678.3	453.1	776.6	1 143.5	649.7	325.1	377.8
National Savings Certificates:												
5yr Fixed Interest - Principal	KQNQ	1 455.3	1 193.4	647.9	1 292.6	843.0	840.1	1 838.8	2 256.2	1 934.3	1 182.2	..
- Accrued Interest	KQNR	991.0	738.7	417.4	670.9	437.2	474.8	937.0	1 021.4	645.6	391.6	..
Total	GQRJ	..	..	..	..	..	..	..	..	..	..	1 980
5yr Index-linked - Principal	KQNS	412.9	418.8	448.2	913.5	761.7	1 419.7	1 432.7	1 803.5	1 520.1	1 200.5	..
- Accrued Interest/ Index-linking, etc.	KQNT	403.3	396.6	378.5	598.1	425.8	672.0	613.6	703.1	527.5	373.7	..
Total	GQRK	..	..	..	..	..	..	..	..	..	..	2 476
2yr Fixed Interest - Principal	ZCFD	..	..	..	..	..	..	..	..	..	3.1	..
- Accrued Interest	ZCFE	..	..	..	..	..	..	..	..	..	–	..
Total	GQRL	..	..	..	..	..	..	..	..	..	..	20.0
2yr Index-linked - Principal	ZCFF	..	..	..	..	..	..	..	..	..	1.5	..
- Accrued Interest/ Total	GQRM	..	..	..	..	..	..	..	..	..	..	17
Yearly Plan:												
Principal	KQNU	124.2	106.5	98.4	89.5	77.0	102.0	96.3	119.5	111.8	118.4	–
Interest	KQNV	43.2	40.9	35.7	30.3	26.2	42.1	39.2	43.6	30.6	32.6	–
Total rep	GQRN	..	..	..	..	..	..	..	..	..	..	38.2
Save As You Earn:												
Fixed Interest - Principal	KQNW	59.3	74.4	88.7	86.1	85.0	96.7	69.1	67.4	35.9	35.2	..
- Accrued Interest	KQNX	13.3	16.0	18.2	18.1	19.2	21.9	17.9	18.5	9.1	7.9	..
Index-linked - Principal	KQNY	24.2	29.4	26.5	9.3	7.4	1.8	0.9	0.8	0.6	0.5	..
- Accrued Interest/ Index-linking	KQNZ	27.1	38.5	38.9	14.3	12.2	3.3	1.6	1.5	1.2	1.0	..
Total reps	GQRO	..	..	..	..	..	..	..	..	..	..	4
Income bonds	KQOA	824.2	719.9	956.0	1 000.3	1 180.1	1 256.2	1 392.0	1 141.9	880.7	1 685.1	855.0
First Option bonds	KHYY	–	–	4.8	375.8	288.4	126.5	139.1	335.2	205.5	283.8	217.0
Investment Account	KQOB	1 904.0	1 803.9	1 780.0	1 677.1	1 777.2	1 797.2	1 856.0	2 177.1	1 981.6	1 888.2	1 625.0
Premium Savings bonds	KQOC	193.4	153.7	153.4	181.0	333.0	590.4	869.0	1 203.1	1 398.4	1 683.0	1 888.0
Ordinary Account	KQOD	700.9	663.7	658.1	674.7	676.8	676.5	692.3	703.4	684.6	676.4	662.0
Children's Bonus bonds	KHCV	–	0.1	0.9	1.2	1.8	2.6	30.8	39.8	52.4	69.5	95.0
5yr Pensioners' bonds	KJRE	..	..	..	..	56.7	104.8	172.5	331.4	903.1	922.1	1 959.0
2yr Pensioners' bonds	ZCFH	..	..	..	..	..	..	..	..	..	8.4	30.0
1yr Pensioners' bonds	GQRP	..	..	..	..	..	..	..	..	..	–	4
Deposit bonds	KQOE	137.7	85.3	79.8	72.4	72.2	73.5	65.5	76.6	79.0	67.1	72.0
Indexed-income bonds	KQOF	2.2	1.0	0.6	0.5	0.6	1.7	6.5	2.6	–	–	–
Treasurer's Account	KXCZ	–	–	–	–	–	–	1.1	11.6	14.0	15.8	14.0
ISA's	ZCFI	..	..	..	..	..	..	..	..	..	12.4	41.0
Fixed Rate Savings Bond	ZCFJ	..	..	..	..	..	..	..	..	..	3.0	67.0

17.9 National savings
Year ending 31 March
continued

£ millions

		1990 /91	1991 /92	1992 /93	1993 /94	1994 /95	1995 /96	1996 /97	1997 /98	1998 /99	1999 /00	2000 /01
Department for National Savings												
Interest accruing												
Capital bonds	KQOO	42.0	76.8	130.8	223.1	218.8	214.6	249.9	172.0	146.9	126.6	102.0
National Savings Certificates:												
5yr Fixed Interest	KQOP	525.7	443.3	521.2	604.2	622.2	703.7	787.6	557.8	485.3	432.5	360.0
5yr Index-linked	KQOQ	477.0	351.7	267.8	303.9	458.5	655.2	671.9	690.3	502.7	344.1	500.0
2yr Fixed Interest	ZCFK	..	..	..	..	..	..	..	..	..	1.1	40.0
2yr Index-linked	ZCFL	..	..	..	..	..	..	..	..	..	1.0	19.0
Yearly Plan	KQOR	40.9	36.7	32.5	30.5	34.1	37.5	38.0	28.3	17.2	16.0	3.0
Save As You Earn:												
Fixed Interest (1st, 2nd and 4th issues)	KQOS	14.4	18.3	18.8	18.3	18.0	18.3	14.6	11.7	5.7	4.9	..
Index-linked (3rd issue)	KQOT	21.1	8.8	1.1	0.3	0.9	0.4	0.5	0.5	0.5	0.1	..
Total	GQRQ	..	..	..	..	..	..	..	..	..	..	−5
Premium Bonds	GQRR	..	..	..	..	..	..	..	..	..	..	66
First Option bonds	KIAJ	–	–	–	70.7	40.4	31.8	40.4	54.8	48.4	40.1	25.0
Investment Account	KQOU	1 007.8	864.4	657.7	541.8	529.1	518.5	509.0	497.8	464.5	335.7	375.0
Ordinary Account	KQOV	60.9	58.2	57.3	44.6	42.8	35.5	36.2	29.4	30.6	15.7	25.0
Childrens Bonus bonds	KHCW	–	–	9.3	14.4	19.2	27.0	98.9	73.7	66.6	72.0	75.0
Deposit Bonds	KQOW	95.4	77.9	59.8	46.4	41.4	39.4	38.3	37.2	31.5	22.9	21.0
Treasurer's Account	KXDA	–	–	–	–	–	–	–	–	–	6.2	3.0
ISA's	ZCFM	..	..	..	..	..	..	..	..	..	6.0	31.0
Fixed Rate Savings Bond	ZCFN	..	..	..	..	..	..	..	..	..	1.2	15.0
Total	KQOX	2 285.2	1 936.1	1 756.3	1 898.2	2 025.4	2 281.9	2 485.3	2 153.5	1 799.9	1 426.1	1 622.0
Amounts remaining invested												
Capital bonds	KQOY	694.7	1 094.9	1 680.5	2 124.7	2 176.4	2 438.4	2 394.4	2 006.5	1 741.8	1 572.5	1 325.0
National Savings Certificates												
5yr Fixed Interest - Principal	KQOZ	5 120.6	6 046.8	7 293.6	7 930.1	8 170.7	8 850.4	8 817.5	8 314.7	7 554.8	7 076.7	..
- Accrued Interest	KQPA	2 193.4	1 898.0	2 001.8	1 935.1	2 120.1	2 349.0	2 199.6	1 736.0	1 575.7	1 616.6	..
Total	GQRS											7 681
5yr Index-linked - Principal	KQPB	4 013.5	5 095.5	6 247.3	6 768.7	7 090.2	7 620.3	8 059.4	8 896.3	9 110.3	8 461.7	..
- Accrued Interest,												
Index-linking, etc.	KQPC	1 500.1	1 455.2	1 344.5	1 050.3	1 083.0	1 066.2	1 124.5	1 111.7	1 086.9	1 057.3	..
Total	GQRT											7 972
2yr Fixed interest - Principal	ZCFO	..	..	..	..	..	..	..	..	..	434.9	..
- Accrued Interest	ZCFP	..	..	..	..	..	..	..	..	..	1.0	..
Total	GQRU	..	..	..	..	..	..	..	..	..	..	1 506
2yr Index-linked - Principal	ZCFQ	..	..	..	..	..	..	..	..	..	284.1	..
- Accrued Interest/												
Index-linking, etc.	ZCFR	..	..	..	..	..	..	..	..	..	1.0	..
Total	GQRV	..	..	..	..	..	..	..	..	..	..	1 563
Yearly Plan:												
Principal	KQPD	441.1	423.9	441.2	469.9	510.4	505.4	409.8	290.3	178.5	61.0	..
Interest	KQPE	73.1	68.9	65.7	65.9	73.8	69.2	68.0	52.7	39.3	29.8	..
Total	GQRW	..	..	..	..	..	..	..	..	..	..	45
Save As You Earn:												
Fixed Interest - Principal	KQPF	208.8	228.5	225.3	216.1	197.8	151.0	115.3	68.2	43.5	16.1	..
- Accrued Interest	KQPG	22.5	24.8	25.4	25.6	24.4	20.8	17.5	10.7	7.3	4.4	..
Index-linked - Principal	KQPH	92.0	62.6	36.1	26.8	19.4	17.6	16.7	15.9	15.3	13.5	..
- Accrued Interest/												
Index-linking, etc.	KQPI	108.0	78.3	40.5	26.5	15.2	12.3	11.2	10.2	9.5	9.2	..
Total	GQRX	..	..	..	..	..	..	..	..	..	..	22
Register (DNS only)	KQPJ	963.1	1 026.2	1 180.3	1 198.6	1 392.7	1 530.7	1 541.1	1 468.5	–	..	..
Income bonds	KQPK	8 963.2	9 599.2	9 884.4	10 833.0	10 881.8	10 428.0	10 299.6	10 205.2	10 689.9	9 647.0	9 560.0
First Option bonds	KIAK	–	–	880.2	822.1	669.7	769.3	1 068.9	937.7	890.7	672.1	480.0
Investment Account	KQPL	8 626.5	8 934.7	8 919.8	9 177.4	9 322.4	9 342.9	9 474.2	9 065.0	8 593.3	7 959.4	7 628.0
Premium Savings bonds	KQPM	2 326.3	2 430.1	2 661.2	3 478.4	4 971.6	6 456.9	8 166.0	10 162.5	12 387.0	13 847.0	15 312.0
Ordinary Account	KQPN	1 474.3	1 434.8	1 438.4	1 444.4	1 446.0	1 432.3	1 419.3	1 398.3	1 366.6	1 347.6	1 380.0
Children's Bonus bonds	KHCX	–	135.4	234.3	340.1	474.3	643.6	836.0	979.6	1 067.2	1 127.0	1 158.0
5yr Pensioners' bonds	KJRG	–	–	–	895.0	1 926.8	4 158.1	6 637.0	7 409.8	6 705.8	6 016.9	4 132.0
2yr Pensioners' bonds	ZCFS	..	..	..	..	..	..	..	..	..	365.2	767.0
1yr Pensioners'bonds	GQRY	..	..	..	..	..	..	..	..	..	..	192
Deposit bonds	KQPO	737.4	730.0	710.0	684.0	653.2	619.1	591.9	552.5	505.0	460.8	410.5
Indexed-income bonds	KQPP	16.9	15.9	15.3	14.8	14.2	12.5	6.0	–	–	–	–
National Savings stamps and gift tokens	KQPR	1.9	1.8	1.8	1.7	1.7	1.6	1.6	1.6	1.6	1.6	1.6
Treasurer's Account	KXDB	–	–	–	–	–	–	20.8	47.2	49.7	53.3	54.9
ISA's	ZCFT	..	..	..	..	..	..	..	..	..	249.6	534.0
Fixed Rate Savings Bond	ZCFU	..	..	..	..	..	..	..	..	..	170.5	439.0
Total administered by DNS	KQPS	37 577.4	40 785.5	45 327.6	49 529.2	53 235.8	58 495.6	63 296.3	64 741.1	63 619.7	62 548.0	62 163.0

Source: Department for National Savings: 020 7605 9314

17.10 Income tax: allowances and reliefs
United Kingdom

£

		1991/92	1992/93	1993/94	1994/95	1995/96	1996/97	1997/98	1998/99	1999/00	2000/01	2001/02
Personal allowances												
Personal allowance	KDZP	3 295	3 445	3 445	3 445	3 525	3 765	4 045	4 195	4 335	4 385	4 535
Married couples allowance	KDZR	1 720	1 720	1 720	1 720	1 720	1 790	1 830	1 900	1 970	..	..
Age allowance:												
Personal (aged 65-74)	KSOH	4 020	4 200	4 200	4 200	4 630	4 910	5 220	5 410	5 720	5 790	5 990
Personal (aged 75 or over)	KSOI	4 180	4 370	4 370	4 370	4 800	5 090	5 400	5 600	5 980	6 050	6 260
Married couple's (either partner between 65-74 but neither partner 75 or over)[1]	KEDI	2 355	2 465	2 465	2 665	2 995	3 115	3 185	3 305	5 125	5 185	5 365
Married couples (either partner 75 or over)	KEIY	2 395	2 505	2 505	2 705	3 035	3 155	3 225	3 345	5 195	5 255	5 435
Income limit	KEOO	13 500	14 200	14 200	14 200	14 600	15 200	15 600	16 200	16 800	17 100	17 600
Marginal fraction		1/2	1/2	1/2	1/2	1/2	1/2	1/2	1/2	1/2	1/2	1/2
Additional personal allowance	KEPG	1 720	1 720	1 720	1 720	1 720	1 790	1 830	1 900	1 970	..	..
Widow's bereavement allowance	KEPH	1 720	1 720	1 720	1 720	1 720	1 790	1 830	1 900	1 970	..	..
Blind person's allowance												
Single or married (one spouse blind)	KSOJ	1 080	1 080	1 080	1 200	1 200	1 250	1 280	1 330	1 380	1 400	1 450
Married (both spouses blind)	KSOK	2 160	2 160	2 160	2 400	2 400	2 500	2 560	2 660	2 760	2 800	2 900
Life Assurance Relief (Percentage of gross premium)	KFDR	12.5 or Nil	12.5 or Nil	12.5 or Nil	12.5 or Nil	12.5 or Nil	12.5 or Nil	12.5 or Nil	12.5 or Nil	12.5 or Nil	12.5 or Nil	12.5 or Nil

1 At least one of the partners must be aged 65 before April 2000 to be entitled to the MCA. This means that only people born before 6 April 1935 are entitled to MCA

Source: Board of Inland Revenue: 020 7438 4335

17.11 Rates of Income tax
United Kingdom

	1992/93		1993/94		1994/95		1995/96		1996/97	
	Bands of taxable income (£)[1]	Rate of tax (%)	Bands of taxable income (£)[1]	Rate of tax (%)	Bands of taxable income (£)[1]	Rate of tax (%)	Bands of taxable income (£)[1]	Rate of tax (%)	Bands of taxable income (£)[1]	Rate of tax (%)
Lower rate	1 - 2000	20	1 - 2 500	20	1 - 3 00	20	1 - 3 200	20	1 - 3 900	20
Basic rate	2 001 - 23 700	25	2 501 - 23 700	25[2]	3 001 - 23 700	25[2]	3 201 - 24 300	25[2]	3 901 - 25 500	24[3]
Higher rate	over 23 700	40	over 23 700	40	over 23 700	40	over 24 300	40	over 25 500	40

	1997/98		1998/99		1999/00		2000/01		2001/02	
	Bands of taxable income (£)[1]	Rate of tax (%)	Bands of taxable income (£)[1]	Rate of tax (%)	Bands of taxable income (£)[1]	Rate of tax (%)	Bands of taxable income (£)[1]	Rate of tax (%)	Bands of taxable income (£)[1]	Rate of tax (%)
Lower rate	1 - 4 100	20	1 - 4 300	20	1 - 1 500	10[4]	1 - 1 520	10[4]	1 - 1 880	10[4]
Basic rate	4 101 - 26 100	23[3]	4 301 - 27 100	23[3]	1 501 - 28 000	23[5]	1 520 - 28 400	22[5]	1 880 - 29 400	22[5]
Higher rate	over 26 100	40	over 27 100	40	over 28 000	40[6]	over 28 400	40[6]	over 29 400	40[6]

1 Taxable income is defined as gross income for income tax purposes less any allowances and reliefs available at the taxpayer's marginal rate.
2 The basic rate of tax on dividend income is 20%.
3 The basic rate of tax on dividends and savings income is 20%.
4 The starting rate also applies to savings.
5 The basic rate of tax on dividends is 10% and savings income is 20%
6 The higher rate of tax on dividends is 32.5%.

Source: Board of Inland Revenue: 020 7438 4335

17.12 Rateable values
England and Wales
At 1 April in each year

		Unit	1991	1992	1993	1994	1995	1996	1997	1998	1999	2000	2001
Number of properties		Thousands											
Total - all classes	KMIH	"	1 709	1 734	1 737	1 734	1 723	1 726	1 725	1 719	1 720	1 729	1 740
Commercial: total	KMIN	"	1 211	1 227	1 230	1 227	1 223	1 228	1 225	1 223	1 219	1 223	1 230
Shops and cafes	KMIO	"	572	570	567	565	562	497	491	488	484	478	476
Offices	KMIP	"	234	243	248	251	252	255	255	257	258	261	269
Other	KMIQ	"	405	413	415	411	409	476	479	478	477	484	485
On-licensed premises: total	KMIR	"	55	55	55	55	60	59	59	59	60	61	61
Entertainment and recreational: total	KMIS	"	95	94	93	92	87	87	87	81	80	79	79
Cinemas	KMIT	"	1	1	1	1	1	1	1	1	1	1	1
Theatres and music-halls	KMIU	"	1	1	1	1	1	1	1	1	1	1	1
Other	KMIV	"	94	93	92	91	86	85	86	80	79	76	76
Public utility: total	KMIW	"	15	15	15	15	9	8	8	9	9	8	8
Educational and cultural: total	KMIX	"	42	42	42	41	41	41	41	41	41	41	42
Miscellaneous: total	KMIY	"	53	59	58	58	56	55	55	56	61	67	70
Industrial: total	KMIZ	"	237	241	244	247	248	249	249	250	250	250	251
Value of assessments		£ million											
Total - all classes	KMHA	"	34 214	35 608	35 263	34 129	33 912	34 245	34 299	33 909	33 649	42 985	43 626
Commercial: total	KMHG	"	20 659	21 440	21 336	20 662	19 626	19 822	19 859	19 733	19 652	26 320	27 255
Shops and cafes	KMHH	"	7 382	7 472	7 335	7 068	7 780	6 094	5 959	5 860	5 840	6 801	6 972
Offices	KMHI	"	7 545	8 093	8 239	8 027	5 587	5 630	5 641	5 624	5 575	8 625	9 191
Other	KMHJ	"	5 732	5 876	5 762	5 568	6 260	8 098	8 259	8 249	8 237	10 894	11 092
On-licensed premises: total	KMHK	"	691	698	679	642	968	969	970	980	997	1 311	1 347
Entertainment and recreational: total	KMHL	"	994	1 025	1 022	988	1 009	1 018	1 033	1 040	1 045	1 310	1 369
Cinemas	KMHM	"	21	24	25	24	32	32	36	39	45	79	92
Theatres and music-halls	KMHN	"	21	22	21	19	21	21	21	21	20	24	25
Other	KMHO	"	951	979	975	946	956	965	975	979	980	1 207	1 252
Public utility: total	KMHP	"	3 493	3 518	3 505	3 424	3 455	3 469	3 488	3 380	3 361	3 828	3 411
Educational and cultural: total	KMHQ	"	1 994	1 970	1 883	1 813	1 873	1 883	1 894	1 773	1 672	1 829	1 872
Miscellaneous: total	KMHR	"	823	1 375	1 367	1 319	1 429	1 500	1 494	1 464	1 439	2 142	2 172
Industrial: total	KMHS	"	5 559	5 583	5 470	5 280	5 550	5 584	5 561	5 540	5 463	6 249	6 202

Source: Board of Inland Revenue: 020 7438 6314

17.13 Local authorities: gross loan debt outstanding[1]
At 31 March in each year

£ millions

		1991	1992	1993	1994	1995	1996	1997	1998	1999	2000	2001
United Kingdom												
Total debt	KQBR	57 985	56 331	55 943	55 869	..	..	..	..	..	..	..
Public Works Loan Board	KQBS	48 001	48 717	41 447	40 803	40 388	40 445	41 683	42 901	44 701	46 044	47 073
Northern Ireland Consolidated Fund	KQBT	239	93	109	126	138	157	175	220	..	..	..
Other debt	KQBU	9 745	..	..	..	..	..	..	..	..	..	..
England and Wales												
Total debt	KQBV	49 914	48 187	47 357	46 695	..	..	..	..	..	..	..
of which Public Works Loan Board	KQBW	*41 025*	*41 501*	*34 082*	*33 132*	*32 448*	*32 617*	*33 660*	*34 606*	*36 049*	*37 172*	*38 013*
Scotland												
Total debt[2]	KQBX	7 948	8 005	8 429	8 999	9 984	10 850	..	..	..	..	..
of which Public Works Loan Board	KQBY	*6 976*	*7 216*	*7 365*	*7 671*	*7 940*	*7 828*	*8 023*	*8 295*	*8 652*	*8 872*	*9 060*
Northern Ireland												
Total debt	KQBZ	123	139	157	175	186	183	211	225	250	..	..

1 The sums shown exclude inter-authority loans and debt transfers, and temporary loans and overdrafts obtained for the purpose of providing for current expenses. No deduction has been made in respect of sums held in sinking funds for the repayment of debt.

2 The data for 1991 is taken from information supplied by the Chartered Institute of Public Finance and Accountancy. Data for 1996 is before transfer of responsibility for Water & Sewerage and the Scottish Childrens Reporters Administration.

Sources: Department for Transport, Local Government and the Regions.;
Public Works Loan Board: 020 7270 3874;
Department of the Environment for Northern Ireland: 028 9054 0707;
Chartered Institute of Public Finance and Accountancy (England and Wales, 1991)

17.14 Revenue expenditure of local authorities

	1998/99 outturn £m	1999/00 outturn £m	2000/01 budget[1] £m	2000/01 adjusted budget[2,3] £m	2001/02 budget[4] £m	Difference 2001/02 over 2000/01 adjusted budget[5]	
						£m	%
England							
Education	19 946	22164	23531	23 470	25 813	2 343	10.0
Personal social services	9 059	10 050	10 288	10 257	11 076	820	8.0
Police	6 693	7 034	7 304	7 468	7 861	393	5.3
Fire	1 402	1 473	1 543	1 543	1 615	72	4.7
Highway maintenance	1 621	1 645	1 879	1 879	1 842	-37	-2.0
EPC services	14 751	14 751	16 294	15 904	16 865	961	6.0
Comprising:							
Civil defence and other Home office	558	594	612	160	105	-55	-34.5
Magistrates courts	309	316	323	323	324	1	0.4
Parking and public transport	695	669	786	840	972	132	15.7
Housing benefit and council tax administration[6]	5 520	5 757	5 990	5 990	6 167	177	3.0
Non-HRA housing	400	420	434	441	434	-7	-1.5
Libraries and art galleries	881	1 056	1 114	1 114	1 201	87	7.8
Sports and recreation centres	562	563	542	542	557	15	2.8
Local environmental services	3 675	3 561	4 202	4 202	4 696	494	11.7
Other[3]	2 150	2 150	2 291	2 292	2 410	118	5.1
Net current expenditure	53 471	57 872	60 838	60 518	65 073	4 555	7.5
Capital charges	1 968	1 927	2 038	2 038	2 050	12	0.6
CERA[7]	717	628	658	658	699	41	6.2
Interest receipts	-1 143	-877	-788	-788	-809	-21	2.7
Other non-current[8]	3 992	2 223	2 349	2 349	2 378	29	1.2
Gross revenue expenditure[9]	59 005	61 774	65 094	64 774	69 390	4 616	7.1
Specific grants outside AEF	-8 816	-8 122	-8 205	-7 886	-8 119	-233	3.0
Revenue expenditure	50 189	53 651	56 889	56 888	61 270	4 382	7.7
Specific and special grants inside AEF	-2 334	-2 921	-3 485	-3 657	-5 431	-1 774	48.5
Net revenue expenditure	47 855	50 730	53 404	53 232	55 839	2 607	4.9
Other adjustments	-67	-35	-31	-31	-25	7	-21.0
Use of reserves	243	-157	-550	-550	-479	71	-13.0
Budget requirement	48 030	50 539	52 823	52 651	55 336	2 685	5.1
SSA reduction grant	-102	-68	-18	-18	-2	16	-89.7
Police grant	-3 375	-3 505	-3 627	-3 627	-3 798	-171	4.7
Revenue support grant	-19 480	-19 875	-19 437	-19 265	-21 086	-1 821	9.5
Central Support Protection Grant	-	-51	-34	-34	-1	33	-96.0
Council Tax Benefit Subsid Limitation Scheme	-	31	54	54	83	29	53.1
Non-domestic rates	-12 531	-13 612	-15 406	-15 406	-15 143	263	-1.7
Greater London Authority Grant	-	-	-22	-22	-23	-1	5
Other items	-211	-181	-132	-132	-119	13	-9.7
Precepts/demand on collection fund	12 332	13 278	14 200	14 200	15 245	1 046	7.4
Scotland							
Net revenue expenditure on general fund	6 732	7019	7 235	..	7 663	428	2.0

17.14 Revenue expenditure of local authorities
continued

£ millions

	1994/95 outturn	1995/96 outturn	1996/97 outturn	1997/98 outturn	1998/99 outturn	1999/00 outturn	2000/01 budget	2001/02 budget
Wales[10]								
Education	1 283	1 300	1 307	1 328	1 385	1 407	1 476	1 586
Personal social services	430	486	528	560	595	632	668	717
Police	285	307	321	344	353	370	395	426
Fire	69	74	78	81	88	94	98	103
Other law, order and protective services	50	50	58	58	60	56	57	35
Roads and transport	164	172	164	157	159	160	166	192
Local environmental services[11]	240	256	231	238	244	259	273	294
Libraries, culture, heritage, sport and recreation	84	90	87	89	102	107	106	123
Non-HRA housing, including housing benefit[12]	224	246	260	260	259	266	279	280
Council tax benefit and administration	10	11	13	12	12	14	14	14
Debt financing costs	192	209	219	243	248	249	263	257
Other revenue services[13]	117	139	143	139	133	157	167	198
Total gross revenue expenditure[14]	3 147	3 340	3 409	3 510	3 639	3 770	3 963	4 224
Specific grants outside AEF	-392	-408	-419	-389	-392	-346	-330	-366
Revenue expenditure	2 755	2 932	2 990	3 121	3 246	3 424	3 633	3 858
Specific grants inside AEF	-73	-70	-73	-75	-84	-80	-81	-94
Net revenue expenditure	2 682	2 862	2 918	3 046	3 163	3 344	3 551	3 764
Appropriations to/from financial reserves	16	-74	-7	-21	7	-1	-11	-7
Other adjustments	-	-1	-3	-4	-8	-	-	-
Budget requirement	2 699	2 786	2 908	3 022	3 162	3 343	3 540	3 757
Discretionary non-domestic rate relief	1	1	1	2	1	2	2	2
Council tax reduction scheme	-	-	-45	-17	-31	-22	-17	-4
Police grant	-142	-156	-166	-171	-180	-181	-186	-195
Revenue support grant	-1 739	-1 717	-1 790	-1 769	-1 798	-1 890	-2 031	-2 147
Redistributed non-domestic rates	-464	-520	-459	-584	-612	-656	-638	-697
Aggregate of precepts/demand on collection fund	354	394	449	483	542	596	670	716
Northern Ireland								
Total expenditure[15]								
Capital	65.3	47.4	73.7	65.2	77.2	..	..	..
Other	227.8	251.7	294.6	304.3	324.6	359.1	..	..
Total income	251.3	243.5	301.1	370.4	407.3	359.1	..	..

1 For Scotland figure for 2000/2001 is a provisional outrun figure not a budget figure
2 Adjustments made for transfers of responsibilities of various services out of local authority responsibility, changes of funds between SSAs and specific grants and for changes in the level of specific grants and other minor function changes.
3 Includes other income for licence fees etc.
4 Scotland figure for 2000/2001 is a budget estimate, not an actual budget.
5 For Scotland, the difference is between the 2001/2002 budget over 2000/2001 provisional outrun.
6 Administration and payment of housing benefit and administration of Council Tax
7 Capital Expenditure charged to the Revenue Account
8 Includes:
(i) Gross expenditure on council tax benefit.
(ii) Expenditure on council tax reduction scheme.
(iii) Discretionary (non-domestic) rate relief.
(iv) Flood defence payments to the National Rivers Authority (now Environment Agency).
(v) Payments in respect of grant maintained schools.
(vi) Bad debt provision.
9 This measure of expenditure is referred to as 'Gross Revenue Expenditure' on local authority returns, but is actually net of expenditure met by sales fees, charges and interest receipts, and excludes most expenditure on the housing revenue account and on trading services.

10 For definitions of the below please e-mail: LGFS.Transfer@Wales.gsi.gov.uk
11 Includes waste management, environmental health, cemeteries and crematoria, parks and open spaces, planning, economic development, community safety and local tax collection.
12 Excludes costs associated with local authority housing stock which is covered by the housing revenue account (HRA)
13 Includes community council spending, agricultural services, consumer protection, capital expenditure charged to the revenue account, and corporate and democratic services.
14 Gross revenue expenditure is total authority revenue expenditure on services, including debt financing costs, excluding that financed by income from sales, fees and charges, but including that financed by specific government grants.
15 'Capital and Other' figures cannot be added to give 'Total' figure because of double counting of loan charges, which are recorded as both 'Capital' and 'Other' expenditure.

Sources: Department for Transport, Local Government and the Regions: 020 7944 4163;
Scottish Executive, Economic Advice & Statistics: 0131 244 7033;
National Assembly for Wales: 029 2082 5355;
Department of the Environment for Northern Ireland: 028 9054 0707

17.15 Funding of revenue expenditure
Years ending 31 March

£ millions

		Community charge system			Council tax system								
		1990 /91	1991[1] /92	1992 /93	1993 /94	1994 /95	1995 /96	1996 /97	1997 /98	1998 /99	1999 /00	2000[2] /01	2001[2] /02
England													
Revenue expenditure[3]													
1999/00 prices £m[4]	KRTM	49 068	50 898	52 471	50 490	52 304	52 271	52 568	51 914	53 605	56 027	58 311	61 270
Cash £m	KRTN	35 851	39 472	42 020	41 506	43 602	44 827	46 532	47 256	50 189	53 651	56 889	61 270
Government grants[5]													
Cash £m	KRTO	12 927	18 620	20 968	21 685	23 679	23 335	23 003	23 840	25 291	26 421	26 600	30 318
Per cent	KRTP	36	47	50	52	54	52	49	50	50	49	47	49
Non- domestic rates[6]													
Cash £m	KRTQ	10 429	12 408	12 306	11 584	10 692	11 361	12 743	12 034	12 531	13 619	15 407	15 144
Per cent	KRTR	29	32	29	28	25	25	27	25	25	25	27	25
Community charges and council taxes[7]													
Cash £m	KRTS	12 251	8 533	9 521	8 912	9 239	9 777	10 461	11 241	12 332	13 278	14 200	15 245
Per cent	KRTT	34	22	23	21	21	22	22	24	24	25	25	25
Wales													
Revenue expenditure	ZBXH	2 217	2 473	2 644	2 624	2 755	2 932	2 990	3 121	3 246	3 424	3 633	3 858
General government grants[1,8]	ZBXI	1 250	1 660	1 753	1 807	1 881	1 873	2 001	1 957	2 009	2 093	2 234	2 345
Specific government grants[1,9]	ZBXG	59	64	69	70	73	70	73	75	84	80	81	94
Share of redistributed non- domestic rates	ZBXJ	443	525	536	470	464	520	459	584	612	656	638	697
Community charge/council tax income[10]	ZBXK	477	231	299	323	354	394	449	483	542	596	670	716
Other[11]	ZBXL	−12	−7	−12	−46	−17	75	9	22	–	−2	9	5

1 In 1991-92, a grant of £140 per taxpayer was given to local authorities in Wales to reduce community charge bills. Although identified separately from general government grants in 1991-92 it has been included under that heading as it was added into revenue support grant in subsequent years.

2 Budget figures

3 'Revenue expenditure to compare with TSS' ie. expenditure financed from revenue support grants, specific grants within Aggregate External Finance, special grants, non domestic rates, community charges/council taxes and balances. Also include spending met by community charge grant (1991-92), and additional grant for teacher pay (1992-93), SSA reduction grant (1994/95 onwards), police grant (1995/96 onwards), Central Support Reduction Grant (1999/00 onwards) and Greater London Local Authority Grant (2000/01 onwards). This line is not the total of the others. The difference is due to funding by balances and other adjustments.

4 Revenue expenditure at 2001/02 prices have been calculated using the GDP deflator. Major function changes include:
(i) Increased responsibilities as a result of care in the community since 1 April 1993.
(ii) Funding for colleges of further education and sixth form colleges transferred to the Further Education Funding Council (FEFC) on 1 April 1993.

5 Revenue support grants, specific and special grants within AEF, community charge grant (1991/92), teachers' pay award additional grant (1995/96 onward) and Central Support Protection Grant (1999/00) and Greater London Authority Grant (2000/01 onwards).

6 1990/91 onwards: distributables amount from non-domestic rate pool. 1993/94 onwards: includes City Offset.

7 1990/91 to 1992/93: gross of community charge benefit community charge transitional relief/community charge reduction scheme grant. 1993/94 to 1995/96: council tax transitional reduction scheme.

8 Includes all hypothecated grants, namely revenue support grant, police grant, council tax reduction scheme grant and the adjustment to reverse the transfer out of nursery voucher monies in 1997-98.

9 Comprises specific and supplementary grants within aggregate external finance, excluding police grant.

10 This includes community council precepts, and income covered by community charge/council tax benefit grant, but excludes council tax reduction scheme grant.

11 This includes use of, or contributions to, local authority reserves and other minor adjustments.

Sources: Department for Transport, Local Government and the Regions: 020 7944 4163;
National Assembly for Wales: 029 2082 5355

17.16 Local authority capital expenditure and receipts[1]
Years ending 31 March

£ millions

		1995	1996	1997	1998	1999	2000
England		1995/96 final outturn	1996/97 final outturn	1997/98 final outturn	1998/99 final outturn	1999/00 final outturn	2000/01 provisional outturn[2]
Expenditure[3]							
Education	KRUD	793	807	857	995	1 139	1 468
Personal Social Services	KRUE	200	194	150	140	134	149
Transport	KRUC	1 399	1 194	1 114	1 053	1 086	1 412
Housing	KRUB	2 712	2 529	2 346	2 513	2 406	2 775
Arts and libraries	GEKZ	61	69	130	150	195	143
Agriculture and fisheries	GELA	60	64	55	57	48	20
Sport and recreation	KRUH	203	217	205	235	241	259
Other[4]	GELB	1 075	1 006	1 121	1 140	1 299	1 535
Fire and civil defence	GELC	63	49	50	49	50	44
Police and probation	GELD	260	262	253	263	286	280
Magistrates courts	GELE	81	28	19	33	28	29
Total	KRUR	6 911	6 419	6 298	6 630	6 912	8 114
Receipts							
Education	KRUT	75	120	133	82	102	103
Personal social services	KRUV	40	57	43	52	51	42
Transport	KRUU	39	132	34	64	105	62
Housing	KRUS	1 351	1 169	1 438	1 630	2 249	2 458
Arts and libraries	GELF	3	1	2	6	2	5
Agriculture and fisheries	GELG	49	63	64	51	48	43
Sport and recreation	KRUX	14	9	13	10	8	10
Other[4]	GELH	364	545	544	687	960	654
Fire and civil defence	GELI	3	5	9	3	5	8
Police and probation	GELJ	56	82	70	76	118	95
Magistrates court	GELK	1	–	1	–	2	2
Total	KRVB	1 995	2 183	2 349	2 662	3 651	3 482

1 'Total capital expenditure' in this table includes acquisition of share or loan capital. Similarly 'Total capital receipts' in this table include the disposal of share or loan capital and disposal of other investments.

2 The figures shown here have been adjusted based on historical differences between provisional and final outturn

3 Expenditure funded by Regeneration (including SRB) resources is included in gross expenditure.

4 'Other' covers other environmental services, consumer protection and employment services.

Source: Department for Transport, Local Government and the Regions: 020 7944 4076

17.17 Capital expenditure and income

£ millions

	Expenditure			Income				
	Expenditure on land works, etc	Capital assigned to repayment of debt	All expenditure	Loans	Government grants	Miscellaneous	All income	Gross debt at end of year
Financial year								
	KRVC	KRVD	KRVE	KRVF	KRVG	KRVH	KRVI	KRVJ
1970/71	1 792	150	1 942	1 516	106	349	1 970	13 384
1971/72	1 938	170	2 109	1 605	116	421	2 143	14 450
1972/73	2 418	213	2 631	2 030	122	531	2 682	16 105
1973/74	3 286	225	3 511	2 781	143	619	3 544	18 300
1974/75[1]	3 712	127	3 839	3 209	128	498	3 835	18 884
1975/76	3 917	198	4 115	3 285	177	647	4 109	21 930
1976/77	3 783	312	4 095	3 097	249	803	4 149	24 534
1977/78	3 487	352	3 839	2 677	255	981	3 913	26 282
1978/79	3 621	390	4 011	2 627	351	1 139	4 117	27 103
1979/80	4 249	331	4 580	2 992	385	1 367	4 745	30 187
1980/81	4 476	413	4 889	2 900	492	1 864	5 256	32 076
1981/82	4 061	563	4 623	2 527	470	2 177	5 174	34 069
1982/83	5 090	634	5 724	3 358	416	3 100	6 874	36 231
1983/84	5 890	562	6 452	3 538	379	3 294	7 211	38 698
1984/85	6 352	515	6 867	3 381	327	3 283	6 991	40 554
1985/86	5 748	348	6 096	3 008	360	3 239	6 607	40 138
1986/87	5 899	328	6 227	2 814	388	3 878	7 081	43 033
1987/88	6 091	486	6 577	2 953	297	4 286	7 536	44 904
1988/89	7 166	658	7 824	2 985	270	6 122	9 376	47 295
1989/90	9 590	474	10 064	2 919	440	6 110	9 469	48 695

		Income					Capital receipts set aside[2]	Credit ceiling[3]	Provision for credit liabilities[3]
	Gross capital expenditure	Credit approvals used	Government grants	Capital receipts	Other income	Total income			
Financial year									
At 1 April 1990	-	-	-	-	-	-	4 241	42 167	4 241
	KRVK	KRVL	KRVM	KRVN	KRVO	KRVP	KRVQ	KRVR	KRVS
1990/91	6 869	2 786	907	3 165	542	7 400	2 022	41 125	5 677
1991/92	6 572	3 140	1 041	2 251	674	7 106	1 353	41 234	6 502
1992/93	6 567	3 229	1 210	2 110	619	7 168	908	37 051	6 282
1993/94	7 124	2 948	1 279	3 310	651	8 188	356	37 941	6 041
1994/95	6 950	2 722	1 176	2 458	724	7 080	1 409	37 673	6 921
1995/96	6 910	2 264	1 484	1 966	1 278	6 992	1 160	37 103	7 677
1996/97	6 420	2 120	1 388	2 183	1 132	6 823	1 039	37 261	8 520
1997/98	6 298	2 099	1 262	2 349	1 129	6 839	1 186	36 711	8 594
1998/99	6 630	2 334	1 160	2 662	1 413	7 569	1 130	36 791	7 274
1999/00	6 912	2 301	1 168	3 651	1 480	8 600	1 483	36 317	7 470

1 Reorganisation of local government in April 1974 transferred responsibility for various services to regional health and water authorities.
2 Excluding Social Housing Grant and European Regional Development Fund (ERDF) grants.
3 At end of year.

Source: Department for Transport, Local Government and the Regions: 020 7944 4076

17.18 Expenditure of local authorities
Scotland
Year ending 31 March

£ thousand

		Out of revenue [1]									
		1990/91	1991/92	1992/93	1993/94	1994/95	1995/96	1996/97	1997/98	1998/99	1999/00
Total	KQTA	7 429 771	7 985 137	8 560 071	8 713 471	9 111 751	9 690 424	9 196 125	9 566 936	10 033 985	10 435 726
General Fund Services:	KQTB	5 650 719	6 093 642	6 542 916	6 589 420	6 904 228	7 324 381	7 151 759	6 679 396	7 021 038	7 430 529
Education	KQTC	2 390 134	2 564 363	2 757 058	2 537 582	2 563 049	2 654 158	2 629 961	2 512 725	2 649 170	2 855 945
Libraries, museums and galleries	KQTD	103 489	109 181	117 243	125 791	132 055	149 427	138 483	121 387	124 648	131 696
Social work	KQTE	668 792	733 067	806 613	914 436	1 045 638	1 222 693	1 289 928	1 315 387	1 394 142	1 519 191
Law, order and protective services	KQTF	653 197	704 943	763 917	804 616	828 480	866 567	816 315	931 795	952 940	1 006 000
Roads[2]	KQTG	561 522	589 564	633 874	650 555	684 452	676 116	716 570	440 712	546 945	527 921
Environmental services	KQTH	264 507	283 968	305 645	322 534	330 039	351 689	329 674	343 565	349 413	373 050
Planning	KQTI	162 566	174 380	188 753	202 027	211 346	226 073	210 827	163 380	179 078	198 285
Leisure and recreation	KQTJ	338 532	362 560	383 081	396 874	405 083	451 952	426 422	364 853	368 023	375 579
Other services	KQTL	383 221	445 968	456 198	516 842	580 561	591 766	562 462	456 219	430 790	435 155
Other general fund expenditure[3]	KQTM	124 759	125 648	130 534	118 163	123 525	133 940	31 117	29 373	25 889	7 707
Housing	KQTN	1 473 950	1 573 590	1 672 566	1 738 427	1 806 022	1 924 930	2 000 684	1 658 935	1 754 686	1 821 380
Trading services:	KQTO	429 861	443 553	475 123	503 787	525 026	575 053	74 799	75 976	79 644	87 300
Water supply	KQTP	188 478	203 847	218 864	239 291	255 081	274 773	–	–	–	–
Sewerage	KQTQ	176 449	185 216	194 576	200 036	209 323	233 525	–	–	–	–
Passenger transport	KQTR	560	603	859	681	685	794	2 849	1 524	121	315
Ferries	KQTS	6 596	4 508	8 336	7 203	7 574	7 744	6 831	7 512	8 930	9 709
Harbours, docks and piers	KQTT	23 428	28 008	27 811	16 215	16 804	15 301	13 482	12 884	15 697	15 923
Road bridges	KQTV	9 277	9 629	9 508	10 948	7 579	11 755	12 759	16 064	16 408	8 231
Slaughterhouses	KQTW	2 737	1 427	1 282	985	976	1 000	794	850	228	4
Markets	KQTX	..	6 086	8 145	8 462	8 615	10 336	14 278	13 479	13 161	14 106
Other trading services	KQTY	22 336	4 229	5 742	19 966	18 389	19 825	23 806	23 663	25 099	39 012
Loan charges:[4] Total	KQTZ	1 267 466	1 327 639	1 343 768	1 346 433	1 383 167	1 451 179	1 121 448	1 126 637	1 152 728	1 104 224
Allocated to :											
General Fund services	KMHV	567 143	607 867	631 479	649 212	677 377	710 801	639 380	651 982	710 371	696 360
Housing	KMHW	530 566	542 248	528 488	505 407	499 904	504 162	475 507	471 274	438 556	402 936
Trading services	KMHX	169 757	177 524	183 801	191 814	205 886	236 216	6 561	3 381	3 801	4 928

		On capital works [5]									
		1990/91	1991/92	1992/93	1993/94	1994/95	1995/96	1996/97	1997/98	1998/99	1999/00
Total	KQUA	1 249 744	1 276 006	1 344 250	1 428 545	1 518 362	1 528 167	889 572	813 900	815 981	816 473
General Fund Services:	KQUB	589 921	620 287	650 779	699 250	760 564	767 795	540 127	540 096	541 769	557 119
Education	KQUC	75 166	81 007	92 584	85 619	113 121	114 128	101 898	112 753	125 341	136 508
Libraries, museums & galleries	KQUD	7 223	9 225	15 319	11 077	12 822	16 757	11 602	9 974	13 231	10 261
Social work	KQUE	25 797	26 017	32 940	29 040	29 067	30 298	20 658	19 660	22 554	22 097
Law, order and protective services	KQUF	23 378	19 903	28 230	32 951	33 635	35 847	41 326	37 701	37 727	37 132
Roads	KQUG	159 467	164 333	179 275	189 525	198 178	187 988	116 881	108 227	113 954	108 500
Environmental services	KQUH	12 738	12 798	13 239	18 905	16 595	14 580	10 226	21 193	18 397	14 936
Planning	KQUI	55 899	84 900	69 065	76 477	102 152	103 221	51 182	69 648	50 854	52 045
Leisure and recreation	KQUJ	43 872	51 490	44 774	74 563	65 411	57 243	36 232	29 692	40 926	52 365
Administrative buildings & equipment	KQUK	32 251	29 996	24 980	17 888	23 994	14 693	40 014	45 374	35 107	35 824
Other services	KQUL	154 130	140 618	150 373	163 205	165 589	193 040	110 108	85 814	83 678	87 451
Housing	KQUM	504 378	485 131	460 140	467 811	497 997	517 593	345 713	270 005	268 135	255 019
Trading Services:	KQUN	155 445	170 588	233 331	261 484	259 801	242 779	3 732	3 799	6 077	4 335
Water supply	KQUO	63 872	77 000	109 655	128 081	123 564	107 064	–	–	–	–
Sewerage	KQUP	77 096	88 035	113 998	127 047	130 634	131 684	–	–	–	–
Passenger Transport	KQUQ	–	–	–	–	–	–	–	–	–	–
Ferries	KQUR	846	773	18	–	376	355	521	770	268	1 030
Harbours, docks and piers	KQUS	8 444	336	5 020	2 300	1 982	1 218	934	1 175	1 626	1 389
Airports	KQUT	14	2	2	184	173	763	1 149	439	–	–
Road bridges	KQUU	237	380	694	799	830	805	277	973	2 791	600
Slaughterhouses	KQUV	73	56	87	1 068	139	63	112	69	54	12
Other trading services	KMHY	4 863	4 006	3 857	2 005	2 103	827	739	373	1 338	1 304

1 Gross expenditure less inter-authority and inter-account transfers.
2 Including general fund support for transport (LA and NON-LA).
3 General fund contributions to Housing and Trading services (excluding transport), are also included in the expenditure figures for these services. From 1996/97 water and sewerage are excluded from other general fund expenditure.
4 From 1997/98 loan charges are not included within individual service totals
5 Expenditure out of loans, government grants and other capital receipts.

Source: Scottish Executive, Economic Advice & Statistics: 0131 244 7033

17.19
Income of local authorities: classified according to source
Scotland

Year ending 31 March

£ thousand

		1989 /90	1990 /91	1991 /92	1992 /93	1993 /94	1994 /95	1995 /96	1996 /97	1997 /98	1998 /99	1999 /00
Revenue account												
Rates[1]	KQXA	1 265 922	1 351 627	1 414 346	1 336 395	1 258 863	1 198 575	1 310 721	1 313 531	1 326 129	1 437 646	1 440 522
Community charges	KQXB	867 519	890 645	802 005	932 994	–	–	–	–	–	–	–
Council tax	KPUC	–	–	–	–	822 830	918 502	976 465	968 153	1 070 405	1 146 366	1 193 639
Government grants												
RSG:	KQXC	2 346 281	2 495 840	2 706 629	3 546 958	3 582 127	3 741 567	3 716 567	3 649 694	3 520 461	3 483 815	3 537 043
Rate rebate grant	KQXG	24 164	30 941	37 304	33 741	41 772	39 860	4 456	496	–	–	–
Community charge grant[2]	KIMJ	..	..	437 105	15 512	–	–	–	–	–	–	–
Community charge rebate grants	KQXH	187 182	192 378	112 904	153 231			–	–	–	–	–
Council tax rebate grants	KPUD	–	–	–	–	166 015	186 219	193 937	226 132	260 424	274 940	275 789
Other grants and subsidies	KQXI	808 535	882 296	951 871	1 049 899	1 118 978	1 179 327	1 236 160	1 347 706	1 480 890	1 642 045	1 778 216
Sales	KQXJ	49 439	50 001	45 134	54 399	61 970	59 182	64 284	59 059	46 874	39 595	43 660
Fees and charges	KQXK	1 185 303	1 288 728	1 410 355	1 435 951	1 421 565	1 471 320	1 528 270	1 539 611	1 625 952	1 668 223	1 682 385
Other income	KQXL	123 212	132 009	161 791	184 581	194 151	209 819	207 005	162 825	189 496	190 934	236 946
Capital account												
Sale of fixed assets	KQXM	446 097	416 838	415 475	413 083	441 600	529 528	500 838	499 143	327 569	335 037	303 582
Loans	KQXN	682 767	..	..	..	..	..	..	..	..	..	..
Revenue contributions to capital	KQXP	11 812	48 997	73 896	111 710	163 228	134 156	197 606	119 641	149 423	204 982	213 564
Transfer from special funds	KMHZ	1 513	2 196	1 218	1 751	7 902	10 679	9 035	2 652	36 929	26 959	125 365
Other receipts	KMGV	23 156	24 649	23 110	42 631	32 554	38 736	29 571	45 067	32 118	45 028	39 014

1 Excluding government grants towards rate rebates and domestic element of rate support grant (RSG). Including domestic water rate receipts.
2 Payment to local authorities in respect of the £140 reduction in community charge awarded.

Source: Scottish Executive, Economic Advice & Statistics: 0131 244 7033

17.20
Income of local authorities from government grants[1]
Scotland

Year ending 31 March

£ thousand

		1989 /90	1990 /91	1991 /92	1992 /93	1993 /94	1994 /95	1995 /96	1996 /97	1997 /98	1998 /99	1999 /00
General fund services	KQYA	295 169	339 619	368 717	403 437	428 927	450 056	468 660	487 734	557 536	690 569	818 537
Education	KQYB	11 510	17 809	17 699	20 439	21 791	17 452	17 186	18 324	61 960	92 368	225 668
Libraries, museums and galleries	KQYC	57	80	106	154	108	247	123	137	326	627	507
Social work	KQYD	8 311	10 561	24 817	32 626	36 734	48 091	50 230	57 576	59 892	62 167	71 611
Law, order and protective services	KQYE	211 304	235 477	253 548	274 149	288 835	295 600	312 812	330 767	359 811	366 961	382 246
Transport[2]	KQYF	4 127	4 580	3 325	3 540	1 993	4 315	4 788	403	237	97 649	68 429
Environmental services	KQYG	150	50	56	50	84	82	42	119	159	89	71
Planning	KQYH	4 144	971	947	785	1 310	867	3 030	3 337	4 885	2 695	4 311
Leisure and recreation	KQYI	1 522	1 739	1 503	1 396	1 476	1 609	1 830	1 509	1 856	1 509	1 491
Central administration[3]	KQYJ	867	–	–	–	–	–	–	–	–	–	–
Other services	KQYK	53 177	68 352	66 716	70 298	76 596	81 793	78 619	75 562	68 410	66 504	64 203
Housing	KQYL	510 201	538 042	577 321	640 127	684 519	723 604	762 172	856 435	920 700	948 232	959 276
Trading services	KQYM	3 165	4 024	4 739	5 405	4 954	4 009	4 557	–	–	–	403
Water supply	KQYN	3 132	3 998	4 139	4 255	4 823	4 009	4 459	–	–	–	–
Ferries	KQYO	–	–	1	46	47	–	–	–	–	–	–
Other trading services	KQYP	33	26	599	1 104	84	–	98	–	–	–	403
Grants not allocated to specific services[4]	KMGY	2 557 627	2 719 159	3 293 942	3 749 442	3 789 914	3 781 426	3 721 023	3 650 190	3 520 461	3 483 815	3 537 043
Total	KMGZ	..	3 600 844	4 244 719	4 798 411	4 908 314	4 959 095	4 956 412	4 994 362	4 998 697	5 122 616	5 315 259

1 Including grants for capital works.
2 The significant increase in 1998/99 is due to the different reporting of a grant in aid of expenditure on rail passenger services in the Strathclyde Passenger Transport area.
3 From 1990/91 Central Administration income is included in the relevant service income.
4 Revenue support grant, community charge grant and rate and community charge rebate grants.

Source: Scottish Executive, Economic Advice & Statistics: 0131 244 7033

17.21 Expenditure of local authorities
Northern Ireland
Years ending 31 March

£ thousand

Out of revenue and special funds

		1989 /90	1990 /91	1991 /92	1992 /93	1993 /94	1994 /95	1995 /96	1996 /97	1997 /98	1998 /99	1999 /00
Total	KQVA	179 404	193 450	203 650	214 107	230 666	251 737	252 794	294 563	304 305	413 698	281 030
Libraries, museums and art galleries	KQVB	3 606	3 881	4 030	4 644	5 647	7 214	8 481	10 956	13 928	14 571	14 565
Environmental health services:												
Refuse collection and disposal	KQVC	26 366	29 363	32 131	33 582	39 952	42 109	41 284	52 267	56 246	56 360	48 228
Public baths	KQVD	1 457	1 571	1 808	1 505	1 562	1 648	1 703	1 838	2 585	2 634	513
Parks, recreation grounds, etc	KQVE	63 284	68 593	74 439	80 601	91 258	101 319	100 418	111 884	115 302	118 396	119 987
Other sanitary services	KQVF	24 990	24 237	26 251	27 593	32 074	34 582	35 706	39 545	39 682	42 923	37 956
Housing (grants and small dwellings acquisition)[1]	KQVG	1 008	1 130	860	792	873	553	472	489	545	358	2
Trading services:												
Gas supply	KQVH	7 997	3 472	–	–	–	–	–	..	..	..	..
Cemeteries	KQVI	4 335	4 492	4 908	5 044	5 352	5 984	5 489	5 120	5 626	5 887	3 648
Other trading services (including markets, fairs and harbours)	KQVJ	6 491	7 340	7 778	7 335	7 123	6 587	4 254	8 672	7 016	10 779	3 741
Miscellaneous	KQVK	39 870	49 371	51 445	53 011	46 825	51 741	54 987	63 792	63 375	161 790	52 390
Total loan charges	KQVL	18 154	19 430	20 226	21 693	19 194	20 797	21 122	24 363	34 823	26 413	..
Loan charges included in terms of expenditure above:												
Allocated to rate fund services	KQVM	13 216	15 155	16 777	18 785	..	..	..	..	..	..	..
Allocated to trading services	KQVN	4 513	3 904	3 102	2 689	..	..	..	..	..	..	..
Not allocated	KQVO	425	371	347	219	..	..	..	..	..	..	..

On capital works[1]

		1989 /90	1990 /91	1991 /92	1992 /93	1993 /94	1994 /95	1995 /96	1996 /97	1997 /98	1998 /99
Total	KQVP	34 955	37 800	42 005	52 908	63 870	56 031	60 629	72 910	69 159	81 869
Libraries, museums and art galleries	KQVQ	683	997	919	2 008	3 833	1 225	1 466	890	1 158	4 019
Environmental health services:											
Refuse collection and disposal	KQVR	3 917	7 254	6 363	4 629	7 013	8 907	8 772	10 401	9 136	8 831
Public baths	KQVS	73	189	225	156	35	143	213	1 000	2 669	8 107
Parks, recreation grounds, etc	KQVT	14 343	18 654	19 239	29 205	26 736	20 914	23 732	26 749	28 884	32 033
Other sanitary services	KQVU	1 666	1 844	2 053	2 094	1 657	1 883	2 233	1 894	2 739	1 716
Housing (including small dwellings acquisition)[1]	KQVV	84	254	441	164	–	18	–	–	192	224
Trading services:											
Gas supply	KQVW	22	–	–	–	–	–	–	–	–	–
Cemeteries	KQVX	597	795	690	673	267	198	714	322	167	689
Other trading services (including markets, fairs and harbours)	KQVY	4 493	2 762	4 738	3 043	4 231	2 954	357	5 456	6 145	4 438
Miscellaneous	KQVZ	9 077	5 051	7 337	10 936	20 098	19 789	23 142	26 198	18 069	21 812

1 Expenditure met out of loans, government grants for capital works, sales of property and other capital receipts.

Source: Department of the Environment for Northern Ireland: 028 9054 0707

18 External trade and investment

External trade and investment

External trade *(Table 18.1 and 18.3 to 18.6)*
The statistics in Table 18.1 are on a Balance of Payments (BoP) basis; all other statistics in this section are on an Overseas Trade Statistics (OTS) basis, compiled from information provided to HM Customs and Excise by importers and exporters, which values exports 'f.o.b.' (free on board) and imports 'c.i.f.' (including insurance and freight). In addition to deducting these freight costs and insurance premiums from the OTS figures, coverage adjustments are made to convert the OTS data to a BoP basis. Adjustments are also made to the level of all exports and EU imports to take account of estimated under-recording. The adjustments are set out and described in the annual ONS *'Pink Book' (United Kingdom Balance of Payments)*. These adjustments are made to conform to the definitions in the 5th edition of the IMF Balance of Payments Manual.

Aggregate estimates of trade in goods, seasonally adjusted and on a BoP basis are published monthly in the ONS First Release UK Trade. More detailed figures are available from the ONS Databank and are also published in the Monthly Review of External Trade Statistics (Business Monitor MM24). Detailed figures for EU and non-EU trade on an OTS basis are published by The Stationery Office in Overseas Trade Statistics of the United Kingdom.

A fuller description of how trade statistics are compiled can be found in Statistics on Trade in Goods (Government Statistical Service Methodological Series).

Import penetration and export sales ratios *(Table 18.2)*
The ratios were first introduced in the August 1977 edition of *Economic Trends* in an article 'The Home and Export Performance of United Kingdom Industries'. The article described the conceptual and methodological problems involved in measuring such variables as import penetration.

The industries are grouped according to the 1992 Standard Industrial Classification. The four different ratios are defined as follows:

Ratio 1: percentage ratio of imports to home demand
Ratio 2: percentage ratio of imports to (home demand plus exports)
Ratio 3: percentage ratio of exports to total manufacturers' sales
Ratio 4: percentage ratio of exports to (total manufacturers' sales plus imports)

Home demand is defined as total manufacturers' sales plus imports minus exports.

Ratio 1 is commonly used to describe the import penetration of the home market. Allowance is made for the extent of a domestic industry's involvement in export markets by using Ratio 2; this reduces as exports increase.

Similarly Ratio 3 is the measure normally used to relate exports to total sales by UK producers and Ratio 4 makes an allowance for the extent that imports of the same product are coming into the UK.

International trade in services *(Tables 18.7 and 18.8)*
These data relate to overseas trade in services and cover both production and non-production industries (excluding the Public Sector). In terms of types of services traded this equates to trade in royalties, various forms of consultancy, computing and telecommunications services, advertising and market research and other business services. A separate inquiry covers the Film and Television industries. The surveys cover receipts from the provision of services to residents of other countries (exports) and payments to residents of other countries for services rendered (imports). "Residents of other countries" is defined as companies, governments and individuals.

Sources of data
The ITIS surveys (which consist of a quarterly component addressed to the largest businesses and an annual component for the remainder) are based on a sample of companies derived from the Inter-departmental Business register. The companies are asked to show the amounts for their imports and exports against the geographical area to which they were paid or from which they were received - irrespective of where they were first earned.

The purpose of the ITIS survey is to record international transactions which impact on the UK's Balance of Payments, hence companies are asked to exclude from their earnings trade expenses such as the cost of services purchased abroad. Trade in service exports or imports which are included in invoices for the export or import of goods are excluded as they are already counted in the estimates for trade in goods. However, earnings from third country trade, i.e. from arranging the sale of goods between two countries other than the UK and where the goods never physically enter the UK (known as merchanting), are included. Earnings from commodity trading are also included. Together these two comprise "Trade Related Services".

"Royalties" are the largest part of the total trade in services collected in the ITIS survey: these cover transactions for items such as printed matter, sound recordings, performing rights, patents, licences, trademarks, designs, copyrights, manufacturing rights, the use of technical "know-how" and technical assistance.

Balance of payments *(Tables 18.9 to 18.12)*
Tables 18.9 to 18.12 in this section are derived from *United Kingdom Balance of Payments 2001 edition - the ONS Pink Book*. The following general notes to the tables provide brief definitions and explanations of the figures and terms used. Further notes are included in the *Pink Book*.

Summary of Balance of Payments
The Balance of Payments consists of the current account, the capital account, the financial account and the International Investment Position. The **current account** consists of trade in goods and services, income and current transfers. **Income** consists of investment income and a new category compensation of employees. The **capital account** mainly consists of

capital transfers and the **financial account** covers financial transactions. The **International Investment Position** covers balance sheet levels of UK external assets and liabilities. Every credit entry in the balance of payments accounts should, in theory, be matched by a corresponding debit entry so that total current, capital and financial account credits should be equal to, and therefore offset by, total debits. In practice there is a discrepancy termed **net errors and omissions**.

The Current Account

Trade in goods

The goods account covers exports and imports of goods. Imports of motor cars from Japan, for example, are recorded as debits in the trade in goods account whereas exports of vehicles manufactured in the UK are recorded as credits. Trade in goods forms a component of the expenditure measure of Gross Domestic Product (GDP).

Trade in services

The services account covers exports and imports of services (eg, civil aviation). Passenger tickets for travel on UK aircraft sold abroad, for example, are recorded as credits in the services account whereas the purchases of airline tickets from foreign airlines by UK passengers are recorded as debits. Trade in services, along with trade in goods, forms a component of the expenditure measure of Gross Domestic Product (GDP).

Income

The income account consists of compensation of employees and investment income and is dominated by the latter. Compensation of employees covers employment income from cross-border and seasonal workers which is less significant in the UK than in other countries. Investment income covers earnings (eg, profits, dividends and interest payments and receipts) arising from foreign investment in financial assets and liabilities. For example, earnings on foreign bonds and shares held by financial institutions based in the UK are recorded as credits in the investment income account, whereas earnings on UK company securities held abroad are recorded as investment income debits. Investment income forms a component of Gross National Income (GNI) but not Gross Domestic Product (GDP).

Current transfers

Current transfers are composed of central government transfers (eg, taxes and payments to and receipts from the European Union) and other transfers (eg, gifts in cash or kind received by private individuals from abroad or receipts from the EU, where the UK government acts as an agent for the ultimate beneficiary of the transfer). Current transfers do not form a component either of Gross Domestic Product (GDP) or of Gross National Income (GNI). For example payments to the UK farming industry under the EU Agricultural Guarantee Fund are recorded as credits in the current transfers account while payments of EU agricultural levies by the UK farming industry are recorded as debits in the current transfers account.

Capital Account

Capital account transactions involve transfers of ownership of fixed assets, transfers of funds associated with acquisition or disposal of fixed assets, and cancellation of liabilities by creditors without any counterparts being received in return. The main components are migrants transfers, EU transfers relating to fixed capital formation (regional development fund and agricultural guidance fund) and debt forgiveness. Funds brought into the UK by new immigrants would, for example, be recorded as credits in the capital account, while funds sent abroad by UK residents emigrating to other countries would be recorded as debits in the capital account. The magnitude of capital account transactions are quite minor compared with the current and financial accounts.

Financial Account

While investment income covers earnings arising from overseas investments in financial assets and liabilities, the financial account of the balance of payments covers the flows of such investments. Earnings on foreign bonds and shares held by financial institutions based in the UK are, for example, recorded as credits in the investment income account, but the acquisition of such foreign securities by UK based financial institutions are recorded as net debits in the financial account or portfolio investment abroad. Similarly the acquisitions of UK company securities held by foreign residents are recorded in the financial account as net credits or portfolio investment in the UK.

International Investment Position

While the financial account covers the flows of foreign investments and financial assets and liabilities, the International Investment Position records the levels of external assets and liabilities. While the acquisition of foreign securities by UK based financial institutions are recorded in the financial account, as net debits, the total holdings of foreign securities by UK based financial institutions are recorded as levels of UK external assets. Similarly the holdings of UK company securities held by foreign residents are recorded as levels of UK liabilities.

Foreign direct investment
(Tables 18.13 to 18.18)

Direct investment refers to investment that adds to, deducts from or acquires a lasting interest in an enterprise operating in an economy other than that of the investor, the investor's purpose being to have an effective voice in the management of the enterprise. (For the purposes of the statistical inquiry, an effective voice is taken as equivalent to a holding of 10 per cent or more in the foreign enterprise.) Other investments in which the investor does not have an effective voice in the management of the enterprise are mainly portfolio investments and these are not covered here. Cross-border investment by public corporations or in property (which is regarded as direct investment in the national accounts) is not covered here, but is shown in the balance of payments. Similarly foreign direct investment earnings data are shown net of tax in Tables 18.15 and 18.18 but are gross of tax in the balance of payments.

External trade and investment

Direct investment is a financial concept and is not the same as capital expenditure on fixed assets. It covers only the money invested in a related concern by the parent company and the concern will then decide how to use the money. A related concern may also raise money locally without reference to the parent company.

The investment figures are published on a net basis, that is, they consist of investments net of disinvestments by a company into its foreign subsidiaries, associate companies and branches.

Definitional changes from 1997
The new European System of Accounts (ESA(95)) definitions were introduced from the 1997 estimates. The changes were as follows:

i) Previously for the measurement of direct investment, an effective voice in the management of an enterprise was taken as the equivalent of a 20 per cent shareholding. This is now 10 per cent.

ii) The Channel Islands (Jersey, Guernsey etc.) and the Isle of Man have been excluded from the definition of the economic territory of the UK. Prior to 1987 these islands were considered to be part of the United Kingdom.

iii) Interest received or paid was replaced by interest accrued in the figures on earnings from direct investment. There is deemed to be little or no impact arising from this definitional change on the estimates.

The definitional changes have been introduced from 1997 only. The data prior to 1997 have not been reworked in Tables 18.13 to 18.18. For clarity, the Offshore Islands are identified separately on the tables. The breaks in the series for the other definitional changes are not quantified but are relatively small. More detailed information on the effect of these changes was in the business monitor, MA4 – Overseas Direct Investment 1999 published in February 2000.

Sources of data
The figures in Tables 18.13 to 18.18 are based on annual inquiries into foreign direct investment for 1999. These were sample surveys which involved sending around 900 forms to UK businesses investing abroad and 1700 forms to UK businesses in which foreign parents and associates had invested. The tables also contain some revisions to 1998 as a result of new information coming to light in the course of conducting the 1999 annual inquiries. Further details from the 1999 annual inquiries, including analyses by industry and by components of direct investment, were published in February 2000 in MA4, Overseas Direct Investment 1999, one of the ONS Business Monitor series of publications. Figures for 2000 and revised 1999 and 1998 data were published on the ONS website in a first release "Foreign Direct Investment 2000" in December 2001. The more detailed MA4, Foreign Direct Investment 2000 business monitor publication is due for release on the ONS website in February 2002.

Country allocation
The analysis of inward investment is based on the country of ownership of the immediate parent company. Thus, inward investment in a UK company may be attributed to the country of the intervening overseas subsidiary, rather than the country of the ultimate parent. Similarly, the country analysis of outward investment is based on the country of ownership of the immediate subsidiary. As an example, to the extent that overseas investment in the UK is channelled through holding companies in the Netherlands, the underlying flow of investment from this country is overstated and the inflow from originating countries is understated.

Further information
More detailed statistics on foreign direct investment are available on request from Simon Harrington, Office for National Statistics, Financial International & Innovations Inquiries Division, Room D.245, Government Buildings, Cardiff Road, Newport, South Wales, United Kingdom, NP10 8XG. Telephone: 01633 813314, Fax: 01633 812855, e-mail simon.harrington@ons.gov.uk.

18.1 Trade in goods United Kingdom
On a balance of payments basis[1]

		1990	1991	1992	1993	1994	1995	1996	1997	1998	1999	2000
Value(£ millions)												
Exports of goods	BOKG	102 313	103 939	107 863	122 229	135 143	153 577	167 196	171 923	164 056	166 198	187 656
Imports of goods	BOKH	121 020	114 162	120 913	135 295	146 269	165 600	180 918	184 265	185 869	193 722	218 036
Balance on trade in goods	BOKI	−18 707	−10 223	−13 050	−13 066	−11 126	−12 023	−13 722	−12 342	−21 813	−27 524	−30 380
Price index numbers 1995 = 100												
Exports of goods	BQKR	81.7	82.8	84.5	95.0	96.9	100.0	100.7	95.3	90.3	89.5	92.9
Imports of goods	BQKS	81.2	82.2	82.9	91.2	94.3	100.0	99.8	93.2	87.6	86.4	90.1
Terms of trade[2]	BQKT	100.6	100.7	101.9	104.2	102.8	100.0	100.9	102.3	103.1	103.6	103.1
Volume index numbers 1995 = 100												
Exports of goods	BQKU	77.2	78.0	79.9	83.1	91.3	100.0	107.6	116.7	118.2	123.3	137.3
Imports of goods	BQKV	86.5	81.9	87.3	90.5	94.5	100.0	109.5	120.3	131.1	141.3	158.2

1 Statistics of trade in goods on a balance of payments basis are obtained by making certain adjustments in respect of valuation and coverage to the statistics recorded in the *Overseas Trade Statistics.* These adjustments are described in detail in *The Pink Book 2001.*

2 Export price index as a percentage of the import price index.

Source: Office for National Statistics: 020 7533 6064

18.2 Import penetration and export sales ratios for products of manufacturing industry [1,2]

United Kingdom: SIC 92

			1997	1998	1999
Ratio 1 Imports/Home Demand					
Description		*SIC Division*			
Total of divisions below	**BAZY**		47	47	47
Mining of Metal Ores[3]	**BAZZ**	13	..	..	..
Other Mining and Quarrying	**BBAM**	14	126	98	128
Food products and beverages	**BBAN**	15	21	21	21
Tobacco products	**BBAO**	16	12	9	8
Textiles	**BAZJ**	17	55	53	57
Wearing Apparel: Dressing and dyeing of fur	**BAZK**	18	77	71	81
Tanning and dressing of leather:luggage, handbags, saddlery, harness and footwear	**BBAP**	19	83	83	86
Wood products of wood and cork (except furniture) articles of straw and plaiting materials	**BBAQ**	20	35	33	36
Pulp, paper and paper products	**BBAR**	21	37	38	38
Publishing, printing and reproduction of recorded media[1]	**BBAS**	22	6	6	6
Chemicals and chemical products	**BAZL**	24	56	63	63
Rubber and plastic products[1]	**BBAT**	25	28	28	28
Other non metallic mineral products	**BBAU**	26	20	20	19
Basic metals [1]	**BBAV**	27	64	64	59
Fabricated metal products (except machinery and equipment)[1]	**BBAW**	28	19	20	20
Machinery and equipment not elsewhere classified	**BBAX**	29	60	59	59
Office machinery and computers	**BBAY**	30	105	85	91
Electrical machinery not elsewhere classified	**BBAZ**	31	55	56	57
Radio, television and communication equipment and apparatus	**BBBA**	32	93	88	85
Medical, precision and optical instruments, watches and clocks	**BBBB**	33	74	71	69
Motor vehicles, trailers and semi-trailers	**BBBC**	34	56	56	57
Other transport equipment	**BBBD**	35	62	65	60
Furniture and manufacturing not elsewhere classified	**BBBE**	36	52	52	50
Ratio 2 Imports/Home Demand plus Exports					
Description		*SIC Division*			
Total of divisions below	**BBBF**		33	33	34
Mining of Metal Ores[3]	**BBBG**	13	..	..	..
Other Mining and Quarrying	**BBBH**	14	54	52	61
Food products and beverages	**BBBI**	15	18	19	19
Tobacco products	**BBBJ**	16	7	6	5
Textiles	**BAZN**	17	41	41	43
Wearing Apparel: Dressing and dyeing of fur	**BAZO**	18	52	55	63
Tanning and dressing of leather:luggage, handbags, saddlery, harness and footwear	**BBBK**	19	62	64	67
Wood products of wood and cork (except furniture) articles of straw and plaiting materials	**BBBL**	20	34	32	34
Pulp, paper and paper products	**BBBM**	21	32	33	33
Publishing, printing and reproduction of recorded media[1]	**BBBN**	22	6	6	6
Chemicals and chemical products	**BAZP**	24	35	37	36
Rubber and plastic products[1]	**BBBO**	25	23	23	23
Other non metallic mineral products	**BBBP**	26	16	17	16
Basic metals[1]	**BBBQ**	27	43	45	41
Fabricated metal products (except machinery and equipment)[1]	**BBBR**	28	16	16	17
Machinery and equipment not elsewhere classified	**BBBS**	29	35	35	36
Office machinery and computers	**BBBT**	30	54	55	58
Electrical machinery not elsewhere classified	**BBBU**	31	37	37	38
Radio, television and communication equipment and apparatus	**BBBV**	32	50	47	48
Medical, precision and optical instruments, watches and clocks	**BBBW**	33	40	40	40
Motor vehicles, trailers and semi-trailers	**BBBX**	34	40	40	41
Other transport equipment	**BBBY**	35	35	37	35
Furniture and manufacturing not elsewhere classified	**BBBZ**	36	39	40	40

18.2

Import penetration and export sales ratios for products of manufacturing industry [1],[2]

continued

United Kingdom: SIC 92

			1997	1998	1999
Ratio 3 Exports/Sales					
Description		*SIC Division*			
Total of divisions below	BBCK			44	42	41
Mining of Metal Ores[3]	BBCL	13	..	..	..
Other Mining and Quarrying	BBCM	14	124	97	134
Food products and beverages	BBCN	15	15	15	14
Tobacco products	BBCO	16	46	42	41
Textiles	BAZR	17	44	39	43
Wearing Apparel:Dressing and dyeing of fur	BAZS	18	68	50	62
Tanning and dressing of leather:luggage, handbags, saddlery, harness and footwear	BBCP	19	66	64	68
Wood products of wood and cork (except furniture) articles of straw and plaiting materials	BBCQ	20	7	7	8
Pulp, paper and paper products	BBCR	21	21	21	20
Publishing, printing and reproduction of recorded media[1]	BBCS	22	10	9	8
Chemicals and chemical products	BAZT	24	56	66	66
Rubber and plastic products[1]	BBCT	25	26	25	24
Other non metallic mineral products	BBCU	26	21	20	18
Basic metals[1]	BBCV	27	57	55	52
Fabricated metal products (except machinery and equipment)[1]	BBCW	28	18	19	18
Machinery and equipment not elsewhere classified	BBCX	29	64	62	60
Office machinery and computers	BBCY	30	106	79	86
Electrical machinery not elsewhere classified	BBDK	31	53	53	55
Radio, television and communication equipment and apparatus	BBDL	32	92	89	84
Medical, precision and optical instruments, watches and clocks	BBDM	33	76	72	70
Motor vehicles, trailers and semi-trailers	BBDN	34	48	47	47
Other transport equipment	BBDO	35	66	67	63
Furniture and manufacturing not elsewhere classified	BBDP	36	41	40	36
Ratio 4 Exports/Sales plus Imports					
Description		*SIC Division*			
Total of divisions below	BBDQ			30	28	27
Mining of Metal Ores[3]	BBDR	13	..	..	..
Other Mining and Quarrying	BBDS	14	57	47	52
Food products and beverages	BBDT	15	12	12	11
Tobacco products	BBDU	16	43	40	39
Textiles	BAZV	17	26	23	24
Wearing Apparel: Dressing and dyeing of fur	BAZW	18	33	23	23
Tanning and dressing of leather: luggage, handbags, saddlery, harness and footwear	BBDV	19	25	23	23
Wood products of wood and cork (except furniture) articles and straw and plaiting materials	BBDW	20	5	5	5
Pulp, paper and paper products	BBDX	21	14	14	14
Publishing, printing and reproduction of recorded media[1]	BBDY	22	9	9	8
Chemicals and chemical products	BAZX	24	36	42	42
Rubber and plastic products[1]	BBDZ	25	20	19	18
Other non-metallic mineral products	BBEA	26	18	17	15
Basic metals[1]	BBEB	27	33	31	30
Fabricated metal products (except machinery and equipment)[1]	BBEC	28	15	16	15
Machinery and equipment not elsewhere classified	BBED	29	42	40	38
Office machinery and computers	BBEE	30	48	36	37
Electrical machinery not elsewhere classified	BBEF	31	34	33	34
Radio, television and communication equipment and apparatus	BBEG	32	46	47	44
Medical, precision and optical instruments, watches and clocks	BBEH	33	45	43	42
Motor vehicles, trailers and semi-trailers	BBEI	34	29	28	28
Other transport equipment	BBEJ	35	43	42	41
Furniture and manufacturing not elsewhere classified	BBEK	36	25	24	22

1 Previously included duplicate trade data for certain headings.
2 Division 23 (coke, refined petroleum products and nuclear fuel) and SIC 24610 (manufacture of explosives) are excluded from the analysis. SIC 27100 (basic iron and steel and ferro-alloys) is not incorporated in PRODCOM and therefore also does not form part of the analysis.
3 Division 13 (mining of metal ores) has not been published since 1995.

Source: Office for National Statistics: 01633 813065

18.3 United Kingdom exports, by commodity[1]

£ million BOP-consistent basis seasonally adjusted

		1991	1992	1993	1994	1995	1996	1997	1998	1999	2000
0. Food and live animals	BOGG	4 657	5 276	5 869	6 305	7 079	6 997	6 581	6 279	5 918	5 819
Of which:											
01. Meat and meat preparations	BOGS	666	829	997	1 229	1 466	1 081	925	745	658	636
02. Dairy products and eggs	BQMS	445	534	658	692	820	732	745	745	688	655
04 & 08. Cereals and animal feeding stuffs	BQMT	1 393	1 545	1 600	1 523	1 702	2 008	1 800	1 710	1 560	1 597
05. Vegetables and fruit	BQMU	294	332	315	398	456	470	455	407	433	402
1. Beverages and tobacco	BQMZ	2 997	3 401	3 304	3 734	4 113	4 331	4 522	3 937	4 029	4 078
11. Beverages	BQNB	2 225	2 435	2 656	2 865	2 986	3 138	3 305	2 879	3 007	3 067
12. Tobacco	BQOW	772	966	648	869	1 127	1 193	1 217	1 058	1 022	1 011
2. Crude materials	BQOX	1 914	1 865	2 158	2 397	2 725	2 583	2 489	2 269	2 086	2 446
Of which:											
24. Wood, lumber and cork	BQOY	25	25	22	45	46	52	52	57	69	75
25. Pulp and waste paper	BQOZ	38	39	22	50	66	57	64	48	55	79
26. Textile fibres	BQPA	466	486	508	571	636	611	568	493	447	492
28. Metal ores	BQPB	530	458	628	663	771	657	642	556	517	757
3. Fuels	BOPN	7 637	7 479	9 075	9 492	9 942	11 578	11 016	7 513	9 878	17 087
33. Petroleum and petroleum products	ELBL	7 284	7 172	8 624	9 079	9 384	10 928	10 239	7 018	9 072	15 615
32, 34 and 35. Coal, gas and electricity	BOQI	353	307	451	413	558	650	777	495	806	1 472
4. Animal and vegetable oils and fats	BQPI	94	85	118	171	221	207	264	243	198	156
5. Chemicals	ENDG	13 700	14 931	17 742	18 806	20 999	22 166	21 901	22 102	23 071	24 919
Of which:											
51. Organic chemicals	BQPJ	3 450	3 692	4 484	4 731	4 923	5 152	4 974	4 913	5 487	5 664
52. Inorganic chemicals	BQPK	991	1 179	1 249	1 120	1 236	1 190	1 183	1 160	1 135	1 492
53. Colouring materials	CSCE	1 212	1 277	1 455	1 479	1 618	1 641	1 578	1 542	1 540	1 566
54. Medicinal products	BQPL	2 542	2 983	3 784	4 010	4 926	5 333	5 416	5 857	6 279	7 218
55. Toilet preparations	CSCF	1 292	1 466	1 702	2 012	2 124	2 409	2 569	2 449	2 462	2 597
57 & 58. Plastics	BQQA	2 110	2 129	2 530	2 800	3 276	3 294	3 166	3 192	3 149	3 349
6. Manufactures classified chiefly by material	BQQB	15 495	15 427	17 760	19 574	22 459	23 142	22 675	21 243	20 302	22 661
Of which:											
63. Wood and cork manufactures	BQQC	117	129	133	170	189	228	250	254	275	252
64. Paper and paperboard manufactures	BQQD	1 613	1 726	1 882	2 049	2 350	2 343	2 309	2 199	2 021	2 102
65. Textile manufactures	BQQE	2 337	2 444	2 661	2 950	3 282	3 471	3 421	3 261	3 018	3 055
67. Iron and steel	BQQF	2 994	2 996	3 220	3 660	4 345	4 059	3 637	3 317	2 582	2 839
68. Non-ferrous metals	BQQG	1 966	1 748	1 955	2 233	2 864	2 680	2 774	2 436	2 133	3 171
69. Metal manufactures	BQQH	2 155	2 192	2 319	2 648	3 086	3 346	3 368	3 586	3 540	3 590
7. Machinery and transport equipment[2]	BQQI	42 860	43 768	49 443	55 852	65 353	73 366	79 002	78 021	78 955	87 638
71 - 716, 72, 73 & 74. Mechanical machinery	BQQK	13 425	13 921	15 179	16 272	18 337	20 481	22 329	22 699	21 885	22 142
716, 75, 76 & 77. Electrical machinery	BQQL	15 391	16 042	21 110	24 900	30 652	32 939	34 252	34 463	36 006	42 378
78. Road vehicles	BQQM	8 341	8 679	8 520	9 654	11 644	14 278	14 811	14 555	15 082	15 605
79. Other transport equipment	BQQN	5 703	5 126	4 634	5 026	4 720	5 668	7 610	6 304	5 982	7 513
8. Miscellaneous manufactures[2]	BQQO	12 749	13 580	15 101	17 315	18 859	20 873	21 530	20 552	20 265	21 167
Of which:											
84. Clothing	CSCN	1 874	2 035	2 377	2 717	3 056	3 356	3 259	2 982	2 807	2 722
85. Footwear	CSCP	309	332	417	479	519	595	605	539	533	514
87 & 88. Scientific and photographic	BQQQ	4 155	4 351	4 824	5 357	5 900	6 594	6 974	6 712	6 736	7 334
9. Other commodities and transactions	BOQL	1 836	2 051	1 659	1 497	1 827	1 953	1 943	1 897	1 496	1 685
TOTAL UK EXPORTS	BOKG	103 939	107 863	122 229	135 143	153 577	167 196	171 923	164 056	166 198	187 656

1 The numbers on the left hand side of the table refer to the code numbers of the *Standard International Trade Classification*, Revision 3, which was introduced in January 1988.

2 Sections 7 and 8 are shown by broad economic category in table G2 of the *Monthly Review of External Trade Statistics*.

Source: Office for National Statistics: 020 7533 6064

18.4 United Kingdom imports, by commodity[1]

£ million BOP-consistent basis seasonally adjusted

		1991	1992	1993	1994	1995	1996	1997	1998	1999	2000
0. Food and live animals	BQQR	9 779	10 701	11 219	11 660	12 923	14 030	13 318	13 185	13 287	13 242
Of which:											
01. Meat and meat preparations	BQQS	1 752	1 920	1 913	1 884	2 237	2 540	2 231	2 003	2 135	2 332
02. Dairy products and eggs	BQQT	827	1 060	1 007	1 092	1 077	1 194	1 101	1 107	1 160	1 167
04 & 08. Cereals and animal feeding stuffs	BQQU	1 364	1 628	1 768	1 682	1 781	1 915	1 991	1 807	1 716	1 761
05. Vegetables and fruit	BQQV	2 826	2 919	3 033	3 285	3 820	4 173	3 898	4 008	4 027	3 884
1. Beverages and tobacco	BQQW	1 830	1 912	2 081	2 228	2 638	3 392	3 593	4 065	4 601	4 807
11. Beverages	EGAT	1 398	1 488	1 667	1 829	2 065	2 479	2 610	2 897	3 077	2 962
12. Tobacco	EMAI	432	424	414	399	573	913	983	1 168	1 524	1 845
2. Crude materials	ENVB	4 230	4 228	4 620	5 041	5 893	5 859	5 670	5 077	4 860	5 827
Of which:											
24. Wood, lumber and cork	ENVC	943	930	1 053	1 300	1 142	1 202	1 239	1 100	1 087	1 201
25. Pulp and waste paper	EQAH	556	569	505	578	979	656	572	480	510	765
26. Textile fibres	EQAP	411	435	454	576	636	639	590	448	416	413
28. Metal ores	EHAA	1 084	1 030	1 053	1 028	1 358	1 474	1 460	1 316	1 307	1 819
3. Fuels	BQAT	7 623	7 123	7 473	6 342	6 161	7 284	6 824	4 892	5 592	9 955
33. Petroleum and petroleum products	ENXO	6 010	5 562	6 012	5 142	5 061	6 118	5 679	3 976	4 839	8 984
32, 34 and 35. Coal, gas and electricity	BPBI	1 613	1 561	1 461	1 200	1 100	1 166	1 145	916	753	971
4. Animal and vegetable oils and fats	EHAB	358	388	457	498	561	686	603	554	569	493
5. Chemicals	ENGA	10 599	11 205	12 980	14 156	17 481	18 095	17 405	17 379	18 620	20 598
Of which:											
51. Organic chemicals	EHAC	2 528	2 695	3 109	3 421	4 670	4 719	4 462	4 512	4 788	5 322
52. Inorganic chemicals	EHAE	995	914	983	1 063	1 086	1 233	1 107	1 017	1 055	1 050
53. Colouring materials	CSCR	599	661	870	788	930	1 000	975	1 005	959	1 007
54. Medicinal products	EHAF	1 328	1 603	2 021	2 254	2 785	3 061	3 100	3 308	4 122	4 717
55. Toilet preparations	CSCS	773	913	1 014	1 193	1 364	1 477	1 506	1 621	1 771	2 010
57 & 58. Plastics	EHAG	2 932	2 936	3 311	3 672	4 597	4 338	4 168	3 905	3 822	4 136
6. Manufactures classified chiefly by material	EHAH	19 792	19 905	21 697	23 844	27 760	28 700	28 007	27 695	26 931	29 279
Of which:											
63. Wood and cork manufactures	EHAI	780	801	872	997	1 037	1 078	1 083	1 086	1 148	1 251
64. Paper and paperboard manufactures	EHAJ	3 742	3 674	3 763	4 180	5 200	4 961	4 550	4 504	4 322	4 422
65. Textile manufactures	EHAK	3 586	3 778	3 974	4 401	4 806	5 075	5 003	4 864	4 382	4 368
67. Iron and steel	EHAL	2 538	2 433	2 574	2 905	3 620	3 604	3 337	3 205	2 473	2 743
68. Non-ferrous metals	EHAM	2 439	2 473	2 848	2 915	3 753	3 720	3 625	3 709	2 943	3 718
69. Metal manufactures	EHAN	2 412	2 460	2 546	2 812	3 239	3 492	3 561	3 738	3 778	4 060
7. Machinery and transport equipment[2]	EHAO	41 417	45 577	53 353	59 993	68 044	76 120	80 518	83 308	88 423	99 192
71 - 716, 72, 73 & 74. Mechanical machinery	EHAQ	10 568	11 142	11 802	13 095	15 148	16 540	17 037	17 155	17 328	17 855
716, 75, 76 & 77. Electrical machinery	EHAR	17 467	19 154	23 559	26 146	31 487	35 299	35 792	36 901	40 747	50 692
78. Road vehicles	EHAS	9 786	11 616	14 463	15 893	17 831	20 238	21 704	22 482	24 007	23 186
79. Other transport equipment	EHAT	3 596	3 665	3 529	4 859	3 578	4 043	5 985	6 770	6 341	7 459
8. Miscellaneous manufactures[2]	EHAU	16 618	18 103	19 989	21 325	22 522	24 987	26 568	27 910	29 038	32 796
Of which:											
84. Clothing	CSDR	3 927	4 256	4 699	4 779	5 178	6 059	6 630	7 026	7 483	8 500
85. Footwear	CSDS	1 115	1 102	1 233	1 427	1 514	1 770	1 912	1 864	2 041	1 995
87 & 88. Scientific and photographic	EHAW	3 889	4 051	4 620	4 837	5 382	6 001	6 067	6 106	6 178	7 261
9. Other commodities and transactions	BQAW	1 916	1 771	1 426	1 182	1 617	1 765	1 759	1 804	1 801	1 847
TOTAL UK IMPORTS	BOKH	114 162	120 913	135 295	146 269	165 600	180 918	184 265	185 869	193 722	218 036

1 The numbers on the left hand side of the table refer to the code numbers of the *Standard International Trade Classification,* Revision 3, which was introduced in January 1988.

2 Sections 7 and 8 are shown by broad economic category in table G2 of the *Monthly Review of External Trade Statistics.*

Source: Office for National Statistics: 020 7533 6064

18.5 United Kingdom exports, by area

£ million BOP-consistent basis seasonally adjusted

		1991	1992	1993	1994	1995	1996	1997	1998	1999	2000
European Union:	ENOF	63 118	64 976	69 402	76 876	89 536	95 758	96 048	95 690	97 804	107 600
EMU members:	QAKW	59 280	60 984	64 884	71 644	83 271	89 124	89 504	89 240	91 722	101 094
Germany	ENYO	14 513	15 185	16 097	17 339	20 242	20 715	20 686	20 593	20 453	22 701
Greece	CHNT	661	776	929	933	1 038	1 147	1 046	1 033	1 139	1 229
France	ENYL	11 739	11 493	12 215	13 655	15 265	17 093	16 602	16 451	16 901	18 512
Italy	CHNO	6 111	6 137	6 094	6 836	7 883	8 027	8 214	8 609	7 830	8 394
Netherlands	CHNP	8 166	8 491	8 121	9 593	12 346	13 484	13 923	12 985	13 627	15 109
Belgium and Luxembourg	CHNQ	5 819	5 706	7 150	7 367	8 298	8 522	8 450	8 446	9 237	10 286
Irish Republic	CHNS	5 234	5 733	6 369	7 163	7 794	8 661	9 357	9 605	10 779	12 329
Portugal	CHNU	1 075	1 164	1 376	1 259	1 469	1 677	1 752	1 722	1 711	1 654
Spain	CHNV	4 354	4 509	4 494	5 131	6 098	6 725	6 745	7 172	7 525	8 275
Finland	CHMZ	845	995	1 121	1 316	1 716	1 810	1 570	1 434	1 353	1 464
Austria	CHMY	763	795	918	1 052	1 122	1 263	1 159	1 190	1 167	1 141
Non-EMU members	QAKZ	3 838	3 992	4 518	5 232	6 265	6 634	6 544	6 450	6 082	6 506
Sweden	CHNA	2 444	2 435	2 900	3 411	4 157	4 420	4 451	4 393	4 031	4 198
Denmark	CHNR	1 394	1 557	1 618	1 821	2 108	2 214	2 093	2 057	2 051	2 308
Other Western Europe:	HCJD	4 559	4 298	5 317	5 772	6 417	7 332	7 850	7 673	6 513	7 486
Of which:											
Norway	EPLX	1 329	1 409	1 505	2 047	2 002	2 051	2 607	2 689	2 064	2 030
Switzerland	EPLV	2 124	1 839	2 282	2 480	2 729	3 185	2 958	2 902	2 754	3 085
Turkey	EOBA	742	690	1 047	821	1 149	1 554	1 734	1 614	1 216	1 813
Iceland	EPLW	97	92	148	110	138	152	153	161	157	194
North America:	HBZQ	13 645	14 741	17 779	19 722	20 450	22 357	23 871	24 793	27 888	33 845
Of which:											
USA	EOBB	11 550	12 640	15 403	17 081	17 901	19 761	20 900	21 721	24 312	29 390
Canada	EOBC	1 729	1 637	1 848	1 935	1 804	1 970	2 147	2 178	2 553	3 503
Mexico	EPJX	280	302	336	393	277	317	428	545	584	676
Other OECD countries:	HCII	5 242	5 371	6 677	7 843	9 467	11 121	10 784	8 875	9 159	10 931
Of which:											
Japan	EOBD	2 246	2 172	2 673	3 047	3 814	4 295	4 177	3 151	3 302	3 682
Australia	EPMA	1 341	1 340	1 611	1 957	2 140	2 488	2 457	2 218	2 164	2 708
South Korea	ERDM	780	644	805	987	1 162	1 313	1 228	675	951	1 357
Poland	ERDR	351	589	732	716	953	1 364	1 355	1 188	1 181	1 314
New Zealand	EPMB	259	258	335	422	440	475	409	340	326	306
Czech Republic	FKML	..	..	290	383	571	722	712	699	741	936
Hungary	QALC	133	157	209	263	296	349	438	487	489	619
Oil exporting countries:	HDII	5 758	6 051	6 589	5 811	6 296	7 933	9 404	7 313	5 550	6 056
Of which:											
Dubai	QALI	486	548	681	624	701	750	866	833	790	974
Saudi Arabia	ERDI	2 213	1 969	1 844	1 534	1 621	2 436	3 656	2 614	1 489	1 566
Indonesia[1]	FKMR	202	315	333	371	518	813	674	368	388	404
Kuwait	QATB	175	264	313	319	548	569	486	327	295	338
Nigeria	QATE	554	625	641	467	430	425	410	454	452	527
Rest of the World	HCHW	11 620	12 427	16 461	19 122	21 413	22 695	23 962	19 713	19 282	21 739
Of which:											
Brazil	FKMO	331	270	422	539	679	851	1 030	927	750	782
China	ERDN	316	425	755	868	832	744	924	861	1 219	1 480
Egypt	QALL	275	251	347	378	385	432	501	505	545	504
Hong Kong	ERDG	1 357	1 597	2 177	2 356	2 664	2 942	3 223	2 680	2 328	2 698
India	ERDJ	988	937	1 155	1 340	1 689	1 717	1 575	1 247	1 463	2 078
Israel	ERDL	518	583	895	1 060	1 113	1 274	1 180	1 082	1 306	1 532
Malaysia	ERDK	577	633	985	1 346	1 192	1 169	1 210	679	948	919
Pakistan	FKMU	266	308	336	362	342	347	270	235	226	211
Philippines	FKMX	143	202	313	364	436	397	601	303	241	276
Russia	ERDQ	..	..	561	728	871	1 016	1 234	932	546	675
Singapore	ERDH	997	1 137	1 459	1 811	2 072	2 159	2 049	1 604	1 610	1 639
South Africa	EPME	1 001	1 071	1 149	1 452	1 837	1 892	1 637	1 534	1 291	1 426
Taiwan	ERDP	511	552	681	752	965	949	1 035	875	871	1 025
Thailand	ERDO	456	473	677	769	838	981	866	390	467	591

1 Includes East Timor.

Source: Office for National Statistics: 020 7533 6064

18.6 United Kingdom imports, by area

£ million BOP-consistent basis seasonally adjusted

		1991	1992	1993	1994	1995	1996	1997	1998	1999	2000
European Union:	ENOS	65 463	69 910	74 434	82 448	94 059	100 628	100 516	102 261	105 113	111 188
EMU members	QAKX	60 213	64 383	68 735	76 082	87 323	93 399	93 514	95 745	98 294	103 924
Germany	ENYS	17 312	18 588	19 891	21 860	26 234	27 583	25 602	25 094	26 460	27 724
Greece	CHOB	381	370	315	348	429	402	398	360	397	439
France	ENYP	10 771	11 945	13 430	15 037	16 457	16 869	18 001	17 957	18 154	18 227
Italy	CHNW	6 237	6 609	6 660	7 496	8 264	8 897	9 537	9 743	9 318	9 438
Netherlands	CHNX	9 802	9 676	8 973	10 064	11 516	12 592	12 314	13 409	13 394	15 111
Belgium and Luxembourg	CHNY	5 350	5 601	6 678	7 121	8 130	9 063	9 491	10 109	10 575	11 631
Irish Republic	CHOA	4 310	4 945	5 449	5 897	7 045	7 340	7 384	7 802	8 478	9 508
Portugal	CHOC	1 017	1 141	1 235	1 283	1 467	1 685	1 758	1 790	1 817	1 715
Spain	CHOD	2 646	2 952	3 266	3 678	4 356	5 115	5 095	5 740	5 892	5 989
Finland	CHNC	1 490	1 636	1 880	2 271	2 500	2 681	2 541	2 328	2 357	2 748
Austria	CHNB	897	920	958	1 027	925	1 172	1 393	1 413	1 452	1 394
Non-EMU members:	QALA	5 250	5 527	5 699	6 366	6 736	7 229	7 002	6 516	6 819	7 264
Sweden	CHND	3 073	3 201	3 566	4 196	4 537	4 837	4 688	4 360	4 594	4 910
Denmark	CHNZ	2 177	2 326	2 133	2 170	2 199	2 392	2 314	2 156	2 225	2 354
Other Western Europe:	HBTS	8 481	8 407	9 489	9 374	10 341	11 387	10 802	9 759	10 628	13 165
Of which:											
Norway	EPMX	4 138	3 798	4 027	3 711	4 175	4 790	4 685	3 431	3 563	5 592
Switzerland	EPMV	3 641	3 830	4 590	4 677	4 981	5 210	4 668	4 770	5 329	5 512
Turkey	EOBU	391	446	515	610	768	898	993	1 105	1 213	1 456
Iceland	EPMW	233	233	242	233	244	257	229	250	284	367
North America:	HCRB	15 457	15 298	17 960	19 379	22 293	24 910	27 311	27 919	28 100	33 591
Of which:											
USA	EOBV	13 336	13 221	15 886	17 233	19 615	22 069	24 355	24 892	24 425	28 525
Canada	EOBW	1 869	1 824	1 805	1 827	2 300	2 407	2 485	2 518	3 022	4 021
Mexico	EPJY	143	149	160	233	288	322	372	366	397	617
Other OECD countries:	HDJQ	8 808	9 911	11 421	12 312	13 762	13 780	14 591	15 023	15 882	18 071
Of which:											
Japan	EOBX	6 269	7 051	8 140	8 584	9 276	8 584	9 043	9 121	9 222	10 191
Australia	EPNA	808	953	954	1 035	1 068	1 239	1 319	1 366	1 351	1 539
South Korea	ERDY	857	890	1 029	1 068	1 505	1 949	2 153	2 201	2 813	3 410
Poland	ERED	293	338	429	533	616	573	598	654	672	903
New Zealand	EPNB	362	405	474	527	555	604	554	518	572	542
Czech Republic	FKMM	..	..	234	271	312	356	450	551	578	798
Hungary	QALD	97	112	145	232	358	404	466	533	664	681
Oil exporting countries:	HCPC	2 565	2 857	3 600	3 049	2 930	3 263	3 327	3 183	3 262	4 281
Of which:											
Dubai	QALJ	90	175	123	123	169	207	284	337	437	404
Saudi Arabia	ERDU	879	900	1 208	757	649	656	838	789	791	985
Indonesia[1]	FKMS	387	501	665	728	814	855	860	868	937	1 088
Kuwait	QATC	33	116	204	223	133	159	166	165	121	318
Nigeria	QATF	223	149	110	117	163	257	102	124	112	91
Rest of the World	HCIF	13 390	14 534	18 391	19 704	22 215	26 948	27 719	27 726	30 732	37 740
Of which:											
Brazil	FKMP	714	830	872	891	936	941	911	884	971	1 118
China	ERDZ	657	891	1 279	1 592	1 843	2 112	2 384	2 820	3 403	4 838
Egypt	QALM	122	130	180	245	235	269	258	278	255	413
Hong Kong	ERDS	1 995	2 242	2 894	2 988	3 364	3 900	4 153	4 370	4 935	5 929
India	ERDV	725	808	1 050	1 249	1 363	1 542	1 550	1 384	1 430	1 656
Israel	ERDX	424	454	530	555	659	797	841	875	1 004	1 027
Malaysia	ERDW	849	1 032	1 350	1 166	1 414	2 277	1 931	1 896	1 963	2 296
Pakistan	FKMV	297	256	312	348	344	372	362	338	321	364
Philippines	FKMY	214	225	266	237	335	857	727	855	988	1 160
Russia	EREC	..	..	792	781	916	1 218	1 416	1 393	1 314	1 476
Singapore	ERDT	1 050	1 113	1 558	1 836	2 101	2 463	2 588	2 342	2 360	2 399
South Africa	EPNE	897	811	964	941	1 058	1 165	1 325	1 352	1 578	2 570
Taiwan	EREB	1 184	1 305	1 561	1 535	1 640	2 000	2 237	2 219	2 640	3 570
Thailand	EREA	591	600	746	884	987	1 137	1 167	1 263	1 298	1 606

1 Includes East Timor.

Source: Office for National Statistics: 020 7533 6064

18.7 Services supplied (exports) and purchased (imports)[1]: 1999

£ millions

	Exports	Imports	Net
Business services			
Legal	1 005	241	763
Accounting	605	101	504
Management consulting	1 033	287	746
Advertising	863	579	284
Market research	219	89	129
Research and development	2 340	651	1 689
Insurance: premiums	-	64	-64
claims	11	-	11
Financial Services	265	152	113
Property	25	26	-1
Other business services	2 880	1 192	1 688
Telecommunications services			
Communications	1 429	1 449	-20
Computer	1 912	533	1 379
Information	346	90	256
Technical services			
Architectural	71	12	59
Engineering (consulting, process etc.)	2 521	816	1 705
Surveying	45	14	31
Construction	253	94	159
Agriculture	42	24	18
Mining	11	34	-23
Other technical	1 016	383	633
Miscellaneous services			
Operational leasing	89	57	32
Cultural services			
TV and radio services	95	20	76
Music services (excluding royalties)	64	9	55
Other cultural	101	63	38
Royalties	4 279	3 250	1 029
Trade related services			
Own account earning	746	44	702
Commission	783	466	317
Commodity trading	581	221	360
Management services to affiliated companies	1 064	709	355
All other services	1 243	428	815
WORLD TOTAL	25 935	12 097	13 838

1 Due to rounding, the sum of constituent items may not always equal the total shown. Data excludes the following industries: Financial, Film and TV, Travel and Transport, Public Sector (including Education) and Law Society members.

Source: Office for National Statistics

18.8 International trade in services[1] by country: 1999

£ millions

	Exports	Imports	Net
European Union	9 655	4 836	4 819
Austria	104	52	52
Belgium/Luxembourg	1 041	453	588
Denmark	259	204	54
Finland	244	69	175
France	1 199	973	226
Germany	2 030	1 111	918
Greece	103	44	60
Irish Republic	1 152	347	805
Italy	567	342	225
Netherlands	1 831	791	1 040
Portugal	154	60	94
Spain	509	212	297
Sweden	453	174	279
EU Institutions	..	..	6
EFTA	1 439	643	795
Iceland	5	1	3
Liechtenstein	..	..	3
Norway	505	177	328
Switzerland	920	460	461
Other European countries	1 125	448	677
Czech Republic	52	19	33
Poland	60	24	37
Russia	65	27	39
Channel Islands	100	29	71
Isle of Man	29	5	24
Turkey	75	44	31
Rest of Europe	210	64	146
Europe Unallocated	534	237	297
Africa	768	212	556
South Africa	248	46	203
Rest of Africa	440	117	323
Africa Unallocated	80	49	30
America	7 442	4 139	3 303
Brazil	77	27	49
Canada	440	139	301
Mexico	47	27	20
USA	6 323	3 755	2 568
Rest of America	342	95	248
America Unallocated	214	96	117
Asia	4 998	1 580	3 418
China	164	42	122
Hong Kong	270	149	121
India	92	102	-10
Indonesia	52	16	35
Israel	173	57	116
Japan	1 010	407	603
Malaysia	109	14	96
Pakistan	78	35	43
Phillippines	45	20	25
Saudi Arabia	1 430	357	1 074
Singapore	682	43	639
South Korea	130	21	109
Taiwan	28	29	-1
Thailand	34	15	20
Rest of Asia	568	169	399
Asia Unallocated	132	104	28
Australia and Oceania	433	194	239
Australia	314	126	189
New Zealand	62	25	38
Rest of Australia and Oceania	21	6	14
Oceania Unallocated	36	38	-2
Rest of World Unallocated	73	41	32
International Orgainisations	-	-	-
WORLD TOTAL	25 934	12 096	13 839
Economic Zones			
OCED	19 213	10 011	9 201
NAFTA	6 624	3 921	2 703
Central and Eastern Europe	223	75	148
OPEC	1 924	473	1 451
ASEAN	940	111	829
CIS	196	53	143
NICs1	1 110	243	867
Offshore Financial centres	1 248	296	952
ACP	390	93	297

1 Due to rounding, the sum of constituent items may not always equal the total
shown. Data excludes the following industries: Financial, Film and TV,
Travel and Transport, Public Sector (including Education) and Law Society
members.

Source: Office for National Statistics

18.9 Summary of balance of payments in 2000
United Kingdom

£ millions

	Credits	Debits
1. Current account		
A. Goods and services	265 305	281 024
1. Goods	187 656	218 036
2. Services	77 649	62 988
2.1. Transportation	12 829	15 280
2.2. Travel	14 406	25 332
2.3. Communications	1 653	1 525
2.4. Construction	199	55
2.5. Insurance	4 311	657
2.6. Financial	12 149	2 052
2.7. Computer and information	2 439	759
2.8. Royalties and licence fees	4 867	4 039
2.9. Other business	22 504	10 808
2.10. Personal, cultural and recreational	1 119	591
2.11. Government	1 173	1 890
B. Income	133 997	127 880
1. Compensation of employees	1 014	871
2. Investment income	132 983	127 009
2.1 Direct investment	43 773	26 981
2.2 Portfolio investment	32 438	32 234
2.3 Other investment (including earnings on reserve assets)	56 772	67 794
C. Current transfers	13 582	22 405
1. Central government	2 628	8 015
2. Other sectors	10 954	14 390
Total current account	**412 884**	**431 309**
2. Capital and financial accounts		
A. Capital account	2 811	838
1. Capital transfers	2 644	708
2. Acquisition/disposal of non-produced, non-financial assets	167	130
B. Financial account	532 621	506 246
1. Direct investment	88 652	165 673
Abroad		165 673
1.1. Equity capital		150 521
1.2. Reinvested earnings		27 076
1.3. Other capital[1]		−11 924
In United Kingdom	88 652	
1.1. Equity capital	64 380	
1.2. Reinvested earnings	16 146	
1.3. Other capital[2]	8 126	
2. Portfolio investment	165 045	63 046
Assets		63 046
2.1. Equity securities		21 387
2.2. Debt securities		41 659
Liabilities	165 045	
2.1. Equity securities	113 608	
2.2. Debt securities	51 437	
3. Financial derivatives (net)		−1 553
4. Other investment	278 924	275 165
Assets		275 165
4.1 Trade credits		−288
4.2 Loans		54 138
4.3 Currency and deposits		221 262
4.4 Other assets		53
Liabilities	278 924	
4.1. Trade credits	−	
4.2. Loans	78 783	
4.3. Currency and deposits	199 133	
4.4. Other liabilities	1 008	
5. Reserve assets		3 915
5.1. Monetary gold		−883
5.2. Special drawing rights		−73
5.3. Reserve position in the IMF		−478
5.4. Foreign exchange		5 299
Total capital and financial accounts	**535 432**	**507 084**
Total current, capital and financial accounts	**948 316**	**938 393**
Net errors and omissions	−9 923	

1 Other capital transaction on direct investment abroad represents claims on affiliated enterprises less liabilities to affiliated enterprises
2 Other capital transactions on direct investment in the United Kingdom represents liabilities to direct investors less claims on direct investors

Source: Office for National Statistics

18.10 Summary of balance of payments
Balances (credits less debits)
United Kingdom

£ millions

				Current account							
	Trade in goods	Trade in services	Total goods and services	Compensation of employees	Investment income	Total income	Current transfers	Current balance	Capital account	Financial account	Net errors & omissions
	LQCT	KTMS	KTMY	KTMP	HMBM	HMBP	KTNF	HBOG	FKMJ	HBNT	HHDH
1947	−358	−197	−555	−19	140	121	123	−311	−21	552	−220
1948	−152	−64	−216	−20	223	203	96	83	−17	−58	−8
1949	−137	−43	−180	−20	206	186	29	35	−12	−103	80
1950	−54	−4	−58	−21	378	357	39	338	−10	−447	119
1951	−692	32	−660	−21	322	301	29	−330	−15	426	−81
1952	−272	123	−149	−22	231	209	169	229	−15	−229	15
1953	−244	123	−121	−25	207	182	143	204	−13	−177	−14
1954	−210	115	−95	−27	227	200	55	160	−13	−174	27
1955	−315	42	−273	−27	149	122	43	−108	−15	34	89
1956	50	26	76	−30	203	173	2	251	−13	−250	12
1957	−29	121	92	−32	223	191	−5	278	−13	−313	48
1958	34	119	153	−34	261	227	4	384	−10	−411	37
1959	−116	118	2	−37	233	196	–	198	−5	−68	−125
1960	−404	39	−365	−35	201	166	−6	−205	−6	−7	218
1961	−144	51	−93	−35	223	188	−9	86	−12	23	−97
1962	−104	50	−54	−37	301	264	−14	196	−12	−195	11
1963	−123	4	−119	−38	364	326	−37	170	−16	−30	−124
1964	−551	−34	−585	−33	365	332	−74	−327	−17	392	−48
1965	−263	−66	−329	−34	405	371	−75	−33	−18	49	2
1966	−111	44	−67	−39	358	319	−91	161	−19	22	−164
1967	−601	157	−444	−39	354	315	−118	−247	−25	179	93
1968	−708	341	−367	−48	303	255	−119	−231	−26	688	−431
1969	−214	392	178	−47	468	421	−109	490	−23	−794	327
1970	−18	455	437	−56	527	471	−89	819	−22	−818	21
1971	205	590	795	−63	481	418	−90	1 123	−23	−1 330	230
1972	−736	665	−71	−52	407	355	−142	142	−35	477	−584
1973	−2 573	760	−1 813	−68	1 074	1 006	−336	−1 143	−39	1 031	151
1974	−5 241	1 065	−4 176	−92	1 184	1 092	−302	−3 386	−34	3 185	235
1975	−3 245	1 393	−1 852	−102	518	416	−313	−1 749	−36	1 569	216
1976	−3 930	2 465	−1 465	−140	1 100	960	−534	−1 039	−12	507	544
1977	−2 271	3 219	948	−152	−280	−432	−889	−373	11	−3 286	3 648
1978	−1 534	3 679	2 145	−140	138	−2	−1 420	723	−79	−2 655	2 011
1979	−3 326	3 965	639	−130	155	25	−1 777	−1 113	−103	864	352
1980	1 329	3 717	5 046	−82	−1 683	−1 765	−1 653	1 628	−4	−2 157	533
1981	3 238	3 834	7 072	−66	−1 058	−1 124	−1 219	4 729	−79	−5 312	662
1982	1 879	3 069	4 948	−95	−1 273	−1 368	−1 476	2 104	6	−1 233	−877
1983	−1 618	3 941	2 323	−89	280	191	−1 391	1 123	75	−3 287	2 089
1984	−5 409	4 341	−1 068	−94	1 284	1 190	−1 566	−1 444	107	−7 130	8 467
1985	−3 416	6 619	3 203	−120	−877	−997	−2 924	−718	185	−1 657	2 190
1986	−9 617	6 505	−3 112	−156	1 850	1 694	−2 094	−3 512	135	−122	3 499
1987	−11 698	6 813	−4 885	−174	1 091	917	−3 570	−7 538	333	10 764	−3 559
1988	−21 553	4 450	−17 103	−64	817	753	−3 500	−19 850	235	17 201	2 414
1989	−24 724	3 643	−21 081	−138	−654	−792	−4 448	−26 321	270	18 001	8 050
1990	−18 707	4 337	−14 370	−110	−2 869	−2 979	−4 932	−22 281	497	15 083	6 701
1991	−10 223	4 102	−6 121	−63	−3 244	−3 307	−1 231	−10 659	290	5 269	5 100
1992	−13 050	5 482	−7 568	−49	177	128	−5 534	−12 974	421	5 089	7 464
1993	−13 066	6 581	−6 485	35	−226	−191	−5 243	−11 919	309	11 330	280
1994	−11 126	6 379	−4 747	−170	3 518	3 348	−5 369	−6 768	33	2 126	4 609
1995	−12 023	8 481	−3 542	−296	2 397	2 101	−7 574	−9 015	533	4 964	3 518
1996	−13 722	9 597	−4 125	93	1 111	1 204	−5 788	−8 709	736	5 515	2 458
1997	−12 342	12 528	186	83	3 823	3 906	−5 812	−1 720	804	−5 066	5 982
1998	−21 813	12 666	−9 147	−10	12 568	12 558	−8 225	−4 814	473	245	4 096
1999	−27 524	11 660	−15 864	201	3 818	4 019	−7 246	−19 091	808	21 462	−3 179
2000	−30 380	14 661	−15 719	143	5 974	6 117	−8 823	−18 425	1 973	26 375	−9 923

Source: Office for National Statistics

18.11 Balance of Payments: current account
United Kingdom

£ millions

		1990	1991	1992	1993	1994	1995	1996	1997	1998	1999	2000
Credits												
Exports of goods and services												
Exports of goods	LQAD	102 313	103 939	107 863	122 229	135 143	153 577	167 196	171 923	164 056	166 198	187 656
Exports of services	KTMQ	31 574	32 001	36 228	41 411	45 365	49 932	55 895	59 699	64 745	70 522	77 649
Total exports of goods and services	KTMW	133 887	135 940	144 091	163 640	180 508	203 509	223 091	231 622	228 801	236 720	265 305
Income												
Compensation of employees	KTMN	543	551	551	595	681	887	911	1 007	840	960	1 014
Investment income	HMBN	77 663	75 073	66 153	72 333	73 702	87 132	91 621	95 337	102 945	99 312	132 983
Total income	HMBQ	78 206	75 624	66 704	72 928	74 383	88 019	92 532	96 344	103 785	100 272	133 997
Current transfers												
Central government	FJUM	2 050	4 892	2 180	2 826	2 138	1 730	2 828	2 173	1 943	3 733	2 628
Other sectors	FJUN	7 376	9 281	10 295	9 565	9 454	10 751	16 088	10 929	10 500	9 537	10 954
Total current transfers	KTND	9 426	14 173	12 475	12 391	11 592	12 481	18 916	13 102	12 443	13 270	13 582
Total	HBOE	**221 519**	**225 737**	**223 270**	**248 959**	**266 483**	**304 009**	**334 539**	**341 068**	**345 029**	**350 262**	**412 884**
Debits												
Imports of goods and services												
Imports of goods	LQBL	121 020	114 162	120 913	135 295	146 269	165 600	180 918	184 265	185 869	193 722	218 036
Imports of services	KTMR	27 237	27 899	30 746	34 830	38 986	41 451	46 298	47 171	52 079	58 862	62 988
Total imports of goods and services	KTMX	148 257	142 061	151 659	170 125	185 255	207 051	227 216	231 436	237 948	252 584	281 024
Income												
Compensation of employees	KTMO	653	614	600	560	851	1 183	818	924	850	759	871
Investment income	HMBO	80 532	78 317	65 976	72 559	70 184	84 735	90 510	91 514	90 377	95 494	127 009
Total income	HMBR	81 185	78 931	66 576	73 119	71 035	85 918	91 328	92 438	91 227	96 253	127 880
Current transfers												
Central government	FJUO	2 125	3 450	3 812	4 343	4 977	5 022	5 297	5 260	6 787	7 482	8 015
Other sectors	FJUP	12 233	11 954	14 197	13 291	11 984	15 033	19 407	13 654	13 881	13 034	14 390
Total current transfers	KTNE	14 358	15 404	18 009	17 634	16 961	20 055	24 704	18 914	20 668	20 516	22 405
Total	HBOF	**243 800**	**236 396**	**236 244**	**260 878**	**273 251**	**313 024**	**343 248**	**342 788**	**349 843**	**369 353**	**431 309**
Balances												
Trade in goods and services												
Trade in goods	LQCT	−18 707	−10 223	−13 050	−13 066	−11 126	−12 023	−13 722	−12 342	−21 813	−27 524	−30 380
Trade in services	KTMS	4 337	4 102	5 482	6 581	6 379	8 481	9 597	12 528	12 666	11 660	14 661
Total trade in goods and services	KTMY	−14 370	−6 121	−7 568	−6 485	−4 747	−3 542	−4 125	186	−9 147	−15 864	−15 719
Income												
Compensation of employees	KTMP	−110	−63	−49	35	−170	−296	93	83	−10	201	143
Investment income	HMBM	−2 869	−3 244	177	−226	3 518	2 397	1 111	3 823	12 568	3 818	5 974
Total income	HMBP	−2 979	−3 307	128	−191	3 348	2 101	1 204	3 906	12 558	4 019	6 117
Current transfers												
Central government	FJUQ	−75	1 442	−1 632	−1 517	−2 839	−3 292	−2 469	−3 087	−4 844	−3 749	−5 387
Other sectors	FJUR	−4 857	−2 673	−3 902	−3 726	−2 530	−4 282	−3 319	−2 725	−3 381	−3 497	−3 436
Total current transfers	KTNF	−4 932	−1 231	−5 534	−5 243	−5 369	−7 574	−5 788	−5 812	−8 225	−7 246	−8 823
Total (Current balance)	HBOG	**−22 281**	**−10 659**	**−12 974**	**−11 919**	**−6 768**	**−9 015**	**−8 709**	**−1 720**	**−4 814**	**−19 091**	**−18 425**

Source: Office for National Statistics

18.12 Balance of payments: summary of international investment position, financial account and investment income

United Kingdom

£ billions

		1990	1991	1992	1993	1994	1995	1996	1997	1998	1999	2000
Investment abroad												
International investment position												
Direct investment	HBWD	122.5	128.1	151.8	172.6	176.1	203.7	201.6	223.3	299.6	434.1	617.8
Portfolio investment	HHZZ	207.0	260.6	327.2	469.8	429.8	499.3	548.2	651.0	704.6	790.2	872.5
Other investment	HLXV	549.6	528.4	639.7	684.4	708.6	808.1	851.0	1 066.6	1 104.2	1 136.6	1 431.5
Reserve assets	APDD	22.5	26.0	28.3	29.7	30.7	31.8	27.3	22.8	23.3	22.2	..
Total	HBQA	901.5	943.1	1 146.9	1 356.5	1 345.2	1 542.9	1 628.1	1 963.7	2 131.8	2 383.1	2 950.6
Financial account transactions												
Direct investment	–HJYP	10.9	9.3	11.3	18.2	22.7	28.7	22.3	38.2	73.3	128.7	165.7
Portfolio investment	–HHZC	15.9	32.3	28.6	89.6	–21.8	39.3	59.6	51.9	31.9	24.9	63.0
Other investment	–XBMM	52.7	–20.2	31.7	45.3	27.8	47.5	137.1	168.2	17.2	56.7	275.2
Reserve assets	–AIPA	0.1	2.7	–1.4	0.7	1.0	–0.2	–0.5	–2.4	–0.2	–0.6	7.3
Total	–HBNR	79.6	24.1	68.9	153.5	27.3	113.6	217.6	254.9	125.4	206.9	506.2
Investment income												
Direct investment	HJYW	16.1	13.2	13.8	17.4	21.9	24.8	28.5	29.4	29.8	32.8	43.8
Portfolio investment	HLYX	8.2	9.7	12.6	16.7	16.4	19.7	20.2	23.8	29.0	25.6	32.4
Other investment	AIOP	51.6	50.5	38.4	36.8	33.8	41.0	41.3	40.7	43.0	39.8	55.8
Reserve assets	HHCB	1.7	1.7	1.5	1.5	1.6	1.7	1.6	1.4	1.1	1.2	1.0
Total	HMBN	77.7	75.1	66.2	72.3	73.7	87.1	91.6	95.3	102.9	99.3	133.0
Investment in the UK												
International investment position												
Direct investment	HBWI	121.0	128.6	130.8	135.9	129.9	146.2	152.6	173.7	213.6	257.9	348.8
Portfolio investment	HLXW	189.2	208.8	247.1	306.9	320.0	406.3	480.0	583.3	694.4	840.7	1 008.1
Other investment	HLYD	604.0	608.3	756.3	882.3	877.4	1 013.0	1 064.9	1 282.1	1 359.0	1 417.9	1 711.4
Total	HBQB	914.1	945.7	1 134.2	1 325.1	1 327.3	1 565.5	1 697.5	2 039.1	2 267.0	2 516.5	3 068.2
Financial account transactions												
Direct investment	HJYU	19.1	9.2	9.4	10.9	7.1	13.8	17.6	22.8	45.1	54.1	88.7
Portfolio investment	HHZF	12.9	9.8	9.6	28.8	30.7	37.3	43.0	26.7	20.9	112.3	165.0
Other investment	XBMN	62.7	10.3	55.0	125.2	–8.3	67.4	162.5	200.3	59.6	61.9	278.9
Total	HBNS	94.7	29.4	74.0	164.9	29.5	118.6	223.1	249.8	125.6	228.3	532.6
Investment income												
Direct investment	HJYX	7.8	4.9	5.6	11.1	10.6	13.8	16.6	14.9	8.8	18.7	27.0
Portfolio investment	HLZC	15.4	14.4	13.3	14.2	17.2	20.6	23.7	26.6	29.2	28.2	32.2
Other investment	HLZN	57.4	58.9	47.1	47.2	42.5	50.3	50.1	50.0	52.5	48.6	67.8
Total	HMBO	80.5	78.3	66.0	72.6	70.2	84.7	90.5	91.5	90.4	95.5	127.0
Net Investment												
International investment position												
Direct investment	HBWQ	1.5	–0.6	20.9	36.7	46.2	57.5	49.0	49.5	85.9	176.2	269.1
Portfolio investment	CGNH	17.8	51.8	80.1	162.9	109.8	93.0	68.2	67.7	10.2	–50.4	–135.6
Other investment	CGNG	–54.3	–79.8	–116.6	–197.9	–168.8	–204.9	–213.9	–215.5	–254.7	–281.3	–279.9
Reserve assets	APDD	22.5	26.0	28.3	29.7	30.7	31.8	27.3	22.8	23.3	22.2	..
Net investment position	HBQC	–12.6	–2.6	12.8	31.4	17.9	–22.6	–69.4	–75.5	–135.2	–133.4	–117.7
Financial account transactions												
Direct investment	HJYV	8.2	–0.1	–1.8	–7.2	–15.6	–14.9	–4.7	–15.4	–28.3	–74.5	–77.0
Portfolio investment	HHZD	–3.0	–22.5	–19.1	–60.8	52.5	–2.0	–16.6	–25.3	–11.0	87.4	102.0
Other investment	HHYR	10.0	30.6	23.3	79.8	–36.1	19.9	25.4	32.1	42.4	5.3	3.8
Reserve assets	AIPA	–0.1	–2.7	1.4	–0.7	–1.0	0.2	0.5	2.4	0.2	0.6	–7.3
Net transactions	HBNT	15.1	5.3	5.1	11.3	2.1	5.0	5.5	–5.1	0.2	21.5	26.4
Investment income												
Direct investment	HJYE	8.3	8.3	8.2	6.2	11.4	10.9	11.9	14.5	21.1	14.0	16.8
Portfolio investment	HLZX	–7.1	–4.8	–0.7	2.5	–0.8	–0.9	–3.5	–2.8	–0.2	–2.6	0.2
Other investment	CGNA	–5.8	–8.4	–8.7	–10.4	–8.7	–9.4	–8.8	–9.3	–9.5	–8.8	–12.0
Reserve assets	HHCB	1.7	1.7	1.5	1.5	1.6	1.7	1.6	1.4	1.1	1.2	1.0
Net earnings	HMBM	–2.9	–3.2	0.2	–0.2	3.5	2.4	1.1	3.8	12.6	3.8	6.0

Source: Office for National Statistics

18.13 Net outward foreign direct investment by UK companies analysed by area and main country [1,2]

£ millions

		1989	1990	1991	1992	1993	1994	1995	1996	1997	1998	1999
Europe	GQBX	5 620	5 844	3 978	4 911	6 171	9 241	9 184	13 321	19 964	22 899	43 625
EU	CAUU	5 941	5 103	3 919	4 613	6 146	8 278	9 457	13 432	17 368	11 459	38 031
Austria	CBJD	32	58	45	16	13	102	90	102	16	22	9
Belgium and Luxembourg	CAUV	301	−211	316	−191	160	132	438	991	1 536	−147	56
Denmark	CAUW	105	43	66	47	237	64	416	−176	47	−114	122
Finland	CBJE	13	4	−1	7	10	26	112	28	−5	96	307
France	CAUX	1 484	1 158	486	628	471	423	1 515	2 375	2 380	−101	2 322
Germany	CAUY	797	187	155	536	1 333	1 261	1 478	1 184	1 078	1 418	1 389
Greece	CAUZ	52	42	37	167	44	84	163	106	302	221	−34
Irish Republic	CAVA	299	144	388	895	1 082	100	776	755	450	1 057	..
Italy	CAVB	358	548	258	222	282	298	406	421	447	548	240
Netherlands	CAVC	1 644	2 258	985	1 585	2 436	4 615	2 953	6 577	9 804	7 750	5 565
Portugal	CAVD	202	159	61	237	25	169	159	56	112	−11	92
Spain	CAVE	573	699	982	217	−31	460	431	735	864	197	525
Sweden	CBJG	82	15	141	249	84	546	522	277	335	527	..
EFTA of which	CAVG	−163	497	−42	163	−84	645	−594	−12	2 195	8 794	3 634
Norway	CBJF	170	32	35	156	92	662	−255	96	1 997	773	84
Switzerland	CBJH	−333	465	−74	−1	−177	−16	−338	−110	197	8 013	3 548
Other European Countries of which	GQBY	−159	244	100	135	110	317	322	−97	402	2 646	1 960
Russia[3]	GLAA	..	2	−2	..	11	115	39	132	448	−170	257
UK offshore islands	GLAC	−	−	−	−	−	−	−	−	−933	2 445	890
America of which	GQBZ	13 000	2 181	2 628	2 657	8 673	8 464	13 460	3 277	13 953	48 863	76 379
Bermuda	CBKZ	25	276	−438	506	586	349	291	142	−43	469	1 443
Brazil	CBLA	269	211	89	121	38	291	473	692	337	323	942
Canada	CAVK	542	894	318	−106	5	−4	244	−159	823	393	933
Chile	GQCA	49	19	80	−22	101	76	220	89	168	168	−672
Colombia	GQCB	48	20	−264	..	−245	204	123	100	241	346	332
Mexico	GLAD	−136	27	39	114	44	42	79	110	760	151	113
Panama	GLAE	−14	−13	100	211	−100	94	75	103	..	310	−18
USA	CAVJ	11 676	47	2 235	1 321	7 975	6 549	11 840	1 837	10 509	46 066	70 759
Asia	GQCI	798	888	853	959	1 596	2 049	1 657	2 823	2 251	1 671	5 005
Near and Middle East Countries of which	CBKF	−7	244	489	44	−239	253	154	28	350	1 678	−864
Gulf Arabian countries[4]	GQCC	−47	239	476	27	−236	250	116	30	260	1 622	−595
Other Asian Countries of which	GQCD	806	644	364	915	1 834	1 796	1 503	2 794	1 901	−6	5 870
Hong Kong	CAVN	−161	−250	−245	−18	456	128	734	730	−359	1 537	626
India	GLAF	38	42	2	−27	139	87	61	110	171	206	155
Indonesia	GLAG	32	−46	74	−59	69	92	−28	155	170	93	1
Japan	CAVM	230	235	−4	13	−49	245	169	378	383	10	1 996
Malaysia	CBKN	−32	159	140	272	363	286	28	184	731	619	201
Singapore	CBKQ	509	344	232	569	528	590	−48	535	352	−2 479	1 340
South Korea	GLAH	27	4	20	37	44	27	47	32	−26	279	130
Thailand	GLAI	67	40	24	51	103	177	245	194	103	87	94
Australasia and Oceania of which	GQCE	783	999	1 239	1 280	658	959	2 596	1 843	827	202	925
Australia	CBJO	654	913	1 089	989	655	625	2 258	1 472	737	216	814
New Zealand	CBJP	76	−24	66	110	71	264	67	244	255	−112	177
Africa of which	GQCF	1 290	196	606	300	262	327	707	561	623	−95	1 267
Kenya	GLAJ	30	47	22	23	33	9	67	24	73	38	59
Nigeria	CBJY	..	−12	227	138	347	−197	−271	−94	234	−144	159
South Africa	CAVO	414	22	151	72	314	170	466	−25	401	−212	405
Zimbabwe	CBKD	51	52	72	59	36	28	16	25	1	36	74
World Total	CDQD	21 491	10 108	9 304	10 107	17 358	21 040	27 604	21 823	37 619	73 539	127 202
OECD	GQCG	18 868	7 731	7 673	7 343	14 864	16 880	23 686	17 545	33 212	67 758	116 518
Central and Eastern Europe[5]	GQCH	5	2	18	37	41	168	194	201	214	457	219

1 Net investment includes unremitted profits.
2 Minus sign indicates net disinvestment overseas.
3 Prior to 1995 Russia covers other former USSR countries, the Baltic States and Albania.
4 Includes Abu Dhabi, Bahrain, Dubai, Iraq, Kuwait, Oman, Other Gulf States, Qatar, Saudi Arabia and Yemen.
5 Includes Albania, Belarus, Bulgaria, Croatia, Czech Republic, Estonia, Hungary, Latvia, Lithuania, Poland, Romania, Serbia and Montenegro, Slovakia and Slovenia.

Sources: ONS Foreign Direct Investment Inquiries: 01633 813314; Bank of England

18.14 UK outward foreign direct international investment position - book value of net assets analysed by area and main country at year end

£ millions

		1989	1990	1991	1992	1993	1994	1995	1996	1997	1998	1999
Europe	GQCJ	30 626	34 450	37 272	44 213	57 853	66 705	76 434	87 582	99 263	115 142	169 002
EU	CDLN	27 826	31 610	34 312	40 620	53 914	61 674	72 808	83 902	92 072	94 894	150 158
Austria	CDLZ	244	336	384	371	379	454	734	578	461	492	745
Belgium and Luxembourg	CDLO	1 814	1 590	2 505	3 804	2 687	3 189	3 172	5 326	5 701	5 421	10 933
Denmark	CDLP	778	757	739	863	1 301	1 538	2 803	2 273	2 123	2 258	3 075
Finland	CDMA	101	102	80	122	104	117	271	215	217	255	541
France	CDLQ	6 173	6 898	7 290	8 043	8 619	10 357	12 913	13 128	11 368	9 889	12 904
Germany	CDLR	4 303	4 217	3 998	3 804	5 974	8 442	9 215	8 943	8 328	9 956	10 860
Greece	CDLS	189	159	156	288	294	203	500	465	366	506	425
Irish Republic	CDLT	1 659	2 048	2 743	3 333	4 169	4 436	4 587	6 282	6 182	7 517	27 164
Italy	CDLU	1 941	2 093	2 400	2 427	2 287	2 475	2 698	3 196	3 064	3 092	3 069
Netherlands	CDLV	6 442	8 287	8 369	11 980	23 190	25 228	29 906	37 676	48 240	49 678	69 033
Portugal	CDLW	739	865	1 032	1 171	1 195	932	1 210	1 190	1 023	1 020	985
Spain	CDLX	2 737	3 498	3 796	3 471	2 820	3 157	3 399	3 477	3 748	3 149	3 593
Sweden	CDMD	707	761	821	942	894	1 146	1 401	1 154	1 250	1 663	6 831
EFTA	CDLY	2 495	2 511	2 545	2 968	3 303	4 113	2 522	2 161	1 533	10 506	7 144
of which												
Norway	CDMC	549	522	542	736	803	1 513	1 244	1 171	1 116	428	1 391
Switzerland	CDME	1 943	1 989	2 003	2 232	2 500	2 594	1 279	988	415	10 073	5 750
Other European Countries	GQCK	306	329	415	626	636	918	1 103	1 520	5 658	9 742	11 700
of which												
Russia[1]	GQAA	10	9	10	20	7	26	120	238	401	200	282
UK offshore islands	GQAB	–	–	–	–	–	–	–	–	2 690	6 940	8 520
America	GQCU	66 515	62 381	62 939	74 868	77 003	75 390	83 275	67 592	80 324	137 860	207 212
of which												
Bermuda	CDOA	2 589	4 630	4 628	5 382	4 869	5 403	5 504	5 295	4 942	4 688	6 669
Brazil	CDOB	1 452	1 250	1 345	1 880	1 963	2 059	2 323	2 421	2 214	1 604	2 633
Canada	CDML	6 516	6 219	6 253	6 766	7 162	4 919	5 395	4 563	5 748	4 889	5 687
Chile	GQCT	252	207	363	416	481	439	666	670	970	1 099	1 075
Colombia	GQCS	..	..	594	1 109	839	1 071	1 207	1 274	1 197	558	977
Mexico	GQAC	314	405	428	504	419	334	350	553	1 327	797	1 035
Panama	GQAD	169	100	232	630	435	507	467	744	..	..	121
USA	CDMM	50 933	45 532	45 367	54 688	57 380	55 174	62 159	49 170	59 083	120 382	185 363
Asia	GQCL	7 996	8 285	9 633	12 230	14 118	16 095	18 038	19 916	19 389	20 777	25 319
Near and Middle East Countries	CDNH	373	314	749	748	698	754	788	676	917	2 646	1 064
of which												
Gulf Arabian countries[2]	GQCM	294	229	657	592	617	660	704	586	658	2 375	660
Other Asian Countries	GQCR	7 623	7 970	8 884	11 482	13 419	15 341	17 250	19 239	18 472	18 131	24 254
of which												
Hong Kong	CDNN	2 059	1 654	1 895	2 753	3 569	3 373	4 033	4 636	4 406	5 271	6 334
India	GQAE	312	341	302	245	490	601	498	532	703	700	868
Indonesia	GQAF	281	264	316	222	272	295	418	391	801	638	747
Japan	CDMP	1 398	1 591	1 674	1 998	1 936	2 613	2 397	2 437	1 605	1 844	3 679
Malaysia	CDNQ	690	706	845	1 285	1 750	2 119	1 813	2 164	2 411	1 900	2 076
Singapore	CDNT	2 134	2 449	2 691	3 516	3 706	4 445	5 287	5 822	5 186	5 600	5 964
South Korea	GQAG	45	57	69	114	155	183	250	238	154	218	555
Thailand	GQAH	138	205	253	359	404	511	920	1 053	1 009	621	564
Australasia and Oceania	GQCN	11 284	9 951	10 210	11 222	12 287	13 517	13 985	14 636	13 312	12 117	11 928
of which												
Australia	CDMO	9 979	8 924	9 057	9 605	10 299	11 153	11 365	12 213	10 598	9 017	9 387
New Zealand	CDMQ	1 069	696	700	930	1 443	1 689	1 670	1 640	1 663	1 617	1 749
Africa	GQCQ	4 526	3 868	4 039	4 080	4 570	5 409	4 955	4 876	5 873	4 254	9 884
of which												
Kenya	GQAI	246	267	233	249	165	673	276	237	361	414	454
Nigeria	CDNA	639	325	419	490	754	681	335	321	1 060	462	505
South Africa	CDMR	2 296	2 012	2 239	2 311	2 622	2 202	2 827	2 429	2 527	1 693	6 552
Zimbabwe	CDNF	435	402	324	411	248	331	262	200	192	114	154
World Total	CDOO	120 948	118 935	124 093	146 613	165 831	177 116	196 687	194 601	218 162	290 150	423 343
OECD	GQCO	100 632	97 637	100 517	118 430	136 247	142 332	159 476	157 652	175 434	246 158	366 007
Central & Eastern Europe[3]	GQCP	3	9	36	123	106	460	427	622	1 782	2 129	1 521

1 Prior to 1995 Russia covers other former USSR countries, the Baltic States and Albania.
2 Includes Abu Dhabi, Bahrain, Dubai, Iraq, Kuwait, Oman, Other Gulf States, Qatar, Saudi Arabia and Yemen.
3 Includes Albania, Belarus, Bulgaria, Croatia, Czech Republic, Estonia, Hungary, Latvia, Lithuania, Poland, Romania, Serbia and Montenegro, Slovakia and Slovenia.

Sources: ONS Foreign Direct Investment Inquiries: 01633 813314; Bank of England

18.15 Net earnings from foreign direct investment overseas by UK companies analysed by area and main country [1,2]

£ millions

		1989	1990	1991	1992	1993	1994	1995	1996	1997	1998	1999
Europe	GQCV	4 548	4 727	4 182	3 315	5 182	7 033	8 289	9 700	10 440	10 938	14 116
EU	CAWG	4 045	4 198	3 721	2 499	4 450	6 138	7 251	8 557	8 994	9 445	11 230
Austria	CBLQ	36	49	43	54	35	52	73	82	65	45	57
Belgium and Luxembourg	CAWH	299	165	259	404	412	387	308	358	297	608	362
Denmark	CAWI	86	91	71	115	207	115	286	208	191	207	227
Finland	CBLR	17	9	–	24	22	30	43	–	36	56	96
France	CAWJ	805	688	598	279	50	607	619	999	1 036	934	1 245
Germany	CAWK	595	623	617	260	381	834	1 032	951	844	755	1 235
Greece	CAWL	34	22	12	50	58	−202	−106	172	122	76	167
Irish Republic	CAWM	171	265	414	393	669	516	639	847	1 112	1 195	1 367
Italy	CAWN	173	220	175	75	113	219	272	327	268	319	411
Netherlands	CAWO	1 449	1 674	1 141	758	2 459	2 986	3 248	3 748	4 143	4 381	5 207
Portugal	CAWP	135	124	93	83	53	162	188	184	96	154	155
Spain	CAWQ	178	219	197	−5	39	234	338	493	561	429	391
Sweden	CBLT	68	50	103	12	−48	200	310	188	224	285	310
EFTA of which	CAWS	451	476	433	740	639	792	899	963	991	835	1 426
Norway	CBLS	114	242	214	281	119	267	224	311	242	123	245
Switzerland	CBLU	337	233	219	459	520	524	675	652	747	703	1 180
Other European Countries of which	GQCW	52	53	28	75	95	103	139	180	454	658	1 461
Russia[3]	GQAJ	..	1	..	..	2	3	12	24	−30	−214	4
UK offshore islands	GQAK	–	–	–	–	–	–	–	–	225	681	979
America of which	GQCX	7 525	6 962	4 624	5 530	6 126	8 007	10 254	10 698	11 867	11 820	12 964
Bermuda	CBNK	376	269	449	562	428	446	509	506	70	440	464
Brazil	CBNL	366	227	87	182	193	348	432	650	380	321	120
Canada	CAWW	650	464	189	175	283	357	374	571	913	832	879
Chile	GQCY	44	35	88	118	139	195	263	265	236	146	141
Colombia	GQCZ	41	64	21	−40	16	−22	28	23	53	2	76
Mexico	GQAL	8	12	−2	41	43	48	52	74	145	95	179
Panama	GQAM	11	54	17	−27	69	51	45	67	..	180	36
USA	CAWV	5 499	5 402	3 255	4 065	4 621	5 894	7 803	8 034	9 339	9 534	9 968
Asia	GQDA	1 873	2 114	2 355	2 636	2 792	3 449	2 501	3 776	3 249	4 086	2 741
Near and Middle East Countries of which	CBMS	221	235	303	342	283	297	262	241	475	920	493
Gulf Arabian countries[4]	GQDB	234	249	300	317	273	293	260	212	424	875	444
Other Asian Countries of which	GQDC	1 652	1 879	2 053	2 293	2 509	3 152	2 239	3 536	2 774	3 166	2 248
Hong Kong	CAYB	485	439	440	846	972	1 427	1 362	1 463	623	932	869
India	GQAN	63	88	77	−2	−190	121	100	81	124	192	189
Indonesia	GQAO	29	25	71	18	60	48	71	87	143	110	111
Japan	CAWY	125	72	115	182	142	199	212	281	313	164	443
Malaysia	CBNA	152	182	197	229	248	221	248	332	360	246	344
Singapore	CBND	611	967	1 010	839	977	781	−144	883	795	1 286	72
South Korea	GQAP	14	7	10	5	8	29	40	34	17	33	10
Thailand	GQAQ	30	34	17	28	78	84	75	101	95	17	134
Australasia and Oceania of which	GQDD	1 627	854	541	960	1 233	2 131	2 044	2 269	1 950	1 516	1 500
Australia	CBMB	1 590	925	535	809	991	1 776	1 587	1 747	1 503	1 078	1 152
New Zealand	CBMC	15	−98	5	73	213	302	322	319	278	145	283
Africa of which	GQDE	1 035	869	986	844	1 465	737	807	1 055	965	654	1 097
Kenya	GQAR	47	47	36	41	34	41	46	35	94	78	83
Nigeria	CBML	197	159	273	280	498	−27	−35	61	46	49	64
South Africa	CAWZ	595	410	425	280	488	366	438	503	521	395	641
Zimbabwe	CBMQ	80	73	81	77	54	58	58	50	58	53	73
World Total	GLAB	16 608	15 526	12 688	13 285	16 796	21 355	23 894	27 498	28 470	29 014	32 419
OECD	GQDF	12 425	11 486	8 279	8 624	11 454	15 578	18 567	20 621	22 601	22 244	25 857
Central & Eastern Europe[5]	GQDG	1	2	1	7	11	−24	16	15	118	70	294

1 A minus sign indicates net losses.
2 Net earnings equal profits of overseas branches plus UK companies' receipts of interest and their share of profits of overseas subsidiaries and associates. Earnings are after deducting provisions for depreciation and overseas tax on profits, dividends and interest.
3 Prior to 1995 Russia covers other former USSR countries, the Baltic States and Albania.

4 Includes Abu Dhabi, Bahrain, Dubai, Iraq, Kuwait, Oman, Other Gulf States, Qatar, Saudi Arabia and Yemen.
5 Includes Albania, Belarus, Bulgaria, Croatia, Czech Republic, Estonia, Hungary, Latvia, Lithuania, Poland, Romania, Serbia and Montenegro, Slovakia and Slovenia.

Sources: ONS Foreign Direct Investment Inquiries: 01633 813314;
Bank of England

18.16 Net inward Foreign direct investment in the UK analysed by area and main country [1,2]

£ millions

		1989	1990	1991	1992	1993	1994	1995	1996	1997	1998	1999
Europe	GQDH	7 971	8 042	4 910	4 044	2 202	3 065	4 626	6 931	8 394	21 455	32 298
EU	CAYO	5 617	7 628	4 578	3 433	1 589	3 367	3 555	4 673	6 905	11 407	32 772
Austria	CBOB	1	62	11	–45	13	60	21	20	18	126	–
Belgium and Luxembourg	CAYP	853	296	201	65	–427	357	520	6	174	1 008	464
Denmark	CAYQ	198	154	122	91	97	76	68	151	228	195	313
Finland	CBOC	56	36	8	54	–42	32	–36	2	193	130	230
France	CAYR	1 870	1 551	1 333	802	–37	310	1 004	1 321	2 647	649	3 717
Germany	CAYS	460	1 610	396	1 261	656	71	2 090	835	1 123	60	26 132
Greece	CAYT	..	..	..	..	..	..	..	..	..	..	..
Irish Republic	CAYU	230	229	137	–32	49	224	–35	221	1 127	663	174
Italy	CAYV	26	–42	45	–37	80	177	328	–184	–32	43	–12
Netherlands	CAYW	1 613	2 085	2 335	1 135	1 244	1 915	–633	2 610	1 180	8 609	837
Portugal	CAYX	..	..	..	..	..	..	..	..	..	..	..
Spain	CAYY	130	3	–11	3	14	21	17	66	71	81	153
Sweden	CBOE	185	1 658	5	129	–56	119	184	–379	147	–155	754
EFTA of which	CAZB	2 310	431	327	674	550	–176	1 036	2 211	1 512	9 703	–712
Norway	CBOD	–52	201	–71	–34	49	–131	124	1 060	182	–123	–510
Switzerland	CBOF	2 363	229	399	710	501	–44	912	1 151	1 320	9 822	–206
Other European Countries of which	GQDI	44	–17	5	–62	64	–125	36	47	–21	345	239
Russia[3]	GQAS	28	–26	–11	..	49	–	19	61	19	..	..
UK offshore islands	GQAT	–	–	–	–	–	–	–	–	–74	395	185
America of which	GQDJ	7 019	6 266	1 898	3 720	5 993	2 344	8 750	7 210	10 615	18 142	21 748
Canada	CAZF	610	–264	265	–45	33	–246	–438	444	374	–69	382
USA	CAZE	6 415	5 095	1 879	3 748	5 142	2 138	9 293	6 742	10 045	17 809	20 540
Asia	GQDK	1 378	1 931	255	630	570	186	–189	412	402	1 293	–2 745
Near and Middle East Countries	GQAU	114	–54	137	251	115	78	58	64	103	66	110
Other Asian Countries of which	GQAV	1 264	1 986	118	380	456	110	–248	348	299	1 227	–2 855
Hong Kong	GQAW	10	10	53	280	106	45	–124	10	15	42	168
Japan	CAZH	1 238	2 091	48	–21	277	4	–379	209	288	898	–2 999
Singapore	GQAX	4	9	7	9	14	2	40	1	41	7	–1
South Korea	GQAY	..	..	..	..	43	2	85	–8	–78	182	–122
Australasia and Oceania of which	GQDL	990	852	1 328	323	995	387	–647	992	714	931	–226
Australia	CBOJ	846	957	937	340	995	260	–708	1 096	721	1 045	..
New Zealand	CBOK	..	–105	391	–17	–	127	60	–104	–6	–113	..
Africa of which	GQAZ	47	64	27	99	111	63	117	118	170	801	194
South Africa	CAZJ	..	38	30	85	58	50	125	109	149	584	183
World Total	CBDH	17 405	17 155	8 418	8 816	9 871	6 046	12 654	15 662	20 296	42 622	51 266
OECD	GQBA	17 188	15 727	8 428	8 221	8 636	5 346	12 511	15 235	19 758	40 864	49 632
Central & Eastern Europe[4]	GQBB	4	–	–	–7	–	–141	15	–19	14	–2	1

1 Net investment includes unremitted profits.
2 A minus sign indicates net disinvestment in the UK.
3 Prior to 1995 Russia covers other former USSR countries, the Baltic States and Albania.
4 Includes Albania, Belarus, Bulgaria, Croatia, Czech Republic, Estonia, Hungary, Latvia, Lithuania, Poland, Romania, Serbia and Montenegro, Slovakia and Slovenia.

Sources: ONS Foreign Direct Investment Inquiries: 01633 813314;
Bank of England

309

18.17 UK inward foreign direct international investment position - book value of net liabilities analysed by area and main country at year end

£ millions

		1989	1990	1991	1992	1993	1994	1995	1996	1997	1998	1999
Europe	GQDM	37 610	40 606	45 205	46 928	47 770	47 281	52 144	55 856	58 037	73 385	113 741
EU	CDOT	28 711	33 707	38 036	39 547	40 266	39 998	43 493	43 774	44 927	62 225	103 695
Austria	CDPF	40	104	103	−30	93	428	412	280	79	175	57
Belgium and Luxembourg	CDOU	1 357	1 634	1 812	1 817	1 801	2 221	2 170	1 233	1 856	2 399	3 578
Denmark	CDOV	696	685	701	877	1 339	1 072	1 127	850	927	1 276	1 509
Finland	CDPG	291	423	364	437	300	356	352	334	444	623	796
France	CDOW	6 148	7 427	9 000	8 749	7 880	7 728	8 289	9 147	13 880	14 870	19 063
Germany	CDOX	2 543	4 239	4 597	5 627	5 921	5 589	8 854	9 508	10 078	10 173	34 814
Greece	CDOY	..	..	..	..	..	..	..	..	..	..	..
Irish Republic	CDOZ	491	1 069	840	865	681	956	686	703	1 837	2 357	2 580
Italy	CDPA	623	597	649	845	875	839	1 223	988	824	1 033	1 099
Netherlands	CDPB	14 571	14 182	16 547	16 715	18 477	18 511	17 173	18 692	12 131	26 089	35 704
Portugal	CDPC	..	..	..	..	..	..	..	..	..	..	..
Spain	CDPD	194	318	329	356	346	178	164	78	247	338	935
Sweden	CDPI	1 732	3 025	3 058	3 274	2 542	2 105	2 908	1 871	2 521	2 769	3 377
EFTA of which	CDPE	8 248	6 794	7 040	7 308	7 225	7 111	8 188	11 735	12 379	8 426	8 594
Norway	CDPH	725	748	661	647	701	506	665	1 571	1 866	1 481	476
Switzerland	CDPJ	7 521	6 044	6 375	6 657	6 519	6 605	7 523	10 164	10 422	6 868	8 038
Other European Countries of which	GQDN	651	105	129	73	280	172	463	348	731	2 734	1 453
Russia[1]	GQBC	374	18	18	−51	43	24	80	212	..	..	190
UK offshore islands	GQBD	−	−	−	−	−	−	−	−	341	2 257	970
America of which	GQDU	43 591	49 721	49 682	50 910	55 209	55 918	59 420	62 253	77 408	96 833	100 804
Canada	CDPM	4 935	4 104	4 427	4 065	4 101	4 593	2 652	3 517	4 129	3 653	6 677
USA	CDPN	37 093	43 784	44 434	46 001	49 537	49 829	55 129	55 956	70 270	89 255	90 155
Asia	GQDO	5 729	7 184	7 378	6 935	7 655	7 782	7 934	8 072	9 166	9 058	4 893
Near and Middle East Countries	GQBE	1 119	1 110	1 372	1 099	1 427	2 027	1 324	1 274	1 450	1 287	944
Other Asian Countries of which	GQBF	4 609	6 073	6 006	5 836	6 228	5 755	6 609	6 797	7 715	7 771	3 949
Hong Kong	GQBG	402	406	200	422	262	233	19	31	56	216	245
Japan	CDPQ	3 965	5 648	5 346	4 929	5 427	5 105	5 542	5 888	6 562	6 505	3 145
Singapore	GQBH	29	47	..	..	415	421	500	503	757	407	83
South Korea	GQBI	..	..	−43	−28	−3	−203	12	−206	−305	−99	−242
Australasia and Oceania of which	GQDP	6 297	7 937	8 715	9 135	9 560	9 644	8 527	7 707	7 354	7 491	6 879
Australia	CDPP	6 081	6 799	7 655	8 083	8 598	7 968	7 021	6 169	6 003	5 654	4 977
New Zealand	CDPR	..	912	832	824	844	1 676	1 506	1 538	1 351	1 492	1 030
Africa of which	GQBJ	357	313	393	501	811	712	861	766	991	1 595	1 116
South Africa	CDPS	..	263	342	438	618	549	665	578	743	1 220	941
World Total	CDPZ	93 554	105 760	111 373	114 409	121 005	121 336	128 885	134 654	152 956	188 362	227 433
OECD	GQBK	89 287	101 702	107 814	110 816	116 082	116 171	123 761	128 475	145 336	177 147	218 081
Central & Eastern Europe[2]	GQBL	238	29	29	24	21	10	258	14	24	53	78

1 Prior to 1995 Russia covers other former USSR countries, the Baltic States and Albania.
2 Includes Albania, Belarus, Bulgaria, Croatia, Czech Rebuplic, Estonia, Hungary, Latvia, Lithuania, Poland, Romania, Serbia and Montenegro, Slovakia and Slovenia.

Sources: ONS Foreign Direct Investment Inquiries: 01633 813314; Bank of England

18.18 Net earnings from foreign direct investment in the UK analysed by area and main country [1,2]

£ millions

		1989	1990	1991	1992	1993	1994	1995	1996	1997	1998	1999
Europe	GQDQ	2 734	2 007	1 243	2 482	4 833	3 661	5 432	6 401	5 746	729	7 715
EU	ÇBDJ	2 256	1 689	1 025	1 932	3 556	3 659	4 657	5 631	5 231	2 231	7 463
Austria	CBOR	−3	−8	..	..	−5	94	30	55	13	8	14
Belgium and Luxembourg	CBDK	72	−3	−53	−1	224	272	249	209	139	375	294
Denmark	CBDL	117	88	42	−17	92	18	152	137	171	236	212
Finland	CBOS	−10	−43	−71	−36	−52	2	88	74	80	63	95
France	CBDM	297	420	377	340	633	227	836	705	1 239	561	1 593
Germany	CBDN	117	169	22	221	576	507	700	706	563	−468	−350
Greece	CBDO	..	..	..	..	..	..	..	..	..	22	8
Irish Republic	CBDP	78	−4	−27	−12	74	92	155	141	222	357	435
Italy	CBDQ	30	−73	−55	−24	97	246	196	318	430	220	131
Netherlands	CBDR	1 443	1 148	927	1 731	1 820	2 076	2 070	3 053	2 034	510	4 631
Portugal	CBDS	..	..	..	..	..	..	..	..	..	−8	−1
Spain	CBDT	28	−	−29	−5	55	17	42	69	106	72	112
Sweden	CBOU	112	13	−56	−177	46	107	127	146	219	286	291
EFTA of which	CBDW	464	316	146	846	1 188	−33	685	709	408	−1 471	233
Norway	CBOT	42	17	−14	−35	27	12	11	−58	121	−182	−220
Switzerland	CBOV	423	301	338	885	1 161	−45	675	768	277	−1 294	448
Other European Countries of which	GQDR	13	2	−104	−296	88	36	89	60	108	−30	19
Russia[3]	GQBM	9	2	..	..	55	1	15	31	..	..	11
UK offshore islands	GQBN	−	−	−	−	−	−	−	−	33	25	−44
America of which	GQDV	6 072	5 131	2 948	2 391	4 917	4 992	5 824	7 589	6 775	5 912	7 836
Canada	CBEA	448	273	199	47	234	506	228	281	65	166	220
USA	CBDZ	5 492	4 602	2 951	2 284	4 441	4 372	5 606	6 986	6 512	5 436	7 754
Asia	GQDS	481	102	193	107	106	172	459	300	−332	−699	428
Near and Middle East Countries	GQBO	29	−119	−89	−31	16	−8	112	89	96	38	110
Other Asian Countries of which	GQBP	453	222	283	139	90	181	347	211	−428	−737	318
Hong Kong	GQBQ	−27	−23	47	207	52	4	−2	28	21	−195	182
Japan	CBEC	456	261	246	−41	45	171	334	151	−502	−462	137
Singapore	GQBS	2	−12	3	−2	4	1	5	−	41	−83	59
South Korea	GQBT	..	..	..	..	7	15	−6	−6	−11	−23	−68
Australasia and Oceania of which	GQDT	−185	−302	74	211	418	327	472	594	860	597	384
Australia	CBOZ	−194	−168	92	222	410	330	479	566	830	576	..
New Zealand	CBPA	9	−134	−18	..	8	−1	−6	28	..	..	..
Africa of which	GQBU	56	−6	3	..	19	25	49	44	55	4	127
South Africa	CBED	65	−6	−1	6	9	21	38	35	46	−24	111
World Total	CBEV	9 158	6 932	4 461	5 197	10 293	9 176	12 235	14 928	13 103	6 542	16 490
OECD	GQBV	8 844	6 831	4 878	5 371	9 998	9 118	12 081	14 388	12 583	6 550	16 164
Central & Eastern Europe[4]	GQBW	−	−	−	2	1	24	60	13	18	−13	5

1 A minus sign indicates net losses.
2 Net earnings equal profits of UK branches plus overseas investors' receipts of interest and their share of the profits of UK subsidiaries and associates. Earnings are after deducting provisions for depreciation and UK tax on profits and interest.

3 Prior to 1995 Russia covers other former USSR countries, the Baltic States and Albania.
4 Includes Albania, Belarus, Bulgaria, Croatia, Czech Republic, Estonia, Hungary, Latvia, Lithuania, Poland, Romania, Serbia and Montenegro, Slovakia and Slovenia.

Sources: ONS Foreign Direct Investment Inquiries: 01633 813314;
Bank of England

19 Research and development

Research and development

Research and development
(Tables 19.1 to 19.5)

Research and experimental development (R&D) is defined for statistical purposes as 'creative work undertaken on a systematic basis in order to increase the stock of knowledge, including knowledge of man, culture and society, and the use of this stock of knowledge to devise new applications'.

R&D is financed and carried out mainly by businesses, the Government, and institutions of higher education. A small amount is performed by non-profit-making bodies. Gross Expenditure on R&D (GERD) is an indicator of the total amount of R&D performed within the UK: it has been approximately 2 per cent of GDP in recent years. Detailed figures are reported each year in a First Release published in March and the August edition of the ONS's *Economic Trends*. Table 19.1 shows the main components of GERD.

The ONS conducts an annual survey of expenditure and employment on R&D performed by Government, and of Government funding of R&D. The survey collects data on outturn and planning years. Until 1993 the detailed results were reported in the *Annual Review of Government Funded R&D* produced by the Office of Science and Technology (OST). From 1997 the results have appeared in OST's *Science, Engineering and Technology Statistics* publication. Table 19.2 gives some broad totals for gross expenditure by Government (expenditure before deducting funds received by Government for R&D). Table 19.3 gives a breakdown of net expenditure (receipts are deducted).

The ONS conducts an annual survey of R&D in business. Tables 19.4 and 19.5 give a summary of the main trends up to 1999. The latest set of results from the survey will be available in a First Release dated 16 November 2001 and a Business Monitor (MA14) to be published in January 2002.

Statistics on expenditure and employment on R&D in Higher Education Institutions (HEIs) are based on information collected by Higher Education Funding Councils and HESA (Higher Education Statistics Agency). In 1994 a new methodology was introduced to estimate expenditure on R&D in HEIs. This is based on the allocation of various Funding Council Grants. Full details of the new methodology are contained in SET 2001 available on the Office of Science and Technology Web Site at http://www.dti.gov.uk/ost/

The most comprehensive international comparisons of resources devoted to R&D appear in Main Science and Technology Indicators published by the organisation for Economic Co-operation and Development (OECD). The Statistical Office of the European Union and the United Nations, also compile R&D statistics based on figures supplied by member states.

To make international comparisons more reliable the OECD have published a series of manuals giving guidance on how to measure various components of R&D inputs and outputs. The most important of these is the Frascati Manual which defines R&D and recommends how resources for R&D should be measured. The UK follows the Frascati Manual as far as possible.

For information on available aggregated data on Research and Development please contact Jane Morgan on 01633 813109, (e-mail jane.morgan@ons.gov.uk).

19.1 Cost of research and development: analysis by sector
United Kingdom

	Work performed within each sector													
	1993		1994		1995		1996		1997		1998		1999	
	£m	%	£m	%	£m	%	£m	%	£m	%	£m	%	£m	%
Sector carrying out the work (£m cash terms)														
Government	1 928	15	2 051	15	1 462	10	1 495	10	1 427	10	1 487	10	1 178	7
Research Councils	-	-	-	-	581	4	575	4	590	4	591	4	622	4
Business enterprise	8 717	66	8 842	65	9 116	65	9 297	65	9 556	65	10 133	66	11 302	68
Higher education	2 312	18	2 623	19	2 696	19	2 792	19	2 893	20	3 040	20	3 324	20
Private non-profit	232	2	168	1	177	1	177	1	190	1	203	1	231	1
Total	13 189	100	13 684	100	14 034	100	14 336	100	14 656	100	14 455	100	16 657	100

	Finance provided by each sector													
	1993		1994		1995		1996		1997		1998		1999	
	£m	%	£m	%	£m	%	£m	%	£m	%	£m	%	£m	%
Sector providing the funds (£m cash terms)														
Government	4 236	32	4 479	33	2 513	18	2 401	17	2 331	16	2 523	16	2 316	14
Research Councils	-	-	-	-	1 078	8	1 092	8	1 135	8	1 128	7	1 195	7
Higher Education Funding Councils	-	-	-	-	1 018	7	1 027	7	1 033	7	1 085	7	1 157	7
Higher education	103	1	116	1	119	1	120	1	123	1	130	1	143	1
Business enterprise[1]	6 840	52	6 905	50	6 766	48	6 818	48	7 321	50	7 356	48	8 216	49
Private non-profit	451	3	495	4	511	4	546	4	578	4	621	4	701	4
Abroad	1 560	12	1 690	12	2 029	14	2 332	16	2 136	15	2 610	17	2 930	18
Total	13 189	100	13 684	100	14 034	100	14 336	100	14 656	100	15 455	100	16 657	100

1 Including research associations and public corporations.

Source: Office for National Statistics: 01633 813109

19.2 Gross Central Government expenditure on research and development
United Kingdom

£ millions

	1994/95		1995/96		1996/97		1997/98		1998/99		1999/00	
	Intra-mural	Extra-mural[1]	Intra-mural	Extra-mural[1]	Intra-mural	Extra-mural[1]	Intra-mural	Extra-mural[1]	Intra-mural	Extra-mural[1]	Intra-mural	Extra-mural[1]
Defence	707	1451	692	1562	804	1429	774	1 639	818	1 436	520	1 979
Research councils	589	783	599	823	592	851	608	852	608	865	644	894
Higher Education Institutes	-	1 017	-	1 018	-	1 027	-	1 033	-	1 085	-	1 157
Other programmes	414	552	374	572	290	628	253	681	266	714	274	810
Total (excluding NHS)	1 710	3 803	1 665	3 975	1 686	3 935	1 635	4 205	1 692	4 100	1 439	4 840

1 Including work performed overseas and excluding monies spent with other government departments.

Source: Office for National Statistics: 01633 813109

19.3 Net central government expenditure on research and development, using European Union objectives for R&D expenditure

United Kingdom

£ millions

		1989 /90	1990 /91	1991 /92	1992 /93	1993 /94	1994 /95	1995 /96	1996 /97	1997 /98	1998 /99	1999 /00
Exploration and exploitation of the earth	KDVP	123.7	145.2	143.9	120.5	98.8	106.8	105.2	95.4	81.3	78.5	79.4
Infrastructure and general planning of land-use	KDVQ	71.7	74.1	64.2	85.6	96.7	98.1	94.1	98.8	98.9	103.5	104.4
Control of environmental pollution	KDVR	53.0	70.3	71.9	69.5	108.7	117.2	131.8	128.7	136.2	142.8	147.0
Protection and promotion of human health (ex NHS)	KDVS	264.1	292.0	298.4	341.5	383.1	397.2	416.0	427.4	444.8	450.1	519.5
Production, distribution and rational utilisation of energy	KDVT	157.7	141.7	133.0	120.0	96.8	55.5	52.3	43.2	41.0	28.0	29.0
Agricultural production and technology	KDVU	197.7	198.6	216.2	261.1	284.6	263.4	281.9	257.0	268.9	255.5	260.6
Industrial production and technology	KDVV	455.2	478.8	399.0	394.1	458.7	184.4	165.8	144.6	116.9	61.6	56.5
Social structures and relationships	KDVW	101.6	110.8	115.5	141.9	149.1	141.9	137.1	120.7	113.8	154.7	217.6
Exploration and exploitation of space	KDVX	146.3	155.2	134.2	149.1	187.4	161.5	153.0	164.1	164.4	142.5	142.7
Research financed from General University Funds	KDVY	799.0	835.0	919.1	963.3	968.4	1 017.9	1 018.6	1 027.5	1 033.3	1 085.1	1 157.1
Non-oriented research	KDVZ	257.3	287.6	287.6	337.1	267.3	612.5	653.5	680.5	671.0	677.0	700.5
Other civil research	KDWA	11.9	11.0	35.5	23.8	34.0	22.2	24.7	20.5	21.6	25.8	20.6
Defence	KDWB	2 132.7	2 154.7	2 208.8	2 071.1	2 268.6	2 021.9	2 098.9	2 143.5	2 312.1	2 099.5	2 346.8
Total (excluding NHS)	KDWC	4 771.8	4 955.1	5 027.4	5 078.6	5 402.3	5 200.4	5 332.9	5 351.8	5 504.2	5 304.5	5 781.6

Source: Office for National Statistics: 01633 813109

19.4 Intramural expenditure on business enterprise R&D At Current Prices and Constant Prices

United Kingdom

£ millions

		(i) Current Prices										
		Total				Civil				Defence		
		1997	1998	1999		1997	1998	1999		1997	1998	1999
Total	KDWD	9 556	10 133	11 302	KDWN	8 112	8 600	9 626	KDWX	1 443	1 533	1 675
Manufacturing Total	KDWE	7 383	7 909	8 783	KDWO	6 079	6 491	7 164	KDWY	1 304	1 417	1 618
Chemicals	KDWF	2 831	2 926	3 253	KDWP	2 829	2 926	3 252	KDWZ	2	–	1
Mechanical engineering	KDWG	709	730	712	KDWQ	407	455	434	KDXA	302	276	279
Electrical machinery	KJRT	1 181	1 320	1 335	KJTC	803	916	1 013	KJUL	377	404	322
Aerospace	KDWJ	893	1 039	1 237	KDWT	412	485	535	KDXD	481	554	701
Transport equipment	KDWK	990	1 020	1 235	KDWU	979	983	1 159	KDXE	11	36	77
Other manufacturing	KDWL	779	874	1 010	KDWV	648	727	771	KDXF	131	147	239
Services	KDWM	2 172	2 224	2 519	KDWW	2 034	2 108	2 462	KDXG	139	116	57

		(ii) 1995 Prices										
		Total				Civil				Defence		
		1997	1998	1999		1997	1998	1999		1997	1998	1999
Total	KDXH	9 003	9 276	10 089	KDXR	7 643	7 872	8 593	KDYB	1 359	1 403	1 495
Manufacturing Total	KDXI	6 956	7 240	7 841	KDXS	5 727	5 942	6 395	KDYC	1 229	1 297	1 444
Chemicals	KDXJ	2 667	2 678	2 904	KDXT	2 665	2 678	2 903	KDYD	2	–	1
Mechanical engineering	KDXK	668	668	636	KDXU	383	416	387	KDYE	285	253	249
Electrical machinery	KKKJ	1 113	1 208	1 192	KKKK	757	838	904	KKKX	355	370	287
Aerospace	KDXN	841	951	1 104	KDXX	388	444	478	KDYH	453	507	626
Transport equipment	KDXO	933	934	1 102	KDXY	922	900	1 035	KDYI	10	33	69
Other manufacturing	KDXP	734	800	902	KDXZ	610	665	688	KDYJ	123	135	213
Services	KDXQ	2 046	2 036	2 249	KDYA	1 916	1 930	2 198	KDYK	131	106	51

Source: Office for National Statistics: 01633 813109

19.5 Sources of funds for R&D within Business Enterprises in the United Kingdom

		Total				Civil				Defence		
		1997	1998	1999		1997	1998	1999		1997	1998	1999
Funds for Business Enterprise R&D £m cash terms												
Total	KDYL	9 556	10 133	11 302	KDYT	8 112	8 600	9 626	KDZB	1 443	1 533	1 675
Government funds	KDYM	915	1 094	1 157	KDYU	198	307	316	KDZC	717	787	841
Overseas funds	KDYN	1 800	2 238	2 570	KDYV	1 475	1 857	2 092	KDZD	325	381	478
Mainly own funds	KDYO	6 840	6 800	7 575	KDYW	6 439	6 435	7 219	KDZE	401	365	356
Funds for Business Enterprise R&D Percentage												
Total	KDYP	100	100	100	KDYX	100	100	100	KDZF	100	100	100
Government funds	KDYQ	10	11	10	KDYY	2	4	3	KDZG	50	51	50
Overseas funds	KDYR	19	22	23	KDYZ	18	22	22	KDZH	22	25	29
Mainly own funds	KDYS	72	67	67	KDZA	79	75	75	KDZI	28	24	21

Source: Office for National Statistics: 01633 813109

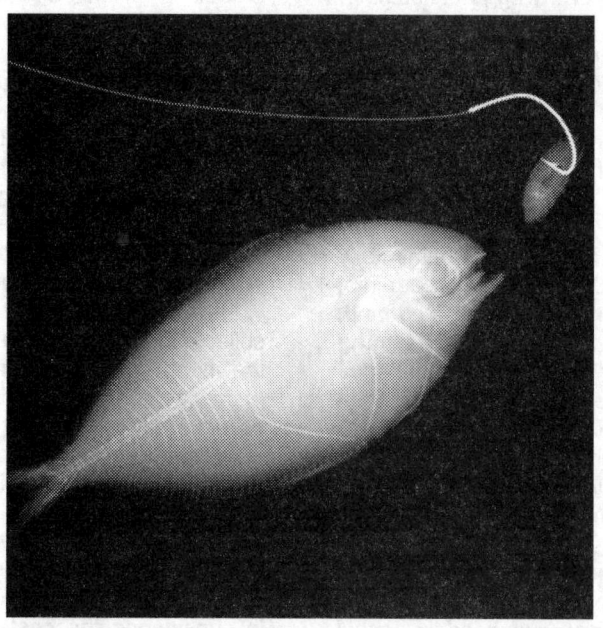

20 Agriculture, fisheries and food

Agriculture, fisheries and food

Output and input *(Tables 20.1 and 20.2)*
For both tables, output is a net of VAT collected on the sale of non-edible products. Figures for total output include subsidies on products, but not other subsidies.

Unspecified crops include turf, other minor crops and arable area payments for fodder maize. Eggs include the value of duck eggs and exports of eggs for hatching. Landlords' expenses are included within farm maintenance, miscellaneous expenditure and depreciation of buildings and works. Also included within "other farming costs" are livestock and crop costs, water costs, insurance premia, bank charges, professional fees, rates, and other farming costs.

Other subsidies
Agri-Environment schemes include Environmentally and Nitrate Sensitive Areas, Countryside Stewardship, Countryside Premium, Tir Cymen, Tir Gofal, Moorland, Habitat, Farm Woodland and Organic Farming Schemes. Included in "other" subsidies are guidance premium for beef and sheepmeat production, Pilot Beef and Sheep Extensification Scheme, non-agricultural horse grazing and farm accounts grant as well as historic data for fertiliser and lime grant and payments to small scale cereal producers.

Compensation of employees and interest charges
Total compensation of employees excludes the value of work done by farm labour on own account capital formation in buildings and work. "Interest" relates to interest charges on loans for current farming purposes and buildings and less interest on money held on short term deposit.

Rent
Rent paid (after deductions) is the rent paid on all tenanted land including "conacre" land in Northern Ireland, less landlords' expenses and the benefit value of dwellings on that land. Rent received (after deductions) is the rent received by farming landowners from renting of land to other farmers, less landlords' expenses and the benefit value of dwellings on that land. Total net rent is the net rent flowing out of the agricultural sector paid to non farming landowners, including that part of tenanted land in Northern Ireland. (Although there has been some updating of the technical procedures for calculating this figure, it corresponds with the previous net rent variable.)

Agricultural censuses and surveys
(Tables 20.3, 20.5 and 20.13)
The coverage for holdings includes all main and minor holdings for each country. Scotland now includes minor holdings and Northern Ireland data is now based on all active farm business, therefore data here will differ from previous editions.

Estimated quantity of crops and grass harvested *(Table 20.4)*
The estimated yields of sugar beet and hops are obtained from production figures supplied by British Sugar plc, and the main hop producers in England and Wales. In Great Britain potato yields are estimated in consultation with the British Potato Council.

Forestry *(Table 20.6)*
Statistics for state forestry are from the Annual Reports and Accounts of Forest Enterprise in Great Britain and the Forest Service in Northern Ireland.

For private forestry in Great Britain, statistics on new planting and restocking are based on records of the Woodland Grant Scheme, and timber removals are estimated from a survey of the largest timber harvesting companies. Productive woodland is based on data obtained from censuses of woodlands and adjusted to reflect subsequent changes. Figures are based on results from the 1995 National Inventory of Woodlands.

Average weekly earnings and hours of agricultural and horticultural workers *(Tables 20.7 and 20.8)*
Since 1998, data on the Earnings and Hours of Agricultural and Horticultural workers has been collected via an annual telephone survey. This annual survey collects information for a snapshot in time, relating to the month of September. The survey covers seven main categories of workers and in 1999 data was collected on about 1,200 workers. Prior to 1998, data was collected from a monthly postal survey, which mainly covered male full-time workers.

The survey provides data which is used by the Agricultural Wages Board when considering wage claims and by the Department for Environment, Food and Rural Affairs in considering the cost of labour in agriculture and horticulture.

Fisheries *(Tables 20.14 and 20.15)*
Data relating to the weight and value of landings of fish in the United Kingdom (Table 20.14) is generally obtained from sales notes completed at fish market auctions.

Fishing fleet information (Table 20.15) is obtained from vessel registers maintained by the Department for Environment, Food and Rural Affairs in England and Wales and the Scottish Executive Agriculture and Fisheries Department.

Estimated average household food consumption in Great Britain - National Food Survey *(Table 20.16)*

The sample
The National Food Survey results are derived from the responses of a random sample of private households throughout Great Britain. Although the survey was extended to include Northern Ireland in 1996, the results given are for Great Britain in order to preserve continuity. The person most responsible for the catering arrangements of the household is designated as the main diary keeper; he or she records details of all items of food for human consumption brought into the home during the course of a week. Until 1997 about 8,000 households in Great Britain participated in the Survey. From 1997 a more efficient sample design was introduced and the sample for Great Britain was reduced to around 6,000 households. A description of the sampling methods is given in the annual reports; the latest is *National Food Survey* 2000.

Household

A group of persons living in the same dwelling and sharing common catering arrangements. The size of the household is defined in terms of the number of persons who spend at least four nights in the household during the week of the survey and also have at least one meal a day from the household food supply on at least four days. The head of the household and the main diary keeper are regarded as 'persons' in all cases.

Food obtained for consumption

Purchases of selected foods for home consumption during the Survey week (including purchases in bulk and, exceptionally, school milk) plus any garden or allotment produce, etc, consumed during the week. For a few minor miscellaneous items, expenditure is recorded but not the quantity (eg artificial sweeteners). The survey also includes information on confectionery and soft and alcoholic drinks brought home and, published from 1994, on food and drink consumed outside the home.

Although the quantity of food purchased or obtained free during the survey week will differ from the actual consumption of an individual household, the average quantity of food for a large number of households will equal the average consumption if there is no general change in the level of larder stocks.

20.1 Outputs, inputs and income at current prices
United Kingdom
Calendar years

£ millions

		1990	1991	1992	1993	1994	1995	1996	1997	1998	1999	2000[1]
Outputs												
Cereals:												
wheat	KFKA	1 426	1 689	1 682	1 783	1 723	2 079	2 315	1 851	1 652	1 525	1 585
barley	KFKB	776	714	855	845	846	1 109	1 183	977	781	735	693
oats	KFKC	53	52	58	72	81	89	86	71	61	58	65
rye, mixed corn and triticale	KFKD	4	3	4	6	7	9	9	9	8	8	8
1. Total production of cereals	KFKF	2 259	2 458	2 599	2 704	2 657	3 285	3 593	2 907	2 502	2 326	2 350
Other crops:												
oilseed rape	KFKG	240	357	288	411	376	380	422	409	410	365	250
linseed	KIBT	13	40	84	183	39	40	40	52	67	132	34
sugar beet	KFKH	276	310	386	353	343	355	358	329	299	277	253
hops	KFKI	15	21	18	21	20	17	20	20	15	13	11
peas and beans for stockfeed	KFKJ	117	107	124	186	147	135	129	129	112	115	111
hay and dried grass	KFKK	29	28	24	25	27	30	29	28	23	24	24
grass and clover seed	KFKL	18	15	15	14	16	15	21	23	20	20	11
straw	LUJX	213	165	116	219	249	321	222	169	184	188	218
unspecified crops	LUJY	40	44	33	46	55	56	61	52	51	53	54
2. Total production of other crops	KFKN	961	1 086	1 087	1 458	1 271	1 348	1 301	1 210	1 181	1 185	965
3. Total production of potatoes	KFKO	574	527	533	390	710	1 095	636	390	630	750	501
Horticulture:												
vegetables	KFKP	1 019	986	916	915	998	1 064	1 080	960	984	956	974
fruit	KFKQ	253	282	280	271	245	257	291	199	242	259	250
ornamentals	KFKR	506	524	526	567	605	630	678	671	659	719	714
fruit, vegetables and tomato seeds	KFKS	6	6	9	8	7	7	7	7	7	7	7
4. Total production of horticulture	KFKT	1 790	1 798	1 731	1 760	1 855	1 959	2 056	1 836	1 893	1 941	1 945
Livestock												
finished cattle and calves	KFKU	1 944	2 051	1 999	2 372	2 468	2 580	2 546	2 276	1 982	2 058	2 011
finished sheep and lambs	KFKV	1 013	1 138	1 159	1 245	1 235	1 334	1 295	1 194	1 130	1 001	982
finished pigs	KFKW	1 072	1 023	1 149	1 043	1 037	1 177	1 373	1 203	887	787	826
poultry	KFKX	1 079	1 084	1 128	1 268	1 362	1 353	1 523	1 491	1 366	1 273	1 298
other livestock	KFKY	112	119	125	128	130	134	143	148	147	149	152
5. Total production of livestock	KFLA	5 220	5 415	5 560	6 055	6 231	6 578	6 879	6 312	5 512	5 267	5 268
Livestock products:												
milk	KFLB	2 793	2 790	2 925	3 187	3 288	3 498	3 495	3 154	2 709	2 654	2 340
eggs	KFLC	430	398	387	413	412	383	453	415	381	344	368
clip wool	KFLD	49	43	41	30	46	46	40	35	24	21	22
unspecified livestock products	KFLE	26	21	23	24	22	24	23	25	21	25	23
6. Total production of livestock products	KFLF	3 298	3 251	3 376	3 654	3 768	3 951	4 011	3 628	3 135	3 045	2 794
Capital formation in livestock												
cattle	KUJZ	314	265	426	624	568	414	297	391	295	201	141
sheep	LUKA	167	129	139	134	151	149	150	198	154	55	61
pigs	LUKB	15	16	18	14	14	16	20	15	5	6	7
poultry	LUKC	106	110	114	117	111	122	130	130	135	125	127
7. Total capital formation in livestock	KFLI	602	520	698	889	844	701	596	735	588	387	336

20.1
continued

Outputs, inputs and income at current prices
United Kingdom
Calendar years

£ millions

		1990	1991	1992	1993	1994	1995	1996	1997	1998	1999	2000[1]
Other agricultural activities												
contract work	LUKD	392	413	437	471	502	553	608	575	572	613	650
leasing out milk quota	LUKE	44	32	42	104	127	136	169	120	99	92	29
leasing out ewe premium	LUKF	–	–	–	5	6	6	5	4	4	4	4
leasing out suckler cow premium	LUKG	–	–	–	1	1	1	1	1	6	3	3
8. Total other agricultural activities	LUOS	419	445	479	580	635	697	783	700	681	712	686
9. Total inseparable non-agricultural activities	LUOT	225	246	267	294	321	325	360	369	432	441	479
10. Gross output at basic prices	KFLT	15 365	15 747	16 331	17 784	18 294	19 938	20 214	18 087	16 560	16 053	15 324
11. Total subsidies (less taxes) on product	LUOU	448	660	805	1 763	1 686	2 107	2 782	2 588	2 437	2 383	2 226
12. Output at market prices (10-11)	LUOV	14 917	15 087	15 527	16 021	16 608	17 832	17 432	15 499	14 123	13 670	13 098
of which												
transactions within the agricultural industry	LUNP	..	..	..	..	..	..	..	..	..	..	..
feed wheat	LUNQ	62	95	114	81	75	55	67	77	80	65	48
feed barley	LUNR	228	255	265	233	201	199	206	193	164	148	136
feed oats	LUNS	19	22	19	21	22	17	16	12	12	14	12
seed potatoes	LUNT	25	17	23	13	14	41	34	10	12	25	9
straw	LUNU	203	156	109	207	236	308	212	160	173	176	205
contract work	LUNV	392	413	437	471	502	553	608	575	572	613	650
leasing of quota	LUNW	44	32	42	109	133	144	175	124	109	99	36
total capital formation in livestock	LUNX	602	520	698	889	844	701	596	735	588	387	336
Intermediate consumption (expenditure net of reclaimed VAT)												
Feedingstuffs												
compounds[2]	LUNY	1 761	1 734	1 671	1 764	1 689	1 806	1 960	1 772	1 524	1 402	1 287
straights[2]	LUNZ	771	763	796	834	888	963	937	750	667	632	685
feed purchased from other farms	LUOA	308	371	399	336	297	271	289	282	254	226	196
other costs	LUOB	–	–	69	72	76	84	80	71	68	69	..
13. Total feedingstuffs	KFMB	2 841	2 868	2 865	2 934	2 875	3 040	3 185	2 804	2 444	2 260	2 167
Seeds												
cereals	KFMC	121	123	114	114	112	121	124	103	84	94	87
other	KFMD	205	189	201	183	213	262	256	234	250	240	209
14. Total seeds	KFME	326	312	315	297	326	384	380	337	334	334	296
15. Total fertilisers and lime	KFMM	924	912	836	760	798	916	1 040	990	827	752	826
16. Pesticides	KFMN	516	546	531	548	558	590	647	675	653	618	543
Farm maintenance												
occupier	KCOZ	201	202	226	248	282	304	295	292	250	248	239
landlord	KCPA	63	64	64	64	64	64	69	72	71	69	66
17. Total farm maintenance	KCPB	264	265	291	312	346	368	364	364	321	317	305
Miscellaneous expenditure												
machinery repairs	KFMO	579	612	601	638	631	722	706	678	659	645	625
machinery fuel and oil	KFMP	324	335	328	349	343	354	400	397	369	401	539
veterinary expenses and medicines	KCPC	211	222	231	253	274	289	298	308	290	276	271
power and fuel (mainly electricity)	KCPD	213	252	245	246	245	240	250	233	224	217	237
imported livestock	LUOC	40	31	37	35	33	25	19	23	14	18	..
straw for bedding	LUOD	203	156	109	207	236	308	212	160	173	176	205
contract work	LUOE	392	413	437	471	502	553	608	575	572	613	650
leasing of quota	LUOF	44	32	42	109	133	144	175	124	109	99	36
other farming costs	KCPG	1 267	1 439	1 593	1 645	1 697	1 718	1 883	2 006	1 974	1 999	1 979
18. Total miscellaneous expenses	KCPH	2 696	2 874	3 012	3 323	3 473	3 734	3 880	3 852	3 777	3 807	3 766

20.1 Outputs, inputs and income at current prices
United Kingdom

continued   Calendar years

£ millions

		1990	1991	1992	1993	1994	1995	1996	1997	1998	1999	2000[1]
19. Total intermediate consumption	KCPM	8 103	8 363	8 422	8 768	8 962	9 626	10 146	9 651	8 949	8 705	8 678
20. Gross value added at basic prices (10-19)	LUOG	7 262	7 284	7 910	9 016	9 331	10 313	10 069	8 435	7 610	7 348	6 646
Consumption of Fixed Capital												
buildings and works	LUOH	691	636	568	568	582	640	637	632	626	616	601
landlord	KCPP	123	115	105	105	110	120	95	85	83	78	76
other	KCPQ	568	520	463	463	472	520	542	547	543	537	525
plant, machinery and vehicles	KCPR	1 062	1 098	1 110	1 142	1 180	1 230	1 250	1 253	1 235	1 212	1 181
cattle	LUOI	283	318	330	577	529	416	314	393	316	210	246
sheep	LUOJ	150	148	120	137	141	174	189	155	106	68	91
pigs	LUOK	14	16	18	14	15	17	18	15	9	8	8
poultry	LUOL	103	109	118	108	108	121	130	123	147	137	129
21. Total Consumption of Fixed Capital	KCPS	2 302	2 325	2 263	2 546	2 554	2 598	2 539	2 572	2 438	2 251	2 257
22. Net value added (at basic prices)(20-21)	KCPT	4 960	5 059	5 647	6 470	6 777	7 715	7 530	5 864	5 172	5 097	4 389
Other subsidies												
animal disease compensation	LUOM	6	7	6	10	7	7	5	15	15	23	29
set-aside	LUON	–	–	–	142	206	198	160	90	88	170	130
Agri-Environment schemes	ZBXC	10	14	23	36	56	80	85	103	132	166	193
other	LUOO	–	–	–	–	–	–	–	–	–	–	–
vehicle licenses	ZBXD	27	32	34	40	42	46	54	56	59	59	58
23. Total other subsidies less taxes	LUOP	–37	–30	–25	125	201	212	169	125	145	269	263
24. Net value added at factor cost(22+23)	LUOQ	4 923	5 029	5 622	6 595	6 978	7 927	7 699	5 989	5 317	5 366	4 652
25. Total compensation of employees	LUOR	1 715	1 779	1 784	1 787	1 828	1 836	1 881	1 930	1 978	2 015	1 853
26. Interest	KCPU	1 010	837	715	525	539	590	556	626	688	608	689
Rent												
net rent paid	ZBXE	151	161	175	179	182	176	303	336	331	321	299
net rent received[3]	ZBXF	..	..	..	..	..	..	74	80	81	82	71
27. Net rent expenditure	KCPV	151	161	175	179	182	176	229	256	250	239	228
28. Total income from farming (24-25-26-27)	KCQB	2 047	2 253	2 948	4 105	4 430	5 325	5 033	3 177	2 401	2 505	1 882

1 Provisional
2 For years prior to 1992 the split between compounds and straights has been estimated based on the split present in later years.
3 This series starts in 1996 following a revision to the methodology of calculating net rent.

Source: Department for Environment, Food and Rural Affairs: 01904 455089

20.2 Output and input volume indices
United Kingdom
Calendar years

1995=100

		1990	1991	1992	1993	1994	1995	1996	1997	1998	1999	2000
Outputs[1]												
Cereals:												
wheat	LUKH	95	103	98	90	93	100	111	105	108	104	115
barley	LUKI	104	95	108	88	88	100	115	112	101	94	96
oats	LUKJ	77	74	76	73	89	100	93	92	90	82	97
rye, mixed corn and triticale	LUKK	96	79	90	86	91	100	96	95	89	106	118
1. Total production of cereals	LUKL	97	99	100	89	91	100	112	107	105	100	108
Other crops:												
oilseed rape	LUKM	80	105	99	90	100	100	113	122	126	138	96
linseed	LUKN	77	202	279	239	116	100	107	132	178	352	137
sugar beet	LUKO	94	103	120	115	113	100	124	131	119	126	111
hops	LUKP	112	146	116	128	108	100	126	120	82	70	64
peas and beans for stockfeed	LUKQ	134	115	119	160	128	100	101	123	116	124	129
hay and dried grass	LUKR	129	129	107	109	104	100	102	97	82	84	83
grass and clover seed	LUKS	176	136	126	116	133	100	98	107	97	103	76
straw	LUKT	87	75	65	74	78	100	85	74	71	63	66
unspecified crops[2]	LUKU	57	55	53	62	65	100	104	103	102	111	108
2. Total production of other crops	LUKV	93	102	104	104	97	100	107	113	110	120	98
3. Total production of potatoes	LUKW	100	97	122	105	99	100	108	102	90	106	92
Horticulture:												
vegetables	LUKX	104	107	111	107	107	100	106	101	99	100	96
fruit	LUKY	109	114	128	106	104	100	104	77	94	96	109
ornamentals	LUKZ	92	92	96	96	97	100	95	89	87	90	91
fruit, vegetable and tomato seeds	LULA	104	106	114	98	98	100	98	96	97	93	88
4. Total production of horticulture	LULB	101	103	108	103	103	100	102	94	94	96	97
Livestock												
finished cattle and calves	LULC	101	105	97	92	99	100	75	75	77	78	83
finished sheep and lambs	LULD	100	103	100	100	99	100	95	92	98	100	96
finished pigs	LULE	97	101	101	103	106	100	101	110	112	103	89
poultry	LULF	96	86	87	92	98	100	104	107	108	105	106
other livestock	LULG	96	95	102	99	98	100	101	103	103	103	103
5. Total production of livestock	LULH	95	99	96	96	100	100	90	92	94	93	93
Livestock products:												
milk	LULI	103	100	99	100	101	100	100	101	99	101	98
eggs[3]	LULJ	101	105	102	101	101	100	100	103	105	101	104
clip wool	LULK	110	105	105	100	97	100	95	97	103	95	93
unspecified	LULL	131	102	112	111	92	100	85	90	80	95	83
6. Total production of livestock products	LULM	103	101	100	100	101	100	99	101	100	101	98
Capital formation in livestock:												
cattle	LULN	103	101	100	100	101	100	99	101	100	101	98
sheep	LULO	115	78	119	99	135	100	84	131	141	105	86
pigs	LULP	173	169	184	168	144	100	182	191	31	35	27
poultry	LULQ	95	93	89	102	101	100	101	109	100	94	96
7. Total capital formation in livestock	LULR	107	84	120	115	119	100	95	115	112	107	82
Other agricultural activities												
contract work	LULS	93	91	91	93	96	100	105	108	114	122	127
leasing out milk quota	LULT	57	65	68	79	91	100	103	112	120	130	66
leasing out ewe premium	LULU	87	87	87	87	91	100	72	51	60	61	60
leasing out suckler cow premium	LULV	52	52	52	52	51	100	76	62	417	189	145
8. Total other non-agricultural activities	LULW	87	87	87	90	94	100	104	108	115	123	119
9. Total inseparable non-agricultural activities	LULX	84	86	90	96	102	100	108	110	123	124	131

Source: Department for Environment, Food and Rural Affairs: 01904 455080

20.2 Output and input volume indices
United Kingdom
continued Calendar years

1995=100

		1990	1991	1992	1993	1994	1995	1996	1997	1998	1999	2000
10. Gross output (at basic prices)[4]	LULY	97	99	100	98	100	100	100	100	101	102	100
of which												
transactions within the agricultural industry												
feed wheat	LULZ	112	161	190	141	146	100	122	180	212	177	148
feed barley	LUMA	109	121	124	107	105	100	105	126	124	114	112
feed oats	LUMB	97	113	94	95	119	100	89	82	89	98	92
seed potatoes	LUMC	117	104	132	121	88	100	119	93	96	87	93
straw	LUMD	86	74	64	73	78	100	85	73	70	61	64
contract work	LUME	93	91	91	93	96	100	105	108	114	122	127
leasing of quota	LUMF	57	65	69	79	91	100	101	109	121	127	68
total capital formation in livestock	LUMG	107	84	120	115	119	100	95	115	112	107	82
Intermediate Consumption (formerly known as inputs) (Expenditure net of reclaimed VAT)												
Feedingstuffs:												
compounds	LUMH	95	94	95	98	100	100	101	97	95	98	91
straights	LUMI	87	85	87	86	113	100	92	86	87	88	92
feed purchased from other farms	LUMJ	109	128	135	113	114	100	108	134	140	126	118
other costs	LUMK	94	94	94	97	100	100	99	98	100	..	..
13. Total feedingstuffs	LUML	94	95	96	96	101	100	99	97	96	97	94
Seeds:												
cereals	LUMM	111	107	93	96	95	100	104	95	87	97	93
other	LUMN	105	100	104	103	99	100	101	95	94	93	92
14. Total seeds	LUMO	108	103	100	100	98	100	102	95	92	94	92
15. Total fertilisers and lime	LUMP	103	101	100	97	102	100	99	111	108	102	100
16. Pesticides	LUMQ	102	99	95	97	93	100	103	106	110	106	106
Farm maintenance:[5]												
occupier	LUMR	76	74	82	87	97	100	95	96	83	82	79
landlord	LUMS	105	105	105	104	102	100	97	97	95	93	92
17. Total farm maintenance	LUMT	81	80	86	90	98	100	95	96	85	84	82
Miscellaneous expenditure:												
machinery repairs	LUMU	102	102	93	94	90	100	98	94	92	90	87
machinery fuel and oil	LUMV	100	102	100	102	103	100	100	101	99	95	91
veterinary expenses and medicines	LUMW	80	81	82	89	96	100	101	103	94	89	89
power and fuel (mainly electricity)	LUMX	95	107	99	100	102	100	99	98	103	98	103
imported livestock	LUMY	240	181	209	125	124	100	85	108	76	..	..
straw for bedding	LUMZ	86	74	64	73	78	100	85	73	70	61	64
contract work	LUNA	93	91	91	93	96	100	105	108	114	122	127
leasing of quota	LUNB	57	65	69	79	91	100	101	109	121	127	68
other farming costs[5,6]	LUNC	93	96	102	101	102	100	107	108	107	108	105
18. Total miscellaneous expenses	LUND	93	93	93	94	96	100	102	102	101	102	100
19. Total intermediate consumption (formerly known as Gross input)	LUNE	95	95	95	96	98	100	100	101	100	99	97
20. Gross Value Added (10-19)	LUNF	100	102	106	100	101	100	99	99	101	105	103
Consumption of fixed capital:												
buildings and works	LUNG	99	100	100	100	100	100	99	99	98	96	94
landlord[5]	LUNH	113	106	96	95	95	100	97	102	79	77	77
other		97	98	101	101	101	100	100	98	102	101	98
plant, machinery and vehicles	LUNI	104	102	100	99	99	100	101	102	101	99	96
cattle	LUNJ	82	96	79	88	87	100	105	94	89	91	97
sheep	LUNK	83	77	82	86	102	100	97	79	81	92	94
pigs	LUNL	92	103	104	101	110	100	92	101	111	101	88
poultry	LUNM	95	94	96	92	98	100	103	103	110	104	99
21. Total consumption of Fixed Capital	LUNN	96	97	94	95	97	100	101	99	98	97	95
22. Net value added (at basic prices)	LUNO	101	104	111	101	102	100	98	99	103	108	107

1 Output is net of VAT collected on the sale of non-edible products. Figures for total output include subsidies on products, but not other subsidies.
2 Includes turf, other minor crops and arable area payments for fodder maize.
3 Includes the value of duck eggs and exports of eggs for hatching.
4 Gross Output at basic prices includes subsidies (less taxes) on products.

5 Landlords' expenses are included within farm maintenance, miscellaneous expenditure and depreciation of buildings and works.
6 Includes livestock and crop costs, water costs, insurance premia, bank charges, professional fees, rates, vehicle licence costs and other farming costs.

Source: Department for Environment, Food and Rural Affairs: 01904 455080

20.3 Agriculture land-use
United Kingdom
Area at the June census[1]

Thousand hectares

		1990	1991	1992	1993	1994	1995	1996	1997	1998	1999	2000
Total Agricultural area	KFEU	18 884	18 853	18 849	18 890	18 850	18 746	18 750	18 653	18 604	18 579	18 304
Crops	KSJA	5 015	4 957	4 982	4 520	4 470	4 544	4 722	4 990	4 971	4 709	4 665
Bare fallow	KIJQ	68	67	53	50	46	43	37	29	34	33	37
Total tillage	KIJR	5 082	5 024	5 035	4 569	4 516	4 586	4 759	5 020	5 005	4 742	4 702
All grass under 5 years old	KFEM	1 606	1 608	1 584	1 582	1 456	1 407	1 395	1 405	1 301	1 226	1 226
Total arable land	KFEN	6 689	6 632	6 618	6 152	5 972	5 993	6 154	6 425	6 306	5 968	5 928
All grasses 5 years old and over	KFEO	5 316	5 327	5 279	5 274	5 388	5 375	5 354	5 282	5 364	5 449	5 364
Total tillage and grass	KFEP	12 005	11 959	11 897	11 426	11 360	11 368	11 507	11 706	11 671	11 417	11 292
Sole right rough grazing	KFEQ	4 965	4 950	4 943	4 879	4 825	4 785	4 760	4 657	4 621	4 575	4 437
Set aside[2]	KSJB	72	97	160	677	728	633	509	306	313	572	567
All other land on agricultural holdings including woodland	KSJC	607	614	618	680	712	734	751	763	773	789	779
Total land on agricultural holdings	KSJD	17 648	17 620	17 619	17 661	17 626	17 520	17 527	17 432	17 377	17 352	17 075
Common rough grazing (estimated)	KFER	1 236	1 233	1 230	1 229	1 224	1 226	1 223	1 221	1 227	1 227	1 229
Crops	KSJE	5 015	4 957	4 982	4 520	4 470	4 544	4 722	4 990	4 971	4 709	4 665
Cereals	KSJF	3 660	3 501	3 489	3 033	3 043	3 182	3 359	3 514	3 418	3 141	3 348
Wheat	KFDA	2 014	1 981	2 067	1 759	1 811	1 859	1 976	2 036	2 045	1 847	2 086
Barley	KFDB	1 518	1 395	1 299	1 166	1 108	1 193	1 269	1 359	1 253	1 179	1 128
Oats	KFDC	107	104	100	92	109	112	96	100	98	92	109
Mixed corn	KFDD	4	4	4	3	3	3	3	2	2	2	2
Rye[3]	KFDE	8	9	8	6	7	8	8	9	10	8	7
Triticale[4]	KIHX	9	10	11	7	6	7	7	8	11	13	16
Other arable crops (excluding potatoes)	KSJG	970	1 074	1 115	1 128	1 073	1 003	996	1 126	1 193	1 211	979
Oilseed rape	KFEH	390	440	421	377	404	354	356	445	507	417	332
Sugar beet not for stock feeding[3]	KFEG	194	196	197	197	195	196	199	196	189	183	173
Hops[5]	KIHZ	4	4	4	3	3	3	3	3	3	3	2
Peas for harvesting dry and field beans	KSJH	216	203	208	244	228	195	178	197	213	202	208
Linseed[6]	KSJI	34	92	144	150	58	54	49	73	100	209	71
Other crops	KSJJ	132	141	141	157	185	201	211	211	211	197	192
Potatoes	KGRS	177	177	181	171	164	172	178	166	164	178	166
Horticultural	KSJK	208	204	198	188	189	187	189	184	180	179	172
Vegetables grown in the open	KSJL	142	139	135	126	127	130	132	126	125	126	119
Orchard fruit	KSJM	34	34	33	32	32	28	28	30	30	28	28
Soft fruit	KSJN	15	15	14	13	13	12	12	11	10	9	10
Ornamentals[7]	KSJO	14	14	14	14	14	15	14	14	13	12	14
Glasshouse crops	KFEP	2	2	2	2	2	2	2	2	2	2	2

1 Includes estimates for minor holdings for all countries. In previous editions minor holdings were excluded for Scotland and therefore data here will differ from previous editions. Also, Northern Ireland data are now based on all active farm business.
2 Figures are for England only in 1990 and 1991 and Great Britain only in 1992.
3 Figures are for England and Wales only.
4 Figures are for Great Britain only.
5 Figures are for England only
6 Figures are for England and Wales only in 1990 and 1991 and Great Britain only in 1992
7 Includes non-commercial orchards.

Source: Agricultural Departments: 01904 455332

20.4 Estimated quantity of crops and grass harvested[1,2]
United Kingdom

Thousand tonnes

		1990	1991	1992	1993	1994	1995	1996	1997	1998	1999	2000
Cereals												
Wheat	KFQA	14 035	14 362	14 095	12 890	13 320	14 310	16 100	15 020	15 450	14 870	16 700
Barley	KFQB	7 911	7 632	7 368	6 050	5 950	6 840	7 790	7 830	6 620	6 580	6 490
Oats	KFQC	520	522	503	480	600	615	590	575	585	540	640
Mixed corn for threshing	KFQD	17	15	16	14	13	16	12	11	7	11	13
Rye for threshing	KFQE	40	49	37	30	43	43	51	53	55	43	44
Maize for threshing	KFQF	1 035	1 695	1 975	2 730	..	..	..	..	..	..	..
Potatoes												
Early crop	KFQG	437	359	411	426	337	373	325	386	336	341	..
Main crop	KFQH	6 106	6 000	7 402	6 647	6 203	6 033	6 900	6 739	6 081	6 759	..
Fodder crops												
Beans for stockfeeding	KFQI	474	423	445	612	454	319	318	377	378	397	450
Turnips, swedes	KFQJ	920	835	760	620	..	..	..	..	..	..	..
Fodder beet and mangolds	KFQK	640	715	710	655	..	..	..	..	..	..	..
Maize for threshing or stock-feeding	KFQL	..	..	..	..	..	..	..	..	..	..	..
Kale, cabbage, savoys and kohl rabi	KFQN	535	610	515	485	..	..	..	..	..	..	..
Peas harvested dry for stock-feeding	KFQP	320	224	209	266	246	229	239	297	259	286	253
Other crops												
Sugar beet[3]	KFQQ	7 902	8 701	10 148	9 666	8 720	8 431	10 420	11 084	10 002	10 584	9 335
Rape grown for oilseed	KFQR	1 258	1 278	1 166	1 100	1 243	1 224	1 415	1 527	1 566	1 737	1 129
Hops	KFQS	5	6	5	6	5	4	6	5	4	..	..
Horticultural crops												
Vegetables grown in the open												
Brussels sprouts	KFQW	91	100	98	102	93	74	83	74	71	79	63
Cabbage (including savoys and spring greens)	KFQX	406	395	379	381	356	377	348	280	286	268	251
Cauliflowers	KFQY	295	317	309	312	268	247	217	191	192	168	152
Carrots	KFQZ	492	536	532	605	567	525	679	591	626	702	455
Parsnips	KFRA	46	50	56	69	65	66	88	92	99	95	77
Turnips and swedes	KFRB	143	156	161	141	137	124	136	107	121	126	106
Beetroot	KFRC	87	83	104	84	89	72	72	72	66	61	72
Onions, Dry bulb	KFRD	224	231	216	322	245	254	313	329	376	406	379
Onions, Salad	KFRE	23	26	24	25	25	25	30	25	25	27	14
Leeks	KFRF	64	72	66	60	57	61	44	49	55	46	40
Broad beans	KFRG	13	20	17	11	12	11	10	10	13	12	13
Runner beans including French	KFRH	28	37	39	46	36	30	35	35	30	24	22
Peas, Green for market	KFRI	8	8	6	6	6	8	7	8	7	7	7
Peas, Green for processing	KFRJ	238	223	211	209	181	198	216	168	152	143	174
Celery	KFRK	46	49	44	41	42	39	38	39	35	40	36
Lettuce	KFRL	198	193	174	145	179	192	187	158	152	156	138
Rhubarb	KFRM	27	21	20	22	20	20	20	18	21	23	19
Protected crops												
Tomatoes	KFRN	134	133	122	110	108	113	117	115	109	117	113
Cucumbers	KFRO	101	104	90	104	83	88	86	82	84	84	80
Lettuce	KFRP	50	47	44	37	33	30	27	24	21	20	19
Fruit crops												
Total Dessert Apples	KFRQ	179.0	148.3	164.7	167.1	175.9	138.5	105.4	96.0	97.8	133.9	101.3
Total Culinary Apples	KFRR	125.7	157.2	161.8	158.7	130.2	134.9	118.5	91.1	85.9	112.4	99.5
Pears	KFRS	34.1	36.0	30.8	30.7	32.5	29.7	35.8	33.0	26.3	22.7	26.6
Plums	KFRT	7.2	21.5	21.1	11.8	11.0	14.4	19.6	12.1	6.4	9.3	5.3
Cherries	KFRU	1.5	1.0	3.8	2.4	1.3	3.5	3.6	0.6	0.9	1.3	0.4
Soft fruit	KFRV	102.4	102.2	94.1	94.5	77.4	76.5	81.6	59.4	60.5	65.9	60.7

1 For vegetables; output marketed for the calendar year; for horticultural crops output marketed for the crop year.

2 Except for sugar beet and hops, the production area for England and Wales is the area returned at the June census together with estimates for very small holdings (known as minor holdings). In Scotland and Northern Ireland the area returned at June is also the production area except that estimates for minor holdings are included in Scotland for potatoes and in Nothern Ireland for barley, oats and potatoes.

3 From 1991 figures are adjusted to constant 16% sugar content.

Source: Agricultural Departments: 01904 455332

20.5 Cattle, sheep, pigs and poultry on agricultural holdings[1]
United Kingdom

At June each year

Thousands

		1990	1991	1992	1993	1994	1995	1996	1997	1998	1999	2000
Total cattle and calves	**KFSB**	12 192	12 003	11 924	11 851	11 954	11 857	12 040	11 637	11 519	11 423	11 133
of which:												
dairy cows	**KFCT**	2 848	2 771	2 683	2 668	2 716	2 603	2 587	2 478	2 439	2 440	2 336
beef cows	**KFCU**	1 632	1 700	1 731	1 784	1 809	1 840	1 864	1 862	1 947	1 924	1 842
heifers in calf	**KFCV**	763	738	768	803	775	775	818	848	787	763	717
Total sheep and lambs	**KFSG**	44 469	44 166	44 540	44 436	43 813	43 304	42 086	42 823	44 471	44 656	42 261
of which:												
ewes and shearlings	**KSJP**	20 787	20 665	20 732	20 881	20 861	20 830	20 550	20 696	21 260	21 458	20 447
lambs under one year old	**KFSF**	22 380	22 213	22 607	22 394	21 758	21 350	20 443	21 032	22 138	22 092	20 855
Total pigs	**KFSQ**	7 548	7 695	7 707	7 853	7 892	7 627	7 590	8 072	8 146	7 284	6 482
of which:												
sows in pig and other sows for breeding	**KSJQ**	671	690	683	698	691	654	649	683	675	603	537
gilts in pig	**KSJR**	110	109	110	117	106	101	107	116	103	85	73
Total fowls	**KFSV**	125 357	128 025	124 842	131 093	126 653	127 035	..	..	..	149 867	154 503
of which:												
table fowls including broilers	**KFSU**	73 944	76 111	73 748	79 940	75 696	77 177	..	106 937	98 244	101 625	105 688
laying fowls[2]	**KFSS**	33 624	33 416	33 348	32 965	32 682	31 837	..	34 286	29 483	29 258	28 686
growing pullets	**KFSR**	10 530	11 102	10 849	10 750	10 388	10 210	..	11 510	9 860	9 583	9 461

1 Includes estimates for minor holdings for all countries. In previous editions minor holdings were excluded for Scotland and therefore data here will differ from previous editions. Also Northern Ireland data are now based on all active farm business.

2 Excludes fowls laying eggs for hatching.

Source: DEFRA Farming Statistics: 01904 455332

20.6 Forestry

Area-thousand hectares, volume-thousand m³ overbark standing

	1980	1990	1998	1999	2000	2001
Woodland area[1]						
United Kingdom	2 175	2 400	2 758	2 775	2 793	2 790
England[2]	948	958	1 093	1 097	1 103	1 100[3]
Scotland[2]	920	1 120	1 298	1 308	1 318	1 317[3]
Wales[2]	241	248	286	288	289	289
Northern Ireland	67	74	81	82	83	83
Forestry Commission / Forest Service	946	956	895	891	886	861[3]
Other[4]	1 230	1 443	1 863	1 884	1 907	1 929
Conifer	1 372	1 576	1 651	1 656	1 663	1 660
Broadleaved[5]	804	824	1 107	1 120	1 131	1 130

	1990/91	1991/92	1992/93	1993/94	1994/95	1995/96	1996/97	1997/98	1998/99	1999/00	2000/01
New Planting[6]											
United Kingdom	20.2	18.0	19.0	18.6	19.9	16.4	17.2	16.7	16.7	17.4	18.3
England	4.4	4.0	5.1	6.2	5.1	4.4	4.4	4.1	4.9	5.5	5.5
Scotland	14.0	12.7	12.1	10.5	13.4	10.6	11.7	11.4	10.5	10.4	11.7
Wales	0.5	0.4	0.4	0.6	0.6	0.4	0.4	0.5	0.6	0.7	0.4
Northern Ireland	1.2	0.9	1.3	1.3	0.9	1.0	0.8	0.6	0.7	0.8	0.7
Forestry Commission / Forest Service	4.1	3.4	2.8	1.8	1.2	0.6	0.6	0.2	0.2	0.3	0.3
Other[7]	16.1	14.6	16.2	16.8	18.7	15.8	16.6	16.4	16.5	17.2	18.0
Conifer	13.5	11.6	10.1	7.4	9.4	7.4	7.7	7.0	6.6	6.5	5.2
Broadleaved	6.7	6.5	8.9	11.2	10.5	8.9	9.5	9.7	10.1	10.9	13.2
Restocking[6]											
United Kingdom	15.2	16.6	17.0	16.8	14.6	13.9	15.0	14.1	14.0	15.1	15.2
England	6.5	6.9	6.7	6.4	4.9	4.2	4.3	4.3	4.0	3.8	3.8
Scotland	6.5	6.8	7.5	7.6	6.6	6.8	7.2	6.3	6.3	8.0	8.0
Wales	1.8	2.4	2.4	2.4	2.6	2.3	3.0	2.7	3.0	2.6	2.2
Northern Ireland	0.5	0.5	0.5	0.5	0.6	0.6	0.6	0.7	0.6	0.6	1.1
Forestry Commission / Forest Service	8.1	8.7	8.9	8.4	8.4	8.4	8.4	8.5	8.5	8.8	8.9
Other[7]	7.1	7.8	8.1	8.5	6.2	6.6	6.6	5.6	5.6	6.3	6.2
Conifer	10.4	11.8	11.5	11.5	11.0	10.9	11.4	11.2	11.3	11.9	12.2
Broadleaved	4.8	4.8	5.5	5.3	3.6	3.0	3.4	2.9	2.8	3.2	2.9

	1994	1995	1996	1997	1998	1999	2000
Wood Production (Volume)							
United Kingdom	8 540	8 690	8 650	9 340	9 160	9 740	10 430
Great Britain							
Softwood	7 350	7 440	7 510	8 170	8 070	8 660	9 310
Forestry Commission	4 320	4 130	4 290	4 570	4 830	5 440	5 530
Private Woodland	3 030	3 310	3 220	3 600	3 250	3 210	3 780
Hardwood[8]	950	990	880	910	800	760	740
Northern Ireland[9]	250	250	250	260	290	320	380

1 Areas as at 31 March.
2 For England, Scotland and Wales, 1980 woodland area figures are the published results from the 1979-1982 Census of Woodlands and Trees and figures for 1990 are adjusted to reflect subsequent changes. From 1998 onwards they are based on results from the 1995-1999 National Inventory of Woodlands and Trees, adjusted to reflect subsequent changes.
3 The apparent fall in woodland cover in 2001 is due to the reclassification of Forestry Commission open land within the forest.
4 "Other" is private woodland and non-Forestry Commission / Forest Service public woodland.

5 Broadleaved includes coppice. For data based on 1979-82 Census, all scrub and other non-plantation woodland has been assumed to be broadleaved.
6 Figures shown are for the areas of new planting and restocking in the year to 31 March.
7 "Other" figures are for grant aided planting on non-Forestry Commission / Forest Service woodland. They exclude areas planted without the aid of grants.
8 Hardwood is timber from broadleaved species. Most hardwood production comes from private woodlands; the figures are estimates based on reported deliveries to wood processing industries.
9 Most Northern Ireland production is from the Forest Service. The figures shown include Forest Service estimates of private sector production.

Sources: Forest Service Agency;
Department of Agriculture and Rural Development (Northern Ireland);
Forestry Commission: 0131 334 0303

20.7 Average weekly earnings and hours of male agricultural workers[1,2,3]
England and Wales
At September in each year

		1995	1996	1997	1998	1999	2000
Average weekly earnings (£)	LQML	272.27	288.33	286.01	301.24	301.22	298.24
95% confidence interval		(+/-£10.02)	(+/-£13.59)	(+/-£11.57)	(+/-£12.69)	(+/-£11.88)	(+/-£13.84)
Average weekly hours worked	LQMM	50.5	52.4	50.9	50.7	50.9	49.0
95% confidence interval		(+/-1.4)	(+/-1.8)	(+/-1.3)	(+/-1.5)	(+/-1.4)	(+/-1.4)
Average earnings/hours (£)	LQMN	5.39	5.50	5.62	5.94	5.92	6.09
95% confidence interval		(+/-£0.10)	(+/-£0.12)	(+/-£0.12)	(+/-£0.18)	(+/-£0.15)	(+/-£0.18)
Number of workers in the sample		239	172	244	274	292	234

1 Total earnings of regular full-time male workers, including all payments-in-kind, valued where applicable in accordance with the Agricultural Wages Order.
2 Aged 19 and over.
3 Results exclude earnings and hours of hire farm managers.
Source: Department for Environment, Food and Rural Affairs: 01904 455332

20.8 Average weekly earnings and hours of different types of agricultural workers[1,2]
England and Wales
At September 2000

	Full-time		Part-time[3]		Casual[4]		
	Male	Female	Male	Female	Male	Female	Managers
Average weekly earnings (£)	298.24	237.77	110.42	106.80	163.40	113.75	422.04
95% confidence interval	(+/-£13.84)	(+/-£14.19)	(+/-£10.68)	(+/-£9.41)	(+/-£16.11)	(+/-£12.30)	(+/-£31.34)
Average weekly hours worked	49.0	42.7	21.0	22.2	32.0	25.6	..
95% confidence interval	(+/-1.4)	(+/-1.2)	(+/-1.7)	(+/-1.7)	(+/-2.7)	(+/-2.4)	
Average earnings/hour (£)	6.09	5.57	5.27	4.80	5.10	4.45	..
95% confidence interval	(+/-£0.18)	(+/-£0.29)	(+/-£0.25)	(+/-£0.14)	(+/-£0.21)	(+/-£0.20)	
Number of workers in the sample	234	83	122	132	166	126	151

1 Total earnings of workers, including all payments-in-kind, valued where applicable in accordance with the Agricultural Wages Order.
2 Aged 19 and over.
3 Part-time workers are defined as working less than 39 basic hours per week.
4 Casual workers are employed on a temporary basis.
Source: Department for Environment, Food and Rural Affairs: 01904 455332

20.9 Sales for food of agricultural produce and livestock
United Kingdom

		Unit	1990	1991	1992	1993	1994	1995	1996	1997	1998	1999	2000
Cereals:		Thousand											
Wheat[1,2]	KCQK	tonnes	4 347	4 269	4 212	3 865	4 234	4 668	4 842	4 737	4 676	4 826	4 707
Barley	KCQL	"	3 791	3 849	3 599	2 762	3 190	3 776	3 692	3 411	3 483	3 412	3 750
Oats[3]	KCQM	"	222	215	222	208	215	216	235	259	273	270	263
Potatoes[4]	KCQN	"	5 924	5 800	6 008	6 382	6 519	5 961	6 146	6 279	5 997	6 210	6 379
Milk[5]:													
Milk utilised for liquid consumption	KCQO	Million litres	6 892	6 893	6 966	7 026	6 926	6 922	6 838	6 748	6 739	6 853	6 768
Milk utilised for manufacture	KCQP	Million litres	7 489	7 022	6 876	6 880	7 134	6 918	6 934	7 059	6 875	7 041	6 550
Total milk available for domestic use[6]	KCQQ	Million litres	14 751	14 282	14 189	14 228	14 420	14 255	14 194	14 258	13 973	14 238	13 738
Hen eggs in shell	KCQR	Million dozens	804	818	806	791	787	774	775	794	792	743	752
Animals slaughtered:													
Cattle and calves:													
Cattle	KCQS	Thousands	3 478	3 568	3 355	2 944	3 089	3 266	2 291	2 264	2 297	2 217	2 280
Calves	KCQT	"	46	49	33	19	22	26	24	20	32	75	153
Total	KCQU	"	3 524	3 617	3 387	2 963	3 112	3 292	2 315	2 284	2 329	2 292	2 433
Sheep and lambs	KCQV	"	20 012	20 918	19 428	18 864	18 962	19 311	18 049	16 660	18 688	19 116	18 381
Pigs:													
For bacon:													
Used wholly[7]	KCQW	"	1 903	14 091	14 143	14 265	14 681	14 021	13 897	15 132	15 872	14 350	12 369
Used in part	KCQX	"	3 281	..	..	..	..	..	..	..	..	..	..
Other uses	KCQY	"	8 694	..	..	..	..	..	..	..	..	..	..
Sows and boars	KCQZ	"	325	366	373	356	389	355	324	363	415	379	321
Total	KCRA	"	14 203	14 457	14 515	14 620	15 069	14 376	14 221	15 496	16 286	14 728	12 691
Poultry:[8] slaughtered	KCRB	Millions	676	700	696	721	761	783	823	850	856	848	843

Note: The figures for cereals and for animals slaughtered relate to periods of 52 weeks

1 Flour millers' receipts of home-grown wheat.
2 Following the receipt of additional data, figures have been revised back to 1992 and are not strictly comparable with those for earlier years.
3 Oatmeal millers' receipts of home-grown oats.
4 Total sales for human consumption in the UK.

5 Data to 1994 sourced from the Milk Marketing Boards. Data from 1995 sourced from surveys run by the agricultural departments. 1994 includes two months of data sourced from the surveys run by the agricultural departments.
6 The totals of liquid consumption and milk used for manufacture may not add up to the total available for domestic use because of adjustments for dairy wastage, stock changes and other uses, such as farmhouse consumption, milk fed to stock and on farm waste.
7 From 1991, data series quotes the number of clean pigs slaughtered for all pig meat.
8 Total fowls, ducks, geese and turkeys.

Source: Department for Environment, Food and Rural Affairs: 01904 455332

20.10 Stocks of food and feedingstuffs[1]
United Kingdom

At end-December in each year

Thousand tonnes

		1990	1991	1992	1993	1994	1995	1996	1997	1998	1999	2000
Wheat and flour (as wheat)	KCRC	860	1 461	1 839	1 255	1 236	1 036	1 012	984	1 047	848	..
Barley (GB only)	KCRD	1 120	1 489	2 028	1 401	1 375	1 542	1 502	1 441	1 224	1 373	..
Maize	KCRE	41	36	109	23	32	33	25	45	67	43	..
Oilcake and meal[2]	KCRF	153	93	107	92	108	103	89	79	69	72	..
Oilseeds and nuts (crude oil equivalent)	KCRG	25	18	11	17	28	34	25	18	12	18	..
Vegetable oil (as crude oil)	KCRI	109	89	94	90	109	96	100	99	98	97	..
Marine oil (as crude oil)	KCRJ	9	9	8	8	18	17	10	4	–	–	..
Butter[3]	KCRK	74.0	65.0	63.0	34.0	19.0	11.0	14.0	7.0	11.0	22.1	17.0
Meat and offal[4]	KCRL	150.8	212.0	218.2	198.7	102.5	76.9	129.5	161.9	156.8	84.1	53.7
Raw coffee[5]	KCRM	11	10	10	12	13	11	8	7	8	7	8
Tea[6]	KCRN	48	43	40	44	43	38	39	37	38	38	28
Sugar	KCRO	824	824	888	1 069	1 016	766	807	1 003	928	..	..

1 Recorded stocks, including stocks in bond or held by the main processors.
2 Excluding castor meal, cocoa cake and meal.
3 In addition to stocks in public cold stores surveyed by DEFRA, closing stocks include all intervention stocks in private cold stores.

4 Stocks of imported and home-produced meat and offal held in public cold stores, excluding poultrymeat, bacon and ham.
5 Including manufacturers' stocks and additional public warehouses.
6 Covering stocks held by primary wholesalers and held in public/private warehouses.

Source: Department for Environment, Food and Rural Affairs: 01904 455332

20.11 Processed food and animal feedingstuffs: production
United Kingdom

Thousand tonnes

		1990	1991	1992	1993	1994	1995	1996	1997	1998	1999	2000
Flour milling:												
Wheat milling: total[1]	KFTA	4 875	4 796	5 022	5 236	5 290	5 338	5 501	5 535	5 707	5 668	5 617
Home produced[1]	KFTB	4 273	4 185	4 192	3 781	4 106	4 598	4 772	4 667	4 582	4 701	4 609
Imported	KFTC	605	611	830	1 455	1 184	740	729	868	1 125	966	1 008
Flour produced[1]	KFTD	3 879	3 851	3 975	4 120	4 232	4 294	4 454	4 439	4 526	4 497	4 486
Offals produced[1]	KFTE	999	968	1 045	1 123	1 078	1 079	1 111	1 111	1 221	1 181	1 148
Oat milling:												
Oats milled by oatmeal millers	KFTF	231	216	225	207	209	217	250	259	272	266	261
Products of oat milling	KFTG	132	124	124	105	102	110	123	129	154	157	155
Seed crushing:												
Oilseeds and nuts processed	KFTH	1 877	1 710	1 807	1 903	2 035	2 122	2 466	2 587	2 683	2 398	2 380
Crude oil produced, including production of maize oil	KFTI	630	583	636	658	739	779	862	909	915	832	820
Oilcake and meal produced, excluding castor meal, cocoa cake and meal	KFTJ	1 193	1 081	1 125	1 187	1 242	1 305	1 541	1 614	1 687	1 484	1 475
Production of home-killed meat: total including meat subsequently canned	KFTK	2 376	2 455	2 392	2 262	2 381	2 394	2 095	2 162	2 278	2 142	2 069
Beef	KFTL	1 000	1 018	970	858	915	973	701	695	704	675	704
Veal	KFTM	2	2	1	1	1	1	1	1	1	2	4
Mutton and lamb	KFTN	370	385	362	349	352	364	345	321	356	361	359
Pork	KFTO	735	772	786	783	807	761	778	875	937	829	731
Offal[2]	KFTP	270	278	274	270	307	295	269	270	279	274	270
Production of poultry meat[3]	KFTQ	1 148	1 211	1 226	1 289	1 344	1 397	1 461	1 502	..	..	..
Production of bacon and ham, including meat subsequently canned	KFTR	191	193	189	216	233	245	241	239	236	233	209
Production of milk products:												
Butter[4]	KFTS	151	132	127	141	148	133	130	139	137	141	132
Cheese (including farmhouse)	KFTT	320	309	332	338	341	362	377	377	366	368	340
Condensed milk: includes skim concentrate and condensed milk used in manufacture of chocolate crumb	KFTU	204	198	206	191	196	181	206	214	192	177	162
Milk powder: excluding buttermilk and whey powder												
Full cream	KFTV	70	79	84	71	83	90	83	96	97	102	..
Skimmed	KFTW	166	143	106	132	142	117	108	109	107	102	..
Cream, fresh and sterilised; including farm cream[4]	KFTX	230	254	240	255	274	281	281	268	266	275	..
Sugar: production from home-grown sugar-beet (as refined sugar)	KFTY	1 241	1 220	1 472	1 433	1 263	1 469	1 324	1 524	1 557	..	..
Production of compound fats:												
Margarine and other table spreads	KFTZ	486	481	477	493	487	490	491	461	448	421	388
Solid cooking fats	KFUA	122	117	116	129	109	110	123	109	131	125	135
Production of other processed foods:												
Jam and marmalade	KFUB	–	..	..	..	..	..	..	..	..	..	..
Syrup and treacle[5]	KFUC	51	51	49	52	50	48	–	–	..	..	..
Chocolate confectionery	KSJS	539	534	532	563	573	592	608	569	567	553	544
Sugar confectionery	KSJT	320	303	300	302	322	322	351	345	337	317	307
Cocoa beans excluding re-exports	KFVX	125	148	159	171	163	160	189	174	172	168	..
Soups, canned and powdered	KFUF	..	..	..	..	..	..	..	..	..	..	..
Canned meat	KFUG	91	147	..	..	..	..	..	..	..	..	..
Breakfast cereals, other than oatmeal and oatmeal flakes	KFUJ	286	290	303	302	325	335	343	359	349	354	334
Glucose	KFUM	546	557	568	580	593	607	642	637	644	630	657
Production of soft drinks (million litres):												
Concentrated	KFUN	557	..	..	..	..	..	..	..	..	..	..
Unconcentrated	KFUO	4 316	..	..	..	..	..	..	..	..	..	..
Compound feedingstuffs: total[6]	KFUP	10 564	10 374	10 514	11 141	11 402	11 609	11 801	11 304	11 206	11 404	10 612
Cattle food[6]	KFUQ	3 909	3 798	4 098	4 271	4 347	4 476	4 430	3 926	3 844	4 264	4 039
Calf food[6]	KFUR	324	280	242	261	286	307	277	227	198	187	190
Pig food[6]	KFUS	2 276	2 361	2 489	2 561	2 547	2 453	2 566	2 659	2 740	2 435	2 089
Poultry food[7]	KFUT	3 212	3 062	2 737	3 123	3 179	3 243	3 280	3 324	3 213	3 139	3 063
Other compounds[6]	KFUU	843	873	948	925	1 043	1 130	1 249	1 168	1 210	1 378	1 231

Note: The figures relate to periods of 52 weeks (53 weeks in 1992 and 1998) with the following exceptions which are on a calendar year basis: butter, cheese, cream, canned meat, soft drinks, condensed milk and milk powder, canned vegetables, canned and bottled fruit, jam and marmalade, and soups.

Please note production of Poultry Feed by Integrated Poultry Units has been;
1992 = 2,556,000 tonnes
1993 = 2,679,000 tonnes
1994 = 2,767,000 tonnes
1995 = 2,892,000 tonnes
1996 = 3,012,000 tonnes
1997 = 3,072,000 tonnes
1998 = 3,105,000 tonnes
1999 = 2,940,000 tonnes
2000 = 2,974,000 tonnes
These figures have been revised following the receipt of more up-to-date information.

1 Following the receipt of additional data, figures have been revised back to 1992 and are not strictly comparable with those for earlier years.

2 Including poultry offal.

3 Total of fowl, ducks, geese and turkeys (carcase weight).

4 Includes cream from the residual elements of low fat milk production.

5 This survey ceased at the end of 1995.

6 Figures from 1992 onwards have been revised to include data on blended cattle and sheep feeds and are therefore not strictly comparable with earlier years. In 1996, mainly as a result of the introduction of the Beef Assurance Scheme, the Ministry became aware of a number of feed mills that it had not been surveying. Data from these mills has now been included in these figures back to 1992. Total production from these mills has been in the range of 110,000 to 135,000 tonnes each year.

7 It was found that data for Poultry food had previously contained some mills whose production or part of their production should have been recorded against the Integrated Poultry Unit (IPU) series. Production for these sites has now been moved from the Poultry food series to the IPU series. This data was available from 1992 onwards. Earlier years have been estimated in order to make the Poultry food series comparable.

Source: Department for Environment, Food and Rural Affairs: 01904 455332

20.12 Food and animal feedingstuffs: disposals

Thousand tonnes

		1990	1991	1992	1993	1994	1995	1996	1997	1998	1999	2000
Flour[1]	KFPU	3 830	3 798	3 932	4 076	4 200	4 293	4 457	4 434	4 529	4 487	4 489
Sugar (as refined sugar): total disposals	KFPV	2 332	2 297	2 319	2 154	2 196	2 177	2 200	2 040	2 143	..	..
For food in the United Kingdom[2]	KFPW	2 320	2 280	2 292	2 123	2 165	2 157	2 180	2 007	2 106	..	..
Syrup and treacle[3]	KFPX	51	51	49	52	50	48	–	–	..	..	..
Meat and fish:												
Fresh and frozen meat and offal, including usage for canning:												
Beef and veal	KFPY	1 104	1 130	1 145	1 094	1 228	1 206	804	865	872	942	922
Mutton and lamb	KFPZ	517	511	497	470	474	504	501	468	496	497	494
Pork	KFVA	814	847	877	895	922	926	963	1 039	1 116	1 062	1 001
Offal[4]	KFVB	329	324	335	316	351	354	312	320	315	322	328
Poultry-meat[5,6]	KFVC	1 208	1 247	1 328	1 361	1 459	1 500	1 581	1 560	1 649	1 696	1 707
Bacon and ham, including usage for canning	KFVD	451	446	428	453	457	473	502	477	468	461	477
Dairy products:												
Butter	KFVI	245	245	258	279	284	255	240	256	238	244	255
Cheese	KFVJ	515	509	560	523	559	577	617	614	632	645	595
Condensed milk[7]	KFVK	218	211	218	202	208	195	217	229	205	190	177
Milk powder, excluding buttermilk and whey powder:												
Full cream	KFVM	76	81	91	75	91	97	94	105	107	112	117
Skimmed	KFVN	170	157	136	144	149	138	95	103	91	127	162
Hen eggs in shell[8]	KFVO	864	853	831	821	837	818	833	838	819	795	827
Oils (as crude oil):												
Vegetable oil	KFVP	1 501	1 465	1 488	1 492	1 567	1 905	1 960	2 010	1 780	2 449	..
Marine oil for the manufacture of margarine and compound fat	KFVQ	..	115	114	95	91	105	100	52	31	8	8
Potatoes	KFVR	7 177	7 068	7 876	8 288	7 835	7 055	7 661	7 938	7 626	7 584	7 997
Other foods:												
Chocolate confectionery	KFVT	603	621	640	667	696	674	698	672	697	680	685
Sugar confectionery, excluding medicated	KFVU	366	362	367	366	382	380	410	420	415	401	400
Tea excluding re-exports	KFVV	145	152	147	157	149	141	148	152	145	133	144
Raw coffee	KFVW	104	101	108	116	119	105	116	118	122	115	109
Barley:[9]												
For brewing and distilling and for food	KFVY	3 858	3 917	3 436	2 682	3 092	3 574	3 579	3 439	3 502	3 324	3 646
Maize (including maize meal): total disposals	KFVZ	1 659	1 510	1 433	1 414	1 382	1 409	1 372	1 429	1 445	1 238	..
Animal feed	KCRT	292	145	148	152	173	154	156	174	194	198	206
Oilcake and meal	KCRQ	3 569	3 470	3 646	3 891	4 152	4 462	4 429	4 041	3 677	4 035	..
Wheat milling offals	KCRR	1 133	1 064	1 086	1 170	1 121	1 131	1 157	1 158	1 273	1 209	1 176
Fish and poultry meal for animal feed,[10] figures relate to sales	KCRS	394	383	430	382	385	378	257	233	216	194	193

Note: The figures relate to periods of 52 weeks with the following exceptions which are on a calendar year basis: fish and potatoes; condensed milk; milk powder; butter and sugar.

1 Following the receipt of additional data, figures have been revised back to 1992 and are not strictly comparable with those for previous years.
2 Including sugar used in the manufacture of other foods subsequently exported. Excluding sugar in imported manufactured foods.
3 This survey ceased at the end of 1995.
4 Including poultry offal.
5 Carcase weight.

6 Total of fowls, ducks, geese and turkeys.
7 Includes skim concentrate and condensed milk used in the manufacture of chocolate crumb.
8 Million dozen eggs
9 From 1992 figures exclude sales of barley and barley screenings and are not strictly comparable with those from earlier years.
10 Before a ban on 29 March 1996 this included poultry meat as well as mammalian meat and bonemeal.

Source: Department for Environment, Food and Rural Affairs: 01904 455332

20.13 Number of workers employed in agriculture [1,2]
United Kingdom
At June in each year

Thousands

| | Regular workers | | | | | Seasonal or casual workers | | | All workers | | | Salaried managers[3] |
| | Whole - time | | Part - time | | | | | | | | | |
	Total	Male	Female	Male	Female	Total	Male	Female	Total	Male	Female	
	KAXV	KAXW	KAXX	KAXY	KAXZ	KAYA	KAYB	KAYC	KAYD	KAYE	KAYF	KAYG
1990	183.3	109.7	15.7	29.9	28.0	90.5	55.6	35.0	273.8	195.2	78.6	8.1
1991	176.9	104.7	15.0	29.7	27.4	86.6	53.8	32.8	263.5	188.2	75.3	7.9
1992	169.9	99.9	14.8	29.1	26.1	86.2	54.4	31.9	256.2	183.3	72.8	7.8
1993	165.3	96.5	13.7	29.8	25.3	85.4	55.0	30.4	250.7	181.3	69.4	7.6
1994	161.0	93.6	13.2	30.0	24.2	82.2	53.9	28.4	243.2	177.5	65.7	7.8
1995	157.4	90.4	13.0	30.0	24.1	83.7	56.5	27.2	241.2	176.8	64.3	7.7
1996	156.4	89.2	12.6	31.2	23.4	81.5	55.6	25.8	237.9	176.0	61.9	7.8
1997	154.2	87.5	12.5	31.2	22.9	80.9	55.4	25.6	235.0	174.1	61.0	7.8
1998[4,5]	154.6	87.6	13.0	29.5	24.5	78.4	53.9	24.5	233.0	171.0	62.0	12.1
1999	143.8	82.3	11.8	27.2	22.5	72.0	51.0	21.0	215.8	160.5	55.3	13.8
2000	129.0	73.4	10.3	24.6	20.6	64.4	45.9	18.5	193.3	143.9	49.4	11.1

1 Includes estimates for minor holdings for all countries. In previous editions minor holdings were excluded for Scotland and therefore data here will differ from previous editions. Also, Northern Ireland data are now based on all active business.
2 Figures exclude school children, farmers, partners, directors and their spouses and most trainees.
3 Great Britain only.

4 Results from 1998 onwards are not comparable with previous years, due to changes in the labour questions on the June Agricultural and Horticultural Census in England, Wales and Scotland.
5 From 1998, all farmers managing holdings for limited companies or other institutions in England and Wales were asked to classify themselves as salaried managers.

Source: DEFRA Farming Statistics: 01904 455332

20.14 Landings of fish by United Kingdom vessels: live weight and value into United Kingdom

		Quantity (thousand tonnes)							Value (£ thousand)					
		1995	1996	1997	1998	1999	2000		1995	1996	1997	1998	1999	2000
Total all species	KSJU	725.6	635.9	593.3	552.5	506.5	464.7	KSLN	478 209	491 045	467 694	484 005	464 131	422 063
Total wet fish	KSJV	601.0	504.3	467.2	428.3	389.8	337.6	KSLO	333 174	343 045	314 712	323 297	297 831	268 816
Brill	KSJX	0.5	0.5	0.5	0.4	0.3	0.4	KSLP	2 201	2 639	2 244	1 674	1 405	1 839
Catfish	KSJY	1.0	1.1	1.0	0.8	0.7	0.8	KSLQ	1 474	1 449	1 152	1 070	1 006	1 081
Cod	KSJZ	74.4	75.7	71.0	72.7	46.8	37.0	KSLR	65 772	69 752	67 641	79 450	62 587	50 635
Dogfish	KSKA	10.9	9.7	8.6	7.4	6.9	7.3	KSLS	7 684	7 002	5 586	5 535	5 295	5 862
Haddock	KSKB	85.3	89.1	82.6	82.8	71.3	50.3	KSLT	54 734	54 333	44 778	57 131	59 286	51 181
Hake	KSKC	3.1	2.8	2.7	2.5	3.9	3.5	KSLU	7 361	7 346	6 375	5 117	7 839	6 941
Lemon Soles	KSKD	4.6	5.1	5.2	4.7	4.5	4.0	KSLV	10 115	11 897	11 786	10 620	10 374	9 934
Ling	KSKE	9.8	9.2	9.4	10.0	8.8	7.6	KSLW	7 483	6 945	6 568	8 291	8 502	7 571
Megrims	KSKF	5.1	6.0	6.0	5.3	5.0	5.0	KSLX	9 227	10 430	9 467	8 573	9 326	8 914
Monks or Anglers	KSKG	22.2	29.7	25.6	18.5	15.5	14.7	KSLY	39 451	51 468	45 947	38 540	35 591	33 609
Plaice	KSKH	15.5	12.5	12.9	11.5	9.5	8.6	KSLZ	17 573	16 013	15 484	13 185	12 549	9 869
Pollack (Lythe)	KSKI	3.3	2.9	3.0	2.6	2.3	2.5	KSMA	2 935	2 563	2 491	2 423	2 734	3 197
Saithe	KSKJ	12.8	13.3	12.3	10.1	10.4	10.2	KSMB	5 625	5 674	4 894	4 971	4 878	4 089
Sand Eels	KSKK	7.3	9.3	14.5	11.6	6.8	9.7	KSMC	398	505	815	742	283	400
Skates and Rays	KSKL	7.6	8.3	7.2	6.8	5.6	5.5	KSMD	6 543	7 451	6 215	6 403	5 380	5 677
Soles	KSKM	2.8	2.5	2.3	2.0	2.0	1.9	KSME	14 200	14 068	14 800	13 960	13 829	11 295
Turbot	KSKN	0.8	0.8	0.7	0.6	0.5	0.5	KSMF	4 667	5 006	4 263	3 614	2 918	2 859
Whiting	KSKO	39.8	37.3	34.5	26.7	25.4	23.3	KSMG	18 918	18 962	15 939	13 380	14 010	14 317
Whiting, Blue	KSKP	3.4	3.5	12.4	27.8	38.4	17.7	KSMH	180	190	693	2 003	1 476	743
Whitches	KSKQ	2.3	2.3	2.3	1.9	2.2	2.4	KSMI	2 915	3 068	2 263	1 587	2 202	2 352
Other Demersal	KSKR	12.9	13.3	13.2	12.7	15.7	14.6	KSMJ	17 028	16 614	16 000	15 612	18 559	16 025
Total Demersal[1]	KSKS	325.4	334.8	327.9	319.3	282.6	227.3	KSMK	296 485	313 377	285 402	293 882	280 028	248 392
Herring[2]	KSKT	95.9	72.3	57.4	39.5	45.3	39.5	KSML	11 105	8 742	6 430	4 897	5 057	4 073
Horse Mackerel	KSKU	26.2	22.0	5.5	5.1	2.1	2.7	KSMM	2 636	2 966	878	783	304	440
Mackerel[2]	KSKV	140.4	60.8	63.2	54.4	41.3	54.6	KSMN	20 860	15 645	19 822	21 754	9 544	13 848
Pilchards	KSKW	6.8	6.8	4.7	4.7	3.5	2.9	KSMO	680	959	696	765	550	602
Sprats	KSKX	5.9	7.2	8.3	5.0	14.3	8.3	KSMP	1 080	1 175	1 386	1 112	2 053	1 040
Tuna	KSKY	0.1	..	..	..	0.1	..	KSMQ	246	66	46	44	111	20
Other Pelagic	KSKZ	0.2	0.3	0.1	0.2	0.6	2.3	KSMR	82	116	52	60	184	401
Total Pelagic	KSLA	275.6	169.5	139.3	108.9	107.2	110.3	KSMS	36 689	29 668	29 309	29 416	17 803	20 424
Cockles	KSLB	25.4	24.2	19.5	12.1	14.2	20.3	KSMT	3 544	3 266	3 632	4 162	2 526	2 953
Crabs	KSLC	21.7	20.3	22.5	27.2	23.0	25.7	KSMU	21 346	22 226	24 264	32 290	26 983	28 036
Lobsters	KSLD	1.3	1.3	1.5	1.6	1.8	1.2	KSMV	11 896	11 888	13 060	14 489	14 928	12 458
Mussels	KSLE	9.5	12.3	9.6	12.7	8.4	7.5	KSMW	2 976	4 574	3 102	3 502	2 107	1 442
Nephrops	KSLF	31.1	29.0	31.1	28.6	31.1	28.3	KSMX	60 704	57 164	63 480	56 810	74 327	60 778
Periwinkles	KSLG	2.4	2.4	2.9	2.0	1.2	1.1	KSMY	1 954	2 046	2 735	1 892	1 165	1 089
Queens	KSLH	2.9	2.3	5.6	8.1	5.9	5.3	KSMZ	1 929	1 225	1 954	2 887	2 563	2 292
Scallops	KSLI	15.7	17.1	18.5	20.1	19.1	19.7	KSNA	24 279	27 036	27 576	30 156	29 145	30 741
Shrimps/Prawns	KSLJ	2.7	2.7	1.0	2.2	2.0	1.6	KSNB	3 517	3 257	960	2 594	2 931	2 062
Squid	KSLK	1.6	1.4	1.6	2.2	2.1	1.4	KSNC	3 783	2 987	4 044	4 362	4 190	2 716
Other shellfish	KSLL	10.4	18.7	12.2	7.6	8.0	14.8	KSND	9 106	12 332	8 176	7 564	5 434	8 680
Total shellfish	KSLM	124.6	131.6	126.1	124.2	116.7	127.0	KSNE	145 034	148 001	152 983	160 708	166 299	153 247

1 Includes fish roes.
2 Includes transshipments i.e. caught by UK boats but not actually landing at UK ports. These quantities are transshipped to foreign vessels in coastal waters and are later recorded as exports.

Source: Department for Environment, Food and Rural Affairs: 01904 455332

20.15 United Kingdom fishing fleet
At 31 December each year[1]

Numbers

		1992	1993	1994	1995	1996	1997	1998	1999	2000
By size										
10m and under	KSNF	7 376	7 666	7 195	6 320	5 606	5 474	5 487	5 409	5 273
10.01 - 12.19m	KSNG	1 450	1 361	1 167	1 016	800	732	628	577	547
12.20 - 17.00m	KSNH	787	751	680	622	540	523	491	468	467
17.01 - 18.29m	KSNI	232	220	193	187	164	162	154	154	131
18.30 - 24.38m	KSNJ	697	657	610	574	509	471	443	414	406
24.39 - 30.48m	KSNK	200	210	211	212	223	227	226	224	219
30.49 - 36.58m	KSNL	120	124	126	127	114	104	89	80	77
over 36.58m	KSNM	117	119	116	117	117	119	121	122	122
Total over 10m	KSNN	3 603	3 442	3 103	2 855	2 467	2 338	2 152	2 039	1 969
Total UK fleet (excluding Islands)	KSNO	10 979	11 108	10 297	9 174	8 073	7 812	7 639	7 448	7 242
By segment										
Pelagic gears	KSNP	76	69	68	67	58	49	50	46	44
Beam trawl	KSNQ	227	240	212	220	215	153	123	114	111
Demersal trawls and seines	KXET	..	..	..	..	1 040	..	..	..	..
Demersal trawls	KSIX	1 039	988	854	856	..	..	..	..	..
Nephrop trawls	KSIY	566	560	593	528	411	..	..	..	..
Seines	KSIZ	255	203	197	165	..	..	..	..	..
Demersal, Seines and Nephrops	JZCI	..	..	..	..	..	1 428	1 318	1 235	1 208
Lines and Nets	KSNR	339	329	300	267	224	214	187	172	165
Shellfish: mobile	KSNS	214	181	206	194	265	227	241	243	211
Shellfish: fixed	KSNT	306	312	305	283	339	352	311	301	297
Distant water	KSNU	16	14	13	12	15	13	14	12	13
Under 10m	KSNV	7 831	8 128	7 607	6 757	6 091	6 022	6 027	5 920	5 769
Non-active/non-TAC	KSNW	692	668	472	371	–	–	–	–	–
Other: Mussel Dredgers	JZCJ	..	..	..	..	..	3	2	2	2
Total UK fleet[2]	KSNX	11 561	11 692	10 827	9 720	8 658	8 461	8 271	8 104	7 820

1 Prior to 1990 the figures referred to vessels that were active; after 1990 the figures refer to vessels in the registered fleet for which the data are currently under review.
2 The UK figures here include Channel Islands and Isle of Man.

Source: Department for Environment, Food and Rural Affairs: 01904 455332

20.16 Estimated household food consumption by all households in Great Britain

Grammes per person per week

		1990	1991	1992	1993	1994	1995	1996	1997	1998	1999	2000
Liquid wholemilk[1] (ml)	KPQM	1 232	1 104	995	898	870	812	776	712	693	634	664
Fully skimmed (ml)	KZBH	193	198	213	217	207	204	137	158	164	167	164
Semi skimmed (ml)	KZBI	516	579	752	814	863	899	935	978	945	958	975
Other milk and cream (ml)	KZBJ	228	247	262	249	252	255	259	248	243	248	278
Cheese	KPQO	113	117	114	109	106	108	111	109	104	104	110
Butter	KPQP	46	44	41	40	39	36	39	38	39	37	39
Margarine	KPQQ	91	89	79	70	43	41	36	26	26	20	21
Low and reduced fat spreads	KZBK	45	47	51	52	74	72	79	77	69	71	68
All other oils and fats (ml for oils)	KPQR	67	60	74	69	70	69	71	62	62	58	58
Eggs (number)	KPQS	2.20	2.25	2.08	1.92	1.86	1.85	1.87	1.78	1.74	1.68	1.75
Preserves and honey	KPQT	48	51	45	42	43	39	41	41	38	33	33
Sugar	KPQU	171	167	156	151	144	136	144	128	119	107	105
Beef and veal	KPQV	149	152	141	133	131	121	101	110	109	110	124
Mutton and lamb	KPQW	83	86	71	66	54	54	66	56	59	57	55
Pork	KPQX	84	82	72	80	77	71	73	75	76	69	68
Bacon and ham, uncooked	KPQY	86	85	77	77	77	76	77	72	76	68	71
Bacon and ham, cooked (including canned)	KPQZ	32	33	33	35	38	39	33	41	40	39	41
Poultry uncooked	JZCH	211	202	216	222	209	215	233	221	218	201	214
Cooked poultry (not purchased in cans)	KYBP	15	14	15	16	20	22	23	33	33	35	39
Other cooked and canned meats	KPRB	62	60	68	60	63	63	62	52	49	48	51
Offals	KPRC	14	13	12	11	9	9	7	7	5	5	5
Sausages, uncooked	KPRD	68	62	61	60	61	63	63	63	60	58	60
Other meat products	KPRE	163	173	183	194	203	211	207	209	216	221	239
Fish, fresh and processed (including shellfish)	KPRF	69	65	67	71	71	68	72	70	70	70	67
Canned fish	KPRG	29	30	32	30	30	29	31	31	29	31	32
Fish and fish products, frozen	KPRH	47	43	43	44	44	46	50	46	46	42	44
Potatoes (excluding processed)	KPRI	996	959	901	875	812	803	805	745	715	673	707
Fresh green vegetables	KPRJ	277	259	250	240	245	225	233	251	246	245	240
Other fresh vegetables	KPRK	459	461	475	477	464	470	489	497	486	500	492
Frozen potato products	KYBQ	73	82	92	98	103	99	113	106	111	113	120
Other frozen vegetables	KPRL	112	117	106	105	107	101	94	94	88	87	80
Potato products not frozen	JZCF	62	59	75	80	82	89	92	90	89	86	82
Canned beans	KPRM	124	123	120	112	111	117	125	122	118	112	114
Other canned vegetables (excl. potatoes)	KPRN	117	120	124	114	103	110	113	104	99	92	97
Other processed vegetables (excl. potatoes)	LQZH	41	43	50	52	55	48	55	52	54	59	54
Apples	KPRO	201	190	187	179	180	183	175	179	181	169	180
Bananas	KPRP	125	129	144	151	162	176	185	195	198	202	206
Oranges	KPRQ	81	76	72	62	65	66	63	62	63	50	54
All other fresh fruit	KPRR	198	216	216	224	238	247	263	276	274	290	304
Canned fruit	KPRS	52	52	51	48	46	45	43	44	37	38	38
Dried fruit, nuts and fruit and nut products	KPRT	36	39	38	39	36	34	36	35	34	30	35
Fruit juices (ml)	KPRU	202	250	222	236	240	244	258	277	304	284	303
Flour	KPRV	91	81	81	82	62	57	70	54	55	56	67
Bread	KPRW	797	752	755	757	758	756	752	746	742	717	720
Buns, scones and teacakes	KPRX	34	39	40	39	38	36	47	43	41	40	43
Cakes and pastries	KPRY	70	79	76	79	85	85	87	93	88	87	89
Biscuits	KPRZ	149	147	148	142	138	135	150	138	137	132	141
Breakfast cereals	KPSA	127	134	132	129	134	135	140	135	136	134	143
Oatmeal and oat products	KPSB	15	19	15	14	11	11	13	16	11	13	15
Other cereals and cereal products	JZCG	187	204	217	218	218	251	304	293	270	284	291
Tea	KPSC	43	42	39	36	38	39	38	36	35	32	34
Instant coffee	KPSD	14	15	14	13	13	12	13	11	12	11	11
Canned soups	KPSE	68	69	70	66	68	64	72	70	71	67	71
Pickles and sauces	KPSF	67	69	72	77	77	80	84	92	96	91	107

1 Including also school and welfare milk.

Sources: Department for Environment, Food and Rural Affairs;
(National Food Survey): 020 7270 8563

21 Production

Production

Annual Business Inquiry *(Table 21.1)*

The Annual Business Inquiry (ABI) estimates cover all UK businesses registered for Value Added Tax (VAT) and/ or Pay As You Earn (PAYE), classified to the 1992 Standard Industrial Classification (SIC(92)) headings listed in the tables. The ABI obtains details on these businesses from the ONS Inter-Departmental Business Register (IDBR).

As with all its statistical inquiries, the ONS is concerned to minimise the form-filling burden of individual contributors and as such the ABI is a sample inquiry. The sample was designed as a stratified random sample of about 70,500 businesses, the inquiry population is stratified by SIC(92) and employment using the information from the register.

The inquiry results are grossed up to the total population, so that they relate to all active UK businesses on the IDBR for the sectors covered.

The results meet a wide range of needs for government, economic analysts and the business community at large. In official statistics the inquiry is an important source for the national accounts and input-output tables, but also provides weights for the indices of production and producer prices. Inquiry results also enable the United Kingdom to meet statistical requirements of the European Union.

Data from 1995 and 1996 were calculated on a different basis from those for 1997 and later years. In order to provide a link between the two data series, the 1995 and 1996 data have been reworked to provide estimates on a consistent basis.

Revised Annual Business Inquiry results at SIC(92) 3 digit group level, for 1995-1999, giving both analysis and tabular detail are now available free of charge from the ONS Website at http://www.statistics.gov.uk/abi/, with further extracts and bespoke analyses available on request. This service replaces existing publications.

Manufacturers' sales by industry *(Table 21.2)*

This table shows the total manufacturers' sales for products classified to the 1992 Standard Industrial Classification and collected under the PRODCOM (Products of the European Community) Inquiry since its introduction in 1993. Some data is not available for confidentiality reasons or where data has not been published for a given period. Detailed product sales data together with exports and imports data are available in the Product Sales and Trade quarterly and annual reports (PRQ and PRA series).

Number of local units in manufacturing industries in 2001 *(Table 21.3)*

This table shows the number of local units (sites) in manufacturing by employment sizebands. The class-ification breakdown is at division level (2 digit) as classified to the 1992 Standard Industrial Classification held on the Inter-Departmental Business Register (IDBR). This register became fully operational in 1995 and combines information on VAT traders and PAYE employers in a statistical register comprising 2 million enterprises (businesses), representing nearly 99% of economic activity. Business Monitor PA1003 - Size

Analysis of United Kingdom Businesses 2001 provides further details and contains detailed information on enterprises in the UK including size, classification and location. Additionally, this information is available for manufacturing local units.

For further information on the IDBR see the National Statistics website at www.statistics.gov.uk/themes/commerce/services/idbr.asp.

Total inland energy consumption *(Table 21.4)*

This table shows energy consumption by fuel and final energy consumption by fuel and class of consumer. Primary energy consumption covers consumption of all primary fuels for energy purposes. Primary fuels are coal, natural gas (including colliery methane, landfill gas and sewage gas), oil and primary electricity (i.e. electricity generated by hydro, nuclear and wind stations and also electricity imported from France through the interconnector). This measure of energy consumption includes energy that is lost by converting primary fuels into secondary fuels, i.e. the energy lost burning coal to generate electricity or the energy used by refineries to separate crude oil into fractions, in addition to losses in distribution. The other common way of measuring energy consumption is to measure the energy content of the fuels supplied to consumers. This is called final energy consumption. It is net of fuel used by the energy industries, conversion, transmission and distribution losses. The figures are presented on a common basis, measured as energy supplied and expressed in million tonnes of oil equivalent. Estimates of the gross calorific values used for converting the statistics for the various fuels to these are given in the *Digest of UK Energy Statistics* (published by The Stationery Office and available on the Internet at www.dti.gov.uk/epa/dukes). So far as practicable the user categories have been grouped on the basis of the SIC92 although the methods used by each of the supply industries to identify end users are slightly different. Chapter 1 of the *Digest of UK Energy Statistics* gives more information on these figures.

Coal *(Table 21.5)*

Since 1995, aggregate data on coal production has been obtained from the Coal Authority. In addition main coal producers provide data in response to an annual DTI inquiry which covers production (deepmined and opencast), trade, stocks and disposals. HM Customs and Excise also provide trade data for solid fuels. The DTI collects information on the use of coal from Iron and Steel Statistics Bureau and consumption of coal for electricity generation is covered by data provided by the electricity generators.

Gas *(Table 21.6)*

Production figures, covering the production of gas from the UKCS offshore and onshore gas fields and gas obtained during the production of oil, are obtained from returns made under the DTI's Petroleum Production Reporting System. Additional information is used on imports and exports of gas and details from the operators of gas terminals in the UK to complete the picture.

It is no longer possible to present information on fuels input into the gas industry and gas output and sales in the same format as in previous editions of this table. As such, users are directed to Chapter 4 of the 2000 edition of the *Digest of UK Energy Statistics*, where more detailed information on gas production and consumption in the UK is available.

DTI carry out an annual survey of gas suppliers to obtain details of gas sales to the various categories of consumer. Estimates are included for the suppliers with the smallest market share since the DTI inquiry covers only the largest suppliers (i.e. those more than about 0.5% per cent share of the UK market).

Electricity *(Tables 21.7 - 21.9)*
The electricity Tables 21.7 to 21.9 cover all generators and suppliers of electricity in the United Kingdom.

The relationship between generation, supply, availability and consumption is as follows:

Electricity generated
less	electricity used on works
equals	electricity supplied (gross)
less	electricity used in pumping at pumped storage stations
equals	electricity supplied (net)
plus	imports (net of exports) of electricity
equals	electricity available
less	losses and statistical differences
equals	electricity consumed.

In table 21.7 'major power producers' are those generating companies corresponding to the old public sector supply system, ie. AES Electric Ltd., Anglian Power Generation, Barking Power Ltd., BNFL Magnox, British Energy plc., Coolkeeragh Power Ltd., Corby Power Ltd., Coryton Energay Company Ltd., Deeside Power, Derwent Cogeneration Ltd., Edison Mission Energy Ltd., Enfield Energy Centre Ltd., Entergy Power Group Ltd., Fellside Heat and Power Ltd., Fibrogen Ltd., Fibropower Ltd., Fibrothetford Ltd., Fife Power Ltd., Humber Power Ltd., Innology plc., International Power plc., Killingholme Power Ltd., Lakeland Power Ltd., London Electricity plc., Medway Power Ltd., Midlands Power Ltd., NIGEN, Peterborough Power Ltd., PowerGen plc., Premier Power Ltd., Regional Power Generators Ltd., Rocksavage Power Company Ltd., Sita Tyre Recycling Ltd., Scottish Power plc., Scottish and Southern Energy plc., Seabank Power Ltd., SELCHP Ltd. (South East London Combined Heat & Power Ltd.), South Coast Power Ltd., South Western Electricity, Sutton Bridge Power Ltd., Teesside Power Ltd., TXU Europe Power Ltd.

In Table 21.9 all fuels are converted to the common unit of million tonnes of oil equivalent, i.e. the amounts of oil which would be needed to produce the output of electricity generated from those fuels.

More detailed statistics on energy are given in the *Digest of United Kingdom Energy Statistics 2001*. Readers may wish to note that the production and consumption of fuels are presented using commodity balances. A commodity balance shows the flows of an individual fuel through from production to final consumption, showing its use in transformation and energy industry own use.

Oil and oil products *(Tables 21.10 - 21.12)*
The data on the production of crude oil, condensates and natural gases given in Table 21.10 are collected by the DTI direct from the operators of production facilities and terminals situated on UK territory, either on land or on the UK continental shelf. Data is also collected from the companies on their trade in oil and oil products. This data is used in preference to the foreign trade as recorded by HM Customs & Excise in the Overseas Trade Statistics.

Data on the internal UK oil industry (i.e. on the supply, refining and distribution of oil and oil products in the UK) is collected by the UK Petroleum Industry Association. This data, reported by individual refining companies and wholesalers and supplemented where necessary by data from other sources, provides the contents of Tables 21.11 and 21.12. The data is presented in terms of deliveries to the inland UK market. This is regarded as an acceptable proxy for actual consumption of products. The main shortcoming is that whilst changes in stocks held by companies in central storage areas are taken into account, changes in the levels of stocks further down the retail ladder (such as stocks held on petrol station forecourts) are not. This is not thought to result in a significant degree of difference in the data.

Iron and steel *(Tables 21.13 - 21.15)*

Iron and steel industry
The general definition of the UK iron and steel industry is based on groups 271 "ECSC iron and steel", 272 "Tubes", and 273 "Primary Transformation" of the UK Standard Industrial Classification (1992), except those parts of groups 272 and 273 which cover cast iron pipes, drawn wire, cold formed sections and Ferro alloys.

The definition excludes certain products which may be made by works within the industry such as refined iron, finished steel castings, steel tyres, wheels, axles and rolled rings, open and closed die forgings,colliery arches and springs. Iron foundries and steel stockholders are also considered to be outside of the industry.

Statistics
The statistics for the UK iron and steel industry are compiled by ISSB Ltd. from data collected from UK steel producing companies with the exception of trade data which is based on HM Customs data.

Crude steel is the total of usable ingots, usable continuously cast semi-finished products and liquid steel for castings.

Production of finished products is the total production at the mill of that product after deduction of any material which is immediately scrapped.

Deliveries are based on invoiced tonnages and will include deliveries made to steel stockholders and service centres by the UK steel industry.

Production

For more detailed information on definitions etc please contact ISSB Ltd. on 020 7343 3900.

Construction *(Tables 21.21 - 21.22)*
Table 21.21 shows the value of contractors' output in the construction industry in Great Britain. Contractors' output is defined as the amount chargeable to customers for building and civil engineering work done in the relevant period. The data comes from surveys run by the Department for Transport , Local Government and the Regions (DTLR). As well as being an important input to the National Accounts, it is used by the government and the construction industry in their efforts to fully understand the industry, and also by Eurostat.

Table 21.22 shows the value of new orders in the construction industry; this is also collected by DTLR. This information relates to contracts for new construction work awarded to main contractors by clients in both the public and private sectors; it also includes speculative work, undertaken on the initiative of the firm, where no contract is awarded. New orders are used as a good indicator of future output.

Motor vehicle production *(Table 21.25)*
The figures represent the output of United Kingdom based manufacturers classified to Class 34.10 (motor vehicles) of the Standard Industrial Classification 1992. They are derived from the Motor Vehicle Production Inquiry (MVPI).

These figures include vehicles produced in the form of kits for assembly. The value of the kit must be 50% or more of the value of a corresponding complete vehicle.

Drink and tobacco *(Tables 21.26 and 21.27)*
Data for these tables are derived by Customs and Excise from the systems for collecting excise duties. Alcoholic drinks and tobacco products become liable to duty when released for consumption in the UK. Figures for releases include both home-produced products and commercial imports. Production figures are also available for potable spirits distilled and beer brewed in the UK.

Alcoholic drink *(Table 21.26)*
The figures for Imported and other spirits released for home consumption include gin and other UK produced spirits, for which a breakdown is not available.

Since June 1993 beer duty has been charged when the beer leaves the brewery or other registered premises. Previously duty was chargeable at an earlier stage (the worts stage) in the brewing process, and an allowance was made for wastage. Figures for years prior to 1994 include adjustments to bring them into line with current data. The change in June 1993 also led to the availability of data on the strength; a series in hectolitres of pure alcohol is shown from 1994.

Made wine with alcoholic strength from 1.2% to 5.5% is termed 'coolers'. Included in coolers are alcoholic lemonade and similar products of appropriate strength.

Tobacco Products *(Table 21.27)*
Releases of cigarettes and other tobacco products tend to be higher in the period before a Budget. Products may then be stocked, duty paid, before being sold.

21.1

Production and construction: summary table
United Kingdom

	Estimates for all firms (£ million)					
			Stocks and work in progress			
	Total turnover	Gross value added	At end of year	Change during year	Capital expenditure *less* disposals	Total employment costs
Standard Industrial Classification: Revised 1992						
Production and construction Sections C-F[3]						
	ZIYQ	KSCD	KSCE	KSCF	KSCG	AWKC
1995	589 269	..	75 248	6 067	29 539	98 919
1996	617 803	209 942	71 573	605	29 363	101 392
1997	635 402	215 385	71 978	−138	32 024	108 034
1998	633 423	213 228	70 025	407	34 086	112 063
1999	647 552	220 867	66 992	1 909	29 869	114 901
Production industries (Revised definitions) Sections C-E[3]						
	ZIYR	KSCL	KSCM	KSCN	KSCO	AWKH
1995	496 847	171 258	59 350	4 964	27 998	83 592
1996	523 632	179 432	56 675	122	27 943	85 213
1997	538 678	181 569	58 371	−1 150	30 149	89 323
1998	530 981	178 629	55 309	−559	32 267	93 426
1999	536 213	182 078	55 059	571	28 007	94 094
Mining and quarrying Section C[3]						
	ZIYS	KSCT	KSCU	KSCV	KSCW	AWKI
1995	23 922	14 925	591	−86	4 775	2 534
1996	27 507	18 633	658	14	4 977	2 533
1997	26 791	16 530	1 214	17	4 799	2 577
1998	24 139	13 421	1 044	57	6 275	2 538
1999	26 426	15 375	1 150	15	3 965	2 438
Mining and quarrying of energy producing materials Subsection CA[3]						
	ZIYT	KSDB	KSDC	KSDD	KSDE	KSDF
1995	20 380	13 363	368	−103	4 531	1 939
1996	23 320	16 796	372	−13	4 597	1 829
1997	22 961	14 759	926	−9	4 537	1 929
1998	19 660	11 631	758	28	5 940	1 827
1999	22 129	13 753	861	−	3 645	1 734
Mining and quarrying except energy producing materials Subsection CB						
	ZIYU	KSDJ	KSDK	KSDL	KSDM	KSDN
1995	3 541	1 562	223	18	244	595
1996	4 187	1 837	285	26	380	703
1997	3 830	1 771	288	26	262	647
1998	4 479	1 790	286	29	335	711
1999	4 298	1 623	289	14	320	705
Manufacturing (Revised definition) Section D						
	ZIYV	KSDR	KSDS	KSDT	KSDU	AWKL
1995	425 963	139 927	56 994	5 153	18 136	76 337
1996	450 177	144 001	54 560	129	18 565	78 764
1997	468 525	148 691	55 701	−1 143	20 248	82 894
1998	462 640	149 896	52 735	−604	20 505	86 818
1999	463 030	151 038	52 154	654	18 050	87 653

21.1 Production and construction: summary table
United Kingdom

			Estimates for all firms (£ million)			
			Stocks and work in progress			
		Gross value added	At end of year	Change during year	Capital expenditure *less* disposals	Total employment costs
	Total turnover					

Standard Industrial Classification: Revised 1992

Manufacture of food; beverages and tobacco
Subsection DA

	ZIYM	KSDZ	KSEA	KSEB	KSEC	AWKM
1995	73 749	17 926	6 824	388	2 538	8 441
1996	76 868	19 610	7 049	517	2 429	8 593
1997	77 320	20 041	7 616	259	2 665	9 243
1998	73 400	19 368	8 060	−230	2 761	9 337
1999	71 198	19 720	6 984	−121	2 642	9 821

Manufacture of textile and textile products
Subsection DB

	ZIYX	KSEH	KSEI	KSEJ	KSEK	AWKN
1995	17 679	6 810	3 016	197	474	4 172
1996	18 135	7 182	2 911	17	584	4 341
1997	18 874	7 664	3 046	29	506	4 607
1998	17 364	6 699	2 906	−140	552	4 476
1999	16 156	5 909	2 608	−66	460	4 055

Manufacture of leather and leather products
Subsection DC

	ZIYY	KSEP	KSEQ	KSER	KSES	AWKO
1995	2 343	824	365	25	65	635
1996	2 395	900	389	5	53	487
1997	2 152	787	409	45	49	478
1998	1 987	671	410	−10	42	461
1999	1 837	715	368	26	38	360

Manufacture of wood and wood products
Subsection DD

	ZIYZ	KSEX	KSEY	KSEZ	KSFA	AWKP
1995	6 158	1 978	763	12	157	1 222
1996	6 010	1 930	675	−7	169	1 233
1997	6 145	2 218	667	15	237	1 267
1998	5 797	2 270	593	6	255	1 360
1999	5 839	2 074	510	−13	238	1 250

Manufacture of pulp, paper and paper products; publishing and printing
Subsection DE

	ZIZA	KSFF	KSFG	KSFH	KSFI	AWKQ
1995	40 700	17 269	3 275	460	2 187	8 781
1996	42 637	17 495	2 947	−207	1 843	9 403
1997	42 166	17 717	3 035	−44	2 087	9 762
1998	42 721	18 296	2 660	−28	1 957	10 277
1999	43 563	19 395	2 613	68	1 730	10 270

Manufacture of coke, refined petroleum products and nuclear fuel
Subsection DF

	ZIZB	KSFN	KSFO	KSFP	KSFQ	AWKR
1995	21 566	2 895	1 178	215	776	785
1996	24 755	2 442	1 076	−94	738	828
1997	25 593	2 024	1 171	−175	704	787
1998	25 609	2 289	885	−196	730	923
1999	27 726	2 866	1 305	410	777	998

21.1
continued

Production and construction: summary table
United Kingdom

	Total turnover	Gross value added	Estimates for all firms (£ million)		Capital expenditure *less* disposals	Total employment costs
			Stocks and work in progress			
			At end of year	Change during year		

Standard Industrial Classification: Revised 1992

Manufacture of chemicals, chemical products and man-made fibres
Subsection DG

	ZIZC	KSFV	KSFW	KSFX	KSFY	AWKS
1995	43 846	15 471	5 771	453	2 337	6 618
1996	44 988	15 392	5 692	267	2 779	6 589
1997	46 722	14 582	5 595	−44	2 917	6 852
1998	44 688	14 081	5 705	96	3 285	7 085
1999	46 371	14 600	6 025	56	2 786	7 776

Manufacture of rubber and plastic products
Subsection DH

	ZIZD	KSGD	KSGE	KSGF	KSGG	AWKT
1995	18 147	6 713	1 837	175	960	4 102
1996	19 347	7 187	1 911	28	995	4 349
1997	20 323	7 834	1 908	34	1 072	4 631
1998	20 420	8 062	2 021	54	1 102	4 855
1999	19 406	7 526	1 885	26	1 080	4 927

Manufacture of other non-metallic mineral products
Subsection DI

	ZIZE	KSGL	KSGM	KSGN	KSGO	AWKU
1995	12 051	5 201	1 495	126	619	2 810
1996	11 565	5 102	1 471	98	672	2 730
1997	11 866	5 092	1 527	17	571	2 798
1998	11 346	4 904	1 420	29	656	2 771
1999	11 738	4 872	1 366	−104	747	2 758

Manufacture of basic iron and of ferro-alloys
Subsection DJ

	ZIZF	KSGT	KSGU	KSGV	KSGW	AWKV
1995	44 440	16 623	4 856	521	1 517	9 794
1996	45 158	15 878	4 624	14	1 749	10 066
1997	43 401	16 335	4 289	−23	1 744	9 988
1998	44 399	17 330	4 255	−130	2 024	10 739
1999	41 689	16 359	4 034	88	1 429	10 548

Manufacture of machinery and equipment not elsewhere specified
Subsection DK

	ZIZG	KSHB	KSHC	KSHD	KSHE	AWKW
1995	34 039	12 316	5 742	374	1 117	7 802
1996	35 118	12 591	5 277	63	1 223	7 780
1997	36 045	13 373	5 483	96	1 109	8 345
1998	35 580	13 412	5 086	46	978	8 636
1999	33 499	12 339	5 038	−221	950	8 351

Manufacture of electrical and optical equipment
Subsection DL

	ZIZH	KSHJ	KSHK	KSHL	KSHM	AWKX
1995	51 434	17 437	7 577	770	2 592	9 583
1996	56 485	18 069	7 180	−224	2 386	10 147
1997	61 008	18 964	7 337	16	2 792	10 766
1998	61 037	19 203	6 832	−10	2 688	11 568
1999	64 961	20 183	7 079	132	1 939	11 873

21.1
continued

Production and construction: summary table
United Kingdom

	Estimates for all firms (£ million)					
			Stocks and work in progress			
	Total turnover	Gross value added	At end of year	Change during year	Capital expenditure *less* disposals	Wages and salaries
Standard Industrial Classification: Revised 1992						
Manufacture of transport equipment Subsection DM						
	ZIZI	KSHR	KSHS	KSHT	KSHU	AWKY
1995	46 256	13 689	12 565	1 323	2 361	8 534
1996	52 714	14 991	11 716	−437	2 488	9 020
1997	61 465	16 204	11 729	−1 427	3 237	9 876
1998	62 933	17 157	10 330	−200	2 948	10 840
1999	62 964	18 231	10 507	302	2 750	10 859
Manufacture not elsewhere classified Subsection DN						
	ZIZJ	KSHZ	KSIA	KSIB	KSIC	AWKZ
1995	13 555	4 774	1 729	114	437	3 057
1996	14 001	5 231	1 641	88	457	3 199
1997	15 443	5 856	1 890	62	557	3 494
1998	15 356	6 153	1 574	110	528	3 493
1999	16 082	6 248	1 831	70	483	3 808
Electricity, gas and water supply Section E						
	ZIZK	KSIH	KSII	KSIJ	KSIK	AWLA
1995	46 961	16 045	1 765	−104	5 086	4 722
1996	45 948	16 797	1 458	−21	4 402	3 916
1997	43 361	16 348	1 456	−25	5 102	3 852
1998	44 202	15 312	1 529	−13	5 487	4 070
1999	46 757	15 666	1 754	−98	5 993	4 002
Construction Section F						
	ZIZL	KSIP	KSIQ	KSIR	KSIS	AWLB
1995	92 423	..	15 897	1 103	1 541	15 327
1996	94 171	30 510	14 898	483	1 420	16 179
1997	96 724	33 816	13 607	1 012	1 875	18 711
1998	102 441	34 600	14 716	966	1 819	18 636
1999	111 339	38 789	11 934	1 338	1 862	20 807

Source: Office for National Statistics: 01633 812435

21.2 Manufacturers' sales by industry[1]
United Kingdom

£ millions

Industry		SIC (92)	1996	1997	1998	1999
Other mining and quarrying						
Quarrying of stone for construction	KSPF	14110	..	..	..	..
Quarrying of limestone, gypsum and chalk	KSPG	14120	..	..	..	..
Quarrying of slate	KSPH	14130	..	..	..	..
Operation of gravel and sand pits	KSPJ	14210	..	..	..	..
Mining of clays and kaolin	KSPK	14220	..	..	..	..
Mining of chemical and fertilizer minerals	KSPL	14300	141	60	151	
Production of salt	KSPM	14400	..	..	..	..
Other mining and quarrying n.e.c.	KSPN	14500	55	65	89	..
Manufacture of food products and beverages						
Production and preserving of meat	KSPO	15110	3 650	3 671	3 390	3 314
Production and preserving of poultry meat	KSPP	15120	1 675	1 650	1 568	1 601
Bacon and ham production	KSPQ	15131		..	..	874
Other meat and poultry meat processing	KSPR	15139[2]	3 452	3 548	3 714	3 691
Processing and preserving of fish and fish products	KSPS	15200	1 531	1 387	1 377	1 532
Processing and preserving of potatoes	KSPT	15310	..	1 148	..	..
Fruit and vegetable juice	KSPU	15320	488	..	..	473
Processing and preserving of fruit and vegetables n.e.c.	KSPV	15330	2 005	1 955	1 954	1 981
Crude oils and fats	KSPW	15410	525	587	635	476
Refined oils and fats	KSPX	15420	567	486	489	462
Margarine and similar edible fats	KSPY	15430	478	465	443	442
Operation of dairies	KTEH	15510	..	5 794	5 756	5 593
Ice cream	KSPZ	15520	567	..	530	484
Grain mill products	KSQA	15610	2 927	2 827	2 681	2 707
Starches and starch products	KSQB	15620	482	441	376	378
Prepared feeds for farm animals	KSPI	15710	2 558	2 987	3 488	3 489
Prepared pet foods	KSQC	15720	..	1 458	1 321	1 142
Bread; fresh pastry goods and cakes	KSQD	15810	3 785	3 861	4 198	3 877
Rusks and biscuits; preserved pastry goods and cakes	KSQE	15820	3 249	..	3 062	..
Sugar	KSQF	15830	1 383	1 308	1 205	..
Cocoa; chocolate and sugar confectionery	KSQG	15840	3 139	3 333	3 312	3 323
Macaroni, noodles, couscous and similar farinaceous products	KSQH	15850	374	..	..	..
Processing of tea and coffee	KSQI	15860	1 349	1 384	1 484	..
Condiments and seasonings	KSQJ	15870	..	..	..	..
Homogenised food preparations and dietetic foods	KSQK	15880	113	123	..	..
Manufacture of other food products n.e.c.	KSQL	15890	..	1 519	1 848	1 871
Distilled potable alcoholic beverages	KSQM	15910	2 263	2 068	2 110	2 181
Production of ethyl alcohol from fermented materials	KSQN	15920	..	..	104	101
Wines	KSQO	15930	..	..	160	96
Cider and other fruit wines	KSQP	15940	..	..	465	527
Other non-distilled fermented beverages	KSQQ	15950	–	–	–	–
Beer	KSQR	15960	5 458	5 455	4 719	..
Malt	KSQS	15970	433	365	296	257
Mineral waters and soft drinks	KSQT	15980	..	..	..	2 718
Manufacture of tobacco products						
Tobacco products	KSQU	16000	2 616	2 622	2 482	2 440
Manufacture of textiles						
Preparation and spinning of textile fibres	KSQV	17100	1 482	837	999	892
Textile weaving	KSQW	17200	1 320	518	1 083	972
Finishing of textiles	KSQX	17300	..	778	715	630
Soft furnishings	KSQY	17401	451	723	494	448
Canvas goods, sacks etc	KSQZ	17402	181	145	127	161
Household textiles	KSRA	17403	..	926	896	897
Carpets and rugs	KSRB	17510	..	1 103	1 083	1 031
Cordage, rope, twine and netting	KSRC	17520	81	100	83	80

21.2

Manufacturers' sales by industry[1]
United Kingdom

continued

£ millions

Industry		SIC (92)	1996	1997	1998	1999
Manufacture of textiles continued						
Nonwovens and articles made from nonwovens, except apparel	KSRD	17530	145	141	145	158
Lace	KSRE	17541	105	88	62	39
Narrow fabrics	KSRF	17542	255	..	236	223
Other textiles n.e.c.	KSRG	17549[3]	603	598	524	499
Knitted and crocheted fabrics	KSRH	17600	625	608	..	..
Knitted and crocheted hosiery	KSRI	17710	546	495	451	357
Knitted and crocheted pullovers, cardigans and similar	KSRJ	17720	922	1 007	771	664
Manufacture of wearing apparel; dressing and dyeing of fur						
Leather clothes	KSRK	18100	25	16	20	15
Workwear	KSRL	18210	269	..	290	284
Men's outerwear	KSRM	18221	1 051	894	759	620
Other women's outerwear	KSRN	18222	1 716	1 460	1 302	1 003
Men's underwear	KSRO	18231	557	581	572	437
Women's underwear	KSRP	18232	1 025	902	938	777
Hats	KSRQ	18241	97	..	71	63
Other wearing apparel and accessories	KSRR	18249[4]	748	212	661	605
Dressing/dyeing of fur; articles of fur	KSRS	18300	25	19	7	6
Tanning and dressing of leather; manufacture of luggage, handbags, saddlery, harness and footwear						
Tanning and dressing of leather	KSRT	19100	444	365	363	323
Luggage, handbags and the like, saddlery and harness	KSRU	19200	239	248	238	262
Footwear	KSRV	19300	1 295	1 026	899	764
Manufacture of wood and of products of wood and cork, except furniture; manufacture of articles of straw and plaiting materials						
Sawmilling and planing of wood, impregnation of wood	KSRW	20100	710	663	619	678
Veneer sheets	KSRX	20200	815	783	709	705
Builders' carpentry and joinery	KSRY	20300	1 972	1 972	2 038	1 832
Wooden containers	KSRZ	20400	567	515	500	449
Other products of wood	KSSA	20510	428	319	383	362
Articles of cork, straw and plaiting materials	KSSB	20520	35	29	..	28
Manufacture of pulp, paper and paper products						
Paper and paperboard	KSSC	21120	3 972	3 582	3 338	3 055
Corrugated paper and paperboard, sacks and bags	KSSD	21211	624	..	..	521
Cartons, boxes, cases and other containers	KSSE	21219[5]	3 683	3 524	3 447	3 274
Household and sanitary goods and toilet requisites	KSSF	21220	1 699	1 431	..	..
Paper stationery	KSSG	21230	928	813	739	685
Wallpaper	KSSH	21240	..	..	302	291
Other articles of paper and paperboard n.e.c.	KSSI	21250	841	784	799	781
Publishing, printing and reproduction of recorded media						
Publishing of books	KSSJ	22110	3 001	2 815	2 973	3 294
Publishing of newspapers	KSSK	22120	3 131	3 455	3 573	3 574
Publishing of journals and periodicals	KSSL	22130	5 649	5 754	6 164	6 652
Publishing of sound recordings	KSSM	22140	132	..	..	147
Other publishing	KSSN	22150	423	417	476	527
Printing of newspapers	KSSO	22210	239	212	..	..
Printing n.e.c.	KSSP	22220	9 384	9 043	9 127	9 413
Bookbinding and finishing	KSSQ	22230	419	383	369	387
Composition and plate-making	KSSR	22240	852	711	538	539
Other activities related to printing	KSSS	22250	410	519	651	704
Reproduction of sound recording	KSST	22310	371	..	336	..
Reproduction of video recording	KSSU	22320	..	..	193	..
Reproduction of computer media	KSSV	22330	119	92	118	..
Manufacture of chemicals and chemical products						
Industrial gases	KSSW	24110	827	535	600	530
Dyes and pigments	KSSX	24120	1 727	1 114	1 031	1 058
Other inorganic basic chemicals	KSSY	24130	2 305	1 538	1 366	1 251
Other organic basic chemicals	KSSZ	24140	7 014	4 810	4 045	4 094
Fertilizers and nitrogen compounds	KSTA	24150	1 053	764	631	734

21.2
continued

Manufacturers' sales by industry[1]
United Kingdom

£ millions

Industry	SIC (92)	1996	1997	1998	1999
Manufacture of chemicals and chemical products continued					
Plastics in primary forms	KSTB 24160	4 772	..	3 342	3 493
Synthetic rubber in primary forms	KSTC 24170	368	207	349	..
Pesticides and other agro-chemical products	KSTD 24200	1 874	1 159	..	726
Paints, varnishes and similar coatings, printing ink and mastic	KSTE 24300	2 807	2 229	2 482	2 614
Basic pharmaceutical products	KSTF 24410	1 042	624	515	521
Pharmaceutical preparations	KSTG 24420	6 283	5 969	6 029	7 292
Soap and detergents, cleaning and polishing preparations	KSTH 24510	2 405	1 889	1 840	1 924
Perfumes and toilet preparations	KSTI 24520	2 533	..	2 471	2 549
Explosives	KSTJ 24610	118	122	112	107
Glues and gelatines	KSTK 24620	402	397	449	353
Essential oils	KSTL 24630	314	432	466	497
Photographic chemical material	KSTM 24640	1 645	1 158	1 209	..
Prepared unrecorded media	KSTN 24650	297	..	137	141
Other chemical products n.e.c.	KSTO 24660	2 645	2 193	2 230	2 324
Man-made fibres	KSTP 24700	1 463	..	756	671
Manufacture of rubber and plastic products					
Rubber tyres and tubes	KSTQ 25110	1 118	1 006	1 014	972
Retreading and rebuilding of rubber tyres	KSTR 25120	180	..	..	124
Other rubber products	KSTS 25130	1 687	1 740	1 802	1 717
Plastic plates, sheets, tubes and profiles	KSTT 25210	3 351	3 312	3 196	3 158
Plastic packing goods	KSTU 25220	2 827	2 677	2 682	2 646
Builders' ware of plastic	KSTV 25230	3 084	3 074	3 251	3 155
Other plastic products	KSTW 25240	3 793	3 867	3 918	4 191
Manufacture of other non-metallic mineral products					
Flat glass	KSTX 26110	271	168	159	..
Shaping and processing of flat glass	KSTY 26120	646	738	812	790
Hollow glass	KSTZ 26130	730	744	721	..
Glass fibres	KSUA 26140	349	320	314	298
Manufacturing and processing of other glass including technical glassware	KSUB 26150	208	..	328	..
Ceramic household and ornamental articles	KSUC 26210	774	740	655	587
Ceramic sanitary fixtures	KSUD 26220	172	..	..	..
Ceramic insulators and insulating fittings	KSUE 26230	..	..	23	23
Other technical ceramic products	KSUF 26240	26	..	..	29
Other ceramic products	KSUG 26250	17	15	22	..
Refractory ceramic products	KSUH 26260	515	496	475	443
Ceramic tiles and flags	KSUI 26300	93	118	103	92
Bricks, tiles and construction products in baked clay	KSUJ 26400	603	601	..	656
Cement	KSUK 26510	..	706	..	774
Lime	KSUL 26520	..	..	..	..
Plaster	KSUM 26530	..	..	..	104
Concrete products for construction purposes	KSUN 26610	1 442	1 647	1 587	..
Plaster products for construction purposes	KSUO 26620	..	258	281	..
Ready mixed concrete	KSUP 26630	981	..	1 047	..
Mortars	KSUQ 26640	111	..	..	69
Fibre cement	KSUR 26650	105	..	96	99
Other articles of concrete, plaster and cement	KSUS 26660	135	127	..	122
Cutting, shaping and finishing of stone	KSUT 26700	206	205	216	197
Abrasive products	KSUU 26810	239	245	239	220
Other non-metallic mineral products n.e.c.	KSUV 26820	775	772	746	675
Manufacture of basic metals					
Cast iron tubes	KSUW 27210	..	154	127	121
Steel tubes	KSUX 27220	1 471	1 398	1 486	1 321
Cold drawing	KSUY 27310	232	222	..	..

21.2 continued

Manufacturers' sales by industry[1]
United Kingdom

£ millions

Industry		SIC (92)	1996	1997	1998	1999
Manufacture of basic metals continued						
Cold rolling of narrow strip	KSUZ	27320	134	124	126	105
Cold forming or folding	KSVA	27330	166	156	159	122
Wire drawing	KSVB	27340	353	369	331	301
Other first processing of iron and steel n.e.c.	KSVC	27350	84	98	86	..
Precious metals production	KSVD	27410	252	285	234	267
Aluminium production	KSVE	27420	2 270	2 314	2 160	..
Lead, zinc and tin production	KSVF	27430	492	435	389	363
Copper production	KSVG	27440	..	1 046	856	751
Other non-ferrous metal production	KSVH	27450	671	634	605	505
Casting of iron	KSVI	27510	853	815	757	647
Casting of steel	KSVJ	27520	228	226	185	151
Casting of light metals	KSVK	27530	257	302	318	279
Casting of other non-ferrous metals	KSVL	27540	498	478	464	..
Manufacture of fabricated metal products, except machinery and equipment						
Metal structures and parts of structures	KSVM	28110	4 172	4 579	4 649	4 783
Builders' carpentry and joinery of metal	KSVN	28120	777	813	807	872
Tanks, reservoirs and containers of metal	KSVO	28210	..	412	..	..
Central heating radiators and boilers	KSVP	28220	588	635	646	624
Steam generators, except central heating hot water boilers	KSVQ	28300	643	531	530	567
Forging, pressing, stamping and roll forming of metal	KSVR	28400	2 393	2 250	2 207	2 068
Treatment and coating of metals	KSVS	28510	1 052	1 072	1 156	1 123
General mechanical engineering	KSVT	28520	2 818	2 829	2 853	3 053
Cutlery	KSVU	28610	241	206	220	..
Tools	KSVV	28620	1 106	1 086	1 024	941
Locks and hinges	KSVW	28630	703	723	663	680
Steel drums and similar containers	KSVX	28710	210	..	184	190
Light metal packaging	KSVY	28720	1 415	1 297	1 234	1 167
Wire products	KSVZ	28730	656	609	569	521
Fasteners, screw machine products, chain and spring	KSWA	28740	866	797	782	684
Other fabricated metal products n.e.c.	KSWB	28750	1 651	1 661	1 726	1 678
Manufacture of machinery and equipment not elsewhere classified						
Engines and turbines, except aircraft, vehicles and cycle engines	KSWC	29110	1 356	1 444	..	1 566
Pumps	KSWD	29121	1 031	1 048	1 024	1 049
Compressors	KSWE	29122	1 184	1 190	1 224	1 221
Taps and valves	KSWF	29130	1 393	1 296	1 377	1 171
Bearings, gears, gearing and driving elements	KSWG	29140	1 206	1 167	1 115	1 016
Furnaces and furnace burners	KSWH	29210	374	..	411	310
Lifting and handling equipment	KSWI	29220	2 737	2 641	2 753	2 759
Non-domestic cooling and ventilation equipment	KSWJ	29230	2 296	2 403	2 651	2 516
Other general purpose machinery n.e.c.	KSWK	29240	2 252	2 125	2 313	2 144
Agricultural tractors	KSWL	29310	..	1 047	1 060	920
Other agricultural and forestry machinery	KSWM	29320	602	592	619	619
Machine tools	KSWN	29400	1 906	2 090	2 025	1 900
Machinery for metallurgy	KSWO	29510	141	105	92	79
Machinery for mining	KSWP	29521	426	487	545	422
Earth-moving equipment	KSWQ	29522	913	1 006	999	..
Equipment for concrete crushing and screening and roadworks	KSWR	29523	587	497	543	..
Machinery for food, beverage and tobacco processing	KSWS	29530	893	780	656	661
Machinery for textile, apparel and leather production	KSWT	29540	391	400	683	255
Machinery for paper and paperboard production	KSWU	29550	393	286	318	234
Other special purpose machinery n.e.c.	KSWV	29560	2 216	2 277	2 129	1 963
Weapons and ammunition	KSWW	29600	2 086	1 673	1 724	1 503

21.2
Manufacturers' sales by industry[1]
United Kingdom
continued

£ millions

Industry	SIC (92)	1996	1997	1998	1999
Manufacture of machinery and equipment not elsewhere classified continued					
Electric domestic appliances	KSYR 29710	1 923	2 025	1 870	1 744
Non-electric domestic appliances	KSWX 29720	498	515	..	495
Manufacture of office machinery and computers					
Office machinery	KSWY 30010	1 005	1 040	1 165	..
Computers and other information processing equipment	KSWZ 30020	11 968	9 974	9 801	9 291
Manufacture of electrical machinery and apparatus not elsewhere classified					
Electric motors, generators and transformers	KSXA 31100	2 635	2 719	2 324	2 236
Electricity, distribution and control apparatus	KSXB 31200	2 510	2 657	2 522	2 552
Insulated wire and cable	KSXC 31300	..	..	..	1 313
Accumulators, primary cells and batteries	KSXD 31400	526	499	482	500
Lighting equipment and electric lamps	KSXE 31500	1 348	1 333	1 293	1 267
Electrical equipment for engines and vehicles n.e.c.	KSXF 31610	..	1 161	1 144	1 065
Other electrical equipment n.e.c.	KSXG 31620	2 162	1 917	1 745	1 608
Manufacture of radio, television and communication equipment and apparatus					
Electronic valves and tubes and other electronic components	KSXH 32100	3 830	4 099	4 489	3 948
Telegraph and telephone apparatus and equipment	KSXI 32201	..	3 174	3 465	4 518
Radio and electronic capital goods	KSXJ 32202	2 290	2 984	3 004	4 194
Television and radio receivers, sound or video recording etc	KSXK 32300	3 488	3 717	3 400	3 371
Manufacture of medical, precision and optical instruments, watches and clocks					
Medical and surgical equipment and orthopaedic appliances	KSXL 33100	1 811	1 719	1 696	1 748
Instruments and appliances for measuring, checking, testing etc	KSXM 33200	4 817	4 950	4 880	4 894
Industrial process control equipment	KSXN 33300	655	771	865	858
Optical instruments and photographic equipment	KSXO 33400	876	926	939	989
Watches and clocks	KSXP 33500	89	92	92	96
Manufacture of motor vehicles, trailers and semi-trailers					
Motor vehicles	KSXQ 34100	20 383	20 839	20 868	21 877
Bodies (coachwork) for motor vehicles (excluding caravans)	KSXR 34201	800	781	906	818
Trailers and semi-trailers	KSXS 34202	1 050	962	961	891
Caravans	KSXT 34203	386	392	343	377
Parts and accessories for motor vehicles and their engines	KSXU 34300	8 248	8 036	8 729	8 621
Manufacture of other transport equipment					
Building and repairing of ships	KSXV 35110	4 118	..	1 538	2 115
Building and repairing of pleasure and sporting boats	KSXW 35120	394	398	436	458
Railway and tramway locomotives and rolling stock	KSXX 35200	978	976	996	..
Aircraft and spacecraft	KSXY 35300	10 191	11 827	..	13 911
Motorcycles	KSXZ 35410	..	..	..	..
Bicycles	KSYA 35420	148	159	115	112
Invalid carriages	KSYB 35430	..	96	..	..
Other transport equipment n.e.c.	KSYC 35500	..	71	..	72
Manufacture of furniture; manufacturing not elsewhere classified					
Chairs and seats	KSYD 36110	2 348	2 300	2 421	2 373
Other office and shop furniture	KSYE 36120	1 429	1 296	1 286	1 294
Other kitchen furniture	KSYF 36130	920	1 026	908	1 076
Other furniture	KSYG 36140	2 104	2 160	1 950	2 234
Mattresses	KSYH 36150	390	467	493	491
Striking of coins and medals	KSYI 36210	131	..	..	..
Jewellery and related articles n.e.c.	KSYJ 36220	618	554	518	..
Musical instruments	KSYK 36300	63	..	62	55
Sports goods	KSYL 36400	292	264	269	266
Games and toys	KSYM 36500	601	507	465	448
Imitation jewellery	KSYN 36610	46	33	33	33
Brooms and brushes	KSYO 36620	179	192	174	175
Miscellaneous stationers' goods	KSYP 36631	284	287	267	269
Other manufacturing n.e.c.	KSYQ 36639[6]	474	500	507	518

1 The data are collected under the PRODCOM inquiry which was introduced in 1993. The inquiry replaced the previous QSI/ASI inquiries.
2 Previously 15132.
3 Previously 17543.
4 Previously 18242.
5 Previously 21212.
6 Previously 36632.

Source: Office for National Statistics: 01633 813065

351

21.3 Number of local units in manufacturing industries in 2001[1]
United Kingdom
Standard Industrial Classification 1992 Division by Employment Sizeband

					Employment size				Total
		1 - 9	10 - 19	20 - 49	50 - 99	100 - 199	200 - 499	500 - 999	1,000+	

Number of local units

Division

		1 - 9	10 - 19	20 - 49	50 - 99	100 - 199	200 - 499	500 - 999	1,000+	Total
15/16	Food products; beverages and tobacco	6 070	1 725	1 180	600	495	455	130	45	10 700
17	Textiles and textile products	3 705	705	655	330	245	110	15	-	5 765
18	Wearing apparel; dressing and dyeing of fur	4 200	845	615	195	115	70	10	-	6 055
19	Leather and leather products	645	125	115	70	40	20	-	-	1 020
20	Wood and wood products	6 810	885	535	150	65	20	5	-	8 475
21	Pulp, paper and paper products	1 560	345	425	235	195	90	10	-	2 860
22	Publishing, printing and reproduction of recorded media	24 440	2 930	1 680	630	330	185	40	10	30 245
23	Coke, refined petroleum products and nuclear fuel	155	35	40	25	10	10	10	5	285
24	Chemicals, chemical products and man-made fibres	2 355	520	570	365	265	190	75	25	4 365
25	Rubber and plastic products	4 335	1 220	1 105	530	335	165	25	5	7 725
26	Other non-metallic mineral products	4 935	750	580	305	170	100	15	-	6 855
27	Basic metals	1 465	315	350	195	140	85	25	5	2 585
28	Fabricated metal products, except machinery and equipment	21 745	3 870	2 575	900	380	145	30	-	29 640
29	Machinery and equipment not elsewhere classified	8 890	1 975	1 635	725	400	245	50	20	13 950
30	Office machinery and computers	960	120	95	65	40	30	10	10	1 325
31	Electrical machinery and apparatus not elsewhere classified	3 750	695	625	330	205	165	35	5	5 805
32	Radio, television and communication equipment and apparatus	1 835	275	275	130	110	75	40	20	2 765
33	Medical, precision and optical instruments, watches and clocks	3 220	645	560	285	165	75	25	-	4 970
34	Motor vehicles, trailers and semi-trailers	1 520	365	380	210	155	160	50	25	2 860
35	Other transport equipment	1 635	240	205	100	90	65	30	35	2 405
36/37	Manufacturing not elsewhere classified	16 860	1 710	990	430	205	120	20	-	20 340
Total manufacturing (15/37)		121 095	20 290	15 200	6 810	4 160	2 585	640	220	171 000

1 The data in this table is taken from the NS publication, Business Monitor *PA1003 - Size Analysis of United Kingdom Businesses* 2001 edition. The count of units refers to local units, i.e. individual sites, rather than whole businesses. All counts have been rounded to avoid disclosure.

Source: Office for National Statistics: 01633 813269

21.4 Total inland energy consumption
United Kingdom
Heat supplied basis

Million tonnes of oil equivalent

		1990	1991	1992	1993	1994	1995	1996	1997	1998	1999	2000
Inland energy consumption of primary fuels and equivalents[1]	KLWA	213.6	219.5	216.7	220.7	217.5	218.4	230.3	226.1	230.7	230.7	232.5
Coal[2,3]	KLWB	66.9	67.1	63.0	55.0	51.3	48.9	45.7	40.8	41.0	36.7	38.1
Petroleum[4]	KLWC	77.2	77.1	77.5	78.1	76.7	75.4	77.8	75.4	76.0	75.9	75.2
Primary electricity	KLWD	17.7	19.2	20.4	23.4	23.1	23.1	23.8	24.8	25.0	24.0	21.4
Natural gas	KLWE	51.2	55.4	55.1	62.9	64.9	69.2	80.9	82.7	86.2	91.4	94.9
less Energy used by fuel producers and losses in conversion and distribution	KLWF	66.3	67.7	65.6	68.0	65.0	68.0	73.0	71.7	74.3	72.0	72.4
Total consumption by final users[1]	KLWG	147.3	151.8	151.1	152.7	152.5	150.4	157.3	154.4	156.4	158.7	160.1
Final energy consumption by type of fuel												
Coal (direct use)[3]	KLWH	8.1	8.6	8.1	7.6	6.9	5.3	4.5	4.4	3.8	3.9	2.6
Coke and breeze	KLWI	4.3	4.0	3.9	3.8	3.9	3.9	1.0	0.8	0.9	0.9	0.9
Other solid fuel[3]	KLWJ	0.8	0.8	0.7	0.8	0.8	0.7	0.8	0.7	0.7	0.6	0.6
Coke oven gas	KLWK	0.6	0.6	0.5	0.6	0.6	0.6	0.6	0.6	0.4	0.4	0.4
Natural gas (direct use)	KLWL	46.1	49.7	48.4	49.3	49.9	50.1	56.6	54.2	56.4	57.6	60.0
Electricity	KLWM	23.6	24.2	24.2	24.6	24.4	25.3	26.2	26.6	27.2	27.8	28.3
Petroleum (direct use)[5]	KLWN	63.3	63.5	64.6	65.4	65.2	63.7	66.1	65.4	66.0	66.5	66.5
Final energy consumption by class of consumer												
Agriculture	KLWP	1.3	1.4	1.4	1.4	1.4	1.3	1.4	1.3	1.4	1.3	1.2
Iron and steel industry	KLWQ	6.9	6.6	6.5	7.0	7.7	7.7	4.1	4.2	4.0	4.1	3.9
Other industries	KLWR	31.7	31.6	30.2	29.5	30.0	28.6	30.6	30.7	31.0	32.2	32.2
Railways[6]	KLWS	1.1	1.1	1.2	1.3	1.3	1.3	1.3	1.2	1.3	1.2	1.2
Road transport	KLWT	38.8	38.5	39.4	39.5	39.7	39.3	40.8	41.3	41.0	41.4	41.1
Water transport	KLWU	1.4	1.4	1.4	1.3	1.2	1.2	1.3	1.3	1.2	1.1	1.0
Air transport	KLWV	7.3	6.9	7.4	7.9	8.1	8.5	8.9	9.3	10.2	11.0	11.9
Domestic	KLWW	40.8	44.8	44.1	45.5	43.9	42.7	48.1	44.8	46.1	46.1	46.8
Public administration	KLWX	7.6	8.5	9.1	8.1	8.3	8.5	8.9	8.6	8.2	8.1	8.1
Commercial and other services	KLWY	10.3	11.0	10.5	11.2	11.0	11.4	12.0	11.7	12.0	12.2	12.6

1 Includes small amounts of primary heat sources (solar, geothermal, etc.).
2 Includes net trade and stock change in other solid fuels.
3 Includes solid renewable sources (wood, waste, etc.).
4 Refinery throughput of crude oil, *plus* net foreign trade and stock change in petroleum products. Petroleum products not used as fuels (chemical feedstock, industrial and white spirits, lubricants, bitumen and wax) are excluded.

5 Includes briquettes, ovoids, Phurnacite, Coalite, etc, and wood, waste etc used for heat generation.
6 Includes fuel used at transport premises.

Source: Department of Trade and Industry: 020 7215 5187

21.5 Coal: supply and demand[1]
United Kingdom

Million tonnes

		1990	1991	1992	1993	1994	1995	1996	1997	1998	1999	2000
Supply												
Production of deep-mined coal	KLXA	72.9	73.4	65.8	50.5	31.9	35.2	32.2	30.3	25.5	20.9	17.2
Production of opencast coal	KLXB	18.1	18.6	18.2	17.0	16.8	16.4	16.3	16.7	14.5	15.3	13.4
Total	KLXC	91.0	92.0	84.0	67.5	48.7	51.5	48.5	47.0	40.0	36.2	30.6
Recovered slurry, fines, etc	KLXD	1.7	2.2	0.5	0.7	0.1	1.5	1.7	1.5	1.1	0.9	0.6
Imports	KLXE	14.8	19.6	20.3	18.4	15.1	15.9	17.8	19.8	21.2	20.3	23.4
Total	KLXF	107.5	113.8	104.8	86.6	64.9	68.9	68.0	68.3	62.4	57.4	54.6
Change in colliery stocks	KLXG	–0.9	2.8	2.2	1.8	–4.2	–4.2	–3.0	0.7	–0.2	0.6	–3.5
Change in stocks at opencast sites	KLXH (KSOL)	–0.1	–0.8	0.6	0.5	–0.5						
Total supply	KLXI	108.5	111.8	102.0	84.5	69.6	73.1	70.9	67.6	62.7	56.8	58.1
Home consumption												
Total home consumption	KLXW	108.3	107.5	100.6	86.6	81.7	76.9	71.4	63.1	63.1	55.7	58.9
Overseas shipments and bunkers	KLXX	2.5	1.7	1.0	1.1	1.2	0.9	1.0	1.1	1.0	0.8	0.7
Total consumption and shipments	KLXY	110.8	109.2	101.6	87.7	82.9	77.8	72.4	64.2	64.1	56.5	59.6
Change in distributed stocks[2]	KLXZ	–0.4	3.6	1.2	–3.6	–13.9	–4.4	–0.9	3.0	–1.2	0.6	–1.5
Balance[3]	KLYA	1.9	–1.0	–0.8	0.4	0.6	–0.3	–0.5	0.3	–0.3	–0.3	0.1
Stocks at end of year												
Distributed[2]	KLYB	28.7	32.3	33.5	29.9	16.0	11.6	10.8	13.8	12.6	13.2	11.6
At collieries	KLYC	6.0	8.8	10.9	12.7	8.5	7.1	4.2	4.8	4.6	5.2	1.6
At opencast sites	KLYD (KSOM)	3.0	2.2	2.8	3.3	2.8						
Total stocks	KLYE	37.8	43.3	47.2	45.9	27.3	18.7	14.9	18.6	17.2	18.3	13.3

1 Figures relate to periods of 52 weeks. For 1990, figures relate to 52 weeks estimate for period ended 29 December 1990.
2 Great Britain. Stock change excludes industrial and domestic stocks.

3 This is the balance between supply and consumption, shipments and changes in known distributed stocks.

Source: Department of Trade and Industry: 020 7215 2717

21.6 Fuel input and gas output: gas sales[1]
United Kingdom
Public supply

Giga-watt hours

		1990	1991	1992	1993	1994	1995	1996	1997	1998	1999	2000
Analysis of gas sales												
Fuel producers												
Power stations[2]	KIKK	6 404	6 561	17 894	81 778	114 575	145 790	190 691	250 155	260 631	307 818	312 545
Coal extraction and												
manufacture of solid fuels	KIKL	338	630	1 042	415	266	368	344	193	67	14	6
Coke ovens	KIKM	91	62	108	191	1	1	–	–	–	–	–
Petroleum refineries	KIKN	272	279	1 940	2 449	1 933	2 922	3 118	3 122	4 318	4 775	5 300
Nuclear fuel production	KIKO	422	496	508	565	550	467	874	923	989	1 021	1 272
Production and distribution												
of other energy	KIKP	145	270	447	178	114	352	437	487	549	629	619
Total final producers	KIKQ	7 672	8 298	21 939	85 576	117 439	149 900	195 464	254 880	266 554	314 256	319 742
Final users:												
Iron and steel industry	KIKR	13 594	12 565	13 908	15 577	20 327	19 988	21 159	20 577	20 139	21 838	21 331
Other industries	KIKS	146 122	139 488	132 936	132 719	143 979	150 697	165 922	13 888	15 060	15 231	15 656
Domestic	KIKT	300 410	333 963	330 100	340 162	329 710	326 010	375 841	345 532	355 895	358 066	369 909
Public administration	KIKU	35 376	40 030	43 817	38 725	41 119	46 308	51 411	53 203	52 441	51 861	54 432
Agriculture	KIKV	1 001	1 087	1 286	1 277	1 227	1 210	1 420	1 443	1 344	1 486	1 475
Miscellaneous	KIKW	48 844	59 394	54 769	58 917	58 790	61 502	66 504	59 022	64 442	66 523	70 882
Total final users	KIKX	545 347	586 527	576 816	587 377	595 152	605 715	682 257	493 665	509 321	515 005	533 685
Total sales	KIKY	553 019	594 825	598 755	672 952	712 592	755 615	877 721	748 545	775 875	829 261	853 427

1 The breakdown of consumption by industrial users is made according to the
1980 Standard Industrial Classification.
2 Includes auto-production of electricity.

Source: Department of Trade and Industry: 020 7215 2717

21.7 Electricity: generation, supply and consumption
United Kingdom

Gigawatt-hours

		1990	1991	1992	1993	1994	1995	1996	1997	1998	1999	2000
Electricity generated												
Major power producers: total	KLUA	298 495	301 490	300 177	305 434	306 726	313 958	327 843	323 973	333 702	336 486	341 785
Conventional thermal and other[1]	AWLC	..	..	..	..	175 187	170 056	162 496	133 591	134 009	118 762	131 032
Combined cycle gas turbine stations	KJCS	..	312	2 991	22 811	36 971	48 720	65 880	86 974	93 832	114 620	117 965
Nuclear stations	KLUC	65 749	70 543	76 807	89 353	88 282	88 964	94 671	98 146	99 486	95 133	85 063
Hydro-electric stations:												
Natural flow	KLUE	4 393	3 777	4 591	3 522	4 317	4 096	2 801	3 337	4 237	4 431	4 331
Pumped storage	KLUF	1 982	1 523	1 697	1 437	1 463	1 552	1 556	1 486	1 624	2 902	2 694
Renewables other than hydro	KLUG	4	3	45	165	506	570	439	439	514	638	700
Other generators: total	KLUH	21 244	21 385	20 864	17 669	18 252	20 084	22 703	24 478	29 018	31 878	33 115
Conventional thermal and other[1]	AWLD	..	..	..	..	14 263	15 387	19 098	19 993	22 698	21 074	19 985
Combined cycle gas turbine stations	KJCT	292	310	409	607	1 505	2 126	1 232	1 500	2 848	6 533	8 693
Hydro-electric stations (natural flow)	KLUK	814	847	840	780	777	742	592	832	880	930	779
Renewables other than hydro	KILA	683	784	1 028	1 417	1 707	1 829	1 781	2 153	2 592	3 341	3 658
All generating companies: total	KLUL	319 739	322 875	321 043	323 102	324 978	334 042	350 546	348 451	362 720	368 364	374 900
Conventional thermal and other[1]	AWYH	..	..	..	..	189 451	185 443	181 594	153 584	156 707	139 836	151 017
Combined cycle gas turbine stations	KJCU	292	622	3 400	23 418	38 475	50 846	67 112	88 474	96 680	121 153	126 658
Nuclear stations	KLUN	65 749	70 543	76 807	89 353	88 282	88 964	94 671	98 146	99 486	95 133	85 063
Hydro-electric stations:												
Natural flow	KLUP	5 207	4 624	5 431	4 302	5 094	4 838	3 393	4 169	5 117	5 361	5 110
Pumped storage	KLUQ	1 982	1 523	1 697	1 437	1 463	1 552	1 556	1 486	1 624	2 902	2 694
Renewables other than hydro	KLUR	687	787	1 073	1 582	2 213	2 399	2 220	2 592	3 106	3 979	4 358
Electricity used on works: Total	KLUS	19 611	20 111	20 237	19 287	17 491	17 411	17 703	16 503	17 362	16 693	16 260
Major generating companies	KLUT	17 891	18 424	18 485	17 391	16 696	16 510	16 674	15 404	16 078	15 338	14 953
Other generators	KLUU	1 720	1 687	1 752	1 896	795	901	1 029	1 099	1 284	1 355	1 307
Electricity supplied (gross)												
Major power producers: total	KLUV	280 604	283 066	281 692	287 264	290 780	299 000	311 169	308 569	317 624	321 148	326 832
Conventional thermal and other[1]	AWYI	..	..	..	..	167 866	163 818	155 086	127 419	127 788	112 920	124 829
Combined cycle gas turbine stations	KJCV	..	309	2 964	22 611	36 815	48 525	65 604	86 682	93 005	112 768	116 110
Nuclear stations	KLUX	58 664	62 761	69 135	80 979	79 962	80 598	85 820	89 341	90 590	87 672	78 334
Hydro-electric stations:												
Natural flow	KLUZ	4 384	3 767	4 579	3 513	4 265	4 051	2 763	3 299	4 225	4 410	4 316
Pumped storage	KLVA	1 892	1 465	1 635	1 388	1 417	1 502	1 507	1 439	1 569	2 804	2 603
Renewables other than hydro	KLVB	3	3	37	136	455	506	389	389	447	574	640
Other generators: total	KLVC	19 524	19 698	19 112	16 522	18 207	20 909	21 674	23 379	27 734	30 523	31 808
Conventional thermal and other[1]	AWYJ	..	..	..	..	14 333	16 338	18 253	19 131	21 758	20 285	19 124
Combined cycle gas turbine stations	KJCW	280	298	394	584	1 466	2 100	1 180	1 425	2 706	6 207	8 424
Hydro-electric stations (natural flow)	KLVF	806	839	832	772	769	733	585	823	869	917	766
Renewables other than hydro	KIKZ	656	753	987	1 360	1 639	1 738	1 656	2 000	2 401	3 114	3 494
All generating companies: total	KLVG	300 128	302 764	300 804	303 815	308 987	319 909	332 843	331 948	345 358	351 671	358 640
Conventional thermal and other[1]	AWYK	..	..	..	..	182 199	180 156	173 339	146 550	149 546	133 205	143 953
Combined cycle gas turbine stations	KJCX	280	607	3 358	23 195	38 281	50 625	66 784	88 107	95 711	118 975	124 534
Nuclear stations	KLVI	58 664	62 761	69 135	80 979	79 962	80 598	85 820	89 341	90 590	87 672	78 334
Hydro-electric stations:												
Natural flow	KLVK	5 190	4 666	5 411	4 285	5 034	4 784	3 348	4 122	5 094	5 327	5 082
Pumped storage	KLVL	1 892	1 465	1 635	1 388	1 417	1 502	1 507	1 439	1 569	2 804	2 603
Renewables other than hydro	KLVM	659	756	1 024	1 496	2 094	2 244	2 045	2 389	2 848	3 688	4 134
Electricity used in pumping												
Major power producers	KLVN	2 626	2 109	2 257	1 948	2 051	2 282	2 430	2 477	2 594	3 774	3 499
Electricity supplied (net): Total	KLVO	297 502	300 654	298 547	301 868	306 936	317 627	330 413	329 471	341 734	345 568	355 141
Major power producers	KLVP	277 978	280 956	279 435	285 316	288 729	296 718	308 739	306 092	315 030	317 374	323 333
Other generators	KLVQ	19 524	19 698	19 112	16 552	18 207	20 909	21 674	23 379	27 734	30 523	31 808
Net imports	KGEZ	11 990	16 408	16 694	16 716	16 887	16 313	16 755	16 574	12 468	14 244	14 174
Electricity available	KGIZ	309 408	317 062	315 241	318 584	323 830	333 940	347 168	346 045	355 232	362 141	369 315
Losses in transmission etc	KGKW	24 988	26 221	23 788	22 838	31 000	30 020	31 295	26 949	29 672	29 789	30 796
Electricity consumption: Total	KGKX	284 420	290 841	291 453	295 746	292 830	303 920	315 868	319 101	325 560	332 352	338 519
Fuel industries	KGKY	9 986	9 794	9 984	9 615	7 518	8 070	8 850	8 290	8 411	8 310	8 426
Final users: total	KGKZ	274 434	281 048	281 468	286 130	285 310	295 849	307 024	310 802	317 149	324 042	330 093
Industrial sector	KGLZ	100 643	99 570	95 277	96 842	96 120	101 780	104 320	106 160	108 503	112 128	114 674
Domestic sector	KGMZ	93 793	98 098	99 482	100 456	101 407	102 210	107 513	104 455	109 410	110 308	111 842
Other sectors	KGNZ	79 997	83 380	86 711	88 833	87 790	91 860	95 190	100 190	99 236	101 606	103 577

1 Includes electricity supplied by gas turbines and oil engines.

Source: Department of Trade and Industry: 020 7215 5190

21.8 Electricity: plant capacity and demand
United Kingdom

Megawatts

		At end of March						At end of December[1]				
		1992	1993	1994	1995	1996		1996	1997	1998	1999	2000
Major power producers[2]:												
Total declared net capability	KGON	66 956	63 997	64 901	64 923	66 100	GUFY	69 090	68 288	68 390	70 057	72 531
Conventional steam stations	KGOO	48 309	44 860	41 143	38 453	38 242	GUFZ	38 230	37 395	35 081	35 427	35 221
Combined cycle gas turbine stations	KJCZ	229	1 129	5 463	8 364	9 034	GUGA	12 052	12 252	14 638	16 110	19 349
Nuclear stations[3,4]	KGOP	11 353	11 353	11 894	12 037	12 762	GUGB	12 916	12 946	12 956	12 956	12 486
Gas turbines and oil engines	KGOQ	2 968	2 539	2 248	1 895	1 890	GUGC	1 721	1 526	1 492	1 333	1 243
Hydro-electric stations:												
Natural flow	KGOR	1 308	1 314	1 314	1 314	1 314	GUGD	1 313	1 311	1 327	1 327	1 327
Pumped storage	KGOS	2 787	2 787	2 787	2 788	2 788	GUGE	2 788	2 788	2 788	2 788	2 788
Renewables other than hydro	KGOT	2	15	52	72	71	GUGF	70	70	108	117	117
Other generators:												
Total capacity of own generating plant[5]	KGOU	3 590	3 502	3 622	3 818	4 025	GUGG	4 181	4 577	4 943	5 349	6 360
Conventional steam stations[6]	KGOV	3 211	3 037	3 096	3 257	3 234	GUGH	3 192	3 485	3 496	3 571	3 616
Combined cycle gas turbine stations	KJDA	102	150	150	153	343	GUGI	410	464	710	948	1 742
Hydro-electric stations (natural flow)	KGOX	122	110	111	111	118	GUGJ	142	145	148	150	158
Renewables other than hydro	KILB	155	205	265	297	330	GUGK	437	483	589	680	844
All generating companies: Total capacity[5]	KGOY	70 546	67 499	68 523	68 741	70 126	GUGL	73 271	72 865	73 333	75 406	78 891
Conventional steam stations[6]	KGOZ	51 520	47 897	44 239	41 710	41 476	GUGM	41 422	40 880	38 577	38 998	38 837
Combined cycle gas turbine stations	KJDC	331	1 279	5 613	8 517	9 377	GUGN	12 462	12 716	15 348	17 058	21 091
Nuclear stations[3]	KGPM	11 353	11 353	11 894	12 037	12 762	GUGO	12 916	12 946	12 956	12 956	12 486
Gas turbines and oil engines	KGPN	2 968	2 539	2 248	1 895	1 890	GUGP	1 721	1 526	1 492	1 333	1 243
Hydro-electric stations:												
Natural flow	KGPO	1 430	1 424	1 425	1 425	1 432	GUGQ	1 455	1 456	1 475	1 477	1 485
Pumped storage	KGPP	2 787	2 787	2 787	2 788	2 788	GUGR	2 788	2 788	2 788	2 788	2 788
Renewables other than hydro	KGPQ	157	220	317	369	401	GUGS	507	553	697	797	961
Major power producers[2]:												
Simultaneous maximum load met[7]	KGPR	54 472	51 663	54 848	52 362	55 611	GUGT	56 815	56 965	56 312	57 849	58 452
System load factor[8] (percentage)	KGQY	62.9	66.6	63.8	67.3	65.4	GUGU	66.3	65.7	67.4	66.7	67.4

1 From 1996 data are on a calendar year basis.
2 See chapter text.
3 The 1995 figure includes 300 MW of the 1,188 MW capacity of Sizewell B which began to produce electricity in March 1995.
4 Nuclear generators are now included under "major power producers" only.
5 Capacity figures for other generators are as at end-December of the previous year.

6 For other generators, conventional steam stations cover all types of stations not separately listed.
7 Maximum load in year to end of March.
8 The average hourly quantity of electricity available during the year ended March expressed as a percentage of the maximum demand.

Source: Department of Trade and Industry: 020 7215 5190

21.9 Electricity: fuel used in generation
United Kingdom

Million tonnes of oil equivalent

		1990	1991	1992	1993	1994	1995	1996	1997	1998	1999	2000
Major power producers[1]: total all fuels	KGPS	72.20	72.90	71.30	72.32	71.65	72.72	74.61	73.17	74.96	73.61	74.38
Coal	FTAJ	49.00	49.00	46.00	38.30	35.90	35.00	32.40	27.70	28.70	24.50	27.80
Oil[2]	FTAK	6.80	5.90	5.00	4.40	3.60	3.10	3.00	1.40	0.80	0.80	0.80
Gas[3]	KGPT	–	–	1.0	6.3	9.1	11.4	15.2	19.2	20.3	24.2	24.4
Nuclear[4]	FTAL	16.30	17.40	18.50	21.60	21.20	21.30	22.20	23.00	23.40	22.20	19.60
Hydro (natural flow)	FTAM	0.40	0.30	0.40	0.30	0.40	0.40	0.20	0.30	0.40	0.40	0.40
Other fuels used by UK companies[3]	KGPU	–	–	–	0.1	0.1	0.1	0.1	0.1	0.2	0.2	0.2
Net imports	KGPV	1.0	1.4	1.4	1.4	1.5	1.4	1.4	1.4	1.1	1.2	1.2
Other generators: total all fuels	KGPW	5.2	5.4	6.7	4.5	3.5	5.8	6.0	6.5	6.6	6.6	6.9
Transport undertakings												
Gas	KGPX	0.2	0.2	0.2	0.2	0.2	0.2	0.2	0.2	0.2	0.2	0.2
Undertakings in industrial sector												
Coal	KGPY	1.0	1.0	1.0	1.3	1.2	1.3	1.2	1.3	1.2	0.9	0.9
Oil	KGPZ	1.6	1.7	3.1	1.4	0.5	1.0	1.0	0.9	0.7	0.7	0.6
Gas	KGQM	0.3	0.3	0.3	0.8	0.6	1.6	1.8	2.1	1.9	2.0	2.3
Hydro (natural flow)	KGQO	0.1	0.1	0.1	0.1	0.1	0.1	0.1	0.1	0.1	0.1	0.1
Other fuels	KGQP	1.8	1.9	1.1	1.0	1.0	1.7	1.8	1.9	2.6	2.7	2.8
All generating companies: total fuels	KGQQ	77.4	78.3	78.0	76.8	75.2	78.6	80.6	79.7	81.5	80.2	81.3
Coal	KGQR	50.0	50.0	46.9	39.6	37.1	36.3	33.6	29.0	29.9	25.4	28.6
Oil	KGQS	8.4	7.6	8.1	5.8	4.1	4.1	4.0	2.3	1.5	1.5	1.4
Gas[3]	KGQT	0.6	0.6	1.5	7.0	9.9	13.3	17.2	21.5	22.4	26.5	26.9
Nuclear[4]	KGQU	16.3	17.4	18.5	21.6	21.2	21.3	22.2	23.0	23.4	22.2	19.6
Hydro (natural flow)	KGQV	0.4	0.4	0.5	0.4	0.4	0.4	0.3	0.4	0.4	0.5	0.4
Other fuels used by UK companies[3,5]	KGQW	1.8	0.9	1.1	1.0	1.1	1.8	1.9	2.1	2.8	2.9	3.1
Net imports	KGQX	1.0	1.4	1.4	1.4	1.5	1.4	1.4	1.4	1.1	1.2	1.2

1 See chapter text.
2 Includes oil used in gas turbine and diesel plant for lighting up coal fired boilers and Orimulsion.
3 For 1990 and 1991 gas used by major power producers was included with other fuels for reasons of confidentiality.

4 Nuclear generators are now included under "major power producers" only.
5 Main fuels included are coke oven gas, blast furnace gas, waste products from chemical processes and sludge gas.

Source: Department of Trade and Industry: 020 7215 5190

21.10 Indigenous production, refinery receipts, imports and exports of oil[1]

Thousand tonnes

		1990	1991	1992	1993	1994	1995	1996	1997	1998	1999	2000
Total indigenous petroleum production[2]	KMBA	91 064	91 260	94 251	100 188	126 812	129 894	129 742	128 234	132 363	137 099	126 245
Crude petroleum[3]:												
Refinery receipts total	KMBB	89 735	92 523	92 789	97 400	93 771	93 572	96 660	97 023	93 797	88 286	88 014
Foreign trade[4]												
Imports	KMBF	52 710	57 084	57 683	61 701	53 096	48 749	50 099	49 994	47 958	44 869	54 387
Exports	AXRB	56 999	55 131	57 627	64 415	83 205	84 578	81 563	79 400	84 610	91 797	92 918
Net imports	AXRC	−4 289	1 953	56	−2 714	−30 109	−35 829	−31 464	−29 406	−36 652	−46 928	−38 531
Petroleum products												
Foreign trade[5]												
Imports[4]	KMBI	11 005	10 140	10 567	10 064	10 441	9 878	9 315	8 706	11 418	13 896	14 212
Exports[4]	AXRD	16 899	19 351	20 250	23 060	22 157	21 614	23 681	26 755	24 375	21 730	20 677
Net imports[4]	AXRE	−5 894	−9 211	−9 683	−12 996	−11 716	−11 736	−14 366	−18 049	−12 957	−7 834	−6 465
International marine bunkers	KMBL	2 538	2 486	2 546	2 478	2 313	2 465	2 664	2 961	3 080	2 329	2 079

1 The term 'indigenous' is used in this table for convenience to include oil from the UK Continental Shelf as well as the small amounts produced on the mainland.

2 Crude oil *plus* condensates and petroleum gases derived at onshore treatment plants.

3 Includes process(partly refined) oils.

4 Foreign trade as recorded by the petroleum industry and may differ from figures published in *Overseas Trade Statistics*.

5 The trade data has been revised to more closely follow the format used in the energy statistics published by the DTI. This change reallocates some product data to be counted in with crude oil and other upstream products. This change has been worked back the whole period of the table to provide a consistent series from 1990 onwards.

Source: Department of Trade and Industry: 020 7215 5184

21.11 Throughput of crude and process oils and output of refined products from refineries[1]

United Kingdom

Thousand tonnes

		1990	1991	1992	1993	1994	1995	1996	1997	1998	1999	2000
Throughput of crude and process oils	KMAU	88 692	92 001	92 334	96 274	93 162	92 743	96 661	97 024	93 797	88 285	88 013
less: Refinery fuel[2]:	KMAA	5 838	6 058	6 080	6 383	6 256	6 481	6 623	6 572	6 468	5 976	5 402
Losses	KMAB	568	467	471	308	261	129	152	86	233	324	−128
Total output of refined products	KMAC	82 286	85 476	85 783	89 583	86 645	86 133	89 885	90 366	87 096	81 985	82 739
Gases:												
Butane and propane	KMAE	1 514	1 664	1 583	1 575	1 605	1 815	1 828	1 950	1 978	2 002	1 957
Other petroleum	KMAF	106	134	172	162	132	133	144	139	200	209	169
Naphtha and other feedstock	KMAG	2 139	2 515	3 040	2 696	2 794	2 711	2 824	2 854	2 335	2 465	3 145
Aviation spirit	KMAH	–	–	–	–	–	–	–	–	–	16	31
Motor spirit	KMAJ	26 724	27 793	27 980	28 394	27 562	27 254	28 046	28 260	27 392	25 587	23 929
Industrial and white spirit	KMAK	121	136	150	159	143	143	136	128	136	130	124
Kerosene:												
Aviation turbine fuel	KMAL	7 541	7 037	7 681	8 341	7 697	7 837	8 305	8 342	7 942	7 352	6 620
Burning oil	KMAM	2 344	2 446	2 450	2 707	2 967	2 924	3 510	3 336	3 471	3 603	3 141
Gas/diesel oil	KMAN	23 402	26 057	25 650	27 361	27 137	27 169	28 903	28 778	27 859	26 226	28 879
Fuel oil	KMAO	13 805	13 205	12 388	13 183	11 378	10 969	11 479	11 747	11 066	10 289	10 302
Lubricating oil	KMAP	974	973	1 163	1 264	1 296	1 261	1 111	1 231	1 134	920	717
Bitumen	KMAQ	2 454	2 302	2 336	2 450	2 569	2 459	2 189	2 258	2 190	1 667	1 468
Petroleum wax	KMAR	40	37	62	59	64	46	41	65	59	264	445
Petroleum coke	KMAS	586	555	535	621	679	759	714	598	694	648	857
Other products	KMAT	536	620	593	613	623	653	655	680	640	607	955

1 Crude and process oils comprise all feedstocks, other than distillation benzines, for treatment at refinery plants. Refinery production does not cover further treatment of finished products for special grades such as in distillation plant for the preparation of industrial spirits.

2 Comprising 2,681 thousand tonnes gases, 2,079 thousand tonnes fuel oil and 1,216 thousand tonnes other products in 1999.

Source: Department of Trade and Industry: 020 7215 5184

21.12 Deliveries of petroleum products for inland consumption
United Kingdom

Thousand tonnes

		1990	1991	1992	1993	1994	1995	1996	1997	1998	1999	2000
Total (including refinery fuel)	KMCA	79 781	80 564	81 550	82 173	81 213	80 175	82 013	79 073	78 437	77 985	76 635
Total (excluding refinery fuel)	KMCB	73 943	74 506	75 470	75 970	74 957	73 694	75 390	72 501	71 969	72 009	71 233
Gases:												
Butane and propane:												
For gas works	KMCC	37	42	40	41	47	43	48	45	46	52	40
Other uses	KMCD	1 009	1 172	1 049	1 094	1 153	1 158	1 272	1 148	1 108	1 109	1 064
Other gases:												
Other uses	KMCF	48	63	58	48	88	98	101	73	69	74	80
Feedstock:												
For petroleum chemical plants	KMCG	5 115	5 935	5 970	5 921	6 199	6 227	6 228	6 088	6 322	6 793	5 881
Aviation spirit	KMCI	26	24	27	27	29	29	32	37	36	45	52
Dealers:												
4 star	KMCK	15 586	13 793	12 481	11 049	9 503	7 973	7 043	6 138	4 595	2 728	1 462
3 star	KMCL	915	1 158	1 401	1 439	1 323	925	698	506	409	473	403
2 star	KMCM	7 145	8 429	9 542	10 754	11 536	12 604	14 228	15 188	16 432	18 307	19 008
Unleaded	KMCN	8 060	9 587	10 943	12 193	12 859	13 529	14 926	15 694	16 841	18 780	19 411
Commercial consumers:												
4 star	KMCO	472	360	294	217	178	149	135	112	91	61	44
3 star	KMCP	10	15	22	25	26	17	11	9	4	6	6
2 star	KMCQ	185	267	304	286	277	285	294	298	318	311	480
Unleaded	KMCR	195	282	326	311	303	302	305	307	322	317	486
Motor spirit: total	BHOD	24 313	24 022	24 044	23 770	22 843	21 953	22 409	22 251	21 849	21 886	21 403
Industrial and white spirits	KMCS	171	162	159	164	170	178	184	195	179	174	170
Kerosene:												
Aviation turbine fuel	BHOE	6 589	6 176	6 666	7 106	7 284	7 660	8 049	8 411	9 241	9 939	10 698
Burning oil	KMCT	2 058	2 383	2 472	2 625	2 655	2 774	3 336	3 343	3 575	3 633	3 748
Gas/diesel oil:												
Derv fuel	BHOI	10 652	10 694	11 132	11 806	12 914	13 457	14 365	14 976	15 143	15 088	15 631
Other	BHOJ	8 046	8 031	7 871	7 782	7 491	7 227	7 631	7 326	7 244	6 667	6 542
Fuel oil	BHOK	11 997	11 948	11 481	10 770	9 275	7 975	6 854	3 936	2 935	2 415	1 833
Lubricating oils	BHOL	822	759	786	806	795	895	864	872	813	790	801
Bitumen	BHOM	2 491	2 514	2 555	2 523	2 595	2 420	2 146	2 015	1 967	1 928	1 975
Petroleum wax	KMCU	55	49	47	48	47	44	44	44	18	37	32
Petroleum coke	KMCV	112	154	682	778	911	1 008	1 210	1 095	887	660	776
Miscellaneous products	KMCW	402	378	431	661	461	548	617	646	537	719	507

Source: Department of Trade and Industry: 020 7215 5184

21.13 Iron and steel[1]
Summary of steel supplies, deliveries and stocks
United Kingdom

		Finished product weight - thousand tonnes										
		1990	1991	1992	1993	1994	1995	1996	1997	1998	1999	2000
Supply, disposal and consumption												
UK producers' home deliveries	KLTA	9 711	7 951	7 315	7 567	7 827	8 257	8 383	8 626	8 260	7 652	7 255
Imports excluding steelworks receipts	KLTB	4 446	4 509	4 418	4 132	5 012	5 384	5 147	5 894	6 466	6 014	6 387
Total deliveries to home market (a)	KLTC	14 157	12 460	11 733	11 698	12 839	13 641	13 530	14 520	14 726	13 748	13 642
Total exports (producers, consumers, merchants)	KLTD	6 550	7 444	7 718	7 621	8 120	8 228	8 917	9 060	8 008	7 538	7 442
Exports by UK producers	KLTE	6 370	7 082	7 587	7 536	7 873	7 828	8 305	8 534	7 876	7 416	7 163
Derived consumers' and merchants' exports (b)	KLTF	180	362	131	85	247	400	612	526	132	122	279
Net home disposals (a)-(b)	KLTG	13 977	12 098	11 602	11 614	12 592	13 241	12 918	13 994	14 594	13 545	13 363
Consumers' and merchants' stock change	KLTH	−290	−400	60	60	390	..	..	..	..	..	..
Estimated home consumption	KLTI	14 267	12 498	11 542	11 554	12 202	13 241	12 918	13 994	14 594	13 545	13 363
Stocks												
Producers												
- ingots & semis	KLTJ	1 245	1 035	933	1 005	946	1 068	767	946	717	747	727
- finished steel	KLTK	1 563	1 719	1 573	1 425	1 389	1 274	1 515	1 358	1 495	1 318	1 066
Consumers	KLTL	1 590	1 400	1 410	1 300	1 470	..	..	..	..	..	..
Merchants	KLTM	1 050	840	890	1 060	1 280	..	..	..	..	..	..

		Crude steel equivalent - million tonnes										
		1990	1991	1992	1993	1994	1995	1996	1997	1998	1999	2000
Estimated home consumption												
Crude steel production[2]	KLTN	17.84	16.47	16.21	16.62	17.28	17.60	17.99	18.50	17.32	16.28	15.16
Producers' stock change	KLTO	−0.08	−0.07	−0.30	−0.09	−0.12	0.01	−0.07	0.03	−0.11	−0.19	−0.27
Re-usable material	KLTP	0.10	0.07	0.06	0.08	0.09	0.08	0.07	0.06	0.02	..	..
Total supply from home sources	KLTQ	18.02	16.61	16.57	16.79	17.49	17.67	18.13	18.53	17.45	16.47	15.43
Total imports[3]	KLTR	5.96	6.21	5.99	5.44	6.58	7.05	7.01	7.49	8.38	7.81	8.43
Total exports[3]	KLTS	7.66	8.72	9.07	8.95	9.55	9.63	10.26	10.43	9.25	8.70	8.61
Net home disposals	KLTT	16.32	14.10	13.49	13.28	14.52	15.09	14.88	15.59	16.58	15.58	15.25
Consumers' and merchants' stock change	KLTU	−0.37	−0.50	0.07	0.07	0.48	..	..	..	..	..	..
Estimated home consumption	KLTV	16.69	14.60	13.42	13.21	14.04	15.09	14.88	15.59	16.58	15.58	15.25

1 The figures relate to periods of 52 weeks (53 weeks in 1992).
2 Includes liquid steel for castings.
3 Based on HM Customs Statistics, reflecting total trade rather than producers' trade.

Source: Iron and Steel Statistics Bureau: 020 8686 9050 ext 126

21.14 Iron and steel[1]
Iron ore, manganese ore, pig iron and iron and steel scrap
United Kingdom

Thousand tonnes

		1990	1991	1992	1993	1994	1995	1996	1997	1998	1999	2000
Iron ore												
Jurassic	KLOA	53	57	29	–	–	–	–	–	–	–	–
Hematite	KLOB	–	–	–	–	–	–	–	–	–	–	–
Production: total	KLOC	53	57	29	–	–	–	–	–	–	–	–
Home produced	KLOD	53	57	29	–	–	–	–	–	–	–	–
Imported	KLOE	17 935	17 833	17 235	17 507	18 161	18 670	19 720	20 820	19 532	18 739	16 955
Consumption: total	KLOF	17 988	17 890	17 264	17 507	18 161	18 670	19 720	20 820	19 532	18 739	16 955
Manganese ore												
Consumption	KLOG	340	383	308	152	64	32	48	37	22	14	36
Pig iron (and blast furnace ferro-alloys)												
Average number of furnaces in blast during period	KLOH	10	8	8	8	8	8	9	9	9	9	8
Production												
Steelmaking iron	KLOI	12 218	11 834	11 469	11 534	11 943	12 236	12 830	13 054	12 746	12 139	10 890
Foundry iron	KLOJ	102	50	73	–	–	–	–	–	–	–	–
Speigeleisen and ferro-manganese	KLOK	143	178	137	45	–	–	–	–	–	–	–
In blast furnaces: total	KLOL	12 463	12 062	11 679	11 579	11 943	12 236	12 830	13 054	12 746	12 139	10 890
In steel works and steel foundries	KLOM	12 358	11 836	11 463	11 554	11 889	12 121	12 753	13 044	12 746	12 139	10 890
In iron foundries	KLON	195	181	214	..	..	..	..	..	..	..	..
Consumption of pig iron: total	KLOO	12 553	12 017	11 677	11 554	11 889	12 121	12 753	13 044	12 746	12 139	10 890
Iron and steel scrap												
Steelworks and steel foundries												
Circulating scrap	KLOQ	2 489	2 332	2 449	2 303	2 326	2 390	2 639	2 459	2 380	2 488	2 287
Purchased receipts	KLOR	4 730	3 694	3 739	4 149	4 533	4 688	4 130	5 418	4 045	3 433	3 327
Consumption	KLOS	7 251	6 085	6 190	6 550	6 874	7 012	6 828	7 207	6 408	5 884	5 675
Stocks (end of period)	KLOT	430	365	365	267	253	319	260	236	253	290	229
Iron foundries												
Arisings	KLOU	693	582	587	..	..	..	..	..	..	..	..
Consumption	KLOV	1 609	1 457	1 556	..	..	..	..	..	..	..	..

1 The figures relate to periods of 52 weeks (53 weeks in 1992).

Source: Iron and Steel Statistics Bureau: 020 8686 9050 ext 126

21.15 Iron and steel[1]
Number of furnaces and production of steel
United Kingdom

		1990	1991	1992	1993	1994	1995	1996	1997	1998	1999	2000
Steel furnaces												
(Number in existence at end of period)[2]												
Total	KLPA	214	209	206	202	202	192	192	192	190	181	181
Oxygen converters	KLPC	14	14	11	11	11	11	11	11	11	11	11
Electric	KLPD	200	195	195	191	191	181	181	181	179	170	170
Production of crude steel												
(thousand tonnes)												
Total	KLPF	17 841	16 474	16 212	16 625	17 286	17 604	17 992	18 499	17 315	16 284	15 155
by process												
Oxygen converters	KLPH	13 169	12 540	12 092	12 330	12 909	13 082	13 758	13 986	13 426	12 634	11 551
Electric	KLPI	4 672	3 934	4 120	4 295	4 377	4 522	4 234	4 513	3 889	3 664	3 604
by cast method												
Cast to ingot	KLPK	2 692	2 201	2 083	2 140	2 033	2 174	1 892	1 660	784	534	539
Continuously cast	KLPL	14 909	14 085	13 958	14 319	15 079	15 250	15 912	16 653	16 346	15 636	14 470
Steel for castings	KLPM	240	189	171	166	174	180	188	186	185	128	146
by quality												
Non alloy steel	KLPN	16 641	15 496	15 195	15 558	16 062	16 243	16 708	17 193	16 145	15 263	14 004
Stainless and other alloy steel	KLPO	1 200	978	1 017	1 067	1 224	1 361	1 284	1 306	1 170	1 035	1 151
Production of finished steel products												
(all quantities)[3] (thousand tonnes)												
Rods and bars for reinforce-												
ment (in coil and lengths)	KLPP	1 241	1 151	1 130	1 229	1 269	1 154	1 182	1 118	1 133	893	812
Wire rods and other rods and												
bars in coil	KLPQ	1 407	1 272	1 327	1 427	1 524	1 642	1 536	1 565	1 492	1 407	1 408
Hot rolled bars in lengths	KLPR	1 336	1 192	1 178	1 140	1 275	1 311	1 499	1 716	1 791	1 542	1 545
Bright steel bars[4]	KLPS	318	257	281	295	363	424	357	385	336	311	337
Light sections other than rails	KLPT	325	324	349	294	306	286	298	302	318	264	183
Heavy and light rails and												
accessories	KGQZ KLPU	2 583	2 297	2 361	2 408	2 412	2 549	2 557	2 397	2 346	2 303	1 915
Other heavy sections	KLPV											
Hot rolled plates, sheets and												
strip in coil and lengths	KLPW	8 089	7 270	7 145	7 230	7 715	8 077	8 512	8 956	8 454	7 893	7 278
Cold rolled plates and sheets												
in coil and lengths	KLPX	3 749	3 592	3 532	3 635	3 835	4 100	4 221	4 437	4 288	3 914	3 612
Cold rolled strip[4]	KLPZ	357	286	222	229	243	267	246	255	259	233	218
Tinplate	KLQW	855	742	805	829	767	791	739	754	772	736	753
Other coated sheet	KLQX	1 657	1 647	1 795	1 865	2 021	2 306	2 366	2 534	2 610	2 475	2 471
Tubes and pipes[4]	KLQY	1 465	1 260	1 187	1 155	1 136	1 183	1 317	1 310	1 276	1 100	1 061
Forged bars[4]	KLQZ	16	7	4	2	2	3	3	3	3	2	1

1 The figures relate to periods of 52 weeks (53 weeks in 1992).
2 Includes steel furnaces at steel foundries.
3 Includes material for conversion into other products listed in the table.
4 Based on producers' deliveries.

Source: Iron and Steel Statistics Bureau: 020 8686 9050 ext 126

21.16 Non-ferrous metals
United Kingdom

		1989	1990	1991	1992	1993	1994	1995	1996	1997	1998	1999
Copper												
Production of refined copper:												
Primary	KLAA	48.6	47.0	16.6	10.4	10.7	11.1	12.0	13.0	9.1	6.4	1.7
Secondary	KLAB	70.4	74.6	53.5	31.7	35.9	35.6	43.0	43.6	51.3	47.4	48.6
Home consumption:												
Refined	KLAC	324.7	317.2	269.4	308.3	325.0	377.3	397.9	396.0	408.3	374.1	305.3
Scrap (metal content)	KLAD	129.7	126.3	118.5	83.2	77.9	88.0	81.0	81.0	69.0	64.6	112.5
Stocks (end of period)[1,2]	KLAE	14.5	11.7	9.3	9.7	9.3	8.1	7.5	6.6	12.8	7.5	7.3
Analysis of home consumption												
(refined and scrap):[3] total	KLAF	454.4	443.5	387.9	391.5	403.0	468.0	493.2	477.3	477.4	438.7	417.7
Wire[4]	KLAG	221.7	220.2	191.9	247.0	253.9	306.2	321.4	309.4	312.5	287.2	276.1
Rods, bars and sections	KLAH	55.5	54.4	52.7	51.5	53.2	54.9	59.0	58.3	58.3	53.6	46.9
Sheet, strip and plate	KLAI	59.2	54.4	37.1	31.0	30.7	33.0	37.1	34.0	36.5	30.5	27.7
Tubes	KLAJ	77.7	73.0	65.5	62.0	65.2	73.9	75.7	75.6	70.1	67.4	67.1
Castings and miscellaneous	KLAK	40.4	41.5	40.7	..	..	..	..	..	..	..	..
Zinc												
Slab zinc:												
Production	KLAL	79.8	93.3	100.7	96.8	102.4	101.3	106.0	96.9	107.7	99.6	132.8
Home consumption	KLAM	194.5	193.0	183.7	190.1	195.9	196.5	198.4	195.7	194.8	187.9	198.9
Stocks (end of period)	KLAN	13.9	12.2	11.2	11.4	11.4	10.5	9.8	10.5	10.1	10.6	10.9
Other zinc (metal content):												
Consumption	KLAO	49.6	52.4	49.5	46.7	45.4	45.0	46.8	41.3	41.5	37.3	41.6
Analysis of home consumption												
(slab and scrap): total	KLAP	244.1	245.4	233.2	236.8	241.3	241.5	245.2	237.1	236.3	226.2	236.7
Brass	KLAQ	51.1	51.4	47.2	40.9	41.6	42.6	45.2	39.1	41.6	36.6	33.6
Galvanized products	KLAR	104.3	104.7	96.6	103.4	105.1	107.4	110.7	110.3	108.4	103.8	116.6
Zinc sheet and strip	KLAS	4.0	3.6	3.6	4.1	4.0	4.6	3.0	3.0	3.3	3.3	3.3
Zinc alloy die castings	KLAT	43.1	44.4	45.4	45.2	46.5	46.5	46.5	46.5	46.5	46.5	46.5
Zinc oxide	KLAU	21.7	21.1	20.3	22.5	20.7	21.6	21.6	20.7	20.6	20.4	21.1
Other products	KLAV	19.8	20.2	20.2	20.8	23.4	18.8	18.2	17.5	16.1	11.0	11.0
Refined lead												
Production[5,6]	KLAW	350.0	329.4	311.0	346.8	363.8	352.5	320.7	351.4	384.1	349.7	347.6
Home consumption[6,7]												
Refined lead	KLAX	301.3	301.6	263.8	263.6	263.6	267.6	285.4	272.8	270.4	275.5	283.3
Scrap and remelted lead[6]	KLAY	35.0	32.5	33.6	38.7	35.2	38.5	41.6	43.4	39.1	38.4	32.2
Stocks (end of period)[8]												
Lead bullion	KLAZ	17.0	18.0	22.8	36.3	20.7	10.2	9.5	32.9	15.5	20.9	17.1
Refined soft lead at consumers	KLBA	25.7	22.3	21.8	24.5	25.0	23.5	24.9	28.8	29.1	27.4	25.7
In LME Warehouses (UK)	KLBB	11.0	12.1	8.0	9.0	9.5	6.1	0.4	3.0	2.4	–	0.1
Analysis of home consumption												
(refined and scrap): total	KLBC	336.4	334.0	297.4	302.3	298.8	306.1	327.0	316.2	309.5	313.9	315.5
Cables	KLBD	12.6	10.4	8.6	9.3	8.9	9.3	9.8	9.8	9.7	9.7	9.7
Batteries (excluding oxides)	KLBE	50.5	51.0	51.9	53.4	48.7	52.5	52.7	52.3	54.7	51.6	47.4
Oxides and compounds:												
Batteries	KLBF	51.7	52.8	54.2	53.1	53.9	55.2	56.2	54.9	56.1	54.4	53.1
Other uses	KLBG	72.6	73.7	55.0	55.6	56.3	53.9	53.8	56.1	54.5	56.4	57.0
Sheets and pipes	KLBH	98.1	96.8	79.8	82.8	82.7	84.6	101.2	94.1	91.1	96.1	94.9
Solder	KLBJ	9.1	8.0	7.7	7.4	7.4	7.4	7.4	7.4	7.4	7.4	7.4
Alloys	KLBK	13.4	14.0	12.2	14.7	14.1	15.3	15.9	12.1	9.4	9.4	11.9
Other uses	KLBL	28.4	27.5	28.0	26.2	26.8	27.9	30.0	29.5	26.6	28.9	34.1

21.16
continued

Non-ferrous metals
United Kingdom

		1990	1991	1992	1993	1994	1995	1996	1997	1998	1999	2000
Tin												
Tin ore (metal content):												
Production	KLBM	3.4	2.3	2.0	2.2	1.9	2.1	2.3	0.4	–	–	..
Tin metal[9]:												
Production[10]	KLBO	12.0	5.2	–	–	–	–	–	–	..	..	..
Home consumption[10]	KLBT	10.4	10.3	10.4	10.4	10.4	10.5	10.5	10.1	9.6	10.0	..
Exports and re-exports[11]	KLBQ	5.7	2.9	0.2	0.3	1.2	2.7	0.6	0.3	0.1	0.1	..
Stocks (end of period):												
Consumers	KLBR	1.0	1.0	1.0	1.0	1.0	1.0	1.0	1.0	1.0	1.0	..
Analysis of home consumption (excluding scrap): total	KLBT	10.4	10.3	10.4	10.4	10.4	10.5	10.5	10.1	9.6	10.0	..
Tinplate	KLBU	3.6	3.6	3.6	3.6	3.6	3.6	3.6	3.6	2.6	3.0	..
Alloys	KLBV	3.4	3.3	3.4	3.4	3.3	3.4	3.5	3.6	3.6	3.6	..
Solder	KLBW	1.0	1.1	1.1	1.1	1.1	1.1	1.1	1.1	1.1	1.1	..
Other uses	KLBX	2.4	2.3	2.3	2.3	2.4	2.4	2.3	2.3	2.3	2.3	..
Primary aluminium[12]												
Production	KLBY	289.8	293.5[13]	244.2	239.1	231.2	237.9	240.0	247.7	258.4	269.7	305.1
Despatches to consumers	KLBZ	520.2	485.4	587.2	815.3	610.6	459.4	593.7	456.4	648.5	480.1	234.4
Secondary aluminium												
Production	KLCA	201.4	195.1	197.3	236.2	224.3	229.7	260.0	242.7	274.8	285.3	237.7
Exports	KLCC	59.7	64.8	83.5	98.3	124.8	145.8	152.2	153.3	156.6	143.1	84.2
Fabricated aluminium												
Total despatches[13]	KLCD	547.7	518.0	598.2	592.0	643.1	648.3	633.5	663.6	668.5	668.7	738.7
Rolled products[14]	KLCE	261.0	269.4	328.9	309.3	346.4	359.2	327.9	350.4	352.5	349.7	419.1
Extrusions and tubes[15]	KLCF	157.9	129.1	132.8	136.2	142.7	142.1	149.6	160.8	168.0	181.7	184.7
Castings	KLCH	111.3	97.3	116.3	133.0	143.4	147.0	156.0	152.4	148.0	137.3	134.9
Refined nickel												
Production (including ferro-nickel)	KLCM	26.5	28.6	28.0	28.0	28.4	35.1	42.0	36.6	39.1	39.5	..

1 Unwrought copper (electrolytic, fire refined and blister).
2 Reported stocks of refined copper held by consumers and those held in London Metal Exchange (LME) warehouses in the United Kingdom.
3 Copper content.
4 Consumption for high-conductivity copper and cadmium copper wire represented by consumption of wire rods, production of which for export is also included.
5 Lead reclaimed from secondary and scrap material and lead refined from bullion and domestic ores.
6 Figures for production and consumption of refined lead include antimonial lead, and for scrap and remelted lead, exclude secondary antimonial lead.
7 Including toll transactions involving fabrication.
8 Excluding government stocks.

9 Including production from imported scrap and residues refined on toll.
10 Primary and secondary metal.
11 Including re-exports on toll transactions.
12 Including primary alloys. Despatches to consumers are calculated as the despatches by UK industry plus imports, minus exports but deliveries to LME warehouses are not included.
13 Includes wrought, cast products, and excludes foil products.
14 Includes foil stock and excludes foil products.
15 Excluding forging bars, wirebars, and almost two-thirds of despatches of hot rolled rod.

Sources: World Bureau of Metal Statistics: 01920 461274;
Aluminium Federation: 0121 456 1103

21.17 Cotton, man-made fibres and wool[1]

		Unit	1988	1989	1990	1991	1992	1993	1994	1995	1996	1997	1998
Raw cotton													
Imports[2]	KLKC	Thousand	48	43	32	23	24	24	..	..	..	..	..
Home consumption: total	BKCA	tonnes	42	37	30	20	14	6	..	..	..	..	..
Stocks (end of period)	BKCB	"	4	3	1	1	–	1	..	..	..	..	..
Cotton waste													
Imports	KLKD	"	28.4	29.2	36.1	31.3	35.2	25.3	..	..	..	..	..
Cotton linters													
Imports	KLKE	"	13.6	18.0	13.7	16.1	19.0	5.2	..	..	..	..	..
Man-made fibres[3]													
Production: total	KLKF	"	280.1	272.5	273.2	267.4	261.9	240.6	206.9	195.3	..	..	..
Continuous filament yarn	KLKG	"	105.3	108.5	101.7	92.6	93.8	86.7	67.1	68.1	68.2	..	..
Staple fibre	KLKH	"	174.9	164.0	171.5	174.8	168.1	153.9	139.8	127.2	115.5	..	..
Cotton and man-made fibre yarn (including waste spinning)													
Production of single yarn[4]:													
100% Cotton	KJEK	"	33.2	25.9	20.4	11.2	6.4	7.3	5.3	5.5	5.8	4.8	3.9
Predominantly Cotton	KJEL	"	2.2	2.4	2.2	1.4	2.3	7.3	8.0	7.1	7.0	5.2	4.9
100% man-made fibre	KJEM	"	17.1	13.1	11.0	8.1	7.6	10.2	10.4	9.1	7.8	6.8	5.1
Mixtures including 50/50 blends	KJEN	"	29.8	26.6	24.4	21.3	19.3	16.3	16.4	15.9	15.5	14.1	13.3
Spindle activity (includes waste spinning)	KJEO	Millions	1.00	0.83	0.52	0.42	0.33	0.28	0.27	0.26	0.23	0.19	0.15
Yarn consumption:													
Cotton and predominantly Cotton yarns	KJEP	Thousand	31.5	30.6	28.0	24.1	23.6	20.7	19.1	17.9	19.0	11.8	10.8
100% man-made fibre spun yarns	KJEQ	tonnes	2.9	2.7	2.8	2.5	2.1	2.6	2.6	2.5	2.3	..	..
Spun mixture yarns	KJER	"	26.2	24.2	25.5	24.7	23.9	21.7	20.0	34.1	35.8	..	..
Continuous filament													
Man-made fibre yarn	KJES	"	34.6	35.2	34.4	31.8	33.0	33.0	32.0	30.2	33.0	..	..
Other	KJET	"	3.2	3.2	3.0	1.5	0.4	0.2	0.2	0.2	–	..	..
Other	LQYW	"	..	..	..	..	..	..	..	..	..	22.0	18.5
Cotton and man-made fibre weaving		Million linear											
Production of woven cloth:		metres											
Cotton	KLKV	"	219	206	169	154	142	109	86	80	83	78	74
Man-made fibres	KLKW	"	212.5	217.4	223.4	197.1	195.8	191.3	187.8	179.6	184.6	161.5	152.4
Cotton/man-made fibre mixtures	KLKX	"	44.6	35.7	36.5	35.1	34.3	30.7	29.6	28.9	26.9	22.7	19.4
Loom activity													
Average number of looms running on cotton and man-made fibres	KLKY	Thousands	11.6	10.6	8.9	7.9	7.6	6.8	5.9	5.9	5.6	5.0	4.6
Wool													
Virgin wool (clean weight):		Million kilo-											
Production[5]	KLKZ	grammes	44	47	48	47	47	44	..	..	..	..	..
Imports[2]	KLLA	"	89	77	88	93	102	67	..	..	..	..	..
Exports[6]	KLLB	"	34	33	23	40	32	19	..	..	..	..	..
Stocks at 31 August	KLLC	"	21	21	20	28	26	19	..	..	..	..	..
Consumption:													
Wool	KLLD	"	104.5	97.2	93.6	87.9	92.3	89.6	86.5	84.4	79.9	..	..
Hair	KLLE	"	7.0	6.5	5.9	5.6	5.0	3.5	2.3	0.9	1.1	..	..
Man-made fibres	KLLF	"	53.9	45.9	40.6	37.7	36.4	38.8	39.6	31.7	37.3	..	..
Other fibres[7]	KLLG	"	10.0	8.9	6.4	5.6	5.7	5.9	5.4	7.0	6.7	..	..
Tops													
Production: total	KLLH	"	80.0	69.1	60.5	61.9	64.3	61.5	63.4	52.8	52.3	..	..
Wool and hair	KLLI	"	42.8	38.7	34.2	36.0	38.6	36.4	38.2	32.9	29.2	..	..
Man-made fibres	KLLJ	"	37.2	30.4	26.3	25.9	25.7	25.1	25.2	19.9	23.1	..	..
Worsted yarns[2]:													
Production	KLLK	"	60.2	52.4	47.2	44.8	47.0	44.4	43.0	39.1	40.3	..	..
Semi-worsted yarns[8]:													
Production	KLLL		13.5	12.7	11.4	7.6	7.0	6.8	7.1	5.5	5.0	..	..
Woollen yarn:													
Production	KLLM	"	78.3	74.9	72.7	66.1	68.2	67.0	68.1	63.7	62.6	..	..
Woven woollen and worsted fabrics[9]:		Million square											
Deliveries	KLLN	metres	89.0	85.4	79.0	72.1	71.8	70.4	75.9	68.3	68.6	..	..
Blankets:													
Deliveries	KLLO	"	7.2	7.0	7.3	6.2	5.4	5.7	4.7	5.4	6.0	..	..

1 Figures for consumption of raw cotton, and production and consumption of cotton and man-made fibre yarn are for periods of 52 weeks.
2 From 1993 trade data does not include UK trade with other EU Member States.
3 Figures are based on returns from producers (excluding waste) and include all man-made fibres in commercial production.
4 Includes waste spinning.
5 Estimated.

6 Including imported wool and wool from imported skins, scoured, etc in the United Kingdom.
7 Including noils, broken tops, wastes, mungo and shoddy.
8 Including all yarn spun on the worsted system.
9 Includes mixture and man-made fibre fabrics classified as wool or worsted, but excludes blankets.

Sources: British Man-made Fibres Federation;
Textile Statistics Bureau: 0161 620 7272

Production

21.18 Fertilisers
Deliveries to UK agriculture by Members of the Fertiliser Manufacturers' Association
Years ending 30 June

Thousand tonnes

		1990	1991	1992	1993	1994	1995	1996	1997	1998	1999	2000
Nutrient Content												
N (nitrogen):												
Straight	KGRM	707	628	587	537	553	602	685	615	664	618	637
Compounds	KGRN	483	462	378	377	413	449	444	420	406	430	398
P_2O_5 (phosphate)	KGRO	318	278	227	218	236	272	284	287	296	291	253
K_2O (potash)	KGRP	417	364	287	284	299	343	353	356	360	357	309
Compounds - total product	KGRQ	2 967	2 742	2 254	2 216	2 378	2 656	2 688	2 664	2 620	2 727	2 523

Source: Fertiliser Manufacturers' Association: 01780 720422

21.19 Minerals: production

Thousand tonnes

Great Britain

		1990	1991	1992	1993	1994	1995	1996	1997[4,8]	1998[5,8]	1999[6,7]	2000
Limestone	KLEA	9 775	91 999	86 000	90 069	102 844	90 933	82 442	84 252	85 382	82 714	80 810
Sandstone	KLEB	14 952	12 928	11 586	12 100	13 494	15 017	12 581	12 457	13 545	11 870	12 056
Igneous rock	KLEC	49 542	46 008	48 630	49 209	50 014	49 641	43 731	42 370	39 838	45 294	44 633
Clay/shale	KLED	15 864	13 038	12 155	10 891	12 464	13 930	11 804	11 322	12 230	11 355	10 838
Industrial sand	KLEE	4 132	4 201	3 615	3 587	4 038	4 344	4 861	4 704	4 662	4 092	4 095
Chalk	KLEF	13 129	10 317	9 171	9 076	10 236	9 949	9 239	9 550	9 934	9 667	9 213
Fireclay	KLEG	892	867	572	479	679	708	536	338	577	545	595
Barium sulphate	KLEH	68	86	77	33	34	74	93	57	64	59	54
Calcium fluoride	KLEI	119	78	76	70	50	46	..	58	52	46	21
Copper	KLEJ	1.0	0.2	–	–	–	–	–	–	–	–	–
Lead	KLEK	1	–	..	..	2	..	..	..	1	1	–
Tin	KLEL	3.4	2.3	2.0	2.2	1.9	2.0	2.1	2.0	–	–	–
Zinc	KLEM	6.7	1.0	..	..	..	..	..	–	–	–	–
Iron ore: crude	KLEN	4	..	4	..	2	2	1	2	2	1	1
Iron ore: iron content	KLEO	2	..	2	1	1	1	1	1	1	1	1
Calcspar	KLEP	34	8	4	3	..	..	..	13	15	..	..
China clay	KLEQ / KILC	4 042	3 744	2 732	2 852	2 977	3 076	2 654	2 798	2 866	2 841	2 779
Ball clay	KIMS			..	..	913	..	..	..	..	..	..
Chert and flint	KLER	14	5	..	..	..	..	..	..	..	6	..
Fuller's earth	KLES	228	202	203	153	193	150	183	162	111	83	103
Lignite	KLET	5	3	3	3	2	–	–	–	–	–	–
Rock salt	KLEU	815	2 088	..	..	..	..	..	..	..	..	..
Salt from brine	KLEV	..	1 319	..	..	..	..	..	..	..	..	..
Salt in brine	KLEW	..	..	3 401	4 076	4 009	3 548	3 512	3 561	..	..	..
Anhydrite	KLEX	..	..	..	..	..	..	–	–	–	–	–
Dolomite	KLEY	20 674	19 454	18 539	17 985	17 616	17 966	16 555	17 282	15 632	13 698	13 069
Gypsum	KLEZ	..	..	..	..	..	..	..	..	..	..	..
Slate[1]	KLFA	359	360	326	462	402	275	408	347	425	361	479
Soapstone and talc	KLFB	15	11	5	5	5	4	5	5	5	6	5
Sand and gravel (land-won)	KLFC	98 993	85 479	78 341	79 380	86 341	78 031	70 489	74 362	73 016	74 785	74 877
Sand and gravel (marine dredged)	KLFD	17 179	12 439	10 557	10 090	11 331	11 625	11 508	12 004	12 952	13 424	14 356

Northern Ireland

		1990	1991	1992	1993	1994	1995	1996	1997	1998	1999	2000
Sand and gravel	KLFG	4 030	3 832	3 697	4 318	5 109	5 262	7 684	5 138	5 300	5 517	5 073
Basalt and igneous rock (other than granite)	KLFH	7 691	7 787	9 024	8 557	6 480	7 564	6 974	6 286	6 107	7 861	9 480
Limestone	KLFI	2 866	2 861	3 398	3 236	..	3 703	4 122	3 500	3 892	4 219	3 538
Sandstone[2]	KLFJ	3 090	3 679	3 304	3 959	5 480	4 779	4 941	6 042	6 584	3 615	2 844
Granite	KLFL	..	..	..	..	..	..	–	–	–	–	–
Others[3]	KLFN	..	..	..	647	896	812	1 392	625	473	1 579	3 098

1 Includes waste used for constructional fill, and powder and granules used in manufacturing.
2 Prior to 1993 the 'Sandstone' heading was called 'Grit and conglomerate'. The new heading is all encompassing and was confirmed as correct with the Geological Survey in Northern Ireland.
3 Rock salt, Chalk, Diatomite and Fireclay.

Source: Office for National Statistics: 01633 812082

21.20 Building materials and components: production
Great Britain

		Unit	1990	1991	1992	1993	1994	1995	1996	1997	1998	1999	2000
Building bricks[1]	KLGA	Millions	3 802	3 212	3 000	2 639	3 114	3 256	3 046	2 997	3 000	2 939	2 864
Common bricks	GRTD	"	878	642	497	436	464	480	401	422	385	367	342
Facing bricks	GRTE	"	2 690	2 340	2 266	1 978	2 421	2 546	2 430	2 386	2 411	2 369	2 287
Engineering bricks	GRTF	"	233	230	237	225	229	230	216	190	204	204	235
Clay bricks (including sand-lime)	GRTG	"	3 521	2 999	2 819	2 447	2 900	3 065	2 880	2 828	2 830	2 759	2 694
Concrete bricks	GRTH	"	281	213	181	192	214	191	166	169	171	180	170
Cement (grey Portland)[2]	KLGB	Thousand tonnes	14 740	12 297	11 006	11 039	12 307	11 805	12 214	12 638	12 409	12 697	12 452
Sand and gravel	GRTI	"	116 172	97 918	88 898	89 470	97 672	89 656	81 997	86 366	85 968	88 209	89 234
Building sand[3]	KLGC	"	20 948	18 079	16 769	17 406	18 534	17 389	14 655	15 337	13 810	13 941	14 219
Concreting sand	KLGD	"	37 213	31 239	28 573	28 021	30 977	29 390	28 659	30 130	30 244	31 730	31 167
Gravel[4]	KLGE	"	58 010	48 598	43 557	44 043	48 162	42 877	38 683	40 899	41 914	42 538	43 847
Crushed rock	GRTJ	"	161 615	148 007	143 967	149 576	161 757	150 838	132 894	133 787	131 716	132 598	130 307
Coated roadstone	KLGF	"	26 430	26 387	26 647	27 238	28 512	28 972	26 270	23 906	23 131	22 260	21 785
Uncoated roadstone	KLGG	"	61 742	60 748	53 471	54 412	51 121	49 307	40 893	40 186	36 816	38 114	36 509
Fill and ballast	KLGH	"	54 640	45 669	48 919	52 141	65 779	56 140	50 982	51 396	51 623	52 144	53 417
Concrete aggregate	KLGI	"	18 804	15 203	14 929	15 786	16 345	16 419	14 748	18 300	20 146	20 080	18 595
Ready mixed concrete[2]	GRXA	Thousand m³	26 782	22 527	20 776	20 771	22 931	21 676	20 892	22 327	22 983	23 550	23 043
Concrete building blocks	GRTK	Thousand m²	91 154	74 631	68 194	74 287	87 548	78 287	75 866	82 537	84 662	87 767	90 219
Dense aggregate	KLGN	"	39 297	32 456	29 732	30 116	36 997	36 933	34 996	37 250	39 439	38 439	37 629
Lightweight aggregate	KLGO	"	23 768	18 581	17 479	19 235	22 048	18 147	16 316	17 783	19 110	20 830	22 991
Aerated concrete	KLGP	"	28 089	23 594	20 984	24 936	28 503	23 207	24 554	27 505	26 113	28 497	29 599
Concrete roofing tiles	KLGM	"	31 510	26 359	21 490	24 574	28 149	26 118	24 651	24 958	24 981	25 972	26 316
Roofing & architectural slates	GRXB	tonnes	44 113	41 025	41 615	37 321	44 910	42 030	48 474	44 578	46 159	46 998	41 214
Fibre cement products	KLGK	Thousand tonnes	234.7	133.7	121.1	128.7	154.1	160.5	146.2	163.5	160.9	156.2	..

1 Excluding refractory and glazed bricks.
2 United Kingdom.
3 Includes sand and gravel used for coating.
4 Includes hoggin.

Source: Department of Trade & Industry: 020 7944 5593

21.21 Construction: Value of output in Great Britain[1]

£ millions

		1990	1991	1992	1993	1994	1995	1996	1997	1998	1999	2000
All work: total	FGAY	55 307	51 115	47 472	46 323	49 439	52 643	55 243	58 352	62 060	65 704	69 527
New work: total	BLAB	30 762	27 726	24 814	23 556	25 086	26 672	27 926	29 928	32 491	35 587	37 510
New housing: total	KLQA	6 680	5 796	6 084	6 628	7 417	7 135	7 013	7 983	8 430	8 419	9 946
For public sector	BLAC	934	793	1 243	1 415	1 671	1 660	1 421	1 232	1 069	1 012	1 313
For private sector	BLAD	5 746	5 003	4 841	5 213	5 746	5 475	5 592	6 751	7 361	7 406	8 633
Infrastructure: total	KIAM	4 965	6 062	5 716	5 544	5 149	5 660	6 338	6 311	6 182	6 200	6 427
Other new work: total (excluding infrastructure)	KLQB	19 118	15 867	13 015	11 384	12 521	13 877	14 575	15 635	17 878	20 969	21 138
For public sector	BLAE	4 414	4 142	4 181	4 045	4 384	4 661	4 441	3 756	4 151	4 919	4 835
For private sector	KLQC	14 704	11 725	8 834	7 339	8 137	9 217	10 134	11 879	13 727	16 049	16 303
Private Industrial	BLAF	3 394	2 622	2 234	2 208	2 489	3 008	3 119	3 491	3 810	3 973	3 702
Private Commercial	BLAG	11 310	9 103	6 600	5 131	5 648	6 209	7 015	8 388	9 917	12 076	12 601
Repair and maintenance: total	BLAH	24 544	23 389	22 658	22 767	24 353	25 971	27 317	28 423	29 569	30 117	32 016
Housing: total	KLQD	13 839	13 001	12 586	12 809	13 767	14 595	15 035	15 755	16 202	16 370	16 907
For public sector	BLBK	5 384	4 938	4 991	5 439	5 963	6 465	6 637	6 629	6 506	6 485	6 552
For private sector	BLBL	8 455	8 063	7 595	7 370	7 804	8 130	8 398	9 126	9 696	9 885	10 354
Public other work	BLAJ	5 488	5 291	5 087	4 916	5 211	5 398	5 252	5 079	5 220	5 371	5 685
Private other work	BLAK	5 218	5 098	4 985	5 042	5 375	5 978	7 030	7 590	8 147	8 376	9 424

1 Output by contractors, including unrecorded estimates by small firms and self-employed workers, and output by public sector direct labour departments - classified to construction in the *1992 Standard Industrial Classification.*

Source: Department for Transport, Local Government and the Regions: 020 7890 5583

21.22 Construction: Value of new orders obtained by contractors[1]
Great Britain

£ millions

		1990	1991	1992	1993	1994	1995	1996	1997	1998	1999	2000
New work: total	FHAA	22 491	19 455	17 493	19 965	21 285	22 065	22 834	24 806	27 477	26 079	28 114
Public housing	BLBC	683	875	1 246	1 668	1 386	1 182	1 073	995	933	969	915
Private housing[2]	BLBD	4 855	4 552	4 016	4 874	5 721	4 905	5 416	6 253	5 997	5 901	6 085
New housing: total	FGAU	5 538	5 427	5 263	6 542	7 106	6 087	6 487	7 248	6 930	6 869	7 000
Infrastructure:												
Water	KIBV	321	509	669	421	412	500	640	733	957	760	1 078
Sewerage	KIBW	491	429	469	447	389	394	481	656	737	789	380
Electricity	KIBX	187	301	281	211	170	218	294	382	359	254	244
Roads	KIBY	1 425	1 415	1 322	1 435	1 356	1 531	1 710	928	821	957	1 450
Gas, communications, air	KIBZ	391	441	554	642	494	904	745	693	745	713	1 090
Railways	KIDP	160	125	200	623	412	351	524	416	573	471	540
Harbours	KIDQ	216	203	252	220	218	273	270	182	287	250	216
Total	KIDR	3 190	3 423	3 746	3 998	3 451	4 170	4 664	3 991	4 479	4 195	4 999
of which												
- Public	KIDS	2 029	2 090	1 690	2 472	2 211	2 327	1 671	1 352	1 505	1 495	1 434
- Private	KIDT	1 161	1 333	2 056	1 525	1 240	1 843	2 993	2 639	2 974	2 700	3 565
Other public non-housing:												
Factories	KIDU	149	89	128	111	111	94	91	72	84	72	64
Warehouses	KIDV	14	14	54	23	38	29	14	27	20	24	12
Oil, steel, coal	KIDW	81	13	47	30	12	13	4	4	2	5	1
Schools and colleges	KIDX	527	584	584	655	658	710	708	749	770	791	996
Universities	KIDY	146	150	203	353	376	373	355	273	405	345	336
Health	KIDZ	663	578	644	697	752	717	674	491	769	635	686
Offices	KIFP	570	492	499	684	469	393	381	391	292	390	294
Entertainment	KIFQ	283	250	189	281	308	285	253	342	432	435	361
Garages	KIFR	56	44	28	42	49	51	28	34	19	36	44
Shops	KIFS	24	25	23	26	14	21	11	35	35	29	34
Agriculture	KIFT	5	17	14	44	22	12	8	33	17	9	14
Miscellaneous	KIFU	601	421	351	450	844	508	419	441	660	503	998
Total	KIFV	3 117	2 677	2 763	3 397	3 654	3 206	2 945	2 894	3 504	3 273	3 840
Private industrial:[2]												
Factories	KIFW	2 094	1 830	1 006	1 221	1 451	2 055	1 603	2 184	1 878	1 698	1 448
Warehouses	KIFX	648	438	426	429	498	594	663	901	1 014	821	1 109
Oil, steel, coal	KIFY	108	79	72	27	51	76	71	64	79	38	34
Total	KIFZ	2 850	2 347	1 503	1 677	1 999	2 725	2 337	3 149	2 971	2 558	2 591
Private commercial:[2]												
Schools, universities	KIHP	169	175	121	134	115	105	156	189	351	393	572
Health	KIHQ	271	369	193	179	255	288	277	356	651	411	453
Offices	KIHR	4 215	2 215	1 691	1 471	1 777	2 123	2 169	2 506	3 472	3 566	4 358
Entertainment	KIHS	1 195	1 111	747	751	928	940	1 407	1 847	2 244	2 224	1 857
Garages	KIHT	364	261	234	308	300	301	265	344	315	266	170
Shops	KIHU	1 345	1 222	1 034	1 278	1 453	1 871	1 795	1 937	2 154	1 901	1 894
Agriculture	KIBN	127	105	94	108	120	124	123	148	146	100	77
Miscellaneous	KIBO	109	123	103	122	127	126	198	198	259	321	304
Total	KIBP	7 796	5 581	4 218	4 351	5 075	5 877	6 390	7 525	9 593	9 184	9 684

1 Classified to construction in the *1992 Standard Industrial Classification.*
2 Figures for private sector include work to be carried out by contractors on their own initiative for sale.

Source: Department for Transport, Local Government and the Regions: 020 7890 5583

21.23 Total engineering
Total turnover of UK based manufacturers[1,2,3]
Standard Industrial Classification 1992

£ millions

Activity heading	Product group		1995	1996	1997	1998	1999	2000
Class 29: Manufacture of machinery and equipment not elsewhere classified								
2911	Manufacture of engines and turbines except aircraft, vehicle and cycle engines	BBEM	1 764	1 662	1 457	1 534	1 396	1 474
2912	Manufacture of pumps and compressors	BBEN	2 780	2 697	2 657	2 852	2 736	2 820
2913	Manufacture of taps and valves	BBEO	1 589	1 485	1 454	1 560	1 263	1 396
2914	Manufacture of bearings, gears, gearing and driving elements	BBEP	1 616	1 736	1 588	1 581	1 439	1 372
2922	Manufacture of lifting and handling equipment	BBEQ	3 453	3 878	3 488	3 551	3 673	3 487
2923	Manufacture of non-domestic cooling and ventilation equipment	BBER	2 925	3 314	3 541	3 629	3 329	3 414
2924	Manufacture of other general purpose machinery not elsewhere classified	BBES	2 474	2 323	2 504	2 494	2 715	2 700
2940	Manufacture of machine tools	BBET	2 301	2 136	2 221	2 155	1 981	1 969
2952	Manufacture of machinery for mining, quarrying and construction	BBEU	2 231	2 906	2 375	2 450	2 339	2 435
2953	Manufacture of machinery for food, beverage and tobacco processing	BBEV	1 343	998	967	860	723	760
2954	Manufacture of machinery for textile, apparel and leather production	BBEW	495	460	419	382	260	267
2956	Manufacture of other special purpose machinery not elsewhere classified	BBEX	2 163	3 190	2 910	2 781	2 610	2 381
2971	Manufacture of electric domestic appliances	BBEY	2 233	2 019	2 051	2 062	1 975	2 012
	Total	BBEZ	27 367	34 262	33 971	33 843	31 896	31 583
Class 30 : Manufacture of electrical and optical equipment								
3001	Manufacture of office machinery	BBFA	1 232	1 449	1 279	1 354	1 448	1 571
3002	Manufacture of computers and other information processing equipment	BBFB	12 105	12 166	13 518	13 745	13 281	12 626
	Total	BBFC	13 337	13 615	14 797	15 099	14 729	14 196
Class 31 : Manufacture of electrical machinery and apparatus not elsewhere classified								
3110	Manufacture of electric motors, generators and transformers	BBFD	2 057	2 462	2 490	2 457	2 676	2 834
3120	Manufacture of electricity distribution and control apparatus	BBFE	3 428	3 863	3 656	3 561	3 814	4 226
3130	Manufacture of insulated wire and cable	BBFF	2 384	2 739	2 284	1 988	1 814	1 829
3140	Manufacture of accumulators, primary cells and primary batteries	BBFG	613	695	685	632	588	603
3150	Manufacture of lighting equipment and electric lamps	BBFH	1 589	1 772	1 709	1 611	1 639	1 599
3161	Manufacture of other electrical equipment for engines and vehicles not otherwise classified	BBFI	1 247	1 457	1 364	1 266	1 069	1 031
3162	Manufacture of other electrical equipment not elsewhere classified	BBFJ	2 808	2 961	2 898	3 216	3 231	2 588
	Total	BBFK	14 126	15 949	15 086	14 731	14 830	14 709
Class 32 : Manufacture of radio, television and communication equipment and apparatus								
3210	Manufacture of electronic valves and tubes and other electronic components	BBFL	6 362	6 031	5 869	5 876	4 924	7 087
3220	Manufacture of television and radio transmitters and apparatus for line telephony and line telegraphy	BBFM	6 616	6 815	7 029	7 786	11 871	15 242
3230	Manufacture of television and radio receivers, sound or video recording or reproducing apparatus and associated goods	BBFN	4 257	4 922	4 654	4 375	4 243	4 485
	Total	BBFO	17 235	17 768	17 552	18 037	21 038	26 814
Class 33 : Manufacture of medical, precision and optical instruments, watches and clocks								
3310	Manufacture of medical and surgical equipment and orthopaedic appliances	BBFP	2 015	2 156	1 942	1 880	2 094	2 170
3320	Manufacture of instruments and appliances for measuring, checking, testing, navigating and other purposes, except industrial process control equipment	BBFQ	6 066	7 086	6 818	6 508	6 238	6 516
3340	Manufacture of optical instruments and photographic equipment	BBFR	1 233	1 393	1 431	1 512	1 331	1 421
	Total	BBFS	9 314	11 785	11 168	10 974	10 687	11 031

1 The figures shown represent the output of UK based manufacturers classified to Subsections DK and DL of the Standard Industrial Classification 1992. The figures shown are derived from the monthly production inquiry (MPI) and include estimates for non-responders and for establishments which are not sampled.

2 Orders on hand figures are given for the end of the period to which they relate.
3 The data on this table are not seasonally adjusted.

Source: Office for National Statistics: 01633 812786

21.24 Volume index numbers of turnover and orders for the engineering industries
United Kingdom

	Total			Home			Export		
	Orders on hand end of period (1995 average = 100)	1995 average monthly sales = 100		Orders on hand end of period (1995 average = 100)	1995 average monthly sales = 100		Orders on hand end of period (1995 average = 100)	1995 average monthly sales = 100	
		New orders[1]	Turnover		New orders[1]	Turnover		New orders[1]	Turnover
Total Engineering industries *SIC 1992 Class 29, 30, 31,32 and 33*									
	FGWA	FGWB	FGVT	FGVU	FGVV	FGVW	FGVX	FGVY	FGVZ
1992	94.9	84.6	86.0	90.3	85.7	87.7	102.0	83.1	83.5
1993	95.6	87.5	87.3	92.0	92.6	92.1	101.3	80.4	80.7
1994	105.0	98.1	95.4	105.6	103.1	99.0	104.2	91.2	90.4
1995	98.4	98.0	100.0	100.0	98.3	100.0	95.9	97.7	100.0
1996	94.3	102.4	103.6	94.6	98.2	99.8	93.9	108.4	109.0
1997	97.3	107.0	106.1	97.9	101.8	100.8	96.2	114.2	113.6
1998	94.6	110.3	111.1	90.0	100.7	103.1	101.6	123.8	122.3
1999	105.7	118.6	115.3	104.5	113.0	108.6	107.7	126.4	124.7
2000	118.6	128.0	124.2	118.3	115.5	115.5	119.0	139.7	136.6
Manufacture of Machinery and Equipment *SIC 1992 Class 29*									
	FGVB	FGVD	FGVF	FGVH	FGVJ	FGVL	FGVN	FGVP	FGVR
1992	94.4	94.2	97.4	82.9	95.1	99.4	112.7	92.8	93.9
1993	95.0	96.4	96.2	84.9	100.9	100.2	111.0	88.9	89.5
1994	107.1	104.3	99.9	107.9	111.1	103.1	105.8	92.6	94.6
1995	97.9	96.7	100.0	97.9	96.5	100.0	97.8	97.0	100.0
1996	96.1	98.6	99.2	99.8	97.2	96.5	89.8	101.1	103.9
1997	100.6	99.1	97.5	106.0	97.4	95.2	91.4	102.1	101.6
1998	86.0	92.3	97.5	86.8	86.6	93.2	84.4	102.3	104.8
1999	87.9	92.8	92.1	92.0	91.7	89.9	81.1	94.8	96.0
2000	92.4	93.0	91.4	94.1	87.4	86.6	89.5	102.7	99.7
Manufacture of Electrical and Optical Equipment *SIC 1992 Class 30, 31,32 and 33*									
	FGVC	FGVE	FGVG	FGVI	FGVK	FGVM	FGVO	FGVQ	FGVS
1992	95.4	79.1	79.3	96.6	79.5	80.0	93.7	78.5	78.6
1993	96.2	82.4	82.2	98.0	87.1	86.8	93.7	76.4	76.4
1994	103.3	94.6	92.8	103.6	97.8	96.3	102.9	90.5	88.4
1995	98.8	98.8	100.0	101.8	99.5	100.0	94.4	98.0	100.0
1996	92.9	104.7	106.2	90.2	98.9	102.0	96.8	112.0	111.4
1997	94.6	111.7	111.3	91.0	104.9	104.6	99.8	120.2	119.6
1998	101.6	121.0	119.2	92.8	110.3	109.8	114.5	134.4	131.0
1999	120.0	134.0	129.2	115.0	127.6	121.4	127.2	141.9	138.9
2000	139.6	149.0	143.9	139.0	141.7	135.1	140.5	158.0	154.8

1 Net of cancellations.

Source: Office for National Statistics: 01633 812786

21.25 Motor vehicle production[1]
United Kingdom

Numbers

		1990	1991	1992	1993	1994	1995	1996	1997	1998	1999	2000
Motor vehicles												
SIC 1992, Class 34-10 Passenger cars: total	JCYM	1 295 610	1 236 900	1 291 880	1 375 524	1 466 823	1 532 084	1 686 134	1 698 001	1 748 258	1 786 623	1 641 452
1 000 c.c. and under	GKAB	93 039	26 621	22 037	98 034	98 178	95 198	108 645	119 894	112 044	113 204	96 043
Over 1 000 c.c. but not over 1 600c.c.	GKAD	809 219	830 530	793 307	709 615	729 397	814 873	845 084	829 079	814 595	776 111	676 438
Over 1 600 c.c. but not over 2 800 c.c.	GKAF	325 116	338 877	437 951	515 487	573 357	528 444	635 861	653 147	720 556	758 478	723 294
Over 2 800 c.c.	GKAH	68 236	40 872	38 585	52 388	65 891	93 569	96 544	95 881	101 063	138 830	145 677
Commercial vehicles: total	JCYG	270 346	217 141	248 453	193 467	227 815	233 001	238 314	237 706	227 379	185 905	172 442
Of which: Light commercial vehicles Trucks:	GKDH	230 510	105 633	216 477	171 141	197 285	199 346	205 372	210 942	203 629	162 176	104 730
Under 7.5 tonnes	GKDJ	10 515	5 379	9 558	4 755	8 154	9 523	8 913	6 254	5 006	4 107	3 026
Over 7.5 tonnes	GKDL	13 674	7 673	11 113	8 269	10 016	11 717	10 128	7 932	7 002	6 443	3 854
Motive units for articulated vehicles	GKCV	3 327	1 444	2 788	2 283	2 794	3 476	2 631	2 574	2 492	2 739	1 569
Buses, coaches and mini buses	GKDN	12 320	5 593	8 517	7 019	9 566	8 939	11 270	10 004	9 250	10 440	10 305

1 Figures for motor vehicles relate to periods of 52 weeks (53 weeks in 1993).

Source: Office for National Statistics: 01633 812963

Production

21.26 Alcoholic drink
United Kingdom

			1990	1991	1992	1993	1994	1995	1996	1997	1998	1999	2000
Spirits[1]		Thousand hectolitres of alcohol											
Production	KMEA	"	4 743	4 476	4 219	3 974	4 114	4 507	4 868	5 297	5 145	4 705	4 210
Released for home consumption													
Home produced whisky	KMEE	"	413	383	356	374	383	310	321	312	289	323	314
Imported and other	KMEG	"	567	529	505	504	531	481	495	533	505	596	615
Total	KMEH	"	980	912	861	878	914	791	815	845	794	919	929
Beer[2]		Thousand hectolitres											
Production	KMEI	"	61 783	59 552	57 616	56 746	58 333	56 800	58 072	59 139	56 652	57 854	55 279
Released for home consumption	KMEL	"	65 184	63 038	60 973	59 177	60 575	59 129	59 894	61 114	58 835	58 917	57 007
		Thousand hectolitres of pure alcohol											
Production	JYXJ		..	..	..	..	2 345	2 298	2 360	2 406	2 333	2 364	2 299
Released for home consumption	JYXK		..	..	..	..	2 453	2 410	2 448	2 504	2 439	2 428	2 382
Wine of fresh grapes													
Released for home consumption		Thousand hectolitres											
Fortified	KMEM	"	378	357	345	335	329	330	331	323	370	316	289
Still table	KMEN	"	5 893	5 910	6 166	6 471	6 759	6 577	6 995	7 653	7 979	8 391	8 864
Sparkling	KMEO	"	365	316	292	296	297	315	358	382	416	576	543
Total	KMEP	"	6 636	6 583	6 803	7 102	7 385	7 221	7 683	8 358	8 765	9 284	9 696
Made-wine													
Released for home consumption													
Other than coolers	KMEQ	"	521	436	439	505	470	516	513	485	406	416	431
Coolers[3]	KJDD	"	185	263	433	485	549	903	1 781	1 153	1 244	1 802	2 800
Cider and perry													
Released for home consumption	KMER	"	3 666	3 713	4 398	4 496	4 811	5 575	5 656	5 513	5 548	6 022	6 006

1 Potable spirits distilled.
2 A new system was introduced for beer duty in June 1993. The figures in this table include adjustments to data prior to this date to bring them into line with current data.

3 Made wine with alcoholic strength 1.2% to 5.5%. Includes alcoholic lemonade of appropriate strength and similar product.

Source: HM Customs and Excise: 020 7865 5249

21.27 Tobacco products: released for home consumption
United Kingdom

			1990	1991	1992	1993[1]	1994	1995	1996	1997	1998	1999	2000
Cigarettes:		Thousand million											
Home produced	KMFA	"	87.4	85.3	76.4	85.8	82.4	70.8	73.8	71.1	67.8	28.2	49.3
Imported	KMFB	"	10.3	10.3	9.3	9.5	10.2	9.5	9.5	9.9	7.5	6.0	7.3
Total	KMFC	"	97.8	95.6	85.7	95.2	92.6	80.3	83.3	81.0	75.3	34.2	56.6
Cigars:		Million kg.											
Home produced	KMFD	"	2.1	1.9	1.8	1.7	1.6	1.5	1.4	1.3	1.2	0.9	1.0
Imported	KMFE	"	0.3	0.1	0.1	0.1	0.1	0.1	0.1	0.1	0.1	0.1	0.1
Total	KMFF	"	2.3	2.1	1.9	1.8	1.7	1.6	1.5	1.4	1.3	1.0	1.1
Hand-rolling tobacco:													
Home produced	KMFG	"	4.1	4.1	3.7	3.5	3.0	2.4	2.1	1.8	1.7	2.0	2.1
Imported	KMFH	"	–	0.1	0.1	0.1	0.1	0.1	0.1	0.1	0.1	0.1	–
Total	KMFI	"	4.1	4.2	3.8	3.6	3.2	2.6	2.3	1.9	1.8	2.0	2.2
Other smoking and chewing tobacco:													
Home produced	KMFJ	"	2.1	2.0	1.8	1.8	1.5	1.3	1.2	1.1	1.0	0.6	0.7
Imported	KMFK	"	0.2	0.1	0.2	0.1	0.1	0.1	0.1	0.1	0.1	0.1	0.1
Total	KMFL	"	2.2	2.1	2.0	1.9	1.6	1.4	1.3	1.2	1.1	0.7	0.8

1 1993 contained two Budgets, in March and November.

Source: HM Customs and Excise: 020 7865 5249

22 Banking, insurance etc

Banking, insurance etc

Other banks' balance sheet (Table 22.3)
The implementation of the review of banking statistics at end-September 1997 has resulted in several changes to this table:

(a)   The table now includes the business of all monthly and quarterly reporting banks in the UK; it formerly covered only the business of monthly reporting institutions.

(b)   The Channel Islands and Isle of Man are no longer treated as part of the UK for statistical purposes. Banking institutions in the Channel Islands and Isle of Man no longer have the option of being within the UK banking sector and their business, along with the business of offshore island branches of UK mainland banks, is now excluded from the figures within this table. Additionally, the business of the UK banking sector with offshore island residents and entities has been reclassified from UK residents to non-residents.

(c)   The table now contains more comprehensive detail of business with building societies. This business was previously included indistinguishably within the UK private sector elements of the table.

(d)   The aggregate balance sheet of the banking sector has been inflated because it is now reported on an accrual basis rather than a cash basis (accrued amounts payable/ receivable are shown under liabilities and assets respectively). Additionally, acceptances have been brought onto the balance sheet and are shown under both liabilities and assets.

With effect from 1998, the balance sheet of the Banking Department of the Bank of England is excluded from this table, and other banks' business with the Issue Department is reclassified from "UK public sector" to "UK banks".

Bank lending to, and bank deposits from, UK residents (Tables 22.4 and 22.5)
These are series of statistics based on the Standard Industrial Classification 1992.

Table 22.4 comprises loans, advances (including under reverse repos), finance leasing, acceptances, facilities and holdings of sterling and euro commercial paper. It includes lending under the Department of Trade and Industry special scheme for domestic shipbuilding. Holdings of investments and bills and adjustments for transit items are not included.

Table 22.5 includes borrowing under sale and repurchase agreements (repro). Adjustments for transit items are not included.

Figures for both tables are supplied by monthly reporting banks and grossed to cover quarterly reporters. They exclude lending to building societies and to residents of the Channel Islands and Isle of Man.

Capital issues and redemptions (Table 22.14)
The estimates in this table relate to new money raised on the stock market by issues of ordinary, preference and loan capital (public issues, offers for sale, issues by tender, placings and issues to shareholders and employees) by non-resident borrowers split between central government, state and local governments and companies.

The estimates include UK local government negotiable bonds (of not less than one year) issue to or through the agency of banks, discount houses, issuing houses or brokers. Mortgages, bank advances and any other loans redeemable in less than twelve months are excluded; so also are loans from UK government funds (including the former Industrial Reorganisation Corporation and the National Enterprise Board) but not government subscriptions to company issues made *pari passu* with the market. Issues to shareholders are included only if the sole or principal share register is maintained in the United Kingdom.

Estimates of issues are based on the prices at which securities are offered to the market. Subscriptions are recorded under the periods in which they are due to be paid. Redemptions exclude share buy-backs. They relate to fixed interest securities of the kinds included as issues; conversion issues in lieu of cash repayment are included in the gross figures of both issues and redemptions. These figures include issues of debentures and loan stock carrying the right of conversion into, or subscription to, equity capital.

The division between the United Kingdom and non-resident company borrowers is determined by the location of the registered office. The industrial classification of companies is according to the primary occupation of the borrowing company or group. Until 1982 it is based on the Standard Industrial Classification (SIC) 1968, from 1983 to 1995 on SIC 1983 and subsequently on SIC 92.

The estimates exclude issues on the unlisted securities market which was launched by the Stock Exchange in November 1980. These issues are mainly of ordinary shares by industrial and commercial companies. Estimates of new money raised are: 1990 364; 1991 261.

Consumer credit (Table 22.16)
Figures for net lending refer to changes in amounts outstanding adjusted to remove distortions caused by revaluations of debt outstanding, such as write-offs. Lending by retailers refers to self-financed credit advanced by food retailers, clothing retailers, household goods retailers, mixed business retailers (other than co-operative societies) and general mail order houses. Class 3 loans are advanced under the terms of the Building Societies' Act 1986. Loans on personal accounts exclude loans for house purchase and bridging finance.

Data relating to the narrower coverage covers finance houses and other specialist credit grantors, bank credit cards (operated under the VISA and Mastercard systems), and secured loans by building societies. A high proportion of credit advanced in certain types of agreement, notably on credit cards, is repaid within a month. This reflects use of such agreements as a method of payment rather than a way of obtaining credit.

22.1 Bank of England

£ millions

						December						
		1990	1991	1992	1993	1994	1995	1996	1997	1998	1999	2000
Issue Department												
Liabilities:												
Notes in circulation	AEFA	17 283	17 466	17 542	18 218	20 055	21 262	22 407	23 715	24 573	27 232	29 412
Notes in Banking Department	AEFB	7	4	8	12	5	7	12	5	7	8	8
Assets:												
Government securities[1]	AEFC	14 672	11 791	7 808	6 816	11 468	14 552	16 524	16 416	15 826	17 264	13 498
Other securities[2]	AEFD	2 618	5 679	9 742	11 414	8 592	6 717	5 896	7 304	8 754	9 976	15 921
Banking Department												
Liabilities:												
Total[3]	AEFE	8 613	5 825	5 623	11 095	6 192	7 114	6 229	7 221	6 802	52 072	10 397
Public deposits[4]	AEFF	44	104	97	6 205	938	1 159	1 001	1 192	237	195	391
Bankers' deposits[5]	AEFH	1 842	1 813	1 553	1 700	1 855	2 001	2 021	2 800	1 388	1 357	1 520
Reserves and other accounts[6]	AEFI	6 713	3 894	3 959	3 175	3 385	3 941	3 193	3 214	5 163	50 506	8 471
Assets:												
Total	KCYT	8 615	5 825	5 623	11 095	6 192	7 114	6 229	7 221	6 802	..	..
Government securities	AEFJ	1 432	1 346	1 237	1 174	1 050	1 090	1 232	1 373	1 352	1 444	1 504
Advances and other accounts	AEFK	2 146	2 443	3 935	9 411	4 696	5 499	2 339	5 388	3 302	46 895	6 533
Premises, equipment and other securities[6]	AEFL	5 030	2 031	443	498	441	518	2 646	455	2 141	3 724	2 352
Notes and coin	AEFM	7	5	8	12	5	7	12	5	7	8	8

1 Including the historic liability of the Treasury of £11 million until 1993.
2 Including gilt and Treasury bill repurchase agreements (from 1994 - previously in "Government securities")
3 The only liability not shown separately is the Bank's capital (held by the Treasury) which has been constant at £14.6 million.
4 Excluding local government and public corporations' deposits which are included under Reserves and other accounts.

5 These consist of operational deposits held mainly by the clearing banks and non-operational cash ratio deposits for which institutions authorised under the Banking Act, deposit - taking UK branches of "European Authorised Institutions" and (from 1998) building societies are liable.
6 Large increases from 1999 arise from the Bank of England's role in TARGET, as a result of which other European central banks may hold substantial credit balances or overdrafts with the Bank.

Source: Bank of England: 020 7601 3236

22.2 Value of inter-bank clearings[1]

£ billions

		1990	1991	1992	1993	1994	1995	1996	1997	1998	1999	2000
Bulk paper clearings												
Cheque (formerly general)	KCYY	1 089	1 084	1 052	1 065	1 075	1 097	1 161	1 196	1 214	1 225	1 214
Credit (formerly credit clearing)	KCYZ	109	104	101	97	93	92	94	94	92	88	82
High-value clearings												
Town	KCZA	4 776	2 228	1 387	1 069	681	59	–	–	–	–	–
CHAPS	KCZB	18 880	19 050	20 929	23 545	25 052	26 719	28 881	36 032	41 501	44 704	49 146
Electronic clearing	KCZC	668	772	803	836	941	1 055	1 251	1 432	1 602	1 761	1 922

1 Excludes inter-branch clearings and clearings in Scotland and Northern Ireland.

Source: Association of Payment Clearing Services (APACS): 020 7601 4340

22.3 Other banks' balance sheet[1]

£ millions

		1991	1992	1993	1994	1995	1996	1997	1998	1999[2]	2000
Sterling liabilities											
Notes outstanding & cash loaded cards	TBFA	1 840	2 084	2 186	2 456	2 576	2 717	2 832	2 929	3 311	3 359
Sight deposits											
UK banks	TBFB	10 229	14 243	14 768	16 222	16 983	20 138	44 573	37 839	33 463	40 054
UK building societies	TBFC	..	..	..	..	..	..	950	1 277	841	1 168
UK public sector	TBFD	2 953	2 952	3 335	3 301	3 824	3 641	3 781	3 003	3 449	3 402
Other UK residents	TBFE	144 516	148 011	161 907	164 451	192 297	211 179	271 232	295 069	325 392	372 726
Non-residents	TBFF	14 466	15 094	15 075	16 425	18 690	17 707	37 730	43 528	44 581	55 489
Time deposits											
UK banks	TBFG	72 344	78 640	68 531	75 629	90 044	95 798	99 783	111 970	112 530	110 955
UK building societies	TBFH	–	–	–	–	–	–	5 682	4 362	4 254	4 688
UK public sector	TBFI	2 885	3 193	4 223	4 908	7 896	6 087	9 060	9 749	8 064	8 241
Other UK residents	TBFJ	154 223	157 979	162 053	166 505	190 707	210 045	284 630	295 925	282 789	301 007
of which TESSAs	TBFK	2 453	4 331	5 896	7 517	10 314	9 389	20 393	21 568	22 868	24 265
of which SAYE	TBFL	–	–	–	–	–	–	2 255	2 604	2 840	2 726
Non-residents	TBFM	57 718	58 550	58 583	62 905	68 274	63 995	91 040	97 954	116 967	134 843
Acceptances granted	TBFN	–	–	–	–	–	–	19 952	16 659	12 854	10 012
Liabilities under sale and repurchase agreements											
of which British govt. securities	TBFU	–	–	–	–	–	22 668	47 297	55 561	56 145	83 819
UK banks	TBFP	–	–	–	–	–	13 718	29 089	43 314	48 213	56 408
UK building societies	TBFQ	..	..	..	..	..	..	20	32	200	36
UK public sector	TBFR	–	–	–	–	–	2 279	6 044	–	–	14 351
Other UK residents	TBFS	–	–	–	–	–	7 703	18 114	20 918	17 165	22 974
Non-residents	TBFT	–	–	–	–	–	683	5 664	5 469	5 542	9 849
CDs and other short-term paper issued	TBFV	52 307	50 912	52 783	63 880	70 277	96 390	119 266	138 248	158 826	151 153
Total sterling deposits	TBFW	511 641	529 575	541 260	574 224	658 993	749 364	1 046 610	1 125 314	1 175 131	1 297 357
Sterling items in suspense and transmission	TBFX	11 349	10 317	11 011	8 412	10 423	12 120	16 055	15 714	17 307	15 262
Net derivatives	TBFY	..	..	..	..	..	..	8 186	8 342	8 324	10 992
Accrued amounts payable	TBFZ	..	..	..	..	..	..	20 713	24 632	22 122	23 726
Sterling capital and other internal funds	TBGA	65 908	68 640	71 833	78 775	82 160	90 464	103 463	103 867	100 576	133 435
Total sterling liabilities	TBGB	590 738	610 616	626 290	663 868	754 152	854 666	1 197 858	1 280 799	1 326 770	1 484 131
Foreign currency liabilities											
Sight and time deposits											
UK banks	TBGC	76 901	89 532	95 921	105 813	104 769	91 314	90 858	77 128	77 685	99 448
UK building societies	TBGD	..	..	..	..	..	..	1 027	639	681	233
UK public sector	TBGE	..	..	..	..	..	..	226	149	127	1 808
Other UK residents	TBGF	..	..	..	..	..	..	64 188	60 513	65 202	79 627
Non-residents	TBGG	432 000	543 883	580 951	618 769	696 380	605 439	716 573	766 934	736 792	914 889
Acceptances granted	TBGH	..	..	..	..	..	..	743	730	619	686
Sale and repurchase agreements											
UK banks	TBGJ	–	–	–	–	–	17 114	21 311	30 669	25 169	38 900
UK building societies	TBGK	..	..	..	..	..	..	22	–	–	468
UK public sector	TBGL	..	..	..	..	..	..	22	–	–	468
Other UK residents	TBGM	..	..	..	..	..	..	25 716	26 742	21 997	35 146
Non-residents	TBGN	–	–	–	–	–	61 307	100 935	118 909	115 357	139 656
CDs and other short-term paper issued	TBGO	65 648	73 814	61 017	67 869	89 032	101 005	131 620	124 151	151 009	199 510
Total foreign currency deposits	TBGP	608 685	754 851	790 361	851 856	972 832	975 619	1 153 220	1 206 562	1 194 637	1 510 371
Items in suspense and transmission	TBGQ	5 637	11 261	20 714	14 779	13 881	21 272	35 713	25 027	30 547	46 677
Net derivatives	TBGR	..	..	..	..	..	..	8 653	2 657	3 704	–4 472
Accrued amounts payable	TBGS	..	..	..	..	..	..	21 996	25 184	18 081	18 568
Capital and other internal funds	TBGT	18 697	20 833	21 581	21 081	26 430	25 535	31 676	46 952	69 797	89 360
Total foreign currency liabilities	TBGU	633 019	786 945	832 656	887 716	1 013 143	1 022 426	1 251 258	1 306 381	1 316 766	1 660 504
Total liabilities	TBGV	1 223 757	1 397 561	1 458 946	1 551 584	1 767 295	1 877 092	2 449 116	2 587 180	2 643 536	3 144 635

Banking, insurance etc.

22.3 Other banks' balance sheet[1]

continued

£ millions

		1991	1992	1993	1994	1995	1996	1997	1998	1999[2]	2000
Sterling assets											
Notes and coins	TBGW	3 920	4 454	4 711	4 983	5 357	4 812	5 225	6 698	9 047	8 007
With UK central bank											
Cash ratio deposits	TBGX	1 576	1 402	1 415	1 490	1 682	1 888	2 566	1 068	1 141	1 275
Other	TBGY	27	−42	183	103	113	533	217	383	676	117
Market loans											
UK banks	TBGZ	77 568	87 691	79 281	88 582	103 006	109 500	139 996	148 139	144 537	149 173
UK bank CDs	TBHB	19 661	20 620	19 028	23 632	26 767	36 922	62 584	65 510	75 070	65 156
UK bank commercial paper	TBHC							29	130	208	8
UK building societies CDs etc and deposits	TBHD	3 673	4 433	5 360	5 358	4 387	4 891	4 241	4 505	5 093	4 748
Non-residents	TBHE	23 978	33 734	43 571	44 582	47 470	50 585	79 367	84 162	74 403	94 381
Acceptances granted											
UK building societies	TBHF	..	..	..	..	..	..	−	−	−	−
UK public sector	TBHG	..	..	..	..	..	..	−	−	−	−
Other UK residents	TBHH	..	..	..	..	..	..	18 573	15 395	11 934	9 496
Non-residents	TBHI	..	..	..	..	..	..	1 379	1 264	920	516
Bills											
Treasury bills	TBHJ	4 045	1 952	1 561	4 166	10 404	1 652	554	779	2 750	1 613
UK bank bills	TBHA	..	..	..	..	..	..	18 221	14 110	11 426	7 011
UK building societies	TBHK	..	..	..	..	..	..	−	−	−	−
Other UK	TBHL	..	..	..	..	..	..	1 117	1 220	818	1 202
Non-residents	TBHM	..	..	..	..	..	..	309	207	206	288
Claims under sale and repurchase agreements											
of which British govt. securities	TBHT	−	−	−	−	−	26 030	47 158	56 639	64 943	86 362
UK banks	TBHO	−	−	−	−	−	16 853	27 611	41 969	39 667	46 088
UK building societies	TBHP	..	..	..	..	..	..	345	134	91	116
UK public sector	TBHQ	..	..	..	..	..	..	..	−	−	9 067
Other UK residents	TBHR	..	..	..	..	..	..	21 283	23 803	30 338	35 058
Non-residents	TBHS	..	..	..	..	..	..	6 873	5 907	6 310	7 266
Advances											
UK public sector	TBHU	1 788	2 397	3 309	3 526	3 549	2 912	3 872	3 402	2 566	2 746
Other UK residents	TBHV	366 459	366 096	371 086	380 615	426 936	460 107	636 162	672 812	732 649	823 786
Non-residents	TBHW	13 825	12 336	12 268	12 163	13 403	16 759	21 102	21 040	23 364	24 494
Banking dept. lending to central govt. (net)	TBNU	1 526	1 277	−5 407	−947	−1 801	948	−2 741	−	−	−
Investments											
British government stocks	TBHX	3 873	4 848	13 753	14 366	17 135	19 910	23 078	14 714	9 242	2 866
Other public sector	TBHY	334	236	204	303	409	303	282	215	124	88
UK banks	TBHZ	..	..	..	..	..	..	11 922	13 415	13 584	22 935
UK building societies	TBIA	3 966	4 767	5 492	4 769	4 639	4 898	2 875	2 222	2 506	2 251
Other UK residents	TBIB	..	..	..	..	..	..	45 133	48 780	57 391	77 647
Non-residents	TBIC	..	..	..	..	..	..	9 342	11 833	13 775	20 571
Items in suspense and collection	TBID	17 356	16 426	17 135	16 477	17 613	19 830	23 526	23 888	23 441	21 983
Accrued amounts receivable	TBIE	..	..	..	..	..	..	15 003	17 351	15 172	15 919
Other assets	TBIF	12 346	11 724	11 146	10 242	10 525	10 267	12 218	12 593	13 036	12 654
Total sterling assets	TBIG	597 389	617 158	630 527	668 960	755 937	852 075	1 192 263	1 257 650	1 321 485	1 468 526
Foreign currency assets											
Market loans and advances											
UK banks	TBIH	72 961	87 596	96 129	99 885	98 305	83 920	90 367	72 262	74 250	93 270
UK banks' CDs etc.	TBII	11 081	11 239	8 642	7 226	9 345	7 793	13 634	11 064	14 363	13 171
UK building societies CDs etc. and deposits	TBIJ	..	..	..	..	..	..	83	259	451	173
UK public sector	TBIK	29	4 061	3 421	28	38	36	25	45	21	30
Other UK residents	TBIL	59 592	65 836	71 326	76 538	102 061	72 213	76 356	83 968	88 848	107 707
Non-residents	TBIM	412 552	504 567	489 439	534 589	604 783	505 953	598 541	616 832	599 145	743 782
Claims under sale and repurchase agreement											
UK banks	TBIO	−	−	−	−	21 189	24 184	31 900	28 008	41 801
UK building societies	TBIP	..	..	..	..	..	..	−	−	−	−
UK public sector	TBIQ	..	..	..	..	..	..	22	−	−	737
Other UK residents	TBIR	..	..	..	..	..	..	55 945	39 764	33 027	57 876
Non-residents	TBIS	−	−	−	−	75 376	121 101	147 562	146 756	199 989
Acceptances granted	TBIT							743	729	618	689
Bills	TBIU	7 835	11 784	15 398	10 490	14 429	9 660	12 728	15 240	19 508	21 878
Investments											
British government stocks	TBIV	..	..	..	..	..	..	3 453	4 755	4 473	3 518
Other public sector	TBIW	..	..	..	..	..	..	..	..	..	..
UK banks	TBIX	..	..	..	..	..	..	2 850	4 310	8 607	11 707
UK building societies	TBIY	335	701	889	997	728	701	414	526	631	939
Other UK residents	TBIZ	..	..	..	..	..	..	4 055	4 584	5 679	12 298
Non-residents	TBJA	53 940	79 547	114 904	128 507	154 398	161 045	186 289	234 564	243 147	297 404
Items in suspense and collection	TBJB	4 557	9 981	19 371	15 572	17 598	21 664	40 175	30 228	29 705	44 884
Accrued amounts receivable	TBJC	..	..	..	..	..	..	23 672	27 820	20 163	21 279
Other assets	TBJD	1 370	1 586	2 791	1 868	1 817	1 809	2 214	3 111	4 647	2 978
Total foreign currency assets	TBJE	626 368	780 403	828 419	882 624	1 011 358	1 025 017	1 256 850	1 329 525	1 322 045	1 676 112
Total assets	TBJF	1 223 757	1 397 561	1 458 946	1 551 584	1 767 295	1 877 092	2 449 113	2 587 175	2 643 530	3 144 638
Holdings of own sterling acceptances	TBJG	19 081	21 988	21 814	18 274	18 721	21 521	1 823	2 137	1 724	1 231
Holdings of own FC acceptances	TBJH	5 474	1 439	914	640	1 153	1 031	291	170	146	126
Eligible banks' total sterling acceptances	TBJI	18 870	21 812	21 726	18 168	18 476	21 220	21 411	18 753	14 458	10 565
Eligible liabilities	TBJJ	401 451	406 885	425 353	440 032	507 279	564 648	768 082	807 803	849 290	952 063

1 The implementation of the review of banking statistics at end-September 1997 has resulted in several changes to this table. Details are given in the chapter text.

2 Data for 1999 reflect the acquisition of Birmingham Midshires Building Society by Halifax plc during that year.

Source: Bank of England: 020 7601 3236

22.4 Industrial analysis of bank lending to UK residents[1]

£ millions

	UK residents		Agriculture, hunting and forestry	Fishing	Mining & quarrying	Manufacturing			Pulp, paper, publishing & printing
	Total to	of which sterling				Total	Food, beverages & tobacco	Textiles & leather	
Amounts outstanding (sterling & other currencies)									
Loans & advances (including under repo & sterling commercial paper)									
	TBOA	TBOB	TBOC	TBOD	TBOE	TBOF	TBOG	TBOH	TBOI
1999	887 815	765 839	7 479	360	4 672	57 903	10 598	2 027	7 321
2000	1 037 954	871 164	7 734	401	4 182	58 391	11 014	1 849	8 055
Acceptances									
	TBQA	TBQB	TBQC	TBQD	TBQE	TBQF	TBQG	TBQH	TBQI
1999	12 252	11 934	20	–	456	3 541	1 568	111	212
2000	9 839	9 496	27	–	687	2 708	1 106	89	132
Total									
	TBSA		TBSC	TBSD	TBSE	TBSF	TBSG	TBSH	TBSI
1999	900 067		7 499	361	5 128	61 444	12 166	2 138	7 532
2000	1 047 793		7 761	401	4 870	61 099	12 120	1 939	8 187
of which in sterling									
	TBUA		TBUC	TBUD	TBUE	TBUF	TBUG	TBUH	TBUI
1999	777 772		7 425	354	2 634	41 372	9 563	1 685	5 121
2000	880 660		7 674	370	3 192	41 055	9 451	1 568	5 568
Facilities granted									
	TCAA		TCAC	TCAD	TCAE	TCAF	TCAG	TCAH	TCAI
1999	1 134 379		9 627	441	10 452	115 494	26 172	3 416	12 919
2000	1 299 398		9 918	486	10 093	114 621	26 520	3 120	13 765
of which in sterling									
	TCCA		TCCC	TCCD	TCCE	TCCF	TCCG	TCCH	TCCI
1999	932 209		9 498	430	3 782	71 189	15 772	2 805	7 953
2000	1 049 619		9 799	439	4 415	67 451	15 260	2 628	8 599

	Manufacturing					Electricity, gas and water supply		Construction
	Chemicals, man-made fibres, rubber & plastics	Non-metallic mineral products & metals	Machinery, equipment & transport equipment	Electrical, medical & optical equipment	Other manufacturing	Electricity, gas & heated water	Cold water purification & supply	
Amounts outstanding (sterling & other currencies)								
Loans & advances (including under repo & sterling commercial paper)								
	TBOJ	TBOK	TBOL	TBOM	TBON	TBOO	TBOP	TBOQ
1999	7 261	6 673	9 320	8 644	6 061	7 041	794	9 177
2000	6 847	7 715	9 205	7 209	6 496	11 594	1 379	11 517
Acceptances								
	TBQJ	TBQK	TBQL	TBQM	TBQN	TBQO	TBQP	TBQQ
1999	317	427	468	195	242	525	10	85
2000	325	240	488	200	128	186	10	188
Total								
	TBSJ	TBSK	TBSL	TBSM	TBSN	TBSO	TBSP	TBSQ
1999	7 577	7 100	9 788	8 839	6 303	7 566	804	9 261
2000	7 172	7 956	9 693	7 408	6 624	11 780	1 389	11 706
of which in sterling								
	TBUJ	TBUK	TBUL	TBUM	TBUN	TBUO	TBUP	TBUQ
1999	4 767	4 892	6 637	4 052	4 656	7 014	602	8 078
2000	4 475	5 226	6 560	3 766	4 442	8 194	1 178	10 725
Facilities granted								
	TCAJ	TCAK	TCAL	TCAM	TCAN	TCAO	TCAP	TCAQ
1999	16 173	13 270	17 780	15 770	9 995	17 625	3 369	15 575
2000	15 848	12 926	17 574	14 088	10 781	21 934	4 532	20 091
of which in sterling								
	TCCJ	TCCK	TCCL	TCCM	TCCN	TCCO	TCCP	TCCQ
1999	9 515	8 843	11 713	7 272	7 316	12 881	2 262	13 672
2000	8 134	8 485	11 380	6 150	6 814	13 575	3 021	18 031

22.4 continued Industrial analysis of bank lending to UK residents[1]

£ millions

	Wholesale and retail trade						Real estate, renting, computer and other business activities		
	Total	Sale & repair of motor vehicles & fuel	Other wholesale trade	Other retail trade & repair	Hotels and restaurants	Transport, storage & communication	Total	Development, buying, selling, renting of real estate	Renting of machinery & equipment
Amounts outstanding (sterling & other currencies)									
Loans & advances (including under repo & sterling commercial paper)									
	TBOR	TBOS	TBOT	TBOU	TBOV	TBOW	TBOX	TBOY	TBPA
1999	34 307	9 216	12 810	12 281	12 690	18 853	64 158	45 005	4 302
2000	36 366	8 745	13 645	13 977	15 409	19 093	81 023	56 520	5 797
Acceptances									
	TBQR	TBQS	TBQT	TBQU	TBQV	TBQW	TBQX	TBQY	TBRA
1999	2 012	378	953	681	94	119	300	64	66
2000	1 580	170	890	520	11	58	902	711	26
Total									
	TBSR	TBSS	TBST	TBSU	TBSV	TBSW	TBSX	TBSY	TBTA
1999	36 319	9 593	13 763	12 963	12 784	18 972	64 459	45 069	4 368
2000	37 947	8 915	14 535	14 497	15 420	19 151	81 925	57 231	5 823
of which in sterling									
	TBUR	TBUS	TBUT	TBUU	TBUV	TBUW	TBUX	TBUY	TBVA
1999	29 339	9 161	8 537	11 641	11 500	15 345	60 622	43 964	3 879
2000	30 377	8 542	8 569	13 266	13 951	14 891	77 361	56 120	5 426
Facilities granted									
	TCAR	TCAS	TCAT	TCAU	TCAV	TCAW	TCAX	TCAY	TCBA
1999	58 945	13 664	21 687	23 593	16 490	50 783	87 620	58 154	5 241
2000	58 292	12 264	21 837	24 191	19 681	57 018	108 925	72 907	6 848
of which in sterling									
	TCCR	TCCS	TCCT	TCCU	TCCV	TCCW	TCCX	TCCY	TCDA
1999	46 095	12 229	14 178	19 688	14 172	26 555	81 025	56 183	4 557
2000	45 916	11 317	13 918	20 681	16 854	32 956	100 638	70 519	6 215

	Real estate, renting, computer and other business activities				Recreational, personal & community service activities		Financial intermediation (excl. insurance & pension funds)	
	Computer & related activities	Legal, accountancy, consultancy & other business activities	Public administration & defence	Education	Health & social work	Recreational, cultural & sporting activities	Personal & community services activities	Total	Financial leasing corporations
Amounts outstanding (sterling & other currencies)									
Loans & advances (including under repo & sterling commercial paper)									
	TBPB	TBPC	TBPD	TBPE	TBPF	TBPH	TBPG	TBPI	TBPJ
1999	1 939	12 912	2 301	2 894	6 868	5 764	3 636	203 765	39 633
2000	2 938	15 491	12 140	3 102	6 933	7 279	4 563	246 482	35 565
Acceptances									
	TBRB	TBRC	TBRD	TBRE	TBRF	TBRH	TBRG	TBRI	TBRJ
1999	22	148	–	–	1	78	4	4 593	1 547
2000	22	143	–	–	–	69	6	3 150	638
Total									
	TBTB	TBTC	TBTD	TBTE	TBTF	TBTH	TBTG	TBTI	TBTJ
1999	1 961	13 060	2 301	2 894	6 869	5 842	3 640	208 358	41 180
2000	2 960	15 634	12 140	3 102	6 933	7 348	4 569	249 632	36 204
of which in sterling									
	TBVB	TBVC	TBVD	TBVE	TBVF	TBVH	TBVG	TBVI	TBVJ
1999	1 439	11 340	2 285	2 870	6 743	5 049	3 349	132 870	39 998
2000	2 346	13 218	11 431	3 072	6 834	6 648	4 221	139 975	35 087
Facilities granted									
	TCBB	TCBC	TCBD	TCBE	TCBF	TCBH	TCBG	TCBI	TCBJ
1999	3 730	20 494	3 975	3 519	8 394	9 418	4 969	231 212	44 509
2000	4 765	24 377	14 306	3 734	8 426	12 083	5 896	273 886	39 856
of which in sterling									
	TCDB	TCDC	TCDD	TCDE	TCDF	TCDH	TCDG	TCDI	TCDJ
1999	2 812	17 474	3 858	3 491	8 159	7 597	4 551	145 827	43 087
2000	3 777	20 126	13 445	3 693	8 248	9 841	5 373	155 146	38 018

22.4
continued **Industrial analysis of bank lending to UK residents[1]**

£ millions

Financial intermediation (excl. insurance & pension funds)

	Non-bank credit grantors, excl. credit unions	Credit unions	Factoring corporations	Mortgage & housing credit corporations	Investment & unit trusts excl. money market mutual funds	Money market mutual funds	Bank holding companies	Securities dealers (f)	Other financial intermediaries
Amounts outstanding (sterling & other currencies)									
Loans & advances (including under repo & sterling commercial paper)									
	TBPK	TBPL	TBPM	TBPN	TBPO	TBPP	TBPQ	TBPR	TBPS
1999	12 350	1	2 031	16 138	5 070	14	7 631	87 695	33 202
2000	11 989	3	2 416	15 333	7 286	–	12 585	118 841	47 205
Acceptances									
	TBRK	TBRL	TBRM	TBRN	TBRO	TBRP	TBRQ	TBRR	TBRS
1999	1 199	–	92	44	43	–	1	187	1 480
2000	664	–	126	14	133	–	13	127	1 433
Total									
	TBTK	TBTL	TBTM	TBTN	TBTO	TBTP	TBTQ	TBTR	TBTS
1999	13 549	1	2 123	16 182	5 113	14	7 632	87 882	34 681
2000	12 653	3	2 542	15 347	7 420	–	12 598	118 968	48 638
of which in sterling									
	TBVK	TBVL	TBVM	TBVN	TBVO	TBVP	TBVQ	TBVR	TBVS
1999	12 393	1	2 012	16 182	3 302	14	7 404	29 717	21 847
2000	11 530	3	2 236	15 347	4 225	–	11 644	33 748	30 891
Facilities granted									
	TCBK	TCBL	TCBM	TCBN	TCBO	TCBP	TCBQ	TCBR	TCBS
1999	15 322	23	2 193	17 024	8 123	54	7 724	92 051	44 190
2000	14 420	62	2 689	16 896	12 078	37	12 798	124 202	55 675
of which in sterling									
	TCDK	TCDL	TCDM	TCDN	TCDO	TCDP	TCDQ	TCDR	TCDS
1999	13 614	23	2 058	16 910	5 514	14	7 440	31 166	26 002
2000	12 837	45	2 356	16 886	7 613	–	11 845	35 501	34 820

	Activities auxiliary to financial intermediation			Individuals & individual trusts		
	Insurance companies & pension funds	Fund management activities	Other	Total	Lending secured on dwellings inc. bridging finance	Other loans & advances
Amounts outstanding (sterling & other currencies)						
Loans & advances (including under repo & sterling commercial paper)						
	TBPT	TBPU	TBPV	TBPW	TBPX	TBPY
1999	16 407	3 547	4 805	420 392	337 899	82 493
2000	19 758	4 384	10 332	471 321	377 088	94 233
Acceptances						
	TBRT	TBRU	TBRV			
1999	336	31	47			
2000	208	40	8			
Total						
	TBTT	TBTU	TBTV	TBTW	TBTX	TBTY
1999	16 743	3 578	4 852	420 392	337 899	82 493
2000	19 966	4 424	10 340	471 321	377 088	94 233
of which in sterling						
	TBVT	TBVU	TBVV	TBVW	TBVX	TBVY
1999	15 883	2 236	2 043	420 159	337 867	82 292
2000	18 440	3 225	2 322	470 963	377 051	93 912
Facilities granted						
	TCBT	TCBU	TCBV	TCBW	TCBX	TCBY
1999	24 387	5 765	5 995	450 322	349 535	100 788
2000	26 834	6 917	11 567	505 530	390 364	115 165
of which in sterling						
	TCDT	TCDU	TCDV	TCDW	TCDX	TCDY
1999	21 255	2 935	2 923	450 053	349 495	100 559
2000	23 007	4 837	3 257	505 097	390 326	114 772

1 Data for 1999 reflect the acquisition of the Birmingham Midshires Building Society by Halifax plc during that year.

Source: Bank of England: 020 7601 3236

22.5 Industrial analysis of bank deposits from UK residents[1]

£ millions

	Total from UK residents	Agriculture, hunting and forestry	Fishing	Mining & quarrying	Manufacturing Total	Food, beverages & tobacco	Textiles & leather	Pulp, paper, publishing & printing
Amounts outstanding (sterling & other currencies)								
Deposit liabilities (including under repos)								
	TDAA	TDAB	TDAC	TDAD	TDAE	TDAF	TDAG	TDAH
1999	724 185	2 940	114	3 504	32 203	3 343	1 335	3 490
2000	839 750	3 049	103	4 317	33 126	3 453	1 257	4 538
of which in sterling								
	TDCA	TDCB	TDCC	TDCD	TDCE	TDCF	TDCG	TDCH
1999	636 859	2 900	104	2 236	25 062	2 598	1 103	2 948
2000	722 701	3 003	94	1 853	24 774	2 666	1 070	3 863

	Manufacturing					Electricity, gas and water supply		
	Chemicals, man-made fibres, rubber & plastics	Non-metallic mineral products & metals	Machinery, equipment & transport equipment	Electrical, medical & optical equipment	Other manufacturing	Electricity, gas & heated water	Cold water purification & supply	Construction
Amounts outstanding (sterling & other currencies)								
Deposit liabilities (including under repos)								
	TDAI	TDAJ	TDAK	TDAL	TDAM	TDAN	TDAO	TDAP
1999	4 816	3 570	6 123	5 776	3 749	3 737	1 074	8 369
2000	5 094	3 273	6 383	5 715	3 413	3 813	1 178	8 855
of which in sterling								
	TDCI	TDCJ	TDCK	TDCL	TDCM	TDCN	TDCO	TDCP
1999	2 907	3 129	4 696	4 513	3 169	3 580	1 041	8 122
2000	3 156	2 719	4 754	3 937	2 609	3 512	853	8 544

	Wholesale and retail trade						Real estate, renting, computer and other business activities		
	Total	Sale & repair of motor vehicles & fuel	Other wholesale trade	Other retail trade & repair	Hotels and restaurants	Transport, storage & communication	Total	Development, buying, selling, renting of real estate	Renting of machinery & equipment
Amounts outstanding (sterling & other currencies)									
Deposit liabilities (including under repos)									
	TDAQ	TDAR	TDAS	TDAT	TDAU	TDAV	TDAW	TDAX	TDAY
1999	21 911	2 406	9 550	9 955	2 830	14 475	52 711	14 236	1 150
2000	22 153	2 694	10 101	9 358	3 192	16 691	60 348	15 366	1 307
of which in sterling									
	TDCQ	TDCR	TDCS	TDCT	TDCU	TDCV	TDCW	TDCX	TDCY
1999	18 738	2 316	7 124	9 298	2 788	12 277	48 560	13 859	1 080
2000	18 684	2 470	7 439	8 775	3 100	13 737	55 688	15 106	1 180

22.5 Industrial analysis of bank deposits from UK residents[1]
continued

£ millions

	Real estate, renting, computer and other business activities					Recreational, personal & community service activities		Financial intermediation (excl. insurance & pension funds)	
	Computer & related activities	Legal, accountancy, consultancy & other business activities	Public administration & defence	Education	Health & social work	Recreational, cultural & sporting activities	Personal & community services activities	Total	Financial leasing corporations
Amounts outstanding (sterling & other currencies)									
Deposit liabilities (including under repos)									
	TDAZ	TDBA	TDBB	TDBC	TDBD	TDBF	TDBE	TDBG	TDBH
1999	5 366	31 960	9 483	4 109	6 382	5 579	9 560	113 149	4 263
2000	7 621	36 054	27 046	4 552	6 307	6 852	10 262	147 247	2 485
of which in sterling									
	TDCZ	TDDA	TDDB	TDDC	TDDD	TDDF	TDDE	TDDG	TCDJ
1999	4 450	29 170	9 373	4 018	6 236	5 022	9 226	64 234	43 087
2000	6 698	32 703	24 822	4 427	6 059	6 262	9 905	80 354	38 018

Financial intermediation (excl. insurance & pension funds)

	Non-bank credit grantors, excl. credit unions	Credit unions	Factoring corporations	Mortgage & housing credit corporations	Investment & unit trusts excl. money market mutual funds	Money market mutual funds	Bank holding companies	Securities dealers	Other financial intermediaries
Amounts outstanding (sterling & other currencies)									
Deposit liabilities (including under repos)									
	TDBI	TDBJ	TDBK	TDBL	TDBM	TDBN	TDBO	TDBP	TDBQ
1999	2 556	108	156	901	13 155	408	3 841	53 856	33 904
2000	3 511	302	390	1 367	17 596	403	7 494	68 040	45 660
of which in sterling									
	TDDI	TDDJ	TDDK	TDDL	TDDM	TDDN	TDDO	TDDP	TDDQ
1999	1 913	93	134	901	10 719	395	3 450	19 975	23 071
2000	2 525	302	349	1 366	14 337	400	5 860	24 341	28 904

	Insurance companies & pension funds	Activities auxiliary to financial intermediation		Individuals & individual trusts
		Placed by fund managers	Other	
Amounts outstanding (sterling & other currencies)				
Deposit liabilities (including under repos)				
	TDBR	TDBS	TDBT	TDBU
1999	49 501	22 340	11 785	348 431
2000	57 517	29 423	14 287	379 431
of which in sterling				
	TDDR	TDDS	TDDT	TDDU
1999	43 394	16 109	6 793	347 046
2000	50 142	21 704	7 382	377 802

1 Data for 1999 reflect the acquisition of Birmingham Midshires Building Society by Halifax plc during that year.

Source: Bank of England: 020 7601 3236

22.6 Public sector net cash requirement and other counterparts to changes in money stock during the year
Not seasonally adjusted

£ millions

		1990	1991	1992	1993	1994	1995	1996	1997	1998	1999	2000
Public sector net cash requirement (surplus-)	ABEN	−2 365	7 659	28 670	42 514	37 888	35 118	25 000	12 412	−6 400	−1 782	−36 958
Sales(-) of public sector debt to M4 private sector	KHGZ		−767	−5 685	−20 268	−30 799	−23 426	−21 688	−19 241	−16 121	−1 517	−1 255	13 240
M4 lending[1]	AVBS		70 556	37 092	25 605	22 685	31 567	57 736	59 129	68 311	63 929	78 087	111 230
External and foreign currency finance of the public sector	KHJP		2 947	−3 058	−12 647	−10 768	654	−3 640	−10 885	−2 493	−4 711	6 188	7 333
Other external and foreign currency flows[2]	AVBW		−12 248	1 199	8 842	14 305	−7 692	−3 521	17 917	24 922	13 665	−46 872	6 800
Net non-deposit liabilities (increase-)	AVBX		−8 443	−8 564	−12 013	−14 850	−15 064	−8 377	−12 213	−6 187	−7 903	−2 243	30 824
Money stock (M4)	AUZI		50 356	27 941	17 955	23 931	25 386	55 957	59 395	80 287	60 095	32 106	67 068

1 Bank and building society lending, plus holdings of commercial bills by the Issue Department of the Bank of England.
2 Including sterling lending to non-residents sector.

Source: Bank of England: 020 7601 5468

22.7 Money stock and liquidity

£ millions

		1990	1991	1992	1993	1994	1995	1996	1997	1998	1999	2000
Amounts outstanding at end-year												
Notes and coin in circulation with the M4 private sector[1]	VQKT	15 253	15 690	16 770	17 795	18 749	20 007	20 843	22 491	23 705	26 269	28 184
UK private sector sterling non-interest bearing sight deposits[2,3]	AUYA	29 282	29 388	28 659	34 515	33 487	35 435	38 433	38 936	37 261	43 011	46 604
Money stock (M2)[3,4]	VQXV	309 810	335 928	373 243	394 510	410 469	437 102	460 294	484 842	515 005	559 214	598 270
Money stock M4[3]	AUYM	477 128	504 113	517 919	544 097	567 195	623 542	682 999	722 213	783 238	814 557	882 685
Changes during the year[5]												
Notes and coin in circulation with the M4 private sector[1]	VQLU	−102	437	1 087	1 025	954	1 256	836	1 660	1 506	2 582	1 974
UK private sector sterling non-interest bearing sight deposits[2,3]	AUZA	−2 056	−781	−322	4 203	1 084	1 783	3 527	5 366	−632	5 769	3 365
Money stock (M2)[3,4]	AUZE	18 339	22 988	9 811	18 851	17 614	26 570	24 358	36 019	30 601	42 404	38 972
Money stock M4[3]	AUZI	50 356	27 941	17 955	23 931	25 386	55 957	59 395	80 287	60 095	32 106	67 068

1 The estimates of levels of coin in circulation include allowance for wastage, hoarding, etc.

2 Non-interest bearing deposits are confined to those with institutions included in the United Kingdom banks sector (See Table 22.3).

3 Revised rules on netting of customers' credit balances against their borrowing increased the UK private sector's outstanding balances of deposits and borrowing by £2.5bn at end-December 1993. Within retail deposit, £1.7bn of the increase was in NIB bank deposits. Re-netting during 1994 amounted to £1.7bn. Changes data have been adjusted to exclude these effects. Building societies' data from 1992 onwards are affected by the revised treatment of building society transit items within M4.

4 With effect from the flow for December 1992, M2 comprises the UK non-monetary financial institutions and non-public sector, i.e. M4 private sector's holdings of notes and coin together with its sterling denominated retail deposits with UK monetary financial institutions.

5 As far as possible the changes exclude the effect of changes in the number of contributors to the series, and also of the introduction of new statistical returns. Changes are not seasonally adjusted.

Source: Bank of England: 020 7601 5468

22.8 Selected retail banks' base rate[1]
Percentage rates operative between dates shown

Rates

Date of change	New rate	Date of change	New rate	Date of change	New rate
1986 Jan 9	12.50	Jul 5	10.00	Feb 3	6.75
Mar 19	11.50	Jul 18	10.00-10.50	Dec 13	6.50
Apr 8	11.00-11.50	Jul 19	10.50		
Apr 9	11.00	Aug 8	10.50-11.00	1996 Jan 18	6.25
Apr 21	10.50	Aug 9	11.00	Mar 8	6.00
May 23	10.00-10.50	Aug 25	11.00-12.00	Jun 6	5.75
May 27	10.00	Aug 26	12.00	Oct 30	5.75-6.00
Oct 14	10.00-11.00	Nov 25	13.00	Oct 31	6.00
Oct 15	11.00				
		1989 May 24	14.00	1997 May 6	6.25
1987 Mar 10	10.50	Oct 5	15.00	Jun 6	6.25-6.50
Mar 18	10.00-10.50			Jun 9	6.50
Mar 19	10.00	1990 Oct 8	14.00	Jul 10	6.75
Apr 28	9.50-10.00			Aug 7	7.00
Apr 29	9.50	1991 Feb 13	13.50	Nov 6	7.25
May 11	9.00	Feb 27	13.00		
Aug 6	9.00-10.00	Mar 22	12.50	1998 Jun 4	7.50
Aug 7	10.00	Apr 12	12.00	Oct 8	7.25
Oct 23	9.50-10.00	May 24	11.50	Nov 5	6.75
Oct 29	9.50	Jul 12	11.00	Dec 10	6.25
Nov 4	9.00-9.50	Sep 4	10.50		
Nov 5	9.00			1999 Jan 7	6.00
Dec 4	8.50	1992 May 5	10.00	Feb 4	5.50
		Sep 16[1]	12.00	Apr 8	5.25
1988 Feb 2	9.00	Sep 17[1]	10.00-12.00	Jun 10	5.00
Mar 17	8.50-9.00	Sep 18	10.00	Sep 8	5.00-5.25
Mar 18	8.50	Sep 22	9.00	Sep 10	5.25
Apr 11	8.00	Oct 16	8.00-9.00	Nov 4	5.50
May 17	7.50-8.00	Oct 19	8.00		
May 18	7.50	Nov 13	7.00	2000 Jan 13	5.75
Jun 2	7.50-8.00			Feb 10	6.00
Jun 3	8.00	1993 Jan 26	6.00		
Jun 6	8.00-8.50	Nov 23	5.50	2001 Feb 8	5.75
Jun 7	8.50			Apr 5	5.50
Jun 22	8.50-9.00	1994 Feb 8	5.25	May 10	5.25
Jun 23	9.00	Sep 12	5.75	Aug 2	5.00
Jun 28	9.00-9.50	Dec 7	6.25	Sep 18	4.75
Jun 29	9.50			Oct 4	4.50
Jul 4	9.50-10.00	1995 Feb 2[1]	6.25-6.75	Nov 8	4.00

1 Data obtained from Barclays Bank, Lloyds TSB Bank, HSBC, National Westminster Bank whose rates are used to compile this series. Where all the rates did not change on the same day a spread is shown.

Source: Bank of England: 020 7601 4342

22.9 Average three month sterling money market rates[1]

	1991	1992	1993	1994	1995	1996	1997	1998	1999	2000	2001
Treasury bills:[2] KDMM											
January	13.00	9.97	6.05	4.88	5.93	6.08	6.01	6.84	5.28	5.72	5.49
February	12.39	9.80	5.37	4.76	6.16	5.96	5.81	6.88	5.04	5.83	5.46
March	11.64	10.10	5.38	4.83	6.09	5.81	5.92	6.95	4.92	5.86	5.23
April	11.25	9.97	5.33	4.88	6.30	5.80	6.09	7.02	4.90	5.90	5.12
May	10.84	9.42	5.30	4.81	6.20	5.82	6.15	6.99	4.93	5.95	4.98
June	10.72	9.42	5.19	4.88	6.37	5.58	6.37	7.29	4.76	5.85	4.98
July	10.52	9.43	5.13	5.09	6.62	5.49	6.60	7.22	4.76	5.83	5.01
August	10.20	9.65	5.06	5.34	6.59	5.54	6.81	7.19	4.85	5.80	4.72
September	9.66	9.16	5.16	5.39	6.52	5.54	6.88	6.94	5.08	5.80	..
October	9.86	7.47	5.15	5.44	6.57	5.55	6.94	6.54	5.25	5.75	..
November	9.98	6.49	4.95	5.63	6.44	6.02	7.09	6.31	5.20	5.69	..
December	10.10	6.39	4.87	5.87	6.21	6.08	7.04	5.72	5.49	5.63	..
Eligible bill:[3] KDMY											
January	13.34	10.08	6.43	5.07	6.41	6.18	6.15	7.28	5.63	5.90	5.64
February	12.55	9.87	5.59	4.95	6.54	6.00	5.99	7.24	5.28	6.01	5.56
March	11.75	10.14	5.62	4.90	6.40	5.87	6.01	7.25	5.11	5.98	5.37
April	11.44	10.18	5.66	4.93	6.44	5.83	6.26	7.24	5.02	6.05	5.21
May	11.05	9.56	5.67	4.92	6.54	5.85	6.31	7.20	5.08	6.09	5.06
June	10.78	9.52	5.62	4.94	6.44	5.66	6.50	7.41	4.94	6.03	5.08
July	10.61	9.59	5.63	5.01	6.66	5.57	6.80	7.49	4.89	5.97	5.07
August	10.39	9.80	5.59	5.44	6.64	5.60	6.95	7.40	4.94	5.97	4.82
September	9.85	9.43	5.58	5.54	6.55	5.63	7.02	7.20	5.16	5.95	..
October	10.02	7.78	5.50	5.74	6.58	5.76	7.10	6.91	5.42	5.92	..
November	10.09	6.70	5.31	5.89	6.49	6.10	7.27	6.52	5.43	5.88	..
December	10.21	6.69	5.04	6.12	6.29	6.18	7.31	6.05	5.59	5.78	..
Interbank rate:[4] AMIJ											
January	13.97	10.65	6.94	5.39	6.56	6.36	6.32	7.48	5.80	6.06	5.76
February	13.25	10.37	6.16	5.22	6.75	6.16	6.19	7.46	5.43	6.15	5.69
March	12.40	10.62	5.98	5.16	6.66	6.05	6.20	7.48	5.30	6.15	5.47
April	11.95	10.62	5.98	5.21	6.67	6.00	6.38	7.44	5.23	6.21	5.33
May	11.53	10.06	5.97	5.17	6.72	6.02	6.45	7.41	5.25	6.23	5.17
June	11.24	9.98	5.89	5.13	6.64	5.85	6.66	7.63	5.12	6.14	5.19
July	11.09	10.15	5.95	5.20	6.80	5.73	6.96	7.71	5.07	6.11	5.19
August	10.89	10.35	5.84	5.53	6.79	5.75	7.15	7.66	5.18	6.14	4.93
September	10.29	9.99	5.91	5.67	6.72	5.77	7.21	7.38	5.32	6.12	..
October	10.40	8.32	5.76	5.91	6.73	5.94	7.26	7.14	5.94	6.08	..
November	10.48	7.21	5.57	6.06	6.64	6.30	7.54	6.89	5.78	6.00	..
December	10.78	7.15	5.33	6.37	6.49	6.35	7.62	6.38	5.97	5.89	..
Certificate of deposits:[4] KOSA											
January	13.86	10.53	6.82	5.29	6.48	6.31	6.27	7.44	5.74	6.02	5.73
February	13.18	10.27	6.00	5.14	6.67	6.11	6.14	7.42	5.38	6.10	5.66
March	12.33	10.51	5.87	5.09	6.59	6.01	6.15	7.43	5.26	6.09	5.44
April	11.86	10.50	5.84	5.12	6.62	5.96	6.33	7.40	5.19	6.17	5.30
May	11.44	9.95	5.86	5.10	6.66	5.98	6.39	7.37	5.22	6.19	5.15
June	11.13	9.89	5.77	5.06	6.56	5.79	6.62	7.59	5.09	6.10	5.16
July	10.99	10.04	5.81	5.11	6.72	5.69	6.92	7.66	5.03	6.08	5.17
August	10.79	10.21	5.71	5.45	6.73	5.71	7.12	7.61	5.14	6.09	4.90
September	10.21	9.83	5.79	5.58	6.66	5.74	7.17	7.34	5.28	6.08	..
October	10.30	8.17	5.65	5.81	6.68	5.89	7.22	7.09	5.86	6.05	..
November	10.37	7.04	5.46	5.97	6.58	6.25	7.50	6.82	5.72	5.98	..
December	10.67	7.02	5.23	6.25	6.44	6.29	7.57	6.32	5.89	5.85	..
Local authority deposits:[4] KDPX											
January	13.94	10.61	6.84	5.30	6.52	6.31	6.27	7.43	5.76	6.03	5.73
February	13.24	10.34	6.09	5.12	6.69	6.13	6.15	7.40	5.38	6.09	5.62
March	12.45	10.57	5.93	5.08	6.59	6.02	6.14	7.40	5.27	6.08	5.39
April	11.89	10.59	5.95	5.14	6.60	5.98	6.33	7.38	5.17	6.12	5.26
May	11.50	10.02	5.94	5.12	6.68	6.00	6.38	7.34	5.19	6.14	5.13
June	11.23	9.94	5.86	5.08	6.58	5.80	6.57	7.56	5.07	6.09	5.10
July	11.05	10.10	5.90	5.18	6.76	5.69	6.90	7.64	5.01	6.04	5.12
August	10.88	10.24	5.80	5.44	6.74	5.71	7.11	7.55	5.11	6.06	4.86
September	10.32	9.82	5.85	5.62	6.65	5.72	7.19	7.35	5.19	6.05	..
October	10.45	8.28	5.70	5.84	6.68	5.86	7.21	7.08	5.83	6.03	..
November	10.44	7.17	5.51	5.99	6.60	6.24	7.49	6.85	5.64	5.96	..
December	10.75	7.08	5.26	6.32	6.43	6.30	7.56	6.35	5.88	5.80	..

1 Working day average of the mean bid and offer yield.
2 A full definition of these series is given in Section 7 of the ONS Financial Statistics Explanatory Handbook.

3 Average rate of discount at weekly (Friday) tender.
4 Working day average of the mean of the bid and offer discount rate.

Source: Bank of England: 020 7601 4342

22.10 Average foreign exchange rates[1]

	1991	1992	1993	1994	1995	1996	1997	1998	1999	2000	2001
Sterling exchange rate index (1990 = 100) AJHX											
January	103.0	99.6	88.8	92.0	88.5	83.2	95.9	104.7	99.6	108.5	104.4
February	103.0	99.7	84.7	90.4	87.4	83.8	97.4	104.7	100.8	108.4	104.1
March	101.9	98.9	86.4	89.8	85.6	83.5	97.4	106.8	102.8	108.4	105.0
April	101.6	100.2	88.9	89.2	84.5	83.8	99.5	107.1	103.4	110.1	105.8
May	100.9	101.7	89.0	88.9	84.3	84.6	99.0	103.4	104.2	108.5	106.6
June	99.5	101.7	88.3	89.1	84.1	86.0	100.4	105.4	104.7	104.6	106.8
July	99.6	101.2	90.5	87.9	83.6	85.7	104.5	105.3	103.5	105.6	107.2
August	99.9	100.5	90.3	87.8	84.4	84.7	102.5	104.6	103.3	107.4	105.1
September	100.1	96.5	89.8	88.1	84.8	86.1	100.4	103.3	104.7	106.2	106.1
October	99.6	88.7	89.4	89.1	84.3	88.4	101.1	100.7	105.4	109.2	..
November	99.9	86.2	90.2	89.1	83.3	92.0	103.8	100.6	105.7	107.3	..
December	100.0	88.2	91.0	89.1	82.9	93.8	104.4	100.4	106.7	106.4	..
Sterling/US Dollar AJFA											
January	1.9348	1.8127	1.5325	1.4940	1.5747	1.5306	1.6587	1.6353	1.6509	1.6402	1.4769
February	1.9655	1.7781	1.4386	1.4799	1.5720	1.5364	1.6246	1.6407	1.6276	1.5998	1.4529
March	1.8265	1.7238	1.4625	1.4917	1.6005	1.5271	1.6063	1.6620	1.6220	1.5802	1.4454
April	1.7502	1.7576	1.5472	1.4837	1.6074	1.5145	1.6295	1.6733	1.6105	1.5837	1.4350
May	1.7252	1.8109	1.5481	1.5029	1.5868	1.5152	1.6334	1.6366	1.6154	1.5075	1.4259
June	1.6499	1.8556	1.5099	1.5252	1.5949	1.5418	1.6446	1.6507	1.5950	1.5089	1.4014
July	1.6503	1.9186	1.4963	1.5463	1.5953	1.5539	1.6702	1.6437	1.5748	1.5088	1.4139
August	1.6841	1.9412	1.4911	1.5427	1.5681	1.5502	1.6034	1.6320	1.6073	1.4910	1.4365
September	1.7249	1.8559	1.5261	1.5651	1.5584	1.5597	1.6015	1.6822	1.6243	1.4355	1.4635
October	1.7226	1.6577	1.5037	1.6057	1.5779	1.5862	1.6329	1.6952	1.6571	1.4511	..
November	1.7787	1.5275	1.4806	1.5886	1.5623	1.6626	1.6890	1.6620	1.6214	1.4256	..
December	1.8258	1.5536	1.4904	1.5595	1.5398	1.6647	1.6597	1.6705	1.6132	1.4625	..
Sterling/Deutsche Mark AJFH											
January	2.920	2.856	2.475	2.604	2.409	2.236	2.660	2.971	2.784	3.169	3.081
February	2.908	2.877	2.362	2.567	2.360	2.252	2.722	2.974	2.843	3.179	3.087
March	2.931	2.865	2.407	2.523	2.249	2.256	2.725	3.036	2.915	3.203	3.110
April	2.979	2.895	2.468	2.520	2.218	2.282	2.788	3.032	2.944	3.272	3.146
May	2.963	2.936	2.488	2.491	2.239	2.323	2.782	2.904	2.970	3.257	3.189
June	2.940	2.917	2.496	2.484	2.232	2.356	2.840	2.958	3.007	3.106	3.214
July	2.947	2.860	2.566	2.426	2.214	2.336	2.992	2.954	2.974	3.139	3.214
August	2.936	2.816	2.529	2.413	2.264	2.298	2.950	2.919	2.962	3.223	3.121
September	2.925	2.683	2.472	2.424	2.276	2.349	2.863	2.860	3.023	3.222	..
October	2.911	2.455	2.463	2.441	2.232	2.424	2.868	2.778	3.030	3.324	..
November	2.884	2.424	2.517	2.446	2.215	2.513	2.926	2.795	3.072	3.259	..
December	2.856	2.455	2.549	2.451	2.218	2.583	2.952	2.788	3.120	3.188	..

1 Working day average. A full definition of these series is given in Section 7 of the ONS Explanatory Handbook.

Source: Bank of England: 020 7601 4342

22.11 Average FTSE Actuaries share indices[1]

	1991	1992	1993	1994	1995	1996	1997	1998	1999	2000	2001
FTSE 100 AJNO											
January	2 106.64	2 520.19	2 790.29	3 431.29	3 028.27	3 715.78	4 166.48	5 242.10	5 975.84	6 471.60	6 193.48
February	2 278.36	2 543.31	2 840.17	3 396.40	3 051.68	3 738.08	4 316.57	5 657.73	6 010.79	6 178.51	6 118.41
March	2 449.81	2 495.24	2 897.07	3 206.10	3 078.24	3 697.50	4 349.78	5 861.80	6 168.55	6 541.46	5 713.40
April	2 514.14	2 549.44	2 837.45	3 130.94	3 198.38	3 792.32	4 312.51	5 974.51	6 459.86	6 312.71	5 767.89
May	2 493.32	2 702.34	2 830.13	3 089.23	3 288.31	3 758.41	4 622.62	5 936.72	6 322.04	6 210.24	5 877.82
June	2 495.14	2 604.44	2 874.70	2 980.32	3 351.55	3 734.02	4 649.40	5 847.04	6 425.82	6 450.25	5 753.06
July	2 530.10	2 443.25	2 850.73	3 036.57	3 426.50	3 707.21	4 843.16	5 987.19	6 422.83	6 433.31	5 462.43
August	2 600.50	2 344.11	3 019.28	3 178.50	3 486.95	3 841.75	4 945.56	5 555.77	6 210.91	6 480.01	5 444.36
September	2 622.16	2 452.41	3 028.12	3 098.35	3 534.27	3 927.10	5 010.35	5 171.92	6 116.94	6 462.63	4 887.19
October	2 580.86	2 587.09	3 125.15	3 046.77	3 531.80	4 020.99	5 145.13	5 063.84	6 071.20	6 293.60	..
November	2 505.09	2 712.92	3 111.59	3 086.85	3 580.31	3 969.54	4 846.24	5 595.58	6 487.49	6 362.19	..
December	2 410.50	2 777.08	3 313.68	3 026.62	3 650.05	4 038.89	5 087.53	5 695.61	6 718.34	6 243.13	..
FT Non-Financials AJMG											
January	1 115.00	1 353.77	1 496.94	1 818.98	1 631.29	1 919.36	2 104.75	2 455.76	2 778.42	3 245.63	2 915.36
February	1 204.72	1 374.45	1 522.74	1 818.96	1 631.03	1 941.86	2 150.64	2 586.40	2 815.82	3 148.44	2 888.49
March	1 308.69	1 354.06	1 552.97	1 745.46	1 631.47	1 953.49	2 178.24	2 708.91	2 877.41	3 351.94	2 726.80
April	1 342.30	1 387.84	1 522.32	1 708.89	1 690.67	2 021.61	2 149.68	2 776.91	2 988.44	3 156.97	2 717.69
May	1 331.16	1 476.08	1 522.69	1 690.44	1 738.74	2 013.00	2 219.45	2 847.14	2 970.83	3 093.98	2 782.39
June	1 330.25	1 419.66	1 539.22	1 618.42	1 767.52	1 999.60	2 231.81	2 833.04	3 020.57	3 216.08	2 714.57
July	1 342.46	1 319.06	1 521.63	1 642.28	1 806.86	1 958.89	2 284.21	2 859.68	3 064.76	3 220.07	2 570.25
August	1 379.55	1 258.02	1 614.52	1 726.77	1 846.24	2 002.27	2 326.86	2 658.60	2 983.93	3 192.66	2 529.94
September	1 404.22	1 301.02	1 623.43	1 680.38	1 868.17	2 043.06	2 369.90	2 480.53	2 944.00	3 165.81	2 295.62
October	1 387.17	1 364.42	1 653.67	1 639.72	1 851.30	2 069.12	2 439.08	2 413.68	2 901.63	3 047.93	..
November	1 353.28	1 425.57	1 643.34	1 654.73	1 854.75	2 040.44	2 332.02	2 630.55	3 090.84	3 041.11	..
December	1 299.58	1 473.45	1 733.10	1 622.39	1 879.54	2 056.24	2 401.00	2 651.00	3 269.95	2 957.69	..
Financials AMAA											
January	1 333.92	1 385.89	1 718.78	2 619.71	2 084.15	2 916.24	3 674.44	4 968.04	5 145.56	5 280.33	6 637.23
February	1 464.83	1 384.60	1 822.76	2 607.79	2 125.71	2 942.72	3 919.61	5 542.60	5 263.96	4 884.58	6 601.49
March	1 591.19	1 346.68	1 888.45	2 324.02	2 170.51	2 837.38	3 876.31	5 732.81	5 566.39	5 109.08	5 969.68
April	1 594.89	1 353.29	1 901.37	2 240.03	2 264.66	2 866.93	3 825.30	5 801.80	5 598.23	5 267.23	6 131.70
May	1 548.06	1 505.57	1 926.91	2 164.18	2 350.00	2 898.78	4 331.40	5 497.77	5 762.20	5 319.47	6 314.55
June	1 507.79	1 452.21	2 011.94	2 111.15	2 411.52	2 867.16	4 281.17	5 274.89	5 837.41	5 530.31	6 277.57
July	1 513.55	1 352.32	2 065.80	2 129.92	2 466.78	2 886.69	4 468.02	5 352.53	5 734.03	5 585.71	5 965.94
August	1 584.38	1 267.47	2 175.74	2 197.58	2 526.20	3 078.43	4 647.61	4 914.36	5 575.43	5 997.42	6 162.30
September	1 605.07	1 348.16	2 174.42	2 181.71	2 599.72	3 149.04	4 634.33	4 410.37	5 489.99	6 147.05	..
October	1 531.22	1 483.95	2 310.58	2 137.44	2 691.46	3 292.82	4 787.52	4 319.56	5 388.54	6 084.93	..
November	1 455.47	1 622.84	2 289.99	2 188.27	2 805.33	3 300.68	4 407.61	4 877.76	5 765.55	6 417.09	..
December	1 348.81	1 645.58	2 502.99	2 134.40	2 879.80	3 418.82	4 756.91	4 955.84	5 706.70	6 443.77	..
Investments Trusts DEPG											
January	1 497.25	1 822.17	2 064.63	3 058.15	2 609.12	3 079.31	3 198.05	3 436.17	3 649.01	4 966.17	5 147.77
February	1 642.43	1 825.74	2 217.35	3 056.69	2 604.17	3 142.90	3 328.88	3 635.46	3 712.94	5 029.95	5 143.56
March	1 835.51	1 808.41	2 244.24	2 901.35	2 583.43	3 106.91	3 340.35	3 855.17	3 812.75	5 403.93	4 658.99
April	1 863.97	1 826.01	2 225.74	2 844.45	2 648.57	3 216.41	3 234.90	3 935.37	–	5 044.26	4 645.29
May	1 864.72	1 945.40	2 256.79	2 812.57	2 762.00	3 237.58	3 377.50	4 036.89	–	5 035.94	4 874.87
June	1 859.45	1 837.53	2 330.08	2 709.20	2 791.09	3 170.26	3 422.71	3 976.40	4 112.19	5 327.88	4 751.66
July	1 854.11	1 726.09	2 372.09	2 725.64	2 874.20	3 075.76	3 453.98	3 960.55	4 319.87	5 474.11	4 312.46
August	1 885.60	1 626.22	2 563.16	2 882.04	2 938.91	3 147.91	3 512.81	3 606.48	4 258.92	5 596.02	4 233.41
September	1 926.31	1 688.05	2 549.64	2 831.12	2 969.59	3 182.58	3 493.30	3 166.36	4 251.66	5 818.74	..
October	1 905.34	1 801.19	2 663.51	2 732.79	2 924.52	3 204.46	3 534.96	3 118.92	4 122.35	5 439.58	..
November	1 834.04	1 933.38	2 669.09	2 732.46	2 932.60	3 137.47	3 275.77	3 478.60	4 510.47	5 374.91	..
December	1 747.99	2 000.31	2 880.07	2 686.29	2 998.07	3 129.25	3 370.41	3 480.98	4 910.85	5 158.18	..
FTSE All Share AJMA											
January	1 010.79	1 203.08	1 351.60	1 710.35	1 501.87	1 818.72	2 041.99	2 455.05	2 715.41	3 072.11	2 979.84
February	1 095.30	1 218.70	1 384.99	1 709.09	1 506.17	1 839.78	2 105.82	2 624.19	2 757.57	2 947.10	2 955.31
March	1 190.90	1 199.04	1 415.40	1 619.80	1 511.04	1 836.04	2 121.89	2 740.51	2 841.78	3 126.10	2 759.72
April	1 217.27	1 225.16	1 393.70	1 582.06	1 566.98	1 892.47	2 092.74	2 799.69	2 976.58	3 000.08	2 771.56
May	1 203.75	1 310.73	1 397.10	1 559.27	1 614.69	1 889.96	2 203.40	2 814.73	2 935.82	2 959.31	2 841.85
June	1 198.76	1 260.28	1 419.94	1 497.44	1 643.59	1 875.05	2 207.24	2 775.66	2 982.44	3 076.22	2 786.32
July	1 208.52	1 171.62	1 413.38	1 517.70	1 680.80	1 844.67	2 269.94	2 804.19	3 000.90	3 085.70	2 640.55
August	1 244.49	1 114.82	1 498.55	1 591.47	1 718.13	1 899.46	2 324.27	2 597.71	2 920.81	3 114.63	2 633.13
September	1 265.42	1 156.91	1 505.06	1 554.01	1 743.26	1 938.37	2 357.80	2 397.79	2 880.46	3 112.47	2 356.57
October	1 245.25	1 221.44	1 544.80	1 516.65	1 739.84	1 973.94	2 422.75	2 338.00	2 835.95	3 015.93	..
November	1 210.28	1 284.96	1 535.11	1 533.46	1 755.17	1 951.91	2 293.45	2 571.19	3 024.26	3 050.28	..
December	1 156.90	1 324.08	1 628.88	1 502.42	1 783.30	1 976.41	2 388.17	2 595.88	3 146.68	2 989.69	..

1 Working day average. A full definition of these series is given in Section 7 of
the ONS Explanatory Handbook.

Source: Bank of England: 020 7601 4342

22.12 Average Zero Coupon Yields[1]

	1991	1992	1993	1994	1995	1996	1997	1998	1999	2000	2001
Nominal Five Year Yield ZBRG											
January	10.47	9.54	7.46	5.89	8.63	6.85	7.15	6.18	4.30	6.28	5.07
February	9.97	9.34	7.06	6.23	8.53	7.12	6.82	6.10	4.46	6.13	5.04
March	10.04	9.71	6.94	6.96	8.45	7.45	7.07	6.09	4.69	5.89	4.86
April	10.06	9.53	7.23	7.58	8.25	7.52	7.28	5.93	4.66	5.80	4.96
May	10.15	9.08	7.47	7.97	7.95	7.53	6.94	5.95	4.95	5.82	5.14
June	10.33	9.10	7.34	8.45	7.77	7.46	6.96	6.04	5.28	5.61	5.25
July	10.15	9.08	7.02	8.27	7.89	7.30	7.01	6.12	5.49	5.58	5.26
August	9.93	9.45	6.62	8.47	7.70	7.19	6.97	5.80	5.75	5.65	5.03
September	9.57	9.18	6.59	8.71	7.47	7.18	6.72	5.32	6.00	5.65	..
October	9.65	8.06	6.43	8.64	7.56	6.97	6.51	4.94	6.25	5.46	..
November	9.70	7.46	6.35	8.49	7.21	7.18	6.69	4.92	5.86	5.33	..
December	9.72	7.65	5.89	8.49	6.88	7.20	6.46	4.51	5.90	5.14	..
Nominal Ten Year Yield ZBRH											
January	10.19	9.21	8.51	6.39	8.57	7.46	7.52	5.96	4.24	5.62	4.75
February	9.84	9.08	8.25	6.78	8.50	7.80	7.15	5.91	4.39	5.44	4.75
March	10.05	9.40	7.95	7.43	8.45	8.08	7.41	5.85	4.60	5.18	4.64
April	9.95	9.15	8.06	7.79	8.31	8.06	7.58	5.69	4.53	5.14	4.90
May	10.13	8.82	8.32	8.24	8.07	8.10	7.08	5.73	4.83	5.23	5.05
June	10.31	8.90	8.11	8.65	8.04	8.09	7.04	5.60	5.07	5.05	5.11
July	10.00	8.79	7.74	8.47	8.20	7.96	6.92	5.65	5.24	5.09	5.10
August	9.77	9.04	7.23	8.54	8.07	7.86	6.97	5.41	5.25	5.18	4.87
September	9.43	8.99	7.09	8.77	7.93	7.86	6.70	5.03	5.51	5.25	..
October	9.50	8.78	7.00	8.64	8.09	7.56	6.37	4.93	5.68	5.09	..
November	9.53	8.42	6.97	8.51	7.78	7.56	6.46	4.83	5.11	4.98	..
December	9.41	8.46	6.45	8.43	7.52	7.52	6.22	4.44	5.19	4.80	..
Nominal Twenty Year Yield ZBRI											
January	9.28	..	9.19	6.57	8.23	7.89	7.74	5.94	4.36	4.45	4.33
February	9.10	8.67	8.97	6.88	8.16	8.19	7.39	5.88	4.44	4.38	4.42
March	9.22	8.94	8.67	7.45	8.15	8.37	7.59	5.78	4.60	4.25	4.45
April	9.15	8.81	8.63	7.69	8.09	8.30	7.73	5.61	4.53	4.35	4.76
May	9.30	8.57	8.74	7.98	7.92	8.38	7.16	5.67	4.75	4.40	4.87
June	9.47	8.61	8.51	8.18	7.98	8.41	7.08	5.42	4.77	4.37	4.98
July	9.35	8.43	8.12	8.08	8.24	8.34	6.80	5.45	4.67	4.38	4.90
August	..	8.55	7.56	8.15	8.14	8.26	6.86	5.30	4.53	4.49	4.69
September	..	8.72	7.37	8.29	8.05	8.27	6.64	4.91	4.62	4.63	..
October	..	9.37	7.27	8.23	8.30	7.98	6.36	4.87	4.56	4.61	..
November	..	9.09	7.20	8.18	7.98	7.81	6.37	4.73	4.07	4.39	..
December	..	9.00	6.63	8.08	7.80	7.67	6.17	4.47	4.20	4.30	..
Real Ten Year Yield ZBRJ											
January	4.10	4.29	3.56	2.73	3.87	3.42	3.45	3.10	2.00	2.10	2.22
February	4.12	4.22	3.19	2.86	3.86	3.54	3.27	3.06	1.91	2.17	2.27
March	4.11	4.33	3.01	3.09	3.87	3.67	3.43	3.00	1.85	2.05	2.33
April	4.04	4.51	3.07	3.25	3.79	3.63	3.56	2.91	1.70	2.08	2.56
May	4.05	4.43	3.23	3.48	3.57	3.72	3.57	2.92	1.91	2.14	2.57
June	4.17	4.38	3.25	3.76	3.56	3.77	3.66	2.85	1.89	2.12	2.54
July	4.27	4.50	3.19	3.84	3.58	3.70	3.62	2.77	1.90	2.14	2.56
August	4.32	4.77	3.15	3.78	3.48	3.58	3.60	2.65	2.19	2.25	2.42
September	4.16	4.67	3.09	3.81	3.45	3.57	3.52	2.59	2.31	2.28	..
October	4.14	3.77	3.02	3.82	3.63	3.41	3.23	2.67	2.26	2.33	..
November	4.17	3.42	2.95	3.81	3.52	3.43	3.25	2.40	2.05	2.34	..
December	4.33	3.67	2.79	3.83	3.43	3.42	3.11	2.11	1.98	2.23	..
Real Twenty Year Yield ZBRK											
January	..	..	3.84	3.07	3.89	..	3.67	3.06	2.07	2.01	1.88
February	..	..	3.68	3.23	3.89	3.79	3.49	3.05	1.99	1.95	1.89
March	..	..	3.53	3.45	3.88	3.81	3.59	2.98	1.93	1.78	1.99
April	..	4.52	3.54	3.51	3.80	3.75	3.68	2.85	1.81	1.84	2.25
May	..	4.40	3.63	3.68	3.64	3.82	3.66	2.83	1.99	1.91	2.31
June	..	4.32	3.59	3.91	3.69	3.86	3.69	2.63	1.97	1.87	2.27
July	..	4.40	3.52	3.93	3.71	3.81	3.57	2.58	2.00	1.90	2.24
August	..	4.55	3.35	3.84	3.62	3.75	3.57	2.53	2.14	1.96	2.16
September	..	4.48	3.25	3.88	3.61	3.76	3.48	2.49	2.26	1.96	..
October	..	3.98	3.19	3.87	3.73	3.61	3.22	2.59	2.22	1.99	..
November	..	3.82	3.21	3.85	3.61	3.62	3.18	2.36	1.92	1.94	..
December	..	3.96	3.08	3.87	3.56	3.62	3.06	2.14	1.87	1.87	..

1 Working day average. Calculated using the Variable Roughness Penalty (VRP) model.

Source: Bank of England: 020 7601 4342

22.13 Average Rates on Representative British Government Stocks[1]

	1991	1992	1993	1994	1995	1996	1997	1998	1999	2000	2001
5 Year Conventional Rate KORP											
January	10.66	9.57	6.88	5.76	8.61	6.78	7.19	6.33	4.25	6.36	5.17
February	10.16	9.34	6.72	6.05	8.52	7.02	6.86	6.24	4.41	6.23	5.13
March	10.22	9.75	6.62	6.72	8.44	7.56	7.08	6.26	4.65	6.01	4.94
April	10.23	9.54	6.91	7.33	8.26	7.43	7.30	6.11	4.66	5.95	4.97
May	10.27	9.09	7.10	7.74	7.96	7.61	6.98	6.14	4.93	5.97	5.15
June	10.41	9.12	7.01	8.22	7.79	7.52	7.01	6.31	5.27	5.78	5.32
July	10.25	9.13	6.70	8.06	7.90	7.35	7.09	6.14	5.49	5.75	5.34
August	10.04	9.50	6.35	8.31	7.69	7.21	7.02	5.84	5.80	5.81	5.09
September	9.67	9.13	6.34	8.61	7.45	7.20	6.78	5.34	6.04	5.81	..
October	9.74	7.80	6.17	8.57	7.54	7.01	6.59	4.88	6.24	5.66	..
November	9.79	7.15	6.09	8.44	7.16	7.22	6.79	4.86	5.89	5.50	..
December	9.83	7.38	5.66	8.49	6.83	7.26	6.60	4.45	5.91	5.27	..
10 year Conventional Rate KORQ											
January	10.42	9.47	8.22	6.23	8.66	7.42	7.53	6.07	4.16	5.75	4.86
February	10.11	9.32	7.91	6.61	8.59	7.75	7.17	6.02	4.32	5.56	4.88
March	10.25	9.67	7.66	7.29	8.53	8.05	7.41	5.97	4.54	5.29	4.75
April	10.17	9.43	7.82	7.68	8.39	8.05	7.60	5.81	4.48	5.25	4.95
May	10.32	9.06	8.06	8.13	8.12	8.08	7.13	5.85	4.77	5.35	5.13
June	10.53	9.14	7.87	8.54	8.08	8.04	7.10	5.77	5.02	5.15	5.09
July	10.24	9.08	7.49	8.37	8.23	7.91	7.01	5.67	5.20	5.18	5.16
August	10.00	9.35	6.98	8.52	8.10	7.81	7.05	5.56	5.24	5.27	4.92
September	9.65	9.17	6.90	8.80	7.92	7.80	6.77	5.10	5.52	5.32	..
October	9.72	8.68	6.81	8.70	8.08	7.51	6.47	4.93	5.70	5.15	..
November	9.76	8.26	6.77	8.57	7.75	7.56	6.59	4.87	5.16	5.06	..
December	9.69	8.38	6.29	8.53	7.45	7.54	6.34	4.49	5.24	4.88	..
20 Year Conventional Rate KORR											
January	10.06	9.23	8.74	6.53	8.45	7.73	7.71	6.04	4.36	4.91	4.52
February	9.75	9.12	8.44	6.88	8.43	8.04	7.35	5.98	4.47	4.80	4.58
March	9.89	9.44	8.19	7.49	8.40	8.28	7.58	5.90	4.64	4.64	4.56
April	9.81	9.25	8.42	7.81	8.30	8.26	7.74	5.73	4.58	4.71	4.84
May	10.00	8.93	8.58	8.18	8.09	8.31	7.21	5.79	4.83	4.77	4.98
June	10.20	8.99	8.36	8.48	8.08	8.31	7.15	5.59	4.92	4.68	5.10
July	9.98	8.85	7.98	8.35	8.30	8.21	6.93	5.63	4.88	4.70	5.05
August	9.78	9.06	7.46	8.46	8.19	8.12	6.98	5.43	4.82	4.79	4.83
September	9.44	9.08	7.31	8.65	8.06	8.11	6.74	5.02	4.97	4.90	..
October	9.50	9.15	7.18	8.56	8.26	7.84	6.45	4.92	4.97	4.84	..
November	9.57	8.78	7.12	8.46	7.93	7.77	6.50	4.79	4.46	4.64	..
December	9.46	8.78	6.57	8.39	7.70	7.67	6.32	4.49	4.56	4.51	..
10 Year Index-Linked Rate KORS											
January	4.19	4.29	3.60	2.70	3.89	3.42	3.44	3.01	2.00	2.11	2.21
February	4.19	4.18	3.23	2.81	3.87	3.57	3.23	2.94	1.94	2.16	2.30
March	4.19	4.29	3.07	3.07	3.86	3.70	3.41	2.89	1.90	2.06	2.34
April	4.09	4.47	3.11	3.25	3.79	3.66	3.55	2.80	1.74	2.08	2.55
May	4.14	4.41	3.30	3.51	3.58	3.74	3.52	2.83	1.96	2.15	2.61
June	4.28	4.40	3.31	3.78	3.58	3.80	3.62	2.81	1.93	2.13	2.56
July	4.34	4.51	3.22	3.85	3.61	3.82	3.68	2.67	1.93	2.14	2.57
August	4.34	4.76	3.16	3.82	3.52	3.59	3.59	2.55	2.20	2.25	2.45
September	4.18	4.68	3.09	3.85	3.46	3.57	3.47	2.59	2.32	2.29	..
October	4.16	3.82	3.03	3.84	3.65	3.41	3.17	2.66	2.26	2.33	..
November	4.19	3.40	2.96	3.84	3.54	3.42	3.23	2.39	2.03	2.32	..
December	4.34	3.61	2.75	3.85	3.45	3.41	3.01	2.11	1.99	2.20	..
20 Year Index-Linked rate KORT											
January	4.23	4.34	3.84	2.96	3.91	3.58	3.62	3.01	2.06	2.01	1.96
February	4.23	4.32	3.64	3.11	3.89	3.70	3.43	3.01	1.97	1.98	1.99
March	4.25	4.49	3.50	3.35	3.89	3.82	3.55	2.92	1.93	1.83	2.09
April	4.17	4.59	3.51	3.45	3.81	3.77	3.65	2.80	1.81	1.90	2.35
May	4.23	4.42	3.62	3.64	3.64	3.84	3.61	2.79	1.99	1.97	2.41
June	4.35	4.35	3.57	3.88	3.67	3.88	3.65	2.61	1.97	1.94	2.38
July	4.40	4.42	3.48	3.90	3.71	3.72	3.68	2.56	1.97	1.96	2.36
August	4.40	4.61	3.32	3.83	3.62	3.75	3.54	2.51	2.12	2.03	2.25
September	4.25	4.55	3.22	3.87	3.60	3.74	3.43	2.51	2.23	2.04	..
October	4.25	4.00	3.15	3.86	3.74	3.60	3.17	2.58	2.18	2.08	..
November	4.27	3.77	3.14	3.85	3.62	3.59	3.16	2.35	1.91	2.02	..
December	4.39	3.94	2.98	3.86	3.55	3.58	3.02	2.12	1.88	1.94	..

1 Working day average.

Source: Bank of England: 020 7601 4342

22.14 Capital issues and redemptions[1]

£ millions

		1990	1991	1992	1993	1994	1995	1996	1997	1998	1999	2000
Total issues and redemptions												
Gross issues	KDSF	18 821	26 735	20 649	40 615	37 110	25 929	38 354	38 217	33 000	54 989	75 891
Gross redemptions	KDSG	5 359	3 765	7 011	11 399	11 866	10 367	14 123	14 579	11 607	12 661	10 472
Issues *less* redemptions: total	KDSH	13 462	22 970	13 638	29 216	25 244	15 562	24 231	23 638	21 393	42 328	65 419
Loan capital	KDSI	13 001	11 498	12 744	22 560	24 640	20 788	29 493	29 960	28 624	37 639	55 409
Preference shares	DEDO	781	1 245	589	1 700	603	2 875	710	−881	−330	−438	275
Ordinary shares	DEDF	3 449	10 849	6 224	16 671	14 620	9 777	10 273	8 614	4 637	10 127	19 517
UK borrowers: total	DEDX	13 462	22 970	13 638	29 216	25 244	15 562	24 231	23 638	21 393	42 328	65 419
Local government	DEEA	–	1	1	−1	–	–	–	–	–	–	–
Listed public companies	KDSN	13 462	22 969	13 637	29 217	25 244	15 562	24 231	23 638	21 393	42 328	65 419
Non-resident borrowers: total	KDSO	2 878	5 132	1 829	9 237	3 285	2 153	9 452	10 790	3 935	3 356	7 390
Central government[2]	KIMI / KDSP	1 142	2 956	2 001	5 525	749	652	1 929	2 724	2 889	2 080	5 766
State, local government[2]	KDSQ											
Companies[3]	KHDR	1 736	2 176	−172	3 712	2 536	1 501	7 523	8 066	1 046	1 276	1 624
UK listed public companies												
All companies: total	KDSN	13 462	22 969	13 637	29 217	25 244	15 562	24 231	23 638	21 393	42 328	65 419
Loan capital	KDSS	9 232	10 875	6 824	10 846	10 021	2 910	13 248	15 905	17 086	32 639	45 627
Preference shares	KDST	781	1 245	589	1 700	603	2 875	710	−881	−330	−438	275
Ordinary shares	KDSU	3 449	10 849	6 224	16 671	14 620	9 777	10 273	8 614	4 637	10 127	19 517
Financial corporations: total	DEEC	6 737	7 815	5 427	12 523	11 774	−341	11 030	6 711	6 830	16 104	26 120
Loan capital	KDSW	5 868	6 027	3 898	7 455	6 972	−4 005	7 508	4 142	6 190	13 191	22 267
Preference shares	KDSX	214	660	459	1 221	138	1 538	868	−536	175	−438	292
Ordinary shares	DELC	655	1 128	1 070	3 847	4 664	2 126	2 654	3 105	465	3 351	3 561
Other companies: total	DEEB	6 725	15 154	8 210	16 694	13 470	15 903	13 201	16 927	14 563	26 224	39 299
Loan capital	KDTA	3 364	4 848	2 926	3 391	3 049	6 915	5 740	11 763	10 896	19 448	23 360
Preference shares	KDTB	567	585	130	479	465	1 337	−158	−345	−505	–	−17
Ordinary shares	DEEY	2 794	9 721	5 154	12 824	9 956	7 651	7 619	5 509	4 172	6 776	15 956
UK listed public companies												
Financial companies: total	KDTD	6 735	7 817	5 426	12 519	11 774	−342	11 032	8 172	6 828	16 106	26 119
Monetary financial institutions	KDTE	4 614	2 856	1 972	4 764	3 763	−648	9 618	22	2 161	2 312	14 231
Insurance corporations	DELR	−157	63	394	1 694	501	578	1 007	1 805	617	1 843	85
Investment trust companies	DELS	439	841	709	3 027	4 118	1 415	1 537	927	427	231	2 396
Other[4]	KDTH	1 839	4 057	2 351	3 034	3 392	−1 687	−1 130	5 418	3 623	11 720	9 407
Other companies: total	DEEB	6 725	15 154	8 210	16 694	13 470	15 903	13 201	16 927	14 563	26 224	39 299
Manufacturing industries: total	KDTJ	2 522	5 611	4 460	7 133	4 814	9 536	1 888	1 849	−413	3 637	6 129
Minerals and metal manufacture	DEKN	209	1 170	1 116	447	76	534	−947	−549	−325	637	822
Chemicals and allied industries	DEKO	628	338	51	2 043	283	1 759	1 124	854	−295	393	−419
Metal goods, engineering and vehicles	DEKP	612	1 165	1 197	1 441	1 535	1 097	365	676	94	987	498
Electrical and electronic engines	DEKQ	104	219	339	119	376	868	447	451	145	167	4 086
Food, drink and tobacco	DEKR	40	1 289	561	1 136	1 242	3 730	−112	−279	−474	876	−396
Other manufacturing	DEKS	929	1 430	1 196	1 947	1 302	1 548	1 011	696	442	577	1 538
Energy	DEKT	704	817	539	1 413	1 173	948	1 821	1 781	1 829	3 255	1 409
Water	DEKU	87	724	168	212	251	648	354	509	1 025	1 642	210
Construction	DEKV	533	852	238	662	1 284	53	623	703	54	258	203
Distribution, hotels and repairs	DEKW	1 048	3 121	1 064	2 191	1 137	901	854	1 481	1 242	1 291	2 603
Transport and communications	DEKX	499	843	418	872	912	1 134	3 744	4 769	6 946	10 220	16 381
Property companies	DEKY	338	1 402	212	2 007	1 873	1 370	1 907	2 798	1 196	1 605	1 704
Services	DEKZ	993	1 782	1 118	2 207	2 025	1 310	2 011	3 039	2 689	4 322	10 660

1 Components of aggregated series may not always sum to the total due to rounding discrepancies.
2 Series now combined.
3 Non-resident companies including public corporations.

4 'Other' includes special finance agencies (listed public companies engaged in the provision of medium and long-term finance to industry eg ICFC) and those finance houses and other consumer credit grantors not included under banks and building societies.

Source: Bank of England: 020 7601 5949

22.15 Building societies[1]
United Kingdom

		1991	1992	1993	1994	1995[2]	1996[2]	1997[2]	1998[2]	1999[2]	2000[3]
Number and balance sheets											
Societies on register (number)	KRNA	110	105	101	96	94	88	82	78	72	68
Share investors (thousands)	KRNB	37 925	37 533	37 809	38 150	38 998	37 768	19 234	21 195	21 774	22 237
Depositors (thousands)	KRNC	4 698	3 879	3 686	5 369	6 143	6 718	882	820	642	660
Borrowers (thousands)	KRND	6 998	7 055	7 140	7 222	6 906	6 586	2 703	2 934	2 868	2 925
Assets and liabilities (£ million)											
Liabilities:											
Shares	KRNE	177 519.4	187 108.4	194 975.1	201 812.2	200 682.0	196 546.4	90 092.8	103 289.8	109 137.7	119 298.5
Deposits and loans	KRNF	49 516.6	57 067.5	62 301.2	69 925.2	67 513.8	73 919.1	31 033.7	33 311.2	34 746.6	44 262.4
Taxation and other	KRNG	3 093.9	2 559.5	2 565.7	2 939.2	3 306.2	3 727.4	1 338.8	1 586.4	1 665.4	1 664.0
General reserves	KRNH	11 430.4	12 634.4	14 269.5	16 312.3	17 218.3	17 940.3	7 331.2	7 926.4	8 301.5	8 987.1
Other Capital	KRNI	2 419.4	3 144.7	3 900.9	4 125.7	3 498.0	4 762.3	1 643.9	1 550.7	1 529.2	1 861.0
Assets: total	KRNJ	243 979.7	262 514.5	278 012.4	295 114.6	292 218.3	296 895.5	131 440.4	147 664.5	155 380.4	176 073.0
Mortgages	KRNK	196 945.6	210 994.5	221 237.6	240 297.2	236 841.0	241 472.9	107 531.5	118 288.4	123 183.4	137 072.3
Investments / Cash	KHVZ KRNL / KRNM	39 513.6	42 909.1	47 174.2	50 786.7	50 894.1	51 016.7	21 869.8	27 102.0	29 917.8	36 574.2
Other	KRNN	7 520.5	8 610.1	9 600.6	4 030.7	4 483.2	4 405.9	2 039.1	2 274.1	2 279.2	2 426.6
Current transactions (£ million)											
Mortgage advances	KRNU	42 948.0	34 989.0	32 259.0	34 829.0	34 673.0	38 488.0	28 771.7	21 988.3	23 997.9	28 233.6
Management expenses	KRNX	2 591.0	2 723.7	2 952.5	3 136.7	3 352.6	3 555.3	2 270.5	1 501.7	1 573.8	1 640.7

1 The figures for each year relate to accounting years ending on dates between 1 February of that year and 31 January of the following year.

2 The societies which have converted to the banking sector, namely Cheltenham & Gloucester (August 1995), National & Provincial (August 1996), Alliance & Leicester (April 1997), Halifax (June 1997), Woolwich (July 1997), Bristol & West (July 1997), Northern Rock (October 1997), and Birmingham Midshires (April 1999) have been included in flow figures (using flows up to the date of conversion), but have been excluded from the end of year balances.

3 Bradford & Bingley, which converted to the banking sector in December 2000, is included within flow figures and the end of year balances.

Source: Financial Services Authority: 020 7676 1000

22.16 Consumer credit

£ millions

		1990	1991	1992	1993	1994	1995	1996	1997	1998	1999	2000
Total amount outstanding	AILA	52 578	53 555	52 609	52 330	..	..	..	..	..	..	..
	VZRD	53 471[9]	54 416[9]	53 486[9]	53 295[9]	58 051[9]	68 205[9]	77 494	88 100	102 222	115 402	127 298
Total net lending	-AIKL	4 439	2 245	284	2 423	..	..	..	..	..	..	..
	VZQC	4 616	2 318	484	2 653	5 743	8 234	11 215	12 013	14 490	14 486	14 241
Retailers	AAPP	50	37	25	69	83	−133	75	208	7	103	−285
Building societies' class 3 loans	ALPY	223	−45	−65	46	89	238	383	120	−22	10	107
Banks	AIKN	3 765	2 523	792	843	3 704	5 606	7 682	9 027	11 711	10 998	13 198
of which Credit cards	VTFY	1 761	774	126	700	..	..	..	..	..	..	..
	VZQS	1 761	774	138	719	1 483	2 103	3 029	3 507	4 854	6 615	6 377
Loans on personal accounts	VTGA	1 981	1 805	615	156	..	..	..	..	..	..	..
Other	VZQT	2 855	1 544	346	1 934	4 261	6 132	8 186	8 505	9 636	7 871	7 864
Insurance companies	-AIKQ	156	68	29	165	..	..	..	..	..	..	..
	RSBK	157	69	29	170	−178	39	−81	4	−16	−65	−111
Non-bank credit companies	-AGSJ	254	−417	−483	1 332	1 856	2 222	2 805	2 287	2 409	2 928	676
Other specialist lenders	VZQQ	421	−266	−297	1 525	2 045	2 485	3 156	2 654	2 810	3 439	1 333
Total gross lending	VZQG	13 299	12 530	11 913	54 094	75 079	89 115	103 215	116 134	133 886	146 879	160 227
Narrower coverage[1]												
Total amount outstanding	RLWE	30 255	30 624	30 120	32 204	37 027	..	..	..	..	..	..
Total net lending	RLWF	3 683	1 060	367	3 042	5 515	..	..	..	..	..	..
Total new credit advanced	RLBY	46 336	47 098	48 865	54 859	62 050	..	..	..	..	..	..

1 Data no longer available from 1995.

Source: Office for National Statistics: 01633 812789

22.17 End-year assets and liabilities of investment trust companies, unit trusts[1] and property unit trusts[2]

£ millions

		1990	1991	1992	1993	1994	1995	1996	1997	1998	1999	2000
Investment trust companies												
Short-term assets and liabilities (net):	CBPL	1 070	730	390	623	273	627	1 076	1 426	2 263	71	423
Cash and UK bank deposits	AHAG	642	397	340	387	443	1 009	1 087	1 577	2 647	1 227	2 202
Other short-term assets	CBPN	657	711	645	1 030	772	738	794	1 714	1 734	1 097	1 082
Short-term liabilities	−CBPS	−229	−378	−595	−794	−942	−1 120	−805	−1 865	−2 118	−2 253	−2 861
Medium and long-term liabilities and capital:	−CBPO	−20 382	−23 417	−28 895	−36 140	−40 180	−43 882	−50 911	−54 821	−49 985	−57 616	−60 412
Issued share and loan capital	−CBPQ	−5 193	−5 076	−4 827	−8 286	−10 978	−13 250	−8 330	−9 350	−8 837	−8 565	−8 934
Foreign currency borrowing	−CBPR	−119	−135	−407	−473	−354	−1 061	−638	−658	−607	−880	−994
Other borrowing	−CBQA	−596	−733	−802	−849	−1 354	−622	−823	−1 296	−1 723	−1 716	−2 503
Reserves and provisions, etc	−AHBC	−14 474	−17 473	−22 859	−26 532	−27 494	−28 949	−41 120	−43 517	−38 818	−46 455	−47 981
Investments:	CBPM	19 108	22 392	28 586	35 300	39 586	43 410	50 034	51 618	46 575	56 491	59 948
British government securities	AHBF	326	415	996	1 013	2 490	1 194	1 422	1 255	815	1 217	821
UK company securities:												
Loan capital and preference shares	CBGZ	687	720	814	854	1 000	846	832	1 320	1 359	1 425	1 654
Ordinary and deferred shares	CBGY	9 878	10 637	12 825	14 892	15 926	19 384	25 046	27 916	24 729	28 010	33 456
Overseas company securities:												
Loan capital and preference shares	CBHA	257	355	514	533	896	740	279	1 165	773	979	963
Ordinary and deferred shares	AHCC	7 392	9 105	11 943	16 886	17 873	19 485	21 047	17 747	17 844	23 330	21 355
Other investments	CBPT	568	1 160	1 494	1 122	1 401	1 761	1 408	1 631	1 055	1 530	1 699
Unit trusts												
Short-term assets and liabilities:	CBPU	2 315	1 698	2 099	2 673	3 266	3 116	3 822	4 627	6 883	5 894	8 340
Cash and UK bank deposits	AGYE	1 864	1 318	1 793	2 579	3 102	3 326	3 895	4 731	6 020	4 797	6 969
Other short-term assets	CBPW	710	628	920	1 013	1 364	986	1 201	467	1 343	1 545	2 319
Short-term liabilities	−CBPX	−259	−248	−614	−919	−1 200	−1 196	−1 274	−571	−480	−448	−948
Foreign currency borrowing	−AGYK	−31	−47	−8	−39	−21	−1	–	–	–	–	–
Investments:	CBPZ	41 608	50 459	58 785	88 479	83 495	104 069	125 841	143 108	163 048	213 553	222 844
British government securities	CBHT	411	523	664	959	1 414	1 774	2 716	3 087	3 771	3 627	4 693
UK company securities:												
Loan capital and preference shares	CBHU	1 337	1 337	1 664	2 906	2 970	3 298	5 029	6 494	9 290	13 322	14 654
Ordinary and deferred shares	RLIB	25 529	29 546	33 356	49 657	43 335	59 122	67 509	85 742	93 410	119 496	116 808
Overseas company securities:												
Loan capital and preference shares	CBHV	347	516	570	864	1 001	2 145	1 288	1 834	1 801	3 032	3 212
Ordinary and deferred shares	RLIC	13 791	18 124	21 862	32 904	33 473	36 062	47 346	42 898	51 119	70 256	79 601
Other assets	CBQE	193	413	669	1 189	1 302	1 668	1 953	2 593	3 657	3 820	3 876
Property unit trusts												
Short-term assets and liabilities (net)	AGVC	136	86	73	212	253	186	343	351	254	205	285
Property	CBQG	948	1 241	1 373	1 492	2 197	1 807	2 582	3 875	2 740	2 722	3 488
Other assets	AGVL	21	–	34	60	11	11	11	167	197	436	380
Long-term borrowing	−AGVM	−6	−8	−42	−42	–	−131	−45	−246	−106	−75	−391

Note: Assets are shown as positive: liabilities as negative.

1 Including open ended investment companies (OEICs).
2 Investments are at market value.

Source: Office for National Statistics: 01633 812789

22.18 Self-administered pension funds: market value of assets
United Kingdom

End year

£ millions

		1992	1993	1994	1995	1996	1997	1998	1999
Total pension funds[1]									
Total net assets	AHVA	381 997	480 547	443 467	508 581	543 879	656 874	699 191	776 614
Short-term assets	RYIQ	18 492	20 279	22 617	26 114	31 521	35 368	39 005	27 365
British government securities	AHVK	25 188	34 279	41 854	52 659	57 783	80 533	91 084	82 181
UK local authority long-term debt	AHVO	34	81	250	81	89	156	183	138
Overseas government securities	AHVT	10 529	11 044	11 092	11 721	11 800	13 079	15 493	13 722
UK company securities									
Ordinary shares	AHVP	202 311	251 099	219 189	256 625	276 001	339 687	334 648	398 121
Other	AHVQ	5 905	5 758	3 935	7 064	6 180	5 618	8 168	7 480
Overseas company securities									
Ordinary shares	AHVR	63 276	84 118	74 813	82 164	84 163	104 187	108 884	121 514
Other	AHVS	1 787	2 103	3 045	1 184	4 909	3 851	3 842	3 769
UK loans and mortgages	RLDQ	232	260	44	34	83	160	22	12
UK land, property and ground rent	AHWA	19 914	21 932	24 353	21 317	21 637	24 176	24 355	24 660
Authorised unit trust units	AHVU	8 569	13 188	13 345	15 212	21 767	21 979	30 596	30 367
Property unit trusts	AHVW	1 745	1 905	2 463	2 485	2 666	3 219	3 211	5 429
Other assets	RKPL	28 794	38 761	31 318	36 352	30 628	32 978	47 136	68 998
Total liabilities	GQFX	4 781	4 261	4 852	4 412	5 347	8 118	7 436	7 142

1 These figures cover funded schemes only and therefore exclude the main superannuation arrangements in the central government sector.

Source: Office for National Statistics: 01633 812729

22.19 Insurance companies: balance sheet
Market values
End year

£ millions

		1991	1992	1993	1994	1995	1996	1997	1998	1999
Long-term insurance companies										
Assets										
Total current assets (gross)	RYEW	15 303	18 101	16 925	16 690	24 171	31 699	42 795	46 165	56 360
Agents' and reinsurance balances (net)	AHNY	788	799	457	−209	−157	−232	155	1 383	508
Other debtors[1]	RKPN	4 070	4 198	4 368	4 562	7 565	12 982	15 708	18 210	18 613
British government securities	AHNJ	36 584	50 970	72 575	64 921	80 268	90 996	107 847	127 903	126 223
UK local authority securities etc	AHNN	577	667	772	815	1 322	1 088	914	1 722	1 456
UK company securities[2]	RKPO	145 590	172 204	237 020	217 034	272 554	304 587	386 734	438 666	539 834
Overseas company securities	RKPP	28 120	32 101	49 087	48 195	59 950	62 378	73 428	82 122	120 665
Overseas government securities	AHNS	5 996	8 793	8 874	6 871	8 793	7 554	8 471	17 515	18 494
Loans and mortgages	RKPQ	7 771	8 345	7 885	6 833	7 305	6 653	8 271	11 027	10 914
UK land, property and ground rent	AHNX	32 185	30 074	33 939	35 914	35 596	36 209	42 275	45 903	50 387
Overseas land, property and ground rent	RGCP	160	124	144	151	118	114	98	252	206
Other investments	RKPR	1 447	2 663	3 096	4 644	2 162	3 886	3 416	5 654	8 334
Total	RFXN	278 591	329 039	435 142	406 421	499 647	557 914	690 112	796 522	951 994
Net value of direct investment in:										
Non-insurance subsidiaries and associate companies in the United Kingdom	RYET	3 044	2 569	2 288	2 547	2 773	3 033	3 426	3 035	3 045
UK associate and subsidiary insurance companies and insurance holding companies	RYEU	345	639	1 186	504	701	575	−239	148	2 245
Overseas subsidiaries and associates	RYEV	471	773	1 016	1 034	987	986	1 104	1 087	3 638
Total assets	RKBI	282 451	333 020	439 632	410 506	504 108	562 508	694 403	800 792	960 922
Liabilities										
Borrowing:										
Borrowing from UK banks	RGDF	1 701	1 162	1 234	1 570	1 907	2 234	3 027	3 252	6 064
Other UK borrowing	RGDE	1 372	1 007	553	982	796	1 349	786	1 040	3 070
Borrowing from overseas	RGDD	292	603	381	176	79	90	104	148	159
Long-term business:										
Funds	RKDC	238 145	280 276	354 711	357 263	424 866	470 893	581 009	669 301	800 184
Claims admitted but not paid	RKBM	927	951	1 035	1 085	1 419	1 441	1 436	1 712	2 032
Provision for taxation net of amounts receivable:										
UK authorities	RYPI	−907	−1 119	−141	−470	502	2 568	4 207	5 443	6 344
Overseas authorities	RYPJ	−13	−14	−20	29	−11	9	25	67	314
Provision for recommended dividends	RYPK	145	46	83	76	195	276	368	359	201
Other creditors and liabilities	RYPL	3 642	3 763	4 020	4 399	5 979	6 303	8 083	12 509	17 042
Excess of assets over above liabilities:										
Excess of value of assets over liabilities in respect of long-term funds	RKBR	36 032	43 511	74 160	42 608	63 255	71 817	89 790	96 456	116 951
Minority interests in UK subsidiary companies	RKTI	–	30	30	–	3	–	2	–	25
Shareholders' capital and reserves in respect of general business	RKBS	414	1 952	890	1 143	2 050	2 576	3 862	6 299	6 139
Other reserves including profit and loss account balances	RKBT	701	852	2 696	1 645	3 068	2 952	1 704	4 206	2 396
Total liabilities	RKBI	282 451	333 020	439 632	410 506	504 108	562 508	694 403	800 792	960 922

22.19
continued

Insurance companies: balance sheet
Market values
End year

£ millions

		1991	1992	1993	1994	1995	1996	1997	1998	1999
Other than long-term insurance companies										
Assets										
Total current assets (gross)	RYME	5 774	6 523	6 467	7 426	8 318	11 559	12 628	8 524	10 468
Agents' and reinsurance balances (net)	AHMX	5 796	6 380	5 887	6 123	7 494	11 569	9 405	10 528	12 177
Other debtors[1]	RKPS	2 833	1 765	1 847	2 118	3 403	6 097	5 998	6 277	7 059
British government securities	AHMJ	6 359	8 378	11 474	12 320	14 363	16 893	15 666	16 409	15 938
UK local authority securities etc	AHMN	33	49	59	50	56	42	16	14	10
UK company securities[2]	RKPT	9 877	10 480	14 533	14 312	17 425	17 825	18 845	18 440	18 800
Overseas company securities	RKPU	3 776	3 747	4 163	3 578	4 422	5 072	6 594	8 676	6 284
Overseas government securities	AHMS	3 534	4 660	5 324	5 064	6 511	9 546	8 215	10 459	7 980
Loans and mortgages	RKPV	1 166	1 147	1 234	1 321	1 337	1 593	1 385	1 335	1 070
UK land, property and ground rent	AHMW	3 034	2 398	2 375	2 121	2 100	2 077	2 842	1 146	1 085
Overseas land, property and ground rent	RYNK	91	185	80	89	128	120	149	107	83
Other investments	RKPW	673	633	418	536	665	716	2 465	2 366	2 638
Total	RKAL	42 946	46 345	53 861	55 058	66 222	83 106	84 208	84 281	83 592
Net value of direct investment in:										
Non-insurance subsidiaries and associate companies in the United Kingdom	RYNR	1 724	2 617	2 214	2 474	2 449	3 195	6 950	5 553	7 074
UK associate and subsidiary insurance companies and insurance holding companies	RYNS	682	1 087	1 835	1 738	1 642	7 170	4 204	6 424	5 617
Overseas subsidiaries and associates	RYNT	8 534	9 908	12 275	11 854	15 485	14 859	16 402	14 239	17 775
Total assets	RKBY	53 886	59 957	70 185	71 124	85 798	108 330	111 764	110 750	114 058
Liabilities										
Borrowing:										
Borrowing from UK banks	RYMB	910	434	721	1 382	1 584	1 524	3 029	1 825	1 392
Other UK borrowing	RYMC	1 208	1 677	1 989	2 354	2 370	2 536	2 996	1 551	3 186
Borrowing from overseas	RYMD	1 202	1 296	1 103	1 626	1 876	1 976	1 202	1 600	3 045
General business technical reserves	RKCT	33 832	38 005	39 746	42 374	47 493	58 618	59 527	60 775	59 455
Long-term business:										
Funds	RKTF	–	–	–	–	–	–	–	–	–
Claims admitted but not paid	RKTK	–	–	–	–	–	–	–	–	–
Provision for taxation net of amounts receivable:										
UK authorities	RYPO	−148	−295	235	397	841	807	1 253	1 197	939
Overseas authorities	RYPP	18	24	14	22	16	22	7	11	11
Provision for recommended dividends	RYPQ	635	650	794	874	1 098	1 407	2 048	1 318	1 817
Other creditors and liabilities	RYPR	2 180	1 921	1 987	2 551	2 955	3 886	3 873	3 793	4 981
Excess of assets over above liabilities:										
Excess of value of assets over liabilities in respect of long-term funds	RKCG	–	–	–	–	–	–	–	–	–
Minority interests in UK subsidiary companies	RKCH	17	33	80	52	22	24	60	68	29
Shareholders' capital and reserves in respect of general business	RKCI	13 035	14 552	21 355	17 628	25 545	35 069	35 172	34 397	34 938
Other reserves including profit and loss account balances	RKCJ	997	1 660	2 161	1 864	1 998	2 461	2 597	4 215	4 265
Total liabilities	RKBY	53 886	59 957	70 185	71 124	85 798	108 330	111 764	110 750	114 058

1 Including outstanding interest, dividends and rents (net).
2 Including authorised unit trust units.

Source: Office for National Statistics: 01633 812729

22.20 Individual insolvencies

Numbers

		1989	1990	1991	1992	1993	1994	1995	1996	1997	1998	1999	2000
England and Wales													
Bankruptcies[1]	AIHW	8 138	12 058	22 632	32 106	31 016	25 634	21 933	21 803	19 892	19 647	21 611	21 550
Individual voluntary arrangements[2,3]	AIHI	1 227	1 929	3 008	4 688	5 687	5 105	4 386	4 468	4 549	4 902	7 195	7 978
Total	AIHK	9 365	13 987	25 640	36 794	36 703	30 739	26 319	26 271	24 441	24 549	28 806	29 528
Scotland													
Sequestrations[4]	KRHA	2 301	4 350	7 665	10 845	6 828	2 182	2 188	2 503	2 502	3 016	3 195	2 965
Northern Ireland													
Bankruptcies[5]	KRHB	238	286	367	406	474	438	399	415	393	394	401	347
Individual voluntary arrangements[3,6]	KJRK	..	..	2	42	67	84	64	101	84	122	173	260
Total	KRHD	238	286	369	448	541	522	463	516	477	516	574	607

1 Comprises receiving and administration orders under the Bankruptcy Act 1914 and bankruptcy orders under the Insolvency Act 1986. Orders later consolidated or rescinded are included in these figures.
2 Introduced under the Insolvency Act 1986.
3 For statistical purposes deeds of arrangement are now included with individual voluntary arrangements.
4 Sequestrations awarded but not brought into operation are included in these figures.

5 Comprises bankruptcy adjudication orders, arrangement protection orders and orders for the administration of estates of deceased insolvents. Orders later set aside or dismissed are included in these figures.
6 Introduced under the Insolvency Northern Ireland order 1989.

Source: Department of Trade and Industry: 020 7215 3291/3305

22.21 Company insolvencies

Numbers

		1989	1990	1991	1992	1993	1994	1995	1996	1997	1998	1999	2000
England and Wales													
Compulsory liquidations	AIHR	4 020	5 977	8 368	9 734	8 244	6 597	5 519	5 080	4 735	5 216	5 209	4 925
Creditors' voluntary liquidations	AIHS	6 436	9 074	13 459	14 691	12 464	10 131	9 017	8 381	7 875	7 987	9 071	9 392
Total	AIHQ	10 456	15 051	21 827	24 425	20 708	16 728	14 536	13 461	12 610	13 203	14 280	14 317
Scotland													
Compulsory liquidations	KRGA	229	251	304	310	286	242	252	266	254	338	364	344
Creditors' voluntary liquidations	KRGB	199	219	312	360	265	202	189	175	223	228	208	239
Total	KRGC	428	470	616	670	551	444	441	441	477	566	572	583
Northern Ireland													
Compulsory liquidations	KRGD	69	73	112	79	73	69	72	68	60	53	58	83
Creditors' voluntary liquidations	KRGE	75	55	71	77	85	52	37	54	53	46	45	53
Total	KRGF	144	128	183	156	158	121	109	122	113	99	103	136

Source: Department of Trade and Industry: 020 7215 3291/3305

22.22 Industry analysis: bankruptcies and deeds of arrangement[1]
England and Wales

Numbers

		1990	1991	1992	1993	1994	1995	1996	1997	1998	1999	2000
Industry												
Self-employed												
Agriculture and horticulture	KRFY	198	266	313	277	231	218	168	155	157	183	173
Manufacturing:												
Food, drink and tobacco	KRFZ	31	48	56	34	33	30	31	18	21	17	18
Chemicals	KRLA	4	12	9	7	23	8	5	5	7	4	2
Metals and engineering	KRLB	240	424	634	612	523	396	411	413	378	385	306
Textiles and clothing	KRLC	63	152	174	160	95	114	91	76	81	87	81
Timber and furniture	KRLD	116	233	317	207	176	158	118	98	96	94	90
Paper, printing and publishing	KRLE	80	143	205	161	142	142	117	104	101	112	80
Other	KRLF	67	120	125	169	133	146	117	116	110	111	84
Total	KRLG	601	1 132	1 520	1 350	1 125	994	890	830	794	810	661
Construction and transport:												
Construction	KRLH	2 348	3 812	4 692	4 361	3 362	2 783	2 713	2 182	1 919	1 911	1 741
Transport and communication	KRLI	953	1 620	2 038	1 754	1 402	1 138	1 227	1 162	1 060	1 187	1 120
Total	KHGP	3 301	5 432	6 730	6 115	4 764	3 921	3 940	3 344	2 979	3 098	2 861
Wholesaling:												
Food, drink and tobacco	KRLJ	57	68	114	114	94	103	77	62	53	45	49
Motor vehicles	KRLK	8	21	48	21	28	33	36	28	20	22	29
Other	KRLL	81	122	220	191	160	122	101	78	92	83	83
Total	KHGQ	146	211	382	326	282	258	214	168	165	150	161
Retailing:												
Food, drink and tobacco	KRLM	595	895	1 001	1 107	981	782	662	546	514	438	424
Motor vehicles and filling stations	KRLN	155	362	399	412	343	316	327	276	238	241	237
Other	KRLO	807	1 442	2 159	2 087	1 615	1 566	1 268	1 048	971	1 032	801
Total	KHGR	1 557	2 699	3 559	3 606	2 939	2 664	2 257	1 870	1 723	1 711	1 462
Services:												
Financial institutions	KRLP	143	247	266	292	241	185	125	105	79	54	45
Business services	KRLQ	662	1 284	1 859	1 843	1 537	1 354	1 176	1 117	1 057	1 162	1 127
Hotels and catering	KRLR	867	1 481	2 366	2 437	2 102	1 956	1 736	1 603	1 309	1 376	1 263
Total	KHGS	1 672	3 012	4 491	4 572	3 880	3 495	3 037	2 825	2 445	2 592	2 435
Other	KHGT	1 014	1 857	2 530	2 315	1 893	1 732	2 161	2 077	2 157	2 179	2 199
Total: self-employed	KRLT	8 489	14 609	19 525	18 561	15 114	13 282	12 667	11 269	10 420	10 723	9 952
Other individuals												
Employees	KRLU	1 172	1 639	2 588	2 507	2 279	1 981	2 471	2 625	3 141	4 357	4 601
No occupation and unemployed	KRLV	1 107	2 811	4 325	4 816	3 696	2 859	3 294	3 051	3 384	4 457	4 856
Directors and promoters of companies	KRLW	427	667	965	862	628	484	368	310	272	330	296
Occupation unknown	KRLX	865	2 906	4 703	4 270	3 917	3 327	3 003	2 637	2 430	1 744	1 845
Total: other individuals	KRLY	3 571	8 023	12 581	12 455	10 520	8 651	9 136	8 623	9 227	10 888	11 598
Total bankruptcies and deeds of arrangements[1]	KRLZ	12 060	22 632	32 106	31 016	25 634	21 933	21 803	19 892	19 647	21 611	21 550

1 From January 1991 Industrial Analysis excludes Deeds of Arrangement.

Source: Department of Trade and Industry: 020 7215 3291/3305

22.23 Industry analysis: company insolvencies[1]
England and Wales

		1990	1991	1992	1993	1994	1995	1996	1997	1998	1999	2000
Industry												
Agriculture and horticulture	KRMA	111	135	191	157	166	99	89	51	65	75	67
Manufacturing:												
Food, drink and tobacco	KRMB	109	171	215	213	142	130	163	93	89	67	104
Chemicals	KRMC	97	134	141	91	108	69	65	31	57	35	61
Metals and engineering	KRMD	972	1 344	1 621	1 381	932	681	658	591	594	698	683
Textiles and clothing	KRME	921	1 052	1 120	917	736	567	568	596	526	419	423
Timber and furniture	KRMF	391	527	508	333	252	267	249	181	149	190	187
Paper, printing and publishing	KRMG	552	856	830	777	579	452	438	364	426	387	386
Other	KRMH	792	939	1 014	878	859	681	599	613	652	780	678
Total	KRMI	3 834	5 023	5 449	4 590	3 608	2 847	2 740	2 469	2 493	2 576	2 522
Construction and transport:												
Construction	KRMJ	2 445	3 373	3 830	3 189	2 401	1 844	1 610	1 419	1 325	1 529	1 474
Transport and communication	KRMK	932	1 246	1 261	1 082	774	706	682	540	504	443	526
Total	KHGU	3 377	4 619	5 091	4 271	3 175	2 550	2 292	1 959	1 829	1 972	2 000
Wholesaling:												
Food, drink and tobacco	KRML	235	287	388	231	244	205	183	158	139	187	150
Motor vehicles	KRMM	107	152	186	142	112	83	95	41	60	38	29
Other	KRMN	724	841	672	639	638	678	429	340	364	394	391
Total	KHGV	1 066	1 280	1 246	1 012	994	966	707	539	563	619	570
Retailing:												
Food, drink and tobacco	KRMO	244	291	406	388	299	246	236	219	186	193	200
Motor vehicles and filling stations	KRMP	174	245	339	229	226	195	227	132	120	142	141
Other	KRMQ	1 181	1 578	1 732	1 388	1 186	1 127	956	891	847	919	853
Total	KHGW	1 599	2 114	2 477	2 005	1 711	1 568	1 419	1 242	1 153	1 254	1 194
Services:												
Financial institutions	KRMR	303	394	563	421	259	198	222	111	101	118	57
Business services	KRMS	1 558	2 396	2 788	2 415	1 807	1 525	1 500	1 528	1 617	1 831	1 605
Hotels and catering	KRMT	489	748	1 010	912	777	692	708	609	626	562	530
Total	KJRS	2 350	3 538	4 361	3 748	2 843	2 415	2 430	2 248	2 344	2 511	2 192
Other	KHGX	2 714	5 118	5 610	4 925	4 231	4 091	3 784	4 102	4 756	5 273	5 772
Total company insolvencies	KHGY	15 051	21 827	24 425	20 708	16 728	14 536	13 461	12 610	13 203	14 280	14 317

1 Including partnerships.

Source: Department of Trade and Industry: 020 7215 3291/3305

23 Service industry

Service industry

Annual Business Inquiry *(Tables 23.1, 23.3 and 23.4)*
For details of the Annual Business Inquiry, see the text accompanying table **21.1**.

Retail trade: index numbers of value and volume *(Table 23.2)*
The main purpose of the Retail Sales Inquiry (RSI) is to provide up to date information on short period movements in the level of retail sales. In principle, the RSI covers the retail activity of every business classified in the retail sector (Division 52 of the 1992 Standard Industrial Classification) in Great Britain. A business will be classified to the retail sector if its main activity is one of the individual 4 digit SIC categories within Division 52. The retail activity of a business is then defined by its retail turnover i.e. the sale of all retail goods (note that petrol, for example, is not a retail good).

The RSI is compiled from the information returned to the statutory monthly retail trades inquiry. The inquiry is addressed to a stratified sample of 5000 businesses classified to the retail sector, the stratification being by 'type of store' (the individual 4 digit SIC categories within Division 52) and by size. The sample structure is designed to ensure that the inquiry estimates are as accurate as possible. In terms of the selection, this means that:

- each of the individual 4 digit SIC categories are represented, their coverage depending upon the relative size of the category and the variability of the data.

- within each 4 digit SIC category, the larger retailers tend to be fully enumerated with decreasing proportions of medium and smaller retailers.

The structure of the inquiry is updated every two or three years at the time of rebasing, by reference to the more comprehensive results of the Annual Retail Inquiry (ARI). The inquiry estimates are benchmarked to the ARI results at the same time. The monthly inquiry also incorporates a rotation element for the smallest retailers. This helps to spread the burden more fairly, as well as improving the representativeness between successive benchmarks.

During 1998, the retail sales index was rebased using detailed information from the 1995 annual retailing inquiry. The reference year is now set at 1995=100. Details of the work, together with revised figures for January 1990 to December 1997, were published in *ONS News Release* (98) 349 on 21 October 1998.

The latest summary statistics are published each month by *First Release*. More disaggregated value indices (not seasonally adjusted) are published each month in *Business Monitor SDM28*, available from NS Direct Sales or via the National Statistics Website: www.statistics.gov.uk.

23.1 Retail businesses
United Kingdom
All currency values are £ million

		1996[1]	1997	1998	1999
Number of businesses	ZABE	211 062	218 333	216 000	216 826
Total turnover[2]	ZABL	201 951	207 489	221 267	230 478
Value added tax in total turnover	ZABM	19 523	20 410	21 778	22 585
Retail turnover[2]	ZABN	189 726	193 928	202 538	209 079
Non-retail turnover[2]	ZABO	12 226	13 561	18 729	21 399
Other income					
Value of commercial insurance claims received	ZABP	..	..	117	87
Subsidies received from UK government sources and the EC	ZAEN	..	..	13	23
Employment costs[3]	ZABQ	19 103	21 178	22 958	25 136
Gross wages and salaries	ZABR	17 342	19 165	20 552	22 438
Redundancy and severance payments	ZABS	..	..	145	332
Employers' National Insurance contributions	ZABT	1 761	2 013	1 514	1 577
Contributions to pension funds[4]	ZABU	..	..	747	789
Stocks	ZABV				
Increase during year		1 154	1 387	1 204	1 264
Value at end of year	ZABW	18 129	19 593	19 849	20 765
Total turnover[3] divided by end-year stocks (Quotient)	ZABX	10.1	9.5	10.1	10.0
Purchases of goods, materials and services[3]	ZABY	145 472	148 254	157 694	162 752
Goods bought for resale without processing	ZABZ	124 937	126 833	134 241	137 500
Energy and water products for own consumption[5]	ZACA	2 483	2 568	1 832	1 816
Goods and materials[5]	ZACB	..	..	3 035	2 937
Hiring, leasing or renting of plant, machinery and vehicles	ZACC	436	677	662	612
Commercial insurance premiums	ZACD	598	617	554	569
Road transport services	ZACE	1 830	2 051	1 847	1 818
Telecommunication services	ZACF	416	468	474	512
Computer and related services	ZACG	361	484	534	642
Advertising and marketing services	ZACH	2 162	2 491	2 429	2 890
Other services	ZACI	12 250	12 066	12 085	13 457
Taxes, duties and levies	ZACJ	2 678	3 534	3 823	4 100
National non-domestic (business) rates	ZACK	2 405	2 965	3 116	3 308
Other amounts paid for taxes, duties and levies	ZACL	273	569	707	792
Capital expenditure					
Cost of acquisitions	ZACM	6 327	7 722	8 264	8 301
Proceeds from disposals	ZACN	704	1 438	1 141	2 274
Net capital expenditure	ZACO	5 623	6 284	7 123	6 027
Amount included in acquisitions for assets under finance leasing arrangements	ZACP	..	..	..	..
Work of a capital nature carried out by own staff (included in acquisitions)	ZACQ	58	77	80	81
Gross margin					
Amount	ZACR	58 645	61 633	65 837	70 460
As a percentage of adjusted turnover[6]	ZACS	32.1	32.9	33.0	30.6
Approximate gross value added at basic prices	ZACT	37 895	39 719	42 502	45 885

23.1

continued

Retail businesses
United Kingdom
All currency values are £ million

£ million

		1996[1]	1997	1998	1999
Total turnover	ZABL	201 951	207 489	221 267	230 478
Retail turnover	ZABN	189 726	193 928	202 538	209 079
1 Fruit and vegetables	ZACU	6 562	6 752	7 383	7 359
2 Meat, poultry and game	ZACV	8 735	8 494	9 047	8 225
3 Fish, crustaceans and molluscs	ZACW	1 389	1 580	1 587	1 595
4 Bread, cakes, flour and sugar confectionery	ZACX	7 755	8 168	8 204	9 254
5 Alcoholic drink	ZACY	8 076	8 569	9 116	9 875
6 Soft drinks	ZACZ	3 490	3 434	3 426	3 913
7 Tobacco and smokers' requisites	ZADA	9 256	8 749	8 868	9 007
8 Dairy products and eggs	ZADB	7 422	7 196	7 472	7 468
9 Canned and packaged foods[7]	ZADC	..	7 800	8 558	9 252
10 Other food for human consumption[7]	ZADD	21 884	13 769	15 066	14 140
11 Pharmaceutical preparations	ZADE	1 985	1 666	1 791	1 765
12 National Health Service receipts	ZADF	5 221	5 262	5 588	5 771
13 Medical and orthopaedic goods	ZADG	817	831	943	877
14 Perfumes, cosmetics and toilet articles	ZADH	8 666	7 106	7 421	8 062
15 Clothing fabrics, haberdashery etc.	ZADI	499	526	544	614
16 Household textiles	ZADJ	1 611	1 518	1 665	1 766
17 Men's wear and accessories[8]	ZADK	6 388	6 802	6 772	6 840
18 Ladies' wear and accessories[8]	ZADL	14 839	13 261	13 861	14 892
19 Adult clothing of fur and leather accessories	ZADM	315	361	363	399
20 Boys', girls' and infants' wear[9]	ZADN	2 845	2 790	3 003	3 118
21 Footwear[10]	ZADO	4 332	4 172	3 924	3 688
22 Leather and travel goods	ZADP	493	530	587	603
23 Domestic gas appliances	ZADQ	429	516	447	305
24 Soft furnishings	ZADR	1 341	1 503	1 605	1 742
25 Other household articles	ZADS	3 945	4 495	4 913	5 293
26 Domestic furniture	ZADT	6 316	7 299	7 558	7 866
27 Domestic electrical appliances	ZADU	3 787	4 168	4 135	4 138
28 Audio and visual equipment[11]	ZADV	3 926	3 708	3 580	3 673
29 Audio and video tape, records, compact discs etc.	ZADW	3 008	3 488	3 333	3 570
30 Home computers and computer software[12]	ZADX	..	2 516	2 739	2 831
31 Decorators and DIY supplies	ZADY	5 432	5 165	5 378	5 906
32 Wallpaper	ZADZ	489	566	414	387
33 Lawnmowers	ZAEA	247	246	270	253
34 Books, newspapers and periodicals	ZAEB	5 302	5 737	5 612	5 685
35 Stationery	ZAEC	1 553	1 913	1 873	1 908
36 Floor coverings	ZAED	2 367	2 537	2 759	2 887
37 Photographic and optical goods; spectacles and contact lenses	ZAEE	2 664	2 736	1 961	2 405
38 Office and telecommunications equipment[11]	ZAEF	2 682	1 143	1 373	1 578
39 Jewellery, silverware and plate; watches and clocks	ZAEG	2 766	3 246	2 809	2 791
40 Souvenirs, gifts and novelties	ZAEH	2 864	2 830	2 827	3 150
41 Prints and picture frames; works of art[13]	ZAEI	580	784	523	543
42 Stamps and coins; toys and games; sports and camping; cycles[14]	ZAEJ	5 545	6 805	8 098	8 103
43 Antiques and other second-hand goods[15]	ZAEK	1 173	1 416	1 715	1 754
44 Other goods not elsewhere specified	ZAEL	10 042	10 878	12 532	13 005
45 Hire and repair of personal and household goods[16]	ZAEM	687	899	896	820

1 Data for 1996 were calculated on a different basis from those of subsequent year (see chapter introduction).
2 Inclusive of VAT.
3 Exclusive of VAT.
4 Previously combined with employers' National Insurance contributions for 1995 to 1997.
5 Previously combined with purchases of energy, water and materials for 1995 to 1997.
6 Turnover is adjusted to take out VAT.
7 "Canned and packaged foods" were combined with "Other food for human consumption" in 1996.
8 Excludes sports clothing and second-hand clothes.

9 Excludes sports clothing.
10 Excludes sports shoes.
11 Includes computers and computer software in 1996 but excludes them in 1997, 1998 and 1999.
12 Included in commodities 28 and 38 in 1996.
13 Includes prams in 1996 but excludes them in 1997, 1998 and 1999.
14 Excludes prams in 1996 but includes them in 1997, 1998 and 1999; excludes sports clothing and footwear in 1996 but includes them in 1997, 1998 and 1999.
15 Excludes second-hand clothes in 1996 but includes them in 1997, 1998 and 1999.
16 The commodity values for 1996 cover hire and repair whilst those for 1997, 1998 and 1999 only cover repair.

Source: Office for National Statistics: 01633 812435

23.2 Retail trade: Index numbers of value and volume of sales
Great Britain

Weekly average 1995 = 100, not seasonally adjusted

Value		Sales in 1995 £million	1990	1991	1992	1993	1994	1995	1996	1997	1998	1999	2000
All retailing: total	EAFY	166 681	80.5	84.1	87.3	92.0	96.3	100.0	105.4	112.0	116.4	120.3	124.7
All retailing: large	EAFZ	119 937	74	78	83	89	94	100	107	115	121	126	132
All retailing: small	EAGA	46 743	99	100	100	101	102	100	102	103	104	104	106
Predominantly food stores: total	EAFS	74 914	74.1	80.2	85.7	90.1	94.4	100.0	105.3	110.7	116.3	120.3	124.4
Predominantly food stores: large	EAGK	57 713	68	75	82	87	93	100	107	113	120	125	129
Predominantly food stores: small	EAGL	17 201	100	102	102	102	100	100	100	102	103	105	109
Non specialised food stores: total	EAGB	60 602	68	75	81	87	93	100	107	113	119	124	128
Non specialised food stores: large	EAGC	54 878	66	73	80	86	92	100	107	114	121	125	130
Non specialised food stores: small	EAGD	5 724	91	95	96	97	98	100	102	104	104	108	112
Specialised food stores	EAPP	14 311	101	103	105	105	102	100	100	101	103	105	107
Retail sale of fruit and vegetables	EAOZ	1 283	117	115	108	102	98	100	100	102	112	104	108
Retail sale of meat and meat products	EAPA	2 515	132	129	122	116	107	100	97	92	89	91	96
Retail sale of fish, crustaceans and molluscs	EAPB	266	157	147	128	123	109	100	95	91	78	61	61
Retail sale of bread cakes and confectionery	EAPC	1 796	91	95	99	102	102	100	100	103	109	108	111
Retail sale of alcohol and other beverages	EAPD	3 208	89	90	95	95	96	100	101	104	105	110	100
Retail sale of tobacco products	EAPE	3 944	97	102	108	109	106	100	100	103	106	111	118
Other specialised food stores	EAPF	1 296	107	108	105	110	105	100	97	100	102	111	117
Predominantly non-food stores: total	EAFT	83 184	84.2	85.8	87.2	92.4	97.0	100.0	105.8	113.6	116.8	120.7	126.0
Predominantly non-food stores: large	EAGM	55 351	78	81	83	89	95	100	107	118	122	128	136
Predominantly non-food stores: small	EAGN	27 832	97	97	96	100	102	100	104	105	107	106	106
Non specialised predominantly non-food stores: total	EAGE	15 035	80.7	84.5	88.1	93.4	96.4	100.0	108.2	115.5	116.9	120.2	126.6
Non specialised predominantly non-food stores: large	EAGF	12 070	80	84	87	92	95	100	108	115	117	121	128
Non specialised predominantly non-food stores: small	EAGG	2 964	83	91	98	106	103	100	109	116	115	115	120
Pharmaceutical, medical, cosmetic and toilet goods	EAPQ	3 165	74	81	89	97	97	100	102	109	113	116	120
Textiles, clothing, footwear and leather: total	EAFU	26 100	84.7	85.8	87.2	91.2	96.8	100.0	104.2	111.8	112.4	114.9	118.4
Textiles clothing footwear and leather: large	EAGO	20 352	77	80	84	89	95	100	106	116	118	121	125
Textiles clothing footwear and leather: small	EAGP	5 746	118	111	101	102	103	100	97	96	93	92	94
Retail sale of textiles	EAPG	699	105	105	106	127	117	100	99	105	106	108	113
Retail sale of clothing: total	EAGH	21 535	83	85	87	90	96	100	106	113	115	118	122
Retail sale of clothing: large	EAGI	17 606	77	80	84	89	95	100	108	118	120	124	128
Retail sale of clothing: small	EAGJ	3 928	110	106	99	99	101	100	95	92	92	91	92
Retail sale of footwear and leather goods	EAPH	3 864	96	91	87	92	100	100	97	105	98	99	101
Household goods stores: total	EAFV	19 770	84.1	85.9	86.9	92.9	97.0	100.0	107.9	118.3	124.8	130.3	138.4
Household goods stores: large	EAGQ	13 273	70	75	81	87	94	100	109	122	130	138	150
Household goods stores: small	EAGR	6 496	115	108	101	106	104	100	106	112	114	115	115
Retail sale of furniture, lighting, etc.	EAPI	6 400	96	94	94	101	103	100	108	122	128	127	133

23.2 Retail trade: Index numbers of value and volume of sales
Great Britain
continued

Weekly average 1995 = 100, not seasonally adjusted

		Sales in 1995 £million	1990	1991	1992	1993	1994	1995	1996	1997	1998	1999	2000
Retail sale of electrical household appliances	EAPJ	7 727	79	80	79	86	91	100	108	119	124	132	141
Retail sale of hardware paint and glass	EAPK	5 642	81	87	91	96	100	100	107	114	122	131	141
Other specialised non-food stores: total	EAFW	22 280	85.4	86.3	87.1	92.5	97.3	100.0	104.1	110.0	114.8	119.3	123.4
Other specialised non-food stores: large	EAGS	9 655	89	85	81	89	94	100	103	119	124	137	150
Other specialised non-food stores: small	EAGT	12 624	83	87	92	95	100	100	105	103	108	106	103
Retail sale of books newspapers and periodicals	EAPL	4 078	84	88	92	97	99	100	104	109	117	118	118
Retail sale of floor covering	EAPM	1 045	93	91	92	98	99	100	107	116	99	90	94
Photo, optical and precision equipment office supplies and equipment	EAWH	2 676	113	112	111	97	97	100	104	103	104	115	124
Other retail sale in specialised stores not elsewhere specified	EAWK	10 201	89	87	83	90	95	100	105	112	120	128	130
Second-hand goods stores	EAQA	1 112	68	67	68	74	105	100	94	104	102	97	117
Other retail sale (non-store) and repair: total	EAFX	8 583	97.4	99.0	99.3	102.1	104.3	100.0	102.8	107.7	113.9	115.9	114.0
Other retail sale (non-store) and repair: large	EAGU	6 872	89	90	91	97	102	100	104	112	122	126	122
Other retail sale (non-store) and repair: small	EAGV	1 710	116	119	118	114	110	100	96	90	82	75	80
Retail sale via mail order houses	EAPN	6 629	87	89	92	98	103	100	103	109	117	123	121
Non-store retail excl. mail order	EAPO	1 544	113	113	110	107	106	100	100	102	101	87	88
Repair of personal and household goods	EAPR	408	84	99	106	115	106	100	104	110	110	106	105
Volume													
All retailing	EAHC	166 681	93.0	91.8	92.4	95.3	98.8	100.0	103.1	108.5	111.7	115.6	120.8
Predominantly food stores	EAGW	74 914	89.4	90.4	93.1	95.0	98.1	100.0	101.8	105.9	108.8	110.8	113.6
Predominantly non-food stores	EAGX	83 184	93.9	91.0	90.3	94.2	98.4	100.0	104.4	111.2	114.3	119.9	127.9
Non specialised predominantly non-food stores	EAHI	15 035	94.3	92.9	93.6	97.0	99.0	100.0	106.0	111.5	111.5	114.7	122.2
Textiles,clothing, footwear and leather	EAGY	26 100	89.9	88.0	89.1	92.3	97.5	100.0	104.3	111.2	112.0	117.1	124.7
Household goods stores	EAGZ	19 770	89.7	87.0	86.5	92.2	97.3	100.0	106.8	117.2	125.2	135.2	148.6
Other specialised non-food stores	EAHA	22 280	102.5	97.1	93.8	96.7	100.1	100.0	101.4	105.7	109.2	113.2	117.0
Other retail sale (non-store) and repair	EAHB	8 583	109.4	105.7	103.8	105.0	106.1	100.0	101.4	105.7	111.6	115.2	115.6

Source: Office for National Statistics: 01633 812609

23.3 Motor trades[1,2]
United Kingdom

	Number of businesses	Total turnover	Motor trades turnover	Retail sales of		Sales to other dealers of		Gross sales of used motor vehicles and motorcycles	Turnover from sales of petrol, diesel, oil and other petroleum products	Other motor trades sales and receipts (including parts and accessories, workshop receipts)	Non-motor trades turnover
				New cars	Other new motor vehicles and motorcycles	New cars	Other new motor vehicles and motorcycles				
	Number	£ million	£ million	£ million	£ million	£ million	£ million	£ million	£ million	£ million	£ million

Sale, maintenance and repair of motor vehicles and motorcycles; retail sale of automotive fuel (SIC 92 50.00)

	MKEQ	CMRH	CMRI	CMRJ	CMRK	CMRL	CMRM	CMRN	CMRO	CMRP	CMRQ
1995	70 278	100 742	97 579	18 169	3 177	14 123	2 444	23 101	11 847	24 718	3 163
1996	71 119	108 805	105 489	19 888	3 246	16 085	2 328	25 558	11 698	26 686	3 316
1997	72 527	119 069	115 445	23 119	3 311	15 762	2 395	28 328	12 871	29 656	3 624
1998	72 105	123 130	119 817	24 492	3 626	16 922	2 547	27 327	13 445	31 457	3 314
1999	72 298	128 662	125 520	25 734	3 555	16 769	2 935	28 027	15 436	33 063	3 142

Sale of motor vehicles (SIC 92 50.10)

	MKER	EWRI	FDFZ	FDGA	FDGB	FDGC	FDGD	FDGE	FDGF	FDGG	FDHJ
1995	39 473	69 177	68 425	16 517	2 740	14 076	2 352	20 839	1 328	10 573	752
1996	36 383	76 920	76 009	18 877	2 878	16 053	2 225	23 793	1 271	10 912	911
1997	34 664	84 395	83 548	22 554	2 890	15 737	2 255	26 910	1 182	12 020	846
1998	31 196	87 035	86 122	23 897	3 125	16 896	2 435	26 124	1 379	12 266	913
1999	29 761	87 996	87 323	24 817	2 934	16 742	2 621	25 860	1 326	13 024	673

Maintenance and repair of motor vehicles (SIC 92 50.20)

	MKES	FDHK	FDHL	FDHM	FDHN	FDHO	FDHP	FDHQ	FDHR	FDHS	FDHT
1995	17 363	8 930	8 698	1 238	169	31	1	1 467	741	5 051	232
1996	19 709	8 263	8 147	796	129	19	1	1 021	550	5 631	116
1997	22 027	8 011	7 832	417	78	20	5	662	286	6 361	179
1998	24 680	8 975	8 862	297	54	17	–	312	343	7 839	114
1999	26 089	11 116	10 949	724	61	22	8	1 416	655	8 062	167

Sale of motor vehicle parts and accessories (SIC 92 50.30)

	MKET	FDIW	FDIX	FDIY	FDIZ	FDJA	FDJB	FDJC	FDJD	FDJE	FDJF
1995	4 801	9 437	9 101	223	99	10	–	259	130	8 380	336
1996	5 829	10 066	9 806	70	24	9	–	118	78	9 507	260
1997	6 583	10 741	10 567	9	21	–	–	70	79	10 388	175
1998	7 187	10 962	10 808	8	5	–	–	89	111	10 595	154
1999	7 630	11 602	11 539	46	34	1	–	111	147	11 200	64

Sale, maintenance and repair of motorcycles and related parts and accessories (SIC 92 50.40)

	MKEU	FDKI	FDKJ	FDKK	FDKL	FDKM	FDKN	FDKO	FDKP	FDKQ	FDKR
1995	1 276	1 054	1 024	95	168	4	91	291	10	365	30
1996	1 231	1 019	996	15	214	–	102	342	3	320	23
1997	1 522	1 248	1 225	–	322	–	135	344	2	422	23
1998	1 782	1 274	1 196	–	441	–	112	281	1	361	78
1999	2 077	1 665	1 625	17	526	–	306	342	3	432	40

Retail sale of automotive fuel (SIC 92 50.50)

	MKEV	FDLV	FDLW	FDLX	FDLY	FDLZ	FDMA	FDMB	FDMC	FDMD	FDME
1995	7 365	12 144	10 331	96	1	2	–	245	9 638	349	1 813
1996	7 967	12 537	10 531	130	1	4	–	284	9 796	316	2 006
1997	7 701	14 674	12 273	139	–	5	–	342	11 322	465	2 400
1998	7 260	14 884	12 829	290	1	9	–	521	11 611	396	2 056
1999	6 741	16 283	14 084	130	–	5	1	298	13 306	346	2 199

23.3 Motor trades[1,2]
United Kingdom
continued

	Total purchases	Energy, water and materials	Used motor vehicles and motorcycles	Parts used solely in repair and servicing activities	Other goods for resale	Hiring, leasing and renting of plant, machinery and vehicles	Commercial insurance premiums	Road transport services	Telecommun- ication services	Computer and related services	Advertising and marketing services	Other services
	£ million	£ million	£ million	£ million	£ million	£ million	£ million	£ million	£ million	£ million	£ million	£ million

Sale, maintenance and repair of motor vehicles and motorcycles; retail sale of automotive fuel (SIC 92 50.00)

	CMNR	CMRS	COBU	CMRT	CMRU	CMRV	CMRW	CMRX	CMRY	CMRZ	CMSA	CMSB
1995	87 908	..	20 751	..	57 452	..	..	..	..	..	..	..
1996	94 753	505	23 001	5 739	59 599	183	328	299	226	132	1 316	3 425
1997	102 470	643	25 327	5 615	64 809	245	361	327	245	130	1 190	3 579
1998	106 434	1 638	24 673	6 237	67 545	228	343	326	250	186	1 464	3 545
1999	111 024	1 226	25 246	6 361	71 519	249	360	379	282	231	1 631	3 540

Sale of motor vehicles (SIC 92 50.10)

	FDGH	FDGI	FDGJ	FDGK	FDGL	FDGM	FDGN	FDGO	FDGP	FDGQ	FDGR	FDGS
1995	61 540	..	18 733	..	37 447	..	..	..	..	..	..	..
1996	68 655	248	21 483	3 048	39 869	86	163	202	123	88	1 110	2 235
1997	74 662	298	24 065	2 803	43 307	106	179	191	133	88	998	2 495
1998	77 395	975	23 604	2 592	46 218	90	156	205	126	99	1 233	2 097
1999	78 041	632	23 240	2 828	47 244	75	176	216	149	140	1 367	1 976

Maintenance and repair of motor vehicles (SIC 92 50.20)

	FDHU	FDHV	FDHW	FDHX	FDHY	FDHZ	FDIA	FDIB	FDIC	FDID	FDIE	FDIF
1995	6 623	..	1 324	..	2 576	..	..	..	..	..	..	..
1996	5 703	115	900	2 266	1 583	59	89	21	45	17	89	519
1997	5 103	176	604	2 291	1 235	97	102	37	49	18	70	423
1998	5 667	292	300	3 171	846	86	112	23	54	21	74	688
1999	7 238	298	1 151	3 081	1 591	115	116	33	66	35	92	662

Sale of motor vehicle parts and accessories (SIC 92 50.30)

	FDJG	FDJH	FDJI	FDJJ	FDJK	FDJL	FDJM	FDJN	FDJO	FDJP	FDJQ	FDJR
1995	7 826	..	226	..	6 664	..	..	..	..	..	..	..
1996	8 107	69	101	291	7 044	31	42	69	40	21	82	317
1997	8 336	74	68	328	7 186	31	46	89	46	21	92	355
1998	8 625	169	144	346	7 089	43	50	88	53	42	111	489
1999	9 208	205	102	296	7 715	51	38	78	49	40	129	506

Sale, maintenance and repair of motorcycles and related parts and accessories (SIC 92 50.40)

	FDKT	FDKU	FDKV	FDKW	FDKX	FDKY	FDKZ	FDLA	FDLB	FDLC	FDLD	FDLE
1995	884	..	247	..	543	..	..	..	..	..	..	..
1996	856	3	271	29	489	1	5	4	2	2	14	36
1997	1 059	17	293	43	629	1	8	4	4	1	11	49
1998	1 089	46	226	29	731	1	4	3	2	1	21	24
1999	1 423	10	313	55	958	1	7	6	4	3	22	44

Retail sale of automotive fuel (SIC 92 50.50)

	FDMF	FDMG	FDMH	FDMI	FDMJ	FDMK	FDML	COBV	COBW	COBX	COBY	COBZ
1995	11 035	..	221	..	10 222	..	..	..	..	..	..	..
1996	11 432	70	246	105	10 614	6	29	3	16	4	21	318
1997	13 311	78	297	149	12 452	10	26	6	13	2	19	258
1998	13 657	154	399	98	12 661	8	21	7	14	23	25	247
1999	15 115	82	440	101	14 013	8	23	46	15	13	21	353

23.3 Motor trades[1,2]
United Kingdom
continued

	Taxes, duties and levies			Capital Expenditure			
	Total taxes and levies	National (non-domestic business) rates	Other amounts paid for taxes, duties and levies	Cost of acquisitions	Cost of disposals	Net capital expenditure	Work of a capital nature carried out by own staff (included in acquisitions)
	£ million	£ million	£ million	£ million	£ million	£ million	£ million

Sale, maintenance and repair of motor vehicles and motorcycles; retail sale of automotive fuel (SIC 92 50.00)

	CMSC	CMSD	CMSE	CMSF	CMSG	CMSH	CMSI
1995	..	..	..	825	338	487	..
1996	598	467	131	827	354	473	7
1997	691	499	192	1 550	569	981	14
1998	951	497	454	2 035	836	1 198	39
1999	984	561	423	1 995	1 115	880	21

Sale of motor vehicles (SIC 92 50.10)

	FDGT	FDGU	FDGV	FDGW	FDGX	FDGY	FDGZ
1995	..	..	..	566	275	291	..
1996	330	216	114	617	311	306	5
1997	373	277	96	934	398	535	7
1998	610	240	370	1 232	655	577	27
1999	587	245	343	1 228	554	674	13

Maintenance and repair of motor vehicles (SIC 92 50.20)

	FDIG	FDIH	FDII	FDIJ	FDIK	FDIL	FDIM
1995	..	..	..	70	14	56	..
1996	106	103	3	72	14	58	1
1997	141	84	58	266	38	228	4
1998	141	114	28	437	97	340	2
1999	172	132	39	390	86	304	7

Sale of motor vehicle parts and accessories (SIC 92 50.30)

	FDJS	FDJT	FDJU	FDJV	FDJW	FDJX	FDJY
1995	..	..	..	96	17	79	..
1996	111	104	7	92	15	77	1
1997	105	80	25	239	81	158	3
1998	100	73	27	181	43	138	6
1999	101	89	12	204	105	99	1

Sale, maintenance and repair of motorcycles and related parts and accessories (SIC 92 50.40)

	FDLF	FDLG	FDLH	FDLI	FDLJ	FDLK	FDLL
1995	..	..	..	11	2	9	..
1996	8	6	2	11	2	9	..
1997	12	11	1	24	6	18	..
1998	17	10	6	26	10	16	4
1999	18	7	11	23	3	20	1

Retail sale of automotive fuel (SIC 92 50.50)

	COCA	COCB	COCC	COCD	COCE	COCF	COCG
1995	..	..	..	82	30	52	..
1996	43	38	5	35	12	23	..
1997	60	48	12	88	47	41	..
1998	83	59	24	158	31	128	..
1999	107	89	18	151	367	−216	..

23.3 Motor trades[1,2]
United Kingdom
continued

	Stocks			Employment costs			Gross margin		
	Increase during year	Value at end of year	Total turnover divided by end-year stocks	Total employment costs	Gross wages and salaries paid	National insurance and pension contributions	Amount	As a percentage of adjusted turnover	Approximate gross value added at basic prices
	£ million	£ million	Quotient	£ million	£ million	£ million	£ million	Percentage	£ million

Sale, maintenance and repair of motor vehicles and motorcycles; retail sale of automotive fuel (SIC 92 50.00)

	CMSJ	CMSK	CMSL	CMSM	COBP	COBQ	COBR	COBS	COBT
1995	953	10 294	9.8	5 683	5 082	601	23 492	23.3	13 787
1996	888	11 127	9.8	6 206	5 564	642	21 354	20.7	14 816
1997	1 388	12 079	9.9	6 982	6 229	753	24 703	21.8	17 804
1998	1 133	12 861	9.6	7 660	6 801	859	25 809	22.1	17 463
1999	1 030	13 897	9.3	8 167	7 284	883	26 332	21.5	18 718

Sale of motor vehicles (SIC 92 50.10)

	FDHA	FDHB	FDHC	FDHD	FDHE	FDHF	FDHG	FDHH	FDHI
1995	729	8 003	8.6	3 068	2 728	340	13 726	19.9	8 366
1996	748	8 786	8.8	3 381	3 024	357	13 268	18.0	8 904
1997	1 213	9 494	8.9	3 765	3 349	417	15 433	18.9	10 856
1998	948	10 233	8.5	4 048	3 594	454	15 569	18.4	10 273
1999	985	10 894	8.1	4 270	3 802	468	15 522	18.2	10 970

Maintenance and repair of motor vehicles (SIC 92 50.20)

	FDIN	FDIO	FDIP	FDIQ	FDIR	FDIS	FDIT	FDIU	FDIV
1995	57	645	13.8	1 221	1 100	121	5 087	57.0	2 364
1996	30	558	14.8	1 366	1 230	136	3 544	59.1	2 588
1997	46	544	14.7	1 436	1 273	162	3 924	68.6	2 901
1998	28	515	17.4	1 718	1 517	201	4 687	80.7	3 318
1999	−3	747	14.9	1 931	1 726	205	5 288	65.8	3 895

Sale of motor vehicle parts and accessories (SIC 92 50.30)

	FDJZ	FDKA	FDKB	FDKC	FDKD	FDKE	FDKF	FDKG	FDKH
1995	129	1 136	8.3	939	842	97	2 676	28.4	1 740
1996	81	1 231	8.2	1 018	911	107	2 711	27.7	2 034
1997	66	1 329	8.1	1 231	1 104	127	3 225	31.0	2 450
1998	53	1 332	8.2	1 291	1 141	149	3 436	32.4	2 374
1999	31	1 464	7.9	1 299	1 155	144	3 479	30.8	2 422

Sale, maintenance and repair of motorcycles and related parts and accessories (SIC 92 50.40)

	FDLM	FDLN	FDLO	FDLP	FDLQ	FDLR	FDLS	FDLT	FDLU
1995	15	187	5.6	85	76	9	279	26.5	185
1996	16	216	4.7	69	61	8	246	24.8	177
1997	26	263	4.7	93	83	10	309	25.6	214
1998	77	333	3.8	102	90	11	365	29.3	259
1999	−24	291	5.7	128	115	13	314	19.5	218

Retail sale of automotive fuel (SIC 92 50.50)

	COCH	COCI	COCJ	COCK	COCL	COCM	COCN	CMQN	CMQO
1995	23	323	37.6	370	336	34	1 724	14.2	1 132
1996	13	336	37.3	372	338	34	1 585	12.7	1 113
1997	37	449	32.7	456	420	36	1 812	12.5	1 388
1998	27	449	33.1	501	458	43	1 752	11.8	1 240
1999	42	501	32.5	539	486	53	1 729	10.7	1 212

1 Figures are exclusive of VAT.
2 Data for 1995 and 1996 were collected on a different basis from those for 1997 onwards.

Source: Office for National Statistics: 01633 812435

23.4 Catering and allied trades[1]
United Kingdom

			Taxes and levies[1]			Capital expenditure[1]			
	Number of businesses	Total turnover[2]	Total taxes and levies	National (non-domestic business) rates	Other amounts paid for taxes duties and levies	Capital acquisitions	Capital disposals	Net capital expenditure	Work of a capital nature carried out by your own staff (included in acquisitions)
	Number	£ million	£ million	£ million	£ million	£ million	£ million	£ million	£ million

Total catering and allied trades (SIC 92 55.00)

	MKEK	CMKX	CMLM	CMLJ	CMLL	CMLP	CMLQ	CMLK	CMLR
1995	112 398	39 057	..	..	..	2 822	551	2 271	..
1996	110 583	41 666	979	787	192	2 991	445	2 546	14
1997	110 245	45 844	1 082	899	183	3 909	465	3 444	14
1998	111 815	48 680	1 215	1 053	162	4 453	519	3 934	30
1999	114 353	51 014	1 282	1 144	139	4 794	642	4 152	51

Hotels and motels (SIC 92 55.11 and 55.12)

	MKEL	CMLW	CMML	CMMI	CMMK	CMMO	CMMP	CMMJ	CMMQ
1995	12 563	8 226	..	..	..	612	125	487	..
1996	12 163	8 933	244	226	18	782	195	587	3
1997	11 555	9 589	255	228	28	1 116	99	1 018	8
1998	11 374	10 333	259	254	5	1 221	105	1 116	3
1999	11 381	10 637	257	248	9	1 258	197	1 061	8

Camping sites and other provision of short-stay accommodation (SIC 92 55.21 to 55.23)

	MKEM	CMMV	CMNK	CMNH	CMNJ	CMNN	CMNO	CMNI	CMNP
1995	3 065	1 440	..	..	..	194	22	172	..
1996	3 094	1 620	43	43	..	159	15	144	1
1997	3 289	1 945	59	50	9	253	36	216	2
1998	3 435	2 071	67	62	6	261	37	224	2
1999	3 688	1 978	61	54	7	275	38	237	7

Restaurants or cafes, take-away food shops (SIC 92 55.30)

	MKEN	CMNU	CMOJ	CMOG	CMOI	CMOM	CMON	CMOH	CMOO
1995	46 575	11 071	..	..	..	651	83	568	..
1996	46 379	11 643	246	225	21	625	66	559	1
1997	46 984	12 660	272	250	22	720	62	657	2
1998	48 362	13 710	305	290	15	971	122	849	1
1999	49 955	14 613	386	360	26	960	137	823	9

Licensed clubs with entertainment, independent, tenanted, managed public houses or wine bars (SIC 92 55.40)[4]

	MKEO	CMOT	CMPI	CMPF	CMPH	CMPL	CMPM	CMPG	CMPN
1995	46 395	14 868	..	..	..	1 300	310	990	..
1996	45 134	15 484	423	270	153	1 364	164	1 200	8
1997	44 198	16 792	451	336	115	1 734	265	1 470	2
1998	44 283	17 820	559	429	130	1 910	251	1 658	12
1999	44 647	18 414	551	459	92	2 195	263	1 932	25

Canteen operator, catering contractor (SIC 92 55.51 and 55.52)

	MKEP	CMPS	CMQH	CMQE	CMQG	CMQK	CMQL	CMQF	CMQM
1995	3 800	3 452	..	..	..	65	11	54	..
1996	3 813	3 986	23	23	..	61	5	56	1
1997	4 219	4 858	44	35	9	86	3	83	–
1998	4 361	4 748	24	19	5	91	5	87	12
1999	4 682	5 372	28	23	5	106	8	99	2

23.4 Catering and allied trades[1]
United Kingdom
continued

	Stocks[1]		Purchases of goods and services[1]									
	Increase during year	Value at end of year	Total purchases	Energy, water and materials	Goods for resale	Hiring, leasing of plant, machinery etc.	Commercial insurance premiums	Road transport services	Telecommun-ication services	Computer and related services	Advertising and marketing services	Other services
	£ million	£ million	£ million	£ million	£ million	£ million	£ million	£ million	£ million	£ million	£ million	£ million

Total catering and allied trades (SIC 92 55.00)

	CMLN	CMLO	CMLI	CMKZ	CMLA	CMLB	CMLC	CMLD	CMLE	CMLF	CMLG	CMLH
1995	37	767	19 951	..	8 476	..	..	..	..	..	..	..
1996	38	787	19 966	6 108	7 971	208	281	62	154	36	477	4 669
1997	48	840	21 371	8 053	7 338	234	285	89	187	50	546	4 589
1998	43	969	22 702	9 335	7 094	273	271	51	189	62	581	4 846
1999	65	1 082	23 985	8 726	8 086	309	274	99	214	104	580	5 592

Hotels and motels (SIC 92 55.11 and 55.12)

	CMMM	CMMN	CMMH	CMLY	CMLZ	CMMA	CMMB	CMMC	CMMD	CMME	CMMF	CMMG
1995	3	115	3 467	..	706	..	..	..	..	..	..	..
1996	−10	130	3 413	1 211	548	66	83	14	64	15	173	1 239
1997	−1	137	3 532	1 487	506	68	73	27	60	17	162	1 132
1998	1	157	3 702	1 633	512	54	72	11	58	17	169	1 178
1999	−5	202	3 978	1 735	445	66	70	23	62	35	172	1 369

Camping sites and other provision of short-stay accommodation (SIC 92 55.21 to 55.23)

	CMNL	CMNM	CMNG	CMMX	CMMY	CMMZ	CMNA	CMNB	CMNC	CMND	CMNE	CMNF
1995	3	56	705	..	265	..	..	..	..	..	..	..
1996	4	65	761	165	252	8	27	6	10	3	47	243
1997	8	87	887	172	278	11	23	5	10	5	55	327
1998	−1	91	932	212	265	11	22	3	15	6	76	321
1999	4	93	925	216	251	5	24	10	10	6	62	341

Restaurants or cafes, take-away food shops (SIC 92 55.30)

	CMOK	CMOL	CMOF	CMNW	CMNX	CMNY	CMNZ	CMOA	CMOB	CMOC	CMOD	CMOE
1995	10	179	5 669	..	1 783	..	..	..	..	..	..	..
1996	6	185	5 725	2 212	1 679	21	66	15	30	5	119	1 578
1997	14	206	6 175	2 926	1 538	27	78	22	41	7	159	1 376
1998	16	231	6 683	3 197	1 611	49	66	10	43	11	159	1 537
1999	24	298	6 918	2 936	1 974	53	70	31	61	19	170	1 605

Licensed clubs with entertainment, independent, tenanted, managed public houses or wine bars (SIC 92 55.40)[4]

	CMPJ	CMPK	CMPE	CMOV	CMOW	CMOX	CMOY	CMOZ	CMPA	CMPB	CMPC	CMPD
1995	18	359	8 440	..	5 367	..	..	..	..	..	..	..
1996	29	338	8 203	1 298	5 143	86	93	17	41	4	125	1 396
1997	15	340	8 665	2 042	4 800	95	96	17	64	13	158	1 379
1998	21	408	9 147	2 796	4 389	96	96	15	62	17	160	1 517
1999	29	397	9 442	2 056	4 916	149	92	15	68	28	162	1 957

Canteen operator, catering contractor (SIC 92 55.51 and 55.52)

	CMQI	CMQJ	CMQD	CMPU	CMPV	CMPW	CMPX	CMPY	CMPZ	CMQA	CMQB	CMQC
1995	3	58	1 670	..	355	..	..	..	..	..	..	..
1996	9	69	1 864	1 222	349	27	12	10	9	9	13	213
1997	12	71	2 111	1 427	216	32	14	18	11	9	11	374
1998	7	82	2 237	1 497	317	63	16	12	11	10	18	293
1999	12	92	2 721	1 784	500	35	17	21	14	15	14	321

23.4 Catering and allied trades[1]
United Kingdom
continued

	Employment costs[1]			Gross margin[5]			Accommodation	
	Total employment costs	Gross wages and salaries paid	National insurance and pension contributions	Amount	As a percentage of turnover	Value added at basic prices[5]	Number of establishments	Letting bedplaces
	£ million	£ million	£ million	£ million	Percentage	£ million	Number	Number
Total catering and allied trades (SIC 92 55.00)								
	CMKY	CMKV	CMKW	CMQP	CMQQ	CMQR	CMLS	CMLT
1995	7 742	7 133	609	24 950	74.7	13 475	..	..
1996	8 214	7 570	644	27 634	77.3	15 639	..	..
1997	9 200	8 493	707	32 088	81.1	18 055	23 207	1 591 979
1998	10 261	9 461	799	34 870	82.9	19 333	23 962	1 672 755
1999	11 011	10 175	836	35 849	81.3	20 189	..	..
Hotels and motels (SIC 92 55.11 and 55.12)								
	CMLX	CMLU	CMLV	CMQS	CMQT	CMQU	CMMR	CMMS
1995	2 059	1 887	172	6 354	90.0	3 593	–	–
1996	2 179	1 998	181	7 047	92.5	4 182	–	–
1997	2 257	2 071	186	7 663	93.6	4 636	13 505	727 016
1998	2 460	2 251	209	8 284	94.2	5 101	12 995	694 150
1999	2 564	2 356	207	8 633	94.8	5 139	..	..
Camping sites and other provision of short-stay accommodation (SIC 92 55.21 to 55.23)								
	CMMW	CMMT	CMMU	CMQV	CMQW	CMQX	CMNQ	CMRR
1995	237	217	20	1 000	79.2	560	–	–
1996	255	235	20	1 181	82.7	672	–	–
1997	312	293	19	1 456	84.0	846	4 598	770 397
1998	350	326	24	1 574	85.4	913	5 074	868 867
1999	356	331	25	1 484	84.1	847	..	..
Restaurants or cafes, take-away food shops (SIC 92 55.30)								
	CMNV	CMNS	CMNT	CMQY	CMQZ	CMRA	CMOP	CMOQ
1995	2 000	1 850	150	7 710	81.3	3 824	..	..
1996	2 095	1 946	149	8 316	83.1	4 270	..	..
1997	2 404	2 231	174	9 352	85.8	4 715	655	29 815
1998	2 787	2 590	196	10 258	86.5	5 223	654	31 124
1999	3 018	2 791	226	10 617	84.1	5 746	..	..
Licensed clubs with entertainment, independent, tenanted, managed public houses or wine bars (SIC 92 55.40)[4]								
	CMOU	CMOR	CMOS	CMRB	CMRC	CMRD	CMPO	CMPP
1995	2 305	2 131	174	7 310	57.7	4 237	–	–
1996	2 418	2 227	191	7 937	60.1	4 877	..	–
1997	2 657	2 451	205	9 494	66.0	5 629	4 449	64 751
1998	2 982	2 752	230	10 793	70.6	6 052	5 239	78 614
1999	3 212	2 981	231	10 766	68.2	6 324	..	..
Canteen operator, catering contractor (SIC 92 55.51 and 55.52)								
	CMPT	CMPQ	CMPR	CMRE	CMRF	CMRG		
1995	1 141	1 048	93	2 576	88.0	1 261		
1996	1 267	1 164	103	3 153	90.3	1 638		
1997	1 569	1 447	122	4 132	95.1	2 228		
1998	1 681	1 541	140	3 962	93.0	2 044		
1999	1 862	1 715	146	4 349	89.9	2 133		

1 Exclusive of VAT.
2 Inclusive of VAT.
3 Data for 1995 and 1996 were collected on a different basis from those for 1997 onwards.
4 Includes figures for managed public houses owned by breweries.
5 The 1995, 1996 and 1997 total turnover figure used to calculate these data excludes VAT.

Source: Office for National Statistics: 01633 812435

SOURCES

This index of sources gives the titles of official publications or other sources containing statistics allied to those in the tables of this *Annual Abstract*. These publications provide more detailed analyses than are shown in the *Annual Abstract*. This index includes publications to which reference should be made for short-term (monthly or quarterly) series. No entry is made in this index for items where the data have been obtained from departmental records. Further advice on published statistical sources is available from the National Statistics Public Enquiry Service on the numbers provided on page ii.

Subject	Table number in *Abstract*	Government department or other organisation	Official publication or other source
1. Area			
	1.1	Ordnance Survey Ordnance Survey of Northern Ireland Office for National Statistics	Regional Trends (annual, The Stationery Office (TSO))
2. Parliamentary elections			
Elections	2.1	University of Plymouth for the Electoral Commission	British Electoral Facts 1832-1999 (Ashgate) Dod's Parliamentary Companion (annual)
By-elections	2.2	University of Plymouth for the Electoral Commission	Vachers Parliamentary Companion (quarterly) **Social Trends (annual, TSO)**
3. International development			
	3.1, 3.2	Department for International Development	Statistics on International Development (annual)
4. Defence			
	4.1 - 4.12	Ministry of Defence/ DASA	UK Defence Statistics 2001 (TSO)
5. Population and vital statistics			
Population	5.1 - 5.3, 5.5, 5.6	Office for National Statistics	*England and Wales*: Census reports 1911, 1921, 1931, 1951, 1961, 1971, 1981 and 1991 Census 1991, Key Population and Vital Statistics; Great Britain Digest of Welsh Statistics (annual, National Assembly for Wales)
		General Register Office (Scotland)	*Scotland*: Census reports 1951, 1961, 1971, 1981 and 1991 Census 1991, Key statistics for urban areas: Scotland
		General Register Office (Northern Ireland)	*Northern Ireland*: Census of population 1951, 1961, 1966 and 1971, 1981 and 1991
		Office for National Statistics	*England and Wales*: Series FM (Family statistics), DH (Deaths), MB (Morbidity), PP (Population estimates and projections), MN (Migration) and VS (Key population and vital statistics) Series PP1, Population estimates: The Registrar General's estimates of the population of regions and local government areas of England and
Wales			Population Trends (quarterly TSO) Health Statistics Quarterly (TSO)
		General Register Office (Scotland)	*Scotland*: Annual report of the Registrar General for Scotland Annual estimate of the population of Scotland
		General Register Office (Northern Ireland)	*Northern Ireland*: Annual report of the Registrar General
Projections	5.1 - 5.3	Government Actuary's Department Office for National Statistics	Series PP2, Population projections - national figures
Migration	5.7, 5.8	Office for National Statistics	Series MN (International migration) Population Trends (quarterly, TSO)
	5.9, 5.10	Home Office	Control of immigration statistics United Kingdom (annual)
Vital statistics	5.4, 5.11 - 5.21	Office for National Statistics	*England and Wales*: Series FM (Births, marriages and divorce statistics), DH (Deaths), MB (Morbidity), PP (Population estimates and projections), MN (International migration) and VS (Key population and vital statistics) Population Trends (quarterly, TSO)

SOURCES

Subject	Table number in *Abstract*	Government department or other organisation	Official publication or other source
	5.4, 5.11 - 5.20	General Register Office (Scotland)	*Scotland*: Annual report of the Registrar General for Scotland Quarterly return of births, deaths and marriages
		General Register Office (Northern Ireland)	*Northern Ireland*: Annual report of the Registrar General Quarterly return of births, deaths and marriages
	5.13	Northern Ireland Court Service	Northern Ireland Judicial Statistics (annual)
	5.17	Scottish Executive	
	5.22	Government Actuary's Department	*England and Wales*: Interim Life Table *Scotland*: Interim Life Table *Northern Ireland*: Annual Report of the Registrar General

6. Education

Subject	Table number in *Abstract*	Government department or other organisation	Official publication or other source
	6.1 - 6.11	Department for Education and Skills	Education and Training Statistics for the United Kingdom (annual, TSO)
		National Assembly for Wales	Digest of Welsh Statistics (annual) Statistics of Education and Training in Wales (annual, NAfW)
		Scottish Executive	Scottish Educational Statistics (annual and ad-hoc, SE) Scottish Social Statistics (annual)
		Department of Education; Northern Ireland Department for Employment and Learning	Annual Abstract of Statistics, Northern Ireland (annual) Northern Ireland Education Statistics (annual and ad-hoc, DENI, DELNI)

7. Labour market

Subject	Table number in *Abstract*	Government department or other organisation	Official publication or other source
Labour Force Survey	7.1 - 7.3, 7.6, 7.9, 7.10, 7.12, 7.15 - 7.17	Office for National Statistics	Labour Market Trends (monthly, TSO)
	7.4, 7.5	Office for National Statistics	
	7.7	Cabinet Office	Civil Service Statistics (annual) Monthly Digest of Statistics (TSO)
	7.8	Office for National Statistics Home Office Scottish Executive	Labour Market Trends (monthly, TSO)
Claimant count	7.11, 7.13 7.14, 7.27	Office for National Statistics	Labour Market Trends (monthly, TSO)
	7.18	Office for National Statistics	Labour Market Trends (monthly TSO) Monthly Digest of Statistics (TSO)
New Earnings Survey	7.19, 7.20, 7.23, 7.25	Office for National Statistics	New Earnings Survey (annual, ONS)
Average Earnings Index	7.21, 7.22	Office for National Statistics	Labour Market Trends (monthly, TSO) Monthly Digest of Statistics (TSO)
	7.24	Department of Enterprise, Trade and Investment (Northern Ireland)	New Earnings Survey Northern Ireland (annual) (some details in Northern Ireland Annual Abstract of Statistics)
	7.26	Department of Trade and Industry	Labour Market Trends (monthly, TSO)

8. Personal income, expenditure and wealth

Subject	Table number in *Abstract*	Government department or other organisation	Official publication or other source
	8.1	Office for National Statistics	Economic Trends, March (monthly, TSO)
	8.2	Board of Inland Revenue	Inland Revenue Statistics (annual, TSO) Economic Trends (monthly, TSO)
	8.3 - 8.5	Office for National Statistics	Family Expenditure Survey, (annual) (1990 onwards edition-Family Spending) (annual, TSO)

9. Health

Subject	Table number in *Abstract*	Government department or other organisation	Official publication or other source
National health service	9.1	Department of Health	Appropriation Accounts (annual) Health and Personal Social Services Statistics for England (annual)
		National Assembly for Wales	Health and Personal Social Services Statistics for Wales (annual)

Subject	Table number in *Abstract*	Government department or other organisation	Official publication or other source
	9.2	Scottish Health Service, Common Services Agency	
	9.3	Central Services Agency (Northern Ireland) Department, Health and Social Services and Public Safety (Northern Ireland)	Summary of Health and Personal Social Services Accounts (annual) Hospital Statistics (annual)
	9.4	Department of Health Scottish Health Service, Common Services Agency National Assembly for Wales	Health and Personal Social Services Statistics for England (annual)
Public health	9.5	PHLS Communicable Disease Surveillance Centre	Communicable Disease Statistics Series MB2 (annual) Annual Review of Communicable Diseases
		Scottish Health Service, Common Services Agency	Scottish Health Statistics (annual)
		General Register Office (Northern Ireland)	Annual report of the Registrar General Northern Ireland Quarterly return of births, deaths and marriages
	9.6 - 9.8	Health and Safety Executive	Health and Safety Statistics (annual)

10. Social protection

Subject	Table number in *Abstract*	Government department or other organisation	Official publication or other source
Social security pensions, benefits and allowances	10.1, 10.2,	Department for Work and Pensions	National Insurance Fund Account (annual)
	10.4	Board of Inland Revenue	
	10.3, 10.5, 10.6 - 10.16	Department for Work and Pensions Department of Health and Social Services (Northern Ireland)	Social Security Statistics (annual, TSO) Health and Personal Social Services Statistics for England (annual) Welsh Office: Health and Personal Social Services Statistics for Wales (annual)
Working Family Tax Credit	10.12	Board of Inland Revenue	Quarterly Enquiry United Kingdom (quarterly)
Social services	10.17 - 10.21	Office for National Statistics Department for Education and Skills	Appropriation Accounts (annual) Northern Ireland Annual Abstract of Statistics
Housing	10.22	Office for National Statistics	

11. Crime and justice

Subject	Table number in *Abstract*	Government department or other organisation	Official publication or other source
	11.1	Home Office	Monthly Digest of Statistics (TSO)
	11.2	Home Office	*England and Wales*: Report of Her Majesty's Chief Inspector of Constabulary (annual)
		Scottish Executive Justice Department The Police Force of Northern Ireland	*Scotland*: Report of Her Majesty's Chief Inspector of Constabulary for Scotland (annual) The Chief Constable's Annual Report
	11.3 - 11.11	Home Office	Criminal Statistics, England and Wales (annual) (TSO) Prison statistics, England and Wales (annual) Digest of Welsh Statistics (annual, Welsh Office)
	11.12 - 11.17	Home Office	HM Prison Service Annual Report and Accounts April 2000 - March 2001
		Scottish Executive Justice Department	Recorded Crime in Scotland, 2000
	11.18, 11.19	Scottish Executive Justice Department	Prison Statistics Scotland, 2000 Scottish Prison Service Annual Report and Accounts 2000-01
	11.20 - 11.23	Northern Ireland Office	

SOURCES

Subject	Table number in *Abstract*	Government department or other organisation	Official publication or other source
12. Lifestyles			
	12.1	Department for Culture, Media and Sport	Department for Culture, Media and Sport Annual Report 2001
	12.2	Department for Culture, Media and Sport	
	12.3	Office for National Statistics	GB Cinema Exhibitors News Release Monthly Digest of Statistics (TSO)
	12.4	Department for Culture, Media and Sport	British Film Institute Film and Television Handbook
	12.5	Office for National Statistics	Travel Trends (annual, TSO) Overseas Travel and Tourism First Release Monthly Digest of Statistics (TSO)
		English Tourism Council	The UK Tourist: Statistics (annual) Sightseeing in the UK (annual) Visits to Tourist attractions (annual) www.staruk.org.uk
	12.6	Office for National Statistics	Living in Britain: Results from the General Household Survey
	12.7	Department for Culture, Media and Sport Gaming Board for Great Britain	The Gaming Board for Great Britain Annual Report
Households	12.8	Office for National Statistics General Register Office (Scotland)	Census 1991 National Report Great Britain Part II 1991 Census. Household & Family Composition (10%) G.B.
13. Environment, water and housing			
Environment	13.1 - 13.7 13.9 -13.18	Department for Environment, Food and Rural Affairs	Digest of Environmental Statistics (annual, www.defra.gov.uk/environment/statistics/des) The Environment in your Pocket (annual)
	13.9, 13.10	Scottish Executive	
Water	13.8	Office of Water Services (OFWAT)	1999-2000 report on tariff structure and charges (annual)
Housing	13.19 - 13.21	Department for Transport, Local Government and the Regions (DTLR)	Housing Statistics, Great Britain (quarterly, TSO)
	13.20 - 13.21	National Assembly for Wales Scottish Executive	Welsh Housing Statistics (annual, NAfW) Statistical Bulletins on Housing (SE)
	13.21	Department for Social Development, Northern Ireland	Northern Ireland Housing Statistics (annual)
14. Transport and communications			
General	14.1, 14.2, 14.4	DTLR	
	14.3	Office for National Statistics	
Road transport	14.5 - 14.11	DTLR	Transport Statistics Great Britain (annual, TSO) Vehicle Licensing Statistics (annual, TSO) Monthly Digest of Statistics (TSO) Road accidents in Great Britain (annual, TSO) Road accidents Wales (annual, National Assembly for Wales)
	14.12, 14.13	Department of the Environment for Northern Ireland	Transport Statistics NI
Rail transport	14.19, 14.20	DTLR	Transport Statistics Great Britain (annual, TSO) Health and Safety Executive: Industry and Services (annual) Bulletin of Rail Statistics (quarterly)
	14.21, 14.22	Department of the Environment for Northern Ireland	Northern Ireland Annual Abstract of Statistics

Subject	Table number in *Abstract*	Government department or other organisation	Official publication or other source
Air transport	14.23 - 14.27	Civil Aviation Authority	Monthly Digest of Statistics (TSO) Civil Aviation Authority; Annual Statements of Movements, Passengers and Cargo Civil Aviation Authority; Monthly Statements of Movements, Passengers and Cargo Accidents to aircraft on the British Register (annual)
Sea transport	14.28, 14.29	DTLR	Maritime Statistics (annual, TSO) Monthly Digest of Statistics (TSO)
Passenger movement	14.30	DTLR Civil Aviation Authority	Monthly Digest of Statistics (TSO)
Communications	14.31	Royal Mail Parcel Force Subscription Services Ltd Post Office Counters Ltd	Monthly Digest of Statistics (TSO) Post Office report and accounts (annual)

15. National accounts

	15.1 - 15.22	Office for National Statistics	United Kingdom National Accounts (annual, TSO) Monthly Digest of Statistics (TSO) Economic Trends (monthly, TSO) UK Economic Accounts (quarterly, TSO) Consumer Trends (quarterly, TSO)

16. Prices

Producer prices	16.1, 16.2	Office for National Statistics	Producer Price Index Press Notice (monthly) Business Monitor MM22, Producer Price Indices (monthly, TSO) Monthly Digest of Statistics (TSO)
Consumer prices	16.3 - 16.5	Office for National Statistics	Monthly Digest of Statistics (TSO) Labour Market Trends (monthly, TSO) Business Monitor MM23, Consumer Price Indices (monthly, TSO)
	16.6, 16.7	Department for Environment, Food and Rural Affairs	Agricultural Census Statistics, United Kingdom (annual) Indices (Monthly) Monthly Digest of Statistics (TSO)
	16.8	Department for Environment, Food and Rural Affairs	Agriculture in the UK (annual)

17. Government finance

Central government	17.1 - 17.3	Office for National Statistics	Financial Statistics (monthly, TSO)
	17.4 - 17.7	HM Treasury Office for National Statistics	Consolidated Fund and National Loans Fund Accounts Financial Statistics (monthly, TSO)
	17.8	Bank of England	
Saving	17.9	Department for National Savings	Accounts of National Savings Bank Investment Deposit Accounts (annual) Ordinary Deposit Accounts (annual)
Central government	17.10, 17.11	Board of Inland Revenue	Inland Revenue Statistics (annual, TSO)
Rateable values	17.12	Board of Inland Revenue	Rates and Rateable values in England and Wales (annual)
Local authorities	17.13, 17.14	Department for Transport, Local Government and the Regions	Local government financial statistics (England)(annual)
		National Assembly for Wales	Welsh local government financial statistics (annual)
		Public Works Loan Board	Annual report of the Public Works Loan Board
		Scottish Executive, Economic Advice and Statistics	Local financial returns (Scotland) (annual)
		Department of the Environment for Northern Ireland	
		Chartered Institute of Public Finance and Accountancy	
	17.15, 17.16	Department for Transport,	Local government financial statistics (England) (annual)

SOURCES

Subject	Table number in *Abstract*	Government department or other organisation	Official publication or other source
		Local Government and the Regions National Assembly for Wales	Welsh local government financial statistics (annual)
	17.17	Department for Transport, Local Government and the Regions	Local government financial statistics (England) (annual)
	17.18 - 17.20	Scottish Executive, Economic Advice and Statistics	Local financial returns (Scotland) (annual)
	17.21	Department of the Environment for Northern Ireland	District Council - Summary of Statement of Accounts (annual)

18. External trade and investment

Subject	Table number in *Abstract*	Government department or other organisation	Official publication or other source
	18.1 - 18.8	Office for National Statistics	Business Monitor MM24, Monthly Review of External Trade Statistics (monthly, TSO) Overseas Trade Analysed in Terms of Industries MQ10 (quarterly, TSO) Monthly Digest of Statistics (monthly, TSO) HM Customs & Excise: Overseas Trade Statistics of the UK (monthly, quarterly and annual)
	18.9 - 18.18	Office for National Statistics Bank of England	United Kingdom Balance of Payments (annual, TSO) Quarterly figures: UK Economic Accounts Financial Statistics (monthly, TSO)

19. Research and development

Subject	Table number in *Abstract*	Government department or other organisation	Official publication or other source
	19.1 - 19.5	Office for National Statistics	Business Monitor MA14, Research and Development in UK Business (annual, ONS)

20. Agriculture, fisheries and food

Subject	Table number in *Abstract*	Government department or other organisation	Official publication or other source
Agriculture	20.1, 20.2	Department for Environment, Food and Rural Affairs	Agriculture in the United Kingdom (annual)
	20.3 - 20.5	Department for Environment, Food and Rural Affairs	Agricultural Statistics; United Kingdom (annual) Scottish Agricultural Economics (annual) Welsh Agricultural Statistics (annual, National Assembly for Wales)
	20.6	Forestry Commission	Great Britain: Annual Report and Accounts of the Forestry Commission
		Department of Agriculture and Rural Development (Northern Ireland)	Northern Ireland Annual Abstract of Statistics
	20.7, 20.8	Department for Environment, Food and Rural Affairs	
Food	20.9 - 20.12	Department for Environment, Food and Rural Affairs	Monthly Digest of Statistics (TSO)
	20.13	Department for Environment, Food and Rural Affairs	Agricultural Statistics, United Kingdom (annual) As for notes 20.3 - 20.5
Fisheries	20.14, 20.15	Department of Environment, Food and Rural Affairs; Scottish Executive Agricultural Departments	*England and Wales*: Sea fisheries statistical tables (annual) *Scotland*: Fisheries of Scotland report (annual) Scottish Sea fisheries statistics (annual, TSO)
Food consumption	20.16	Department for Environment, Food and Rural Affairs	National Food Survey

21. Production

Subject	Table number in *Abstract*	Government department or other organisation	Official publication or other source
Production and construction	21.1	Office for National Statistics	Annual Business Inquiry
Manufacturers sales	21.2	Office for National Statistics	Product Sales and Trade PRA1 to 92 and PRQ1 to 33 (ONS)
	21.3	Office for National Statistics	Size analysis of United Kingdom Businesses (Business Monitor PA1003) (annual, ONS)
Energy	21.4 - 21.12	Department of Trade and Industry (Energy Policy, Technology Analysis and Coal Unit)	Digest of United Kingdom Energy Statistics (annual) Energy Trends (monthly) PACSTAT (CD-ROM) (annual, ONS)

Subject	Table number in *Abstract*	Government department or other organisation	Official publication or other source
Iron and steel	21.13 - 21.15	Iron and Steel Statistics Bureau	Iron and steel industry: annual statistics published by the Iron and Steel Statistics Bureau Corporation Regional Trends (annual, TSO)
Industrial materials	21.16	World Bureau of Metal Statistics Aluminium Federation	World Metal Statistics (monthly) PACSTAT (CD-ROM) (annual, ONS)
	21.17, 21.18	British man-made fibres Federation Textile Statistics Bureau Fertiliser Manufacturers' Association	Monthly Digest of Statistics (TSO) PACSTAT (CD-ROM) (Annual, ONS)
	21.19	Office for National Statistics	Minerals (Business Monitor PA 1007) (annual, ONS) Natural Environment Research Council: United Kingdom Minerals Yearbook
		Department of Economic Development (Northern Ireland)	Northern Ireland Annual Abstract of Statistics
Building and construction	21.20	Office for National Statistics DETR	Minerals (Business Monitor PA 1007) (annual, ONS) Monthly Digest of Statistics (TSO) Housing and Construction Statistics (quarterly and annual)
	21.21, 21.22	DETR	Housing and Construction Statistics (quarterly and annual)
Engineering	21.23, 21.24	Office for National Statistics	PACSTAT (CD-ROM) (annual, ONS)
Motor vehicle production	21.25	Office for National Statistics	Business Monitor PM 34.10, (monthly, ONS) PACSTAT (CD-ROM) (annual, ONS) Sector Review- Motor Trades (formerly Business Monitor SDA27) (annual, TSO)
Drink and tobacco	21.26, 21.27	HM Customs and Excise	Annual report of the Commissioners of HM Customs and Excise
		Office for National Statistics	Monthly Digest of Statistics (TSO)

22. Banking, insurance, etc

Subject	Table number in *Abstract*	Government department or other organisation	Official publication or other source
Banking	22.1	Bank of England	Bank of England Annual Report and Accounts
	22.2	Association of Payment Clearing Services	Annual report of the Bankers' Clearing House
	22.3 - 22.5	Bank of England	Bank of England Quarterly Bulletin
	22.6	Bank of England	Financial Statistics (monthly, TSO)
	22.7	Bank of England	Bank of England Quarterly Bulletin
	22.8	Bank of England	Bank of England Quarterly Bulletin
	22.9 - 22.13	Bank of England	Monthly Digest of Statistics (TSO) Financial Statistics (monthly, TSO)
	22.14	Bank of England	Financial Statistics (monthly, TSO), tables E2.1 to E2.10
Other financial institutions	22.15	Building Societies Commission	Report of the Chief Registrar incorporating the Report of the Industrial Assurance Commissioner (annual)
	22.16	Office for National Statistics	Business Monitor SDQ7, Assets and Liabilities of Finance Houses and Other Credit Companies (quarterly, ONS)
	22.17	Office for National Statistics	Financial Statistics (monthly, TSO) Monthly Digest of Statistics (TSO) Business Monitor MQ5, Insurance Companies; Pension Funds and Trusts Investments (quarterly, ONS) First Release
	22.18, 22.19	Office for National Statistics	Financial Statistics (monthly, TSO) Business Monitor MQ5, Insurance Companies; Pension Funds and Trusts Investments (quarterly, ONS)
Insolvency	22.20 - 22.23	Department of Trade and Industry	Insolvency Annual Report (DTI) Companies (DTI) Financial Statistics (monthly, TSO)

SOURCES

Subject	Table number in *Abstract*	Government department or other organisation	Official publication or other source
23. Service industry			
Retail trades	23.1	Office for National Statistics	Annual Business Inquiry
	23.2	Office for National Statistics	Business Monitor SDM 28, Retail Sales (monthly, ONS) Monthly Digest of Statistics (TSO)
Motor trades	23.3	Office for National Statistics	Annual Business Inquiry
Catering	23.4	Office for National Statistics	Annual Business Inquiry

INDEX

Figures indicate table numbers

INDEX

Figures indicate table numbers

INDEX

Figures indicate table numbers

INDEX

425

Figures indicate table numbers

INDEX

Figures indicate table numbers

INDEX

Printed in the United Kingdom for The Stationery Office
Id 80116   C45   688824   1/02   19585